CONTEMPORARY Management

CONTEMPORARY Management

2024 Release

Jennifer M. George
Rice University

Mc Graw Hill

CONTEMPORARY MANAGEMENT

Some ancillaries, including electronic and print components, may not be available to customers outside the United States.

This book is printed on acid-free paper.

1 2 3 4 5 6 7 8 9 LWI 29 28 27 26 25 24

ISBN 978-1-266-80294-2
MHID 1-266-80294-0

Cover Image: *Hilch/Shutterstock*

mheducation.com/highered

BRIEF CONTENTS

AUTHOR

Courtesy of Jennifer George

Jennifer George is the Mary Gibbs Jones Professor of Management and Professor of Psychology in the Jesse H. Jones Graduate School of Business at Rice University. She received her BA in Psychology/Sociology from Wesleyan University, her MBA in Finance from New York University, and her PhD in Management and Organizational Behavior from New York University. Prior to joining the faculty at Rice University, she was a professor in the Department of Management at Texas A&M University.

Professor George specializes in organizational behavior and is well known for her research on mood and emotion in the workplace, their determinants, and their effects on various individual and group-level work outcomes. She is the author of many articles in leading peer-reviewed journals such as the *Academy of Management Journal*, the *Academy of Management Review*, the *Journal of Applied Psychology*, *Organizational Behavior and Human Decision Processes*, *Journal of Personality and Social Psychology*, *Organization Science*, and *Psychological Bulletin*. One of her papers won the Academy of Management's Organizational Behavior Division Outstanding Competitive Paper Award, and another paper won the *Human Relations* Best Paper Award. She is, or has been, on the editorial review boards of the *Journal of Applied Psychology*, *Academy of Management Journal*, *Academy of Management Review*, *Administrative Science Quarterly*, *Journal of Management*, *Organizational Behavior and Human Decision Processes*, *Organization Science*, *International Journal of Selection and Assessment*, and *Journal of Managerial Issues*; was a consulting editor for the *Journal of Organizational Behavior*; was a member of the SIOP *Organizational Frontiers Series* editorial board; and was an associate editor of the *Journal of Applied Psychology*. She is a fellow in the Academy of Management, the American Psychological Association, the American Psychological Society, and the Society for Industrial and Organizational Psychology and a member of the Society for Organizational Behavior. She also has coauthored a textbook titled *Understanding and Managing Organizational Behavior*.

PREFACE

In the 2024 Release of *Contemporary Management,* I continue to focus on providing the most up-to-date account of the changes taking place in the world of management and management practices while maintaining emphasis on keeping the text relevant and interesting to students. The increased focus on the challenges and opportunities facing businesses large and small and integrated timely examples bring management issues to life for students.

The issues facing managers today are unprecedented, as the world continues to recover from the global coronavirus pandemic, which over the past several years killed nearly 7 million people worldwide (and more than 1.3 million in the United States alone). With incredible speed, major industries such as airlines, hotels, restaurants, and entertainment venues, among others, were shuttered, millions of employees (and managers) were laid off or furloughed, and still others were forced to work remotely and communicate with colleagues and customers via online platforms. As vaccines were developed at breakneck speed and governments subsidized businesses and individuals to help keep them afloat, companies and managers who were able to pivot quickly to address this crisis seemed to weather the pandemic with new lessons on how to survive and recover while continuing to do business.

In addition, the ongoing revolution in technology continues to transform how managers make decisions across all levels of a company's hierarchy and across its functions and divisions, both domestic and international. The 2024 Release addresses these ongoing challenges as technology continues to evolve quickly, especially in the areas of artificial intelligence, data analytics, and remote work.

Other major challenges I continue to address in the 2024 Release include the impact of the steadily increasing diversity in the workforce and how this increasing diversity makes it imperative for managers to understand how and why people differ so they can manage effectively and reap the performance benefits of diversity and inclusion. To that end, I have expanded the scope of the "Focus on Diversity" features to acknowledge the importance of equity, inclusion, and belonging in the workplace, renaming the boxes "Focus on DEI&B."

Seven new DEI&B features describe efforts to promote diversity at Electronic Arts (Chapter 1); to employ workers with disabilities at a North Carolina coffee shop business (Chapter 4); to provide affordable housing in Los Angeles's Black and Brown neighborhoods (Chapter 7); to implement strategies to drive corporate values at UPS (Chapter 8); to set diversity goals as a way of improving research at Genentech (Chapter 9); to measure bias that may affect organizational performance (Chapter 11); and to lead effectively across the divide between right- and left-leaning political opinions (Chapter 14).

Finally, I have added a new chapter on Starting a New Business (Chapter 19) because entrepreneurial endeavors have become a large part of the overall business environment in the United States, particularly as a result of the pandemic. I believe more than ever that managers, whether they work in a large organization or for a startup company, need to understand that businesses thrive because they are led by effective managers.

Major Content Changes

Encouraged by the number of instructors and students who use each new release of the book, and based on the reactions and suggestions of both users and reviewers, I have revised and updated the book in several ways. First, just as I have included new research concepts as appropriate, so too have I been careful to eliminate outdated or marginal management concepts. As usual, my goal has been to streamline the presentation and keep the focus on the changes taking place that have the most impact on managers and organizations. In today's world of instant sound bites, videos, text messaging, and tweets, providing the best content is much more important than providing excessive content—especially when some of the students are burdened by time pressures stemming from the need to work long hours at paying jobs and meeting personal commitments and obligations.

Second, I have added new management content and have reinforced its importance by using both small and large company examples in the chapter-opening cases titled "A Manager's Challenge"; in the many boxed examples featuring managers and employees in companies both large and small in each chapter; and in the "Case in the News" closing cases.

Chapter 1

- New "A Manager's Challenge" on how Airbnb CEO Brian Chesky made difficult decisions to keep the company afloat during the global pandemic.
- Updated statistics on managerial wages and projected growth rate in managerial job opportunities between now and 2031.
- New "Manager as a Person" about Bernard Kim, CEO of Match Group, and how he uses his experience and skills to perform the four managerial functions of planning, organizing, leading, and controlling.

- New "Managing Globally" describes the efforts of Blue Power CEO Salma Okonkwo to make solar power installations and sustainable energy available in her home country of Ghana.
- Updated statistics on global spending on technology.
- New text discussion on how the COVID-19 pandemic forced companies to send employees home to work remotely and recent research about the effects of remote work on productivity, employee engagement, and work-life balance.
- New "Focus on DEI&B" profiles Laura Miele, chief operating officer at Electronic Arts, and Miele's efforts to promote diversity within the organization.
- New "Case in the News" about GE CEO Larry Culp and his managerial decision to split the global conglomerate into three separate companies to streamline costs and increase profits.

Chapter 2

- New "A Manager's Challenge" about Google's struggles to lead its workforce back to the office after the pandemic.
- New text example about a recent startup, Syndio, whose software is used by companies to analyze and resolve pay equity issues.
- New "Managing Globally" on how global events such as the recent pandemic, supply chain disruptions, and the war in Ukraine are reshaping the role of the manager.
- New "Case in the News" about RIOS and how their intelligent machines are reshaping processes in small- and medium-sized manufacturing businesses.

Chapter 3

- Updated statistics on the number of Fortune 500 companies using Myers-Briggs Type personality assessments.
- New discussion on job satisfaction levels among U.S. workers, particularly during the recent pandemic, and how companies are increasing their efforts to attract and retain top workers, as many have quit their jobs and taken new positions with higher salaries, flexible work options, and better benefits as the economy recovers from the pandemic at an accelerated pace.
- New "Management Insight" on the hazards of employee and manager burnout, especially during the pandemic.
- New text example about IBM hiring its first director of transformation and culture, whose major task is to rethink Big Blue's organizational culture and HR systems.
- New "Case in the News" on Instacart's CEO and how she brings a unique perspective to the organization.

Chapter 4

- New "A Manager's Challenge" on the president of the UPS Foundation and how she aligns the foundation's work with UPS's overall corporate vision by contributing to local communities the global delivery giant serves.
- Revised discussion on how ethics change over time, including several relevant examples.
- New text example about MacKenzie Scott (former wife of Amazon's Jeff Bezos) pledging to give away most of her wealth to philanthropic organizations.
- New "Ethics in Action" about billing the poor for hospital care.
- Updated discussion on how managers struggle with the difficult decision of laying off or terminating employees, especially during a global pandemic.
- Updated discussion on the compensation packages for U.S. CEOs compared to those of the average worker.
- New text example about the city of Chicago suing food delivery services over their unethical practices.
- New "Manager as a Person" on how managers can nudge employees to do the right thing.
- New "Focus on DEI&B" on how the owners of Bitty & Beau's Coffee take a proactive approach to social responsibility by hiring people with disabilities to help them become accepted and included in the local community.
- New "Managing Ethically" exercise about Unilever's apparent double standard in ice cream ingredients in China.
- New "Case in the News" about McDonald's and its decision to walk away from business in Russia after the country invaded Ukraine.

Chapter 5

- New "A Manager's Challenge" about the NFL's diversity initiatives.
- Updated statistics on female CEOs of Fortune 500 companies.
- Updated statistics on the increasing diversity of the U.S. workforce.
- Updated "Focus on DEI&B" about Latinos' impact on the U.S. economy.
- New statistics on the number of religious discrimination complaints filed in the United States.
- Updated discussion on U.S. employers recognized for employing people with disabilities.
- New statistics on the U.S. poverty rate–before, during, and after the start of the pandemic.

- Updated discussion on U.S. employers recognized as the best places to work for LGBTQ equality.
- New text example about The Coca-Cola Company's efforts to ensure a diverse workforce within the organization.
- New "Management Insight" about what gets in the way of women being promoted.
- New "Case in the News" about how Nike keeps score on its diversity efforts, including tying diversity, equity, and inclusion initiatives to executives' compensation.

Chapter 6

- New "A Manager's Challenge" about BMW and its global expansion, especially to China.
- New discussion about managers' approach to the task environment in light of recent global supply chain disruptions.
- New discussion and examples about companies' recent decisions to bring back manufacturing jobs to the United States.
- Updated ranking of world's largest PC makers.
- Updated example of recent real estate acquisitions by Amazon to expand the number of distribution centers.
- Updated text discussion about Brexit (the UK's departure from the European Union) and its impact on the country as well as companies doing business in the UK and in Europe.
- Updated text discussion about the possibility that the United States will rejoin the CPTPP during the Biden administration; CPTPP is the new name for the Trans-Pacific Partnership (TPP).
- New text discussion about the four approaches companies use to expand internationally (content moved from Chapter 8).
- Updated text discussion on steel and aluminum tariffs on Chinese imports.
- New "Managing Globally" on the effects of global supply disruptions.
- New "Case in the News" about Netflix and its global reach.

Chapter 7

- New "A Manager's Challenge" about the CEO of CVS Health and her bold corporate decisions.
- New "Management Insight" on the flexible approach to decision making associated with workers returning to the office during the pandemic.
- New "Focus on DEI&B" on how a for-profit company in Los Angeles provides affordable housing for low-income residents.
- Revised discussion on the importance of intrapreneurs within an organization.
- New "Case in the News" about Zara and its use of technology in the retail industry to make effective business decisions.

Chapter 8

- New "A Manager's Challenge" about Marriott International's CEO and his strategies for planning a new way forward as the pandemic wanes and consumers begin to travel again.
- New text example about planning and the impact of a global shutdown that caused panic buying by consumers.
- Updated running text example about General Mills and its planning strategies.
- New "Manager as a Person" about Walgreen's CEO Roz Brewer and her corporate strategies for growth.
- New text discussion added about the use of SMART goals by managers and their organizations.
- Updated SWOT analysis discussion about Amazon and Walmart.
- Updated text example about Toys R Us and its new partnership with Macy's to open shops within the retailer's store locations.
- New "Focus on DEI&B" on UPS's CEO and her strategies to drive values at the global organization.
- New "Ethics in Action" on Gotham Greens and its focus on diversifying in an environmentally thoughtful way.
- New "Case in the News" on GM's strategies for electric vehicles.

Chapter 9

- New text discussion about a company's supply chain in comparison to its value chain.
- New text discussion about artificial intelligence and its role in a company's value chain process.
- New "Management Insight" on using artificial intelligence to improve customer experiences.
- New "Focus on DEI&B" on Genentech's efforts to set diversity goals as a way of improving the quality of its research.
- New "Case in the News" about two disc golf companies and their approach to quality and responsiveness to customers as their business grew exponentially during the pandemic.

Chapter 10

- New "A Manager's Challenge" about how Phoenix-based Banner Health restructured facilities management functions across its member hospitals to lower energy expenses and make processes more efficient.
- Updated running text example about the Home Depot and its organizational structure.
- Updated text example about Glaxo Smith Kline (GSK) and the spin-off of its consumer health care business.
- New "Management Insight" describes how the CEO of Wells Fargo streamlined the company's structure.
- New "Manager as a Person" profiles NASA's administrator and his strategies for maintaining an active organizational culture at the federal agency.
- New text discussion about the competing values framework, which describes four different types of company cultures.
- New "Ethics in Action" about Roblox, the Internet gaming platform, and whether it can enforce community standards that include civility and the safety of users.
- New "Case in the News" on how Volkswagen aligned its organizational structure with its corporate strategies.

Chapter 11

- New "A Manager's Challenge" about Delta Airlines and how listening to customers helped the airline implement changes that kept them flying during the global pandemic.
- New "Focus on DEI&B" describes the importance of measuring bias that may affect organizational performance.
- New "Management Insight" describes the skills employers are looking for in recent college grads.
- New "Ethics in Action" on whether bureaucratic controls could have saved cryptocurrency company FTX.
- New text discussion about former Disney CEO Bob Iger returning to run the company after the board fired his successor, Bob Chapek.
- New "Case in the News" describes the controls put in place by Procter & Gamble as a result of the pandemic, supply chain disruptions, and inflation.

Chapter 12

- New "A Manager's Challenge" on the importance of the HR function in recruiting and retaining truck drivers.
- New text discussion about the lingering effects of the COVID-19 pandemic with regard to recruiting efforts by both large and small companies.
- New text example about Medical Solutions, a health care staffing company, rated the best training program for employees by *Training* magazine.
- New "Management Insight" on how some companies have implemented apprenticeship programs to train new and less-experienced workers.
- Updated statistics on how much more U.S. CEOs earn than the average worker.
- Updated statistics on the number of employers who offer wellness programs for their workers.
- Updated statistics on union members in the United States.
- New text discussion about more employees seeking union membership as a result of their work experiences during the pandemic.
- New "Manager as a Person" about Bobbie, a provider of organic infant formula, and the company's decision to offer paid parental leave to its employees.

Chapter 13

- New "A Manager's Challenge" about Chieh Huang, CEO of bulk-shopping retailer Boxed, and his approach to motivating employees.
- New text discussion about managers boosting employees' expectancy levels and motivation during the recent era of "the great resignation."
- New text discussion related to employees' need for work–life balance during the pandemic, when most were trying to do their jobs from home.
- New "Manager as a Person" about a physician whose motivation to help those suffering from COVID-19 led him to set up oxygen-producing facilities in Kenya.
- New text discussion about the importance of showing appreciation to colleagues and other employees within organizations.
- New "Case in the News" about Unilever and the company's approach to motivating its global workforce.

Chapter 14

- New "A Manager's Challenge" about Accenture CEO Julie Sweet and her leadership strategies at the global consulting firm.
- New "Focus on DEI&B" on the challenges of leading in a business environment influenced by ongoing political and social debate.
- New text discussion about empowerment and employees' desire for flexibility in how they work.

- Updated statistics on women in senior executive and corporate officer positions.
- New "Case in the News" about people-first leadership at WM (formerly Waste Management).

Chapter 15

- New "A Manager's Challenge" about the CEO of NI (formerly National Instruments) and his strategies for improving teamwork within the organization.
- New text discussion about how the use of teams led to increased collaboration and talent retention during the pandemic.
- New text discussion highlighting recent research about the shift to virtual work during the pandemic and management challenges regarding how widely to extend virtual/remote work options for employees as the pandemic wanes.
- New "Manager as a Person" on ways to build strong relationships among virtual team members.
- New "Case in the News" about Novartis, a global pharmaceutical company, and how it used project teams to accelerate R&D efforts.

Chapter 16

- New "A Manager's Challenge" provides insights into how managers can communicate effectively as new media tools become available.
- New text discussion about recent research regarding how company leaders now view online communication methods and remote work as the pandemic continues to fade.
- New text discussion about communication via software, such as Zoom, Slack, and Microsoft Teams.
- New "Manager as a Person" about the fallout from a CEO using Zoom to lay off hundreds of employees in the same meeting.
- Updated statistics on worldwide Internet usage.
- New text discussion about the possibility of more companies using a hybrid work model that includes limited office time on a weekly basis.
- New "Case in the News" about ExxonMobil's communication strategies during recent turbulent times.

Chapter 17

- New "A Manager's Challenge" about Daymond John, founder of the FUBU clothing line and potential investor on TV's Shark Tank, and his negotiation skills.
- Updated "Case in the News" about Boeing and the disastrous conflict surrounding the 737 MAX airplane.

Chapter 18

- Updated "A Manager's Challenge" about the use of AI in the workplace.
- New text discussion about future technology trends.
- New text discussion about the top worries among global business leaders.
- New text example about the massive data breach experienced by T-Mobile and its customers.
- New text example about the Internet of Things and possible hacks.
- New text example about Starbucks and the coffee shortage the company experienced recently.
- Updated statistics on B2B and B2C e-commerce sales.
- Updated statistics on supply-chain spending by U.S. firms.
- New text discussion about the top companies for remote workers.

Flexible Organization

Another factor of interest to instructors is how I have designed the grouping of chapters to allow instructors to teach the chapter material in the order that best suits their needs. For example, the more micro-oriented instructor can follow Chapters 1 through 5 with Chapters 12 through 16 and then use the more macro chapters. The more macro-oriented professor can follow Chapters 1 and 2 with Chapters 6 through 11, jump to 16 through 18, and then use the micro chapters, 3 through 5 and 12 through 15.

The sequencing of parts and chapters gives instructors considerable freedom to design the course that best suits their needs. Instructors are not tied to the planning, organizing, leading, and controlling framework, even though our presentation remains consistent with this approach.

Education for all

McGraw Hill works directly with Accessibility Services departments and faculty to meet the learning needs of all students. Please contact your Accessibility Services Office, and ask them to email **accessibility@mheducation.com**, or visit **mheducation.com/about/accessibility** for more information.

Affordable solutions, added value

Make technology work for you with LMS integration for single sign-on access, mobile access to the digital textbook, and reports to quickly show you how each of your students is doing. And with our Inclusive Access program, you can provide all these tools at the lowest available market price to your students. Ask your McGraw Hill representative for more information.

Solutions for your challenges

A product isn't a solution. Real solutions are affordable, reliable, and come with training and ongoing support when you need it and how you want it. Visit **supportateverystep.com** for videos and resources both you and your students can use throughout the term.

Updated and relevant content

Our new Evergreen delivery model provides the most current and relevant content for your course, hassle-free. Content, tools, and technology updates are delivered directly to your existing McGraw Hill Connect® course. Engage students and freshen up assignments with up-to-date coverage of select topics and assessments, all without having to switch editions or build a new course.

COURSE DESIGN AND DELIVERY

CREATE Instructors can now tailor their teaching resources to match the way they teach! With McGraw Hill Create, **www.mcgrawhillcreate.com,** instructors can easily rearrange chapters, combine material from other content sources, and quickly upload and integrate their own content, such as course syllabi or teaching notes. Find the right content in Create by searching through thousands of leading McGraw Hill textbooks. Arrange the material to fit your teaching style. Order a Create book and receive a complimentary print review copy in three to five business days or a complimentary electronic review copy via email within one hour. Go to **www.mcgrawhillcreate.com** today and register.

Tegrity: Lectures 24/7 Tegrity in Connect is a tool that makes class time available 24/7 by automatically capturing every lecture. With a simple one-click start-and-stop process, you capture all computer screens and corresponding audio in a format that is easy to search, frame by frame. Students can replay any part of any class with easy-to-use, browser-based viewing on a PC, Mac, tablet, or other mobile device.

Educators know that the more students can see, hear, and experience class resources, the better they learn. In fact, studies prove it. Tegrity's unique search feature helps students efficiently find what they need, when they need it, across an entire semester of class recordings. Help turn your students' study time into learning moments immediately supported by your lecture. With Tegrity, you also increase intent listening and class participation by easing students' concerns about note-taking. Using Tegrity in Connect will make it more likely you will see students' faces, not the tops of their heads.

BLACKBOARD® PARTNERSHIP McGraw Hill Education and Blackboard have teamed up to simplify your life. Now you and your students can access Connect and Create right from within your Blackboard course–all with one single sign-on. The grade books are seamless, so when a student completes an integrated Connect assignment, the grade for that assignment automatically (and instantly) feeds your Blackboard grade center. Learn more at www.omorenow.com.

MCGRAW HILL CAMPUS™ McGraw Hill Campus is a new one-stop teaching and learning experience available to users of any learning management system. This institutional service allows faculty and students to enjoy single sign-on (SSO) access to all McGraw Hill Higher Education materials, including the award-winning McGraw Hill Connect platform, from directly within the institution's website. With McGraw Hill Campus, faculty receive instant access to teaching materials (eTextbooks, test banks, PowerPoint slides, animations, learning objectives, etc.), allowing them to browse, search, and use any instructor ancillary content in our vast library at no additional cost to instructor or students. In addition, students enjoy SSO access to a variety of free content (quizzes, flash cards, narrated presentations, etc.) and subscription-based products (e.g., McGraw Hill Connect). With McGraw Hill Campus enabled, faculty and students will never need to create another account to access McGraw Hill products and services. Learn more at **www.mhcampus.com.**

ASSURANCE OF LEARNING READY Many educational institutions today focus on the notion of *assurance of learning,* an important element of some accreditation standards. *Contemporary Management* is designed specifically to support instructors' assurance of learning initiatives with a simple yet powerful solution. Each test bank question for *Contemporary Management* maps to a specific chapter learning objective listed in the text.

AACSB TAGGING McGraw Hill Education is a proud corporate member of AACSB International. Understanding the importance and value of AACSB accreditation, *Contemporary Management* recognizes the curricula guidelines detailed in the AACSB standards for business accreditation by connecting selected questions in the text and the test bank to the eight general knowledge and skill guidelines in the AACSB standards. The statements contained in *Contemporary Management* are provided only as a guide for the users of this product. The AACSB leaves content coverage and assessment within the purview of individual schools, the mission of the school, and the faculty. While the *Contemporary Management* teaching package makes no claim of any specific AACSB qualification or evaluation, we have within *Contemporary Management* labeled selected questions according to the eight general knowledge and skills areas.

MCGRAW HILL CUSTOMER EXPERIENCE GROUP CONTACT INFORMATION At McGraw Hill Education, we understand that getting the most from new technology can be challenging. That's why our services don't stop after you purchase our products. You can email our Product Specialists 24 hours a day to get product training online. Or you can search our knowledge bank of Frequently Asked Questions on our support website. For Customer Support, call **800-331-5094** or visit **www.mhhe.com/support.** One of our Technical Support Analysts will be able to assist you in a timely fashion.

ACKNOWLEDGMENTS

Finding a way to integrate and present the rapidly growing literature about contemporary management and make it interesting and meaningful for students is not an easy task. In writing and revising the various drafts of *Contemporary Management,* I have been fortunate to have the assistance of several people who have contributed greatly to the book's final form. First, I are grateful to Michael Ablassmeir, our director, for his ongoing support and commitment to the project and for always finding ways to provide the resources that I needed to continually improve and refine the book. Second, I are grateful to Haley Burmeister, my product developer, for so ably coordinating the book's progress; and to Debbie Clare, my marketing manager, for providing concise and timely feedback and information from professors and reviewers that have allowed me to shape the book to the needs of its intended market. We also thank Sherry Kane for coordinating the production process. I am also grateful to the many colleagues and reviewers who provided useful and detailed feedback and perceptive comments and valuable suggestions for improving the manuscript.

Producing any competitive work is a challenge. Producing a truly market-driven textbook requires tremendous effort beyond simply obtaining reviews of a draft manuscript. The goal was simple with the development of *Contemporary Management:* to be the most customer-driven principles of management text and supplement package ever published! With the goal of exceeding the expectations of both faculty and students, I executed one of the most aggressive product development plans ever undertaken in textbook publishing. Hundreds of faculty have taken part in developmental activities ranging from regional focus groups to manuscript and supplement reviews and surveys. Consequently, I am confident in assuring you and your students that every aspect of the text and support package reflects your advice and needs.

I extend my special thanks to the faculty who provided detailed chapter-by-chapter feedback during the development of this product:

Jerry Alley, Aspen University
M. Ruhul Amin, Bloomsburg University of Pennsylvania
Lindy Archambeau, University of Florida
Amy S. Banta, Ohio University
Kelly Barbour-Conerty, Parkland College
Gerald Baumgardner, Pennsylvania College of Technology
Charles W. Beem, Bucks County Community College
James D. Bell, Texas State University
Danielle R. Blesi, Hudson Valley Community College
Susan Blumen, Montgomery College Department of Business and Economics
Jennifer P. Bott, Ball State University
Edwin L. Bowman, Principal, Manhattanville College, Purchase, NY
Charley Braun, Marshall University
Reginald Bruce, College of Business, University of Louisville
Murray Brunton, Central Ohio Technical College
Charles Buchanan, The Ohio State University
Judith G. Bulin, Monroe Community College, Rochester, New York
Barry Bunn, Valencia Community College
Aaron Butler, Warner Pacific College ADP
Gerald Calvasina, Southern Utah University
Glen Edward Chapuis, Saint Charles Community College
Bruce H. Charnov, Hofstra University
Alexander Chen, University of Central Arkansas
Jay Christensen-Szalanski, University of Iowa
Jason W. Coleman, Wesley College
Joy Colarusso, Daytona State College
Renee Y. Cooper, Fashion Institute of Technology
Robert Cote, Lindenwood University
C. Brad Cox, Midlands Technical College
Marian Cox Crawford, University of Arkansas–Little Rock
Susie S. Cox, University of Arkansas–Little Rock
Cheryl Cunningham, Embry-Riddle Aeronautical University–Daytona Beach
Teresa A. Daniel, Marshall University
Justin Davis, University of West Florida
Thomas W. Deckelman, Owens Community College
Richard S. DeFrank, University of Houston
Lauryn De George, University of Central Florida
Fred J. Dorn, University of Mississippi
D. Harold Doty, University of Southern Mississippi
Max E. Douglas, Indiana State University
Sandra Edwards, Northeastern State University
Stewart W. Edwards, Northern VA Community College–Annandale
William Eichenauer, Northwest State Community College
Scott Elston, Iowa State University
Richard Estrella, California Polytechnic University
Tracy Ethridge, Tri-County Technical College
Valerie Evans, Kansas State University
Bagher Fardanesh, Piaget Consulting
Carla C. Flores, Ball State University
Andrea Foster, John Tyler Community College
Caren Fullerton, Texas Tech University
Dane L. Galden, Columbus State Community College

Justin Gandy, Dallas Baptist University
Shahbaz Gill, University of Illinois-Urbana Champaign
Jim Glasgow, Instructor, Villanova School of Business
Monica Godsey, University of Nebraska
Selina Griswold, The University of Toledo
Kathy Hastings, Greenville Technical College
Karen H. Hawkins, Miami Dade College
Travis Lee Hayes, Chattanooga State Technical Community College
Samuel Hazen, Tarleton State University
Kim Hester, Arkansas State University
Perry Hidalgo, Gwinnett Technical College
Dwight Hite, East Central University
Anne Kelly Hoel, University of Wisconsin-Stout
Robert C. Hoell, Georgia Southern University
Jenni Hunt, Southern Illinois University-Edwardsville
Irene Joanette-Gallio, Western Nevada College
Paul D. Johnson, University of Mississippi
Carol Larson Jones, Cal Poly Pomona, California
Coy A. Jones, The University of Memphis
Gwendolyn Jones, University of Akron
Kathleen Jones, University of North Dakota
Rusty Juban, Southeastern Louisiana University
Jordan J. Kaplan, Long Island University School of Business
Joanne E. Kapp, Siena College
Renee N. King, Eastern Illinois University
Deanna R. Knight, Daytona State College
Mike Knudstrup, Florida Southern College
Susan Kowalewski, D'Youville College
Cynthia J. Lanphear, University of the Ozarks
Marcie Lensges, Xavier University
John E. Lewis, Midlands Technical College
Jim Long, Southwestern Oklahoma State University
Joyce Lopez, Missouri State University
Margaret Lucero, Texas A&M-Corpus Christi
Nicholas Mathys, DePaul University
Daniel W. McAllister, University of Nevada-Las Vegas
Erin McLaughlin, University of Alabama Hunstville
Christy McLendon Corey, University of New Orleans
Chrisann Merriman, University of Mary Hardin-Baylor
Douglas L. Micklich, Illinois State University
Sandra Jeanquart Miles, Murray State University
Carol T. Miller, Community College of Denver
Dan Morrell, Middle Tennessee State University
Don C. Mosley Jr., University of South Alabama
Liz Muhlenbeck, Andrews University
Clive Muir, Stetson University
Troy V. Mumford, Colorado State University
Bahaudin G. Mujtaba, Nova Southeastern University
Jane Murtaugh, College of DuPage
Renee Nelms King, Eastern Illinois University
Nanci D. Newstrom, Eastern Illinois University
Catherine Nowicki, International Business College
John Overby, The University of Tennessee at Martin
Karen Overton, Houston Community College
Eren Ozgen, Troy University, Dothan Campus
Fernando A. Pargas, James Madison University
Marc Pendel, Miller College of Business, Ball State University
Susan A. Peterson, Scottsdale Community College
Ronald Purser, San Francisco State University
Kenneth Rasheed, Chattahoochee Technical College
Gary Renz, Webster University
Bruce Wayne Richardson, Northeastern State University-Broken Arrow Campus
L. Jeff Seaton, University of Tennessee-Martin
Gregory J. Schultz, Carroll University
Marc Siegall, California State University-Chico
Randi L. Sims, Nova Southeastern University
Michaeline Skiba, Monmouth University-Leon Hess Business School
Frederick J. Slack, Indiana University of Pennsylvania
M. James Smas, Kent State University
Gerald Smith, University of Northern Iowa
Marjorie Smith, Mountain State University
Howard Stanger, Canisius College
Susan D. Steiner, The University of Tampa
Steven A. Stewart, Georgia Southern University
Warren Stone, University of Arkansas at Little Rock
Cynthia L. Sutton, Metropolitan State College of Denver
Laurie Taylor-Hamm, California State University, Fresno
Sabine Turnley, Kansas State University
Isaiah O. Ugboro, North Carolina A&T State University
Barbara VanderWerf, Palm Beach Atlantic University
Debbie Vance, Tri-County Technical College
Valerie Wallingford, Bemidji State University
Velvet Weems, Landingham, Kent State University
John Weiss, Daytona State College
William K. Wesley, Golden Gate University
Christopher Whelpley, Virginia Commonwealth University
W. Alexander Williams Jr., Texas A&M University-Commerce
Elizabeth Wilson, Georgia Southwestern State University
Doula Zaharopoulos, Ottowa University
Jan Zantinga, University of Georgia
Ivana Zilic, DePaul University

Finally, I am grateful to two incredibly wonderful children, Nicholas and Julia, for being all that they are and for the joy they bring to all who know them.

Jennifer M. George
Rice University

CONTENTS

Part One | Management

Chapter 3

Part Two | The Environment of Management

Chapter 4

Chapter 5

Part Four | Organizing and Controlling

Chapter 12
Human Resource Management 336

Part Five | Leading Individuals and Groups

Chapter 13
Motivation and Performance 370

Chapter 14
Leadership 402

Chapter 15
Effective Groups and Teams 432

Part Six | Managing Critical Organizational Processes

Chapter 16
Promoting Effective Communication 464

Chapter 17
Managing Conflict, Politics, and Negotiation 492

Chapter 18 Using Advanced Information Technology to Increase Performance 518

Chapter 19 Starting a New Business 546

CONTEMPORARY Management

CHAPTER 1

Managers and Managing

Luis Alvarez/Getty Images

Learning Objectives

After studying this chapter, you should be able to:

LO1-1 Describe what management is, why management is important, what managers do, and how managers use organizational resources efficiently and effectively to achieve organizational goals.

LO1-2 Distinguish among planning, organizing, leading, and controlling (the four principal managerial functions), and explain how managers' ability to handle each one affects organizational performance.

LO1-3 Differentiate among three levels of management, and understand the tasks and responsibilities of managers at different levels in the organizational hierarchy.

LO1-4 Distinguish among three kinds of managerial skill, and explain why managers are divided into different departments to perform their tasks more efficiently and effectively.

LO1-5 Discuss some major changes in management practices today that have occurred as a result of globalization and the use of advanced technologies.

LO1-6 Discuss the principal challenges managers face in today's increasingly competitive global environment.

A MANAGER'S CHALLENGE

How Airbnb's CEO Manages in a Turbulent Economy

How do managers contribute to their organization's success? COVID-19 hit a lot of businesses hard, and Airbnb was one of them. During the first two months of the pandemic, the company's revenues dived by 80%. Airbnb's chief executive officer, Brian Chesky, describes that time as a "near-death business experience" and "the most defining year" of his career—even more significant than working with two other cofounders to start the business. In 2020, Airbnb had thousands of employees and worldwide brand recognition; Chesky was determined to find a way to lead his people through the pandemic, and two years later, a leaner, more agile Airbnb was enjoying a resurgence of business.[1]

When pandemic-related measures all but shut down business travel and tourism, Chesky took stock of his role at the head of the company, recognizing that others would take their cues from him. He considered that optimism rooted in reality would be most likely to inspire his employees' best efforts. Drawing on his creativity (Chesky's degree is in industrial design), he reviewed the organizational structure of Airbnb to make it more efficient without losing its capacity to innovate. He cut Airbnb's 10 departments down to a few basic functions, put new initiatives on hold, slashed the marketing budget, and laid off 1,900 people.[2]

At the head of a now-leaner company, Chesky put the focus on innovation, with twice-a-year upgrades to the service. For example, Airbnb's search tool originally generated lists of properties based on location, and the company made it possible to search on a traveler's specific interests. Chesky also monitored the rapidly changing business environment, focusing on changes in travel patterns. Initial reactions to the pandemic were to stay put: Where possible, companies told employees to work from home and avoid business trips. Computer connections replaced in-person interaction for months. As travel restrictions eased, businesspeople were among the first to hit the road and the skies, often for extended stays. Then tourism rebounded. Two years after the pandemic began, Airbnb's bookings and revenues rose above their previous highs.[3]

This period also provided what became a unique opportunity. Chesky observed that when Airbnb's employees began working remotely, their productivity rose. He surmised that if employees didn't need to work in offices, their remote work could take place anywhere, and Airbnb was well positioned to provide almost-unlimited choices of location. He became his

The global pandemic forced Airbnb's CEO Brian Chesky to make difficult decisions to keep the company afloat. He consolidated departments, slashed budgets, and laid off thousands of employees, strategies that helped Airbnb weather turbulent times over the past few years.
Jeff Chiu/AP Images

own research subject, booking Airbnb sites in various states and Canada, traveling from site to site with his laptop and golden retriever, Sophie Supernova. Chesky determined that he worked effectively—and that spreading the word about the potential of remote work could only enhance demand for Airbnb. So he took the practice to the next level, establishing a work-from-anywhere policy for his employees. Chesky maintains that such a policy makes a company more attractive to potential employees and also promotes diversity by expanding the locations employees can be drawn from. At the same time, Chesky acknowledges that in-person interaction is better for building trust and deepening relationships, so Airbnb requires in-office time for one week each quarter.[4]

Beyond Airbnb's relations with employees, Chesky also sees significance in the company's relations with the communities within which it operates. One initiative that leverages Airbnb's strengths has been to offer temporary housing for displaced people. The first initiative, in 2012, involved housing people affected by Superstorm Sandy in New York. More recent efforts have helped refugees from Afghanistan and Ukraine. On a personal level, Chesky supports programs that get young people interested in and equipped for technology careers.[5]

Overview

Managing today's organizations is a complex affair, and leaders like Brian Chesky face multiple challenges from within and outside their organizations. To make decisions and lead others successfully, managers must possess a complex set of skills, knowledge, and abilities that help them interpret cues from the environment and respond accordingly.

In this chapter we consider what managers do and the skills, knowledge, and abilities they must possess to lead their organizations effectively. We also identify the different kinds of managers that organizations rely on to help guide them. Finally, we consider some of the challenges that managers must overcome to help their organizations prosper.

What Is Management?

LO1-1 Describe what management is, why management is important, what managers do, and how managers use organizational resources efficiently and effectively to achieve organizational goals.

When you think of a manager, what kind of person comes to mind? Do you think of an executive like Brian Chesky, who helps direct Airbnb? Or do you see a manager at a fast-food restaurant, who engages directly with employees and customers? Perhaps you think of a supervisor at a manufacturing company? Regardless of how we view managers, they all share important characteristics. First, they all work in organizations. **Organizations** are collections of people who work together and coordinate their actions to achieve a wide variety of goals or desired future outcomes. Second, as managers, they are the people responsible for supervising and making the most of an organization's human and other resources to achieve its goals.

Management, then, is the planning, organizing, leading, and controlling of human and other resources to achieve organizational goals efficiently and effectively. An organization's *resources* include assets such as people and their skills, know-how, and experience; machinery; raw materials; computers and information technology; and patents, financial capital, and loyal customers and employees.

organizations Collections of people who work together and coordinate their actions to achieve a wide variety of goals or desired future outcomes.

management The planning, organizing, leading, and controlling of human and other resources to achieve organizational goals efficiently and effectively.

Achieving High Performance: A Manager's Goal

One of the key goals that organizations try to achieve is to provide goods and services that customers value and desire. Brian Chesky's principal goal is to manage Airbnb so that the company can meet travelers' and remote workers' needs for a place to sleep, work, relax, and/or seek out adventure. Likewise, the principal goal of fast-food managers is to produce tasty and convenient food that customers enjoy and come back to buy. And manufacturing managers must balance the quality needs of their consumers against the pressure to be cost effective.

organizational performance A measure of how efficiently and effectively a manager uses resources to satisfy customers and achieve organizational goals.

efficiency A measure of how well or how productively resources are used to achieve a goal.

effectiveness A measure of the appropriateness of the goals an organization is pursuing and the degree to which the organization achieves those goals.

Organizational performance is a measure of how efficiently and effectively managers use available resources to satisfy customers and achieve organizational goals. Organizational performance increases in direct proportion to increases in efficiency and effectiveness, as Figure 1.1 shows. What are efficiency and effectiveness?

Efficiency is a measure of how productively resources are used to achieve a goal.[6] Organizations are efficient when managers minimize the amount of input resources (such as labor, raw materials, and component parts) or the amount of time needed to produce a given output of goods or services. For example, Wendy's develops ever more efficient fat fryers that not only reduce the amount of oil used in cooking but also speed up the cooking of french fries. UPS develops new work routines to reduce delivery time, such as instructing drivers to leave their truck doors open when going short distances.

To encourage efficiency, for example, the CEO of Momentive (formerly SurveyMonkey), Zander Lurie, led the retooling of some of the company's products and services after he took over the top job in 2016. Lurie eliminated an unsuccessful business while expanding others and continues to foster a collaborative environment in which he encourages employees to stay curious, which has helped spur the company's growth.[7]

Effectiveness is a measure of the *appropriateness* of the goals that managers have selected for the organization to pursue and the degree to which the organization achieves those goals. Organizations are effective when managers choose appropriate goals and then achieve them. Some years ago, for example, managers at McDonald's decided on the goal of providing breakfast service to attract more customers. The choice of this goal proved smart: Several years ago, McDonald's management made the decision to offer the breakfast menu all day long, a strategy that has been successful and well received by consumers. After COVID-19 shut down most fast-food restaurants for an extended period of time, McDonald's announced they would resume an all-day breakfast menu tailored to specific consumer tastes in various regions of the country.[8] High-performing organizations such as Apple, Amazon, Walmart, Home Depot, Accenture, and Habitat for Humanity are simultaneously efficient and effective. Effective managers are those who choose the right organizational goals to pursue and have the skills to utilize resources efficiently.

Figure 1.1

Efficiency, Effectiveness, and Performance in an Organization

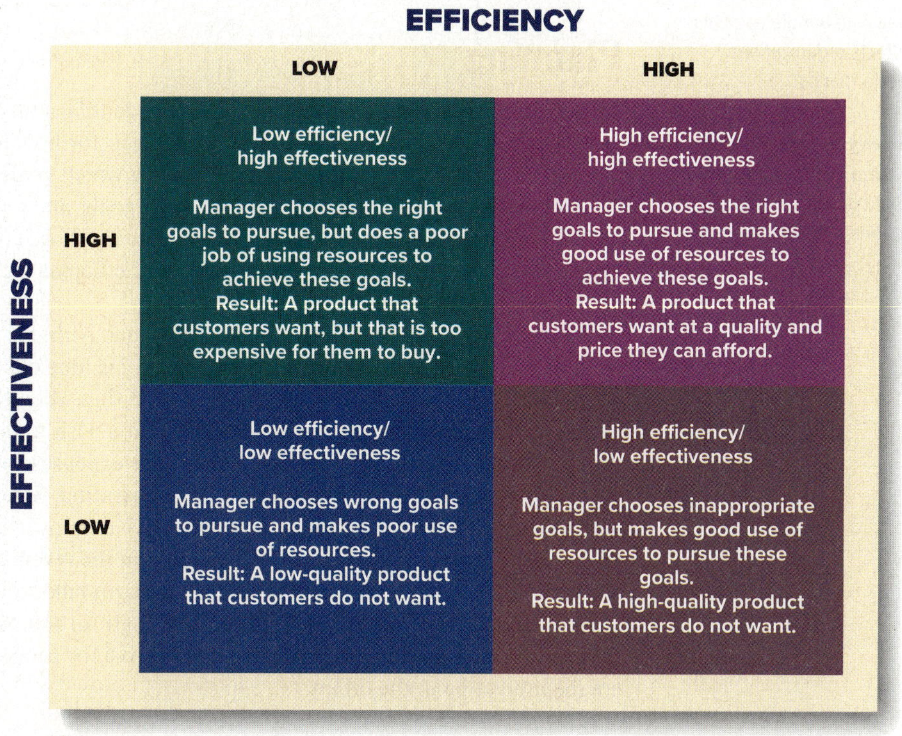

High-performing organizations are efficient *and* effective.

Why Study Management?

The dynamic and complex nature of modern work means that managerial skills are in demand. Organizations need people like you who can understand this complexity, respond to environmental contingencies, and make decisions that are ethical and effective. Studying management helps equip you to accomplish each of these tasks.

We generally learn through personal experience or the experiences of others. By studying management in school, you are exposing yourself to the lessons others have learned. The advantage of such social learning is that you are less likely to repeat the mistakes others have made in the past. Furthermore, by studying and practicing the behaviors of good managers and high-performing companies, you will equip yourself to help your future employer succeed.

The economic benefits of becoming a good manager are also impressive. In the United States, general managers earn a median wage of $97,970, with a projected growth in job openings of between 4% and 7% between now and 2031.[9]

Finally, learning management principles can help you make good decisions in nonwork contexts. If you're coaching a child's baseball team, organizing a charity 5K run, planning your financial budget, or starting a new business, good management principles will help you understand others, make quality decisions, and improve your personal success.

Essential Managerial Functions

The job of management is to help an organization make the best use of its resources to achieve its goals. How do managers accomplish this objective? They do so by performing four essential managerial functions: *planning, organizing, leading,* and *controlling.* The arrows linking these functions in Figure 1.2 suggest the sequence in which managers typically perform them. French manager Henri Fayol first outlined the nature of these managerial activities around the turn of the 20th century in *General and Industrial Management,* a book that remains the classic statement of what managers must do to create a high-performing organization.[10]

LO1-2 Distinguish among planning, organizing, leading, and controlling (the four principal managerial functions), and explain how managers' ability to handle each one affects organizational performance.

Managers at all levels and in all departments–whether in small or large companies, for-profit or not-for-profit organizations, or organizations that operate in one country or throughout the world–are responsible for performing these four functions, which we look at next. How well managers perform these functions determines how efficient and effective their organizations are.

Planning

planning Identifying and selecting appropriate goals; one of the four principal functions of management.

To perform the **planning** function, managers identify and select appropriate organizational goals and courses of action; they develop *strategies* for how to achieve high performance. The three steps involved in planning are (1) deciding which goals the organization will pursue, (2) deciding what strategies to adopt to attain those goals, and (3) deciding how to allocate organizational resources to pursue the strategies that attain those goals. How well managers plan and develop strategies determines how effective and efficient the organization is–its performance level.[11]

As an example of planning in action, consider Airbnb's policy of allowing employees to work from anywhere. CEO Brian Chesky tested his idea of "live on Airbnb" and concluded it was feasible, at least for some. He also observed that when the company's employees learned of Chesky's experience, many of them expressed a wish to do the same. In preparing the new policy, Chesky determined that it would require expenses for administering payroll and helping employees manage more complex tax preparation. The company weighed these factors against the upside of becoming a more attractive employer in the labor market and widening their pool of job candidates. They also factored in the revenue potential of pioneering this new level of remote work: Other companies facing a tight labor market might allow their employees to travel and perhaps book long-term stays through Airbnb. And the company determined that they would need to establish worthwhile objectives for people to meet during the periods they are required to be in the office.[12]

Figure 1.2
Four Functions of Management

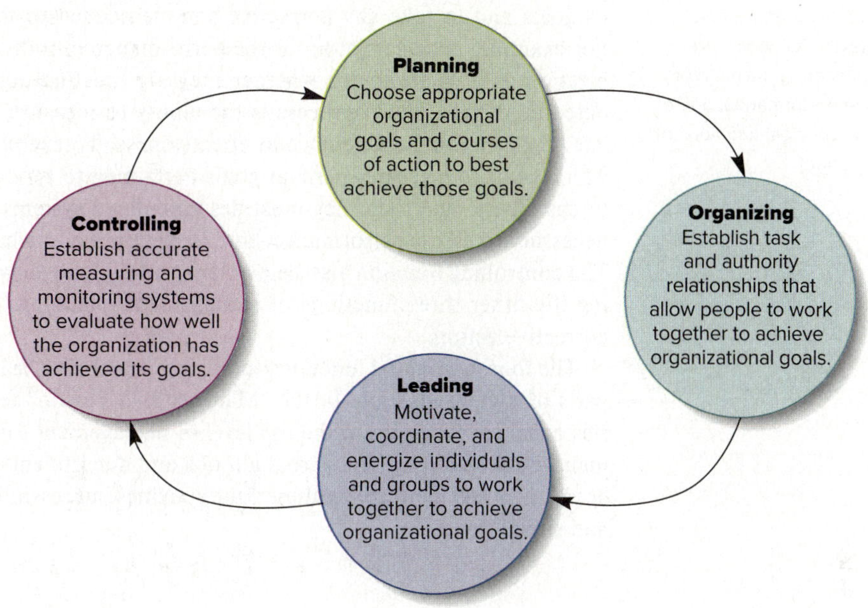

Organizing

organizing Structuring working relationships in a way that allows organizational members to work together to achieve organizational goals; one of the four principal functions of management.

organizational structure A formal system of task and reporting relationships that coordinates and motivates organizational members so they work together to achieve organizational goals.

Organizing is structuring working relationships so organizational members interact and cooperate to achieve organizational goals. Organizing people into departments according to the kinds of job-specific tasks they perform lays out the lines of authority and responsibility between different individuals and groups. Managers must decide how best to organize resources, particularly human resources.

The outcome of organizing is the creation of an **organizational structure**, a formal system of task and reporting relationships that coordinates and motivates members so they work together to achieve organizational goals. Organizational structure determines how an organization's resources can be best used to create goods and services. As discussed in "A Manager's Challenge," Airbnb's CEO realized he needed to rethink the company's organizational structure during the global pandemic when revenues plummeted because people were not traveling for business or pleasure. Consolidating departments and reducing operations to basic business functions helped Airbnb stay lean while COVID-19 vaccines were developed and the world began to slowly return to a normal way of life.[13] We examine the organizing process in detail in Chapters 10 through 12.

Leading

leading Articulating a clear vision and energizing and enabling organizational members so they understand the part they play in achieving organizational goals; one of the four principal functions of management.

An organization's *vision* is a short, succinct, and inspiring statement of what the organization intends to become and the goals it is seeking to achieve–its desired future state. In **leading**, managers articulate a clear organizational vision for the organization's members to accomplish, and they energize and enable employees so everyone understands the part they play in achieving organizational goals. Leadership involves managers using their power, personality, influence, persuasion, and communication skills to coordinate people and groups so their activities and efforts are in harmony. Leadership revolves around encouraging all employees to perform at a high level to help the organization achieve its vision and goals. Another outcome of leadership is a highly motivated and committed workforce. Airbnb's employees appreciate the core values of their leadership, especially CEO Chesky's creative way of handling the company's policy about working remotely–from anywhere. We discuss the issues involved in managing and leading individuals and groups in Chapters 13 through 16.

Controlling

controlling Evaluating how well an organization is achieving its goals and taking action to maintain or improve performance; one of the four principal functions of management.

In **controlling**, the function of managers is to evaluate how well an organization has achieved its goals and to take any corrective actions needed to maintain or improve performance. For example, managers monitor the performance of individuals, departments, and the organization as a whole to see whether they are meeting desired performance standards. The outcome of the control process is the ability to measure performance accurately and regulate organizational efficiency and effectiveness. To exercise control, managers must decide which goals to measure—perhaps goals pertaining to productivity, quality, or responsiveness to customers—and then they must design control systems that will provide the information necessary to assess performance—that is, determine to what degree the goals have been met. The controlling function also helps managers evaluate how well they themselves are performing the other three functions of management—planning, organizing, and leading—and take corrective action.

The four managerial functions—planning, organizing, leading, and controlling—are essential parts of a manager's job. In the "Manager as a Person" feature, read how Bernard Kim carries out these functions at the top level of management for Match Group. At all levels in the managerial hierarchy, and across all jobs and departments in an organization, effective management means performing these four activities successfully—in ways that increase efficiency and effectiveness.

MANAGER AS A PERSON

New CEO's Skills a Perfect Fit for Match

Bernard Kim's flexible and practical approach to planning, organizing, leading, and controlling helps guide the Match Group during challenging times.
FREDERIC J. BROWN/Getty Images

Bernard Kim is no stranger to managerial challenges, and he brings strong skills to the Match Group as the company tries to refocus its business strategies post-pandemic. Kim became the CEO of Match Group in May 2022, replacing Shar Dubey, who stepped down after two years as CEO. (Dubey remains on the company's board of directors.) The Match Group owns a portfolio of popular online dating apps, including Tinder, Match, OKCupid, and Hinge.[14]

For more than six years, Kim was president of Zynga, the mobile gaming company, famous for *Words with Friends* and *FarmVille,* with additional managerial experience as head of mobile publishing at Electronic Arts and a stint with the Walt Disney Company as director of sales and channel strategy for Disney Mobile. At Zynga, Kim was responsible for several key functions, including global marketing, consumer insights, data science, product management, and communications, which made him a top candidate for the CEO position at Match.[15]

As the world turns the corner from the global pandemic, Kim and his management team at Match are working hard to reset their planning strategies to entice more subscribers to sign up for its apps and to recover some of the share-price valuation lost over the past several years. In addition, Kim's extensive experience in mobile gaming will help Match grow its business beyond traditional matchmaking and into a potential dating metaverse—where online daters can meet in a virtual space to engage in conversations.[16]

The organizing function at Match continues to evolve. Kim recently announced that Tinder's CEO was stepping down and leaving the company after disappointing revenue results and missteps in product development. Kim also suggested the management team would take some time to review future plans for Tinder with the goal of driving sustainable growth over the next year.[17]

An important performance measure for any manager is the pace of innovation and openness to global expansion. Kim's experience preparing Zynga for expansion and acquisition by Take-Two Interactive (maker of *Grand Theft Auto*) in a recent $12 billion deal spurs him to look for business beyond the United States. For example, Match recently launched the Hinge app in Germany. Hinge has thrived in English-speaking markets outside the United States over the past few years. In addition, Match's recent acquisition of Hyperconnect, a South Korean video chat company, continues to reap rewards: paying users in Asia increased more than 12% in a recent quarter.[18]

Despite his relatively short time as Match's new CEO, Kim is quick to point out that cost controls continue to be an important part of ongoing business operations, especially in the areas of workforce and marketing expenses due to soaring inflation and the effects of a strong U.S. dollar overseas. Implementing cost controls across the organization while still looking to innovate with new products and services will help ensure the company's financial turnaround as it grows its paid subscriber base to more than 16 million worldwide.[19]

Performing Managerial Tasks: Mintzberg's Typology

So far, our discussion of management has presented it as an orderly process in which one carefully weighs information before making the best possible decision. Henry Mintzberg was one of the first to show that management is often chaotic, marked by quick decisions in a tense and sometimes emotional environment. Quick, immediate reactions to situations, rather than deliberate thought and reflection, are an important aspect of managerial action. Mintzberg, a professor at McGill University, has spent most of his life researching management in an attempt to help organizations better achieve their goals in an ethical manner. Some of his most important research examined the different roles that managers play in organizations and directly informs our discussion in this chapter. Often managers are overloaded with responsibilities, and they do not have time to analyze every nuance of a situation; they therefore make decisions in uncertain conditions, not knowing which outcomes will be best.[20] Moreover, top managers face constantly changing situations, and a decision that seems right today may prove to be wrong tomorrow. The range of problems that managers face is enormous; managers usually must handle many problems simultaneously, and they often must make snap decisions using the intuition and experience gained through their careers to perform their jobs to the best of their abilities.[21] Henry Mintzberg, by following managers and observing what they actually *do* hour by hour and day by day, identified 10 kinds of specific roles, or sets of job responsibilities, that capture the dynamic nature of managerial work.[22] He grouped these roles according to whether the responsibility is primarily decisional, interpersonal, or informational; they are described in Table 1.1.

Given the many complex, difficult job responsibilities managers have, it is no small wonder that many claim they are performing their jobs well if they are right just half of the time.[23] And it is understandable that many experienced managers accept their employees' failure as a normal part of the learning experience and a rite of passage to becoming an effective manager. Managers and their employees learn from both their successes and their failures.

Table 1.1
Managerial Roles Identified by Mintzberg

Type of Role	Specific Role	Examples of Role Activities
Decisional	Entrepreneur	Commit organizational resources to develop innovative goods and services; decide to expand internationally to obtain new customers for the organization's products.
	Disturbance handler	Move quickly to take corrective action to deal with unexpected problems facing the organization from the external environment, such as a crisis like an oil spill, or from the internal environment, such as producing faulty goods or services.
	Resource allocator	Allocate organizational resources among different tasks and departments of the organization; set budgets and salaries of middle and first-level managers.
	Negotiator	Work with suppliers, distributors, and labor unions to reach agreements about the quality and price of input, technical, and human resources; work with other organizations to establish agreements to pool resources to work on joint projects.
Interpersonal	Figurehead	Outline future organizational goals to employees at company meetings; open a new corporate headquarters building; state the organization's ethical guidelines and the principles of behavior employees are to follow in their dealings with customers and suppliers.
	Leader	Provide an example for employees to follow; give direct commands and orders to employees; make decisions concerning the use of human and technical resources; mobilize employee support for specific organizational goals.
	Liaison	Coordinate the work of managers in different departments; establish alliances between different organizations to share resources to produce new goods and services.
Informational	Monitor	Evaluate the performance of managers in different tasks and take corrective action to improve their performance; watch for changes occurring in the external and internal environments that may affect the organization in the future.
	Disseminator	Inform employees about changes taking place in the external and internal environments that will affect them and the organization; communicate to employees the organization's vision and purpose.
	Spokesperson	Launch a national advertising campaign to promote new goods and services; give a speech to inform the local community about the organization's future intentions.

Levels and Skills of Managers

To perform the four managerial functions efficiently and effectively, organizations group or differentiate their managers in two main ways—by level in hierarchy and by type of skill. First, they differentiate managers according to their level or rank in the organization's hierarchy of authority. The three levels of managers are first-line managers, middle managers, and top managers—arranged in a hierarchy. Typically, first-line managers report to middle managers, and middle managers report to top managers.

Second, organizations group managers into different departments (or functions) according to their specific job-related skills, expertise, and experiences, such as a manager's engineering

department A group of people who work together and possess similar skills or use the same knowledge, tools, or techniques to perform their jobs.

skills, marketing expertise, or sales experience. A **department**, such as the manufacturing, accounting, engineering, or sales department, is a group of managers and employees who work together because they possess similar skills and experience or use the same kind of knowledge, tools, or techniques to perform their jobs. Within each department are all three levels of management. Next we examine why organizations use a hierarchy of managers and group them, by the jobs they perform, into departments.

Levels of Management

LO1-3 Differentiate among three levels of management, and understand the tasks and responsibilities of managers at different levels in the organizational hierarchy.

Organizations normally have three levels of management: first-line managers, middle managers, and top managers (see Figure 1.3). Managers at each level have different but related responsibilities for using organizational resources to increase efficiency and effectiveness.

At the base of the managerial hierarchy are **first-line managers**, often called *supervisors*. They are responsible for daily supervision of the nonmanagerial employees who perform the specific activities necessary to produce goods and services. First-line managers work in all departments or functions of an organization. Examples of first-line managers include the supervisor of a work team in the manufacturing department of a car plant, the head nurse in the obstetrics department of a hospital, and the chief mechanic overseeing a crew of mechanics in the service function of a new car dealership.

first-line manager A manager who is responsible for the daily supervision of nonmanagerial employees.

middle manager A manager who supervises first-line managers and is responsible for finding the best way to use resources to achieve organizational goals.

Supervising the first-line managers are **middle managers**, responsible for finding the best way to organize human and other resources to achieve organizational goals. To increase efficiency, middle managers find ways to help first-line managers and nonmanagerial employees better use resources to reduce manufacturing costs or improve customer service. To increase effectiveness, middle managers evaluate whether the organization's goals are appropriate and suggest to top managers how goals should be changed. Often the suggestions that middle managers make to top managers can dramatically increase organizational performance. A major part of the middle manager's job is developing and fine-tuning skills and know-how, such as manufacturing or marketing expertise, that allow the organization to be efficient and effective. Middle managers make thousands of specific decisions about the production of goods and services: Which first-line supervisors should be chosen for this particular project? Where can we find the highest-quality resources? How should employees be organized to allow them to make the best use of resources?

Figure 1.3
Levels of Managers

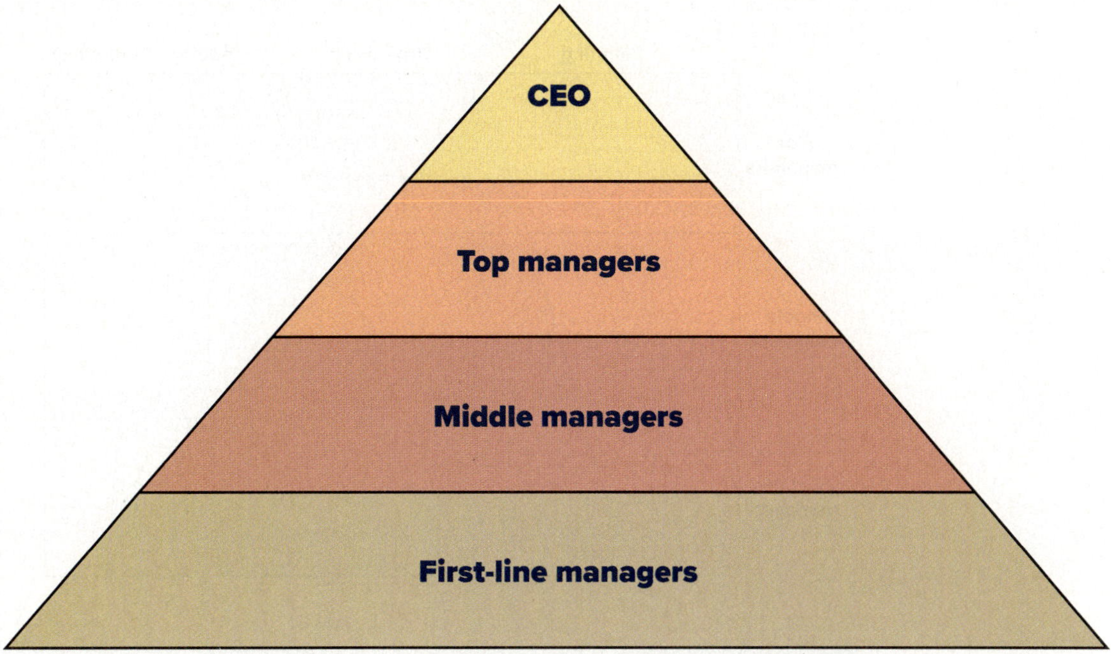

Behind a top-notch sales force, look for the middle managers responsible for training, motivating, and rewarding the salespeople. Behind a committed staff of high school teachers, look for the principal who energizes them to find ways to obtain the resources they need to do outstanding and innovative jobs in the classroom.

top manager A manager who establishes organizational goals, decides how departments should interact, and monitors the performance of middle managers.

In contrast to middle managers, **top managers** are responsible for the performance of *all* departments. They have *cross-departmental responsibility.* Top managers establish organizational goals, such as which goods and services the company should produce; they decide how the different departments should interact; and they monitor how well middle managers in each department use resources to achieve goals.[24] Top managers are ultimately responsible for the success or failure of an organization, and their performance is continually scrutinized by people inside and outside the organization, such as other employees and investors.[25]

The *chief executive officer (CEO)* is a company's most senior and important manager, the one all other top managers report to. Today the term *chief operating officer (COO)* often refers to top managers who are being groomed to assume CEO responsibilities when the current CEO retires, leaves the company, or assumes other responsibilities. Together the CEO and COO are responsible for developing good working relationships among the top managers of various departments (manufacturing and marketing, for example); usually, these top managers have the title "vice president." A central concern of the CEO is the creation of a smoothly functioning **top management team**, a group composed of the CEO, the COO, and the vice presidents most responsible for achieving organizational goals.[26]

top management team A group composed of the CEO, the COO, and the vice presidents most responsible for achieving organizational goals.

The relative importance of planning, organizing, leading, and controlling–the four principal managerial functions–to any manager depends on the manager's position in the managerial hierarchy.[27] The amount of time managers spend planning and organizing resources to maintain and improve organizational performance increases as they ascend the hierarchy (see Figure 1.4).[28] Top managers devote most of their time to planning and organizing, the functions so crucial to determining an organization's long-term performance. The lower managers' positions are in the hierarchy, the more time they spend leading and controlling first-line managers or nonmanagerial employees.

Figure 1.4

Relative Amount of Time Managers Spend on the Four Managerial Functions

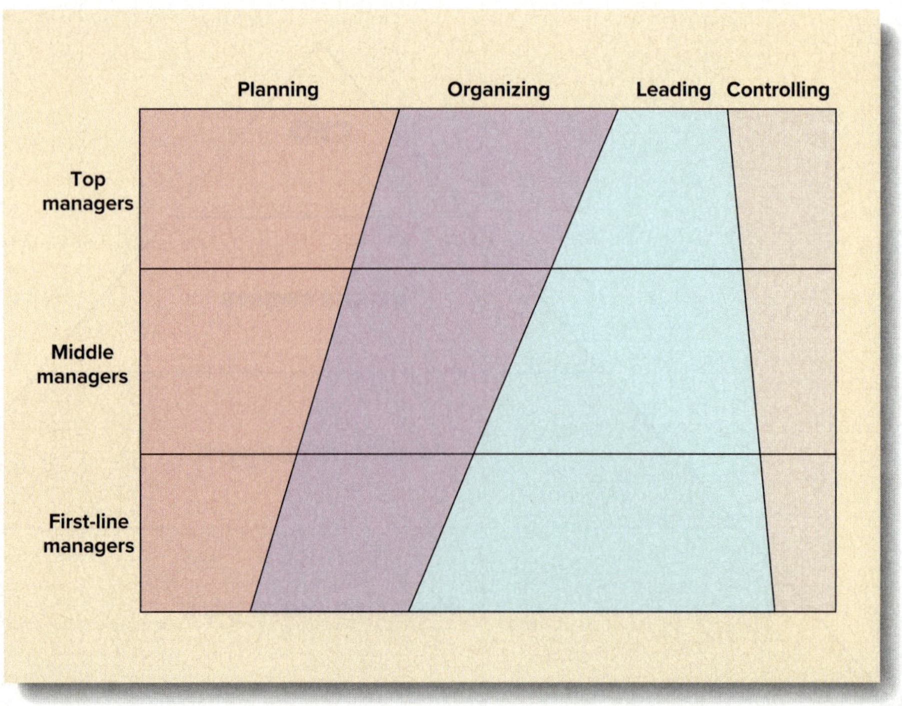

Types of Managerial Skills

LO1-4 Distinguish among three kinds of managerial skill, and explain why managers are divided into different departments to perform their tasks more efficiently and effectively.

Both education and experience enable managers to recognize and develop the personal skills they need to put organizational resources to their best use. Research has shown that education and experience help managers acquire and develop three types of skills: *conceptual, human,* and *technical.*[29]

Conceptual skills are demonstrated in the general ability to analyze and diagnose a situation and to distinguish between cause and effect. Top managers require the best conceptual skills because their primary responsibilities are planning and organizing.[30] Managers like Brian Chesky must constantly identify new opportunities and mobilize organizational resources to take advantage of those opportunities.

conceptual skills The ability to analyze and diagnose a situation and to distinguish between cause and effect.

Formal education and training are important in helping managers develop conceptual skills. Business training at the undergraduate and graduate (MBA) levels provides many of the conceptual tools (theories and techniques in marketing, finance, and other areas) that managers need to perform their roles effectively. The study of management helps develop the skills that allow managers to understand the big picture confronting an organization. The ability to focus on the big picture lets managers see beyond the immediate situation and consider choices while keeping in mind the organization's long-term goals. To learn how a business owner in Ghana developed and used impressive conceptual skills, see the "Managing Globally" feature.

MANAGING GLOBALLY

Blue Power CEO Is Fueling Ghana's Growth

Ghanaian businesswoman Salma Okonkwo is CEO of Blue Power Energy, which she started in 2018 to bring renewable energy to her home country. Before Blue Power, Okonkwo founded UBI Group, an oil and gas distribution company, where she now chairs the board of directors (which oversees the company's performance). Her career journey to UBI and Blue Power reflect her vision of contributing to the sustainable development of Ghana. Okonkwo observed that foreign investors in Ghana and other African countries often established operations to extract resources from these countries without investing in infrastructure that could build wealth within them. Okonkwo determined that she would, through her determination and skills, provide some of that infrastructure.[31]

Like most business managers, Okonkwo developed her skills through a combination of formal and informal learning. At age 18, she left Ghana to attend Loyola Marymount University in the United States, where she earned a degree in business. She worked through college and afterward, seeing business opportunities whenever she returned home for visits. After several years, she received the job offer that would enable her return (with her husband and children) to Ghana: Sahara Group, an energy and infrastructure corporation, hired her to work on importing and selling crude oil. She took the position to learn about meeting energy needs but chafed at her employer's reluctance to consider her ideas for infrastructure investments and cleaner fuels.[32]

Then, taking what she had learned in school and at Sahara Group, Okonkwo started her own company, UBI Group, aiming to distribute liquefied petroleum gas (LPG), which pollutes less than gasoline. However, she found that the infrastructure did not exist in her intended markets, so she pivoted to distributing gasoline. Revenues began flowing in, but profits were less than expected. An investigation uncovered poor oversight that taught Okonkwo lessons about policies, procedures, and controls for hiring and accounting. Reforms put the company on a more solid footing, eventually enabling UBI to invest in LPG infrastructure. Okonkwo found a company interested in purchasing a large stake in UBI, which freed Okonkwo to start a business that truly fits her aspirations for herself and her country: Blue Power, which is building solar power installations to make affordable, sustainable energy available in the long term. She anticipates that her business can help her country build industrial strength without some of the environmental consequences endured during earlier waves of industrialization.[33]

Today continuing management education and training, including training in advanced technology, are an integral part of building managerial skills because new theories and techniques are constantly being developed to improve organizational effectiveness, such as total quality management, global supply chain management, and cloud computing and virtual business-to-business (B2B) networks. A quick scan through a magazine such as *Bloomberg Businessweek* or *Fortune* reveals a host of seminars on topics such as advanced marketing, finance, leadership, and human resource management that are offered to managers at many levels in the organization, from the most senior corporate executives to middle managers. Microsoft, IBM, Oracle, and many other organizations designate a portion of each manager's personal budget to be used at the manager's discretion to attend management development programs.

In addition, organizations may wish to develop a particular manager's abilities in a specific skill area–perhaps to learn an advanced component of departmental skills, such as international bond trading, or to learn the skills necessary to implement a total quality management program or to develop systems for the use of artificial intelligence (AI) in business operations. The organization thus pays for managers to attend specialized programs to develop these skills. Indeed, one signal that a manager is performing well is an organization's willingness to invest in that manager's skill development. Similarly, many nonmanagerial employees who are performing at a high level (because they have studied management) are often sent to intensive management training programs to develop their management skills and to prepare them for promotion to first-level management positions.

human skills The ability to understand, alter, lead, and control the behavior of other individuals and groups.

Human skills include the general ability to understand, alter, lead, and control the behavior of other individuals and groups. The ability to communicate, to coordinate, to motivate, and to mold individuals into a cohesive team distinguishes effective from ineffective managers. Like conceptual skills, human skills can be learned through education and training and developed through experience.[34] Organizations increasingly use advanced programs in leadership skills and team leadership as they seek to capitalize on the advantages of self-managed teams.[35] To manage personal interactions effectively, each person in an organization must learn how to empathize with other people–to understand their viewpoints and the problems they face. One way to help managers to understand their personal strengths and weaknesses is to have their superiors, peers, and employees provide feedback about their job performance. Thorough and direct feedback allows managers to develop their human skills.

technical skills The job-specific knowledge and techniques required to perform an organizational role.

Technical skills are the *job-specific* skills required to perform a particular type of work or occupation at a high level. Examples include a manager's specific manufacturing, accounting, marketing, and technological skills. Managers need a range of technical skills to be effective. The array of technical skills managers need depends on their position in their organizations. The manager of a restaurant, for example, may need cooking skills to fill in for an absent cook, accounting and bookkeeping skills to keep track of receipts and costs and to administer the payroll, and aesthetic skills to keep the restaurant looking attractive for customers.

As noted earlier, managers and employees who possess the same kinds of technical skills typically become members of a specific department and are known as, for example, marketing managers or manufacturing managers.[36] Managers are grouped into different departments because a major part of a manager's responsibility is to monitor, train, and supervise employees so their job-specific skills and expertise increase. Obviously this is easier to do when employees with similar skills are grouped into the same department because they can learn from one another and become more skilled and productive at their jobs.

To be a successful manager, individuals need to develop their conceptual, human, and technical skills.
Erik Isakson/Getty Images

Figure 1.5 shows how an organization groups managers into departments on the basis of their job-specific skills. It also shows that inside each department, a managerial hierarchy of first-line, middle, and top managers emerges. These managers work together on similar tasks in departments. For example, middle and frontline managers may specialize in areas such as marketing and sales, human resource management, accounting, engineering, or production. When the

Figure 1.5
Types and Levels of Managers

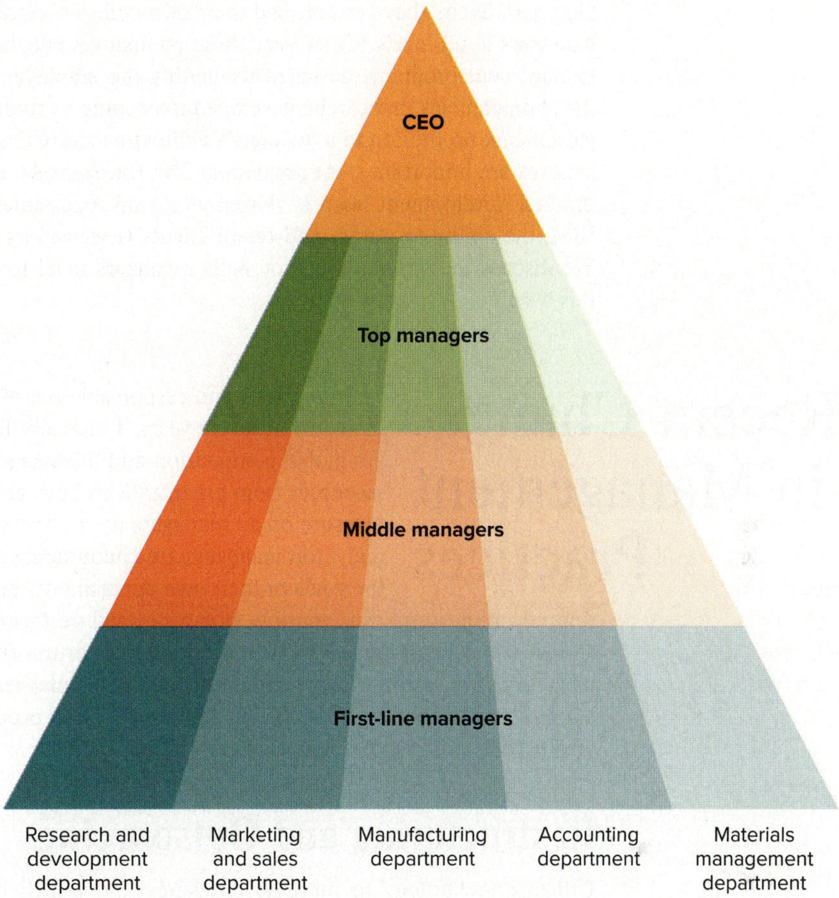

head of manufacturing finds that they have no time to supervise computer assembly, they may recruit experienced manufacturing middle managers from other companies to assume this responsibility.

core competency The specific set of departmental skills, knowledge, and experience that allows one organization to outperform another.

Today the term **core competency** is often used to refer to the specific set of departmental skills, knowledge, and experience that allows one organization to outperform its competitors. In other words, departmental skills that create a core competency give an organization a *competitive advantage.* Dell, for example, was the first PC maker to develop a core competency in materials management that allowed it to produce PCs at a much lower cost than its competitors–a major source of competitive advantage. Google is well known for its core competency in research and development (R&D) that allows it to innovate new products and services at a faster rate than its competitors. From AI to self-driving cars, Google has been pioneering the development of technology for the masses.

Effective managers need all three kinds of skills–conceptual, human, and technical–to help their organizations perform more efficiently and effectively. The absence of even one type of managerial skill can lead to failure. One of the biggest problems that people who start small businesses confront, for example, is their lack of appropriate conceptual and human skills. Someone who has the technical skills to start a new business does not necessarily know how to manage the venture successfully. Similarly, one of the biggest problems that scientists or engineers who switch careers from research to management confront is their lack of effective human skills. Ambitious managers or prospective managers are constantly in search of the latest educational contributions to help them develop the conceptual, human, and technical skills they need to perform at a high level in today's changing and increasingly competitive global environment.

Developing new and improved skills through education and training has become a priority for both aspiring managers and the organizations they work for. Many people are enrolling in advanced management courses, and many companies–such as Walgreens, Enterprise, and Goldman Sachs–have established their own colleges to train and develop their employees and managers at all levels. Every year these companies put thousands of their employees through management programs designed to identify the employees whom the company believes have the competencies that can be developed to become its future top managers. Most organizations closely link promotion to a manager's ability to acquire the competencies a particular company believes are important.[37] At Apple and 3M, for example, the ability to successfully lead a new product development team is viewed as a vital requirement for promotion; at Accenture and IBM, the ability to attract and retain clients is viewed as a skill its consultants must possess. We discuss the various kinds of skills managers need to develop in most of the chapters of this book.

Recent Changes in Management Practices

The functions and responsibilities of managers have been changing dramatically in recent years. Two major factors that have led to these changes are global competition and advances in technology. Stiff competition for resources from organizations both at home and abroad has put increased pressure on all managers to improve efficiency and effectiveness. Increasingly, top managers are encouraging lower-level managers to look beyond the goals of their own departments and take a cross-departmental view to find new opportunities to improve organizational performance. Technology gives managers at all levels and in all areas access to more and better information and improves their ability to plan, organize, lead, and control. It also gives employees more job-related information and allows them to become more skilled, specialized, and productive, which can lead to increased employee engagement.[38]

Restructuring and Outsourcing

Utilizing technology to increase efficiency and effectiveness, CEOs and top management teams have restructured organizations and outsourced specific organizational activities to reduce the number of employees on the payroll and make more productive use of the remaining workforce.

restructuring Downsizing an organization by eliminating the jobs of large numbers of top, middle, and first-line managers and nonmanagerial employees.

Restructuring involves simplifying, shrinking, or downsizing an organization's operations to lower operating costs, as Macy's, 3M, and Airbnb have been forced to do. The global pandemic in 2020 forced most companies–large and small, and profit and nonprofit–to find ways to reduce costs because their customers spent less money, so their revenues decreased. Restructuring can be done by eliminating product teams, shrinking departments, and reducing levels in the hierarchy, all of which result in the loss of large numbers of jobs of top, middle, or first-line managers, as well as nonmanagerial employees. Technology's ability to improve efficiency has increased the amount of downsizing in recent years because technology makes it possible for fewer employees to perform a given task. Technology also increases each person's ability to process information and make decisions more quickly and accurately, for example. In 2023, global spending on technology is projected to top $4.6 trillion, including increased spending on digital technologies to improve overall efficiency and effectiveness.[39] We discuss the many effects of information technology on management in Chapter 18 and throughout the book.

Restructuring, however, can produce some powerful negative outcomes. It can reduce the morale of remaining employees, who worry about their own job security or become frustrated with management's inability to hire additional help and look elsewhere for new jobs. And top managers of many downsized organizations realize that they have downsized too far when their employees complain they are overworked and when increasing numbers of customers complain about poor service.[40]

outsourcing Contracting with another company, usually abroad, to have it perform an activity the organization previously performed itself.

Outsourcing involves contracting with another company, usually in a low-cost country abroad, to have it perform a work activity the organization previously performed itself, such as manufacturing, marketing, or customer service. Outsourcing increases efficiency because it lowers operating costs, freeing up money and resources that can be used in more effective ways–for example, to develop new products.

Low-cost global competition dramatically increased outsourcing in the early 2000s, and that trend continues today. The Philippines, India, and Malaysia are rated as the top outsourcing countries. Companies primarily sent jobs offshore to control costs and gain access to unavailable resources while freeing up internal ones. Thousands of high-paying technology jobs have also moved abroad, to countries such as India, Ukraine, and China, where programmers work for one-third the salary of those in the United States.[41]

empowerment The expansion of employees' knowledge, tasks, and decision-making responsibilities.

self-managed work teams Groups of employees who assume responsibility for organizing, controlling, and supervising their own activities and monitoring the quality of the goods and services they provide.

Large for-profit organizations today typically employ 10–20% fewer people than they did 10 years ago because of restructuring, outsourcing, and advances in new technologies. Ford, IBM, AT&T, and Amazon are among the thousands of organizations that have streamlined their operations to increase efficiency and effectiveness. The argument is that the managers and employees who have lost their jobs will find employment in new and growing U.S. companies where their skills and experience will be better utilized. For example, the millions of manufacturing jobs that have been lost overseas will be replaced by higher-paying U.S. jobs in the service sector, which are made possible because of the growth in global trade. At the same time, many companies continue to experience outsourcing problems in Asia, as well as increasing wages in that part of the world.

Empowerment and Self-Managed Teams

LO1-5 Discuss some major changes in management practices today that have occurred as a result of globalization and the use of advanced technologies.

The second principal way managers have sought to increase efficiency and effectiveness is by empowering lower-level employees and moving to self-managed teams. **Empowerment** is a management technique that involves giving employees more authority and responsibility over how they perform their work activities. Many companies, from startups to well-established organizations, have embraced empowerment as a key corporate strategy. One by-product of fostering an empowered workforce may include a flatter organizational structure. For example, Valve Corporation, a billion-dollar company in Bellevue, Washington, does not believe in managers. Started more than 20 years ago, Valve is a video game developer that has gained a reputation for a dynamic organizational culture. At Valve, there is no hierarchy or top-down control, and innovation permeates the company environment. There is no "reporting" structure at Valve, and employees pick their own projects, which typically are high profile and complex. While this may seem daunting to some employees, others thrive in this environment in which they are empowered to be the CEOs of their own work. In addition, bonuses, hirings, and firings are all determined by peer review, not managers.[42]

At Valve Corporation in Bellevue, Washington, there are no managers and no reporting structure. Employees are encouraged to become the CEOs of their own work.
Adam Hester/Blend Images

The use of technology increasingly empowers employees because it expands employees' job knowledge and broadens the scope of their job responsibilities. Often technology allows one employee to perform a task that was previously performed by several employees. As a result, the employee has more autonomy and responsibilities. Technology has also expanded the use of **self-managed work teams**, groups of employees who assume collective responsibility for organizing, supervising, and controlling their own work activities. Using technology provides team members with real-time information about each member's performance and helps the team accomplish a task more quickly and effectively. In addition, self-managed teams assume many tasks and responsibilities previously performed by first-line managers, so a company can better utilize its workforce.[43] With self-managed teams, first-line managers act as coaches or mentors whose job is not to tell employees what to do, but to provide advice and guidance and to help teams find new ways to perform their tasks more efficiently. Using the same technology, middle managers can easily monitor what is happening in these teams and make better decisions regarding resource allocation and the workforce.

remote workers Employees who work from their homes or other outside workspaces on a regular basis.

A related trend is the use of **remote workers** by organizations. These are usually employees of a company who work outside of the office several times a week, if not the entire workweek. Working remotely has become commonplace for many employees as a result of the COVID-19 pandemic. When companies sent their employees home to work early in 2020, they soon found out that overall productivity increased, and many workers decided they would rather work remotely than commute to corporate offices on a daily basis. According to recent statistics, before the pandemic nearly 75% of the U.S. workforce did not work remotely at all, with only 6% primarily working from home. As the pandemic started to fade in 2022, many organizations started to reopen their offices; however, many workers balked at returning to the office. A 2022 survey by Pew Research Center suggests that nearly 60% of U.S. workers prefer to work remotely because they believe they are more productive and because it provides better work-life balance. In contrast, the same survey also reveals that 60% of workers believe working from home has made them feel less connected to coworkers.[44]

Challenges for Management in a Global Environment

LO1-6 Discuss the principal challenges managers face in today's increasingly competitive global environment.

Because the world continues to change more rapidly than ever before, managers and other employees throughout an organization must perform at higher and higher levels. In the last 20 years, rivalry between organizations competing domestically (in the same country) and globally (in countries abroad) has increased dramatically. The rise of **global organizations**, organizations that operate and compete in more than one country, has pressured many organizations to identify better ways to use their resources and improve their performance. The successes of the German pharmaceutical conglomerate Bayer, Italian furniture manufacturer Natuzzi, Korean electronics companies Samsung and LG, Brazilian plane maker Embraer, and Europe's Airbus Industries are putting pressure on companies in other countries to raise their level of performance to compete successfully against these global organizations.

global organizations Organizations that operate and compete in more than one country.

Even in the not-for-profit sector, global competition is spurring change. Schools, universities, police forces, and government agencies are reexamining their operations because looking at how activities are performed in other countries often reveals better ways to do them. For example, many curriculum and teaching changes in the United States have resulted from the study of methods that Japanese and European school systems use. Similarly, European and Asian health care systems have learned much from the U.S. system—which may be the most effective, though not the most efficient, in the world.

Today managers who make no attempt to learn from and adapt to changes in the global environment find themselves reacting rather than innovating, and their organizations often become uncompetitive and fail. Five major challenges stand out for managers in today's world: building a competitive advantage, maintaining ethical standards, managing a diverse workforce, utilizing new information systems and technologies, and practicing global crisis management.

Building Competitive Advantage

What are the most important lessons for managers and organizations to learn if they are to reach and remain at the top of the competitive environment of business? The answer relates to the use of organizational resources to build a competitive advantage. **Competitive advantage** is the ability of one organization to outperform other organizations because it produces desired goods or services more efficiently and effectively than its competitors. The four building blocks of competitive advantage are superior *efficiency, quality, innovation and flexibility,* and *responsiveness to customers,* as Figure 1.6 shows.

competitive advantage The ability of one organization to outperform other organizations because it produces desired goods or services more efficiently and effectively than they do.

Organizations increase their efficiency when they reduce the quantity of resources (such as people and raw materials) they use to produce goods or services. In today's competitive environment, organizations continually search for new ways to use their resources to improve efficiency.

Figure 1.6
Building Blocks of Competitive Advantage

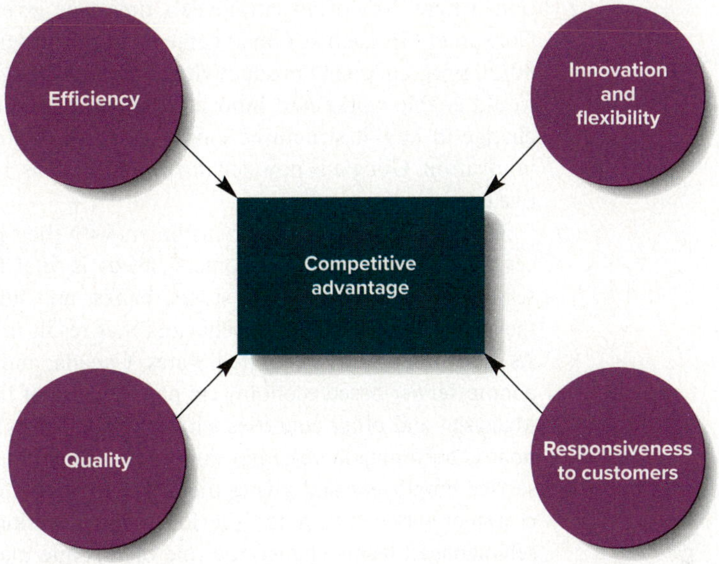

Many organizations are training their workforces in the new skills and techniques needed to operate heavily computerized assembly plants. Similarly, cross-training gives employees the range of skills they need to perform many different tasks, and organizing employees in new ways, such as in self-managed teams, lets them make good use of their skills. These are important steps in the effort to improve productivity. Japanese and German companies invest far more in training employees than do American or Italian companies.

Managers must improve efficiency if their organizations are to compete successfully with companies operating in Mexico, Malaysia, and other countries where employees are paid comparatively low wages. New methods must be devised either to increase efficiency or to gain some other competitive advantage–higher-quality goods, for example–if outsourcing and the loss of jobs to low-cost countries are to be prevented.

The challenge from global organizations such as Korean electronics manufacturers, Mexican agricultural producers, and European design and financial companies also has increased pressure on companies to develop the skills and abilities of their workforces in order to improve the quality of their goods and services. One strategy to improving quality has been to introduce the quality-enhancing techniques known as *total quality management (TQM).* Employees involved in TQM are often organized into quality control teams and are responsible for finding new and better ways to perform their jobs; they also must monitor and evaluate the quality of the goods they produce. We discuss ways of managing TQM successfully in Chapter 9.

Today companies can win or lose the competitive race depending on their *speed*–how fast they can bring new products to market–or their *flexibility*–how easily they can change or alter the way they perform their activities to respond to actions of their competitors. Companies that have speed and flexibility are agile competitors: Their managers have superior planning and organizing abilities; they can think ahead, decide what to do, and then speedily mobilize their resources to respond to a changing environment. We examine how managers can build speed and flexibility in their organizations in later chapters. Agile companies are adept at responding to changes in their environments, including change from technological, regulatory, and economic sources.

innovation The process of creating new or improved goods and services or developing better ways to produce or provide them.

Innovation, the process of creating new or improved goods and services that customers want or developing better ways to produce or provide goods and services, poses a special challenge. Managers must create an organizational setting in which people are encouraged to be innovative. Typically, innovation takes place in small groups or teams; management decentralizes control of work activities to team members and creates an organizational culture that rewards risk taking. Innovation doesn't happen by itself; companies have to devote resources that enable innovation. These investments are a delicate balancing act. Consider Google. More than a decade ago, Google won praise for its 80/20 work allocation, where 20% of an employee's time was given to work on individual "pet projects." Consumer hits such as Gmail came from this program. But the company has eliminated the 80/20 program due to productivity concerns. Google had banked on the idea that slack time would enable workers to innovate, but economic realities and productivity needs meant a change in how it structured employee work. Instead of a more autonomous approach to innovation, Google is now relying on its X lab as a formal means of maintaining a competitive edge.[45]

Organizations compete for customers with their products and services, so training employees to be responsive to customers' needs is vital for all organizations, but particularly for service organizations. Retail stores, banks, and hospitals, for example, depend entirely on their employees to perform behaviors that result in high-quality service at a reasonable cost. As many countries (the United States, Canada, and Switzerland are just a few) move toward a more service-based economy (in part because of the loss of manufacturing jobs to Vietnam, Malaysia, and other countries with low labor costs), managing behavior in service organizations is becoming increasingly important. Many organizations are empowering their customer service employees and giving them the authority to take the lead in providing high-quality customer service. As noted previously, empowering nonmanagerial employees and creating self-managed teams change the role of first-line managers and lead to more efficient use of organizational resources.

turnaround management
The creation of a new vision for a struggling company based on a new approach to planning and organizing to make better use of a company's resources and allow it to survive and prosper.

Sometimes the best efforts of managers to revitalize their organizations' fortunes fail; faced with bankruptcy, the directors of these companies are forced to appoint a new CEO who has a history of success in rebuilding a company. **Turnaround management** is the creation of a new vision for a struggling company using a new approach to planning and organizing to make better use of a company's resources and allow it to survive and eventually prosper—something Apple's Steve Jobs excelled at. It involves developing radical new strategies, such as how to reduce the number of products sold or change how they are made and distributed, or closing corporate and manufacturing operations to reduce costs. Organizations that appoint turnaround CEOs are generally experiencing a crisis because they have become inefficient or ineffective; sometimes this is because of ineffective management over a continuing period, or sometimes it occurs because a competitor introduces a new product or technology that makes their own products unattractive to customers. For example, fast-casual food chain Chipotle was flying high until food-safety scares in recent years caused the company to lose customers, market share, and consumers' confidence in the chain's reputation for quality. Founder and CEO Steve Ells, who ran the chain since its start in 1993, stepped aside as CEO in 2018 and moved into the chairperson's role until he left the company altogether in 2020. Ells was replaced by Brian Niccol, former CEO of Taco Bell. Under Niccol's guidance, Chipotle has made a strong comeback, with its stock trading at an all-time high, same-store sales accelerating quarter after quarter, and consumers feeling confident the chain has overcome its food-safety issues.[46]

Achieving a competitive advantage requires that managers use all their skills and expertise, as well as their companies' other resources, to find new and better ways to improve efficiency, quality, innovation, and responsiveness to customers. We revisit this theme often as we examine the ways managers plan strategies, organize resources and activities, and lead and control people and groups to increase efficiency and effectiveness.

Maintaining Ethical and Socially Responsible Standards

Managers at all levels are under considerable pressure to make the best use of resources to increase the level at which their organizations perform.[47] For example, top managers feel pressure from shareholders to increase the performance of the entire organization to boost its stock price, improve profits, or raise dividends. In turn, top managers may pressure middle managers to find new ways to use organizational resources to increase efficiency or quality and, thus, attract new customers and earn more revenues–and then middle managers pressure their departments' supervisors.

Pressure to increase performance can be healthy for an organization because it leads managers to question how the organization is working, and it encourages them to find new and better ways to plan, organize, lead, and control. However, too much pressure to perform can be harmful. It may induce managers to behave unethically, and even illegally, when dealing with people and groups inside and outside the organization.[48]

A purchasing manager for a nationwide retail chain, for example, might buy inferior clothing as a cost-cutting measure or ignore the working conditions under which products are made to obtain low-priced products. These issues faced the managers of companies that made footwear and clothing in the 1990s, when customers learned about the unfair conditions in which garment and shoe workers around the world labored. Today companies such as Nike, Walmart, and Apple are trying to stop sweatshop practices and prevent managers abroad from adopting work practices that harm their workers. They now employ hundreds of inspectors who police the overseas factories that make the products they sell and who can terminate contracts with suppliers when they behave in an unethical or illegal way.

Similarly, to secure a large foreign contract, a sales manager in a large company, such as in the defense or electronics industry, might offer bribes to foreign officials to obtain lucrative contracts–even though this is against the law. For example, Airbus recently paid more than $3.9 billion to the United States, United Kingdom, and French authorities for bribing government officials and airplane executives around the world. Other companies, such as Goldman Sachs, Novartis Pharmaceuticals, and Glencore have paid millions in penalties to resolve international bribery charges.[49]

The temptation to gain from practices such as these can get companies into legal trouble. Harmful and illegal actions also can hurt a company's reputation with its suppliers and customers, as well as with the communities in which it operates. Furthermore, people of good character do not want to manage or work for such organizations. For all of these reasons, organizations need managers who will uphold ethical standards, as will be described in Chapter 3.

The issue of social responsibility, discussed in Chapter 4, centers on deciding what obligations a company has toward the people and groups affected by its activities–such as employees, customers, or the cities in which it operates. Some companies have strong views about social responsibility; their managers believe they should protect the interests of others. Socially responsible companies put this view into action when they set goals for reducing wasted resources and pollution, treating workers with dignity and respect, and promoting community development.

Managing a Diverse Workforce

A major challenge for managers everywhere is to recognize the ethical need and legal requirement to treat human resources fairly and equitably. Today the age, gender, race, ethnicity, religion, sexual orientation, and socioeconomic composition of the workforce presents new challenges for managers. To create a highly trained and motivated workforce, as well as to avoid lawsuits, managers must establish human resource management (HRM) procedures and practices that are legal and fair and do not discriminate against any organizational members.[50] Today most organizations understand that to motivate effectively and take advantage of the talents of a diverse workforce, they must make promotion opportunities available to every employee. Managers must recognize the performance-enhancing possibilities of a diverse workforce, such as the ability to take advantage of the skills and experiences of different kinds of people from different generations.[51] Laura Miele's career illustrates the value of a manager who both promotes and embodies diversity in the electronic game industry. See the "Focus on DEI&B" feature for more information.

FOCUS ON DEI&B

A Bold Model for Diversity in Video Games

Laura Miele, whom *Businessweek* called "the most powerful woman in gaming," says the excitement of her career has outweighed its awkward moments.[52] Miele has loved games since she played board games as a child in Northern California. When she left college for a position as a project manager for video game developer Westwood Studios, coworkers expected her to take notes during meetings and clean up the table after they adjourned. Nevertheless, Miele was so enthusiastic about contributing to a great game-playing experience that she persevered and won greater authority as she learned to speak up for herself. She told an interviewer, "It has been the passion and engagement of our players that has kept me in the industry."[53] Notably, almost half of those players are female.

As one of the few female executives in video game development, EA's Laura Miele continues to lead efforts to increase diversity in the company's workforce and its video games.
Eugene Gologursky/Getty Images

A fast learner and bold innovator, Miele made a significant impact, eventually running the company's marketing efforts. In 1998, Electronic Arts (EA) acquired Westwood and tasked Miele with improving decision making. Her team replaced monthly forecasts based on handmade spreadsheets with advanced analytics that could create alternative scenarios on demand. Another transformation came years later when Miele noted a mismatch between advertising budgets and buying behavior. While 80% of EA's ad spending went to TV ads, gamers were online, not watching television. She slashed TV's share of ad spending for *Battlefield 3* to 30%, redirecting the money to digital. Some executives fretted, but when *Battlefield 3* became EA's fastest-selling game, Miele's daring move became the standard. With these and other successes, Miele moved up to chief studios officer and then to the number-two role, chief operating officer, managing more than 25 studios creating products for half a billion players worldwide.[54]

As one of the few female executives in video game development, Miele sees the need for equity and inclusion firsthand. She has led efforts to increase diversity in EA's workforce and its games. She founded the EA Women's Ultimate Team, an employee resource group focused on gender diversity and equity.[55] Throughout Miele's career, several people took an interest in her, modeled leadership skills, and advocated for her, and she now wants to offer others access to similar mentoring, including EA's support for organizations like Black Girls Code and Girls Who Code. As Miele describes it, her outlook has evolved from planning her own career to investing in her team's and company's success.[56]

A company known for leveraging the potential of its diverse workforce is Accenture, a global management consulting company that serves the needs of thousands of client companies in over 120 countries around the world. A major driving force behind Accenture's core organizational vision is to manage and promote diversity in order to improve employee performance and client satisfaction. At Accenture, managers at all levels realize their consultants bring distinct experiences, talents, and values to their work, and a major management initiative is to take advantage of that diversity to encourage collaboration between consultants to

Global management consulting firm Accenture provides hundreds of diversity programs to its employees each year in an effort to promote individual and organizational performance.
Tinpixels/Getty Images

improve the service Accenture provides each of its clients. Because Accenture's clients are also diverse by country, religion, ethnicity, and so forth, it tries to match its teams of consultants to the attributes of its diverse clients.

Accenture provides hundreds of diversity management training programs to its consultants each year. Several years ago, Accenture became the first large consulting firm to publish its race and gender statistics in an effort to increase transparency when it comes to diversity and inclusion among its employees. More than 46% of its global workforce is composed of women, and a little more than half of its employees are white and a third Asian. Julie Sweet, Accenture's CEO, believes the company needs to make progress in hiring more African Americans, Latinos, and military veterans. Accenture works to accommodate employees with disabilities and promotes an inclusionary environment for LGBTQ employees.[57] The firm also provides diversity training programs to its suppliers and prospective suppliers around the world to show them how diversity can increase their efficiency and effectiveness. In all these ways, Accenture uses its expertise in managing diversity to promote individual and organizational performance—one reason it has become the most successful and fast-growing consultancy company in the world. Accenture recently earned the top spot for the third time in recent years on the Refinitiv's Diversity & Inclusion Index, which identifies the 100 publicly traded companies with the most diverse and inclusive workplaces.[58]

Managers who value their diverse workforce not only invest in developing these employees' skills and capabilities, but also succeed best in promoting performance over the long run. Today more organizations are realizing that people are their most important resource and that developing, protecting, and retaining employees is one of the most important challenges managers face in a competitive global environment. To underscore the importance of diversity in today's workplace, *Forbes* initiated an annual list of America's best employers for diversity, based on a survey of 60,000 U.S. employees working for firms or institutions with 1,000 or more employees. The top five employers on the 2022 list were Progressive, VMware, Booz Allen Hamilton, Cummins, and Interpublic Group (IPG).[59] We discuss the many issues surrounding the management of a diverse workforce in Chapter 5.

Utilizing New Technologies

As we have discussed, another important challenge for managers is to continually use efficient and effective technologies that can link and enable managers and employees to better perform their jobs, regardless of their role in the organization. One example of pushing the technology envelope is UPS's ORION (On-Road Integrated Optimization and Navigation) tool. On average, a UPS driver makes at least 100 deliveries a day, and figuring out the quickest way to navigate all of those stops is a problem with financial indications for the global shipping giant. UPS estimates that a driver with 25 packages could choose from *15 trillion* different routes![60]

ORION blends GPS navigation and learning to help UPS drivers optimize their routes every day. Of course, UPS drivers must also balance promised delivery times, traffic, weather, and other factors into their decisions, meaning ORION is a critical technological competency helping UPS to work effectively and efficiently. According to the company, now that ORION has been fully implemented, the system helps reduce miles driven annually by 100 million—that's a reduction of 10 million gallons of fuel and 100,000 metric tons of carbon dioxide emissions. In addition, reducing just one mile per driver per day can save UPS more than $50 million.[61] UPS has also developed a chatbot powered by artificial intelligence that mimics human conversation and can respond to customer queries through text or voice commands via mobile devices, and EDGE technology used for internal operations that is driven by real-time data, which helps employees make decisions, reduce costs, and optimize operations.[62]

Increasingly, new kinds of technology—such as AI, quantum computing, 5G and 6G, robotics, biometrics, and virtual/augmented reality—enable not just individual employees, but also self-managed teams by giving them important, real-time information and encouraging virtual interactions around the world.[63] Increased global collaboration and coordination also help improve quality and increase the pace of innovation. The importance of technology is discussed throughout the text, and you will find examples of how technology is changing the way companies operate and employees do their work.

Practicing Global Crisis Management

Today another challenge facing managers and organizations is global crisis management. The causes of global crises or disasters fall into two main categories: natural causes and human causes. Crises that arise because of natural causes include the hurricanes, wildfires, earthquakes, famines, and diseases that have devastated so many countries over the past few years.

Meanwhile, human-created crises result from factors such as industrial pollution, inattention to employee safety, the destruction of natural habitat or environment, geopolitical tension and terrorism, and the recent global pandemic. Human-created crises, such as global warming due to emissions of carbon dioxide and other gases, may intensify the effects of natural disasters. For example, increasing global temperatures and acid rain may have increased the intensity of hurricanes, led to unusually strong rains, and contributed to lengthy droughts. Scientists believe that global warming is responsible for the rapid destruction of coral reefs, forests, animal species, and the natural habitat in many parts of the world. The shrinking polar ice caps are expected to raise sea level by a few critical inches.

Increasing geopolitical tensions, which reflect increased globalization, have upset the balance of world power as nations have jockeyed to protect their economic and political interests. For example, global cyberattacks and rising inflation, tensions between the United States and North Korea, and Russia's invasion of Ukraine—all could play a part in global instability and result in the need for managers who can interpret and respond to often unpredictable situations in a global marketplace.[64]

Management has an important role to play in helping people, organizations, and countries respond to global crises; such crises provide lessons in how to plan, organize, lead, and control the resources needed to both forestall and respond effectively to a crisis. Crisis management involves making important choices about how to (1) create teams to facilitate rapid decision making and communication, (2) establish the organizational chain of command and reporting relationships necessary to mobilize a fast response, (3) recruit and select the right people to lead and work in such teams, and (4) develop bargaining and negotiating strategies to manage the conflicts that arise whenever people and groups have different interests and objectives. How well managers make such decisions determines how quickly an effective response to a crisis can be implemented, and it sometimes can prevent or reduce the severity of the crisis itself.

Summary and Review

LO1-1 **WHAT IS MANAGEMENT?** A manager is a person responsible for supervising the use of an organization's resources to meet its goals. An organization is a collection of people who work together and coordinate their actions to achieve a wide variety of goals. Management is the process of using organizational resources to achieve organizational goals effectively and efficiently through planning, organizing, leading, and controlling. An efficient organization makes the most productive use of its resources. An effective organization pursues appropriate goals and achieves these goals by using its resources to create goods or services that customers want.

LO1-2 **ESSENTIAL MANAGERIAL FUNCTIONS** The four principal managerial functions are planning, organizing, leading, and controlling. Managers at all levels of the organization and in all departments perform these functions. Effective management means managing these activities successfully.

LO1-3, 1-4 **LEVELS AND SKILLS OF MANAGERS** Organizations typically have three levels of management. First-line managers are responsible for the day-to-day supervision of nonmanagerial employees. Middle managers are responsible for developing and utilizing organizational resources efficiently and effectively. Top managers have cross-departmental responsibility. Three main kinds of managerial skills are conceptual, human, and technical. The need to develop and build technical skills leads organizations to divide managers into departments according to their job-specific responsibilities. Top managers must establish appropriate goals for the entire organization and verify that department managers are using resources to achieve those goals.

LO1-5 **RECENT CHANGES IN MANAGEMENT PRACTICES** To increase efficiency and effectiveness, many organizations have altered how they operate. Managers have restructured and downsized operations and outsourced activities to reduce costs. Companies are also empowering their workforces and using self-managed teams to increase efficiency and effectiveness. In addition, the global pandemic has caused managers at all levels to revise their thinking when it comes to employees working remotely on a more frequent basis. Managers are increasingly using technology and other advances to increase productivity.

LO1-6 **CHALLENGES FOR MANAGEMENT IN A GLOBAL ENVIRONMENT** Today's competitive global environment presents many interesting challenges to managers. One of the main challenges is building a competitive advantage by increasing efficiency; quality; speed, flexibility, and innovation; and responsiveness to customers. Other challenges include behaving in an ethical and socially responsible way toward people inside and outside the organization, managing a diverse workforce, utilizing new technologies, and practicing global crisis management.

Management in Action

Topics for Discussion and Action

Discussion

1. Describe the difference between efficiency and effectiveness, and identify real organizations that you think are, or are not, efficient and effective. **[LO1-1]**

2. In what ways can managers at each of the three levels of management contribute to organizational efficiency and effectiveness? **[LO1-3]**

3. Identify an organization that you believe is high-performing and one that you believe is low-performing. Give five reasons you think the performance levels of the two organizations differ so much. **[LO1-2, 1-4]**

4. What are the building blocks of competitive advantage? Why is obtaining a competitive advantage important to managers? **[LO1-5]**

5. In what ways do you think managers' jobs have changed the most over the last 10 years? Why have these changes occurred? **[LO1-6]**

Action

6. Choose an organization such as a school or a bank; visit it; then list the different organizational resources it uses. How do managers use these resources to maintain and improve its performance? **[LO1-2, 1-4]**

7. Visit an organization, and talk to first-line, middle, and top managers about their respective management roles in the organization and what they do to help the organization be efficient and effective. **[LO1-3, 1-4]**

8. Ask a middle or top manager, perhaps someone you already know, to give examples of how they perform the managerial functions of planning, organizing, leading, and controlling. How much time do they spend in performing each function? **[LO1-3]**

9. Like Mintzberg, try to find a cooperative manager who will allow you to follow them around for a day. List the roles the manager plays, and indicate how much time they spend performing these roles. **[LO1-3, 1-4]**

Building Management Skills

Thinking about Managers and Management [LO1-2, 1-3, 1-4]

Think of an organization that has provided you with work experience and the manager to whom you report (or talk to someone who has had extensive work experience); then answer these questions:

1. Think about your direct supervisor. Of what department are they a member, and at what level of management is this person?

2. How do you characterize your supervisor's approach to management? For example, which management functions and roles does this person perform most often? What kinds of management skills does this manager have?

3. Are the tasks, roles, and skills of your supervisor appropriate for the particular job they perform? How could this manager improve their task performance? How can IT affect this?

4. How does your supervisor's approach to management affect your attitudes and behavior? For example, how well do you perform as an employee, and how motivated are you?

5. Think about the organization and its resources. Do its managers use organizational resources effectively? Which resources contribute most to the organization's performance?

6. Describe how the organization treats its human resources. How does this treatment affect the attitudes and behaviors of the workforce?

7. If you could give your manager one piece of advice or change one management practice in the organization, what would it be?

8. How attuned are the managers in the organization to the need to increase efficiency, quality, innovation, or responsiveness to customers? How well do you think the organization performs its prime goals of providing the goods or services that customers want or need the most?

Managing Ethically [LO1-1, 1-3]

Think about an example of unethical behavior that you observed recently. The incident could be something you experienced as an employee or customer or something you observed informally.

Questions

1. Either by yourself or in a group, give three reasons you think the behavior was unethical. For example, what rules or norms were broken? Who benefited or was harmed by what took place? What was the outcome for the people involved?
2. What steps might you take to prevent such unethical behavior and encourage people to behave in an ethical way?

Small Group Breakout Exercise

Opening a New Restaurant [LO1-2, 1-3, 1-4]

Form groups of three or four people, and appoint one group member as the spokesperson who will communicate your findings to the entire class when called on by the instructor. Then discuss the following scenario:

You and your partners have decided to open a restaurant in your local community; it will be open from 7 a.m. to 3 p.m. daily to serve breakfast and lunch. Each of you is investing $50,000 in the venture, and together you have secured a bank loan for $300,000 to begin operations. You and your partners have little experience in managing a restaurant beyond serving meals or eating in restaurants, and you now face the task of deciding how you will manage the restaurant and what your respective roles will be.

1. Decide what each partner's managerial role in the restaurant will be. For example, who will be responsible for the necessary departments and specific activities? Describe your managerial hierarchy.
2. Which building blocks of competitive advantage do you need to establish to help your restaurant succeed? What criteria will you use to evaluate how successfully you are managing the restaurant?
3. Discuss the most important decisions that must be made about (a) planning, (b) organizing, (c) leading, and (d) controlling to allow you and your partners to use organizational resources effectively and build a competitive advantage.
4. For each managerial task, list the issues to solve, and decide which roles will contribute the most to your restaurant's success.

Be the Manager [LO1-2, 1-5]

Rapid Growth Causes Problems

You have just been called in to help managers at Achieva, a fast-growing Internet software company that specializes in business-to-business (B2B) network software. Your job is to help Achieva solve some management problems that have arisen because of its rapid growth.

Customer demand to license Achieva's software has boomed so much in just two years that more than 50 new programmers have been added to help develop a new range of software products. Achieva's growth has been so swift that the company still operates informally, its organizational structure is loose and flexible, and programmers are encouraged to find solutions to problems as they go along. Although this structure worked well in the past, you have been told that problems are arising.

There have been increasing complaints from employees that good performance is not being recognized in the organization and that they do not feel they are being treated fairly. Moreover, there have been complaints about getting managers to listen to their new ideas and to act on them. A bad atmosphere is developing in the company, and recently several talented employees left. Your job is to help Achieva's managers solve these problems quickly and keep the company on the fast track.

Questions

1. What kinds of organizing and controlling problems is Achieva suffering from?
2. What kinds of management changes need to be made to solve these problems?

Case in the News [LO1-1, 1-2, 1-3, 1-6]

Larry Culp Redefines Success at GE

When Larry Culp became the 12th chief executive officer of General Electric, he was the first CEO to be brought in from outside the company, and GE desperately needed a fresh perspective. The company, formed in the 1890s to deliver electricity to cities, later grew by adding a variety of businesses until it became a giant conglomerate. By 2000, GE seemed unstoppable: Its total stock value exceeded that of any other corporation, and observers concluded that great management was enabling GE to thrive in businesses as diverse as jet engines, entertainment, power generation, and consumer finance. Then a financial crisis hit in 2008, and excessive risk in the financial-services division nearly caused the company to collapse under the weight of its debt. Ten years and two CEOs later, when Culp joined GE, the company was still struggling to remain relevant. The supposed advantage of being a conglomerate—that thriving business lines could keep the company going when other businesses hit headwinds—had become a liability, because this approach meant executives weren't consistently allocating funds where they could generate the most value.

Culp arrived with a track record of wins over 14 years at Danaher Corporation, a manufacturing company that, like GE, had grown through a series of acquisitions but, unlike GE, had maintained a focus on pursuing efficiency in a couple of industries it could manage effectively. Within weeks, Culp was leading an extensive investigation into each division's performance. His experience, coupled with an education in business administration, enabled Culp to assess which companies consistently generated cash and where expenses were out of control.

One of Culp's passions, going back to his years at Danaher, is to make processes lean by cutting unnecessary expenses and activities. At GE, he visited facilities to inspect operations and ask workers about their processes. A factory making turbines, for example, was moving the giant parts three miles around the facility over an 85-day production process. Upgrading machinery and rearranging the layout shortened the process to 165 feet and about 50 days. At an aviation facility, he observed a team studying ways to improve on-time deliveries of a military engine. During the week he was there, teams cut costs by $2 million and timelines by 62 days.

In his first few years on the job, Culp's focus remained on improving operations so divisions could generate profits to help pay down the corporate debt burden. To generate more cash for debt reduction, he also cut dividends paid to shareholders and sold divisions including aircraft leasing and biopharmaceuticals. His predecessors had also sold off businesses but far less aggressively; Culp's moves pulled GE completely out of consumer-facing businesses such as appliances and home mortgages and left the company with four main businesses—aviation, health care (hospital equipment), renewable energy (wind turbines), and power (equipment for fossil-fuel power generation). GE's aviation business is an industry leader, and health care has been reliably profitable. Orders and revenues for renewable-power equipment have exceeded those on the fossil-fuel side, and GE found it had overestimated the extent to which its customers would continue to pursue natural-gas solutions. In addition to these changes, Culp moved many corporate functions (for example, IT and human resources) to the business divisions and made each business responsible for its own performance, rather than expecting some businesses to prop up others.

Recently Culp determined that the divisions were profitable enough for him to announce his big move: GE would split into three parts: health care, power (fossil-fuel and renewables), and aviation. The intent was that the divisions on their own would be more flexible at responding to market changes and more attractive to investors knowledgeable about each industry. At the time of the announcement, the plan was to spin off GE's strongest division, health care, in early 2023. In the meantime, it would combine its fossil-fuel power unit with its renewable-energy unit to create one power unit, aiming to sell in 2024. With those deals complete, GE would retain the aviation unit and try to maintain its leadership position.

Questions for Discussion

1. List three examples of Larry Culp using organizational resources to achieve organizational goals.
2. What is something Culp planned? What is an organizational change he made? When was he engaged in controlling? How would effective leadership help him carry out these tasks?
3. At GE, Larry Culp is a top manager. How would the work of a middle manager at GE differ from Culp's work?

Sources: "H. Lawrence 'Larry' Culp: Chairman and Chief Executive Officer, GE," *Business Roundtable*, www.businessroundtable.org, accessed January 4, 2023; T. Gryta, "GE CEO Larry Culp to Also Run Aviation Business," *The Wall Street Journal*, www.wsj.com, June 27, 2022; R. Clough and R. Beene, "Can GE Divide and Conquer?" *Bloomberg Businessweek*, November 15, 2021, 21–22; J. Zweig, "GE and the Belief in Management Magic," *The Wall Street Journal*, www.wsj.com, November 13, 2021; T. Gryta, T. Mann, and C. Lombardo, "Larry Culp Rewired GE; Then He Unwound It," *The Wall Street Journal*, www.wsj.com, November 13, 2021; A. Sen and R. Kumar Singh, "How GE's Larry Culp Split the Empire Jack Welch Built," *Reuters*, www.reuters.com, November 10, 2021; M. Heller, "GE to Split into Three Public Companies," *CFO*, www.cfo.com, November 9, 2021; A. Peacher, "Friendly Breakup: After 129 Years, GE Plans Future as Three Smaller Companies," *Marketplace*, www.marketplace.org, November 9, 2021; T. Gryta, "'The End of the GE We Knew': Breakup Turns a Page in Modern Business History," *The Wall Street Journal*, www.wsj.com, November 9, 2021; R. Beene, "After 129 Years of Carbon, GE Seeks a Cleaner Path," *Bloomberg Businessweek*, COP26 Guide, Fall 2021, 16–20.

Notes

1. J. Vincent, "Why More Creatives Should Lead Major Companies: The Story of Airbnb as told by Cofounder and CEO Brian Chesky," *Fast Company*, www.fastcompany.com, October 6, 2022; M. Lev-Ram, "The Conversation: Brian Chesky," *Fortune*, June/July 2022, 17–20; D. Abril, "Future of Work: 'The Office as We Knew It Is Over,' Airbnb CEO Says," *Washington Post*, www.washingtonpost.com, May 18, 2022; K. Ryssdal and M. Hollenhorst, "Airbnb's Brian Chesky on Repositioning the Company for a New Era of Travel," *Marketplace*, www.marketplace.org, May 11, 2022.
2. Ryssdal and Hollenhorst, "Airbnb's Brian Chesky"; Lev-Ram, "The Conversation"; Vincent, "Why More Creatives Should Lead."
3. Vincent, "Why More Creatives Should Lead."
4. Lev-Ram, "The Conversation"; K. Linebaugh, "Why Airbnb Is Letting Employees Work Anywhere," interview with Brian Chesky, *The Journal* (podcast), www.wsj.com, April 29, 2022.
5. Lev-Ram, "The Conversation."
6. J.P. Campbell, "On the Nature of Organizational Effectiveness," in P.S. Goodman, J.M. Pennings, et al., *New Perspectives on Organizational Effectiveness* (San Francisco: Jossey-Bass, 1977).
7. Z. Lurie, "How I Did It: SurveyMonkey's CEO on Creating a Culture of Curiosity," *Harvard Business Review*, January-February 2019, 35–39.
8. "Let There Be Breakfast: McDonald's Serving All Day Breakfast Starting Oct. 6," https://corporate.mcdonalds.com, accessed January 3, 2023.
9. "Summary Report: 11-1021.00—General and Operations Manager," *O*NET OnLine*, www.onetonline.org, accessed January 3, 2023.
10. H. Fayol, *General and Industrial Management* (New York: IEEE Press, 1984). Fayol actually identified five different managerial tasks, but most scholars today believe these four capture the essence of Fayol's ideas.
11. P.F. Drucker, *Management Tasks, Responsibilities, and Practices* (New York: Harper & Row, 1974).
12. Linebaugh, "Why Airbnb Is Letting Employees Work Anywhere."
13. Vincent, "Why More Creatives Should Lead."
14. Match Group, "Who We Are," https://ir.mtch.com, accessed January 3, 2023; Reuters, "Match Group's Shar Dubey to Step Down as CEO," *Reuters*, www.reuters.com, May 3, 2022.
15. Match Group, "Leadership: Bernard Kim, Chief Executive Officer," https://mtch.com, accessed January 3, 2023; S. Perez, "Match Names Zynga President Bernard Kim as CEO, Replacing Shar Dubey," *Tech Crunch*, https://techcrunch.com, May 3, 2022.
16. S. Perez, "Match Group Details Plans for a Dating 'Metaverse,' Tinder's Virtual Goods-Based Economy," *Tech Crunch*, https://techcrunch.com, November 3, 2021.
17. D. Jacob, "Match Splits with Tinder CEO as Earnings Fall Short," *The Wall Street Journal*, www.wsj.com, August 2, 2022.
18. S. Shahidullah, "Match Shares Climb on Quarterly Sales, Cost-Control Pledge," *Bloomberg*, www.bloomberg.com, November 1, 2022; "San Francisco-Based Zynga Acquired by 'Grand Theft Auto' Maker Take-Two Interactive in $12.7B Deal," *CBS News* (San Francisco), www.cbsnews.com, January 10, 2022.
19. Shahidullah, "Match Shares Climb"; Match Group, "Who We Are."
20. L. Hill, *Becoming a Manager: Mastery of a New Identity* (Boston: Harvard Business School Press, 1992).
21. Ibid.
22. H. Mintzberg, "The Manager's Job: Folklore and Fact," *Harvard Business Review*, July-August 1975, 56–62.
23. H. Mintzberg, *The Nature of Managerial Work* (New York: Harper & Row, 1973).
24. A.I. Kraul, P.R. Pedigo, D.D. McKenna, and M.D. Dunnett, "The Role of the Manager: What's Really Important in Different Management Jobs," *Academy of Management Executive* (November 1989), 286–93; C.P. Hales, "What Do Managers Do? A Critical Review of the Evidence," *Journal of Management Studies* (January 1986), 88–115.
25. A.K. Gupta, "Contingency Perspectives on Strategic Leadership," in D.C. Hambrick, ed., *The Executive Effect: Concepts and Methods for Studying Top Managers* (Greenwich, CT: JAI Press, 1988), 147–78.
26. D.G. Ancona, "Top Management Teams: Preparing for the Revolution," in J.S. Carroll, ed., *Applied Social Psychology and Organizational Settings* (Hillsdale, NJ: Erlbaum, 1990); D.C. Hambrick and P.A. Mason, "Upper Echelons: The Organization as a Reflection of Its Top Managers," *Academy of Management Journal* 9 (1984), 193–206.
27. L. Gomez-Mejia, J. McCann, and R.C. Page, "The Structure of Managerial Behaviors and Rewards," *Industrial Relations* 24 (1985), 147–54.
28. W.R. Nord and M.J. Waller, "The Human Organization of Time: Temporal Realities and Experiences," *Academy of Management Review* 29 (January 2004), 137–40.
29. R.L. Katz, "Skills of an Effective Administrator," *Harvard Business Review*, September-October 1974, 90–102.
30. Ibid.
31. S. Okonkwo, "The Founder of UBI Group on Leading a Transition to Renewable Energy in Africa," *Harvard Business Review*, https://hbr.org, accessed January 3, 2023; "Salma Okonkwo Defends Why Africa Will Industrialize at 2022 Clinton Global Initiative," *Ghana Web*, www.ghanaweb.com, October 3, 2022.
32. C. Sorvino, "Why This 48-Year-Old Woman Is Building Ghana's Biggest Solar Farm," *Forbes*, www.forbes.com, July 31, 2018.
33. "Salma Okonkwo Defends Why Africa Will Industrialize"; Sorvino, "Why This 48-Year-Old Woman Is Building."
34. P. Tharenou, "Going Up? Do Traits and Informal Social Processes Predict Advancing in Management?" *Academy of Management Journal* 44 (October 2001), 1005–18.
35. C.J. Collins and K.D. Clark, "Strategic Human Resource Practices, Top Management Team Social Networks, and Firm Performance: The Role of Human Resource Practices in Creating Organizational Competitive Advantage," *Academy of Management Journal* 46 (December 2003), 740–52.
36. R. Stewart, "Middle Managers: Their Jobs and Behaviors," in J.W. Lorsch, ed., *Handbook of Organizational Behavior* (Englewood Cliffs, NJ: Prentice-Hall, 1987), 385–91.
37. S.C. de Janasz, S.E. Sullivan, and V. Whiting, "Mentor Networks and Career Success: Lessons for Turbulent Times," *Academy of Management Executive* 17 (November 2003), 78–92.
38. "7 Ways Technology Can Drive Higher Employee Engagement," *HR Cloud*, www.hrcloud.com, August 19, 2022.
39. "Gartner Forecasts Worldwide IT Spending to Grow 5.1% in 2023," www.gartner.com, October 19, 2022.
40. B. Morgan, "15 Stats about Post-Covid Consumer Customer Service," *Forbes*, www.forbes.com, March 15, 2022.

41. D. Gunn, "10 Best Countries to Outsource Software Development (Analysis)," *Code in WP,* www.codeinwp.com, September 14, 2022.

42. "Valve Handbook for New Employees," www.valvesoftware.com, accessed January 4, 2023; S. Wagreich, "A Billion Dollar Company with No Bosses? Yes, It Exists," *Inc.,* www.inc.com, accessed February 22, 2018; E. Jansen, "What's Going On with Employee Empowerment?" https://shift.newco.co, March 2, 2017; R. Peters, "Success Through Self-Governing Teams," *LinkedIn,* www.linkedin.com, February 2, 2016.

43. R. Starr, "What Are Self-Managed Teams and How Can They Serve Your Business," *Small Business Trends,* https://smallbiztrends.com, accessed February 5, 2020.

44. K. Parker, J.M. Horowitz, and R. Minkin, "COVID-19 Pandemic Continues to Reshape Work in America," *Pew Research Center,* www.pewresearch.org, February 16, 2022.

45. A. Davies, "Inside X, the Moonshot Factory Racing to Build the Next Google," *Wired,* www.wired.com, accessed February 5, 2020.

46. "Chipotle Announces Third Quarter 2022 Results," https://ir.chipotle.com, accessed November 14, 2022; A. Lucas, "Chipotle Founder Steve Ells Steps Down from Board, CEO Niccol Adds Chairman Title," *CNBC,* www.cnbc.com, March 6, 2020.

47. C. Manibog and S. Foley, "The Long and Winding Road to Economic Recovery," *Financial Times,* www.ft.com, August 9, 2017.

48. W.H. Shaw and V. Barry, *Moral Issues in Business,* 6th ed. (Belmont, CA: Wadsworth, 1995).

49. H. Cassin, "Mining and Commodities Giant Lands on the FCPA Blog Top Ten List," *The FCPA Blog,* https://fcpablog.com, May 31, 2022; W. Wysong and A. Pan, "The Top Ten Asia-Pacific FCPA Enforcement Actions of 2020," *Steptoe,* www.steptoe.com, January 27, 2021.

50. D. Meinert, "Creating an Ethical Workplace," www.shrm.org, accessed February 6, 2020.

51. D. Rock and H. Grant, "Why Diverse Teams Are Smarter," *Harvard Business Review,* https://hbr.org, November 4, 2016.

52. "Laura Miele, Chief Studios Officer at Electronic Arts (EA)," *Online Education,* www.onlineeducation.com, accessed January 4, 2023; O. Kharif, "Laura Miele Is Listening," *Bloomberg Businessweek,* May 24, 2021, 21–23.

53. *Online Education,* "Laura Miele."

54. J. Peters, "EA Promotes Laura Miele to COO, Making Her One of the Most Powerful Women in Gaming," *The Verge,* www.theverge.com, September 30, 2021; D. Takahashi, "EA's Laura Miele: Making Games Is Hard, and It Keeps Changing," *Venture Beat,* https://venturebeat.com, April 29, 2021.

55. "Laura Miele: COO, Electronic Arts," Speakers, WSJ Tech, https://techlive.wsj.com, accessed January 4, 2023.

56. *Online Education,* "Laura Miele."

57. "A Global Commitment to Transparency," www.accenture.com, accessed January 4, 2023; M. McGrath, "The World's Most Powerful Women 2021: Julie Sweet," *Forbes,* www.forbes.com, accessed January 4, 2023; K. Bellstrom, "Exclusive: Accenture Is the First Big Consulting Firm to Publish Race and Gender Stats," *Fortune,* https://fortune.com, February 8, 2016.

58. "Accenture Ranked No. 1 on Refinitiv Index of World's Most Diverse and Inclusive Companies," https://newsroom.accenture.com, September 29, 2022.

59. J. Council, "America's Best Employers for Diversity," *Forbes,* www.forbes.com, April 26, 2022.

60. R.V. Zicari, "Big Data at UPS: Interview with Jack Levis," *ODBMS Industry Watch,* www.odbsm.org, August 1, 2017.

61. "ORION Backgrounder," www.pressroom.ups.com, accessed February 6, 2020.

62. B. Marr, "The Brilliant Ways UPS Uses Artificial Intelligence, Machine Learning and Big Data," *Forbes,* www.forbes.com, accessed February 6, 2020.

63. N. Duggal, "Top 18 New Technology Trends for 2023," *Simpli Learn,* www.simplilearn.com, November 7, 2022.

64. BlackRock Investment Institute, "Geopolitical Risk Indicator: September 2022," www.blackrock.com, accessed January 4, 2023.

CHAPTER 2

The Evolution of Management Thought

Luis Alvarez/Getty Images

Learning Objectives

After studying this chapter, you should be able to:

LO2-1 Describe how the need to increase organizational efficiency and effectiveness has guided the evolution of management theory.

LO2-2 Explain the principle of job specialization and division of labor, and tell why the study of person–task relationships is central to the pursuit of increased efficiency.

LO2-3 Identify the principles of administration and organization that underlie effective organizations.

LO2-4 Trace the changes in theories about how managers should behave to motivate and control employees.

LO2-5 Explain the contributions of management science to the efficient use of organizational resources.

LO2-6 Explain why the study of the external environment and its impact on an organization has become a central issue in management thought.

A MANAGER'S CHALLENGE

Google Searches for the Best Way to Work

What is the best way to maintain a competitive edge? Google and its parent company, Alphabet, expanded substantially during the COVID-19 pandemic, when it hired about one-third of its 165,000 employees.[1] In a time when most of its people were working remotely, managers had to find ways to direct work, inspire innovation, and ensure collaboration. Then, almost as quickly, the stakes changed again as tech companies faced headwinds and talk of recession. To meet the challenge, Google's chief executive, Sundar Pichai, urged employees to work with "more hunger."[2]

Pichai's message relayed an ever-present objective of managers: to serve customers well while keeping costs under control. Companies that achieve this kind of efficiency are well positioned to sustain profitable growth. Google's revenue and profits growth had slowed when Pichai addressed employees, so he called on them to be "more mission-focused, more focused on our products, more customer focused."[3]

Words alone are not enough. Managers traditionally pursue objectives like efficiency and quality by structuring work and keeping a close eye on workers. That can be difficult in a high-tech organization like Google. Managers also need knowledge about what kinds of people are likely to be high performers and what conditions will enable them to excel. Much of the responsibility for this has fallen on Fiona Cicconi, Google's chief people officer, who was one of the pandemic-era hires. She had been working from home, managing human resources for pharmaceutical company AstraZeneca, when she negotiated for the Google position by video conference. It would be months before travel restrictions lifted, allowing her to relocate.[4]

Cicconi's primary challenge has been to lead Google's transition away from remote work, considered necessary to create the conditions for a focused workforce. According to managers, it was difficult to mentor and acclimate new employees remotely, and employees working in separate locations had trouble resolving conflicts. However, employees also grew accustomed to remote work. Before the pandemic, Google had been noted for enhancing work life with free food, on-site massages, and other perks, but during the pandemic-related distancing, employees enjoyed different comforts, like sleeping later and lunching on the back porch. Google's plan for a solution was to establish "hybrid" working as the norm: employees would work from the office three days a week and remotely on the other two. To enable collaboration, in-office days were designated according to

Like many other organizations, Google continues to struggle with the issue of employees being required to work in offices or allowed to work remotely.
REUTERS/Alamy Stock Photo

the employee's product area. Recognizing that not every job demands the same amount of interaction, the company allows employees to apply for permission to work only remotely.[5]

As Cicconi led the transition to hybrid work, she had data to inform her decisions. Google prides itself on using data and advanced analytics to improve decision making. The data don't always make Cicconi's job easy. In surveys asking employees how often they wanted to work at the office, responses varied widely. One complicating factor is that Google adjusts pay rates to reflect the local cost of living. During the pandemic, some employees moved to lower-stress, lower-cost locations; to continue remote work in those locations, they would have to take a pay cut. Also, some managers have objected to being put in the position of deciding who may continue to work remotely—another issue where employees are highly attuned to fairness.[6]

Still, Cicconi sees signs that the transition can succeed. When employees began working remotely during the pandemic, productivity initially dipped and then improved, suggesting that employees are adaptable. Also, employees have been far less likely than expected to pursue the option of full-time remote work.[7] In the meantime, Google will continue the search for the optimal way (or ways) of working.

Overview

When a company such as Google is facing a difficult problem, many factors are in play. Does the solution come from changes to people, processes, technology, or reporting relationships? Compared with managers a century ago, Google's managers have a significant advantage: They can apply the knowledge gained by the researchers, consultants, and businesspeople who have studied management, constructing and testing theories about what gets results.

In this chapter we examine how management thought has evolved in modern times and the central concerns that have guided ongoing advances in management theory. First we examine the so-called classical management theories that emerged around the turn of the 20th century. These include scientific management, which focuses on matching people and tasks to maximize efficiency, and administrative management, which focuses on identifying the principles that will lead to the creation of the most efficient system of organization and management. Next we consider behavioral management theories, developed both before and after World War II; these focus on how managers should lead and control their workforces to increase performance. Then we discuss management science theory, which developed during World War II and has become increasingly important as researchers have developed rigorous analytical and quantitative techniques to help managers measure and control organizational performance. Finally, we discuss changes in management practices from the middle to the late 20th century and focus on the theories developed to help explain how the external environment affects the way organizations and managers operate.

By the end of this chapter you will understand how management thought and theory have evolved over time. You will also understand how economic, political, and cultural forces have affected the development of these theories and how managers and their organizations have changed their behavior as a result. In Figure 2.1 we summarize the chronology of the management theories discussed in this chapter.

Scientific Management Theory

The evolution of modern management began in the closing decades of the 19th century, after the Industrial Revolution had swept through Europe and America. In the new economic climate, managers of all types of organizations–political, educational, and economic–were trying to find better ways to satisfy customers' needs. Many major economic, technical, and cultural changes were taking place. The introduction of steam power and the development of sophisticated machinery and equipment changed

Figure 2.1
The Evolution of Management Theory

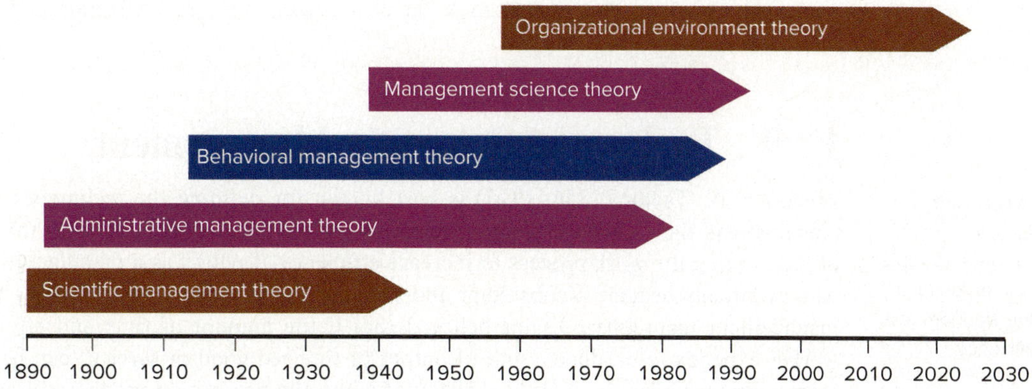

LO2-1 Describe how the need to increase organizational efficiency and effectiveness has guided the evolution of management theory.

how goods were produced, particularly in the weaving and clothing industries. Small workshops run by skilled workers who produced hand-manufactured products (a system called *crafts production*) were being replaced by large factories in which sophisticated machines controlled by hundreds or even thousands of unskilled or semiskilled workers made products. For example, raw cotton and wool, which in the past had been spun into yarn by families or whole villages working together, were now shipped to factories, where workers operated machines that spun and wove large quantities of yarn into cloth.

Owners and managers of the new factories found themselves unprepared for the challenges accompanying the change from small-scale crafts production to large-scale, mechanized manufacturing. Moreover, many managers and supervisors in these workshops and factories were engineers who had only a technical orientation. They were unprepared for the social problems that occur when people work together in large groups in a factory or shop system. Managers began to search for new techniques to manage their organizations' resources, and soon they started focusing on ways to increase the efficiency of the worker-task mix.

Job Specialization and the Division of Labor

LO2-2 Explain the principle of job specialization and division of labor, and tell why the study of person–task relationships is central to the pursuit of increased efficiency.

Initially, management theorists were interested in why the new machine shops and factory system were more efficient and produced greater quantities of goods and services than older, crafts-style production operations. Nearly 200 years before, Adam Smith had been one of the first writers to investigate the advantages associated with producing goods and services in factories. A famous economist, Smith journeyed around England in the 1700s, studying the effects of the Industrial Revolution.[8] In a study of factories that produced various pins or nails, Smith identified two different manufacturing methods. The first was similar to crafts-style production, in which each worker was responsible for all the 18 tasks involved in producing a pin. The other had each worker performing only one or a few of these 18 tasks.

Smith found that the performance of the factories in which workers specialized in only one or a few tasks was much greater than the performance of the factory in which each worker performed all 18 pin-making tasks. In fact, Smith found that 10 workers specializing in a particular task could make 48,000 pins a day, whereas those workers who performed all the tasks could make only a few thousand.[9] Smith reasoned that this performance difference occurred because the workers who specialized became much more skilled at their specific tasks and as a group were thus able to produce a product faster than the group of workers who each performed many tasks. Smith concluded that increasing the level of **job specialization**—the process by which a division of labor occurs as different workers specialize in tasks—improves efficiency and leads to higher organizational performance.[10]

job specialization The process by which a division of labor occurs as different workers specialize in different tasks over time.

Armed with the insights gained from Adam Smith's observations, other managers and researchers began to investigate how to improve job specialization to increase performance. Management practitioners and theorists focused on how managers should organize and control the work process to maximize the advantages of job specialization and the division of labor.

F. W. Taylor and Scientific Management

scientific management The systematic study of relationships between people and tasks for the purpose of redesigning the work process to increase efficiency.

Frederick W. Taylor (1856–1915) is best known for defining the techniques of **scientific management**, the systematic study of relationships between people and tasks for the purpose of redesigning the work process to increase efficiency. Taylor was a manufacturing manager who eventually became a consultant and taught other managers how to apply his scientific management techniques. Taylor believed that if the amount of time and effort that each worker expends to produce a unit of output (a finished good or service) can be reduced by increasing specialization and the division of labor, the production process will become more efficient. According to Taylor, the way to create the most efficient division of labor could best be determined by scientific management techniques rather than by intuitive or informal, rule-of-thumb knowledge. Based on his experiments and observations as a manufacturing manager in a variety of settings, he developed four principles to increase efficiency in the workplace:

- Principle 1: *Study the way workers perform their tasks, gather all the informal job knowledge that workers possess, and experiment with ways of improving how tasks are performed.*

To discover the most efficient method of performing specific tasks, Taylor studied in great detail and measured the ways different workers went about performing their tasks. One of the main tools he used was a time-and-motion study, which involves the careful timing and recording of the actions taken to perform a particular task. Once Taylor understood the existing method of performing a task, he then experimented to increase specialization. He tried different methods of dividing and coordinating the various tasks necessary to produce a finished product. Usually, this meant simplifying jobs and having each worker perform fewer, more routine tasks, as at a pin factory or on a car assembly line. Taylor also sought to find ways to improve each worker's ability to perform a particular task–for example, by reducing the number of motions workers made to complete the task, by changing the layout of the work area or the type of tools workers used, or by experimenting with tools of different sizes.

- Principle 2: *Codify the new methods of performing tasks into written rules and standard operating procedures.*

Once the best method of performing a particular task was determined, Taylor specified that it should be recorded so this procedure could be taught to all workers performing the same task. These new methods further standardized and simplified jobs–essentially making jobs even more routine. In this way efficiency could be increased throughout an organization.

- Principle 3: *Carefully select workers who possess skills and abilities that match the needs of the task, and train them to perform the task according to the established rules and procedures.*

To increase specialization, Taylor believed workers had to understand the tasks that were required and be thoroughly trained to perform the tasks at the required level. Workers who could not be trained to this level were to be transferred to a job where they were able to reach the minimum required level of proficiency.[11]

- Principle 4: *Establish a fair or acceptable level of performance for a task, and then develop a pay system that rewards performance above the acceptable level.*

To encourage workers to perform at a high level of efficiency, and to give them an incentive to reveal the most efficient techniques for performing a task, Taylor advocated that workers benefit from any gains in performance. They should be paid a bonus and receive some percentage of the performance gains achieved through the more efficient work process.[12]

By 1910 Taylor's system of scientific management had become nationally known and in many instances was faithfully and fully practiced.[13] However, managers in many organizations chose to implement the new principles of scientific management selectively. This decision ultimately resulted in problems. For example, some managers using scientific management

Frederick W. Taylor, founder of the scientific management movement, was one of the first people to study the behavior and performance of people at work.
Bettmann/Getty Images

obtained increases in performance, but rather than sharing performance gains with workers through bonuses, as Taylor had advocated, they simply increased the amount of work that each worker was expected to do. Many workers experiencing the reorganized work system found that as their performance increased, managers required that they do more work for the same pay. Workers also learned that performance increases often meant fewer jobs and a greater threat of layoffs, because fewer workers were needed. In addition, the specialized, simplified jobs were often monotonous and repetitive, and many workers became dissatisfied with their jobs.

Scientific management brought many workers more hardship than gain and a distrust of managers who did not seem to care about workers' well-being.[14] These dissatisfied workers resisted attempts to use the new scientific management techniques and at times even withheld their job knowledge from managers to protect their jobs and pay. It is not difficult for workers to conceal the true potential efficiency of a work system to protect their interests. Experienced machine operators, for example, can slow their machines in undetectable ways by adjusting the tension in the belts or misaligning the gears.

Unable to inspire workers to accept the new scientific management techniques for performing tasks, some organizations increased the mechanization of the work process. For example, one reason Henry Ford introduced moving conveyor belts in his factory was the realization that when a conveyor belt controls the pace of work (instead of workers setting their own pace), workers can be pushed to perform at higher levels—levels that they may have thought were beyond their reach. Charlie Chaplin captured this aspect of mass production in one of the opening scenes of his famous movie *Modern Times* (1936). In the film Chaplin caricatured a new factory employee fighting to work at the machine-imposed pace but losing the battle to the machine. Henry Ford also used the principles of scientific management to identify the tasks that each worker should perform on the production line and, thus, to determine the most effective division of labor to suit the needs of a mechanized production system.

From a performance perspective, the combination of the two management practices—(1) achieving the right worker–task specialization and (2) linking people and tasks by the speed of the production line—makes sense. It produces the huge cost savings and dramatic output increases that occur in large, organized work settings. For example, in 1908 managers at the Franklin Motor Company using scientific management principles redesigned the work process, and the output of cars increased from 100 cars a *month* to 45 cars a *day;* workers' wages, however, increased by only 90%.[15]

The Gilbreths

Two prominent followers of Taylor were Frank Gilbreth (1868–1924) and Lillian Gilbreth (1878–1972), who refined Taylor's analysis of work movements and made many contributions to time-and-motion study.[16] Their aims were to (1) analyze every individual action necessary to perform a particular task and break it into each of its component actions, (2) find better ways to perform each component action, and (3) reorganize each of the component actions so that the action as a whole could be performed more efficiently—at less cost in time and effort.

This scene from the 2003 version of the movie *Cheaper by the Dozen* illustrates how "efficient families" such as the Gilbreths use formal family courts to solve problems, such as assigning chores to different family members.
Collection Christophel/Alamy Stock Photo

The Gilbreths often filmed a worker performing a task and then separated the task actions, frame by frame, into their component movements. Their goal was to maximize the efficiency with which each task was performed so that gains across tasks would add up to enormous savings of time and effort. Their attempts to develop improved management principles were captured—at times quite humorously—in the movie *Cheaper by the Dozen,* a new version of which appeared in 2003, which depicts how the Gilbreths (with their 12 children) tried to live their own lives according to these efficiency principles and apply them to daily actions such as shaving, cooking, and even raising a family.[17]

Eventually, the Gilbreths became increasingly interested in the study of fatigue. They studied how physical characteristics of the workplace contribute to job stress that often leads to fatigue and thus poor performance. They isolated factors that result in worker fatigue, such as lighting, heating, the color of walls, and the design of tools and machines. Their pioneering studies paved the way for new advances in management theory.

In workshops and factories, the work of the Gilbreths, Taylor, and many others had a major effect on the practice of management. In comparison with the old crafts system, jobs in the new system were more repetitive, boring, and monotonous as a result of the application of scientific management principles, and workers became increasingly dissatisfied. Often the management of work settings became a game between workers and managers: Managers tried to initiate work practices to increase performance, and workers tried to hide the true potential efficiency of the work setting to protect their own well-being.

Administrative Management Theory

LO2-3 Identify the principles of administration and organization that underlie effective organizations.

While scientific managers were studying the person–technology mix to increase efficiency, other managers and researchers were focusing on **administrative management**, the study of how to create an organizational structure and control system that leads to high efficiency and effectiveness. *Organizational structure* is the system of task and authority relation ships that controls how employees use resources to achieve the organization's goals. Two of the most influential early views regarding the creation of efficient systems of organizational administration were developed in Europe: Max Weber, a German sociology professor, developed one theory, and Henri Fayol, the French manager who developed the model of management introduced in Chapter 1, developed the other.

administrative management The study of how to create an organizational structure and control system that leads to high efficiency and effectiveness.

bureaucracy A formal system of organization and administration designed to ensure efficiency and effectiveness.

The Theory of Bureaucracy

Max Weber (1864–1920) wrote at the turn of the 20th century, when Germany was undergoing its industrial revolution.[18] To help Germany manage its growing industrial enterprises while it was striving to become a world power, Weber developed the principles of **bureaucracy**—a formal system of organization and administration designed to ensure efficiency and effectiveness. A bureaucratic system of administration is based on the five principles summarized in Figure 2.2.

Figure 2.2
Weber's Principles of Bureaucracy

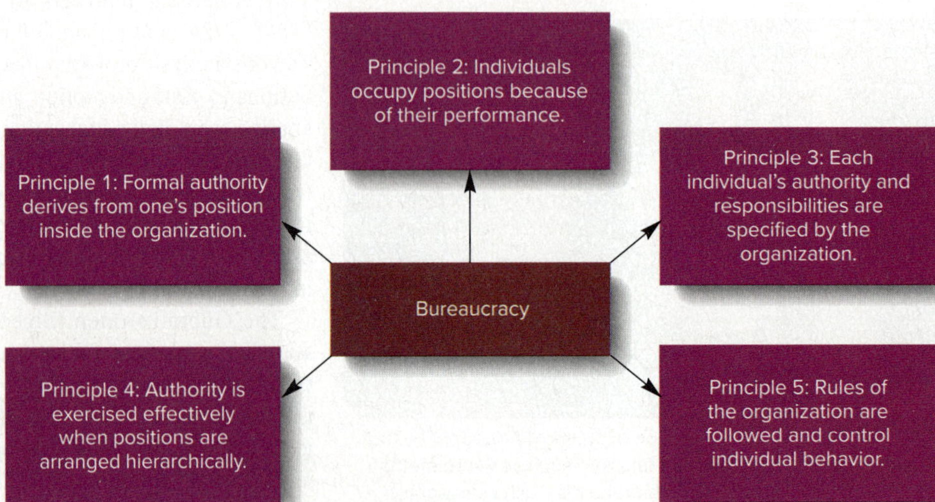

- Principle 1: *In a bureaucracy, a manager's formal authority derives from the position they hold in the organization.*

authority The power to hold people accountable for their actions and to make decisions concerning the use of organizational resources.

Authority is the power to hold people accountable for their actions and to make decisions concerning the use of organizational resources. Authority gives managers the right to direct and control their employees' behavior to achieve organizational goals. In a bureaucratic system of administration, obedience is owed to a manager not because of any personal qualities–such as personality, wealth, or social status–but because the manager occupies a position that is associated with a certain level of authority and responsibility.[19]

- Principle 2: *In a bureaucracy, people should occupy positions because of their performance, not because of their social standing or personal contacts.*

This principle was not always followed in Weber's time and is often ignored today. Some organizations and industries are still affected by social networks in which personal contacts and relations, not job-related skills, influence hiring and promotion decisions.

- Principle 3: *The extent of each position's formal authority and task responsibilities, and its relationship to other positions in an organization, should be clearly specified.*

When the tasks and authority associated with various positions in the organization are clearly specified, managers and workers know what is expected of them and what to expect from each other. Moreover, an organization can hold all its employees strictly accountable for their actions when they know their exact responsibilities.

- Principle 4: *Authority can be exercised effectively in an organization when positions are arranged hierarchically so employees know whom to report to and who reports to them.*

Managers must create an organizational hierarchy of authority that makes it clear who reports to whom and to whom managers and workers should go if conflicts or problems arise. This principle is especially important in the military, the FBI, the CIA, and other organizations that deal with sensitive issues involving possible major repercussions. It is vital that managers at high levels of the hierarchy be able to hold employees accountable for their actions.

- Principle 5: *Managers must create a well-defined system of rules, standard operating procedures, and norms so they can effectively control behavior within an organization.*

rules Formal, written instructions that specify actions to be taken under different circumstances to achieve specific goals.

standard operating procedures (SOPs) Specific sets of written instructions about how to perform a certain aspect of a task.

norms Unwritten, informal codes of conduct that prescribe how people should act in particular situations and are considered important by most members of a group or an organization.

Rules are formal, written instructions that specify actions to be taken under different circumstances to achieve specific goals (for example, if A happens, do B). **Standard operating procedures (SOPs)** are specific sets of written instructions about how to perform a certain aspect of a task. A rule might state that at the end of the workday employees are to leave their machines in good order, and a set of SOPs would specify exactly how they should do so, itemizing which machine parts must be oiled or replaced. **Norms** are unwritten, informal codes of conduct that prescribe how people should act in particular situations and are considered important by most members of a group or an organization. For example, an organizational norm in a restaurant might be that waiters should help each other if time permits.

Rules, SOPs, and norms provide behavioral guidelines that improve the performance of a bureaucratic system because they specify the best ways to accomplish organizational tasks. Companies such as McDonald's and Walmart have developed extensive rules and procedures to specify the behaviors required of their employees, such as, "Always greet the customer with a smile." For example, Walmart, the world's largest retailer, automatically tracks inventory levels of products at its stores. When inventory is too low, the retailer sends an automatic request to a supplier to purchase an item and have it shipped. These items are then routed as efficiently as possible to the store where they are needed. Thus, Walmart incorporates bureaucratic controls in its operations to make employees as efficient as possible.[20]

Weber believed organizations that implement all five principles establish a bureaucratic system that improves organizational performance. The specification of positions and the use of rules and SOPs to regulate how tasks are performed make it easier for managers to organize and control the work of employees. Similarly, fair and equitable selection and promotion systems improve managers' feelings of security, reduce stress, and encourage organizational members to act ethically and further promote the interests of the organization.

If bureaucracies are not managed well, however, many problems can result. Sometimes managers allow rules and SOPs, so-called bureaucratic red tape, to become so cumbersome

Max Weber developed the principles of bureaucracy during Germany's burgeoning industrial revolution to help organizations increase their efficiency and effectiveness.
akg-images/Newscom

that decision making is slow and inefficient and organizations cannot change. When managers rely too much on rules to solve problems and not enough on their own skills and judgment, their behavior becomes inflexible. A key challenge for managers is to use bureaucratic principles to benefit, rather than harm, an organization.

Fayol's Principles of Management

Henri Fayol (1841–1925) was the CEO of Comambault Mining. Working at the same time as Weber, but independently, Fayol identified 14 principles (summarized in Table 2.1) that he believed essential to increasing the efficiency of the management process.[21] We discuss these principles in detail here because, although they were developed at the turn of the 20th century, they remain the bedrock on which much of recent management theory and research are based.

DIVISION OF LABOR A champion of job specialization and the division of labor for reasons already mentioned, Fayol was nevertheless among the first to point out the downside of too much specialization: boredom–a state of mind likely to diminish product quality, worker initiative, and flexibility. As a result, Fayol advocated that workers be given more job duties to perform or be encouraged to assume more responsibility for work outcomes–a principle increasingly applied today in organizations that empower their workers. Modern grocery stores, like Publix, use division of labor in their operations. For example, in the bakery and deli, employees focus on creating cakes, pies, and ready-to-eat meals. By using division of labor, Publix employees are able to develop expertise they might not otherwise gain.[22]

Table 2.1

Fayol's 14 Principles of Management

Division of labor Job specialization and the division of labor should increase efficiency, especially if managers take steps to lessen workers' boredom.

Authority and responsibility Managers have the right to give orders and the power to exhort their employees for obedience.

Unity of command An employee should receive orders from only one superior.

Line of authority The length of the chain of command that extends from the top to the bottom of an organization should be limited.

Centralization Authority should not be concentrated at the top of the chain of command.

Unity of direction The organization should have a single plan of action to guide managers and workers.

Equity All organizational members are entitled to be treated with justice and respect.

Order The arrangement of organizational positions should maximize organizational efficiency and provide employees with satisfying career opportunities.

Initiative Managers should allow employees to be innovative and creative.

Discipline Managers need to create a workforce that strives to achieve organizational goals.

Remuneration of personnel The system that managers use to reward employees should be equitable for both employees and the organization.

Stability of tenure of personnel Long-term employees develop skills that can improve organizational efficiency.

Subordination of individual interests to the common interest Employees should understand how their performance affects the performance of the whole organization.

Esprit de corps Managers should encourage the development of shared feelings of comradeship, enthusiasm, or devotion to a common cause.

AUTHORITY AND RESPONSIBILITY Like Weber, Fayol emphasized the importance of authority and responsibility. Fayol, however, went beyond Weber's formal authority, which derives from a manager's position in the hierarchy, to recognize the *informal* authority that derives from personal expertise, technical knowledge, moral worth, and the ability to lead and to generate commitment from their employees.

unity of command A reporting relationship in which an employee receives orders from, and reports to, only one superior.

UNITY OF COMMAND The principle of **unity of command** specifies that an employee should receive orders from, and report to, only one superior. Fayol believed that *dual command,* the reporting relationship that exists when two supervisors give orders to the same employee, should be avoided except in exceptional circumstances. Dual command confuses employees, undermines order and discipline, and creates havoc within the formal hierarchy of authority. For example, the U.S. Army maintains unity of command for its soldiers. Clearly defined ranks range from private to five-star general, and each soldier answers to a commanding officer with a higher rank. While operating in the field, it is critical that soldiers understand their objectives, and consistent unity of command enables each soldier to know exactly whom they should follow to get the job done.[23]

line of authority The chain of command extending from the top to the bottom of an organization.

LINE OF AUTHORITY The **line of authority** is the chain of command extending from the top to the bottom of an organization. Fayol was one of the first management theorists to point out the importance of limiting the length of the chain of command by controlling the number of levels in the managerial hierarchy. The more levels in the hierarchy, the longer communication takes between managers at the top and bottom and the slower the pace of planning and organizing. Restricting the number of hierarchical levels to lessen these communication problems lets an organization act quickly and flexibly.

Fayol also pointed out that when organizations are split into different departments or functions, each with its own hierarchy, it is important to allow middle and first-line managers in each department to interact with managers at similar levels in other departments. This interaction helps speed decision making because managers know each other and know whom to go to when problems arise. For cross-departmental integration to work, Fayol noted the importance of keeping one's superiors informed about what is taking place so that lower-level decisions do not harm activities taking place in other parts of the organization.

centralization The concentration of authority at the top of the managerial hierarchy.

CENTRALIZATION Fayol also was one of the first management writers to focus on **centralization**, the concentration of authority at the top of the managerial hierarchy. Fayol believed authority should not be concentrated at the top of the chain of command. One of the most significant issues that top managers face is how much authority to centralize at the top of the organization and what authority to decentralize to managers and workers at lower hierarchical levels. This important issue affects the behavior of people at all levels in the organization.

If authority is very centralized, only managers at the top make important decisions, and employees simply follow orders. This arrangement gives top managers great control over organizational activities and helps ensure that the organization is pursuing its strategy, but it makes it difficult for the people who are closest to problems and issues to respond to them in a timely manner. It also can reduce the motivation of middle and first-line managers and make them less flexible and adaptable because they become reluctant to make decisions on their own, even when doing so is necessary. They get used to others making decisions. The pendulum is now swinging toward decentralization as organizations seek to empower middle managers and create self-managed teams that monitor and control their own activities, both to increase organizational flexibility and to reduce operating costs and increase efficiency.

unity of direction The singleness of purpose that makes possible the creation of one plan of action to guide managers and workers as they use organizational resources.

UNITY OF DIRECTION Just as there is a need for unity of command, there is also a need for **unity of direction**, the singleness of purpose that makes possible the creation of one plan of action to guide managers and workers as they use organizational resources. An organization without a single guiding plan becomes inefficient and ineffective; its activities become unfocused, and individuals and groups work at cross-purposes. Successful planning starts with top managers working as a team to craft the organization's strategy, which they communicate to middle managers, who decide how to use organizational resources to implement the strategy.

equity The justice, impartiality, and fairness to which all organizational members are entitled.

EQUITY As Fayol wrote, "For personnel to be encouraged to carry out their duties with all the devotion and loyalty of which they are capable, they must be treated with respect for their own sense of integrity, and equity results from the combination of respect and justice."[24] **Equity**–the justice, impartiality, and fairness to which all organizational members are entitled–is receiving much attention today; the desire to treat employees fairly is a primary concern of managers. (Equity theory is discussed in Chapter 13.)

order The methodical arrangement of positions to provide the organization with the greatest benefit and to provide employees with career opportunities.

ORDER Like Taylor and the Gilbreths, Fayol was interested in analyzing jobs, positions, and individuals to ensure that the organization was using resources as efficiently as possible. To Fayol, **order** meant the methodical arrangement of positions to provide the organization with the greatest benefit and to provide employees with career opportunities that satisfied their needs. Thus Fayol recommended the use of organizational charts to show the position and duties of each employee and to indicate which positions an employee might move to or be promoted into in the future. He also advocated that managers engage in extensive career planning to help ensure orderly career paths.

initiative The ability to act on one's own without direction from a superior.

INITIATIVE Although order and equity are important means to fostering commitment and loyalty among employees, Fayol believed managers must also encourage employees to exercise **initiative**, the ability to act on their own without direction from a superior. Used properly, initiative can be a major source of strength for an organization because it leads to creativity and innovation. Managers need skill and tact to achieve the difficult balance between the organization's need for order and employees' desire for initiative. Fayol believed the ability to strike this balance was a key indicator of a superior manager.

discipline Obedience, energy, application, and other outward marks of respect for a superior's authority.

DISCIPLINE In focusing on the importance of **discipline**–obedience, energy, application, and other outward marks of respect for a superior's authority–Fayol was addressing the concern of many early managers: how to create a workforce that was reliable and hardworking and would strive to achieve organizational goals. According to Fayol, discipline results in respectful relationships between organizational members and reflects the quality of an organization's leadership and a manager's ability to act fairly and equitably.

REMUNERATION OF PERSONNEL Fayol proposed reward systems, including bonuses and profit-sharing plans, that are increasingly used today as organizations seek ways to motivate employees. Convinced from his own experience that an organization's payment system has important implications for organizational success, Fayol believed effective reward systems should be equitable for both employees and the organization, encourage productivity by rewarding well-directed effort, not be subject to abuse, and be uniformly applied to employees. For example, Syndio is a recent startup whose software is used by companies to analyze and resolve pay equity issues due to gender, race, or other issues and to provide strategies for fixing the disparities among employees. More than 200 companies work with Syndio, including Salesforce, Nordstrom, NerdWallet, and others.[25]

STABILITY OF TENURE OF PERSONNEL Fayol also recognized the importance of long-term employment, and this idea has been echoed by contemporary management gurus such as Tom Peters, Jeff Pfeffer, and Jim Collins. When employees stay with an organization for extended periods, they develop skills that improve the organization's ability to use its resources.

SUBORDINATION OF INDIVIDUAL INTERESTS TO THE COMMON INTEREST The interests of the organization as a whole must take precedence over the interests of any individual or group if the organization is to survive. Equitable agreements must be established between the organization and its members to ensure that employees are treated fairly and rewarded for their performance and to maintain the disciplined organizational relationships so vital to an efficient system of administration.

esprit de corps Shared feelings of comradeship, enthusiasm, or devotion to a common cause among members of a group.

ESPRIT DE CORPS As this discussion of Fayol's ideas suggests, the appropriate design of an organization's hierarchy of authority and the right mix of order and discipline foster cooperation and commitment. Likewise, a key element in a successful organization is the development of **esprit de corps**, a French expression that refers to shared feelings of comradeship, enthusiasm, or devotion to a common cause among members of a group. (Today the term *organizational culture* is used to refer to these shared feelings; this concept is discussed at length in Chapter 3.)

Some of the principles that Fayol outlined have faded from contemporary management practices, but the basic concerns that motivated Fayol continue to inspire management theorists.[26] The principles that Fayol and Weber set forth still provide clear and appropriate guidelines that managers can use to create a work setting that efficiently and effectively uses organizational resources. These principles remain the bedrock of modern management theory; recent researchers have refined or developed them to suit modern conditions. For example, Weber's and Fayol's concerns for equity and for establishing appropriate links between performance and reward are central themes in contemporary theories of motivation and leadership. Consider also how their principles apply to the example of E Source in the "Management Insight" feature.

MANAGEMENT INSIGHT

E Source's Approach to Employee Satisfaction and Productivity

Knowledge, insights, and human relations are all wired into E Source's business. The Colorado-based company started in the 1980s with a mission to help people use less electricity, and its founders soon realized they could achieve the best results if they also worked with utilities to develop energy-efficiency programs. Now E Source is a firm that conducts research and provides consulting to utilities and large-scale users of electricity, aimed at helping utilities efficiently meet their customers' needs for reliable energy.[27]

At a company that uses market research to answer questions about customer experience, it was only natural that management would be curious about its own employees' experiences. So E Source asked them how working there compared with their ideals. They learned that some disconnects existed: Managers didn't feel that their work was clearly connected with what other groups were doing, and employees didn't understand how their work related to any overarching company objectives.[28]

E Source's leaders understood that they needed to build commitment to a common cause, which they expected would also result in greater enthusiasm for daily work, both of which are essentials in Fayol's idea of esprit de corps. The company began holding monthly social gatherings of department managers, with the expectation that as they talked more among themselves, they would build relationships and share ideas. E Source also took a more structured approach to goal setting, starting with organization-level goals, which are then linked to departmental and personal goals. Laying out the structure of goals along lines of authority enables people to align their work with the common interest and see how their contributions contribute to success.[29]

In other efforts, E Source has moved beyond some of Fayol's thinking. Whereas Fayol addresses management from a perspective of managers having authority and giving orders, E Source's approach to management takes more account of employees' creativity and expertise–but still in the service of business goals. So, for example, the company instituted a policy that employees who complete their assignments on time while working four days a week can take Fridays off. The company found that employees became creative about working more efficiently, so the policy is a win for both employees and the company.[30]

Behavioral Management Theory

LO2-4 Trace the changes in theories about how managers should behave to motivate and control employees.

Because the writings of Weber and Fayol were not translated into English and published in the United States until the late 1940s, American management theorists in the first half of the 20th century were unaware of the contributions of these European pioneers. American management theorists began where Taylor and his followers left off. Although their writings were different, these theorists all espoused a theme that focused on **behavioral management**, the study of how managers should personally behave to motivate employees and encourage them to perform at high levels and be committed to achieving organizational goals.

behavioral management The study of how managers should behave to motivate employees and encourage them to perform at high levels and be committed to the achievement of organizational goals.

The Work of Mary Parker Follett

Another important researcher in the field of management theory was Mary Parker Follett (1868–1933). Much of her writing about management and about the way managers should behave toward workers was a response to her concern that Taylor was ignoring the human side of the organization. She pointed out that management often overlooks the multitude of ways in which employees can contribute to the organization when managers allow them to participate and exercise initiative in their everyday work lives.[31] Taylor, for example, never proposed that managers should involve workers in analyzing their jobs to identify better ways to perform tasks or should even ask workers how they felt about their jobs. Instead he used time-and-motion experts to analyze workers' jobs for them. Follett, in contrast, argued that because workers know the most about their jobs, they should be involved in job analysis and managers should allow them to participate in the work development process.

Follett proposed that "authority should go with knowledge . . . whether it is up the line or down." In other words, if workers have the relevant knowledge, then workers, rather than managers, should be in control of the work process itself, and managers should behave as coaches and facilitators–not as monitors and supervisors. In making this statement, Follett anticipated the current interest in self-managed teams and empowerment. She also recognized the importance of having managers in different departments communicate directly with each other to speed decision making. She advocated what she called "cross-functioning": members of different departments working together in cross-departmental teams to accomplish projects–an approach that is increasingly used today.[32]

Fayol also mentioned expertise and knowledge as important sources of managers' authority, but Follett went further. She proposed that knowledge and expertise, not managers' formal authority deriving from their position in the hierarchy, should decide who will lead at any particular moment. She believed, as do many management theorists today, that power is fluid and should flow to the person who can best help the organization achieve its goals. Follett took a horizontal view of power and authority, in contrast to Fayol, who saw the formal line of authority and vertical chain of command as being most essential to effective management. Follett's behavioral approach to management was very radical for its time.

Mary Parker Follett, an early management thinker who advocated, "Authority should go with knowledge . . . whether it is up the line or down."
Regina A. Greenwood, from the Ronald G. Greenwood Collection

The Hawthorne Studies and Human Relations

Probably because of its radical nature, Follett's work was unappreciated by managers and researchers until quite recently. Most continued to follow in the footsteps of Taylor and the Gilbreths. To increase efficiency, they studied ways to improve various characteristics of the work setting, such as job specialization or the kinds of tools workers used. One series of studies was conducted from 1924 to 1932 at the Hawthorne Works of the Western Electric Company.[33] This research, now known as the *Hawthorne studies,* began as an attempt to investigate how characteristics of the work setting–specifically, the level of lighting, or illumination–affect worker fatigue and performance. The researchers conducted an experiment in which they systematically measured worker productivity at various levels of illumination.

Workers in a telephone manufacturing plant in 1931. Around this time, researchers at the Hawthorne Works of the Western Electric Company began to study the effects of work-setting characteristics, such as lighting and rest periods, on employee productivity. To their surprise, they discovered that workers' productivity was affected more by the attention they received from researchers than by characteristics of the work setting—a phenomenon that became known as the Hawthorne effect.
Fox Photos/Hulton Archive/Getty Images

The experiment produced some unexpected results. The researchers found that regardless of whether they raised or lowered the level of illumination, productivity increased. In fact, productivity began to fall only when the level of illumination dropped to the level of moonlight—a level at which workers could presumably no longer see well enough to do their work efficiently.

The researchers found these results puzzling and invited a noted Harvard psychologist, Elton Mayo, to help them. Mayo proposed another series of experiments to solve the mystery. These experiments, known as the *relay assembly test experiments,* were designed to investigate the effects of other aspects of the work context on job performance, such as the effect of the number and length of rest periods and hours of work on fatigue and monotony.[34] The goal was to increase productivity.

During a two-year study of a small group of female workers, the researchers again observed that productivity increased over time, but the increases could not be solely attributed to the effects of changes in the work setting. Gradually, the researchers discovered that, to some degree, the results they were obtaining were influenced by the fact that the researchers themselves had become part of the experiment. In other words, the presence of the researchers was affecting the results because the workers enjoyed receiving attention and being the subject of study and were willing to cooperate with the researchers to produce the results they believed the researchers desired.

Hawthorne effect The finding that a manager's behavior or leadership approach can affect workers' level of performance.

human relations movement A management approach that advocates the idea that supervisors should receive behavioral training to manage employees in ways that elicit their cooperation and increase their productivity.

Subsequently, it was found that many other factors also influence worker behavior, and it was not clear what was actually influencing the Hawthorne workers' behavior. However, this particular effect—which became known as the **Hawthorne effect**—seemed to suggest that workers' attitudes toward their managers affect the level of workers' performance. In particular, the significant finding was that each manager's personal behavior or leadership approach can affect performance. This finding led many researchers to turn their attention to managerial behavior and leadership. If supervisors could be trained to behave in ways that would elicit cooperative behavior from their employees, productivity could be increased. From this view emerged the **human relations movement**, which advocates that supervisors be behaviorally trained to manage employees in ways that elicit their cooperation and increase their productivity.

The importance of behavioral, or human relations, training became even clearer to its supporters after another series of experiments—the *bank wiring room experiments.* In a study of workers making telephone switching equipment, researchers Elton Mayo and F. J. Roethlisberger discovered that the workers, as a group, had deliberately adopted a norm of output restriction to protect their jobs. Workers who violated this informal production norm were subjected to sanctions by other group members. Those who violated group performance norms and performed above the norm were called "ratebusters"; those who performed below the norm were called "chiselers."

The experimenters concluded that both types of workers threatened the group as a whole. Ratebusters threatened group members because they revealed to managers how fast the work could be done. Chiselers were looked down on because they were not doing their share of the work. Work group members disciplined both ratebusters and chiselers to create a pace of work that the workers (not the managers) thought was fair. Thus, a work group's influence over output can be as great as the supervisors' influence. Because the work group can influence the behavior of its members, some management theorists argue that supervisors should be trained to behave in ways that gain the goodwill and cooperation of workers so that supervisors, not workers, control the level of work group performance.

informal organization The system of behavioral rules and norms that emerge in a group.

One implication of the Hawthorne studies was that the behavior of managers and workers in the work setting is as important in explaining the level of performance as the technical aspects of the task. Managers must understand the workings of the **informal organization**, the system of behavioral rules and norms that emerge in a group, when they try to manage or change behavior in organizations. Many studies have found that as time passes, groups often develop elaborate procedures and norms that bond members together, allowing unified action either to cooperate with management to raise performance or to restrict output and thwart the attainment of organizational goals. The Hawthorne studies demonstrated the importance of understanding how the feelings, thoughts, and behavior of work group members and managers affect performance. It was becoming increasingly clear to researchers that understanding behavior in organizations is a complex process that is critical to increasing performance.[35] Indeed, the increasing interest in the area of management known as **organizational behavior**, the study of the factors that have an impact on how individuals and groups respond to and act in organizations, dates from these early studies.

organizational behavior The study of the factors that have an impact on how individuals and groups respond to and act in organizations.

Theory X and Theory Y

Several studies after World War II revealed how assumptions about workers' attitudes and behavior affect managers' behavior. Perhaps the most influential approach was developed by Douglas McGregor. He proposed two sets of assumptions about how work attitudes and behaviors not only dominate the way managers think but also affect how they behave in organizations. McGregor named these two contrasting sets of assumptions *Theory X* and *Theory Y* (see Figure 2.3).[36]

Theory X A set of negative assumptions about workers that leads to the conclusion that a manager's task is to supervise workers closely and control their behavior.

THEORY X According to the assumptions of **Theory X**, the average worker is lazy, dislikes work, and will try to do as little as possible. Moreover, workers have little ambition and wish to avoid responsibility. Thus, the manager's task is to counteract workers' natural tendencies to avoid work. To keep workers' performance at a high level, the manager must supervise workers closely and control their behavior by means of "the carrot and stick"–rewards and punishments.

Managers who accept the assumptions of Theory X design and shape the work setting to maximize their control over workers' behaviors and minimize workers' control over the pace of work. These managers believe workers must be made to do what is necessary for the success of the organization, and they focus on developing rules, SOPs, and a well-defined system of rewards and punishments to control behavior. They see little point in giving workers autonomy to solve their own problems because they think the workforce neither expects nor desires cooperation. Theory X managers see their role as closely monitoring workers to ensure that they contribute to the production process and do not threaten product quality. Henry Ford, who closely supervised and managed his workforce, fits McGregor's description of a manager who holds Theory X assumptions.

Figure 2.3

Theory X versus Theory Y

THEORY X	THEORY Y
The average employee is lazy, dislikes work, and will try to do as little as possible.	Employees are not inherently lazy. Given the chance, employees will do what is good for the organization.
To ensure that employees work hard, managers should closely supervise employees.	To allow employees to work in the organization's interest, managers must create a work setting that provides opportunities for workers to exercise initiative and self-direction.
Managers should create strict work rules and implement a well-defined system of rewards and punishments to control employees.	Managers should decentralize authority to employees and make sure employees have the resources necessary to achieve organizational goals.

Source: D. McGregor, *The Human Side of Enterprise.* Copyright © McGraw-Hill Education. Reprinted with permission.

Inspired by its cofounder, the late Herb Kelleher, Southwest Airlines continues to operate with an open-door policy that empowers employees to solve problems quickly and emphasizes a culture of fun and creativity.
The Washington Post/Contributor/Getty Images

THEORY Y In contrast, **Theory Y** assumes that workers are not inherently lazy, do not naturally dislike work, and, if given the opportunity, will do what is good for the organization. According to Theory Y, the characteristics of the work setting determine whether workers consider work to be a source of satisfaction or punishment, and managers do not need to closely control workers' behavior to make them perform at a high level because workers exercise self-control when they are committed to organizational goals. The implication of Theory Y, according to McGregor, is that "the limits of collaboration in the organizational setting are not limits of human nature but of management's ingenuity in discovering how to realize the potential represented by its human resources." It is the manager's task to create a work setting that encourages commitment to organizational goals and provides opportunities for workers to be imaginative and to exercise initiative and self-direction.

Theory Y A set of positive assumptions about workers that leads to the conclusion that a manager's task is to create a work setting that encourages commitment to organizational goals and provides opportunities for workers to be imaginative and to exercise initiative and self-direction.

When managers design the organizational setting to reflect the assumptions about attitudes and behavior suggested by Theory Y, the characteristics of the organization are quite different from those of an organizational setting based on Theory X. Managers who believe workers are motivated to help the organization reach its goals can decentralize authority and give more control over the job to workers, both as individuals and in groups. In this setting, individuals and groups are still accountable for their activities; however, the manager's role is not to control employees but to provide support and advice, to make sure employees have the resources they need to perform their jobs, and to evaluate them on their ability to help the organization meet its goals. Henri Fayol's approach to administration more closely reflects the assumptions of Theory Y rather than Theory X. Companies such as 3M, Apple, and Google exemplify those that follow Theory Y.

Southwest Airlines has long been the envy of the airline industry, and Southwest's leadership cites their Theory Y culture as a driving force. Inspired by cofounder and former CEO the late Herb Kelleher, Southwest Airlines emphasizes a culture of fun, creativity, and camaraderie.[37] Southwest employees note how Kelleher maintained an open-door policy of contact, which enabled him to stay in touch with problems facing the airline and to find solutions faster. That policy is still the norm today.

Employees have highly flexible job descriptions that enable them to chip in and help where needed. Unlike many of its competitors, which use highly regimented and formalized employee roles, Southwest employees are encouraged to help solve problems where they see them. Thus, it's not uncommon to see a Southwest manager helping move passenger luggage into aircraft or check in passengers at a gate.

Southwest also gives its employees significant discretion, enabling them to solve problems quickly. In an industry dominated by tight schedules and narrow windows to resolve problems, these actions enable employees to serve customers better.

management science theory An approach to management that uses rigorous quantitative techniques to help managers make maximum use of organizational resources.

Finally, Southwest Airlines views its unions as partners rather than adversaries, although fallout from the COVID-19 pandemic has tested these relationships. It works with independent unions to ensure that employees are compensated and treated fairly, and it solicits input from its employees on how to improve operations.[38] As a result of this innovative culture dominated by Theory Y thinking, Southwest Airlines has become one of the most consistently profitable companies among its competitors.

Management Science Theory

LO2-5 Explain the contributions of management science to the efficient use of organizational resources.

Management science theory is a contemporary approach to management that focuses on the use of rigorous quantitative techniques to help managers make maximum use of organizational resources to produce goods and services. In essence, management science theory is a contemporary extension of scientific management, which, as developed by Taylor, also took a quantitative approach to measuring the worker–task mix to raise efficiency. There are many branches of management science, and technology, which has a significant impact on all kinds of management practices, continues to affect the tools managers use to make decisions.[39] Each branch of management science deals with a specific set of concerns:

- *Quantitative management* uses mathematical techniques–such as linear and nonlinear programming, modeling, simulation, queuing theory, and chaos theory–to help managers decide, for example, how much inventory to hold at different times of the year, where to locate a new factory, and how best to invest an organization's financial capital. Technology offers managers new and improved ways of handling information so they can make more accurate assessments of the situation and better decisions.
- *Operations management* gives managers a set of techniques they can use to analyze any aspect of an organization's production system to increase efficiency. Technology, through the Internet and through the increasing use of cloud computing, is transforming how managers acquire inputs and distribute finished products.
- *Management information systems (MISs)* give managers details about events occurring inside the organization as well as in its external environment–information that is vital for effective decision making. Technology helps managers access more and better information and allows more managers at all levels to participate in the decision-making process.

All these subfields of management science, enhanced by sophisticated technology, provide tools and techniques that managers can use to help improve the quality of their decision making and increase efficiency and effectiveness. For example, Toyota applied management science theory with its Toyota Production System (TPS). The TPS emphasizes continuous improvement in quality and the reduction of waste through learning. TPS was a major catalyst for the "lean revolution" in global manufacturing, and manufacturing companies worldwide have embraced this philosophy and adapted it for their own operations.[40] We discuss many important developments in management science theory in this book. In particular, Chapter 9 focuses on how to use operations management and the principle of total quality management (TQM) to improve quality, efficiency, and responsiveness to customers.

Organizational Environment Theory

LO2-6 Explain why the study of the external environment and its impact on an organization has become a central issue in management thought.

An important milestone in the history of management thought occurred when researchers went beyond the study of how managers can influence behavior within organizations to consider how managers control the organization's relationship with its external environment, or **organizational environment**–the set of forces and conditions that operate beyond an organization's boundaries but affect a manager's ability to acquire and utilize resources. Resources in the organizational environment include the raw materials and skilled people that an organization requires to produce goods and services, as well as the support of groups, including customers who buy these goods and services and provide the organization with big data critical to the firm's overall financial success. One way of determining the relative success of an organization is to consider how effective its managers are at obtaining scarce and valuable resources.[41] The importance of studying the environment became clear after the development of open-systems theory and contingency theory during the 1960s and other more recent theories, including dynamic capabilities.

organizational environment The set of forces and conditions that operate beyond an organization's boundaries but affect a manager's ability to acquire and utilize resources.

The Open-Systems View

One of the most influential views of how an organization is affected by its external environment was developed by Daniel Katz, Robert Kahn, and James Thompson in the 1960s.[42] These theorists viewed the organization as an **open system**–a system that takes in resources from its external environment and converts or transforms them into goods and services that are sent back to that environment, where they are bought by customers (see Figure 2.4).

open system A system that takes in resources from its external environment and converts them into goods and services that are then sent back to that environment for purchase by customers.

At the *input stage,* an organization acquires resources such as raw materials, money, and skilled workers to produce goods and services. Once the organization has gathered the necessary resources, conversion begins. At the *conversion stage,* the organization's workforce, using appropriate tools, techniques, and machinery, transforms the inputs into outputs of finished goods and services such as cars, hamburgers, or flights to Hawaii. At the *output stage,* the

Figure 2.4

The Organization as an Open System

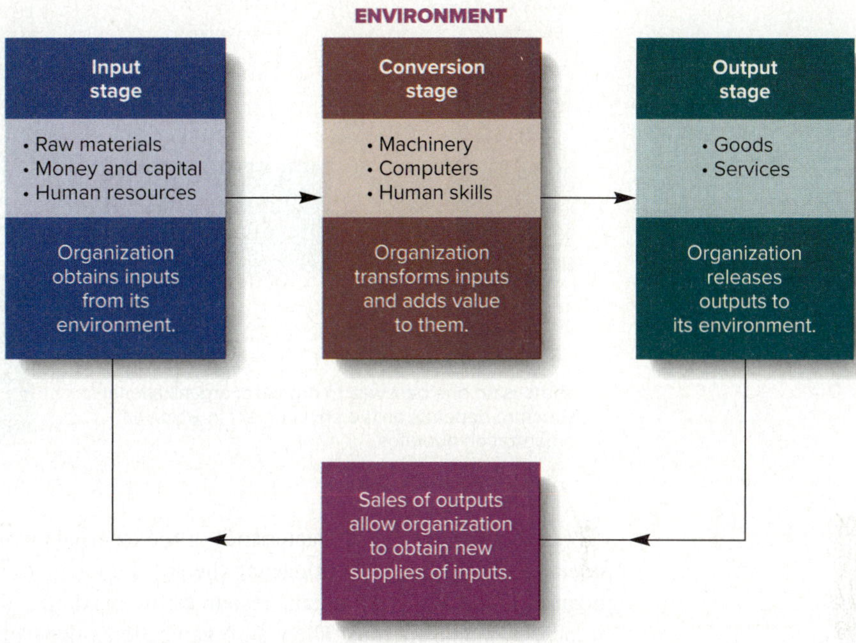

organization releases finished goods and services to its external environment, where customers purchase and use them to satisfy their needs. The money the organization obtains from the sales of its outputs allows the organization to acquire more resources so the cycle can begin again.

The system just described is said to be open because the organization draws from and interacts with the external environment in order to survive; in other words, the organization is open to its environment. A **closed system**, in contrast, is a self-contained system that is not affected by changes in its external environment. Organizations that operate as closed systems, that ignore the external environment, and that fail to acquire inputs are likely to experience **entropy**, which is the tendency of a closed system to lose its ability to control itself and thus to dissolve and disintegrate.

closed system A system that is self-contained and thus not affected by changes occurring in its external environment.

entropy The tendency of a closed system to lose its ability to control itself and thus to dissolve and disintegrate.

Management theorists can model the activities of most organizations by using the open-systems view. For example, manufacturing companies, like Ford and Caterpillar, buy inputs such as component parts, skilled and semiskilled labor, and robots and computer-controlled manufacturing equipment; then at the conversion stage they use their manufacturing skills to assemble inputs into outputs of cars and heavy equipment. As we discuss in later chapters, competition between organizations for resources is one of several major challenges to managing the organizational environment.

Researchers using the open-systems view are also interested in how the various parts of a system work together to promote efficiency and effectiveness. Systems theorists like to argue that the whole is greater than the sum of its parts; they mean that an organization performs at a higher level when its departments work together rather than separately. **Synergy**, the performance gains that result from the *combined* actions of individuals and departments, is possible only in an organized system. The strategy of using teams composed of people from different departments reflects systems theorists' interest in designing organizational systems to create synergy and thus increase efficiency and effectiveness.

synergy Performance gains that result when individuals and departments coordinate their actions.

Contingency Theory

contingency theory The idea that the organizational structures and control systems managers choose depend on (are contingent on) characteristics of the external environment in which the organization operates.

Another milestone in management theory was the development of **contingency theory** in the 1960s by Tom Burns and G. M. Stalker in Britain and Paul Lawrence and Jay Lorsch in the United States.[43] The crucial message of contingency theory is that *there is no one best way to organize:* The organizational structures and the control systems that managers choose depend

Figure 2.5

Contingency Theory of Organizational Design

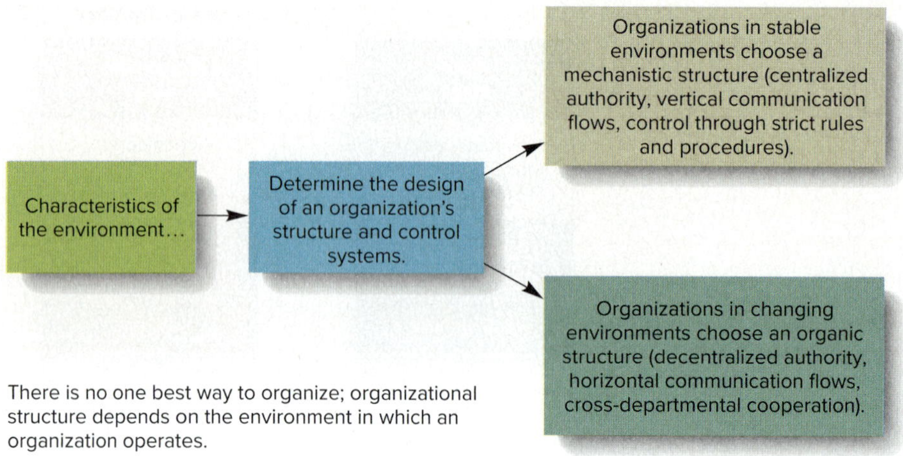

on (are contingent on) characteristics of the external environment in which the organization operates. According to contingency theory, the characteristics of the environment affect an organization's ability to obtain resources; to maximize the likelihood of gaining access to resources, managers must allow an organization's departments to organize and control their activities in ways most likely to allow them to obtain resources, given the constraints of the environment they face. In other words, how managers design the organizational hierarchy, choose a control system, and lead and motivate their employees is contingent on the characteristics of the organizational environment (see Figure 2.5).

An important characteristic of the external environment that affects an organization's ability to obtain resources is the degree to which the environment is changing. Changes in the organizational environment include changes in technology, which can lead to the creation of new products (such as Amazon Echo) and result in the obsolescence of existing products (Blu-ray players); the entry of new competitors (such as foreign organizations that compete for available resources); and unstable economic conditions. In general, the more quickly the organizational environment is changing, the greater the problems are associated with gaining access to resources, and the greater is managers' need to find ways to coordinate the activities of people in different departments to respond to the environment quickly and effectively. Recent years have seen an extraordinary degree of change; for examples of how recent changes have forced organizations to respond, see the "Managing Globally" feature.

MANAGING GLOBALLY

Changing Up the Manager's Role

Perhaps more than ever, global forces are reshaping the role of the manager. A pandemic shook up whole industries and forced companies to rethink where people can and should work. Pent-up consumer demand that erupted even as some regions and companies were keeping workers at home contributed to disrupted supply chains. Russia's invasion of Ukraine and the global response to it have added fuel to the fire of demand-driven inflation and forced some companies to re-evaluate their global footprint. Ongoing trends, such as the rapid adoption of digital technology, are automating work once considered the exclusive domain of humans. Employers also find themselves competing for talent in a labor market that is tight because of slowing birth rates and pandemic-related challenges to being at work.[44]

These and other conditions have changed the mix of skills that managers need. Today's managers spend less time on routine tasks that computers can handle. In a tight labor market, they must increasingly focus on retaining employees by providing meaningful work and career development, including one-on-one coaching. For organizations to be flexible and innovative, their people need to learn new technology and take on a wider scope of responsibility. It often falls to managers to prepare their people for these roles.[45]

The turbulent environment and multiple skill sets required for adapting to it can be frustrating, exhausting, and overwhelming. And it is happening after years of company initiatives to become more efficient and agile by eliminating layers of management. In other words, managers have to develop new skill sets even as the number of people reporting to them increases.[46]

Organizations therefore need to adjust so they support managers and employees with the right structure and systems. At some companies, this will mean a commitment to developing next-generation managers through a variety of learning opportunities. Other organizations are redefining managers' roles. In Australia, for example, Telstra divided managers' work into two different positions. Leaders of people focus on human resource planning, employee selection, and career development to ensure the company has the talent it needs. And leaders of work take charge of project teams, with responsibility for budgets, timelines, and project delivery. Managers appreciate the ability to focus on their strengths, and employees see advantages in having one manager interested in their personal development and another who is clear about how to succeed on specific projects.[47]

MECHANISTIC AND ORGANIC STRUCTURES Drawing on Weber's and Fayol's principles of organization and management, Burns and Stalker proposed two basic ways in which managers can organize and control an organization's activities to respond to characteristics of its external environment: They can use a *mechanistic structure* or an *organic structure*.[48] As you will see, a mechanistic structure typically rests on Theory X assumptions, and an organic structure typically rests on Theory Y assumptions.

mechanistic structure An organizational structure in which authority is centralized, tasks and rules are clearly specified, and employees are closely supervised.

When the environment surrounding an organization is stable, managers tend to choose a mechanistic structure to organize and control activities and make employee behavior predictable. In a **mechanistic structure**, authority is centralized at the top of the managerial hierarchy, and the vertical hierarchy of authority is the main means used to control employees' behavior. Tasks and roles are clearly specified, employees are closely supervised, and the emphasis is on strict discipline and order. Everyone knows their place, and there is a place for everyone. A mechanistic structure provides the most efficient way to operate in a stable environment because it allows managers to obtain inputs at the lowest cost, giving an organization the most control over its conversion processes and enabling the most efficient production of goods and services with the smallest expenditure of resources. McDonald's restaurants operate with a mechanistic structure. Supervisors make all important decisions; employees are closely supervised and follow well-defined rules and standard operating procedures.

organic structure An organizational structure in which authority is decentralized to middle and first-line managers and tasks and roles are left ambiguous to encourage employees to cooperate and respond quickly to the unexpected.

In contrast, when the environment is changing rapidly, it is difficult to obtain access to resources, and managers need to organize their activities in a way that allows them to cooperate, to act quickly to acquire resources (such as new types of inputs to produce new kinds of products), and to respond effectively to the unexpected. In an **organic structure**, authority is decentralized to middle and first-line managers to encourage them to take responsibility and act quickly to pursue scarce resources. Departments are encouraged to take a cross-departmental or functional perspective, and cross-functional teams composed of people from different departments are formed. As in Follett's model, the organization operates in an organic way because authority rests with the individuals, departments, and teams best positioned to control the current problems the organization is facing. As a result, managers in an organic structure can react more quickly to a changing environment than can managers in a mechanistic structure. However, an organic structure is generally more expensive to operate because it requires that more managerial time, money, and effort be spent on coordination. So it is used only when needed–when the organizational environment is unstable and changing rapidly.[49] Google, Apple, and 3M are examples of companies that operate with organic structures.

Dynamic Capabilities

dynamic capabilities Theory that organizations have the ability to build, integrate, and reconfigure processes to address rapidly changing internal and external environments.

Over the past few decades, other management theories have emerged, which have had a significant impact on how organizations function, including total quality management (discussed in Chapter 9), organizational learning (described in Chapter 7), and dynamic capabilities. David Teece, a professor at UC-Berkeley's Haas School of Business, came up with the theory of **dynamic capabilities** in the late 1990s to explain how companies must be stable enough to deliver value to customers yet resilient and flexible enough to shift focus when situations demand a different approach.[50] Unlike best practices, which typically are learned capabilities and activities undertaken by one or two companies that spread to an entire industry, dynamic capabilities are unique to each company and are more than likely rooted in the organization's past experiences.[51]

According to Teece, three types of managerial activities can help make a process or activity dynamic: sensing, seizing, and transforming. *Sensing* refers to identifying and assessing opportunities outside the company. For example, Steve Jobs recognized consumers wanted a smaller, more attractive mp3 player than what was available in the marketplace. *Seizing* describes the action of mobilizing company resources to capture value for the organization from these opportunities. Acting on its assessment of the competition, Apple seized the opportunity to design and produce the iPod, a sleek alternative to bulky mp3 devices. *Transforming* is an organization's ability to continue making changes as needed to maintain success. Once Apple created the iPod, the company shifted its focus from solely producing computers to expanding its product line to consumer electronics and, eventually, music and original content streaming. In 2022, Apple topped the *Forbes* annual list of the world's most valuable brands for the tenth consecutive year, worth more than $482 billion.[52]

In addition, technological advances, such as artificial intelligence and data analytics, among others, have prompted managers to devise processes and innovative tools to take advantage of opportunities while staying ahead of the competition. For example, big data, information gathered via social media and other digital platforms, can be analyzed and categorized into useful patterns and data sets, which companies use to change or refine internal processes, develop and introduce new products and services, and create efficiencies in managing customers and suppliers.[53] These technologies and dynamic capabilities can be tested, scaled, and adapted quickly, giving organizations tremendous competitive advantage.[54]

Summary and Review

In this chapter we examined the evolution of management theory and research over the last century. Much of the material in the rest of this book stems from developments and refinements of this work. Indeed, the rest of this book incorporates the results of the extensive research in management that has been conducted since the development of the theories discussed here.

LO2-1, 2-2 **SCIENTIFIC MANAGEMENT THEORY** The search for efficiency started with the study of how managers could improve person–task relationships to increase efficiency. The concept of job specialization and division of labor remains the basis for the design of work settings in modern organizations. New developments such as lean production and total quality management are often viewed as advances on the early scientific management principles developed by Taylor and the Gilbreths.

LO2-3 **ADMINISTRATIVE MANAGEMENT THEORY** Max Weber and Henri Fayol outlined principles of bureaucracy and administration that are as relevant to managers today as they were when developed at the turn of the 20th century. Much of modern management research refines these principles to suit contemporary conditions. For example, the use of cross-departmental teams and the empowerment of workers are issues that managers also faced a century ago.

LO2-4 **BEHAVIORAL MANAGEMENT THEORY** Researchers have described many different approaches to managerial behavior, including Theories X and Y. Often the managerial behavior that researchers suggest reflects the context of their own historical eras and cultures. Mary

Parker Follett advocated managerial behaviors that did not reflect accepted modes of managerial behavior at the time, and her work was largely ignored until conditions changed.

LO2-5 **MANAGEMENT SCIENCE THEORY** The various branches of management science theory provide rigorous quantitative techniques that give managers more control over each organization's use of resources to produce goods and services.

LO2-6 **ORGANIZATIONAL ENVIRONMENT THEORY** A main focus of contemporary management research is to find methods to help managers improve how they use organizational resources and compete in the global environment. The importance of studying the organization's external environment became clear after the development of open-systems and contingency theories during the 1960s. More recent management approaches have emerged, including dynamic capabilities.

Management in Action

Topics for Discussion and Action

Discussion

1. Choose a fast-food restaurant, a fitness club, or some other organization with which you are familiar, and describe the division of labor and job specialization it uses to produce goods and services. How might this division of labor be improved? **[LO2-1, 2-2]**
2. Apply Taylor's principles of scientific management to improve the performance of the organization you chose in question 1. **[LO2-2]**
3. In what ways are Weber's and Fayol's ideas about bureaucracy and administration similar? How do they differ? **[LO2-3]**
4. Which of Weber's and Fayol's principles seem most relevant to the creation of an ethical organization? **[LO2-4, 2-6]**
5. How are companies using management science theory to improve their processes? Is this theory equally applicable for manufacturing and service companies? If so, how? **[LO2-4, 2-5]**
6. What is contingency theory? What kinds of organizations familiar to you have been successful or unsuccessful in dealing with contingencies from the external environment? **[LO2-6]**
7. Why are mechanistic and organic structures suited to different organizational environments? **[LO2-4, 2-6]**

Action

8. Question a manager about their views of the relative importance of Fayol's 14 principles of management. **[LO2-3, 2-4]**
9. Visit at least two organizations in your community, and identify those that seem to operate with a Theory X or a Theory Y approach to management. **[LO2-4]**

Building Management Skills

Managing Your Own Business [LO2-2, 2-4]

Now that you understand the concerns addressed by management thinkers over the last century, use this exercise to apply your knowledge to developing your management skills.

Imagine that you are the founder of a software company that specializes in developing games for mobile devices. Customer demand for your games has increased so much that over the last year your company has grown from a busy one-person operation to one with 16 employees. In addition to yourself, you employ six software developers to produce the software, three graphic artists, two computer technicians, two marketing and sales personnel, and two assistants. In the next year you expect to hire 30 new employees, and you are wondering how best to manage your growing company.

1. Use the principles of Weber and Fayol to decide on the system of organization and management that you think will be most effective for your growing organization. How many levels will the managerial hierarchy of your organization have? How much authority will you decentralize to your employees? How will you establish the division of labor between employees? Will your employees work alone and report to you or work in teams?
2. Which management approach (for example, Theory X or Y) do you propose to use to run your organization? In 50 or fewer words, write a statement describing the management approach you believe will motivate and coordinate your employees, and tell why you think this style will be best.

Managing Ethically [LO2-3, 2-4]

How Unethical Behavior Shut Down a Meatpacking Plant

By all appearances the Westland/Hallmark Meat Co. based in Chico, California, was considered to be an efficient and sanitary meatpacking plant. Under the control of its owner and CEO, Steven Mendell, the plant regularly passed inspections by the U.S. Department of Agriculture (USDA). Over 200 workers were employed to slaughter cattle and prepare the beef for shipment to fast-food restaurants such as Burger King and Taco Bell. Also, millions of pounds of meat the plant produced yearly were delivered under contract to one of the federal government's most coveted accounts: the National School Lunch Program.[55]

When the Humane Society turned over a videotape (secretly filmed by one of its investigators, who had taken a job as a plant employee) to the San Bernardino County district attorney, showing major violations of health procedures, an uproar followed. The videotape showed two workers dragging sick cows up the ramp that led to the slaughterhouse using metal chains and forklifts, and shocking them with electric prods and shooting streams of water in their noses and faces. Not only did the tape show inhumane treatment of animals, but it also provided evidence that the company was flouting the ban on allowing sick animals to enter the food supply chain—something that federal regulations explicitly outlaw because of concerns for human health and safety.

Once the USDA was informed that potentially contaminated beef products had entered the supply chain—especially the one to the nation's schools—it issued a notice for the recall of the 143 million pounds of beef processed in the plant over the last two years, the largest recall in history. In addition, the plant was shut down as the investigation proceeded. CEO Steven Mendell was subpoenaed to appear before a subcommittee of the House Energy and Commerce Committee. He denied that these violations had taken place and that diseased cows had entered the food chain. However, when panel members demanded that he view the videotape, which he claimed he had not seen, he was forced to acknowledge that inhumane treatment of animals had occurred.[56] Moreover, federal investigators turned up evidence that as early as 1996 the plant had been cited for overuse of electric prods to speed cattle through the plant and had been cited for other violations since, suggesting that these abuses had been going on for a long period.

Not only were consumers and schoolchildren harmed by these unethical actions, but the plant itself was permanently shut down and all 220 workers lost their jobs. In addition, the employees directly implicated in the video were prosecuted and one, who pleaded guilty to animal abuse, was convicted and sentenced to six months in prison.[57] Clearly, all the people and groups affected by the meatpacking plant have suffered from its unethical and inhumane organizational behaviors and practices.

Questions

1. Use the theories discussed in the chapter to debate the ethical issues involved in the way the Westland/Hallmark Meat Co. business operated.
2. Use the theories to discuss the ethical issues involved in the way the meatpacking business is being conducted today.
3. Search the Internet for changes occurring in the meatpacking industry.

Small Group Breakout Exercise

Modeling an Open System [LO2-6]

Form groups of three to five people, and appoint one group member as the spokesperson who will communicate your findings to the class when called on by the instructor. Then discuss the following scenario:

Think of an organization with which you are all familiar, such as a local restaurant, store, or bank. After choosing an organization, model it from an open-systems perspective. Identify its input, conversion, and output processes, and identify forces in the external environment that help or hurt the organization's ability to obtain resources and dispose of its goods or services.

Be the Manager [LO2-2, 2-4]

How to Manage a Luxury Hotel

You have been called in to advise the owners of an exclusive new luxury hotel. For the venture to succeed, hotel employees must focus on providing customers with the highest-quality service possible. The challenge is to devise a way of organizing and controlling employees that will promote high-quality service, that will encourage employees to be committed to the hotel, and that will reduce the level of employee turnover and absenteeism—which are typically high in the hotel business.

Questions

1. How do the various management theories discussed in this chapter offer clues for organizing and controlling hotel employees?
2. Which parts would be the most important for an effective system to organize and control employees?

Case in the News [LO2-1, 2-2, 2-5, 2-6]

RIOS Intelligent Machines Will Rent You the Future

Bernard Casse applies his scientific knowledge (he holds a PhD in physics from the National University of Singapore) and experience in research and development (he has worked for Brookhaven National Laboratories and the Xerox PARC, among other R&D leaders) to bring the latest digital technology to small- and medium-size manufacturers. In 2018, Casse cofounded RIOS Intelligent Machines to offer these businesses robots that use artificial intelligence (AI).

RIOS, based in California's Silicon Valley, aims to transform manufacturing at a time when demand is spiking beyond many companies' ability to fill orders, especially given stiff competition for labor and upward pressure on wages. According to Casse, the company's CEO, the mission of RIOS is to "completely transform labor-intensive factories into smart factories of the future powered by robotics and AI." The company serves manufacturers by automating their product assembly, packaging, and shipping.

RIOS is among a handful of companies pioneering "robots as a service." The idea is that only the largest companies can afford to invest in robots and other elements of a high-tech production system—not to mention the technology experts needed to maintain it. So RIOS develops basic robot designs that can be tailored to customers' needs by tweaking the hardware and software, and it hires experts in maintaining robotic systems. Then RIOS signs rental agreements to bring in the necessary equipment and set up a customized work cell using its robots. The company's experts monitor information from sensors in the system so they can handle questions and problems, even from a distance. As soon as the system is installed, the customer can begin running the equipment and reaping the benefits.

Those benefits can be considerable, especially when it comes to productivity. RIOS says its robots can reduce labor costs by up to 60% and reduce interruptions to work flow. Further, a digital system can deliver data on machines' performance and outputs. The data can enable further savings by, for example, notifying users to perform maintenance that could prevent breakdowns or recommending adjustments that could improve efficiency. Robotic systems that reduce risky or repetitive motions also can prevent injuries and their associated costs. According to RIOS, some of its customers have more than doubled their productivity.

Companies have the option to pass along some or all of the benefits to their workers. Thomson Plastics, located in Georgia, rents robots to move plastic parts from molding machines to a conveyor belt for quality inspections. Instead of one worker moving parts from each molding machine, a worker can oversee parts removal from three machines. As output has tripled, the company has increased starting wages by $7 an hour.

According to Casse, more than two-thirds of the tasks performed in the world's factories are performed by humans rather than machines, and many of these jobs are physically difficult but pay only minimum wage. Filling such jobs—and then keeping the employees onboard—has become increasingly difficult for employers. Therefore, Casse maintains that RIOS and similar providers of robotic systems are addressing labor shortages and turnover, not taking away jobs from workers.

Ideally, robots as a service will improve rather than eliminate work. For example, Ramar Foods, a Northern California maker of Filipino food, was intrigued by RIOS robots that could perform the delicate task of moving dumplings from a conveyor to a steam tray. They signed an agreement to rent a robot, which works as fast as two employees. PJ Quesada, a company vice president, says the machinery is sparing the employees repetitive lower-back movements, and employees are freed up for other kinds of work. Quesada sees no layoffs resulting from the use of the robots, as the company is trying to fill two dozen positions.

In the context of management theories, it's interesting to note that the introduction of robots is changing work to a degree that the earlier pursuit of efficiency through scientific management did not. In the earlier approach, studying workers' movements led to more efficient ways to oversee the same people doing similar tasks in new ways. But a worker who is monitoring robots is performing a kind of oversight almost like supervision, rather than the original job. Furthermore, as robots help workers get more done, their jobs might get less taxing physically but more difficult mentally. The management of the work likely will change as well. Instead of watching workers do repeated physical tasks, the manager will need other ways of preparing employees and evaluating their results.

Questions for Discussion

1. Review Fayol's management principles in Table 2.1. Choose two that you think are relevant for RIOS's customers (the companies that rent RIOS's systems). Briefly describe how a manufacturer implementing "robots as a service" should try to apply these two principles.
2. How could management science help managers decide whether to enter robots-as-a-service agreements with RIOS? What would be the limitations of relying only on management science? What else should the managers consider to ensure automation will achieve its objectives?
3. Using the examples of automation at Thomson Plastics and Ramar Foods, how could the theory of dynamic capabilities guide management as they implement their new systems?

Sources: RIOS website, https://www.rios.ai, accessed January 4, 2023; "RIOS: Heralding the Dawn of Intelligent Machines of the Future," *Manufacturing Technology Insights*, www.manufacturingtechnologyinsights.com, accessed November 9, 2022; RIOS Intelligent Machines: "Re-industrializing America with Best-in-Class American Technology," interview with Bernard Casse, *Global Business Leaders*, https://globalbusinessleadersmag.com, accessed November 9, 2022; B. Orrell and J. Easter, "Rent-a-Robot and Our Tight Labor Market," *The Bulwark*, May 25, 2022, https://www.thebulwark.com; T. Black, "Robots for the Little Guy," *Bloomberg Businessweek*, April 4, 2022, 8–11.

Notes

1. B. Kowitt, "Google's Search for the Hybrid Holy Grail," *Fortune*, June/July 2022, 93–99.
2. H. Weber, "Google Tells Staff to Act 'More Entrepreneurial'; Translation: Work Harder, or Else," *Tech Crunch*, www.techcrunch.com, July 12, 2022.
3. "Inside Alphabet's Performance Improvement Plan," *People Matters*, www.peoplematters.com, August 15, 2022.
4. Kowitt, "Google's Search for the Hybrid Holy Grail."
5. C. Cutter, K. Bindley, and K. Dill, "The War to Define What Work Looks Like," *The Wall Street Journal*, www.wsj.com, October 22, 2022; D. Abril, "Hybrid Work for Many Is Messy and Exhausting," *Washington Post*, www.washingtonpost.com, April 5, 2022; J. Corrigan, "Google's Hybrid Work Policy Isn't Popular amongst Employees," *Human Resources Director*, www.hrdmag.com, March 18, 2022.
6. Kowitt, "Google's Search for the Hybrid Holy Grail"; Corrigan, "Google's Hybrid Work Policy"; Cutter et al, "The War to Define What Work Looks Like."
7. Kowitt, "Google's Search for the Hybrid Holy Grail."
8. A. Smith, *The Wealth of Nations* (London: Penguin, 1982).
9. Ibid., 110.
10. J.G. March and H.A. Simon, *Organizations* (New York: Wiley, 1958).
11. L.W. Fry, "The Maligned F.W. Taylor: A Reply to His Many Critics," *Academy of Management Review* 1 (1976), 124–29.
12. F.W. Taylor, *Shop Management* (New York: Harper, 1903); F.W. Taylor, *The Principles of Scientific Management* (New York: Harper, 1911).
13. J.A. Litterer, *The Emergence of Systematic Management as Shown by the Literature from 1870–1900* (New York: Garland, 1986).
14. H.R. Pollard, *Developments in Management Thought* (New York: Crane, 1974).
15. D. Wren, *The Evolution of Management Thought* (New York: Wiley, 1994), 134.
16. F.B. Gilbreth, *Primer of Scientific Management* (New York: Van Nostrand Reinhold, 1912).
17. F.B. Gilbreth Jr. and E.G. Gilbreth, *Cheaper by the Dozen* (New York: Crowell, 1948).
18. M. Weber, *From Max Weber: Essays in Sociology*, eds. H.H. Gerth and C.W. Mills (New York: Oxford University Press, 1946); M. Weber, *Economy and Society*, ed. G. Roth and C. Wittich (Berkeley: University of California Press, 1978).
19. C. Perrow, *Complex Organizations*, 2nd ed. (Glenview, IL: Scott, Foresman, 1979).
20. Z. Riaz, "What Is Walmart's Inventory Management System?" *URTasker*, www.urtasker.com, August 23, 2022.
21. H. Fayol, *General and Industrial Management* (New York: IEEE Press, 1984).
22. "Company Overview," http://corporate.publix.com, accessed January 4, 2023.
23. U.S. Department of Defense (DOD), *DOD Dictionary of Military and Associated Terms*, https://irp.fas.org, accessed January 4, 2023.
24. Fayol, *General and Industrial Management*, 79.
25. "About Us," https://synd.io, accessed January 4, 2023; K. Schlosser, "Pay-Equity Startup Syndio Raises $50M as More Companies Broaden Analysis of Workplace Fairness," *GeekWire*, www.geekwire.com, March 15, 2022.
26. R.E. Eccles and N. Nohira, *Beyond the Hype: Rediscovering the Essence of Management* (Boston: Harvard Business School Press, 1992).
27. "About E Source," www.esource.com, accessed January 3, 2023; J. Nobile, "Align Capital Buys Colorado Energy Research and Advisory Firm E Source," *Crain's Cleveland Business*, June 24, 2019, www.crainscleveland.com.
28. G. Dutton, "Taking Employee Satisfaction from Bust to Boom," *Training*, July/August 2019, 20–22.

29. Dutton, "Taking Employee Satisfaction from Bust to Boom," 21.
30. Ibid.
31. P. Graham, *M.P. Follett–Prophet of Management: A Celebration of Writings from the 1920s* (Boston: Harvard Business School Press, 1995).
32. M.P. Follett, *Creative Experience* (London: Longmans, 1924).
33. E. Mayo, *The Human Problems of Industrial Civilization* (New York: Macmillan, 1933); F.J. Roethlisberger and W.J. Dickson, *Management and the Worker* (Cambridge: Harvard University Press, 1947).
34. D.W. Organ, "Review of *Management and the Worker,* by F.J. Roethlisberger and W.J. Dickson," *Academy of Management Review* 13 (1986), 460–64.
35. For an analysis of the problems in distinguishing cause from effect in the Hawthorne studies and in social settings in general, see A. Carey, "The Hawthorne Studies: A Radical Criticism," *American Sociological Review* 33 (1967), 403–16.
36. D. McGregor, *The Human Side of Enterprise* (New York: McGraw-Hill, 1960).
37. "Corporate Citizenship at Southwest," www.southwest.com, accessed January 4, 2023.
38. J. Kunzler, "Labor Relations at Southwest Airlines Are Becoming More Turbulent," *Simple Flying*, https://simpleflying.com, October 5, 2022.
39. R. Clayton, "7 Big Ways Technology Has Reshaped the Modern Workplace," *Charge Spot*, www.chargespot.com, accessed January 4, 2023.
40. "Toyota Production System," https://global.toyota/en/company/vision-and-philosophy/production-system/, accessed January 4, 2023.
41. J.D. Thompson, *Organizations in Action* (New York: McGraw-Hill, 1967).
42. D. Katz and R.L. Kahn, *The Social Psychology of Organizations* (New York: Wiley, 1966); Thompson, *Organizations in Action.*
43. T. Burns and G.M. Stalker, *The Management of Innovation* (London: Tavistock, 1961); P.R. Lawrence and J.R. Lorsch, *Organization and Environment* (Boston: Graduate School of Business Administration, Harvard University, 1967).
44. D. Gherson and L. Gratton, "Managers Can't Do It All," *Harvard Business Review,* March-April 2022, 96–105; K. Dill, "Your Next Boss: More Harmony, Less Authority," *The Wall Street Journal,* www.wsj.com, January 12, 2021.
45. N. Nohria, "As the World Shifts, So Should Leaders," *Harvard Business Review,* July-August 2022, 59–61.
46. Gherson and Gratton, "Managers Can't Do It All."
47. Ibid.
48. Burns and Stalker, *The Management of Innovation.*
49. C.W.L. Hill and G.R. Jones, *Strategic Management: An Integrated Approach,* 8th ed. (Florence, KY: Cengage, 2010).
50. A. Kleiner, "The Dynamic Capabilities of David Teece," *Strategy+ Business,* www.strategy-business.com, accessed February 3, 2020.
51. D.J. Teece, "Explicating Dynamic Capabilities: The Nature and Microfoundations of (Sustainable) Enterprise Performance," *Strategic Management Journal* 28 (August 2007), 1319–50.
52. M. Faithfull, "Luxury Soars But Apple Named Best Global Brand for Tenth Year Running," *Forbes*, www.forbes.com, November 3, 2022.
53. G. George, M.R. Haas, and A. Pentland, "Big Data and Management," *Academy of Management Journal,* 57 (2014), 321–26.
54. G. George and Y. Lin, "Analytics, Innovation, and Organizational Adaptation," *Innovation* 19, no. 1 (2017), 16–22.
55. E. Werner, "Slaughterhouse Owner Acknowledges Abuse," www.pasadenastarnews.com, March 13, 2008.
56. C. Tasci, "Former Chico Meat Packers Settle Suit over Mistreatment of Downer Cows," *Daily Bulletin,* www.dailybulletin.com, accessed February 7, 2020.
57. "Owners of Infamous Calif. Slaughterhouse Pay Millions to Settle Government Fraud Case," *The Humane Society,* www.humanesociety.org, November 27, 2013; "Worker Sentenced in Slaughterhouse Abuse," www.yahoo.com, March 22, 2008.

CHAPTER 3

Values, Attitudes, Emotions, and Culture: The Manager as a Person

Fizkes/Shutterstock

Learning Objectives

After studying this chapter, you should be able to:

LO3-1 Describe the various personality traits that affect how managers think, feel, and behave.

LO3-2 Explain what values and attitudes are, and describe their impact on managerial action.

LO3-3 Appreciate how moods and emotions influence all members of an organization.

LO3-4 Describe the nature of emotional intelligence and its role in management.

LO3-5 Define organizational culture, and explain how managers both create and are influenced by organizational culture.

A MANAGER'S CHALLENGE

Strong Values Guide John Hancock CEO

What qualities does a successful manager possess? For many examples, consider Marianne Harrison, CEO of John Hancock, a U.S. life insurance company owned by Toronto-based Manulife Financial. Her appointment as CEO made her the first woman to hold John Hancock's top job.[1]

Harrison found her career path because she is open to challenges and driven to succeed. In college, she was an English major with a talent for numbers and a willingness to accept advice to study business. She earned a degree in finance, passed her CPA exam, and became an accountant. She then moved into banking and insurance, gaining experience for management roles at John Hancock, which provides life insurance and other financial products to about 10 million Americans. Openness to experience entails risks, which Harrison has embraced. Moving to John Hancock involved relocating herself, her children, and her husband from Toronto to Boston so she could run the entire long-term care insurance business. For Harrison, that was "everything I wanted to do."[2]

Harrison embraces hard work. She describes herself as being in control of her actions and owing her success to her efforts. In every position, she says, she has done her best, and as soon as a role became comfortable, she began looking for the next challenge. While she was still an accountant, she learned of an open position in another city, which would involve serving the firm's largest client. She asked a manager if she might be considered for the role, and he said yes but that he hadn't expected her to relocate with three children, not to mention a husband running his own business. While some might have been discouraged, Harrison took away a lesson in the importance of speaking up for oneself. Likewise, in the year Harrison relocated to Boston to work for John Hancock, the financial crisis hit, and her job got drastically tougher. She seized the chance to try new management techniques as she rallied her team and adjusted her strategy—and actually enjoyed herself.[3]

When Harrison describes her work, her tone is positive. She explains her job satisfaction by saying that work in financial services lets her make a significant difference for people—for example, helping them make decisions so they can become financially secure. She also loves the difficulties of her work, saying challenges give her energy.[4]

Significantly, Harrison's joy in her work tends to involve helping others. The focus on others has helped her succeed not only in empowering customers, but also in motivating employees. She is committed to fostering diversity of ideas by hiring—and then listening to—people of varied races, genders, and physical abilities.

Marianne Harrison, CEO of John Hancock, shapes the values of her organization by showing concern for others, fostering diverse ideas, and demonstrating a willingness to step outside her comfort zone.
Scott Eisen/Stringer/Getty Images

She willingly steps outside her comfort zone to share personal stories and to give others a platform for sharing theirs.[5]

Harrison's concern for others informs her business strategy. She takes John Hancock into new territory for insurance companies, thinking more about how to help customers improve their lives than how to create and sell sophisticated products. New offerings include a wellness tool called Vitality, which delivers rewards and savings to customers for making healthy choices, and John Hancock Aspire—life insurance for people with diabetes combined with coaching in disease management. The company is also using technology to simplify the claims process.[6]

Harrison shapes the values of her organization. She had her sales team spend a month answering phone calls from customers. This sensitized them to what matters to customers, which in turn embedded customer focus as a company value. Harrison says the refreshed culture at John Hancock has attracted management talent and sharpened the focus on both customers and shareholders.[7]

Overview

Like people everywhere, Marianne Harrison has her own distinctive personality, values, ways of viewing things, and personal challenges and disappointments. In this chapter we focus on the manager as a feeling, thinking human being. We start by describing enduring characteristics that influence how managers work and how they view other people, their organizations, and the world around them. We also discuss how managers' values, attitudes, and moods play out in organizations, shaping organizational culture. By the end of this chapter you will appreciate how the personal characteristics of managers influence the process of management in general—and organizational culture in particular.

Enduring Characteristics: Personality Traits

LO3-1 Describe the various personality traits that affect how managers think, feel, and behave.

All people, including managers, have certain enduring characteristics that influence how they think, feel, and behave both on and off the job. These characteristics are **personality traits**: particular tendencies to feel, think, and act in certain ways that can be used to describe the personality of every individual. It is important to understand the personalities of managers because their personalities influence their behavior and their approach to managing people and resources.

personality traits Enduring tendencies to feel, think, and act in certain ways.

Some managers are demanding, difficult to get along with, and highly critical of other people. Other managers may be as concerned about effectiveness and efficiency as highly critical managers but are easier to get along with, are likable, and often praise the people around them. Both management styles may produce excellent results, but their effects on employees are quite different. Do managers deliberately decide to adopt one of these approaches to management? Although they may do so part of the time, in all likelihood their personalities account for their different approaches. Indeed, research suggests that the way people react to different conditions depends, in part, on their personalities.[8]

The Big Five Personality Traits

We can think of one's personality as being composed of five general traits or characteristics: extraversion, negative affectivity, agreeableness, conscientiousness, and openness to experience. Researchers often consider these the Big Five personality traits.[9] Each of them can be viewed as a continuum along which every person or, more specifically, every manager falls (see Figure 3.1).

Some managers may be at the high end of one trait continuum, others at the low end, and still others somewhere in between. An easy way to understand how these traits can affect a person's approach to management is to describe what people are like at the high and low

Figure 3.1

The Big Five Personality Traits

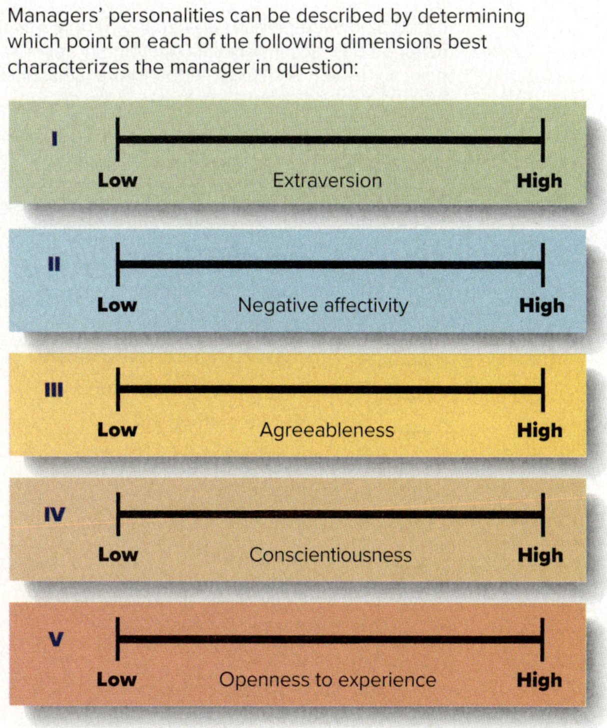

ends of each trait continuum. As will become evident as you read about each trait, no single trait is right or wrong for being an effective manager. Rather, effectiveness is determined by a complex interaction between the characteristics of managers (including personality traits) and the nature of the job and organization in which they are working. Moreover, personality traits that enhance managerial effectiveness in one situation may impair it in another. Recent studies suggest that personality traits may even predict job performance in certain situations. For example, researchers found that extraversion better predicted performance in jobs requiring social skills, while agreeableness was less positively related to job performance in competitive environments.[10]

extraversion The tendency for individuals to be outgoing, sociable, and energetic in their behavior.

EXTRAVERSION **Extraversion** is the tendency for people to be outgoing, sociable, and energetic in their behavior. Managers who are high on the extraversion continuum (often called extraverts) tend to be friendly and enjoy social interactions. Managers who are low on the extraversion continuum (often called introverts) tend to be less inclined toward social interactions and prefer to spend more time alone. Being high on extraversion may be an asset for managers whose jobs entail especially high levels of social interaction. Managers who are low on extraversion may nevertheless be highly effective and efficient, especially when their jobs do not require much social interaction. Their quieter approach may enable them to accomplish quite a bit of work in a limited amount of time. See Figure 3.2 for an example of a scale that can be used to measure a person's level of extraversion.

negative affectivity The tendency to experience negative emotions and moods, to feel distressed, and to be critical of oneself and others.

NEGATIVE AFFECTIVITY **Negative affectivity** is the tendency to experience negative emotions and moods, feel distressed, and be critical of oneself and others. Managers high on this trait may often feel angry and dissatisfied and complain about their own and others' lack of progress. Managers who are low on negative affectivity do not tend to experience as many negative emotions and moods and are less pessimistic and critical of themselves and others. On the plus side, the critical approach of a manager high on negative affectivity may sometimes spur both the manager and others to improve their performance. Nevertheless, it is probably more pleasant to work with a manager who is low on negative affectivity; the better working relationships that such a manager is likely to cultivate also can be an important asset.

Figure 3.2

Measures of Extraversion, Agreeableness, Conscientiousness, and Openness to Experience

Listed below are phrases describing people's behaviors. Please use the rating scale below to describe how accurately each statement describes *you*. Describe yourself as you generally are now, not as you wish to be in the future. Describe yourself as you honestly see yourself, in relation to other people you know of the same sex as you are and roughly your same age.

1	2	3	4	5
Very inaccurate	Moderately inaccurate	Neither inaccurate nor accurate	Moderately accurate	Very accurate

____ **1.** Am interested in people.
____ **2.** Have a rich vocabulary.
____ **3.** Am always prepared.
____ **4.** Am not really interested in others.*
____ **5.** Leave my belongings around.*
____ **6.** Am the life of the party.
____ **7.** Have difficulty understanding abstract ideas.*
____ **8.** Sympathize with others' feelings.
____ **9.** Don't talk a lot.*
____ **10.** Pay attention to details.
____ **11.** Have a vivid imagination.
____ **12.** Insult people.*
____ **13.** Make a mess of things.*
____ **14.** Feel comfortable around people.
____ **15.** Am not interested in abstract ideas.*
____ **16.** Have a soft heart.
____ **17.** Get chores done right away.
____ **18.** Keep in the background.*
____ **19.** Have excellent ideas.
____ **20.** Start conversations.
____ **21.** Am not interested in other people's problems.*
____ **22.** Often forget to put things back in their proper place.*
____ **23.** Have little to say.*
____ **24.** Do not have a good imagination.*
____ **25.** Take time out for others.
____ **26.** Like order.
____ **27.** Talk to a lot of different people at parties.
____ **28.** Am quick to understand things.
____ **29.** Feel little concern for others.*
____ **30.** Shirk my duties.*
____ **31.** Don't like to draw attention to myself.*
____ **32.** Use difficult words.
____ **33.** Feel others' emotions.
____ **34.** Follow a schedule.
____ **35.** Spend time reflecting on things.
____ **36.** Don't mind being the center of attention.
____ **37.** Make people feel at ease.
____ **38.** Am exacting in my work.
____ **39.** Am quiet around strangers.*
____ **40.** Am full of ideas.

* Item is reverse-scored: 1 = 5, 2 = 4, 4 = 2, 5 = 1
Scoring: Sum responses to items for an overall scale.
Extraversion = sum of items 6, 9, 14, 18, 20, 23, 27, 31, 36, 39
Agreeableness = sum of items 1, 4, 8, 12, 16, 21, 25, 29, 33, 37
Conscientiousness = sum of items 3, 5, 10, 13, 17, 22, 26, 30, 34, 38
Openness to experience = sum of items 2, 7, 11, 15, 19, 24, 28, 32, 35, 40

Source: L. R. Goldberg, Oregon Research Institute, http://ipip.ori.org/ipip/.

agreeableness The tendency to get along well with other people.

AGREEABLENESS **Agreeableness** is the tendency to get along well with others. Managers who are high on the agreeableness continuum are likable, tend to be affectionate, and care about other people. Managers who are low on agreeableness may be somewhat distrustful of others, unsympathetic, uncooperative, and even at times antagonistic. Being high on agreeableness may be especially important for managers whose responsibilities require that they develop good, close relationships with others. Nevertheless, a low level of agreeableness may be an asset in managerial jobs that actually require that managers be antagonistic, such as drill sergeants and some other kinds of military managers. See Figure 3.2 for an example of a scale that measures a person's level of agreeableness.

conscientiousness The tendency to be careful, scrupulous, and persevering.

CONSCIENTIOUSNESS **Conscientiousness** is the tendency to be careful, scrupulous, and persevering.[11] Managers who are high on the conscientiousness continuum are organized and self-disciplined; those who are low on this trait might sometimes appear to lack direction and self-discipline. Conscientiousness has been found to be a good predictor of performance in many kinds of jobs, including managerial jobs in a variety of organizations.[12] Entrepreneurs who start their own companies often are high on conscientiousness, and their persistence and determination help them overcome obstacles and turn their ideas into successful new ventures. Figure 3.2 provides an example of a scale that measures conscientiousness.

openness to experience The tendency to be original, have broad interests, be open to a wide range of stimuli, be daring, and take risks.

OPENNESS TO EXPERIENCE **Openness to experience** is the tendency to be original, have broad interests, be open to a wide range of stimuli, be daring, and take risks.[13] Managers who are high on this trait continuum may be especially likely to take risks and be innovative in their planning and decision making. Marianne Harrison, discussed in this chapter's opening feature, continues to explore new ways for her company John Hancock to grow, innovate, and succeed–a testament to her high level of openness to experience. Managers who are low on openness to experience may be less prone to take risks and more conservative in their planning and decision making. In certain organizations and positions, this tendency might be an asset. The manager of the fiscal office in a public university, for example, must ensure that all university departments and units follow the university's rules and regulations pertaining to budgets, spending accounts, and reimbursements of expenses. Figure 3.2 provides an example of a measure of openness to experience.

These personality traits do not, of course, exist in a vacuum. They combine with each other and with a person's values and culture. Consider the example of Eileen Huntington, the business founder described in the "Manager as a Person" feature. Her agreeableness, conscientious, and openness to experience combine with a high value placed on learning and her professional knowledge. As you read about Huntington's experience as a business founder and manager, look for examples of her personality traits in action.

MANAGER AS A PERSON

Eileen Huntington *(left)*, pictured here with husband Ray and daughter Anne, exhibits personality traits that have helped her become a successful manager and business owner.
Gonzalo Marroquin/Contributor/Getty Images

Making the Grade as a Business Founder

Eileen Huntington is the cofounder of Huntington Learning Center along with her husband, Ray Huntington. They owe their success in part to knowledge and skills from Eileen's career as a high school history teacher and Ray's as a business analyst.[14] However, Eileen demonstrates that not only skills but also personality traits play a role. Openness to experience inspired her to see a new way to teach one-on-one and to risk starting a business. Conscientiousness propelled her through the difficult early years. And caring about others (a measure of agreeableness) gave her a vision that guides her people.

As a high school teacher, Huntington observed with concern that some students were falling behind because they lacked key skills. She concluded that what would help them most would be one-on-one tutoring in the skills they could use to succeed. She identified that this need presented a business opportunity, so she crafted the idea of learning centers that would test students to identify what skills they needed and then provide tutoring in those skills. She and her husband rented an office in Oradell, New Jersey, quit their jobs, and opened the first Huntington Learning Center, paid for with personal loans.[15]

With cash flow from the first center, they opened a second one 10 months later. Huntington focused on developing training systems and recruiting teachers to work in the centers. Over the next seven years, they opened 16 more locations, using revenues from existing centers to pay for the expansion. Then they began offering franchises, where centers are owned and run by people who pay to use the Huntington name and tutoring program. The pace of growth–opening more than 300 centers over four decades–was controlled but demanded considerable effort.[16]

Huntington told a reporter that the company's competitive advantage is its concern for students. "Every business decision we make," she said, "we make with the student in mind."[17] The average student enrolled at a Huntington Learning Center for three months moves up two grade levels in math and reading skills, and Huntington is motivated by seeing students gain skills and confidence in themselves. She applies a similar attitude to her role as a manager; she tries to make a positive difference in the experience of her employees by listening carefully and practicing empathy. All of this is directed toward the company's official mission: to give every student the best education possible.[18]

Successful managers occupy a variety of positions on the Big Five personality trait continuum. One highly effective manager may be high on extraversion and negative affectivity; another, equally effective manager may be low on both these traits; and still another may be somewhere in between. Members of an organization must understand these differences among managers because they can shed light on how managers behave and on their approach to planning, leading, organizing, or controlling. If employees realize, for example, that their manager is low on extraversion, they will not feel slighted when the manager seems to be aloof because they will realize that by nature the manager is simply not outgoing.

Managers themselves also need to be aware of their own personality traits and the traits of others, including those of their employees and fellow managers. A manager who knows that they have a tendency to be highly critical of other people might try to tone down their negative approach. Similarly, a manager who realizes that a chronically complaining employee tends to be so negative because of their personality may realize that things probably aren't as bad as this employee says they are.

In order for all members of an organization to work well together and with people outside the organization, such as customers and suppliers, they must understand each other. Such understanding comes, in part, from an appreciation of some fundamental ways in which people differ from one another–that is, an appreciation of personality traits.

Other Personality Traits That Affect Managerial Behavior

Many other traits in addition to the Big Five describe people's personalities. Here we look at traits that are particularly important for understanding managerial effectiveness: locus of control, self-esteem, and the needs for achievement, affiliation, and power.

LOCUS OF CONTROL People differ in their views about how much control they have over what happens to and around them. The locus of control trait captures these beliefs.[19] People with an **internal locus of control** believe they themselves are responsible for their own fate; they see their own actions and behaviors as being major and decisive determinants of important outcomes such as attaining levels of job performance, being promoted, or being turned down for a choice job assignment. Some managers with an internal locus of control see the success of a whole organization resting on their shoulders. One example is Marianne Harrison, CEO of John Hancock, described in "A Manager's Challenge." An internal locus of control also helps to ensure ethical behavior and decision making in an organization because people feel accountable and responsible for their own actions.

internal locus of control
The tendency to locate responsibility for one's fate within oneself.

People with an **external locus of control** believe that outside forces are responsible for what happens to and around them; they do not think their own actions make much of a difference. As such, they tend not to intervene to try to change a situation or solve a problem, leaving it to someone else.

external locus of control
The tendency to locate responsibility for one's fate in outside forces and to believe one's own behavior has little impact on outcomes.

Managers need an internal locus of control because they *are* responsible for what happens in organizations; they need to believe they can and do make a difference. Moreover, managers are responsible for ensuring that organizations and their members behave in an ethical fashion, and for this as well they need an internal locus of control–they need to know and feel they can make a difference.

self-esteem The degree to which individuals feel good about themselves and their capabilities.

SELF-ESTEEM **Self-esteem** is the degree to which people feel good about themselves and their capabilities. People with high self-esteem believe they are competent, deserving, and capable of handling most situations. People with low self-esteem have poor opinions of themselves, are unsure about their capabilities, and question their ability to succeed at different endeavors.[20] Research suggests that people tend to choose activities and goals consistent with their levels of self-esteem. High self-esteem is desirable for managers because it facilitates their setting and keeping high standards for themselves, pushes them ahead on difficult projects, and gives them the confidence they need to make and carry out important decisions.

need for achievement The extent to which an individual has a strong desire to perform challenging tasks well and to meet personal standards for excellence.

need for affiliation The extent to which an individual is concerned about establishing and maintaining good interpersonal relations, being liked, and having other people get along.

need for power The extent to which an individual desires to control or influence others.

NEEDS FOR ACHIEVEMENT, AFFILIATION, AND POWER Psychologist David McClelland has extensively researched the needs for achievement, affiliation, and power.[21] The **need for achievement** is the extent to which an individual has a strong desire to perform challenging tasks well and to meet personal standards for excellence. People with a high need for achievement often set clear goals for themselves and like to receive performance feedback. The **need for affiliation** is the extent to which one is concerned about establishing and maintaining good interpersonal relations, being liked, and having the people around them get along with one another. The **need for power** is the extent to which one wants to control or influence others.[22]

Research suggests that high needs for achievement and for power are assets for first-line and middle managers and that a high need for power is especially important for upper-level managers.[23] One study found that U.S. presidents with a relatively high need for power tended to be especially effective during their terms of office.[24] A high need for affiliation may not always be desirable in managers because it might lead them to try too hard to be liked by others (including their employees) rather than doing all they can to ensure that performance is as high as it can and should be. Although most research on these needs has been done in the United States, some studies suggest that these findings may also apply to people in other countries such as India and New Zealand.[25]

Taken together, these desirable personality traits for managers–an internal locus of control, high self-esteem, and high needs for achievement and power–suggest that managers need to be take-charge people who not only believe their own actions are decisive in determining their own and their organizations' fates but also believe in their own capabilities. Such managers have a personal desire for accomplishment and influence over others.

Additional Personality Assessments

In addition to the Big Five personality factors discussed earlier, several other personality assessments can be effective in helping managers and others identify positive and negative behaviors demonstrated by people in the workplace.

The Myers–Briggs Type Indicator (MBTI) is the most widely used personality instrument around the world–millions of assessments are administered annually. Based on the theories of psychologist Carl Jung, MBTI measures a person's preferences for introversion versus extroversion, sensation versus intuition, thinking versus feeling, and judging versus perceiving. Various combinations of these four preferences result in 16 unique personality types, which can be helpful to individuals who seek to understand not only how they make decisions, but also how they manage their time, solve problems, and deal with stress. In addition, recent research suggests that the four personality dimensions can be linked to various job-related components, including job satisfaction, job performance, motivation, and promotion. More than 88% of *Fortune* 500 companies in 115 countries use this type of assessment to build stronger and healthier organizations.[26]

Another personality measure that can be useful to managers and others in an organization is the DiSC Inventory Profile, which many companies use to assess the personality characteristics of their employees. DiSC is based on the work of William Marston, a psychologist who tried to characterize normal behavior patterns. A person taking the DiSC inventory receives a profile describing their behavioral style, preferred environment, and strategies for effectiveness. Behavior style is described in terms of **d**ominance, **i**nfluence, **s**teadiness, and **c**onscientiousness (DiSC).[27]

Information from these types of assessments help companies better understand their employees' strengths and weaknesses and how people perceive and process information—all factors that contribute to the success of an organization.

Values, Attitudes, and Moods and Emotions

What are managers striving to achieve? How do they think they should behave? What do they think about their jobs and organizations? And how do they actually feel at work? We can find some answers to these questions by exploring managers' values, attitudes, and moods.

LO3-2 Explain what values and attitudes are, and describe their impact on managerial action.

Values, attitudes, and moods and emotions capture how managers experience their jobs as individuals. *Values* describe what managers are trying to achieve through work and how they think they should behave. *Attitudes* capture their thoughts and feelings about their specific jobs and organizations. *Moods and emotions* encompass how managers actually feel when they are managing. Although these three aspects of managers' work experience are highly personal, they also have important implications for understanding how managers behave, how they treat and respond to others, and how, through their efforts, they help contribute to organizational effectiveness through planning, leading, organizing, and controlling.

Values: Terminal and Instrumental

terminal value A lifelong goal or objective that an individual seeks to achieve.

instrumental value A mode of conduct that an individual seeks to follow.

norms Unwritten, informal codes of conduct that prescribe how people should act in particular situations and are considered important by most members of a group or an organization.

value system The terminal and instrumental values that are guiding principles in an individual's life.

The two kinds of personal values are *terminal* and *instrumental.* A **terminal value** is a personal conviction about lifelong goals or objectives; an **instrumental value** is a personal conviction about desired modes of conduct or ways of behaving. Terminal values often lead to the formation of **norms**, which are unwritten, informal codes of conduct, such as behaving honestly or courteously, that prescribe how people should act in particular situations and that are considered important by most members of a group or an organization.

Milton Rokeach, a leading researcher in the area of human values, identified 18 terminal values and 18 instrumental values that describe each person's value system. By rank ordering the terminal values from "1 (most important as a guiding principle in one's life)" to "18 (least important as a guiding principle in one's life)" and then rank ordering the instrumental values from 1 to 18, people can give good pictures of their **value systems**—what they are striving to achieve in life and how they want to behave.[28]

Although Rokeach's research is nearly 50 years old, some of his findings are still applicable today.[29] Several terminal values seem to be especially important for managers, such as a sense of accomplishment, equality, and self-esteem. For example, managers who think a sense of accomplishment is particularly important might focus their energies on making a lasting contribution to an organization by developing a new product or by opening a new foreign subsidiary.

Several of Rokeach's instrumental values are also important modes of conduct for managers, such as being ambitious, open minded, competent, responsible, and self-disciplined.[30] A manager who considers being honest and responsible to be of paramount importance may be a driving force for taking steps to ensure that all members of an organization behave ethically.

All in all, managers' value systems signify what managers as individuals are trying to accomplish and become in their personal lives and at work. Thus, managers' value systems are fundamental guides to their behavior and efforts at planning, leading, organizing, and controlling.

Attitudes

attitude A collection of feelings and beliefs.

An **attitude** is a collection of feelings and beliefs. Like everyone else, managers have attitudes about their jobs and organizations, and these attitudes affect how they approach their jobs. Two of the most important attitudes in this context are job satisfaction and organizational commitment.

Figure 3.3

Sample Items from Two Measures of Job Satisfaction

Sample items from the Minnesota Satisfaction Questionnaire:
People respond to each of the items in the scale by checking whether they are:

[ ] Very dissatisfied
[ ] Dissatisfied
[ ] Can't decide whether satisfied or not
[ ] Satisfied
[ ] Very satisfied

On my present job, this is how I feel about . . .

____ **1.** Being able to do things that don't go against my conscience.

____ **2.** The way my job provides for steady employment.

____ **3.** The chance to do things for other people.

____ **4.** The chance to do something that makes use of my abilities.

____ **5.** The way company policies are put into practice.

____ **6.** My pay and the amount of work I do.

____ **7.** The chances for advancement on this job.

____ **8.** The freedom to use my own judgment.

____ **9.** The working conditions.

____ **10.** The way my coworkers get along with each other.

____ **11.** The praise I get for doing a good job.

____ **12.** The feeling of accomplishment I get from the job.

The Faces Scale
Workers select the face which best expresses how they feel about their job in general.

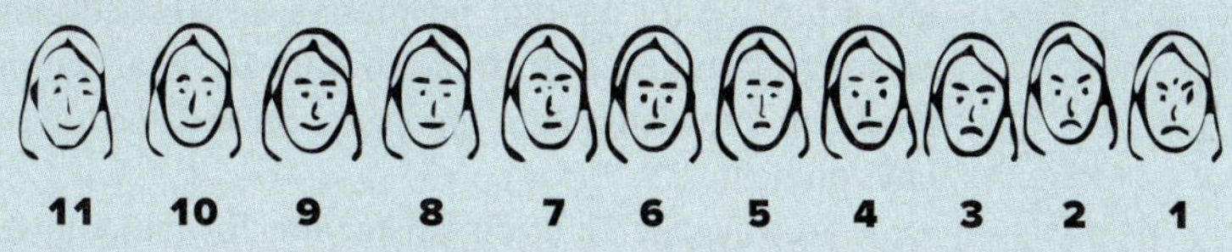

Source: Adapted from D. J. Weiss et al., *Manual for the Minnesota Satisfaction Questionnaire*. Copyrighted by the Vocational Psychology Research, University of Minnesota; copyright © 1975 by the American Psychological Association. Adapted by permission of R.B. Dunham and J.B. Brett. Used with Permission.

job satisfaction The collection of feelings and beliefs that managers have about their current jobs.

JOB SATISFACTION **Job satisfaction** is the collection of feelings and beliefs that managers have about their current jobs. Managers who have high levels of job satisfaction generally like their jobs, feel they are fairly treated, and believe their jobs have many desirable features or characteristics (such as interesting work, good pay and job security, autonomy, or nice coworkers). Figure 3.3 shows sample items from two scales that managers can use to measure job satisfaction. Levels of job satisfaction tend to increase as one moves up the hierarchy in an organization. Upper managers, in general, tend to be more satisfied with their jobs than entry-level employees. Managers' levels of job satisfaction can range from very low to very high.

One might think that in tough economic times, when unemployment is high and layoffs are prevalent, people who have jobs might be relatively satisfied with them. However, this is not necessarily the case. For example, in the middle of the global recession back in 2009, the U.S. unemployment rate was 10%; thousands of jobs disappeared from the economy; and the underemployment rate, which includes people who have given up looking for jobs and those working part-time because they can't find a full-time position, was a staggering 17.3%. During these recessionary conditions, job satisfaction levels in the United States fell to record lows.[31]

The Conference Board has been tracking levels of U.S. job satisfaction since 1987, when 61.1% of workers surveyed indicated they were satisfied with their jobs. In 2009, only 45% of workers surveyed were satisfied with their jobs, an all-time low for the survey.[32] In 2019, 54%

of U.S. workers indicated they were satisfied with their jobs and much more at ease with the prospects of job security. This three-point jump from 2018 satisfaction numbers marked one of the largest single-year gains in the survey's history.

Surprisingly, overall job satisfaction during the pandemic remained high: 56% of 1,000 workers surveyed in November 2020 were satisfied with their jobs and job components. Job satisfaction did, however, vary by age group. Those under age 35 experienced a drop in satisfaction, while those 55 and older experienced an increase. In addition, the percentage of workers reporting they were engaged in their work increased nearly a percentage point during 2020. Interestingly, the survey results showed the job satisfaction of employees working remotely was not significantly different from the satisfaction level of other workers.[33]

As the U.S. economy continued to recover at a feverish pace in 2022 and the country's unemployment rate hit an historic low, job satisfaction continued to be high even as many companies faced a very tight labor market, with many workers quitting their jobs and taking new positions with higher salaries, flexible work options, and better benefits. Managers and their organizations must continue to review compensation packages and overall company strategies in an effort to attract and retain top performers.[34]

In general, it is desirable for managers to be satisfied with their jobs, for at least two reasons. First, satisfied managers may be more likely to exceed expectations for their organizations or perform **organizational citizenship behaviors (OCBs)**–behaviors that are not required of organizational members but that contribute to and are necessary for organizational efficiency, effectiveness, and competitive advantage.[35] Managers who are satisfied with their jobs are more likely to perform these "above and beyond the call of duty" behaviors, which can include putting in long hours when needed, coming up with creative ideas and overcoming obstacles to implement them (even when doing so is not part of the manager's job), or going out of one's way to help a coworker, employee, or superior (even when doing so entails considerable personal sacrifice).[36]

organizational citizenship behaviors (OCBs)
Behaviors that are not required of organizational members but that contribute to and are necessary for organizational efficiency, effectiveness, and competitive advantage.

A second reason it is desirable for managers to be satisfied with their jobs is that satisfied managers may be less likely to quit. A manager who is highly satisfied may never even think about looking for another position; a dissatisfied manager may always be on the lookout for new opportunities. Turnover can hurt an organization because it causes a loss of the experience and knowledge that managers have gained about the company, industry, and business environment.[37]

A growing source of dissatisfaction for many lower-level and middle managers, as well as for nonmanagerial employees, is the threat of unemployment and increased workloads from organizational restructurings, including layoffs. Organizations that try to improve their efficiency through restructuring and layoffs often eliminate a sizable number of first-line and middle management positions. This decision obviously hurts the managers who are laid off, and it can reduce the job satisfaction levels of managers who remain. They might fear being the next to be let go. In addition, the workloads of remaining employees often increase dramatically as a result of restructuring, and this can contribute to dissatisfaction.

How managers and organizations handle layoffs is of paramount importance, not only for the employees let go but also for employees who survive the layoff and keep their jobs. Showing compassion and empathy for layoff victims, giving them as much advance notice as possible about the layoff, providing clear information about severance benefits, and helping them in their job search efforts are a few of the ways in which managers can humanely manage a layoff.[38]

organizational commitment
The collection of feelings and beliefs that managers have about their organization as a whole.

ORGANIZATIONAL COMMITMENT **Organizational commitment** is the collection of feelings and beliefs that managers have about their organization as a whole.[39] Managers who are committed to their organizations believe in what their organizations are doing, are proud of what these organizations stand for, and feel a high degree of loyalty toward their organizations. Committed managers are more likely to go above and beyond the call of duty to help their company and are less likely to quit.[40] Organizational commitment can be especially strong when employees and managers truly believe in organizational values; it also leads to a strong organizational culture.

Organizational commitment is likely to help managers perform some of their figurehead and spokesperson roles (see Chapter 1). It is much easier for a manager to persuade others, both inside and outside the organization, of the merits of what the organization has done and is seeking to accomplish if the manager truly believes in and is committed to the organization.

ATTITUDES IN CONTEXT Attitudes are not, of course, purely a personal characteristic; they can be shaped by external conditions. For example, we can expect working conditions to shape job satisfaction and organizational commitment. As described in the "Management Insight" feature, situations with high stress and low control over outcomes can contribute to dissatisfaction and low levels of organizational commitment.

Likewise, levels of job satisfaction and organizational commitment may vary from country to country in accordance with the opportunities and challenges associated with different economic conditions, laws and regulations, and social norms. For example, levels of organizational commitment may depend on the extent to which countries have legislation affecting firings and layoffs and the extent to which citizens of a country are geographically mobile.

MANAGEMENT INSIGHT

Pandemic Highlights the Hazards of Burnout

Across most industries, the COVID-19 pandemic created conditions associated with burnout: highly demanding work under uncertainty, coupled with a sense of powerlessness to achieve the desired results. The virus mutated and spread faster than researchers could craft new preventive measures and cures, and institutions scrambled to establish safe workplaces as conditions were in flux. Workers found themselves sent home, called in, furloughed, rescheduled, overscheduled, asked to cover for absent colleagues, and expected to balance all this with the needs of their children and other family members. Add to this the shutdowns at some companies and spikes in sales at others, along with disruptions in deliveries of many essential items, and it is no surprise to learn that workers reported increasing levels of stress and dissatisfaction.[41]

Negative attitudes become burnout when the stress at work reaches a point where workers are exhausted, feel detached from or cynical about their work, and no longer can work effectively.[42] During the pandemic, employers blamed stress and burnout for a surge of employees leaving their jobs.[43] The problem was especially troubling in health care, where it resulted in severe shortages of nurses and other frontline workers.[44]

Managers tried to improve conditions for their employees, with varying degrees of success.[45] Some established four-day workweeks or flexible schedules, hoping it would help employees to get more rest and achieve better work–life balance. Others set boundaries limiting when employees were expected to answer email or participate in online meetings. Still others raised salaries or moved dissatisfied employees into higher-paying jobs. However, Gallup's research into worker engagement finds that other actions are more significant: reducing workloads, improving communication, and equipping managers to be more supportive.[46]

The COVID-19 pandemic helped fuel increased stress and burnout in many organizations. Managers were challenged to think outside the box when it came to improving conditions for workers, which included flexible schedules, increased communications, and better work–life balance.
sirikorn thamniyom/Shutterstock

Even as they try to help their teams succeed in challenging conditions, managers are dealing with their own stresses. Gallup finds even higher rates of burnout among managers than among nonmanagement workers.[47] Managers are especially likely to say expectations of them are unclear, performance feedback is unhelpful, their workdays are full of interruptions, and they don't have a chance to spend time doing what they do best. However, managers also have a chance to improve their own conditions—for example, by delegating work, collaborating with others, pursuing opportunities for career development, and having a voice in decisions.

Moods and Emotions

LO3-3 Appreciate how moods and emotions influence all members of an organization.

mood A feeling or state of mind.

emotions Intense, relatively short-lived feelings.

Just as you sometimes are in a bad mood and at other times are in a good mood, so are managers. A **mood** is a feeling or state of mind. When people are in a positive mood, they feel excited, enthusiastic, active, or elated. When people are in a negative mood, they feel distressed, fearful, scornful, hostile, jittery, or nervous.[48] People who score high on negative affectivity are especially likely to experience negative moods. People's situations or circumstances also determine their moods; however, receiving a raise is likely to put most people in a good mood regardless of their personality traits. People who are high on negative affectivity are not always in a bad mood, and people who are low on extraversion still experience positive moods.[49]

Emotions are more intense feelings than moods, are often directly linked to whatever caused the emotion, and are more short-lived.[50] However, once whatever has triggered the emotion has been dealt with, the feelings may linger in the form of a less intense mood.[51] For example, a manager who gets very angry when an employee has engaged in an unethical behavior may find their anger decreasing in intensity once they have decided how to address the problem. Yet they continue to be in a bad mood the rest of the day, even though they are not directly thinking about the unfortunate incident.

Research has found that moods and emotions affect the behavior of managers and everyone else in an organization. For example, research suggests that the employees of managers who experience positive moods at work may perform at somewhat higher levels and be less likely to resign and leave the organization than the employees of managers who do not tend to be in a positive mood at work.[52] Other research suggests that under certain conditions, creativity might be enhanced by positive moods, whereas under other conditions negative moods might push people to work harder to come up with truly creative ideas.[53] Recognizing that both mood states have the potential to contribute to creativity in different ways, recent research suggests that employees may be especially likely to be creative to the extent that they experience both mood states (at different times) on the job and to the extent that the work environment is supportive of creativity.[54]

Other research suggests that moods and emotions may play an important role in ethical decision making. For example, researchers at Princeton University found that when people are trying to solve difficult personal moral dilemmas, the parts of their brains that are responsible for emotions and moods are especially active.[55]

More generally, emotions and moods give managers and all employees important information and signals about what is going on in the workplace.[56] Positive emotions and moods signal that things are going well and thus can lead to more expansive, and even playful, thinking. Negative emotions and moods signal that there are problems in need of attention and areas for improvement. So when people are in negative moods, they tend to be more detail-oriented and focused on the facts at hand.[57] Some studies suggest that critical thinking and devil's advocacy may be promoted by a negative mood, and sometimes especially accurate judgments may be made by managers in negative moods.[58]

Managers and other members of an organization need to realize that how they feel affects how they treat others and how others respond to them, including their employees. For example, an employee may be more likely to approach a manager with a somewhat unusual but potentially useful idea if she thinks the manager is in a good mood. Likewise, when managers are in very bad moods, their employees might try to avoid them at all costs. Figure 3.4 is an example of a scale that can measure the extent to which a person experiences positive and negative moods at work.

Emotional Intelligence

LO3-4 Describe the nature of emotional intelligence and its role in management.

In understanding the effects of managers' and all employees' moods and emotions, it is important to take into account their levels of emotional intelligence. **Emotional intelligence** is the ability to understand and manage one's own moods and emotions and the moods and emotions of other people.[59] Managers with a high level of emotional intelligence are more likely to understand how they are feeling and why, and they are more able to effectively manage their feelings. When managers are experiencing stressful feelings and emotions such as fear or anxiety, emotional intelligence lets them understand why and manage these feelings so they do not get in the way of effective decision making.[60]

Figure 3.4

A Measure of Positive and Negative Mood at Work

People respond to each item by indicating the extent to which the item describes how they felt at work during the past week on the following scale:

1 = Very slightly or not at all	4 = Quite a bit
2 = A little	5 = Very much
3 = Moderately	

____ **1.** Active	____ **7.** Enthusiastic
____ **2.** Distressed	____ **8.** Fearful
____ **3.** Strong	____ **9.** Peppy
____ **4.** Excited	____ **10.** Nervous
____ **5.** Scornful	____ **11.** Elated
____ **6.** Hostile	____ **12.** Jittery

Scoring: Responses to items 1, 3, 4, 7, 9, and 11 are summed for a positive mood score; the higher the score, the more positive mood is experienced at work. Responses to items 2, 5, 6, 8, 10, and 12 are summed for a negative mood score; the higher the score, the more negative mood is experienced at work.

Sources: A. P. Brief, M. J. Burke, J. M. George, B. Robinson, and J. Webster, "Should Negative Affectivity Remain an Unmeasured Variable in the Study of Job Stress?" *Journal of Applied Psychology* 72 (1988), 193–98; M. J. Burke, A. P. Brief, J. M. George, L. Roberson, and J. Webster, "Measuring Affect at Work: Confirmatory Analyses of Competing Mood Structures with Conceptual Linkage in Cortical Regulatory Systems," *Journal of Personality and Social Psychology* 57 (1989), 1091–102.

emotional intelligence The ability to understand and manage one's own moods and emotions and the moods and emotions of other people.

Emotional intelligence also can help managers perform their important roles such as their interpersonal roles (figurehead, leader, and liaison).[61] Understanding how your employees feel, why they feel that way, and how to manage these feelings is central to developing strong interpersonal bonds with them.[62] For work that involves encounters with people from different cultures, this effort is more complex but just as important, as described in the "Managing Globally" feature. In addition, emotional intelligence has the potential to contribute to effective leadership in multiple ways[63] and can help managers make lasting contributions to society. For example, Microsoft CEO Satya Nadella is credited with drastically changing the company's organizational culture from one filled with arrogance and cut-throat rivalries among various departments and functions to a culture filled with openness, collaboration, and innovation by focusing on self-awareness and empathy.[64]

MANAGING GLOBALLY

Emotional Intelligence Varies by Culture

Although definitions of emotional intelligence are based on the work of U.S. researchers, the idea has attracted the interest of managers, psychologists, and educators around the world.[65] While managing and reading emotions is important globally, the specific emotional information tends to vary by culture.

For example, in the United States, people express enthusiasm openly; this is considered both normal and desirable. Hiring managers tend to look favorably on job candidates who express enthusiasm, and people who act excited about a new project or product are admired for being devoted to the company's vision. In other countries, this outward enthusiasm is seen as odd or even annoying or offensive. British businesspeople tend to tone down their emotions, and Chinese people might interpret enthusiastic behavior as showing off rather than fitting in.[66]

Smiling also differs by culture. In North America, people smile often to signal they are friendly and well intentioned. This looks odd in Northern Europe, where smiles have the more limited purpose of signaling happiness. In Japan, a smile is more often a way to cover up embarrassment or unhappiness.[67]

Evidence suggests that differences such as these are less about what people feel (feelings are similar across cultures) and more about what they learn to express around others. Those differences in expression are tied to cultural values.[68] For example, British people value mature self-control, so they don't broadcast enthusiasm. In the United States, enthusiasm is more compatible with the high value placed on individual success and happiness. In much of Asia, group harmony is valued over individuality, so open celebrations of personal success can seem inappropriate. Further, as people practice different culture-based behaviors, they tend to develop different areas of strength in emotional intelligence. Travis Bradberry, president of TalentSmart, compared test scores of U.S. and Chinese managers and found that the Chinese managers scored higher in aspects of emotional intelligence focused on the feelings of others.[69]

Recognizing that emotional expressions vary by culture can build emotional intelligence.[70] A starting point is to recognize that unexpected behavior might indicate that emotions are being expressed differently. For example, if a U.S. manager notices that a Chinese employee seems unenthusiastic about a new project, the manager should check the assumption that absence of enthusiastic behavior signals lack of interest. Follow-up questions can be an effective way to find out. Also, whenever situations involve interacting with people from different cultures, it's worthwhile to learn each culture's emotional norms.

Emotional intelligence helps managers understand and relate well to other people. It also helps managers maintain their enthusiasm and confidence and energize their employees to help the organization attain its goals.[71] Recent theorizing and research suggest that emotional intelligence may be especially important in awakening employee creativity.[72] Managers themselves are increasingly recognizing the importance of emotional intelligence. An example of a scale that measures emotional intelligence is provided in Figure 3.5.

Organizational Culture

LO3-5 Define organizational culture, and explain how managers both create and are influenced by organizational culture.

Personality is a way of understanding why all managers and employees, as individuals, characteristically think and behave in different ways. However, when people belong to the same organization, they tend to share certain beliefs and values that lead them to act in similar ways.[73] **Organizational culture** comprises the shared set of beliefs, expectations, values, norms, and work routines that influence how members of an organization relate to one another and work together to achieve organizational goals. In essence, organizational culture reflects the distinctive ways in which organizational members perform their jobs and relate to others inside and outside the organization. It may, for example, be how customers in a particular hotel chain are treated from the time they are greeted at check-in until they leave, or it may be the shared work routines that research teams use to guide new product development. When organizational members share an intense commitment to cultural values, beliefs, and routines and use them to achieve their goals, a *strong* organizational culture exists.[74] When organizational members are not strongly committed to a shared system of values, beliefs, and routines, organizational culture is weak.

organizational culture The shared set of beliefs, expectations, values, norms, and work routines that influence how individuals, groups, and teams interact with one another and cooperate to achieve organizational goals.

The stronger the culture of an organization, the more one can think about it as being the "personality" of an organization because it influences the way its members behave.[75] Organizations that possess strong cultures may differ on a wide variety of dimensions that determine how their members behave toward one another and perform their jobs. For example, organizations differ in how members relate to each other (formally or informally), how important decisions are made (top-down or bottom-up), willingness to change (flexible or unyielding),

Figure 3.5

A Measure of Emotional Intelligence

Please indicate the extent to which you agree or disagree with each of the following items using the 1–7 scale below:

1	2	3	4	5	6	7
Totally disagree	Disagree	Somewhat disagree	Neither agree nor disagree	Somewhat agree	Agree	Totally agree

_____ **1.** I have a good sense of why I have certain feelings most of the time.

_____ **2.** I always know my friends' emotions from their behavior.

_____ **3.** I always set goals for myself and then try my best to achieve them.

_____ **4.** I am able to control my temper so that I can handle difficulties rationally.

_____ **5.** I have a good understanding of my own emotions.

_____ **6.** I am a good observer of others' emotions.

_____ **7.** I always tell myself I am a competent person.

_____ **8.** I am quite capable of controlling my own emotions.

_____ **9.** I really understand what I feel.

_____ **10.** I am sensitive to the feelings and emotions of others.

_____ **11.** I am a self-motivating person.

_____ **12.** I can always calm down quickly when I am very angry.

_____ **13.** I always know whether or not I am happy.

_____ **14.** I have good understanding of the emotions of people around me.

_____ **15.** I would always encourage myself to try my best.

_____ **16.** I have good control of my own emotions.

Scoring: Self-emotions appraisal = sum of items 1, 5, 9, 13
Others-emotions appraisal = sum of items 2, 6, 10, 14
Use of emotion = sum of items 3, 7, 11, 15
Regulation of emotion = sum of items 4, 8, 12, 16

Sources: K. Law, C. Wong, and L. Song, "The Construct and Criterion Validity of Emotional Intelligence and Its Potential Utility for Management Studies," *Journal of Applied Psychology* 89, no. 3 (June 2004), 496; C. S. Wong and K. S. Law, "The Effects of Leader and Follower Emotional Intelligence on Performance and Attitude: An Exploratory Study," *Leadership Quarterly* 13 (2002), 243–74.

innovation (creative or predictable), and playfulness (serious or serendipitous). In an innovative design firm like IDEO in Silicon Valley, employees are encouraged to adopt a playful attitude toward their work, look outside the organization to find inspiration, and adopt a flexible approach toward product design that uses multiple perspectives.[76] IDEO's culture is vastly different from that of companies such as Citibank and ExxonMobil, in which employees treat each other in a more formal or deferential way, employees are expected to adopt a serious approach to their work, and decision making is constrained by the hierarchy of authority.

Managers and Organizational Culture

While all members of an organization can contribute to developing and maintaining organizational culture, managers play a particularly important part in influencing organizational culture[77] because of their multiple and important roles (see Chapter 1). How managers create

IDEO employees brainstorming—informal communication, casual attire, and flexibility are all hallmarks of this organization.
IDEO Corporation

culture is most vividly evident in startups of new companies. Entrepreneurs who start their own companies are typically also the startups' top managers until the companies grow and become profitable. Often referred to as the firms' founders, these managers literally create their organizations' cultures.

The founders' personal characteristics play an important role in the creation of organizational culture. Benjamin Schneider, a well-known management researcher, developed a model that helps explain the role that founders' personal characteristics play in determining organizational culture.[78] His model, called the **attraction-selection-attrition (ASA) framework**, posits that when founders hire employees for their new ventures, they tend to be attracted to and choose employees whose personalities are similar to their own.[79] These similar employees are more likely to stay with the organization. Although employees who are dissimilar in personality might be hired, they are more likely to leave the organization over time. As a result of these attraction, selection, and attrition processes, people in the organization tend to have similar personalities, and the typical or dominant personality profile of organizational members determines and shapes organizational culture.[80]

attraction–selection–attrition (ASA) framework A model that explains how personality may influence organizational culture.

For example, when David Kelley became interested in engineering and product design challenges in the late 1970s, he realized that who he was as a person meant he would not be happy working in a typical corporate environment. Kelley is high on openness to experience, driven to go where his interests take him, and not content to follow others' directives. Kelley recognized that he needed to start his own business, and with the help of other Stanford-schooled engineers and design experts, IDEO was born.[81]

From the start, IDEO's culture has embodied Kelley's spirited, freewheeling approach to work and design–from colorful and informal workspaces to an emphasis on networking and communicating with as many people as possible to understand a design problem. No project or problem is too big or too small for IDEO; the company designed the Apple Lisa computer and mouse (the precursor of the Mac), the Palm, and more recently worked with the Ford Motor Company to make its new, electrified F-150 truck more customer-centric.[82] Kelley hates rules, job titles, big corner offices, and all the other trappings of large, traditional organizations that stifle creativity. Employees who are attracted to, are selected by, and remain with IDEO value creativity and innovation and embrace one of IDEO's mottos: "Everyone is creative."[83]

Although ASA processes are most evident in small firms such as IDEO, they also can operate in large companies.[84] According to the ASA model, this is a naturally occurring phenomenon to the extent that managers and new hires are free to make the kinds of choices the model specifies. However, while people tend to get along well with others who are similar to themselves, too much similarity in an organization can impair organizational effectiveness. That is, similar people tend to view conditions and events in similar ways and thus can be resistant to change. Moreover, organizations benefit from a diversity of perspectives rather than similarity in perspectives (see Chapter 5). At IDEO, Kelley recognized early on how important it is to take advantage of the diverse talents and perspectives that people with different personalities, backgrounds, experiences, and education can bring to a design team. Hence, IDEO's design teams include not only engineers, but others who might have a unique insight into a problem, such as anthropologists, communications experts, doctors, and users of a product. When new employees are hired at IDEO, they meet many employees who have different backgrounds and characteristics; the focus is not on hiring someone who will fit in but, rather, on hiring someone who has something to offer and can "wow" different kinds of people with their insights.[85]

In addition to personality, other personal characteristics of managers shape organizational culture; these include managers' values, attitudes, moods and emotions, and emotional intelligence.[86] For example, both terminal and instrumental values of managers play a role in determining organizational culture. Managers who highly value freedom and equality, for example, might be likely to stress the importance of autonomy and empowerment in their organizations, as well as fair treatment for all. As another example, managers who highly value being helpful and forgiving might not only tolerate mistakes but also emphasize the importance of organizational members' being kind and helpful to one another.

Managers who are satisfied with their jobs, are committed to their organizations, and experience positive moods and emotions might also encourage these attitudes and feelings in others. The result would be an organizational culture emphasizing positive attitudes and feelings. Research suggests that attitudes like job satisfaction and organizational commitment can be affected by the influence of others. Managers are in a particularly strong position to engage in social influence, given their multiple roles. Moreover, research suggests that moods and emotions can be contagious and that spending time with people who are excited and enthusiastic can increase one's own levels of excitement and enthusiasm.

The Role of Values and Norms in Organizational Culture

Shared terminal and instrumental values play a particularly important role in organizational culture. *Terminal values* signify what an organization and its employees are trying to accomplish, and *instrumental values* guide how the organization and its members achieve organizational goals. In addition to values, shared norms also are a key aspect of organizational culture. Recall that norms are unwritten, informal rules or guidelines that prescribe appropriate behavior in particular situations. For example, norms at IDEO include not being critical of others' ideas, coming up with multiple ideas before settling on one, and developing prototypes of new products.[87]

Managers determine and shape organizational culture through the kinds of values and norms they promote in an organization. Some managers, like David Kelley of IDEO, cultivate values and norms that encourage risk taking, creative responses to problems and opportunities, experimentation, tolerance of failure in order to succeed, and autonomy.[88] Top managers at organizations such as Microsoft and Google encourage employees to adopt such values to support their commitment to innovation as a source of competitive advantage.

Other managers, however, might cultivate values and norms that tell employees they should be conservative and cautious in their dealings with others and should consult their superiors before making important decisions or any changes to the status quo. Accountability for actions and decisions is stressed, and detailed records are kept to ensure that policies and procedures are followed. In settings where caution is needed—nuclear power stations, oil refineries, chemical plants, financial institutions, insurance companies—a conservative, cautious approach to making decisions might be appropriate. In a nuclear power plant, for example, the catastrophic consequences of a mistake make a high level of supervision vital. Similarly, in a bank or mutual fund company, the risk of losing investors' money makes a cautious approach to investing appropriate.

Managers of different kinds of organizations deliberately cultivate and develop the organizational values and norms that are best suited to their task and general environments, strategy, or technology. Organizational culture is maintained and transmitted to organizational members through the values of the founder, the process of socialization, ceremonies and rites, and stories and language (see Figure 3.6).

VALUES OF THE FOUNDER From the ASA model just discussed, it is clear that founders of an organization can have profound and long-lasting effects on organizational culture. Founders' values inspire the founders to start their own companies and, in turn, drive the nature of these new companies and their defining characteristics. Thus, the terminal and instrumental values of an organization's founder have a substantial influence on the values, norms, and standards of behavior that develop over time within the organization.[89] Founders set the scene for

Figure 3.6
Factors That Maintain and Transmit Organizational Culture

the way cultural values and norms develop because their own values guide the building of the company, and they hire other managers and employees who they believe will share these values and help the organization promote them. Moreover, new managers quickly learn from the founder what values and norms are appropriate in the organization and thus what is desired of them. They imitate the style of the founder and, in turn, transmit their values and norms to their employees. Gradually, over time, the founder's values and norms permeate the organization.[90]

A founder who requires a great display of respect from employees and insists on "correctness," such as formal job titles and formal dress, encourages managers to act in this way toward their employees. Often a founder's personal values affect an organization's competitive advantage. For example, McDonald's founder Ray Kroc insisted from the beginning on high standards of customer service and cleanliness at McDonald's restaurants; these became core sources of McDonald's competitive advantage. Similarly, Bill Gates, the cofounder of Microsoft, pioneered certain cultural values in Microsoft. Employees are expected to be creative and to work hard, but they are encouraged to dress informally and to personalize their offices. Gates also established a host of company events such as cookouts, picnics, and sports events to emphasize to employees the importance of being both an individual and a team player.

SOCIALIZATION Over time, organizational members learn from each other which values are important in an organization and the norms that specify appropriate and inappropriate behaviors. Eventually, organizational members behave in accordance with the organization's values and norms–often without realizing they are doing so. This makes culture a significant force in shaping employees' behavior.

organizational socialization The process by which newcomers learn an organization's values and norms and acquire the work behaviors necessary to perform jobs effectively.

Organizational socialization is the process by which newcomers learn an organization's values and norms and acquire the work behaviors necessary to perform jobs effectively.[91] As a result of their socialization experiences, organizational members internalize an organization's values and norms and behave in accordance with them, not only because they think they have to but because they think these values and norms describe the right and proper way to behave.[92]

At Texas A&M University, for example, all new students are encouraged to go to "Fish Camp" to learn how to be an "Aggie" (the traditional nickname of students at the university). They learn about the ceremonies that have developed over time to commemorate significant events or people in A&M's history. In addition, they learn how to behave at football games and in class and what it means to be an Aggie. As a result of this highly organized socialization program, by the time new students arrive on campus and start their first semester, they have been socialized into what a Texas A&M student is supposed to do, and they have relatively few problems adjusting to the college environment.[93]

Most organizations have some kind of socialization program to help new employees learn the ropes–the values, norms, and culture of the organization. The military, for example, is well known for the rigorous socialization process it uses to turn raw recruits into trained soldiers. Organizations such as The Walt Disney Company also put new recruits through a rigorous training program to teach them to perform well in their jobs and play their parts in helping visitors have fun in the company's theme parks. New recruits at Disney are called "cast members" and attend Disney University to learn the Disney culture and their parts in it. Disney's culture emphasizes the values of safety, courtesy, entertainment, and efficiency, and these values are brought to life for newcomers at Disney University. Newcomers also learn about the attraction area they will be joining (such as Adventureland or Fantasyland) at Disney University and then receive on-the-job socialization in the area itself from experienced cast members.[94] Through organizational socialization, founders and managers of an organization transmit to employees the cultural values and norms that shape the behavior of organizational members. Thus, the values and norms of founder Walt Disney live on today as newcomers are socialized into the Disney way.

CEREMONIES AND RITES Another way in which managers can create or influence organizational culture is by developing organizational ceremonies and rites–formal events that recognize incidents of importance to the organization as a whole and to specific employees.[95] The most common rites that organizations use to transmit cultural norms and values to their members are rites of passage, of integration, and of enhancement (see Table 3.1).[96]

Rites of passage determine how individuals enter, advance within, and leave the organization. The socialization programs developed by military organizations (such as the U.S. Army) or by large accountancy and law firms are rites of passage. Likewise, the ways in which an organization prepares people for promotion or retirement are rites of passage.

Rites of integration, such as shared announcements of organizational successes, office parties, and company cookouts, build and reinforce common bonds among organizational members. IDEO uses many rites of integration to make its employees feel connected to one another and special. In addition to having wild "end-of-year" celebratory bashes, groups of IDEO employees periodically take time off to go to a sporting event, movie, or meal or sometimes go on a long bike ride or for a sail. These kinds of shared activities not only reinforce IDEO's culture but also can be a source of inspiration on the job. One 35-member design studio at IDEO has bimonthly lunch fests with no set agenda–anything goes. While enjoying great food, jokes, and camaraderie, studio members often end up sharing ideas for their latest great products, and the freely flowing conversation that results often leads to creative insights.[97]

A company's annual meeting also may be used as a ritual of integration, offering an opportunity to communicate organizational values to managers, other employees, and shareholders.[98] Walmart, for example, makes its annual stockholders' meeting an extravagant ceremony that celebrates the company's success. The company often flies thousands of its highest-performing employees to its annual meeting at its Bentonville, Arkansas, headquarters for a huge weekend entertainment festival complete with star musical performances. Walmart believes that rewarding its supporters with entertainment reinforces the company's high-performance values and culture. The proceedings are shown live over closed-circuit television in all Walmart stores so all employees can join in the rites celebrating the company's achievements.[99]

Rites of enhancement, such as awards dinners, employee promotions, and recognition in press releases and social media posts, let organizations publicly recognize and reward employees' contributions and thus strengthen their commitment to organizational values. By bonding members within the organization, rites of enhancement reinforce an organization's values and norms.

Stories and language also communicate organizational culture. Stories (whether fact or fiction) about organizational heroes and villains and their actions provide important clues about values and norms. Such stories can reveal the kinds of behaviors that are valued by the organization and the kinds of practices that are frowned upon.[100] At the heart of the rich culture

Table 3.1
Organizational Rites

Type of Rite	Example of Rite	Purpose of Rite
Rite of passage	Induction and basic training	Learn and internalize norms and values
Rite of integration	Office holiday party	Build common norms and values
Rite of enhancement	Presentation of annual awards	Motivate commitment to norms and values

Stories about McDonald's founder, Ray Kroc (pictured here), permeate the company's organizational culture.
Bettmann/Getty Images

at McDonald's are hundreds of stories that organizational members tell about founder Ray Kroc. Most of these stories focus on how Kroc established the strict operating values and norms that are at the heart of McDonald's culture. Kroc was dedicated to achieving perfection in McDonald's quality, service, cleanliness, and value for money (QSC&V), and these four central values permeate McDonald's culture. For example, an often retold story describes what happened when Kroc and a group of managers from the Houston region were touring various restaurants. One of the restaurants was having a bad day operationally. Kroc was incensed about the long lines of customers, and he was furious when he realized that the products customers were receiving that day were not up to his high standards. To address the problem, he jumped up and stood on the front counter to get the attention of all customers and operating crew personnel. He introduced himself, apologized for the long wait and cold food, and told the customers they could have freshly cooked food or their money back—whichever they wanted. As a result, the customers left happy; and when Kroc checked on the restaurant later, he found that his message had gotten through to its managers and crew—performance had improved. Other stories describe Kroc scrubbing dirty toilets and picking up litter inside or outside a restaurant. These and similar stories are spread around the organization by McDonald's employees. They are the stories that have helped establish Kroc as McDonald's "hero."

Because spoken language is a principal medium of communication in organizations, the characteristic slang or jargon—that is, organization-specific words or phrases—that people use to frame and describe events provides important clues about norms and values. "McLanguage," for example, is prevalent at all levels of McDonald's. A McDonald's employee described as having "ketchup in their blood" is someone who is truly dedicated to the McDonald's way—someone who has been completely socialized to its culture. McDonald's has an extensive training program that teaches new employees "McDonald's speak," and new employees are welcomed into the family with a formal orientation that illustrates Kroc's dedication to QSC&V.

The concept of organizational language encompasses not only spoken language but how people dress, the offices they occupy, the cars they drive, and the degree of formality they use when they address one another. For example, casual dress reflects and reinforces IDEO's entrepreneurial culture and values. Formal business attire supports the conservative culture found in many banks and other financial institutions, which emphasizes the importance of conforming to organizational norms such as respect for authority and staying within one's prescribed role. When employees speak and understand the language of their organization's culture, they know how to behave in the organization and what is expected of them.

At IDEO, language, dress, the physical work environment, and extreme informality all underscore a culture that is adventuresome, playful, risk-taking, egalitarian, and innovative. For example, when designing products at IDEO, employees refer to taking the consumers' perspective as "being left-handed." Employees dress in T-shirts and jeans, the physical work environment continually evolves and changes depending on how employees wish to personalize their workspace, no one "owns" a fancy office with a window, and rules are almost nonexistent.[101]

Culture and Managerial Action

While founders and managers play a critical role in developing, maintaining, and communicating organizational culture, the same culture shapes and controls the behavior of all employees, including managers themselves. For example, culture influences how managers perform their four main functions: planning, organizing, leading, and controlling. As we consider these

IBM CEO Arvind Krishna has made his mark on the organization by hiring the company's first vice president of transformation and culture to rethink Big Blue's company culture and HR systems.
Stefan Wermuth/Bloomberg/Getty Images

functions, we continue to distinguish between top managers who create organizational values and norms that encourage creative, innovative behavior and top managers who encourage a conservative, cautious approach by their employees. We noted earlier that both kinds of values and norms can be appropriate depending on the situation and type of organization.

PLANNING Top managers in an organization with an innovative culture are likely to encourage lower-level managers to participate in the planning process and develop a flexible approach to planning. They are likely to be willing to listen to new ideas and to take risks involving the development of new products. In contrast, top managers in an organization with conservative values are likely to emphasize formal top-down planning. Suggestions from lower-level managers are likely to be subjected to a formal review process, which can significantly slow decision making. Although this deliberate approach may improve the quality of decision making in a nuclear power plant, it can have unintended consequences in other organizations.

For example, in the past, at conservative IBM, the planning process became so formalized that managers spent most of their time assembling complex slideshows to defend their current positions rather than thinking about what they should do to keep IBM abreast of the changes taking place in the computer industry. When former CEO Lou Gerstner took over, he used every means at his disposal to abolish this culture, even building a brand-new campus-style headquarters to change managers' mind-sets. IBM's culture underwent further changes initiated by its next CEO, Samuel Palmisano. The next CEO, Ginni Rometty, who took over in 2012 and stepped down in 2020, changed the company's culture in her own way, including bringing back thousands of remote workers to IBM regional offices in an effort to improve collaboration and accelerate the pace of work and innovation at the tech giant.[102] Rometty's successor, Arvind Krishna, has already made his own mark on IBM's culture by hiring the company's first senior vice president of transformation and culture, whose first major task is to rethink Big Blue's organizational culture and its human resources systems.[103]

ORGANIZING What kinds of organizing will managers in innovative and in conservative cultures encourage? Valuing creativity, managers in innovative cultures are likely to try to create an organic structure–one that is flat, with few levels in the hierarchy, and one in which authority is decentralized so employees are encouraged to work together to solve ongoing problems. A product team structure may be suitable for an organization with an innovative culture. In contrast, managers in a conservative culture are likely to create a well-defined hierarchy of authority and establish clear reporting relationships so employees know exactly whom to report to and how to react to any problems that arise.

LEADING In an innovative culture, managers are likely to lead by example, encouraging employees to take risks and experiment. They are supportive regardless of whether employees succeed or fail. In contrast, managers in a conservative culture are likely to use management by objectives and to constantly monitor employees' progress toward goals, overseeing their every move. We examine leadership in detail in Chapter 14, when we consider the leadership styles that managers can adopt to influence and shape employee behavior.

CONTROLLING The ways in which managers evaluate and take actions to improve performance differ depending on whether the organizational culture emphasizes formality and caution or innovation and change. Managers who want to encourage risk taking, creativity, and innovation recognize that there are multiple potential paths to success and that failure must be accepted for creativity to thrive. Thus, they are less concerned about employees' performing their jobs in a specific, predetermined manner and in strict adherence to preset goals and more concerned about employees' being flexible and taking the initiative to come up with ideas for improving performance. Managers in innovative cultures are also more concerned about long-term performance than short-term targets because they recognize that real innovation entails much uncertainty that necessitates flexibility. In contrast, managers in cultures that emphasize caution and maintenance of the status quo often set specific, difficult goals for employees, frequently monitor progress toward these goals, and develop a clear set of rules that employees are expected to adhere to.

The values and norms of an organization's culture strongly affect the way managers perform their management functions. The extent to which managers buy into the values and norms of their organization shapes their view of the world and their actions and decisions in particular circumstances. In turn, the actions that managers take can have an impact on the performance of the organization. Thus, organizational culture, managerial action, and organizational performance are all linked together.

While our earlier example of IDEO illustrates how organizational culture can give rise to managerial actions that ultimately benefit the organization, this is not always the case. The cultures of some organizations become dysfunctional, encouraging managerial actions that harm the organization and discouraging actions that might improve performance. Recent corporate scandals at large companies such as Boeing, Google, Facebook, and Wells Fargo, to name a few, show how damaging a dysfunctional culture can be to an organization and its members. For example, Boeing's arrogant "success at all cost" mentality led to fraudulent behavior on the part of top managers and others, which may have indirectly caused two fatal crashes of the 737 MAX and the deaths of 346 people, and led to the firing of Boeing's CEO.[104] We discuss ethics in depth in the next chapter.

Summary and Review

LO3-1 **ENDURING CHARACTERISTICS: PERSONALITY TRAITS** Personality traits are enduring tendencies to feel, think, and act in certain ways. The Big Five general traits are extraversion, negative affectivity, agreeableness, conscientiousness, and openness to experience. Other personality traits that affect managerial behavior include locus of control, self-esteem, and the needs for achievement, affiliation, and power. Several other personality assessments can be effective in helping managers and individuals identify positive and negative behaviors in themselves and others. These include the Myers-Briggs Type Indicator (MBTI) and the DiSC Inventory Profile.

LO3-2, 3-3, 3-4 **VALUES, ATTITUDES, AND MOODS AND EMOTIONS** A terminal value is a personal conviction about lifelong goals or objectives; an instrumental value is a personal conviction about modes of conduct. Terminal and instrumental values have an impact on what managers try to achieve in their organizations and the kinds of behaviors they engage in. An attitude is a collection of feelings and beliefs. Two attitudes important for understanding managerial behaviors include job satisfaction (the collection of feelings and beliefs that managers have about their jobs) and organizational commitment (the collection of feelings and beliefs that managers have about their organizations). A mood is a feeling or state of mind; emotions are intense feelings that are short-lived and directly linked to their causes. Managers' moods and emotions, or how they feel at work on a day-to-day basis, have the potential to impact not only their own behavior and effectiveness but also those of their employees. Emotional intelligence is the ability to understand and manage one's own and other people's moods and emotions.

LO3-5 **ORGANIZATIONAL CULTURE** Organizational culture is the shared set of beliefs, expectations, values, norms, and work routines that influence how members of an organization relate to one another and work together to achieve organizational goals. Founders of new organizations and managers play an important role in creating and maintaining organizational culture. Organizational socialization is the process by which newcomers learn an organization's values and norms and acquire the work behaviors necessary to perform jobs effectively.

Management in Action

Topics for Discussion and Action

Discussion

1. Discuss why managers who have different types of personalities can be equally effective and successful. [LO3-1]
2. Can managers be too satisfied with their jobs? Can they be too committed to their organizations? Why or why not? [LO3-2]
3. Assume that you are a manager of a restaurant. Describe what it is like to work for you when you are in a negative mood. [LO3-3]
4. Why might managers be disadvantaged by low levels of emotional intelligence? [LO3-4]

Action

5. Interview a manager in a local organization. Ask the manager to describe situations in which they are especially likely to act in accordance with their values. Ask the manager to describe situations in which they are less likely to act in accordance with their own values. [LO3-2]
6. Watch a popular television show or a series streaming online and as you watch it, try to determine the emotional intelligence levels of the characters the actors in the show portray. Rank the characters from highest to lowest in terms of emotional intelligence. As you watched the show, what factors influenced your assessments of emotional intelligence levels? [LO3-4]
7. Go to an upscale store in your neighborhood, and go to a store that is definitely not upscale. Observe the behavior of employees in each store as well as the store's environment. In what ways are the organizational cultures in each store similar? In what ways are they different? [LO3-5]

Building Management Skills

Diagnosing Culture [LO3-5]

Think about the culture of the last organization you worked for, your current university, or another organization or club to which you belong. Then answer the following questions:

1. What values are emphasized in this culture?
2. What norms do members of this organization follow?
3. Who seems to have played an important role in creating the culture?
4. In what ways is the organizational culture communicated to organizational members?

Managing Ethically [LO3-1, 3-2]

Some organizations rely on personality and interest inventories to screen potential employees. Other organizations attempt to screen employees by using paper-and-pencil honesty tests.

Questions

1. Either individually or in a group, think about the ethical implications of using personality and interest inventories to screen potential employees. How might this practice be unfair to potential applicants? How might organizational members who are in charge of hiring misuse it?
2. Because of measurement error and validity problems, some relatively trustworthy people may "fail" an honesty test given by an employer. What are the ethical implications of trustworthy people "failing" honesty tests, and what obligations do you think employers should have when relying on honesty tests for screening potential employees?

Small Group Breakout Exercise

Making Difficult Decisions in Hard Times [LO3-2, 3-3, 3-4, 3-5]

Form groups of three or four people, and appoint one member as the spokesperson who will communicate your findings to the whole class when called on by the instructor. Then discuss the following scenario:

You are on the top management team of a medium-size company that manufactures cardboard boxes, containers, and other packaging materials. Your company is facing increasing levels of competition for major corporate customer accounts, and profits have declined significantly. You have tried everything you can to cut costs and remain competitive, with the exception of laying off employees. Your company has had a no-layoff policy for the past 20 years, and you believe it is an important part of the organization's culture. However, you are experiencing mounting pressure to increase your firm's performance, and your no-layoff policy has been questioned by shareholders. Even though you haven't decided whether to lay off employees and thus break with a 20-year tradition for your company, rumors are rampant in your organization that something is going on, and employees are worried. You are meeting today to address this problem.

1. Develop a list of options and potential courses of action to address the heightened competition and decline in profitability that your company has been experiencing.
2. Choose your preferred course of action, and justify why you will take this route.
3. Describe how you will communicate your decision to employees.
4. If your preferred option involves a layoff, justify why. If it doesn't involve a layoff, explain why.

Be the Manager [LO3-1, 3-2, 3-3, 3-4, 3-5]

You have recently been hired as the vice president for human resources in an advertising agency. One problem that has been brought to your attention is the fact that the creative departments at the agency have dysfunctionally high levels of conflict. You have spoken with members of each of these departments, and in each one it seems that a few members of the department are creating all the problems. All these individuals are valued contributors who have many creative ad campaigns to their credit. The high levels of conflict are creating problems in the departments, and negative moods and emotions are much more prevalent than positive feelings. What are you going to do to both retain valued employees and alleviate the excessive conflict and negative feelings in these departments?

Case in the News [LO3-1, 3-2, 3-3, 3-4, 3-5]

Fidji Simo Brings a Unique Perspective to Instacart

Fidji Simo joined Instacart as CEO at a pivotal time in the company's short history. Founded in 2012 to provide rapid delivery of groceries, Instacart contracts with workers to shop and then deliver to consumers' doorsteps. In 2021, when Simo took the reins from founder Apoorva Mehta, the company was figuring out how to maintain significant growth that occurred shortly after the start of the COVID-19 pandemic.

Simo does not fit the usual characteristics of a tech company CEO. The obvious difference is that she is female in an industry where about two-thirds to three-quarters of leaders are men. In addition, Simo is young (in her mid-thirties), came from France, didn't start out in information technology (or retailing), and brings a strong fashion sense to a casual culture. However, her values and attitudes, combined with her intelligence, help explain why she has thrived.

Simo's early years exhibit her impressive drive and adventurousness. She was born near the Mediterranean coast, where her father was a fisherman and her mother owned a clothing boutique. She became the first in her family to complete high school, where she met her husband. The two of them moved to Paris so Simo could attend the prestigious business school known as HEC, and she completed the program with a year at UCLA. With her master's in business, Simo got a strategy job at eBay and then moved over to Facebook to work in marketing. Soon she was fascinated by the product side of the business, where jobs usually require a computer science degree. Undeterred, Simo learned to write product requirements, and her sample documents persuaded management to assign her to a product management position. She led the development of a platform for mobile advertising and the launch of Facebook Live.

At Facebook, colleagues spoke to Simo about company culture. One norm was casual attire—the stereotype of techies in jeans and hoodies. Simo's style is chic dresses, high heels, and vibrant lipstick. More experienced managers warned Simo that engineers would be put off by her appearance. Simo tried dressing down but felt awkward and inauthentic. She decided she had to succeed in her own way. Over the following years, she took that spirit to the next level as she experienced health conditions that are often not discussed—the painful disease endometriosis, a miscarriage, a difficult pregnancy that required bed rest, and a neuroimmune disorder. Through all of this, she was open about her situation and need for accommodations, and her frankness freed others to be more open with her. Simo also developed her ability to deliver negative feedback clearly but in a respectful manner that recipients can accept. Colleagues and board members from Facebook and Instacart have praised Simo for her discipline, self-confidence, knowledge, empathy, willingness to listen, and leadership skills.

Now at Instacart, Simo is identifying and seizing opportunities for the company. When the pandemic arrived in the United States in March 2020, grocery delivery was a small but growing business increasingly dominated by Walmart. Then Instacart's sales quadrupled, putting it on par with Walmart. Although sales quickly softened, they remain above pre-pandemic levels. Simo also is passionate about her company's role in selling groceries, telling an AP reporter that in her French Sicilian family, "the way we show care is always food."

Significant challenges lie ahead. Like other companies with gig workers, Instacart must respond to their pressure for better pay and conditions. With the easing of pandemic restrictions and fears, U.S. consumers are returning to supermarkets. Some large retailers are investing in their own delivery services. Nevertheless, Simo envisions ways to generate revenue growth, such as selling ads, expanding internationally, and offering information services to retail partners. On the cost side, the company is investing in robotics to automate warehouses and speed order fulfillment. Simo anticipates that Instacart can lower costs and delivery prices to a point where 30% of U.S. consumers will opt for delivery.

Simo says as long as leaders keep open minds, they can adapt quickly. Her idea for career success is "iterate yourself," meaning continually try new ideas and ways of working to see what is most authentic and effective. She also embraces her identity as a unique contributor in the workplace. Like other managers who value diversity, Simo describes it as an ingredient that makes work more interesting, creative, and even fun.

Questions for Discussion

1. What personality traits and values do you associate with Fidji Simo's success as a manager?
2. Based on the information in the case, would you describe Simo as having high emotional intelligence? What evidence supports your opinion?
3. How did Simo relate to corporate culture at Facebook? How could her experience influence the way she shapes organizational culture as CEO of Instacart?

Sources: M. Aspan, "Instacart CEO Fidji Simo on How She Found Her Own Leadership Groove," *Fortune,* https://fortune.com, accessed January 8, 2023; J. Wells and S. Silverstein, "Instacart Founder Apoorva Mehta to Exit Company Once It Goes Public," *Grocery Dive,* www.grocerydive.com, July 22, 2022; M. Aspan "Shopping Outside the Aisle," *Fortune,* October/November 2021, 85–90; Associated Press, "Instacart CEO Fidji Simo Says Online Grocery Shopping Has Room to Grow," *TribLive* (Pittsburgh), https://triblive.com, October 11, 2021; J. Kang, "Instacart Goes Deeper into Digital Advertising as Grocery Delivery Shows," *The Wall Street Journal,* www.wsj.com, September 6, 2021; F. Richter, "Women's Representation in Big Tech," *Statista,* www.statista.com, July 10, 2021; A. Achuthan, "Five Questions with Fidji Simo, Director of Product at Facebook," *Medium,* https://medium.com, September 12, 2016.

Notes

1. Company website, "Who We Are: Leadership Profiles," www.johnhancock.com, accessed January 8, 2023; P. La Duke, "Five Things I Wish Someone Told Me before I Became a CEO," interview of Marianne Harrison, *Authority,* https://medium.com/authority-magazine, September 6, 2019.
2. La Duke, "Five Things I Wish Someone Told Me."
3. C.J. Prince, "CEO Harrison: Insurance Can–and Must–Transform," *Chief Executive,* https://chiefexecutive.net, January 8, 2020.
4. La Duke, "Five Things I Wish Someone Told Me."
5. C.J. Prince, "How One CEO Is Changing Culture in a 157-Year-Old Company," *Chief Executive,* https://chiefexecutive.net, January 10, 2020; N.D. Debevoise, "How This CEO's Inclusive Approach Is Growing Her Business," *Forbes,* www.forbes.com, November 7, 2019.
6. La Duke, "Five Things I Wish Someone Told Me"; Prince, "Insurance Can–and Must–Transform."
7. Prince, "Insurance Can–and Must–Transform"; Prince, "How One CEO Is Changing Culture."
8. E. Larson, "Here's How Your Personality Type Affects Your Decision Making at Work," *Forbes,* www.forbes.com, accessed January 8, 2023.
9. J.M. George, "Personality, Five-Factor Model," in S. Clegg and J.R. Bailey, eds., *International Encyclopedia of Organization Studies* (Thousand Oaks, CA: Sage, 2007); J.M. Digman, "Personality Structure: Emergence of the Five-Factor Model," *Annual Review of Psychology* 41(1990), 417-40.
10. T.A. Judge and C.P. Zapata, "The Person-Situation Debate Revisited: Effect of Situation Strength and Trait Activation on the Validity of the Big Five Personality Traits in Predicting Job Performance," *Academy*

of Management Journal 58, no. 4 (2015), 1149–79.

11. L.A. Witt and G.R. Ferris, "Social Skills as Moderator of Conscientiousness–Performance Relationship: Convergent Results across Four Studies," *Journal of Applied Psychology* 88, no. 5 (2003), 809–20; M.J. Simmering, J.A. Colquitte, R.A. Noe, and C.O.L.H. Porter, "Conscientiousness, Autonomy Fit, and Development: A Longitudinal Study," *Journal of Applied Psychology* 88, no. 5 (2003), 954–63.
12. M.R. Barrick and M.K. Mount, "The Big Five Personality Dimensions and Job Performance: A Meta-Analysis," *Personnel Psychology* 44 (1991), 1–26; S. Komar, D.J. Brown, J.A. Komar, and C. Robie, "Faking and the Validity of Conscientiousness: A Monte Carlo Investigation," *Journal of Applied Psychology* 93 (2008), 140–54.
13. Digman, "Personality Structure."
14. "Who Are the Huntingtons?" https://huntingtonfranchise.com, accessed January 8, 2023; D. Stockbridge, "Top of the Class: Eileen Huntington," *CEO,* www.theceomagazine.com, October 31, 2019; M. Fry, "The Numbers Add Up: Huntington Learning Center Has Become $150M Franchise Business," *ROI-NJ,* March 30, 2018, www.roi-nj.com, March 30, 2018.
15. Huntington Learning Center, "Our Story"; Fry, "The Numbers Add Up."
16. Stockbridge, "Top of the Class"; Fry, "The Numbers Add Up."
17. Stockbridge, "Top of the Class."
18. Huntington Learning Center, "Our Story"; Stockbridge, "Top of the Class"; Fry, "The Numbers Add Up."
19. J.B. Rotter, "Generalized Expectancies for Internal versus External Control of Reinforcement," *Psychological Monographs* 80 (1966), 1–28; P. Spector, "Behaviors in Organizations as a Function of Employees' Locus of Control," *Psychological Bulletin* 91 (1982), 482–97.
20. A. Howell, "How to Build Confidence at Work," *Harvard Business Review*, https://hbr.org, August 9, 2021.
21. D.C. McClelland, *Human Motivation* (Glenview, IL: Scott, Foresman, 1985); D.C. McClelland, "How Motives, Skills, and Values Determine What People Do," *American Psychologist* 40 (1985), 812–25; D.C. McClelland, "Managing Motivation to Expand Human Freedom," *American Psychologist* 33 (1978), 201–10.
22. D.G. Winter, *The Power Motive* (New York: Free Press 1973).
23. M.J. Stahl, "Achievement, Power, and Managerial Motivation: Selecting Managerial Talent with the Job Choice Exercise," *Personnel Psychology* 36 (1983), 775–89; D.C. McClelland and D.H. Burnham, "Power Is the Great Motivator," *Harvard Business Review* 54 (1976), 100–10.
24. R.J. House, W.D. Spangler, and J. Woycke, "Personality and Charisma in the U.S. Presidency: A Psychological Theory of Leader Effectiveness," *Administrative Science Quarterly* 36 (1991), 364–96.
25. G.H. Hines, "Achievement, Motivation, Occupations and Labor Turnover in New Zealand," *Journal of Applied Psychology* 58 (1973), 313–17; P.S. Hundal, "A Study of Entrepreneurial Motivation: Comparison of Fast- and Slow-Progressing Small Scale Industrial Entrepreneurs in Punjab, India," *Journal of Applied Psychology* 55 (1971), 317–23.
26. The Myers-Briggs Company, "Myers-Briggs Type Indicator®," www.themyersbriggs.com, accessed January 8, 2023; E. Bajic, "How the MBTI Can Help You Build a Stronger Company," *Forbes*, www.forbes.com, accessed January 8, 2023; A. Furnham and J. Crump, "The Myers-Briggs Type Indicator (MBTI) and Promotion at Work," *Psychology* 6, no. 12 (September 2015) 1510–15.
27. "What Is DiSC?" www.discprofile.com, accessed February 8, 2020.
28. M. Rokeach, *The Nature of Human Values* (New York: Free Press 1973).
29. K. Tuulik, T. Ounapuu, K. Kuimet, and E. Titov, "Rokeach's Instrumental and Terminal Values as Descriptors of Modern Organisation Values," *International Journal of Organizational Leadership* 5 (2016), 151–61.
30. Rokeach, *The Nature of Human Values.*
31. B. Steverman, "Layoffs: Short-Term Profits, Long-Term Problems," *Bloomberg,* www.bloomberg.com, January 13, 2010; P.S. Goodman, "U.S. Job Losses in December Dim Hopes for Quick Upswing," *The New York Times,* www.nytimes.com, January 9, 2010.
32. Conference Board, "U.S. Job Satisfaction at Lowest Level in Two Decades," www.conference-board.org, January 5, 2010.
33. The Conference Board, "Survey: Despite Pandemic, Job Satisfaction Remains High," www.conference-board.org, April 26, 2021.
34. A. Li, C. Rong, S. Hong, and R.L. Ray, "Job Satisfaction 2022: Chartbook," www.conference-board.org, April 5, 2022.
35. C.F. Iam, W.H. Wan, and C.J. Roussin, "Going the Extra Mile and Feeling Energized: An Enrichment Perspective of Organizational Behaviors," *Journal of Applied Psychology* 101, no. 3 (2016), 379–91; D.W. Organ, *Organizational Citizenship Behavior: The Good Soldier Syndrome* (Lexington, MA: Lexington Books, 1988).
36. J.M. George and A.P. Brief, "Feeling Good–Doing Good: A Conceptual Analysis of the Mood at Work–Organizational Spontaneity Relationship," *Psychological Bulletin* 112 (1992), 310–29.
37. A. Kopoulos, "How to Engage Your Managers," *Employee Connect,* www.employeeconnect.com, accessed February 8, 2020.
38. S. M. Heathfield, "Tips for Compassionate Employee Layoffs," *The Balance Careers,* www.thebalancecareers, January 7, 2020; K.W. Freeman, "A Guide to Being Compassionate During Layoffs," *Harvard Business Review,* https://hbr.org, February 25, 2016.
39. N. Solinger, W. van Olffen, and R.A. Roe, "Beyond the Three-Component Model of Organizational Commitment," *Journal of Applied Psychology* 93 (2008), 70–83.
40. J.E. Mathieu and D.M. Zajac, "A Review and Meta-Analysis of the Antecedents, Correlates, and Consequences of Organizational Commitment," *Psychological Bulletin* 108 (1990), 171–94.
41. T.-P. Chen and R. A. Smith, "American Workers Are Burned Out, and Bosses Are Struggling to Respond," *The Wall Street Journal,* www.wsj.com, accessed January 8, 2023.
42. J. Robison, "The Antidote to Manager Burnout," *Gallup,* www.gallup.com, January 22, 2022; World Health Organization, "Burn-Out an 'Occupational Phenomenon': International Classification of Diseases," www.who.int., May 28, 2019.
43. B. Mena, "Workers Quit Jobs at a Record Level in November," *The Wall Street Journal,* www.wsj.com, January 4, 2022.
44. Ibid.
45. R. A. Smith, "These Workers Wanted to Quit, But Promotions Persuaded Them to Stay," *The Wall Street Journal,* www.wsj.com, January 7, 2022.
46. Chen and Smith, "American Workers Are Burned Out."
47. Robison, "The Antidote to Manager Burnout."
48. D. Watson and A. Tellegen, "Toward a Consensual Structure of Mood," *Psychological Bulletin* 98 (1985), 219–35.
49. J.M. George, "The Role of Personality in Organizational Life: Issues and Evidence," *Journal of Management* 18 (1992), 185–213.
50. H.A. Elfenbein, "Emotion in Organizations: A Review and Theoretical Integration," in J.P. Walsh and A.P. Brief, eds., *The Academy of Management Annals,* vol. 1 (New York: Erlbaum, 2008), 315–86.
51. J.P. Forgas, "Affect in Social Judgments and Decisions: A Multi-Process Model," in M. Zamma, ed., *Advances in Experimental and Social Psychology,* vol. 25 (San Diego, CA: Academic Press, 1992), 227–75;

J.P. Forgas and J.M. George, "Affective Influences on Judgments and Behavior in Organizations: An Information Processing Perspective," *Organizational Behavior and Human Decision Processes* 86 (2001), 3–34; J.M. George, "Emotions and Leadership: The Role of Emotional Intelligence," *Human Relations* 53 (2000), 1027–55; W.N. Morris, *Mood: The Frame of Mind* (New York: Springer-Verlag, 1989).

52. J.M. George and K. Bettenhausen, "Understanding Prosocial Behavior, Sales Performance, and Turnover: A Group Level Analysis in a Service Context," *Journal of Applied Psychology* 75 (1990), 698–709.

53. George and Brief, "Feeling Good–Doing Good"; J.M. George and J. Zhou, "Understanding When Bad Moods Foster Creativity and Good Ones Don't: The Role of Context and Clarity of Feelings," paper presented at the Academy of Management Annual Meeting, 2001; A.M. Isen and R.A. Baron, "Positive Affect as a Factor in Organizational Behavior," in B.M. Staw and L.L. Cummings, eds., *Research in Organizational Behavior,* vol. 13 (Greenwich, CT: JAI Press, 1991), 1–53.

54. J.M. George and J. Zhou, "Dual Tuning in a Supportive Context: Joint Contributions of Positive Mood, Negative Mood, and Supervisory Behaviors to Employee Creativity," *Academy of Management Journal* 50 (2007), 605–22; J.M. George, "Creativity in Organizations," in J.P. Walsh and A.P. Brief, eds., *The Academy of Management Annals,* vol. 1 (New York: Erlbaum, 2008), 439–77.

55. J.D. Greene, R.B. Sommerville, L.E. Nystrom, J.M. Darley, and J.D. Cohen, "An FMRI Investigation of Emotional Engagement in Moral Judgment," *Science,* September 14, 2001, 2105–108; L. Neergaard, "Brain Scans Show Emotions Key to Resolving Ethical Dilemmas," *Houston Chronicle,* September 14, 2001, 13A.

56. George and Zhou, "Dual Tuning in a Supportive Context."

57. George and Zhou, "Dual Tuning in a Supportive Context;" J.M. George, "Dual Tuning: A Minimum Condition for Understanding Affect in Organizations?" *Organizational Psychology Review* 2 (2011), 147–64.

58. R.C. Sinclair, "Mood, Categorization Breadth, and Performance Appraisal: The Effects of Order of Information Acquisition and Affective State on Halo, Accuracy, Informational Retrieval, and Evaluations," *Organizational Behavior and Human Decision Processes* 42 (1988), 22–46.

59. D. Goleman, *Emotional Intelligence* (New York: Bantam Books, 1994); J.D. Mayer and P. Salovey, "The Intelligence of Emotional Intelligence," *Intelligence* 17 (1993), 433–42; J.D. Mayer and P. Salovey, "What Is Emotional Intelligence?" in P. Salovey and D. Sluyter, eds., *Emotional Development and Emotional Intelligence: Implications for Education* (New York: Basic Books, 1997); P. Salovey and J.D. Mayer, "Emotional Intelligence," *Imagination, Cognition, and Personality* 9 (1989–1990), 185–211.

60. J. Fabiano, "9 Ways You Should Use Emotional Intelligence at Work," *The Ladders,* www.ladders.com, accessed February 8, 2020.

61. L. Landry, "Why Emotional Intelligence Is Important in Leadership," *Harvard Business School Online,* https://online.hbs.edu, April 3, 2019.

62. P.C. Early and R.S. Peterson, "The Elusive Cultural Chameleon: Cultural Intelligence as a New Approach to Intercultural Training for the Global Manager," *Academy of Management Learning and Education* 3, no. 1 (2004), 100–15.

63. George, "Emotions and Leadership"; S. Begley, "The Boss Feels Your Pain," *Newsweek,* October 12, 1998, 74; D. Goleman, *Working with Emotional Intelligence* (New York: Bantam Books, 1998).

64. J. Thier, "Microsoft CEO Satya Nadella's Son Died at 26. Here's What He Taught the Leader about Empathy," *Fortune,* https://fortune.com, March 2, 2022; N. Lanctot, "How to Lead–and Succeed–with Emotional Intelligence," *Fast Company,* www.fastcompany.com, February 19, 2021.

65. See Daniel Goleman, "Emotional Intelligence," www.danielgoleman.info, accessed January 8, 2023.

66. A. Molinsky, "Emotional Intelligence Doesn't Translate across Borders," *Harvard Business Review,* https://hbr.org, April 20, 2015.

67. P. Surana, "Is Emotional Intelligence Culture Specific?" *LinkedIn,* www.linkedin.com, May 4, 2017.

68. Surana, "Is Emotional Intelligence Culture Specific?"; Molinsky, "Emotional Intelligence Doesn't Translate."

69. P. Gaul, "Travis Bradberry" *TD,* May 2017, 60–61.

70. Molinsky, "Emotional Intelligence Doesn't Translate"; Surana, "Is Emotional Intelligence Culture Specific?"

71. George, "Emotions and Leadership."

72. J. Zhou and J.M. George, "Awakening Employee Creativity: The Role of Leader Emotional Intelligence," *Leadership Quarterly* 14 (2003), 545–68.

73. H.M. Trice and J.M. Beyer, *The Cultures of Work Organizations* (Englewood Cliffs, NJ: Prentice-Hall, 1993).

74. J.B. Sørensen, "The Strength of Corporate Culture and the Reliability of Firm Performance," *Administrative Science Quarterly* 47 (2002), 70–91.

75. "Personality and Organizational Culture," in B. Schneider and D.B. Smith, eds., *Personality and Organizations* (Mahway, NJ: Erlbaum, 2004), 347–69; J.E. Slaughter, M.J. Zickar, S. Highhouse, and D.C. Mohr, "Personality Trait Inferences about Organizations: Development of a Measure and Assessment of Construct Validity," *Journal of Applied Psychology* 89, no. 1 (2004), 85–103.

76. "About IDEO," www.ideo.com, accessed February 9, 2020; T. Kelley, *The Art of Innovation: Lessons in Creativity from IDEO, America's Leading Design Firm* (New York: Random House, 2001).

77. L. Alton, "Why Corporate Culture Is Becoming Even More Important," *Forbes,* www.forbes.com, accessed February 9, 2020.

78. B. Schneider, "The People Make the Place," *Personnel Psychology* 40 (1987), 437–53.

79. "Personality and Organizational Culture."

80. B. Schneider, H.B. Goldstein, and D.B. Smith, "The ASA Framework: An Update," *Personnel Psychology* 48 (1995), 747–73; J. Schaubroeck, D.C. Ganster, and J.R. Jones, "Organizational and Occupational Influences in the Attraction–Selection–Attrition Process," *Journal of Applied Psychology* 83 (1998), 869–91.

81. Kelley, *The Art of Innovation.*

82. "Can't Wait: How Ford Transformed Itself to Take On the Future of Mobility," https://cantwait.ideo.com, accessed January 8, 2023.

83. "Who We Are," www.ideo.com, accessed January 8, 2023.

84. "Personality and Organizational Culture."

85. L. Lamb, "Inside the Creative Office Cultures at Facebook, IDEO, and Virgin America," *Fast Company,* www.fastcompany.com, accessed February 9, 2020.

86. George, "Emotions and Leadership."

87. Lamb, "Inside the Creative Office Cultures at Facebook, IDEO, and Virgin America."

88. Kelley, *The Art of Innovation.*

89. M. McClain, "How Corporate Culture Can Make (or Break) Your Organization," *Forbes,* www.forbes.com, November 6, 2017.

90. H. Schein, "The Role of the Founder in Creating Organizational Culture," *Organizational Dynamics* 12 (1983), 13–28.

91. J.M. George, "Personality, Affect, and Behavior in Groups," *Journal of Applied Psychology* 75 (1990), 107–16.

92. J. Van Maanen, "Police Socialization: A Longitudinal Examination of Job

Attitudes in an Urban Police Department," *Administrative Science Quarterly* 20 (1975), 207–28.

93. Texas A&M University, "Fish Camp," https://fishcamp.tamu.edu, accessed January 8, 2023.

94. "Welcome to the Wiki: Disney University," https://disney.fandom.com, accessed February 9, 2020.

95. K. Zhang, "Want a Killer Culture Like the Top Tech Firms? Start Some Company Rituals," *Entrepreneur,* www.entrepreneur.com, May 23, 2019.

96. H.M. Trice and J.M. Beyer, "Studying Organizational Culture through Rites and Ceremonies," *Academy of Management Review* 9 (1984), 653–69.

97. Kelley, *The Art of Innovation.*

98. H.M. Trice and J.M. Beyer, *The Cultures of Work Organizations* (Englewood Cliffs, NJ: Prentice-Hall, 1993).

99. R. Feloni, "How the Walmart Shareholders Meeting Went from a Few Guys in a Coffee Shop to a 14,000-Person, Star-Studded Celebration," *Business Insider,* www.businessinsider.com, accessed February 9, 2020.

100. Trice and Beyer, "Studying Organizational Culture through Rites and Ceremonies."

101. Kelley, *The Art of Innovation.*

102. J. Simons, "IBM, a Pioneer of Remote Work, Calls Workers Back to the Office," *The Wall Street Journal,* www.wsj.com, May 18, 2017.

103. J. McGregor, "Keeping the Elephant Dancing: IBM's First Head of Culture Explains How He's Working to Keep Its People Focused Like Its Strategy," *Forbes,* www.forbes.com, November 9, 2021.

104. R. Conconi, "With Corporate Scandals on the Rise, People Must Demand Accountability," *Observer,* https://observer.com, accessed January 8, 2023; Agence France-Presse, "Boeing Employees' Emails Bemoan 'Arrogance,'" *Voice of America,* www.voanews.com, January 8, 2023; D. Gelles and N. Kitroeff, "Boeing Fires C.E.O. Dennis Muilenburg," *The New York Times,* www.nytimes.com, December 23, 2019.

CHAPTER 4

Ethics and Social Responsibility

Hero Images/Getty Images

Learning Objectives

After studying this chapter, you should be able to:

LO4-1 Explain the relationship between ethics and the law.

LO4-2 Differentiate between the claims of the different stakeholder groups affected by managers and their companies' actions.

LO4-3 Describe four rules that can help companies and their managers act in ethical ways.

LO4-4 Discuss why it is important for managers to behave ethically.

LO4-5 Identify the four main sources of managerial ethics.

LO4-6 Distinguish among the four main approaches toward social responsibility that a company can take.

A MANAGER'S CHALLENGE

UPS Foundation Delivers What Matters to Global Community

How can doing good help a company do well? UPS offers an example. The company defines its role as not merely earning profits by delivering packages but also enabling economic growth and prosperity worldwide. UPS helps large and small companies and entrepreneurs do business in more than 220 countries. It allocates some of its earnings to the UPS Foundation, which provides financial assistance and employee volunteer support to help build resilient communities and address social and environmental issues around the world. In the view of UPS's leadership, all these efforts to support economic development create both a social benefit and a business environment in which UPS can flourish.[1]

The UPS Foundation, led by Nicole (Nikki) Clifton, aligns its work with UPS's vision, as well as with the Sustainable Development Goals established by the United Nations to guide governments, businesses, and civil society as they work together to address the world's most pressing needs. The Foundation's contributions since its inception more than 70 years ago total more than $3 billion and have a significant impact on communities worldwide in the form of HELP: health and humanitarian relief; equity and economic empowerment; local community engagement; and planet protection.[2]

Research indicates that disaster aid arrives faster and has a longer-term impact on recovery when companies apply relevant expertise and have local ties to the area served. Clifton meets those standards, focusing on applying UPS's expertise in logistics and transportation and its customer relationships. For example, the foundation does not merely respond to emergencies but engages in disaster preparedness, as a good logistics provider does, so it has plans and resources in place.[3]

Because of its presence in many markets, UPS is aware of floods, earthquakes, and other situations that impair deliveries, even when stories don't make the news in the United States, as was the case recently with catastrophic flooding in Pakistan, where more than 33 million people were displaced. This awareness positions the foundation to respond quickly wherever the need arises, creating goodwill in many locales. In 2021, the UPS Foundation gave $23 million in funding, in-kind and technical support in response to more than 30 humanitarian crises globally.[4]

Why would UPS managers care about rapid disaster response? They may, of course, simply believe that helping others is the right thing to do. Helping is also consistent with the company's vision of creating a prosperous economy; when customers are devastated by disasters such as the global COVID-19 pandemic, they will

UPS workers move a shipping container that holds the first shipment of the Pfizer COVID-19 vaccine inside the UPS Worldport Facility in Louisville, Kentucky. As president of the UPS Foundation, Nikki Clifton oversees the logistics company's efforts to reach out to local as well as global communities in times of need.
Michael Clevenger/REUTERS/Alamy Stock Photo

not be shipping many packages. Clifton and her staff take this thinking one step further. The innovation required for effective disaster response also prepares the company to operate more efficiently and meet unfilled needs. Since the pandemic began, UPS helped the global community by providing everyday necessities and critical medical supplies (including test kits, masks, hand sanitizer, and vaccines); opening up dedicated space for FEMA in an expansive health care distribution center in its Louisville Worldport facility; and donating more than $20 million in funding for U.S. organizations and others around the world to help sustain underserved and impacted communities in the areas of food security, health care, education, and financial sustainability. In addition, UPS employees delivered more than 1 billion doses of COVID-19 vaccines in 110 countries.[5]

Recent repeated calls for social justice and equality have been answered by UPS and its foundation in response to the killings of George Floyd, Breonna Taylor, and many others. The foundation allocated more than $3 million for programs that support employment, education, small business, advocacy, and reform. In addition, UPS recorded more than 1 million hours of employee volunteer service around the world in support of mentoring and education programs in disadvantaged Black communities. These initiatives, in conjunction with the company's Equity, Justice & Action Task Force led by Clifton, help promote equity and justice in areas where systemic racism still persists.[6]

Celebrating its 70th anniversary in 2021, the UPS Foundation with Clifton at the helm is dedicated to continuing a legacy of service with the help of its more than 530,000 employees worldwide, long-time business partners, and other organizations to deliver what matters most to the global community.[7]

Overview

As UPS's work in communities worldwide illustrates, management decision making can have far-reaching implications when it comes to doing business in a socially responsible manner. Nikki Clifton and her colleagues at the UPS Foundation work diligently to find solutions to human and ethical challenges around the world, using their expertise as global logistics managers.

Globally, nations, companies, and managers differ enormously in their commitment to various *stakeholders*—groups of people who may benefit or be harmed by how managers make decisions that affect them. Managers of some companies make the need to behave ethically toward stakeholders their main priority. Managers of other companies pursue their own self-interest at the expense of their stakeholders and do harm to them—such as the harm done to the millions of people around the world who live and work in dangerous conditions.

In this chapter, we examine the obligations and responsibilities of managers and the companies they work for toward the people and society that are affected by their actions. First we examine the nature of ethics and the sources of ethical problems. Next we discuss the major stakeholder groups that are affected by how companies operate. We also look at four rules or guidelines managers can use to decide whether a specific business decision is ethical or unethical. Finally, we consider the sources of managerial ethics and the reasons why it is important for a company to behave in a socially responsible manner. By the end of this chapter, you will understand the central role of ethics in shaping the practice of management and the life of a people, society, and nation.

The Nature of Ethics

Suppose you learn from a colleague that the manager of the accounting department is creating fake invoices from an unidentified supplier, issuing company checks to themselves, and cashing the checks for a little extra spending money. Will you take this info to your supervisor and ask them to intervene? Will you persuade your colleague to raise the red flag about this person's behavior to HR? To the CEO? Or do you ignore the situation for fear you could lose your job for taking action?

Ethical Dilemmas

ethical dilemma The quandary people find themselves in when they have to decide if they should act in a way that might help another person or group even though doing so might go against their own self-interest.

The situation just described is an example of an **ethical dilemma**, the quandary people find themselves in when they have to decide if they should act in a way that might help another person or group and is the right thing to do even though doing so might go against their own self-interest.[8] A dilemma may also arise when a person has to choose between two different courses of action, knowing that whichever course they select will harm one person or group even though it may benefit another. The ethical dilemma here is to decide which course of action is the lesser of two evils.

ethics The inner guiding moral principles, values, and beliefs that people use to analyze or interpret a situation and then decide what is the right or appropriate way to behave.

People often know they are confronting an ethical dilemma when their moral scruples come into play and cause them to hesitate, debate, and reflect upon the correctness or goodness of a course of action. Moral scruples are thoughts and feelings that tell a person what is right or wrong; they are a part of a person's ethics. **Ethics** are the inner guiding moral principles, values, and beliefs that people use to analyze or interpret a situation and then decide what is the right or appropriate way to behave. Ethics also indicate what is inappropriate behavior and how a person should behave to avoid harming another person. An organization's culture then, in establishing and promoting certain values, can play a role in defining ethical conduct for members of that organization. For more on making ethical standards part of organizational culture, see the "Management Insight" feature.

The essential problem in dealing with ethical issues, and thus solving moral dilemmas, is that no absolute or indisputable rules or principles can be developed to decide whether an action is ethical or unethical. Put simply, different people or groups may dispute which actions are ethical or unethical depending on their personal self-interest and specific attitudes, beliefs, and values—concepts we discussed in Chapter 3. How are we and companies and their managers and employees to decide what is ethical and so act appropriately toward other people and groups?

MANAGEMENT INSIGHT

Embedding Ethics in Organizational Culture

Organizations have typically approached ethics by devising and teaching rules so employees understand how to behave ethically. However, those who study human behavior have been finding evidence that whether people behave ethically in a situation is more complex.[9] People often know basic principles of fairness, respect, and so on, but even people who believe they follow those principles may be reluctant to act ethically in certain situations. For example, they tend to be more willing to help someone in need if they are the only other person on the scene, and they tend to make ethical choices more often when ethical values are mentioned explicitly.

The powerful implication of this situational approach to ethical behavior is that organizations can create the kinds of situations that promote ethical conduct. These efforts include teaching principles, but to be effective, the principles should be memorable—expressed simply and briefly—and referred to often. For example, when launching a new project, managers should mention how it relates to the company's mission, vision, or values statement. Managers should also embed ethical conversations in decision-making processes to ensure employees are thinking about what they should do, not what they can get away with. Engaging in conversations around ethics is associated with more ethical behavior as people learn from one another how to approach these issues.[10]

Organizations also create an ethical climate when they ensure that rewards and consequences are aligned with ethical values. Besides money, rewards include praise, interesting work, and the knowledge that one's actions matter to others. Consequences involve rewards and punishment, but also the practice of ensuring that employees are working with colleagues who adhere to shared values. Ethical behavior is more likely when employees believe their colleagues generally do the right thing. Rewards and consequences also should be tied to outcomes that realistically can result from ethical behavior. Rewards for impossibly high sales or customer service targets just tempt employees to meet the targets in questionable ways. Conversely, when employees are equipped with resources, training, and mentoring to meet their targets through ethical practices, they are more likely to embrace that way of working.[11]

Finally, the organization's executives need to model the ethical behaviors they seek. In order to promote justice, they should listen to their people. And if they define organizational values, they should practice those values.[12]

Ethics and the Law

LO4-1 Explain the relationship between ethics and the law.

The first answer to this question is that society as a whole, using the political and legal process, can lobby for and pass laws that specify what people can and cannot do. Many different kinds of laws govern business–for example, laws against fraud and deception and laws governing how companies can treat their employees and customers. Laws also specify what sanctions or punishments will follow if those laws are broken. Different groups in society lobby for which laws should be passed based on their own personal interests and beliefs about right and wrong. The group that can summon the most support can pass laws that align with its interests and beliefs. Once a law is passed, a decision about what the appropriate behavior is with regard to a person or situation is taken from the personally determined ethical realm to the societally determined legal realm. If you do not conform to the law, you can be prosecuted; and if you are found guilty of breaking the law, you can be punished. You have little say in the matter; your fate is in the hands of the court and its lawyers.

In studying the relationship between ethics and law, it is important to understand that *neither laws nor ethics are fixed principles* that do not change over time. Ethical beliefs change as time passes; as they do so, laws change to reflect the changing ethical beliefs of a society. It was considered ethical, and it was legal, for example, to acquire and possess enslaved people in ancient Rome and Greece and in the United States until the late 19th century. Ethical views regarding whether slavery was morally right or appropriate changed, however. Slavery was made illegal in the United States when those in power acknowledged that slavery degraded the meaning of being human. Slavery makes a statement about the value or worth of human beings and about their right to life, liberty, and the pursuit of happiness. And if we deny these rights to other people, how can we claim to have any natural rights to these things?

Moreover, what is to stop any person or group that becomes powerful enough to take control of the political and legal process from enslaving us and denying us the right to be free and to own property? In denying freedom to others, one risks losing it oneself, just as stealing from others opens the door for them to steal from us in return. "Do unto others as you would have them do unto you" is a common ethical or moral rule that people apply in such situations to decide what is the right thing to do.

Changes in Ethics over Time

There are many types of behavior–such as murder, assault, rape, robbery, and reckless endangerment of others–that most people believe are unacceptable and unethical and should therefore be illegal. However, the ethics of many other actions and behaviors are open to dispute. Some people might believe a particular behavior–for example, smoking tobacco or collecting guns–is unethical and so should be made illegal. Others might argue that it is up to the individual or group to decide if such behaviors are ethical and thus whether a particular behavior should remain legal.

As ethical beliefs change over time, some people may begin to question whether existing laws that make specific behaviors illegal are still appropriate. They might argue that although a specific behavior is deemed illegal, this does not make it unethical and thus the law should be changed. For example, in 1967, interracial marriages were still illegal in 16 states. In June of that year, the U.S. Supreme Court issued its unanimous *Loving v. Virginia* decision, which struck down state laws that banned interracial marriages as unconstitutional.[13]

As ethical beliefs change, so do laws. Here customers shop for recreational marijuana at Dispensary 33 in Chicago. Illinois is one of 26 U.S. states that have legalized the use of recreational marijuana.
KAMIL KRZACZYNSKI/Contributor/Getty Images

Another example underscores how ethics continue to change over time. Currently, in four states, it is illegal to possess or use marijuana (cannabis). To justify such a law, it is commonly argued that smoking marijuana leads people to try more dangerous drugs. It has been documented medically, however, that marijuana use can help people with certain conditions. For example, for cancer patients undergoing chemotherapy or individuals experiencing epileptic seizures or anxiety disorders, marijuana offers relief from many side effects. Yet, in the United States, it is illegal in some states for physicians to prescribe marijuana for these patients, so their suffering continues. Since 1996, however, 37 states have made it legal to prescribe marijuana for medical purposes. People in many states are currently lobbying for a relaxation of state laws against marijuana's use.[14] While not making the drug legal, decriminalization removes the threat of prosecution even for uses that are not medically related. Initiatives continue in several states to decriminalize the possession of small amounts of marijuana for personal use as well as to make it more widely available to people legally for medical purposes.[15]

The important point to note is that while ethical beliefs lead to the development of laws and regulations to prevent certain behaviors or encourage others, laws themselves change or even disappear as ethical beliefs change. In Britain in 1830, a person could be executed for over 350 different crimes, including sheep stealing. Today the death penalty is no longer legal in Britain. Thus, both ethical and legal rules are *relative:* No absolute or unvarying standards exist to determine how we should behave, and people are caught up in moral dilemmas all the time. Because of this, we have to make ethical choices.

The previous discussion highlights an important issue in understanding the relationship among ethics, law, and business. Throughout the 2010s, many scandals plagued major companies such as JPMorgan Chase, HSBC, Standard Chartered Bank, ING, Barclays, and Wells Fargo. Managers at some of these companies engaged in risky trades, interest rate manipulation, illegal trade facilitation, drug money laundering, and deception of customers.

In other cases, no laws were broken, yet outrage was expressed over perceptions of unethical actions. One example of this is the movement to end gun violence. In 2018, March for Our Lives was founded by student survivors of a mass shooting at Marjory Stoneman Douglas High School in Parkland, Florida, in which 14 students and 3 coaches and teachers were killed. Today, the organization continues to be a leader in the demand for gun reform across the United States, holding marches and protests against gun violence nationwide. As of this writing in late 2022, more than 611 mass shootings (defined as at least 4 people shot, not including the shooter) occurred across the country, including Uvalde, Texas; Buffalo, New York; Colorado Springs, Colorado; and Chesapeake, Virginia.[16]

Stakeholders and Ethics

Just as people have to work out the right and wrong ways to act, so do companies. When the law does not specify how companies should behave, their managers must decide the right or ethical way to behave toward the people and groups affected by their actions. Who are the people or groups that are affected by a company's business decisions? If a company behaves in an ethical way, how does this benefit people and society? Conversely, how are people harmed by a company's unethical actions?

stakeholders The people and groups that supply a company with its productive resources and so have a claim on and a stake in the company.

The people and groups affected by how a company and its managers behave are called its stakeholders. **Stakeholders** supply a company with its productive resources; as a result, they have a claim on and a stake in the company.[17] Because stakeholders can directly benefit or be harmed by its actions, the ethics of a company and its managers are important to them. Who are a company's major stakeholders? What do they contribute to a company, and what do they claim in return? Here we examine the claims of these stakeholders—shareholders; managers; employees; suppliers and distributors; customers; and community, society, and nation-state as Figure 4.1 depicts.

Figure 4.1
Types of Company Stakeholders

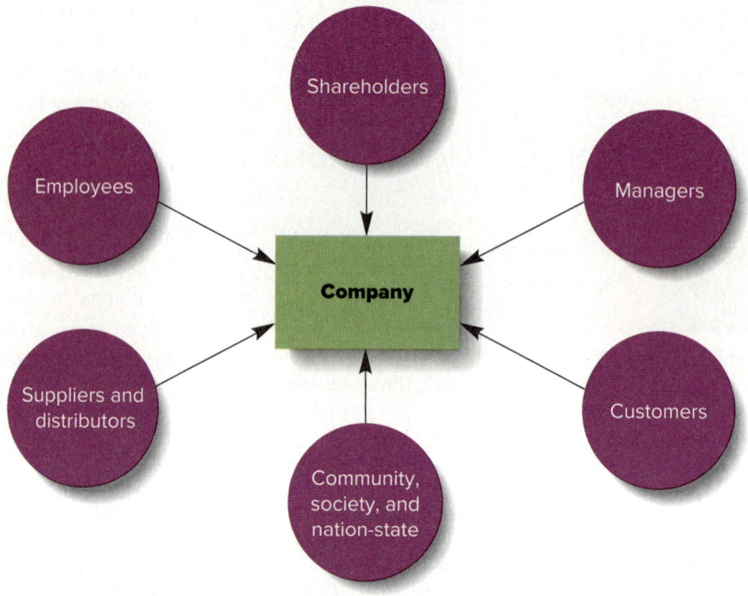

Shareholders

LO4-2 Differentiate between the claims of the different stakeholder groups affected by managers and their companies' actions.

Shareholders have a claim on a company because when they buy its stock or shares they become its owners. When the founder of a company decides to publicly incorporate the business to raise capital, shares of the stock of that company are issued. This stock grants its buyers ownership of a certain percentage of the company and the right to receive any future stock dividends. For example, MacKenzie Scott became one of the world's wealthiest women following her divorce from Amazon founder Jeff Bezos in 2019, which left her with a 4% stake in the global e-commerce giant. Since 2020, Scott has given away more than $14 billion of her estimated $29 billion in personal wealth to "high-impact organizations" focused on various causes, including racial justice, higher education, and domestic violence. In 2022 alone, Scott gave nearly $2 billion to 343 organizations that support underserved communities, including Big Brothers and Big Sisters; Girl Scouts of America; and Friends of the Children, a mentorship program. In addition, Scott signed on to the Giving Pledge, committing to give away at least half of her fortune to charity. The Giving Pledge was started by Warren Buffet and Bill and Melinda Gates more than 12 years ago to encourage the world's wealthiest individuals to distribute their wealth to serve global ethical causes such as climate change, education, malnutrition, malaria, and other health-related concerns.[18]

Shareholders are interested in how a company operates because they want to maximize the return on their investment. Thus, they watch the company and its managers closely to ensure that management is working diligently to increase the company's profitability.[19] Shareholders also want to ensure that managers are behaving ethically and not risking investors' capital by engaging in actions that could hurt the company's reputation. A company's top executives are likely to feel some combination of pressure to increase earnings in the short term and to build long-term value from a good reputation in the eyes of the company's stakeholders. Ethical challenges can arise from trying to balance these sometimes competing pressures, as described in the "Ethics in Action" feature. No company wants the reputation described by the March for Our Lives organization, which alleges that some business organizations value profits over people. However, experts warn businesses not to ignore the movement. They warn that the growing voice and influence of the gun violence movement may continue to single out politicians, companies, and other organizations that do little to reduce gun violence or support gun reform.[20]

ETHICS IN ACTION

Billing the Poor for Hospital Care

Recent studies criticize nonprofit hospitals for providing too little no-cost or reduced-cost care to needy patients. According to one study, nonprofit hospitals spent 2.3% of expenses on charity care, versus 3.8% at for-profit hospitals. In another study, charity care equaled 1.4% or less of operating expenses at half of hospitals. The low rate at nonprofits draws criticism because these hospitals typically have missions to help the poor and because governments exempt nonprofits from taxes in exchange for their service to their communities.[21]

Hospital charity care is also called "required financial benefits" because federal law–the Affordable Care Act (ACA)–requires that nonprofit hospitals provide it. However, the ACA does not specify an amount or eligibility standards. (Some states require financial benefits for poor patients, and some set standards for eligibility.) The ACA requirements include establishing a policy for providing financial assistance; widely publicizing that policy in the hospital, on the hospital's website, and on patient paperwork; and making reasonable efforts to identify whether patients are eligible before sending past-due bills to debt collectors. The broadness of these requirements gives hospitals room to define their mission and determine whether their conduct is ethical.[22]

Hospitals do provide financial benefits to poor patients. Even at the small percentages measured, a large hospital might be providing tens or hundreds of millions of dollars in care it will not be paid for. Typically, hospitals measure their largest contribution to serving the poor as the shortfall in Medicaid payments relative to the cost of serving patients with Medicaid coverage. Charity care amounts are often much less.[23]

What is harder to assess is whether hospitals notify qualified patients of financial assistance programs. Patients have complained about receiving bills exceeding a year of their income with no idea that they can get help to pay these bills. Training materials at some hospitals direct employees to pursue payment by using scripts that avoid any hint that assistance might be available, except as a last resort. Some employees have complained that pressuring patients to pay feels wrong. Even when patients are informed, the hospital may have a time-consuming and difficult application process. Meanwhile, some hospitals generate sizable cash reserves that they invest to fund a variety of possible uses.[24] The Kaufman Hall consulting firm advises hospitals to assess whether their policies and procedures align with legal requirements and their mission statements and whether the organization is following them consistently.[25]

Managers

Managers are a vital stakeholder group because they are responsible for using a company's financial, capital, and human resources to increase its performance and thus its stock price.[26] Managers have a claim on an organization because they bring to it their skills, expertise, and experience. They have the right to expect a good return or reward by investing their human capital to improve a company's performance. Such rewards include good salaries and benefits, the prospect of promotion and a career, and stock options and bonuses tied to company performance.

Managers are the stakeholder group that bears the responsibility to decide which goals an organization should pursue to most benefit stakeholders and how to make the most efficient use of resources to achieve those goals. In making such decisions, managers frequently must juggle the interests of different stakeholders, including themselves.[27] These sometimes difficult decisions challenge managers to uphold ethical values because some decisions that benefit certain stakeholder groups (managers and shareholders) harm other groups (individual workers and local communities). For example, in economic downturns or when a company experiences performance shortfalls, layoffs may help cut costs (thus benefiting shareholders) at the expense of the employees laid off. Many U.S. managers recently faced this difficult decision as COVID-19 caused companies, particularly in the hospitality, travel, and retail industries, to lay off or terminate millions of U.S. workers at the height of the global pandemic. The Congressional Research Service estimates that nonfarm payrolls shed more than 22 million jobs between January and April 2020, with an unemployment rate of 14.8%–the highest rate observed since data collection began in 1948. Fortunately, as more people were vaccinated against the virus and the economy rebounded, most of those jobs were reinstated, with the unemployment rate dropping to 3.7% near the end of 2022.[28]

As we discussed in Chapter 1, managers must be motivated and given incentives to work hard in the interests of shareholders. Their behavior must also be scrutinized to ensure they do not behave illegally or unethically, pursuing goals that threaten shareholders and the company's interests. Unfortunately, we have seen how easy it is for top managers to find ways to ruthlessly pursue their self-interest at the expense of shareholders and employees because laws and regulations are not strong enough to force them to behave ethically.

Essentially the problem has been that in many companies corrupt managers focus not on building the company's capital and shareholders' wealth, but on maximizing their own personal capital and wealth. In an effort to prevent future scandals, the Securities and Exchange Commission (SEC), the government's top business watchdog, has begun to rework the rules governing a company's relationship with its auditor, as well as regulations concerning stock options, and to increase the power of outside directors to scrutinize a CEO. The SEC's goal is to outlaw many actions that were previously classified as merely unethical. For example, companies are now forced to reveal to shareholders the value of the stock options they give their top executives and directors and when they give them these options; this shows how greatly such payments reduce company profits. Managers and directors can now be prosecuted if they disguise or try to hide these payments. In the 2010s, the SEC announced many new rules requiring that companies disclose myriad details of executive compensation packages to investors; already the boards of directors of many companies have stopped giving CEOs perks such as free personal jet travel, membership in exclusive country clubs, and luxury accommodations on "business trips." Also, in 2010, Congress passed new laws preventing the many unethical and illegal actions of managers of banks and other financial institutions that led to the 2009 financial crisis. One of these regulations, the "Volcker Rule," seeks to reduce the chances that banks will put depositors' money at risk. In 2018, however, Wall Street and U.S. banks asked federal regulators to revisit the Volcker Rule in an effort to loosen some of the stricter requirements of the legislation, which could lessen the financial burden put on banking institutions nationwide. Final changes to the Volcker Rule became official in January 2020 and soften regulations, particularly for smaller financial institutions.[29]

Layoff decisions are always difficult. As a result of the global pandemic in 2020, millions of U.S. workers lost their jobs, particularly in the hospitality, travel, and retail industries.
88studio/Shutterstock

Indeed, many experts argue that the rewards given to top managers, particularly the CEO and COO, grew out of control in the 2000s. Top managers are today's "elites," and through their ability to influence the board of directors and raise their own pay, they have amassed personal fortunes worth hundreds of millions of dollars. For example, according to a study by the Economic Policy Institute, U.S. CEOs at the 350 biggest companies now get paid nearly 399 times what the average worker earns–a staggering 1,460% increase since 1978–while the average worker saw an 18% pay hike over the same period. In 2021, the average CEO compensation at these companies was $27.8 million. Remarkably, even with millions of employees out of work during the pandemic, CEOs' compensation jumped 11.1% in the period 2020-2021.[30] We noted in Chapter 1 that besides their salaries, top managers often receive tens of millions in stock bonuses and options–even when their companies perform poorly.

Is it ethical for top managers to receive such vast amounts of money from their companies? Do they earn it? Remember, this money could have gone to shareholders in the form of dividends. It could also have reduced the huge salary gap between those at the top and those at the bottom of the hierarchy. Many people argue that the growing disparity between the rewards given to CEOs and to other employees is unethical and should be regulated. CEO pay has skyrocketed because CEOs are the people who set and control one another's salaries and bonuses; they can do this because they sit on the boards of other companies as outside directors. Others argue that because top managers play an important role in building a company's capital and wealth, they deserve a significant share of its profits. Some recent research has suggested that the companies whose CEO compensation includes a large percentage of stock options tend to experience big share losses more often than big gains, and on average, company performance improves as stock option use declines.[31] The debate over how much money CEOs and other top managers should be paid is still raging, particularly because the financial crisis beginning in 2009 showed how much money the CEOs of troubled financial companies earned even as their companies' performance and stock prices collapsed.

Ethics and Nonprofit Organizations

The issue of what is fair compensation for top managers is not limited to for-profit companies; it is one of many issues facing nonprofits. The many ethics scandals that have plagued companies in recent years might suggest that the issue of ethics is important only for profit-seeking companies, but this is untrue. There are almost 2 million private nonprofit charitable and philanthropic organizations in the United States, and charges that their managers have acted in unethical and even illegal ways have grown. For example, many states and the federal government are investigating the huge salaries that the top executives of charitable institutions earn.

One impetus for this was the revelation that the New York Stock Exchange, which used to be classified as a nonprofit, paid its disgraced top executive, Richard A. Grasso, over $187 million in pension benefits. According to recent research, more than 2,700 executives of nonprofit organizations (including hospitals, universities, and charities) each earn more than $1 million a year in salary, bonus, and other benefits, and the boards of trustees or directors of many of these organizations also enjoy lavish perks and compensation for attendance at board meetings.[32] And unlike for-profit companies, which are required by law to provide detailed reports of their operations to their shareholders, nonprofits do not have shareholders, so the laws governing disclosure are far weaker. As a result, the board and its top managers have considerable latitude to decide how they will spend a nonprofit's resources, and little oversight exists.

To remedy this situation, many states and the federal government are considering new laws that would subject nonprofits to strict Sarbanes–Oxley-type regulations that force the disclosure of issues related to managerial compensation and financial integrity. In fact, the tax reform legislation signed into law by President Trump in late 2017 includes a new 21% excise tax on nonprofit employers for salaries over $1 million.[33]

Experts hope that the introduction of new rules and regulations to monitor and oversee how nonprofits spend their funds will result in much more value being created from the funds given by donors. After all, every cent that is spent administering a nonprofit is a cent not being used to help the people or cause for which the money was intended. Ethical issues are involved because some badly run charities spend 70 cents of every dollar on administration costs. And charges have been leveled against charities such as the Red Cross for mishandling the hundreds of millions of dollars they received in donations after Hurricane Katrina struck; changes have been made in the Red Cross to address these issues. Clearly, the directors and managers of all organizations need to carefully consider the ethical issues involved in their decision making.

Nonprofit organizations, such as the American Red Cross, are under increased scrutiny to make sure their managers act in an ethical and lawful manner.
AB Forces News Collection/Alamy Stock Photo

Employees

A company's employees are the hundreds of thousands of people who work in its various departments and functions, such as research, sales, and manufacturing. Employees expect to receive rewards consistent with their performance. One principal way that a company can act ethically toward employees and meet their expectations is by creating an organizational structure that fairly and equitably rewards employees for their contributions. Companies, for example, need to develop recruitment, training, performance appraisal, and reward systems that do not discriminate against employees and that employees believe are fair.

Suppliers and Distributors

No company operates alone. Every company is in a network of relationships with other companies that supply it with the inputs (such as raw materials, components, contract labor, and clients) that it needs to operate. It also depends on intermediaries such as wholesalers and retailers to distribute its products to the final customers. Suppliers expect to be paid fairly and promptly for their inputs; distributors expect to receive quality products at agreed-upon prices. Once again, many ethical issues arise in how companies contract and interact with their suppliers and distributors.

Many other issues depend on business ethics. For example, numerous products sold in U.S. stores have been outsourced to countries that do not have U.S.-style regulations and laws to protect the workers who make these products. All companies must take an ethical position on the way they obtain and make the products they sell. Commonly, this stance is published on a company's website. Table 4.1 presents part of the Gap's statement about its approach to global ethics (www.gapinc.com).

Customers

Customers are often regarded as the most critical stakeholder group because if a company cannot attract them to buy its products, it cannot stay in business. Thus, managers and employees must work to increase efficiency and effectiveness in order to create loyal customers and attract new ones. They do so by selling customers quality products at a fair price and providing good after-sales service. Not only do these practices meet the needs of customer stakeholders, but they also can have an impact on the communities and nations where customers live and work.

Community, Society, and Nation

The effects of the decisions made by companies and their managers permeate all aspects of the communities, societies, and nations in which they operate. *Community* refers to physical locations like towns or cities or to social milieus like ethnic neighborhoods in which companies are located. A community provides a company with the physical and social infrastructure that allows it to operate; its utilities and labor force; the homes in which its managers and employees live; the schools, colleges, and hospitals that serve their needs; and so on.

Through the salaries, wages, and taxes it pays, a company contributes to the economy of its town or region and often determines whether the community prospers or declines. Similarly, a company affects the prosperity of a society and a nation and, to the degree that a company is involved in global trade, all the countries it operates in and thus the prosperity of the global economy. We have already discussed the many issues surrounding global outsourcing and the loss of jobs in the United States, for example.

Although the individual effects of the way each McDonald's restaurant operates might be small, for instance, the combined effects of how all McDonald's and other fast-food companies do business are enormous. In the United States alone, more than 3.7 million people work in the fast-food industry, and many thousands of suppliers, like farmers, paper cup manufacturers, and builders, depend on it for their livelihood. Small wonder, then, that the ethics of the fast-food business are scrutinized closely. This industry was the major lobbyer against attempts to raise the federal minimum wage (which was raised to $7.25 an hour in 2009, where it remains

Table 4.1

Some Principles from the Gap's Code of Vendor Conduct

As a condition of doing business with Gap Inc., each and every factory must comply with this Code of Vendor Conduct. Gap Inc. will continue to develop monitoring systems to assess and ensure compliance. If Gap Inc. determines that any factory has violated this Code, Gap Inc. may either terminate its business relationship or require the factory to implement a corrective action plan. If corrective action is advised but not taken, Gap Inc. will suspend placement of future orders and may terminate current production.

I. General Principles

Factories that produce goods for Gap Inc. shall operate in full compliance with the laws of their respective countries and with all other applicable laws, rules, and regulations.

II. Environment

Factories must comply with all applicable environmental laws and regulations. Where such requirements are less stringent than Gap Inc.'s own, factories are encouraged to meet the standards outlined in Gap Inc.'s statement of environmental principles.

III. Discrimination

Factories shall employ workers on the basis of their ability to do the job, without regard to race, color, gender, nationality, religion, age, maternity, or marital status.

IV. Forced Labor

Factories shall not use any prison, indentured, or forced labor.

V. Child Labor

Factories shall employ only workers who meet the applicable minimum legal age requirement or are at least 15 years of age, whichever is greater. Factories must also comply with all other applicable child labor laws. Factories are encouraged to develop lawful workplace apprenticeship programs for the educational benefit of their workers, provided that all participants meet both Gap Inc.'s minimum age standard of 15 and the minimum legal age requirement.

VI. Wages & Hours

Factories shall set working hours, wages, and overtime premiums in compliance with all applicable laws. Workers shall be paid at least the minimum legal wage or a wage that meets local industry standards, whichever is greater. While it is understood that overtime is often required in garment production, factories shall carry out operations in ways that limit overtime to a level that ensures humane and productive working conditions.

in 2022, up from $5.15–a figure that had not changed since 1997), for example, because a higher minimum wage would substantially increase its operating costs. However, responding to protests about chickens raised in cages where they cannot move, McDonald's–the largest egg buyer in the United States–issued new ethical guidelines concerning cage size and related matters that its egg suppliers must abide by if they are to retain its business. What ethical rules does McDonald's use to decide its stance toward minimum pay or minimum cage size?

Business ethics are also important because the failure of a company can have catastrophic effects on a community; a general decline in business activity affects a whole nation. The decision of a large company to pull out of a community, for example, can threaten the community's future. Some companies may attempt to improve their profits by engaging in actions that, although not illegal, can hurt communities and nations. One of these actions is pollution. For example, many U.S. companies reduce costs by trucking their waste to Mexico, where it is legal to dump waste in the Rio Grande. The dumping pollutes the river from the Mexican side, but the U.S. side of the river is increasingly experiencing pollution's negative effects.

Rules for Ethical Decision Making

LO4-3 Describe four rules that can help companies and their managers act in ethical ways.

When a stakeholder perspective is taken, questions on company ethics abound.[34] What is the appropriate way to manage the claims of all stakeholders? Company decisions that favor one group of stakeholders, for example, are likely to harm the interests of others.[35] High prices charged to customers may bring high returns to shareholders and high salaries to managers in the short run. If in the long run, customers turn to companies that offer lower-cost products, however, the result may be declining sales, laid-off employees, and the decline of the communities that support the high-priced company's business activity.

When companies act ethically, their stakeholders support them. For example, banks are willing to supply them with new capital, they attract highly qualified job applicants, and new customers are drawn to their products. Thus, ethical companies grow and expand over time, and all their stakeholders benefit. The results of unethical behavior are loss of reputation and resources, shareholders selling their shares, skilled managers and employees leaving the company, and customers turning to the products of more reputable companies.

When making business decisions, managers must consider the claims of all stakeholders. To help themselves and employees make ethical decisions and behave in ways that benefit their stakeholders, managers can use four ethical rules or principles to analyze the effects of their business decisions on stakeholders: the *utilitarian, moral rights, justice,* and *practical* rules (Figure 4.2).[36] These rules are useful guidelines that help managers decide on the appropriate way to behave in situations where it is necessary to balance a company's self-interest and the interests of its stakeholders. Remember, the right choices will lead resources to be used where they can create the most value. If all companies make the right choices, all stakeholders will benefit in the long run.

utilitarian rule An ethical decision is a decision that produces the greatest good for the greatest number of people.

UTILITARIAN RULE The **utilitarian rule** is that an ethical decision is a decision that produces the greatest good for the greatest number of people. To decide which is the most ethical course of business action, managers should first consider how different possible courses of business action would benefit or harm different stakeholders. They should then choose the course of action that provides the most benefits, or, conversely, the one that does the least harm, to stakeholders.[37]

The ethical dilemma for managers is this: How do you measure the benefit and harm that will be done to each stakeholder group? Moreover, how do you evaluate the rights of different stakeholder groups, and the relative importance of each group, in coming to a decision? Because shareholders own the company, shouldn't their claims be held above those of employees? For example, managers might face a choice of using global outsourcing to reduce costs

Figure 4.2
Four Ethical Rules

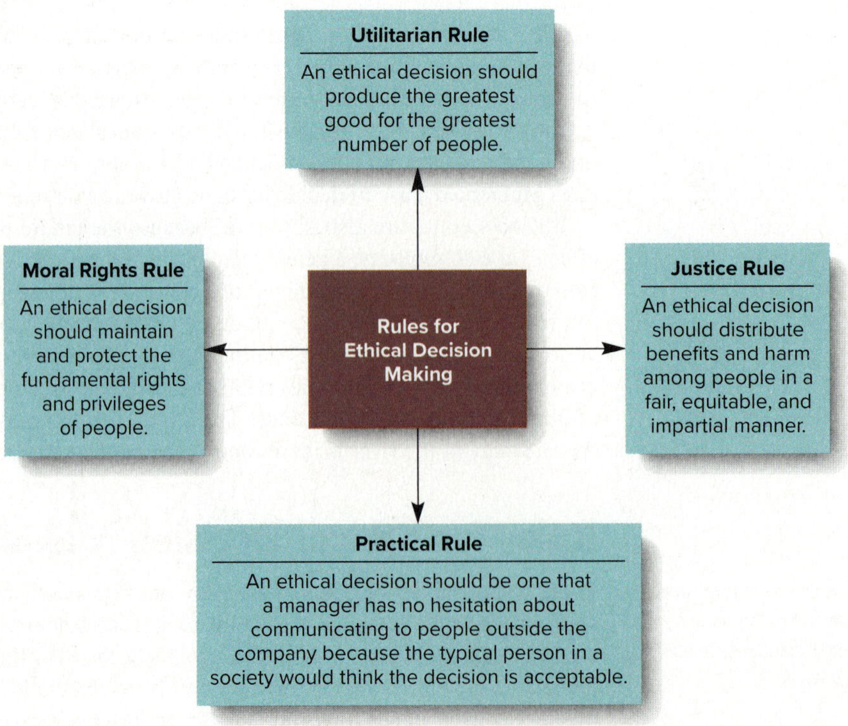

and lower prices or continuing with high-cost production in the United States. A decision to use global outsourcing benefits shareholders and customers but will result in major layoffs that will harm employees and the communities in which they live. Typically, in a capitalist society such as the United States, the interests of shareholders are put above those of employees, so production will move abroad. This is commonly regarded as being an ethical choice because the alternative, home production, might cause the business to collapse and go bankrupt, in which case greater harm will be done to all stakeholders.

moral rights rule An ethical decision is one that best maintains and protects the fundamental or inalienable rights and privileges of the people affected by it.

MORAL RIGHTS RULE Under the **moral rights rule**, an ethical decision is one that best maintains and protects the fundamental or inalienable rights and privileges of the people affected by it. For example, ethical decisions protect people's rights to freedom, life and safety, property, privacy, free speech, and freedom of conscience. The adage "Do unto others as you would have them do unto you" is a moral rights principle that managers should use to decide which rights to uphold. Customers must also consider the rights of the companies and people who create the products they wish to consume.

From a moral rights perspective, managers should compare and contrast different courses of business action on the basis of how each course will affect the rights of the company's different stakeholders. Managers should then choose the course of action that best protects and upholds the rights of *all* stakeholders. For example, decisions that might significantly harm the safety or health of employees or customers would clearly be unethical choices.

The ethical dilemma for managers is that decisions that will protect the rights of some stakeholders often will hurt the rights of others. How should they choose which group to protect? For example, in deciding whether it is ethical to snoop on employees, or search them when they leave work to prevent theft, does an employee's right to privacy outweigh an organization's right to protect its property? Suppose a coworker is having personal problems and is coming in late and leaving early, forcing you to pick up the person's workload. Do you tell your boss even though you know this will probably get that person fired?

justice rule An ethical decision distributes benefits and harms among people and groups in a fair, equitable, or impartial way.

JUSTICE RULE The **justice rule** is that an ethical decision distributes benefits and harms among people and groups in a fair, equitable, or impartial way. Managers should compare and contrast alternative courses of action based on the degree to which they will fairly or equitably distribute outcomes to stakeholders. For example, employees who are similar in their level of skill, performance, or responsibility should receive similar pay; allocation of outcomes should not be based on differences such as gender, race, or religion.

The ethical dilemma for managers is to determine the fair rules and procedures for distributing outcomes to stakeholders. Managers must not give people they like bigger raises than they give to people they do not like, for example, or bend the rules to help their favorites. On the other hand, if employees want managers to act fairly toward them, then employees need to act fairly toward their companies by working hard and being loyal. Similarly, customers need to act fairly toward a company if they expect it to be fair to them.

PRACTICAL RULE Each of these rules offers a different and complementary way of determining whether a decision or behavior is ethical, and all three rules should be used to sort out the ethics of a particular course of action. Ethical issues, as we just discussed, are seldom clear-cut, however, because the rights, interests, goals, and incentives of different stakeholders often conflict. For this reason many experts on ethics add a fourth rule to determine whether a business decision is ethical: The **practical rule** is that an ethical decision is one that a manager has no hesitation or reluctance about communicating to people outside the company because the typical person in a society would think it is acceptable. A business decision is probably acceptable on ethical grounds if a manager can answer yes to each of these questions:

practical rule An ethical decision is one that a manager has no reluctance about communicating to people outside the company because the typical person in a society would think it is acceptable.

1. Does my decision fall within the accepted values or standards that typically apply in business activity today?
2. Am I willing to see the decision communicated to all people and groups affected by it—for example, by having it reported on TV or via social media?
3. Would the people with whom I have a significant personal relationship, such as family members, friends, or even managers in other organizations, approve of the decision?

Applying the practical rule to analyze a business decision ensures that managers are taking into account the interests of all stakeholders.[38] After applying this rule, managers can judge if they have chosen to act in an ethical or unethical way, and they must abide by the consequences.

Why Should Managers Behave Ethically?

LO4-4 Discuss why it is important for managers to behave ethically.

Why is it so important that managers, and people in general, act ethically and temper their pursuit of self-interest by considering the effects of their actions on others? The answer is that the relentless pursuit of self-interest can lead to a collective disaster when one or more people start to profit from being unethical because this encourages other people to act in the same way.[39] As more and more people act in their own interests, soon everybody is trying to manipulate the situation to serve their personal ends with no regard for the effects of their action on others. This is called the "tragedy of the commons."

Suppose that in an agricultural community there is common land that everybody has an equal right to use. Pursuing self-interest, each farmer acts to make the maximum use of the free resource by grazing their own cattle and sheep. Collectively, all the farmers overgraze the land, which quickly becomes worn out. Then a strong wind blows away the exposed topsoil, so the common land is destroyed. The pursuit of person self-interest with no consideration of societal interests leads to disaster for each individual and for the whole society because scarce resources are destroyed.[40]

We can look at the effects of unethical behavior on business activity in another way. Suppose companies and their managers operate in an unethical society, meaning one in which stakeholders routinely try to cheat and defraud one another. If stakeholders expect each other to cheat, how long will it take them to negotiate the purchase and shipment of products? When they do not trust each other, stakeholders will probably spend hours bargaining over fair prices, and this is a largely unproductive activity that reduces efficiency and effectiveness.[41] The time and effort that could be spent improving product quality or customer service are lost to negotiating and bargaining. Thus, unethical behavior ruins business commerce, and society has a lower standard of living because fewer goods and services are produced, as Figure 4.3 illustrates.

trust The willingness of one person or group to have faith or confidence in the goodwill of another person, even though this puts them at risk.

On the other hand, suppose companies and their managers operate in an ethical society, meaning stakeholders believe they are dealing with others who are basically moral and honest. In this society stakeholders have a greater reason to trust others. **Trust** is the willingness of one person or group to have faith or confidence in the goodwill of another person, even though this puts them at risk (because the other might act in a deceitful way). When trust exists, stakeholders are likely to signal their good intentions by cooperating and providing information that makes it easier to exchange and price goods and services. When one person acts in a trustworthy way, this encourages others to act in the same way. Over time, as greater trust between stakeholders develops, they can work together more efficiently and effectively, which raises company performance (see Figure 4.3). As people see the positive results of acting in an honest way, ethical behavior becomes a valued social norm, and society in general becomes increasingly ethical.

As noted in Chapter 1, a major responsibility of managers is to protect and nurture the resources under their control. Any organizational stakeholders–managers, workers, shareholders, suppliers–who advance their own interests by behaving unethically toward other stakeholders, either by taking resources or by denying resources to others, waste collective resources. If other individuals or groups copy the behavior of the unethical stakeholder, the rate at which collective resources are misused increases, and eventually few resources are available to produce goods and services. Unethical behavior that goes unpunished creates incentives for people to put their unbridled self-interests above the rights of others.[42] When this happens, the benefits that people reap from joining together in organizations disappear quickly.

reputation The esteem or high repute that individuals or organizations gain when they behave ethically.

An important safeguard against unethical behavior is the potential for loss of reputation.[43] **Reputation**, the esteem or high repute that people or organizations gain when they behave ethically, is an important asset. Stakeholders have valuable reputations, which they must protect because their ability to earn a living and obtain resources in the long run depends on how they behave.

Figure 4.3
Some Effects of Ethical and Unethical Behavior

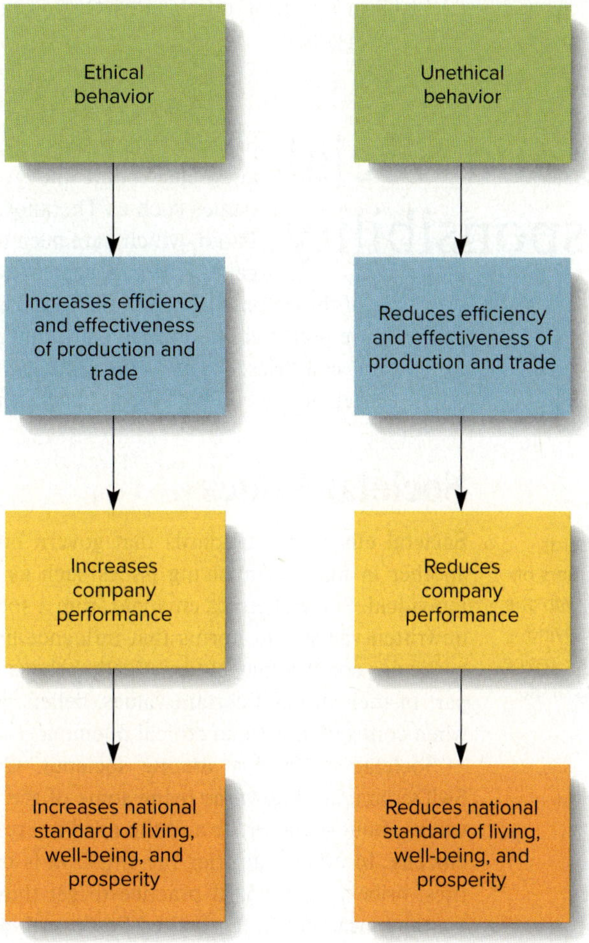

If a manager misuses resources and other parties regard that behavior as being at odds with acceptable standards, the manager's reputation will suffer. Behaving unethically in the short run can have serious long-term consequences. A manager who has a poor reputation will have difficulty finding employment with other companies. Shareholders who see managers behaving unethically may refuse to invest in their companies, and this will decrease the stock price, undermine the companies' reputations, and ultimately put the managers' jobs at risk.[44]

All stakeholders have reputations to lose. Suppliers who provide shoddy inputs find that organizations learn over time not to deal with them, and eventually they go out of business. Powerful customers who demand ridiculously low prices find that their suppliers become less willing to deal with them, and resources ultimately become harder for them to obtain. Workers who shirk responsibilities on the job find it hard to get new jobs when they are fired. In general, if a manager or company is known for being unethical, other stakeholders are likely to view that individual or organization with suspicion and hostility, creating a poor reputation. But a manager or company known for ethical business practices will develop a good reputation.[45]

In summary, in a complex, diverse society, stakeholders, and people in general, need to recognize they are part of a larger social group. How they make decisions and act not only affects them personally but also affects the lives of many other people. Unfortunately, for some people, the daily struggle to survive and succeed or their total disregard for others' rights can lead them to lose that bigger connection to other people. We can see our relationships to our families and friends, school, church, and so on. But we must go further and keep in mind the effects of our actions on other people—people who will be judging our actions and whom we might harm by acting unethically. Our moral scruples are like those "other people" but are inside our heads.

Ethics and Social Responsibility

LO4-5 Identify the four main sources of managerial ethics.

Some companies, like Accenture, Best Buy, Colgate-Palmolive, Microsoft, and PepsiCo, are known for their ethical business practices.[46] Other companies such as Theranos, which is out of business, or Siemens and Wells Fargo, which have been totally restructured, repeatedly engaged in unethical and illegal business activities. What explains such differences between the ethics of these companies and their managers?

There are four main determinants of differences in ethics among people, employees, companies, and countries: *societal ethics*, *occupational ethics*, *individual ethics*, and *organizational ethics*—especially the ethics of a company's top managers[47] (see Figure 4.4).

Societal Ethics

societal ethics Standards that govern how members of a society should deal with one another in matters involving issues such as fairness, justice, poverty, and the rights of the individual.

Societal ethics are standards that govern how members of a society should deal with one another in matters involving issues such as fairness, justice, poverty, and the rights of the individual. Societal ethics emanate from a society's laws, customs, and practices and from the unwritten values and norms that influence how people interact with each other. People in a particular country may automatically behave ethically because they have *internalized* (made a part of their morals) certain values, beliefs, and norms that specify how they should behave when confronted with an ethical dilemma.

Societal ethics vary among societies. Countries like Denmark, Iceland, Sweden, and Switzerland are known as being some of the most ethical countries in the world, with strong values about social order and the need to create a society that protects the welfare of all their citizens. In other countries the situation is different. In many economically struggling countries, bribery is standard practice to get things done—such as getting lighting installed or a contract awarded. In the United States and other economically advanced countries, bribery is considered unethical and has been made illegal.

Figure 4.4
Sources of Ethics

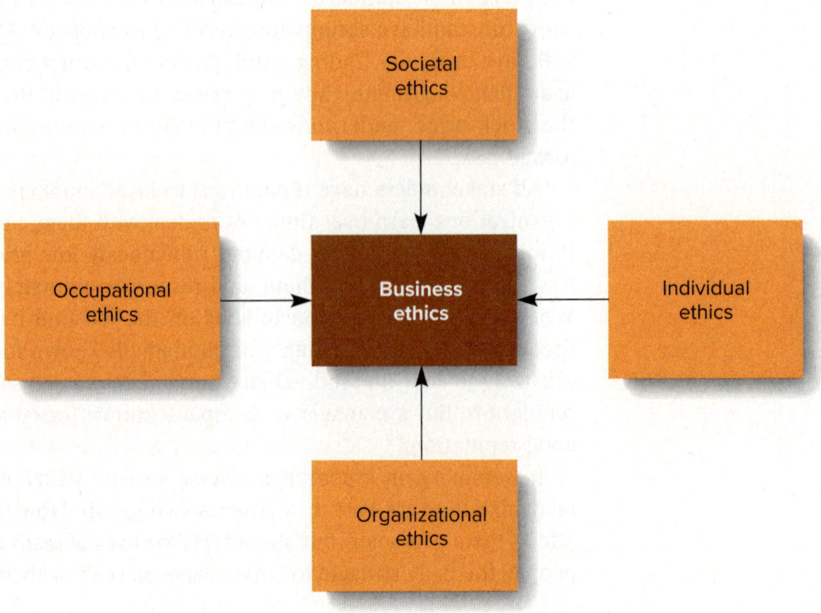

But even in countries with high marks on the ethical scale, corruption still happens. For example, in Iceland, which is lauded as one of the world's most ethical countries, a massive bribery scheme undertaken by Samherji, one of the country's largest fishing conglomerates, reached the shores of Africa. The Icelandic organization allegedly bribed government officials in Namibia and Angola for rights for massive fishing quotas in local waters. Samherji established shell companies in tax havens like United Arab Emirates, Mauritius, and Cyprus to launder the proceeds of corrupt deals.[48]

Occupational Ethics

occupational ethics Standards that govern how members of a profession, trade, or craft should conduct themselves when performing work-related activities.

Occupational ethics are standards that govern how members of a profession, trade, or craft should conduct themselves when performing work-related activities.[49] For example, medical ethics govern how doctors and nurses should treat their patients. Doctors are expected to perform only necessary medical procedures and to act in the patient's interest, not their own self-interest. The ethics of scientific research require that scientists conduct their experiments and present their findings in ways that ensure the validity of their conclusions. Like society at large, most professional groups can impose punishments for violations of ethical standards.[50] Doctors and lawyers can be prevented from practicing their professions if they disregard professional ethics and put their own interests first.

Within an organization, occupational rules and norms often govern how employees such as lawyers, researchers, and accountants should make decisions to further stakeholder interests. Employees internalize the rules and norms of their occupational group (just as they do those of society) and often follow them automatically when deciding how to behave. Because most people tend to follow established rules of behavior, people often take ethics for granted. However, when occupational ethics are violated, such as when engineers alter software to disguise the harmful effects of products, ethical issues come to the forefront. For example, in 2017 Volkswagen was ordered to pay a $2.8 billion criminal penalty for its diesel emission scandal in which the company was caught rigging some of its diesel engines to pass U.S. emissions tests. As part of its settlement with the U.S. Justice Department, Volkswagen incurred costs of more than $35 billion, a figure that included the price of buying back nearly 500,000 diesel vehicles sold in the United States. In addition, at least eight current and former Volkswagen employees have been charged with crimes connected with the scandal. To date, this is the largest fine ever handed out to any automaker.[51] Table 4.2 lists some failures or lapses in professional ethics according to the type of functional manager.

Individual Ethics

individual ethics Personal standards and values that determine how people view their responsibilities to others and how they should act in situations when their own self-interests are at stake.

Individual ethics are personal standards and values that determine how people view their responsibilities to other people and groups and, thus, how they should act in situations when their own self-interests are at stake.[52] Sources of individual ethics include the influence of one's family, peers, and upbringing in general. The experiences gained over a lifetime–through membership in social institutions such as schools and religions, for example–also contribute to the development of the personal standards and values that a person uses to evaluate a situation and decide what is the morally right or wrong way to behave. However, suppose you are the son or daughter of a mobster, and your upbringing and education take place in an organized crime context; this affects how you evaluate a situation. You may come to believe that it is ethical to do anything and perform any act, up to and including murder, if it benefits your family or friends. These are your ethics. They are obviously not the ethics of the wider society, and so they are subject to sanction. In a similar way, managers and employees in an organization may come to believe that actions they take to promote or protect their organization are more important than any harm these actions may cause other stakeholders. So they behave unethically or illegally, and when this is discovered, they could be sanctioned.

Recently the city of Chicago sued both DoorDash and Grubhub for allegedly deceiving customers and using unfair business practices. In the complaint, the city reiterates claims from restaurant owners that the platforms advertise delivery services for their businesses without the owners' consent and conceal lower prices that restaurants offer directly to customers outside

Table 4.2
Some Failures in Professional Ethics

For manufacturing and materials management managers:
- Releasing products that are not of a consistent quality because of defective inputs
- Producing product batches that may be dangerous or defective and harm customers
- Compromising workplace health and safety to reduce costs (for example, to maximize output, employees are not given adequate training to maintain and service machinery and equipment)

For sales and marketing managers:
- Knowingly making unsubstantiated product claims
- Engaging in sales campaigns that use covert persuasive or subliminal advertising to create customer need for the product
- Marketing to target groups such as older adults, underrepresented minority groups, or children to build demand for a product
- Sponsoring ongoing campaigns of unsolicited junk mail, spam, door-to-door, or telephone selling

For accounting and finance managers:
- Engaging in misleading financial analysis involving creative accounting or "cooking the books" to hide salient facts
- Authorizing excessive expenses and perks to managers, customers, and suppliers
- Hiding the level and amount of top management and director compensation

For human resource managers:
- Failing to act fairly, objectively, and in a consistent manner toward different employees or kinds of employees because of personal factors such as personality and beliefs
- Excessively encroaching on employee privacy through non-job-related surveillance or personality, ability, and drug testing
- Failing to respond to employee observations and concerns surrounding health and safety violations, hostile workplace issues, or inappropriate or even illegal behavior by managers or employees

of the delivery platforms. Chicago also claims that the two delivery services use a "bait and switch" process to attract customers with low delivery fees, only to add additional fees when customers were about to place their orders. Both DoorDash and Grubhub called the lawsuits "baseless." As of this writing, the lawsuits are still pending but have moved forward in the court system. Chicago recently announced it had reached a $10 million settlement with Uber Eats for similar unethical practices.[53]

In general, many decisions or behaviors that one person finds unethical, such as using animals for cosmetics testing, may be acceptable to another person. If decisions or behaviors are not illegal, individuals may agree to disagree about their ethical beliefs, or they may try to impose their own beliefs on other people and make those ethical beliefs the law. In all cases, however, people should develop and follow the ethical criteria described earlier to balance their self-interests against those of others when determining how they should behave in a particular situation.

Organizational Ethics

organizational ethics The guiding practices and beliefs through which a particular company and its managers view their responsibility toward their stakeholders.

Organizational ethics are the guiding practices and beliefs through which a particular company and its managers view their responsibility toward their stakeholders. The individual ethics of a company's founders and top managers are especially important in shaping the organization's code of ethics. Organizations whose founders had a vital role in creating a highly ethical code of organizational behavior include UPS, Procter & Gamble, Johnson & Johnson, and the Prudential Insurance Company. Johnson & Johnson's code of ethics—its credo—reflects a well-developed concern for its stakeholders (see Figure 4.5). Company credos, such as that of Johnson & Johnson, are meant to deter self-interested, unethical behavior; to demonstrate to managers and employees that a company will not tolerate people who, because of their own poor ethics, put their personal interests above the interests of other organizational stakeholders and ignore the harm they are inflicting on others; and to demonstrate that those who act unethically will be punished.

Figure 4.5

Johnson & Johnson's Credo

Our Credo

We believe our first responsibility is to the patients, doctors and nurses, to mothers and fathers and all others who use our products and services. In meeting their needs everything we do must be of high quality. We must constantly strive to provide values, reduces our costs and maintain reasonable prices. Customer's orders must be serviced promptly and accurately. Our business partners must have an opportunity to make a fair profit.

We are responsible to our employees who work with us throughout the world. We must provide an inclusive work environment where each person must be considered as an individual. We must respect their diversity and dignity and recognize their merit. They must have a sense of security, fulfillment and purpose in their jobs. Compensation must be fair and adequate and working conditions clean, orderly and safe. We must support the health and well-being of our employees and help them fulfill their family and other personal responsibilities. Employees must feel free to make suggestions and complaints. There must be equal opportunity for employment, development and advancement for those qualified. We must provide highly capable leaders and their actions must be just and ethical.

We are responsible to the communities in which we live and work and to the world community as well. We must help people be healthier by supporting better access and care in more places around the world. We must be good citizens — support good works and charities, better health and education, and bear our fair share of taxes. We must maintain in good order the property we are privileged to use, protecting the environment and natural resources.

Our final responsibility is to our stockholders. Business must make a sound profit. We must experiment with new ideas. Research must be carried on, innovative programs developed, investments made for the future and mistakes paid for. New equipment must be purchased, new facilities provided and new products launched. Reserve must be created to provide for adverse times. Where we operate according to these principles, the stockholders should realize a fair return.

Johnson & Johnson

Managers or workers may behave unethically if they feel pressured to do so by the situation they are in and by unethical top managers. People typically confront ethical issues when weighing their personal interests against the effects of their actions on others. Suppose a manager knows that promotion to vice president is likely if they can secure a $100 million contract, but getting the contract requires bribing the contract giver with $1 million. The manager reasons that performing this act will ensure their career and future, and what harm would it do, anyway? Bribery is common, and the manager knows that even if they decide not to pay the bribe, someone else surely will. So what to do? Research seems to suggest that people who realize they have the most at stake in a career sense or a monetary sense are the ones most likely to act unethically. And it is exactly in this situation that a strong code of organizational ethics can help people behave in the right or appropriate way. *The New York Times* detailed code of ethics, for example, was crafted by its editors to ensure the integrity and honesty of its journalists as they report sensitive information.

If a company's top managers consistently endorse the ethical principles in its corporate credo, they can prevent employees from going astray. Managers should model the behavior expected from their employees, as well as educate employees in the ethical behavior the organization expects. As described in the "Manager as a Person" feature, companies also can consider ways to embed ethical behavior in their processes. Employees are much more likely to act unethically when a credo does not exist or is disregarded. Accounting firm Arthur Andersen, for example, did not follow its credo at all; its unscrupulous partners ordered middle managers to shred records that showed evidence of their wrongdoing. Although the middle managers knew this was wrong, they followed the orders because they responded to the personal power and status of the partners and not the company's code of ethics. They were afraid they would lose their jobs if they did not behave unethically, but their actions cost them their jobs anyway, when the company was forced to close its doors as a result of its unethical practices.[54]

MANAGER AS A PERSON

Do People Just Need a Nudge?

Organizations often assume pursuing ethical behavior involves simply teaching ethical standards and punishing violations of the standards. Certainly, employees must know the standards, and bad behavior should have consequences, but education and punishment alone often fail. Why? Sometimes employees work within systems where the immediate rewards of unethical behavior outweigh the rewards of ethical alternatives. An employee who closes a sale may receive immediate and enthusiastic praise, but any investigation of how the employee closed the deal might happen much later, if at all.[55]

Increasingly, managers seeking alternatives consider "nudging" employees–that is, making a desired action easier to choose. An often-cited example involves retirement savings plans in which employers match employee contributions. Companies were concerned that many employees did not choose to participate, perhaps because enrolling would shrink their paychecks, even though the amounts saved would grow substantially by retirement. At companies that tried nudging employees by making participation the default (so employees wanting to opt out had to request it), more employees participated.[56] Could nudges also promote ethical behavior?

Experience suggests that nudges can help, but a simplistic view of nudging can fail or even backfire. Consider a company wanting to conserve resources. If it nudges people with email reminders, these are likely to interest only environmentally conscious employees. Frequent reminders might annoy employees, so they resist the appeal. Furthermore, employees may view some nudges–such as those targeted to recipients based on detailed data about them without their knowledge and consent–as unethical, thus undermining the whole effort to promote ethics.[57]

Still, nudges may have an important role when they are part of a deeper and more comprehensive use of behavioral science. This approach to promoting ethical conduct, often called behavioral risk management, uses various research methods to understand how a company's systems and processes shape employee behavior. The analysis looks for red flags, such as blaming employees personally when a situation goes wrong, distributing rewards unfairly, or a lack of trust in colleagues. Solutions could include nudges. At an insurance company, for example, employees felt like they and their coworkers had competing goals. One measure that improved their team spirit was to create email signature panels including the names, faces, and titles of all the members on the team serving a particular client. Every time an employee sent an email, that person would see a reminder that they represent a team.[58]

Top managers play a crucial role in determining a company's ethics. It is clearly important, then, that when making appointment decisions, the board of directors should scrutinize the reputations and ethical records of top managers. It is the responsibility of the board to decide whether a prospective CEO has the maturity, experience, and integrity needed to head a company and be entrusted with the capital and wealth of the organization, on which the fate of all its stakeholders depends. Clearly, a track record of success is not enough to decide whether a top manager is capable of moral decision making; a manager might have achieved this success through unethical or illegal means. It is important to investigate prospective top managers and examine their credentials. Although the best predictor of future behavior is often past behavior, the board of directors needs to be on guard against unprincipled executives who use unethical means to rise to the top of the organizational hierarchy. For this reason it is necessary that a company's directors continuously monitor the behavior of top executives. This increased scrutiny led to the dismissal of many top executives for breaking ethical rules concerning issues such as excessive personal loans, stock options, inflated expense accounts, and even sexual misconduct.

Approaches to Social Responsibility

LO4-6 Distinguish among the four main approaches toward social responsibility that a company can take.

A company's ethics are the result of differences in societal, organizational, occupational, and individual ethics. In turn, a company's ethics determine its stance on social responsibility. A company's stance on **social responsibility** is the way its managers and employees view their duty or obligation to make decisions that protect, enhance, and promote the welfare and well-being of stakeholders and society as a whole. As we noted earlier, when no laws specify how a company should act toward stakeholders, managers must decide the right, ethical, and socially responsible thing to do. Differences in business ethics can lead companies to diverse positions or views on their responsibility toward stakeholders.

social responsibility The way a company's managers and employees view their duty or obligation to make decisions that protect, enhance, and promote the welfare and well-being of stakeholders and society as a whole.

Many kinds of decisions signal a company's beliefs about its obligations to make socially responsible business decisions (see Table 4.3). The decision to spend money on training and educating employees–investing in them–is one such decision; so is the decision to minimize or avoid layoffs whenever possible. The decision to act promptly and warn customers when a batch of defective merchandise has been accidentally sold is another one. Companies that try to hide such problems show little regard for social responsibility. In the past, both GM and Ford tried to hide the fact that several of their vehicles had defects that made them dangerous to drive; the companies were penalized with hundreds of millions of dollars in damages for their unethical behavior, and today they move more quickly to recall vehicles to fix problems. Several years ago, General Motors CEO Mary Barra admitted that the automaker did not react fast enough when fault was found with an ignition switch that triggered the recall of eventually more than 10 million cars worldwide.[59] On the other side, Fitbit voluntarily recalled its activity tracking wrist band, the Fitbit Force, due to skin rash issues. The company offered to send consumers a return kit and promised a reimbursement check or exchange within two to six weeks of receipt.[60] The way a company announces business problems or admits its mistakes provides strong clues about its stance on social responsibility.

Table 4.3
Forms of Socially Responsible Behavior

Managers are being socially responsible and showing their support for their stakeholders when they

- Provide severance payments to help laid-off workers make ends meet until they can find another job.
- Give workers opportunities to enhance their skills and acquire additional education so they can remain productive and do not become obsolete because of changes in technology.
- Allow employees to take time off when they need to and provide health care and other benefits for employees.
- Contribute to charities or support various civic-minded activities in the cities or towns in which they are located (Target and Levi Strauss both contribute a percentage of their profits to support schools, charities, the arts, and other good works).
- Decide to keep open a factory whose closure would devastate the local community.
- Decide to keep a company's operations in the United States to protect the jobs of American workers rather than move abroad.
- Decide to spend money to improve a new factory so it will not pollute the environment.
- Decline to invest in countries that have poor human rights records.
- Choose to help poor countries develop an economic base to improve living standards.

Four Different Approaches

obstructionist approach Companies and their managers choose *not* to behave in a socially responsible way and instead behave unethically and illegally.

The strength of companies' commitment to social responsibility can range from low to high (see Figure 4.6). At the low end of the range is an **obstructionist approach**, in which companies and their managers choose *not* to behave in a socially responsible way. Instead they behave unethically and often illegally and do all they can to prevent knowledge of their behavior from reaching other organizational stakeholders and society at large. Managers at the Manville Corporation adopted this approach when they sought to hide evidence that asbestos causes lung damage; so, too, did tobacco companies when they sought to hide evidence that cigarette smoking causes lung cancer. In 2010, it was revealed that the managers of Lehman Brothers, whose bankruptcy helped propel the 2008–2009 financial crisis, used loopholes in UK law to hide billions of dollars of worthless assets on its balance sheet to disguise its poor financial condition.

Top managers at Enron also acted in an obstructionist way when they prevented employees from selling Enron shares in their pension funds while they sold hundreds of millions of dollars' worth of their own Enron stock. Most employees lost all their retirement savings. Senior partners at Arthur Andersen who instructed their employees to shred files chose an obstructionist approach that caused not only a loss of reputation but devastation for the organization and for all stakeholders involved. These companies are no longer in business.

defensive approach Companies and their managers behave ethically to the degree that they stay within the law and strictly abide by legal requirements.

A **defensive approach** indicates at least some commitment to ethical behavior. Defensive companies and managers stay within the law and abide strictly by legal requirements but make no attempt to exercise social responsibility beyond what the law dictates; thus, they can and often do act unethically. These are the kinds of companies, like Computer Associates, World Com, and Merrill Lynch, that gave their managers large stock options and bonuses even as company performance was declining rapidly. The managers are the kind who sell their stock in advance of other shareholders because they know their company's performance is about to fall. Although acting on inside information is illegal, it is often hard to prove because top managers have wide latitude regarding when they sell their shares. The founders of most tech companies took advantage of this legal loophole to sell billions of dollars of their company shares before their stock prices collapsed. When making ethical decisions, such managers put their own interests first and commonly harm other stakeholders.

accommodative approach Companies and their managers behave legally and ethically and try to balance the interests of different stakeholders as the need arises.

An **accommodative approach** acknowledges the need to support social responsibility. Accommodative companies and managers agree that organizational members ought to behave legally and ethically, and they try to balance the interests of different stakeholders so the claims of shareholders are seen in relation to the claims of other stakeholders. Managers adopting this approach want to make choices that are reasonable in the eyes of society and want to do the right thing.

This approach is the one taken by the typical large U.S. company, which has the most to lose from unethical or illegal behavior. Generally, the older and more reputable a company, the more likely its managers are to curb attempts by their employees to act unethically. Large companies, like GM, Intel, 3M, and Dell, seek every way to build their companies' competitive advantage. Nevertheless, they rein in attempts by their managers to behave unethically or illegally, knowing the grave consequences such behavior can have on future profitability. Sometimes they fail, however, such as in 2013 when SAC Capital Advisors (among others)

Figure 4.6

Four Approaches to Social Responsibility

agreed to pay $1.8 billion and plead guilty to criminal insider trading charges. To date, this is the biggest insider trading settlement in history.[61]

proactive approach Companies and their managers actively embrace socially responsible behavior, going out of their way to learn about the needs of different stakeholder groups and using organizational resources to promote the interests of all stakeholders.

Companies and managers taking a **proactive approach** actively embrace the need to behave in socially responsible ways. They go out of their way to learn about the needs of different stakeholder groups and are willing to use organizational resources to promote the interests not only of shareholders, but also of the other stakeholders such as their employees and communities. U.S. steelmaker Nucor is one such company. In 1977, its visionary CEO Ken Iverson announced that throughout its history Nucor had never laid off one employee, and even though a major recession was raging, it did not plan to start now. In 2009, Nucor CEO Daniel R. DiMicco announced that Nucor again would not start layoffs despite the fact its steel mills were operating at only 50% of capacity (compared to 95% just months earlier) because customers had slashed orders due to the recession. While rivals laid off thousands of employees, Nucor remained loyal to its employees. However, even though there were no layoffs, both managers and employees took major cuts in pay and bonuses to weather the storm together, as they always had, and they searched for ways to reduce operating costs so they would all benefit when the economy recovered, and by 2012 their sacrifice had paid off: Nucor was doing well again. In 2022, Nucor paid out a cash dividend to shareholders for the 198th consecutive quarter.[62]

Proactive companies are often at the forefront of campaigns for causes such as a pollution-free environment; recycling and conservation of resources; the minimization or elimination of the use of animals in drug and cosmetics testing; and the reduction of crime, illiteracy, and poverty. For example, companies such as McDonald's, Google, REI, Whole Foods, and Target all have reputations for being proactive in the support of stakeholders such as their suppliers or the communities in which they operate. For a more detailed example of a company that is proactive about employee diversity, see the "Focus on DEI&B" feature.

FOCUS ON DEI&B

Bitty & Beau's Commitment to Human Rights

The owners of Bitty & Beau's Coffee take a proactive approach to social responsibility with their vision of hiring individuals with disabilities to provide a way for them to become more accepted and included in every community.
sturti/Getty Images

Bitty & Beau's Coffee calls itself "a human rights movement disguised as a coffee shop."[63] The original location, in Wilmington, North Carolina, employed 19 people with intellectual and developmental disabilities. Six years later, the company has 400 employees in 23 Bitty & Beau's franchises in a dozen states and operates several more shops inside corporations' headquarters.[64]

The husband-and-wife owners, Amy and Ben Wright, founded their business for personal reasons. Of their four children, one has autism and two—Beau and Bitty—have Down syndrome. In considering their children's future, the Wrights observed an 80% unemployment rate for persons with intellectual and developmental disabilities and concluded they could change that number by starting a business. Their vision, displayed on Bitty & Beau's website, is to create "a path for people with disabilities to become more valued, accepted and included in every community." From the beginning, they sought profitability—and say they achieved it.[65]

In hiring nonmanagement employees, Bitty & Beau's chooses people with intellectual and developmental disabilities. The Wrights say this gives them an advantage in today's tight labor market. People with disabilities are an underused source of talent, so job applicants actively seek out the company. Furthermore, turnover is almost nonexistent, as workers are dedicated and enthusiastic. Store managers have devised clever ways to structure the work so employees can succeed at it. For example, employees may use a deck of playing cards to identify each order, handing a card to the customer. Calling out the number and suit of the playing card is easier than figuring out how to read customers' names.[66]

Bitty & Beau's has an impressive impact on employees and local communities. For example, Kyle, a Pennsylvania employee with autism, found a sense of community at work and developed an outgoing manner; Sydney, a North Carolina employee with Down syndrome, appreciates the dignity of earning a paycheck. Consistent with its mission, Bitty & Beau's pays at least minimum wage and provides employee benefits. The coffee shops draw school field trips and families because the environment is fun (karaoke and dancing are encouraged) and because the employees demonstrate what people with disabilities can accomplish and experience when given the chance. The company's owners expect that as more and more people visit Bitty & Beau's, the number of employers who can imagine hiring these highly committed workers will grow, and opportunities will arise nationwide.[67]

Why Be Socially Responsible?

Several advantages result when companies and their managers behave in a socially responsible manner. First, demonstrating its social responsibility helps a company build a good reputation. Reputation is the trust, goodwill, and confidence others have in a company that lead them to want to do business with it. The rewards for a good company reputation are increased business and improved ability to obtain resources from stakeholders. Reputation thus can enhance profitability and build shareholder wealth, and behaving responsibly socially is the economically right thing to do because companies that do so benefit from increasing business and rising profits.

A second major reason for companies to act responsibly toward employees, customers, and society is that, in a capitalist system, companies as well as the government, have to bear the costs of protecting their stakeholders, providing health care and income, paying taxes, and so on. So if all companies in a society act responsibly, the quality of life as a whole increases.

Moreover, how companies behave toward their employees determines many of a society's values and norms and the ethics of its citizens, as already noted. It has been suggested that if all organizations adopted a caring approach and agreed that their responsibility is to promote the interests of their employees, a climate of caring would pervade the wider society. Experts point to Japan, Sweden, Germany, the Netherlands, and Switzerland as countries where organizations are highly socially responsible and where, as a result, crime, poverty, and unemployment rates are relatively low, literacy rates are relatively high, and sociocultural values promote harmony between different groups of people. Business activity affects all aspects of people's lives, so how business behaves toward stakeholders affects how stakeholders behave toward business.

The Role of Organizational Culture

Although an organization's code of ethics guides decision making when ethical questions arise, managers can go one step further by ensuring that important ethical values and norms are key features of an organization's culture. For example, Herb Kelleher and Coleen Barrett created Southwest Airlines's culture in which promoting employee well-being is a main company priority; this translates into organizational values and norms dictating that layoffs should be avoided and employees should share in the profits the company makes.[68] Google, UPS, and Toyota are among the many companies that espouse similar values. When ethical values and norms such as these are part of an organization's culture, they help organizational members resist self-interested action because they recognize that they are part of something bigger than themselves.[69]

Managers' roles in developing ethical values and standards in other employees are important. Employees naturally look to those in authority to provide leadership, just as a country's citizens look to its political leaders, and managers become ethical role models whose behavior is scrutinized by employees. If top managers are perceived as being self-interested and not ethical, their employees are not likely to behave in an ethical manner. Employees may think that if it's all right for a top manager to engage in dubious behavior, it's all right for them, too, and for employees this might mean slacking off, reducing customer support, and not taking supportive actions to help their company. The actions of top managers such as CEOs and the president of the United States are scrutinized so closely for ethical improprieties because their actions represent the values of their organizations and, in the case of the president, the values of the nation.

ethics officer A manager responsible for communicating and teaching ethical standards to all employees and monitoring their conformity to those standards.

Managers can also provide a visible means of support to develop an ethical culture. Increasingly, organizations are creating the role of **ethics officer**, to monitor their ethical practices and procedures. The ethics officer is responsible for communicating ethical standards to all employees, designing systems to monitor employees' conformity to those standards, and teaching managers and employees at all levels of the organization how to respond to ethical dilemmas appropriately.[70] Because the ethics officer typically has organizationwide authority, organizational members in any department can communicate instances of unethical behavior by their managers or coworkers without fear of retribution. This arrangement makes it easier for everyone to behave ethically. In addition, ethics officers can provide guidance when organizational members are uncertain about whether an action is ethical. Some organizations have an organizationwide ethics committee to provide guidance on ethical issues and help write and update the company code of ethics.

Ethical organizational cultures encourage organizational members to behave in a socially responsible manner. As mentioned earlier in this chapter, one company epitomizing an ethical, socially responsible firm is Johnson & Johnson. The ethical values and norms in Johnson & Johnson's culture, along with its credo, have guided its managers to make the right decision in difficult situations for decades.

Summary and Review

LO4-1 **THE NATURE OF ETHICS** Ethical issues are central to how companies and their managers make decisions, and they affect not only the efficiency and effectiveness of company operations but also the prosperity of the nation. The result of ethical behavior is a general increase in company performance and in a nation's standard of living, well-being, and wealth. An ethical dilemma is the quandary people find themselves in when they have to decide if they should act in a way that might help another person or group and is the right thing to do, even though it might go against their own self-interest. Ethics are the inner guiding moral principles, values, and beliefs that people use to analyze or interpret a situation and then decide what is the right or appropriate way to behave. Ethical beliefs alter and change as time passes, and as they do so, laws change to reflect the changing ethical beliefs of a society.

LO4-2, 4-4 **STAKEHOLDERS AND ETHICS** Stakeholders are people and groups who have a claim on and a stake in a company. The main stakeholder groups are shareholders, managers, employees, suppliers and distributors, customers, and the community, society, and nation. Companies and their managers need to make ethical business decisions that promote the well-being of their stakeholders and avoid doing them harm.

LO4-3, 4-5 **ETHICS AND DECISION MAKING** To determine whether a business decision is ethical, managers can use four ethical rules to analyze it: the utilitarian, moral rights, justice, and practical rules. Managers should behave ethically because this avoids the tragedy of the commons and results in a general increase in efficiency, effectiveness, and company performance. The main determinants of differences in a manager's, company's, and country's business ethics are societal, occupational, individual, and organizational.

LO4-6 **ETHICS AND SOCIAL RESPONSIBILITY** A company's stance on social responsibility is the way its managers and employees view their duty or obligation to make decisions that protect, enhance, and promote the welfare and well-being of stakeholders and society as a whole. There are four main approaches to social responsibility: obstructionist, defensive, accommodative, and proactive. The rewards from behaving in a socially responsible way are a good reputation, the support of all organizational stakeholders, and thus superior company performance.

Management in Action

Topics for Discussion and Action

Discussion

1. What is the relationship between ethics and the law? [LO4-1]
2. Why do the claims and interests of stakeholders sometimes conflict? [LO4-2]
3. Why should managers use ethical criteria to guide their decision making? [LO4-3]
4. As an employee of a company, what are some of the most unethical business practices that you have encountered in its dealings with stakeholders? [LO4-4]
5. What are the main determinants of business ethics? [LO4-5]

Action

6. Find a manager and ask about the most important ethical rules they use to make the right decisions. [LO4-3]
7. Find an example of (a) a company that has an obstructionist approach to social responsibility and (b) one that has an accommodative approach. [LO4-6]

Building Management Skills

Dealing with Ethical Dilemmas [LO4-1, 4-4]

Use the chapter material to decide how you, as a manager, should respond to each of the following ethical dilemmas:

1. You are planning to leave your job to go work for a competitor; your boss invites you to an important meeting where you will learn about new products your company will be bringing out next year. Do you go to the meeting? Explain your reasoning.
2. You're the manager of sales in an expensive sports car dealership. A young executive who has just received a promotion comes in and wants to buy a car that you know is out of their price range. Do you encourage the executive to buy it so you can receive a big commission on the sale or do you persuade them to buy a less-expensive model?
3. You sign a contract to manage a young rock band, and that group agrees to let you produce their next five records, for which they will receive royalties of 5%. Their first record is a smash hit and sells millions. Do you increase their royalty rate on future records? Why or why not?

Managing Ethically [LO4-3, 4-5]

Double Standard in Ingredients?

British conglomerate Unilever recently came under fire from Chinese customers when it was revealed that its Magnum ice creams sold in China contained ingredients that were inferior to ingredients in the same products that were sold in Europe. According to Unilever's officials, the Chinese ice cream products contained milk powder (not condensed milk) and a higher proportion of vegetable oil than the ice cream made for the European market. The backlash about the double standard on ingredients was immediate and intense: With more than 400 million views on Weibo, one of China's leading social media platforms, comments were tagged with topics like "double standards for ingredients."

China is the largest market for Unilever's Magnum ice cream products, and customers there were unhappy with Unilever's explanation for the inferior ingredients. The company indicated that milk powder was used because of the difficulty of transporting fresh milk from Europe to China, and that if milk produced in China were used, it would cause a "supply problem"; they were careful not to discuss whether domestic milk products were inferior in quality. In addition, some Chinese analysts suggested that cost might be an important factor in Unilever's decision to use milk powder and water instead of condensed milk. For example, liquid milk added to skim milk powder is priced at approximately $1,500 US per ton, while condensed milk with the same protein content could cost nearly $2,000 US per ton.

Chinese consumers are known for reading ingredient lists for products they purchase, and it is unclear if the double standard for ingredients will affect the overall sales of Magnum ice cream products in China. Meanwhile, Unilever recently opened an ice cream factory in TaiCang, China, touting the factory's use of new technologies, including digital smart machines and artificial intelligence. No word on whether there will be a change in the ice cream's ingredients.[71]

Questions

1. Why is it that an organization's values and norms can become too strong and lead to unethical behavior?
2. What steps can a company take to prevent this problem—to stop its values and norms from becoming so inwardly focused that managers and employees lose sight of their responsibility to their stakeholders?

Small Group Breakout Exercise

Is Chewing Gum the "Right" Thing to Do? [LO4-1, 4-3]

Form groups of three or four people, and appoint one member as the spokesperson who will communicate your findings to the class when called on by the instructor. Then discuss the following scenario:

In the United States, the right to chew gum is taken for granted. Although it is often against the rules to chew gum in a classroom, church, and so on, it is legal to do so on the street. If you possess or chew gum on a street in Singapore, you can be arrested. Chewing gum has been made illegal in Singapore because those in power believe it creates a mess on pavements; they feel that people cannot be trusted to dispose of their gum properly and, thus, should have no right to use it.

1. What makes chewing gum acceptable in the United States but unacceptable in Singapore?
2. Why can you chew gum on the street but not in a church?
3. How can you use ethical principles to decide when gum chewing is ethical or unethical and if and when it should be made illegal?

Be the Manager [LO4-3]

Creating an Ethical Code

You are an entrepreneur who has decided to go into business and open a steak and chicken restaurant. Your business plan requires that you hire at least 20 people as chefs, waiters, and so on. As the owner, you are drawing up a list of ethical principles that each of these people will receive and must agree to when they accept a job offer. These principles outline your view of what is right or acceptable behavior and what will be expected both from you and from your employees.

Create a list of the five main ethical rules or principles you will use to govern how your business operates. Be sure to spell out how these principles relate to your stakeholders; for example, state the rules you intend to follow in dealing with your employees and customers.

Case in the News [LO4-2, 4-3, 4-4, 4-5, 4-6]

McDonald's Walks Away from Russia

When Russia invaded Ukraine in February 2022, managers around the world faced thorny decisions related to the conflict's impact on their employees, customers, and bottom lines. This was very true for Chris Kempczinski, the chief executive of McDonald's. The company had 108 stores in Ukraine and 853 stores in Russia. Should these continue to operate, and if so, how?

The answer for Ukraine was straightforward. Operating there would be dangerous for employees and customers. McDonald's directed the stores to close, promising to pay employees during the shutdown. This was a familiar move for Kempczinski, who became CEO just ahead of the COVID-19 pandemic. However, it would hurt: The Ukraine business generated 2% of McDonald's global revenues.

Decisions about Russia were more complex. Stakeholders would be affected significantly, and McDonald's was under pressure from all sides. Investors had been eyeing revenue growth, and Russian sales were 7% of worldwide revenues. However, some investors feared remaining in Russia would pose a reputation risk. If consumers in other key markets were sympathetic to Ukraine, they might boycott a company doing business in Russia. Still, leaving could damage the company's image as a global powerhouse.

Employees were a key concern. Most of McDonald's restaurants in Russia were owned by the corporation, not franchisees, so 62,000 people in Russia were corporate employees. McDonald's published values start with, "We put our customers and people first."

Societal pressure to leave Russia affected many Western companies but hit McDonald's hard. The company's move into Russia had been symbolically significant: Customers are immersed in U.S. culture when they enter a McDonald's restaurant, so the brand's presence became linked with Russia's willingness to engage with the West. At Yale University, the Chief Executive Leadership Institute tracked which companies were leaving Russia and which were staying, and it issued critical messages about companies that remained. Following negative press, stock prices dropped for prominent companies, including McDonald's.

The U.S. government established some legal boundaries for decision making when it imposed sanctions on Russia. These included prohibiting the use of Sberbank, the only bank in some of the towns served by McDonald's. In April, additional sanctions prohibited companies from exporting services to Russia or making new investments in Russia.

Kempczinski determined that he would take his time to arrive at the right decision, rather than risk a costly error. Fortunately, he had trusted advisers. Within the company, Kempczinski consulted with his chief financial officer and his board of directors. He also spoke several times a day with Ian Borden, the president of international operations, who had previously worked in Ukraine and Russia for McDonald's.

Kempczinski repeatedly addressed the same set of five questions: Is operating in Russia possible to do legally? Does the company still have the freedom it needs to operate there? Is operating there a plus for the McDonald's brand? Does operating there help the company succeed financially? And does operating there align with the company's values? At first, some questions could be answered yes, but as time passed, they began to flip to no. In March, Kempczinski announced his first decision: McDonald's would pause operations temporarily, publicly acknowledging the "unspeakable suffering" that had resulted from the invasion. The announcement also said McDonald's would continue paying Russian employees during the pause because it had a moral obligation to them—as well as a practical need to keep its workforce intact in case the stores reopened. On the last day before the closing, long lines of customers formed to get their last taste of American-style fast food.

No reopening followed. As hostilities continued, McDonald's paid tens of millions of dollars a month for a business generating zero revenues. By May, the answers to the five questions pointed to the same decision: It was time to leave Russia. But Kempczinski still had to determine how. In Russia, McDonald's owned buildings, machinery, and other large assets, and Kempczinski remained concerned about the Russian workers. McDonald's negotiated a sale of the business to a Russian restaurant operator. The contract requires the new owner to retain the employees, and the restaurants may not use the McDonald's brand. However, selling a business in a country enduring heavy sanctions was expected to result in McDonald's posting a heavy loss on the deal.

McDonald's announced its withdrawal from Russia in May. Public opinion was largely favorable, and the company's stock price dipped only briefly. The owner of the new business asserts that sales are robust despite supply problems, including no way to buy Coca-Cola.

Questions for Discussion

1. Of McDonald's different stakeholders, which of them would most likely benefit from a decision to leave Russia, and which would benefit from the company staying? In your opinion, which stakeholders had the most compelling reasons? Why?
2. Review the four ethical rules in Figure 4.2. Choose one of these approaches to making an ethical decision, and describe how Chris Kempczinski could have applied that approach when deciding whether to stay in Russia.
3. Based on the information provided, do you consider McDonald's decision to leave Russia an ethical decision? Was the process for leaving done ethically? Why or why not?

Sources: McDonald's, "Our Mission and Values," https://corporate.mcdonalds.com, accessed January 10, 2023; C. Rainey, "I'm Leavin' It," *Bloomberg Businessweek*, January 9, 2023, 34–41; J. Askew, "Tasty and That's It: Russia's Knock-Off McDonald's Goes International," *Euronews*, www.euronews.com, November 14, 2022; G. Colvin, "The Long Goodbye: Inside McDonald's Agonizing Decision to Leave Russia," *Fortune*, August/September 2022, 44–51; N. Turak, "Goodbye, American Soft Power: McDonald's Exiting Russia after 32 Years Is the End of an Era," *CNBC*, www.cnbc.com, May 17, 2022; J. Creswell, "McDonald's Coca-Cola and Starbucks Temporarily Stop Sales in Russia," *The New York Times*, www.nytimes.com, March 8, 2022.

Notes

1. The UPS Foundation, "Creating a More Equitable and Just World: 2021 Social Impact Report," https://about.ups.com, accessed January 10, 2023.
2. "Social Impact and the UPS Foundation," https://about.ups.com, accessed January 10, 2023.
3. "UPS Sustainability Highlights," https://about.ups.com, accessed January 10, 2023.
4. Ibid.; "The UPS Foundation Delivers Hope During Times of Crisis," https://about.ups.com, September 27, 2022.
5. "UPS 2021 Social Impact Report"; "Keeping the American and Global Economy Moving," https://about.ups.com, accessed February 6, 2022.
6. "UPS 2021 Social Impact Report"; "Our People" and "The UPS Foundation's Mission and Purpose," https://about.ups.com, accessed January 10, 2023.
7. "The UPS Foundation Celebrates 70 Years" and "Company Facts," https://about.ups.com, accessed January 10, 2023.
8. M. Nink and J. Robinson, "Ethical Dilemmas: What to Do When Employees Stay Silent," *Gallup,* www.gallup.com, May 3, 2022.
9. N. Epley and A. Kumar, "How to Design an Ethical Organization," *Harvard Business Review,* May-June 2019, 145-50.
10. Ibid; V. Cherepanova, "Yes, 'Ethical Culture' Can Be Measured," *FCPA Blog,* https://fcpablog.com, July 22, 2019.
11. Epley and Kumar, "How to Design an Ethical Organization."
12. J. Rosen, "What Factors Influence a Company's Ethical Culture?" *Corporate Compliance Insights,* www.corporatecomplianceinsights.com, September 25, 2019.
13. National Constitutional Center, "On This Day: Supreme Court Rejects Anti-Interracial Marriage Laws," *Constitutional Daily,* https: constitutioncenter.org, June 12, 2021.
14. DISA, "Marijuana Legality by State (as of November 2022)," https://disa.com, accessed January 10, 2023.
15. J. Wu, D. Silva, and N. Chiwaya, "Map: See the States Where Marijuana Is Legal," *NBC News,* www.nbc.com, November 9, 2022.
16. B. Bushard, "611 Mass Shootings Recorded So Far in 2022," *Forbes,* www.forbes.com, November 25, 2022; E. Shapiro, "March for Our Lives Recap," *ABC News,* https://abcnews.go.com, June 11, 2022.
17. R.E. Freeman, *Strategic Management: A Stakeholder Approach* (Marshfield, MA: Pitman, 1984).
18. "About the Giving Pledge," https://givingpledge.org, accessed January 10, 2023; M. Durot, "MacKenzie Scott Just Announced She's Donated $2 Billion to Hundreds of Groups over the Past Seven Months," *Forbes,* www.forbes.com, November 14, 2022; M. Scott, "Of and By," *Medium,* https://mackenzie-scott.medium.com, November 14, 2022.
19. C. Linnane, "Maximizing Shareholder Value Can No Longer Be a Company's Main Purpose: Top CEOs," *Market Watch,* www.marketwatch.com, August 24, 2019.
20. T. Huddleston Jr., "228 High-Powered CEOs–from Lyft to Bain Capital–Are Calling for 'Bold Urgent Action' on Gun Violence," *CNBC,* www.cnbc.com, June 10, 2022.
21. Z. Levinson, S. Hulver, and T. Neuman, "Hospital Charity Care: How It Works and Why It Matters," Kaiser Family Foundation, www.kff.org, November 3, 2022; R. King, "Nonprofit Hospitals Spend Less on Charity Care than For-Profits, Study Finds," *Fierce HealthCare,* www.fierce-healthcare.com, April 7, 2021.
22. A. Wilde Mathews, A. Fuller, and M. Evans, "Hospitals Often Don't Help Needy Patients, Even Those Who Qualify," *The Wall Street Journal,* www.wsj.com, November 17, 2022; S. Singer, E. Wilson, and O. Carare, *Understanding Required Financial Assistance in Medical Care,* Consumer Financial Protection Bureau, July 2022, www.consumerfinance.gov.
23. Levinson et al., "Hospital Charity Care"; S. Goldberg, "More Are Uninsured, Charity Care Is Down," *Crain's Chicago Business,* January 29, 2021, EBSCOhost, https://web.p.ebscohost.com.
24. J. Silver-Greenberg and K. Thomas, "They Were Entitled to Free Care; Hospitals Hounded Them to Pay," *The New York Times,* www.nytimes.com, September 24, 2022; Wilde Mathews et al., "Hospitals Often Don't Help Needy Patients."
25. S. Wiley, "Does Your Approach to Charity Care Live Up to Your Own Standards?" Kaufman Hall, www.kaufmanhall.com, October 26, 2022.
26. C.I. Barnard, *The Functions of the Executive* (Cambridge, MA: Harvard University Press, 1948).
27. Freeman, *Strategic Management.*
28. Bureau of Labor Statistics, "The Employment Situation–November 2022," www.bls.gov, December 2, 2022; T. Henderson, "The US Has Reversed Pandemic Job Losses. Most Individual States Haven't," *Pew,* www.pewtrusts.com, September 21, 2022.
29. K. Ramirez, "Fed Approves Final Changes to Volcker Rule," *Housing Wire,* www.housingwire.com, October 9, 2019.
30. J. Bivens and J. Kandra, "CEO Pay Has Skyrocketed 1,460% Since 1978," *Economic Policy Institute,* www.epi.org, accessed January 10, 2023.
31. D. Baker, J. Bivens, and J. Schieder, "Reining in CEO Compensation and Curbing the Rise of Inequality," *Economic Policy Institute,* www.epi.org, June 4, 2019.
32. J. Novak, "How Tax Reform Will End the Nonprofit Executive Pay Scam," *CNBC,* www.cnbc.com, December 20, 2017.
33. L. DePillis, "Tax Bill Makes Nonprofits Pay Up for Millionaire Execs," *CNN Money,* http://money.cnn.com, December 20, 2017.
34. T.L. Beauchamp and N.E. Bowie, eds., *Ethical Theory and Business* (Englewood Cliffs, NJ: Prentice-Hall, 1929); A. MacIntyre, *After Virtue* (South Bend, IN: University of Notre Dame Press, 1981).
35. R.E. Goodin, "How to Determine Who Should Get What," *Ethics,* July 1975, 310-21.
36. T.M. Jones, "Ethical Decision Making by Individuals in Organization: An Issue Contingent Model," *Academy of Management Journal* 16 (1991), 366-95; G.F. Cavanaugh, D.J. Moberg, and M. Velasquez, "The Ethics of Organizational Politics," *Academy of Management Review* 6 (1981), 363-74.
37. T.M. Jones, "Instrumental Stakeholder Theory: A Synthesis of Ethics and Economics," Academy of Management Review 20 (1995), 404-37.
38. B. Victor and J.B. Cullen, "The Organizational Bases of Ethical Work Climates," *Administrative Science Quarterly* 33 (1988), 101-25.
39. D. Collins, "Organizational Harm, Legal Consequences and Stakeholder Retaliation," *Journal of Business Ethics* 8 (1988), 1-13.
40. R.C. Solomon, *Ethics and Excellence* (New York: Oxford University Press, 1992).
41. T.E. Becker, "Integrity in Organizations: Beyond Honesty and Conscientiousness,"

Academy of Management Review 23 (January 1998), 154–62.

42. S.W. Gellerman, "Why Good Managers Make Bad Decisions," in K.R. Andrews, ed., *Ethics in Practice: Managing the Moral Corporation* (Boston: Harvard Business School Press, 1989).
43. J. Dobson, "Corporate Reputation: A Free Market Solution to Unethical Behavior," *Business and Society* 28 (1989), 1–5.
44. S. Dimmock and W.C. Gerken, "Research: How One Bad Employee Can Corrupt a Whole Team," *Harvard Business Review*, https://hbr.org, March 5, 2018.
45. L.K. Trevino, "Ethical Decision Making in Organizations: A Person-Situation Interactionist Model," *Academy of Management Review* 11, no. 3 (1986), 283–98.
46. Ethisphere, "The 2022 World's Most Ethical Companies Honorees List," https://worldsmostethicalcompanies.com, accessed January 10, 2023.
47. A.S. Waterman, "On the Uses of Psychological Theory and Research in the Process of Ethical Inquiry," *Psychological Bulletin* 103, no. 3 (1988), 283–98.
48. Transparency International, "CPI 2019: Trouble at the Top," www.transparency.org, January 23, 2020.
49. M.S. Frankel, "Professional Codes: Why, How and with What Impact?" *Ethics* 8 (1989), 109–15.
50. J. Van Maanen and S.R. Barley, "Occupational Communities: Culture and Control in Organizations," in B. Staw and L. Cummings, eds., *Research in Organizational Behavior*, vol. 6 (Greenwich, CT: JAI Press, 1984), 287–365.
51. K. Matussek, "VW Diesel Fraud Starts over Scandal That Won't Go Away," *Bloomberg*, www.bloomberg.com, accessed January 10, 2023.
52. Jones, "Ethical Decision Making."
53. A. Selvam and N. Waxman, "Uber Eats and Chicago Reach a $10 Million Settlement over Deceptive Practices," *Eater Chicago*, https://chicago.eater.com, accessed January 10, 2023; A. Gordon, "As Chicago's Lawsuits against DoorDash and Grubhub Progress, San Francisco Settles," *Local Today News* (Illinois), https://localtoday.news, July 28, 2022; L. Feinder, "Chicago Sues DoorDash, Grubhub for Allegedly Deceiving Customers," *CNBC*, www.cnbc.com, August 27, 2021.
54. M. Maurer, "Arthur Andersen's Legacy, 20 Years after Its Demise Is Complicated," *The Wall Street Journal*, www.wsj.com, August 31, 2022.
55. M. Osman, "Nudges: Four Reasons to Doubt Popular Techniques to Shape People's Behaviour," *The Conversation*, https://theconversation.com, January 10, 2022; H. Engler, "Behavioral-Risk Management an Evolving, Complex Journey as Practice Spreads at Big Banks," *Reuters*, www.reuters.com, September 28, 2021.
56. Osman, "Nudges: Four Reasons to Doubt"; Engler, "Behavioral-Risk Management."
57. W. Scholten, F. de Vries, and T. Besieux, "A Better Approach to Avoiding Misconduct," *Harvard Business Review*, May-June 2022, 105–11.
58. Ibid.
59. "GM: Steps to a Recall Nightmare," *CNN Money*, http://money.cnn.com, accessed February 8, 2020.
60. M. Maslakovic, "Fitness Tracker Rash: How to Avoid Getting a Rash from Your Fitness Tracker," https://gadgetsand wearables.com, January 26, 2018; "Fitbit Force Skin Irritation FAQs," https://help.fitbit.com, February 26, 2014.
61. C. English: "Conviction Upheld in Biggest Insider-Trading Case in History," *New York Post*, https://nypost.com, August 23, 2017.
62. "Nucor Announces 198th Consecutive Cash Dividend," *PR Newswire*, www.prnewswire.com, September 15, 2022.
63. Bitty & Beau's website, www.bittyandbeauscoffee.com, accessed January 10, 2023.
64. A.L. Jackson, "A Cup with a Cause," *Bloomberg Businessweek*, April 18, 2022, 36–37; A.J. Hare, "Bitty & Beau's Serves More than Just Coffee," *Pride*, www.pridemagazine.com, June 28, 2022.
65. Jackson, "A Cup with a Cause"; A. Kaplan, "Bitty & Beau's Coffee: Embracing Disabilities, Changing the Workforce," *Brown and White*, https://thebrownandwhite.com, October 29, 2022.
66. Jackson, "A Cup with a Cause"; Kaplan, "Bitty & Beau's Coffee"; Hare, "Bitty & Beau's Serves More than Just Coffee."
67. Jackson, "A Cup with a Cause"; Hare, "Bitty & Beau's Serves More than Just Coffee."
68. "2021 Southwest Airlines One Report," www.southwest.com, accessed January 10, 2023.
69. G.R. Jones, Organizational Theory: Text and Cases (Englewood Cliffs, NJ: Prentice-Hall, 2008).
70. Indeed, "How to Become an Ethics Officer (with Job Duties and Skills)," www.indeed.com, accessed January 10, 2023.
71. C. Liubing, "Differing Ingredients for Unilever Ice Cream in China and Europe Generate Controversy," *China Daily*, www.chinadaily.com.cn, accessed January 10, 2023; B. Ferrer, "Unilever's Chinese Ice Cream Factory Joins Consortium of Smart, Digitized Supply Chains," *Food Ingredients First*, www.foodingredientsfirst.com, September 28, 2021; M. Tanner, "Mark Tanner Traces Unilever's Clever Marketing of Its Magnum Ice Cream Products in China, and How It Was Undone by a Product That Delivered Different Ingredients to What Savvy Consumers Expected," *Interest.co.nz*, www.interest.co.nz., August 25, 2021.

CHAPTER 5

Managing Diverse Employees in a Multicultural Environment

Rawpixel.com/Shutterstock

Learning Objectives

After studying this chapter, you should be able to:

LO5-1 Discuss the increasing diversity of the workforce and the organizational environment.

LO5-2 Explain the central role that managers play in the effective management of diversity.

LO5-3 Explain why the effective management of diversity is both an ethical and a business imperative.

LO5-4 Discuss how perception and the use of schemas can result in unfair treatment.

LO5-5 List the steps managers can take to manage diversity effectively.

LO5-6 Identify the two major forms of sexual harassment and how they can be eliminated.

A MANAGER'S CHALLENGE

How the NFL Is Tackling Diversity Head On

What steps can an organization take to ensure diversity among its workforce? The National Football League wants its staff and teams to be drawn broadly from the people who play the game and cheer for their teams. To achieve this, the NFL analyzes data on the race, ethnicity, gender, and generational categories of its employees. For example, it found that 39% of its coaches in 2021 were members of a racial or ethnic minority, up from 35% the year before. However, the number of minority head coaches was unchanged at 9%, and the number of minority offensive coordinators actually declined during the same period.[1]

The NFL's playbook for more wins on diversity emphasizes hiring goals for managers and staff. For example, a recent set of goals includes a requirement that all NFL teams employ an offensive assistant who is a woman or a member of an ethnic or racial minority. This requirement aims to address the problem of few women and minorities in leadership positions; past promotions to head coach have drawn heavily from candidates with experience in coaching the offense. Hiring more minorities and women as offensive assistants should position them to be considered when teams are looking for coaches and, eventually, head coaches.[2]

Besides filling the talent pipeline, the NFL seeks to achieve more diversity in hiring by setting requirements for the hiring process. Since 2003, the NFL's so-called Rooney Rule says teams seeking to hire a head coach must interview at least two external candidates from a racial or ethnic minority group. The league recently added a requirement that key decision makers in the hiring of coaches and general managers must be trained in inclusive hiring.[3]

In 2022, the NFL extended its diversity effort to include sports medicine. The league partnered with the NFL Physicians Society and the Professional Football Athletic Trainer Society to bring diversity into its medical staff. In its first year, the initiative focused on recruiting Black medical students by recruiting from historically Black colleges and universities for 16 internships with 8 of its teams. As it continues and expands, the program to more underrepresented groups, the league hopes to build a more diverse pipeline of medical professionals with experience in sports medicine and knowledge of health issues facing football players. The league also referred to research showing that health outcomes of diverse patients tend to be better when medical care is provided by diverse professionals. It expects that its diversity goals will therefore enhance the well-being of its players.[4]

The National Football League's diversity initiatives include setting hiring goals for managers and staff; recruiting Black medical students to intern on teams' training staffs; and requiring all NFL teams to employ an offensive assistant who is a woman or a member of an underrepresented ethnic or racial group.
NurPhoto/Getty Images

The NFL has been able to report some areas of progress. Along with the percentage of racial and ethnic minorities, the percentage of female coaches has risen. However, just 9% of head coaches are Black (compared with 58% of players), and a recent 25% increase in number of female coaches at training camp represented a change from just 12 women to 15. One obstacle to greater diversity might be that the NFL has focused too narrowly on hiring a more diverse workforce. Fully embracing diversity will require more than just targets. In organizations that value diversity well enough to benefit from diverse employees' strengths and contributions, those employees are fully included and heard, not just recruited and hired.[5]

Overview

As described in "A Manager's Challenge," effective management of diversity and inclusion means more than hiring diverse employees. It means learning to appreciate and respond appropriately to the needs, attitudes, beliefs, and values that diverse people bring to an organization. It also means correcting misconceptions about why and how various kinds of employee groups differ from one another and finding the most effective way to use the skills and talents of diverse employees.

In this chapter, we focus on the effective management of diversity in an environment that is becoming increasingly diverse in all respects. Not only are the diversity and integration of the global workforce increasing, but suppliers and customers are also becoming increasingly diverse. Managers need to manage diversity proactively to attract and retain the best employees and compete effectively in a global environment. For example, managers at the audit and consulting firm Deloitte have instituted a program to encourage suppliers who belong to a minority ethnic group to compete for its business, and the firm sponsors schools and colleges that supply a stream of well-trained recruits.[6]

diversity Dissimilarities or differences among people due to age, gender, race, ethnicity, religion, sexual orientation, socioeconomic background, education, experience, physical appearance, capabilities/disabilities, and any other characteristic that is used to distinguish among people.

Sometimes well-intentioned managers inadvertently treat various groups of employees differently, even though there are no performance-based differences between them. This chapter explores why differential treatment occurs and the steps managers and organizations can take to ensure that diversity, in all respects, is effectively managed for the good of all organizational stakeholders.

The Increasing Diversity of the Workforce and the Environment

LO5-1 Discuss the increasing diversity of the workforce and the organizational environment.

One of the most important management issues to emerge over the last 40 years has been the increasing diversity of the workforce. **Diversity** is dissimilarities–differences–among people due to age, gender, race, ethnicity, religion, sexual orientation, socioeconomic background, education, experience, physical appearance, capabilities/disabilities, and any other characteristic that is used to distinguish among people (see Figure 5.1).

Diversity raises important ethical issues and social responsibility issues (see Chapter 4). It is also a critical issue for organizations–one that if not handled well can bring an organization to its knees, especially in our increasingly global environment. There are several reasons that diversity continues to be such a pressing concern and an issue, both in the popular press and for managers and organizations:

- There is a strong ethical imperative in many societies that minorities and other underrepresented groups must receive equal opportunities and be treated fairly and justly. Unfair treatment is also illegal.
- Effectively managing a diverse team of employees can improve organizational effectiveness. When managers effectively manage diversity, they not only encourage other managers to treat diverse members of an organization fairly and justly but also realize that diversity is an important organizational resource that can help an organization gain a competitive advantage.[7] Current research suggests there are specific situations in which diversity can enhance performance, for example, in teams. However, simply having a diverse workforce may not guarantee higher performance.[8] This last point is important as

Figure 5.1

Sources of Diversity in the Workplace

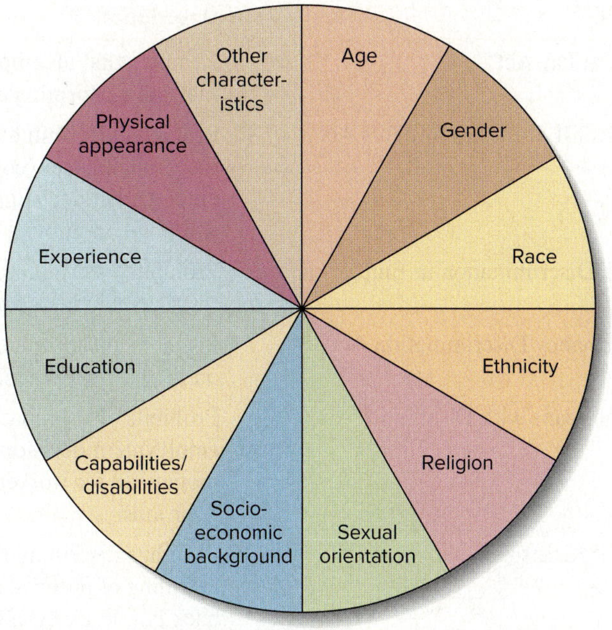

managers continue to explore the impact of diversity on the workplace and the challenges of moving employees and organizations forward in an effective manner.

- There is substantial evidence that diverse individuals continue to experience unfair treatment in the workplace as a result of biases, stereotypes, and overt discrimination. In a recent review of multiple studies, evidence suggests that hiring discrimination against African Americans has not changed significantly over the past 25 years in the United States, and Latinos have experienced only a moderate drop in discrimination.[9] In addition, a recent survey of U.S. workers suggests that "pay secrecy" within companies in the private sector may contribute to reducing women's bargaining power when it comes to salaries and may also be a factor in the ongoing gender wage gap.[10]

glass ceiling A metaphor alluding to the invisible barriers that prevent minorities and women from being promoted to top corporate positions.

- Finally, the **glass ceiling**—the invisible barrier that prevents women and minorities from being promoted to top corporate positions—is beginning to crack, though much work still needs to be done. For example, in November 2022, only 32 leaders of Fortune 500 companies were women (6.4%); there are currently only two Black women running top organizations: Roz Brewer, CEO of Walgreens Boots Alliance, and Thasunda Brown Duckett, CEO of TIAA.[11]

Before we can discuss the multitude of issues surrounding the effective management of diversity, we must document just how diverse the U.S. workforce is becoming.

Age

According to data from the U.S. Census Bureau, the median age of a person in the United States is the highest it has ever been, at 38.8 years. Moreover, it is projected that by 2060, close to 24% of the U.S. population will be 65 or older. The Age Discrimination in Employment Act of 1967 prohibits age discrimination.[12] Although we discuss federal employment legislation in more depth in, major equal employment opportunity legislation that prohibits discrimination among diverse groups is summarized in Table 5.1.

The aging of the population suggests that managers need to be vigilant to ensure that employees are not discriminated against because of age. Moreover, managers need to ensure that the policies and procedures they have in place treat all workers fairly, regardless of their ages. In addition, effectively managing diversity means employees of different ages can learn from each other, work well together, and take advantage of the unique perspective each has to offer.

Table 5.1

Major Equal Employment Opportunity Laws Affecting Human Resources Management

Year	Law	Description
1963	Equal Pay Act	Requires that all employees, regardless of gender, be paid equally if they are performing equal work.
1964	Title VII of the Civil Rights Act	Prohibits discrimination in employment decisions on the basis of race, religion, sex, color, or national origin; covers a wide range of employment decisions, including hiring, firing, pay, promotion, and working conditions.
1967	Age Discrimination in Employment Act	Prohibits discrimination against workers over the age of 40 and restricts mandatory retirement.
1978	Pregnancy Discrimination Act	Prohibits discrimination against women in employment decisions on the basis of pregnancy, childbirth, and related medical decisions.
1990	Americans with Disabilities Act	Prohibits discrimination against individuals with a disability in employment decisions and requires that employers make accommodations for workers with a disability to enable them to perform their jobs.
1991	Civil Rights Act	Prohibits discrimination (as does Title VII) and allows for the awarding of punitive and compensatory damages, in addition to back pay, in cases of intentional discrimination.
1993	Family and Medical Leave Act	Requires that employers provide 12 weeks of unpaid leave for medical and family reasons, including paternity and illness of a family member.
1994	Uniformed Services Employment and Reemployment Rights Act	Protects the civilian employment of active and reserve military personnel called to active duty; prohibits discrimination on the basis of military status and military service obligations; also provides certain reemployment rights following military service.

Gender

Women and men both have substantial participation rates in the U.S. workforce (approximately 56.5% women and 68.0% men), yet women's median weekly earnings continue to trail men's earnings ($968 for women compared to $1,166 for men).[13] Although the gender wage gap has narrowed in recent years, it continues to be an issue, just like the glass ceiling. According to Catalyst, a nonprofit organization that researches women in business, while women compose about 40.9% of employees in managerial and professional positions, only around 29.1% of executive officers in S&P 500 companies are women, and only 11% of the top earners in these companies are women.[14] These women, such as Mary Barra of GM, Roz Brewer of Walgreens, and Michele Buck of the Hershey Company, stand out among their male peers and often receive a disparate amount of attention in the media. Women are also underrepresented on companies' boards of directors–they currently hold roughly 32% of the board seats on S&P 500 companies.[15]

Additionally, research conducted by consulting firms suggests that female executives outperform their male colleagues in skills such as motivating others, promoting good communication, turning out high-quality work, and being good listeners. For example, in a recent analysis of thousands of 360-degree performance reviews, women consistently outscored men in 17 of 19 key leadership capabilities, including taking initiative, driving for results, exhibiting bold leadership, and championing change within organizations.[16] Results of a study conducted by Catalyst found that organizations with higher proportions of women in top management positions had significantly better financial performance than organizations with lower proportions of female top managers.[17] Another study conducted by Credit Suisse found that companies with one or more women on their boards of directors performed better in terms of returns on

A female executive enjoying the company plane is not as rare a sight today as it used to be. Nevertheless, the glass ceiling remains a real barrier to women, minorities, and other underrepresented groups in the business workforce.
4 PM production/Shutterstock

equity, sales, and invested capital than companies with fewer or no women on their boards.[18] Studies such as these make one wonder why the glass ceiling continues to hamper the progress of women in business (a topic we address later in the chapter).

Race and Ethnicity

The U.S. Census Bureau distinguished among the following races in the 2020 census: white, Black or African American, American Indian or Alaska Native, Asian, Native Hawaiian or Other Pacific Islander, and Some Other Race. Additional groups were used in the diversity calculations of the 2020 census: Hispanic; white alone, non-Hispanic; Black or African American alone, non-Hispanic; American Indian and Alaska Native alone, non-Hispanic; Asian alone, non-Hispanic; Native Hawaiian and Other Pacific Islander alone, non-Hispanic; Some Other Race alone, non-Hispanic; and Multiracial, non-Hispanic. Although *ethnicity* refers to a grouping of people based on some shared characteristic such as national origin, language, or culture, the U.S. Census Bureau treats ethnicity in terms of whether a person is Hispanic or Latino or Not Hispanic or Latino.[19] For the 2020 census, the government conducted extensive research to fine-tune the various ethnic groups tracked in the national census survey. More than ever before, many people see themselves as multiracial with various ethnicities.[20]

The racial and ethnic diversity of the U.S. population continues to change, as does the diversity of the workforce. According to the U.S. Census Bureau, approximately one of every three U.S. residents belongs to a minority group (is not a non-Hispanic white). More specifically, 18.9% of the population is Hispanic or Latino, 80.6% is not Hispanic or Latino, and 59.3% of the population is white alone (that is, white and not Hispanic or Latino). For those individuals self-identifying as one race in the 2020 census, approximately 75.8% are white, 13.6% are Black or African American, 1.3% are American Indian or Alaska Native, 6.1% are Asian, 0.3% are Native Hawaiian and Other Pacific Islander alone. In addition, 2.9% of the population self-identifies as two or more races.[21] According to projections released by the U.S. Census Bureau, the composition of the U.S. population in 2060 will be quite different from its composition today: In 2060, the U.S. population is projected to be close to 56% minority.[22] For more on the impact that one minority group–those who identify themselves as Hispanic or Latino–is already having on U.S. businesses, see the "Focus on DEI&B" feature.

FOCUS ON DEI&B

Latinos' Impact on the U.S. Economy

The share of the U.S. population counted as Hispanic or Latino includes those with ancestry or country of origin in any of 27 countries in Europe (Spain), North America (Mexico), Central America, South America, and the Caribbean. This diverse category includes native-born Americans and immigrants–people who speak English, Spanish, or some combination of the two. As a whole, they have been and are forecast to continue contributing disproportionately to the growth of the U.S. economy.[23]

One cause of their large impact is faster growth in their numbers relative to the overall U.S. population. The Hispanic population has been rising by 16% a year, versus 3% for non-Hispanics. The primary reason is a higher birth rate, although immigration plays a role.[24]

Not only are Hispanics a growing share of the U.S. labor force, but they are also starting their own businesses at a higher-than-average rate.
Ariel Skelley/Blend Images LLC

Because of the higher birth rate, the Hispanic population is relatively young. This results in relatively high labor-force participation because as people get older, they more often choose not to work or cannot work. High population growth and greater labor-force participation increase the number of wage earners, contributing to economic growth. In addition, by adding to the supply of workers, Hispanics enable more output from businesses. Without the increase in the Hispanic population, U.S. economic growth would be slower. An economic analysis suggests U.S. Latinos' contribution to the country's gross domestic product in 2020 was worth $2.8 trillion.[25]

Not only are Hispanics a growing share of the labor force, but they are starting their own businesses at a higher-than-average rate. In 2020, Latinos accounted for 52% of new employer businesses. According to the Latino Donor Cooperative, Latinos' contributions to the U.S. economy would be equal to the fifth largest economy in the world. Because startups are associated with growth and innovation, they give an added boost to the economy.[26]

Another qualitative way in which Hispanics contribute involves cultural diversity. To varying degrees, Hispanic Americans have been navigating two or more cultures, and many find that this gives them cultural agility that is an asset in the workplace. For example, Patricia Mota, CEO of the Hispanic Alliance for Career Advancement, says her experience as the daughter of Mexican immigrants taught her traditional values of hard work, family, and faith, and her work experience taught her values of independence and strategic thinking. She combines them to operate in way that is adaptable and inclusive.[27]

The increasing racial and ethnic diversity of the workforce and the population as a whole underscores the importance of effectively managing diversity. Data compiled by the Bureau of Labor Statistics suggest that much needs to be done in terms of ensuring that all employees have equal opportunities. For example, median weekly earnings for Black men are approximately 81% of median earnings for white men; median weekly earnings for Black women are approximately 83% of median earnings for white women.[28] In the remainder of this chapter, we focus on the fair treatment of all employees and explore why this is such an important challenge and what managers can do to meet it. We begin by taking a broader perspective and considering how increasing racial and ethnic diversity in an organization's environment (such as customers and suppliers) affects decision making and organizational effectiveness.

At a general level, managers and organizations are increasingly being reminded that stakeholders are diverse and expect organizational decisions and actions to reflect this diversity. For example, many advocacy groups continue to lobby the entertainment industry to increase the diversity in TV programming, acting, writing, and producing.[29] The need for such increased diversity is more than apparent. For example, while Hispanics make up more than 19% of the U.S. population (more than 62 million potential TV viewers), less than 8% of the characters in prime-time TV shows are Hispanics, according to a recent Hollywood diversity report by UCLA's College of Social Sciences.[30] Pressure continues to mount on networks, streaming services, and the media in general to increase diversity within their ranks to reflect the diversity of the population as a whole.[31]

Religion

Title VII of the Civil Rights Act prohibits discrimination based on religion (as well as based on race/ethnicity, country of origin, and sex; see Table 5.1 and Chapter 12). In addition to enacting Title VII, in 1997 the federal government issued "The White House Guidelines on

Religious Exercise and Expression in the Federal Workplace." These guidelines, while technically applicable only in federal offices, also are frequently relied on by large corporations. The guidelines require that employers make reasonable accommodations for religious practices, such as observances of holidays, as long as doing so does not entail major costs or hardships.[32]

A key issue for managers in recognizing different religions is being aware of different religions and their beliefs, with particular attention being paid to when religious holidays fall. For example, critical meetings should not be scheduled during a holy day for members of a certain faith, and managers should be flexible in allowing people to have time off for religious observances. When managers acknowledge, respect, and make even small accommodations for religious diversity, employee loyalty is often enhanced. For example, allowing employees to leave work early on certain days instead of taking a lunch break or posting holidays for different religions on the company calendar can go a long way toward making people of diverse religions feel respected and valued as well as enabling them to practice their faith.[33] According to recent data gathered by the U.S. Equal Employment Opportunity Commission, the number of religious discrimination complaints and settlement amounts have increased by more than 50% over the past 20 years.[34]

Capabilities/Disabilities

The Americans with Disabilities Act (ADA) of 1990 prohibits discrimination against persons with disabilities and requires that employers make reasonable accommodations to enable these people to effectively perform their jobs. On the surface, few would argue with the intent of this legislation. However, as managers try to implement policies and procedures to comply with the ADA, they face a number of challenges. For example, some people hesitate to reveal their disabilities to employers, foregoing the accommodations they need to do their jobs effectively. A key challenge for managers is to promote an environment in which employees who need accommodation feel comfortable disclosing their needs.[35]

In addressing this challenge, often managers must educate both themselves and their employees about the disabilities. According to recent statistics, the unemployment rate for workers with a disability is twice that of workers without disabilities. However, many companies are committed to hiring workers with disabilities and recognize that diversity and inclusion are two strategies vital to their overall business success. In 2022, the American Association of People with Disabilities and Disability:IN recognized 241 companies with their "Best Places to Work" award, including Airbnb, Best Buy, Hilton, Starbucks, and Target. These companies scored 100% on the Disability Equality Index, a benchmarking tool that provides organizations with an objective score on their disability and inclusion policies and practices.[36]

Socioeconomic Background

The term *socioeconomic background* typically refers to a combination of social class and income-related factors. From a management perspective, socioeconomic diversity (and, in particular, diversity in income levels) requires that managers be sensitive and responsive to the needs and concerns of individuals who might not be as wealthy as others. U.S. welfare reform in the middle to late 1990s emphasized the need for single mothers and others receiving public assistance to join or return to the workforce. In conjunction with a strong economy, this led to record declines in the number of families, households, and children living below the poverty level, according to the 2000 U.S. Census.[37]

According to statistics released by the U.S. Census Bureau, the U.S. poverty rate in 2018 was 13.9%. Fast forward to 2020, when the poverty level sat at an astounding 9.1% due to government assistance in the form of stimulus checks, enhanced unemployment insurance payments and eligibility, supplemental nutrition assistance program (SNAP) payments, and refundable child tax credits, which was necessary to help stabilize the economy during the COVID-19 pandemic. It is estimated that governments at both the state and federal levels contributed more than $1 trillion in benefits to low-income Americans–more than four times what the governments paid out in 2018. These stimulus payments moved more than 11 million people out of poverty (with an overall poverty rate of 12.8% in 2021), according to the Census

Bureau. However, with child tax credits ending at the end of 2021, more than 3.7 million children slipped back into poverty in early 2022.[38]

The Census Bureau relies on predetermined threshold income figures, based on family size and composition, adjusted annually for inflation, to determine the nation's poverty level. Families whose income falls below the threshold level are considered poor. For example, in 2022, a family of four was considered poor if their annual income fell below $27,750.[39] When workers earn less than $15 per hour, it is often difficult, if not impossible, for them to meet their families' needs.[40] Moreover, increasing numbers of families face the challenge of finding suitable child care arrangements.

This certainly was the case at the height of the COVID-19 pandemic. As companies sent employees home to work, and many schools shut down for lengthy periods of time with children trying to learn remotely, people were faced with working from home while taking care of children and other family members who were also at home. This situation was particularly difficult for workers who had no other options for child care while they struggled to keep working remotely. In a recent survey of working parents, nearly 20% of those surveyed had to leave work or reduce their hours solely due to the lack of available child care. It is estimated that more than 2 million women left the U.S. labor force during the pandemic to care for children at home learning remotely. In 2022, many of these women went back into the job market as the pandemic eased, schools reopened, and high inflation persisted.[41]

Socioeconomic diversity suggests that managers need to be sensitive and responsive to the needs and concerns of workers who may be less fortunate than themselves in terms of income and financial resources, child care and older adult care options, housing opportunities, and the existence of sources of social and family support. Moreover—and equally important—managers should try to give such persons opportunities to learn, advance, and make meaningful contributions to their organizations while improving their economic well-being.

Sexual Orientation

According to a recent Gallup report, an estimated 7.1% of Americans self-identified as lesbian, gay, bisexual, transgender, or queer (LGBTQ) in 2021, which is two times the percentage in 2012 when Gallup first measured it.[42] In 2015, the Equal Employment Opportunity Commission pronounced that workplace discrimination on the grounds of sexual orientation is illegal, according to federal law. In that same year, the U.S. Supreme Court declared same-sex marriage legal in all 50 states.[43] More and more companies are recognizing the inclusion of LGBTQ employees, affirming their rights to fair and equal treatment and providing benefits to their partners and/or spouses. In the Corporate Equality Index (CEI) 2022, an annual report published by the Human Rights Campaign Foundation, 842 U.S. employers earned a 100% rating and the designation of being a "best place to work for LGBTQ equality." (Two decades ago, the first CEI index recognized only 13 top-rated companies.) The index's rating criteria focus on four key components: (1) non-discrimination policies across business entities, (2) equitable benefits for LGBTQ workers and their families, (3) an inclusive organizational culture; and (4) a commitment to corporate social responsibility. Some of the companies named as best places to work include Apple, Amazon, AT&T, CVS Health, General Mills, Kroger, Sephora, Walmart, and Macy's.[44]

Amazon employees raise awareness about diversity and equality at San Francisco's Pride Parade. Corporate support can go a long way toward making sure the workplace environment is safe and respectful for everyone.
Sundry Photography/Alamy Stock Photo

Other Kinds of Diversity

Other kinds of diversity are important in organizations, are critical for managers to deal with effectively, and are potential sources of unfair treatment. For example, organizations and teams need members with diverse backgrounds and experiences. This is clearly illustrated by the prevalence of cross-functional teams in organizations whose members might come from various departments such as marketing, production, finance, and sales (teams are covered in depth in Chapter 15). A team responsible for developing and introducing a new product, for example, often needs the expertise of employees not only from research and design and engineering but also from marketing, sales, production, and finance.

Other types of diversity can affect how employees are treated in the workplace. For example, employees differ from each other in physical appearance, and it has no bearing on their job performance unless they have jobs in which physical appearance plays a role, such as modeling. Yet sometimes these physical sources of diversity affect advancement rates and salaries. For example, according to a recent survey, when 500 hiring professionals were shown a picture of a larger-bodied woman, only 15.6% of them said they would hire her. In another study, biased workers viewed larger-bodied people as less competent.[45] Clearly, managers need to ensure that all employees are treated fairly, regardless of their physical appearance.

Managers and the Effective Management of Diversity

LO5-2 Explain the central role that managers play in the effective management of diversity.

The increasing diversity of the environment—which, in turn, increases the diversity of an organization's workforce—increases the challenges managers face in effectively managing diversity. Each of the kinds of diversity just discussed presents a particular set of issues managers need to appreciate before they can respond to them effectively. Understanding these issues is not always a simple matter, as many informed managers have discovered. Research on how different groups are currently treated and the unconscious biases that might adversely affect them is vital because it helps managers become aware of the many subtle ways in which diverse employee groups can come to be treated unfairly over time. Managers can take many more steps to become sensitive to the ongoing effects of diversity in their organizations, take advantage of all the contributions diverse employees can make, and prevent employees from being unfairly treated.

Critical Managerial Roles

In each of their managerial roles (see Chapter 1), managers can either promote the effective management of diversity or derail such efforts; thus, they are critical to this process. For example, in their interpersonal roles, managers can convey that the effective management of diversity is a valued goal and objective (figurehead role), can serve as a role model and institute policies and procedures to ensure that all organizational members are treated fairly (leader role), and can enable diverse individuals and groups to coordinate their efforts and cooperate with each other both inside the organization and at the organization's boundaries (liaison role). Table 5.2 summarizes ways in which managers can ensure that diversity is effectively managed as they perform their different roles. For an example, read the "Manager as a Person" feature and see if you can identify the roles filled by Stryker's CEO, Kevin Lobo.

Given the formal authority that managers have in organizations, they typically have more influence than rank-and-file employees. When managers commit to supporting diversity, as is the case within the National Football League as discussed in "A Manager's Challenge," their authority and positions of power and status influence other members of an organization to make a similar commitment. Research on social influence supports such a link: People are likely to be influenced and persuaded by others who have high status.[46]

MANAGER AS A PERSON

Stryker CEO Promotes Diversity

Stryker is a global medical technology company based in Kalamazoo, Michigan. Its businesses are medical/surgical equipment (including surgical power tools), orthopedics (for example, knee and hip implants), and neurotechnology (such as products for treating strokes). Its stated mission is to work with its customers—hospitals

Stryker CEO Kevin Lobo's commitment to diversity is reflected in various company policies and practices, including measurable goals for managers related to diversity and inclusion and flexible work arrangements to enable family caregiving.
Mark Bugnaski/AP Images

and doctors–to "make healthcare better."[47] Such a high-impact organization needs talent to provide the necessary innovation and quality.

Stryker's Chair and CEO, Kevin Lobo, sees diversity and inclusion as a part of the strategy for carrying out the company's mission. His attitude is that the company should reflect the diversity of its customers and patients for the simple reasons that this "is the right way to treat people" and "leads to better business results." So far, the company is moving in that direction, with 35% of its workforce being women, 26% being a group inclusive of multiple races and genders, and 2% being people with disabilities.[48]

A highly visible way in which Lobo has demonstrated his attitude toward diversity has been in doubling the number of women on Stryker's board of directors from two when he was appointed to four today. In fact, to appoint one of the female members when all positions were filled, he expanded the size of the board from 9 to 10 members. Lobo directly speaks of the value of hiring for diversity when he says, "If you hire from the same area over and over, you are not getting the best talent." Lobo also serves as a role model by involving himself with employee resource groups that promote inclusiveness and encourages his executives to do the same.[49]

Lobo's commitment to diversity shows up in various organizational policies and practices. The company's website describes diversity and inclusion as "a business imperative that aligns with our mission and values." Top managers have measurable goals for diversity and inclusion, and progress toward these goals counts in performance assessments. Stryker's employment policies include flexible work arrangements, such as part-time or remote work, in order to enable family caregiving, and these are applied equally across genders. The company also invites employees to form and participate in employee resource groups to promote inclusion. Examples of such groups are Stryker's African Ancestry Network, Stryker's Veterans Association, and Stryker's Allies for Equality, which supports LGBTQ employees.[50]

Table 5.2
Managerial Roles and the Effective Management of Diversity

Type of Role	Specific Role	Example
Interpersonal	Figurehead	Conveys that the effective management of diversity is a valued goal and objective.
	Leader	Serves as a role model and institutes policies and procedures to ensure that all members are treated fairly.
	Liaison	Enables diverse individuals to coordinate their efforts and cooperate with one another.
Informational	Monitor	Evaluates the extent to which all employees are treated fairly.
	Disseminator	Informs employees about diversity policies and initiatives and the refusal to tolerate discrimination.
	Spokesperson	Supports diversity initiatives in the wider community and speaks to diverse groups to interest them in career opportunities.
Decisional	Entrepreneur	Commits resources to develop new ways to effectively manage diversity and eliminate biases and discrimination.
	Disturbance handler	Takes quick action to correct inequalities and curtail discriminatory behavior.
	Resource allocator	Allocates resources to support and encourage the effective management of a diverse workforce.
	Negotiator	Works with organizations (for example, suppliers) and groups (for example, labor unions) to support and encourage the effective management of diversity.

When managers commit to diversity, their commitment legitimizes the diversity management efforts of others.[51] In addition, resources are devoted to such efforts, and all members of an organization believe that their diversity-related efforts are supported and valued. Consistent with this reasoning, top management commitment and rewards for the support of diversity are often cited as critical ingredients in the success of diversity management initiatives.[52] Additionally, seeing managers express confidence in the abilities and talents of diverse employees causes other organizational members to be similarly confident and helps reduce any prejudice they have as a result of ignorance or stereotypes.[53]

Two other important factors emphasize why managers are so central to the effective management of diversity. The first factor is that women, African Americans, Hispanics, and other underrepresented groups often start out at a slight disadvantage due to how they are perceived by others in organizations, particularly in work settings where they are a numerical minority. As Virginia Valian, a psychologist at Hunter College who studies gender, indicates, "In most organizations women begin at a slight disadvantage. A woman does not walk into the room with the same status as an equivalent man, because she is less likely than a man to be viewed as a serious professional."[54]

The second factor is that research suggests that slight differences in treatment can accumulate and result in major disparities over time. Even small differences–such as a small favorable bias toward men for promotions–can lead to major differences in the number of male and female managers over time. Thus, while women and other minorities are sometimes advised not to complain when they have been treated unfairly, research conducted by Valian and others suggests that differences in how people are treated based on irrelevant distinctions such as race, gender, or ethnicity can turn into major disparities over time in important outcomes such as promotions if these situations are ignored.[55] Once again, managers have the obligation, from both an ethical and a business perspective, to prevent any disparities in treatment and outcomes due to irrelevant distinctions such as race or ethnicity.

The Ethical Imperative to Manage Diversity Effectively

LO5-3 Explain why the effective management of diversity is both an ethical and a business imperative.

Effectively managing diversity not only makes good business sense (which is discussed in the next section) but also is an ethical imperative in U.S. society. Two moral principles guide managers in their efforts to meet this imperative: distributive justice and procedural justice.

distributive justice A moral principle calling for fair distribution of pay, promotions, and other organizational resources based on meaningful contributions that individuals have made and not personal characteristics over which they have no control.

DISTRIBUTIVE JUSTICE The principle of **distributive justice** dictates fair distribution of pay, promotions, job titles, interesting job assignments, office space, and other organizational resources among members of an organization. These outcomes should be distributed according to the meaningful contributions that individuals have made to the organization (such as time, effort, education, skills, abilities, and performance levels) and not irrelevant personal characteristics over which individuals have no control (such as gender, race, or age).[56] Managers have an obligation to ensure that distributive justice exists in their organizations. This does not mean that all members of an organization receive identical or similar outcomes; rather, it means that members who receive more favorable outcomes than others have made substantially higher or more significant contributions to the organization.

Is distributive justice common in organizations in corporate America? Probably the best way to answer this question is to say things are getting better. Fifty years ago, overt discrimination against a group that is inclusive of multiple races and genders was common; today organizations are inching closer toward the ideal of distributive justice. Statistics comparing the treatment of a group that is inclusive of multiple races and genders with the treatment of other employees suggest that most managers need to take a proactive approach to achieve distributive justice in their organizations.[57] For example, across occupations, women consistently earn less than men (see Table 5.3), according to data collected by the U.S. Bureau of Labor Statistics.[58] Even in occupations dominated by women, such as sales and office occupations, men tend to earn more than women.

In many countries, managers have not only an ethical obligation to strive to achieve distributive justice in their organizations but also a legal obligation to treat all employees fairly. They risk

Table 5.3

Median Weekly Earnings for Full-Time Workers by Sex and Occupation in 2023

Occupation	Men	Women	Women's Earnings as a Percentage of Men's
Management, professional, and related	$1,726	$1,284	74%
Service	767	643	84
Sales and office	1,019	810	74
Natural resources, construction, and maintenance	979	700	71
Production, transportation, and material moving	891	694	78

Source: Bureau of Labor Statistics, "Household Data Annual Averages: Table 39. Median Weekly Earnings of Full-Time Wage and Salary Workers by Detailed Occupation and Sex," www.bls.gov, January 25, 2023.

being sued by employees who believe they are not being fairly treated. That is precisely what more than 30 female Ford workers did when they experienced racial bias and sexual discrimination.[59]

procedural justice A moral principle calling for the use of fair procedures to determine how to distribute outcomes to organizational members.

PROCEDURAL JUSTICE The principle of **procedural justice** requires that managers use fair procedures to determine how to distribute outcomes to organizational members.[60] This principle applies to typical procedures such as appraising employees' performance, deciding who should receive a raise or a promotion, and deciding whom to lay off when an organization is forced to downsize. Procedural justice exists, for example, when managers (1) carefully appraise an employee's performance; (2) take into account any environmental obstacles to high performance beyond the employee's control, such as lack of supplies, machine breakdowns, or dwindling customer demand for a product; and (3) ignore irrelevant personal characteristics such as the employee's age or ethnicity. Like distributive justice, procedural justice is necessary not only to ensure ethical conduct but also to avoid costly lawsuits.

Effectively Managing Diversity Makes Good Business Sense

Diverse organizational members can be a source of competitive advantage, helping an organization provide customers with better goods and services.[61] The variety of points of view and approaches to problems and opportunities that diverse employees provide can improve managerial decision making. Suppose a frozen food company is trying to come up with creative ideas for new frozen meals that will appeal to health-conscious, time-conscious customers tired of the same old frozen food options. Which group do you think is likely to come up with the most creative ideas: a group of white women with marketing degrees from Yale University who grew up in upper-middle-class families in the Northeast, or a group that is inclusive of multiple races and genders who grew up in families with varying income levels in different parts of the country and attended a variety of geographically dispersed business schools? Most people would agree that the diverse group is likely to have a wider range of creative ideas. Although this example is simplistic, it underscores one way in which diversity can lead to a competitive advantage.

Just as the workforce is becoming increasingly diverse, so are the customers who buy an organization's goods or services. In an attempt to suit local customers' needs and tastes, organizations like IKEA often vary the selection of products available in stores in different cities and regions.[62]

Employees with diverse backgrounds are likely to be attuned to what goods and services diverse segments of the market want and do not want. Automakers, for example, are increasingly assigning women to their design teams to ensure that the needs and desires of female customers are taken into account in new car design.

Another way that effective management of diversity can improve profitability is by increasing retention of valued employees, which decreases the costs of hiring replacements for those who quit and ensures that all employees are highly motivated. In terms of retention, given the current legal environment, more and more organizations are attuned to the need to emphasize the importance of diversity in hiring. Once hired, if diverse employees think they are being unfairly treated, however, they will be likely to seek opportunities elsewhere. Thus, recruiting a diverse workforce has to be followed with ongoing effective management of diversity to retain valued organizational members.

If a diverse workforce is not effectively managed and turnover rates are higher for members of groups who are not treated fairly, profitability will suffer on several counts. Not only are the future contributions of employees with diverse backgrounds lost when they quit, but the organization also has to bear the costs of hiring replacement workers, which may be a challenge if the organization gains a reputation that management does not consider minorities and other members of underrepresented groups important members of the organization.[63] According to a recent report, it costs employers an average of two times the amount of that employee's salary to hire a replacement if the employee leaves the organization. In addition, the company experiences substantial indirect costs associated with the new hire, which can include knowledge lost when an experienced worker leaves, time spent finding a replacement, and time the new employee needs to get up to speed in the new job.[64]

Effectively managing diversity makes good business sense for another reason. More and more, managers and organizations concerned about diversity are insisting that their suppliers also support diversity.[65]

Finally, from both business and ethical perspectives, effective management of diversity is necessary to avoid costly lawsuits. In 2000, the Coca-Cola Company settled a class-action suit brought by African American employees at a cost of $192 million. The damage such lawsuits cause goes beyond the monetary awards to the injured parties; it can tarnish a company's image. One positive outcome of Coca-Cola's 2000 settlement was the company's recognition of the need to commit additional resources to diversity management initiatives. More than 20 years later, the company has redoubled its efforts to ensure a diverse workforce as its progress has been thwarted by a "sense of complacency." According to company officials, only 8% of its executives are Black, and representation of Black employees among U.S. salaried staff is now at approximately 15%–5 percentage points lower than when the discrimination lawsuit was filed back in 2000. The company recently announced a 10-year internal and external recruiting program for people of color with an emphasis on Black executives. In addition, the company has added training for company leaders on recognizing bias; a new HR position focusing on diversity in executive recruitment; and a commitment to recruit talent not only for current job openings but also for future career paths at the company.[66]

By now it should be clear that effectively managing diversity is a necessity on both ethical and business grounds. This brings us to the question of why diversity presents managers and all of us with so many challenges–a question we address in the next section, on perception.

Perception

LO5-4 Discuss how perception and the use of schemas can result in unfair treatment.

Most people tend to think that the decisions managers make in organizations and the actions they take are the result of objective determination of the issues involved and the surrounding situation. However, each manager's interpretation of a situation or even of another person is precisely that–an interpretation. Nowhere are the effects of perception more likely to lead to different interpretations than in the area of diversity. This is because each person's interpretation of a situation, and subsequent response to it, is affected by their own age, race, gender, religion, socioeconomic status, capabilities, and sexual orientation. For example, different managers may see the same 21-year-old Black male, gay, gifted, and talented employee in different ways: One may see a creative maverick with a great future in the organization, while another may see a potential troublemaker who needs to be watched closely.

perception The process through which people select, organize, and interpret what they see, hear, touch, smell, and taste to give meaning and order to the world around them.

Perception is the process through which people select, organize, and interpret sensory input–what they see, hear, touch, smell, and taste–to give meaning and order to the world around them.[67] All decisions and actions of managers are based on their subjective perceptions. When these perceptions are relatively accurate–close to the true nature of what is actually being perceived–good decisions are likely to be made and appropriate actions taken. Managers of fast-food restaurant chains such as McDonald's, Pizza Hut, and Wendy's accurately perceived that their customers were becoming more health-conscious in the 1980s and 1990s and added salad bars and low-fat items to their menus. Managers at Kentucky Fried Chicken, Jack-in-the-Box, and Burger King took much longer to perceive this change in what customers wanted.

One reason that McDonald's is so successful is that its managers go to great lengths to make sure their perceptions of what customers want are accurate. McDonald's has more than 38,000 restaurants in more than 100 countries that generate billions of dollars in revenue. Key to McDonald's success in these diverse markets are managers' efforts to perceive accurately a country's culture and taste in food and to act on these perceptions. For example, McDonald's serves corn pies in Thailand and seafood burgers in Hong Kong.[68]

When managers' perceptions are relatively inaccurate, managers are likely to make bad decisions and take inappropriate actions that hurt organizational effectiveness. Bad decisions concerning diversity for reasons of age, ethnicity, or sexual orientation include (1) not hiring qualified people, (2) failing to promote top-performing employees, who subsequently may take their skills to competing organizations, and (3) promoting poorly performing managers because they have the same "diversity profile" as the manager or managers making the decision.

Factors That Influence Managerial Perception

Several managers' perceptions of the same person, event, or situation are likely to differ because managers differ in personality, values, attitudes, and moods (see Chapter 3). Each of these factors can influence how someone perceives a person or situation. An older middle manager who is high on openness to experience is likely to perceive the recruitment of able young managers as a positive learning opportunity; a similar middle manager who is low on openness to experience may perceive able younger employees as a threat. A manager who has high levels of job satisfaction and organizational commitment may perceive a job transfer to another department or geographic location that has very different employees (age, ethnicity, and so on) as an opportunity to learn and develop new skills. A dissatisfied, uncommitted manager may perceive the same transfer as a demotion.

schema An abstract knowledge structure that is stored in memory and makes possible the interpretation and organization of information about a person, an event, or a situation.

Managers' and all organizational members' perceptions of one another also are affected by their past experiences with and acquired knowledge about people, events, and situations–information that is organized into preexisting schemas. **Schemas** are abstract knowledge structures stored in memory that allow people to organize and interpret information about a person, an event, or a situation.[69] Once a person develops a schema for a kind of person or event, any newly encountered person or situation that is related to the schema activates it, and information is processed in ways consistent with the information stored in the schema. Thus, people tend to perceive others by using the expectations or preconceived notions contained in their schemas.[70] Once again, these expectations are derived from past experience and knowledge.

People tend to pay attention to information that is consistent with their schemas and to ignore or discount inconsistent information. Thus, schemas tend to be reinforced and strengthened over time because the information attended to is seen as confirming the schemas. This also results in schemas being resistant to change.[71] This does not mean schemas never change; if that were the case, people could never adapt to changing conditions and learn from their mistakes. Rather, it suggests that schemas are slow to change and that for people to change their schemas, they need to encounter a considerable amount of contradictory information.

Schemas that accurately depict the true nature of a person or situation are functional because they help people make sense of the world around them. People typically confront so much information that it is not possible to make sense of it without relying on schemas. Schemas are dysfunctional when they are inaccurate because they cause managers and all members of an organization to perceive people and situations inaccurately and assume certain things that are not necessarily true.

gender schemas Preconceived beliefs or ideas about the nature of men and women and their traits, attitudes, behaviors, and preferences.

Psychologist Virginia Valian refers to inaccurate preconceived notions of men and women as gender schemas. **Gender schemas** are a person's preconceived notions about the nature of men and women and their traits, attitudes, behaviors, and preferences.[72] Research suggests that among white middle-class Americans, the following gender schemas are prevalent: Men are action-oriented, assertive, independent, and task-focused; women are expressive, nurturing, and oriented toward and caring of other people.[73] Any schemas such as these–which assume that a single visible characteristic such as gender causes a person to possess specific traits and tendencies–are bound to be inaccurate. For example, not all women are alike and not all men are alike, and many women are more independent and task-focused than men. Gender schemas can be learned in childhood and are reinforced in a number of ways in society. For instance, while young girls may be encouraged by their parents to play with toy trucks and tools (stereotypically masculine toys), boys generally are not encouraged to, and sometimes are actively discouraged from, playing with dolls (stereotypically feminine toys).[74] As children grow up, they may learn that occupations dominated by men have higher status than occupations dominated by women.

Perception as a Determinant of Unfair Treatment

Even though most people would agree that distributive justice and procedural justice are desirable goals, diverse organizational members are sometimes treated unfairly, as previous examples illustrate. Why is this problem occurring? One important overarching reason is inaccurate perceptions. To the extent that managers and other members of an organization rely on inaccurate information, such as gender schemas, to guide their perceptions of each other, unfair treatment is likely to occur.

stereotype Simplistic and often inaccurate belief about the typical characteristics of particular groups of people.

Gender schemas are a kind of **stereotype**, which is composed of simplistic and often inaccurate beliefs about the typical characteristics of particular groups of people. Stereotypes are usually based on a visible characteristic such as a person's age, gender, or race.[75] Managers who allow stereotypes to influence their perceptions assume erroneously that a person possesses a whole host of characteristics simply because the person happens to be an Asian woman, a white man, or a lesbian, for example. African American men are often stereotyped as good athletes, Hispanic women as subservient.[76] Obviously, there is no reason to assume that every African American man is a good athlete or that every Hispanic woman is subservient. Stereotypes, however, lead people to make such erroneous assumptions. A manager who accepts stereotypes might, for example, decide not to promote a highly capable Hispanic woman into a management position because the manager thinks she will not be assertive enough to supervise others. Similar stereotypes related to age can also result in unfair treatment, as detailed in the "Ethics in Action" feature.

ETHICS IN ACTION

Are Older Tech Workers the Victims of Stereotypes?

What kind of person comes to mind when you think of an information technology worker at an innovative high-tech company? It would need to be someone intelligent and creative, perhaps with a lot of drive and energy to put in long hours on big projects. Would such a person be 50 years old, or 60?

According to IT professionals in the upper age bracket, companies are saying older workers do not fit the schema for a desirable tech worker. Hiring patterns suggest they have a point. Workers aged 22 to 44 are overrepresented in the IT industry: They are 49% of the total workforce but hold 61% of IT jobs. Workers 45 and older are underrepresented, at 44% of the workforce but just 38% of IT jobs. Analysis of hiring patterns in the tech industry finds behavior supporting this outcome: Hiring decisions favor younger workers.[77] And anecdotally, tech workers in their forties and older tell of discomfort in groups of young workers and of going to great lengths, from fashion makeovers to plastic surgery, to appear a decade or two younger than they are.[78]

Companies that value diversity recognize a team of well-trained tech workers of different ages can provide a competitive edge.
Kostiantyn Voitenko/Shutterstock

The ethical question is whether these patterns result from applying unfair stereotypes or from making reasonable business decisions. Older workers expect to earn more than someone with a year or two of experience. And the tech sector values knowledge of the latest technology, such as artificial intelligence, above years of experience or networks of contacts. Some employees focus on applying existing skills so that as they add experience and as technology advances, they actually lessen their value to employers. At the same time, companies find they can fill jobs economically by tapping highly educated recent graduates overseas.[79]

Even if these points are true, they rely on stereotypes about what older workers know and can contribute. Companies that value diversity are finding ways to meet their need for talent with more experienced workers. Some provide training to keep employees' skills aligned with talent needs, and many older employees are eager for the chance to keep up. These companies tend to appreciate that although an older employee may need to learn new technical skills, this person has spent years developing problem-solving skills. A team of well-trained tech workers of different ages can deliver a competitive edge.[80]

A recent study suggests that stereotypes might hamper the progress of mothers in their organizations when they are seeking to advance in positions that are traditionally held by men, especially as the global pandemic recedes. According to the study, based on gender stereotypes, people tend to view mothers as less competent in terms of skills and capabilities related to advancing in such positions.[81]

People with disabilities might also be unfairly treated due to stereotypes.[82] Although the ADA requires (as mentioned previously) that organizations provide employees who have a disability with accommodations, employment rates of people with disabilities tend to be low. That is, around 19% of people with disabilities are employed compared to 64% of people with disabilities.[83]

Inaccurate perceptions leading to unfair treatment of diverse members of an organization also can be due to biases. **Biases** are systematic tendencies to use information about others in ways that result in inaccurate perceptions. Because of the way biases operate, people often are unaware that their perceptions of others are inaccurate.

bias The systematic tendency to use information about others in ways that result in inaccurate perceptions.

Implicit bias is defined as the attitudes or stereotypes that affect our understanding, actions, and decisions in an unconscious manner. These tendencies are activated involuntarily and without awareness. Research into this type of bias suggests that it is pervasive in many areas of daily life, such as employment, education, and criminal justice, among others.[84] The concept of implicit bias is important to managers because it can lead to unfair treatment of diverse employees simply because they are different from the managers who are perceiving them, evaluating them, and making decisions that affect their future in the organization.[85] Some organizations are implementing hiring processes aimed at combating implicit bias in their hiring practices. For example, some companies use a cross-functional interview team as part of the hiring process to reduce biases. The team meets after the interview to discuss the candidate so that any team members' biases can also be explored and vetted.[86]

Managers (particularly top managers) are likely to be white men. Although these managers may endorse the principles of distributive and procedural justice, they may unintentionally fall into the trap of perceiving other white men more positively than they perceive women and others in underrepresented groups. Being aware of this bias as well as using objective information about employees' capabilities and performance as much as possible in decision making about job assignments, pay raises, promotions, and other outcomes can help managers avoid implicit bias.

Social status–a person's real or perceived position in a society or an organization–can also be a source of implicit bias. This is the tendency to perceive individuals with high social status more positively than we perceive those with low social status. A high-status person may be perceived as smarter and more believable, capable, knowledgeable, and responsible than a low-status person, even in the absence of objective information about either person.

Imagine being introduced to two people at a company holiday party. Both are white men in their late thirties, and you learn that one is a member of the company's top management team and the other is a supervisor in the mailroom. From this information alone, you might assume that the top manager is smarter, more capable, more responsible, and even more interesting than the mailroom supervisor. Because women and others in underrepresented groups have traditionally had lower social status than white men, the social status effect may lead some people to perceive women and others less positively than they perceive white men.

Have you ever stood out in a crowd? Maybe you were the only man in a group of women, or maybe you were dressed formally for a social gathering but everyone else was in jeans. Salience (that is, conspicuousness) is another source of implicit bias. The *salience effect* is the tendency to focus attention on those who are conspicuously different from others in a group; the salience effect results in extra attention being focused on a person who stands out from the group mold. When people are salient, they often feel as though all eyes are watching them, and this perception is not far from the mark. Salient persons are more often the object of attention than are other members of a work group, for example. A manager who has six white employees and one Hispanic employee reporting to them may inadvertently pay more attention to the Hispanic employee in group meetings because of the salience effect. Individuals who are salient are often perceived to be primarily responsible for outcomes and operations and are evaluated more extremely in either a positive or a negative direction.[87] Thus, when the Hispanic employee does a good job on a project, they receive excessive praise, and when they miss a deadline, they are excessively chastised. Part of being a good manager includes being aware of these sorts of tendencies and actively working against them.

Overt Discrimination

overt discrimination Knowingly and willingly denying diverse individuals access to opportunities and outcomes in an organization.

Inaccurate schemas and perceptual biases can lead well-meaning managers and organizational members to unintentionally discriminate against others. On the other hand, **overt discrimination**, or knowingly and willingly denying diverse individuals access to opportunities and outcomes in an organization, is intentional and deliberate. Overt discrimination is both unethical and illegal. Unfortunately, just as some managers steal from their organizations, others engage in overt discrimination.

Overt discrimination is a clear violation of the principles of distributive and procedural justice. Moreover, when managers are charged with overt discrimination, costly lawsuits can ensue. Organizations including, Walmart, Tesla, Facebook, and others have settled or face pending lawsuits alleging overt workplace discrimination.[88] Whereas in the past, lawsuits due to overt workplace discrimination focused on unfair treatment of women and minority group members, given the aging of the U.S. workforce, increasing numbers of discrimination cases are being brought by older workers who believe they were unfairly dismissed from their jobs due to their age.[89]

Despite all the advances that have been made, allegations of overt discrimination based on gender, race, age, and other forms of diversity continue to occur in the United States. For example, a married couple, both employees of the Michigan correctional system, were awarded more than $11 million recently on their claims of racial discrimination, hostile work environment, and retaliation. In court filings, the woman said she was subjected to a "culture of racism" while working for the state's department of corrections, which included racial slurs and coworkers showing her racist videos. She also said attempts to file a meaningful complaint about the situation were thwarted by the harassment counselor for the department, whom filings described as very friendly with the staff about whom she filed the complaints. Her husband allegedly was forced into retirement from his deputy warden position with the state when phony disciplinary charges were brought against him.[90]

Overt discrimination continues to be a problem in other countries as well. For example, although Japan passed its first Equal Employment Opportunity Law in 1985 and Japanese women are increasingly working in jobs once dominated by men, professional Japanese women have continued to find it difficult to advance in their careers and assume managerial positions. Women make up almost half of the Japanese workforce, but only around 11% of managerial positions in business and government are occupied by women.[91]

Age-related discrimination complaints have been at record highs over the last decade.[92] Although this might be due to the fact that there were more older employees in the workforce than in previous years, some suggest that the rise in age discrimination allegations could also be due to the fact that older workers tend to be paid more and have better benefits. For example, a jury in Los Angeles awarded more than $15 million to an *LA Times* sports columnist for discrimination because of his age and health issues. In 2013, T.J. Simers was demoted after 22 years with the paper from columnist to writer when he developed health problems.[93] In the lawsuit, Simers claimed the *Times* cut back his column and tried to pressure him to leave after he suffered a ministroke while covering baseball spring training. In another recent example, four former salaried employees filed a lawsuit against Ford Motor Company, alleging the company deprived them of retirement benefits during a global restructuring they claim was based on their age and how close they were to obtaining full pensions from the company.[94]

How to Manage Diversity Effectively

Various kinds of barriers arise to managing diversity effectively in organizations. Some barriers originate in the person doing the perceiving; others are based on the information and schemas that have built up over time concerning the person being perceived. To overcome these barriers and effectively manage diversity, managers (and other organizational members) must possess or develop certain attitudes and values as well as the skills needed to change other people's attitudes and values.

Steps in Managing Diversity Effectively

LO5-5 List the steps managers can take to manage diversity effectively.

Managers can take a number of steps to change attitudes and values and promote the effective management of diversity. Here we describe these steps (listed in Table 5.4), some of which we have referred to previously.

SECURE TOP MANAGEMENT COMMITMENT As mentioned earlier in the chapter, top management's commitment to diversity is crucial for the success of any diversity-related initiatives. Top managers need to develop the correct ethical values and performance- or business-oriented attitudes that allow them to make appropriate use of their human resources.

STRIVE TO INCREASE THE ACCURACY OF PERCEPTIONS One aspect of developing the appropriate values and attitudes is to take steps to increase the accuracy of perceptions. Managers should consciously attempt to be open to other points of view and perspectives, seek them out, and encourage their employees to do the same.[95] Organizational members who are open to other perspectives put their own beliefs and knowledge to an important reality test and will be more inclined to modify them when necessary. Managers should not be afraid to change their views about a person, an issue, or an event; moreover, they should encourage their employees to be open to changing their views in the light of disconfirming evidence. Additionally, managers and all other members of an organization should strive to avoid making snap

Table 5.4
Promoting the Effective Management of Diversity

- Secure top management commitment.
- Increase the accuracy of perceptions.
- Increase diversity awareness.
- Increase diversity skills.
- Encourage flexibility.
- Pay close attention to how employees are evaluated.
- Consider the numbers.
- Empower employees to challenge discriminatory behaviors, actions, and remarks.
- Reward employees for effectively managing diversity.
- Provide training, utilizing a multi-pronged, ongoing approach.
- Encourage mentoring of employees with diverse backgrounds.

judgments about people; rather, judgments should be made only when sufficient and relevant information has been gathered.[96]

INCREASE DIVERSITY AWARENESS It is natural for managers and other members of an organization to view other people from their own perspective because their own feelings, thoughts, attitudes, and experiences guide their perceptions and interactions. The ability to appreciate diversity, however, requires that people become aware of other perspectives and the various attitudes and experiences of others. Many diversity awareness programs in organizations strive to increase managers' and workers' awareness of (1) their own attitudes, biases, and stereotypes and (2) the differing perspectives of diverse managers, employees, coworkers, and customers. Diversity awareness programs often have these goals:[97]

- Providing organizational members with accurate information about diversity
- Uncovering personal biases and stereotypes
- Assessing personal beliefs, attitudes, and values and learning about other points of view
- Overturning inaccurate stereotypes and beliefs about different groups
- Developing an atmosphere in which people feel free to share their differing perspectives and points of view–even going so far as to mentally walk in other people's shoes
- Improving understanding of others who are different from oneself

Sometimes simply taking the time to interact with someone who is different in some way can increase awareness. Often when employees and managers are at social functions or just having lunch with a coworker, they interact with the people with whom they feel most comfortable. If all members of an organization make an effort to interact with people they ordinarily would not, mutual understanding is likely to be enhanced.

In large organizations, top managers are often far removed from entry-level employees–they may lack an understanding and appreciation for what these employees do day in and day out, the challenges and obstacles they face, and the steps that can be taken to improve effectiveness. Recognizing this fact, some managers have taken concrete steps to improve their understanding of the experiences, attitudes, and perspectives of frontline employees.

INCREASE DIVERSITY SKILLS Efforts to increase diversity skills focus on improving how managers and their employees interact with each other and improving their ability to work with different kinds of people.[98] An important issue here is being able to communicate with diverse employees. Diverse organizational members may have different communication styles, may differ in their language fluency, may use words differently, may differ in the nonverbal signals they send through facial expressions and body language, and may differ in how they perceive and interpret information. Managers and their employees must learn to communicate effectively with one another if an organization is to take advantage of the skills and abilities of its entire workforce. Educating organizational members about differences in ways of communicating is often a good starting point.

Diversity education can help managers and employees gain a better understanding of how people may interpret certain kinds of comments. Diversity education also can help employees learn how to resolve misunderstandings. Organizational members should feel comfortable enough to solve communication difficulties and misunderstandings as they occur rather than letting problems grow and fester without acknowledgment.

ENCOURAGE FLEXIBILITY Managers and their employees must learn how to be open to different approaches and ways of doing things. This does not mean organizational members have to suppress their personal styles. Rather, it means they must be open to, and not feel threatened by, different approaches and perspectives and must have the patience and flexibility to understand and appreciate diverse perspectives.[99]

To the extent feasible, managers should also be flexible enough to incorporate the differing needs of diverse employees. Earlier we mentioned that religious diversity suggests that people of certain religions might need time off for holidays that are traditionally workdays in the United States; managers need to anticipate and respond to such needs with flexibility (perhaps letting people skip the lunch hour so they can leave work early). Moreover, flexible work hours, the option to work from home, and cafeteria-style benefit plans (see Chapter 12) are just a few of the many ways in which managers can respond to the differing needs of diverse employees while enabling those employees to be effective contributors to an organization.

PAY CLOSE ATTENTION TO HOW ORGANIZATIONAL MEMBERS ARE EVALUATED Whenever feasible, it is desirable to rely on objective performance indicators (see Chapter 12) because they are less subject to bias. When objective indicators are not available or are inappropriate, managers should ensure that adequate time and attention are focused on the evaluation of employees' performance and that evaluators are held accountable for their evaluations. Vague performance standards should be avoided.[100]

CONSIDER THE NUMBERS Looking at the numbers of members of different minority groups and women in various positions, at various levels in the hierarchy, in locations that differ in their desirability, and in any other relevant categorizations in an organization can tell managers important information about potential problems and ways to rectify them.[101] If members of certain groups are underrepresented in particular kinds of jobs or units, managers need to understand why this is the case and resolve any problems they uncover. To explore examples of ideas that can surface from analyzing employment data, read the "Management Insight" feature.

MANAGEMENT INSIGHT

What Gets in the Way of Promoting Women?

Although companies have pursued equal opportunity for years, women continue to be underrepresented in management. The disparity begins at the first level of management: 87 women are promoted to first-line management for every 100 men receiving similar promotions. The pattern accelerates, and in upper management, only one-fourth of the positions are held by women. Companies have set diversity goals, conducted training in unconscious biases, and encouraged female employees to be more assertive about seeking promotions, but they continue missing out on female employees' leadership potential.[102]

Recent research suggests some reasons why. A trio of Australian economists observed that organizations with management positions to fill tend to invite candidates to put themselves forward. Women are much less likely than men with comparable experience to speak up, yet asking female employees to be assertive doesn't help much if they have been raised to value modesty or to avoid risk. Another researcher, at MIT's Sloan School of Management, investigated promotions at a large retail chain where the percentage of women declined from one level of the hierarchy to the next. She observed that performance evaluations ranked men and women differently on average: The rankings said women outscored men on performance but ranked lower than men on "potential." Promotions were highly correlated with high rankings on potential. This was a missed opportunity for the retailer, because when women and men had the same scores for potential, those women on average went on to outperform those men. In other words, promotions were based on scores that undervalued the female employees.[103]

The research findings suggest ideas for making promotion decisions that not only treat employees more equitably but also place the best candidates in management positions. Organizations that invite expressions of interest in management jobs could replace this opt-in method with an opt-out approach. They could say that everyone with a given set of experience and accomplishments will be considered, unless they ask to be excluded. Research on decision making has shown that people are less likely to pass up an opportunity if they have to opt out. For the problem of undervaluing women's potential, organizations should improve these assessments. Often "potential" is a vague concept; to be a valid basis for significant decisions, it needs a precise and relevant definition. Employers can benefit from keeping data on assessment measures, promotions, and subsequent performance to look for patterns that can inform better assessments and promotions in the future.[104]

EMPOWER EMPLOYEES TO CHALLENGE DISCRIMINATORY BEHAVIORS, ACTIONS, AND REMARKS When managers or employees witness another organizational member being unfairly treated, they should be encouraged to speak up and rectify the situation. Top managers can make this happen by creating an organizational culture (see Chapter 3) that has zero tolerance for discrimination. As part of such a culture, organizational members should feel empowered to challenge discriminatory behavior, whether the behavior is directed at them or they witness it being directed at another employee.[105]

REWARD EMPLOYEES FOR EFFECTIVELY MANAGING DIVERSITY If effective management of diversity is a valued organizational objective, then employees should be rewarded for their contributions to this objective. For example, after settling a major race discrimination lawsuit, the Coca-Cola Company now ties managers' pay to their achievement of diversity goals. Examples of other companies that tie managers' compensation to diversity goals include McDonald's, General Motors, and Dentsu.[106]

PROVIDE TRAINING UTILIZING A MULTIPRONGED, ONGOING APPROACH Many managers use a multipronged approach to increase diversity awareness and skills in their organizations; they use films and printed materials supplemented by experiential exercises to uncover hidden biases and stereotypes. Sometimes simply providing a forum for people to learn about and discuss their differing attitudes, values, and experiences can be a powerful means of increasing awareness. Also useful are role-plays that enact problems resulting from lack of awareness and show the increased understanding that comes from appreciating others' viewpoints. Accurate information and training experiences can debunk stereotypes. Group exercises, role-plays, and diversity-related experiences can help organizational members develop the skills they need to work effectively with a variety of people. Many organizations hire outside consultants to provide diversity training, in addition to utilizing their own in-house diversity experts.[107]

ENCOURAGE MENTORING OF DIVERSE EMPLOYEES Unfortunately, African Americans and other underrepresented groups continue to be less likely to attain high-level positions in their organizations, and for those who do attain them, the climb up the corporate ladder typically takes longer than it does for white men. David Thomas, formerly a professor at Harvard Business School and currently the president of Morehouse College in Atlanta, has studied the careers of underrepresented groups in corporate America. One of his major conclusions is that mentoring is very important for underrepresented groups, most of whom have reached high levels in their organizations by having a solid network of mentors and contacts.[108] **Mentoring** is a process by which an experienced member of an organization (the mentor) provides advice and guidance to a less experienced member (the protégé) and helps the less experienced member learn how to advance in the organization and in their career.

mentoring A process by which an experienced member of an organization (the mentor) provides advice and guidance to a less experienced member (the protégé) and helps the less experienced member learn how to advance in the organization and in their career.

According to Thomas, effective mentoring is more than providing instruction, offering advice, helping build skills, and sharing technical expertise. Of course, these aspects of mentoring are important and necessary. However, equally important is developing a high-quality, close, and supportive relationship with the protégé. Emotional bonds between a mentor and a protégé can enable a protégé, for example, to express fears and concerns, and sometimes even reluctance to follow a mentor's advice. The mentor can help the protégé build their confidence and feel comfortable engaging in unfamiliar work behaviors.[109]

Sexual Harassment

LO5-6 Identify the two major forms of sexual harassment and how they can be eliminated.

Sexual harassment seriously damages both the people who are harassed and the reputation of the organization in which it occurs. It also can cost organizations billions. For example, in late 2017, a new social campaign called the #MeToo movement began after Hollywood entertainment mogul Harvey Weinstein was accused of sexual harassment and assault by many women in the film industry over the previous three decades.[110] Women were encouraged to tweet about their harassment experiences, and within the first 24 hours of the movement, the #MeToo hashtag was used more than 12 million times.[111] In 2020, Weinstein was convicted of rape and criminal sexual assault in New York and is currently serving a 23-year prison sentence there. Weinstein also was recently found guilty of three of seven charges in a sex crimes trial in Los Angeles (while serving the New York prison sentence).[112]

But sexual harassment is not limited to the entertainment industry. According to recent research, here are some sobering statistics:

- Most women (between 54% and 81%) report experiencing some level of sexual harassment at work.
- Despite these numbers, between 58% and 72% of female victims do not report instances of workplace sexual harassment.
- Although 75% of adults surveyed believe their companies take sexual harassment seriously, only 30% of women strongly agreed that their employers handled the harassment incidents properly. Interestingly, 56% of men surveyed believed that reported workplace sexual harassment goes unpunished.[113]

Despite victims' reluctance to report sexual harassment, the EEOC recovered nearly $300 million on behalf of victims between 2018 and 2021.[114]

Sexual harassment victims can be of any gender, and their harassers do not necessarily have to be of the opposite sex.[115] However, women are the most frequent victims of sexual harassment, particularly those in male-dominated occupations or those who occupy positions stereotypically associated with certain gender relationships, such as a female employee reporting to a male manager. Sexual harassment is not only unethical but also illegal. Managers have an ethical obligation to ensure that they, their coworkers, and their employees never engage in sexual harassment, even unintentionally.

Forms of Sexual Harassment

quid pro quo sexual harassment Asking or forcing an employee to perform sexual favors in exchange for receiving some reward or avoiding negative consequences.

hostile work environment sexual harassment Telling lewd jokes, displaying pornography, making sexually oriented remarks about someone's personal appearance, and other sex-related actions that make the work environment unpleasant.

There are two basic forms of sexual harassment: quid pro quo sexual harassment and hostile work environment sexual harassment. **Quid pro quo sexual harassment** occurs when a harasser asks or forces an employee to perform sexual favors to keep a job, receive a promotion, receive a raise, obtain some other work-related opportunity, or avoid receiving negative consequences such as demotion or dismissal.[116] This "Sleep with me, or you're fired" form of harassment is the more extreme type and leaves no doubt in anyone's mind that sexual harassment has taken place. Claims of this type of sexual harassment fall under Title VII of the Civil Rights Act.[117]

Hostile work environment sexual harassment can be more subtle. It occurs when organizational members face an intimidating, hostile, or offensive work environment because of their sex.[118] Lewd jokes, sexually oriented comments or innuendos, vulgar language, displays of pornography, displays or distribution of sexually oriented objects, and sexually oriented remarks about one's physical appearance are examples of hostile work environment sexual harassment.[119] A hostile work environment interferes with organizational members' ability to perform their jobs effectively and has been deemed illegal by the courts. Managers who engage in hostile work environment harassment or allow others to do so risk costly lawsuits for their organizations.

The courts have also recognized other forms of hostile work environment harassment in addition to sexual harassment. For example, a federal court in California recently decided that Tesla must pay $137 million to an ex-worker over a hostile work environment and racism he faced while he worked at the company. The worker told the court that colleagues at the company used language to denigrate him and other Black workers and left a racist drawing in his workspace. Tesla's attorneys appealed the judgment, which was eventually reduced to $3.2 million.[120]

The #MeToo movement continues to help bring the issue of sexual harassment out of the shadows and into the mainstream and to increase public awareness about this serious topic.
Sundry Photography/Shutterstock

Steps Managers Can Take to Eradicate Sexual Harassment

Managers, in collaboration with the HR staff, have an ethical obligation to eradicate sexual harassment in their organizations. There are many ways to accomplish this objective. Here are four steps managers can take to deal with the problem:[121]

- *Develop and clearly communicate a sexual harassment policy endorsed by top management.* This policy should include prohibitions against both quid pro quo and hostile work environment sexual harassment. It should contain (1) examples of types of behavior that are unacceptable, (2) a procedure for employees to use to report instances of harassment, (3) a discussion of the disciplinary actions that will be taken when harassment has taken place, and (4) a commitment to educate and train organizational members about sexual harassment.
- *Use a fair complaint procedure to investigate charges of sexual harassment.* Such a procedure should (1) be managed by a neutral third party, (2) ensure that complaints are dealt with promptly and thoroughly, (3) protect and fairly treat victims, and (4) ensure that alleged harassers are fairly treated.
- *When it has been determined that sexual harassment has taken place, take corrective actions as soon as possible.* These actions can vary depending on the severity of the harassment. When harassment is extensive, prolonged, of a quid pro quo nature, or severely objectionable in some other manner, corrective action may include firing the harasser.
- *Provide sexual harassment education and training to all organizational members, including managers.* The majority of *Fortune* 500 firms currently provide this education and training for their employees.

The Purple Campaign is an organization whose mission is to address workplace harassment by implementing stronger corporate policies, establishing better laws, and empowering people to create real and lasting change within their own work environments and communities. The organization's corporate partners include Amazon, Expedia, General Electric, Airbnb, Instacart, Lyft, Uber, and Spotify.[122]

Summary and Review

LO5-1 **THE INCREASING DIVERSITY OF THE WORKFORCE AND THE ENVIRONMENT** Diversity is dissimilarity or differences among people. Diversity is a pressing concern for managers and organizations for business and ethical reasons. There are multiple forms of diversity such as age, gender, race and ethnicity, religion, capabilities/disabilities, socioeconomic background, sexual orientation, and physical appearance.

LO5-2, 5-3 **MANAGERS AND THE EFFECTIVE MANAGEMENT OF DIVERSITY** Both the workforce and the organizational environment are increasingly diverse, and effectively managing this diversity is an essential component of management. In each of their managerial roles, managers can encourage the effective management of diversity, which is both an ethical and a business imperative.

LO5-4 **PERCEPTION** Perception is the process through which people select, organize, and interpret sensory input to give meaning and order to the world around them. It is inherently subjective. Schemas guide perception; when schemas are based on a single visible characteristic such as race or gender, they are inaccurate stereotypes that lead to unfair treatment. Unfair treatment also can result from biases and overt discrimination.

LO5-5 **HOW TO MANAGE DIVERSITY EFFECTIVELY** Managers can take many steps to manage diversity effectively, an ongoing process that requires frequent monitoring.

LO5-6 **SEXUAL HARASSMENT** Two forms of sexual harassment are quid pro quo sexual harassment and hostile work environment sexual harassment. Steps that managers can take to eradicate sexual harassment include development and communication of a sexual harassment policy endorsed by top management, use of fair complaint procedures, prompt corrective action when harassment occurs, and sexual harassment training and education.

Management in Action

Topics for Discussion and Action

Discussion

1. Discuss why violations of the principles of distributive and procedural justice continue to occur in modern organizations. What can managers do to uphold these principles in their organizations? [LO5-2, 5-3, 5-4, 5-5]
2. Sometimes employees with disabilities experience discrimination in the workplace. As a manager, what would you do to ensure such discrimination is eliminated? [LO5-1, 5-4]
3. Some workers might resent accommodations made for employees with disabilities. As a manager, what could you do to ensure all employees are treated fairly? [LO5-1, 5-4]
4. Discuss the ways in which schemas can be functional and dysfunctional. [LO5-4]
5. Discuss an occasion when you may have been treated unfairly because of stereotypical thinking. What stereotypes were applied to you? How did they result in your being treated unfairly? [LO5-4]
6. How does implicit bias influence your own behavior and decisions? [LO5-4]
7. Why is mentoring particularly important for members of underrepresented groups? [LO5-5]
8. Why is it important to consider the numbers of different groups of employees at various levels in an organization's hierarchy? [LO5-5]
9. Think about a situation in which you would have benefited from mentoring but a mentor was not available. What could you have done to try to get the help of a mentor in this situation? [LO5-5]

Action

10. Choose a *Fortune* 500 company not mentioned in the chapter. Conduct research to determine what steps this organization has taken to manage diversity effectively. [LO5-2, 5-5, 5-6]

Building Management Skills

Solving Diversity-Related Problems [LO5-1, 5-2, 5-3, 5-4, 5-5, 5-6]

Think about the last time that you (1) were treated unfairly because you differed from a decision maker on a particular dimension of diversity or (2) observed someone else being treated unfairly because that person differed from a decision maker on a particular dimension of diversity. Then answer these questions:

1. Why do you think the decision maker acted unfairly in this situation?
2. In what ways, if any, were biases, stereotypes, or overt discrimination involved in this situation?
3. Was the decision maker aware that they were acting unfairly?
4. What could you or the person who was treated unfairly have done to improve matters and rectify the injustice on the spot?
5. Was any sexual harassment involved in this situation? If so, what kind was it?
6. If you had authority over the decision maker (that is, if you were their manager or supervisor), what steps would you take to ensure that the decision maker stops treating people unfairly?

Managing Ethically [LO5-1, 5-2, 5-3, 5-5]

Some companies require that their employees work long hours and travel extensively. Employees with young children, employees taking care of older relatives, and employees who have interests outside the workplace sometimes find that their careers are jeopardized if they try to work more reasonable hours or limit their work-related travel. Some of these employees feel that it is unethical for their managers to expect so much of them in the workplace and not understand their needs as parents and caregivers.

Questions

1. Either individually or in a group, think about the ethical implications of requiring long hours and extensive amounts of travel for some jobs.
2. What obligations do you think managers and companies have to enable employees to have balanced lives and meet nonwork needs and demands?

Small Group Breakout Exercise

Determining If a Problem Exists [LO5-1, 5-2, 5-3, 5-4, 5-5]

Form groups of three or four people, and appoint one member as the spokesperson who will communicate your findings to the whole class when called on by the instructor. Then discuss the following scenario:

You and your partners own and manage a local chain of restaurants, with moderate to expensive prices, that are open for lunch and dinner during the week and for dinner on weekends. Your staff is diverse, and you believe that you are managing diversity effectively. Yet on visits to the different restaurants, you have noticed that your African American employees tend to congregate together and communicate mainly with each other. The same is true for your Hispanic employees and your white employees. You are meeting with your partners today to discuss this observation.

1. Discuss why the patterns of communication that you observed might be occurring in your restaurants.
2. Discuss whether your observation reflects an underlying problem. If so, why? If not, why not?
3. Discuss whether you should address this issue with your staff and in your restaurants. If so, how and why? If not, why not?

Be the Manager [LO5-1, 5-2, 5-3, 5-4, 5-5]

You are Maria Herrera and have been recently promoted to the position of director of financial analysis for a medium-sized consumer goods firm. During your first few weeks on the job, you took the time to have lunch with each of your employees to try to get to know them better. You have 12 direct reports, junior and senior financial analysts who support different product lines. Susan Epstein, one of the female financial analysts you had lunch with, made the following statement: "I'm so glad we finally have a woman in charge. Now, hopefully, things will get better around here." You pressed Epstein to elaborate, but she clammed up. She indicated that she didn't want to unnecessarily bias you and that the problems were pretty self-evident. In fact, Epstein was surprised that you didn't know what she was talking about and jokingly mentioned that perhaps you should spend some time undercover, observing her group and their interactions with others.

You spoke with your supervisor and the former director, who had been promoted and volunteered to be on call if you had any questions. Neither man knew of any diversity-related issues in your group. In fact, your supervisor's response was, "We've got a lot of problems, but fortunately that's not one of them."

What are you going to do to address this issue?

Case in the News [LO5-1, 5-2, 5-3, 5-5]

How Nike Keeps Score on Diversity

In 2020, reports of Black people killed by police officers shined a light on racial bias and inequality, sparking widespread efforts to learn more and bring about change. Community members broadened their concern beyond policing to include issues of inequity in the workplace. These community members, who are also customers and stockholders, have been asking what companies are doing to promote diversity, equity, and inclusion (DEI). Investors who are aware of research associating diversity with higher performance may study companies' diversity performance when deciding on stock purchases.

One company feeling the pressure is Nike. The maker of athletic wear and sports equipment defines its market broadly (its mission statement says, "If you have a body, you are an athlete"), so it sees diversity as a valuable tool for knowing the market and generating creative ideas. In early 2021, Nike announced five-year DEI goals aimed at opportunities for women and people of color. Globally, the company aims for females to represent 50% of its corporate workforce and 45% of executive positions (vice president and higher) by 2025. For its U.S. workforce, the company also set a target of 35% racial and ethnic minorities.

In addition to setting goals, Nike is one of the few companies that tie DEI goals to executive compensation. By one calculation, just 3% of companies in the Russell 3000 (an index of the 3,000 largest U.S. businesses by total stock value) have set at least one diversity goal for at least one executive. At Nike, a portion of executives' long-term bonuses are tied to meeting the five-year diversity targets.

The percentage of total compensation is small, but it can amount to a six- or seven-figure pay cut if the targets aren't met. In this way, said CEO John Donahoe, Nike redefined "what responsible leadership looks like."

To achieve these goals, Nike planned to invest $10 million in historically Black colleges and universities and schools serving major Hispanic student populations, anticipating that these schools would become key sources of new interns and employees. Nike also partnered with tennis great Serena Williams on an apprenticeship program for designers, which provides another pool of diverse talent. In addition, Nike supports organizations with missions to enable women and people of color to participate more fully in the workforce and society at large. For example, Nike has contributed to National Urban League programs that promote job opportunities for formerly incarcerated workers and financial education for first-time home buyers, and it has donated to smaller local organizations that promote economic empowerment and social justice.

When Nike announced its five-year DEI goals, it was already close to its target for female employees. Women's share of the global workforce had edged up from 48% in 2015 to 49.5% in 2020. The company also had been increasing its share of employees of color in the United States: 29% in 2020, up from 15.9% in 2015. Nike pointed to its 2020 intern class—with 55% women and 49% racial and ethnic minorities—as a hopeful sign of a diverse future workforce.

Before this, to achieve greater equity across gender and racial lines, Nike had increased 7,000 workers' salaries and amended its bonus plan. According to the company, women in 2020 were earning a dollar for every dollar earned by men globally, and in the United States, employees of color were earning a dollar for every dollar earned by white employees. In other words, pay at Nike did not vary based on race or gender. Nike's five-year plan now includes a commitment to maintain this pay equity.

Despite Nike's efforts, some stockholders continue to press for more. At Nike's 2021 shareholder meeting, a group of stockholders submitted a resolution that Nike publish an annual report of progress on DEI measures. These stockholders pointed to past complaints of discrimination and harassment, while Nike argued that such reporting was unnecessary because the company was already making progress and providing information in its annual report on the company's social impact. Backers of the initiative said the company's report omitted key information, such as data on hiring, retention, and promotion, but the initiative was defeated.

Nike credits its DEI efforts and culture of innovation with contributing to continued growth despite the COVID-19 pandemic. CEO Donahoe acknowledges that Nike is not perfect but insists the company is committed to continuous improvement, as expressed in its slogan "There is no finish line."

Questions for Discussion

1. How have stockholders influenced Nike's approach to diversity, equity, and inclusion?
2. What ethical principles support having a goal of maintaining pay equity? What other measures of equity should Nike managers consider?
3. Do you think Nike benefits from measuring DEI performance and adjusting executives' compensation accordingly? Why or why not?

Sources: Nike, "Diversity, Equity & Inclusion," https://purpose.nike.com, accessed January 14, 2023; Nike, "How Nike Is Building on Diversity and Inclusion to Advance Sustainability," https://news.nike.com, accessed January 14, 2023; P. Verry, "How Nike Is Progressing with Its Diversity, Equity and Inclusion Commitments and Its Goals for 2025," *Footwear News*, https://footwearnews.com, March 22, 2022; M. Kish, "John Donahoe Came to Nike as an Industry Outsider. Two Years Later, Employees Weigh in on Decisions That Have Defined the CEO's Tenure," *Business Insider*, www.businessinsider.com, January 24, 2022; L. Sumagaysay, "Nike Investors Won't Force Company to Show Results of Diversity Efforts," *MarketWatch*, www.marketwatch.com, updated October 7, 2021; J.E. Palmieri, "Nike Says It's Doubling Down on Internal Racial, Gender Goals as It Votes Down Shareholder Proposals on Diversity," *WWD*, https://wwd.com, October 6, 2021; B. Moore, "Serena Williams, Nike Hatch Diverse Design Incubator," *WWD*, https://wwd.com, October 6, 2021; S. Ciment, "Nike Shareholders Want More Proof of Diversity and Inclusion Advancements," *Footwear News*, https://footwearnews.com, August 11, 2021; E. Glazer and T. Francis, "CEO Pay Increasingly Tied to Diversity Goals," *The Wall Street Journal*, www.wsj.com, June 2, 2021; P. Wahba, "Want Progress on Diversity? Link It to Pay," *Fortune*, https://fortune.com, April 6, 2021; L. Thomas, "Nike Sets Fresh Diversity Targets for 2025, and Ties Executive Compensation to Hitting Them," *CNBC*, www.cnbc.com, March 11, 2021; S. McDonald, "How Nike Is Faring with Its Bold Diversity Commitments—and the 'Aggressive' Plans It Will Pursue Next," *Footwear News*, https://footwearnews.com, March 10, 2021.

Notes

1. National Football League (NFL), "League Announces Enhancements, Updates to Diversity, Equity, Inclusion Efforts," press release, www.nfl.com, October 18, 2022; "NFL Launches Initiatives to Increase Diversity in Sports Medicine," press release, www.nfl.com, May 24, 2022; A. Archie, "NFL Is Requiring Teams to Hire Women or Minorities as Coaches for 2022 Season," *NPR*, www.npr.org, March 29, 2022.
2. NFL, "League Announces Enhancements"; Archie, "NFL Is Requiring Teams to Hire Women or Minorities."
3. Ibid.
4. NFL, "NFL Launches Initiative to Increase Diversity in Sports Medicine"; M. Abrams, "NFL Unveils HBCU Sports Medicine Initiative," *Modern Healthcare*, June 6, 2022, EBSCOhost, https://web.s.ebscohost.com.
5. NFL, "League Announces Enhancements"; A. Epting, "What Business Leaders Can Learn from the NBA and NFL," *Leadership Excellence*, August 2022, 27–30.
6. Deloitte, "Our Commitment to Supplier Diversity," www2deloitte.com, accessed January 12, 2023.
7. McKinsey & Company, "Diversity Wins: How Inclusion Matters," www.mckinsey.com, accessed January 12, 2023.

8. S. Tasheva and A. Hillman, "Integrating Diversity at Different Levels: Multi-Level Human Capital, Social Capital, and Demographic Diversity and Their Implications for Team Effectiveness," *Academy of Management Review,* January 19, 2018.
9. Q. Fottrell, "White Workers Are More Likely than Black or Latino Americans to Have a Good Job—Even with the Same Level of Education," *Market Watch,* www.marketwatch.com, October 21, 2019.
10. "Private Sector Workers Lack Transparency," Institute for Women's Policy Research, https://iwpr.org, accessed February 11, 2020.
11. Catalyst, "Women CEOs of the S&P 500 (List)," www.catalyst.org, November 30, 2022; "Women CEOs in Underrepresented Groups (List)," www.catalyst.org, March 29, 2022.
12. "Age Discrimination," www.eeoc.gov, accessed January 12, 2023; U.S. Census Bureau, "Nation Continues to Age as It Becomes More Diverse," www.census.gov, June 30, 2022.
13. U.S. Department of Labor, "Labor Force Status of Women & Men, November 2022," www.dol.gov, accessed December 5, 2022; U.S. Bureau of Labor Statistics, "Usual Weekly Earnings of Wage and Salary Workers, Third Quarter 2022," www.bls.gov, October 18, 2022.
14. Catalyst, "Pyramid: Women in the United States Workforce (Infographic)," www.catalyst.org, accessed January 12, 2023.
15. J. Green, "Women Reach 32% of S&P 500 Board Seats for the First Time," *Bloomberg,* www.bloomberg.com, December 21, 2022.
16. J. Zenger and J. Folkman, "Research: Women Score Higher than Men in Most Leadership Skills," *Harvard Business Review,* https://hbr.org, June 25, 2019.
17. "Catalyst Study Reveals Financial Performance Is Higher for Companies with More Women at the Top," www.catalyst.org, accessed January 12, 2023.
18. "100 Women: Do Women on Boards Increase Company Profits?" *BBC,* www.bbc.com, accessed January 12, 2023.
19. U.S. Census Bureau, "Measuring Racial and Ethnic Diversity for the 2020 Census," www.census.gov, August 4, 2021.
20. Census 2020, "Race/Ethnicity and the 2020 Census," www.census2020now.org, March 23, 2019.
21. U.S. Census Bureau, "Quick Facts: Population Estimates, July 1, 2021," www.census.gov, accessed January 12, 2023.
22. U.S. Census Bureau, "Table 11: Percent Distribution of the Projected Population by Hispanic Origin and Race for the United States, 2015 to 2060," www.census.gov, accessed January 12, 2023.
23. P. Mota, "Three Reasons Why a Latinx/a/o Talent Strategy Drives an Inclusive Culture," *Diversity Best Practices,* www.diversitybestpractices.com, October 1, 2019; J. A. Eisenbach and R. Kulick, *The Latino Contribution to U.S. Economic Dynamism,* NERA Economic Consulting, www.nera.com, March 2019; L. Dishman, "This Is What It's Like to Be One of the Few Hispanic Women Leading a Company in 2018," *Fast Company,* www.fastcompany.com, October 15, 2018.
24. Forbes Councils, "This Leadership Coach Says the Future of the U.S. Economy Depends on a Growing Latino Workforce," *Forbes,* www.forbes.com, September 30, 2019.
25. C. Villegas, "U.S. Latinos' Economic Power Is Bigger than U.K., India," *Spectrum News,* https://spectrumnews.1.com, October 11, 2022.
26. Villegas, "U.S. Latinos Economic Power"; Forbes Councils, "This Leadership Coach."
27. Mota, "Three Reasons Why"; Dishman, "This Is What It's Like"; Forbes Councils, "This Leadership Coach."
28. Bureau of Labor Statistics, "Table 3: Median Usual Weekly Earnings of Full-Time Wage and Salary Workers by Age and Race, Third Quarter 2022," www.bls.gov, accessed January 12, 2023.
29. C. Li, "Why Diversity Is Critical to Media and Entertainment—and How to Achieve It," *World Economic Forum,* www.weforum.org, accessed January 12, 2023.
30. D. Hunt and A.-C. Ramon, "Hollywood Diversity Report 2022: Part 2: Television," https://socialsciences.ucla.edu, accessed January 12, 2023.
31. Li, "Why Diversity Is Critical."
32. U.S. Department of Labor, "Religious Discrimination and Accommodation in the Workplace," www.dol.gov, accessed January 13, 2023.
33. Society for Human Resource Management (SHRM), "Navigating Religious Beliefs in the Workplace," www.shrm.org, accessed January 13, 2023.
34. D. Gerdeman, "Religion in the Workplace: What Managers Need to Know," *Working Knowledge* (Harvard Business School), https://hbswk.hbs.edu, accessed January 13, 2023.
35. L. R. Roepe, "How Managers Can Move Employees with Disabilities into Leadership," *Society for Human Resource Management,* www.shrm.org, October 12, 2021.
36. Disability:IN, "Disability Equality Index: 2022 Best Places to Work," https://disabilityin.org, accessed January 13, 2023.
37. R. Brownstein, "Honoring Work Is Key to Ending Poverty," *Detroit News,* October 2, 2001; G. Koretz, "How Welfare to Work Worked," *BusinessWeek,* September 24, 2001 (*BusinessWeek* Archives).
38. C. Benson, "Poverty Rate of Children Higher Than National Rate, Lower for Older Populations," www.census.gov, October 4, 2022; J. Stein, "Child Poverty Spiked by 41 Percent in January after Biden Benefit Program Expired," *The Washington Post,* www.washingtonpost.com, February 17, 2022; H. Long and A. Goldstein, "Poverty Fell Overall in 2020 Due to Massive Stimulus Checks and Unemployment Aid, U.S. Census Says," *The Washington Post,* www.washingtonpost.com, September 14, 2021.
39. "HHS Poverty Guidelines for 2022," https://aspe.hhs.gov, accessed December 7, 2022.
40. A. Glasmeier and A. Omens, "$15 an Hour Isn't Enough: U.S. Workers Need a Living Wage," *Fortune,* https://fortune.com, September 6, 2021.
41. S. Horsley, "Women Are Returning to (Paid) Work after the Pandemic Forced Many to Leave Their Jobs," *NPR,* www.npr.org, September 28, 2022; A.S. Modestino, J.J. Ladge, A. Swartz, and A. Lincoln, "Childcare Is a Business Issue," *Harvard Business Review,* https://hbr.org, April 29, 2021.
42. J.M. Jones, "LGBT Identification in U.S. Ticks Up to 7.1%," *Gallup,* https://news.gallup.com, accessed January 13, 2023.
43. D. Wiessner, "U.S. Appeals Court Says Title VII Covers Discrimination Based on Sexual Orientation," *Reuters,* www.reuters.com, accessed February 10, 2020; B. Chappell, "Supreme Court Declares Same-Sex Marriage Legal in All 50 States," NPR, www.npr.org, June 26, 2015.
44. Human Rights Campaign Foundation, "Corporate Equity Index 2022," www.hrc.org, accessed January 14, 2023.
45. J. Richman, "Why 'Inclusive' Workplaces Still Make Fat People Feel Invisible," *Fast Company,* www.fastcompany.com, August 13, 2019.
46. V. Valian, *Why So Slow? The Advancement of Women* (Cambridge, MA: MIT Press, 1997); S.T. Fiske and S.E. Taylor, *Social Cognition,* 2nd ed. (New York: McGraw-Hill, 1991).
47. Company website, "Fact Sheet," https://investors.stryker.com, accessed January 14, 2023.
48. "100 Best Companies to Work For: Stryker," *Fortune,* https://fortune.com, accessed January 14, 2023; H. Hitson, "The Best Workplaces for Diversity," *Fortune,* January 2020, 15; "Stryker Honored by Women's Forum for Work toward Gender Parity in the Boardroom," news release, www.stryker.com, September 4, 2019.
49. Hitson, "The Best Workplaces for Diversity"; "Stryker Honored by Women's Forum."
50. "Stryker Honored by Women's Forum"; "Careers," https://careers.stryker.com, accessed January 14, 2023.

51. Valian, *Why So Slow?*
52. G. Cox and D. Lancefield, "5 Strategies to Infuse D&I into Your Organization," *Harvard Business Review,* https://hbr.org, May 19, 2021.
53. V. Brown and F.L. Geis, "Turning Lead into Gold: Leadership by Men and Women and the Alchemy of Social Consensus," *Journal of Personality and Social Psychology* 46 (1984), 811–24; Valian, *Why So Slow?*
54. Valian, *Why So Slow?*
55. J. Cole and B. Singer, "A Theory of Limited Differences: Explaining the Productivity Puzzle in Science," in H. Zuckerman, J.R. Cole, and J.T. Bruer, eds., *The Outer Circle: Women in the Scientific Community* (New York: Norton, 1991), 277–310; M.F. Fox, "Sex, Salary, and Achievement: Reward Dualism in Academia," *Sociology of Education* 54 (1981), 71–84; J.S. Long, "The Origins of Sex Differences in Science," *Social Forces* 68 (1990), 1297–1315.
56. R. Folger and M.A. Konovsky, "Effects of Procedural and Distributive Justice on Reactions to Pay Raise Decisions," *Academy of Management Journal* 32 (1989), 115–30; J. Greenberg, "Organizational Justice: Yesterday, Today, and Tomorrow," *Journal of Management* 16 (1990), 399–402; O. Janssen, "How Fairness Perceptions Make Innovative Behavior More or Less Stressful," *Journal of Organizational Behavior,* 25 (2004), 201–15.
57. V. Valian, *Why So Slow? The Advancement of Women* (Cambridge, MA: MIT Press, 1997); S.T. Fiske and S.E. Taylor, *Social Cognition,* 2nd ed. (New York: McGraw-Hill, 1991).
58. Bureau of Labor Statistics, "Household Data Annual Averages: Table 39. Median Weekly Earnings of Full-Time Wage and Salary Workers by Detailed Occupation and Sex," www.bls.gov, January 20, 2022.
59. A. Elejalde-Ruiz, "Ford Settles Sexual, Racial Harassment Claims at Chicago Plants for $10 Million," *Chicago Tribune,* www.chicagotribune.com, August 17, 2017.
60. Greenberg, "Organizational Justice"; M.G. Ehrhart, "Leadership and Procedural Justice Climate as Antecedents of Unit-Level Organizational Citizenship Behavior," *Personnel Psychology* 57 (2004), 61–94; A. Colella, R.L. Paetzold, and M.A. Belliveau, "Factors Affecting Coworkers' Procedural Justice Inferences of the Workplace Accommodations of Employees with Disabilities," *Personnel Psychology* 57 (2004), 1–23.
61. S. Todd, "Why Diversity Gives Businesses a Competitive Advantage," *Forbes,* www.forbes.com, May 5, 2019.
62. K Schwab, "You Can't Take Anything Home from Ikea's New Store," *Fast Company,* www.fastcompany.com, April 10, 2019.
63. A. Lamb, "The Importance of Diversity and Inclusion in Recruiting," *Blue Signal,* https://bluesignal.com, accessed January 14, 2023.
64. J.D. Farrugia, "7 Statistics on Employee Turnover in 2022 Every HR Manager Should Be Aware Of," *Workforce,* https://workforce.com, September 13, 2022.
65. G. Stengel, "Supplier Diversity Benefits Both Small and Large Businesses," *Forbes,* www.forbes.com, May 29, 2019.
66. J. Maloney and L. Weber, "Coke's Elusive Goal: Boosting Its Black Employees," *The Wall Street Journal,* www.wsj.com, accessed January 14, 2023.
67. H.R. Schiffmann, *Sensation and Perception: An Integrated Approach* (New York: Wiley, 1990).
68. "Welcome to McDonald's Franchising," https://corporate.mcdonalds.com, accessed January 14, 2023; "Special McDonald's Menu Items from Around the World," *Love Food,* www.lovefood.com, accessed January 14, 2023.
69. S.T. Fiske and S.E. Taylor, *Social Cognition* (Reading, MA: Addison-Wesley, 1984).
70. J.S. Bruner, "Going beyond the Information Given," in H. Gruber, G. Terrell, and M. Wertheimer, eds., *Contemporary Approaches to Cognition* (Cambridge, MA: Harvard University Press, 1957); Fiske and Taylor, *Social Cognition.*
71. Fiske and Taylor, *Social Cognition.*
72. Valian, *Why So Slow?*
73. D. Bakan, *The Duality of Human Existence* (Chicago: Rand McNally, 1966); J.T. Spence and R.L. Helmreich, *Masculinity and Femininity: Their Psychological Dimensions, Correlates, and Antecedents* (Austin: University of Texas Press, 1978); J.T. Spence and L.L. Sawin, "Images of Masculinity and Femininity: A Reconceptualization," in V.E. O'Leary, R.K. Unger, and B.B. Wallston, eds., *Women, Gender, and Social Psychology* (Hillsdale, NJ: Erlbaum, 1985), 35–66; Valian, *Why So Slow?*
74. Valian, *Why So Slow?*
75. P.R. Sackett, C.M. Hardison, and M.J. Cullen, "On Interpreting Stereotype Threat as Accounting for African American–White Differences on Cognitive Tests," *American Psychologist* 59, no. 1 (January 2004), 7–13; C.M. Steele and J.A. Aronson, "Stereotype Threat Does Not Live by Steele and Aronson (1995) alone," *American Psychologist* 59, no. 1 (January 2004), 47–48; P.R. Sackett, C.M. Hardison, and M.J. Cullen, "On the Value of Correcting Mischaracterizations of Stereotype Threat Research," *American Psychologist* 59, no. 1 (January 2004), 48–49; D.M. Amodio, E. Harmon-Jones, P.G. Devine, J.J. Curtin, S.L. Hartley, and A.E. Covert, "Neural Signals for the Detection of Unintentional Race Bias," *Psychological Science* 15, no. 2 (2004), 88–93.
76. M. Loden and J.B. Rosener, *Workforce America! Managing Employee Diversity as a Vital Resource* (Burr Ridge, IL: Irwin, 1991).
77. A. Loten, "Older IT Workers Left Out despite Tech Talent Shortage," *The Wall Street Journal,* www.wsj.com, November 25, 2019; W. R. Kerr, "The Plight of the Graying Tech Worker," *MIT Sloan Management Review,* March 28, 2019, https://sloanreview.mit.edu, March 28, 2019.
78. P. Holley, "In Silicon Valley, Some Men Say Cosmetic Procedures Are Essential to a Career," *Washington Post,* www.washingtonpost.com, January 9, 2020.
79. Loten, "Older IT Workers Left Out."
80. Kerr, "The Plight of the Graying Tech Worker"; A. Nova, "How Older Workers Can Push Back Against the Reality of Ageism," *CNBC,* www.cnbc.com, March 20, 2022.
81. S. Savat, "Mothers May Face Increased Work Discrimination Post-Pandemic, Research Warns," *The Source,* https://source.wustl.edu, July 20, 2021.
82. L. Roberson, B.M. Galvin, and A.C. Charles, "Chapter 13, When Group Identities Matter: Bias in Performance Appraisal," in J.P. Walsh and A.P. Brief, eds., *The Academy of Management Annals* vol. 1 (New York: Erlbaum, 2008), 617–50.
83. Bureau of Labor Statistics, "Persons with a Disability: Labor Force Characteristics–2021," www.bls.gov, February 24, 2022.
84. A. Cooks-Campbell, "Implicit Bias: How Unconscious Attitudes Affect Everything," *BetterUp,* www.betterup.com, September 22, 2021.
85. I. Bohnet, A. van Geen, and M. Bazerman, "When Performance Trumps Gender Bias: Joint vs. Separate Evaluation," *Management Science* 62, no. 5 (2015), 1225–34.
86. Forbes Coaches Council, "11 Steps to Reduce Unconscious Bias in Hiring Processes," *Forbes,* www.forbes.com, accessed January 14, 2023.
87. Fiske and Taylor, *Social Cognition.*
88. E. Bachman, "Massive $125 Million Verdict Against Walmart in Disability Discrimination Case," *Forbes,* www.forbes.com, accessed January 14, 2023; D. Wiessner, "Tesla Loses Bid for New Trial in Factory Worker's Race Bias Case," *Reuters,* www.reuters.com, June 21, 2022.
89. U.S. Equal Employment Opportunity Commission, "Lilly USA Sued by EEOC for Nationwide Discrimination," www.eeoc.gov, September 26, 2022; C. Dolmetsch and K. Gemmell, "All About

Age Discrimination at Work and Why Successful Lawsuits Are Rare," *Bloomberg,* www.bloomberg.com, September 12, 2022.

90. L. Burden, "Couple Wins $11.4M Jury Award in Race Discrimination Case," *HR Dive,* www.hrdive.com, September 27, 2019.
91. Catalyst, "Women in the Workforce: Japan (Quick Take)," www.catalyst.com, accessed January 14, 2023.
92. U.S. Equal Employment Opportunity Commission, "Lilly USA Sued by EEOC."
93. Associated Press, "Former L.A. Times Columnist T.J. Simers Awarded Nearly $15.5 Million in Bias Lawsuit," *Market Watch,* www.marketwatch.com, August 19, 2019.
94. I. Thibodeau, "Fired Salaried Workers Sue Ford for Age Discrimination," *The Detroit News,* www.detroitnews.com, June 28, 2019.
95. A.G. Greenwald and M. Banaji, "Implicit Social Cognition: Attitudes, Self-Esteem, and Stereotypes, *Psychological Review* 102 (1995), 4–27.
96. "How to Increase Workplace Diversity," *The Wall Street Journal,* http://guides.wsj.com, accessed January 14, 2023.
97. A. Lindsey, E. King, A. Membere, and H.K. Cheung, "Two Types of Diversity Training That Really Work," *Harvard Business Review,* https://hbr.org, accessed February 11, 2020; A.P. Carnevale and S.C. Stone, "Diversity: Beyond the Golden Rule," *Training & Development,* October 1994, 22–39.
98. J. Rampton, "Why You Need Diversity on Your Team, and 8 Ways to Build It," *Entrepreneur,* www.entrepreneur.com, September 6, 2019.
99. W.B. Swann Jr., J.T. Polzer, D.C. Seyle, and S.J. Ko, "Finding Value in Diversity: Verification of Personal and Social Self-Views in Diverse Groups," *Academy of Management Review* 29, no. 1 (2004), 9–27.
100. L. Mackenzie, J. Wehner, and S.J. Correll, "Why Most Performance Evaluations Are Biased, and How to Fix Them," *Harvard Business Review,* https://hbr.org, January 11, 2019.
101. A.P. Brief, R.T. Buttram, R.M. Reizenstein, S.D. Pugh, J.D. Callahan, R.L. McCline, and J.B. Vaslow, "Beyond Good Intentions: The Next Steps toward Racial Equality in the American Workplace," *Academy of Management Executive,* November 1997, 59–72.
102. McKinsey & Company, *Women in the Workplace 2022,* www.mckinsey.com, October 2022; M. Somers, "Women Are Less Likely than Men to Be Promoted: Here's One Reason Why," *Ideas Made to Matter* (MIT Sloan), https://mitsloan.mit.edu, April 12, 2022; N. Erkal, L. Gangadharan, and E. Xiao, "Beyond 'Lean In': Women in Leadership," *Pursuit* (University of Melbourne), https://pursuit.unimelb.edu.au, March 7, 2019.
103. Erkal et al., "Beyond 'Lean In'"; A. Cohen, "The Way to More Women Bosses," *Bloomberg Businessweek,* April 11, 2022, 32.
104. Somers, "Women Are Less Likely"; Cohen, "The Way to More Women Bosses."
105. Brief et al., "Beyond Good Intentions."
106. M. Costa, "Is Tying C-Suite Bonuses to DEI Targets the Answer to Greater Workplace Equity?" *Worklife,* www.worklife.news, July 7, 2022.
107. S. Rinderle, "8 Things to Expect from a Highly Competent Diversity Consultant," *Workforce,* www.workforce.com, accessed February 11, 2020.
108. M.B. Arthur, "A Life Worth Living: David A. Thomas, President of Morehouse College, Enters a New Career Stage," *Forbes,* www.forbes.com, February 28, 2019; D.A. Thomas, "Race Matters: The Truth about Mentoring Minorities," *Harvard Business Review,* April 2001, 99–107.
109. Thomas, "Race Matters."
110. J. Kantor and M. Twohey, "Harvey Weinstein Paid Off Sexual Harassment Accusers for Decades," *The New York Times,* www.nytimes.com, October 5, 2017.
111. N. Smartt, "Sexual Harassment in the Workplace in a #MeToo World," *Forbes,* www.forbes.com, December 20, 2017.
112. M. Del Barco, "Harvey Weinstein Found Guilty on 3 of 7 Charges in LA Sex Crimes Trial," *NPR,* www.npr.org, December 19, 2022; L. Herstik, "Inside the Harvey Weinstein Rape Trial in Los Angeles," *The New York Times,* www.nytimes.com, November 1, 2022.
113. C. Kolmar, "17 Distressing Sexual Harassment Statistics in the Workplace (2022)," *Zippia,* www.zippia.com, November 2, 2022.
114. EEOC Data Highlights, "Sexual Harassment in Our Nation's Workplaces (April 2022)," www.eeoc.gov, accessed January 14, 2023.
115. R. DiGiacomo, "More Men Report Sexual Harassment at Work," *Monster,* www.monster.com, accessed February 11, 2020.
116. Thomson Reuters, "What Is Quid Pro Quo Harassment in the Workplace?" https://legal.thomsonreuters.com, accessed January 14, 2023.
117. B. Zoller, "Harvey Weinstein and Top Sexual Harassment Mistakes Employers Make," *Xpert HR Blog,* www.xperthr.com, October 18, 2017.
118. A.M. O'Leary-Kelly, R.L. Paetzold, and R.W. Griffin, "Sexual Harassment as Aggressive Action: A Framework for Understanding Sexual Harassment," paper presented at the annual meeting of the Academy of Management, Vancouver, August 1995.
119. B.S. Roberts and R.A. Mann, "Sexual Harassment in the Workplace: A Primer," www3.uakron.edu/lawrev/robert1.html, May 1, 2004.
120. D. Wiessner, "Tesla Ordered to Pay $3.2 Million to Black Ex-Worker in US Race Bias Case," *Reuters,* April 3, 2023, https://www.reuters.com.
121. C. Zillman, "From #MeToo to Now What? Actions That Could Actually Stop Sexual Harassment," *Fortune,* http://fortune.com, October 20, 2017.
122. The Purple Campaign, "Our Mission" and "Corporate Engagement," www.purplecampaign.org, accessed January 14, 2023.

CHAPTER 6

Managing in the Global Environment

oneinchpunch/Shutterstock

Learning Objectives

After studying this chapter, you should be able to:

LO6-1 Explain why the ability to perceive, interpret, and respond appropriately to the global environment is crucial for managerial success.

LO6-2 Differentiate between the global task and global general environments.

LO6-3 Identify the main forces in the global task and general environments, and describe the challenges that each force presents to managers.

LO6-4 Explain why the global environment is becoming more open and competitive, and identify the forces behind the process of globalization that increase the opportunities, complexities, challenges, and threats managers face.

LO6-5 Discuss why national cultures differ and why it is important that managers be sensitive to the effects of falling trade barriers and regional trade associations on the political and social systems of nations around the world.

A MANAGER'S CHALLENGE

BMW's Global Expansion Focuses on China

What opportunities and challenges can managers find in going global? Many Americans would be surprised to learn that the largest U.S. automotive exporter, by value, is BMW. The German-based maker of passenger vehicles exported more than 250,000 U.S.-made vehicles worth a total of $10.1 billion in 2021, maintaining the top spot for the eighth year in a row. The top destination for BMW's U.S. exports was China, which received almost 25% of the total, followed by Germany, South Korea, Canada, Great Britain, and more than a hundred other countries.[1]

Most of those vehicles were made by the 11,000 people working at BMW's plant in Spartanburg, South Carolina. At the headquarters in Munich, BMW Group identifies Spartanburg as its "center of competence" for its X line of vehicles, including the BMW X3 and X5, Motorsport X models, and plug-in hybrid electric X models.[2] The company hires and trains with the goal of staffing the facility with world-class talent. In 2021, despite disruptions in the market for auto parts and components, Spartanburg set a production record of almost 434,000 vehicles.

BMW Group's managers view China as much more than the largest market for its U.S.-made vehicles. For several years, China has been BMW's largest market globally, surpassing the United States to take the lead several years ago. The Chinese market now accounts for almost 40% of the company's sales. Chinese interest in BMW's electrified vehicles is especially strong, growing almost 70% in 2021.[3]

China also is part of BMW's manufacturing network; the company's Chinese production facilities made 700,000 vehicles in 2021. Recently, BMW announced plans for the factories to begin producing the X5 midsize luxury SUV, a model that has been imported from Spartanburg. The additional production is to meet demand growth, so BMW plans no cuts to production in Spartanburg. In fact, BMW already has been making X5 vehicles for China in Thailand, beginning when China imposed tariffs on U.S. imports. The company also is increasing its investment in China in response to changes in the country's regulations on foreign companies. In 2018, China's government announced that it would phase out rules requiring foreign companies to partner with Chinese owners and own no more than half of any venture located there. Investing more to become a majority owner requires renegotiating deals with existing venture partners and securing a license from the government. BMW announced that it would take majority control of its Chinese joint venture in 2022. This gives BMW Group's leadership more control over the business and is expected to enhance its earnings.[4]

Many of these BMW X5 vehicles on the production line in Spartanburg, South Carolina, are destined for China and other foreign markets, as the global automaker expands its reach.
Mark Elias/Bloomberg/Getty Images

BMW Group serves the international demand for vehicles as a German company with a global outlook, operations in several countries, and sales made locally. The company has built its success on superior engineering and premium product quality, so it establishes standard processes and structures, which it applies across its production network of 31 facilities located in 15 countries. The production network employs the latest in manufacturing technologies, including artificial intelligence, 3D printing, virtual reality, and the Internet of Things. BMW also has a global sales network operating in more than 140 countries.[5]

Overview

Top managers of a global company like BMW operate in an environment where they compete with other companies for scarce and valuable resources. Managers of companies large and small have found that to survive and prosper in the 21st century, most organizations must become **global organizations** that operate and compete not only domestically, at home, but also globally, in countries around the world. Operating in the global environment is uncertain and unpredictable because it is complex and changes constantly.

global organizations Organizations that operate and compete in more than one country.

If organizations are to adapt successfully to this changing environment, their managers must learn to understand the forces that operate in it and how these forces give rise to opportunities and threats. In this chapter, we examine why the environment, both domestically and globally, has become more open, vibrant, and competitive. We examine how forces in the task and general environments affect global organizations and their managers. competitive. We also discuss the four approaches used by organizations to expand internationally. By the end of this chapter, you will appreciate the changes that are taking place in the environment and understand why it is important for managers to develop a global perspective as they strive to increase organizational efficiency and effectiveness.

LO6-1 Explain why the ability to perceive, interpret, and respond appropriately to the global environment is crucial for managerial success.

What Is the Global Environment?

The **global environment** is a set of forces and conditions in the world outside an organization's boundary that affects how it operates and shapes its behavior.[6] These forces change over time and thus present managers with *opportunities* and *threats.* Some changes in the global environment, such as the development of efficient new production technology, the availability of lower-cost components, or the opening of new global markets, create opportunities for managers to make and sell more products, obtain more resources and capital, and thereby strengthen their organization. In contrast, the rise of new global competitors, a global economic recession, or an oil shortage poses threats that can devastate an organization if managers cannot sell its products. The ability of managers to understand forces in the global environment and to respond appropriately to those forces, such as BMW's ability to make and sell vehicles that customers around the world want to buy, are critical factors affecting organizational performance.

LO6-2 Differentiate between the global task and global general environments.

global environment The set of global forces and conditions that operates beyond an organization's boundaries but affects a manager's ability to acquire and utilize resources.

In this chapter, we explore the nature of these forces and consider how managers can respond to them. To identify opportunities and threats caused by forces in the environment, it is helpful for managers to distinguish between the *task environment* and the more encompassing *general environment* (see Figure 6.1).

The **task environment** is the set of forces and conditions that originates with global suppliers, distributors, customers, and competitors; these forces and conditions affect an organization's ability to obtain inputs used to manufacture and sell its products or services. The task environment contains the forces that have the most *immediate* and *direct* effect on managers because they pressure and influence managers daily. For example, the recent disruptions in the global supply chain were caused in part by the COVID-19 pandemic, which increased consumer demand for products worldwide. A shortage of workers had managers in both domestic and global organizations scrambling to keep critical supplies and components moving to their final destinations.[7]

task environment The set of forces and conditions that originates with suppliers, distributors, customers, and competitors and affects an organization's ability to obtain inputs used to manufacture and sell its products or services.

Figure 6.1
Forces in the Global Environment

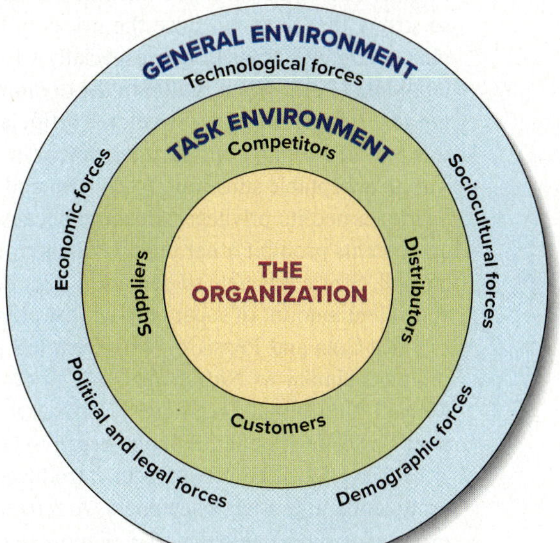

general environment The wide-ranging global, economic, technological, sociocultural, demographic, political, and legal forces that affect an organization and its task environment.

The **general environment** includes the wide-ranging global, economic, technological, sociocultural, demographic, political, and legal forces that affect the organization and its task environment. For the individual manager, opportunities and threats resulting from changes in the general environment are often more difficult to identify and respond to than are events in the task environment. However, changes in these forces can have major impacts on managers and their organizations.

The Task Environment

Forces in the task environment result from the actions of suppliers, distributors, customers, and competitors both at home and abroad (see Figure 6.1). These four groups affect a manager's ability to obtain resources and dispose of outputs daily, weekly, and monthly and thus have a significant impact on short-term decision making.

Suppliers

suppliers Individuals and organizations that provide an organization with the input resources it needs to produce goods and services.

Suppliers are the individuals and companies that provide an organization with the input resources (such as raw materials, component parts, or employees) it needs to produce goods and services. In return, the suppliers receive payment for those goods and services. An important aspect of a manager's job is to ensure a reliable supply of input resources.

Consider Dell Technologies–a leading PC and information technology company–as an example. Dell has many suppliers of component parts such as microprocessors (Intel) and disk drives (Nvidia and AMD). It also has suppliers of preinstalled software, including the operating systems and specific application software (Microsoft and Adobe). Dell's providers of capital, such as banks and other financial institutions, are also key suppliers.

LO6-3 Identify the main forces in the global task and general environments, and describe the challenges that each force presents to managers.

Dell has several suppliers of labor. One source is the educational institutions that train future Dell employees and therefore provide the company with skilled workers. Another is trade unions, organizations that represent employee interests and can control the supply of labor by exercising the right of unionized workers to strike. Unions also can influence the terms and conditions under which labor is employed. In organizations and industries where unions are prevalent, an important part of a manager's job is negotiating and administering agreements with unions and their representatives.

Changes in the nature, number, or type of suppliers produce opportunities and threats to which managers must respond if their organizations are to prosper. For example, a major supplier-related threat that confronts managers arises when suppliers' bargaining positions are so strong that they can raise the prices of the inputs they supply to the organization. A supplier's bargaining position is especially strong when (1) the supplier is the sole source of an input and (2) the input is vital to the organization.[8] For example, for 17 years G. D. Searle was the sole supplier of NutraSweet, the artificial sweetener used in most diet soft drinks. Not only was NutraSweet an important ingredient in diet soft drinks, but it also was one for which there was no acceptable substitute (saccharin and other artificial sweeteners raised health concerns). Searle earned its privileged position because it invented and held the patent for NutraSweet, and patents prohibit other organizations from introducing competing products for 17 years. As a result, Searle was able to demand a high price for NutraSweet, charging twice the price of an equivalent amount of sugar; paying that price raised the costs of soft drink manufacturers such as Coca-Cola and PepsiCo. When Searle's patent expired, many other companies introduced products similar to NutraSweet, and prices fell.[9] In the 2000s, Splenda, which was made by McNeil Nutritionals, replaced NutraSweet as the artificial sweetener of choice, and NutraSweet's price fell further; Splenda began to command a high price from soft drink companies.[10]

However, a natural sweetener introduced less than a decade ago has gained market share on Splenda and other sweeteners. A zero-calorie sweetener extracted from the stevia plant is expected to have a global market of more than $1.6 billion in 2030, according to recent research, replacing many artificial sweeteners in soft drinks, other beverages, and food products.[11]

In contrast, when an organization has many suppliers for a particular input, it is in a relatively strong bargaining position with those suppliers and can demand low-cost, high-quality inputs from them. Often an organization can use its power with suppliers to force them to reduce their prices, as Dell often does. Dell, for example, is constantly searching for low-cost suppliers abroad to keep its prices competitive. At a global level, organizations can buy products from suppliers overseas or become their own suppliers by manufacturing their products abroad.

It is important that managers recognize the opportunities and threats associated with managing the global supply chain. Gaining access to low-cost products made abroad represents an opportunity for U.S. companies to lower their input costs.[12] Conversely, they have less control over production processes carried out by contractors located far away. This poses a threat to the brand if the suppliers deliver poor quality. Buying from countries with fewer protections for workers and much lower wages also involves a threat related to social responsibility: If stakeholders determine that suppliers aren't meeting minimum standards for ethical treatment of their workers, the company's reputation may be damaged. To see how Levi Strauss has addressed this issue, read the "Ethics in Action" feature.

ETHICS IN ACTION

Levi Strauss Insists Global Suppliers Treat Their Workers Well

When Levi Strauss & Company began sourcing work from low-wage countries in the 1990s, it was concerned about poor working conditions. In response, the global retailer prepared a code of conduct–its Terms of Engagement, requiring measures to meet workers' basic needs and protect their rights and the environment.[13] A supplier wanting to sell to Levi's had to meet those terms. Eventually, this innovation became the norm in the clothing industry. But despite efforts to enforce the terms with suppliers, violations continued. CEO Chip Bergh decided that lasting change required a shift in managers' attitudes.

Levi's launched an initiative it calls Worker Well-Being.[14] Its goal is to improve the experience of workers at Levi's suppliers, leading to greater efficiency and reliability, thereby creating a stronger supply network. Caring for workers' interests thus generates a win for all. Levi's provides funds and guidance, but each supplier plans how to achieve worker well-being. The basic approach is to survey workers; learn what they need to be healthy, productive, and engaged at work; identify the company's labor-related areas of improvement; and work with nonprofit partners to meet those needs. Because "well-being" is a broad objective, Levi's partnered with Harvard's Center for Health and the Global Environment to develop success measures that connect worker well-being with business performance.[15] Ultimately, the measures should demonstrate to factory managers why worker well-being matters to the company.

Early participants in the well-being initiative included the 1,200-worker Apparel International (AI) factory in Nazareno, Mexico.[16] AI's president, Oscar González Franch, and CEO Tomas Bello Garza were uncertain how to start, but they already had a track record of innovating to improve the factory's environmental impact. After a company-provided survey didn't illuminate worker needs, they partnered with a nongovernment organization, which created tools more appropriate for the community. They learned that the key issues were lack of access to health care and poor communication between managers and workers. AI trained its supervisors in communicating respectfully and creating a healthier work environment. As attitudes and productivity improved, González Franch and Bello Garza began using company resources to improve health conditions in the community.

In the first five years, Levi's rolled out the program to facilities in 12 countries with 100,000 workers.[17] In Egypt, health education reduced absenteeism and turnover among female employees, and in Turkey, changes to the work schedule did the same. Levi's set a timetable for the program to cover the factories producing 80% of its products by 2020–and to cover all suppliers' workers by 2025.

The purchasing activities of global companies have become increasingly complicated. Hundreds of suppliers around the world produce parts for Boeing's 787 Dreamliner.
Thor Jorgen Udvang/Shutterstock

A common problem facing managers of large, global companies such as Ford, Caterpillar, and Dell is managing the development of a global supplier network that will allow their companies to keep costs down and quality high. For example, Boeing's 777 jet was originally built using many components from more than 500 global suppliers. Boeing chose these suppliers because they were the best in the world at performing their particular activities, and Boeing's goal was to produce a high-quality final product.[18] Pleased with the outcome, Boeing decided to outsource a greater percentage of components to global suppliers when it designed the Boeing 787 Dreamliner; however, many serious problems delayed the introduction of the new aircraft for several years.[19]

The purchasing activities of global companies have become increasingly complicated as a result of the development of a whole range of skills and competencies in different countries around the world and the global impact of the COVID-19 pandemic. It is clearly in companies' interests to search out the lowest-cost, best-quality suppliers. Advances in technology and the global reach of the Internet continue to make it easier for companies to coordinate complicated long-distance exchanges involving the purchasing of inputs and the disposal of outputs–something many global companies have taken advantage of as they consolidate the number of suppliers to reduce costs.

global outsourcing The purchase or production of inputs or final products from overseas suppliers to lower costs and improve product quality or design.

Global outsourcing occurs when a company contracts with suppliers in other countries to make the various inputs or components that go into its products or to assemble the final products to reduce costs. For example, Apple contracts with companies in Taiwan and China to make inputs such as the chips, batteries, and LCD displays that power its digital devices; then it contracts with outsourcers such as Foxconn to assemble its final products–such as iPhones and iPads. Apple also outsources the distribution of its products around the world by contracting with companies such as FedEx or UPS. Due to global supply-chain disruptions caused by COVID-19 outbreaks in China, Apple recently announced that chips for the company's devices will now be made at a new plant in Arizona.[20]

Global outsourcing has grown enormously to take advantage of national differences in the cost and quality of resources such as labor or raw materials that can significantly reduce manufacturing costs or increase product quality or reliability. Today such global exchanges are becoming so complex that some companies specialize in managing other companies' global supply chains. Global companies use the services of overseas intermediaries or brokers, which are located close to potential suppliers, to find the suppliers that can best meet the needs of a particular company. They can design the most efficient supply chain for a company to outsource the component and assembly operations required to produce its final products. Because these suppliers are located in thousands of cities in many countries, finding them is difficult. Li & Fung, based in Hong Kong, is one broker that has helped hundreds of major U.S. companies to outsource their component or assembly operations to suitable overseas suppliers, especially suppliers in mainland China.[21]

Although outsourcing to take advantage of low labor costs has helped many companies perform better, its risks have also become apparent, especially during the recent global pandemic, when supply-chain disruptions led to extensive delays in producing many different products and components. Consequently, some companies started to bring back jobs to the United States. According to a recent report by Deloitte, more than 60% of executives surveyed at U.S. transport and manufacturing companies expect to reshore some of their production capabilities over the next few years.[22]

Other companies do not outsource manufacturing; they prefer to establish their own assembly operations and factories in countries around the world to protect their proprietary technology. For example, most global automakers own their production operations in China and Mexico to retain control over their global decision making and keep their operations secret.

Distributors

distributors Organizations that help other organizations sell their goods or services to customers.

Distributors are organizations that help other organizations sell their goods or services to customers. The decisions managers make about how to distribute products to customers can have important effects on organizational performance. For example, package delivery companies such as FedEx, UPS, and the U.S. Postal Service have become vital distributors for the millions of items bought online and shipped to customers by Internet retailers, both at home and abroad.

The changing nature of distributors and distribution methods can bring opportunities and threats for managers. If distributors become so large and powerful that they can control customers' access to a particular organization's goods and services, they can threaten the organization by demanding that it reduce the prices of its goods and services. For example, retail giant Walmart controls its suppliers' access to millions of customers and, thus, can demand that its suppliers reduce their prices to keep its business. If an organization such as Procter & Gamble refuses to reduce its prices, Walmart might respond by buying products only from Procter & Gamble's competitors–companies such as Unilever and Colgate. Walmart recently used its power as a distributor to put more pressure on suppliers to deliver more goods on time and in full to Walmart warehouses with shipments 98% complete or face fines of 3% on the cost of the delayed goods. This strategy is an effort to keep inventory low and shelves stocked as Walmart competes head-on with Amazon.[23]

Customers

customers Individuals and groups that buy the goods and services an organization produces.

Customers are the individuals and groups that buy the goods and services an organization produces. For example, Dell's customers can be segmented into several distinct groups: (1) individuals who purchase PCs for home use, (2) small companies, (3) large companies, and (4) government agencies and educational institutions. Changes in the number and types of customers or in customers' tastes and needs create opportunities and threats. An organization's success depends on its responsiveness to customers—whether it can satisfy their needs. In the PC industry, customers are demanding smaller computers, longer battery life, new apps, and lower prices—and PC makers must respond to the changing types and needs of customers, such as by introducing tablets and other mobile devices. A school, too, must adapt to the changing needs of its customers. For example, if more non-native students enroll, additional classes for the English language learner may need to be scheduled. A manager's ability to identify an organization's main customer groups, and to make the products that best satisfy their needs, is a crucial factor affecting organizational and managerial success.

The most obvious opportunity associated with expanding into the global environment is the prospect of selling goods and services to millions or billions of new customers, as Amazon's founder, Jeff Bezos, discovered when he expanded his company's operations in many countries. Similarly, Accenture and Capgemini, two large consulting companies, established regional operating centers around the globe, and they recruit and train thousands of overseas consultants to serve the needs of customers in their respective world regions.

Today many products have gained global customer acceptance. This consolidation is occurring both for consumer goods and for business products and has created enormous opportunities for managers. The worldwide acceptance of Coca-Cola, Apple iPads, McDonald's hamburgers, and Samsung smartphones is a sign that the tastes and preferences of customers in different countries may not be so different after all. Likewise, large, global markets exist for business products such as telecommunications equipment, electronic components, and computer and financial services. Thus, Cisco and Siemens sell their telecommunications equipment; Intel, its microprocessors; and Oracle and SAP, their business systems management software, to customers all over the world.

Competitors

competitors Organizations that produce goods and services that are similar to a particular organization's goods and services.

potential competitors Organizations that currently are not in a task environment but can enter if they so choose.

One of the most important forces an organization confronts in its task environment is competitors. **Competitors** are organizations that produce goods and services similar and comparable to a particular organization's goods and services. In other words, competitors are organizations trying to attract the same customers. Dell's competitors include other domestic PC makers (such as Apple and Microsoft) as well as overseas competitors (such as Sony and Toshiba in Japan, Lenovo in China, and Acer in Taiwan). Similarly, online stockbroker E*Trade has other competitors such as Fidelity and Charles Schwab.

Rivalry between competitors is potentially the most threatening force managers must deal with. A high level of rivalry typically results in price competition, and falling prices reduce customer revenues and profits. In the early 2000s, competition in the PC industry became intense because Dell was aggressively cutting costs and prices to increase its global market share. IBM had to exit the PC business after it lost billions in its battle against low-cost rivals, and HP also suffered losses while Dell's profits soared. By 2006, however, HP's fortunes had recovered because it had found ways to lower its costs and offer stylish new PCs, and Apple was growing rapidly, so Dell's profit margins continued to shrink. In 2009, HP overtook Dell to become the largest global PC maker. After a long and harsh battle with investors over the future of Dell, founder Michael Dell took the company private and shifted its focus to becoming more of an all-around technology company with less reliance on PC sales. In 2022, China's Lenovo retained its top position as the world's largest PC maker, followed by HP, Dell, Apple, and Asus. However, PC sales dropped dramatically in 2022 due to a cooling demand and an uneven supply of machines.[24]

Competition among PC makers continues to be strong as consumers look for the best prices and features, whether in retail stores or online.
97/Getty Images

Although extensive rivalry between existing competitors is a major threat to profitability, so is the potential for new competitors to enter the task environment. **Potential competitors** are organizations that are not currently in a task environment but have the resources to enter if they so choose. Ten years ago, for example, Amazon was not in the furniture or

Figure 6.2

Barriers to Entry and Competition

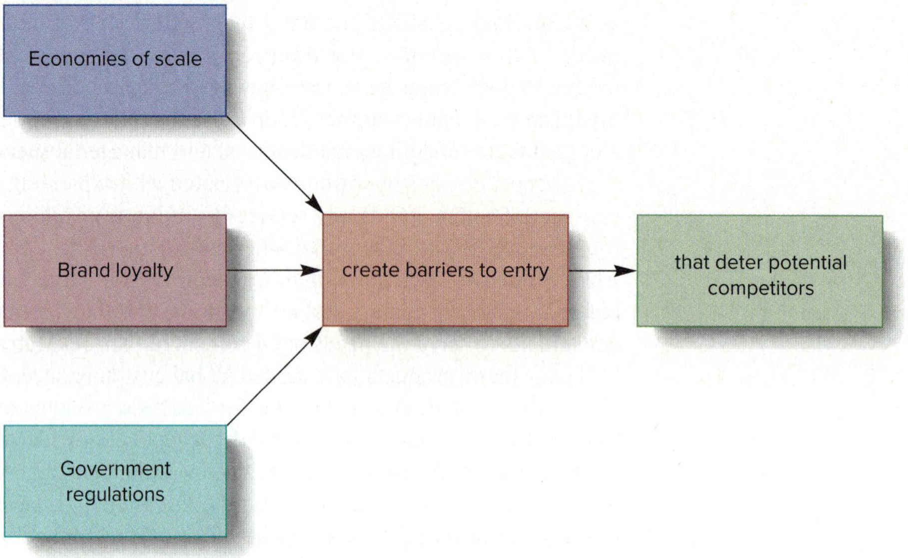

large appliance business, but it could enter these businesses if its managers decided it could profitably sell such products online–and today, the e-commerce giant sells furniture and appliances. When new competitors enter an industry, competition increases and prices and profits decrease–as furniture and electronics stores such as Best Buy have discovered as they continue to do battle with Amazon.

barriers to entry Factors that make it difficult and costly for an organization to enter a particular task environment or industry.

BARRIERS TO ENTRY In general, the potential for new competitors to enter a task environment (and thus increase competition) is a function of barriers to entry. **Barriers to entry** are factors that make it difficult and costly for a company to enter a particular task environment or industry.[25] In other words, the more difficult and costly it is to enter the task environment, the higher are the barriers to entry. The higher the barriers to entry, the fewer the competitors in an organization's task environment and, thus, the lower the threat of competition. With fewer competitors, it is easier to obtain customers and keep prices high.

economies of scale Cost advantages associated with large operations.

Barriers to entry result from three main sources: economies of scale, brand loyalty, and government regulations that impede entry (see Figure 6.2). **Economies of scale** are the cost advantages associated with large operations. Economies of scale result from factors such as manufacturing products in very large quantities, buying inputs in bulk, or making more effective use of organizational resources than do competitors by fully utilizing employees' skills and knowledge. If organizations already in the task environment are large and enjoy significant economies of scale, their costs are lower than the costs that potential entrants will face, and newcomers will find it expensive to enter the industry. Amazon, for example, enjoys significant economies of scale relative to its competitors because of its highly efficient and expansive distribution system. The company recently purchased several huge parcels of land in Niagara, New York; Ontario, California; and Loveland, Colorado to build distribution centers.[26]

brand loyalty Customers' preference for the products of organizations currently existing in the task environment.

Brand loyalty is customers' preference for the products of organizations currently in the task environment. If established organizations enjoy significant brand loyalty, a new entrant will find it difficult and costly to obtain a share of the market. Newcomers must bear huge marketing costs to build customer awareness of the goods or services they intend to provide. Today Apple, Google, Samsung, and Amazon enjoy a high level of brand loyalty and have some of the highest website hit rates, which allows them to increase their marketing revenues.

In some cases, *government regulations* function as a barrier to entry at both the industry and the country levels. Many industries that were deregulated, such as air transport, trucking, utilities, and telecommunications, experienced a high level of new entry after deregulation; this forced existing companies in those industries to operate more efficiently or risk being put out of business. At the national and global levels, administrative barriers are government policies

Now that Japan imports rice from other countries, including the United States, Japanese rice farmers, who can't compete against lower-priced imports, have been forced to leave their fields idle or grow less profitable crops.
MAHATHIR MOHD YASIN/Shutterstock

that create barriers to entry and limit imports of goods by overseas companies. Japan is well known for the many ways in which it tries to restrict the entry of overseas competitors or lessen their impact on Japanese firms. Japan has come under intense pressure to relax and abolish regulations such as those governing the import of rice, for example.

The Japanese rice market, like many other Japanese markets, was closed to overseas competitors until 1993 to protect Japan's thousands of high-cost, low-output rice farmers. Rice cultivation is expensive in Japan because of the country's mountainous terrain, and Japanese consumers have always paid high prices for rice. Under overseas pressure, the Japanese government opened the market, but overseas competitors were allowed to export to Japan only 8% of its annual rice consumption, to protect its farmers.

In the 2000s, however, an alliance between organic rice grower Lundberg Family Farms of California and the Nippon Restaurant Enterprise Co. found a new way to break into the Japanese rice market. Because there is no tariff on rice used in processed foods, Nippon converts the U.S. organic rice into "O-bento," an organic hot boxed lunch packed with rice, vegetables, chicken, beef, and salmon, all imported from the United States. The lunches became very popular, and Japanese rice farmers protested to the government because the entry of U.S. rice growers into the Japanese market forced them to leave their fields idle or grow less profitable crops. Recently, Japan experienced a severe shortage of reasonably priced rice for its food service sector due to the country's strict policy on growing rice for animal feed. This resulted in a higher demand for U.S. rice, which accounted for roughly 58% of Japan's rice imports in 2021. However, recent trade talks between the United States and Japan have broken down, including discussions about Japan importing U.S. rice, because of the U.S. withdrawal from the Trans-Pacific Partnership (TTP). Several countries in the TTP that export rice could provide strong competition for the United States in Japan's rice import business, including Australia.[27]

In summary, intense rivalry among competitors creates a task environment that is highly threatening and makes it increasingly difficult for managers to gain access to the resources an organization needs to make goods and services. Conversely, low rivalry results in a task environment where competitive pressures are more moderate and managers have greater opportunities to acquire the resources they need to make their organizations effective.

The General Environment

Economic, technological, sociocultural, demographic, political, and legal forces in the general environment often have important effects on forces in the task environment that determine an organization's ability to obtain resources–effects that managers may not be aware of. For example, the sudden, dramatic upheavals in the mortgage and banking industry that started in 2007 were brought about by a combination of the development of complex new financial lending instruments called derivatives; a speculative boom in commodities and housing prices; and lax government regulation that allowed unethical bankers and financial managers to exploit the derivatives to make immense short-term profits. These events triggered the economic crisis that peaked in 2008 but continued to ripple through the world economy for years, causing stock markets around the world to plummet, devastating the retirement savings of hundreds of millions of ordinary people, and causing layoffs of millions of employees as companies slashed their workforces because customers reduced their spending. Fortunately, sound economic policies put in place during the recession helped the economy rebound strongly over the past few years, although the effects of the COVID-19 pandemic continue to take their toll on the global economy.

The implication is clear: Managers must continuously analyze forces in the general environment because these forces affect ongoing decision making and planning. How well managers can perform this task determines how quickly an organization can respond to the changes taking place. Next we discuss the major forces in the general environment and examine their impact on an organization's task environment.

Economic Forces

economic forces Interest rates, inflation, unemployment, economic growth, and other factors that affect the general health and well-being of a nation or the regional economy of an organization.

Economic forces affect the general health and well-being of a country or world region. They include interest rates, inflation, unemployment, and economic growth. Economic forces produce many opportunities and threats for managers. Low levels of unemployment and falling interest rates give people more money to spend, and as a result organizations can sell more goods and services. Good economic times affect the supply of resources that become easier or more inexpensive to acquire, and organizations have an opportunity to flourish. High-tech companies enjoyed this throughout the 1990s when computer and electronics companies, like Sony, made record profits as the global economy boomed because of advances in technology and growing global trade. For creative businesspeople, economic times can be good in a region or nation with a less-developed economy, as long as people can see the opportunities that exist in that environment. For an example, see the "Management Insight" feature.

In contrast, worsening macroeconomic conditions, like those in 2020–2021 during the global pandemic, pose a major threat because they reduce managers' ability to gain access to the resources their organizations need to survive and prosper. Profit-seeking organizations such as hotels and retail stores have fewer customers during economic downturns. For example, in 2020, hotel occupancy plummeted by more than 70%, and several major retailers shut their doors for good, as the spread of COVID-19 restricted travel and in-person shopping. In addition, nonprofits such as charities and universities also saw donations decline by double digits due to the economic downturn.

Poor economic conditions make the environment more complex and managers' jobs more difficult and demanding. Companies often need to reduce the number of their managers and employees, streamline their operations, and identify ways to acquire and use resources more efficiently and effectively. Successful managers realize the important effects that economic forces have on their organizations, and they pay close attention to what is occurring in the economy at the national and regional levels to respond appropriately.

MANAGEMENT INSIGHT

Nollywood's a Hit in a Developing Economy

What filmmaking center produces 1,500 movies per year, is worth over $3 billion, and employs a million people? For now, Americans might be forgiven for not knowing the answer: It's Nollywood, the nickname of the Nigerian film industry.[28]

The industry had a modest beginning. In 1992, an electronics salesman named Kenneth Nnebue made a deal to buy a large quantity of blank videocassettes, which he knew would sit on store shelves. His customers had no way to use a blank cassette. Instead, he worked with the seller to record something on them. They wrote a script; hired a producer, director, and actors; and made a movie that sold hundreds of thousands of copies in Nigeria and other African countries. Nnebue wisely recognized that the local market had no movie theaters but plenty of people who enjoyed a good story on film. His early profitability encouraged bank lending and created a market for this kind of entertainment. The demand for videos led to demand for film actors and the establishment of film schools in the country.[29]

In the years since then, Nollywood has grown rapidly, becoming the second-largest center of film production in terms of output, after Bollywood in India. As it expanded its audience beyond Nigeria to the rest of Africa, it kept up with economic conditions and advances in technology. Competitors in this marketplace continue to find opportunities in what might seem like impossible conditions. For example, piracy of intellectual property is an ongoing problem, so a popular movie can actually lose money as consumers snap up illegally produced DVDs. Recently, however, the Nigerian film studio EbonyLife Films got around this problem with DVD sales by making Nollywood's first deal with Netflix to stream its hit *Chief Daddy* to a global market of 149 million customers in 190 countries. Netflix also recently acquired its first original Nollywood movie, *Lionheart.*[30]

The Nollywood story provides lessons for managers evaluating the economic environment. A developing nation may lack much that a business is thought to need: a transportation network, a trustworthy court system, supportive financial institutions, and so on. But what Nnebue saw was a business opportunity that could generate the prosperity needed to change the environment. Instead of entering an existing market, he helped create one by focusing on the particular needs of his local community and offering an affordable product.[31]

Technological Forces

technology The combination of skills and equipment that managers use in designing, producing, and distributing goods and services.

technological forces Outcomes of changes in the technology managers use to design, produce, or distribute goods and services.

Technology is the combination of tools, machines, computers, skills, information, and knowledge that managers use to design, produce, and distribute goods and services; **technological forces** are outcomes of changes in that technology. The overall pace of technological change has accelerated greatly in the last decades because technological advances in microprocessors and computer hardware and software have spurred technological advances in most businesses and industries. The effects of changing technological forces are still increasing in magnitude.

Technological forces can have profound implications for managers and organizations. Technological change can make established products obsolete–for example, cathode-ray tube (CRT) computer monitors and televisions, bound sets of encyclopedias, and newspapers and magazines–forcing managers to find new ways to satisfy customer needs. Although technological change can threaten an organization, it also can create a host of new opportunities for designing, making, or distributing new and better kinds of goods and services. For example, in 2022, AMD launched a new generation of Ryzen processors for use in both desktop units and ultrathin and gaming laptops. Features of the new products include "Zen" architecture for high performance, top-notch graphics for gaming, and longer battery life for mobile use. Innovations like these continue to push technological boundaries and spur demand for all kinds of new digital devices and services, which affect the competitiveness of today's companies.[32]

Changes in technology are altering the nature of work itself within organizations, including that of the manager's job. Today telecommuting, videoconferencing, and cloud computing are everyday activities that let managers supervise and coordinate geographically dispersed employees. Employees in many companies now work from home offices and commute electronically to work. They communicate with other employees through companywide electronic communication networks using smartphones and other mobile devices to orchestrate "face-to-face" meetings with coworkers across the country or globe.

Sociocultural Forces

sociocultural forces Pressures emanating from the social structure of a country or society or from the national culture.

social structure The traditional system of relationships established between people and groups in a society.

national culture The set of values that a society considers important and the norms of behavior that are approved or sanctioned in that society.

Sociocultural forces are pressures emanating from the social structure of a country or society or from the national culture, such as the concern for diversity, discussed in the previous chapter. Pressures from both sources can either constrain or facilitate the way organizations operate and managers behave. **Social structure** is the traditional system of relationships established between people and groups in a society. Societies differ substantially in social structure. In societies that have a high degree of social stratification, there are many distinctions among individuals and groups. Caste systems in India and Tibet and the recognition of numerous social classes in Great Britain and France produce a multilayered social structure in each of those countries. In contrast, social stratification is lower in relatively egalitarian New Zealand and in the United States, where the social structure reveals few distinctions among people. Most top managers in France come from the upper classes of French society, but top managers in the United States come from all strata of American society.

Societies also differ in the extent to which they emphasize the individual over the group. Such differences may dictate how managers need to motivate and lead employees.

National culture is the set of values that a society considers important and the norms of behavior that are approved or sanctioned in that society. Societies differ substantially in the values and norms they emphasize. For example, in the United States, individualism is highly valued, but in Korea and Japan individuals are expected to conform to group expectations.[33] National culture, discussed at length later in this chapter, also affects how managers motivate and coordinate employees and how organizations do business. Ethics, an important aspect of national culture, were discussed in detail in Chapter 4.

Social structure and national culture not only differ across societies but also change within societies over time. In the United States, attitudes toward the roles of women, sex, marriage, and the LGBTQ community changed in each past decade. Many people in Asian countries such as Hong Kong, Singapore, Korea, and even China think the younger generation is far more individualistic than previous generations. Currently, throughout much of Eastern Europe, new values that emphasize individualism and entrepreneurship are replacing communist values based on collectivism and obedience to the state. The pace of change continues to accelerate.

Individual managers and organizations must be responsive to changes in, and differences among, the social structures and national cultures of all the countries in which they operate. In today's increasingly integrated global economy, managers are likely to interact with people from several countries, and many managers live and work abroad. Effective managers are sensitive to differences between societies and adjust their behavior accordingly.

Blue Apron is one of many online meal-kit delivery companies offering complete meals to consumers, delivered to their front door.
Scott Eisen/Stringer/Getty Images

Managers and organizations also must respond to social changes within a society. In the last decades, for example, Americans have become increasingly interested in their personal health and fitness. Managers who recognized this trend early and took advantage of the opportunities that resulted from it were able to reap significant gains for their organizations, such as organic food and meal-kit delivery services. The organic produce industry has been growing for the past decade due to people's interest in healthy and organic food. Many companies offer weekly deliveries of organic fruits, vegetables, and meats to consumers' homes; while others sell complete meal kits for delivery, taking the stress and time required to menu plan and shop out of the equation.[34] But getting portioned meal ingredients delivered to your front door is not cheap–a recent study determined that purchasing meal kits was five times more expensive than food shopping at a local store.[35]

Demographic Forces

demographic forces
Outcomes of changes in, or changing attitudes toward, the characteristics of a population, such as age, gender, ethnic origin, race, sexual orientation, and social class.

Demographic forces are outcomes of changes in, or changing attitudes toward, the characteristics of a population, such as age, gender, ethnic origin, race, sexual orientation, and social class. Like the other forces in the general environment, demographic forces present managers with opportunities and threats and can have major implications for organizations. We examined the nature of these challenges in depth in our discussion of diversity in Chapter 5.

Today most industrialized nations are experiencing the aging of their populations as a consequence of falling birth and death rates and the aging of the Baby Boomer generation. Consequently, the absolute number of older people has increased substantially, which has generated opportunities for organizations that cater to older people, such as the home health care, recreation, and medical industries, which have seen an upswing in demand for their services. The aging of the population also has several implications for the workplace. Most significant are a relative decline in the number of young people joining the workforce and an increase in the number of active employees who are postponing retirement beyond the traditional age of 65. Indeed, the financial crisis in the late 2000s made it impossible for millions of older people to retire because their savings were all but wiped out. These changes suggest that organizations need to find ways to motivate older employees and use their skills and knowledge–an issue that many Western societies continue to tackle.

Political and Legal Forces

political and legal forces Outcomes of changes in laws and regulations, such as deregulation of industries, privatization of organizations, and increased emphasis on environmental protection.

Political and legal forces are outcomes of changes in laws and regulations. They result from political and legal developments that take place within a nation, within a world region, or across the world and significantly affect managers and organizations everywhere. Political processes shape a nation's laws and the international laws that govern the relationships between nations. Laws constrain the operations of organizations and managers and thus create both opportunities and threats.[36] For example, throughout much of the industrialized world there has been a strong trend toward deregulation of industries previously controlled by the state and privatization of organizations once owned by the state, such as airlines, railways, and utility companies.

Another important political and legal force affecting managers and organizations is the political integration of countries that has been taking place during the last decades. Increasingly, nations are forming political unions that allow free exchange of resources and capital. The growth of the European Union (EU) is one example: Common laws govern trade and commerce between EU member countries, and the European Commission has the right to examine the business of any global organization and to approve any proposed mergers between overseas companies that operate inside the EU. For example, Apple's proposed acquisition of Shazam, a UK-based app, was reviewed by the European Commission because of its potential threat to competition among music-sharing platforms in Europe. The Shazam app uses a microphone on a smartphone or computer to identify almost any song playing nearby and then directs users to places where they can listen to the music, such as Apple Music or Spotify. Acquiring Shazam would help Apple embed that capability deeper into its music offerings, which might push more consumers to sign on with Apple Music. The Commission took up the review at the request of several EU members, including Austria, Italy, and Sweden. After a detailed review, the Commission gave Apple the green light to purchase Shazam, saying that the acquisition did not violate antitrust laws in the European Union.[37]

Another political and legal issue that has implications for managers around the world is the departure of the United Kingdom from the EU, the so-called Brexit, a move that occurred in January 2020, nearly five years after UK voters decided the country should leave the EU. Preliminary outcomes from Brexit suggest that the UK economy appears to be less open and less global than it was when the country was part of the European Union. For example, the UK's departure has brought significant disruption to trade, especially for UK exports to EU countries, due to new border rules and required paperwork. In addition, tighter immigration rules and the departure of many European workers from Britain have contributed to a shortage of workers to fill jobs in the country, not to mention the ongoing economic fallout from the global pandemic. A recent report shows reductions in trade from UK to EU by 16% and from EU to UK by 20% relative to pre-Brexit years. Only time will tell whether the vote to leave the EU will be viewed as a success for the United Kingdom.[38]

Indeed, international agreements to abolish laws and regulations that restrict and reduce trade between countries have been having profound effects on global organizations. The falling legal trade barriers create enormous opportunities for companies to sell goods and services internationally. But by allowing overseas companies to compete in a nation's domestic market for customers, falling trade barriers also pose a serious threat because they increase competition in the task environment. For example, the Obama administration negotiated for several years for the United States to join the Trans-Pacific Partnership (TPP), a trade agreement between the United States and 11 other countries. In 2017, however, in the early days of his presidency, Donald Trump issued an executive order pulling the country out of the TPP, taking a stand against foreign competitors as part of his "America First" strategy. The TPP trade agreement was recently renamed the Comprehensive and Progressive Agreement for Trans-Pacific Partnership (CPTPP) to better reflect the 11 countries' commitment to further integrate their economies and provide fair trade throughout the region. As of this writing, the Biden Administration has yet to decide whether the United States will rejoin the trade alliance; however, China, Taiwan, and the United Kingdom have recently submitted requests to join the organization.[39]

Deregulation, privatization, and the removal of legal barriers to trade are just a few of the many ways in which changing political and legal forces can challenge organizations and managers. Others include increased emphasis on environmental protection and the preservation of endangered species, increased emphasis on workplace safety, and legal constraints against discrimination on the basis of race, gender, or age. Managers face major challenges when they seek to take advantage of the opportunities created by changing political, legal, and economic forces.

The Changing Global Environment

The 21st century has banished the idea that the world is composed of distinct national countries and markets that are separated physically, economically, and culturally. Managers need to recognize that companies compete in a truly global marketplace, which is the source of the opportunities and threats they must respond to. Managers continually confront the challenges of global competition such as establishing operations in a country abroad, obtaining inputs from suppliers abroad, or managing in a different national culture.[40]

LO6-4 Explain why the global environment is becoming more open and competitive, and identify the forces behind the process of globalization that increase the opportunities, complexities, challenges, and threats managers face.

In essence, as a result of falling trade barriers, managers view the global environment as open—that is, as an environment in which companies are free to buy goods and services from, and sell goods and services to, whichever companies and countries they choose. They also are free to compete against each other to attract customers around the world. All large companies must establish an international network of operations and subsidiaries to build global competitive advantage. Coca-Cola and PepsiCo, for example, have competed aggressively for decades to develop the strongest global beverage empire, just as Toyota and Honda have built hundreds of car plants around the world to provide the vehicles that global customers like.

In this section, we first explain how this open global environment is the result of globalization and the flow of capital around the world. Then we discuss the four approaches companies use to expand internationally. Next we examine how specific economic, political, and legal changes, such as the lowering of barriers to trade and investment, have increased globalization and led to greater interaction and exchanges between organizations and countries. Then we discuss how declining barriers of distance and culture have also increased the pace of globalization, and we consider the specific implications of these changes for managers and organizations. Finally, in the last section of the chapter, we note that nations still differ widely from each other because they have distinct cultural values and norms and that managers must appreciate these differences to compete successfully across countries.

The Process of Globalization

globalization The set of specific and general forces that work together to integrate and connect economic, political, and social systems across countries, cultures, or geographic regions so that nations become increasingly interdependent and similar.

Perhaps the most important reason the global environment has become more open and competitive is the increase in globalization. **Globalization** is the set of specific and general forces that work together to integrate and connect economic, political, and social systems across countries, cultures, or geographic regions. The result of globalization is that nations and peoples become increasingly interdependent because the same forces affect them in similar ways. The fates of peoples in different countries become interlinked as the world's markets and businesses become increasingly interconnected. And as nations become more interdependent, they become more similar to one another in the sense that people develop a similar liking for products as diverse as cell phones, iPads, blue jeans, soft drinks, sports teams, electric vehicles, and foods such as curry, green tea, and Colombian coffee.

But what drives or spurs globalization? What makes companies like IKEA, Toyota, or Microsoft want to venture into an uncertain global environment? The answer is that the path of globalization is shaped by the ebb and flow of *capital*—valuable wealth-generating assets or resources that people move through companies, countries, and world regions to seek their greatest returns or profits. Managers, employees, and companies like Hyundai and Samsung are motivated to try to profit or benefit by using their skills to make products customers around the world want to buy. The four principal forms of capital that flow between countries are these:

- *Human capital:* the flow of people around the world through immigration, migration, and emigration
- *Financial capital:* the flow of money capital across world markets through overseas investment, credit, lending, and aid
- *Resource capital:* the flow of natural resources, parts, and components between companies and countries, such as metals, minerals, lumber, energy, food products, microprocessors, and auto parts
- *Political capital:* the flow of power and influence around the world using diplomacy, persuasion, aggression, and force of arms to protect the right or access of a country, world region, or political bloc to the other forms of capital

Despite recent headwinds, caused in part by the global pandemic, Africa's overall economic outlook continues to be positive, with a projected growth expected to exceed 3% in the coming year. African countries continue to face economic, political, social, and environmental challenges as globalization accelerates changes to business and everyday life in cities such as Lagos, Nigeria, pictured here.
Pius Utomi Ekpei/AFP/Getty Images

Most of the economic advances associated with globalization are the result of these four capital flows and the interactions between them, as nations compete on the world stage to protect and increase their standards of living and to further the political goals and social causes that are espoused by their societies' cultures. The next sections look at the factors that have increased the rate at which capital flows between companies and countries. In a positive sense, the faster the flow, the more capital is being used where it can create the most value, such as people moving to where their skills earn more money, or investors switching to the stocks or bonds that give higher dividends or interest, or companies finding lower-cost sources of inputs. In a negative sense, however, a fast flow of capital also means that individual countries or world regions can find themselves in trouble when companies and investors move their capital to invest it in more productive ways in other countries or world regions–often those with lower labor costs or rapidly expanding markets. When capital leaves a country, the results are higher unemployment, recession, and a lower standard of living for its people.

International Expansion

As if planning whether to vertically integrate, diversify, or concentrate on the core business were not a difficult enough task, corporate-level managers also must decide on the appropriate way to compete internationally. A basic question confronts the managers of any organization that needs to sell its products abroad and compete in more than one national market: To what extent should the organization customize features of its products and marketing campaign to different national conditions?

global strategy Selling the same standardized product and using the same basic marketing approach in each national market.

multidomestic strategy Customizing products and marketing strategies to specific national conditions.

If managers decide that their organization should sell the same standardized product in each national market in which it competes, and use the same basic marketing approach, they adopt a **global strategy**. Such companies undertake little, if any, customization to suit the specific needs of customers in different countries. But if managers decide to customize products and marketing strategies to specific national conditions, they adopt a **multidomestic strategy**. Panasonic has traditionally pursued a global strategy, selling the same basic TVs, camcorders, and DVD and MP3 players in every country in which it does business and often using the same basic marketing approach. Unilever, the European food and household products company, has pursued a multidomestic strategy. Thus, to appeal to German customers, Unilever's German division sells a different range of food products and uses a different marketing approach than its North American division.

Both global and multidomestic strategies have advantages and disadvantages. The major advantage of a global strategy is the significant cost savings associated with not having to customize products and marketing approaches to different national conditions. For example, Rolex watches, Ralph Lauren or Tommy Hilfiger clothing, Chanel or Armani clothing or accessories or perfume, Apple computers, Chinese-made plastic toys, and U.S.-grown rice and wheat are all products that can be sold using the same marketing across many countries by simply changing the language. Thus, companies can save a significant amount of money. Organizations that serve business customers often adopt a global strategy because customer needs such as improving quality and lowering costs are consistent from place to place. Expanding beyond national borders certainly can be a huge success for companies. However, even a surge in demand can pose management challenges, as described in the "Managing Globally" feature.

MANAGING GLOBALLY

When Growth Becomes a Problem

In 2020, when the COVID-19 pandemic arrived in the United States, a chief economic worry was that lockdowns and physical distancing would trigger massive layoffs and widespread business failures, leading to a recession. However, businesses were more agile and resilient than feared, and the federal government provided support that helped households and companies stay afloat. While economic well-being was out of reach for some, the overall U.S. economy quickly bounced back, and spending soared–but not always through the same channels. Many consumers made more of their purchases online or shifted from entertainment to home goods or from travel to electronics in their buying decisions as they were stuck at home.

These sudden changes led to major headaches for companies with global networks of suppliers and distributors. U.S. ports, many of which have not been expanded or upgraded in years, experienced backups of ships bringing in parts and products from Asia. Shortages of semiconductors led automakers to pause assembly of vehicles. Appliance maker Whirlpool, which had built a system of producing goods based on sales forecasts and orders received, had to shift to building whatever products it could make with the parts on hand. Similarly, Volvo Construction Equipment's Pennsylvania plant constantly had to reschedule production based on which parts made their way into inventory from 17 different countries, which sometimes involved pausing production for hours or even a day at a time.[41]

The difficulties have been especially significant for makers of electric vehicles, which are also swept up by waves of technological and social change. Demand for all-electric and hybrid vehicles is rising faster than the supply of materials for making batteries for these vehicles. U.S. automakers have been investing in battery factories, but investments in materials are still in early stages. Furthermore, a majority of the production of key battery components and materials occurs in China, where the government hopes to maintain the country's dominance of the industry.[42]

For companies trying to cope with a supply shortage and demand surge, the options are limited. Production of semiconductors is already near capacity. Building new capacity to fabricate semiconductors, mine nickel, or process lithium can take months or years and requires a major investment. To accelerate access to the goods and technology, General Motors and other U.S. companies are forming partnerships or acquiring businesses overseas. Manufacturers, construction businesses, and distributors are also coping in the short term by purchasing whenever they can, which typically involves higher prices and greater storage costs.[43]

The major disadvantage of pursuing a global strategy is that by ignoring national differences, managers may leave themselves vulnerable to local competitors that differentiate their products to suit local tastes. Global food makers Kellogg's and Nestlé learned this when they entered the Indian processed food market, which is worth over $300 billion a year. These companies did not understand how to customize their products to the tastes of the Indian market and initially suffered large losses. When Kellogg's launched its breakfast cereals in India, for example, it failed to understand that most Indians eat cooked breakfasts because milk is normally not pasteurized. Today, with the growing availability of pasteurized or canned milk, it offers exotic cereals made from basmati rice and flavored with mango to appeal to customers. Similarly, Nestlé's Maggi noodles failed to please Indian customers until it gave them a "marsala" or mixed curry spice flavor; today its noodles have become a staple in Indian diets.[44]

The advantages and disadvantages of a multidomestic strategy are the opposite of those of a global strategy. The major advantage of a multidomestic strategy is that by customizing product offerings and marketing approaches to local conditions, managers may be able to gain market share or charge higher prices for their products. The major disadvantage is that customization raises production costs and puts the multidomestic company at a price disadvantage because it often has to charge prices higher than the prices charged by competitors pursuing a global strategy. Obviously, the choice between these two strategies calls for trade-offs.

CHOOSING A WAY TO EXPAND INTERNATIONALLY As we have discussed, a more competitive global environment has proved to be both an opportunity and a threat for organizations and managers. The opportunity is that organizations that expand globally can open new markets, reach more customers, and gain access to new sources of raw materials and to low-cost suppliers of inputs. The threat is that organizations that expand globally are likely to encounter new competitors in the foreign countries they enter and must respond to new political, economic, and cultural conditions.

Before setting up foreign operations, managers of companies such as Amazon, Lands' End, GE, P&G, and Boeing needed to analyze the forces in the environment of a particular country (such as Korea or Brazil) to choose the right method to expand and respond to those forces in the most appropriate way. In general, four basic ways to operate in the global environment are exporting and importing, licensing and franchising, strategic alliances, and wholly owned foreign subsidiaries. We briefly discuss each one, moving from the lowest level of foreign involvement and investment required of a global organization and its managers, and the least amount of risk, to the high end of the spectrum (see Figure 6.3).[45]

exporting Making products at home and selling them abroad.

importing Selling products at home that are made abroad.

EXPORTING AND IMPORTING The least complex global operations are exporting and importing. A company engaged in **exporting** makes products at home and sells them abroad. An organization might sell its own products abroad or allow a local organization in the foreign country to distribute its products. Few risks are associated with exporting because a company does not have to invest in developing manufacturing facilities abroad. It can further reduce its investment abroad if it allows a local company to distribute its products.

A company engaged in **importing** sells products at home that are made abroad (products it makes itself or buys from other companies). For example, many of the products that HomeGoods sells to its customers are made abroad. In many cases the appeal of a product—Irish crystal, French wine, Italian furniture, or Indian silk—is that it is made abroad. The Internet has made it much easier for companies to tell potential foreign buyers about their products; detailed product specifications and features are available online, and informed buyers can communicate easily with prospective sellers.

licensing Allowing a foreign organization to take charge of manufacturing and distributing a product in its country or world region in return for a negotiated fee.

franchising Selling to a foreign organization the rights to use a brand name and operating know-how in return for a lump-sum payment and a share of the profits.

LICENSING AND FRANCHISING In **licensing**, a company (the licenser) allows a foreign organization (the licensee) to take charge of both manufacturing and distributing one or more of its products in the licensee's country or world region in return for a negotiated fee. Chemical maker DuPont might license a local factory in India to produce nylon or Teflon. The advantage of licensing is that the licenser does not have to bear the development costs associated with opening up in a foreign country; the licensee bears the costs. The risks associated with this strategy are that the company granting the license has to give its foreign partner access to its technological know-how and so risks losing control of its secrets.

Whereas licensing is pursued primarily by manufacturing companies, franchising is pursued primarily by service organizations. In **franchising**, a company (the franchisor) sells to a foreign organization (the franchisee) the rights to use its brand name and operating know-how in return for a lump-sum payment and share of the franchiser's profits. Hilton Hotels might sell a franchise to a local company in Chile to operate hotels under the Hilton name in return for a franchise payment. The advantage of franchising is that the franchiser does not have to bear the development costs of overseas expansion and avoids the many problems associated with setting up foreign operations. The downside is that the organization that grants the franchise may lose control over how the franchisee operates, and product quality may fall. In this way franchisers, such as Hilton, Avis, and McDonald's, risk losing their good names. American customers who buy McDonald's hamburgers in Korea may reasonably expect those burgers to be as good as the ones they get at home. If they are not, McDonald's reputation will suffer over time. Once again, the Internet facilitates communication between partners and allows them to better meet each other's expectations.

Figure 6.3

Four Ways to Expand Internationally

STRATEGIC ALLIANCES One way to overcome the loss-of-control problems associated with exporting, licensing, and franchising is to expand globally by means of a strategic alliance. In a **strategic alliance**, managers pool or share their organization's resources and know-how with those of a foreign company, and the two organizations share the rewards or risks of starting a new venture in a foreign country. Sharing resources allows a U.S. company, for example, to take advantage of the high-quality skills of foreign manufacturers and the specialized knowledge of foreign managers about the needs of local customers and to reduce the risks involved in a venture. At the same time, the terms of the alliance give the U.S. company more control over how the good or service is produced or sold in the foreign country than it would have as a franchiser or licenser.

strategic alliance An agreement in which managers pool or share their organization's resources and know-how with a foreign company, and the two organizations share the rewards and risks of starting a new venture.

A strategic alliance can take the form of a written contract between two or more companies to exchange resources, or it can result in the creation of a new organization. A **joint venture** is a strategic alliance between two or more companies that agree to jointly establish and share the ownership of a new business.[46] An organization's level of involvement abroad increases in a joint venture because the alliance normally involves a capital investment in production facilities abroad in order to produce goods or services outside the home country. Risk, however, is reduced. The Internet and global teleconferencing provide the increased communication and coordination necessary for global partners to work together. For example, General Mills participates in two international joint ventures. Cereal Partners Worldwide (CPW) is a 50-50 joint venture between General Mills and Nestlé, which markets breakfast cereals in more than 130 countries. CPW combines the expertise of General Mills–the second-largest cereal manufacturer in North America–with the worldwide presence and distribution strength of global giant Nestlé. General Mills' other joint venture is Häagen-Dazs Japan. In fiscal year 2022, these joint ventures accounted for more than $2.1 billion in sales for General Mills.[47]

joint venture A strategic alliance among two or more companies that agree to jointly establish and share the ownership of a new business.

WHOLLY OWNED FOREIGN SUBSIDIARIES When managers decide to establish a **wholly owned foreign subsidiary**, they invest in establishing production operations in a foreign country independent of any local direct involvement. Many Japanese car component companies, for example, have established their own operations in the United States to supply U.S.-based Japanese carmakers such as Toyota and Honda with high-quality car components.

wholly owned foreign subsidiary Production operations established in a foreign country independent of any local direct involvement.

Operating alone, without any direct involvement from foreign companies, an organization receives all of the rewards and bears all of the risks associated with operating abroad.[48] This method of international expansion is much more expensive than the others because it requires a higher level of foreign investment and presents managers with many more threats. However, investment in a foreign subsidiary or division offers significant advantages: It gives an organization high potential returns because the organization does not have to share its profits with a foreign organization, and it reduces the level of risk because the organization's managers have full control over all aspects of their foreign subsidiary's operations. Moreover, this type of investment allows managers to protect their technology and know-how from foreign organizations. Large, well-known companies like DuPont, GM, and P&G, which have plenty of resources, make extensive use of wholly owned subsidiaries.

Declining Barriers to Trade and Investment

One of the main factors that has speeded globalization by freeing the movement of capital has been the decline in barriers to trade and investment, discussed earlier. During the 1920s and 1930s, many countries erected formidable barriers to international trade and investment in the belief that this was the best way to promote their economic well-being. Many of these barriers were high tariffs on imports of manufactured goods. A **tariff** is a tax that a government imposes on goods imported into one country from another. The aim of import tariffs is to protect domestic industries and jobs, such as those in the auto or steel industry, from overseas competition by raising the price of these products from abroad. For example, in May 2018, Donald Trump announced a 25% tariff on imported steel and a 10% tariff on imported aluminum, which caused a global outcry from other countries and received mixed reviews from U.S. business leaders. As of this writing, most of the tariffs are still in place, although steel and aluminum products from Canada and Mexico are now exempt from tariffs as part of the renegotiated NAFTA deal, which we discuss in the next section of the chapter. In addition, tariffs were lifted on steel and aluminum imported from European Union countries. President Biden

tariff A tax that a government imposes on imported or, occasionally, exported goods.

recently commented he was "not ready" to lift U.S. tariffs on Chinese imports because China fell far short of a deal signed during the Trump administration to buy $200 billion in additional goods and services.[49]

The reason for removing tariffs is that, very often, when one country imposes an import tariff, others follow suit, and the result is a series of retaliatory moves as countries progressively raise tariff barriers against each other. In the 1920s, this behavior depressed world demand and helped usher in the Great Depression of the 1930s and massive unemployment. Beginning with the 2009 economic crisis, the governments of most countries have worked hard in the 2010s not to fall into the trap of raising tariffs to protect jobs and industries in the short run because they know the long-term consequences of this would be the loss of even more jobs. Governments of countries that resort to raising tariff barriers ultimately reduce employment and undermine the economic growth of their countries because capital and resources will always move to their most highly valued use–wherever that is in the world.

GATT AND THE RISE OF FREE TRADE After World War II, advanced Western industrial countries, having learned from the Great Depression, committed themselves to the goal of removing barriers to the free flow of resources and capital between countries. This commitment was reinforced by the acceptance of the principle that free trade, rather than tariff barriers, was the best way to foster a healthy domestic economy and low unemployment.[50]

free-trade doctrine The idea that if each country specializes in the production of the goods and services that it can produce most efficiently, this will make the best use of global resources.

The **free-trade doctrine** predicts that if each country agrees to specialize in the production of the goods and services that it can produce most efficiently, this will make the best use of global capital resources and will result in lower prices.[51] For example, if Indian companies are highly efficient in the production of textiles and U.S. companies are highly efficient in the production of computer software, then, under a free-trade agreement, capital would move to India and be invested there to produce textiles, while capital from around the world would flow to the United States and be invested in its innovative software companies. Consequently, prices of both textiles and software should fall because each product is being produced where it can be made at the lowest cost, benefiting consumers and making the best use of scarce capital. This doctrine is also responsible for the increase in global outsourcing and the loss of millions of U.S. jobs in textiles and manufacturing as capital has been invested in factories in Asian countries such as China and Malaysia. However, millions of U.S. jobs have also been created because of new capital investments in the high-tech and service sectors, which in theory should offset manufacturing job losses in the long run.

Historically, countries that accepted this free-trade doctrine set as their goal the removal of barriers to the free flow of goods, services, and capital between countries. They tried to achieve this through an international treaty known as the General Agreement on Tariffs and Trade (GATT). In the years since World War II, there have been multiple rounds of GATT negotiations aimed at lowering tariff barriers. For example, the Uruguay Round involved 117 countries and succeeded in lowering tariffs by more than 30% from the previous level. It also led to the dissolution of GATT and its replacement by the World Trade Organization (WTO), which continues the struggle to reduce tariffs and has more power to sanction countries that break global agreements. The latest round of negotiations, called the Doha Round, effectively ended in 2015, when trade ministers failed to agree to keep the negotiations and discussions alive. It seems that many of the key countries (United States, China, India, and EU members) were unwilling or unable to make fundamental concessions.[52]

Declining Barriers of Distance and Culture

Historically, barriers of distance and culture also closed the global environment and kept managers focused on their domestic market. The management problems Unilever, the global consumer goods company now with more than 400 brands, experienced at the turn of the 20th century illustrate the effect of these barriers.

Founded in London during the 1880s by William Lever, a Quaker, Unilever had a worldwide reach by the early 1900s and operated subsidiaries in most major countries of the British Empire, including India, Canada, and Australia. Lever had a very hands-on, autocratic management style and found his far-flung business empire difficult to control. The reason for Lever's control problems was that communication over great distances was difficult. It took six weeks to reach India by ship from England, and international telephone and telegraph services were unreliable.

Another problem Unilever encountered was the difficulty of doing business in societies that were separated from Britain by barriers of language and culture. Different countries have different sets of national beliefs, values, and norms, and Lever found that a management approach that worked in Britain did not necessarily work in India or Persia (now Iran). As a result, management practices had to be tailored to suit each unique national culture. After Lever's death in 1925, top management at Unilever lowered or *decentralized* decision-making authority to the managers of the various national subsidiaries so they could develop a management approach that suited the country in which they were operating. One result of this strategy was that the subsidiaries grew distant and remote from one another, which reduced Unilever's performance.[53]

Since the end of World War II, a continuing stream of advances in communications and transportation technology has worked to reduce the barriers of distance and culture that affected Unilever and all global organizations. Over the last decades, global communication has been revolutionized by developments in satellites, digital technology, the Internet and global computer networks, and video teleconferencing that allow transmission of vast amounts of information and make reliable, secure, and instantaneous communication possible between people and companies anywhere in the world. This revolution has made it possible for a global organization–a tiny garment factory in Li & Fung's network or a huge company such as IKEA or Unilever–to do business anywhere, anytime and to search for customers and suppliers around the world.

One of the most important innovations in transportation technology that has opened the global environment has been the growth of commercial jet travel. New York is now closer in travel time to Tokyo than it was to Philadelphia in the days of the 13 colonies–a fact that makes control of far-flung international businesses much easier today than in William Lever's era. In addition to speeding travel, modern communications and transportation technologies have also helped reduce the cultural distance between countries. The Internet and its millions of websites facilitate the development of global communications networks and media that are helping to create a worldwide culture that, in some cases, has diluted unique national cultures. Moreover, entertainment and news networks such as CNN, MTV, ESPN, BBC, and HBO can now be received in many countries, and Hollywood films and other original content are streamed via the Internet across the globe.

Effects of Free Trade on Managers

The lowering of barriers to trade and investment and the decline of distance and culture barriers have created enormous opportunities for companies to expand the market for their goods and services through exports and investments in overseas countries. The shift toward a more open global economy has created not only more opportunities to sell goods and services in markets abroad but also the opportunity to buy more from other countries. A manager's job is more challenging in a dynamic global environment because of the increased intensity of competition that goes hand in hand with the lowering of barriers to trade and investment.

REGIONAL TRADE AGREEMENTS The growth of regional trade agreements, such as the North American Free Trade Agreement (NAFTA), and more recently the Central American Free Trade Agreement (CAFTA), also presents opportunities and threats for managers and their organizations. In North America, NAFTA, which became effective in 1994, had the aim of abolishing the tariffs on 99% of the goods traded between Mexico, Canada, and the United States by 2004. Although it did not achieve this lofty goal, NAFTA removed most barriers on the cross-border flow of resources, giving, for example, financial institutions and retail businesses in Canada and the United States unrestricted access to the Mexican marketplace. After NAFTA was signed, there was a flood of investment into Mexico from the United States, as well as from many other countries such as Japan. Walmart, Costco, Ford, and many major U.S. retail chains expanded their operations in Mexico; Walmart, for example, is stocking many more products from Mexico in its U.S. stores, and its Mexican store chain is also expanding rapidly.

The establishment of free-trade areas creates an opportunity for manufacturing organizations because it lets them reduce their costs. They can do this either by shifting production to the lowest-cost location within the free-trade area (for example, U.S. auto and textile companies shifting production to Mexico) or by serving the whole region from one location rather than establishing separate operations in each country. Some managers, however, view regional free-trade agreements as a threat because they expose a company based in one member country to increased competition from companies based in the other member countries. NAFTA has had this effect; today Mexican managers in some industries face the threat of head-to-head competition against efficient U.S. and Canadian companies. But the opposite is true as well: U.S. and Canadian managers are experiencing threats in labor-intensive industries, such as the flooring tile, roofing, and textile industries, where Mexican businesses have a cost advantage.

Over the past several years, negotiating teams from the United States, Mexico, and Canada have worked through more than seven rounds of meetings to renegotiate and modernize NAFTA. The new agreement–the United States-Mexico-Canada Agreement (USMCA)–has been ratified by all three countries and went into effect on July 1, 2020. USMCA includes major changes on car manufacturing rules; new policies on labor and environmental standards; intellectual property and digital trade protections; and increased access to the Canadian dairy market by U.S. farmers.[54]

There are many regional trade agreements around the world. For example, founded in 1999, the African Union's purpose is both political and economic. Its goals include removing any remnants of colonization and apartheid, as well as creating cooperation for development. Complementing the role of the African Union is the Southern African Development Community, a 16-country group whose goals include socioeconomic development and poverty eradication. Another trade agreement is the Cooperation Council for the Arab States of the Gulf, which is made up of several countries, including Qatar, Oman, Bahrain, the United Arab Emirates, Kuwait, and Saudi Arabia. As part of the agreement, countries work on regional cooperation and economic relations.[55] These trade agreements are designed to allow managers to take advantage of opportunities that other members of the agreements can provide.

The Role of National Culture

Despite evidence that countries are becoming more similar because of globalization and that the world may become "a global village," the cultures of different countries still vary widely because of vital differences in their values, norms, and attitudes. As noted earlier, national culture includes the values, norms, knowledge, beliefs, moral principles, laws, customs, and other practices that unite the citizens of a country. National culture shapes individual behavior by specifying appropriate and inappropriate behavior and interaction with others. People learn national culture in their everyday lives by interacting with those around them. This learning starts at an early age and continues throughout their lives.

Cultural Values and Norms

values Ideas about what a society believes to be good, right, desirable, or beautiful.

The basic building blocks of national culture are values and norms. **Values** are beliefs about what a society considers to be good, right, desirable, or beautiful–or their opposites. They provide the basic underpinnings for notions of individual freedom, democracy, truth, justice, honesty, loyalty, social obligation, collective responsibility, gender roles, love, sex, marriage, and so on. Values are more than merely abstract concepts; they are invested with considerable emotional significance. People argue, fight, and even die over values such as freedom or dignity.

Although deeply embedded in society, values are not static; they change over time, but change is often the result of a slow and painful process. For example, the value systems of many former communist states such as Georgia, Hungary, and Romania have undergone significant changes as these countries have moved away from values that emphasize state control toward values that emphasize individual freedoms. Social turmoil often results when countries undergo major changes in their values, as is happening today in Asia, South America, and the Middle East.

norms Unwritten, informal codes of conduct that prescribe how people should act in particular situations and are considered important by most members of a group or an organization.

mores Norms that are considered to be central to the functioning of society and to social life.

Norms are unwritten, informal codes of conduct that prescribe appropriate behavior in particular situations and are considered important by most members of a group or organization. They shape the behavior of people toward one another. Two types of norms play a major role in national culture: mores and folkways. **Mores** are norms that are considered to be of central importance to the functioning of society and to social life. Accordingly, the violation of mores brings serious retribution. Mores include proscriptions against murder, theft, adultery, and incest. In many societies, mores have been enacted into law. Thus, all advanced societies have laws against murder and theft. However, there are many differences in mores from one society to another. In the United States, for example, drinking alcohol is widely accepted, but in Saudi Arabia consumption of alcohol is viewed as a serious violation of social mores and is punishable by imprisonment or even death.

folkways The routine social conventions of everyday life.

Folkways are the routine social conventions of everyday life. They concern customs and practices such as dressing appropriately for particular situations, having good social manners, eating with the correct utensils, and engaging in neighborly behavior. Although folkways define how people are expected to behave, violation of folkways is not a serious or moral matter. People who violate folkways are often thought to be eccentric or ill-mannered, but they are not usually considered immoral or wicked. In many countries, strangers are usually excused for violating folkways because they are unaccustomed to local behavior, but if they repeat the violation, they are censured because they are expected to learn appropriate behavior—hence the importance of managers working in countries abroad to gain wide experience.

Hofstede's Model of National Culture

LO6-5 Discuss why national cultures differ and why it is important that managers be sensitive to the effects of falling trade barriers and regional trade associations on the political and social systems of nations around the world.

Researchers have spent considerable time and effort identifying similarities and differences in the values and norms of different countries. One model of national culture was developed by Geert Hofstede.[56] As a psychologist for IBM, Hofstede collected data on employee values and norms from more than 100,000 IBM employees in 64 countries. Based on his research, Hofstede developed five dimensions along which national cultures can be placed.[57]

INDIVIDUALISM VERSUS COLLECTIVISM The first dimension, which Hofstede labeled "individualism versus collectivism," has a long history in human thought. **Individualism** is a worldview that values individual freedom and self-expression and adherence to the principle that people should be judged by their individual achievements rather than by their social background. In Western countries, individualism usually includes admiration for personal success, a strong belief in individual rights, and high regard for individual entrepreneurs.[58]

In contrast, **collectivism** is a worldview that values subordination of the individual to the goals of the group and adherence to the principle that people should be judged by their contribution to the group. Collectivism was widespread in communist countries but has become less prevalent since the collapse of communism in most of those countries. Japan is a noncommunist country where collectivism is highly valued.

individualism A worldview that values individual freedom and self-expression and adherence to the principle that people should be judged by their individual achievements rather than by their social background.

Managers must realize that organizations and organizational members reflect their national culture's emphasis on individualism or collectivism. Indeed, one of the major reasons Japanese and American management practices differ is that Japanese culture values collectivism and U.S. culture values individualism.[59]

collectivism A worldview that values subordination of the individual to the goals of the group and adherence to the principle that people should be judged by their contribution to the group.

POWER DISTANCE By **power distance**, Hofstede meant the degree to which societies accept the idea that inequalities in the power and well-being of their citizens are due to differences in individuals' physical and intellectual capabilities and heritage. This concept also encompasses the degree to which societies accept the economic and social differences in wealth, status, and well-being that result from differences in individual capabilities.

Societies in which inequalities are allowed to persist or grow over time have *high power distance.* In high-power-distance societies, workers who are professionally successful amass wealth and pass it on to their children, and, as a result, inequalities may grow over time. In such societies, the gap between rich and poor, with all the attendant political and social consequences, grows very large. In contrast, in societies with *low power distance,* large inequalities between citizens are not allowed to develop. In low-power-distance countries, the government uses taxation and social welfare programs to reduce inequality and improve the welfare of the least fortunate. These societies are more attuned to preventing a large gap between rich and poor and minimizing discord between different classes of citizens.

power distance The degree to which societies accept the idea that inequalities in the power and well-being of their citizens are due to differences in individuals' physical and intellectual capabilities and heritage.

Advanced Western countries such as the United States, Germany, the Netherlands, and the United Kingdom have relatively low power distance and high individualism. Economically poor Latin American countries such as Guatemala and Panama, and Asian countries such as Malaysia and the Philippines, have high power distance and low individualism.[60] These findings suggest that the cultural values of richer countries emphasize protecting the rights of individuals and, at the same time, provide a fair chance of success to every member of society.

achievement orientation A worldview that values assertiveness, performance, success, and competition.

nurturing orientation A worldview that values the quality of life, warm personal friendships, and services and care for the weak.

uncertainty avoidance The degree to which societies are willing to tolerate uncertainty and risk.

long-term orientation A worldview that values thrift and persistence in achieving goals.

short-term orientation A worldview that values personal stability or happiness and living for the present.

ACHIEVEMENT VERSUS NURTURING ORIENTATION Societies that have an **achievement orientation** value assertiveness, performance, success, competition, and results. Societies that have a **nurturing orientation** value the quality of life, warm personal relationships, and services and care for the weak. Japan and the United States tend to be achievement-oriented; the Netherlands, Sweden, and Denmark are more nurturing-oriented.

UNCERTAINTY AVOIDANCE Societies as well as individuals differ in their tolerance for uncertainty and risk. Societies low on **uncertainty avoidance** (such as the United States and Hong Kong) are easygoing, value diversity, and tolerate differences in personal beliefs and actions. Societies high on uncertainty avoidance (such as Japan and France) are more rigid and skeptical about people whose behaviors or beliefs differ from the norm. In these societies, conformity to the values of the social and work groups to which a person belongs is the norm, and structured situations are preferred because they provide a sense of security.

LONG-TERM VERSUS SHORT-TERM ORIENTATION The last dimension that Hofstede described is orientation toward life and work.[61] A national culture with a **long-term orientation** rests on values such as thrift (saving) and persistence in achieving goals. A national culture with a **short-term orientation** is concerned with maintaining personal stability or happiness and living for the present. Societies with a long-term orientation include Taiwan and Hong Kong, well known for their high rate of per capita savings. The United States and France have a short-term orientation, and their citizens tend to spend more and save less.

The GLOBE Project

In Asian countries such as Japan where collectivism is highly valued, coworkers identify strongly with being part of a group.
imtmphoto/Shutterstock

Hofstede's research has inspired other major international research projects, including the GLOBE Project, which extends Hofstede's work by looking at additional cultural dimensions. Conceived in the early 1990s by Professor Robert J. House of the University of Pennsylvania, the GLOBE (Global Leadership and Organizational Behavior Effectiveness) Project is an ongoing international research endeavor involving more than 200 researchers who have collected data from more than 17,000 managers in 62 countries.[62] The GLOBE Project looks at nine cultural dimensions:

1. *Performance orientation:* The degree to which individuals in a society are rewarded for performance improvement and excellence.
2. *Assertiveness:* The degree to which members of organizations are confrontational and aggressive in their relationships with others.
3. *Future orientation:* The extent to which individuals engage in behaviors such as planning, investing in the future, and delaying gratification.
4. *Humane orientation:* The degree to which an organization encourages and rewards individuals for being fair, altruistic, generous, caring, and kind to others.
5. *Institutional collectivism:* The degree to which organizational and societal practices encourage and reward collective distribution of resources and collective action.
6. *In-group collectivism:* The degree to which individuals express pride, loyalty, and cohesiveness in their organizations or families.
7. *Gender egalitarianism:* The degree to which an organization minimizes gender inequality.
8. *Power distance:* The extent to which the community accepts and endorses authority, unequal distribution of power, and status privileges.
9. *Uncertainty avoidance:* The extent to which a society or organization uses rules, regulations, and procedures to alleviate the unpredictability of future events.[63]

Based on the data, countries receive an average score on the nine cultural dimensions. For example, Russia scores high on power distance, Singapore scores low on humane orientation, and China scores high on gender differentiation. Managers can also use GLOBE data to cluster countries based on similar cultural values, which would give people working in foreign countries a research-based starting point on how individuals from these cultural clusters are likely to behave.[64]

National Culture and Global Management

Differences among national cultures have important implications for managers. First, because of cultural differences, management practices that are effective in one country might be troublesome in another. General Electric's managers learned this while trying to manage Tungsram, a Hungarian lighting products company GE acquired for $150 million. GE was attracted to Tungsram, widely regarded as one of Hungary's best companies, because of Hungary's low wage rates and the possibility of using the company as a base from which to export lighting products to Western Europe. GE transferred some of its best managers to Tungsram and hoped it would soon become a leader in Europe. Unfortunately, many problems arose.

One problem resulted from major misunderstandings between the American managers and the Hungarian workers. The Americans complained that the Hungarians were lazy; the Hungarians thought the Americans were pushy. The Americans wanted strong sales and marketing functions that would pamper customers. In the prior command economy, sales and marketing activities were unnecessary. In addition, Hungarians expected GE to deliver Western-style wages, but GE went to Hungary to take advantage of the country's low wage structure.[65] As Tungsram's losses mounted, GE managers had to admit that because of differences in basic attitudes between countries, they had underestimated the difficulties they would face in turning Tungsram around. Nevertheless, these problems were eventually solved, and the increased efficiency of GE's Hungarian operations made General Electric a major player in the European lighting market for more than a decade, until GE sold its overseas lighting division in 2018.[66]

Often management practices must be tailored to suit the cultural contexts within which an organization operates. An approach effective in the United States might not work in Japan, Hungary, or Mexico because of differences in national culture. For example, U.S.-style pay-for-performance systems that emphasize the performance of individuals might not work well in Japan, where individual performance in pursuit of group goals is the value that receives emphasis.

Managers doing business with people from another country must be sensitive to the value systems and norms of that country and behave accordingly. For example, Friday is the Islamic Sabbath. Thus, it would be impolite and inappropriate for a U.S. manager to schedule a busy day of activities for Saudi Arabian managers on a Friday.

A culturally diverse management team can be a source of strength for an organization participating in the global marketplace. Compared to organizations with culturally homogeneous management teams, organizations that employ managers from a variety of cultures have a better appreciation of how national cultures differ, and they tailor their management systems and behaviors to the differences.[67] Indeed, one advantage that many Western companies have over their Japanese competitors is greater willingness to create global teams composed of employees from different countries around the world who can draw on and share their different cultural experiences and knowledge to provide service that is customized to the needs of companies in different countries. For example, because technology services account for more than half of IBM's annual revenues, it has been searching for ways to better use its talented workforce to both lower costs and offer customers unique, specialized kinds of services that its competitors cannot. IBM has developed several kinds of techniques to accomplish this.[68]

IBM's competency centers customize teams of workers who have just the right mix of skills to address a specific client's business needs.
ColorBlind Images/Blend Images LLC

In the 2000s, IBM created "competency centers" around the world, staffed by employees who share the same specific technology skill. Most of IBM's employees are concentrated in competency centers located in the countries in which IBM has the most clients and does the most business. These employees have a wide variety of skills, developed from their previous work experience, and the challenge facing IBM is to use these experts efficiently. To accomplish this, IBM used its own expertise to develop sophisticated software that allows it to create self-managed teams composed of IBM experts who have the optimum mix of skills to solve a client's particular problems. First, IBM programmers analyze the skills and experience of its 80,000 global employees and enter the results into the software program. Then they analyze and code the nature of a client's specific problem and input that information. IBM's program matches each specific client problem to the skills of IBM's experts and identifies a list of "best fit" employees. One of IBM's senior managers narrows this list and decides on the actual composition of the self-managed team.

Once selected, team members, from wherever they happen to be in the world, assemble as quickly as possible and go to work analyzing the client's problem. Together, team members use their authority. This lets IBM create an ever-changing set of global self-managed teams that form to develop the software and service packages necessary to solve the problems of IBM's global clients. At the same time, IBM's technology also optimizes the use of its whole talented workforce because each employee is placed in their "most highly valued use"–that is, in the team where the employee's skills can best increase efficiency and effectiveness.

Summary and Review

LO6-1 **WHAT IS THE GLOBAL ENVIRONMENT?** The global environment is the set of forces and conditions that operates beyond an organization's boundaries but affects a manager's ability to acquire and use resources. The global environment has two components: the task environment and the general environment.

LO6-2, 6-3 **THE TASK ENVIRONMENT** The task environment is the set of forces and conditions that originates with global suppliers, distributors, customers, and competitors and influences managers daily. The opportunities and threats associated with forces in the task environment become more complex as a company expands globally.

LO6-2, 6-3 **THE GENERAL ENVIRONMENT** The general environment comprises wide-ranging global economic, technological, sociocultural, demographic, political, and legal forces that affect an organization and its task environment.

LO6-4, 6-5 **THE CHANGING GLOBAL ENVIRONMENT** In recent years, there has been a marked shift toward a more open global environment in which capital flows more freely as people and companies search for new opportunities to create profit and wealth. This has hastened the process of globalization. Globalization is the set of specific and general forces that work together to integrate and connect economic, political, and social systems across countries, cultures, or geographic regions so that nations become increasingly interdependent and similar. Should companies want to expand internationally, they can import/export products; develop a licensing/franchising opportunity for their business; enter into strategic alliances or joint ventures; and create wholly owned subsidiaries in other countries. The process of globalization has been furthered by declining barriers to international trade and investment and declining barriers of distance and culture.

Management in Action

Topics for Discussion and Action

Discussion

1. Why is it important for managers to understand the forces in the global environment that are acting on them and their organizations? [LO6-1]

2. Which organization is likely to face the most complex task environment—a biotechnology company trying to develop a cure for cancer or a large retailer such as The Gap or Macy's? Why? [LO6-2, 6-3]

3. The population is aging because of declining birth rates, declining death rates, and the aging of the Baby Boomer generation. What might some of the implications of this demographic trend be for (a) a pharmaceutical company and (b) the home construction industry? [LO6-1, 6-2, 6-3]

4. How do political, legal, and economic forces shape national culture? What characteristics of national culture do you think have the most important effect on how successful a country is in doing business abroad? [LO6-3, 6-5]

5. After the passage of NAFTA, many companies shifted production operations to Mexico to take advantage of lower labor costs and lower standards for environmental and worker protection. As a result, they cut their costs and were better able to survive in an increasingly competitive global environment. Was their behavior ethical—that is, did the ends justify the means? [LO6-4]

Action

6. Choose an organization, and ask a manager in that organization to list the number and strengths of forces in the organization's task environment. Ask the manager to pay particular attention to identifying opportunities and threats that result from pressures and changes in customers, competitors, and suppliers. [LO6-1, 6-2, 6-3]

Building Management Skills

Analyzing an Organization's Environment [LO6-1, 6-2, 6-3]

Pick an organization with which you are familiar. It can be an organization in which you have worked or currently work or one that you interact with regularly as a customer (such as the college you are attending). For this organization, do the following:

1. Describe the main forces in the global task environment that are affecting the organization.

2. Describe the main forces in the global general environment that are affecting the organization.

3. Explain how environmental forces affect the job of an individual manager within this organization. How do they determine the opportunities and threats that its managers must confront?

Managing Ethically [LO6-4, 6-5]

Home Depot misjudged the Chinese market for its products and services. The world's largest home improvement chain entered China in 2006 and left six years later. The company was unable to sell its do-it-yourself brand to Chinese consumers. Cheap labor in China means many people can hire someone else to do home improvement work for them, so Chinese consumers are not very interested in DIY projects. In addition, apartment or high-rise living is prevalent in China, which means demand for extensive DIY projects is not extensive among Chinese consumers.[69]

Questions

1. What could Home Depot have done to avoid its mistake?

2. In what cultures might Home Depot find better success?

Small Group Breakout Exercise

How to Enter the Copying Business [LO6-1, 6-2]

Form groups of three to five people, and appoint one group member as the spokesperson who will communicate your findings to the whole class when called on by the instructor. Then discuss the following scenario:

You and your partners have decided to open a small printing and copying business in a college town of 100,000 people. Your business will compete with companies like FedEx Office. You know that over 50% of small businesses fail in their first year, so to increase your chances of success, you have decided to perform a detailed analysis of the task environment of the copying business to discover what opportunities and threats you will encounter.

1. Decide what you must know about (a) your future customers, (b) your future competitors, and (c) other critical forces in the task environment if you are to be successful.
2. Evaluate the main barriers to entry into the copying business.
3. Based on this analysis, list some steps you would take to help your new copying business succeed.

Be the Manager [LO6-1, 6-2]

The Changing Environment of Retailing

You are the new manager of a major clothing store that is facing a crisis. This clothing store has been the leader in its market for the last 15 years. In the last 3 years, however, two other major clothing store chains have opened, and they have steadily been attracting customers away from your store—your sales are down 30%. To find out why, your store surveyed former customers and learned that they perceive your store as not keeping up with changing fashion trends and new forms of customer service. In examining how the store operates, you found out that the 10 purchasing managers who buy the clothing and accessories for the store have been buying from the same clothing suppliers and have become reluctant to try new ones. Moreover, salespeople rarely, if ever, make suggestions for changing how the store operates, and they don't respond to customer requests; the culture of the store has become conservative and risk-averse.

Questions

1. Analyze the major forces in the task environment of a retail clothing store.
2. Devise a program that will help other managers and employees to better understand and respond to their store's task environment.

Case in the News [LO6-1, 6-3, 6-4, 6-5]

How Netflix Is Growing (Almost) Everywhere

Netflix started in the 1990s as an online alternative to renting video cassettes from a store. As Internet speeds increased, the company pivoted to streaming movies in 2007, then began streaming original content in 2013. Companies including Apple and Disney soon launched their own streaming services, and Netflix faced its first serious competition. Millions of members signed up for Netflix during the early years, followed by a noticeable jump in subscribers during the COVID-19 pandemic's stay-at-home orders. As more viewing options proliferate and COVID restrictions loosen, Netflix's growth and revenues have stalled, especially in North America.

To address the market saturation, Netflix has pursued international markets, where it now sees the strongest growth. The company operates in almost 200 countries, excluding China; it withdrew from Russia in 2022 in response to the invasion of Ukraine. Its strategy for international expansion is to enter the market by targeting young, affluent consumers in large cities. This population segment has the means to pay for content, is likely to have Internet access, and may be open to watching shows from other countries. Netflix then expands its market by hiring local people to enter into licensing agreements with local content producers, such as movie and television directors. In exchange for funding and creative freedom, the content creators give Netflix the right to stream their work.

The approach has yielded global hits such as *Squid Game* (South Korea),

Sacred Games (India), *Stranger Things* (the United States), and *Narcos* (Colombia). Netflix often succeeds because it can quickly navigate different laws, cultures, and languages. Paradoxically, as Netflix CEO Reed Hastings expresses, the product may also be a global one: "Great stories can be made anywhere and loved everywhere." The company is far ahead of its competitors in commissioning non-U.S. original shows and movies, which it is doing in more than 50 countries.`

In Latin America, an early international market for Netflix, the company is moving at top speed to license non-English programming, including Portuguese content for Brazil and Spanish content for Mexico, the two countries with the most Netflix subscribers in the region. By 2022, Netflix originals represented more than half of its catalog in Latin America. Recently, however, the show with the most unique viewers was *Stranger Things.*

In Japan, there is a distinctive cultural style called anime, which 9 in 10 Japanese viewers watch on Netflix. To meet the demand, Netflix expanded its catalog of originals from one anime feature in 2015 to 40 in 2022. Netflix faces stiff competition in Japan's mature economy but hopes to maintain an edge through deep partnerships with local studios, artists, and other creators.

Europe challenges Netflix with "content quotas" requiring that at least 30% of the content streamed in each market be produced locally. Netflix's early moves and expansion strategy help; the company has already met the 30% mark in most European countries. Companies that are further behind will have to move faster with local content or make deeper cuts in their non-local offerings.

Netflix was particularly hopeful about its prospects in India, given the country's enormous population (the world's second largest, after China), expanding middle class, and existing film industry. Less than three years after entering India, Netflix successfully launched *Sacred Games,* but its hopes for 100 million subscribers were far from realized, reaching about 5.5 million, so the company had to scale back its activities in India. One hurdle there has been pricing. Netflix usually charges $8 to $10 a month, but India's pay TV subscribers already get other services for $2 or $3 a month. Netflix tried setting its price in India at $7.50, but after disappointing enrollment, it offered a lower-priced option for viewing only on mobile devices. Another challenge is that India is a diverse market whose ethnic groups speak more than 20 different languages.

International expansion is only one piece of Netflix's strategy for a maturing product. The company is pursuing other ways to keep its service fresh, including the acquisition of studios producing video games. Netflix recently launched a lower-priced subscription tier delivering an ad-supported service called Netflix Basic with ads. Before the launch, Netflix tested the service in Latin American markets, which are smaller than its U.S. market but at a similar stage of subscriber growth. The ad-supported service launched in November 2022, beginning in the United States. The day after Netflix announced Basic with ads, the price of Netflix stock rose 12%—the market's way of applauding management decisions.

Questions for Discussion

1. Why was it important for Netflix to become a global organization? What do you think would have happened to the company if it had restricted its activities to North America?
2. Would you describe Netflix's strategy for business expansion as global or multidomestic? Explain your reasoning.
3. What are the advantages to Netflix of licensing content to stream, rather than making its own content? Competitors such as Disney+ do create their own content; would you advise the same for Netflix? Why or why not?

Sources: Netflix, "Long-Term View: Streaming Entertainment Is Replacing Linear TV," https://ir.netflix.net, accessed January 17, 2023; "Why Lat Am Originals Are Netflix's Next Big Growth Opportunity," *Television Business International,* https://tbvision.com, November 21, 2022; D. Chmielewski and L. Richwine, "Netflix Targets Global TV Ad Market as Next Business to Disrupt," *Reuters,* www.reuters.com, October 19, 2022; J. Kay, "Netflix Reports 2.41M Global Subs Gain in Q3, First Increase of 2022," *Screen Daily,* www.screendaily.com, October 18, 2022; S. Roxborough, "Netflix's Executive Shake-Up in Europe May Point to Broader Strategic Shift," *Hollywood Reporter,* www.hollywoodreporter.com, October 4, 2022; A. Weprin, "Netflix Rest: After Layoffs, Reed Hastings Promises 'Significant' Investments, but Where?" *Hollywood Reporter,* www.hollywoodreporter.com, June 24, 2022; E. Keslassy, "Netflix Meets 30% European Content Quota in Almost All Markets on Continent," *Variety,* https://variety.com, June 7, 2022; L. Shaw, "Netflix's Indian Drama," *Bloomberg Businessweek,* April 4, 2022, 16–18; P. Brzeski, "Netflix's Head of Anime Says Half of Global Subscribers Watch Japanese Animation, Bullish on Growth," *Hollywood Reporter,* www.hollywoodreporter.com, April 3, 2022; A. Levy, "This Is a $6 Billion Opportunity for Netflix," *Motley Fool,* www.fool.com, March 23, 2022; C. Sinha, "Netflix Suspends Service in Russia," *Vulture,* www.vulture.com, March 6, 2022; D. Butler, "History of Netflix: Timeline and Facts," *The Street,* www.thestreet.com, updated October 5, 2020.

Notes

1. BMW Group, "Eight Years in a Row, BMW Manufacturing Is Largest Automotive Exporter in the United States," news release, www.bmwgroup.com, accessed December 12, 2022.
2. Ibid.
3. W. Boston, "BMW Takes Control of China Venture, Sees Big Profit Gains," *The Wall Street Journal,* www.wsj.com, February 11, 2022; G. Nica, "China Accounts for Nearly 40 Percent of All BMW Sales in 2021," BMW Blog, www.bmwblog.com, January 12, 2022.
4. Boston, "BMW Takes Control of China Venture"; V. Waldersee, "BMW Pays $4.2 Billion to Take Control of Chinese JV," *Reuters,* www.reuters.com, February 11, 2022; "BMW Adds to X5 Production in China–Spokesperson," *Reuters,* www.reuters.com, December 13, 2021.

5. BMW Group, "Eight Years in a Row."
6. L.J. Bourgeois, "Strategy and Environment: A Conceptual Integration," *Academy of Management Review* 5 (1985), 25–39.
7. B. Murray, "Just Get Me a Box: Inside the Brutal Realities of Supply Chain Hell," *Bloomberg Businessweek*, www.bloomberg.com, accessed January 16, 2023.
8. M.E. Porter, *Competitive Strategy* (New York: Free Press, 1980).
9. "Coca-Cola versus Pepsi-Cola and the Soft Drink Industry," Harvard Business School Case 9-391-179.
10. www.splenda.com, accessed February 13, 2020.
11. Emergen Research, "Stevia Market Size, Share, Trends and by Region Forecast," www.emergenresearch.com, accessed January 16, 2023.
12. A.K. Gupta and V. Govindarajan, "Cultivating a Global Mind-Set," *Academy of Management Executive* 16 (February 2002), 116–27.
13. Levi Strauss & Co., "2021 Sustainability Report," www.levistrauss.com, accessed January 16, 2023; E. Fry, "Can Levi's Make Life Better for Garment Workers?" *Fortune*, https://fortune.com, September 8, 2017; A. Peters, "How Levi's Is Building Well-Being Programs Where They Matter the Most," *Fast Company*, www.fastcompany.com, October 13, 2016.
14. Fry, "Can Levi's Make Life Better for Garment Workers?"
15. Harvard School of Public Health, Center for Health and the Global Environment, "Worker Health and Well-Being in the Supply Chain," https://chge.hsph.harvard.edu, accessed January 16, 2023.
16. Fry, "Can Levi's Make Life Better for Garment Workers?"
17. Levi Strauss & Co., "2021 Sustainability Report"; Peters, "How Levi's Is Building."
18. "Boeing's Worldwide Supplier Network," *Seattle Post-Intelligencer*, April 9, 1994, 13; I. Metthee, "Playing a Larger Part," *Seattle Post-Intelligencer*, April 9, 1994, 13.
19. J. Johnsson, "Boeing Falls as Analyst Deems 787 Cost Recoup 'Unachievable,'" *Bloomberg*, www.bloomberg.com, April 20, 2016.
20. P. Prakash, "Apple's Tim Cook Celebrates a 'New Era of Advanced Manufacturing' and Says the Company Will Use U.S.-Made Chips for the First Time in a Decade," *Fortune*, https://fortune.com, December 7, 2022.
21. "About Li & Fung," www.lifung.com, accessed January 16, 2023.
22. B. Baschuk, "US Manufacturers 'Pumped Up' about Supply-Chain Reshoring Trend," Bloomberg, www.bloomberg.com, accessed January 16, 2023.
23. K. Souza, "Walmart Demands All Suppliers Comply with 98% On-Time In-Full Shipment Rule," *TB&P*, https://talkbusiness.net, accessed January 16, 2023.
24. IDC, "Worldwide PC Shipments Decline Another 15% in the Third Quarter of 2022, According to IDC Tracker," www.idc.com, October 9, 2022.
25. For views on barriers to entry from an economics perspective, see Porter, *Competitive Strategy*. For the sociological perspective, see J. Pfeffer and G. R. Salancik, *The External Control of Organization: A Resource Dependence Perspective* (New York: Harper & Row, 1978).
26. L. Young, "Amazon's Plans for Massive Warehouses Go Forward amid Logistics Review," *The Wall Street Journal*, www.wsj.com, July 28, 2022.
27. "Where Does Japan Import Rice From?" *Trend Economy*, https://trendeconomy.com, accessed January 16, 2023; T. Simmons, "U.S. Exports to Japan Fall Short; Implications for TPP Unsettles Industry," *Ag Watch Network*, https://agwatchnetwork.com, accessed February 13, 2020; Bloomberg, "Rice Excluded from Trade Accord U.S. and Japan Aim to Ink Soon," *Japan Times*, www.japantimes.co.jp, September 18, 2019.
28. W. McBain, "Canal+ and Netflix Eye Nollywood Opportunities," *African Business*, https://africanbusinessmagazine.com, October 24, 2019; C. M. Christensen, "Cracking Frontier Markets," *Harvard Business Review*, January–February 2019, 90–101.
29. McBain, "Canal+ and Netflix Eye Nollywood Opportunities."
30. K. Leach, "Nollywood Goes Netflix," *Bloomberg Businessweek*, May 27, 2019, 16–18.
31. S. Collins, "Explained: Inside Nollywood, the Fastest Growing Film Industry in the World," *Movie Web*, https://movieweb.com, March 13, 2022.
32. "AMD Unveils New Ryzen Mobile Processors Uniting 'Zen 3+' Core with AMD RDNA 2 Graphics in Powerhouse Design," www.amd.com, accessed January 16, 2023.
33. N. Goodman, *An Introduction to Sociology* (New York: HarperCollins, 1991); C. Nakane, *Japanese Society* (Berkeley: University of California Press, 1970).
34. "Global Meal Kit Delivery Service Market Worth USD 8.94 Billion by 2020: Hexa Research," *PR Newswire*, www.prnewswire.com, March 13, 2019.
35. M. Le Fort, "You Are Going Broke Because You Are Too Lazy to Cook," *Medium*, https://medium.com, September 20, 2018; "How Much Money Do You Save by Cooking at Home?" *Wellio*, www.getwellio.com, June 7, 2018.
36. For a detailed discussion of the importance of the structure of law as a factor explaining economic change and growth, see D.C. North, *Institutions, Institutional Change, and Economic Performance* (Cambridge: Cambridge University Press, 1990).
37. I. Lunden, "Apple Closes Its $400M Shazam Acquisition and Says the Music Recognition App Will Soon Become Ad Free," *Tech Crunch*, https://techcrunch.com, September 24, 2018.
38. "Brexit Is Weighing on UK Economy, Bank of England Officials Say," *Reuters*, www.reuters.com, November 16, 2022; Economic & Social Research Institute (ESRI), "Brexit Reduced Overall EU-UK Goods Trade Flows by Almost One-Fifth," www.esri.ie, October 19, 2022.
39. B. Allen-Ebrahimian, "U.S. Looks to Rejoin Asia Trade Game," *Axios*, www.axios.com, May 10, 2022; C. Grabow, "5 Years Later the United States Is Still Paying for Its TPP Blunder," *Cato at Liberty*(blog), www.cato.org, February 10, 2022.
40. M.A. Carpenter and J.W. Fredrickson, "Top Management Teams, Global Strategic Posture, and the Moderating Role of Uncertainty," *Academy of Management Journal* 44 (June 2001), 533–46.
41. A. Swanson and C. Edmonson, "US Survey of Firms Finds 'Alarming' Chip Shortages," *Chicago Tribune*, www.chicagotribune.com, January 26, 2022; M. Dorning, "Expect Delays," *Bloomberg Businessweek*, August 9, 2021, 34–37; B. Murray, E. Curran, and K. Chipman, "F.O.R.O.: Fear of Running Out," *Bloomberg Businessweek*, May 24, 2021, 15–17.
42. S. Wilmot, "The Real Brake on America's Electric-Vehicle Revolution," *The Wall Street Journal*, www.wsj.com, January 28, 2022; J. Wong, "EV Makers' Next Headache: Scarce Battery Chemicals, Made in China," *The Wall Street Journal*, www.wsj.com, January 21, 2022.
43. W. Shih, "Why Are Automotive Chips Still in Short Supply?" *Forbes*, www.forbes.com, November 20, 2022; Murray et al., "F.O.R.O."
44. Imarc Group, "India Food Processing Market: Industry Trends, Share, Size, Growth, Opportunity and Forecast 2023–2028," www.imarcgroup.com, accessed January 17, 2023; A. Rakshit, "New Price Points, Smaller Packs: How Kellogg Plans to Double India Revenue," *Business Standard*, www.business-standard.com, July 28, 2019; Penguin India Blog, "8 Things Every Maggi-Lover Should Know about Maggi's Journey to India," https://penguin.co.in, August 6, 2018.
45. R.E. Caves, *Multinational Enterprise and Economic Analysis* (Cambridge: Cambridge University Press, 1982).
46. B. Kogut, "Joint Ventures: Theoretical and Empirical Perspectives," *Strategic Management Journal* 9 (1988), 319–33.

47. General Mills, *2022 Annual Report,* https://s29.q4cdn.com, accessed January 17, 2023.
48. N. Hood and S. Young, *The Economics of the Multinational Enterprise* (London: Longman, 1979).
49. R. Newcomb, N. Bolin, M. Schaefermeier, and M. Larson, "US Lifts Section 232 Tariffs on Steel and Aluminum from the EU January 1, 2022—Continues Similar Negotiations with Japan," *DLA Piper,* www.diapiper.com, accessed January 17, 2023; Reuters, "Biden Says 'Not There Yet' on Possible Easing of Tariffs on Chinese Goods," *U.S. News & World Report,* https://money.usnews.com, January 19, 2022; E. Martin and J. Deaux, "Biden Commerce Chief Says Steel, Aluminum Tariffs 'Effective,'" *Bloomberg,* www.bloomberg.com, March 4, 2021.
50. For a summary of these theories, see P. Krugman and M. Obstfeld, *International Economics: Theory and Policy* (New York: HarperCollins, 1991). Also see C.W.L. Hill, *International Business* (New York: McGraw-Hill, 1997), Chapter 4.
51. A.M. Rugman, "The Quest for Global Dominance," *Academy of Management Executive* 16 (August 2002), 157–60.
52. "The Doha Round," www.wto.org, accessed February 14, 2020; K. Amadeo, "Doha Round of Trade Talks: The Real Reason Why It Failed," *The Balance,* www.thebalance.com, June 25, 2019.
53. C.A. Bartlett and S. Ghoshal, *Managing across Borders* (Boston: Harvard Business School Press, 1989).
54. Office of the U.S. Trade Representative, "United States–Mexico–Canada Trade Fact Sheet," https://ustr.gov, accessed January 17, 2023; J. Kirby, "USMCA, Trump's New NAFTA Deal, Explained in 600 Words," *Vox,* www.vox.com, February 4, 2020.
55. Organization websites: "About the African Union," https://au.int; "Member States," www.sadc.int; "Area of Cooperation Achievements," www.gcc-sg.org, all accessed January 17, 2023.
56. G. Hofstede, B. Neuijen, D.D. Ohayv, and G. Sanders, "Measuring Organizational Cultures: A Qualitative and Quantitative Study Across Twenty Cases," *Administrative Science Quarterly* 35 (1990), 286–316.
57. M.H. Hoppe, "Introduction: Geert Hofstedes Culture's Consequences: International Difference in Work-Related Values," *Academy of Management Executive* 19 (February 2004), 73–75.
58. R. Bellah, *Habits of the Heart: Individualism and Commitment in American Life* (Berkeley: University of California Press, 1985).
59. C. Nakane, *Japanese Society.* University of California Press, 1970.
60. G. Hofstede, "The Cultural Relativity of Organizational Practices and Theories," *Journal of International Business Studies,* (Fall 1983), 75–89.
61. Hofstede et al., "Measuring Organizational Cultures."
62. R. House, M. Javidan, P. Hanges, and P. Dorfman, "Understanding Cultures and Implicit Leadership Theories Across the Globe: An Introduction to Project GLOBE," *Journal of World Business,* no. 37 (2002), 3–10.
63. R.J. House et al., *Culture, Leadership, and Organizations: The GLOBE Studies of 62 Societies* (Los Angeles: Sage Publishing, 2004).
64. M. Javidan and A. Dastmalchian, "Managerial Implications of the GLOBE Project: A Study of 62 Societies," *Asia Pacific Journal of Human Resources* 47, no. 1 (2009), 41–58.
65. J. Perlez, "GE Finds Tough Going in Hungary," *The New York Times,* July 25, 1994, C1, C3.
66. A. Narayanan, "General Electric Begins Selling One of Its Oldest and Most Iconic Businesses," *Investor's Business Daily,* www.investors.com, February 16, 2018.
67. J. Y-J Cheng and B. Groysberg, "How Corporate Cultures Differ Around the World," *Harvard Business Review,* https://hbr.org, January 8, 2020.
68. "Transform Through a Center of Competency," www.ibm.com, accessed January 17, 2023.
69. K. Shedd, "Why Chinese Consumers Rejected Home Depot (video)," *CNBC,* www.cnbc.com, June 14, 2019.

CHAPTER 7

Decision Making, Learning, Creativity, and Entrepreneurship

Klaus Vedfelt/Digital Vision/Getty Images

Learning Objectives

After studying this chapter, you should be able to:

LO7-1 Understand the nature of managerial decision making, differentiate between programmed and nonprogrammed decisions, and explain why nonprogrammed decision making is a complex, uncertain process.

LO7-2 Describe the six steps managers should take to make the best decisions, and explain how cognitive biases can lead managers to make poor decisions.

LO7-3 Identify the advantages and disadvantages of group decision making, and describe techniques that can improve it.

LO7-4 Explain the role that organizational learning and creativity play in helping managers to improve their decisions.

LO7-5 Describe how managers can encourage and promote entrepreneurship to create a learning organization.

A MANAGER'S CHALLENGE

Karen Lynch's Bold Decisions at CVS Health

How do managers make decisions that add value? Decision making doesn't faze Karen Lynch, chief executive of CVS Health. In an interview with *The New York Times,* she described herself as decisive and explained why. When she was growing up, her aunt (who raised Lynch following her mother's premature death) taught her to think of decisions as a given, along with accepting the outcomes. Lynch told the reporter, "When you make decisions as often as I do, you're going to make a bad call. You just have to readjust."[1] Putting decision making in perspective shapes Lynch's approach to her work.

As the CEO of the fourth-largest U.S. company with almost 10,000 stores, Lynch applies her decision-making skills to corporate strategy. In 2018, CVS, which operates a drugstore chain, acquired Aetna, a provider of health insurance, as part of a strategy to offer health care services. When Lynch became CEO three years later, she had already embraced the strategy and opted to address it boldly. She decided to expand services from vaccinations, testing, and pharmacy to setting up offices for primary care and mental health care, which require hiring physicians and mental health professionals. The goal is not merely a new income stream; Lynch defines it as making health care more widely available—and less costly, which would benefit its Aetna insurance business.[2]

A bricks-and-mortar retailer also needs to make decisions about store locations and types, and Lynch has embraced those decisions too. With an eye on her broader strategy, she identifies three types of stores. First, CVS is investing for the fastest growth in the conversion of stores into physician-staffed primary-care clinics, especially in areas with large Medicare-eligible populations.[3] The second priority is the recently built HealthHUBs, which combine services such as screenings, tests, and other preventive services along with the sale of health care products. And CVS plans to maintain some traditional drugstores with pharmacies and the usual product lines plus a small MinuteClinic.[4]

Lynch decided on a career in a health care–related field because the early deaths of her mother and aunt brought home the importance of access to basic care. She worked for several insurance companies, including Aetna, actively seeking a diversity of experiences and profit-and-loss responsibility. When CVS acquired Aetna, it promoted her to run that business. When the COVID-19 pandemic began, she co-led the response with the company's chief medical officer. Her success led to her appointment as CEO following the retirement of her predecessor.[5]

Lynch's decision-making skill is especially evident in her transition to the CEO role in

CVS Health CEO Karen Lynch (pictured here in the center of a group discussion at Forbes Women's Summit) believes decision-making skills are critical to successful corporate strategies.
Gary Gershoff/WireImage/Getty Images

February 2021—not only in the midst of the pandemic, but just as vaccines were to become widely available. Lynch immediately identified and seized the most significant way to fulfill the company's mission: to be a community source of vaccines and COVID tests while looking out for the well-being of the employees tasked with working on the front lines. Of course, these activities also supported the company's strategy: As new customers came in for tests or shots, they discovered CVS's other offerings. But Lynch was not merely concerned about the bottom line. She says the company immediately made employees' health and safety the top priority: "employees first, customers second."[6] CVS arranged for 90,000 headquarters employees to work from home and ensured that the essential workers in the stores had personal protective equipment. Lynch and her executive team also visited stores during this period, where they acted as greeters so they could see and hear employees' and customers' concerns. In this way, they learned that the pharmacists and pharmacy technicians were already overwhelmed, so the stores set up separately staffed in-store clinics to handle the vaccination traffic.[7] For the second year in a row, Lynch ranked number 1 on *Fortune's* list of the 50 Most Powerful Women in 2022.[8]

Overview

"A Manager's Challenge" illustrates how decision making can have a profound influence on organizational effectiveness. The decisions managers make at all levels in companies large and small can change the growth and prosperity of these companies and the well-being of their employees, customers, and other stakeholders. Yet such decisions can be difficult to make because they are fraught with uncertainty.

LO7-1 Understand the nature of managerial decision making, differentiate between programmed and nonprogrammed decisions, and explain why nonprogrammed decision making is a complex, uncertain process.

In this chapter, we examine how managers make decisions, and we explore how individual, group, and organizational factors affect the quality of the decisions they make and ultimately determine organizational performance. We discuss the nature of managerial decision making and examine some models of the decision-making process that help reveal the complexities of successful decision making. Then we outline the main steps of the decision-making process. In addition, we explore the biases that may cause capable managers to make poor decisions, both as individuals and as members of a group. Next, we examine how managers can promote organizational learning and creativity and improve the quality of decision making throughout an organization. Finally, we discuss the important role of entrepreneurship in promoting organizational creativity. By the end of this chapter, you will appreciate the critical role of management decision making in creating a high-performing organization.

The Nature of Managerial Decision Making

Every time managers plan, organize, direct, or control organizational activities, they make a stream of decisions. In opening a new restaurant, for example, managers have to decide where to locate it, what kinds of food to provide, which people to employ, and so on. Decision making is a basic part of every task managers perform. In this chapter, we study how these decisions are made.

As we discussed in the last three chapters, one of the main tasks facing a manager is to manage the organizational environment. Forces in the external environment give rise to many opportunities and threats for managers and their organizations. In addition, inside an organization, managers must address many opportunities and threats that may arise as organizational resources are used. To deal with these opportunities and threats, managers must make decisions–that is, they must select one solution from a set of alternatives. **Decision making** is the process by which managers respond to opportunities and threats by analyzing the options and making determinations, or *decisions,* about specific organizational goals and courses of action. Good decisions result in the selection of appropriate goals and courses of action that increase organizational performance; bad decisions lower performance.

decision making The process by which managers respond to opportunities and threats by analyzing options and making determinations about specific organizational goals and courses of action.

Decision making in response to opportunities occurs when managers search for ways to improve organizational performance to benefit customers, employees, and other stakeholder groups. As described in "A Manager's Challenge," Karen Lynch seized the opportunity to develop new services that capitalize on CVS Health's strengths. *Decision making in response to threats* occurs when events inside or outside the organization adversely affect organizational performance and managers search for ways to increase performance.[9] Lynch responded to the impact of the COVID-19 pandemic by making sure CVS Health became a community source for vaccines and testing, while at the same time ensuring the well-being of employees who were on the front lines of the fight against the spread of the virus. Decision making is central to being a manager, and whenever managers engage in planning, organizing, leading, and controlling–their four principal tasks–they are constantly making decisions.

Managers are always searching for ways to make better decisions to improve organizational performance. At the same time, they do their best to avoid costly mistakes that will hurt organizational performance. Examples of spectacularly good decisions include Martin Cooper's decision to develop the first cell phone at Motorola and Apple's decision to develop the iPod.[10] Examples of spectacularly bad decisions include the decision by managers at NASA and Morton Thiokol to launch the *Challenger* space shuttle–a decision that killed six astronauts in 1986–and the decision by NASA to launch the *Columbia* space shuttle in 2003, which killed seven astronauts.

Programmed and Nonprogrammed Decision Making

Regardless of the specific decisions a manager makes, the decision-making process is either programmed or nonprogrammed.[11]

programmed decision making Routine, virtually automatic decision making that follows established rules or guidelines.

PROGRAMMED DECISION MAKING **Programmed decision making** is a *routine,* virtually automatic process. Programmed decisions are decisions that have been made so many times in the past that managers have developed rules or guidelines to be applied when certain situations inevitably occur. Programmed decision making takes place when a school principal asks the school board to hire a new teacher whenever student enrollment increases by 40 students; when a manufacturing supervisor hires new workers whenever existing workers' overtime increases by more than 10%; and when an office manager orders basic office supplies, such as paper and pens, whenever the inventory of supplies drops below a certain level. Furthermore, in the last example, the office manager probably orders the same amount of supplies each time.

This decision making is called *programmed* because office managers, for example, do not need to repeatedly make new judgments about what should be done. They can rely on long-established decision rules such as these:

- *Rule 1:* When the storage shelves are three-quarters empty, order more copy paper.
- *Rule 2:* When ordering paper, order enough to fill the shelves.

Managers can develop rules and guidelines to regulate all routine organizational activities. For example, rules can specify how a worker should perform a certain task, and rules can specify the quality standards that raw materials must meet to be acceptable. Most decision making that relates to the day-to-day running of an organization is programmed decision making. Examples include deciding how much inventory to hold, when to pay bills, when to bill customers, and when to order materials and supplies. Programmed decision making occurs when managers have the information they need to create rules that will guide decision making. There is little ambiguity involved in assessing when the stockroom is empty or counting the number of new students in class.

nonprogrammed decision making Nonroutine decision making that occurs in response to unusual, unpredictable opportunities and threats.

NONPROGRAMMED DECISION MAKING Suppose, however, that managers are not certain that a course of action will lead to a desired outcome. Or in even more ambiguous terms, suppose managers are not even sure what they are trying to achieve. Obviously, rules cannot be developed to predict uncertain events.

Nonprogrammed decision making is required for these *nonroutine* decisions. Nonprogrammed decisions are made in response to unusual or novel opportunities and threats. Nonprogrammed decision making occurs when there are no ready-made decision rules that managers can apply to a situation. Rules do not exist because the situation is unexpected or uncertain and managers lack the information they would need to develop rules to cover it. Examples of nonprogrammed decision making include decisions to invest in a new technology, develop a new kind of product, launch a new promotional campaign, enter a new market, expand internationally, or start a new business, like Karen Lynch and CVS Health did with their HealthHUBs, as discussed in the chapter's opening story.

intuition Feelings, beliefs, and hunches that come readily to mind, require little effort and information gathering, and result in on-the-spot decisions.

reasoned judgment A decision that requires time and effort and results from careful information gathering, generation of alternatives, and evaluation of alternatives.

How do managers make decisions in the absence of decision rules? They may rely on their **intuition**–feelings, beliefs, and hunches that come readily to mind, require little effort and information gathering, and result in on-the-spot decisions.[12] Or they may make **reasoned judgments**–decisions that require time and effort and result from careful information gathering, generation of alternatives, and evaluation of alternatives. "Exercising" one's judgment is a more rational process than "going with" one's intuition. For reasons that we examine later in this chapter, both intuition and judgment often are flawed and can result in poor decision making. Thus, the likelihood of error is much greater in nonprogrammed decision making than in programmed decision making.[13] In the remainder of this chapter, when we talk about decision making, we are referring to *nonprogrammed* decision making because it causes the most problems for managers and is inherently challenging.

Sometimes managers have to make rapid decisions and don't have time to carefully consider the issues involved. They must rely on their intuition to respond quickly to a pressing concern. For example, when fire chiefs, captains, and lieutenants manage firefighters battling dangerous, out-of-control fires, they often need to rely on their expert intuition to make on-the-spot decisions that will protect the lives of the firefighters and save the lives of others, contain the fires, and preserve property–decisions made in emergency situations entailing high uncertainty, high risk, and rapidly changing conditions.[14] In other cases, managers do have time to make reasoned judgments, but there are no established rules to guide their decisions, such as when deciding whether to proceed with a proposed merger or how to take a start-up business to a new level.

Nonprogrammed decision making covers areas with no previous benchmarks or rubrics, such as making expert chess moves.
Blend Images/Shutterstock

Regardless of the circumstances, making nonprogrammed decisions can result in effective or ineffective decision making. Managers have to be on their guard to avoid being overconfident in decisions that result from either intuition or reasoned judgment.

The classical and administrative decision-making models reveal many of the assumptions, complexities, and pitfalls that affect decision making. These models help reveal the factors that managers and other decision makers must be aware of to improve the quality of their decision making. Keep in mind, however, that the classical and administrative models are just guides that can help managers understand the decision-making process. In real life, the process is typically not cut-and-dried, but these models can help guide a manager through it.

classical model A prescriptive approach to decision making based on the assumption that the decision maker can identify and evaluate all possible alternatives and their consequences and rationally choose the most appropriate course of action.

optimum decision The most appropriate decision in light of what managers believe to be the most desirable consequences for the organization.

The Classical Model

One of the earliest models of decision making, the **classical model**, is *prescriptive,* which means it specifies how decisions *should* be made. Managers using the classical model make a series of simplifying assumptions about the nature of the decision-making process (see Figure 7.1). The premise of the classical model is that once managers recognize the need to make a decision, they should be able to generate a complete list of *all* alternatives and consequences and make the best choice. In other words, the classical model assumes managers have access to *all* the information they need to make the **optimum decision**, which is the most appropriate decision possible in light of what they believe to be the most desirable consequences for the organization. Furthermore, the classical model assumes managers can easily list their own preferences for each alternative and rank them from least to most preferred to make the optimum decision.

Figure 7.1

The Classical Model of Decision Making

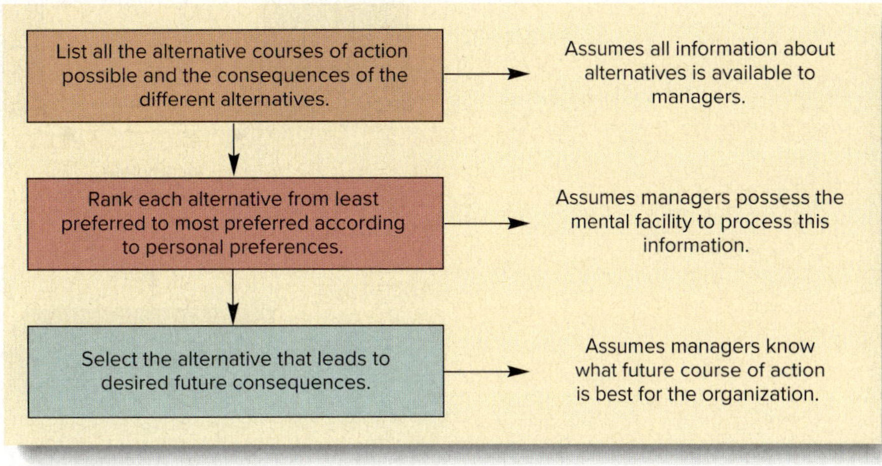

The Administrative Model

James March and Herbert Simon disagreed with the underlying assumptions of the classical model of decision making. In contrast, they proposed that managers in the real world do *not* have access to all the information they need to make a decision. Moreover, they pointed out that even if all information were readily available, many managers would lack the mental or psychological ability to absorb and evaluate it correctly. As a result, March and Simon developed the **administrative model** of decision making to explain why decision making is always an inherently uncertain and risky process—and why managers can rarely make decisions in the manner prescribed by the classical model. The administrative model is based on three important concepts: *bounded rationality, incomplete information,* and *satisficing.*

administrative model An approach to decision making that explains why decision making is inherently uncertain and risky and why managers usually make satisfactory rather than optimum decisions.

BOUNDED RATIONALITY March and Simon pointed out that human decision-making capabilities are bounded by people's cognitive limitations—that is, limitations in their ability to interpret, process, and act on information.[15] They argued that the limitations of human intelligence constrain the ability of decision makers to determine the optimum decision. March and Simon coined the term **bounded rationality** to describe the situation in which the number of alternatives a manager must identify is so great and the amount of information so vast that it is difficult for the manager to even come close to evaluating it all before making a decision.[16]

bounded rationality Cognitive limitations that constrain one's ability to interpret, process, and act on information.

INCOMPLETE INFORMATION Even if managers had unlimited ability to evaluate information, they still would not be able to arrive at the optimum decision because they would have incomplete information. Information is incomplete because the full range of decision-making alternatives is unknowable in most situations, and the consequences associated with known alternatives are uncertain.[17] In other words, information is incomplete because of risk and uncertainty, ambiguity, and time constraints (see Figure 7.2).

RISK AND UNCERTAINTY As we saw in Chapter 6, forces in the organizational environment are constantly changing. **Risk** is present when managers know the possible outcomes of a particular course of action and can assign probabilities to them. For example, managers in the biotechnology industry know that new drugs have a 10% probability of successfully passing advanced clinical trials and a 90% probability of failing. These probabilities reflect the experiences of thousands of drugs that have gone through advanced clinical trials. Thus, when managers in the biotechnology industry decide to submit a drug for testing, they know that there is only a 10% chance that the drug will succeed, but at least they have some information on which to base their decision.

risk The degree of probability that the possible outcomes of a particular course of action will occur.

When **uncertainty** exists, the probabilities of alternative outcomes *cannot* be determined and future outcomes are *unknown.* Managers are working blind. Because the probability of a given outcome occurring is not known, managers have little information to use in making a decision.

uncertainty Unpredictability.

Figure 7.2
Why Information Is Incomplete

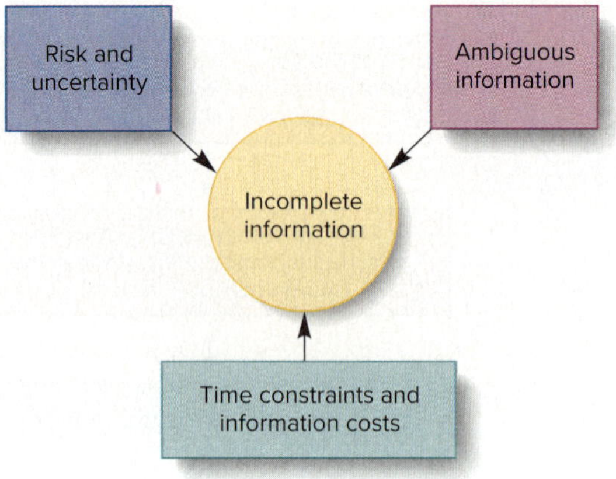

For example, in 1993, when Apple Computer introduced the Newton, its personal digital assistant (PDA), managers had no idea what the probability of a successful product launch for a PDA might be. Because Apple was the first to market this totally new product, there was no body of well-known data that Apple's managers could draw on to calculate the probability of a successful launch. Uncertainty plagues most managerial decision making. Although Apple's initial launch of its PDA was a disaster due to technical problems, an improved version was more successful. The "Ethics in Action" feature describes how people unafraid to take risks can provide both economic and environmental outcomes that are beneficial to many.

ETHICS IN ACTION

Taking Risks to Help Others and the Planet

Discarded plastic containers in oceans are a disturbing problem. Ironically, the major sources of plastic in the ocean are poor nations. These countries consume less plastic but lack efficient systems to collect it and bury or recycle it. What most see as an overwhelming problem looked like an opportunity to David Katz, who was willing to take a risk. The great volume of plastic had economic value, and to release it would require a business–specifically, a way to make money by getting plastic out of the oceans and into recycling plants.[18]

David Katz was willing to take a risk and start a business that would pay locals to collect plastic from oceans and nearby beaches. His idea not only helped clean up the environment, it also provided individuals with a way to participate in the local economy.
Platoo Studio/Shutterstock

Katz's idea was to set up a business that would not just pay for plastic, but do it in a way that enables people to participate more fully in their economy. He founded Plastic Bank, which sets up collection centers run by locals and online bank accounts for collectors. When collectors bring plastic bottles to a center, it credits their Plastic Bank accounts electronically. Collectors can access the amount on their phones, using it to make mobile payments.[19]

The ability to collect small amounts of money in a bank account has tremendous benefits. For the poor in many countries, a few extra dollars means someone can buy a dose of medicine for a headache or save up to repair a roof. Many Plastic Bank account holders are saving for the first time. Since Plastic Bank opened its first recycling centers in Haiti in 2015, it has improved the lives of more than 4,200 families while recovering and recycling more than 1.5 billion pounds of plastic waste. Plastic Bank has expanded to the Philippines, Indonesia, Brazil, and Egypt, as well as Cameroon and Thailand.[20]

A challenge remains: what to do with the bottles. While Katz readily identified a supply of workers for his business, finding a demand for used plastic is more complicated. Virgin plastic costs less to make than recycled plastic, and some countries prohibit the use of recycled plastic for food and beverages. Plastic Bank partners with big global corporations such as S.C. Johnson that want to demonstrate their commitment to sustainability. They fund the recycling centers and commit to using more recycled plastic in their packaging. Local entrepreneurs interested in processing bottles into pellets for resale also seek these commitments, so they can get financing to build their factories.[21] A great idea can come from one person, but to succeed, it may require a group of like-minded people who have the ability to take risks and be comfortable with uncertainty.

ambiguous information Information that can be interpreted in multiple and often conflicting ways.

AMBIGUOUS INFORMATION A second reason information is incomplete is that much of the information managers have at their disposal is **ambiguous information**. Its meaning is not clear–it can be interpreted in multiple and often conflicting ways.[22] Take a look at Figure 7.3. Do you see a young woman or an old woman? In a similar fashion, managers often interpret the same piece of information differently and make decisions based on their own interpretations.

TIME CONSTRAINTS AND INFORMATION COSTS The third reason information is incomplete is that managers have neither the time nor the money to search for all possible alternative solutions and evaluate all the potential consequences of those alternatives. Consider the situation confronting a Ford Motor Company purchasing manager who has one month to choose a supplier for a small engine part. There are 20,000 potential suppliers for this part in the United States alone. Given the time available, the purchasing manager cannot contact all potential suppliers and ask each one for its terms (price, delivery schedules, and so on). Moreover, even if the time were available, the costs of obtaining the information, including the manager's own time, would be prohibitive.

Figure 7.3
Ambiguous Information: Young Woman or Old Woman?

Chronicle of World History/Alamy Stock Photo

SATISFICING March and Simon argued that managers do not try to discover every alternative when faced with bounded rationality, an uncertain future, unquantifiable risks, considerable ambiguity, time constraints, and high information costs. Rather, they use a strategy known as **satisficing**, which is exploring a limited sample of all potential alternatives.[23] When managers satisfice, they search for and choose acceptable, or satisfactory, ways to respond to problems and opportunities rather than trying to make the optimum decision.[24] In the case of the Ford purchasing manager's search, for example, satisficing may involve asking a limited number of suppliers for their terms, trusting that they are representative of suppliers in general, and then making a choice from that set. Although this course of action is reasonable from the perspective of the purchasing manager, it may mean that a potentially superior supplier is overlooked.

satisficing Searching for and choosing an acceptable, or satisfactory, response to problems and opportunities, rather than trying to make the best decision.

March and Simon pointed out that managerial decision making is often more art than science. In the real world, managers must rely on their intuition and judgment to make what seems to them to be the best decision in the face of uncertainty and ambiguity.[25] Moreover, managerial decision making is often fast-paced; managers use their experience and judgment to make crucial decisions under conditions of incomplete information. Although there is nothing wrong with this approach, decision makers should be aware that human judgment is often flawed. As a result, even the best managers sometimes make poor decisions.[26]

Steps in the Decision-Making Process

Using the work of March and Simon as a basis, researchers have developed a step-by-step model of the decision-making process and the issues and problems that managers confront at each step. Perhaps the best way to introduce this model is to examine the real-world nonprogrammed decision making of Scott McNealy at a crucial point in Sun Microsystems's history. McNealy was a founder of Sun Microsystems and was the chairman of the board of directors until Sun was acquired by Oracle in 2010.[27]

LO7-2 Describe the six steps managers should take to make the best decisions, and explain how cognitive biases can lead managers to make poor decisions.

In early August 1985, Scott McNealy, then CEO of Sun Microsystems (a hardware and software computer workstation manufacturer focused on network solutions), had to decide whether to go ahead with the launch of the new Carrera workstation computer, scheduled for September 10. Sun's managers had chosen the date nine months earlier when the development plan for the Carrera was first proposed. McNealy knew it would take at least a month to prepare for the September 10 launch, and the decision could not be put off.

Customers were waiting for the new machine, and McNealy wanted to be the first to provide a workstation that took advantage of Motorola's then-powerful 16-megahertz 68020 microprocessor. Capitalizing on this opportunity would give Sun a significant edge over Apollo, its main competitor in the workstation market. McNealy knew, however, that committing to the September 10 launch date was risky. Motorola was having production problems with the 16-megahertz 68020 microprocessor and could not guarantee Sun a steady supply of these chips. Moreover, the operating system software was not completely free of bugs.

If Sun launched the Carrera on September 10, the company might have to ship some machines with software that was not fully operational, was likely to crash the system, and utilized Motorola's less powerful 12-megahertz 68020 microprocessor instead of the 16-megahertz version.[28] Of course, Sun could later upgrade the microprocessor and operating system software in any machines purchased by early customers, but the company's reputation would suffer. If Sun did not go ahead with the September launch, the company would miss an important opportunity.[29] Rumors were circulating in the industry that Apollo would be launching a new machine of its own that same year in December.

McNealy clearly had a difficult decision to make. He had to decide quickly whether to launch the Carrera, but he did not have all the facts. He did not know, for example, whether the microprocessor or operating system problems could be resolved by September 10; nor did he know whether Apollo was going to launch a competing machine in December. But he could not wait to find these things out—he had to make a decision. We'll see what he decided later in the chapter.

Many managers who must make important decisions with incomplete information face dilemmas similar to McNealy's. Managers should consciously follow six steps to make a good decision (see Figure 7.4).[30] We review these steps in the remainder of this section. As you read

Figure 7.4
Six Steps in Decision Making

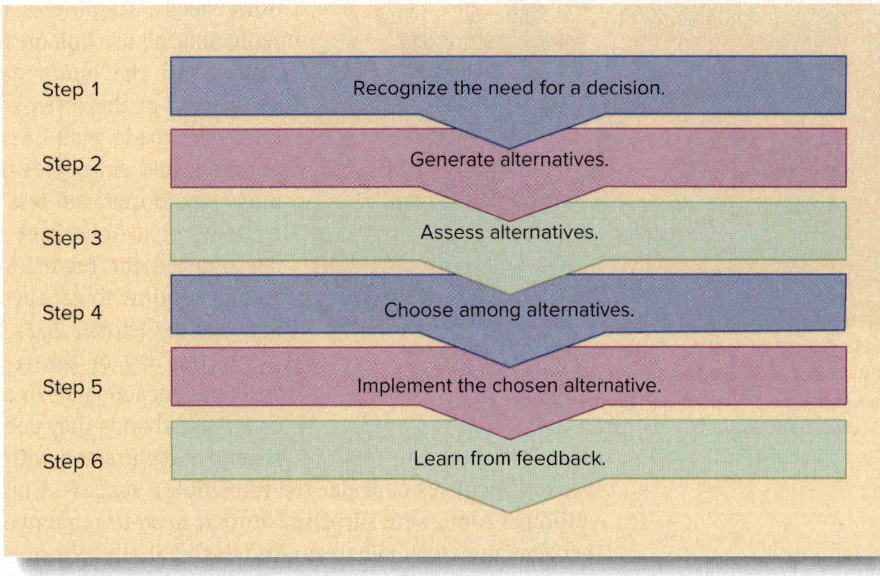

about the steps, keep in mind that, in practice, decision makers may circle back and repeat some steps as conditions change. Different needs may arise, new alternatives may emerge, and the implementation of a decision may uncover issues the decision makers overlooked. The "Management Insight" feature describes this flexible approach to decision making in the rapidly changing conditions associated with workers returning to the office during the COVID-19 pandemic.

MANAGEMENT INSIGHT

Making "Back to Work" Work at Molson Coors

When Molson Coors sent office employees home to work at the start of the COVID-19 pandemic in March 2020, executives already knew they would have to decide when to return, but the decision making would be more complex than expected. They hoped for a few months of remote work, followed by a return to focusing on the big challenges facing Molson, the world's fifth-largest brewing company. CEO Gavin Hattersley's vision to offer a wide variety of beverages was a bold strategy, given that his experience was in the beer industry, whose sales had been declining even before the pandemic shut down bars and restaurants.[31]

The planning to return finally began in early 2021. By then, employees were accustomed to remote work, which raised a new question: Must they be in the office five days a week? Hattersley had assumed they would, but Molson investigated. In surveys, employee forums, and virtual chats with the CEO, employees indicated they were eager to get back, but many said they liked the flexibility of working at home. Some had health concerns, and some worried about child care–common sentiments expressed by employees across the globe about returning to work.[32] Molson's leadership team therefore weighed options of five, four, or three days a week in the office. To enable in-person collaboration, they selected a schedule of three mandatory in-office days: Monday, Tuesday, and Thursday. Employees could choose where to work on the other two days. The team also selected September 7, 2021, as the office-reopening date.[33]

Molson Coors's leadership team worked diligently to ensure that their decision to bring back employees to the office as the pandemic waned worked well for everyone.
Luis Alvarez/Getty Images

Implementation began in April, when Molson announced the in-office schedule, giving employees a few months to plan child care, transportation, and other needs. Employees received memos detailing the reopening plans, tips on hybrid working, and guides to offices (for the hundreds of employees who had not yet worked at the office). Safety concerns persisted, so Hattersley made what he calls his most difficult decision: requiring that employees be vaccinated. He worried that many would quit, but less than 1% did, citing either the mandate or a preference for remote work. Hattersley's decision led the team to rethink the timeline. To give employees time to get vaccinated, they pushed the opening back to October 2021.[34]

On the day of the return, Molson gave employees welcome packets and, in at least one department, color-coded wristbands they could wear to signal whether they wanted to be greeted with a hug, elbow bump, or just a wave. Executives consider the transition a success. Employees expressed satisfaction, although some were surprised at their need to remember basics such as allowing time between in-person meetings. And during it all, Molson stayed on track with deals supporting its diversification strategy.[35]

Recognize the Need for a Decision

The first step in the decision-making process is to recognize the need for a decision. Scott McNealy recognized this need, and he realized a decision had to be made quickly.

Some stimuli usually spark the realization that a decision must be made. These stimuli often become apparent because changes in the organizational environment result in new kinds of opportunities and threats. This happened at Sun Microsystems. The September 10 launch date had been set when it seemed that Motorola chips would be readily available. Later, with the supply of chips in doubt and bugs remaining in the system software, Sun was in danger of failing to meet its launch date.

The stimuli that spark decision making are as likely to result from the actions of managers inside an organization as they are from changes in the external environment.[36] An organization possesses a set of skills, competencies, and resources in its employees and in departments such as marketing, manufacturing, and research and development. Managers who actively pursue opportunities to use these competencies create the need to make decisions. Managers thus can be proactive or reactive in recognizing the need to make a decision, but the important issue is that they must recognize this need and respond in a timely and appropriate way.[37]

Generate Alternatives

Having recognized the need to make a decision, a manager must generate a set of feasible alternative courses of action to take in response to the opportunity or threat. Management experts cite failure to properly generate and consider different alternatives as one reason that managers sometimes make bad decisions.[38] In the Sun Microsystems decision, the alternatives seemed clear: go ahead with the September 10 launch or delay the launch until the Carrera was 100% ready for market introduction. Often, however, the alternatives are not so obvious or so clearly specified.

One major problem is that managers may find it difficult to come up with creative alternative solutions to specific problems. Perhaps some of them are used to seeing the world from a single perspective—they have a certain "managerial mind-set." Many managers find it difficult to view problems from a fresh perspective. According to best-selling management author Peter Senge, we all are trapped within our personal mental models of the world—our ideas about what is important and how the world works.[39] Generating creative alternatives to solve problems and take advantage of opportunities may require that we abandon our existing mindsets and develop new ones—something that usually is difficult to do.

The importance of getting managers to set aside their mental models of the world and generate creative alternatives is reflected in the growth of interest in the work of authors such as Peter Senge and Edward de Bono, who have popularized techniques for stimulating problem solving and creative thinking among managers.[40] Later in this chapter, we discuss the important issues of organizational learning and creativity in detail.

Assess Alternatives

Once managers have generated a set of alternatives, they must evaluate the advantages and disadvantages of each one. The key to a good assessment of the alternatives is to define the opportunity or threat exactly and then specify the criteria that *should* influence the selection of alternatives for responding to the problem or opportunity. One reason for bad decisions is that managers often fail to specify the criteria that are important in reaching a decision.[41] In general, successful managers use four criteria to evaluate the pros and cons of alternative courses of action (see Figure 7.5):

1. *Legality:* Managers must ensure that a possible course of action will not violate any domestic or international laws or government regulations.
2. *Ethicalness:* Managers must ensure that a possible course of action is ethical and will not unnecessarily harm any stakeholder group. Many decisions managers make may help some organizational stakeholders and harm others (see Chapter 4). When examining alternative courses of action, managers need to be clear about the potential effects of their decisions.
3. *Economic feasibility:* Managers must decide whether the alternatives are economically feasible—that is, whether they can be accomplished, given the organization's performance goals. Typically, managers perform a cost-benefit analysis of the various alternatives to determine which one will have the best net financial payoff.
4. *Practicality:* Managers must decide whether they have the capabilities and resources required to implement the alternative, and they must be sure the alternative will not threaten the attainment of other organizational goals. At first glance, an alternative might seem economically superior to other alternatives, but if managers realize it is likely to threaten other important projects, they might decide it is not practical after all.

Figure 7.5

General Criteria for Evaluating Possible Courses of Action

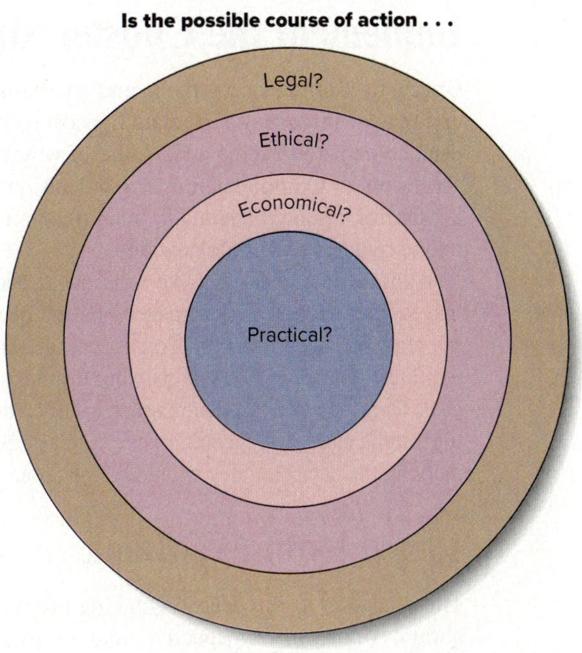

Often a manager must consider these four criteria simultaneously. Scott McNealy framed the problem at hand at Sun Microsystems quite well. The key question was whether to go ahead with the September 10 launch date. Two main criteria were influencing McNealy's choice: the need to ship a machine that was as "complete" as possible (the *practicality* criterion) and the need to beat Apollo to market with a new workstation (the *economic feasibility* criterion). These two criteria conflicted. The first suggested that the launch should be delayed; the second, that the launch should go ahead. McNealy's actual choice was based on the relative importance that he assigned to these two criteria. In fact, Sun Microsystems went ahead with the September 10 launch, which suggests that McNealy thought the need to beat Apollo to market was the more important criterion.

Some of the worst managerial decisions can be traced to poor assessment of the alternatives, such as the decision to launch the *Challenger* space shuttle, mentioned earlier. In that case, the desire of NASA and Morton Thiokol managers to demonstrate to the public the success of the U.S. space program in order to ensure future funding (*economic feasibility*) conflicted with the need to ensure the safety of the astronauts (*ethicalness*). Managers deemed the economic criterion more important and decided to launch the space shuttle even though there were unanswered questions about safety. Tragically, some of the same decision-making problems that resulted in the *Challenger* tragedy led to the demise of the *Columbia* space shuttle 17 years later, killing all seven astronauts on board.[42] In both the *Challenger* and the *Columbia* disasters, safety questions were raised before the shuttles were launched; safety concerns took second place to budgets, economic feasibility, and schedules; top decision makers seemed to ignore or downplay the inputs of those with relevant technical expertise; and speaking up was discouraged.[43] Rather than making safety a top priority, decision makers seemed overly concerned with keeping on schedule and within budget–with catastrophic results.[44]

Choose among Alternatives

Once the set of alternative solutions has been carefully evaluated, the next task is to rank the various alternatives (using the criteria discussed in the previous section) and make a decision. When ranking alternatives, managers must be sure *all* the information available is brought to bear on the problem or issue at hand. As the Sun Microsystems case indicates, however, identifying all *relevant* information for a decision does not mean the manager has *complete* information; in most instances, information is incomplete.

Perhaps more serious than the existence of incomplete information is the often-documented tendency of managers to ignore critical information, even when it is available. We discuss this tendency in detail later when we examine the operation of cognitive biases and groupthink.

Implement the Chosen Alternative

Once a decision has been made and an alternative has been selected, it must be implemented, and many subsequent and related decisions must be made. After a course of action has been decided–say, to develop a new line of women's clothing–thousands of subsequent decisions are necessary to implement it. These decisions would involve recruiting dress designers, obtaining fabrics, finding high-quality manufacturers, and signing contracts with clothing stores and online retailers to sell the new line.

Although the need to make subsequent decisions to implement the chosen course of action may seem obvious, many managers make a decision and then fail to act on it. This is the same as not making a decision at all. To ensure that a decision is implemented, top managers must assign to middle managers the responsibility for making the follow-up decisions necessary to achieve the goal. They must give middle managers sufficient resources to achieve the goal, and they must hold the middle managers accountable for their performance. If the middle managers succeed in implementing the decision, they should be rewarded; if they fail, they should be subject to sanctions.

Learn from Feedback

The final step in the decision-making process is learning from feedback. Effective managers always conduct a retrospective analysis to see what they can learn from past successes or failures. Managers who do not evaluate the results of their decisions do not learn from experience; instead, they stagnate and are likely to make the same mistakes again and again.[45] To avoid this problem, managers must establish a formal procedure with which they can learn from the results of past decisions. The procedure should include these steps:

1. Compare what actually happened to what was expected to happen as a result of the decision.
2. Explore why any expectations for the decision were not met.
3. Derive guidelines that will help in future decision making.

Managers who always strive to learn from past mistakes and successes are likely to continuously improve the decisions they make. A significant amount of learning can take place when the outcomes of decisions are evaluated, and this assessment can produce enormous benefits. For an example of a manager who learns from feedback, see the "Focus on DEI&B" feature.

FOCUS ON DEI&B

SoLa Impact Pursues More than Profits

SoLa Impact invests in affordable housing for low-income residents of Los Angeles, but unlike most organizations providing affordable housing, it operates as a for-profit. SoLa serves majority Black and Brown neighborhoods, where a history of redlining makes the need urgent. (The practice of redlining occurs when companies refuse to loan money or provide insurance to individuals who live in areas deemed to be a poor financial risk.) Home builders in Los Angeles are constructing far fewer units than needed, and rents are too high for many. To address the problem, SoLa has acquired hundreds of properties and become one of Southern California's largest owners of affordable housing units.[46]

SoLa's founder and managing partner, Martin Muoto, grew up in Nigeria, where he learned that his sense of well-being was intertwined with that of his community. This value came with him to the Wharton School of Business. Then, as Muoto developed finance expertise by working for investment firms, he saw in Los Angeles an opportunity to combine community well-being with profits. But when he sought funding, investors hesitated to put money into underserved communities reputed to be dangerous, so Muoto started with his own money. He says he is comfortable in LA's low-income neighborhoods because he is a person of color who learned to navigate West Africa's tough neighborhoods. When he bought a property being used by gang members, Muoto got acquainted with their leader and built support for his vision. Undeterred by a later shooting, he arranged a visible onsite meeting with a city prosecutor.[47]

As SoLa built a track record of generating a return on investment, investors began to fund its expansion. But adequately maintaining long-neglected buildings is hard. While some tenants are satisfied, others complain of living in substandard conditions. Muoto blames the strains of the COVID pandemic, supply chain disruptions, and labor shortages but adds that he is open to learning. As he learns, the community benefits. When SoLa had trouble sourcing enough window frames from China, it set up a shop where metalworkers train unemployed workers in welding, generating local jobs as they fill SoLa's orders.[48]

The challenges led Muoto to decide that existing buildings should be a smaller part of SoLa's portfolio, giving way to new construction. Involvement from the design stage onward gives the company more control over costs. SoLa selects lower-priced options and standardizes designs to speed up construction. It has achieved a cost-per-unit of $250,000, versus $500,000 or more spent by organizations using government funds. Lower costs enable lower rents, so more people can afford housing.[49]

Cognitive Biases and Decision Making

In the 1970s, psychologists Daniel Kahneman and the late Amos Tversky suggested that because all decision makers are subject to bounded rationality, they tend to use **heuristics**, which are rules based on an individual's experience that simplify the process of making decisions.[50] Kahneman and Tversky argued that these rules are often useful because they help decision makers make sense of complex, uncertain, and ambiguous information. Sometimes, however, the use of heuristics can lead to systematic errors in the way decision makers process information about alternatives and make decisions. **Systematic errors** are errors that people make over and over and that result in poor decision making. Because of cognitive biases, which are caused by systematic errors, otherwise capable managers may end up making bad decisions.[51] Four sources of bias that can adversely affect the way managers make decisions are confirmation, representativeness, the illusion of control, and escalating commitment (see Figure 7.6).

heuristics Rules based on an individual's experience that simplify the process of decision making.

systematic errors Errors that people make over and over and that result in poor decision making.

Confirmation Bias

Decision makers who have strong existing beliefs about the relationship between two variables tend to make decisions based on those beliefs *even when presented with evidence that those initial beliefs may be wrong.* In doing so, they fall victim to **confirmation bias**.[52] In addition, decision makers tend to seek and use information consistent with those existing beliefs and to ignore information that contradicts those beliefs. Research suggests that confirmation bias is particularly strong when information is presented sequentially and the person is asked to revisit their decision in light of new information.[53]

confirmation bias A source of cognitive bias that results from the tendency to base decisions on one's existing beliefs even if evidence shows that those beliefs are wrong.

Representativeness Bias

Many decision makers inappropriately generalize from a small sample or even from a single vivid case or episode; these are instances of the **representativeness bias**. Consider the case of a bookstore manager who decided to partner with a local independent school for a "Book Day": Students and parents from the school would be encouraged to buy books at the bookstore as a fund-raiser for the school, and the bookstore would share a small portion of proceeds from these sales with the school. After quite a bit of planning, the Book Day generated lackluster sales and publicity for the store. When other public and independent schools approached the bookstore manager with similar proposals for fund-raising and Book Days, the manager declined based on their initial bad experience. As a result, the manager lost opportunities to expand sales and gain word-of-mouth advertising and publicity for the bookstore. The manager's initial bad experience was the result of a scheduling snafu at the school—an important lacrosse game was scheduled the same day as the Book Day.

representativeness bias A source of cognitive bias that results from the tendency to generalize inappropriately from a small sample or from a single vivid event or episode.

Illusion of Control

Other errors in decision making result from the **illusion of control**, which is the tendency of decision makers to overestimate their ability to control activities and events. Top managers seem particularly prone to this bias. Having worked their way to the top of an organization, they tend to have an exaggerated sense of their own worth and are overconfident about their ability to succeed and to control events.[54] The illusion of control causes managers to

illusion of control A source of cognitive bias that results from the tendency to overestimate one's own ability to control activities and events.

Figure 7.6

Sources of Cognitive Bias at the Individual and Group Levels

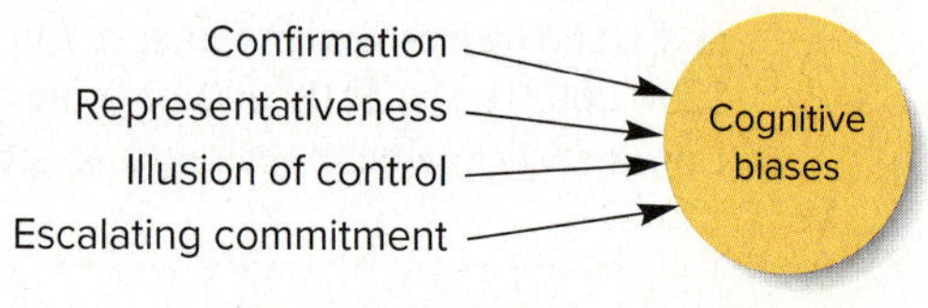

overestimate the odds of a favorable outcome and, consequently, to make inappropriate decisions. According to most studies, 70–90% of mergers and acquisitions fail, yet time and time again, top managers overestimate their abilities to combine companies with vastly different cultures in a successful merger.[55]

Escalating Commitment

escalating commitment A source of cognitive bias that results from the tendency to commit additional resources to a project even if evidence shows that the project is failing.

Having already committed significant resources to a course of action, some managers commit more resources to the project *even if they receive feedback that the project is failing.*[56] Feelings of personal responsibility for a project apparently bias the analysis of decision makers and lead to this **escalating commitment**. The managers decide to increase their investment of time and money in a course of action and even ignore evidence that it is illegal, unethical, uneconomical, or impractical (see Figure 7.5). Often the more appropriate decision would be to cut their losses and run.

Consider the case of Mark Gracin, who owns a landscape company. Gracin had a profitable business doing general landscape work (such as mowing grass, picking up leaves, and fertilizing) for home owners in a large city. To expand his business into landscape design, he hired a landscape designer, advertised landscape design services in local newspapers and on social media, and gave his existing customers free design proposals for their front and back yards. After a few months, Gracin had no landscape design customers. Still convinced that landscape design was a great way to expand his business despite this negative feedback, he decided he needed to do more. He rented a small office for his landscape designer (who used to work from her own home office) to meet with clients, hired an assistant for the designer, had a public relations firm create promotional materials, and started advertising on local TV. These efforts also did not generate sufficient interest in his landscape design services to offset their costs. Yet Gracin's escalating commitment caused him to continue to pour money into trying to drum up business in landscape design. In fact, Gracin reluctantly decided to abandon his landscape design services only when he realized he could no longer afford their mounting costs.

Be Aware of Your Biases

How can managers avoid the negative effects of cognitive biases and improve their decision-making and problem-solving abilities? Managers must become aware of biases and their effects, and they must identify their own personal style of making decisions. One useful way for managers to analyze their decision-making style is to review two decisions that they made recently—one decision that turned out well and one that turned out poorly. Problem-solving experts recommend that managers start by determining how much time to spend on each of the decision-making steps, such as gathering information to identify the pros and cons of alternatives or ranking the alternatives, to make sure they spend sufficient time on each step.[57]

Another recommended technique for examining decision-making style is for managers to list the criteria they typically use to assess and evaluate alternatives—the heuristics they typically employ, their personal biases, and so on—and then critically evaluate the appropriateness of these different factors.

Many managers are likely to have difficulty identifying their own biases, so it is often advisable for managers to scrutinize their own assumptions by working with other managers to help expose weaknesses in their decision-making style. In this context, the issue of group decision making becomes important.

Group Decision Making

Many (or perhaps most) important organizational decisions are made by groups or teams of managers rather than by individuals. Group decision making is superior to individual decision making in several respects. When managers work as a team to make decisions and solve problems, their choices of alternatives are less likely to fall victim to the biases and errors discussed previously. They can draw on the combined skills, competencies, and accumulated knowledge of group members and thereby improve their ability to generate feasible alternatives and make good decisions. Group decision making also allows managers to process more information and to correct one another's errors. And in the implementation phase, all

LO7-3 Identify the advantages and disadvantages of group decision making, and describe techniques that can improve it.

managers affected by the decisions agree to cooperate. When a group of managers makes a decision (as opposed to one top manager making a decision and imposing it on subordinate managers), the probability that the decision will be implemented successfully increases. (We discuss how to encourage employee participation in decision making in Chapter 14.)

Some potential disadvantages are associated with group decision making. Groups often take much longer than individuals to make decisions. Getting two or more managers to agree to the same solution can be difficult because managers' interests and preferences are often different. In addition, just like decision making by individual managers, group decision making can be undermined by biases. A major source of group bias is *groupthink.*

The Perils of Groupthink

groupthink A pattern of faulty and biased decision making that occurs in groups whose members strive for agreement among themselves at the expense of accurately assessing information relevant to a decision.

Groupthink is a pattern of faulty and biased decision making that occurs in groups whose members strive for agreement among themselves at the expense of accurately assessing information relevant to a decision.[58] When managers are subject to groupthink, they collectively embark on a course of action without developing appropriate criteria to evaluate alternatives. Typically, a group rallies around one central manager, such as the CEO, and the course of action that manager supports. Group members become blindly committed to that course of action without evaluating its merits. Commitment is often based on an emotional, rather than an objective, assessment of the optimal course of action.

The decision President Kennedy and his advisers made to launch the unfortunate Bay of Pigs invasion in Cuba in 1962, the decisions made by President Johnson and his advisers from 1964 to 1967 to escalate the war in Vietnam, the decision made by President Nixon and his advisers in 1972 to cover up the Watergate break-in, and the decision made by NASA and Morton Thiokol in 1986 to launch the ill-fated *Challenger* shuttle—all were likely influenced by groupthink. After the fact, decision makers such as these who may fall victim to groupthink are often surprised that their decision-making process and outcomes were so flawed.

When groupthink occurs, pressures for agreement and harmony within a group have the unintended effect of discouraging individuals from raising issues that run counter to majority opinion. For example, when managers at NASA and Morton Thiokol fell victim to groupthink, they convinced each other that all was well and that there was no need to delay the launch of the *Challenger* space shuttle.

Devil's Advocacy and Dialectical Inquiry

The existence of cognitive biases and groupthink raises the question of how to improve the quality of group and individual decision making so managers make decisions that are realistic and are based on thorough evaluation of alternatives. Two techniques known to counteract groupthink and cognitive biases are devil's advocacy and dialectical inquiry (see Figure 7.7).[59]

Figure 7.7

Devil's Advocacy and Dialectical Inquiry

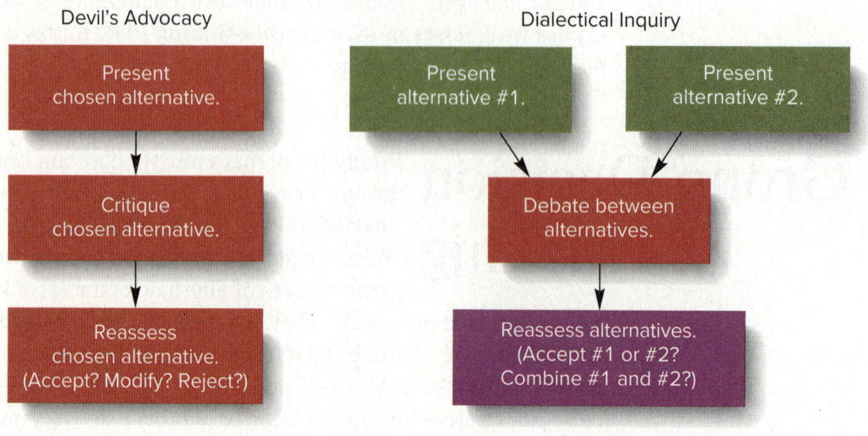

devil's advocacy Critical analysis of a preferred alternative, made in response to challenges raised by a group member who, playing the role of devil's advocate, defends unpopular or opposing alternatives for the sake of argument.

dialectical inquiry Critical analysis of two preferred alternatives in order to find an even better alternative for the organization to adopt.

Devil's advocacy is a critical analysis of a preferred alternative to ascertain its strengths and weaknesses before it is implemented.[60] Typically, one member of the decision-making group plays the role of devil's advocate. The devil's advocate critiques and challenges the way the group evaluated alternatives and chose one over the others. The purpose of devil's advocacy is to identify all the reasons that might make the preferred alternative unacceptable. In this way, decision makers can be made aware of the possible perils of recommended courses of action.

Dialectical inquiry goes one step further. Two groups of managers are assigned to a problem, and each group is responsible for evaluating alternatives and selecting one of them.[61] Top managers hear each group present its preferred alternative, and then each group critiques the other's position. During this debate, top managers challenge both groups' positions to uncover potential problems and perils associated with their solutions. The goal is to find an even better alternative course of action for the organization to adopt.

Both devil's advocacy and dialectical inquiry can help counter the effects of cognitive biases and groupthink.[62] In practice, devil's advocacy is probably easier to implement because it involves less managerial time and effort than does dialectical inquiry.

Diversity among Decision Makers

Another way to improve group decision making is to promote diversity in decision-making groups (see Chapter 5).[63] Bringing together managers from various ethnic, national, and functional backgrounds broadens the range of life experiences and opinions that group members can draw on as they generate, assess, and choose among alternatives. Moreover, diverse groups are sometimes less prone to groupthink because group members already differ from each other and thus are less subject to pressures for uniformity.

Organizational Learning and Creativity

LO7-4 Explain the role that organizational learning and creativity play in helping managers to improve their decisions.

organizational learning The process through which managers seek to improve employees' desire and ability to understand and manage the organization and its task environment.

learning organization An organization in which managers try to maximize the ability of individuals and groups to think and behave creatively and thus maximize the potential for organizational learning to take place.

creativity A decision maker's ability to discover original and novel ideas that lead to feasible alternative courses of action.

The quality of managerial decision making ultimately depends on innovative responses to opportunities and threats. How can managers increase their ability to make nonprogrammed decisions that will allow them to adapt to, modify, and even drastically alter their task environments so they can continually increase organizational performance? The answer is by encouraging organizational learning.[64]

Organizational learning is the process through which managers seek to improve employees' desire and ability to understand and manage the organization and its task environment so employees can make decisions that continuously increase organizational effectiveness.[65] A **learning organization** is one in which managers do everything possible to maximize the ability of individuals and groups to think and behave creatively and thus maximize the potential for organizational learning to take place. At the heart of organizational learning is **creativity**, which is the ability of a decision maker to discover original and novel ideas that lead to feasible alternative courses of action. Encouraging creativity among managers is such a pressing organizational concern that many organizations hire outside experts to help them develop programs to train their managers in the art of creative thinking and problem solving.

Get off email and lose the desk! Giving yourself and your employees the time and space to know that contributions off the beaten track are valued increases the ability to think outside the box.
D. Hurst/Alamy Stock Photo

Creating a Learning Organization

How can managers foster a learning organization? Learning theorist Peter Senge identified five principles for creating a learning organization (see Figure 7.8):[66]

personal mastery Process by which individuals develop a desire for personal learning that may continue indefinitely in the person's daily life, including work activities.

1. For organizational learning to occur, top managers must allow every person in the organization to develop a sense of **personal mastery**, which is the process by which an individual develops the desire for personal learning that will continue throughout the person's life. Managers must understand this process and empower each employee to experiment, create, and explore their own ideas of personal learning, which can have a positive effect on the overall organization.[67]
2. As part of attaining personal mastery, people should think about some of the assumptions they have about how the world works and develop ideas about these so-called *mental models.* Often, however, individuals are unaware of the mental models or assumptions they hold and must look within to understand how they see the world. Once individuals gain perspective on how they view the world, they can use this information to expand their way of thinking not only on a personal level but also at work. Developing complex mental models–sophisticated ways of thinking that challenge them to find new or better ways of performing a task–can help workers and managers to expand the way an organization thinks about how they perform work. To expand thinking in this way requires experimentation, taking risks, and thinking outside the lines, which can help reshape how an organization performs at all levels.[68]
3. Managers must do everything they can to promote creativity within groups. Team members must be encouraged to learn together through exchanging ideas, listening to one another, and working together to solve problems. Ongoing dialog between group members is very important. Senge thought that *team learning* is more important than individual learning as a way to increase organizational learning. He pointed out that most important decisions are made within organization subunits such as groups, functions, and divisions.
4. Managers must emphasize the importance of building a shared vision–meaning that employees share their vision for the future of the organization. Once this shared vision is identified, members of the organization can frame problems and opportunities with the shared vision in mind and work together to achieve common goals that correspond to the vision.
5. Managers must encourage *systems thinking* (a concept drawn from systems theory discussed earlier in Chapter 2). This concept is a way of seeing the whole picture. It is a framework for seeing interrelationships and patterns rather than static "snapshots" within an organization. Systems thinking can be thought of as a conceptual cornerstone that pulls together the other four principles for creating a learning organization.[69]

Building a learning organization requires that managers change their management assumptions radically. Developing a learning organization is neither a quick nor an easy process. Senge worked with Ford Motor Company to help managers make Ford a learning organization. Why would Ford want this? Top management believed that to compete successfully Ford must improve its members' ability to be creative and make the right decisions.

Figure 7.8

Senge's Principles for Creating a Learning Organization

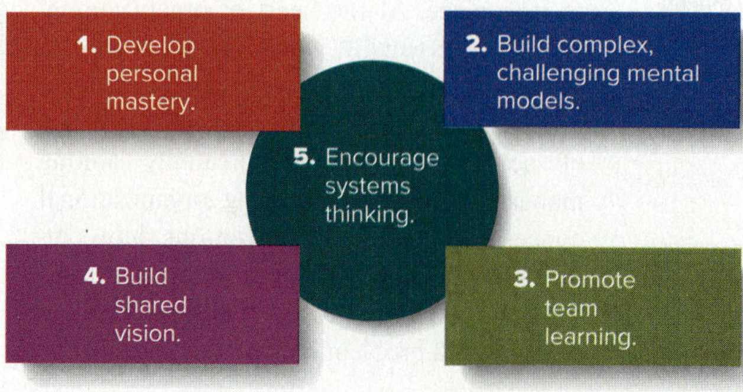

Increasingly, managers are being called on to promote global organizational learning. The "Managing Globally" feature provides one example of such an effort. Likewise, managers at Walmart have used the lessons derived from its failures and successes in one country to promote global organizational learning across the many countries in which it now operates. When Walmart entered Malaysia, it was convinced customers there would respond to its one-stop shopping format. It found, however, that Malaysians enjoy the social experience of shopping in a lively market or bazaar and thus did not like the impersonal efficiency of the typical Walmart store. As a result, Walmart learned the importance of designing store layouts to appeal specifically to the customers of each country in which it operates. Clearly, global organizational learning is essential for companies such as Walmart that have significant operations in multiple countries.

MANAGING GLOBALLY

Western Union Continues to Learn

Western Union (WU) offers a financial lifeline worldwide, sending 130 currencies to recipients in 200-plus countries. When a customer pays, a code is sent to the recipient, who presents it to an agent, who hands over cash minus a processing fee. WU later reimburses the agent. Currency transfers could include support from emigrants to family members back home, help to a stranded traveler overseas, or tuition payments for a child studying abroad. In a recent year, the company processed more than 800 million transactions for its consumer and business clients.[70]

WU outlasted competitors by learning to embrace industry transformations.[71] It started as a telegraph operator, transmitting information to newspapers, banks, brokerages, and even betting parlors. After stumbling by turning down a chance to buy the patent for the telephone, WU learned it must commit to technological advances. It kept communication services up-to-date with teleprinters, faxes, and satellites until anyone could deliver messages from home or work. By then, however, the company had built its money transfer business. Profits accelerated along with immigration into the United States.

Western Union's culture of continuous learning has helped the company and its employees outlast competitors in the global marketplace.
wihtgod/123RF

WU's next focus for learning will be technological, overseen by Harveer Singh, the company's chief data architect and global head of data engineering and architecture.[72] Singh is leading the digital transformation of the company to help compete with more agile start-up businesses. Digital and mobile devices enable easy, low-cost methods of money transfer for Western Union and competitors, including several financial-tech (fintech) startups, which have made some progress in the market. But WU's size is an advantage because millions of daily digital transactions provide valuable data, which allow the company to understand who their customers are.[73]

When the COVID-19 pandemic took hold across the globe, Singh and other WU managers recognized that modernization of the company's processes needed to happen–and happen fast. For example, Western Union moved away from expensive and outdated data warehouses and moved quickly to take the entire data platform to the cloud in less than a year, which reduced the company's costs by 50%. In addition, the pandemic caused the company to refocus their energy on personalized marketing efforts based on the data it collected and to launch an artificial chatbot in many countries to reduce wait times for customers. Recently, Western Union launched a digital banking pilot in Germany and Romania, which offered a multi-currency account and debit card, allowing customers to load, transfer, and use funds in any of 16 currencies. This pilot demonstrated the potential of WU's new technology when the war in Ukraine occurred in early 2022: Although the conflict paralyzed traditional banking operations, customers were able to use the WU network to make money transfers to people in Ukraine without difficulty and without fees.[74]

In December 2021, Devin McGranahan joined Western Union as president and CEO, replacing Hikmet Ersek, who retired after 11 years in the company's top job. McGranahan has more than 25 years of business experience, including extensive work in digital merchant and enterprise platforms. Although financial results in 2022 were disappointing, McGranahan is optimistic that WU's digital bank and ecosystem in Europe will continue to drive growth and gain more digital customers, who tend to do 2.5 times the transactions undertaken by traditional consumers.[75]

Promoting Individual Creativity

Research suggests that when certain conditions are met, managers are more likely to be creative. People must be given the opportunity and freedom to generate new ideas.[76] Creativity declines when managers look over the shoulders of talented employees and try to "hurry up" a creative solution. How would you feel if your boss said you had one week to come up with a new product idea to beat the competition? Creativity results when employees have an opportunity to experiment, to take risks, and to make mistakes and learn from them. And employees must not fear that they will be looked down on or penalized for ideas that might at first seem outlandish; sometimes those ideas yield truly innovative products and services.[77] Highly innovative companies such as Stripe, Microsoft, and SpaceX are well known for the wide degree of freedom they give their managers and employees to experiment and develop innovative goods and services.[78]

Once managers have generated alternatives, creativity can be fostered by giving them constructive feedback so they know how well they are doing. Ideas that seem to be going nowhere can be eliminated and creative energies refocused in other directions. Ideas that seem promising can be promoted, and help from other managers can be obtained.[79]

Top managers must stress the importance of looking for alternative solutions and should visibly reward employees who come up with creative ideas. Being creative can be demanding and stressful. Employees who believe they are working on important, vital issues are motivated to put forth the high levels of effort that creativity demands. Creative people like to receive the acclaim of others, and innovative organizations have many kinds of ceremonies and rewards to recognize creative employees.

Employees on the front line are often in a good position to come up with creative ideas for improvements but may be reluctant to speak up or share their ideas. To encourage frontline employees to come up with creative ideas and share them, some managers have used various types of rewards.[80] These rewards signal the importance of coming up with creative ideas and encouraging employees to share them.

Promoting Group Creativity

To encourage creativity at the group level, organizations can use group problem-solving techniques that promote creative ideas and innovative solutions. These techniques can also prevent groupthink and help managers uncover biases. Here we look at three group decision-making techniques: *brainstorming*, the *nominal group technique*, and the *Delphi technique*.

BRAINSTORMING *Brainstorming* is a group problem-solving technique in which managers meet face-to-face to generate and debate a wide variety of alternatives from which to make a decision.[81] Generally, from 5 to 15 managers meet in a closed-door session and proceed like this:

- One manager describes in broad outline the problem the group is to address.
- Group members share their ideas and generate alternative courses of action.
- As each alternative is described, group members are not allowed to criticize it; everyone withholds judgment until all alternatives have been heard. One member of the group records the alternatives on a flip chart.

- Group members are encouraged to be as innovative and radical as possible. Anything goes; and the greater the number of ideas put forth, the better. Moreover, group members are encouraged to "piggyback," or build on, each other's suggestions.
- When all alternatives have been generated, group members debate the pros and cons of each and develop a short list of the best alternatives.

Brainstorming is one example of a group problem-solving technique that helps promote creative ideas and innovation solutions within an organization.
Fizkes/Shutterstock

Brainstorming is useful in some problem-solving situations—for example, when managers are trying to find a name for a new perfume or car model. But sometimes individuals working alone can generate more alternatives. The main reason for the loss of productivity in brainstorming appears to be **production blocking**, which occurs because group members cannot always simultaneously make sense of all the alternatives being generated, think up additional alternatives, and remember what they were thinking.[82]

production blocking A loss of productivity in brainstorming sessions due to the unstructured nature of brainstorming.

nominal group technique A decision-making technique in which group members write down ideas and solutions, read their suggestions to the whole group, and discuss and then rank the alternatives.

NOMINAL GROUP TECHNIQUE To avoid production blocking, the **nominal group technique** is often used. It provides a more structured way of generating alternatives in writing and gives each manager more time and opportunity to come up with potential solutions. The nominal group technique is especially useful when an issue is controversial and when different managers might be expected to champion different courses of action. Generally, a small group of managers meets in a closed-door session and adopts the following procedures:

- One manager outlines the problem to be addressed, and 30 or 40 minutes are allocated for group members, working individually, to write down their ideas and solutions. Group members are encouraged to be innovative.
- Managers take turns reading their suggestions to the group. One manager writes all the alternatives on a flip chart. No criticism or evaluation of alternatives is allowed until all alternatives have been read.
- The alternatives are then discussed, one by one, in the sequence in which they were proposed. Group members can ask for clarifying information and critique each alternative to identify its pros and cons.
- When all alternatives have been discussed, each group member ranks all the alternatives from most preferred to least preferred, and the alternative that receives the highest ranking is chosen.[83]

Delphi technique A decision-making technique in which group members do not meet face-to-face but respond in writing to questions posed by the group leader.

DELPHI TECHNIQUE Both the nominal group technique and brainstorming require that managers meet to generate creative ideas and engage in joint problem solving. What happens if managers are in different cities or in different parts of the world and cannot meet face-to-face? Videoconferencing is one way to bring distant managers together to brainstorm. Another way is to use the **Delphi technique**, which is a written approach to creative problem solving.[84] The Delphi technique works like this:

- The group leader writes a statement of the problem and a series of questions to which participating managers are to respond.
- The questionnaire is sent to the managers and departmental experts who are most knowledgeable about the problem. They are asked to generate solutions and mail the questionnaire back to the group leader.
- A team of top managers records and summarizes the responses. The results are then sent back to the participants, with additional questions to be answered before a decision can be made.
- The process is repeated until a consensus is reached and the most suitable course of action is apparent.

Entrepreneurship and Creativity

The importance of a learning environment within established organizations cannot be understated. In some instances, managers and other members develop a sense of entrepreneurship within the company that encourages learning and creativity. In a broad sense, entrepreneurship is the process of identifying opportunities to provide customers with new or improved goods and services. In a corporate setting, this process is called intrapreneurship, and, individuals who embrace the spirit of entrepreneurship in a corporate setting are known as intrapreneurs, or *corporate entrepreneurs*.[85]

LO7-5 Describe how managers can encourage and promote entrepreneurship to create a learning organization.

In this section, we discuss how organizational members can use their creativity within a corporate structure to act as entrepreneurs, which is no easy feat given the existing organizational structure and culture already in place.[86] Chapter 19 focuses on how people can become entrepreneurs and start their own businesses and the various requirements for ensuring the success of the new venture, including how managers can play a significant role in an entrepreneur's new business.

Intrapreneurs and Organizational Learning

The intensity of competition today, particularly from agile, small companies, has made it increasingly important for large, established organizations to promote and encourage intrapreneurship to raise their level of innovation and organizational learning. As we discussed earlier, a learning organization encourages all employees to identify opportunities and solve problems, thus enabling the organization to continuously experiment, improve, and increase its ability to provide customers with new and improved goods and services. The higher the level of intrapreneurship, the higher will be the level of learning and innovation. How can organizations promote organizational learning and intrapreneurship?

PRODUCT CHAMPIONS One way to promote intrapreneurship is to encourage someone to assume the role of **product champion**, a manager who takes "ownership" of a project and provides the leadership and vision that take a product from the idea stage to the final customer. 3M, a company well known for its attempts to promote intrapreneurship, encourages all its managers to become product champions and identify new product ideas. A product champion becomes responsible for developing a business plan for the product. Armed with this business plan, the champion appears before 3M's product development committee, a team of senior 3M managers who probe the strengths and weaknesses of the plan to decide whether it should be funded. If the plan is accepted, the product champion assumes responsibility for product development.

product champion A manager who takes "ownership" of a project and provides the leadership and vision that take a product from the idea stage to the final customer.

3M's Audrey Sherman holds the most patents by a female scientist in the organization, with 151, ranking sixth overall in the most patents held by 3M employees. She says the key to successful intrapreneurship is teamwork–collaborating with others who have a deep curiosity and are willing to make connections among concepts that don't seem to be connected. Sherman also suggests building interaction across the organization, bringing in fresh perspectives, and preparing your mind to recognize opportunities within your daily work activities that will help spark innovation and possibly new product ideas.[87]

SKUNKWORKS The idea behind the product champion role is that employees who feel ownership for a project are inclined to act as outside entrepreneurs and go to great lengths to make the project succeed. Using skunkworks and new venture divisions can also strengthen this feeling of ownership. (In Chapter 8, we discuss the "disruptive growth" team within General Mills, the division that also acts as the company's venture capital arm.) A **skunkworks** is a group of intrapreneurs who are deliberately separated from the normal operation of an organization–for example, from the normal chain of command–to encourage them to devote all their attention to developing new products. The idea is that if these people are isolated, they will become so intensely involved in a project that development time will be relatively brief and the quality of the final product will be enhanced. The term *skunkworks* was coined at the Lockheed Corporation, which formed a team of design engineers to develop special aircraft such as the U2 spy plane. The secrecy with which this unit functioned and speculation about its goals led others to refer to it as "the skunkworks."[88] More recently, the Ford Motor Company created a small skunkworks group (called Team Edison) to develop the Mustang Mach-E electric vehicle, which made its debut in 2021 to rave reviews from environmentalists and car enthusiasts alike.[89]

skunkworks A group of intrapreneurs who are deliberately separated from the normal operation of an organization to encourage them to devote all their attention to developing new products.

REWARDS FOR INNOVATION To encourage managers to bear the uncertainty and risk associated with the hard work of entrepreneurship, it is necessary to link performance to rewards. Increasingly, companies are rewarding intrapreneurs on the basis of the outcome of the product development process. Intrapreneurs are paid large bonuses if their projects succeed, or they are granted stock options that can make them millionaires if their products sell well. Both Microsoft and Google, for example, have made hundreds of their employees multimillionaires as a result of the stock options they were granted as part of their reward packages. In addition to receiving money, successful intrapreneurs can expect to receive promotion to the ranks of top management. Most of 3M's top managers, for example, reached the executive suite because they had a track record of successful intrapreneurship. Organizations must reward intrapreneurs equitably if they wish to prevent them from leaving and becoming outside entrepreneurs who might form a competitive new venture. Chapter 19 discusses some key strategies organizations can implement to help retain corporate entrepreneurs.

Summary and Review

LO7-1 **THE NATURE OF MANAGERIAL DECISION MAKING** Programmed decisions are routine decisions made so often that managers have developed decision rules to be followed automatically. Nonprogrammed decisions are made in response to situations that are unusual or novel; they are nonroutine decisions. The classical model of decision making assumes that decision makers have complete information; can process that information in an objective, rational manner; and make optimum decisions. March and Simon argued that managers exhibit bounded rationality, rarely have access to all the information they need to make optimum decisions, and consequently satisfice and rely on their intuition and judgment when making decisions.

LO7-2 **STEPS IN THE DECISION-MAKING PROCESS** When making decisions, managers should take these six steps: recognize the need for a decision, generate alternatives, assess alternatives, choose among alternatives, implement the chosen alternative, and learn from feedback.

LO7-2 **COGNITIVE BIASES AND DECISION MAKING** Most of the time, managers are fairly good decision makers. On occasion, however, problems can result because human judgment can be adversely affected by the operation of cognitive biases that result in poor decisions. Cognitive biases are caused by systematic errors in the way decision makers process information and make decisions. Sources of these errors include confirmation bias, representativeness bias, the illusion of control, and escalating commitment. Managers should undertake a personal decision audit to become aware of their biases and thus improve their decision making.

LO7-3 **GROUP DECISION MAKING** Many advantages are associated with group decision making, but there are also several disadvantages. One major source of poor decision making is groupthink. Afflicted decision makers collectively embark on a dubious course of action without questioning the assumptions that underlie their decision. Managers can improve the quality of group decision making by using techniques such as devil's advocacy and dialectical inquiry and by increasing diversity in the decision-making group.

LO7-4 **ORGANIZATIONAL LEARNING AND CREATIVITY** Organizational learning is the process through which managers seek to improve employees' desire and ability to understand and manage the organization and its task environment so employees can make decisions that continuously raise organizational effectiveness. Managers must take steps to promote organizational learning and creativity at the individual and group levels to improve the quality of decision making.

LO7-5 **ENTREPRENEURSHIP AND CREATIVITY** The importance of a learning environment within established organizations cannot be understated. In some instances, managers and other members develop a sense of entrepreneurship within the company that encourages learning and creativity. In a broad sense, entrepreneurship is the process of identifying opportunities to provide customers with new or improved goods and services. In a corporate setting, this process is called intrapreneurship, and individuals who embrace the spirit of entrepreneurship in a corporate setting are known as intrapreneurs, or corporate entrepreneurs.

Management in Action

Topics for Discussion and Action

Discussion

1. What are the main differences between programmed decision making and nonprogrammed decision making? [LO7-1]
2. In what ways do the classical and administrative models of decision making help managers appreciate the complexities of real-world decision making? [LO7-1]
3. Why do capable managers sometimes make bad decisions? What can individual managers do to improve their decision-making skills? [LO7-1, 7-2]
4. In what kinds of groups is groupthink most likely to be a problem? When is it least likely to be a problem? What steps can group members take to ward off groupthink? [LO7-3]
5. What is organizational learning, and how can managers promote it? [LO7-4]
6. What is the difference between entrepreneurs and intrapreneurs? [LO7-5]

Action

7. Ask a manager to recall the best and the worst decisions they ever made. Try to determine why these decisions were so good or so bad. [LO7-1, 7-2, 7-3]
8. Think about an organization in your community or your university, or an organization that you are familiar with, that is doing poorly. Now think of questions managers in the organization should ask stakeholders to elicit creative ideas for turning around the organization's fortunes. [LO7-4]

Building Management Skills

How Do You Make Decisions? [LO7-1, 7-2, 7-4]

Pick a decision you made recently that has had important consequences for you. It may be your decision about which college to attend, which major to select, whether to take a part-time job, or which part-time job to take. Using the material in this chapter, analyze how you made the decision:

1. Identify the criteria you used, either consciously or unconsciously, to guide your decision making.
2. List the alternatives you considered. Were they all possible alternatives? Did you unconsciously (or consciously) ignore some important alternatives?
3. How much information did you have about each alternative? Were you making the decision on the basis of complete or incomplete information?
4. Try to remember how you reached the decision. Did you sit down and consciously think through the implications of each alternative, or did you make the decision on the basis of intuition? Did you use any rules of thumb to help you make the decision?
5. In retrospect, do you think your choice of alternative was shaped by any of the cognitive biases discussed in this chapter?
6. Having answered the previous five questions, do you think in retrospect that you made a reasonable decision? What, if anything, might you do to improve your ability to make good decisions in the future?

Managing Ethically [LO7-3]

Sometimes groups make extreme decisions—decisions that are either more risky or more conservative than they would have been if persons acting alone had made them. One explanation for the tendency of groups to make extreme decisions is diffusion of responsibility. In a group, responsibility for the outcomes of a decision is spread among group members, so each person feels less than fully accountable. The group's decision is extreme because no one has taken full responsibility for it.

Questions

1. Either alone or in a group, think about the ethical implications of extreme decision making by groups.
2. When group decision making takes place, should each member of a group feel fully accountable for the outcomes of the decision? Why or why not?

Small Group Breakout Exercise

Brainstorming [LO7-3, 7-4]

Form groups of three or four people, and appoint one member as the spokesperson who will communicate your findings to the class when called on by the instructor. Then discuss the following scenario:

You and your partners are trying to decide which kind of restaurant to open in a centrally located shopping center that has just been built in your city. The problem confronting you is that the city already has many restaurants that provide different kinds of food at all price ranges. You have the resources to open any type of restaurant. Your challenge is to decide which type is most likely to succeed.

Use brainstorming to decide which type of restaurant to open. Follow these steps:

1. As a group, spend 5–10 minutes generating ideas about the alternative restaurants that the members think will be most likely to succeed. Each group member should be as innovative and creative as possible, and no suggestions should be criticized.
2. Appoint one group member to write down the alternatives as they are identified.
3. Spend the next 10–15 minutes debating the pros and cons of the alternatives. As a group, try to reach a consensus on which alternative is most likely to succeed.

After making your decision, discuss the pros and cons of the brainstorming method, and decide whether any production blocking occurred.

When called on by the instructor, the spokesperson should be prepared to share your group's decision with the class, as well as the reasons for the group's decision.

Be the Manager [LO7-1, 7-2, 7-3, 7-4, 7-5]

You are a top manager who was recently hired by an oil field services company in Oklahoma to help it respond more quickly and proactively to potential opportunities in its market. You report to the chief operating officer (COO), who reports to the CEO, and you have been on the job for eight months. Thus far, you have come up with three initiatives you carefully studied, thought were noteworthy, and proposed and justified to the COO. The COO seemed cautiously interested when you presented the proposals, and each time he indicated he would think about them and discuss them with the CEO because considerable resources were involved. Each time you never heard back from the COO, and after a few weeks elapsed, you casually asked the COO if there was any news on the proposal in question. For the first proposal, the COO said, "We think it's a good idea, but the timing is off. Let's shelve it for the time being and reconsider it next year." For the second proposal, the COO said, "Julie [the CEO] reminded me that we tried that two years ago and it wasn't well received in the market. I am surprised I didn't remember it myself when you first described the proposal, but it came right back to me once Julie mentioned it." For the third proposal, the COO simply said, "We're not convinced it will work."

You believe your three proposed initiatives are viable ways to seize opportunities in the marketplace, yet you cannot proceed with any of them. Moreover, for each proposal, you invested considerable time and even worked to bring others on board to support the proposal, only to have it shot down by the CEO. When you interviewed for the position, both the COO and the CEO claimed they wanted "an outsider to help them step out of the box and innovate." However, your experience to date has been just the opposite. What are you going to do?

Case in the News [LO7-1, 7-2, 7-3, 7-4]

Decision Making at Fast-Fashion Leader Zara

Globally, the largest fashion retailer is Zara, based in Galicia, Spain. The company pioneered "fast fashion"—lines of low-priced clothing that rapidly change in response to consumer behavior and fashion trends. Zara has enjoyed rapid growth, including a 41% increase in sales between the first half of 2021 and the same period in 2022. Its closest competitor is H&M, based in Sweden. Zara's leadership includes CEO Oscar

García Maceiras and Mara Ortega, chair of Zara's parent company, Inditex. Ortega, a graduate of the European Business School with 15 years of experience at Zara and Inditex, took over at age 38.

A key to Zara's success has been its use of technology to monitor what consumers are buying. Each day, employees on the design floor at headquarters check a computer monitor displaying data from Zara's 1,900-plus stores in 95 countries. Every three minutes, the system ranks the products by sales volume. Together, the employees review the data, ready to adjust their plans based on what is popular. Change is expected: the company creates about 1,000 designs a month. Besides the daily data, the team gets ideas from what is trending on social media, what they notice people wearing, and what store managers observe. The process from idea to product delivery takes roughly a month. In this way, Zara supplies its stores with new products every two weeks—an incentive for consumers to stop in and see the latest. Furthermore, the stores collect data beyond sales: sensors measure store traffic, and shoppers can use a store app to guide them to specific products, thereby delivering additional location information.

Other decisions at Zara are more strategic, such as what channels to use and where to source manufacturing. Channel decisions include whether to sell in stores or online. Zara and H&M do both, with about one-quarter of Zara's sales taking place online. The emphasis on stores was helpful when a spike in fuel costs made shipping packages expensive.

Factory location involves choosing suppliers. To support a low-cost strategy such as fast fashion, apparel companies generally contract with manufacturers located where wages are low. Much of the world's clothing is made in Bangladesh, Myanmar, and Pakistan. While Zara uses this approach for some products, up to half of its merchandise is made at facilities in Europe, Turkey, and Morocco. The diversity of locations has been another advantage for Zara during the recent run-up of transportation costs; for each order, the company has more flexibility in choosing a factory or store to ship from. Choices of supplier location also involve ethical standards. Recently, in response to human rights concerns, some apparel companies ended their use of factories in Myanmar. Zara opted to stay and try to protect human rights through its relationships with suppliers there. This may be difficult to control, but an ethical argument for staying is that many people in Myanmar are poor and desperately need the jobs, even if those jobs aren't always safe.

One of the weightiest issues facing Zara is whether its business model is sustainable for the long term. By its nature, fast fashion treats clothing as disposable, but making, distributing, and disposing of clothing requires substantial resources. Apparel production doubled between 2000 and 2015, reaching 100 billion garments a year, and the number of times people wear an item of clothing is shrinking. Nearly 90% of clothes are not recycled but end up in incinerators or landfills. Faced with these numbers, some governments are looking at regulation—for example, requiring environmentally responsible production methods.

A pure approach to environmental protection would be making durable clothes and convincing consumers to shop less. But rather than abandon its operating model, Zara under Ortega and García Maceiras is exploring ways to make the current model less damaging. This could raise costs, but Zara has maintained a favorable profit margin by expanding its higher-end collections; on average, Zara charges higher prices than H&M. Inditex, in its Sustainability Innovation Hub, is researching lab-grown fibers with features similar to cotton, polyester, and silk. It has also signed a contract to buy fabric made from textile waste and is exploring ways to improve the recycling of fabric. Finally, it is pursuing net-zero carbon emissions and has nearly reached its goal of all stores getting electricity from renewable sources. Management is optimistic that if Zara can solve these problems, its size will make its changes transformative for the whole industry.

Questions for Discussion

1. A persistent problem in management decision making is incomplete information. For Zara's designers making decisions about new products, how does Zara address this problem? Does Zara's approach make the information complete? Why or why not?
2. What are some ethical decisions facing Zara? Choose one, and list some criteria Zara's managers could use to arrive at a well-considered decision.
3. Zara's design team engages in group decision making. For these decisions, how can the team reduce the potential for groupthink?

Sources: Business of Fashion, "Zara," www.businessoffashion.com, accessed January 18, 2023; D. Holger, "Fashion Giants Vow to Buy More Recycled Fibers in Boost to Sustainable-Textile Mills," *WSJ Sustainable Business*, www.wsj.com, November 14, 2022; V. Walt, "Can Zara Be Fast, Cheap—and Green?," *Fortune*, October/November 2022, 93–97; J. Emont, "H&M, Zara's Owner Stick with 'Made in Myanmar' after Coup, but Some Brands Exit," *The Wall Street Journal*, www.wsj.com, October 4, 2022; C. Ryan, "Zara Looks Sharp, but It Is Not the Winter Trend," *The Wall Street Journal*, www.wsj.com, September 14, 2022; C. Ryan, "Inflation Cuts Online Fashion Down to Size," *The Wall Street Journal*, www.wsj.com, June 13, 2022; "H&M versus Zara: Are Premium Fabrics on the Rise?," *Textile World*, March/April 2022, 33–35; "Marta Ortega, the Heiress Taking the Reins of Zara," *RFI*, https://www.rfi.fr, March 30, 2022.

Notes

1. D. Gelles, "The Chief of CVS Health Wants to Be Part of People's 'Everyday Life,'" *The New York Times,* www.nytimes .com, January 21, 2022.
2. Gelles, "The Chief of CVS Health"; "Karen S. Lynch," CVS Health, https:// cvshealth.com, accessed January 20, 2023; S. Tully, "Most Powerful Women: #1 Karen Lynch: CEO, 58, CVS Health," *Fortune,* October/November 2021, 61; E. Hinchliffe, "Vaccine Queen," *Fortune,* June/July 2021, 35.
3. S. Tully, "How the Best Leaders Survive the Worst of Times," *Fortune,* December/ January 2023, 101–102.
4. A. LaVito, "Karen Lynch," *Bloomberg Businessweek,* December 6, 2021, 59.
5. Tully, "#1 Karen Lynch"; Hinchliffe, "Vaccine Queen."
6. LaVito, "Karen Lynch."
7. S. Terlep, "CVS Looks to Add Doctors to Its Payroll," *The Wall Street Journal,* www.wsj.com, November 3, 2021.
8. "The 50 Most Powerful Women 2022: #1 Karen Lynch, CVS Health," *Fortune,* https:// fortune.com, accessed January 20, 2023.
9. C. Gordon and A. Arian, "Threat and Decision Making," *Journal of Conflict Resolution,* vol. 45, no. 2, 2001, 196–215.
10. L. Kahney, "An Illustrated History of the iPod and Its Massive Impact," *Cult of Mac,* www.cultofmac.com, accessed February 19, 2020; T. Anjarwalla, "Inventor of Cell Phone: We Knew Someday Everybody Would Have One," *CNN,* www.cnn.com, accessed February 19, 2020.
11. H.A. Simon, *The New Science of Management* (Englewood Cliffs, NJ: Prentice-Hall, 1977).
12. D. Kahneman, "Maps of Bounded Rationality: A Perspective on Intuitive Judgment and Choice," *Prize Lecture,* December 8, 2002; E. Jaffe, "What Was I Thinking? Kahneman Explains How Intuition Leads Us Astray," *American Psychological Society* 17, no. 5 (May 2004), 23–26; E. Dane and M. Pratt, "Exploring Intuition and Its Role in Managerial Decision Making," *Academy of Management Review* 32 (2007), 33–54.
13. One should be careful not to generalize too much here, however, for as Peter Senge has shown, programmed decisions rely on the implicit assumption that the environment is in a steady state. If environmental conditions change, sticking to a routine decision rule can produce disastrous results. See P. Senge, *The Fifth Discipline: The Art and Practice of the Learning Organization* (New York: Doubleday, 1990).
14. Kahneman, "Maps of Bounded Rationality"; Jaffe, "What Was I Thinking?"
15. H.A. Simon, *Administrative Behavior* (New York: Macmillan, 1947), 79.
16. H.A. Simon, *Models of Man* (New York: Wiley, 1957).
17. K.J. Arrow, *Aspects of the Theory of Risk Bearing* (Helsinki: Yrjo Johnssonis Saatio, 1965).
18. "Who Is Plastic Bank?" https:// plasticbank.com, accessed January 18, 2023; T. Page, "We're Throwing Away a Fortune in Plastic Every Year; This Company Is Cleaning Up," *CNN,* www.cnn .com, December 2, 2019; S. Prasso, "Paying with Plastic," *Bloomberg Businessweek,* November 4, 2019, 46–48.
19. Page, "We're Throwing Away a Fortune"; Prasso, "Paying with Plastic."
20. Plastic Bank, "Frequently Asked Questions," https://plasticbank.com, accessed January 18, 2023.
21. Y. Ibukun, "Lagos Is Facing Its Bottle Problem," *Bloomberg Businessweek,* November 18, 2019, 18–20.
22. R.L. Daft and R.H. Lengel, "Organizational Information Requirements, Media Richness and Structural Design," *Management Science* 32 (1986), 554–71.
23. R. Cyert and J. March, *Behavioral Theory of the Firm* (Englewood Cliffs, NJ: Prentice-Hall, 1963).
24. J.G. March and H.A. Simon, *Organizations* (New York: Wiley, 1958).
25. H.A. Simon, "Making Management Decisions: The Role of Intuition and Emotion," *Academy of Management Executive* 1 (1987), 57–64.
26. M.H. Bazerman, *Judgment in Managerial Decision Making* (New York: Wiley, 1986). Also see Simon, *Administrative Behavior.*
27. "Scott G. McNealy Profile," Forbes.com, http://people.forbes.com/profile/scott-g-mcnealy/75347, February 16, 2010; Sun Oracle, "Overview and Frequently Asked Questions," www.oracle.com, February 16, 2010.
28. R.V. Zicari, "On Innovation: Interview with Scott McNealy," *ODBMS Industry Watch,* www.odbms.org, accessed February 19, 2020; N.J. Langowitz and S.C. Wheelright, "Sun Microsystems, Inc. (A)," Harvard Business School Case, 686–133.
29. R.D. Hof, "How to Kick the Mainframe Habit," *BusinessWeek,* June 26, 1995, 102–4.
30. Bazerman, *Judgment in Managerial Decision Making;* Huber, *Managerial Decision Making;* J.E. Russo and P.J. Schoemaker, *Decision Traps* (New York: Simon & Schuster, 1989).
31. Molson Coors, "About Us," www .molsoncoors.com, accessed January 20, 2023; J. Maloney, "Molson Coors Decided to Reopen Its Offices; Things Got Complicated," *The Wall Street Journal,* www .wsj.com, December 11, 2021; C. Doering, "Molson Coors' CEO Has a Bold Plan to 'Fundamentally Change' the Beer Maker; But Will It Work?" *Food Diver,* www .fooddive.com, June 15, 2021.
32. C. Cutter, "After Covid Closures, a New Quest to Make Offices Less Awful," *The Wall Street Journal,* www.wsj.com, December 9, 2021.
33. Maloney, "Molson Coors Decided to Reopen Its Offices."
34. Ibid.
35. Doering, "Molson Coors' CEO"; A. Holloway, "How Molson Coors Is Finding Its Way Back as a 'Beverage' Company," *Financial Post,* https://financialpost.com, April 19, 2022.
36. M.D. Cohen, J.G. March, and J.P. Olsen, "A Garbage Can Model of Organizational Choice," *Administrative Science Quarterly* 17 (1972), 1–25.
37. Ibid.
38. Bazerman, *Judgment in Managerial Decision Making.*
39. Senge, *The Fifth Discipline.*
40. E. de Bono, *Lateral Thinking* (London: Penguin, 1968); Senge, *The Fifth Discipline.*
41. Bazerman, *Judgment in Managerial Decision Making.*
42. B. Berger, "NASA: One Year after *Columbia*—Bush's New Vision Changes Agency's Course Midstream," *Space News Business Report,* www.space.com/ spacenews/businessmonday_040126.html, January 26, 2004.
43. J. Glanz and J. Schwartz, "Dogged Engineer's Effort to Assess Shuttle Damage," *The New York Times,* September 26, 2003, A1.
44. M.L. Wald and J. Schwartz, "NASA Chief Promises a Shift in Attitude," *The New York Times,* August 28, 2003, A23.
45. Russo and Schoemaker, *Decision Traps.*
46. D. Bakewell, "Doing Well by Doing Good," *L.A. Watts Times,* www.lawattstimes.com, September 22, 2022; P. Waldman, "Cracking the Code on Affordable

Housing," *Bloomberg Businessweek,* July 25, 2022, 48-53; D. Smith, "A For-Profit Mission to House the Poor Gets Praise and Flak," *Los Angeles Times,* www.latimes.com, June 14, 2022.

47. Bakewell, "Doing Well by Doing Good"; Smith, "A For-Profit Mission."
48. Waldman, "Cracking the Code on Affordable Housing"; Smith, "A For-Profit Mission."
49. Bakewell, "Doing Well by Doing Good"; Smith, "A For-Profit Mission."
50. D. Kahneman and A. Tversky, "Judgment under Uncertainty: Heuristics and Biases," *Science* 185 (1974), 1124-31.
51. C.R. Schwenk, "Cognitive Simplification Processes in Strategic Decision Making," *Strategic Management Journal* 5 (1984), 111-28.
52. R.S. Nickerson, "Confirmation Bias: A Ubiquitous Phenomenon in Many Guises," *Review of General Psychology* 2, no. 2 (1998), 175-220.
53. E. Jonas, S. Schulz-Hardt, D. Frey, and N. Thelen, "Confirmation Bias in Sequential Information Search after Preliminary Decisions: An Expansion of Dissonance Theoretical Research on Selective Exposure to Information," *Journal of Personality and Social Psychology* 80, no. 4 (2001), 557-71.
54. An interesting example of the illusion of control is Richard Roll's hubris hypothesis of takeovers. See R. Roll, "The Hubris Hypothesis of Corporate Takeovers," *Journal of Business* 59 (1986), 197-216.
55. C.M. Christensen, R. Alton, C. Rising, and A. Waldeck, "The Big Idea: The New M&A Playbook," *Harvard Business Review,* https://hbr.org, accessed February 19, 2020; D. Garrison, "Most Mergers Fail Because People Aren't Boxes," *Forbes,* www.forbes.com, June 24, 2019.
56. B.M. Staw, "The Escalation of Commitment to a Course of Action," *Academy of Management Review* 6 (1981), 577-87.
57. Russo and Schoemaker, *Decision Traps.*
58. I.L. Janis, *Groupthink: Psychological Studies of Policy Decisions and Disasters,* 2nd ed. (Boston: Houghton Mifflin, 1982).
59. C.R. Schwenk, *The Essence of Strategic Decision Making* (Lexington, MA: Lexington Books, 1988).
60. See R.O. Mason, "A Dialectic Approach to Strategic Planning," *Management Science* 13 (1969), 403-14; R.A. Cosier and J.C. Aplin, "A Critical View of Dialectic Inquiry in Strategic Planning," *Strategic Management Journal* 1 (1980), 343-56; I.I. Mitroff and R.O. Mason, "Structuring III–Structured Policy Issues: Further Explorations in a Methodology for Messy Problems," *Strategic Management Journal* 1 (1980), 331-42.
61. Mason, "A Dialectic Approach to Strategic Planning."
62. D.M. Schweiger and P.A. Finger, "The Comparative Effectiveness of Dialectic Inquiry and Devil's Advocacy," *Strategic Management Journal* 5 (1984), 335-50.
63. A. Hak, "Why Diverse Teams Make Better Business Decisions," *The Next Web,* https://thenextweb.com, accessed February 19, 2020; M.C. Gentile, *Differences That Work: Organizational Excellence through Diversity* (Boston: Harvard Business School Press: 1994).
64. B. Hedberg, "How Organizations Learn and Unlearn," in W.H. Starbuck and P.C. Nystrom, eds., *Handbook of Organizational Design,* vol. 1 (New York: Oxford University Press, 1981), 1-27.
65. Senge, *The Fifth Discipline.*
66. Ibid.
67. P.M. Senge, "The Leader's New Work: Building Learning Organizations," *Sloan Management Review,* Fall 1990, 7-23.
68. Ibid.
69. Senge, "The Leader's New Work," 12, 23.
70. "Moving Money," https://corporate.westernunion.com, accessed February 19, 2020.
71. L. Davison and K. Rajgopal, "Working across Many Cultures at Western Union" (interview with Hikmet Ersek), *McKinsey Quarterly,* www.mckinsey.com, January 2018; D. Bennett and L. Etter, "Give Us Your Tired, Your Poor, Your Huddled Masses Yearning to Send Cash," *Bloomberg Businessweek,* https://Bloomberg.com, June 16, 2017.
72. "Interview with Harveer Singh," *FinTech,* https://fintechmagazine.com, April 25, 2022.
73. Z. Baliva, "Harveer Singh Leads Western Union's Digital Transformation with Data," *Profile Magazine,* https://profilemagazine.com, accessed January 18, 2023.
74. Baliva, "Harveer Singh Leads"; "Supporting Ukraine," www.westernunion.com (blog), accessed January 20, 2023.
75. C. Tyndall, "Western Union Sees Revenues Drop But Sets Out Path for Growth," *FXC Intelligence,* www.fxcintel.com, November 7, 2022; company website, "Western Union Announces Devin B. McGranahan as New Chief Executive Officer," https://ir.westernunion.com, November 15, 2021.
76. J.M George, "Creativity in Organizations," in J.P. Walsh and A.P. Brief, eds., *The Academy of Management Annals,* vol. 1 (New York: Erlbaum, 2008), 439-77.
77. George, "Creativity in Organizations."
78. "The World's Most Innovative Companies of 2022," *Fast Company,* www.fastcompany.com, accessed January 18, 2023.
79. R.W. Woodman, J.E. Sawyer, and R.W. Griffin, "Towards a Theory of Organizational Creativity," *Academy of Management Review* 18 (1993), 293-321.
80. J. Zhou, G.R. Oldham, A. Chuang, R.S. Hsu, "Enhancing Employee Creativity: Effects of Choices, Rewards and Personality," *Journal of Applied Psychology,* https://doi.org/10.1037/apl0000900, accessed January 18, 2023.
81. T.J. Bouchard Jr., J. Barsaloux, and G. Drauden, "Brainstorming Procedure, Group Size, and Sex as Determinants of Problem Solving Effectiveness of Individuals and Groups," *Journal of Applied Psychology* 59 (1974), 135-38.
82. M. Diehl and W. Stroebe, "Productivity Loss in Brainstorming Groups: Towards the Solution of a Riddle," *Journal of Personality and Social Psychology* 53 (1987), 497-509.
83. D.H. Gustafson, R.K. Shulka, A. Delbecq, and W.G. Walster, "A Comparative Study of Differences in Subjective Likelihood Estimates Made by Individuals, Interacting Groups, Delphi Groups, and Nominal Groups," *Organizational Behavior and Human Performance* 9 (1973), 280-91.
84. N. Dalkey, *The Delphi Method: An Experimental Study of Group Decision Making* (Santa Monica, CA: Rand Corp., 1989).
85. T. Chamorro-Premuzic, "Why You Should Become an 'Intrapreneur,'" *Harvard Business Review,* https://hbr.org, accessed January 20, 2023; Wharton School, "Understanding Intrapreneurship," *Wharton on Line,* https://online.wharton.edu, accessed January 20, 2023.
86. L. Grensing-Pophal, "Encouraging Employees to Be Intrapreneurs Pays Off," *Society for Human Resource Management,* www.shrm.org, June 27, 2022.
87. J. MacLachlan, "This Is the Key to Breakthrough Innovation, According to 3M Scientist," *Forbes,* www.forbes.com, April 5, 2022.
88. Lockheed Martin, "Missions Impossible: The Skunk Works® Story," www.lockheedmartin.com, accessed January 20, 2023.
89. P. Fosse, "Ford Mustang Mach-E–Why Ford Made the Right Choices," *Clean Technica,* https://cleantechnica.com, accessed January 20, 2023; A. White, "Tested: 2021 Ford Mustang Mach-E Lives Up to the Hype, if Not the Name," *Car and Driver,* www.caranddriver.com, February 1, 2021.

CHAPTER 8

The Manager as a Planner and Strategist

Piranka/Getty Images

Learning Objectives

After studying this chapter, you should be able to:

LO8-1 Identify the three main steps of the planning process, and explain the relationship between planning and strategy.

LO8-2 Describe some techniques managers can use to improve the planning process so they can better predict the future and mobilize organizational resources to meet future contingencies.

LO8-3 Differentiate among the main types of business-level strategies, and explain how they give an organization a competitive advantage that may lead to superior performance.

LO8-4 Differentiate among the main types of corporate-level strategies, and explain how they are used to strengthen a company's business-level strategy and competitive advantage.

LO8-5 Describe the vital role managers play in implementing strategies to achieve an organization's mission and goals.

A MANAGER'S CHALLENGE

Marriott CEO Plans for Economic Recovery and Growth

What do successful managers consider when they plan a way forward? They forge ahead even when the future seems daunting. Anthony (Tony) Capuano, the recently named CEO at Marriott International, is a good example. Capuano took over CEO duties in February 2021, after the untimely death of Arne Sorenson, who passed away after a two-year battle with pancreatic cancer. For those in the hospitality industry, Sorenson was considered a guiding light for not only Marriott's 730,000 employees, but for many others in the global hotel/restaurant industry.[1] Certainly big shoes for anyone to fill, but Capuano seems energized by the challenge.

Capuano is no stranger to creating competitive strategies, making difficult decisions, or planning for growth within the Marriott organization. He started his Marriott career more than 25 years ago as a member of the market planning and feasibility team. Soon he was leading the company's development efforts in the western United States and Canada. In 2009, Capuano assumed global development responsibilities and added global design and operational duties to his role by 2020. As the largest hotel chain in the world, Marriott has 30 brands, with more than 8,000 properties across 139 countries and territories. With its Starwood acquisition in 2016, Marriott now has the largest customer loyalty program in the world, Bonvoy, with more than 173 million members.[2]

When the pandemic started to spread in early 2020, Capuano was part of the management team that made the decision to lay off tens of thousands of Marriott employees around the world (including at corporate headquarters), shutting down hotels and trying to stop the financial bleeding, as COVID-19 ravaged business operations large and small. At the height of the pandemic, global occupancy for Marriott properties averaged 12%, and revenue per available room, a key hotel performance metric, was down by 90%. In 2020, the company posted a $267 million loss—Marriott's first annual lost since the 2009 global financial crisis.[3] Today, the hotel business is coming back, but Marriott and its competitors still face uncertainty as variants of the coronavirus continue to affect travel, business, and everyday life.

Although business travel may never return to pre-pandemic levels thanks in part to virtual platforms like Zoom and other software collaboration tools, Capuano sees the lines between business and leisure travel continuing to blur, with people combining business with pleasure when they do travel. This has helped the company's growth opportunities in several areas. For example, Marriott recently signed an agreement with Sunwing's Blue Diamond resorts—19 all-inclusive locations in Mexico, Latin America, and the Caribbean. This partnership will double the company's presence in the all-inclusive resorts sector.[4]

Despite overwhelming challenges posed by the global pandemic, Marriott CEO Tony Capuano continues to plan for economic recovery and growth in the hospitality business.
Sylvain Gaboury/Patrick McMullan/Getty Images

Another sector of the travel business is home rentals, one that Marriott first entered several years ago with Homes & Villas by Marriott International. This growing market, which includes competitors like Airbnb and Vrbo, has strong business potential for the company as the pandemic has made travelers somewhat leery of staying in close proximity to strangers. The upscale rental homes in Marriott's portfolio are managed by third-party professionals and provide top-notch properties and amenities that meet Marriott's high standards for quality and service. In addition, Bonvoy members can earn points for each stay.[5]

As progress continues against the pandemic and businesses adapt to a "new normal," Capuano and his colleagues are still in a fight for talent, as many of Marriott's laid-off workers left the hospitality industry altogether. For example, he estimates the company is trying to fill nearly 10,000 job vacancies at the 600 properties it manages in the United States. The need for new hires is particularly critical in states where resort vacations are once again being booked by consumers. Capuano says the company is offering sign-on bonuses and other perks to potential employees as occupancy levels rise across its various properties. He believes it is up to hospitality companies such as Marriott to restore confidence among workers that the travel and tourism industry will come back and be a viable and stable job market, particularly as a result of what organizations learned while operating through the pandemic.[6]

Capuano also credits Marriott franchisees for having a long-term outlook and keeping business development going. Today the company has about 500,000 rooms under construction—a number that remained consistent even during the pandemic. With bookings increasing, Capuano remains optimistic about the future. He is pleased with the momentum he sees in the recovery and hopes for a strong return of travel across Marriott's various brands.[7] And he believes the best way to honor the legacy of his friend and mentor Arne Sorenson is to keep the company on the path Sorenson established: Value the company's culture and remain resilient and adaptable regardless of what crisis occurs in the business environment.[8]

Overview

In a fast-changing, competitive environment, managers must continually evaluate how well their products and services are meeting customer needs, and they must engage in thorough, systematic planning to find new strategies to tailor their products and services to better meet those needs. This chapter explores the manager's role both as planner and as strategist. First, we discuss the nature and importance of planning, the kinds of plans managers develop, and the levels at which planning takes place. Second, we discuss the three major steps in the planning process: (1) determining an organization's mission and major goals, (2) choosing or formulating strategies to realize the mission and goals, and (3) selecting the most effective ways to implement and put these strategies into action. We also examine several techniques, such as scenario planning, SWOT analysis, and SMART goals, that can help managers improve the quality of their planning, and we discuss a range of strategies managers can use to give their companies a competitive advantage over their rivals. By the end of this chapter, you will understand the vital role managers carry out when they plan, develop, and implement strategies to create a high-performing organization.

planning Identifying and selecting appropriate goals and courses of action; one of the four principal tasks of management.

strategy A cluster of decisions about what goals to pursue, what actions to take, and how to use resources to achieve goals.

Planning and Strategy

Planning, as we noted in Chapter 1, is a process managers use to identify and select appropriate goals and courses of action for an organization.[9] The organizational plan that results from the planning process details the goals of the organization and the specific strategies managers will implement to attain those goals. Recall from Chapter 1 that a **strategy** is a cluster of related managerial decisions and actions to help an organization attain one of its goals. Thus, planning is both a goal-making and a strategy-making process.

Figure 8.1
Three Steps in Planning

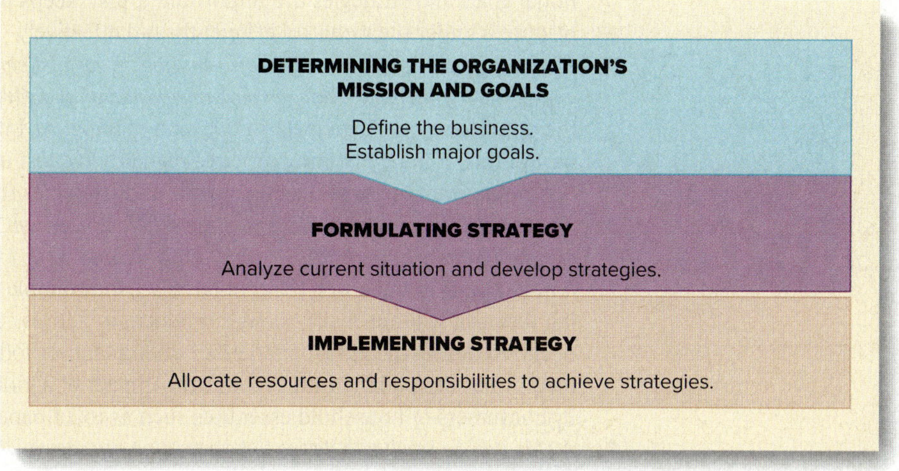

LO8-1 Identify the three main steps of the planning process, and explain the relationship between planning and strategy.

In most organizations, planning is a three-step activity (see Figure 8.1). The first step is determining the organization's mission and goals. A **mission statement** is a broad declaration of an organization's overriding purpose, what it is seeking to achieve from its activities; this statement also identifies what is *unique or important* about its products to its employees and customers; finally, it *distinguishes or differentiates* the organization in some ways from its competitors. For example, the mission statement of Nike is "to bring inspiration and innovation to every athlete in the world."[10]

mission statement A broad declaration of an organization's purpose that identifies the organization's products and customers and distinguishes the organization from its competitors.

The second step is formulating strategy. Managers analyze the organization's current situation and then conceive and develop the strategies necessary to attain the organization's mission and goals. The third step is implementing strategy. Managers decide how to allocate the resources and responsibilities required to implement the strategies among people and groups within the organization.[11] In subsequent sections of this chapter, we look in detail at the specifics of these steps. But first, we examine the general nature and purpose of planning.

The Nature of the Planning Process

Essentially, to perform the planning task, managers (1) establish and discover where an organization is at the *present time;* (2) determine where it should be in the future, its *desired future state;* and (3) decide how to *move it forward* to reach that future state. When managers plan, they must forecast what may happen in the future to decide what to do in the present. The better their predictions, the more effective will be the strategies they formulate to take advantage of future opportunities and counter emerging competitive threats in the environment. As previous chapters noted, however, the external environment is uncertain and complex, and managers typically must deal with incomplete information and "limitations on time, cognitive capacity, and data." This is why planning and strategy making are so difficult and risky, and if managers' predictions are wrong and strategies fail, organizational performance falls.

Why Planning Is Important

Almost all managers participate in some kind of planning because they must try to predict future opportunities and threats and develop a plan and strategies that will result in a high-performing organization. Moreover, the absence of a plan often results in hesitations, false steps, and mistaken changes of direction that can hurt an organization or even lead to disaster. Planning is important for four main reasons:

1. *Planning is necessary to give the organization a sense of direction and purpose.*[12] A plan states what goals an organization is trying to achieve and what strategies it intends to use to achieve them. Without the sense of direction and purpose that a formal plan provides,

managers may interpret their own specific tasks and jobs in ways that best suit them. The result will be an organization that is pursuing multiple and often conflicting goals and a set of managers who do not cooperate and work well together. By stating which organizational goals and strategies are important, a plan keeps managers on track so they use the resources under their control efficiently and effectively.

2. *Planning is a useful way of getting managers to participate in decision making about the appropriate goals and strategies for an organization.* Effective planning gives all managers the opportunity to participate in decision making. At Intel, for example, top managers, as part of their annual planning process, regularly request input from lower-level managers to determine what the organization's goals and strategies should be.
3. *A plan helps coordinate managers of the different functions and divisions of an organization to ensure that they all pull in the same direction and work to achieve the organization's desired future state.* Without a well-thought-out plan, for example, it is possible that the manufacturing function will not make enough products to address consumer demand. This situation occurred during the global pandemic, when planners followed their traditional forecasting data rather than taking into account the impact of a global shutdown and "panic buying" by consumers of household essentials such as toilet paper.[13]
4. *A plan can be used as a device for controlling managers within an organization.* A good plan specifies not only which goals and strategies the organization is committed to but also *who* bears the responsibility for putting the strategies into action to attain the goals. When managers know they will be held accountable for attaining a goal, they are motivated to do their best to make sure the goal is achieved.

Henri Fayol, the originator of the model of management we discussed in Chapter 1, said that effective plans should have four qualities: unity, continuity, accuracy, and flexibility.[14] *Unity* means that at any time only one central, guiding plan is put into operation to achieve an organizational goal; more than one plan to achieve a goal would cause confusion and disorder. *Continuity* means that planning is an ongoing process in which managers build and refine previous plans and continually modify plans at all levels–corporate, business, and functional–so they fit together into one broad framework. *Accuracy* means that managers need to make every attempt to collect and use all available information in the planning process. Of course, managers must recognize that uncertainty exists and that information is almost always incomplete (for reasons we discussed in Chapter 7). Despite the need for continuity and accuracy, however, Fayol emphasized that the planning process should be *flexible* enough so plans can be altered if the situation changes; managers must not be bound to a static plan.

Levels of Planning

In large organizations, planning usually takes place at three levels of management: corporate, business or division, and department or functional. Consider how General Mills operates. The Minneapolis-based global consumer food company has been in business for more than 150 years and has experienced both growth and headwinds over the past several years. Its current CEO, Jeff Harmening, is a company veteran with more than 25 years of experience who took over the top job in 2017.[15] Like many large organizations, General Mills has three main levels of management (see Figure 8.2). At the corporate level are CEO Harmening, his top management team, and their corporate support staff. Together they are responsible for planning and strategy making for the organization as a whole.

Below the corporate level is the business level. At the business level are the different *divisions* or *business units* of the company. Each division or business unit has its own set of *divisional managers* who control planning and strategy for their division or unit. For example, the managers in General Mill's North America Retail division plan how to operate efficiently and keep costs in check while still meeting the shifting tastes of consumers in the United States, Canada, and Mexico.

Organizations routinely review their planning levels as well as their organizational structures in efforts to increase efficiencies. For example, in 2017, General Mills revised its structure to increase operational agility. In 2018, the company added a new business unit to address its growing natural pet food business, which now includes Blue Buffalo Pet Products and Tyson Foods' pet treats business, recently acquired for $1.2 billion. In fiscal year 2022, General Mills

Figure 8.2

Levels of Planning at General Mills

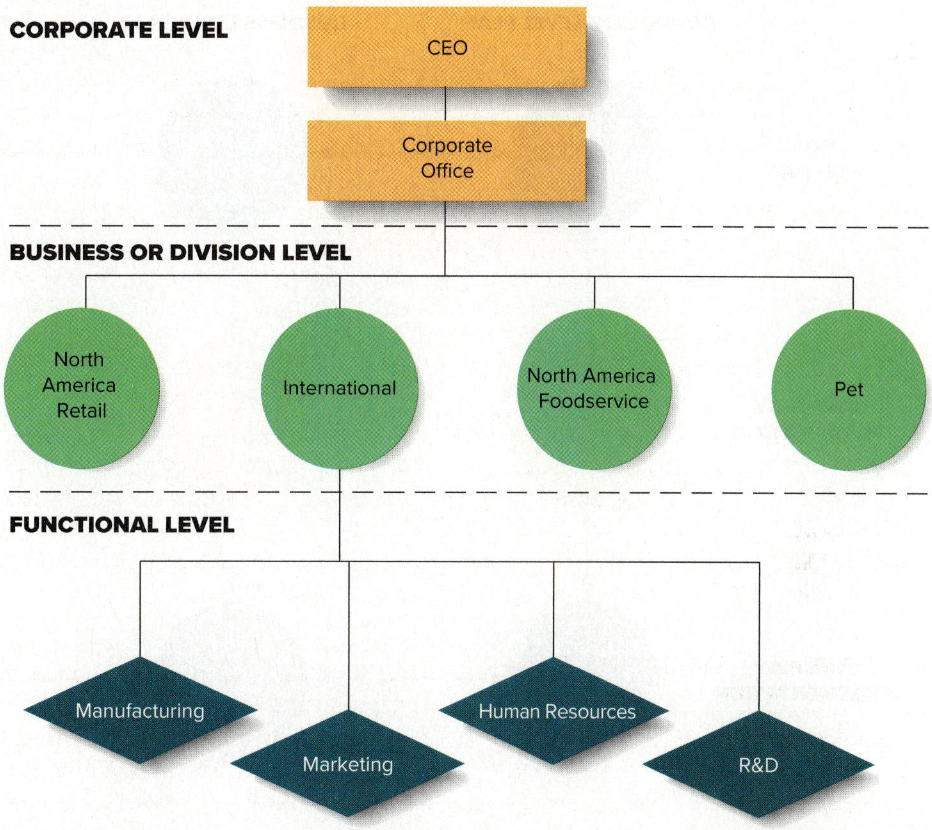

revised its organizational structure again to streamline global operations. As a result of this reorganization, the company now operates four different segments: North America Retail, International, Pet, and North America Foodservice.[16]

Going down one more level, each division has its own set of *functions* or *departments,* such as manufacturing, marketing, human resources, and research and development (R&D). Each division's *functional managers* are responsible for the planning and strategy making required to increase the efficiency and effectiveness of their particular function. For example, the sales managers in General Mills' North America Retail division would be responsible for working with marketing colleagues to ensure various advertising and sales campaigns targeted potential customers in supermarket bakeries.

TYPES OF PLANNING As just discussed, planning at General Mills, as at all other large organizations, takes place at each level. Figure 8.3 shows the link between these three levels and the three steps in the planning and strategy-making process illustrated in Figure 8.1.

corporate-level plan Top management's decisions pertaining to the organization's mission, overall strategy, and structure.

corporate-level strategy A plan that indicates in which industries and national markets an organization intends to compete.

The **corporate-level plan** contains top management's decisions concerning the organization's mission and goals, overall (corporate-level) strategy, and structure (see Figure 8.3). **Corporate-level strategy** specifies in which industries and national markets an organization intends to compete and why. One of the goals stated in General Mills' corporate-level plan is that the company is seeking to increase its market share in the organic/natural food sector. Several years ago, the company set up an internal business segment called 301 Inc. as a way to develop small, disruptive brands within the organization. Recently, this corporate strategy shifted to investing money and expertise in early-stage startup companies outside the organization. This revised strategy, using 301 Inc. as the venture-capital arm of a global food company, allows General Mills to invest in innovative food startups early on, providing them with money, expertise, and access to resources on a global scale. For example, 301 Inc. was an early investor in Beyond Meat, the plant-based product, and recently invested $40 million in Kite Hill, a plant-based yogurt. The company recently announced that 301 Inc. will move into a newly formed "disruptive growth" team within

Figure 8.3

Levels and Types of Planning

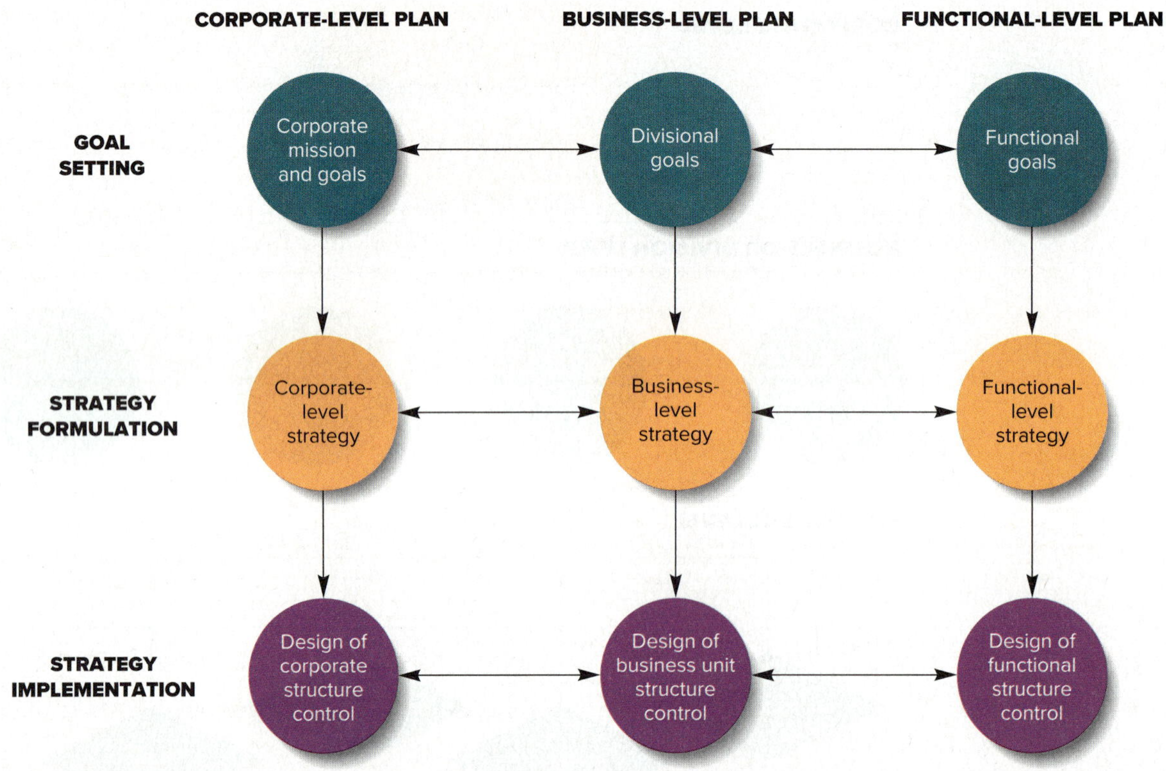

its strategy and growth unit. This move combines the strengths and capabilities of 301 Inc. with the company's internal business incubator (G-Works). In addition, 301 Inc. recently announced a $15 million investment into two venture capital funds that focus on investing in businesses led by minority and female entrepreneurs.[17]

In general, corporate-level planning and strategy are the primary responsibility of top or corporate managers.[18] The corporate-level goal of General Mills is to be the market leader in every business sector in which it competes. Jeff Harmening and his top management team decide which food product sectors General Mills should compete in to achieve this goal. The corporate-level plan provides the framework within which divisional managers create their business-level plans. At the business level, the managers of each division create a **business-level plan** that details (1) the long-term divisional goals that will allow the division to meet corporate goals and (2) the division's business-level strategy and structure needed to achieve divisional goals. **Business-level strategy** outlines the specific methods a division, a business unit, or an organization will use to compete effectively against its rivals in an industry. For example, managers in General Mills' Pet operating unit saw net sales jump 30% in fiscal year 2022 based in part on its acquisition of Tyson's pet treats business. The strategy to acquire this business complements General Mills' existing Blue Buffalo natural pet products and expands its portfolio, generating more than $2.2 billion in nets sales for the company.[19]

business-level plan Divisional managers' decisions pertaining to divisions' long-term goals, overall strategy, and structure.

business-level strategy A plan that indicates how a division intends to compete against its rivals in an industry.

functional-level plan Functional managers' decisions pertaining to the goals that they propose to pursue to help the division attain its business-level goals.

functional-level strategy A plan of action to improve the ability of each of an organization's functions to perform its task-specific activities in ways that add value to an organization's goods and services.

At the functional level, the business-level plan provides the framework within which functional managers devise their plans. A **functional-level plan** states the goals that the managers of each function will pursue to help their division attain its business-level goals, which, in turn, will allow the entire company to achieve its corporate goals. **Functional-level strategy** is a plan of action that managers of individual functions (such as manufacturing or marketing) can follow to improve the ability of each function to perform its task-specific activities in ways that add value to an organization's goods and services and thereby increase the value customers receive. Thus, for example, consistent with the strategy of increasing pet food sales, General Mills might adopt the goal "To increase production by 20% over the next three years," and functional strategies to achieve this goal might include (1) investing in state-of-the-art manufacturing facilities and (2) developing a global supply chain that will increase efficiencies and reduce shipping costs.

In the planning process, it is important to ensure that planning across the three different levels is *consistent*–functional goals and strategies should be consistent with divisional goals and strategies–which, in turn, should be consistent with corporate goals and strategies, and vice versa. When consistency is achieved, the whole company operates in harmony; activities at one level reinforce and strengthen those at the other levels, increasing efficiency and effectiveness. To help accomplish this, each function's plan is linked to its division's business-level plan, which is linked to the corporate plan. With a renewed vigor and detailed business strategies in place at each level of the organization, General Mills continues to review and revise its plans to ensure they are an effective guide to managerial decision making.[20] Likewise, at Walgreens, CEO Roz Brewer is developing business strategies in support of the corporate strategy, as described in the "Manager as a Person" feature.

MANAGER AS A PERSON

Walgreens' CEO Writes Prescription for Growth

Rosalind (Roz) Brewer knows a thing or two about corporate strategies, and she uses her knowledge and experience in her role as CEO at Walgreens Boots Alliance. Hired away from the COO position at Starbucks several years ago, Brewer and her management team continually review and revise business and corporate strategies.[21]

Brewer has a strong track record of getting things done. Trained as a chemist, she worked her way from research technician to the head of global operations for paper manufacturer Kimberly Clark. She left that position to become a vice president at Walmart, eventually becoming the president of Walmart's US East business unit, leading a team responsible for more than $100 billion in annual revenues. Ten years ago, she made history when she was named CEO of Sam's Club, becoming the first woman and first African American to lead the warehouse company owned by Walmart.[22]

As CEO of Walgreens Boots Alliance, Roz Brewer uses her analytical skills and professional experiences to develop, refine, and implement successful business strategies with her management team at the drugstore chain.
Stephen Brashear/Getty Images News/Getty Images

In her five years as Starbucks COO, Brewer led the company's global marketing, technology, supply chain, product innovation, and store development functions. Under her guidance, Starbucks increased its online retail and marketing efforts, beefed up its technology initiatives, and entered a global alliance with Nestle to increase the expansion of Starbucks consumer packaged goods.[23]

Some of Brewer's management hires at Walgreens provide a strong signal as to the corporate strategies and direction the company will take. She recently hired several key executives with backgrounds in health care and retail and is committed to Walgreen's initiative of tech-based health care for its customers.[24] In addition, Brewer is leading the company at a time when it's ready for the next step in digital transformation. The company recently moved more than 100 customized applications for corporate management and planning to the cloud, consolidating apps previously hosted on computers in thousands of Walgreen stores into one single platform. This digital strategy will help speed up inventory management and accounts payable, among other company functions. In addition, Brewer hired a new chief marketing officer, whose charge is to refocus the company's marketing strategies as the pandemic eases and to concentrate on consumers and "everyday living."[25]

Currently only one of two Black women running Fortune 500 companies, Brewer received criticism and death threats while at Sam's Club when she called out the lack of diversity in U.S. companies. She acknowledges that gender and racial bias continue to challenge managers and employees in corporate America today. Her message, particularly to women, is to "stay steadfast and keep using your voice."[26]

Time Horizons of Plans

time horizon The intended duration of a plan.

Plans differ in their **time horizons**, the periods of time over which they are intended to apply or endure. Managers usually distinguish among *long-term plans,* with a time horizon of five years or more; *intermediate-term plans,* with a horizon between one and five years; and *short-term plans,* with a horizon of one year or less.[27] Typically, corporate- and business-level goals and strategies require long- and intermediate-term plans, and functional-level goals and strategies require intermediate- and short-term plans.

Although most companies operate with planning horizons of five years or more, this does not mean that managers undertake major planning exercises only once every five years and then "lock in" a specific set of goals and strategies for that period. Most organizations have an annual planning cycle that is usually linked to the annual financial budget (although a major planning effort may be undertaken only every few years). So a corporate- or business-level plan that extends over several years is typically treated as a *rolling plan*—a plan that is updated and amended every year to take account of changing conditions in the external environment. Thus, the time horizon for an organization's 2024 corporate-level plan might be 2029; for the 2025 plan, it might be 2030; and so on. The use of rolling plans is essential because of the high rate of change in the environment and the difficulty of predicting competitive conditions five years in the future. Rolling plans enable managers to make midcourse corrections if environmental changes warrant or to change the thrust of the plan altogether if it no longer seems appropriate. The use of rolling plans allows managers to plan flexibly without losing sight of the need to plan for the long term.

Standing Plans and Single-Use Plans

LO8-2 Describe some techniques managers can use to improve the planning process so they can better predict the future and mobilize organizational resources to meet future contingencies.

Another distinction often made between plans is whether they are standing plans or single-use plans. Managers create standing and single-use plans to help achieve an organization's specific goals. *Standing plans* are used in situations in which programmed decision making is appropriate. When the same situations occur repeatedly, managers develop policies, rules, and standard operating procedures (SOPs) to control the way employees perform their tasks. A policy is a general guide to action; a rule is a formal, written guide to action; and a standard operating procedure is a written instruction describing the exact series of actions that should be followed in a specific situation. For example, an organization may have a standing plan about ethical behavior by employees. This plan includes a policy that all employees are expected to behave ethically in their dealings with suppliers and customers, a rule that requires any employee who receives from a supplier or customer a gift worth more than $50 to report the gift, and an SOP that obliges the recipient of the gift to make the disclosure in writing within 30 days.

In contrast, *single-use plans* are developed to handle nonprogrammed decision making in unusual or one-of-a-kind situations. Examples of single-use plans include *programs,* which are integrated sets of plans for achieving certain goals, and *projects,* which are specific action plans created to complete various aspects of a program. For instance, NASA worked for several years to develop a rover to investigate the environment on the surface of Mars. Known as Perseverance, the rover landed on Mars in February 2021, after a nearly seven-month journey from Earth. The rover continues to drill and collect rock core samples from the planet's surface and to look for signs of ancient life on the faraway planet.[28]

Scenario Planning

Earlier we noted that effective plans have four qualities: unity, continuity, accuracy, and flexibility. One of the most widely used planning methods or techniques that can help managers create plans that have these qualities is scenario planning. **Scenario planning** (also known as *contingency planning*) is the generation of multiple forecasts of future conditions followed by an analysis of how to respond effectively to each of those conditions.

scenario planning The generation of multiple forecasts of future conditions followed by an analysis of how to respond effectively to each of those conditions.

As noted previously, planning is about trying to forecast the future in order to be able to anticipate future opportunities and threats. The future, however, is inherently unpredictable. How can managers best deal with this unpredictability? This question preoccupied managers at Royal Dutch Shell, the third largest global oil company, in the 1980s. In 1984, oil was $30

As we know all too well, oil and gas prices are unpredictable. Oil industry managers therefore sometimes use scenario planning to deal with this chaotic market.
Robert Clay/Alamy Stock Photo

a barrel, and most analysts and managers, including Shell's, believed it would hit $50 per barrel by 1990. Although these high prices guaranteed high profits, Shell's top managers decided to conduct a scenario-planning exercise. Shell's corporate and divisional managers were told to use scenario planning to generate different future scenarios of conditions in the oil market and then to develop a set of plans that detailed how they would respond to these opportunities and threats if any such scenario occurred.

One scenario assumed that oil prices would fall to $15 per barrel, and managers had to decide what they should do to remain profitable in such a case. Managers went to work with the goal of creating a plan consisting of a series of recommendations. The final plan included proposals to cut oil exploration costs by investing in new technologies, to accelerate investments in cost-efficient oil-refining facilities, and to weed out unprofitable gas stations.[29] In reviewing these proposals, top management came to the conclusion that even if oil prices continued to rise, all of these actions would benefit Shell and increase its profit margin. So they decided to put the cost-cutting plan into action. As it happened, in the mid-1980s oil prices did not rise; they collapsed to $15 a barrel, but Shell, unlike its competitors, had already taken steps to be profitable in a low-oil-price world. Consequently, by 1990, the company was twice as profitable as its major competitors.

As this example suggests, because the future is unpredictable–the $30-a-barrel oil level was not reached again until the early 2000s, for example–the best way to improve planning is first to generate "multiple futures," or scenarios of the future, based on different assumptions about conditions that *might prevail* in the future and then to develop different plans that detail what a company should do if one of these scenarios occurs. Scenario planning is a learning tool that raises the quality of the planning process and can bring benefits to an organization.[30] Over the years, Shell scenario planners have generated more than 30 rounds of scenarios, including one that involved exploring the critical role energy plays in dealing with climate change.[31] A major advantage of scenario planning is its ability not only to anticipate the challenges of an uncertain future but also to educate managers to think about the future–*to think strategically.*

Determining the Organization's Mission and Goals

As we discussed earlier, determining the organization's mission and goals is the first step of the planning process. Once the mission and goals are agreed upon and formally stated in the corporate plan, they guide the next steps by defining which strategies are appropriate.[32] Figure 8.4 presents the mission statements of three Internet-based companies.

Figure 8.4

Mission Statements for Three Internet Companies

COMPANY	MISSION STATEMENT
Facebook	"To give people the power to build community and bring the world closer together."
Twitter	"To give everyone the power to create and share ideas and information instantly, without barriers."
Google	"To organize the world's information and make it universally accessible and useful."

Sources: Facebook's mission: www.facebook.com; Twitter's mission: https://investor.twitterinc.com; Google's mission: www.google.com, accessed January 23, 2023.

Defining the Business

To determine an organization's *mission*–the overriding reason it exists to provide customers with goods or services they value–managers must first *define its business* so they can identify what kinds of value customers are receiving. To define the business, managers must ask three related questions about a company's products: (1) *Who* are our customers? (2) *What* customer needs are being satisfied? (3) *How* are we satisfying customer needs?[33] Managers ask these questions to identify the customer needs that the organization satisfies and how the organization satisfies those needs. Answering these questions helps managers identify not only the customer needs they are satisfying now but also the needs they should try to satisfy in the future and who their true competitors are. All this information helps managers plan and establish appropriate goals.

Establishing Major Goals

Once the business is defined, managers must establish a set of primary goals to which the organization is committed. Developing these goals gives the organization a sense of direction or purpose. In most organizations, articulating major goals is the job of the CEO, although other managers have input into the process. Thus, at General Mills, CEO Harmening's primary goal is still to be one of the top performers in every market in which the company competes, even though this is highly challenging. However, the best statements of organizational goals are ambitious–that is, they *stretch* the organization and require that each of its members work to improve company performance.[34] The role of **strategic leadership**, the ability of the CEO and top managers to convey to their employees a compelling vision of what they want to achieve, is important here. If employees buy into the vision and model their behaviors on their leaders, they develop a willingness to undertake the hard, stressful work that is necessary for creative, risk-taking strategy making.[35]

strategic leadership The ability of the CEO and top managers to convey to their employees a compelling vision of what they want the organization to achieve.

Although goals should be challenging, they should also be realistic and specific. Many organizations establish major goals that are **S**pecific, **M**easurable, **A**ttainable, **R**esults-oriented, and **T**imely–or **SMART goals**:

SMART goals Goals that are specific, measurable, attainable, results-oriented, and timely.

- *Specific:* Goals should include detailed information–for example, "Replacement components for the refrigeration unit should be delivered by March 15, so technicians can install them before the unit goes operational on April 10."
- *Measurable:* Goals should be quantifiable–for example, "At least 95% of employees should complete training within 3 months of their start date." The ability to measure how many new employees completed training will help the organization determine whether planning and execution of training programs align with the company's overall strategy.
- *Attainable:* Goals should be challenging but within reach–for example, "Customer service wait times will be reduced by 15% within 6 months after the new software is operational." Shortening the time customers have to wait by 15% seems to be a goal that could be met once the new software program has been implemented.
- *Results-oriented:* Goals should be able to be met or exceeded–for example, "Increase sales of the new software product by 10% over the next year."
- *Timely:* Goals should include specific timelines or deadlines–for example, "We will acquire two new clients in the building construction sector by the end of the year." Providing sufficient time to accomplish a goal will encourage managers and employees to rethink and revise their processes in an effort to become more efficient.

SMART goals give managers at all levels of an organization incentive to look for ways to improve individual as well as organizational performance.[36] For example, General Mills recently updated its global sustainability goals to include: (1) reducing its greenhouse gas footprint across its value chain by 30% by 2030; (2) committing to advance regenerative agriculture on 1 million acres of farmland by 2030; and (3) reducing the environmental impact of product packaging with a commitment to design 100% recyclable or reusable packaging by 2030.[37]

Formulating Strategy

strategy formulation The development of a set of corporate, business, and functional strategies that allow an organization to accomplish its mission and achieve its goals.

Once the mission and goals of the organization have been set, a strategy to achieve them needs to be formulated. In **strategy formulation**, managers work to develop the set of strategies (corporate, divisional, and functional) that will allow an organization to accomplish its mission and achieve its goals.[38] Strategy formulation begins with managers' systematically analyzing the factors or forces inside an organization and outside in the global environment that affect the organization's ability to meet its goals now and in the future. SWOT analysis and the five forces model are two handy techniques managers can use to analyze these factors.

SWOT Analysis

SWOT analysis A planning exercise in which managers identify organizational strengths (S) and weaknesses (W) and environmental opportunities (O) and threats (T).

SWOT analysis is a planning exercise in which managers identify *internal* organizational strengths (S) and weaknesses (W) and *external* environmental opportunities (O) and threats (T). Based on a SWOT analysis, managers at the different levels of the organization select the corporate, business, and functional strategies to best position the organization to achieve its mission and goals (see Figure 8.5). In Chapter 6, we discussed forces in the task and general environments that have the potential to affect an organization. We noted that changes in these forces can produce opportunities that an organization might take advantage of and threats that may harm its current situation.

The first step in SWOT analysis is to identify an organization's strengths and weaknesses. Table 8.1 lists many important strengths (such as high-quality skills in marketing and in research and development) and weaknesses (such as rising manufacturing costs and outdated technology). The task facing managers is to identify the strengths and weaknesses that characterize the present state of their organization.

The second step in SWOT analysis begins when managers embark on a full-scale SWOT planning exercise to identify potential opportunities and threats in the environment that affect the organization now or may affect it in the future. Examples of possible opportunities and threats that must be anticipated (many of which were discussed in Chapter 6) are listed in Table 8.1. Scenario planning is often used to strengthen this analysis.

With the SWOT analysis completed, and strengths, weaknesses, opportunities, and threats identified, managers can continue the planning process and determine specific strategies for achieving the organization's mission and goals. The resulting strategies should enable the organization to attain its goals by taking advantage of opportunities, countering threats, building strengths, and correcting organizational weaknesses. To appreciate how managers can use SWOT analysis to formulate strategy, consider a recent SWOT analysis comparison between e-tailer Amazon.com and clicks-and-mortar retailer Walmart. Although each company has

Figure 8.5
Planning and Strategy Formulation

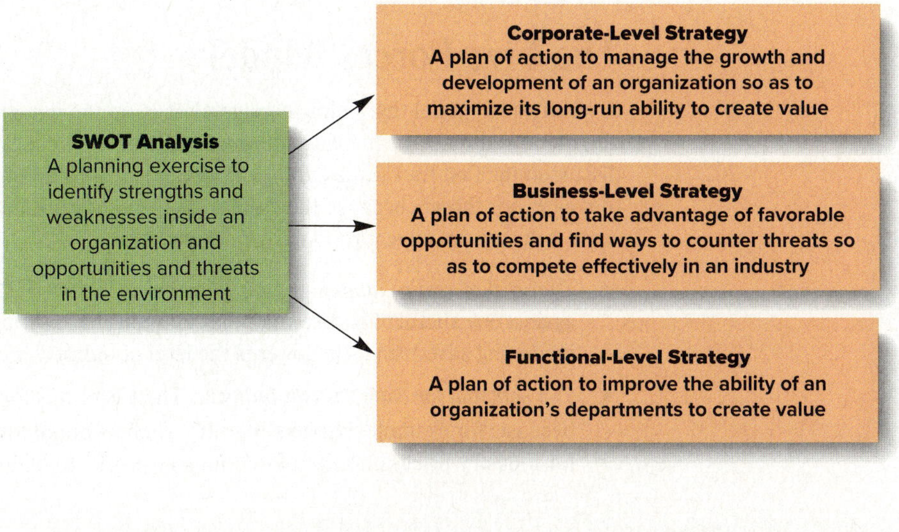

Table 8.1
Questions for SWOT Analysis

Potential Strengths	Potential Opportunities	Potential Weaknesses	Potential Threats
Well-developed strategy? Strong product lines? Broad market coverage? Manufacturing competence? Good marketing skills? Good materials management systems? R&D skills and leadership? Human resource competencies? Brand-name reputation? Cost of differentiation advantage? Appropriate management style? Appropriate organizational structure? Appropriate control systems? Ability to manage strategic change? Other strengths?	Expand core business(es)? Exploit new market segments? Widen product range? Extend cost or differentiation advantage? Diversify into new growth businesses? Expand into foreign markets? Apply R&D skills in new areas? Enter new related businesses? Vertically integrate forward? Vertically integrate backward? Overcome barriers to entry? Reduce rivalry among competitors? Apply brand-name capital in new areas? Seek fast market growth? Other opportunities?	Poorly developed strategy? Obsolete, narrow product lines? Rising manufacturing costs? Decline in R&D innovations? Poor marketing plan? Poor materials management systems? Loss of customer goodwill? Inadequate human resources? Loss of brand name? Growth without direction? Loss of corporate direction? Infighting among divisions? Loss of corporate control? Inappropriate organizational structure and control systems? High conflict and politics? Other weaknesses?	Attacks on core business(es)? Increase in domestic competition? Increase in foreign competition? Change in consumer tastes? Fall in barriers to entry? Rise in new or substitute products? Increase in industry rivalry? New forms of industry competition? Potential for takeover? Changes in demographic factors? Changes in economic factors? Downturn in economy? Rising labor costs? Slower market growth? Other threats?

differing strengths and weaknesses, they both face similar threats and opportunities in the expanding e-commerce market.[39] For example, Walmart's acquisition of several e-commerce companies provides some interesting opportunities for the world's largest retailer to gain market share in the online retail space—as well as some threats to Amazon's position as a top online retailer. In addition, Amazon's acquisition of Whole Food Markets specialty grocery chain and creation of Amazon Go retail stores provide the e-commerce giant with some interesting opportunities in the bricks-and-mortar retail space. Walmart recently announced it would sell its e-commerce technology to small- and medium-sized retailers, which enables the picking and packing of online purchases by employees and the geofencing technology that lets a store know when customers are on their way to pick up their orders. Walmart is working with Adobe to offer these cloud-based services to retailers through a subscription plan.[40]

The Five Forces Model

A well-known model that helps managers focus on the five most important competitive forces, or potential threats, in the external environment is Michael Porter's five forces model.[41] We discussed the first four forces in the following list in Chapter 6. Porter identified these five factors as major threats because they affect how much profit organizations competing within the same industry can expect to make:

- *The level of rivalry among organizations in an industry:* The more that companies compete against one another for customers—for example, by lowering the prices of their products or by increasing advertising—the lower is the level of industry profits (low prices mean less profit).
- *The potential for entry into an industry:* The easier it is for companies to enter an industry—because, for example, barriers to entry, such as brand loyalty, are low—the more likely it is for industry prices and therefore industry profits to be low.

- *The power of large suppliers:* If there are only a few large suppliers of an important input, then suppliers can drive up the price of that input, and expensive inputs result in lower profits for companies in an industry.
- *The power of large customers:* If only a few large customers are available to buy an industry's output, they can bargain to drive down the price of that output. As a result, industry producers make lower profits.
- *The threat of substitute products:* Often the output of one industry is a substitute for the output of another industry (plastic may be a substitute for steel in some applications, for example; similarly, bottled water is a substitute for cola). When a substitute for their product exists, companies cannot demand high prices for it or customers will switch to the substitute, and this constraint keeps their profits low.

Porter argued that when managers analyze opportunities and threats, they should pay particular attention to these five forces because they are the major threats an organization will encounter. It is the job of managers at the corporate, business, and functional levels to formulate strategies to counter these threats so an organization can manage its task and general environments, perform at a high level, and generate high profits.

Sometimes, however, management's review of competitive forces or potential threats cannot keep a company from filing bankruptcy or liquidating its stores. Consider the case of toy retailer Toys "R" Us (TRU). The past decade or so was quite challenging for the retailer—with holiday sales unable to provide the turnaround the company needed to regain profitability. Looking at Porter's framework, TRU experienced a high level of rivalry from other retailers selling the same toys, which pushed down prices when TRU could least likely afford to reduce its margins. By 1998, Walmart began selling more toys than TRU. The potential for entry into the retail toy industry was high and devastating for TRU because there were few barriers to entry—very little brand loyalty for TRU itself from consumers who could buy toys and other items more cheaply and more conveniently from discount retailers and e-commerce websites.

With regard to the power of large suppliers and customers, economies of scale could have played to TRU's advantage; however, the company had been highly leveraged with almost insurmountable debt, and many of its suppliers refused to give the company additional financing or extended credit to purchase the inventory it desperately needed for the all-important holiday season.[42] Lastly, the threat of substitute products was high in the case of TRU, especially if one considers alternative forms of entertainment (such as video games and streaming content) that met the same consumer needs as toys. Analyzing TRU's plight using the five forces model shows the company was vulnerable in several areas, which caused it to reduce its prices to attract shoppers, while trying to pay back enormous amounts of debt. TRU first filed for bankruptcy protection from creditors, and then, in March 2018, started liquidating and closing stores in the United States and abroad, leaving more than 33,000 employees without jobs. Later that year, TRU's controlling lenders canceled a bankruptcy auction amid speculation that they would attempt to revive the TRU brand. In late 2019, Tru Kids, the revitalized brand's parent company, opened two smaller Toys "R" Us stores in New Jersey and Texas, but both closed in early 2021 amid the pandemic. Brand management company WHP Global acquired a controlling interest in Tru Kids shortly thereafter. Tru Kids recently announced they would partner with Macy's and open locations within most Macy's department stores for the holidays and sell merchandise online at macys.com.[43]

Tru Kids, the revitalized brand of Toys "R" Us under new ownership, recently announced a partnership with Macy's to open shops within Macy's locations around the country, as well as to sell merchandise online at the Macy's website.
Seth Wenig/AP Images

hypercompetition Permanent, ongoing, intense competition brought about in an industry by advancing technology or changing customer tastes.

Today competition is tough in most industries, whether companies make cars, soup, computers, or dolls. The term **hypercompetition** applies to industries that are characterized by permanent, ongoing, intense competition brought about by advancing technology or changing customer tastes and fads and fashions.[44] Clearly, planning and strategy formulation are much more difficult and risky when hypercompetition prevails in an industry.

Formulating Business-Level Strategies

LO8-3 Differentiate among the main types of business-level strategies, and explain how they give an organization a competitive advantage that may lead to superior performance.

Michael Porter, the researcher who developed the five forces model, also developed a theory of how managers can select a business-level strategy—a plan to gain a competitive advantage in a particular market or industry.[45] Porter argued that business-level strategy creates a competitive advantage because it allows an organization (or a division of a company) to *counter and reduce* the threat of the five industry forces. That is, successful business-level strategy reduces rivalry, prevents new competitors from entering the industry, reduces the power of suppliers or buyers, and lowers the threat of substitutes—and this raises prices and profits.

According to Porter, to obtain these higher profits, managers must choose between two basic ways of increasing the value of an organization's products: *differentiating the product* to increase its value to customers or *lowering the costs* of making the product. Porter also argues that managers must choose between serving the whole market or serving just one segment of a market. Based on those choices, managers choose to pursue one of four business-level strategies: low-cost, differentiation, focused low-cost, or focused differentiation (see Table 8.2).

Low-Cost Strategy

low-cost strategy Driving the organization's costs down below the costs of its rivals.

With a **low-cost strategy**, managers try to gain a competitive advantage by focusing the energy of all the organization's departments or functions on driving the company's costs down below the costs of its industry rivals. This strategy, for example, would require that manufacturing managers search for new ways to reduce production costs, R&D managers focus on developing new products that can be manufactured more cheaply, and marketing managers find ways to lower the costs of attracting customers. According to Porter, companies pursuing a low-cost strategy can sell a product for less than their rivals sell it and yet still make a good profit because of their lower costs. Thus, such organizations enjoy a competitive advantage based on their low prices. For example, BIC pursues a low-cost strategy: It offers customers razor blades priced lower than Gillette's and ballpoint pens less expensive than those offered by Cross or Waterman. Also, when existing companies have low costs and can charge low prices, it is difficult for new companies to enter the industry because entering is always an expensive process.

Differentiation Strategy

differentiation strategy Distinguishing an organization's products from the products of competitors on dimensions such as product design, quality, or after-sales service.

With a **differentiation strategy**, managers try to gain a competitive advantage by focusing all the energies of the organization's departments or functions on *distinguishing* the organization's products from those of competitors on one or more important dimensions, such as product design, quality, or after-sales service and support. Often the process of making products unique and different is expensive. This strategy, for example, often requires that managers increase spending on product design or R&D to differentiate products, and costs rise as a result. Organizations that successfully pursue a differentiation strategy may be able to charge a *premium price* for their products; the premium price lets organizations pursuing a differentiation strategy

Table 8.2
Porter's Business-Level Strategies

	Number of Market Segments Served	
Strategy	**Many**	**Few**
Low-cost	√	
Focused low-cost		√
Differentiation	√	
Focused differentiation		√

recoup their higher costs. Coca-Cola, PepsiCo, and Procter & Gamble are some of the many well-known companies that pursue a strategy of differentiation. They spend enormous amounts of money on advertising to differentiate, and create a unique image for, their products. Also, differentiation makes industry entry difficult because new companies have no brand name to help them compete, and customers don't perceive other products to be close substitutes, so this also allows premium pricing and results in high profits.

According to Porter's theory, managers cannot simultaneously pursue both a low-cost strategy and a differentiation strategy. Porter identified a simple correlation: Differentiation raises costs and thus necessitates premium pricing to recoup those high costs. For example, if BIC suddenly began to advertise heavily to try to build a strong global brand image for its products, BIC's costs would rise. BIC then could no longer make a profit simply by pricing its blades or pens lower than Gillette or Cross. According to Porter, managers must choose between a low-cost strategy and a differentiation strategy.

More and more, however, exceptions to Porter's ideas about the "either/or" approach to gaining competitive advantage by low cost or differentiation can be found in today's business environment. For example, Southwest Airlines has written its mission statement to say "dedication to the highest quality of customer service delivered with a sense of warmth, friendliness, individual pride, and company spirit."[46] Based on this statement, the company seems to be pursuing a differentiation strategy based on customer service. Yet the average price of a one-way ticket on a Southwest flight continues to be among the lowest, which suggests a cost leadership strategy. Likewise, Apple has a story that mixes cost leadership with differentiation. Apple CEO Tim Cook emphasizes that Apple's strategy is to focus on making great products–a differentiation strategy. He said the company never had the goal of selling a low-cost phone.[47] However, he said, the company did find a way to reach its goal of providing a great experience with a phone while reducing its cost. Cook emphasizes that differentiation was the goal, but low cost also became possible. These examples suggest that although Porter's ideas may be valid in most cases, well-managed companies may pursue both low costs and differentiated products.

Focused Low-Cost and Focused Differentiation Strategies

Both the differentiation strategy and the low-cost strategy are aimed at serving many or most segments of a particular market, such as for cars, toys, foods, or computers. Porter identified two other business-level strategies that aim to serve the needs of customers in only one or a few market segments.[48] Managers pursuing a **focused low-cost strategy** serve one or a few segments of the overall market and aim to make their organization the lowest-cost company serving that segment. By contrast, managers pursuing a **focused differentiation strategy** serve just one or a few segments of the market and aim to make their organization the most differentiated company serving that segment.

focused low-cost strategy Serving only one segment of the overall market and trying to be the lowest-cost organization serving that segment.

focused differentiation strategy Serving only one segment of the overall market and trying to be the most differentiated organization serving that segment.

Companies pursuing either of these strategies have chosen to *specialize* in some way by directing their efforts at a particular kind of customer (such as serving the needs of babies or affluent customers) or even the needs of customers in a specific geographic region (customers on the East or West Coast). Audi, for example, pursues a focused differentiation strategy, producing cars exclusively for higher-income customers. By contrast, Toyota pursues a differentiation strategy and produces cars that appeal to consumers in almost all segments of the car market, from basic transportation (Toyota Corolla) through the middle of the market (Toyota Camry) to the high-income end of the market (Lexus).

Increasingly, smaller companies are finding it easier to pursue a focused strategy and compete successfully against large, powerful low-cost and differentiated companies because of advances in technology that lower costs and enable them to reach and attract customers. By establishing a storefront on the web, thousands of small, specialized companies have been able to carve out a profitable niche against large bricks-and-mortar and virtual competitors.

As discussed in Chapter 7's "Case in the News," Zara is a flagship brand for Spanish global retailer Inditex, whose sales have soared in recent years, and provides an excellent example of the way even a bricks-and-mortar company can use technology to pursue a focused strategy and compete globally.[49] Zara has managed to position itself as the low-price, low-cost leader in the fashion segment of the clothing market, against differentiators like Gucci and H&M, because it has applied technology to its specific needs. Zara has created technology that allows it to manage its design and manufacturing process in a way that minimizes the inventory it has to carry—the major cost borne by a clothing retailer. However, technology also helps give Zara's designers instant feedback on which clothes are selling well and in which countries, and this gives Zara a competitive advantage from differentiation. Specifically, Zara can manufacture more of a particular kind of dress or suit to meet high customer demand, decide which clothing should be sold in its rapidly expanding network of global stores, and constantly change the mix of clothes it offers customers to keep up with fashion—at low cost.

Zara's approach to technology also lets it efficiently manage the interface between its design and manufacturing operations, which work side by side in its corporate headquarters in Arteixo, Spain. Zara sometimes takes only two weeks to design, manufacture, and ship new clothing items to stores across the globe. By contrast, H&M, the trendy Swedish retailer, takes several months to get its advanced orders into the hands of customers.[50] This short time to market gives Zara great flexibility and allows the company to respond quickly to the rapidly changing fashion market, in which fashions can change several times a year. Because of the quick manufacturing-to-sales cycle and just-in-time fashion, Zara offers clothes collections at relatively low prices and still makes profits that are the envy of the fashion apparel industry.

Zara has been able to pursue a focused strategy that is simultaneously low cost and differentiated because it has developed many strengths in functions such as clothing design, marketing, and technology that have given it a competitive advantage. Developing functional-level strategies that strengthen business-level strategy and increase competitive advantage is a vital managerial task. However, we need to go up one planning level and examine how corporate strategy helps an organization achieve its mission and goals.

Formulating Corporate-Level Strategies

LO8-4 Differentiate among the main types of corporate-level strategies, and explain how they are used to strengthen a company's business-level strategy and competitive advantage.

Once managers have formulated the business-level strategies that will best position a company, or a division of a company, to compete in an industry and outperform its rivals, they must look to the future. If their planning has been successful, the company will be generating high profits, and their task now is to plan how to invest these profits to increase performance over time.

Recall that *corporate-level strategy* is a plan of action that involves choosing in which industries and countries a company should invest its resources to achieve its mission and goals. In choosing a corporate-level strategy, managers ask, How should the growth and development of our company be managed to increase its ability to create value for customers (and thus increase its performance) over the long run? Managers of effective organizations actively seek new opportunities to use a company's resources to create new and improved goods and services for customers. Examples of organizations whose product lines are growing rapidly are Google, Intel, Apple, and Toyota, whose managers pursue any feasible opportunity to use their companies' skills to provide customers with new products.

In addition, some managers must help their organizations respond to threats due to changing forces in the task or general environment that have made their business-level strategies less effective and reduced profits. For example, customers may no longer be buying the kinds of goods and services a company is producing, or other organizations may have entered the market and attracted away customers (this happened to Sony in the 2000s after Apple and Samsung began to produce better MP3 players, laptops, and smartphones). Top managers aim to find corporate strategies that can help the organization strengthen its business-level strategies and thus respond to these changes and improve performance.

The principal corporate-level strategies that managers use to help a company grow and keep it at the top of its industry, or to help it retrench and reorganize to stop its decline, include (1) concentration on a single industry, (2) vertical integration, (3) diversification, and (4) international expansion, which we discuss in detail in the global chapter (Chapter 6). An organization will benefit from pursuing any of these strategies only when the strategy helps further increase the value of the organization's goods and services so that more customers buy them. Specifically, to increase the value of goods and services, a corporate-level strategy must help a company, or one of its divisions, either (1) lower the costs of developing and making products or (2) increase product differentiation so that more customers want to buy the products even at high or premium prices. Both of these outcomes strengthen a company's competitive advantage and increase its performance.

Concentration on a Single Industry

concentration on a single industry Reinvesting a company's profits to strengthen its competitive position in its current industry.

Most growing companies reinvest their profits to strengthen their competitive position in the industry in which they are currently operating; in doing so, they pursue the corporate-level strategy of **concentration on a single industry**. Most commonly, an organization uses its functional skills to develop new kinds of products, or it expands the number of locations in which it uses those skills. For example, Apple continuously introduces improved mobile wireless digital devices such as the iPhone and iPad, whereas McDonald's, which began as one restaurant in California, focused all its efforts on using its resources to quickly expand across the globe to become the biggest and most profitable U.S. fast-food company. To learn about corporate-level planning at a company with a concentration strategy, see the "Focus on DEI&B" feature.

On the other hand, when organizations are performing effectively, they often decide to enter *new industries* in which they can use their growing profits to establish new operating divisions to create and make a wider range of more valuable products. Thus, they begin to pursue vertical integration or diversification–such as Coca-Cola, PepsiCo, and Campbell's Soup.

FOCUS ON DEI&B

UPS CEO Uses Experience to Drive Values

In her role as CEO of UPS, Carol Tomé focuses on values, including those related to diversity, equity, and inclusion.
Jonathan Ernst/REUTERS/Alamy Stock Photo

Carol Tomé says it was "easy to say yes" to becoming CEO of UPS.[51] The company has a well-respected brand and delivers about 25 million packages a day. When Tomé assumed the role, she and her leadership team agreed to continue on the same path but with a fresh expression of the values behind it: "Moving our world forward by delivering what matters." In keeping with this mission, UPS would grow through continued concentration on package delivery, providing excellent service and value by empowering employees. The team reviewed all its major projects and prioritized those supporting the mission and strategy.[52]

Tomé's approach worked. UPS increased profit margins through investing in technology and targeting small businesses. Greater profitability led to a rise in stock price, which had been flat for years. UPS also improved on mission-focused measures including a share of customers saying they would recommend UPS as a service and a share of employees saying they would recommend UPS as a place to work. Tomé credits employee empowerment for the company's success, especially in meeting the surge in demand following the onset of the COVID-19 pandemic.[53]

Tomé is an "outsider" CEO. Although she had served on the company's board for more than a decade, she was the first CEO not promoted from within UPS and its first female CEO (she had been chief financial officer at Home Depot previously). Tomé was initially worried about shattering the glass ceiling: Would the people back her up? The answer, fortunately for the company, was yes.[54]

Tomé's focus on values, including those related to diversity, equity, inclusion, and belonging, is an outgrowth of her experience. Early in her career, she accepted that executives should focus mainly on company value, measured by its stock price. Then at Home Depot, she saw that investing in employees–respecting them and seeking their well-being–improved how they took care of customers, which increased the company's overall value. She became UPS's CEO shortly after the video of George Floyd's killing jarred the nation and world. Tomé set aside her original ideas for rallying employees and shared her feelings of anger and shame at the injustice and her commitment to values-based action. UPS has followed up on that message with a salary review to inform pay equity, training in bias avoidance and respect, and a revised dress code that is inclusive of diversity in natural and facial hair. The company also has diversified its board with members who are Asian, Black, and female.[55]

Vertical Integration

vertical integration Expanding a company's operations either backward into an industry that produces inputs for its products or forward into an industry that uses, distributes, or sells its products.

When an organization is performing well in its industry, managers often see new opportunities to create additional value either by producing the inputs it uses to make products or by distributing and selling its products to customers. This process is called vertical integration. **Vertical integration** is a corporate-level strategy in which a company expands its business operations either backward into a new industry that produces inputs for the company's products (*backward vertical integration*) or forward into a new industry that uses, distributes, or sells the company's products (*forward vertical integration*).[56] For example, when Tesla Motors set a corporate goal of mass-producing an electric car that would sell competitively in the $35,000–$40,000 range, management recognized it would need batteries for the vehicle. To meet that need, Tesla decided to become its own battery supplier, building a $5 billion Gigafactory outside Sparks, Nevada. This backward vertical integration not only supplies Tesla's needs for inputs to make the electric car, but it also helped lower the cost of batteries.[57]

Figure 8.6 illustrates the four main stages in a typical raw material to customer value chain; value is added to the product at each stage by the activities involved in each industry. For a company based in the assembly stage, backward integration would involve establishing a new division in the intermediate manufacturing or raw material production industries, and forward integration would involve establishing a new division to distribute its products to wholesalers or a retail division to sell directly to customers. A division at one stage or one industry receives the product produced by the division in the previous stage or industry, transforms it in some way–adding value–and then transfers the output at a higher price to the division at the next stage in the chain.

As an example of how this industry value chain works, consider the cola segment of the soft drink industry. In the raw material industry, suppliers include sugar companies and manufacturers of artificial sweeteners such as NutraSweet and Splenda, which are used in diet beverages. These companies sell their products to companies in the soft drink industry that make concentrate–such as Coca-Cola and PepsiCo–which mix these inputs with others to produce the drink concentrate. In the process, they add value to these inputs. The concentrate producers then sell the concentrate to companies in the bottling and distribution industry, which add carbonated water to the concentrate and package the resulting drinks–again adding value to the concentrate. Next the bottlers distribute and sell the soft drinks to retailers, including stores such as Costco and Walmart and fast-food chains such as McDonald's and Taco Bell. Companies in the retail industry add value by making the product accessible to customers, and they profit from direct sales to customers. Thus, value and profit are added by companies at each stage in the raw material to consumer chain.

Managers pursue vertical integration because it allows them either to add value to their products by making them special or unique or to lower the costs of making and selling them. An example of using forward vertical integration to increase differentiation is Apple's decision

Figure 8.6

Stages in a Vertical Value Chain

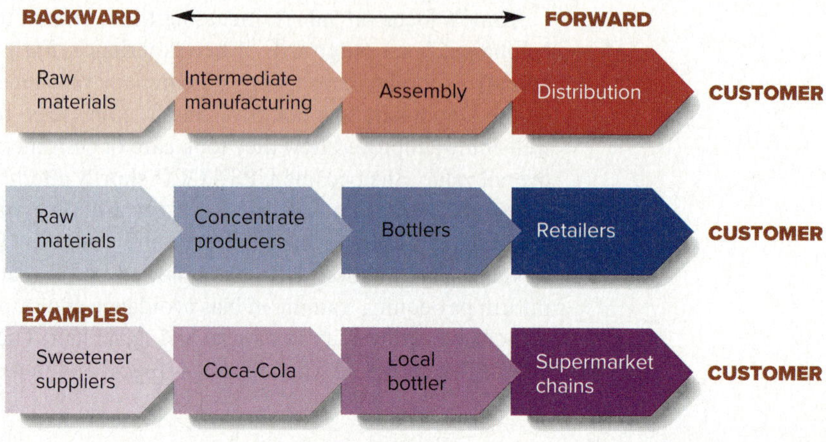

to open its own stores to make its unique products more accessible to customers who could try them out before they bought them. So, too, is PepsiCo's decision to buy its bottlers so they can better differentiate their products and lower costs in the future.

Although vertical integration can strengthen an organization's competitive advantage and increase its performance, it can also reduce its flexibility to respond to changing environmental conditions and create threats that must be countered by changing the organization's strategy. For example, P&G acquired the Gillette Company in 2005. Duracell batteries, a vertical integration for Gillette, came with it. However, Duracell stood out as an oddball among other products in P&G's portfolio, and the company was sold to Warren Buffett's Berkshire Hathaway in 2016.[58]

Thus, when considering vertical integration as a strategy to add value, managers must be careful because sometimes it may *reduce* a company's ability to create value when the environment changes. This is why so many companies have divested themselves of units that draw attention and resources away from an organization's primary purpose.

Diversification

diversification Expanding a company's business operations into a new industry in order to produce new kinds of valuable goods or services.

Diversification is the corporate-level strategy of expanding a company's business operations into a new industry in order to produce new kinds of valuable goods or services.[59] Examples include PepsiCo's diversification into the snack food business with the purchase of Frito Lay and Cisco's diversification into consumer electronics when it purchased Linksys. There are two main kinds of diversification: related and unrelated.

related diversification Entering a new business or industry to create a competitive advantage in one or more of an organization's existing divisions or businesses.

RELATED DIVERSIFICATION **Related diversification** is the strategy of entering a new business or industry to create a competitive advantage in one or more of an organization's existing divisions or businesses. Related diversification can add value to an organization's products if managers can find ways for its various divisions or business units to share their valuable skills or resources so that synergy is created.[60] Although it is in the early stages of diversification, Gotham Greens is looking to expand its business in an environmentally responsible and thoughtful way, as described in the "Ethics in Action" feature.

ETHICS IN ACTION

Healthy Growth for Gotham Greens

Gotham Greens operates greenhouses to grow lettuce and other fresh produce, which it sells to supermarkets. Its 12 climate-controlled greenhouses operate year-round in or near U.S. cities, serving local supermarkets. The company uses hydroponic techniques and applies advanced technology including sensors to ensure that its growing methods conserve water, maximize output, minimize land use and pollution, and ensure plant health and nutrient density.[61]

Founders Viraj Puri and Eric Haley first opened a greenhouse in New York City in 2011. Their next greenhouse opened in 2013, also serving New Yorkers, but with a twist: It was installed on the roof of a Whole Foods Market in Brooklyn. Employees deliver the lettuce by elevator to Whole Foods, as well as to nearby restaurants. Two years later, Gotham Greens entered the Midwest with a greenhouse on Chicago's South Side. Then the company added greenhouses in New York and Chicago and moved into Baltimore, Denver, and Providence, Rhode Island. By 2022, the company had 600,000 square feet of capacity in greenhouses spread across eight states from the East Coast to California.[62]

According to Puri, the company's CEO, Gotham Greens' strategic objective is to grow fresh produce within a day's drive for 90% of U.S. consumers. To that end, the company is continuing its geographic expansion, moving into regions with growing populations, mostly recently adding Georgia and Texas. Gotham Greens also added new retail customers, including the Kroger and Albertsons grocery chains. The company's regional success has opened investors' wallets; with new funding, Gotham Greens plans to accelerate its expansion.[63]

Gotham Greens has committed to being socially responsible and was recently certified as a B Corporation–a business that meets standards for social and environmental performance. Keeping environmental concerns at the heart of its strategy can be difficult. Consumers prefer their lettuce packaged, and that typically means plastic. The company tried compostable fiber containers, but the lettuce quickly wilted. After researching other options, the company settled on #1 PET plastic, the plastic most often recycled, but continues to search for better alternatives.[64]

As Gotham Greens approaches its goal of serving consumers across the United States, the company will need new avenues of growth. Already it is experimenting with product diversification. It has stayed close to its concentration on produce, adding tomatoes and then extending its branding to packaged items such as salad dressings and cooking sauces.[65]

---

synergy Performance gains that result when individuals and departments coordinate their actions.

Synergy is obtained when the value created by two divisions cooperating is greater than the value that would be created if the two divisions operated separately and independently. For example, suppose two or more divisions of a diversified company can use the same manufacturing facilities, distribution channels, or advertising campaigns–that is, share functional activities. Each division has to invest fewer resources in a shared functional activity than it would have to invest if it performed the functional activity by itself. Related diversification can be a major source of cost savings when divisions share the costs of performing a functional activity.[66] Similarly, if one division's R&D skills can improve another division's products and increase their differentiated appeal, this synergy can give the second division an important competitive advantage over its industry rivals–so the company as a whole benefits from diversification.

The way Procter & Gamble's disposable diaper and paper towel divisions cooperate is a good example of the successful production of synergies. These divisions share the costs of procuring inputs such as paper and packaging; a joint sales force sells both products to retail outlets; and both products are shipped using the same distribution system. This resource sharing has enabled both divisions to reduce their costs, and as a result, they can charge lower prices than their competitors and so attract more customers.[67] In addition, the divisions can share the research costs of developing new and improved products, such as finding more absorbent material, that increase both products' differentiated appeal. This is something that is also at the heart of 3M's corporate strategy. From the beginning, 3M has pursued related diversification and created new businesses by leveraging its skills in research and development. Today the company has four business groups that share resources such as technology and marketing. The four groups are safety and industrial, health care, consumer, and transportation and electronics. The company spends about 5.9% of its annual sales on research and development, which helps produce more than 3,500 new patents each year and a steady stream of unique products for consumers and businesses alike.[68] In late July 2022, 3M announced it would spin off its $8 billion health care group into a separate, public company by the end of 2023.[69]

How did we ever survive without Post-it Notes? 3M's intense focus on solving customer problems results in new products that sell well, including countless variations of the original sticky note.
Kuznetsov Alexey/Shutterstock

How does 3M do it? First, the company is a science-based enterprise with a strong tradition of innovation and risk taking. Risk taking is encouraged, and failure is not punished but is seen as a natural part of the process of creating new products and businesses.[70] Second, 3M's management is relentlessly focused on the company's customers and the problems they face. Many of 3M's products have come from helping customers to solve difficult problems. Third, managers set stretch goals that require the company to create new products and businesses at a rapid rate. Fourth, employees are given considerable autonomy to pursue their own ideas; indeed, 15% of employees' time can be spent working on projects of their own choosing without management approval. Many products have resulted from this autonomy, including the ubiquitous Post-it Notes. Fifth, while products belong to business units and business units are responsible for generating profits, the technologies belong to every unit within the company. Anyone at 3M is free to try to develop new applications for a technology developed by its business units. Finally, 3M organizes many companywide meetings where researchers from its different divisions are brought together to share the results of their work.

In sum, to pursue related diversification successfully, managers search for new businesses where they can use the existing skills and resources in their departments and divisions to create synergies, add value to new products and businesses, and improve their competitive position and that of the entire company. In addition, managers may try to acquire a company in a new industry because they believe it possesses skills and resources that will improve the performance of one or more of their existing divisions. If successful, such skill transfers can help an organization to lower its costs or better differentiate its products because they create synergies between divisions.

unrelated diversification Entering a new industry or buying a company in a new industry that is not related in any way to an organization's current businesses or industries.

UNRELATED DIVERSIFICATION Managers pursue **unrelated diversification** when they establish divisions or buy companies in new industries that are *not* linked in any way to their current businesses or industries. One main reason for pursuing unrelated diversification is that sometimes managers can buy a poorly performing company, transfer their management skills to that company, turn around its business, and increase its performance–all of which create value.

Another reason for pursuing unrelated diversification is that purchasing businesses in different industries lets managers engage in *portfolio strategy,* which is apportioning financial resources among divisions to increase financial returns or spread risks among different businesses, much as individual investors do with their own portfolios. For example, managers may transfer funds from a rich division (a "cash cow") to a new and promising division (a "star") and, by appropriately allocating money between divisions, create value. Though used as a popular explanation in the 1980s for unrelated diversification, portfolio strategy ran into increasing criticism in the 1990s because it simply does not work.[71] Why? As managers expand the scope of their organization's operations and enter more and more industries, it becomes increasingly difficult for top managers to be knowledgeable about all of the organization's diverse businesses. Managers do not have the time to process all of the information required to adequately assess the strategy and performance of each division, so the performance of the entire company often falls.

Thus, although unrelated diversification can create value for a company, research evidence suggests that *too much* diversification can cause managers to lose control of their organization's core business. As a result, diversification can reduce value rather than create it.[72] Because of this, during the last decade there has been an increasing trend for diversified companies to divest many of their unrelated, and sometimes related, divisions. Managers in companies like Novartis, Nestlé, and General Electric have sold off numerous divisions and focused on increasing the performance of the businesses that remained–in other words, they went back to a strategy of concentrating on a limited number of industries. In 2022, as part of its turnaround strategy, General Electric continued to dismantle its massive conglomerate structure by splitting into three independent companies, focusing on aviation, health care, and energy.[73]

Planning and Implementing Strategy

LO8-5 Describe the vital role managers play in implementing strategies to achieve an organization's mission and goals.

After identifying appropriate business and corporate strategies to attain an organization's mission and goals, managers confront the challenge of putting those strategies into action. Strategy implementation is a process that typically includes the following steps:

1. Determine responsibility for implementation to the appropriate individuals or groups.
2. Draft detailed action plans that specify how a strategy is to be implemented.
3. Establish a timetable for implementation that includes precise, measurable goals linked to the attainment of the action plan.
4. Allocate appropriate resources to the responsible individuals or groups.

5. Hold specific persons or groups responsible for the attainment of corporate, divisional, and functional goals.
6. Take corrective action as needed throughout the implementation process.
7. Conduct a review of the overall process once the implementation has taken place to evaluate what went right and what went wrong.[74]

The planning process goes beyond just identifying effective strategies; it also includes plans to ensure that these strategies are put into action. Normally, the plan for implementing a new strategy requires the development of new functional strategies, the redesign of an organization's structure, and the development of new control systems; it might also require a new program to change an organization's culture. These are issues we address in subsequent chapters.

Summary and Review

LO8-1, 8-2 **PLANNING** Planning is a three-step process: (1) determining an organization's mission and goals, (2) formulating strategy, and (3) implementing strategy. Managers use planning to identify and select appropriate goals and courses of action for an organization and to decide how to allocate the resources they need to attain those goals and carry out those actions. A good plan builds commitment for the organization's goals, gives the organization a sense of direction and purpose, coordinates the different functions and divisions of the organization, and controls managers by making them accountable for specific goals. In large organizations, planning takes place at three levels: corporate, business or divisional, and functional or departmental. Long-term plans have a time horizon of five years or more; intermediate-term plans, between one and five years; and short-term plans, one year or less.

LO8-1, 8-2, 8-3, 8-4 **DETERMINING MISSION AND GOALS AND FORMULATING STRATEGY** Determining the organization's mission requires that managers define the business of the organization and establish major goals. Many organizations establish corporate goals that are SMART: specific, measurable, attainable, results-oriented, and timely. Strategy formulation requires that managers perform a SWOT analysis and then choose appropriate strategies at the corporate, business, and functional levels. At the business level, managers are responsible for developing a successful low-cost and/or differentiation strategy, either for the whole market or a particular segment of it. At the functional level, departmental managers develop strategies to help the organization either add value to its products by differentiating them or lower the costs of value creation. At the corporate level, organizations use strategies including concentration on a single industry, vertical integration, and related and unrelated diversification to strengthen their competitive advantage by increasing the value of the goods and services provided to customers.

LO8-5 **IMPLEMENTING STRATEGY** Strategy implementation requires that managers allocate responsibilities to appropriate individuals or groups; draft detailed action plans that specify how a strategy is to be implemented; establish a timetable for implementation that includes precise, measurable goals linked to the attainment of the action plan; allocate appropriate resources to the responsible individuals or groups; hold individuals or groups accountable for the attainment of goals; take corrective action as needed throughout the process; and conduct a review of the process to determine what worked and what didn't.

Management in Action

Topics for Discussion and Action

Discussion

1. Describe the three steps of planning. Explain how they are related. [LO8-1]
2. How can scenario planning help managers predict the future? [LO8-2]
3. What is the relationship among corporate-, business-, and functional-level strategies, and how do they create value for an organization? [LO8-3, 8-4]
4. Pick an industry and identify four companies in the industry that pursue one of the four main business-level strategies (low-cost, focused low-cost, and so on). [LO8-2, 8-3]
5. What is the difference between vertical integration and related diversification? [LO8-4]

Action

6. Ask a manager about the kinds of planning exercises they regularly use. What are the purposes of these exercises, and what are their advantages or disadvantages? [LO8-1, 8-2]
7. Ask a manager to identify the corporate- and business-level strategies used by their organization. [LO8-3, 8-4]

Building Management Skills

How to Analyze a Company's Strategy [LO8-3, 8-4]

Pick a well-known business organization that has received recent press coverage and that provides annual reports on its website. From the information in the articles and annual reports, answer these questions:

1. What is (are) the main industry(ies) in which the company competes?
2. What business-level strategy does the company seem to be pursuing in this industry? Why?
3. What corporate-level strategies is the company pursuing? Why?
4. Have there been any major changes in its strategy recently? Why?

Managing Ethically [LO8-2, 8-5]

Recently global advertising giant WPP paid $19 million to resolve U.S. government allegations that the company paid bribes to local officials in several foreign countries in which it owned ad agencies, including India, China, and Brazil. As part of its corporate strategy to expand operations, WPP bought up smaller advertising firms in foreign countries, which were considered high-risk markets, and the acquired firms' founders typically stayed on as CEOs and had broad authority to conduct business as they saw fit.

In India, WPP's subsidiary paid as much as $1 million in bribes to officials through a third party to obtain and retain government business, which resulted in nearly $6 million in additional profit between 2015 and 2017. This occurred despite WPP receiving seven anonymous complaints referring to the payments. According to WPP, those employees involved in the various bribery schemes were terminated.

These types of bribes may not necessarily be illegal in other countries, and managers may insist that paying bribes is part of doing business in the local community. WPP, however, acknowledges that profitability cannot come at the expense of appropriate country controls to identify and root out corrupt behavior.

Questions

1. Either by yourself or in a group, decide if the business practice of paying bribes is ethical or unethical.
2. Should WPP allow its foreign divisions to pay bribes if other companies are doing so?
3. If bribery is common in a particular country, what effect does this likely have on the nation's economy and culture?

Small Group Breakout Exercise

Low-Cost or Differentiation? [LO8-2, 8-3]

Form groups of three or four people, and appoint one member as the spokesperson who will communicate your findings to the class when called on by the instructor. Then discuss the following scenario:

You are a team of managers of a major national clothing chain, and you have been charged with finding a way to restore your organization's competitive advantage. Recently, your organization has been experiencing increasing competition from two sources. First, discount stores such as Walmart and Target have been undercutting your prices because they buy their clothes from low-cost foreign manufacturers, whereas you buy most of yours from high-quality domestic suppliers. Discount stores have been attracting your customers who buy at the low end of the price range. Second, small online retailers provide high-priced designer clothing and are attracting your customers at the high end of the market. Your company has become stuck in the middle, and you have to decide what to do: Should you start to buy abroad so you can lower your prices and pursue a low-cost strategy? Should you focus on the high end of the market and become more of a differentiator? Or should you try to pursue both a low-cost strategy and a differentiation strategy?

1. Using scenario planning, analyze the pros and cons of each alternative.
2. Think about the various clothing retailers in your city and those available online, and analyze the choices they have made about how to compete along the low-cost and differentiation dimensions.

Be the Manager [LO8-2, 8-3]

A group of investors in your city is considering opening a new upscale supermarket to compete with the major supermarket chains that are currently dominating the city's marketplace. They have called you in to help them determine what kind of upscale supermarket they should open. In other words, how can they best develop a competitive advantage against existing supermarket chains?

Questions

1. List the supermarket chains in your city, and identify their strengths and weaknesses.
2. What business-level strategies are these supermarkets currently pursuing?
3. What kind of supermarket would do best against the competition? What kind of business-level strategy should it pursue?

Case in the News [LO8-1, 8-2, 8-3, 8-4]

Can Slow and Steady Give GM the Win?

GM's vision, as expressed by CEO Mary Barra, is a world of zero crashes, zero emissions, and zero congestion. Reducing crashes and congestion involves automating vehicle functions and building vehicles for ride sharing. For this, GM has purchased a majority stake in Cruise, which makes self-driving cars for ride-sharing and rental-car companies. To achieve zero emissions, GM converts its facilities to renewable power sources and develops electric vehicles (EVs). In 2021, GM announced that by 2035, none of the vehicles it sells will be gasoline powered. As of 2022, GM planned to invest $35 billion in EV development (up from $20 billion budgeted in 2017), was making several EV models, and had an interim goal of producing more than a million EVs in North American factories by 2026.

GM's EV strategy requires a broad market, but most EVs, including GM's, are luxury vehicles. After GM's 2016 launch of a compact EV, the Chevy Bolt—which ran into problems and was discontinued—GM pivoted to engineering higher-end models: the GMC Hummer pickup, priced at more than $100,000, followed by the Cadillac Lyriq, a luxury SUV. Choosing the Hummer to lead off the new strategy demonstrated that EVs can be powerhouses. As GM produces and sells high-end vehicles, it learns how to lower costs so it can launch lower-priced models, aiming for a range of 30 EV models by 2025.

Barra insists that time is on the side of GM. Her strategy is a marathon where the company's priority is to develop a platform for EVs and retool factories for making them. These investments should equip GM to expand faster than competitors. Furthermore, in 2021, only about 3% or 4% of cars and trucks sold in the United States were EVs, so all the players are still in early stages. Barra sees GM's size as an advantage. Selling gasoline-powered cars generates profits the company can spend on research and development, efficiency improvements, and talent acquisition, especially in competitive areas of the labor market—software developers, electrical engineers, and electronics technicians.

A key piece of GM's EV strategy is heavy investment in developing a long-lasting, customizable battery. The company spent years developing a modular battery, named Ultium; each Ultium module can be combined with others to create the right battery for any vehicle type—compact cars, pickups, and even commercial trucks. The modular approach is expected to create economies of scale, meaning the cost per unit falls as the number of modules rises, and to cut in half the timeline for developing new models. GM is building factories to produce batteries as it retools vehicle assembly plants. Ultium factories are scheduled to produce batteries for Silverado pickups and Equinox and Blazer SUVs beginning in 2023.

In implementing its strategy, GM faces hurdles that include consumer doubts about EVs, disruptions in supply chains (especially for semiconductors and battery raw materials), and the complexities of engineering good, moderately priced batteries. GM has negotiated large purchase agreements, including several for battery materials sufficient to meet GM's 2025 million-vehicle goal. Challenges also come from GM's competitors—most dramatically Tesla, which has been producing EV batteries already. In addition, Ford outpaced GM in launching an electric pickup truck, the F-150 Lightning, by purchasing batteries from an outside supplier. Still, because batteries are an important and costly feature of an EV, Barra maintains that GM will gain an advantage from its experience with Ultium batteries, eventually cutting battery costs by 30%.

Other factors in GM's business environment are favorable. Demand for EVs is growing rapidly, aided by government policies. In the United States, the Inflation Reduction Act gives companies financial incentives for making batteries and offers consumers tax credits for purchasing EVs. With this support, GM expects it can sell EVs profitably by 2025.

If determined leadership alone could ensure success, the odds would favor GM. Barra has deep industry knowledge, coupled with persistence. Barra first worked for GM as an 18-year-old intern; when she earned her engineering degree, she made her career there. Following her appointment as CEO, she announced that GM's cautious culture would be changing. She pulled GM out of slow-growth, low-profit European markets and didn't let problems with the Bolt dissuade her from pursuing the EV market. During development of the Hummer EV, Barra pressed project managers to cut the time to launch. By yielding to Barra's pressure, the team launched the Hummer EV at about the same time as Rivian introduced an electric truck, so GM remains a contender in the race for EV gold.

Questions for Discussion

1. Is GM's vision to "create a world of zero crashes, zero emissions, and zero congestion" an example of SMART goals? Why or why not?
2. What opportunities and threats is GM facing? What strengths does CEO Mary Barra expect GM can use to address the threats and seize the opportunities?
3. Suppose you are the manager in charge of a new battery production facility at GM. List examples of the kinds of objectives you would need to set so that the facility's accomplishments support GM's vision and corporate strategy. (These can be broad descriptions and need not contain specific numerical targets.)

Sources: General Motors, "Factory ZERO, Our First Fully Dedicated EV Assembly Plant," www.gm.com, accessed January 23, 2023; M. Colias, "GM Outlines Game Plan to Protect Profit in EV Transition," *The Wall Street Journal*, www.wsj.com, November 17, 2022; D. Welch, "Why GM Is Taking the Slow Lane in the EV Race," *Bloomberg Businessweek*, September 26, 2022, 11–13; P. Johnson, "GM Explains Its Electric Vehicle Strategy to Provide 'EVs for Everyone,' Including Pickups, SUVs, Luxury, and Crossovers," *Electrek*, https://electrek.co, September 14, 2022; L. Putre, "GM's Battery Strategy: Finishing Plants, Firming Up Suppliers and Keeping Those Engineers Busy," *Industry Week*, www.industryweek.com, July 26, 2022; J. Trop, "The Electric Car Is Remaking Detroit," *Fortune*, June/July 2022, 127–33; N.E. Boudette, "Mary Barra's 'Long Game': Winning the E.V. Race," *The New York Times*, www.nytimes.com, May 12, 2022.

Notes

1. A. Doyle, "What Marriott's CEO Says About the Prospect of Another Mega-Merger," *Skift*, https://skift.com, accessed January 20, 2023; C. Sperance, "Marriott's New CEO Is Global Development Exec Tony Capuano," *Skift*, https://skift.com, accessed February 24, 2022.
2. Corporate website, "Anthony Capuano," https://news.marriott.com, accessed January 23, 2023; "We Are Marriott International," www.marriott.com, accessed January 23, 2023; "Stephanie Linnartz to Step Down from Marriott International," https://news.marriott.com, December 21, 2022.
3. Sperance, "Marriott's New CEO"; J. Hobson and A. Hagan, "Marriott International CEO Says Business Won't Return to 2019 Levels for 3 Years," *WBUR*, www.wbur.org, September 10, 2020.
4. K. Stankiewicz, "Marriott CEO: Line Between Business and Leisure Is Blurring—That's Good News for Hotels," *CNBC*, www.cnbc.com, May 10, 2021; "Marriott to Double All-Inclusive Portfolio Through Sunwing Agreement," *Hotel Business*, www.hotelbusiness.com, February 9, 2021.
5. L. Najafi, "Marriott Bonvoy Lists Private Vacation Homes to Rent and the Homes Are Spectacular—Here's What to Know about How It Works Plus Our Favorite Rentals," *Business Insider*, www.businessinsider.com, June 17, 2021.
6. A. Hancock, "Marriott Warns of 'Fight for Talent' as Hotels Struggle to Find Staff," *Financial Times*, www.ft.com, September 4, 2021.
7. H. Chipkin, "Hotel Labor Shortage 'Most Significant Challenge,' Says Marriott CEO," *Travel Pulse*, www.travelpulse.com, October 19, 2022; C. Sperance, "Marriott CEO Sees Hotels Bouncing Back Quickly after Delta Variant Slump," *Skift*, https://skift.com, September 9, 2021.
8. "Marriott CEO on Travel Demand, Expanding in China, Hiring Workers (Bloomberg video)," *YouTube*, www.youtube.com, July 14, 2021.
9. A. Chandler, *Strategy and Structure: Chapters in the History of the American Enterprise* (Cambridge, MA: MIT Press, 1962).
10. Nike, "Our Mission," http://about.nike.com, accessed January 23, 2023.
11. Chandler, *Strategy and Structure*.
12. H. Fayol, *General and Industrial Management* (1884; New York: IEEE Press, 1984).
13. S. Banker, "Toilet Paper Shortages, Empty Shelves, and Panic Buying: Just How Bad Was Grocery Store Service in 2020?" *Forbes*, www.forbes.com, October 1, 2021.
14. Fayol, *General and Industrial Management*, 18.
15. "Leadership: Jeffrey L. Harmening," www.generalmills.com, accessed February 20, 2020.
16. General Mills, *2022 Annual Report*, https://investors.generalmills.com, accessed January 23, 2023; T. Wall, "Sales Up 19%, General Mills May Up Dry Pet Food Co-Packing," *Pet Food Industry*, www.petfoodindustry.com, October 3, 2022.
17. Gold Medal Ventures, "Portfolio: 301 Inc.," www.goldmedalventures.com, accessed January 23, 2023; "General Mills Invests $15 Million in Funds for Minority and Female Entrepreneurs," *Business Wire*, www.businesswire.com, April 13, 2022.
18. L. Chevreux, J. Lopez, and X. Mesnard, "The Best Companies Know How to Balance Strategy and Purpose," *Harvard Business Review*, https://hbr.org, November 2, 2017.
19. General Mills, *2022 Annual Report*.
20. General Mills, *2022 Annual Report*.
21. A. Lucas, M. Repko, M. Gilbert, and C.C. Berk, "Walgreens Taps Starbucks Operating Chief Roz Brewer as Its Next CEO," *CNBC*, www.cnbc.com, January 26, 2021.
22. C. Alcorn, "Rosalind Brewer Officially Takes the Helm at Walgreens, Becoming the Only Black Woman Fortune 500 CEO," *CNN Business*, www.cnn.com, March 15, 2021.
23. B. Kowitt, "How Starbucks Got its Buzz Back," *Fortune*, https://fortune.com, accessed January 23, 2023.
24. "Walgreens CEO Roz Brewer to Leaders: Put Your Phones Away and Listen to Employees," *Harvard Business Review*, https://hbr.org, December 9, 2021; B. Japsen, "Walgreens CEO Brewer Begins to Form Her C-Suite," *Forbes*, www.forbes.com, August 21, 2021; B. Japsen, "New Walgreens CEO Sees 'Tech Enabled Healthcare' in Future," *Forbes*, www.forbes.com, July 5, 2021.
25. K. Deighton, "Walgreens Chases Customers It Lost During Covid Focus," *The Wall Street Journal*, www.wsj.com, October 14, 2022.
26. C. Connley, "Walgreen's New CEO Roz Brewer on Bias in the C-Suite: When You're a Black Woman, You Get Mistaken a Lot," *CNBC*, www.cnbc.com, January 27, 2021; S. Terlep, H. Haddon, and S. Nassauer, "Roz Brewer to Bring Pandemic Experience to Walgreens at Pivotal Time," *The Wall Street Journal*, www.wsj.com, January 27, 2021.
27. A. Webb, "How to Do Strategic Planning Like a Futurist," *Harvard Business Review*, https://hbr.org, July 30, 2019; C.W. Hofer and D. Schendel, *Strategy Formulation* (St. Paul, MN: West, 1978).
28. T. Malik, "Perseverance Rover Drops 2nd Sample Tube on Mars, Its Biggest Early Christmas Present Yet for 2033," *Space*, www.space.com, December 23, 2022.
29. J. Andersson, "Ghost in a Shell: The Scenario Tool and the World Making of Royal Dutch Shell," *Business History Review*, vol. 94, no. 4, Winter 2020, 729–51.
30. P. Wack, "Scenarios: Shooting the Rapids," *Harvard Business Review*, November-December 1985, 139–50.
31. "What Are Shell Scenarios?" www.shell.com, accessed January 23, 2023.
32. J.A. Pearce, "The Company Mission as a Strategic Tool," *Sloan Management Review*, Spring 1992, 15–24.
33. D.F. Abell, *Defining the Business: The Starting Point of Strategic Planning* (Englewood Cliffs, NJ: Prentice-Hall, 1980).
34. G. Hamel and C.K. Prahalad, "Strategic Intent," *Harvard Business Review*, May-June 1989, 63–73.
35. D.I. Jung and B.J. Avolio, "Opening the Black Box: An Experimental Investigation of the Mediating Effects of Trust and Value Congruence on Transformational and Transactional Leadership," *Journal of Organizational Behavior*, December 2000, 949–64; B.M. Bass and B.J. Avolio, "Transformational and Transactional Leadership: 1992 and Beyond," *Journal of European Industrial Training*, January 1990, 20–35.
36. Savvy, "Get Inspired by 35 Examples of SMART Goals for Employees," www.savvy.io, accessed January 23, 2023; R. Parnes, "Expert Advice on Setting and Hitting SMART Goals as a Manager," *LinkedIn Learning Blog*, www.linkedin.com, September 26, 2022.
37. General Mills, "Taking Care of Our Planet—from Farm to Fork and Beyond," www.generalmills.com, accessed January 23, 2023.

38. K.R. Andrews, *The Concept of Corporate Strategy* (Homewood, IL: Irwin, 1971).
39. S. Kumar, J. Eiden, and D.N. Perdomo, "Clash of the e-Commerce Titans: A New Paradigm for Consumer Purchase Process Improvement," *International Journal of Productivity and Performance Management* 61, no. 7 (2012), 805–30.
40. P. Wahba, "Walmart to Sell E-Commerce to Smaller Rivals in Latest Challenge to Amazon," *Fortune,* https://fortune.com; July 28, 2021; C.D. Moran, "Study: 59% of US Shoppers See Amazon Go as a Threat to Walmart," *Retail Dive,* March 2, 2021; B. Droesch, "Amazon vs. Walmart: Who's Really Winning Online Grocery?" *eMarketer,* www.emarketer.com, January 27, 2020.
41. M.E. Porter, "How Competitive Forces Shape Strategy," *Harvard Business Review,* March–April 1979.
42. M. Segarra, "Toys R Us and Why the Retail Downturn Is All About Debt," *Marketplace,* www.marketplace.org, March 14, 2018.
43. S. Gardner, "Toys 'R' Us Will Now Be in Every Macy's Store for the Holidays," *Footwear News,* https://footwearnews.com, July 18, 2022; D. Green, "Toys R Us Is Closing or Selling All of Its Stores—Here's Why the Company Couldn't Be Saved," *Business Insider,* www.businessinsider.com, March 15, 2018.
44. R.D. Aveni, *Hypercompetition* (New York: Free Press, 1994).
45. M.E. Porter, *Competitive Strategy* (New York: Free Press, 1980).
46. "About Southwest," https://www.southwest.com, accessed January 23, 2023.
47. S. Grobart, "Tim Cook: The Complete Interview," *Bloomberg Businessweek,* www.bloomberg.com, accessed February 20, 2020.
48. Porter, *Competitive Strategy.*
49. S. Chaudhuri and P. Kowsmann, "Zara Owner Inditex Stays Ahead of the Competition," *The Wall Street Journal,* www.wsj.com, accessed February 20, 2020.
50. H.L. Lee, "How Extreme Agility Put Zara Ahead in Fast Fashion," *Financial Times,* www.ft.com, December 9, 2019.
51. C.B. Tomé, "The CEO of UPS on Taking the Reins Amid Surging Pandemic Demand," *Harvard Business Review,* September-October 2021, 36–39.
52. S. Mehta, "Why UPS CEO Carol Tomé Is Not Worried about Competing with Amazon," *Fast Company,* www.fastcompany.com, September 28, 2021.
53. T. Black, "UPS CEO Solves E-commerce Puzzle with Profit That Wows Investors," *Bloomberg,* https://bloomberg.com, February 1, 2022; D. Gelles, "The CEO of UPS on Voting Rights and Vaccine Delivery," *The New York Times,* www.nytimes.com, June 17, 2021.
54. Gelles, "The CEO of UPS on Voting Rights"; M. Saporta, "Carol Tomé on Becoming CEO of UPS: 'This Was My Calling,'" *Saporta Report,* https://saportareport.com, accessed January 23, 2023.
55. Tomé, "The CEO of UPS on Taking the Reins"; Gelles, "The CEO of UPS on Voting Rights."
56. M.K. Perry, "Vertical Integration: Determinants and Effects," in R. Schmalensee and R.D. Willig, eds., *Handbook of Industrial Organization,* vol. 1 (New York: Elsevier Science, 1989).
57. "Tesla Gigafactory," www.tesla.com, accessed January 23, 2023.
58. R. Klettke, "How Duracell Became Free to Be a Battery Brand," *Sync,* https://syncmagazine.com, accessed February 20, 2020.
59. E. Penrose, *The Theory of the Growth of the Firm* (Oxford: Oxford University Press, 1959).
60. M.E. Porter, "From Competitive Advantage to Corporate Strategy," *Harvard Business Review* 65 (1987), 43–59.
61. Gotham Greens, "Our Story," www.gothamgreens.com, accessed January 23, 2023; R. Gulati, "The Messy but Essential Pursuit of Purpose," *Harvard Business Review,* March-April 2022, 45–52; B.D. Sparks, "Gotham Greens CEO Outlines the Company's Expansion Goals," *Greenhouse Grower,* www.greenhousegrower.com, April 13, 2022.
62. Gotham Greens, "Our Story."
63. Sparks, "Gotham Greens CEO"; B. Heater, "Gotham Greens Just Raised $310 Million to Expand Its Greenhouses Nationwide," *Tech Crunch,* https://techcrunch.com, September 12, 2022.
64. Gulati, "The Messy but Essential Pursuit of Purpose."
65. Sparks, "Gotham Greens CEO."
66. D.J. Teece, "Economies of Scope and the Scope of the Enterprise," *Journal of Economic Behavior and Organization* 3 (1980), 223–47.
67. M.E. Porter, *Competitive Advantage: Creating and Sustaining Superior Performance* (New York: Free Press, 1985).
68. "Business Groups & Roles" and "3M Research & Development," www.3m.com, accessed February 20, 2020; A. Root, "3M's Realignment Could Ease Potential Sales of Divisions," *Barron's,* www.barrons.com, March 18, 2019.
69. A. Park, "3M to Peel Off $8B Healthcare Business into Standalone Public Company," *Fierce Biotech,* www.fiercebiotech.com, July 26, 2022.
70. J. MacLachlan, "This Is the Key to Breakthrough, According to 3M Scientist," *Forbes,* www.forbes.com, April 5, 2022; "Fast Company Names 3M One of 2019's Most Innovative Companies," https://news.3M.com, February 20, 2019.
71. For a review of the evidence, see C.W.L. Hill and G.R. Jones, *Strategic Management,* 5th ed. (Boston: Houghton Mifflin, 2011), Chapter 10.
72. Deloitte, "2022 Global Divestiture Survey," www2deloitte.com, accessed January 23, 2023.
73. M. Chapman, "GE Reveals Identity of 3 Companies after Historic Split," *U.S. News & World Report,* www.usnews.com, July 18, 2022.
74. K. Miller, "A Manager's Guide to Successful Strategy Implementation," *Harvard Business School Insights,* https://online.hbs.edu, accessed January 23, 2023; "What Is Strategy Implementation? (with Steps and Tips)," *Indeed,* www.indeed.com, June 13, 2022.

CHAPTER 9

Value Chain Management: Functional Strategies for Competitive Advantage

Caia Images/Glow Images

Learning Objectives

After studying this chapter, you should be able to:

LO9-1 Explain the role of functional strategy and value chain management in achieving superior quality, efficiency, innovation, and responsiveness to customers.

LO9-2 Describe what customers want, and explain why it is so important for managers to be responsive to their needs.

LO9-3 Explain why achieving superior quality is so important, and understand the challenges facing managers and organizations that seek to implement total quality management.

LO9-4 Explain why achieving superior efficiency is so important, and understand the different kinds of techniques that need to be employed to increase efficiency.

LO9-5 Differentiate between two forms of innovation, and explain why innovation and product development are crucial components of the search for competitive advantage.

A MANAGER'S CHALLENGE

Mattel Adds Value to Stay Relevant

How do managers ensure that activities in their company add value? For Mattel's CEO, Ynon Kreiz, the answer begins with what customers want. Mattel—whose brands include American Girl, Barbie, Fisher-Price, and Hot Wheels, as well as games such as Uno and Pictionary—is making toys and games at a time when more children and adults are seeking their fun online. In recent years, demand for formerly popular items, like Fisher-Price preschool toys and American Girl dolls, has been weak. Upon taking the helm, Kreiz interpreted the company's slumping sales as a sign that Mattel's future would depend on doing two things: making more of what today's consumers want and containing costs while maintaining quality so that the company can remain profitable in a less favorable environment.[1]

Cost containment—that is, efficiency—is essential in a mature market such as toys. Unlike its main competitor, Hasbro, Mattel was operating its own factories, so these operations became an area where efficiency improvements could help the bottom line without reducing product quality. Mattel's management studied the supply chain and identified how it could be simplified, such as by reducing overly complex inventory (150 shades of red paint, for example). Automation, including the creation of an online ordering system for facilities in Europe, has also streamlined work. Information systems make it possible to estimate demand for particular products more accurately.[2]

Product lines are being simplified, eliminating slow-selling items, so not as many factories are needed. Out of more than a dozen factories, Mattel has closed or announced plans to close at least four—in Mexico, China, Indonesia, and Canada. The company also eliminated about one-quarter of its nonmanufacturing workforce to save $150 million a year, meaning the remaining employees will have to work more efficiently to support operations. While employees dread factory closings and layoffs for obvious reasons, Kreiz sees the ethical path as one of communicating clearly and transparently so that employees understand what the plan is and why it is necessary. For the remaining workers, as well as Mattel's investors, he notes that streamlining factory operations has made the company-owned factories a strength, as the factories can quickly change what they produce in response to sales trends.[3]

At the same time, while the toy market overall is mature and slow growing, Kreiz sees opportunity in building excitement with continued innovation, as long as it relates to how children want to play. Kreiz wants the company to move fast in creating new ways for engaging with the company's brands in any format the consumer enjoys—be it a doll, a video game, or a feature-length movie. The company has launched movie

Implementing operational efficiencies has helped Mattel CEO Ynon Kreiz successfully navigate today's turbulent retail industry.
Steven Ferdman/Getty Images

projects with major studios featuring characters such as Barbie and Major Matt Mason. A new video game for mobile devices, called "Hot Wheels: Infinite Loop," takes advantage of the popularity of racing games and has the potential to extend the Hot Wheels brand to older children and teens. Product developers also have created a more diverse line of Barbie dolls and dolls based on the South Korean boy band BTS.[4]

After some shaky quarters under Kreiz, Mattel began to post gains. A major contributor was increased sales for Barbie and Hot Wheels products. International sales got a lift from the BTS dolls. With the greater efficiency, higher sales should translate to higher profits. Stock prices are picking up as investors begin to believe that Mattel is back in the game, despite recent headwinds caused by inflation.[5]

Overview

As "A Manager's Challenge" suggests, organizations must constantly evaluate their business practices in an effort to remain successful. Some organizations may adopt the latest research and methods, while others find different ways to stay competitive.

In this chapter, we focus on the functional-level strategies managers can use to achieve superior efficiency, quality, innovation, and responsiveness to customers and, in doing so, build competitive advantage. We also examine the nature of an organization's value chain and discuss how the combined, or cooperative, efforts of managers across the value chain are required if an organization is to achieve its mission and goal of maximizing the amount of value its products or service provide customers. By the end of this chapter, you will understand the vital role value chain management plays in creating competitive advantage and a high-performing organization.

Functional Strategies, the Value Chain, and Competitive Advantage

LO9-1 Explain the role of functional strategy and value chain management in achieving superior quality, efficiency, innovation, and responsiveness to customers.

As we noted in Chapter 8, managers can use two basic business-level strategies to add value to an organization's products and achieve a competitive advantage over industry rivals. First, managers can pursue a *low-cost strategy* and reduce the costs of creating value to attract customers by keeping product prices as low as or lower than competitors' prices. Second, managers can pursue a *differentiation strategy* and add value to a product by finding ways to make it superior in some way to the products of other companies. If management is successful and customers see greater value in the product, then, like Apple and other top companies, they can charge a premium or higher price for the product. The four specific ways in which managers can lower costs and/or increase differentiation to obtain a competitive advantage were mentioned in Chapter 1 and are reviewed here; how organizations seek to achieve them is the topic of this chapter. (See Figure 9.1.)

1. *Achieve superior efficiency.* Efficiency is a measure of the amount of inputs required to produce a given amount of outputs. The fewer the inputs required to produce a given output, the higher is efficiency and the lower the cost of outputs. For example, Apple has been recognized by Gartner, a U.S. research firm, in the Masters category of its annual rankings for sustained supply chain leadership over the last 10 years. The question remains whether Apple can continue its leadership, as new innovations will be needed from the global tech giant to match its colossal success during the last decade.[6]
2. *Achieve superior quality.* Quality means producing goods and services that have attributes—such as design, styling, performance, and reliability—that customers perceive as being superior to those found in competing products.[7] Providing high-quality products creates a brand-name reputation for an organization's products, and this enhanced reputation allows it to charge higher prices. In the car industry, for example, Toyota's reputation for making reliable vehicles allows it to outperform rival carmakers and gives it a competitive advantage.
3. *Achieve superior innovation, speed, and flexibility.* Anything new or better about the way an organization operates or the goods and services it produces is the result of innovation.

Figure 9.1

Four Ways to Create a Competitive Advantage

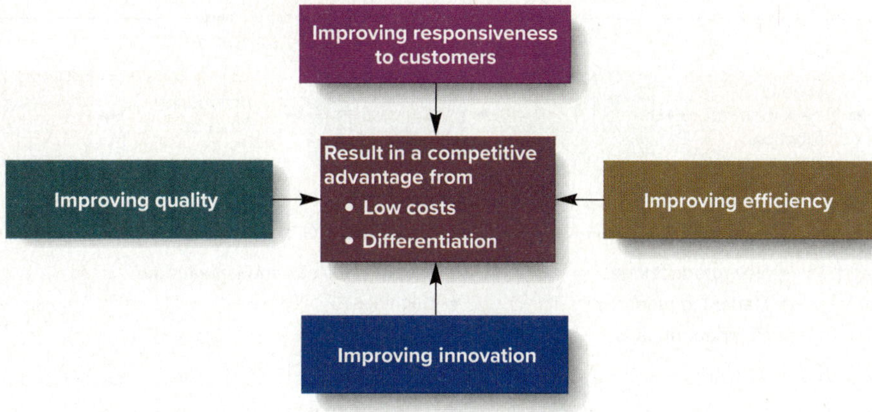

Successful innovation gives an organization something *unique* or different about its products that rivals lack—more attractive, useful, sophisticated products or superior production processes that strengthen its competitive advantage. Innovation adds value to products and allows the organization to further differentiate itself from rivals and attract customers who are often willing to pay a premium price for unique products. For example, Nintendo's competitive advantage in handheld video game devices has completely eroded, now that games are available on mobile devices. The company recently entered the movie industry in an effort to strengthen its overall video content business, announcing that a new film featuring its iconic character Super Mario is under development with Illumination Entertainment, the U.S. animation studio behind the *Despicable Me* film series.[8]

4. *Attain superior responsiveness to customers.* An organization that is responsive to customers tries to satisfy their needs and give them *exactly* what they want. An organization that treats customers better than its rivals do also provides a valuable service some customers may be willing to pay a higher price for. Managers can increase responsiveness by providing excellent after-sales service and support and by working to provide improved products or services to customers in the future. Today smartphone companies such as Samsung, Apple, and Google are searching for ways to better satisfy changing customer needs for higher-quality video, sound, and Internet connection speed.

functional-level strategy A plan of action to improve the ability of each of an organization's functions to perform its task-specific activities in ways that add value to an organization's goods and services.

value chain The coordinated series or sequence of functional activities necessary to transform inputs such as new product concepts, raw materials, component parts, or professional skills into the finished goods or services customers value and want to buy.

value chain management The development of a set of functional-level strategies that support a company's business-level strategy and strengthen its competitive advantage.

Functional Strategies and Value Chain Management

Functional-level strategy is a plan of action to improve the ability of each of an organization's functions or departments (such as manufacturing or marketing) to perform its task-specific activities in ways that add value to an organization's goods and services. A company's **value chain** is the coordinated series or sequence of functional activities necessary to transform inputs such as new product concepts, raw materials, component parts, or professional skills into the finished goods or services customers value and want to buy (see Figure 9.2). Each functional activity along the chain *adds value* to the product when it lowers costs or gives the product differentiated qualities that increase the price a company can charge for it.[9]

Value chain management is the development of a set of functional-level strategies that support a company's business-level strategy and strengthen its competitive advantage. Managers develop the strategies that increase efficiency, quality, innovation, and/or responsiveness to customers and, thus, strengthen an organization's competitive advantage. So the better the fit between functional- and business-level strategies, the greater is the organization's competitive advantage, and the better able the organization is to achieve its mission and goal of maximizing the amount of value it gives customers. Each function along the value chain has an important role to play in value creation.

The concept of a company's value chain has evolved over the years from the broader concept of *operations management,* which is overseeing (or managing) any aspect of the value chain process that transforms inputs into finished goods and services. One important component of

Figure 9.2

Functional Activities and the Value Chain

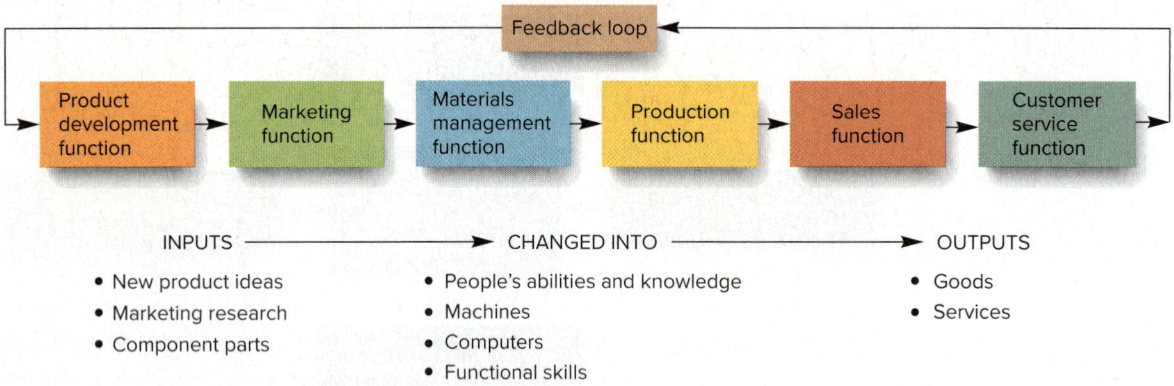

supply chain Network of all individuals, companies, resources, activities, and technology involved in the creation and sale of a product.

the entire process is an organization's supply chain, which is an integral part of the materials management and production functions of the value chain. A **supply chain** is the network of all the individuals, companies, resources, activities, and technology involved in the creation and sale of a product. It includes sourcing raw materials and refining those materials into basic parts or components required to manufacture a product. It is crucial that these items are available to finish the production process in a timely manner.[10]

As Figure 9.2 suggests, the starting point of the value chain is often the search for new and improved products that will better appeal to customers, so the activities of the product development and marketing functions become important. *Product development* is the engineering and scientific research activities involved in innovating new or improved products that add value to a product. For example, Apple has been a leader in developing new kinds of mobile digital devices that have become so popular among buyers that its products are rapidly imitated by its competitors. Once a new product has been developed, the *marketing function's* task is to persuade customers that the product meets their needs and convince them to buy it. Marketing can help create value through brand positioning and advertising that increase customer perceptions of the utility of a company's product. For example, with an aggressive marketing campaign over the last year, online pet retailer Chewy has attracted more than 20 million active clients to its online service.[11]

Even the best-designed product can fail if the marketing function hasn't devised a careful plan to persuade people to buy it and try it out–or to make sure customers really want it. For this reason, marketing often conducts consumer research to discover unmet customer product needs and to find better ways to tailor existing products to satisfy customer needs. As digital technology continues to advance, this research now includes collecting massive amounts of consumer data to enhance marketing activities. Marketing then presents its suggestions to product development, which performs its own research to discover how best to design and make the new or improved products.

At the next stage of the value chain, the *materials management function* controls the movement of physical materials from the procurement of inputs through production and to distribution and delivery to the customer. (This is the first of two stages where the supply chain is critical.) The efficiency with which this is carried out can significantly lower costs and create more value. Walmart has the most efficient materials management function in the retail industry. By tightly controlling the flow of goods from suppliers via its global supply chain through its stores and into the hands of customers, Walmart has eliminated the need to hold large inventories of goods. Lower inventories mean lower costs and hence greater value creation.

The *production function* is responsible for creating, assembling, or providing a good or service–for transforming inputs into outputs. (This is the second stage of the process where a company's supply chain is a key component.) For physical products, when we talk about production, we generally mean manufacturing and assembly. For services such as banking or retailing, production takes place when the service is actually provided or delivered to the customer (for example, when a bank originates a loan for a customer, it is engaged in "production" of the loan). By performing its activities efficiently and making sure critical components and raw materials are on hand, the production function helps to lower costs. For example, the efficient production operations of

Honda and Toyota have made them more profitable than competitors such as Volkswagen and Chrysler. The production function can also perform its activities in a way that is consistent with high product quality, which leads to differentiation (and higher value) and to lower costs.

At the next stage in the value chain, the *sales function* plays a crucial role in locating customers and then informing and persuading them to buy the company's products. Personal selling—that is, direct face-to-face communication by salespeople with existing and potential customers to promote a company's products—is a crucial value chain activity. Which products retailers choose to stock, for example, or which drugs doctors choose to prescribe often depends on the salesperson's ability to inform and persuade customers that their company's product is superior and, thus, the best choice.

Finally, the role of the *customer service function* is to provide after-sales service and support. This function can create a perception of superior value in the minds of customers by solving customer problems and supporting customers after they have purchased the product. For example, UPS can get its customers' parcels to any point in the world within 24 hours, creating value and support for customers' businesses. Customer service controls the electronic systems for tracking sales and inventory, pricing products, selling products, dealing with customer inquiries, and so on, all of which can greatly increase responsiveness to customers. Indeed, an important activity of sales and customer service is to tell product development and marketing why a product is meeting or not meeting customers' needs so the product can be redesigned or improved. Hence, a feedback loop links the end of the value chain to its beginning (see Figure 9.2).

Value Chain Analysis

After identifying the components of its value chain, a company needs to analyze how the value chain is working to meet overall business goals. In his 1985 book, *Competitive Advantage,* management expert Michael Porter described the various components of a company or business, how they are organized, and how they form a value chain. Porter theorized that companies should set up their value chains and link them to the achievement of strategic objectives. In addition, Porter broke down the value chain into primary and support activities. Primary activities directly contribute to the making of a product or service—for example, logistics, operations, marketing, sales, and service. He defined support activities as factors that contribute to creating value but are not directly linked to a product or service—for example, company infrastructure, evolving technology, and human resource management. Porter suggested that once these activities were identified and categorized as primary or support factors, a company could determine which activities provided the most value to the organization and which ones needed to be modified to help meet company objectives.[12]

Using its value chain as a diagnostic tool can provide several benefits to an organization, including increased efficiency, reduced costs, and strengthened collaboration between various functional activities, creating even greater value for the firm.[13] As smart technologies continue to evolve and impact business operations, some researchers suggest that companies must rethink and retool their value chains to maintain competitive advantage in their respective industries.[14]

In the rest of this chapter, we examine the functional strategies used to manage the value chain to improve quality, efficiency, innovation, and responsiveness to customers. Notice, however, that achieving superior quality, efficiency, and innovation is *part* of attaining superior responsiveness to customers. Customers want value for their money, and managers who develop functional strategies that result in a value chain capable of creating innovative, high-quality, low-cost products best deliver this value to customers. For this reason, we begin by discussing how functional managers can increase responsiveness to customers.

Improving Responsiveness to Customers

All organizations produce outputs—goods or services—that are consumed by customers, who, in buying these products, provide the monetary resources most organizations need to survive. Because customers are vital to organizational survival, managers must correctly identify their customers and pursue strategies that result in products that best meet their needs. This is why the marketing function plays such an important part in the value chain, and good value chain management requires that marketing managers focus on defining their company's business in terms of the customer *needs* it is satisfying, not by the *type of products* it makes–or the result can be disaster.[15] For example, Kodak's managers said "no thanks" when the company was offered the rights to "instant photography," which was later marketed by Polaroid. Why did they make this mistake? Because the managers adopted a product-oriented approach to their business that didn't put the needs of customers first. Kodak's managers believed their job was to sell high-quality glossy photographs to people. Why would they want to become involved in instant photography, which results in inferior-quality photographs? In reality, Kodak was not satisfying people's needs for high-quality photographs; it was satisfying the need customers had to *capture and record the images of their lives*–their birthday parties, weddings, graduations, and so on. And people wanted those images quickly so they could share them right away with other people, eventually via their mobile devices. This is why digital photography became the norm and Kodak filed for bankruptcy in 2012.[16]

What Do Customers Want?

LO9-2 Describe what customers want, and explain why it is so important for managers to be responsive to their needs.

Given that satisfying customer demand is central to the survival of an organization, an important question is, "What do customers want?" Although specifying *exactly* what customers want is not possible because their needs vary from product to product, most customers prefer

1. A lower price to a higher price.
2. High-quality products to low-quality products.
3. Quick service and good after-sales service to slow service and poor after-sales support.
4. Products with many useful or valuable features to products with few features.
5. Products that are, as far as possible, customized to their unique needs.

artificial intelligence (AI) Capability of a machine to imitate intelligent human behavior.

To meet those preferences, managers seek data about customers' definitions of high quality and good service, so they can correct any problems and offer what is most valued. To gather such information, more and more companies have turned to **artificial intelligence (AI)** to improve the probability of a successful customer experience. AI can be defined as the capability of a machine to imitate intelligent human behavior, and it has already made it possible to write programs that can solve problems and perform tasks previously handled by humans (see the "Management Insight" feature.)[17] We discuss AI in more detail in Chapter 18.

MANAGEMENT INSIGHT

Using AI to Improve Customer Experiences

Great customer experiences require knowledge of what determines their success. For instance, can customers get their questions answered on the first try? Can they schedule a service call in five minutes or less? Artificial intelligence has potential to improve such experiences, thereby retaining customers and enhancing revenues, often at lower costs to companies. Furthermore, AI can continuously improve the quality of its output by incorporating data from each new transaction. Companies using AI have reported revenue increases of more than 6%, with much of that attributable to personalization.[18]

AI is improving performance across industries. Levi's uses it to personalize online shoppers' experiences, and Johnson & Johnson uses it to give salespeople recommendations for the next action to take during a customer interaction. Brinks Home, which provides smart-home technology, daily tests thousands of possible service scheduling and product recommendations, using test results to personalize customer interactions and improve revenue performance. Comcast logs each customer interaction, including its timing and outcome, using the data to identify poor experiences for the company to correct.[19]

A familiar AI application is chatbots, which use natural language processing to interpret and reply to questions. So far, most chatbots use a text format, but voice functionality is improving. Early chatbots could be frustrating to consumers because they merely served up canned responses linked to a list of possible questions. Aided by AI and larger databases, chatbots are improving. GM's chatbot, Nanci, originally resolved less than 10% of questions from customers, but its AI system "learned" from these experiences, recently attaining a success rate of 60%.[20]

For AI to improve customer experience, it needs sufficient data, appropriate processes, and motivated employees. As much as possible, data should provide a "360-degree view" of customers, with information about their journey from discovering a need to gathering information, weighing alternatives, making a purchase, using the product, and seeking additional product support or service. Processes that rely on AI should put customers first, and the objectives for AI should be realistic–for example, related to the available data. Finally, managers need to consider human factors when implementing AI systems. Employees are more receptive when an AI system handles boring tasks or reconfigures their work to make their role at least as valued as when humans handled customer experiences based on their own wits.[21]

Managers know that the more desired product attributes a company's value chain builds into its products, the higher the price that must be charged to cover the costs of developing and making the product. So what do managers of a customer-responsive organization do? They try to develop functional strategies that allow the organization's value chain to deliver to customers either *more* desired product attributes for the *same price* or the *same* product attributes for a *lower price*.[22] For example, Costco, famously known for its tasty and inexpensive rotisserie chicken, opened its own chicken processing plant in Nebraska in an effort to keep costs in check, while providing the same tasty chicken to its customers. In a recent year, Costco sold 100 million chickens to its loyal shoppers–double the number from a decade earlier.[23]

Managing the Value Chain to Increase Responsiveness to Customers

Because satisfying customers is so important, managers try to design and improve the way their value chains operate so they can supply products or services that have the desired attributes–quality, cost, and features. For example, the need to respond to customer demand for competitively priced, quality cars drove U.S. carmakers like Ford and GM to imitate Japanese companies and copy how Toyota and Honda perform their value chain activities. Today the imperative of satisfying customer needs shapes the activities of U.S. carmakers' materials management and manufacturing functions. As an example of the link between responsiveness to customers and an organization's value chain, consider how Southwest Airlines, one of the most profitable U.S. airlines, operates.[24]

Southwest Airlines' operating system is geared toward satisfying customer demand for low-priced, reliable, and convenient air travel, making it one of the most consistently successful airlines in recent years.
Justin Sullivan/Getty Images

The major reason for Southwest's success is that it has pursued functional strategies that improve how its value chain operates to give customers what they want. Southwest commands high customer loyalty precisely because it can deliver products, such as flights from Houston to Dallas, that have all the desired attributes: reliability, convenience, and low price. In each of its functions, Southwest's strategies revolve around finding ways to lower costs. For example, Southwest offers a no-frills approach to in-flight customer service: No meals are served onboard, and there are no first-class seats. Southwest does not subscribe to the big reservation systems used by travel agents because the booking fees are too costly. Also, the airline flies only one aircraft, the fuel-efficient Boeing 737, which keeps training and maintenance costs down. All this translates into low prices for customers. Additionally, Southwest is one of the few airlines that does not charge baggage fees. Passengers can check two bags for free.[25]

Southwest's reliability derives from the fact that it has the quickest aircraft turnaround time in the industry. A Southwest ground crew needs only 15 minutes to turn around an incoming aircraft and prepare it for departure. This speedy operation helps keep flights on time. Southwest has such a quick turnaround because it has a flexible workforce that has been cross-trained to perform multiple tasks. Thus, the person who checks tickets might also help with baggage loading if time is short.

Southwest's convenience comes from its scheduling multiple flights every day between its popular locations, such as Dallas and Houston, and its use of airports that are close to downtown areas (Hobby at Houston and Love Field at Dallas) instead of using more distant major airports.[26] In sum, Southwest's excellent value chain management has given it a competitive advantage in the airline industry over the past decade.

Although managers must seek to improve their responsiveness to customers by improving how the value chain operates, they should not offer a level of responsiveness to customers that results in costs becoming *too high*—something that threatens an organization's future performance and survival. For example, a company that customizes every product to the unique demands of individual customers is likely to see its costs grow out of control and possibly lead to its demise.

Customer Relationship Management

customer relationship management (CRM) A technique that uses technology to develop an ongoing relationship with customers to maximize the value an organization can deliver to them over time.

One functional strategy managers can use to get close to customers and understand their needs is **customer relationship management (CRM)**. CRM is a technique that uses technology to develop an ongoing relationship with customers to maximize the value an organization can deliver to them over time. By the 2000s, most large companies had installed sophisticated CRM systems to track customers' changing demands for a company's products; this became a vital tool to maximize responsiveness to customers. CRM systems monitor, control, and link each of the functional activities involved in marketing, selling, and delivering products to customers, such as monitoring the delivery of products through the distribution channel, monitoring salespeople's selling activities, setting product pricing, and coordinating after-sales service. CRM systems have three interconnected components: sales and selling, after-sales service and support, and marketing.

Suppose a sales manager has access only to sales data that show the total sales revenue each salesperson generated in the last 30 days. This information does not break down how much revenue came from sales to existing customers versus sales to new customers. What important knowledge is being lost? First, if most revenues are earned from sales to existing customers, this suggests that the money being spent by a company to advertise and promote its products is not attracting new customers and so is being wasted. Second, important dimensions involved in sales are pricing, financing, and order processing. In many companies, to close a deal, a salesperson has to send the paperwork to a central sales office, which handles matters such as approving the customer for special financing and determining specific shipping and delivery dates. In some companies, different departments handle these activities, and it can take a long time to get a response from them; this keeps customers waiting—something that often leads to lost sales. Until CRM systems were introduced, these kinds of problems were widespread and resulted in missed sales and higher operating costs. Today the sales and selling CRM software contains *best sales practices* that analyze this information and then recommend ways to improve how the sales process operates.

Implementing a CRM system has helped Adidas improve its sales and customer service practices across the globe.
Sorbis/Shutterstock

One company that has improved its sales and customer service practices by implementing CRM is global athletic retailer, Adidas. The CRM system has enabled Adidas to transform its sales and customer service approach from a slower, brick-and-mortar focus to an agile online platform customized for the consumer experience. Through the Adidas website, the global brand now offers premium, connected, and personalized experiences delivered by more than 1,100 Adidas "care agents," in a variety of formats–via phone, email, web, or social media–all from a single CRM application. The system allows the care agents to have one view of each Adidas customer and their preferences, tastes, and shopping experience, which allows for agility, speed, and a customized connection to each consumer. In addition, the customer service process becomes more efficient because all customer service agents have access to the same information. The principal benefit of using this CRM approach is that it takes all the guesswork out of accessing key consumer information and data points, allowing customer service agents to focus more on creating a brand experience that will have consumers making more Adidas purchases because of their experience with the company and its front-facing staff.[27]

When a company implements after-sales service and support CRM software, salespeople are required to input detailed information about their follow-up visits to customers. Because the system tracks and documents every customer's case history, salespeople have instant access to a record of everything that occurred during previous phone calls or visits. They are in a much better position to respond to customers' needs and build customer loyalty, so a company's after-sales service improves. For example, cellular service companies, like T-Mobile, require that telephone sales reps collect information about all customers' inquiries, complaints, and requests, and this is recorded electronically in customer logs. The CRM module can analyze the information in these logs to evaluate whether the customer service reps are meeting or exceeding the company's required service standards.

A CRM system can also identify the top 10 reasons for customer complaints. Sales managers can then work to eliminate the sources of these problems and improve after-sales support procedures. The CRM system also identifies the top 10 best service and support practices, which can then be shared with all sales reps.

Finally, as a CRM system processes information about changing customer needs, this improves marketing in many ways. Marketing managers, for example, have access to detailed customer profiles, including data about purchases and the reasons people were or were not attracted to a company's products. Armed with this knowledge, marketing can better identify customers and the specific product attributes they want. Traditional CRM systems were organized by having salespeople input customer information. Now CRM systems can track customers on social media and put them on a company's radar. For example, if a Twitter user posts often about a topic relevant to the company or about the company's product, a CRM system can bring the user to the attention of the company as an important connection, possible influencer, or potential customer.[28] In sum, a CRM system is a comprehensive method of gathering crucial information and data about how customers respond to a company's products. It is a powerful functional strategy used to align a company's products with customer needs.

Improving Quality

LO9-3 Explain why achieving superior quality is so important, and understand the challenges facing managers and organizations that seek to implement total quality management.

As noted earlier, high-quality products have attributes such as superior design, features, reliability, and after-sales support; these products are designed to better meet customer requirements.[29] Quality is a concept that can be applied to the products of both manufacturing and service organizations–goods such as an Apple mobile device or services such as customer service in a Citibank branch. Why do managers seek to control and improve the quality of their organizations' products?[30] There are two reasons (see Figure 9.3).

First, customers usually prefer a higher-quality product to a lower-quality product. So an organization able to provide, *for the same price,* a product of higher quality than a competitor's product is serving its customers better–it is being more responsive to its customers. Often providing high-quality products creates a brand-name reputation for an organization's products. This enhanced reputation may allow the organization to charge more for its products than its competitors can charge, and thus it makes greater profits. For example, in 2022 Lexus won the J. D. Power dependability award for its quality, reliability, and resale value, beating out vehicles from Mercedes-Benz and Volvo.[31] The high quality of Lexus vehicles enables the company to charge higher prices for its cars than the prices charged by rival carmakers.

The second reason for trying to boost product quality is that higher product quality can increase efficiency and thereby lower operating costs and boost profits. Achieving high product quality lowers operating costs because of the effect of quality on employee productivity: Higher

Figure 9.3

The Impact of Increased Quality on Organizational Performance

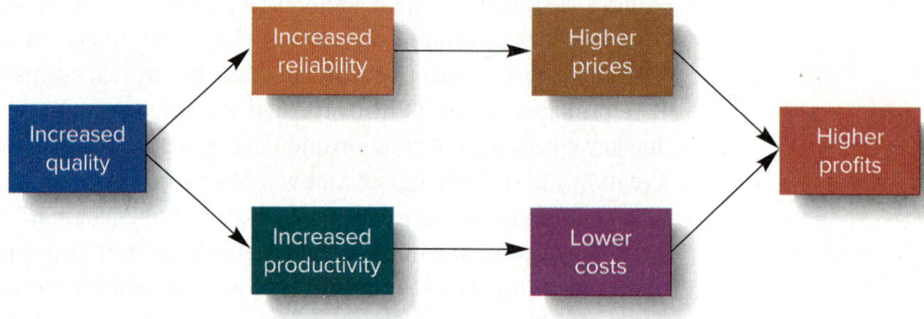

product quality means less employee time is wasted in making defective products that must be discarded or in providing substandard services; thus, less time has to be spent fixing mistakes. This translates into higher employee productivity, which also means lower costs.

Both kinds of quality benefits emerge when companies apply the various management lessons described throughout this book. For example, organizations achieve quality improvements when they hire talented people, lead them in the right direction, and motivate them to contribute, innovate, and excel. Organizations are also coming to realize that diversity, equity, inclusion, and a sense of belonging contribute to a creative environment in which quality flourishes. The "Focus on DEI&B" feature describes how Genentech is applying this principle.

FOCUS ON DEI&B

Genentech Sets Diversity Goals to Improve Research

Genentech, a biotechnology company that now operates independently as a subsidiary of Roche, focuses on discovering and developing new medicines. The company has literally written diversity into its mission statement: "Our mission is to deliver scientific innovations that drive better outcomes for our people, patients, business, and communities by advancing and boldly championing diversity, equity, and inclusion."[32] Key reasons are that management sees a diverse, included workforce as likely to bring new ideas and, furthermore, that serving diverse patient populations will result in more rigorous research.[33]

Genentech management believes that diversity, equity, and inclusion are so important that they have included these goals in the company's mission statement.
Pressmaster/Shutterstock

Like many other companies today, Genentech seeks to build, retain, and develop a diverse workforce. The company sets targets for diversity and inclusion; among these is doubling the number of Black and Latinx directors and top management. It also regularly updates senior leaders on performance and recently began publishing an annual Diversity & Inclusion Report to make Genentech's progress a matter of public record. Quita Highsmith, Genentech's chief diversity officer, explains that the process begins with recruiting and hiring diverse talent and then providing training, development, and career paths. Genentech's Future of Working initiative allows flexible working arrangements, whose objectives include retaining diverse employees.[34]

Genentech sets itself apart in also having DE&I goals to improve the quality of its research data. In a policy the company calls Advancing Inclusive Research, Genentech seeks to address the issue that clinical trials do not always succeed at–or even try to–recruit a diverse population. For a company that, like Genentech, applies genetic data, this means that work on medicines relies on data that reflects only a segment of the world's population. Genentech therefore is reexamining its practices for selecting study sites and identifying ways to recruit study participants more broadly in terms of race, ethnicity, and gender. For example, it recruits more participants from outside Europe and North America, so that the percentage of white participants has fallen from more than 90% to around 75% or less. In addition, the company's efforts to diversify its workforce and suppliers contribute to more diverse research data by improving the company's reputation among people of color, whose relatively low participation in research is partly an outcome of lower-than-average trust of the pharmaceutical industry. The goal of all these efforts is an improved product line: treatments that can be personalized to reflect knowledge about how different kinds of people respond.[35]

Total Quality Management

total quality management (TQM) A management technique that focuses on improving the quality of an organization's products and services.

At the forefront of the drive to improve product quality is a functional strategy known as total quality management.[36] **Total quality management (TQM)** focuses on improving the quality of an organization's products and stresses that *all* of an organization's value chain activities should be directed toward this goal. TQM requires the cooperation of managers in every function of an organization and across functions.[37] To show how TQM works, we next describe the way that Citibank used the technique. Then, using Citibank as an example, we look at the 10 steps that are necessary for managers to implement a successful TQM program.

In the 2000s, Citibank's top managers decided the bank could retain and expand its customer base only if it could increase customer loyalty, so they decided to implement a TQM program to better satisfy customer needs. As the first step in its TQM effort, Citibank identified the factors that dissatisfy its customers. When analyzing the complaints, it found that most concerned the time it took to complete a customer's request, such as responding to an account problem or getting a loan. So Citibank's managers began to examine how they handled each kind of customer request. For each distinct request, they formed a cross-functional team that broke down the request into the steps required, between people and departments, to complete the response. In analyzing the steps, teams found that many of them were unnecessary and could be replaced by using the right information systems. They also found that delays often occurred because employees did not know how to handle a request. They were not being given the right kind of training, and when they couldn't handle a request, they simply put it aside until a supervisor could deal with it.

Citibank's second step to increase its responsiveness was to implement an organizationwide TQM program. Managers and supervisors were charged with reducing the complexity of the work process and finding the most effective way to process each request, such as a customer's request for a loan. Managers were also charged with training employees to answer each specific request. The results were remarkable. For example, in the loan department the TQM program reduced by 75% the number of handoffs necessary to process a request. The department's average response time dropped from several hours to 30 minutes. What are the 10 steps in TQM that made this possible?

1. *Build organizational commitment to quality.* TQM will do little to improve the performance of an organization unless all employees embrace it, and this often requires a change in an organization's culture.[38] At Citibank, the process of changing culture began at the top. First, a group of top managers, including the CEO, received training in TQM from consultants from Motorola, where Six Sigma was founded (Six Sigma is trademarked by Motorola).[39] Each member of the top management group was then given the responsibility of training a group at the next level in the hierarchy, and so on down through the organization until all 100,000 employees had received basic TQM training.
2. *Focus on the customer.* TQM practitioners see a focus on the customer as the starting point.[40] According to TQM philosophy, the customer, not managers in quality control or engineering,

defines what quality is. The challenge is fourfold: (a) to identify what customers want from the good or service that the company provides, (b) to identify what the company actually provides to customers, (c) to identify any gap between what customers want and what they actually get (the quality gap), and (d) to formulate a plan for closing the quality gap. The efforts of Citibank managers to increase responsiveness to customers illustrate this aspect of TQM well.

3. *Find ways to measure quality.* Another crucial element of TQM is the development of a measuring system that managers can use to evaluate quality. Devising appropriate measures is relatively easy in manufacturing companies, where quality can be measured by criteria such as defects per million parts. It is more difficult in service companies, where outputs are less tangible. However, with a little creativity, suitable quality measures can be devised as they were by managers at Citibank. Citibank used customer satisfaction surveys as quality measures and defined a defect as any rating below the two highest ratings.[41]
4. *Set goals and create incentives.* Once a measure has been devised, managers' next step is to set a challenging quality goal and to create incentives for reaching that goal. At Citibank, the CEO set an initial goal of reducing customer complaints by 50%. One way of creating incentives to attain a goal is to link rewards, such as bonus pay and promotional opportunities, to the goal.
5. *Solicit input from employees.* Employees are a major source of information about the causes of poor quality, so it is important that managers establish a system for soliciting employee suggestions about improvements that can be made. At most companies, like Citibank, this is an ongoing endeavor—the process never stops.
6. *Identify defects and trace them to their source.* A major source of product defects is the production system; a major source of service defects is poor customer service procedures. TQM preaches the need for managers to identify defects in the work process, trace those defects back to their source, find out why they occurred, and make corrections so they do not occur again. Today technology makes quality measurement much easier.

inventory The stock of raw materials, inputs, and component parts that an organization has on hand at a particular time.

just-in-time (JIT) inventory system A system in which parts or supplies arrive at an organization when they are needed, not before.

7. *Introduce just-in-time inventory systems.* **Inventory** is the stock of raw materials, inputs, and component parts that an organization has on hand at a particular time. When the materials management function designs a **just-in-time (JIT) inventory system**, parts or supplies arrive at the organization when they are needed, not before. Also, under a JIT inventory system, defective parts enter an organization's operating system immediately; they are not warehoused for months before use. This means defective inputs can be quickly spotted. JIT is discussed more later in the chapter.
8. *Work closely with suppliers.* A major cause of poor-quality finished goods is poor-quality component parts. To decrease product defects, materials managers must work closely with suppliers to improve the quality of the parts they supply. Managers at Xerox worked closely with suppliers to get them to adopt TQM programs, and the result was a huge reduction in the defect rate of component parts. Managers also need to work closely with suppliers to get them to adopt a JIT inventory system, also required for high quality.
9. *Design for ease of production.* The more steps required to assemble a product or provide a service, the more opportunities there are for making mistakes. It follows that designing products that have fewer parts or finding ways to simplify providing a service should be linked to fewer defects or customer complaints. For example, Apple continually redesigns the way it assembles its mobile devices to reduce the number of assembly steps required, and it constantly searches for new ways to reduce the number of components that have to be linked together. The consequence of these redesign efforts was a continuous fall in assembly costs and marked improvement in product quality during the 2000s. At Citibank, defect detection and resolution lead to better performance in process time, cash management, and customer satisfaction.[42]
10. *Break down barriers between functions.* Successful implementation of TQM requires substantial cooperation between the different value chain functions. Materials managers have to cooperate with manufacturing managers to find high-quality inputs that reduce manufacturing costs; marketing managers have to cooperate with manufacturing so that customer problems identified by marketing can be acted on; information systems have to cooperate with all other functions of the company to devise suitable technology training programs; and so on. At Citibank, a cross-functional process mapping method was used to describe the functions involved in each step of a process flow.[43]

In essence, to increase quality, all functional managers need to cooperate to develop goals and spell out exactly how they will be achieved. Managers should embrace the philosophy that mistakes, defects, and poor-quality materials are not acceptable and should be eliminated. Functional managers should spend more time working with employees and providing them with the tools they need to do the job. Managers should create an environment in which employees will not be afraid to report problems or recommend improvements. Output goals and targets need to include not only numbers or quotas but also some indicators of quality to promote the production of defect-free output. Functional managers also need to train employees in new skills to keep pace with changes in the workplace. Finally, achieving better quality requires that managers develop organizational values and norms centered on improving quality.

Six Sigma A technique used to improve quality by systematically improving how value chain activities are performed and then using statistical methods to measure the improvement.

SIX SIGMA One TQM technique called **Six Sigma** has gained increasing popularity in the last decade, particularly because of the well-publicized success GE enjoyed as a result of implementing it across its operating divisions. The goal of Six Sigma is to improve a company's quality to only three defects per million by systematically altering the way all the processes involved in value chain activities are performed, and then carefully measuring how much improvement has been made using statistical methods. Six Sigma shares with TQM its focus on improving value chain processes to increase quality, but it differs because TQM emphasizes top-down organizationwide employee involvement, whereas the Six Sigma approach is to create teams of expert change agents, known as "green belts and black belts," to take control of the problem-finding and problem-solving process and then to train other employees in implementing solutions.

Improving Efficiency

The third goal of value chain management is to increase the efficiency of the various functional activities. The fewer the input resources required to produce a given volume of output, the higher will be the efficiency of the operating system. So efficiency is a useful measure of how well an organization uses all its resources–such as labor, capital, materials, or energy–to produce its outputs, or goods and services.

LO9-4 Explain why achieving superior efficiency is so important, and understand the different kinds of techniques that need to be employed to increase efficiency.

Developing functional strategies to improve efficiency is an extremely important issue for managers because increased efficiency lowers production costs, which lets an organization make a greater profit or attract more customers by lowering its prices. In this way, added value flows to the organization and its customers. Several important strategies are discussed in this section. As you read them, keep in mind that pursuit of efficiency also raises ethical questions such as those discussed in the "Ethics in Action" feature. Consider how companies can pursue efficiency in ways that meet standards of justice; the answers may be complex but can help create the kind of value that sustains the company over the long run.

ETHICS IN ACTION

Does Efficiency Hurt People—and Companies?

Clearly, efficiency is good; you can do more with less, so prosperity increases. But can you have too much of a good thing? Some argue yes because of how prosperity tends to be distributed. Take the case of worker productivity in the United States. During the 1950s and 1970s, productivity rose, and hourly pay rose at about the same rate. The more productive workers were, the more they earned. But from 1970 to 2018, productivity continued its upward trend while hourly pay leveled off.[44] Workers continued getting more productive, but the rewards went elsewhere. From an ethical standpoint, this raises the question of fairness.

Another ethical perspective is to consider who is helped or harmed by efficiency gains. Efficiency gains can generate more and better jobs, but in today's technological environment, automation and artificial intelligence are getting work done faster and more accurately with less human input. Consequently, greater efficiency often eliminates jobs today—especially when organizations seek efficiency by looking only at the immediate cost savings. Managers do have the option to consider the impact on people. For example, when Marlin Steel introduced automation, it also trained its employees in skills needed for working in a highly automated facility, so they could keep their jobs.[45]

Retired professor Roger Martin offers a third and broader perspective. Martin suggests that overemphasizing efficiency damages society as a whole.[46] He notes that in business, successes are not randomly distributed. Rather, a successful company gains resources to dominate and eliminate competitors. Eventually, over time, industries are concentrated in the hands of fewer and fewer companies. While this might seem fair, the resulting situation is unstable. Consider a highly efficient retailer, Amazon. What if it succeeds so well that it becomes the only retailer? Then if a crisis hits the sole retailer—say, its payment system crashes—consumers have nowhere to shop.

In Martin's view, the corrective action to this kind of risk is for businesses to seek resilience. A resilient business and a resilient industry have two qualities that efficiency tries to eliminate: redundancy and slack. An example of a resilient business is a store with adequate resources for handling unexpected shocks to the system (say, enough employees to help unhappy customers or enough inventory to get through a natural disaster). Resilience might sacrifice some efficiency in the short term but positions companies for long-term survival and a favorable reputation among its existing and prospective customers.

Facilities Layout, Flexible Manufacturing, and Efficiency

The strategies managers use to lay out or design an organization's physical work facilities also determine its efficiency. First, the way in which machines and workers are organized or grouped together into workstations affects the efficiency of the operating system. Second, a major determinant of efficiency is the cost associated with setting up the equipment needed to make a particular product. **Facilities layout** is the strategy of designing the machine–worker interface to increase operating system efficiency. **Flexible manufacturing** is a strategy based on the use of technology to reduce the costs associated with the product assembly process or the way services are delivered to customers. For example, this might be how computers are made on a production line or how patients are routed through a hospital.

facilities layout The strategy of designing the machine–worker interface to increase operating system efficiency.

flexible manufacturing The set of techniques that attempt to reduce the costs associated with the product assembly process or the way services are delivered to customers.

FACILITIES LAYOUT The way in which machines, robots, and people are grouped together affects how productive they can be. Figure 9.4 shows three basic ways of arranging workstations: product layout, process layout, and fixed-position layout.

In a *product layout,* machines are organized so that each operation needed to manufacture a product or process a patient is performed at workstations arranged in a fixed sequence. In manufacturing, workers are stationary in this arrangement, and a moving conveyor belt takes the product being worked on to the next workstation so that it is progressively assembled. Mass production is the familiar name for this layout; car assembly lines are probably the best-known example. It used to be that product layout was efficient only when products were created in large quantities; however, the introduction of modular assembly lines controlled by computers is making it efficient to make products in small batches.

In a *process layout,* workstations are not organized in a fixed sequence. Rather, each workstation is relatively self-contained, and a product goes to whichever workstation is needed to perform the next operation to complete the product. Process layout is often suited to manufacturing settings that produce a variety of custom-made products, each tailored to the needs of a different kind of customer. For example, a custom furniture manufacturer might use a process

Figure 9.4

Three Facilities Layouts

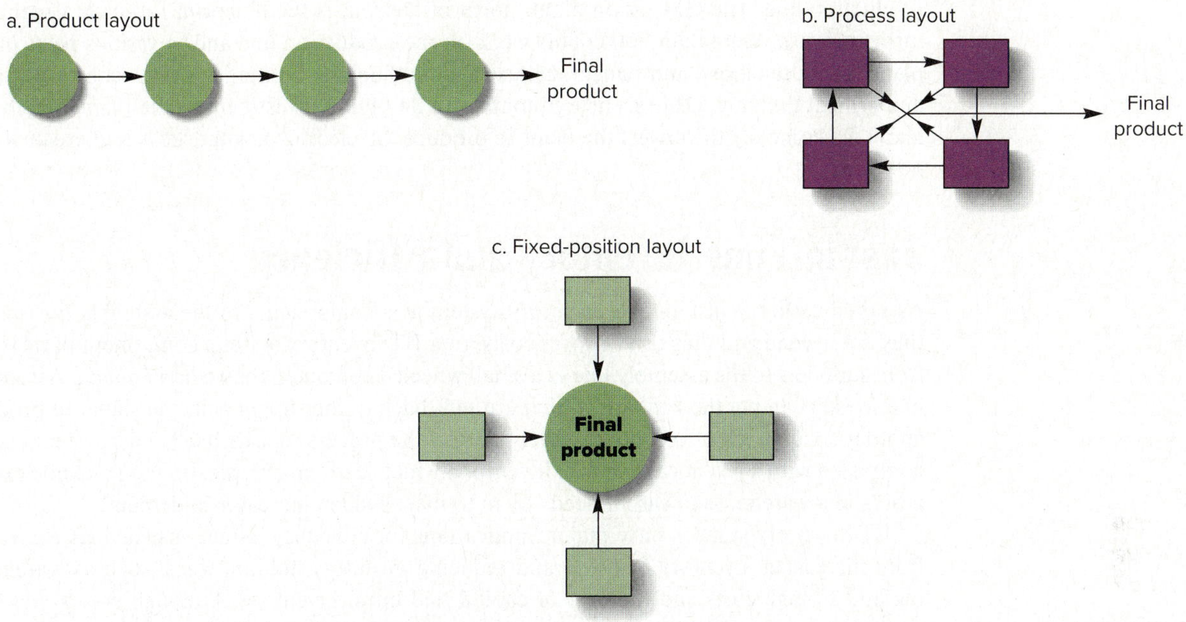

layout so different teams of workers can produce different styles of chairs or tables made from different kinds of woods and finishes. Such a layout also describes how a patient might go through a hospital from emergency room to X-ray room, to operating room, and so on. A process layout provides the flexibility needed to change a product, whether it is a mobile device or a patient's treatment. Such flexibility, however, often reduces efficiency because it is expensive.

In a *fixed-position layout,* the product stays in a fixed position. Its component parts are produced in remote workstations and brought to the production area for final assembly. Increasingly, self-managed teams are using fixed-position layouts. Different teams assemble each component part and then send the parts to the final assembly team, which makes the final product. A fixed-position layout is commonly used for products such as jet airliners, mainframe computers, and gas turbines–products that are complex and difficult to assemble or so large that moving them from one workstation to another would be difficult. Regardless of the layout, facilities need to be designed with efficiency in mind.

FLEXIBLE MANUFACTURING In a manufacturing company, a major source of costs is setting up the equipment needed to make a particular product. One of these costs is that of forgone production because nothing is produced while the equipment is being set up. For example, component manufacturers often need as much as half a day to set up automated production equipment when switching from production of one component part (such as a washer ring for the steering column of a car) to another (such as a washer ring for the steering column of a truck). During this half-day, a manufacturing plant is not producing anything, but employees are paid for this "nonproductive" time.

It follows that if setup times for complex production equipment can be reduced, so can setup costs, and efficiency will rise; that is, the time that employees spend in actually producing something will increase. This simple insight has been the driving force behind the development of flexible manufacturing techniques.

Flexible manufacturing aims to reduce the time required to set up production equipment.[47] By redesigning the manufacturing process so production equipment geared for manufacturing one product can be quickly replaced with equipment geared to make another product, setup times and costs can be reduced dramatically. Another favorable outcome from flexible manufacturing is that a company can produce many more varieties of a product than before in the same amount of time. Thus flexible manufacturing increases a company's ability to be responsive to its customers.

To make flexible manufacturing an effective business strategy, General Motors believes its factories need to have smarter designs, artificial intelligence, and collaborative robots ("cobots") working side by side with humans to produce a wide range of vehicles on the same production line. The GM Orion plant, north of Detroit, is the blueprint for such a manufacturing process. More than 800 cobots work on the production line and in various parts of the plant, doing repetitive and dangerous tasks, while humans do the jobs that require dexterity and critical thinking. GM recently announced a $4 billion investment in the plant, which will allow the company to convert the plant to produce full-electric pickup trucks and create 4,000 new jobs.[48]

Just-in-Time Inventory and Efficiency

As noted earlier, a just-in-time inventory system gets components to the assembly line just as they are needed and thus drives down costs. In a JIT inventory system, component parts travel from suppliers to the assembly line in a small wheeled container known as a *kanban.* Assembly-line workers empty the kanbans, which are sent back to the suppliers as the signal to produce another small batch of component parts, and so the process repeats itself. This system can be contrasted with a just-in-case view of inventory, which leads an organization to stockpile excess inputs in a warehouse in case it needs them to meet sudden increases in demand.

JIT inventory systems have major implications for efficiency. Great cost savings can result from increasing inventory turnover and reducing inventory holding costs, such as warehousing and storage costs and the cost of capital tied up in inventory. Although companies that manufacture and assemble products can obviously use JIT to great advantage, so can service organizations.[49] Walmart, the largest retailer in the world, recently modified its JIT process to one the company calls OTIF (on-time, in full). A recognized concept in supply chain management, OTIF simply means suppliers should deliver their products when and how the buyer needs them. As competition between Walmart and Amazon heats up, the global retailer wants suppliers to ship full trucks of products to deliver orders within a specified two-day window 98% of the time. Suppliers shipping a partial truckload to Walmart stores must hit a 70% on-time threshold, a large jump from the previous target of 50%. Under these rules, suppliers face a fine of 3% of the cost of goods sold for each case that fails to meet Walmart's requirements.[50]

By all measures of performance, JIT systems have been successful—inventory holding costs have fallen sharply, and products are being delivered to customers on time. In addition, the design-to-product cycles for new products have dropped almost in half because suppliers are involved much earlier in the design process so they can supply new inputs as needed. Finally, as Walmart's OTIF process suggests, companies must continue to look for innovative ways to streamline global supply chains, especially because of the time pressures of e-commerce sales and deliveries.[51]

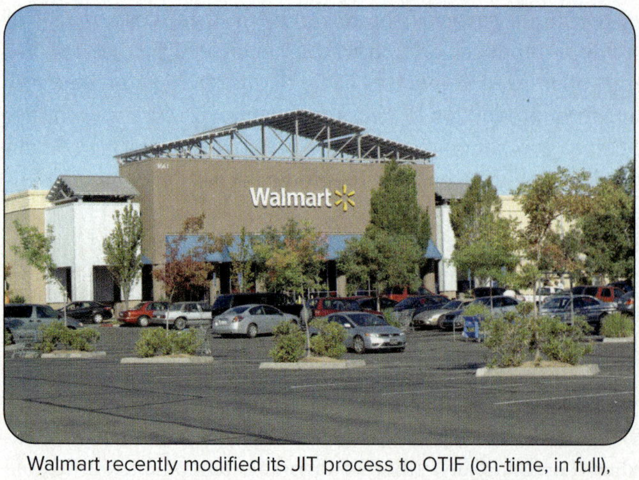

Walmart recently modified its JIT process to OTIF (on-time, in full), which means suppliers should deliver when and how the buyer needs them. A supplier who is early or late with a delivery can be fined by the retailer.
Sergey Yechikov/Shutterstock

Self-Managed Work Teams and Efficiency

Another functional strategy to increase efficiency is the use of self-managed work teams. A typical self-managed team consists of 5 to 15 employees who produce an entire product instead of just parts of it.[52] Team members learn all team tasks and move from job to job. The result is a flexible workforce because team members can fill in for absent coworkers. The members of each team also assume responsibility for scheduling work and vacations, ordering materials, and hiring new members—previously all responsibilities of first-line managers. Because people often respond well to greater autonomy and responsibility, the use of empowered self-managed teams can increase productivity and efficiency. Moreover, cost savings arise from eliminating supervisors and creating a flatter organizational hierarchy, which further increase efficiency.

The effect of introducing self-managed teams is often an increase in efficiency of 30% or sometimes much more. The introduction of self-managed teams at a GE aviation plant in Durham, North Carolina, has produced year-over-year productivity growth, first-time yield quality, and successful on-time delivery rates.[53]

Process Reengineering and Efficiency

process reengineering The fundamental rethinking and radical redesign of business processes to achieve dramatic improvement in critical measures of performance such as cost, quality, service, and speed.

The value chain is a collection of functional activities or business processes that transforms one or more kinds of inputs to create an output that is of value to the customer. **Process reengineering** involves the fundamental rethinking and radical redesign of business processes (and thus the *value chain*) to achieve dramatic improvements in critical measures of performance such as cost, quality, service, and speed.[54] Order fulfillment, for example, can be thought of as a business process: When a customer's order is received (the input), many different functional tasks must be performed as necessary to process the order, and then the ordered goods are delivered to the customer (the output). Process reengineering boosts efficiency when it reduces the number of order fulfillment tasks that must be performed, or reduces the time they take, and so reduces operating costs.

Managers at Ford Motor Company have used process reengineering to improve the efficiency of the company's procurement process. By simplifying the process, Ford has significantly reduced the time spent by accounts payable staff to rectify complex vehicle orders that contain conflicting information.
Robert Clay/Alamy Stock Photo

For an example of process reengineering in practice, consider how Ford used it. One day a manager from Ford was working at its then Japanese partner Mazda and discovered that Mazda had only five people in its accounts payable department. The Ford manager was shocked because Ford's U.S. operation had 500 employees in accounts payable. He reported his discovery to Ford's U.S. managers, who decided to form a task force to study this difference.

Ford managers discovered that procurement began when the purchasing department sent a purchase order to a supplier and sent a copy of the purchase order to Ford's accounts payable department. When the supplier shipped the goods and they arrived at Ford, a clerk at the receiving dock completed a form describing the goods and sent the form to accounts payable. The supplier, meanwhile, sent accounts payable an invoice. Thus accounts payable received three documents relating to these goods: a copy of the original purchase order, the receiving document, and the invoice. If the information in all three was in agreement (most of the time it was), a clerk in accounts payable issued payment. Occasionally, however, all three documents did not agree. And Ford discovered that accounts payable clerks spent most of their time straightening out the 1% of instances in which the purchase order, receiving document, and invoice contained conflicting information.[55]

Ford managers decided to reengineer the procurement process to simplify it. Now when a buyer in the purchasing department issues a purchase order to a supplier, that buyer also enters the order into an online database. As before, suppliers send goods to the receiving dock. When the goods arrive, the clerk at the receiving dock checks a computer terminal to see whether the received shipment matches the description on the purchase order. If it does, the clerk accepts the goods and pushes a button on the terminal keyboard that tells the database the goods have arrived. Receipt of the goods is recorded in the database, and a computer automatically issues and sends a check to the supplier. If the goods do not correspond to the description on the purchase order in the database, the clerk at the dock refuses the shipment and sends it back to the supplier.

Payment authorization, which used to be performed by accounts payable, is now accomplished at the receiving dock. The new process has come close to eliminating the need for an accounts payable department. In some parts of Ford, the size of the accounts payable department has been cut by 95%. By reducing the head count in accounts payable, the reengineering effort reduced the amount of time wasted on unproductive activities, thereby increasing the efficiency of the total organization.

Information Systems, the Internet, and Efficiency

With the rapid spread of computers, the explosive growth of the Internet and corporate intranets, and high-speed digital technology, the information systems function is moving to center stage in the quest for operating efficiencies and a lower cost structure. The impact of information systems on productivity is wide-ranging and potentially affects all other activities of a company. For example, Cisco Systems has been able to realize significant cost savings by moving its ordering and customer service functions online. Cisco Systems designs, manufactures, and sells networking equipment. The company has just 300 service agents handling all its customer accounts, compared to the 900 it would need if sales were not handled online. The difference represents an annual savings of $30 million a year. Moreover, without automated customer service functions, Cisco calculates that it would need at least 1,000 additional service engineers, which would cost around $100 million.

All large companies today use the Internet to manage the value chain, feeding real-time information about order flow to suppliers, which use this information to schedule their own production to provide components on a just-in-time basis. This approach reduces the costs of coordination both between the company and its customers and between the company and its suppliers. Using the Internet to automate customer and supplier interactions substantially reduces the number of employees required to manage these interfaces, which significantly reduces costs. This trend extends beyond high-tech companies. For example, banks and financial service companies are finding that they can substantially reduce costs by moving customer accounts and support functions online. Such a move reduces the need for customer service representatives, bank tellers, stockbrokers, insurance agents, and others. For example, it costs about $1 when a customer executes a transaction at a bank, such as shifting money from one account to another; over the Internet the same transaction costs about $0.01.

Improving Innovation

As discussed in Chapter 6, *technology* comprises the skills, know-how, experience, body of scientific knowledge, tools, machines, computers, and equipment used in the design, production, and distribution of goods and services. Technology is involved in all functional activities, and the rapid advance of technology today is a significant factor in managers' attempts to improve how their value chains innovate new kinds of goods and services or ways to provide them. This section focuses on product innovation, but opportunities to create value from innovation also include companies' processes, as the "Manager as a Person" feature illustrates.

MANAGER AS A PERSON

Amazon's Innovator in Chief

Amazon is one of the world's highest-valued companies in terms of stock price. It started as an online bookseller with an uncertain future; many questioned selling books over the Internet. How could you know what you were buying or find great new titles? Over time, Amazon added automated recommendations based on customer orders; e-books and e-readers; a system for others to sell through its site; and innovations in the speed and efficiency of distribution, using software, robots, and various delivery vehicles. Today Amazon runs the world's largest online sales platform, with a 49% U. S. market share, and the second-largest paid membership program, Amazon Prime, trailing only Netflix for number of paid subscribers.[56]

Amazon's innovation is both a value of founder Jeff Bezos and a consequence of the founder's innovations. During his youth, Bezos was known for experimenting with electronics and engineering. Bezos continues innovating with technology. His name appears on 154 of Amazon's patents, including as sole inventor of 11. This effort was not just to get the company started; his patent activity increased around 2008, a

Thanks to founder Jeff Bezos, Amazon's company processes continue to provide innovative solutions to everyday challenges for both businesses and consumers.
Patrick Semansky/AP/Shutterstock

decade into Amazon's history. Most of Bezos's patents are in e-commerce and logistics, devices and digital content, and computing.[57]

Under Bezos, innovation is part of Amazon's culture. His success as a leader shows up in key measures: Amazon outperforms other companies in number of patent applications and trademark registrations, job postings in advanced technologies, and spending on research and development. The company also abandons patent applications at a high rate, implying innovation efficiency because employees can let go when an idea isn't working or is no longer relevant.[58]

Bezos has even innovated Amazon's innovation process by establishing a process for submitting ideas. Any business idea must be in a memo that meets certain criteria. It must be brief (up to six pages) and in the form of a press release issued in the future, explaining what the company has done. It must identify benefits to customers and say how the idea is superior to existing alternatives. It must include an FAQ page answering likely customer questions. It should spell out what problems remain to be solved–say, the need to create a technology that doesn't yet exist–because identifying a problem spurs creative thinking. Expressing the idea in the form of a press release makes it exciting and easier to imagine.[59]

Two Kinds of Innovation

LO9-5 Differentiate between two forms of innovation, and explain why innovation and product development are crucial components of the search for competitive advantage.

Two principal kinds of innovation can be identified based on the nature of the technological change that brings them about. **Quantum product innovation** results in the development of new, often radically different, kinds of goods and services because of fundamental shifts in technology brought about by pioneering discoveries. Examples include the creation of the Internet and the World Wide Web that have revolutionized the computer, cell phone, and media/music industries, and biotechnology, which has transformed the treatment of illness by creating new, genetically engineered medicines. Panera, Shake Shack, and Chipotle started a restaurant trend in the early 2010s called "fast-casual," which offers rapidly prepared, high-quality food in an upscale dining environment and prices that are typically higher than fast-food chains. And food-delivery companies such as GrubHub, Uber Eats, and DoorDash took a giant leap forward during the COVID-19 pandemic, when millions of consumers ordered takeout meals from restaurants that would have otherwise shut down while the spread of the virus was rampant.[60]

quantum product innovation The development of new, often radically different, kinds of goods and services because of fundamental shifts in technology brought about by pioneering discoveries.

incremental product innovation The gradual improvement and refinement of existing products that occur over time as existing technologies are perfected.

Incremental product innovation results in gradual improvements and refinements of products over time as existing technologies are perfected and functional managers, like those at Apple, Toyota, and McDonald's, learn how to perform value chain activities in better ways–ways that add more value to products. For example, since their debut, Google's staffers have made thousands of incremental improvements to the company's Internet search engine, Chrome, and its Android operating system–changes that have enhanced their capabilities enormously such as giving them the ability to work on all kinds of mobile devices and making them available in many different languages.

Quantum product innovations are relatively rare; most managers' activities focus on incremental product innovations that result from ongoing technological advances. For example, every time Dell puts a new, faster chip into a PC, or Google improves its search engine's capability, the company is making incremental product innovations. Similarly, every time car engineers redesign a car model, and every time McDonald's managers work to improve the flavor and texture of burgers, fries, and breakfast items, their product development efforts are intended to lead to incremental product innovations. Incremental innovation is often as important as–or even more important than–quantum innovation in raising a company's performance. Indeed, as discussed next, it is often managers' ability to successfully manage incremental product development that results in success or failure in an industry.

The need to speed up innovation and quickly develop new and improved products becomes especially important when the technology behind the product is advancing rapidly. This is because the first companies in an industry to adopt the new technology will be able to develop products that better meet customer needs and gain a "first-mover" advantage over their rivals. Indeed, managers who do not quickly adopt and apply new technologies to innovate products may soon find they have no customers for their products–and destroy their organizations. In sum, the greater the rate of technological change in an industry, the more important it is for managers to innovate.

Strategies to Promote Innovation and Speed Product Development

product development The management of the value chain activities involved in bringing new or improved goods and services to the market.

There are several ways in which managers can promote innovation and encourage the development of new products. **Product development** is the management of the value chain activities involved in bringing new or improved goods and services to the market. The steps that Monte Peterson, former CEO of Thermos, took to develop a new barbecue grill show how good product development should proceed. Peterson had no doubt about how to increase Thermos's sales of barbecue grills: motivate Thermos's functional managers to create new and improved models. So Peterson assembled a cross-functional product development team of five functional managers (from marketing, engineering, manufacturing, sales, and finance) and told them to develop a new barbecue grill within 18 months. To ensure that they were not spread too thin, he assigned them to this team only. Peterson also arranged for leadership of the team to rotate. Initially, to focus on what customers wanted, the marketing manager would take the lead; then, when technical developments became the main consideration, leadership would switch to engineering; and so on.

Team members christened the group the "lifestyle team." To find out what people really wanted in a grill, the marketing manager and nine employees spent a month on the road, visiting customers. What they found surprised them. The stereotype of Dad slaving over a smoky barbecue grill was wrong–more women were barbecuing. Many cooks were tired of messy charcoal, and many homeowners did not like rusty grills that spoiled the appearance of their decks. Moreover, environmental and safety issues were increasing in importance. In California, charcoal starter fluid is considered a pollutant and is banned; in many other states, the use of charcoal and gas grills on the balconies of condos and apartments has been prohibited to avoid fires. Based on these findings, the team decided Thermos had to produce a barbecue grill that not only made the food taste good but also looked attractive, used no pollutants, and was safe for balcony use (which meant it had to be electric).

Within one year the basic attributes of the product were defined, and leadership of the team moved to engineering. The critical task for engineering was to design a grill that gave food the cookout taste that conventional electric grills could not provide because they did not get hot enough. To raise the cooking temperature, Thermos's engineers designed a domed vacuum top that trapped heat inside the grill, and they built electric heat rods directly into the surface of the grill. These features made the grill hot enough to sear meat and give it brown barbecue lines and a barbecue taste.

Manufacturing had been active from the early days of the development process, making sure any proposed design could be produced economically. Because manufacturing was involved from the beginning, the team avoided some costly mistakes. At one critical team meeting, the engineers said they wanted tapered legs on the grill. Manufacturing explained that tapered legs would have to be custom-made–and would raise manufacturing costs–and persuaded the team to go with straight legs.

When the new grill was introduced on schedule, it was an immediate success. The study of many product development successes, such as that of Thermos's lifestyle team, suggests three strategies managers can implement to increase the likelihood that their product development efforts will result in innovative and successful new products.

INVOLVE BOTH CUSTOMERS AND SUPPLIERS Many new products fail when they reach the marketplace because they were designed with scant attention to customer needs. Successful product development requires inputs from more than just an organization's members; inputs from customers and suppliers are also needed. Thermos team members spent a month on the road, visiting customers to identify their needs. The revolutionary electric barbecue grill was a direct result of this process. In other cases, companies have found it worthwhile to include customer representatives as peripheral members of their product development teams. Boeing, for example, included its customers, the major airlines, in the design of the 787 Dreamliner. Boeing built a mockup of the aircraft's cabin and then, over a period of months, allowed each airline's representatives to experiment with repositioning the galleys, seating, aisles, and bathrooms to best meet the needs of their particular airline. Boeing learned a great deal from this process.

ESTABLISH A STAGE–GATE DEVELOPMENT FUNNEL One of the most common mistakes managers make in product development is trying to fund too many new projects at any one time. This approach spreads the activities of the different value chain functions too thinly over too many different projects. As a consequence, no single project is given the functional resources and attention required to become a success.

stage–gate development funnel A planning model that forces managers to choose among competing projects so organizational resources are not spread thinly over too many projects.

One strategy for solving this problem is for managers to develop a structured process for evaluating product development proposals and deciding which to support and which to reject. A common solution is to establish a **stage–gate development funnel**, a technique that forces managers to choose among competing projects so functional resources are not spread thinly over too many projects. The funnel gives functional managers control over product development and allows them to intervene and take corrective action quickly and appropriately (see Figure 9.5).

At stage 1, the development funnel has a wide mouth, so top managers initially can encourage employees to come up with as many new product ideas as possible. Managers can create incentives for employees to come up with ideas. Many organizations run "bright-idea programs" that reward employees whose ideas eventually make it through the development process. Other organizations allow research scientists to devote a certain amount of work time to their own projects. Top managers at 3M, for example, have a 15% rule: They expect a research scientist to spend 15% of the workweek working on a project of their own choosing. Ideas may be submitted by individuals or by groups. Brainstorming (see Chapter 7) is a technique that managers often use to encourage new ideas.

New product ideas are written up as brief proposals. The proposals are submitted to a cross-functional team of managers, who evaluate each proposal at gate 1. The cross-functional team considers a proposal's fit with the organization's strategy and its technical feasibility. Proposals

Figure 9.5

A Stage–Gate Development Funnel

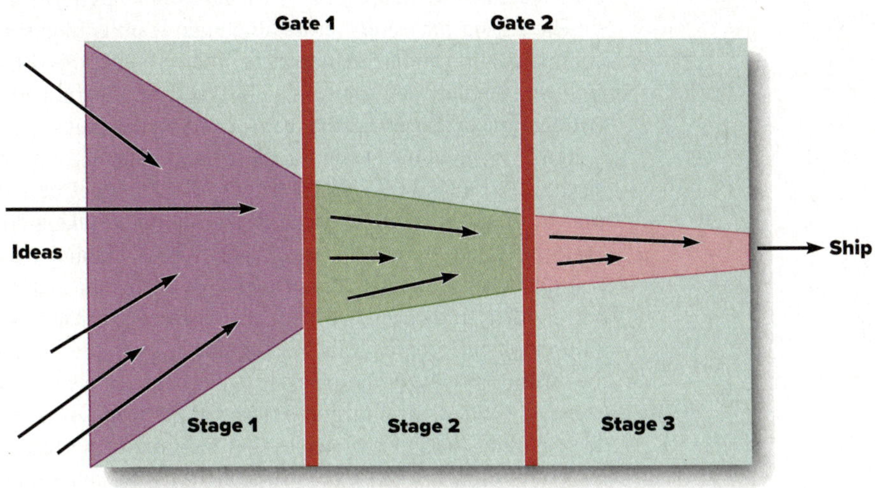

that are consistent with the strategy of the organization and are judged technically feasible pass through gate 1 and into stage 2. Other proposals are turned down (although the door is often left open for reconsidering a proposal later).

product development plan A plan that specifies all of the relevant information that managers need in order to decide whether to proceed with a full-blown product development effort.

The primary goal in stage 2 is to draft a detailed product development plan. The **product development plan** specifies all of the relevant information that managers need to decide whether to go ahead with a full-blown product development effort. The product development plan should include strategic and financial objectives, an analysis of the product's market potential, a list of desired product features, a list of technological requirements, a list of financial and human resource requirements, a detailed development budget, and a time line that contains specific milestones (for example, dates for prototype completion and final launch).

A cross-functional team of managers normally drafts this plan. Good planning requires a good strategic analysis (see Chapter 8), and team members must be prepared to spend considerable time in the field with customers, trying to understand their needs. Drafting a product development plan generally takes about three months. Once completed, the plan is reviewed by a senior management committee at gate 2 (see Figure 9.5). These managers focus on the details of the plan to see whether the proposal is attractive (given its market potential) and viable (given the technological, financial, and human resources that would be needed to develop the product). Senior managers making this review keep in mind all other product development efforts currently being undertaken by the organization. One goal at this point is to ensure that limited organizational resources are used to their maximum effect.

At gate 2, projects are rejected, sent back for revision, or allowed to pass through to stage 3, the development phase. Product development starts with the formation of a cross-functional team that is given primary responsibility for developing the product. In some companies, at the beginning of stage 3 top managers and cross-functional team members sign a **contract book**, a written agreement that details factors such as responsibilities, resource commitments, budgets, time lines, and development milestones. Signing the contract book is viewed as the symbolic launch of a product development effort. The contract book is also a document against which actual development progress can be measured. At 3M, for example, team members and top management negotiate a contract and sign a contract book at the launch of a development effort, thereby signaling their commitment to the objectives contained in the contract.

contract book A written agreement that details product development factors such as responsibilities, resource commitments, budgets, time lines, and development milestones.

The stage 3 development effort can last anywhere from six months to 10 years, depending on the industry and type of product. Some electronics products have development cycles of six months, but it takes from three to five years to develop a new car, about five years to develop a new jet aircraft, and as long as 10 years to develop a new medical drug.

ESTABLISH CROSS-FUNCTIONAL TEAMS A smooth-running cross-functional team also seems to be a critical component of successful product development, as the experience of Thermos suggests. Marketing, engineering, and manufacturing personnel are **core members** of a successful product development team–the people who have primary responsibility for the product development effort. Other people besides core members work on the project when the need arises, but the core members (generally from three to six individuals) stay with the project from inception to completion of the development effort (see Figure 9.6).

core members The members of a team who bear primary responsibility for the success of a project and who stay with a project from inception to completion.

The reason for using a cross-functional team is to ensure a high level of coordination and communication among managers in different functions. Input from both marketing and manufacturing members of Thermos's lifestyle team determined the characteristics of the barbecue grill that the engineers on the team ended up designing.

If a cross-functional team is to succeed, it must have the right kind of leadership and it must be managed effectively. To be successful, a product development team needs a team leader who can rise above a functional background and take a cross-functional view. In addition to having effective leadership, successful cross-functional product development teams have several other key characteristics. Often core members of successful teams are located close to one another, in the same office space, to foster a sense of shared mission and commitment to a development program. Successful teams develop a clear sense of their objectives and how they will be achieved, the purpose again being to create a sense of shared mission. Thermos eventually sold its grill business to the Char-Broil Division of W.C. Bradley Co. But its story demonstrates the three strategies that help ventures succeed: involving customers and suppliers, establishing a stage-gate development funnel, and establishing cross-functional teams.

Figure 9.6
Members of a Cross-Functional Product Development Team

Managing innovation is an increasingly important aspect of a manager's job in an era of dramatic changes in technology. Promoting successful new product development is difficult and challenging, and some product development efforts are much more successful than others. In sum, managers need to recognize that successful innovation and product development cut across roles and functions and require a high level of cooperation among managers in the organization. They should recognize the importance of common values and norms in promoting the high levels of cooperation and cohesiveness necessary to build a culture for innovation. They also should reward successful innovators and make heroes of the employees and teams who develop successful new products. Finally, managers should fully utilize the product development techniques just discussed to guide the process.

Summary and Review

LO9-1 **VALUE CHAIN MANAGEMENT AND COMPETITIVE ADVANTAGE** To achieve high performance, managers try to improve their responsiveness to customers, the quality of their products, and the efficiency of their organization. To achieve these goals, managers can use a number of value chain management techniques to improve the way an organization operates. In addition, analysis of an organization's value chain can provide several benefits, including increased efficiency, reduced costs, and strengthened collaboration between various functional activities.

LO9-2 **IMPROVING RESPONSIVENESS TO CUSTOMERS** To achieve high performance in a competitive environment, it is imperative that the organization's value chain be managed to produce outputs that have the attributes customers want. A central task of value chain management is to develop new and improved operating systems that enhance the ability of the organization to economically deliver more of the product attributes that customers desire for the same price. Techniques such as CRM and TQM, JIT, flexible manufacturing, and process reengineering are popular because they promise to do this. As important as responsiveness to customers is, however, managers need to recognize that there are limits to how responsive an organization can be and still cover its costs.

LO9-3 **IMPROVING QUALITY** Managers seek to improve the quality of their organization's output because doing so enables them to better serve customers, to raise prices, and to lower production costs. Total quality management focuses on improving the quality of an organization's products and services and stresses that all of an organization's operations should be directed toward this goal. Putting TQM into practice requires having an organizationwide commitment to TQM, having a strong customer focus, finding ways to measure quality, setting quality improvement goals, soliciting input from employees about how to improve product quality, identifying defects and tracing them to their source, introducing just-in-time inventory systems, getting suppliers to adopt TQM practices, designing products for ease of manufacture, and breaking down barriers between functional departments.

LO9-4 **IMPROVING EFFICIENCY** Improving efficiency requires one or more of the following: the introduction of a TQM program, the adoption of flexible manufacturing technologies, the introduction of just-in-time inventory systems, the establishment of self-managed work teams, and the application of process reengineering. Top management is responsible for setting the context within which efficiency improvements can take place by, for example, emphasizing the need for continuous improvement. Functional-level managers bear prime responsibility for identifying and implementing efficiency-enhancing improvements in operating systems.

LO9-5 **IMPROVING PRODUCT INNOVATION** When technology is changing, managers must quickly innovate new and improved products to protect their competitive advantage. Some value chain strategies managers can use to achieve this are (1) involving both customers and suppliers in the development process; (2) establishing a stage-gate development funnel for evaluating and controlling different product development efforts; and (3) establishing cross-functional teams composed of individuals from different functional departments, and giving each team a leader who can rise above their functional background.

Management in Action

Topics for Discussion and Action

Discussion

1. Why is it important for managers to pay close attention to value chain management if they wish to be responsive to their customers? [LO9-1, 9-2]
2. What is CRM, and how can it help improve responsiveness to customers? [LO9-2]
3. What are the main challenges in implementing a successful total quality management program? [LO9-3]
4. What is efficiency, and what are some strategies managers can use to increase it? [LO9-4]
5. What is innovation, and what are some strategies managers can use to develop successful new products? [LO9-5]

Action

6. Ask a manager how responsiveness to customers, quality, efficiency, and innovation are defined and measured in their organization. [LO9-1, 9-2]
7. Go to a local store, restaurant, or supermarket; observe how customers are treated; and list the ways in which you think the organization is being responsive or unresponsive to the needs of its customers. How could this business improve its responsiveness to customers? [LO9-1, 9-2]

Building Management Skills

Managing the Value Chain [LO9-1, 9-2]

Choose an organization with which you are familiar—one that you have worked in or patronized or one that has received extensive coverage in the popular press. The organization should be involved in only one industry or business. Answer these questions about the organization:

1. What is the output of the organization?
2. Describe the value chain activities that the organization uses to produce this output.
3. What product attributes do customers of the organization desire?
4. Try to identify improvements that might be made to the organization's value chain to boost its responsiveness to customers, quality, efficiency, and innovation.

Managing Ethically [LO9-1, 9-4]

After implementing efficiency-improving techniques, many companies commonly lay off hundreds or thousands of employees whose services are no longer required. And often the remaining employees must perform more tasks more quickly—a situation that can generate employee stress and other work-related problems. Also, these employees may experience guilt because they stayed while many of their colleagues and friends were fired.

Questions

1. Either by yourself or in a group, think through the ethical implications of using a new functional strategy to improve organizational performance.
2. What criteria would you use to decide which kind of strategy is ethical to adopt and how far to push employees to raise the level of their performance?
3. How big a layoff, if any, is acceptable? If layoffs are acceptable, what could be done to reduce their harm to employees?

Small Group Breakout Exercise

How to Compete in the Sandwich Business [LO9-1, 9-2]

Form groups of three or four people, and appoint one member as the spokesperson who will communicate your findings to the class when called on by the instructor. Then discuss the following scenario:

You and your partners are thinking about opening a new kind of sandwich shop that will compete head-to-head with Subway and Jimmy John's. Because these chains have good brand-name recognition, it is vital that you find some source of competitive advantage for your new sandwich shop, and you are meeting to brainstorm ways of obtaining one.

1. Identify the product attributes that a typical sandwich shop customer wants the most.
2. In what ways do you think you will be able to improve on the operations and processes of existing sandwich shops and increase responsiveness to customers through better product quality, efficiency, or innovation?

Be the Manager [LO9-1, 9-3, 9-4, 9-5]

How to Build Flatscreen Displays

You are the top manager of a start-up company that will produce innovative new flatscreen displays for PC makers like Apple and HP. The flatscreen display market is highly competitive, so there is considerable pressure to reduce costs. Also, PC makers are demanding ever-higher quality and better features to please customers. In addition, they demand that delivery of your product meets their production schedule needs. Functional managers want your advice on how to best meet these requirements, especially because they are in the process of recruiting new workers and building a production facility.

Questions

1. What kinds of techniques discussed in the chapter can help your functional managers to increase efficiency?
2. In what ways can these managers develop a program to increase quality and innovation?
3. What critical lessons do these managers need to learn about value chain management?

Case in the News [LO9-1, 9-2, 9-3, 9-4, 9-5]

Two Disc Golf Companies' Spin on Quality and Responsiveness

On courses laid out in parks, people of all ages are tossing plastic discs into chain-link baskets. They're playing disc golf, which is based on the same principle as golf played with a club: following an 18-hole course, you propel your object (disc or ball) into each target (basket or hole) in as few attempts as possible. The discs are more angular and denser than the Frisbees used for playing catch, and they come in a variety of designs. Enthusiasts buy a variety of discs for different flight paths and distances, plus bags to carry them in. Some compete in tournaments sponsored by the Professional Disc Golf Association (PDGA).

Players can get started with just one or a few $15 discs and park admission fees, if any. With this low cost of entry, the number of players increased steadily at about 10% a year through the late 1990s and 2000s. Videos and social-media posts then accelerated the growth. Now millions of people play the game every year, creating a market for more than 20 million discs. But in 2020, the pandemic completely changed the market dynamics. During social distancing, people were looking for something to do outside without close contact, and disc golf offered a way to have fun with family or friends of all ages. New players bought discs, and membership in the PDGA doubled between 2019 and 2021.

For the providers of equipment, this surge in players was an opportunity combined with all the challenges that have made value chain management difficult. Orders were flooding manufacturers, which added greatly to revenues, but supply chains were disrupted and employees were difficult to hire and keep. Makers of discs scrambled to compete with other kinds of manufacturers for scarce supplies of plastic. Two Michigan-based companies that did all they could to keep customers satisfied were Discraft, the second-largest maker of discs, and MVP Disc Sports, a more recent and smaller industry entrant.

Discraft was founded by a husband-and-wife team in 1978, when the idea of making competition-quality discs was a new concept. The company makes discs for both disc golf and the game of ultimate (soccer played with discs, originally known as ultimate Frisbee). It has reinforced its strong position in the market by negotiating endorsement deals, including one with Paige Pierce, the world's top-rated female pro disc golfer, and a $10 million 10-year deal with five-time PDGA world champion Paul McBeth. When the surge in demand for disc golf hit, Discraft paused manufacturing of ultimate discs to focus on the more distanced sport of disc golf. When finding plastic became difficult, the company bought a machine for recycling used plastic and began converting scrap discs into plastic pellets it could use for making new discs. Discraft also doubled the number of machines it owned and hired as many people as it could find to run three shifts. By running full tilt, it increased disc golf production sixfold. Although it stopped adding new retail customers, Discraft was only able to send existing customers whatever it could make, rather than filling special orders.

MVP Disc Sports is a later entrant in the marketplace and holds a market share of less than 10%. The company was started in 2010 by two brothers who wanted to apply two-step molding processes to make a superior line of discs. MVP skyrocketed in popularity after James Conrad used its Electron Envy disc to make what players still call the "Holy Shot": during the 2021 world championships, the disc sailed 247 feet to the basket, and Conrad won the final round, beating the five-time champion.

Already dealing with pandemic-related challenges, MVP found itself in an operations nightmare. Customers wanted their own Envy discs, and the company had just one mold—a common practice among manufacturers to maintain consistency. Making one disc per minute, the company ran its production process 24 hours a day for three months but couldn't keep up with orders. It increased its payroll to more than 100 employees, up from 20 before the pandemic, and it ordered 15 new disc-manufacturing machines in 2020–21. As orders surged, the company dedicated all its production processes to making existing products, eventually increasing 2021 production tenfold over 2020. According to MVP, it produced more discs in 2021 than in the previous 11 years combined. However, many retailers were disappointed to receive a large share of the discs after the initial surge of enthusiasm among players and other consumers around Electron Envy and the Holy Shot had faded.

Questions for Discussion

1. Based on the description, would you say the managers of Discraft and MVP Disc Sports were successful managing the materials management function during the pandemic years? Why or why not?
2. Discraft and MVP have two kinds of customers: (a) the retailers that sell discs to players and (b) the players themselves. For each kind of customer, list what you think customers wanted from the two companies during the pandemic.
3. How might improving efficiency help Discraft and MVP better provide what their customers want? Describe one measure for improving efficiency that you would recommend to these companies.

Sources: Discraft, "About Us," www.discraft.com, accessed January 29, 2023; MVP Disc Sports, "FAQ & Contact," https://mvpdiscsports.com, accessed January 29, 2023; H. Burns, "Disc Golf Can Turn Your Walk into a Work-out," *The New York Times*, www.nytimes.com, August 18, 2022; V. Bauerlein, "America's Business Challenge Can Be Told in Two Words: Disc Golf," *The Wall Street Journal*, www.wsj.com, March 25, 2022; A. Kostka, "Big Money, More Fans and Budding Stars: Disc Golf (Yes, Disc Golf) Gets Real," *Washington Times*, www.washingtontimes.com, July 28, 2021; D. Gardner, "The Rise of the $10 Million Disc Golf Celebrity," *The Ringer*, www.theringr.com, June 21, 2021; K. Nagl, "Wixom-Based Disc Golf Strikes $10M Sponsor Deal as Disc Golf Soars," *Crain's Detroit Business*, www.crainsdetroit.com, February 26, 2021.

Notes

1. K. Stankiewicz, "The Future of Mattel Is about a Lot More than Making Toys, CEO Says," *CNBC*, www.cnbc.com, December 4, 2019; P. Ziobro, "Barbie, Hot Wheels Go to Hollywood in Mattel CEO's Turnaround Plan," *The Wall Street Journal*, www.wsj.com, April 17, 2019; "Jump in Sales, End of Probe Lift Mattel Stock," *Los Angeles Times*, October 3, 2019, ProQuest, https://search.proquest.com.
2. Stankiewicz, "The Future of Mattel"; P. Ziobro, "Mattel Puts a Lid on Excess Colors," *The Wall Street Journal*, www.wsj.com, January 2, 2020.
3. P. Ziobro, "Mattel Closes Factories as It Revamps Supply Chain," *The Wall Street Journal*, www.wsj.com, February 9, 2020; P. Thomas, "Mattel to Cut More than 2,200 Jobs as Toy Maker Battles Losses," *The Wall Street Journal*, www.wsj.com, July 25, 2018.
4. "Mattel Revenue Beats on Barbie Dolls, BTS K-Pop Band Toys," *Reuters*, www.reuters.com, October 29, 2019; R. Williams, "Mattel Races into Mobile Gaming for Teens with 'Hot Wheels: Infinite Loop,'" *Mobile Marketer*, www.mobilemarketer.com, August 23, 2019.
5. "Mattel Reports Fourth Quarter and Full Year 2022 Financial Results," *The Wall Street Journal*, www.wsj.com, February 8, 2023; D. Hayes, "Mattel CEO Ynon Kreiz Declares 'The Turnaround Is Complete' after Toy Maker Posts Strong Q4 Results and Stock Flirts with 5-Year High," *Deadline*, https://deadline.com, accessed January 28, 2023.

6. "Gartner Announces Rankings of the 2022 Global Supply Chain Top 25," www.gartner.com, May 26, 2022.
7. See D. Garvin, "What Does Product Quality Really Mean?" *Sloan Management Review* 26 (Fall 1984), 25–44; P.B. Crosby, *Quality Is Free* (New York: Mentor Books, 1980); A. Gabor, *The Man Who Discovered Quality* (New York: Times Books, 1990).
8. L. Moore, "New Nintendo Leak Teases More Movies in Development," *Comic Book*, https://comicbook.com, June 7, 2022.
9. T. Stobierski, "What Is a Value Chain Analysis? 3 Steps," *Harvard Business Insights*, https://online.hbs.org, accessed January 28, 2023.
10. R. O'Byrne, "The Supply Chain and the Value Chain: The Same but Different?" *Supply Chain Secrets*, www.supplychain-secrets.com, accessed January 28, 2023; M. Iansiti, "The History and Future of Operations," *Harvard Business Review*, https://hbr.org, accessed January 28, 2023; B. Lutkevich, "What Is a Supply Chain?" *Tech Target*, www.techtarget.com, accessed January 28, 2023.
11. M. Parmar, "The 10 Largest Subscription Companies in the World, and What They Do," *History-Computer*, https://history-computer.com, December 9, 2022; J. Verdon, "Logistics Improvements Boost Chewy's Profits," *Forbes*, www.forbes.com, December 8, 2022.
12. M. E. Porter, *Competitive Advantage: Creating and Sustaining Superior Performance* (New York: Free Press, 1985).
13. K. Robson, *Service-ability: Create a Customer Centric Culture and Achieve Competitive Advantage* (New York: Wiley, 2013).
14. M.E. Porter and J.E. Heppelmann, "How Smart, Connected Products Are Transforming Competition," *Harvard Business Review*, https://hbr.org, accessed January 28, 2023.
15. D.F. Abell, *Defining the Business: The Starting Point of Strategic Planning* (Englewood Cliffs, NJ: Prentice-Hall, 1980).
16. Brand Minds, "Why Did Kodak Fail and What Can You Learn from Its Demise?" *Medium*, https://medium, accessed February 22, 2020.
17. M. K. Pratt, "7 Key Benefits of AI for Business," *Tech Target*, www.techtarget.com, January 24, 2023.
18. D. C. Edelman and M. Abraham, "Customer Experience in the Age of AI," *Harvard Business Review*, March-April 2022, 116–125.
19. Edelman and Abraham, "Customer Experience in the Age of AI"; I. Bousquette, "CIOs Contend with Pushback on AI Rollouts," *The Wall Street Journal*, www.wsj.com, January 5, 2023.
20. S. Lohr, "Customer Service Chatbots Are Starting to Speak Our Lingo," *The New York Times*, www.nytimes.com, April 4, 2022.
21. Edelman and Abraham, "Customer Experience in the Age of AI"; K. C. Kellogg and M. A. Valentine, "Five Mistakes Managers Make When Introducing AI—and How to Fix Them," *The Wall Street Journal*, www.wsj.com, November 5, 2022.
22. According to Richard D'Aveni, the process of pushing price-attribute curves to the right is a characteristic of the competitive process. See R. D'Aveni, *Hypercompetition* (New York: Free Press, 1994).
23. K. Torrella, "Costco's Inflation-Proof \$4.99 Rotisserie Chicken, Explained," *Vox*, www.vox.com, July 18, 2022; A. McDonald, "Costco Sold More Rotisserie Chickens in 2021 as Grocery Prices Hit Record Highs," *Eat This, Not That*, www.eatthis.com, January 14, 2022.
24. V. Utomi, "Top 5 Most Profitable Airlines in the World," *Travel Radar*, https://travelradar.aero, October 21, 2022.
25. "Bags Fly Free!®" www.southwest.com, accessed January 28, 2023.
26. J. Schleckser, "The Secret to the Success of Southwest Airlines, Google, and Ritz Carlton: It's Not What You Think," *Inc.*, www.inc.com, accessed February 22, 2020.
27. "How e-Commerce Became Adidas's Most Important Channel," *Marketing Week*, www.marketingweek.com, May 3, 2019; N. Gilliland, "How Adidas Uses Digital to Enable Powerful Experiences," https://econsultancy.com, May 16, 2017.
28. "TechnologyAdvice Social CRM Software Buyer's Guide," https://technologyadvice.com, February 20, 2020.
29. The view of quality as reliability goes back to the work of Deming and Juran; see Gabor, *The Man Who Discovered Quality*.
30. See Garvin, "What Does Product Quality Really Mean?"; Crosby, *Quality Is Free;* Gabor, *The Man Who Discovered Quality*.
31. "J. D. Power Awards: 2022 Dependability Small Premium SUV Awards," www.jdpower.com, accessed January 28, 2023.
32. Genentech, "Diversity & Inclusion," www.gene.com, accessed January 29, 2023.
33. A. Verasai, "Quita Highsmith on Changing the Face of HR in the Pharmaceutical Industry," *HR Digest*, www.thehrdigest.com, November 10, 2021; M. Alsumidaie, "Clinical Trial Diversity Inclusion Is Becoming a Socially Responsible Initiative," *Clinical Trials*, www.appliedclinicaltrialsonline.com, September 16, 2021.
34. S. K. Corey, "Genentech Aims High with New Diversity Goals, Including Doubling Hires and Spending \$1 Billion with Diverse Suppliers," *Fierce Pharma*, www.fiercepharma.com, April 1, 2021.
35. Genentech, "Advancing Inclusive Research," www.gene.com, accessed January 29, 2023; Coey, "Genentech Aims High"; Alsumidaie, "Clinical Trial Diversity Inclusion."
36. See J.W. Dean and D.E. Bowen, "Management Theory and Total Quality: Improving Research and Practice through Theory Development," *Academy of Management Review* 19 (1994), 392–418.
37. For general background information, see J.C. Anderson, M. Rungtusanatham, and R.G. Schroeder, "A Theory of Quality Management Underlying the Deming Management Method," *Academy of Management Review* 19 (1994), 472–509; "How to Build Quality," *The Economist*, September 23, 1989, 91–92; Gabor, *The Man Who Discovered Quality;* Crosby, *Quality Is Free.*
38. Bowles, "Is American Management Really Committed to Quality?" *Management Review*, April 1992, 42–46.
39. "The History of Six Sigma," www.isixsigma.com, accessed February 22, 2020.
40. Gabor, *The Man Who Discovered Quality*.
41. J. Biolos, "Six Sigma Meets the Service Economy—Six Sigma: It's Not Just for Manufacturing," *Harvard Business School: Working Knowledge Archive*, hbswk.hbs.edu/archive/3278.html, January 27, 2003.
42. S. Kumar, "Six Sigma at Citibank," Sigma Way, www.gosigmaway.com/index.php/easyblog/entry/six-sigma-at-citibank#sthash.15OXtwLH.dpuf, April 2, 2014.
43. R. Rucker, "Six Sigma at Citibank," *Quality Digest*, www.qualitydigest.com/dec99/html/citibank.html.
44. "The Productivity-Pay Gap," Economic Policy Institute, July 2019, https://www.epi.org.
45. T. Mayor, "Ethics and Automation: What to Do When Workers Are Displaced," *Ideas Made to Matter* (blog of MIT Sloan School of Management), July 8, 2019, https://mitsloan.mit.edu.
46. R.L. Martin, "The High Price of Efficiency," *Harvard Business Review*, January–February 2019, 43–55.
47. E. Burr, "Flexible Manufacturing—What Is It?" https://all3dp.com, accessed February 22, 2020.

48. J. Newell, "GM Announces $4 Billion Investment in Orion Assembly Plant," *Lake Orion Review,* https://lakeorionreview.com, January 26, 2022; M. Shirouzu, E. Taylor, and N. Carey, "The Auto Plants of the Future May Have a Surprisingly Human Touch," *Reuters,* www.reuters.com, April 26, 2018.

49. For an interesting discussion of some other dimensions of JIT and other "Japanese" manufacturing techniques, see S.M. Young, "A Framework for Successful Adoption and Performance of Japanese Manufacturing Practices in the United States," *Academy of Management Review* 17 (1992), 677–701.

50. K. Souza, "Walmart Demands All Suppliers Comply with 98% On-Time In-Full Shipment Rule," *TB&P,* https://talkbusiness.net, September 3, 2020.

51. C. Gilliam, "Ecommerce Supply Chain Management: Reducing Cost and Inefficiency," *Web Retailer,* www.webretailer.com, November 18, 2022.

52. See C.W.L. Hill, "Transaction Cost Economizing as a Source of National Competitive Advantage: The Case of Japan," *Organization Science* 2 (1994); M. Aoki, *Information, Incentives, and Bargaining in the Japanese Economy* (Cambridge: Cambridge University Press, 1989).

53. R. Jones, "Teaming at GE Aviation," *Management Innovation eXchange,* www.managementexchange.com, accessed January 29, 2023.

54. M. Hammer and J. Champy, *Reengineering the Corporation* (New York: Harper Business, 1993), 35.

55. Ibid.

56. "74 Amazon Statistics You Must Know: 2023 Market Share Analysis & Data," *Finances Online,* https://financesonline.com, accessed January 29, 2023.

57. T. Gregg and B. Groysberg, "What We Learned from Reading Jeff Bezos' Patents," *Working Knowledge* (Harvard Business School blog), https://hbswk.hbs.edu, February 6, 2020.

58. L. Eadicicco, "This Is the Test Amazon Uses to Decide Which Ideas Are Worth Turning into New Products," *Business Insider,* www.businessinsider.com, October 17, 2019.

59. C. Gallo, "Jeff Bezos Requires Amazon's Leaders to Perform This Powerful Ritual before Launching Anything," *Inc.,* www.inc.com, June 28, 2019.

60. L. Forman, "For Food Delivery, Covid-19 Was a Sugar High," *The Wall Street Journal,* www.wsj.com, April 30, 2021; T. Carman, "Why Fast-Casual Restaurants Became the Decade's Most Important Food Trend," *The Washington Post,* www.washingtonpost.com, December 31, 2019.

CHAPTER 10

Managing Organizational Structure and Culture

Jacob Lund/Shutterstock

Learning Objectives

After studying this chapter, you should be able to:

LO10-1 Identify the factors that influence managers' choice of an organizational structure.

LO10-2 Explain how managers group tasks into jobs that are motivating and satisfying for employees.

LO10-3 Describe the types of organizational structures managers can design, and explain why they choose one structure over another.

LO10-4 Explain why managers must coordinate jobs, functions, and divisions using the hierarchy of authority and integrating mechanisms.

LO10-5 List the four sources of organizational culture, and explain why and how a company's culture can lead to competitive advantage.

A MANAGER'S CHALLENGE

Organizing to Better Manage Banner Health's Facilities

How can an effective organizational structure enable high performance? Phoenix-based Banner Health had a behind-the-scenes problem that could affect its ability to serve patients and other clients. The problem involved facilities management, which is charged with maintaining conditions such as temperature, humidity, and air pressure to efficiently provide an environment that is comfortable and safe for workers and patients in facilities. Across the six states where Banner Health operates, each facility had an automated system, and the organization did not have enough facilities management workers with the high-level skills required to maximize the system's performance. Instead, employees tweaked the systems in various ways, and efficiency tended to deteriorate. Banner Health is a nonprofit, so the consequence of inefficiency is that the 32-hospital organization has less to invest in facilities and technologies to provide more and better care. Furthermore, the independent decision making in the facilities was making it hard for Banner Health to verify that every facility was meeting regulatory requirements and standards of patient care. The challenges would only grow more intense as the organization carried out its ambitious expansion plans.[1]

An opportunity to address the problem comprehensively came along when management decided to undergo a process called *retrocommissioning* at several of its facilities. Retrocommissioning involves inspecting a building to identify deficiencies in systems such as heating, ventilation, and air conditioning, then correcting them to meet goals such as energy efficiency and spending reduction, often using automatic controls and real-time data collection.[2] Banner Health determined that during that process of reviewing the buildings' technology, it would also address the way it organizes the work of facilities management. To maintain more consistent control, the organization would consolidate the processes in a remote operations center, where a highly skilled team would establish standards to ensure high-quality operation of equipment across all facilities. Following these standards, geographically defined clusters of facilities would manage the facilities. In addition, the operations center would use data from the facilities to set priorities for spending on upgrades.[3]

This effort to centralize facilities management quickly yielded benefits. Use of the centralized team has led to a reduction of energy expenses by almost $12 million over the first few years of the program. The center's ability to monitor

While reviewing technology processes in its buildings, Banner Health decided to centralize its facility management practices, which allowed the organization to reduce energy expenses by nearly $12 million in the first years of the program.
David Spates/Shutterstock

equipment performance in real time also lowers maintenance expenses by anticipating problems, rather than repairs happening only after a system breaks down. The center has also met other goals, such as targets for maintaining a comfortable environment (fewer calls about rooms being too hot or too cold) and using pressure controls to prevent the spread of infections. Furthermore, various departments within Banner Health have come to view the staff of the remote operations center as a valuable resource they can consult about spending, construction, and other decisions.[4]

Facilities maintenance may not always be on the minds of doctors, nurses, or the million patients a year using Banner Health's facilities. Nevertheless, the decision to centralize this function has improved Banner Health's ability to maintain its position as a top U.S. health system.[5]

Overview

As the opening story suggests, organizational structure and culture are powerful influences on how employees work. The way an organization's structure is designed also affects employee behavior and how well the organization functions. In a quickly changing business environment, managers at all levels of an organization must identify the best way to organize people and resources to increase efficiency and effectiveness.

In Part 4 of this book, we examine how managers can organize and control human and other resources to create high-performing organizations. To organize and control (two of the four functions of management identified in Chapter 1), managers must design an organizational architecture that makes the best use of resources to produce the goods and services customers want. **Organizational architecture** is the combination of organizational structure, culture, control systems, and human resource management (HRM) systems that determines how efficiently and effectively organizational resources are used.

organizational architecture The organizational structure, control systems, culture, and human resource management systems that together determine how efficiently and effectively organizational resources are used.

By the end of this chapter, you will be familiar not only with various forms of organizational structures and cultures but also with various factors that determine the organizational design choices that managers make. Then, in Chapters 11 and 12, we examine issues surrounding the design of an organization's control systems and HRM systems.

Designing Organizational Structure

Organizing is the process by which managers establish the structure of working relationships among employees to allow them to achieve an organization's goals efficiently and effectively. **Organizational structure** is the formal system of task and job reporting relationships that determines how employees use resources to achieve an organization's goals.[6] *Organizational culture,* discussed in Chapter 3, is the shared set of beliefs, values, and norms that influence how people and groups work together to achieve an organization's goals. **Organizational design** is the process by which managers create a specific type of organizational structure and culture so a company can operate in the most efficient and effective way.[7]

LO10-1 Identify the factors that influence managers' choice of an organizational structure.

Once a company decides what kind of work attitudes and behaviors it wants from its employees, managers create a particular arrangement of task and authority relationships, and promote specific cultural values and norms, to obtain these desired attitudes and behaviors. The challenge facing all companies is to design a structure and a culture that (1) *motivate* managers and employees to work hard and to develop supportive job behaviors and attitudes and (2) *coordinate* the actions of employees, groups, functions, and divisions to ensure they work together efficiently and effectively.

organizational structure A formal system of task and reporting relationships that coordinates and motivates organizational members so they work together to achieve an organization's goals.

As noted in Chapter 2, according to contingency theory, managers design organizational structures to fit the factors or circumstances that are affecting the company the most and causing the most uncertainty.[8] Thus, there is no one best way to design an organization: Design reflects each organization's specific situation, and researchers have argued that stable, mechanistic structures may be most appropriate in some situations, whereas in others flexible, organic structures might be the most effective. Four factors are important determinants of the

Figure 10.1

Factors Affecting Organizational Structure

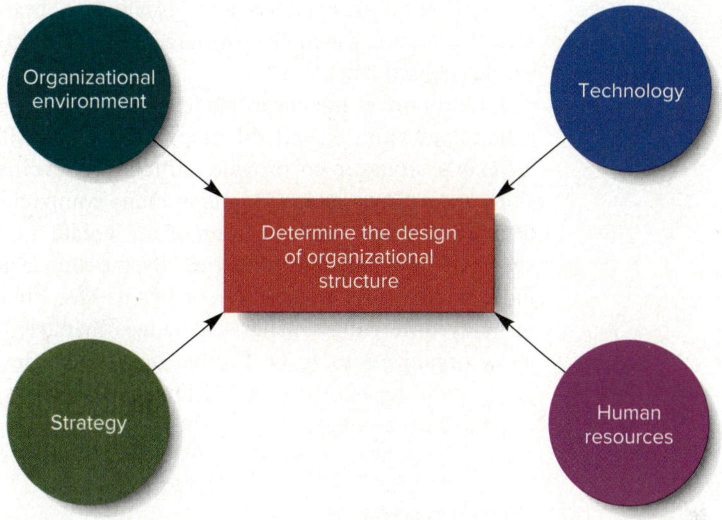

organizational design The process by which managers make specific organizing choices that result in a particular kind of organizational structure.

type of organizational structure or culture managers select: the nature of the organizational environment, the type of strategy the organization pursues, the technology (and particularly information technology) the organization uses, and the characteristics of the organization's human resources (see Figure 10.1).[9]

The Organizational Environment

In general, the more quickly the external environment is changing and the greater the uncertainty within it, the greater are the problems managers face in trying to gain access to scarce resources. In this situation, to speed decision making and communication and make it easier to obtain resources, managers typically make organizing choices that result in more flexible structures and entrepreneurial cultures.[10] They are likely to decentralize authority, empower lower-level employees to make important operating decisions, and encourage values and norms that emphasize change and innovation–a more organic form of organizing.

In contrast, if the external environment is stable, resources are readily available, and uncertainty is low, then less coordination and communication among people and functions are needed to obtain resources. Managers can make organizing choices that bring more stability or formality to the organizational structure and can establish values and norms that emphasize obedience and being a team player. Managers in this situation prefer to make decisions within a clearly defined hierarchy of authority and to use detailed rules, standard operating procedures (SOPs), and restrictive norms to guide and govern employees' activities–a more mechanistic form of organizing.

As we discussed in Chapter 6, change is rapid in today's marketplace, and increasing competition both at home and abroad is putting greater pressure on managers to attract customers and increase efficiency and effectiveness. Consequently, interest in finding ways to structure organizations–such as through empowerment and self-managed teams–to allow people and departments to behave flexibly has been increasing.

Strategy

Chapter 8 suggests that once managers decide on a strategy, they must choose the right means to implement it. Different strategies often call for the use of different organizational structures and cultures. For example, a differentiation strategy aimed at increasing the value customers perceive in an organization's goods and services usually succeeds best in a flexible structure with a culture that values innovation; flexibility facilitates a differentiation strategy because managers can develop new or innovative products quickly—an activity that requires extensive cooperation among functions or departments. In contrast, a low-cost strategy that is aimed at driving down costs in all functions usually fares best in a more formal structure with more conservative norms, which gives managers greater control over the activities of an organization's various departments.[11]

In addition, at the corporate level, when managers decide to expand the scope of organizational activities by vertical integration or diversification, for example, they need to design a flexible structure to provide sufficient coordination among the different business divisions.[12] As discussed in Chapter 8, many companies have been selling off various businesses because managers have been unable to create a competitive advantage to keep them up to speed in fast-changing industries. By moving to a more flexible structure, managers gain more control over their different businesses. Finally, expanding internationally—operating in many different countries—challenges managers to create organizational structures that allow organizations to be flexible on a global level.[13] As we discuss later, managers can group their departments or divisions in several ways to allow them to effectively pursue an international strategy.

Technology

Recall that technology is the combination of skills, knowledge, machines, and computers that are used to design, make, and distribute goods and services. As a rule, the more complicated the technology that an organization uses, the more difficult it is to regulate or control it because more unexpected events can arise. Thus, the more complicated the technology, the greater is the need for a flexible structure and progressive culture to enhance managers' ability to respond to unexpected situations—and give them the freedom and desire to work out new solutions to the problems they encounter. In contrast, the more routine the technology, the more appropriate is a formal structure because tasks are simple and the steps needed to produce goods and services have been worked out in advance.

What makes a technology routine or complicated? One researcher who investigated this issue, Charles Perrow, argued that two factors determine how complicated or nonroutine technology is: task variety and task analyzability.[14] *Task variety* is the number of new or unexpected problems or situations that a person or function encounters in performing tasks or jobs. *Task analyzability* is the degree to which programmed solutions are available to people or functions to solve the problems they encounter. Nonroutine or complicated technologies are characterized by high task variety and low task analyzability; this means many varied problems occur, and solving these problems requires significant nonprogrammed decision making. In contrast, routine technologies are characterized by low task variety and high task analyzability; this means the problems encountered do not vary much and are easily resolved through programmed decision making.

Examples of nonroutine technology are found in the work of scientists in an R&D laboratory who develop new products or discover new drugs, and they are seen in the planning exercises an organization's top management team uses to chart future strategy. Examples of routine technology include typical mass production or assembly operations, where workers perform the same task repeatedly and where managers have already identified the programmed solutions necessary to perform a task efficiently. Similarly, in service organizations such as fast-food restaurants, the tasks that crew members perform in making and serving fast food are routine.

Human Resources

LO10-2 Explain how managers group tasks into jobs that are motivating and satisfying for employees.

Final important factors affecting an organization's choice of structure and culture are the characteristics of the human resources it employs. In general, the more highly skilled its workforce, and the greater the number of employees who work together in groups or teams, the more likely an organization is to use a flexible, decentralized structure and a professional culture based on values and norms that foster employee autonomy and self-control. Highly skilled employees, or employees who have internalized strong professional values and norms of behavior as part of their training, usually desire autonomy and dislike close supervision.

Flexible structures, characterized by decentralized authority and empowered employees, are well suited to the needs of highly skilled people. Similarly, when people work in teams, they must be allowed to interact freely and develop norms to guide their own work interactions, which also is possible in a flexible organizational structure. Thus, when designing organizational structure and culture, managers must pay close attention to the needs of the workforce and to the complexity and kind of work employees perform.

In summary, an organization's external environment, strategy, technology, and human resources are the factors to be considered by managers seeking to design the best structure and culture for an organization. The greater the level of uncertainty in the organization's environment, the more complex its strategy and technologies, and the more highly qualified and skilled its workforce, the more likely managers are to design a structure and a culture that are flexible, can change quickly, and allow employees to be innovative in their responses to problems, customer needs, and so on. The more stable the organization's environment, the less complex and more well understood its strategy or technology, and the less skilled its workforce, the more likely managers are to design an organizational structure that is formal and controlling and a culture whose values and norms prescribe how employees should act in particular situations.

Later in the chapter, we discuss how managers can create different kinds of organizational cultures. First, however, we discuss how managers can design flexible or formal organizational structures. The way an organization's structure works depends on the organizing choices managers make about three issues:

1. How to group tasks into individual jobs.
2. How to group jobs into functions and divisions.
3. How to allocate authority and coordinate or integrate functions and divisions.

Grouping Tasks into Jobs: Job Design

job design The process by which managers decide how to divide tasks into specific jobs.

The first step in organizational design is **job design**, the process by which managers decide how to divide into specific jobs the tasks that have to be performed to provide customers with goods and services. Managers at McDonald's, for example, have decided how best to divide the tasks required to provide customers with fast, cheap food in each McDonald's restaurant. After experimenting with different job arrangements, McDonald's managers decided on a basic division of labor among chefs and food servers. Managers allocated all the tasks involved in actually cooking the food (putting oil in the fryers, opening packages of frozen french fries, putting beef patties on the grill, making salads, and so on) to the job of chef. They allocated all the tasks involved in giving the food to customers (such as greeting customers, taking orders, putting fries and burgers into bags, and taking money) to food servers. In addition, they created other jobs—the job of dealing with drive-through customers, the job of keeping the restaurant clean, and the job of overseeing employees and responding to unexpected events. The result of the job design process is a *division of labor* among employees, one that McDonald's managers have discovered through experience is most efficient.

Establishing an appropriate division of labor among employees is a critical part of the organizing process, one that is vital to increasing efficiency and effectiveness. At McDonald's, the tasks associated with chef and food server were split into different jobs because managers found that, for the kind of food McDonald's serves, this approach was most efficient. It is efficient because when each employee is given fewer tasks to perform (so that each job becomes more specialized), employees become more productive at performing the tasks that constitute each job.

Over the past few years, the job design for McDonald's food servers has undergone significant changes, as more and more self-ordering kiosks for customers and the McDonald's mobile ordering app have become operational at many stores in the United States and abroad. While some critics suggest more jobs will be lost through this automation, others point out that the ordering process has accelerated, eliminating some of the long lines at the counter

The use of self-service kiosks at McDonald's has helped change the job design for many of its employees, which may help food servers learn additional skills to make the customer experience more efficient and satisfying.
Tada Images/Shutterstock

and speeding up overall transactions. In the current tight labor market, the revised job design may help servers learn additional skills to make the customer experience more efficient and satisfying. In addition, during the global pandemic, when many fast-food dining rooms were shuttered, McDonald's mobile app accounted for more than $8 billion in sales in the first half of 2021. Today the fast-food chain has more than 40 million active app users.[15]

At Subway sandwich shops, managers chose a different kind of job design. At Subway there is no division of labor among the people who make the sandwiches, wrap the sandwiches, give them to customers, and take the money. The roles of chef and food server are combined into one. This different division of tasks and jobs is efficient for Subway and not for McDonald's because Subway serves a limited menu of mostly submarine-style sandwiches that are prepared to order. Subway's production system is far simpler than McDonald's; McDonald's menu is much more varied, and its chefs must prepare many different kinds of foods.

Managers of every organization must analyze the range of tasks to be performed and then create jobs that best allow the organization to give customers the goods and services they want. In deciding how to assign tasks to individual jobs, however, managers must be careful not to take **job simplification**, the process of reducing the number of tasks that each worker performs, too far.[16] Too much job simplification may reduce efficiency rather than increase it if workers find their simplified jobs boring and monotonous, become demotivated and unhappy, and as a result, perform at a low level.

job simplification The process of reducing the number of tasks that each worker performs.

Job Enlargement and Job Enrichment

In an attempt to create a division of labor and design individual jobs to encourage workers to perform at a higher level and be more satisfied with their work, several researchers have proposed ways other than job simplification to group tasks into jobs: job enlargement and job enrichment.

job enlargement Increasing the number of different tasks in a given job by changing the division of labor.

Job enlargement is increasing the number of different tasks in a given job by changing the division of labor.[17] For example, because Subway food servers make the food as well as serve it, their jobs are "larger" than the jobs of McDonald's food servers, although automation may help enlarge McDonald's food servers tasks in the near future. The idea behind job enlargement is that increasing the range of tasks performed by a worker will reduce boredom and may increase motivation to perform at a high level–increasing both the quantity and the quality of goods and services provided.

job enrichment Increasing the degree of responsibility a worker has over his or her job.

Job enrichment is increasing the degree of responsibility a worker has over a job by, for example, (1) empowering workers to experiment to find new or better ways of doing the job, (2) encouraging workers to develop new skills, (3) allowing workers to decide how to do the work and giving them the responsibility for deciding how to respond to unexpected situations, and (4) allowing workers to monitor and measure their own performance.[18] The idea behind job enrichment is that increasing workers' responsibility increases their involvement in their jobs and, thus, improves their interest in the quality of the goods they make or the services they provide.

In general, managers who make design choices that increase job enrichment and job enlargement are likely to increase the degree to which people behave flexibly rather than rigidly or mechanically. Narrow, specialized jobs are likely to lead people to behave in predictable ways; workers who perform a variety of tasks and who are allowed and encouraged to discover new and better ways to perform their jobs are likely to act flexibly and creatively. Thus, managers who enlarge and enrich jobs create a flexible organizational structure, and those who simplify jobs create a more formal structure. If workers are grouped into self-managed work teams, the organization is likely to be flexible because team members provide support for each other and can learn from one another.

The Job Characteristics Model

J. R. Hackman and G. R. Oldham's job characteristics model is an influential model of job design that explains in detail how managers can make jobs more interesting and motivating.[19] Hackman and Oldham's model also describes the likely personal and organizational outcomes that will result from enriched and enlarged jobs.

According to Hackman and Oldham, every job has five characteristics that determine how motivating the job is. These characteristics determine how employees react to their work and lead to outcomes such as high performance and satisfaction and low absenteeism and turnover:

- *Skill variety:* The extent to which a job requires that an employee use a wide range of different skills, abilities, or knowledge. Example: The skill variety required by the job of a research scientist is higher than that called for by the job of a food server.
- *Task identity:* The extent to which a job requires that a worker perform all the tasks necessary to complete the job, from the beginning to the end of the production process. Example: A carpenter who takes a piece of wood and transforms it into a custom-made desk has higher task identity than does a worker who performs only one of the numerous operations required to assemble a flat-screen TV.
- *Task significance:* The degree to which a worker feels their job is meaningful because of its effect on people inside the organization, such as coworkers, or on people outside the organization, such as customers. Example: A teacher who sees the effect of their efforts in a well-educated and well-adjusted student enjoys high task significance.
- *Autonomy:* The degree to which a job gives an employee the freedom and discretion needed to schedule different tasks and decide how to carry them out. Example: Salespeople who have to plan their schedules and decide how to allocate their time among different customers have relatively high autonomy compared to assembly-line workers, whose actions are determined by the speed of the production line.
- *Feedback:* The extent to which actually doing a job provides a worker with clear and direct information about how well they have performed the job. Example: An air traffic controller whose mistakes may result in a midair collision receives immediate feedback on job performance; a person who compiles statistics for a marketing research firm often has little idea of when they make a mistake or do a particularly good job.

Hackman and Oldham argue that these five job characteristics affect an employee's motivation because they affect three critical psychological states. The more that employees feel that their work is *meaningful* and that they are *responsible for work outcomes* and *responsible for knowing how those outcomes affect others,* the more motivating work becomes and the more likely employees are to be satisfied and to perform at a high level. Moreover, employees who have jobs that are highly motivating are called on to use their skills more and to perform more tasks, and they are given more responsibility for doing the job. All of these are characteristic of jobs and employees in flexible structures where authority is decentralized and where employees commonly work with others and must learn new skills to complete the range of tasks for which their group is responsible.

Grouping Jobs into Functions and Divisions: Designing Organizational Structure

Once managers have decided which tasks to allocate to which jobs, they face the next organizing decision: how to group jobs together to best match the needs of the organization's environment, strategy, technology, and human resources. Typically, managers first decide to group jobs into departments and then design a *functional structure* to use organizational resources effectively. As an organization grows and becomes more difficult to control, managers must choose a more complex organizational design, such as a divisional structure or a matrix or product team structure. The different ways in which managers can design organizational structure are discussed next. Selecting and designing an organizational structure to increase efficiency and effectiveness is a significant challenge. As noted in Chapter 8, managers reap the rewards of a well-thought-out strategy only if they choose the right type of structure to implement the strategy. The ability to make the right kinds of organizing choices is often what differentiates effective from ineffective managers and creates a high-performing organization.

Functional Structure

LO10-3 Describe the types of organizational structures managers can design, and explain why they choose one structure over another.

A *function* is a group of people, working together, who possess similar skills or use the same kind of knowledge, tools, or techniques to perform their jobs. Manufacturing, sales, and research and development are often organized into functional departments. A **functional structure** is an organizational structure composed of all the departments that an organization requires to produce its goods or services. Figure 10.2 shows the functional structure that the Home Depot, a one-stop home improvement retailer, uses to supply its customers with a range of goods and services that help them build and maintain their homes.[20]

functional structure An organizational structure composed of all the departments that an organization requires to produce its goods or services.

Within Home Depot's organizational structure, the main functions include finance and administration, merchandising (purchasing the goods), supply chain (managing the vendors who supply the goods), outsides sales and services, information technology (managing the IT structure and product development), and human resources. Each job within a function exists because it helps the function perform the activities necessary for high organizational performance. Thus, within the information technology function are all the jobs necessary to keep Home Depot's communications networks operating efficiently across the company's more than 2,200 stores and support centers.

There are several advantages to grouping jobs according to function. First, when people who perform similar jobs are grouped together, they can learn from observing one another and thus become more specialized and can perform at a higher level. The tasks associated with one job often are related to the tasks associated with another job, which encourages cooperation within a function. In Home Depot's merchandising function, for example–which includes all aspects of merchandising, marketing, store environment, pricing, and assortment planning–the person designing the graphics for the company's website and various ad campaigns works closely with the person responsible for designing store layouts and visual displays. As a result, the company can develop strong marketing campaigns to differentiate its products and services.

Second, when people who perform similar jobs are grouped together, it is easier for managers to monitor and evaluate their performance.[21] Imagine if marketing experts, purchasing experts, and real estate experts were grouped together in one function and supervised by a manager from merchandising. Obviously, the merchandising manager would not have the expertise to evaluate all these different people appropriately. A functional structure allows workers to evaluate how well coworkers are performing their jobs, and if some workers are performing poorly, more experienced workers can help them develop new skills.

Finally, managers appreciate functional structure because it lets them create the set of functions they need to scan and monitor the competitive environment and obtain information about how it is changing.[22] With the right set of functions in place, managers are in a good position to develop a strategy that allows the organization to respond to its changing situation. Employees in the marketing group can specialize in monitoring new marketing developments

Figure 10.2
The Functional Structure of the Home Depot

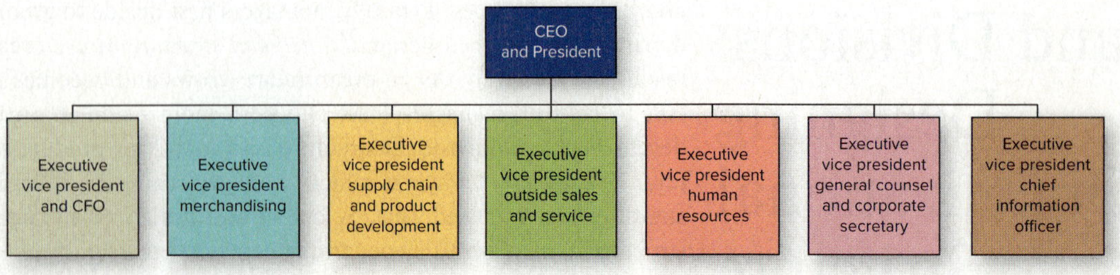

The Home Depot organizes its operations by function, which means that employees can more easily learn from one another and improve the service they provide to customers.
Joe Raedle/Getty Images

that will allow Home Depot to better target its customers and their needs. Employees in merchandising can monitor potential suppliers to find the goods mostly like to appeal to Home Depot's customers.

As an organization grows, and particularly as its task environment and strategy change because it is beginning to produce a wider range of goods and services for different kinds of customers, several problems can make a functional structure less efficient and effective.[23] First, managers in different functions may find it more difficult to communicate and coordinate with one another when they are responsible for several different kinds of products, especially as the organization grows both domestically and internationally. Second, functional managers may become so preoccupied with supervising their own specific departments and achieving their departmental goals that they lose sight of the organization's goals. If that happens, organizational effectiveness will suffer because managers will be viewing issues and problems facing the organization only from their own, relatively narrow departmental perspectives.[24] Both of these problems can reduce efficiency and effectiveness.

Divisional Structures: Product, Market, and Geographic

divisional structure An organizational structure composed of separate business units, within which are the functions that work together to produce a specific kind of product for a specific kind of customer.

As the problems associated with growth and diversification increase over time, managers must search for new ways to organize their activities to overcome the problems associated with a functional structure. Most managers of large organizations choose a **divisional structure** and create a series of business units to produce a specific kind of product for a specific kind of customer. Each *division* is a collection of functions or departments that work together to produce the product. The goal behind the change to a divisional structure is to create smaller, more manageable units within the organization. There are three forms of divisional structure (see Figure 10.3).[25] When managers organize divisions according to the *type of good or service* they provide, they adopt a product structure. When managers organize divisions according to the *area of the country or world* they operate in, they adopt a geographic structure. When managers organize divisions according to *the type of customer* they focus on, they adopt a market structure.

PRODUCT STRUCTURE Imagine the problems that managers at Home Depot would encounter if they decided to diversify into producing and selling cars, fast food, and health insurance–in addition to home-related products and services–and tried to use their existing set of functional managers to oversee the production of all four kinds of products. No manager would have the necessary skills or abilities to oversee those four products. No individual marketing manager, for example, could effectively market cars, fast food, health insurance, and home products and services at the same time. To perform a functional activity successfully, managers must have experience in specific markets or industries. Consequently, if managers decide to diversify into new industries or to expand their range of products, they commonly design a product structure to organize their operations (see Figure 10.3A).

product structure An organizational structure in which each product line or business is handled by a self-contained division.

Using a **product structure**, managers place each distinct product line or business in its own, self-contained division and give divisional managers the responsibility for devising an appropriate business-level strategy to allow the division to compete effectively in its industry or market.[26] Each division is self-contained because it has a complete set of all the functions–marketing, R&D, finance, and so on–that it needs to produce or provide goods or services efficiently and effectively. Functional managers report to divisional managers, and divisional managers report to top or corporate managers.

Figure 10.3

Product, Geographic, and Market Structures

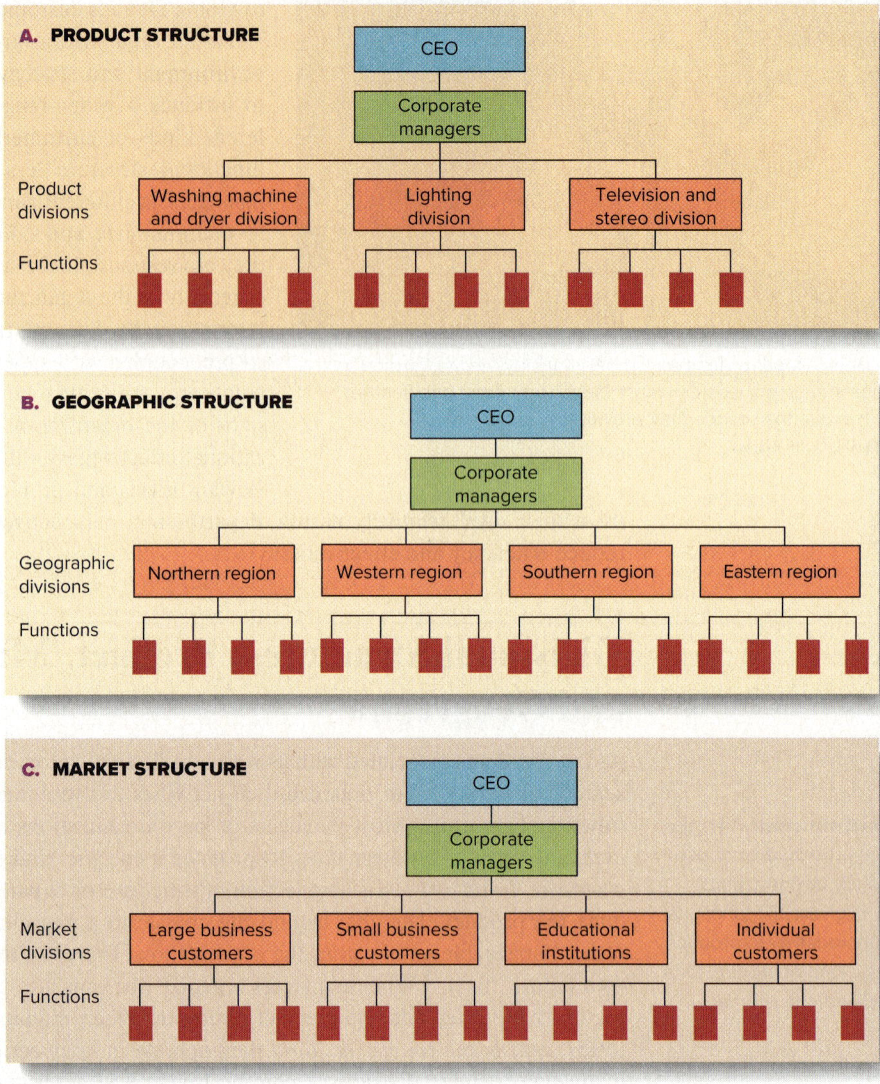

Grouping functions into divisions focused on particular products has several advantages for managers at all levels in the organization. First, a product structure allows functional managers to specialize in only one product area, so they can build expertise and fine-tune their skills in this particular area. Second, each division's managers can become experts in their industry; this expertise helps them choose and develop a business-level strategy to differentiate their products or lower their costs while meeting the needs of customers. Third, a product structure frees corporate managers from the need to supervise directly each division's day-to-day operations; this latitude lets corporate managers create the best corporate-level strategy to maximize the organization's future growth and ability to create value. Corporate managers are likely to make fewer mistakes about which businesses to diversify into or how to best expand internationally, for example, because they can take an organizationwide view.[27] Corporate managers also are likely to evaluate better how well divisional managers are doing, and they can intervene and take corrective action as needed.

The extra layer of management, the divisional management layer, can improve the use of organizational resources. Moreover, a product structure puts divisional managers close to their customers and lets them respond quickly and appropriately to the changing task environment. One pharmaceutical company that successfully adopted a new product structure to better organize its activities is GlaxoSmithKline (GSK). The need to innovate new kinds of prescription drugs to boost performance is a continual battle for pharmaceutical companies. In the 2000s, many of these companies merged to try to increase their research productivity, and one of them, GlaxoSmithKline, was created from the merger between Glaxo Wellcome and SmithKline Beecham. Prior to the merger, both companies experienced a steep decline in the number of new prescription drugs their scientists were able to invent. The problem facing the new company's top managers was how to best use and combine the talents of the scientists and researchers from both of the former companies to allow them to quickly innovate exciting new drugs.

Top managers realized that after the merger there would be enormous problems associated with coordinating the activities of the thousands of research scientists who were working on hundreds of different drug research programs. Understanding the problems associated with large size, the top managers decided to group the researchers into eight product divisions to allow them to focus on particular clusters of diseases such as heart disease or viral infections. The members of each product division were told they would be rewarded based on the number of new prescription drugs they were able to invent and the speed with which they could bring these new drugs to the market. GlaxoSmithKline's new product structure worked well; its research productivity doubled after the reorganization, and a record number of new drugs moved into clinical trials. Under CEO Emma Walmsley, GSK recently reorganized again, dividing into two business units: pharmaceuticals and vaccines. In addition, Walmsley announced GSK would spin off its consumer health care business into a separate company named Haleon in late 2022. Despite pressure from an active shareholder who recently acquired a large stake in the company, Walmsley and the GSK board of directors rejected the investor's demands to sell off the consumer health care business altogether. In this recent reorganization, GSK eliminated hundreds of jobs in its global workforce.[28]

GEOGRAPHIC STRUCTURE When organizations expand rapidly both at home and abroad, functional structures can create special problems because managers in one central location may find it increasingly difficult to deal with the different problems and issues that may arise in each region of a country or area of the world. In these cases, a **geographic structure**, in which divisions are broken down by geographic location, is often chosen (see Figure 10.3B). To achieve the corporate mission of providing next-day delivery service, Fred Smith, founder of FedEx, chose a geographic structure and divided up operations by creating a division in each region. Large retailers such as Macy's, Neiman Marcus, and Nordstrom also use a geographic structure. Because the needs of retail customers differ by region–for example, shorts in California and down parkas in the Midwest–a geographic structure gives retail regional managers the flexibility they need to choose the range of products that best meets the needs of regional customers.

geographic structure An organizational structure in which each region of a country or area of the world is served by a self-contained division.

In adopting a *global geographic structure,* as shown in Figure 10.4A, managers locate different divisions in each of the world regions where the organization operates. Managers are most likely to do this when they pursue a multidomestic strategy because customer needs vary widely by country or world region. If products that appeal to U.S. customers do not sell in Europe, the Pacific Rim, or South America, managers must customize the products to meet the needs of customers in those different world regions; a global geographic structure with global divisions will allow them to do this. For example, food and beverage companies need to customize the taste of their products to closely match the desires of customers in different countries and world regions.

In contrast, to the degree that customers abroad are willing to buy the same kind of product or slight variations thereof, managers are more likely to pursue a global strategy. In this case, they are more likely to use a global product structure. In a *global product structure,* each product division, not the country and regional managers, takes responsibility for deciding where to manufacture its products and how to market them in countries worldwide (see Figure 10.4B). Product division managers manage their own global value chains and decide where to establish foreign subsidiaries to distribute and sell their products to customers in foreign countries.

MARKET STRUCTURE Sometimes the pressing issue facing managers is to group functions according to the type of customer buying the product in order to tailor the products the organization offers to each customer's unique demands. A PC maker such as Dell, for example,

Figure 10.4

Global Geographic and Global Product Structures

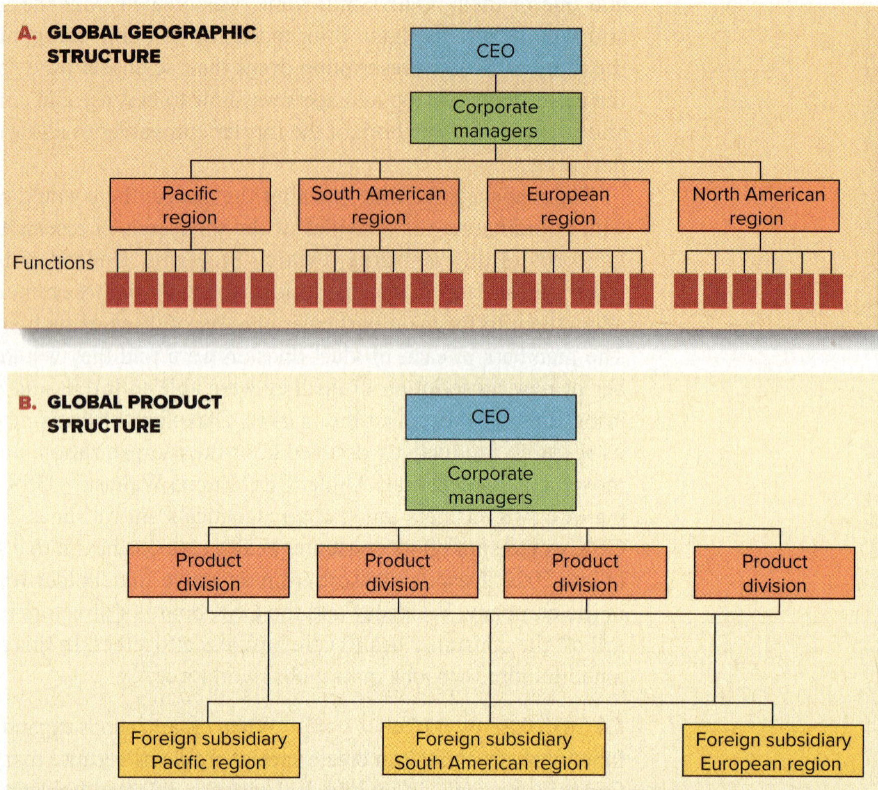

has several kinds of customers, including large businesses (which might demand networks of computers linked to a mainframe computer), small companies (which may need just a few PCs linked together), educational users in schools and universities (which might want thousands of independent PCs for their students), and individual users (who may want a high-quality multimedia PC so they can play the latest video games).

market structure An organizational structure in which each kind of customer is served by a self-contained division; also called *customer structure.*

To satisfy the needs of diverse customers, a company might adopt a **market structure**, which groups divisions according to the particular kinds of customers they serve (see Figure 10.3C). A market structure lets managers respond to the needs of their customers and allows them to act flexibly in making decisions in response to customers' changing needs. To spearhead its turnaround in the PC business, for example, Dell created four streamlined market divisions that each focus on being responsive to one particular type of customer; for example, individual consumers, small businesses, large companies, and government and state agencies.

Matrix and Product Team Designs

Moving to a product, market, or geographic divisional structure allows managers to respond more quickly and flexibly to the particular circumstances they confront. However, when information technology or customer needs are changing rapidly and the environment is uncertain, even a divisional structure may not give managers enough flexibility to respond to the environment quickly. To operate effectively under these conditions, managers must design the most flexible kinds of organizational structure available: a matrix structure or a product team structure (see Figure 10.5).

matrix structure An organizational structure that simultaneously groups people and resources by function and by product.

MATRIX STRUCTURE In a **matrix structure**, managers group people and resources in two ways simultaneously: by function and by product.[29] Employees are grouped by *functions*

Figure 10.5

Matrix and Product Team Structures

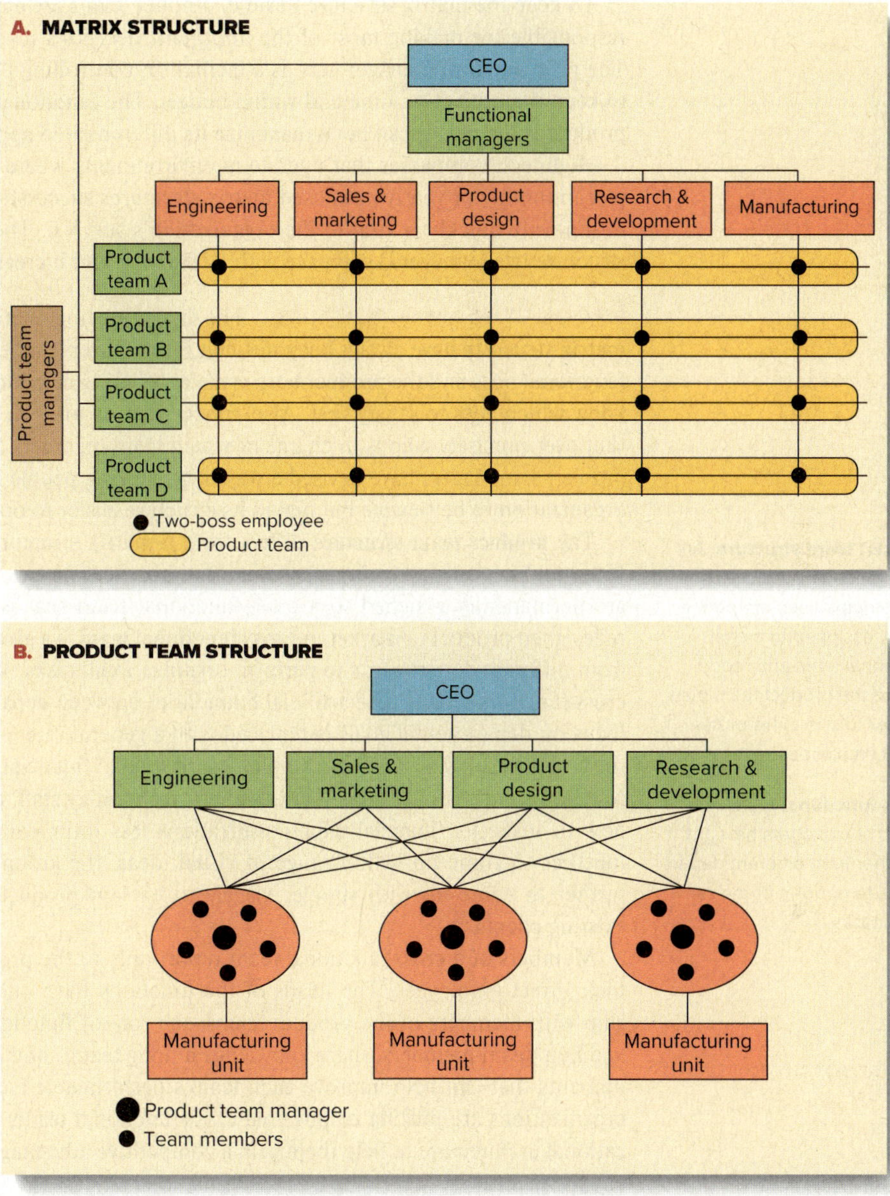

to allow them to learn from one another and become more skilled and productive. In addition, employees are grouped into *product teams* in which members of different functions work together to develop a specific product. The result is a complex network of reporting relationships among product teams and functions that makes the matrix structure very flexible (see Figure 10.5A). Each person in a product team reports to two managers: (1) a functional boss, who assigns individuals to a team and evaluates their performance from a functional perspective, and (2) the boss of the product team, who evaluates their performance on the team. Thus, team members are known as *two-boss employees.* The functional employees assigned to product teams change over time as the specific skills that the team needs change. At the beginning of the product development process, for example, engineers and R&D specialists are assigned to a product team because their skills are needed to develop new products. When a provisional design has been established, marketing experts are assigned to the team to gauge how customers will respond to the new product. Manufacturing personnel join when it is time to find the most efficient way to produce the product. As their specific jobs are completed, team members leave and are reassigned to new teams. In this way the matrix structure makes the most use of human resources.

To keep the matrix structure flexible, product teams are empowered and team members are responsible for making most of the important decisions involved in product development.[30] The product team manager acts as a facilitator, controlling the financial resources and trying to keep the project on time and within budget. The functional managers try to ensure that the product is the best it can be to maximize its differentiated appeal.

High-tech companies that operate in environments where new product development takes place monthly or yearly have used matrix structures successfully for many years, and the need to innovate quickly is vital to the organization's survival. The flexibility afforded by a matrix structure lets managers keep pace with a changing and increasingly complex environment.[31]

PRODUCT TEAM STRUCTURE The dual reporting relationships that are at the heart of a matrix structure have always been difficult for managers and employees to deal with. Often the functional boss and the product boss make conflicting demands on team members, who do not know which boss to satisfy first. Also, functional and product team bosses may come into conflict over precisely who is in charge of which team members and for how long. To avoid these problems, managers have devised a way of organizing people and resources that still allows an organization to be flexible but makes its structure easier to operate: a product team structure.

product team structure An organizational structure in which employees are permanently assigned to a cross-functional team and report only to the product team manager or to one of his or her direct employees.

cross-functional team A group of managers brought together from different departments to perform organizational tasks.

The **product team structure** differs from a matrix structure in two ways: (1) It does away with dual reporting relationships and two-boss employees, and (2) functional employees are permanently assigned to a cross-functional team that is empowered to bring a new or redesigned product to market. A **cross-functional team** is a group of managers brought together from different departments to perform organizational tasks. When managers are grouped into cross-functional teams, the artificial boundaries between departments disappear, and a narrow focus on departmental goals is replaced with a general interest in working together to achieve the organization's goals. For example, insurance and financial services company Northwestern Mutual recently brought together designers, technology staff, and financial planners to explore how to make its financial data visualizations less intimidating to customers. After working together to come up with a range of visual ideas, the group voted on which designs to test further to come up with simpler visuals to explain products and services to potential and existing clients.[32]

Members of a cross-functional team report only to the product team manager or to one of their direct employees. The heads of the functions have only an informal advisory relationship with members of the product teams–the role of functional managers is only to counsel and help team members, share knowledge among teams, and provide new technological developments that can help improve each team's performance (see Figure 10.5B).[33] Increasingly, organizations are making empowered cross-functional teams an essential part of their organizational architecture to help them gain a competitive advantage in fast-changing organizational environments.

Coordinating Functions and Divisions

LO10-4 Explain why managers must coordinate jobs, functions, and divisions using the hierarchy of authority and integrating mechanisms.

The more complex the structure a company uses to group its activities, the greater are the problems of *linking and coordinating* its different functions and divisions. Coordination becomes a problem because each function or division develops a different orientation toward the other groups that affects how it interacts with them. Each function or division comes to view the problems facing the company from its own perspective; for example, it may develop different views about the major goals, problems, or issues facing a company.

At the functional level, the manufacturing function typically has a short-term view; its major goal is to keep costs under control and get the product out the factory door on time. By contrast, the product development function has a long-term viewpoint because developing a new product is a relatively slow process, and high product quality is seen as more important than low costs. Such differences in viewpoint may make manufacturing and product development managers reluctant to cooperate and coordinate their activities to meet company goals. At the divisional level, in a company with a product structure, employees may become concerned more with making *their* division's products a success than with the profitability of the entire company. They may refuse, or simply not see the need, to cooperate and share information or knowledge with other divisions.

The problem of linking and coordinating the activities of different functions and divisions becomes more acute as the number of functions and divisions increases. We look first at how managers design the hierarchy of authority to coordinate functions and divisions so that they work together effectively. Then we focus on integration and examine the integrating mechanisms managers can use to coordinate functions and divisions.

Allocating Authority

authority The power to hold people accountable for their actions and to make decisions concerning the use of organizational resources.

hierarchy of authority An organization's chain of command, specifying the relative authority of each manager.

span of control The number of employees who report directly to a manager.

line manager Someone in the direct line or chain of command who has formal authority over people and resources at lower levels.

staff manager Someone responsible for managing a specialist function, such as finance or marketing.

As organizations grow and produce a wider range of goods and services, the size and number of their functions and divisions increase. To coordinate the activities of people, functions, and divisions and to allow them to work together effectively, managers must develop a clear hierarchy of authority.[34] **Authority** is the power vested in a manager to make decisions and use resources to achieve the organization's goals by virtue of their position in an organization. The **hierarchy of authority** is an organization's *chain of command*–the relative authority that each manager has–extending from the CEO at the top, down through the middle managers and first-line managers, to the nonmanagerial employees who actually make goods or provide services. Every manager, at every level of the hierarchy, supervises one or more employees. The term **span of control** refers to the number of employees who report directly to a manager.

Figure 10.6 shows a simplified picture of the hierarchy of authority at McDonald's Corporation as of April 2023. Chris Kempczinski is McDonald's CEO, a job he took over in 2019. Before being promoted to CEO, Kempczinski was president of McDonald's USA. Kempczinksi is the manager who has the ultimate responsibility for the company's overall performance, and he has the authority to decide how to use organizational resources to benefit McDonald's stakeholders. McDonald's four divisions focus on markets with similar needs, challenges, and opportunities for growth rather than a geographic approach to operations. Also in the top management hierarchy is Sandy Rodriguez, vice president and chief communications officer. Unlike other managers, Rodriguez is not a **line manager**, someone in the direct line or chain of command who has formal authority over people and resources. Rather, Rodriguez is a **staff manager**, responsible for one of McDonald's specialist functions–communications. She reports directly to Kempczinski.[35]

Managers at each level of the hierarchy confer with managers at the next level down the authority hierarchy to decide how to use organizational resources. Accepting this authority, those lower-level managers are accountable for how well they make those decisions. Managers who make the right decisions are typically promoted, and organizations motivate managers with the prospects of promotion and increased responsibility within the chain of command.

Figure 10.6

The Hierarchy of Authority and Span of Control at McDonald's Corporation

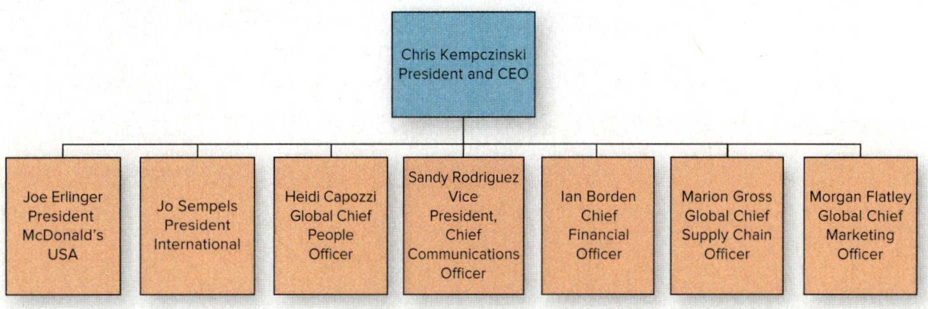

TALL AND FLAT ORGANIZATIONS As an organization grows in size (normally measured by the number of its managers and employees), its hierarchy of authority normally lengthens, making the organizational structure taller. A *tall* organization has many levels of authority relative to company size; a *flat* organization has fewer levels relative to company size (see Figure 10.7).[36] As a hierarchy becomes taller, problems that make the organization's structure less flexible and slow managers' response to changes in the organizational environment may result.

Communication problems may arise when an organization has many levels in the hierarchy. It can take a long time for the decisions and orders of upper-level managers to reach managers further down in the hierarchy, and it can take a long time for top managers to learn how well their decisions worked. Feeling out of touch, top managers may want to verify that lower-level managers are following orders and may require written confirmation from them. Middle managers, who know they will be held strictly accountable for their actions, start devoting too much time to the process of making decisions to improve their chances of being right. They might even try to avoid responsibility by making top managers decide what actions to take.

Another communication problem that can result is the distortion of commands and messages being transmitted up and down the hierarchy, which causes managers at different levels

Figure 10.7

Tall and Flat Organizations

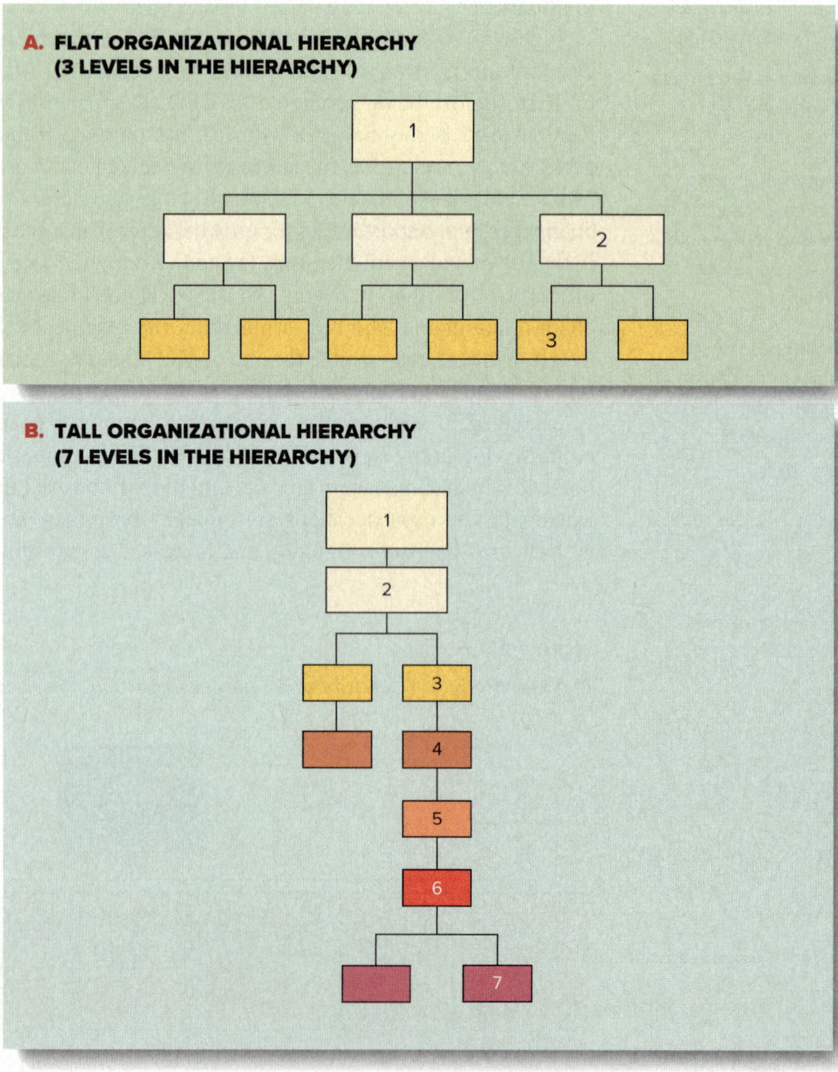

to interpret what is happening differently. Distortion of orders and messages can be accidental, occurring because different managers interpret messages from their own narrow functional perspectives. Or distortion can be intentional, occurring because managers low in the hierarchy decide to interpret information in a way that increases their own personal advantage.

Another problem with tall hierarchies is that they usually indicate that an organization is employing many managers, and managers are expensive. Managerial salaries, benefits, offices, and support staff are a huge expense for organizations. Large companies such as Boeing and GM pay their managers millions of dollars a year. During the global recession more than a decade ago, hundreds of thousands of managers lost their jobs as companies restructured and downsized their workforces to reduce costs. Today, with the economy still recovering from the global pandemic, managers may be key to rethinking the future of work based on what they learned during the COVID-19 crisis when it comes to organizational structure, productivity, remote work, collaboration, reskilling, and the importance of soft skills.[37]

THE MINIMUM CHAIN OF COMMAND To ward off the problems that result when an organization becomes too tall and employs too many managers, top managers need to determine whether they are employing the right number of middle and first-line managers and whether they can redesign their organizational architecture to reduce the number of managers. Top managers might well follow a basic organizing principle—the principle of the minimum chain of command—which states that top managers should always construct a hierarchy with the fewest levels of authority necessary to use organizational resources efficiently and effectively.

Effective managers constantly scrutinize their hierarchies to see whether the number of levels can be reduced—for example, by eliminating one level and giving the responsibilities of managers at that level to managers above and by empowering employees below. One manager recognized for empowering employees is David Novak, former executive chairman and CEO of Yum Brands. Instead of dictating what the company's Taco Bell, KFC, and Pizza Hut brands should do, Novak turned Yum's corporate headquarters into a support center for worldwide operations. Also a best-selling author, Novak recently launched a digital leadership platform that provides online training programs, a leadership podcast and newsletter, and other resource materials to help individuals develop leadership skills that can be important tools in today's workplace environment.[38]

In the United States, over 7 million manufacturing jobs have been lost to factories in low-cost countries abroad since 2000. While many large U.S. manufacturing companies have given up the battle, other companies such as electronics components maker Plexus Corp. have been able to find ways of organizing that allow them to survive and prosper in a low-cost manufacturing world. They have done this by creating empowered work teams among its 15,000 global employees. U.S. companies cannot match the efficiency of manufacturers abroad in producing high volumes of a single product, such as millions of a particular circuit board used in a laptop computer. So Plexus's managers decided to focus their efforts on developing a manufacturing technology, called "low-high," that could efficiently produce low volumes of many different kinds of products. Plexus's managers formed a team to design an organizational structure based on creating "focused factories" in which control over production decisions is given to the workers, whose managers cross-train them so they can perform all the operations involved in making a product in their "factory." Now, when work slows down at any point in the production of a particular product, a worker further along the production process can move back to help solve the problem that has arisen at the earlier stage.[39]

Plexus Corp. uses empowered work teams to help it utilize a "low–high" manufacturing technology that can help produce low volumes of many different kinds of products.
alvarez/Getty Images

Furthermore, managers organized workers into self-managed teams that are empowered to make all the decisions necessary to make a particular product in one of their manufacturing facilities. Because each product is different, the ability of the teams to make rapid decisions and respond to unexpected contingencies is vital on a production line, where time is money. The flexibility brought about by self-managed teams is why Plexus is so efficient and can compete against low-cost manufacturers abroad.

decentralizing authority Giving lower-level managers and nonmanagerial employees the right to make important decisions about how to use organizational resources.

CENTRALIZATION AND DECENTRALIZATION OF AUTHORITY Another way in which managers can keep the organizational hierarchy flat is by **decentralizing authority**—that is, by giving lower-level managers and nonmanagerial employees the right to make important decisions about how to use organizational resources.[40] If managers at higher levels give lower-level employees the responsibility of making important decisions and only *manage by exception,* then the problems of slow and distorted communication noted previously are kept to a minimum. Moreover, fewer managers are needed because their role is not to make decisions but to act as coach and facilitator and to help other employees make the best decisions. In addition, when decision-making authority is low in the organization and near the customer, employees are better able to recognize and respond to customer needs.

Decentralizing authority allows an organization and its employees to behave in a flexible way even as the organization grows and becomes taller. This is why managers are so interested in empowering employees, creating self-managed work teams, establishing cross-functional teams, and even moving to a product team structure. These design innovations help keep the organizational architecture flexible and responsive to complex task and general environments, complex technologies, and complex strategies.

Although more and more organizations are taking steps to decentralize authority, *too much* decentralization has certain disadvantages. If divisions, functions, or teams are given too much decision-making authority, they may begin to pursue their own goals at the expense of the organization's goals. Managers in engineering design or R&D, for example, may become so focused on making the best possible product that they fail to realize that the best product may be so expensive few people are willing or able to buy it. Also, too much decentralization can cause lack of communication among functions or divisions; this prevents the synergies of cooperation from ever materializing, and organizational performance suffers. The "Management Insight" feature describes how Wells Fargo's CEO addressed similar concerns about what he considered to be excessive decentralization.

MANAGEMENT INSIGHT

How Charlie Scharf Streamlined Wells Fargo's Structure

Wells Fargo CEO Charlie Scharf changed the organization's structure to eliminate some of the pitfalls associated with decentralized authority.
Steven Ferdman/Getty Images

A CEO's job is never easy, but the third time Charlie Scharf took a CEO post, it was an especially large—and visible—challenge. Wells Fargo, one of the largest U.S. banks, appointed him to the post in 2019, not long after being rocked by a scandal. The company had avoided trouble during the 2008 financial crisis and quickly pursued growth—too fast, in a sense. Customers began complaining that bankers were opening accounts in their name but without their knowledge and approval. Federal regulators investigated and found mismanagement, resulting in a series of fines and consent orders between 2016 and 2018. Most serious was a limit on assets the bank could hold, imposed by the Federal Reserve Board in 2018.[41]

Scharf was determined to restore Wells Fargo's reputation by transforming the bank so it would never make the same mistake. He replaced much of the top executive team and turned to the nature of Wells Fargo's organizational structure. He found that the company was decentralized to an unusual degree. Instead of a simple chain of command where accountability was clear, many separate businesses operated independently, so the evidence of excessive pressure to sell new accounts was spread broadly enough to escape notice.[42]

Scharf reorganized Wells Fargo to make its structure simpler and its lines of authority unmistakable. He divided it into five divisions, each with a risk officer to ensure everyone in their division was following regulations. At the same time, because of the asset cap, the bank could not grow through its core businesses of consumer and business lending unless it sold off other assets. With his leadership team, Scharf sorted business into "core" and "noncore," then sold off those businesses considered noncore.[43]

Although Wells Fargo hit bumps under Scharf's leadership, it made progress in addressing the regulatory concerns, and the government lifted one of the early consent orders in the fall of 2021. The bank also began to increase its lending as it divested other assets. It improved profitability by cutting costs. For example, it shifted the mix of advisory services more to online advice and independent advisers, rather than a full staff of in-house advisers, and with customers banking more online, it closed low-traffic branches. By the last quarter of 2021, Wells Fargo was posting a gain in share price, signaling investor confidence in Scharf's transformation of the troubled banking giant.[44]

Top managers must seek the balance between centralization and decentralization of authority that best meets the four major contingencies an organization faces (see Figure 10.1). If managers are in a stable environment, are using well-understood technology, and are producing stable kinds of products (such as cereal, canned soup, or books), there is no pressing need to decentralize authority, and managers at the top can maintain control of much of organizational decision making. However, in uncertain, changing environments where high-tech companies are producing state-of-the-art products, top managers must often empower employees and allow teams to make important strategic decisions so the organization can keep up with the changes taking place. No matter what its environment, a company that fails to control the balance between centralization and decentralization will find its performance suffering.

Integrating and Coordinating Mechanisms

Much coordination takes place through the hierarchy of authority. However, several problems are associated with establishing contact among managers in different functions or divisions. As discussed earlier, managers from different functions and divisions may have different views about what must be done to achieve the organization's goals. But if the managers have equal authority (as functional managers typically do), the only manager who can tell them what to do is the CEO, who has the ultimate authority to resolve conflicts. The need to solve everyday conflicts, however, wastes top management time and slows strategic decision making; indeed, one sign of a poorly performing structure is the number of problems sent up the hierarchy for top managers to solve.

integrating mechanisms Organizing tools that managers can use to increase communication and coordination among functions and divisions.

To increase communication and coordination among functions or between divisions and to prevent these problems from emerging, top managers incorporate various **integrating mechanisms** into their organizational architecture. The greater the complexity of an organization's structure, the greater is the need for coordination among people, functions, and divisions to make the organizational structure work efficiently and effectively. Thus when managers adopt a divisional, matrix, or product team structure, they must use complex integrating mechanisms to achieve the organization's goals. Several integrating mechanisms are available to managers to increase communication and coordination.[45] Figure 10.8 lists these mechanisms, as well as examples of the individuals or groups who might use them.

LIAISON ROLES Managers can increase coordination among functions and divisions by establishing liaison roles. When the volume of contacts between two functions increases, one way to improve coordination is to give one manager in each function or division the

Figure 10.8

Types and Examples of Integrating Mechanisms

SIMPLE

Direct contact

Liaison roles Marketing manager and research and development manager meet to brainstorm new product ideas.

Task forces Representatives from marketing, research and development, and manufacturing meet to discuss launch of new product.

Cross-functional teams A cross-functional team composed of all functions is formed to manage product to its launch in the market.

Integrating roles and departments Senior managers provide members of cross-functional team with relevant information from other teams and from other divisions.

COMPLEX

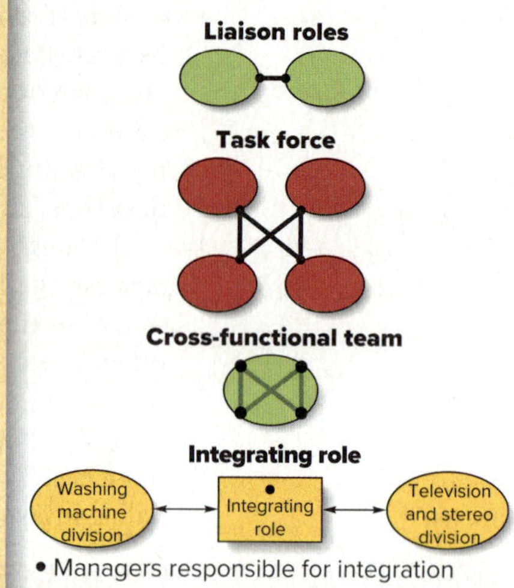

responsibility for coordinating with the other. These managers may meet daily, weekly, monthly, or as needed. A liaison role is illustrated in Figure 10.8; the small dot represents the person within a function who has responsibility for coordinating with the other function. Coordinating is part of the liaison's full-time job, and usually an informal relationship develops between the people involved, greatly easing strains between functions. Furthermore, liaison roles provide a way of transmitting information across an organization, which is important in large organizations whose employees may know no one outside their immediate function or division.

task force A committee of managers from various functions or divisions who meet to solve a specific, mutual problem; also called *ad hoc committee*.

TASK FORCES When more than two functions or divisions share many common problems, direct contact and liaison roles may not provide sufficient coordination. In these cases, a more complex integrating mechanism, a **task force**, may be appropriate (see Figure 10.8). One manager from each relevant function or division is assigned to a task force that meets to solve a specific, mutual problem; members are responsible for reporting to their departments on the issues addressed and the solutions recommended. Task forces are often called *ad hoc committees* because they are temporary; they may meet on a regular basis or only a few times. When the problem or issue is solved, the task force is no longer needed; members return to their normal roles in their departments or are assigned to other task forces. Typically, task force members also perform many of their normal duties while serving on the task force.

CROSS-FUNCTIONAL TEAMS In many cases, the issues addressed by a task force are recurring problems, such as the need to develop new products or find new kinds of customers. To address recurring problems effectively, managers are increasingly using permanent integrating mechanisms such as cross-functional teams. An example of a cross-functional team is a new product development committee that is responsible for the choice, design, manufacturing, and marketing of a new product. Such an activity obviously requires a great deal of integration among functions if new products are to be successfully introduced, and using a complex integrating mechanism such as a cross-functional team accomplishes this. As discussed earlier, in a product team structure people and resources are grouped into permanent cross-functional teams to speed products to market. These teams assume long-term responsibility for all aspects of development and making the product.

INTEGRATING ROLES An integrating role is a role whose only function is to increase coordination and integration among functions or divisions to achieve performance gains from synergies. Usually, managers who perform integrating roles are experienced senior managers who can envisage how to use the resources of the functions or divisions to obtain new synergies. For example, while at PepsiCo, Amy Chen coordinated with several other divisions to help create a program that delivers meals during the summer months to low-income families. The program, Food for Good, now makes healthy meals available year-round to low-income families. To date, Food for Good has delivered more than 245 million healthy meals to people in need. Chen recently left PepsiCo to become chief operating officer at UPSIDE Foods, the leading company in producing cell-cultured meat, poultry, and seafood. In her new role, Chen is responsible for the company's global strategy and commercial functions, as well as scaling the organization as it launches its first commercial products.[46]

In summary, to keep an organization responsive to changes in its task and general environments as it grows and becomes more complex, managers must increase coordination among functions and divisions by using complex integrating mechanisms. Managers must decide on the best way to organize their structures–that is, choose the structure that allows them to make the best use of organizational resources.

Organizational Culture

organizational culture The shared set of beliefs, expectations, values, and norms that influence how members of an organization relate to one another and cooperate to achieve the organization's goals.

The second principal issue in organizational design is to create, develop, and maintain an organization's culture. As we discussed in Chapter 3, **organizational culture** is the shared set of beliefs, expectations, values, and norms that influence how members of an organization relate to one another and cooperate to achieve the organization's goals. Culture influences the work behaviors and attitudes of individuals and groups in an organization because its members adhere to shared values, norms, and expected standards of behavior. Employees *internalize* organizational values and norms and then let these values and norms guide their decisions and actions.[47]

A company's culture is a result of its pivotal or guiding values and norms. A company's *values* are the shared standards that its members use to evaluate whether they have helped the company achieve its vision and goals. The values a company might adopt include any or all of the following standards: excellence, stability, predictability, profitability, economy, creativity, morality, and usefulness. A company's *norms* specify or prescribe the kinds of shared beliefs, attitudes, and behaviors that its members should observe and follow. Norms are informal, but powerful, rules about how employees should behave or conduct themselves in a company if they are to be accepted and help it to achieve its goals. Norms can be equally as constraining as the formal written rules contained in a company's handbook. Companies might encourage workers to adopt norms such as working hard, respecting traditions and authority, and being courteous to others; being conservative, cautious, and a "team player"; being creative and courageous and taking risks; or being honest and frugal and maintaining high personal standards. Norms may also prescribe certain specific behaviors such as keeping one's desk tidy, cleaning up at the end of the day, or taking one's turn to bring doughnuts to the office.

Ideally, a company's norms help the company achieve its values. For example, a new computer company whose culture is based on values of excellence and innovation may try to attain this high standard by encouraging workers to adopt norms about being creative, taking risks, and working hard now and looking long-term for rewards (this combination of values and norms leads to an *entrepreneurial* culture in a company). On the other hand, a bank or an insurance company that has values of stability and predictability may emphasize norms of cautiousness and obedience to authority (the result of adopting these values and norms would be a *stable, conservative* culture in a company).

Over time, members of a company learn from one another how to perceive and interpret various events that happen in the work setting and to respond to them in ways that reflect the company's guiding values and norms. This is why organizational culture is so important: When a strong and cohesive set of organizational values and norms is in place, employees focus on what is best for the organization in the long run–all their decisions and actions become oriented toward helping the organization perform well. For example, a teacher spends personal time after school coaching and counseling students; an R&D scientist works 80 hours a week, evenings, and weekends to help speed up a late project; or a salesclerk at a department store runs after a customer who left a credit card at the cash register.

Where Does Organizational Culture Come From?

LO10-5 List the four sources of organizational culture, and explain why and how a company's culture can lead to competitive advantage.

In managing organizational architecture, some important questions arise: Where does organizational culture come from? Why do different companies have different cultures? Why might a culture that for many years helped an organization achieve its goals suddenly harm the organization?

Organizational culture is shaped by the interaction of four main factors: the personal and professional characteristics of people within the organization, organizational ethics, the nature of the employment relationship, and the design of its organizational structure (see Figure 10.9). These factors work together to produce different cultures in different organizations and cause changes in culture over time.

CHARACTERISTICS OF ORGANIZATIONAL MEMBERS The ultimate source of organizational culture is the people who make up the organization. If you want to know why organizational cultures differ, look at how the characteristics of their members differ. Organizations A, B, and C develop distinctly different cultures because they attract, select, and retain people who have different values, personalities, and ethics.[48] Recall the attraction-selection-attrition model from Chapter 3. People may be attracted to an organization whose values match theirs; similarly, an organization selects people who share its values. Over time, people who do not fit in leave. The result is that people inside the organization become more similar, the values of the organization become more pronounced and clear-cut, and the culture becomes distinct from those of similar organizations.[49]

organizational ethics The moral values, beliefs, and rules that establish the appropriate way for an organization and its members to deal with each other and with people outside the organization.

ORGANIZATIONAL ETHICS The managers of an organization can set out purposefully to develop specific cultural values and norms to control how its members behave. One important class of values in this category stems from **organizational ethics**, which are the moral values, beliefs, and rules that establish the appropriate way for an organization and its members to deal with each other and with people outside the organization. Recall from Chapter 4 that ethical values rest on principles stressing the importance of treating organizational stakeholders fairly and equitably. Managers and employees are constantly making choices about the right, or ethical, thing to do; to help them make ethical decisions, top managers purposefully implant

Figure 10.9

Sources of an Organization's Culture

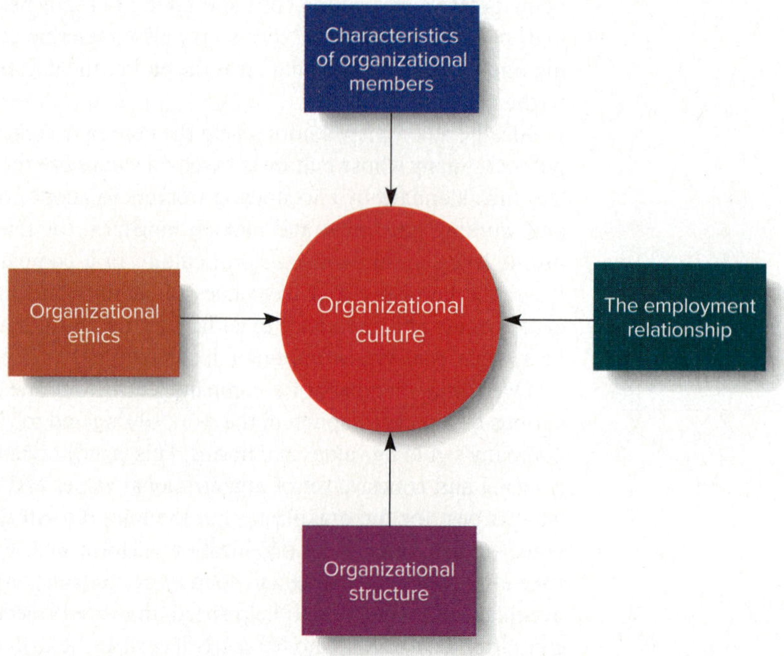

ethical values into an organization's culture.[50] Consequently, ethical values, and the rules and norms that embody them, become an integral part of an organization's culture and determine how its members will manage situations and make decisions.

THE EMPLOYMENT RELATIONSHIP A third factor shaping organizational culture is the nature of the employment relationship a company establishes with its employees via its human resource policies and practices. Recall from Chapter 1 our discussion of the changing relationship between organizations and their employees due to the growth of outsourcing and employment of contingent workers. Like a company's hiring, promotion, and layoff policies, human resource policies, along with pay and benefits, can influence how hard employees will work to achieve the organization's goals, how attached they will be to the organization, and whether they will buy into its values and norms.[51] As we discuss in Chapter 12, an organization's human resource policies are a good indicator of the values in its culture concerning its responsibilities to employees. Consider the effects of a company's promotion policy, for example: A company with a policy of promoting from within will fill higher-level positions with employees who already work for the organization. On the other hand, a company with a policy of promotion from without will fill its open positions with qualified outsiders. What does this say about each organization's culture?

Promoting from within will bolster strong values and norms that build loyalty, align employees' goals with the organization, and encourage employees to work hard to advance within the organization. If employees see no prospect of being promoted from within, they are likely to look for better opportunities elsewhere, cultural values and norms result in self-interested behavior, and cooperation and cohesiveness fall. The tech sector has gone through great turmoil in recent years, and over 2 million U.S. tech employees lost their jobs during the 2000s because of outsourcing and the recession. Apple, HP, and IBM—known for their strong employee-oriented values that emphasized long-term employment and respect for employees—were among the many companies forced to lay off employees, and their cultures have changed as a result. To rebuild their cultures and make their remaining employees feel like "owners," many companies have HRM pay policies that reward superior performance with bonuses and stock options.[52] For example, Southwest Airlines and Google established companywide stock options and profit-sharing systems that encourage their employees to be innovative and responsive to customers. Other companies offer different perks, such as Airbnb's $2,000 annual stipend for each employee to travel and stay in an Airbnb listing anywhere in the world and PwC's $1,200 per year student loan paydown benefit.[53]

ORGANIZATIONAL STRUCTURE We have seen how the values and norms that shape employee work attitudes and behaviors derive from an organization's people, ethics, and HRM policies. A fourth source of cultural values comes from the organization's structure. *Different kinds of structure give rise to different kinds of culture;* thus, to create a certain culture, managers often need to design a particular type of structure. Tall and highly centralized structures give rise to totally different sets of norms, rules, and cultural values than do structures that are flat and decentralized. In a tall, centralized organization, people have little personal autonomy, and norms that focus on being cautious, obeying authority, and respecting traditions emerge because predictability and stability are desired goals. In a flat, decentralized structure, people have more freedom to choose and control their own activities, and norms that focus on being creative and courageous and taking risks appear, giving rise to a culture in which innovation and flexibility are desired goals.

Whether a company is centralized or decentralized also leads to the development of different kinds of cultural values. By decentralizing authority and empowering employees, an organization can establish values that encourage and reward creativity or innovation. In doing this, an organization signals employees that it's okay to be innovative and do things their own way—as long as their actions are consistent with the good of the organization. Conversely, in some organizations it is important that employees do not make decisions on their own and that their actions be open to the scrutiny of superiors. In cases like this, centralization can be used to create cultural values that reinforce obedience and accountability. For example, in nuclear power plants, values that promote stability, predictability, and obedience to authority are deliberately fostered to prevent disasters.[54] Through norms and rules, employees are taught the importance of behaving consistently and honestly, and they learn that sharing information with supervisors, especially information about mistakes or errors, is the only acceptable form of behavior.[55]

An organization that seeks to manage and change its culture must take a hard look at all four factors that shape culture: the characteristics of its members, its ethical values, its human resource policies, and its organizational structure. The "Manager as a Person" feature describes how NASA under Bill Nelson has tried to do this. However, changing a culture can be difficult because of the way these factors interact and affect one another.[56] Often a major reorganization is necessary for a cultural change to occur, as we discuss in Chapter 11.

MANAGER AS A PERSON

NASA Continues Its Winning Ways

For the tenth consecutive year, the National Aeronautics and Space Administration tops the list of the best places to work in the federal government among large agencies, beating out other organizations such as the intelligence community and the Departments of Transportation, Health and Human Services, and Commerce.[57] Measures that placed NASA at the top of the list include employee engagement with their work, effective leadership, teamwork, and innovation.[58]

The factors making NASA a good employer are associated with the agency's culture. NASA has defined an inspirational mission: "to discover and expand knowledge for the benefit of humanity."[59] Its current administrator, Bill Nelson, appointed by President Joe Biden, sees strong commitment to that mission by the agency's nearly 18,000 employees. In the Best Places survey, the agency scored high in employees and senior leaders having the right skills to carry out this mission. HR policies for hiring and training also contribute to this winning culture. NASA regularly gathers and acts on employee feedback, which can contribute to an ethical culture in which employees perceive treatment as fair. One effort involved gathering employees' ideas for removing barriers to innovation. Recommendations included allowing more resources and rewards for innovation and simplifying the requirements for getting an idea through the development process.[60]

When Nelson joined the agency, he brought a background in military and government service. He was a captain in the U.S. Army and a U.S. senator from Florida for 18 years. In addition, he spent six days orbiting the Earth as a payload specialist aboard space shuttle Columbia. This experience gave him a new perspective on the Earth's environment and a greater appreciation for the importance of the country's space exploration program.[61]

NASA Administrator Bill Nelson is committed to making sure that the agency's culture reflects its inspirational mission: to discover and expand knowledge for the benefit of humanity.
Aubrey Gemignani/American Photo Archive/NASA/Alamy Stock Photo

Nelson's experience in Congress should help him navigate the challenges of operating under uncertainty. Priorities for NASA are always in flux as presidential policies and congressional legislation reset priorities with little notice. Nelson says recent commercial "space tourism" flights sponsored by private individuals such as Jeff Bezos and Elon Musk will provide an opportunity for a public/private partnership when it comes to space exploration, new technologies, and the effects of climate change. To that end, Nelson recently announced two new mission directorates: one focusing on systems development for the Artemis program (lunar exploration) and the Moon to Mars exploration missions and one concentrating on launch and space operations, including the International Space Station and commercial space flights.[62]

Types of Organizational Cultures

Many researchers and managers believe that employees of some organizations go out of their way to help the organization because it has a strong and cohesive organizational culture–an adaptive culture that controls employee attitudes and behaviors. *Adaptive cultures* are those whose values and norms help an organization to build momentum and to grow and change as needed to achieve its goals and be effective. By contrast, *inert cultures* are those whose values and norms fail to motivate or inspire employees; they lead to stagnation and, often, failure over time.

Researchers have devised an approach to understanding organizational culture called the *competing values framework* (CVF). The CVF assumes that within any organization, four competing values exist: collaborate, create, control, and compete, which vary along two dimensions (inward versus outward focus and flexibility versus stability). How managers respond to these values and the tensions they create within the organization help shape its culture into four different types: clan, adhocracy, hierarchy, and market.[63]

- **Clan Culture:** Organizations with this type of culture have an internal focus and emphasize collaboration, commitment, community, and communication, valuing flexibility over stability. They embrace the concept of continuous learning and employee development and view customers as partners. Yogurt maker Chobani and Wegman's supermarket chain are examples of a clan culture.
- **Adhocracy Culture:** Organizations with this type of culture have an external focus and emphasize creativity, innovation, adaptability, and entrepreneurship, valuing flexibility over stability. They encourage employees to take risks and experiment with new and different ways of accomplishing tasks. Most tech companies and start-up ventures have this type of culture.
- **Market Culture:** Organizations with this type of culture have an external focus and emphasize competition, making deals, and putting profits over employees, valuing stability over flexibility. They stress getting things done and achieving positive results. Amazon and Tesla are examples of market cultures.
- **Hierarchy Culture:** Organizations with this type of culture have an internal focus and emphasize efficiency, quality, and ongoing improvement of systems, structures, and standards. They insist on adherence to rules and regulations, focusing on preventing mistakes and addressing overall safety concerns. Government agencies, insurance companies, and airlines are examples of hierarchy cultures.

Dimensions of organizational culture play an important role in a company's overall performance, but sometimes those values need to be reviewed and revised to encourage ethical conduct, as discussed in the "Ethics in Action" feature.

ETHICS IN ACTION

Can Roblox Be Creative, Civil, and in Control?

Roblox was launched in 2006 to be more than an Internet game platform. CEO and founder David Baszucki says the original vision was "the next phase of human interaction."[64] Initially, a few dozen people would log in to collaborate on games and learning experiences, with Baszucki and cofounder Erik Cassel moderating to keep interactions positive and civil. More than 16 years later, Roblox has tens of millions of daily users, millions of whom design or improve the experiences. Roblox is for all ages but has attracted mainly young people; before 2021, more than half were under 13. As age diversity increases, Roblox is adding experiences for older users, such as concerts

Enforcing community standards can be a challenge for any gaming platform. For Roblox, thousands of moderators monitor the safety and civility of user conduct and check content users have flagged as inappropriate.
Diego Thomazini/Shutterstock

and fashion shows. During the COVID-19 pandemic, Roblox employees attended weekly town hall meetings on the site, and at the end of 2020, an audience of millions watched a concert by Lil Nas X.[65]

Creativity requires freedom to experiment, so Roblox is structured for flexibility and innovation. In each of its 14 major groups, teams of 10 to 20 collaborate on goals for improving the site. In addition to employees, community members are invited to create enhancements and new activities. These developers contribute much of the new content. They first got involved for fun but eventually could earn money from Roblox or sell to other community members.[66]

To keep employees ethically aligned with Roblox's vision, Baszucki vigorously promotes four core values. First, everyone must treat members of the community with respect. Decision making takes a long-term perspective, rather than chasing short-term profits. Employees should take responsibility, so the organization's systems empower them and respect risk taking. The fourth value, "Get stuff done," refers to continuous improvement. Roblox seeks to employ people who share these values.[67]

To maintain community standards, Roblox cannot rely solely on core values. Thousands of moderators monitor the safety and civility of user conduct and check content users have flagged as inappropriate, supported by algorithms developed to detect misbehavior. Roblox also sets standards for advertisers. Enforcing all these standards is difficult. Roblox has been criticized for using the work of children and for hosting branded experiences not clearly identified as sponsored content. Although Roblox provides a chat tool for developers working in teams, some teams send messages outside the platform. Young developers have reported abusive behavior in these interactions. Roblox tries to maintain safety with, for example, parental controls and age recommendations for experiences.[68] However, some users and developers are not so sure about Roblox's approach.[69]

Summary and Review

LO10-1 **DESIGNING ORGANIZATIONAL STRUCTURE** The four main determinants of organizational structure are the external environment, strategy, technology, and human resources. In general, the higher the level of uncertainty associated with these factors, the more appropriate is a flexible, adaptable structure as opposed to a formal, rigid one.

LO10-2 **GROUPING TASKS INTO JOBS** Job design is the process by which managers group tasks into jobs. To create more interesting jobs, and to get workers to act flexibly, managers can enlarge and enrich jobs. The job characteristics model is a tool that managers can use to measure how motivating or satisfying a particular job is.

LO10-3 **ORGANIZATIONAL STRUCTURE: GROUPING JOBS INTO FUNCTIONS AND DIVISIONS** Managers can choose from many kinds of organizational structures to make the best use of organizational resources. Depending on the specific organizing problems they face, managers can choose from functional, product, geographic, market, matrix, product team, and hybrid structures.

LO10-4 **COORDINATING FUNCTIONS AND DIVISIONS** No matter which structure managers choose, they must decide how to distribute authority in the organization, how many levels to have in the hierarchy of authority, and what balance to strike between centralization and decentralization to keep the number of levels in the hierarchy to a minimum. As organizations grow, managers must increase integration and coordination among functions and divisions. Four integrating mechanisms that facilitate this are liaison roles, task forces, cross-functional teams, and integrating roles.

LO10-5 **ORGANIZATIONAL CULTURE** Organizational culture is the set of values, norms, and standards of behavior that control how individuals and groups in an organization interact with one another and work to achieve the organization's goals. The four main sources of organizational culture are member characteristics, organizational ethics, the nature of the employment relationship, and the design of organizational structure. Based on extensive research, the competing values framework divides organizational culture into four types: clan, adhocracy, market, and hierarchy, along two dimensions (inward versus outward focus and flexibility versus stability).

Management in Action

Topics for Discussion and Action

Discussion

1. Would a flexible or a more formal structure be appropriate for these organizations? (a) a large department store, (b) a Big Four accounting firm, (c) a biotechnology company. Explain your reasoning. **[LO10-1, 10-2]**
2. Using the job characteristics model as a guide, discuss how a manager can enrich or enlarge employees' jobs. **[LO10-2]**
3. How might a salesperson's job or an administrative assistant's job be enlarged or enriched to make it more motivating? **[LO10-2, 10-3]**
4. When and under what conditions might managers change from a functional to (a) a product, (b) a geographic, or (c) a market structure? **[LO10-1, 10-3]**
5. How do matrix structure and product team structure differ? Why is product team structure more widely used? **[LO10-1, 10-3, 10-4]**
6. What is organizational culture, and how does it affect the way employees behave? **[LO10-5]**

Action

7. Find and interview a manager, and identify the kind of organizational structure that their organization uses to coordinate its people and resources. Why is the organization using that structure? Do you think a different structure would be more appropriate? Which one? **[LO10-1, 10-3, 10-4]**
8. With the same or another manager, discuss the distribution of authority in the organization. Does the manager think that decentralizing authority and empowering employees are appropriate? **[LO10-1, 10-3]**
9. Interview some employees of an organization, and ask them about the organization's values and norms, the typical characteristics of employees, and the organization's ethical values and socialization practices. Using this information, try to describe the organization's culture and the way it affects how people and groups behave. **[LO10-1, 10-5]**

Building Management Skills

Understanding Organizing [LO10-1, 10-2, 10-3]

Think of an organization with which you are familiar—perhaps one you have worked for, such as a store, a restaurant, an office, a church, or a school. Then answer the following questions:

1. Which contingencies are most important in explaining how the organization is organized? Do you think it is organized in the best way? Why or why not?
2. Using the job characteristics model, how motivating do you think the job of a typical employee is in this organization?
3. Provide examples of how a typical job could be enlarged or enriched in this organization.
4. What kind of organizational structure does the organization use? If it is part of a chain, what kind of structure does the entire organization use? What other structures discussed in the chapter might allow the organization to operate more effectively? For example, would the move to a product team structure lead to greater efficiency or effectiveness? Why or why not?
5. How many levels are in the organization's hierarchy? Is authority centralized or decentralized? Describe the span of control of the top manager and of middle or first-line managers.
6. Is the distribution of authority appropriate for the organization and its activities? Would it be possible to flatten the hierarchy by decentralizing authority and empowering employees?
7. What are the principal integrating mechanisms used in the organization? Do they provide sufficient coordination among individuals and functions? How might they be improved?
8. Now that you have analyzed the way this organization is structured, what advice would you give its managers to help them improve how it operates?

Managing Ethically [LO10-1, 10-3, 10-5]

Suppose an organization is downsizing and laying off many of its middle managers. Some top managers charged with deciding whom to terminate might decide to keep the employees they like and who are obedient to them, rather than the ones who are difficult or the best performers. They might also decide to lay off the most highly paid employees even if they are high performers. Think of the ethical issues involved in designing a hierarchy, and discuss the following issues.

Questions

1. What ethical rules (see Chapter 4) should managers use to decide which employees to terminate when redesigning their hierarchy?
2. Some people argue that employees who have worked for an organization for many years have a claim on the organization at least as strong as that of its shareholders. What do you think of the ethics of this position—can employees claim to "own" their jobs if they have contributed significantly to the organization's past success? How does a socially responsible organization behave in this situation?

Small Group Breakout Exercise

Bob's Appliances [LO10-1, 10-3]

Form groups of three or four people, and appoint one member as the spokesperson who will communicate your findings to the class when called on by the instructor. Then discuss the following scenario:

Bob's Appliances sells and services household appliances such as washing machines, dishwashers, ranges, and refrigerators. Over the years, the company has developed a good reputation for the quality of its customer service, and many local builders patronize the store. However, large retailers such as Home Depot, Walmart, and Costco are also providing an increasing range of appliances. Moreover, to attract more customers, these stores also carry a complete range of consumer electronics products—TVs, computers, and digital devices. Bob Lange, the owner of Bob's Appliances, has decided that if he is to stay in business, he must widen his product range and compete directly with the chains.

Recently, Bob decided to build a 20,000-square-foot store and service center, and he is now hiring new employees to sell and service the new line of consumer electronics. Because of his company's increased size, Lange is not sure of the best way to organize the employees. Currently, he uses a functional structure; employees are divided into sales, purchasing and accounting, and repair. Bob is wondering whether selling and servicing consumer electronics is so different from selling and servicing appliances that he should move to a product structure (see the accompanying figure) and create separate sets of functions for each of his two lines of business.[70]

You are a team of local consultants whom Bob has called in to advise him as he makes this crucial choice. Which structure do you recommend? Why?

FUNCTIONAL STRUCTURE

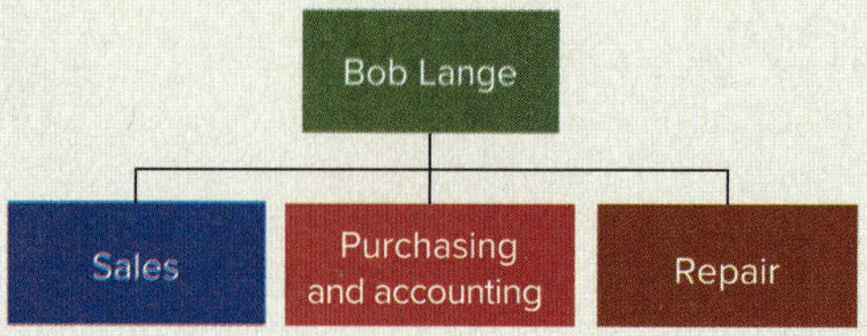

PRODUCT STRUCTURE

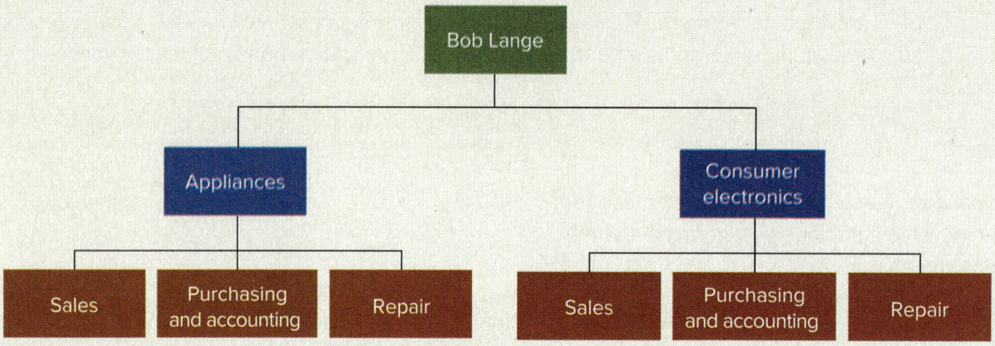

Be the Manager [LO10-1, 10-3, 10-5]

Speeding Up Website Design

You have been hired by a website design, production, and hosting company whose new designs are attracting a lot of attention and many customers. Currently, employees are organized into different functions such as hardware, software design, graphic art, and website hosting, as well as functions such as marketing and human resources. Each function takes its turn to work on a new project from initial customer request to final online website hosting.

The problem the company is experiencing is that it typically takes one year from the initial idea stage to the time a website is up and running; the company wants to shorten this time by half to protect and expand its market niche. In talking to other managers, you discover that they believe the company's current functional structure is the source of the problem—it is not allowing employees to develop websites fast enough to satisfy customers' demands. They want you to design a better structure.

Questions

1. Discuss how you can improve the way the current functional structure operates so it speeds website development.
2. Discuss the pros and cons of moving to a (a) multidivisional, (b) matrix, and (c) product team structure to reduce website development time.
3. Which of these structures do you think is most appropriate, and why?
4. What kind of culture would you help create to make the company's structure work more effectively?

Case in the News [LO10-1, 10-3, 10-4, 10-5]

Volkswagen Group Aligns Structure with Strategy

Along with Toyota, Volkswagen Group is one of the world's two largest carmakers; each sells about 10 million cars a year. Besides its VW brand, Volkswagen Group sells Audis, Lamborghinis, Porsches, Bentleys, and regional European brands. The company also makes commercial vehicles (trucks, buses, and light commercial vehicles) and operates a software subsidiary called CARIAD.

Volkswagen's CEO describes the company's structure as kind of a "conglomerate of brands." Volkswagen is organized into an automotive division and a financial services division. The automotive division is divided into passenger cars and commercial vehicles. The financial services division provides customer financing, leasing, fleet management, and other services. Within the passenger car division, the various brands have their own independently managed marketing strategies. Volkswagen is the leader in volume sales, while Audi and Porsche offer premium brands.

Although brand strategies differ, the business units design their cars using the Volkswagen Group's standard hardware and software, and they all offer the group's financial services. The company seeks to standardize vehicle design via its MQB platform. (A vehicle platform is essentially the hardware that holds the rest of the car—for example, the chassis, axles, engine, powertrain, and suspension system.) VW's volume brands use the same MQB platform for vehicles made around the world, and the company uses an MEB version for electric vehicles. Sharing a platform introduces efficiency, and these platforms are flexible enough that the different brands can vary the appearance and features of the cars.

Recently, Volkswagen, like other carmakers, has run into problems with obtaining needed semiconductors on schedule. Pandemic-related factory shutdowns, weather events, and bottlenecks in transportation caused factories to shut down due to missing parts, especially semiconductors. Volkswagen responded by setting up a logistics task force to investigate the problems in its network of 40,000 suppliers and develop solutions. Options include pausing or rescheduling production, identifying new suppliers, and even rewriting vehicle software to run on whatever chips are available. Volkswagen also has standardized more of its components so that the company can use the same parts across vehicles, therefore placing larger orders and perhaps getting more attention from suppliers. Larger orders also make it more practical to set up networks of regional suppliers, rather than relying on one or a few global suppliers, which often are concentrated in distant regions.

Before Volkswagen's logistics task force had a chance to bring production in line with demand, Russia's military launched attacks on Ukraine, which intensified the supply chain challenges. In the early days of the war, Volkswagen halted production at two of its facilities in Germany because deliveries of components were disrupted. Some of the suppliers to Volkswagen are in Ukraine, and others are in Russia. Without signs of a quick end to the fighting, Volkswagen created another task force, this one responsible for assessing how the Ukraine situation could affect the entire company, including supplier and customer relationships.

Even as the supply chain challenges persist in the present, the company is looking at the longer term, when it expects electric vehicles and autonomous vehicles to redefine transportation. With electric vehicles, the design of the physical vehicle will become less important. The sources of difference in performance and driver experience will have more to do with vehicle software. Already, a car's software is a major part of the cost to make it, and the software is highly complex. Therefore, a company that makes better software and does so more efficiently can differentiate itself from other carmakers.

The growing significance of software in vehicles was the reason Volkswagen launched CARIAD, its software subsidiary. Management wanted to control the process of developing vehicle software that is basically the same across brands yet is highly customizable to meet the needs of each brand and its customers, as well as changes in the business environment such as the recent semiconductor shortage. The company also is looking at expanding by adding new divisions at both ends of its supply chain, including more involvement in semiconductors and vehicle rentals. It also is diversifying its product line, which already includes Ducati motorcycles in the Audi business unit. In these and other ways, Volkswagen aims to refashion itself from a vehicle maker to a "software-driven mobility provider."

Questions for Discussion

1. Volkswagen Group is structured in divisions based on product type. What are some advantages of this type of organization? What, if any, changes would you suggest to make the structure more appropriate for becoming a "software-driven mobility provider"?
2. To meet two major challenges, Volkswagen set up task forces. Do you think this was an appropriate organizational structure for addressing the challenges? Why or why not?
3. Assume that Volkswagen was addressing the semiconductor situation by creating one task force and the turbulence in Ukraine by creating a second task force. What differences and overlaps might arise in their work? What mechanisms would you suggest the company use to integrate and coordinate the work of the two task forces?

Sources: Volkswagen Group, "'New Auto': Volkswagen Reinvents Itself," www.volkswagenag.com, accessed January 25, 2023; O. Storbeck, "Is the VW Structure Too Complex for the Good of Germany?" *Financial Times,* www.ft.com, October 12, 2022; Reuters, "Consensus-Driven Blume Will Usher in New Leadership Era at Volkswagen," *Automotive News Europe,* https://europe.autonews.com, July 23, 2022; W. Boston, "Volkswagen Faces Production Stoppages due to Ukraine Supply Issues," *The Wall Street Journal,* www.wsj.com, March 1, 2022; D. Mihalascu, "VW Halting EV Production This Week amid Ukraine Supply Issues," *Inside EVs,* https://insideevs.com, February 28, 2021; N. Patel, "How Volkswagen Can Reinvent Itself as an EV Company, with Herbert Diess," *Verge,* www.theverge.com, January 18, 2022; M. Raymunt, "VW Sales Drop to Lowest in Decade as Chip Crunch Dents Output," *Bloomberg,* www.bloomberg.com, January 12, 2022; B. Masters and A. Edgecliffe-Johnson, "Supply Chains: Companies Shift from 'Just in Time' to 'Just in Case,'" *Financial Times,* www.ft.com, December 19, 2021; "Volkswagen Expects Chip Supply to Remain Tight in Coming Months," *Reuters,* www.reuters.com, May 1, 2021.

Notes

1. Banner Health, "Banner Health at a Glance," www.bannerhealth.com, accessed January 24, 2023; E.J. Martin, "Centralized Operations Yields Efficiency Upgrade," *Health Facilities Management*, January/February 2022, 24–27.
2. R.K. Calloway, "Energy Improvement Aims High," *Facility Executive*, https://facilityexecutive.com, January 4, 2021.
3. Martin, "Centralized Operations"; American Society for Health Care Engineering (ASHE), "Banner Health Recognized for Excellence in Facility Management," news release, November 8, 2021, www.ashe.org.
4. Martin, "Centralized Operations"; ASHE, "Banner Health Recognized."
5. Banner Health, "Banner Health at a Glance"; Martin, "Centralized Operations."
6. G.R. Jones, *Organizational Theory, Design, and Change: Text and Cases* (Upper Saddle River: Prentice-Hall, 2011).
7. J. Child, *Organization: A Guide for Managers and Administrators* (New York: Harper & Row, 1977).
8. P.R. Lawrence and J.W. Lorsch, *Organization and Environment* (Boston: Graduate School of Business Administration, Harvard University, 1967).
9. R. Duncan, "What Is the Right Organizational Design?" *Organizational Dynamics* (Winter 1979), 59–80.
10. M. Sayyadi, "Improving Performance: Flexible Organizational Structures," *Performance*, www.performancemagazine.org, June 12, 2019.
11. D. Miller, "Strategy Making and Structure: Analysis and Implications for Performance," *Academy of Management Journal* 30 (1987), 7–32.
12. A.D. Chandler, *Strategy and Structure* (Cambridge, MA: MIT Press, 1962).
13. J. Stopford and L. Wells, *Managing the Multinational Enterprise* (London: Longman, 1972).
14. C. Perrow, *Organizational Analysis: A Sociological View* (Belmont, CA: Wadsworth, 1970).
15. H. Russ, "McDonald's Creates New Unit to Focus on Global Digital App," *Reuters*, www.reuters.com, accessed January 24, 2023; D. Klein, "McDonald's Meets Customers in a Suddenly Digital World," *QSR Magazine*, www.qsrmagazine.com, July 29, 2021; H. Johnson, "We Tried the Kiosks That Analysts Say Could Help McDonald's Win Back $2.7 Billion in Sales. Here's the Verdict," *Business Insider*, www.businessinsider.com, accessed February 26, 2020.
16. F.W. Taylor, *The Principles of Scientific Management* (New York: Harper, 1911).
17. R.W. Griffin, *Task Design: An Integrative Approach* (Glenview, IL: Scott, Foresman, 1982).
18. Ibid.
19. J.R. Hackman and G.R. Oldham, *Work Redesign* (Reading, MA: Addison-Wesley, 1980).
20. "The Home Depot Executive Leadership Team," https://corporate.homedepot.com, accessed January 24, 2023.
21. J.R. Galbraith and R.K. Kazanjian, *Strategy Implementation: Structure, System, and Process*, 2nd ed. (St. Paul, MN: West, 1986).
22. Lawrence and Lorsch, *Organization and Environment.*
23. Jones, *Organizational Theory.*
24. Lawrence and Lorsch, *Organization and Environment.*
25. R.H. Hall, *Organizations: Structure and Process* (Englewood Cliffs, NJ: Prentice-Hall, 1972); R. Miles, *Macro Organizational Behavior* (Santa Monica, CA: Goodyear, 1980).
26. Chandler, *Strategy and Structure.*
27. G.R. Jones and C.W.L. Hill, "Transaction Cost Analysis of Strategy-Structure Choice," *Strategic Management Journal* 9 (1988), 159–72.
28. D. Roland, "GSK Spins Off $36 Billion Consumer-Healthcare Business Haleon," *The Wall Street Journal*, www.wsj.com, accessed January 24, 2023; A. King, "Haleon Emerges from GSK Consumer Healthcare Spin-Off," *Chemistry World*, www.chemistryworld.com, July 18, 2022; J. Carroll, "GSK's Vaccines Group—including R&D Faces Heavy Job Cuts in Latest Restructuring," *Endpoints News*, https://endpts.com, February 6, 2020.
29. S.M. Davis and P.R. Lawrence, *Matrix* (Reading, MA: Addison-Wesley, 1977); J.R. Galbraith, "Matrix Organization Designs: How to Combine Functional and Project Forms," *Business Horizons* 14 (1971), 29–40.
30. L.R. Burns, "Matrix Management in Hospitals: Testing Theories of Matrix Structure and Development," *Administrative Science Quarterly* 34 (1989), 349–68.
31. C.W.L. Hill, *International Business* (Homewood, IL: Irwin, 2003).
32. E. Woolery and S. Gonzalez, "How Northwestern Mutual Is Growing Design Collaboratively," www.invisionapp.com, accessed February 28, 2020; "Successful Cross-Functional Teams to Watch in 2019," *Onpoint Consulting*, www.onpoint-consultingllc.com, January 4, 2019.
33. Jones, *Organizational Theory.*
34. P. Blau, "A Formal Theory of Differentiations in Organizations," *American Sociological Review* 35 (1970), 684–95.
35. "Our Leadership," https://corporate.mcdonalds.com, accessed April 23, 2023; D. Bradley, "McDonald's Promotes Michael Gonda, Names Sandy Rodriguez as New CCO," *PR Week*, April 10, 2023, https://www.prweek.com; A. Thompson, "McDonald's Organizational Structure and Its Characteristics—An Analysis," *Panmore Institute*, https://panmore.com, August 7, 2022.
36. Childs, *Organization.*
37. K. Ellingrud, "Future of Work Post Covid-19," *Forbes*, www.forbes.com, accessed January 24, 2023; E.R. McRae and P. Aykens, "9 Future of Work Trends for 2023," *Gartner*, www.gartner.com, December 22, 2022.
38. Corporate website, "How Leaders Lead with David Novak," https://howleaderslead.com, accessed January 24, 2023; Z. Friedman, "'King of Restaurants' David Novak Shares His Best Leadership Advice," *Forbes*, www.forbes.com, March 20, 2019.
39. "Why Choose Plexus?" www.plexus.com, accessed January 25, 2023; "Plexus Expands Facility Footprint in San Jose, Chicago," *Reliable Plant*, www.reliable-plant.com, accessed January 25, 2023.
40. P.M. Blau and R.A. Schoenherr, *The Structure of Organizations* (New York: Basic Books, 1971).
41. R. Mashayekhi, "Busted Stagecoach: Can Charlie Scharf—or Anyone—Fix Wells Fargo?" *Fortune*, February/March 2021, 70–76; P. Rocha, "Wells Fargo's Latest Regulatory Stumble Puts CEO in Hot Seat," *American Banker*, www.american-banker.com, October 14, 2021.
42. Mashayekhi, "Busted Stagecoach."
43. Mashayekhi, "Busted Stagecoach"; N.Z. Hussain and E. Dilts, "Wells Fargo Beats Profit Estimates on Uptick in Loan Demand, Cost Cuts," *Reuters*, www.reuters.com, January 14, 2022.
44. D. Taub and H. Levitt, "Wells Fargo Faces Several Years of Regulatory Work,

Scharf Says," *Bloomberg,* www.bloomberg .com, September 20, 2022; O. McCaffrey, "Wells Fargo's Quarterly Profit Soars 86%," *The Wall Street Journal,* www.wsj .com, January 14, 2022.

45. J.R. Galbraith, *Designing Complex Organizations* (Reading, MA: Addison-Wesley, 1977), chap. 1; Galbraith and Kazanjian, *Strategy Implementation,* Chap. 7.
46. "Food for Good," www.pepsicofood forgood.com, accessed January 25, 2023; D. McCarthy, "One Challenge to Scaling Cultivated Meat? Building a Supply Chain," *Emerging Tech Brew,* www .emergingtechbrew.com, May 23, 2022.
47. S.D.N. Cook and D. Yanow, "Culture and Organizational Learning." *Journal of Management Inquiry* 2 (1993), 373–90.
48. B. Schneider, "The People Make the Place," *Personnel Psychology* 40 (1987), 437–53.
49. J.E. Sheriden, "Organizational Culture and Employee Retention," *Academy of Management Journal* 35 (1992), 657–92.
50. T.L. Beauchamp and N.E. Bowie, eds., *Ethical Theory and Business* (Englewood Cliffs, NJ: Prentice-Hall, 1979); A. Maclntyre, *After Virtue* (Notre Dame, IN: University of Notre Dame Press, 1981).
51. A. Sagie and D. Elizur, "Work Values: A Theoretical Overview and a Model of Their Effects," *Journal of Organizational Behavior* 17 (1996), 503–14.
52. G.R. Jones, "Transaction Costs, Property Rights, and Organizational Culture: An Exchange Perspective," *Administrative Science Quarterly* 28 (1983), 454–67.
53. J. Murphy, "21 Best Employee Perks Your Team Will Love in 2023 (+ 5 Bonus Job & Work Perks)," *Snack Nation,* https:// snacknation.com, accessed January 25, 2023; "Airbnb Benefits," www.levels.fyi, accessed January 25, 2023; PwC, "Student Loan Paydown Benefit," www.pwc.com, accessed January 25, 2023.
54. S.L. Morrow, G.K. Koves, and V.E. Barnes, "Exploring the Relationship between Safety Culture and Safety Performance in U.S. Nuclear Power Operations," *Safety Science* 69 (November 2014), 37–47.
55. H. Mintzberg, *The Structuring of Organizational Structures* (Englewood Cliffs, NJ: Prentice-Hall, 1979).
56. G. Kunda, *Engineering Culture* (Philadelphia: Temple University Press, 1992).
57. Partnership for Pubic Service, "2021 Best Places to Work in the Federal Government Rankings," https:// bestplacetowork.org, accessed January 25, 2023; "NASA Named Best Place to Work, No. 1 for COVID-19 Response," www .nasa.org, June 29, 2021.
58. Partnership for Public Service, "2021 Rankings: #1 NASA," https://bestplaces towork.org, accessed January 25, 2023.
59. "Our Mission and Values," www.nasa.gov, accessed January 25, 2023.
60. "About NASA," www.nasa.org, accessed January 25, 2023; K. Isaacs and D. Ancona, "3 Ways to Build a Culture of Collaborative Innovation," *Harvard Business Review,* https://hbr.org, August 12, 2019.
61. "Bill Nelson Payload Specialist," www.nasa.gov, accessed January 25, 2023.
62. "NASA Leadership Positions Agency for Future," www.nasa.gov, September 21, 2021; D. Ignatius and B. Nelson, "The Path Forward: New Frontiers in Space with NASA Administrator Bill Nelson (transcript)," *The Washington Post,* www.washingtonpost.com, July 22, 2021.
63. J. DeGraff, "Competing Values Assessment: Overview," https:// denverleadership.org, accessed January 25, 2023; K.S. Cameron, R.E. Quinn, J. DeGraff, and A.V. Thakor, *Competing Values Leadership,* Third Edition (Northampton, MA: Edward Elgar, 2022); L. Grensing-Pophal, "4 Distinct Types of Corporate Culture—Which Is Yours?" *HR Daily Advisor,* https://hrdailyadvisor.blr .com, April 12, 2018.
64. D. Baszucki, "The CEO of Roblox on Scaling Community-Sourced Innovation," *Harvard Business Review,* March–April 2022, 30–33.
65. Ibid; M. Sato, "Roblox Is Ready to Grow Up," *The Verge,* www.theverge.com, September 9, 2022; K. Browning, "Roblox, the Gaming Site, Wants to Grow Up without Sacrificing Child Safety," *The New York Times,* www.nytimes.com, updated October 31, 2021.
66. Baszucki, "The CEO of Roblox"; S. Parking, "The Trouble with Roblox, the Video Game Empire Built on Child Labour," *The Guardian,* www.theguardian .com, January 9, 2022.
67. Baszucki, "The CEO of Roblox."
68. Sato, "Roblox Is Ready to Grow Up"; Browning, "Roblox, the Gaming Site, Wants to Grow Up."
69. S. Santos, "Something Needs to Be Done About Roblox," *Screen Rant,* https:// screenrant.com, November 19, 2022.
70. Copyright © 2006, Gareth R. Jones.

CHAPTER 11

Organizational Control and Change

Hero Images/Getty Images

Learning Objectives

After studying this chapter, you should be able to:

LO11-1 Define organizational control, and explain how it increases organizational effectiveness.

LO11-2 Describe the four steps in the control process and the way it operates over time.

LO11-3 Identify the main output controls, and discuss their advantages and disadvantages as means of coordinating and motivating employees.

LO11-4 Identify the main behavior controls, and discuss their advantages and disadvantages as a means of coordinating and motivating employees.

LO11-5 Discuss the relationship between organizational control and change, and explain why managing change is a vital management task.

A MANAGER'S CHALLENGE

How Listening to Passengers Kept Delta Airlines Flying

What controls can managers use to ensure success in turbulent times? March 2020 was an alarming month for airlines. As COVID-19 cases spread from country to country, governments began imposing restrictions on travel, and even when flights were available, most people were too worried to go. Airlines found themselves in the unprecedented situation of recording more cancellations than bookings. Meanwhile, they had equipment to maintain and employees to pay. With no idea how long the situation would last, they needed to preserve what revenues they could.[1]

One of the quickest and most effective responses came at Delta Airlines. That month, it began gathering data on customer attitudes. In calls to corporate clients and surveys of leisure travelers, Delta learned customers felt unsafe sitting near strangers, regardless of any health and safety protocols already in place. Executives prioritized that concern and announced a policy of leaving each plane's middle seats vacant. Flying with empty seats would cut revenues, but the company hoped it would offset that loss by wooing a larger share of people back to airports.[2]

Implementation of this change was complex, including measures such as revisions to ticketing software and communication with employees, travel agents, and prospective passengers. To launch the change quickly, Delta started with simple measures, such as preparing signs to distribute in airports. Then it tackled the harder tasks, such as updating software.[3]

As Delta implemented its policy, it measured performance. In the final months of 2020, leaving middle seats vacant resulted in 9% fewer seats for passengers than on competitors' planes. Still, compared with the average of its closest competitors (American, Southwest, and United), Delta was generating more revenue. Management concluded that Delta's customers were willing to pay more to have a greater sense of safety. In addition, the company's net promoter score (a measure of customers' willingness to recommend Delta) reached an all-time high. Several other airlines blocked off middle seats for weeks or months, but Delta kept the policy in place for an entire year, until COVID vaccines became widely available, and management grew hopeful that travelers were ready to fly again.[4]

Delta's decision had consequences, though not all favorable. During the first months of the pandemic, the airline reported losses larger than those at other major air carriers. However, by March 2021, Delta was close to breaking even. Then hopes that 2021 would

Listening to customers' safety concerns during the pandemic helped Delta Airlines' management team implement operational changes to its business processes, which improved overall service and profitability.
Bing Guan/Bloomberg/Getty Images

bring the end of COVID were dashed first by the delta variant and then the omicron variant. During the December holiday season, illnesses among employees and a series of winter storms wiped out revenue increases. Nevertheless, Delta managed to have two profitable quarters in 2021, had a return to profitability in 2022, and forecasted a strong revenue bump in 2023 as travel demand strengthened. The airline will continue to monitor performance data and make shifts as needed to confront the future changes in its environment.[5]

Overview

As we discussed in Chapter 10, the first task facing managers is to establish a structure of task and job reporting relationships that allows organizational members to use resources most efficiently and effectively. Structure alone, however, does not provide the incentive or motivation for people to behave in ways that help achieve organizational goals. When managers choose how to influence, shape, and regulate the activities of organizational divisions, functions, and employees to achieve the organization's mission and goals, they establish the second foundation of organizational architecture: organizational control. An organization's structure provides the organization with a skeleton, but its control systems give it the muscles, nerves, and sensations that allow managers to regulate and govern its activities. The control systems also give managers specific feedback on how well the organization and its members are performing. As underscored in the opening story about Delta Airlines, the managerial functions of organizing and controlling are inseparable, and effective managers must learn to make them work together in a harmonious way.

In this chapter, we look in detail at the nature of organizational control and describe the main steps in the control process. We also discuss the different types of control systems that are available to managers to shape and influence organizational activities–*output control, behavior control,* and *clan control.*[6] Finally, we discuss the important issue of organizational change, which is possible only when managers have put in place a control system that allows them to adjust the way people and groups behave and change, or transform, the way the organization operates. Control is the essential ingredient needed to bring about and manage organizational change efficiently and effectively. By the end of this chapter, you will appreciate the different forms of control available to managers and understand why developing an appropriate control system is vital to increasing organizational performance.

What Is Organizational Control?

LO11-1 Define organizational control, and explain how it increases organizational effectiveness.

As noted in Chapter 1, *controlling* is the process whereby managers monitor and regulate how efficiently and effectively an organization and its members are performing the activities necessary to achieve organizational goals. As discussed in previous chapters, when planning and organizing, managers develop the organizational strategy and structure that they hope will allow the organization to use resources most effectively to create value for customers. In controlling, managers monitor and evaluate whether the organization's strategy and structure are working as intended, how they can be improved, and how they might be changed if they are not working.

Control, however, does not mean just reacting to events after they have occurred. It also means keeping an organization on track, anticipating events that might occur, and then changing the organization to respond to whatever opportunities or threats have been identified. Control is concerned with keeping employees motivated, focused on the important problems confronting the organization, and working together to make the changes that will help an organization improve its performance over time.

The Importance of Organizational Control

To understand the importance of organizational control, consider how it helps managers obtain superior efficiency, quality, responsiveness to customers, and innovation–the four building blocks of competitive advantage.

To determine how efficiently they are using their resources, managers must be able to accurately measure how many units of inputs (raw materials, human resources, and so on) are being used to produce a unit of output, such as a Toyota vehicle. Managers also must be able to measure how many units of outputs (goods and services) are being produced. A control system contains the measures, or yardsticks, that let managers assess how efficiently the organization is producing goods and services. Moreover, if managers experiment with changing how the organization produces goods and services to find a more efficient way of producing them, these measures tell managers how successful they have been. For example, when Kimberly-Clark, maker of Kleenex and other products, outsourced logistics at a UK plant to a leading lean organization, it reduced long shifts and overtime for its workers. Absenteeism dropped and productivity improved as staff morale went up. Without a control system in place, managers have no idea how well their organization is performing and how its performance can be improved–information that is becoming increasingly important in today's highly competitive environment.

Today much of the competition among organizations centers on increasing the quality of goods and services. In the car industry, for example, cars within each price range compete in features, design, and reliability. Thus, whether a customer buys a Ford Edge, Toyota Camry, or Honda CRV depends significantly on the design and quality of each car. Organizational control is important in determining the quality of goods and services because it gives managers feedback on product quality. If the managers of carmakers consistently measure the number of customer complaints and the number of new cars returned for repairs, or if school principals measure how many students drop out of school or how achievement scores on nationally based tests vary over time, they have a good indication of how much quality they have built into their product–whether it is an educated student or a car that does not break down. Effective managers create a control system that consistently monitors the quality of goods and services so they can continuously improve quality–an approach to change that gives them a competitive advantage.

Effective organizational control can also increase responsiveness to customers. Managers can help make their organizations more responsive to customers, for example, if they develop a control system, such as a CRM system, that allows them to evaluate how well customer-contact employees perform their jobs. Monitoring employee behavior can help managers find ways to increase employees' performance levels, perhaps by revealing areas in which skill training or new procedures can allow employees to perform their jobs better. Also, when employees know their behaviors are being monitored, they have more incentive to be helpful and consistent in how they act toward customers. For example, Caterpillar has a lean initiative to bring employees closer to customers so the employees can provide products and services that match customers' needs. Before Caterpillar introduced its lean manufacturing principle at its Aurora, Illinois, facility, discovering defects on its medium wheel loader value stream was considered normal. Because the defects were discovered, they were fixed before being passed on to the customer. However, the defects were still costing the company lost time and other costs. After the company introduced its lean program at the plant and made it clear that the company was dedicated to eliminating defects, average internal defects fell by 60%.[7]

Finally, controlling can raise the level of innovation in an organization. Successful innovation takes place when managers create an organizational setting in which employees feel empowered to be creative and in which authority is decentralized to employees so they feel free to experiment and take control of their work activities. Deciding on the appropriate control systems to encourage risk taking is an important management challenge; organizational culture is vital in this regard. At Caterpillar, for example, investing in operational excellence and collaborating with employees, especially on the issue of safety, continues to reap rewards. In 2021, the company continued to reduce time lost to injuries from previous years.[8]

Caterpillar's approach to organizational control helped employees eliminate manufacturing defects and increase performance levels.
Rajesh Singh/REUTERS/Newscom

Control Systems and Technology

control systems Formal target-setting, monitoring, evaluation, and feedback systems that provide managers with information about how well the organization's strategy and structure are working.

Control systems are formal target-setting, monitoring, evaluation, and feedback systems that provide managers with information about whether the organization's strategy and structure are working efficiently and effectively.[9] Effective control systems alert managers when something is going wrong and give them time to respond to opportunities and threats. An effective control system has three characteristics: It is flexible enough to allow managers to respond as necessary to unexpected events; it provides accurate information about organizational performance; and it gives managers information in a timely manner because making decisions on the basis of outdated information is a recipe for failure.

Technology has revolutionized control systems because they facilitate the flow of accurate and timely information up and down the organizational hierarchy and between functions and divisions. Today employees at all levels of the organization routinely feed information into a company's information system or network and start the chain of events that affect decision making in some other part of the organization. This could be the department store clerk whose scanning of purchased clothing tells merchandise managers what kinds of clothing need to be reordered or the salesperson in the field who inputs data into a mobile device to inform marketing about customers' changing needs.

feedforward control Control that allows managers to anticipate problems before they arise.

Control and information systems are developed to measure performance at each stage in the process of transforming inputs into finished goods and services (see Figure 11.1). At the input stage, managers use **feedforward control** to anticipate problems before they arise so problems do not occur later during the conversion process.[10] For example, by giving stringent product specifications to suppliers in advance (a form of performance target), an organization can control the quality of the inputs it receives from its suppliers and, thus, avoid potential problems during the conversion process. Also, technology can be used to keep in contact with suppliers and to monitor their progress. Similarly, by screening job applicants, often by viewing their résumés electronically and using several interviews to select the most highly skilled people, managers can lessen the chance that they will hire people who lack the necessary skills or experience to perform effectively. In general, the development of management information systems promotes feedforward control that gives managers timely information about changes in the task and general environments that may impact their organization later on. Effective managers always monitor trends and changes in the external environment to try to anticipate problems.

concurrent control Control that gives managers immediate feedback on how efficiently inputs are being transformed into outputs so managers can correct problems as they arise.

At the conversion stage, **concurrent control** gives managers immediate feedback on how efficiently inputs are being transformed into outputs so managers can correct problems as they arise. Concurrent control through the use of technology alerts managers to the need to react quickly to whatever is the source of the problem, whether it is a defective batch of inputs, a machine that is out of alignment, or a worker who lacks the skills necessary to perform a task efficiently. Concurrent control is at the heart of total quality management programs (discussed in Chapter 9), in which workers are expected to constantly monitor the quality of the goods

Figure 11.1
Three Types of Control

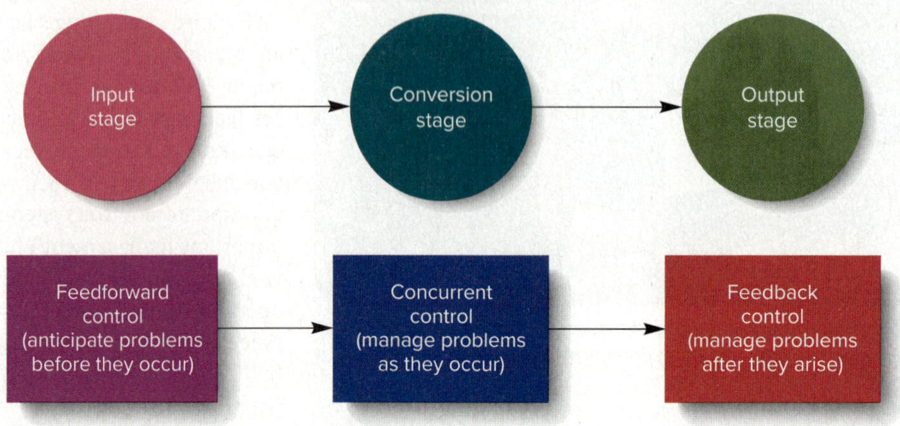

or services they provide at every step of the production process and inform managers as soon as they discover problems. For example, one of the strengths of Toyota's production system is that individual workers have the authority to push a button to stop the assembly line whenever they discover a quality problem. When all the problems have been corrected, the result is a finished product that is much more reliable.

feedback control Control that gives managers information about customers' reactions to goods and services so corrective action can be taken if necessary.

At the output stage, managers use **feedback control** to provide information about customers' reactions to goods and services so corrective action can be taken if necessary. For example, a feedback control system that monitors the number of customer returns alerts managers when defective products are being produced, and a management information system (MIS) that measures increases or decreases in relative sales of different products alerts managers to changes in customer tastes so they can increase or reduce the production of specific products.

The Control Process

LO11-2 Describe the four steps in the control process and the way it operates over time.

The control process, whether at the input, conversion, or output stage, can be broken down into four steps: establishing standards of performance and then measuring, comparing, and evaluating actual performance (see Figure 11.2).[11]

- Step 1: *Establish the standards of performance, goals, or targets against which performance is to be evaluated.*

At step 1 in the control process, managers decide on the standards of performance, goals, or targets that they will use in the future to evaluate the performance of the entire organization or part of it (such as a division, a function, or an individual). The standards of performance that managers select measure efficiency, quality, responsiveness to customers, and innovation.[12] If managers decide to pursue a low-cost strategy, for example, they need to measure efficiency at all levels in the organization.

At the corporate level, a standard of performance that measures efficiency is operating costs, the actual costs associated with producing goods and services, including all employee-related costs. Top managers might set a corporate goal of "reducing operating costs by 10% for the next three years" to increase efficiency. Corporate managers might then evaluate divisional managers for their ability to reduce operating costs within their respective divisions, and divisional managers might set cost-saving targets for functional managers. Thus, performance standards selected at one level affect those at the other levels, and ultimately the performance of individual managers is evaluated in terms of their ability to reduce costs.

The number of standards or indicators of performance that an organization's managers use to evaluate efficiency, quality, and so on can run into the thousands or hundreds of thousands. Managers at each level are responsible for selecting standards that will best allow them to evaluate how well the part of the organization they are responsible for is performing.[13] Managers must be careful to choose standards of performance that let them assess how well they are doing with all

Figure 11.2

Four Steps in Organizational Control

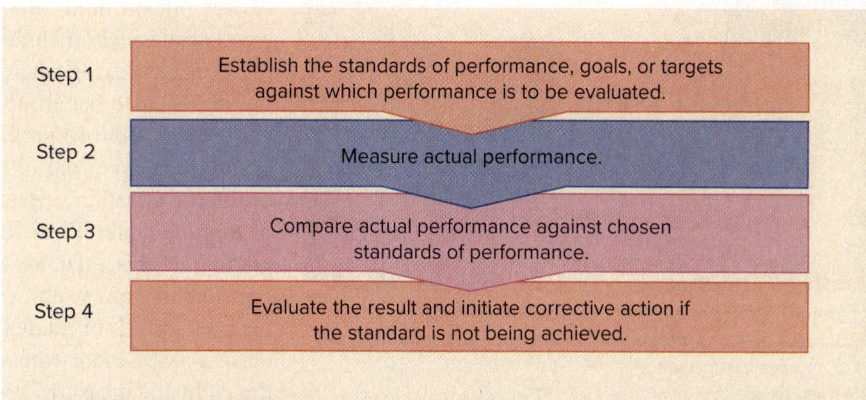

four building blocks of competitive advantage. If managers focus on just one standard (such as efficiency) and ignore others (such as determining what customers really want and innovating a new line of products to satisfy them), managers may end up hurting their organization's performance.

- Step 2: *Measure actual performance.*

Once managers have decided which standards or targets they will use to evaluate performance, the next step in the control process is to measure actual performance. In practice, managers can measure or evaluate two things: (1) the actual *outputs* that result from the behavior of their members and (2) the *behaviors* themselves (hence the terms *output control* and *behavior control* used in this chapter).[14] The "Focus on DEI&B" feature describes the importance and challenges of this step for ensuring consistently excellent customer service.

FOCUS ON DEI&B

Reducing Bias in Customer Service

Many organizations take pride in what they consider to be their excellent customer service; some have inspiring stories about employees going above and beyond to delight customers. However, far fewer companies routinely investigate whether high levels of service extend equitably to different categories of customers.

Researchers have conducted experiments to test for bias in serving customers–for example, by sending actors to shop in the same places for the same items or sending email requests that were identical except for the sender's name. Other studies analyze content posted online. Results include findings that real estate agents avoided certain neighborhoods when customers were Black; department store employees were more likely to accept a returned item if the shopper was female; U.S. hotel concierges were likelier to reply to an email asking for restaurant recommendations if the message was signed by a name that didn't sound "foreign"; customer service reps were less likely to reply to a service complaint on Twitter if the profile indicated the user was Black; and salespeople were less likely to smile and take time to help shoppers who appeared to be obese.[15]

When biases disrupt excellent service, customers complain, and managers may jump to a standard response–say, firing an employee, launching a training program, or hiring a diversity manager. However, this skips a key step in the control process: measuring performance to find out what biases actually exist in the organization. As a starting point, an organization should talk to customers who represent the scope of diversity in its target markets, asking how easy it is to obtain products and how the customers experience interactions with service providers. In addition, most companies have extensive data about transactions; companies should examine the data to look at measures such as how often customers are put on hold, how many customers get perks, or whether messages include polite language.[16]

After identifying where customer service is not provided equitably across consumer groups, organizations can establish controls to improve performance.
vm/E+/Getty Images

After identifying where service is not provided equitably across customer groups, an organization can establish controls to improve performance. A starting point is to ensure employees are often exposed to people inclusive of the organization's customers. This may include review of training materials to verify that all types of customers are fully represented, as well as ensuring diversity within the organization itself. Standardization, such as scripts for interactions or guidelines for distributing extras, can make service more equitable. Making equity something the company measures and rewards also is critical.[17]

Sometimes both outputs and behaviors can be easily measured. Measuring outputs and evaluating behavior is relatively easy in a fast-food restaurant, for example, because employees are performing routine tasks. Managers at Home Depot are rigorous in using output control to measure how fast inventory flows through stores. Similarly, managers of a fast-food restaurant can easily measure outputs by counting how many customers their employees serve, the time each transaction takes, and how much money each customer spends. Managers can easily observe each employee's behavior and quickly take action to solve any problems that may arise.

When an organization and its members perform complex, nonroutine activities that are intrinsically hard to measure, it is more challenging for managers to measure outputs or behavior. For example, it might be simple for a manager at Amazon to measure a customer service representative's effectiveness by examining sales figures and customer satisfaction reports. However, it would be difficult for the managers at the companies that supply Amazon with products to measure a product designer's creativity just by watching the designer's actions.

In general, the more nonroutine or complex organizational activities are, the harder it is for managers to measure outputs or behaviors.[18] Outputs, however, are usually easier to measure than behaviors because they are more tangible and objective. Therefore, the first kind of performance measures that managers tend to use is those that measure outputs. Then managers develop performance measures or standards that allow them to evaluate behaviors to determine whether employees at all levels are working toward organizational goals. Some simple behavior measures are (1) whether employees come to work on time and (2) whether employees consistently follow the established rules for greeting and serving customers. The various types of output and behavior control and how they are used at the different organizational levels–corporate, divisional, functional, and individual–are discussed in detail subsequently.

- Step 3: *Compare actual performance against chosen standards of performance.*

During step 3, managers evaluate whether–and to what extent–performance deviates from the standards of performance chosen in step 1. If performance is higher than expected, managers might decide they set performance standards too low and may raise them for the next period to challenge their employees.[19] Managers at successful companies are well known for the way they try to improve performance in manufacturing settings by constantly raising performance standards to motivate managers and workers to find new ways to reduce costs or increase quality.

However, if performance is too low and standards were not reached, or if standards were set so high that employees could not achieve them, managers must decide whether to take corrective action.[20] It is easy to take corrective action when the reasons for poor performance can be identified–for instance, high labor costs. To reduce costs, managers can search for low-cost overseas suppliers, invest more in technology, or implement cross-functional teams. More often, however, the reasons for poor performance are hard to identify. Changes in the environment, such as the emergence of a new global competitor, a recession, or an increase in interest rates, might be the source of the problem. Within an organization, perhaps the R&D function underestimated the problems it would encounter in developing a new product or the extra costs of doing unforeseen research or perhaps the faulty design of just one component in thousands slipped through the cracks. If managers are to take any form of corrective action, step 4 is necessary.

- Step 4: *Evaluate the result and initiate corrective action (that is, make changes) if the standard is not being achieved.*

The final step in the control process is to evaluate the results and implement change as appropriate. Whether or not performance standards have been met, managers can learn a great deal during this step. If managers decide the level of performance is unacceptable, they must try to change how work activities are performed to solve the problem. Sometimes performance problems occur because the work standard was too high–for example, a sales target was too optimistic and impossible to achieve. In this case, adopting more realistic standards can reduce the gap between actual performance and desired performance.

However, if managers determine that something in the situation is causing the problem, then to raise performance they will need to change how resources are being utilized or shared.[21] Perhaps the latest technology is not being used; perhaps workers lack the advanced training needed to perform at a higher level; perhaps the organization needs to buy its inputs or assemble its products abroad to compete against low-cost rivals; perhaps it needs to restructure itself or reengineer its work processes using Six Sigma to increase efficiency.

Figure 11.3

Three Organizational Control Systems

Type of Control	Mechanisms of Control
Output control	Financial measures of performance Organizational goals Operating budgets
Behavior control	Direct supervision MBO/balanced scorecard Rules and standard operating procedures
Clan control	Values Norms Socialization

The simplest example of a control system is the thermostat in a home. By setting the thermostat, you establish the standard of performance with which actual temperature is to be compared. The thermostat contains a sensing or monitoring device that measures the actual temperature against the desired temperature. Whenever there is a difference between them, the furnace or air-conditioning unit is activated to bring the temperature back to the standard. In other words, corrective action is initiated. This is a simple control system: It is entirely self-contained and the target (temperature) is easy to measure.

Establishing targets and designing measurement systems are much more difficult for managers because the high level of uncertainty in the organizational environment means managers rarely know what might happen in the future. Thus, it is vital for managers to design control systems to alert them to problems quickly so they can be dealt with before they become threatening. Another issue is that managers are not just concerned about bringing the organization's performance up to some predetermined standard; they want to push that standard forward to encourage employees at all levels to find new ways to raise performance.

In the following sections, we consider three important types of control systems that managers use to coordinate and motivate employees to ensure that they pursue superior efficiency, quality, innovation, and responsiveness to customers: output control, behavior control, and clan control (see Figure 11.3). Managers use all three to shape, regulate, and govern organizational activities, no matter what specific organizational structure is in place. However, as Figure 11.3 suggests, an important element of control is embedded in organizational culture, which is discussed later.

Output Control

LO11-3 Identify the main output controls, and discuss their advantages and disadvantages as means of coordinating and motivating employees.

All managers develop a system of output control for their organizations. First they choose the goals or output performance standards or targets that they think will best measure efficiency, quality, innovation, and responsiveness to customers. Then they measure to see whether the performance goals and standards are being achieved at the corporate, divisional, functional, and individual employee levels of the organization. The three main mechanisms that managers use to assess output or performance are financial measures, organizational goals, and operating budgets.

Financial Measures of Performance

Top managers are most concerned with overall organizational performance and use various financial measures to evaluate it. The most common are profit ratios, liquidity ratios, leverage ratios, and activity ratios. They are discussed here and summarized in Table 11.1.[22]

- *Profit ratios* measure how efficiently managers are using the organization's resources to generate profits. *Return on investment (ROI),* an organization's net income before taxes

Table 11.1
Four Measures of Financial Performance

Profit Ratios			
Return on investment	=	$\frac{\text{Net profit before taxes}}{\text{Total assets}}$	Measures how well managers are using the organization's resources to generate profits.
Operating margin	=	$\frac{\text{Total operating profit}}{\text{Sales revenues}}$	Measures how much percentage profit a company is earning on sales; the higher the percentage, the better a company is using its resources to make and sell the product.
Liquidity Ratios			
Current ratio	=	$\frac{\text{Current assets}}{\text{Current liabilities}}$	Measures the availability of resources to meet claims of short-term creditors.
Quick ratio	=	$\frac{\text{Current assets}-\text{inventory}}{\text{Current liabilities}}$	Measures ability to pay off claims of short-term creditors without selling inventory.
Leverage Ratios			
Debt-to-assets ratio	=	$\frac{\text{Total debt}}{\text{Total assets}}$	Measures the extent to which managers have used borrowed funds to finance investments.
Times-covered ratio	=	$\frac{\text{Profit before interest and taxes}}{\text{Total interest charges}}$	Measures how far profits can decline before managers cannot meet interest charges. If this ratio declines to less than 1, the organization is technically insolvent.
Activity Ratios			
Inventory turnover	=	$\frac{\text{Cost of goods sold}}{\text{Inventory}}$	Measures how efficiently managers are turning inventory over so that excess inventory is not carried.
Days sales outstanding	=	$\frac{\text{Current accounts receivable}}{\text{Sales for period divided by days in period}}$	Measures how efficiently managers are collecting revenues from customers to pay expenses.

divided by its total assets, is the most commonly used financial performance measure because it allows managers of one organization to compare performance with that of other organizations. ROI lets managers assess an organization's competitive advantage. *Operating margin* is calculated by dividing a company's operating profit (the amount it has left after all the costs of making the product and running the business have been deducted) by sales revenues. This measure tells managers how efficiently an organization is using its resources; every successful attempt to reduce costs will be reflected in increased operating profit, for example. Also, operating margin is a means of comparing one year's performance to another; for example, if managers discover operating margin has improved by 5% from one year to the next, they know their organization is building a competitive advantage.

- *Liquidity ratios* measure how well managers have protected organizational resources to be able to meet short-term obligations. The *current ratio* (current assets divided by current liabilities) tells managers whether they have the resources available to meet the claims of short-term creditors. The *quick ratio* shows whether they can pay these claims without selling inventory.
- *Leverage ratios,* such as the *debt-to-assets ratio* and the *times-covered ratio,* measure the degree to which managers use debt (borrow money) or equity (issue new shares) to finance ongoing operations. An organization is highly leveraged if it uses more debt than equity. Debt can be risky when net income or profit fails to cover the interest on

the debt–as some people learn too late when they overspend and cannot pay off their credit cards.

- *Activity ratios* show how well managers are creating value from organizational assets. *Inventory turnover* measures how efficiently managers are turning inventory over so excess inventory is not carried. *Days sales outstanding* reveals how efficiently managers are collecting revenue from customers to pay expenses.

The objectivity of financial measures of performance is the reason why so many managers use them to assess the efficiency and effectiveness of their organizations. When an organization fails to meet performance standards such as ROI, revenue, or stock price targets, managers know they must take corrective action. Thus, financial controls tell managers when a corporate reorganization might be necessary, when they should sell off divisions and exit businesses, or when they should rethink their corporate-level strategies.[23] In addition to problem-solving skills, job candidates need teamwork abilities in today's job market, as described in the accompanying "Management Insight" feature.

Although financial information is an important output control, financial information by itself does not tell managers all they need to know about the four building blocks of competitive advantage. Financial results inform managers about the results of decisions they have already made; they do not tell managers how to find new opportunities to build competitive advantage in the future. To encourage a future-oriented approach, top managers must establish organizational goals that encourage middle and first-line managers to achieve superior efficiency, quality, innovation, and responsiveness to customers.

MANAGEMENT INSIGHT

Wanted: Problem-Solving and Teamwork Skills

In today's job market, strong problem-solving and teamwork skills are the top attributes employers are looking for on a college graduate's resume. According to the Job Outlook 2023 Survey by the National Association of Colleges and Employers (NACE), more than 60% of employers responding to the survey say they are looking for evidence of graduates' abilities to solve problems and to work in a team. In addition, more than half of the employers are looking for students to have a strong work ethic, analytical/qualitative skills, written communication skills, and technical skills.[24]

Looking to land a job after graduation? Research suggests employers are looking to hire recent grads who are problem solvers and team players.
Geber86/Getty Images

While past NACE survey results found a student's major the deciding factor between two otherwise qualified candidates, the 2023 survey results suggest that only 37% of those employers surveyed consider a student's GPA as a significant screening tool, which may signal that some employers are rethinking their initial screening procedures. In addition, this result may also suggest the growing awareness that GPA screening might undermine efforts to build an inclusive workforce and might disadvantage students who are balancing school with work and other responsibilities.[25]

As in previous NACE surveys, one of the most influential factors in hiring new college graduates continues to be a candidate's internship experience either within the hiring organization or within the organization's industry, especially when choosing between two equally qualified candidates. This finding underscores employer sentiment that internships provide students with professional experience and opportunities to fine-tune problem-solving, communication, and critical-thinking skills, as well as learn basic workplace etiquette, which may help them hit the ground running on the first day of their new job.[26]

According to NACE, employers plan to hire nearly 15% more new college graduates in 2023, with more than half planning to increase hiring while only 6% of employers surveyed expect to cut back. One factor influencing employers' hiring strategies is the very low national unemployment rate and the need to address worker shortages that began during the pandemic and continue today. Although hiring rates for 2023 are not quite as high as for 2022, employers still rate the job market for 2023 graduates as very good to excellent. Some of the industries where employers will be looking to hire new grads include finance, insurance, real estate, and electronic manufacturing.[27]

Organizational Goals

Once top managers consult with lower-level managers and set the organization's overall goals, they establish performance standards for the divisions and functions. These standards specify for divisional and functional managers the level at which their units must perform if the organization is to achieve its overall goals.[28] Each division is given a set of specific goals to achieve (see Figure 11.4). For example, Jeff Harmening, CEO of General Mills, has established the goal of having each of the company's divisions be first or second in its industry in profit. Divisional managers then develop a business-level strategy (based on achieving superior efficiency or innovation) that they hope will help them to achieve that goal.[29] In consultation with functional managers, they specify the functional goals that the managers of different functions need to achieve to allow the division to achieve its goals. For example, sales managers might be evaluated for their ability to increase sales; materials management managers, for their ability to increase the quality of inputs or lower their costs; R&D managers, for the number of products they innovate or the number of patents they receive. In turn, functional managers establish goals that first-line managers and nonmanagerial employees need to achieve to allow the function to achieve its goals.

Output control is used at every level of the organization, and it is vital that the goals set at each level harmonize with the goals set at other levels so managers and other employees throughout the organization work together to attain the corporate goals that top managers have set.[30] It is also important that goals be set appropriately so managers are motivated to accomplish them. If goals are set at an impossibly high level, managers might work only halfheartedly to achieve them because they are certain they will fail. In contrast, if goals are set so low that they are too easy to achieve, managers will not be motivated to use all their resources as efficiently and effectively as possible. Research suggests that the best goals are specific, difficult goals–goals that challenge and stretch managers' abilities but are not out of reach and

Figure 11.4

Organizationwide Goal Setting

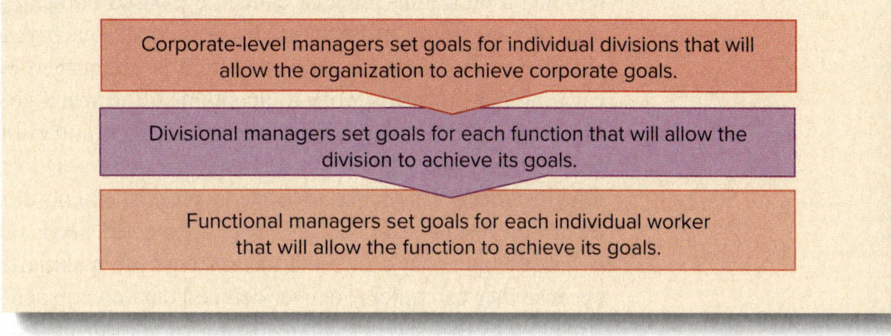

do not require an impossibly high expenditure of managerial time and energy. Such goals are often called *stretch goals.*

Deciding what is a specific, difficult goal and what is a goal that is too difficult or too easy is a skill that managers must develop. Based on their own judgment and work experience, managers at all levels must assess how difficult a certain task is, and they must assess the ability of a particular subordinate manager to achieve the goal. If they do so successfully, challenging, interrelated goals–goals that reinforce one another and focus on achieving overall corporate objectives–will energize the organization.

Operating Budgets

operating budget A budget that states how managers intend to use organizational resources to achieve organizational goals.

Once managers at each level have been given a goal or target to achieve, the next step in developing an output control system is to establish operating budgets that regulate how managers and workers attain their goals. An **operating budget** is a blueprint that states how managers intend to use organizational resources to achieve organizational goals efficiently. Typically, managers at one level allocate to subordinate managers a specific amount of resources to produce goods and services. Once they have been given a budget, these lower-level managers must decide how to allocate money for different organizational activities. They are then evaluated for their ability to stay within the budget and to make the best use of available resources. For example, managers in General Mills' international division might have a budget of $25 million to spend on developing and selling a new line of organic cereal bars in Europe and Southeast Asia. They must decide how much money to allocate to the various functions, such as finance, R&D, production, and sales, so the business unit generates the most customer revenue and makes the biggest profit. The "Managing Globally" feature describes a budgeting method that is helping international companies reduce their expenses.

Large organizations often treat each division as a singular, or stand-alone, responsibility center. Corporate managers then evaluate each division's contribution to corporate performance. Managers of a division may be given a fixed budget for resources and be evaluated on the amount of goods or services they can produce using those resources (this is a cost or expense budget approach). Alternatively, managers may be asked to maximize the revenues from the sales of goods and services produced (a revenue budget approach). Or managers may be evaluated on the difference between the revenues generated by the sales of goods and services and the budgeted cost of making those goods and services (a profit budget approach). Japanese companies' use of operating budgets and challenging goals to increase efficiency is instructive in this context.

MANAGING GLOBALLY

Zero-Based Budgeting Helps Control Expenses

More and more global businesses are telling investors or researchers that they have adopted a budgeting practice called zero-based budgeting (ZBB). With ZBB, the manager of each group or business division creates each year's budget from a blank worksheet. Every amount for every line item is established based on what is necessary for carrying out the year's work to accomplish the year's goals. This may sound basic, but in practice, most managers have saved both time and effort by starting with the previous year's budget and adjusting it upward (or downward) to reflect any changes in goals or circumstances. This tends to leave in place spending done out of habit or provided as a cushion for managers confronting unexpected needs. Creating a budget from scratch is harder, but today's information systems are making the use of ZBB more practical because they can quickly deliver detailed data about spending almost in real time.[31] This strategy was very useful to many organizations during the global pandemic when finance

Many global firms use zero-based budgeting to help control expenses.
Freedomz/Shutterstock

executives were forced to take a more detailed look at company spending to keep costs and expenses in check.[32]

A study by Accenture of large global companies found that the percentage of companies using ZBB has been rising 57% per year during this decade. Among the organizations adopting the method are the Anglo-Dutch company Unilever, the United Kingdom's Tesco supermarket chain, and the U.S.-based food giants Kraft Heinz and Mondelez International.[33]

A chief reason for using ZBB is to cut unnecessary spending in the face of international competition for resources and customers. Unilever, for example, announced expected savings greater than $6 billion in marketing and logistics expenses. In the Accenture survey, the companies using ZBB saved an average of $280 million per year, representing reductions of 15% on average. To be effective, cost cutting should be linked to organizational strategy. Most companies in the Accenture study did this by using savings from ZBB to increase profitability; about half used the savings to free up funds for growth. At Kraft Heinz, the chief information officer used ZBB strategically by emphasizing robotics and artificial intelligence projects, because they could help the company the most in its cost-reduction efforts. The annual routine of ZBB also helps to embed cost consciousness into an organization's culture.[34]

Consultants at Accenture see a bigger future for the principles of ZBB. They believe that the annual process–ground-up planning followed by performance measurement and control–applies to more than budgets. With this mind-set, organizations can look anew at all their processes to see where performance data can help them create a system that does the essentials and does them well.[35]

In summary, three components–objective financial measures, challenging goals and performance standards, and appropriate operating budgets–are the essence of effective output control. Most organizations develop sophisticated output control systems to allow managers at all levels to keep accurate account of the organization so they can move quickly to take corrective action as needed. Output control is an essential part of management.

Problems with Output Control

When designing an output control system, managers must be careful to avoid some pitfalls. For example, they must be sure the output standards they create motivate managers at all levels and do not cause managers to behave in inappropriate ways to achieve organizational goals.

Suppose top managers give divisional managers the goal of doubling profits over a three-year period. This goal seems challenging and reachable when it is jointly agreed upon, and in the first two years profits go up by 70%. In the third year, however, an economic recession hits and sales plummet. Divisional managers think it is increasingly unlikely that they will meet their profit goal. Failure will mean losing the substantial monetary bonus tied to achieving the goal. How might managers behave to try to preserve their bonuses?

Perhaps they might find ways to reduce costs because profit can be increased either by raising sales revenues or reducing costs. Thus, divisional managers might cut back on expensive research activities, delay machinery maintenance, reduce marketing expenditures, and lay off middle managers and workers to reduce costs so that at the end of the year they will make their target of doubling profits and receive their bonuses. This tactic might help them achieve a short-run goal–doubling profits–but such actions could hurt long-term profitability or ROI (because a cutback in R&D can reduce the rate of product innovation, a cutback in marketing will lead to the loss of customers, and so on).

The message is clear: Although output control is a useful tool for keeping managers and employees at all levels motivated and the organization on track, it is only a guide to appropriate action. Managers must be sensitive in how they use output control and must constantly monitor its effects at all levels in the organization–and on customers and other stakeholders.

Behavior Control

LO11-4 Identify the main behavior controls, and discuss their advantages and disadvantages as a means of coordinating and motivating employees.

Organizational structure by itself does not provide any mechanism that motivates managers and nonmanagerial employees to behave in ways that make the structure work–or even improve how it works, hence the need for control. Put another way, managers can develop an organizational structure that has the right grouping of divisions and functions, and an effective chain of command, but it will work as designed *only* if managers also establish control systems that motivate and shape employee behavior in ways that *match* this structure.[36] Output control is one method of motivating employees; behavior control is another method. This section examines three mechanisms of behavior control that managers can use to keep employees on track and make organizational structures work as they are designed to work: direct supervision, management by objectives, and rules and bureaucratic control via standard operating procedures (see Figure 11.3).

Direct Supervision

The most immediate and potent form of behavior control is direct supervision by managers who actively monitor and observe the behavior of their employees, teach them the behaviors that are appropriate and inappropriate, and intervene to take corrective action as needed. Moreover, when managers personally supervise employees, they lead by example and in this way can help employees develop and increase their own skill levels. (Leadership is the subject of Chapter 14.)

Direct supervision allows managers at all levels to become personally involved with their employees and allows them to mentor employees and develop their management skills. Thus, control through personal supervision can be an effective way of motivating employees and promoting behaviors that increase efficiency and effectiveness.[37]

Nevertheless, certain problems are associated with direct supervision. First, it is expensive because a manager can personally manage only a relatively small number of employees effectively. Therefore, if direct supervision is the main kind of control being used in an organization, a lot of managers will be needed, and costs will increase. For this reason, output control is usually preferred to behavior control; indeed, output control tends to be the first type of control that managers at all levels use to evaluate performance. Second, direct supervision can *demotivate* employees. This occurs if employees feel they are under such close scrutiny that they are not free to make their own decisions or if they feel they are not being evaluated in an accurate and impartial way. Team members and other employees may start to pass the buck, avoid responsibility, and cease to cooperate with other team members if they feel their manager is not accurately evaluating their performance and is favoring some people over others.

Third, as noted previously, for many jobs personal control through direct supervision is simply not feasible. The more complex a job is, the more difficult it is for a manager to evaluate how well an employee is performing. The performance of divisional and functional managers, for example, can be evaluated only over relatively long periods (this is why an output control system is developed), so it makes little sense for top managers to continually monitor their performance. However, managers can still communicate the organization's mission and goals to their employees and reinforce the values and norms in the organization's culture through their own personal style.

management by objectives (MBO) A goal-setting process in which a manager and each employee negotiate specific goals and objectives for the employee to achieve and then periodically evaluate the extent to which the employee is achieving employee goals.

Management by Objectives

To provide a framework within which to evaluate employees' behavior and, in particular, to allow managers to monitor progress toward achieving goals, many organizations implement some version of management by objectives. **Management by objectives (MBO)** is a formal system of evaluating employees on their ability to achieve specific organizational goals or

performance standards and to meet operating budgets.[38] Most organizations use some form of MBO system because it is pointless to establish goals and then fail to evaluate whether they are being achieved. Management by objectives involves three specific steps:

- Step 1: *Specific goals and objectives are established at each level of the organization.*

MBO starts when top managers establish overall organizational objectives, such as specific financial performance goals or targets. Then, objective setting cascades down throughout the organization as managers at the divisional and functional levels set their goals to achieve corporate objectives. Finally, first-level managers and employees jointly set goals that will contribute to achieving functional objectives.

- Step 2: *Managers and their employees together determine the employees' goals.*

An important characteristic of management by objectives is its participatory nature. Managers at every level sit down with each of the managers who report directly to them, and together they determine appropriate and feasible goals for the subordinate and bargain over the budget that the person will need to achieve their goals. The participation of employees in the objective-setting process is a way of strengthening their commitment to achieving their goals and meeting their budgets.[39] Another reason it is so important for employees (both individuals and teams) to participate in goal setting is that doing so enables them to tell managers what they think they can realistically achieve.[40]

- Step 3: *Managers and their employees periodically review the employees' progress toward meeting goals.*

Once specific objectives have been agreed on for managers at each level, managers are accountable for meeting those objectives. Periodically, they sit down with their employees to evaluate their progress. Normally, salary raises and promotions are linked to the goal-setting process, and managers who achieve their goals receive greater rewards than those who fall short. (The issue of how to design reward systems to motivate managers and other organizational employees is discussed in Chapter 13.)

In companies that have decentralized responsibility for the production of goods and services to empowered teams and cross-functional teams, management by objectives works somewhat differently. Managers ask each team to develop a set of goals and performance targets that the team hopes to achieve–goals consistent with organizational objectives. Managers then negotiate with each team to establish its final goals and the budget the team will need to achieve them. The reward system is linked to team performance, not to the performance of any one team member.

MBO does not always work out as planned, however. Managers and their employees at all levels must believe that performance evaluations are accurate and fair. Any suggestion that personal biases and political objectives play a part in the evaluation process can lower or even destroy MBO's effectiveness as a control system. This is why many organizations work so hard to protect the integrity of their systems.

Also, when people work in teams, each member's contribution to the team and each team's contribution to the goals of the organization must be fairly evaluated. This is not easy to do. It depends on managers' ability to create an organizational control system that measures performance accurately and fairly and links performance evaluations to rewards so that employees stay motivated and coordinate their activities to achieve the organization's mission and goals.

balanced scorecard A management control system that takes a comprehensive look at an organization's overall performance using four measures: financial, customer service, internal business processes, and the organization's capability for strategic learning and growth.

THE BALANCED SCORECARD In recent years, an extension of the MBO approach to organizational control, which provides a more balanced view of a company's performance, has become popular. Developed by Robert Kaplan and David Norton in the early 1990s, the **balanced scorecard** addresses financial measures as well as three other operational components: customer service, internal business processes, and an organization's potential for learning and growth.[41]

The *financial* component of the scorecard pertains to how well company actions contribute to the organization's overall financial condition; it typically includes measurements such as return on investment and net income. The *customer service* perspective concentrates on how well an organization provides service to its customers; it typically includes a variety of information on customer satisfaction and retention, which can be obtained in several ways, including online surveys. The *internal business processes* component addresses whether the organization's processes and workflow add value to customers and shareholders; it typically includes production and other operational statistics. Finally, the *learning and growth* component focuses on how well company resources, including the workforce, are being managed to ensure a successful future for the company. This effective management tool is used by both large and small businesses as a way to achieve company objectives. Some of the companies that use the balanced scorecard approach include Citibank, Philips Electronics, Apple, UPS, Verizon, and AT&T.[42]

Bureaucratic Control

bureaucratic control Control of behavior by means of a comprehensive system of rules and standard operating procedures.

When direct supervision is too expensive and management by objectives is inappropriate, managers might turn to another mechanism to shape and motivate employee behavior: bureaucratic control. **Bureaucratic control** is control by means of a comprehensive system of rules and standard operating procedures (SOPs) that shapes and regulates the behavior of divisions, functions, and individuals. In Chapter 2 we discussed Weber's theory of bureaucracy and noted that all organizations use bureaucratic rules and procedures, but some use them more than others. Recall that rules and SOPs are formal, written instructions that specify a series of actions that employees should follow to achieve a given end; in other words, if *A* happens, then do *B* and *C*. For example, a supervisor of custodial workers at a health care facility might insist that employees who expect to be late or absent must call by a specific time before their shift starts or face disciplinary action.

Employees demonstrate standardized behavior when they follow the rules that management has developed—actions that are performed the same way time and time again—such as tasks performed on an automobile manufacturing assembly line. This type of bureaucratic control helps maintain quality and increase efficiency.
Monty Rakusen/Cultura/Getty Images

Rules and SOPs guide behavior and specify what employees are to do when they confront a problem that needs a solution. It is the responsibility of a manager to develop rules that allow employees to perform their activities efficiently and effectively. Rules and SOPs also clarify people's expectations about one another and prevent misunderstandings over responsibility or the use of power. Such guidelines can prevent a supervisor from arbitrarily increasing a subordinate's workload and prevent a subordinate from ignoring tasks that are a legitimate part of the job.

When employees follow the rules that managers have developed, their behavior is *standardized*—actions are performed the same way time and time again—and the outcomes of their work are predictable. And to the degree that managers can make employees' behavior predictable, there is no need to monitor the outputs of behavior because *standardized behavior leads to standardized outputs,* such as goods and services of the same uniform quality. Suppose a worker at Toyota comes up with a way to attach exhaust pipes that reduces the number of steps in the assembly process and increases efficiency. Always on the lookout for ways to standardize and improve procedures, managers make this idea the basis of a new rule that says, "From now on, the procedure for attaching the exhaust pipe to the car is as follows." If all workers follow the rule to the letter, every car will come off the assembly line with its exhaust pipe attached in the new way, and there will be no need to check exhaust pipes at the end of the line.

In practice, mistakes and lapses of attention happen, so output control is used at the end of the line, and each car's exhaust system is given a routine inspection. However, the number of quality problems with the exhaust system is minimized because the rule (bureaucratic control) is being followed. Service organizations such as retail stores, fast-food restaurants, and home improvement stores also try to standardize employee behavior, such as customer service quality, by instructing employees in the correct way to greet customers or the appropriate way to serve and bag food. Employees are trained to follow the rules that have proved to be most effective in a particular situation, and the better trained the employees are, the more standardized is their behavior and the more trust managers can have that outputs (such as food quality) will be consistent.

The goal is simple: Use the rules to achieve a quick resolution of a complex issue. If the existing rules don't work, employees must experiment; when they find a solution, it is turned into a new rule to be included in the procedures book to aid the future decision making of all employees in the organization.

Problems with Bureaucratic Control

All organizations make extensive use of bureaucratic control because rules and SOPs effectively control routine organizational activities. (If they don't, the consequences can be severe, as described in the "Ethics in Action" feature.) With a bureaucratic control system in place, managers can manage by exception, intervening and taking corrective action only when necessary. However, managers need to be aware of a number of problems associated with bureaucratic control because such problems can reduce organizational effectiveness.[43]

ETHICS IN ACTION

Could Bureaucratic Controls Have Saved FTX?

Just months after commentators speculated whether FTX founder Sam Bankman-Fried might be the next J. P. Morgan, FTX declared bankruptcy amid accusations of misconduct. The company's business was trading cryptocurrencies (for example, bitcoin and Ethereum's ether). Crypto prices began to tumble in late 2021, and many investors exited the market. Anxiety rose as FTX showed signs it might not be able to give all investors their money, and on November 11, 2022, the company announced its bankruptcy filing and ceased further transactions.[44]

Bankman-Fried, after earning a degree in physics at MIT and becoming a trader of financial securities, started his first business, Alameda, in 2017 as a trading company that borrowed money, bought cryptocurrency, and resold it in markets where the price was higher. Two years later, he started FTX as an exchange where investors could trade crypto securities. While crypto prices soared, the two businesses grew, but when crypto demand fell, both businesses suffered. Paying off Alameda's loans became a problem. A larger exchange, Binance, offered to purchase FTX, but after Binance saw FTX's records, it rescinded the offer, expressing concern about mishandling of funds. Then the day FTX declared bankruptcy, Bankman-Fried resigned.[45]

The CEO who took over was John J. Ray III, who has a 40-year career in leading companies through crises and bankruptcies. Ray characterized FTX as an "unprecedented debacle."[46] It was difficult to see how much money FTX had or where it was going, and apparently some assets were missing. Further, assets of FTX, Alameda, and key individuals, including Bankman-Fried, were entangled to an unusual degree. Ray got to work, hiring a team of lawyers, accountants, consultants, and investigators.[47]

FTX's problem, said Ray, was "an utter failure of corporate controls at every level of the organization."[48] FTX's financial statements did not meet the standards that would apply to a public company of comparable size and scope; these reporting standards do not apply to privately owned companies, including FTX. The board of directors didn't meet good-governance standards of being independent of management and keeping records of meetings. Further, contrary to the standard of care to safeguard clients' assets, senior executives had uncontrolled access to computer systems storing these assets, and Alameda was able to borrow assets from FTX for use in trading or investing.[49] As regulators and the courts continue to sort out the situation, the public is likely to see more consequences of inadequate controls.

First, establishing rules is always easier than discarding them. Organizations tend to become overly bureaucratic over time as managers do everything according to the rule book. If the amount of red tape becomes too great, decision making slows and managers react sluggishly to changing conditions. This can imperil an organization's survival if agile new competitors emerge.

Second, because rules constrain and standardize behavior and lead people to behave in predictable ways, people might become so used to automatically following rules that they stop thinking for themselves. Thus, too much standardization can actually *reduce* the level of learning taking place in an organization and get the organization off track if managers and workers focus on the wrong issues. An organization thrives when its members are constantly thinking of new ways to increase efficiency, quality, and customer responsiveness. By definition, new ideas do not come from blindly following standardized procedures. Similarly, the pursuit of innovation implies a commitment by managers to discover new ways of doing things; innovation, however, is incompatible with extensive bureaucratic control.

Eliminating unnecessary layers in Disney's organizational hierarchy helped Bob Iger foster a successful environment of innovation and creativity.
Matt Baron/Shutterstock

Consider, for example, what happened at The Walt Disney Company when Bob Iger became CEO of the troubled company. Bob Iger had been COO of Disney under CEO Michael Eisner, and he noticed that Disney was plagued by slow decision making that had led to many mistakes in putting its new strategies into action. Its Disney stores were losing money; its Internet properties were flops; and even its theme parks seemed to have lost their luster as few new rides or attractions were introduced. Iger believed one of the main reasons for Disney's declining performance was that it had become too tall and bureaucratic and its top managers were following financial rules that did not lead to innovative strategies.

One of Iger's first moves to turn around performance was to dismantle Disney's central strategic planning office. In this office, several levels of managers were responsible for sifting through all the new ideas and innovations sent up by Disney's different business divisions, such as theme parks, movies, and gaming, and then deciding which ones to present to the CEO. Iger saw the strategic planning office as a bureaucratic bottleneck that reduced the number of ideas coming from below. So he dissolved the office and reassigned its managers back to the different business units.[50]

The result of cutting this unnecessary layer in Disney's hierarchy has been that more new ideas are generated by its different business units. The level of innovation has increased because managers are more willing to speak out and champion their ideas when they know they are dealing directly with the CEO and a top management team searching for innovative ways to improve performance—rather than a layer of strategic planning bureaucrats concerned only with the bottom line.

In 2020, Iger stepped down as CEO, replaced by Bob Chapek, who had served as chairman of Disney parks, experiences, and products. Chapek then reorganized the company to include a new business unit that focused on Disney's direct-to-consumer streaming services, including Hulu, ESPN+, and Disney+. As part of the restructure, Chapek consolidated all content budgeting and strategies for releasing content under a media and distribution unit, which became responsible for the company's continued massive losses on its streaming services—nearly $1.5 billion in the last quarter of 2022, with the company's stock performance plummeting by more than 40% in 2022. In addition, many Disney employees on the creative side of the business reportedly resented Chapek's decision because they believed they had lost their decision-making power.[51] In November 2022, Disney's board of directors fired Chapek and brought back Iger to run the company and refocus its strategies over the next two years to bring costs down, increase stock prices, and welcome back Disney loyalists who were unhappy with the company's direction under the former CEO. As part of his plan, Iger recently announced he would divide the company into three divisions—Disney Entertainment, ESPN, and Parks, Experiences, and Products—and lay off up to 7,000 employees, and cut $5.5 billion in costs as part of the restructuring.[52]

Managers must always be sensitive about the way they use bureaucratic control. It is most useful when organizational activities are routine and well understood and when employees are making programmed decisions–for example, in mass-production settings such as Ford or in routine service settings such as stores like Target or Midas Muffler. Bureaucratic control is much less useful in situations where nonprogrammed decisions have to be made and managers have to react quickly to changes in the task environment.

To use output control and behavior control, managers must be able to identify the outcomes they want to achieve and the behaviors they want employees to perform to achieve those outcomes. For many of the most important and significant organizational activities, however, output control and behavior control are inappropriate for several reasons:

- A manager cannot evaluate the performance of workers such as doctors, research scientists, or engineers by observing their daily behavior.
- Rules and SOPs are of little use in telling a doctor how to respond to an emergency situation or a scientist how to discover something new.
- Output controls such as the amount of time a surgeon takes for each operation or the costs of making a discovery are crude measures of the quality of performance.

How can managers attempt to control and regulate the behavior of their employees when personal supervision is of little use, when rules cannot be developed to tell employees what to do, and when outputs and goals cannot be measured at all or can be measured usefully only over long periods? One solution might be the use of clan control in an organization.

Clan Control

clan control The control exerted on individuals and groups in an organization by shared values, norms, standards of behavior, and expectations.

Increasingly, organizations are using **clan control**, which takes advantage of the power of internalized values and norms to guide and constrain employee attitudes and behavior in ways that increase organizational performance.[53] The first function of a control system is to shape the behavior of organizational members to ensure that they are working toward organizational goals and to take corrective action if those goals are not being met. The second function of control, however, is to keep organizational members focused on thinking about what is best for their organization in the future and to keep them looking for new opportunities to use organizational resources to create value. Clan control serves this dual function of keeping organizational members goal-directed while open to new opportunities because it takes advantage of the power of organizational culture, discussed in Chapter 10.

Organizational culture functions as a kind of control system because managers can deliberately try to influence the kind of values and norms that develop in an organization–values and norms that specify appropriate and inappropriate behaviors and, so, determine the way its members behave. We discussed the sources of organizational culture and the way managers can help create different kinds of cultures in Chapter 10.

Organizational Change

LO11-5 Discuss the relationship between organizational control and change, and explain why managing change is a vital management task.

organizational change The movement of an organization away from its present state and toward some preferred future state to increase its efficiency and effectiveness.

As we have discussed, many problems can arise if an organization's control systems are not designed correctly. One of these problems is that an organization cannot change or adapt in response to a changing environment unless it has effective control over its activities. Companies can lose this control over time, or they can change in ways that make them more effective. **Organizational change** is the movement of an organization away from its present state toward some preferred future state to increase its efficiency and effectiveness.

Interestingly enough, there is a fundamental tension or need to balance two opposing forces in the control process that influences how organizations change. As just noted, organizations and their managers need to be able to control their activities and make their operations routine and predictable. At the same time, however, organizations have to be responsive to the need to change, and managers and employees have to "think on their feet" and realize when they need to depart from routines to be responsive to unpredictable events. In other words, even though adopting the right set of output and behavior controls is essential for improving efficiency, because the environment is dynamic and uncertain, employees also need to feel that they have the autonomy to depart from routines as necessary to increase effectiveness. (See Figure 11.5.)

Figure 11.5

Organizational Control and Change

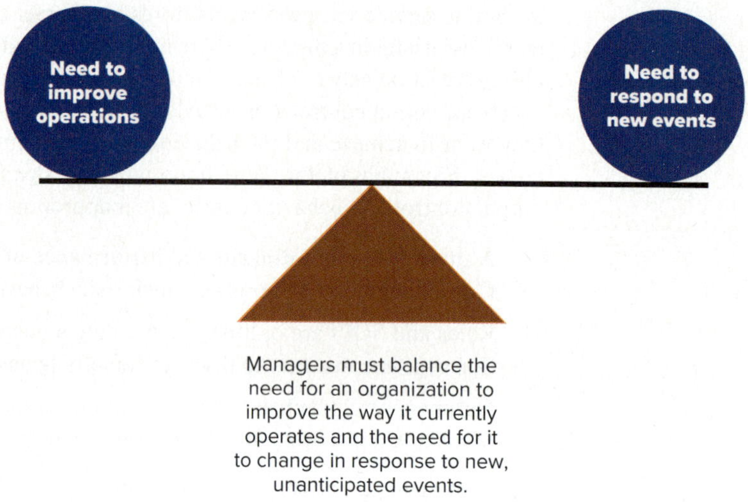

For this reason, many researchers believe that the highest-performing organizations are those that are constantly changing–and thus become experienced at doing so–in their search to become more efficient and effective. Companies like UPS, Toyota, and Walmart are constantly changing the mix of their activities to move forward even as they seek to make their existing operations more efficient. For example, UPS entered the air express parcel market, bought a chain of mailbox stores, and began offering a consulting service. At the same time, the company's ORION on-board technology system, which has increased the efficiency of its delivery process in the United States, is expected to save the company between $300 million and $400 million a year while reducing the average driving route of a UPS driver by close to 8 miles.[54]

Lewin's Force-Field Theory of Change

Researcher Kurt Lewin developed a theory about organizational change. According to his *force-field theory,* a wide variety of forces arise from the way an organization operates–from its structure, culture, and control systems–that make organizations resistant to change. At the same time, a wide variety of forces arise from changing task and general environments that push organizations toward change. These two sets of forces are always in opposition in an organization.[55] When the forces are evenly balanced, the organization is in a state of inertia and does not change. To get an organization to change, managers must find a way to *increase* the forces for change, *reduce* resistance to change, or do *both* simultaneously. Any of these strategies will overcome inertia and cause an organization to change.

Figure 11.6 illustrates Lewin's theory. An organization at performance level P1 is in balance: Forces for change and resistance to change are equal. Management, however, decides that the organization should strive to achieve performance level P2. To get to level P2, managers must *increase* the forces for change (the increase is represented by the lengthening of the up arrows), *reduce* resistance to change (the reduction is represented by the shortening of the down arrows), or both. If managers pursue any of the three strategies successfully, the organization will change and reach performance level P2. Before we look in more detail at the techniques managers can use to overcome resistance and facilitate change, we need to look at the types of change they can implement to increase organizational effectiveness.

Evolutionary and Revolutionary Change

Managers continually face choices about how best to respond to the forces for change. There are several types of change that managers can adopt to help their organizations achieve desired future states.[56] In general, types of change fall into two broad categories: evolutionary change and revolutionary change.[57]

Figure 11.6

Lewin's Force-Field Model of Change

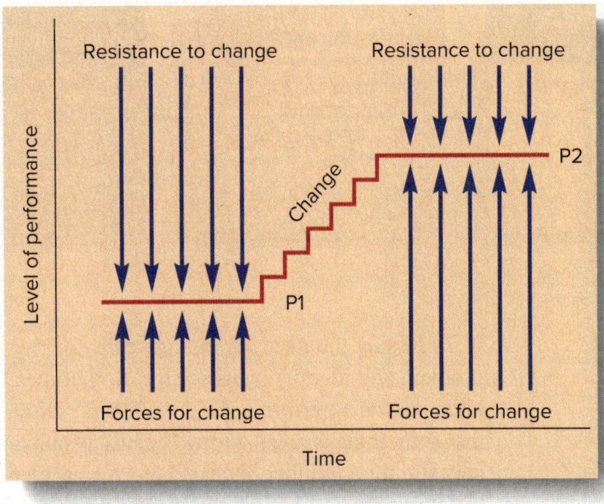

evolutionary change Change that is gradual, incremental, and narrowly focused.

Evolutionary change is gradual, incremental, and narrowly focused. Evolutionary change is not drastic or sudden but, rather, is a constant attempt to improve, adapt, and adjust strategy and structure incrementally to accommodate changes taking place in the environment.[58] Sociotechnical systems theory and total quality management, or kaizen, are two instruments of evolutionary change. Such improvements might entail using technology in a better way or reorganizing the work process.

Some organizations, however, need to make major changes quickly. Faced with drastic, unexpected changes in the environment (for example, a new technological breakthrough) or with an impending disaster resulting from mismanagement, an organization might need to act quickly and decisively. In this case, revolutionary change is called for.

revolutionary change Change that is rapid, dramatic, and broadly focused.

Revolutionary change is rapid, dramatic, and broadly focused. Revolutionary change involves a bold attempt to quickly find new ways to be effective. It is likely to result in a radical shift in ways of doing things, new goals, and a new structure for the organization. The process has repercussions at all levels in the organization–corporate, divisional, functional, group, and individual. Reengineering, restructuring, and innovation are three important instruments of revolutionary change.

Managing Change

The need to constantly search for ways to improve efficiency and effectiveness makes it vital that managers develop the skills necessary to manage change effectively. Several experts have proposed a model of change that managers can follow to implement change successfully–that is, to move an organization away from its present state and toward some desired future state to increase its efficiency and effectiveness.[59] Figure 11.7 outlines the steps in this process. In the rest of this section, we examine each one.

ASSESSING THE NEED FOR CHANGE Organizational change can affect practically all aspects of organizational functioning, including organizational structure, culture, strategies, control systems, and groups and teams, as well as the human resource management system and critical organizational processes such as communication, motivation, and leadership. Organizational change can alter how managers carry out the critical tasks of planning, organizing, leading, and controlling and the ways they perform their managerial roles.

Deciding how to change an organization is a complex matter because change disrupts the status quo and poses a threat, prompting employees to resist attempts to alter work relationships and procedures. Organizational learning–the process through which managers try to increase organizational members' abilities to understand and appropriately respond to changing conditions–can be an important impetus for change and can help all members of an organization, including managers, effectively make decisions about needed changes.

Figure 11.7

Four Steps in the Organizational Change Process

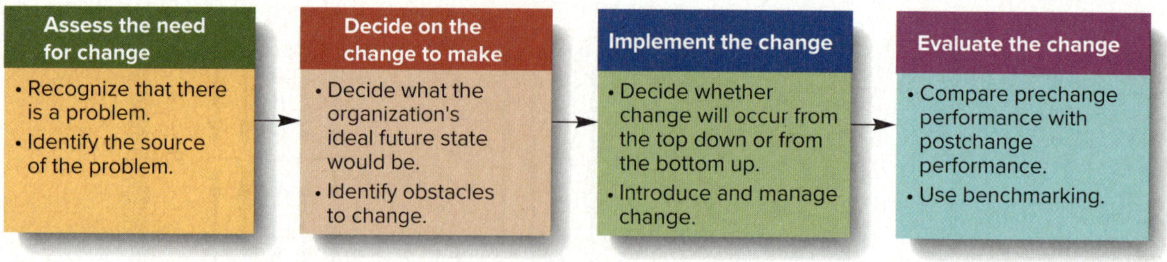

Assessing the need for change calls for two important activities: recognizing that there is a problem and identifying its source. Sometimes the need for change is obvious, such as when an organization's performance is suffering. Often, however, managers have trouble determining that something is going wrong because problems develop gradually; organizational performance may slip for a number of years before a problem becomes obvious. Thus, during the first step in the change process, managers need to recognize that there is a problem that requires change.

Often the problems that managers detect have produced a gap between desired performance and actual performance. To detect such a gap, managers need to look at performance measures–such as falling market share or profits, rising costs, or employees' failure to meet their established goals or to stay within budgets–that indicate whether change is needed. These measures are provided by organizational control systems, discussed earlier in the chapter.

To discover the source of the problem, managers need to look both inside and outside the organization. Outside the organization, they must examine how changing environmental forces may be creating opportunities and threats that are affecting internal work relationships. Perhaps the emergence of low-cost competitors abroad has led to conflict among different departments that are trying to find new ways to gain a competitive advantage. Managers also need to look within the organization to see whether its structure is causing problems between departments.

DECIDING ON THE CHANGE TO MAKE Once managers have identified the source of the problem, they must decide what they think the organization's ideal future state would be. In other words, they must decide where they would like their organization to be in the future–what kinds of goods and services it should be making, what its business-level strategy should be, how the organizational structure should be changed, and so on. During this step, managers also must plan how to attain the organization's ideal future state.

This step in the change process also includes identifying obstacles or sources of resistance to change. Managers must analyze the factors that may prevent the company from reaching its ideal future state. Obstacles to change are found at the corporate, divisional, departmental, and individual levels of the organization.

Organizational change can be a slow and painful process for both managers and employees. Resistance to new processes and other changes can be overcome by improving communication from leadership as to why and how such changes need to be made.
fizkes/Shutterstock

Corporate-level changes in an organization's strategy or structure, even seemingly trivial changes, may significantly affect how divisional and departmental managers behave. Suppose that to compete with low-cost foreign competitors, top managers decide to increase the resources spent on state-of-the-art machinery and reduce the resources spent on marketing or R&D. The power of manufacturing managers would increase, and the power of marketing and R&D managers would fall. This decision would alter the balance of power among departments and might increase conflict as departments fight to retain their status in the organization. An organization's current strategy and structure are powerful obstacles to change.[60]

Whether a company's culture is adaptive or inert facilitates or obstructs change. Organizations with entrepreneurial, flexible cultures, such as high-tech companies, are much easier to change than are organizations with more rigid cultures, such as those sometimes found in large, bureaucratic organizations like the military or GM.

The same obstacles to change exist at the divisional and departmental levels. Division managers may differ in their attitudes toward the changes that top managers propose and, if their interests and power seem threatened, will resist those changes. Managers at all levels usually fight to protect their power and control over resources.[61] Because departments have different goals and time horizons, they may also react differently to the changes other managers propose. When top managers are trying to reduce costs, for example, sales managers may resist attempts to cut back on sales expenditures if they believe that problems stem from manufacturing managers' inefficiencies.

At the individual level, too, people often resist change because it brings uncertainty and stress. For example, individuals may resist the introduction of a new technology because they are uncertain about their abilities to learn it and effectively use it. Or, by their very nature, others may take comfort in the status quo and believe any type of change will require more work on their part, so they resist.[62]

All of these obstacles make organizational change a slow and sometimes painful process. Managers at all levels of the organization must recognize the potential obstacles to change and take them into consideration. Some obstacles can be overcome by improving communication from leadership so all organizational members are aware of the need for change and the nature of the changes being implemented. Empowering employees and inviting them to participate in planning for change may overcome some resistance and allay employees' fears. However, it is also important for managers to listen to employees' sentiment about possible changes, especially when the employees believe they have rational reasons why the change could prove detrimental to the organization. Considering this alternate view of resistance allows organizations to engage in better decision making about which changes to undertake.[63]

IMPLEMENTING THE CHANGE Generally, managers implement–that is, introduce and manage–change from the top down or from the bottom up.[64] **Top-down change** is implemented quickly: Top managers identify the need for change, decide what to do, and then move quickly to implement the changes throughout the organization. For example, top managers may decide to restructure and downsize the organization and then give divisional and departmental managers specific goals to achieve. With top-down change, the emphasis is on making the changes quickly and dealing with problems as they arise; it is revolutionary in nature.

top-down change A fast, revolutionary approach to change in which top managers identify what needs to be changed and then move quickly to implement the changes throughout the organization.

Bottom-up change is typically more gradual or evolutionary. Top managers consult with middle and first-line managers about the need for change. Then, over time, managers at all levels work to develop a detailed plan for change. A major advantage of bottom-up change is that it can co-opt resistance to change from employees. Because the emphasis in bottom-up change is on participation and on keeping people informed about what is going on, uncertainty and resistance are minimized.

bottom-up change A gradual or evolutionary approach to change in which managers at all levels work together to develop a detailed plan for change.

EVALUATING THE CHANGE The last step in the change process is to evaluate how successful the change effort has been in improving organizational performance.[65] Using measures such as changes in market share, profits, or the ability of scientists to innovate new drugs, managers compare how well an organization is performing after the change with how well it was performing before. Managers also can use **benchmarking**, comparing their performance on specific dimensions with the performance of high-performing organizations to decide how successful a change effort has been. For example, when Xerox was performing poorly in the 1980s, it benchmarked the efficiency of its distribution operations against that of L.L.Bean, the efficiency of its central computer operations against that of John Deere, and the efficiency of its marketing abilities against that of Procter & Gamble. Those three companies are renowned for their skills in these different areas, and by studying how they performed, Xerox was able to dramatically increase its own performance. Benchmarking is a key tool in total quality management, an important change program discussed in Chapter 9.

benchmarking The process of comparing one company's performance on specific dimensions with the performance of high-performing organizations.

In summary, organizational control and change are closely linked because organizations operate in environments that are constantly changing, so managers must be alert to the need to change their strategies and structures. Managers of high-performing organizations are attuned to the need to continually modify the way they operate, and they adopt techniques such as empowered work groups and teams, benchmarking, and global outsourcing to remain competitive in a global world.

Summary and Review

LO11-1, 11-2 **WHAT IS ORGANIZATIONAL CONTROL?** Controlling is the process whereby managers monitor and regulate how efficiently and effectively an organization and its members are performing the activities necessary to achieve organizational goals. Controlling is a four-step process: (1) establishing performance standards, (2) measuring actual performance, (3) comparing actual performance against performance standards, and (4) evaluating the results and initiating corrective action if needed.

LO11-3 **OUTPUT CONTROL** To monitor output or performance, managers choose goals or performance standards that they think will best measure efficiency, quality, innovation, and responsiveness to customers at the corporate, divisional, departmental or functional, and individual levels. The main mechanisms that managers use to monitor output are financial measures of performance, organizational goals, and operating budgets.

LO11-4 **BEHAVIOR CONTROL** In an attempt to shape behavior and influence employees to work toward achieving organizational goals, managers use direct supervision, management by objectives, and bureaucratic control by means of rules and standard operating procedures. Direct supervision allows managers to actively monitor and observe the behavior of their employees. Management by objectives (MBO) is a goal-setting process, typically done by a manager with each employee, that provides a framework to evaluate employee performance. An extension of the MBO approach, the balanced scorecard, takes a comprehensive look at an organization's overall performance using four measures: financial, customer service, internal business processes, and the organization's capability for strategic learning and growth. Bureaucratic control is a mechanism that shapes and regulates the behavior of divisions, functions, and individuals within an organization.

CLAN CONTROL Clan control is the control exerted on individuals and groups by shared values, norms, and prescribed standards of behavior. An organization's culture is deliberately fashioned to emphasize the values and norms top managers believe will lead to high performance.

LO11-5 **ORGANIZATIONAL CHANGE** There is a need to balance two opposing forces in the control process that influences the way organizations change. On one hand, managers need to be able to control organizational activities and make their operations routine and predictable. On the other hand, organizations have to be responsive to the need to change, and managers must understand when they need to depart from routines to be responsive to unpredictable events. The four steps in managing change are (1) assessing the need for change, (2) deciding on the changes to make (including identification of possible sources of resistance to change), (3) implementing change, and (4) evaluating the results of change.

Management in Action

Topics for Discussion and Action

Discussion

1. What is the relationship between organizing and controlling? [LO11-1]
2. How do output control and behavior control differ? [LO11-2, 11-3]
3. Why is it important for managers to involve employees in the control process? [LO11-3, 11-4]
4. What kind of controls would you expect to find most used in (a) a hospital, (b) the U.S. Navy, and (c) a city police force? Why? [LO11-2, 11-3, 11-4]
5. What are the main obstacles to organizational change? What techniques can managers use to overcome these obstacles? [LO11-1, 11-5]

Action

6. Ask a manager to list the main performance measures that they use to evaluate how well the organization is achieving its goals. [LO11-1, 11-3, 11-4]
7. Ask the same or a different manager to list the main forms of output control and behavior control that they use to monitor and evaluate employee behavior. [LO11-3, 11-4]

Building Management Skills

Understanding Controlling [LO11-1, 11-3, 11-4]

For this exercise you will analyze the control systems used by a real organization such as a department store, restaurant, hospital, police department, or small business. It can be the organization that you investigated in Chapter 10 or a different one. Your objective is to uncover all the different ways in which managers monitor and evaluate the performance of the organization and employees.

1. At what levels does control take place in this organization?
2. Which output performance standards (such as financial measures and organizational goals) do managers use most often to evaluate performance at each level?
3. Does the organization have a management by objectives system in place? If it does, describe it. If it does not, speculate about why not.
4. How important is behavior control in this organization? For example, how much of managers' time is spent directly supervising employees? How formalized is the organization? Do employees receive a book of rules to teach them how to perform their jobs?
5. What kind of culture does the organization have? What are the values and norms? What effect does the organizational culture have on the way employees behave or treat customers?
6. Based on this analysis, do you think there is a fit between the organization's control systems and its culture? What is the nature of this fit? How could it be improved?

Managing Ethically [LO11-1, 11-5]

Some managers and organizations go to great lengths to monitor their employees' behavior, and they keep extensive records about employees' behavior and performance. Some organizations also seem to possess norms and values that cause their employees to behave in certain ways.

Questions

1. Either by yourself or in a group, think about the ethical implications of organizations' monitoring and collecting information about their employees. What kinds of

information is it ethical or unethical to collect? Why? Should managers and organizations tell employees they are collecting such information? Explain your reasoning.

2. Similarly, some organizations' cultures seem to develop norms and values that cause their members to behave in unethical ways. When and why does a strong norm that encourages high performance become one that can cause people to act unethically? How can organizations keep their values and norms from becoming "too strong"?

Small Group Breakout Exercise

How Best to Control the Sales Force? [LO11-1, 11-3, 11-5]

Form groups of three or four people, and appoint one member as the spokesperson who will communicate your findings to the class when called on by the instructor. Then discuss the following scenario:

You are the regional sales managers of an organization that supplies high-quality windows and doors to building supply centers nationwide. Over the last three years, the rate of sales growth has decreased. There is increasing evidence that, to make their jobs easier, salespeople are primarily servicing large customer accounts and ignoring small accounts. In addition, the salespeople are not dealing promptly with customer questions and complaints, and this inattention has resulted in poor after-sales service. You have talked about these problems, and you are meeting to design a control system to increase both the amount of sales and the quality of customer service.

1. Design a control system that you think will best motivate salespeople to achieve these goals.
2. What relative importance do you put on (a) output control, (b) behavior control, and (c) organizational culture in this design?

Be the Manager [LO11-1, 11-3, 11-4, 11-5]

You have been asked by your company's CEO to find a way to improve the performance of its teams of web design and web hosting specialists and programmers. Each team works on a different aspect of website production; although each is responsible for the quality of its own performance, its performance also depends on how well the other teams perform. Your task is to create a control system that will help to increase the performance of each team separately and facilitate cooperation among the teams. This is necessary because the various projects are interlinked and affect one another, just as the different parts of a car must fit together. Because competition in the website production market is intense, it is imperative that each website be up and running as quickly as possible and incorporate all the latest advances in website software technology.

Questions

1. What kinds of output controls will best facilitate positive interactions both within the teams and among the teams?
2. What kinds of behavior controls will best facilitate positive interactions both within the teams and among the teams?
3. How would you help managers develop a culture to promote high team performance?

Case in the News [LO11-1, 11-3, 11-5]

Procter & Gamble's Controls for Changing Times

Procter & Gamble (P&G), a leading player in consumer packaged goods (CPG), has dozens of brands, including Charmin, Gillette, Swiffer, and Tide. The company has recently dealt with global forces such as a global pandemic, supply chain disruptions, inflation, and digital technology. Through it all, P&G has posted growth, thanks in part to its use of controls.

Like other businesses, P&G sets financial metrics. Its primary ones are organic growth (growth in sales adjusted for changes in foreign-exchange rates), operating margins (difference between revenues and cost of goods), and free cash flow productivity (basically, cash flow relative to earnings from operations). As costs of raw materials and transportation rose, P&G increased prices to protect margins. But to avoid losing so many customers that profits declined, it also pursued lower costs. P&G collaborates with suppliers to fill orders as efficiently as possible, often using automation. The company also reformulates products to improve performance in terms of quality, cost, environmental impact, or other measures.

Quarterly statements show successful performance. P&G's overall profit margin has risen over the past dozen years. In the first quarter of its 2023 fiscal year, P&G posted a 7% increase in sales (despite a 9% average price increase); the volume of sales dipped slightly, but this was mostly the impact of a shrinking presence in Russia. For fiscal year 2021, P&G reported 92% free cash flow productivity, considered a sign of strong operations.

For a CPG company to prosper, marketers must associate its brands with qualities that consumers value. Globally, P&G used to rank first in spending on advertising; now it is in third place after years of spending reductions. Those cuts resulted from efforts to make ad spending more productive. By learning more about which consumers are receiving its messages where, P&G directs more of its spending to media where messages will reach the right people the right number of times while cutting expenses that oversaturate markets already reached. Using marketing terms, P&G's chief financial officer, Andre Schulten, describes this effort as improving advertising's "reach and quality of reach." CEO Jon Moeller says he recently pressed North American executives to focus not just on their spending trends, but on ensuring that spending on each category is helping them meet their objectives for reach.

Advertising efficiency requires that ads be relevant. P&G has a policy of shifting ad dollars to media that can deliver audiences based on spending needs, not just demographic categories like age or income. P&G has defined more than 300 "smart audiences," such as millennial professionals and new homeowners. To reach selected audiences, P&G uses media whose data can identify them—for example, advertising on shows played on connected devices or on retailers' websites. As of 2022, P&G directed 11% of ad spending to such media. The company is not ignoring demographics, however. P&G also recognizes that its markets are diverse, so it identifies messages that do (or don't) work well for, say, a cultural or age group and matches messages to its audiences.

In all these areas, P&G takes advantage of its ability to invest in technology that delivers insights from sophisticated data analytics, especially so the company can predict the best decision, not just study past results. For example, to make ad spending more efficient, P&G tests the impact of spending cuts to learn relationships between spending levels and customer response. The company is also involved in tests of matching audiences with brands' media plans in real time to see if it can place ads in shows as they are being viewed, based on who is viewing. P&G's data and analytics group also provides capabilities to manage spikes in demand with rapid shifts in sourcing, and it contributes to P&G's efforts to reformulate products.

P&G's culture also affects its performance. For example, the company's purpose statement, "Force for Growth. Force for Good," points to P&G's business purpose to grow in value as it meets consumer demand, coupled with a commitment to use that growth in ways that better people's lives. Until recently, "Force for Good" was the first part of the purpose statement, but under pressure from economic and political disruptions, P&G's leadership is now stressing growth as the imperative. Nevertheless, P&G continues to be a force for good through efforts like making packaging more recyclable, developing products whose use is less energy intensive, and choosing responsibly sourced raw materials.

Questions for Discussion

1. What output controls are described in this case? Which do you think are most important for corporate-level managers to focus on? Which would be more relevant for divisional or functional managers?
2. Based on the information given, what norms or values do you see at work in P&G? How would you expect these to influence the behavior of P&G's people?
3. What forces in P&G's environment does this case mention? How is P&G changing—or trying to change—in response to them?

Sources: S. Joseph, "Ad Spending Forecast: Cloudy with a Chance of Recession," *Digiday*, https://digiday.com, December 12, 2022; J. Neff, "Why Brands Like P&G and L'Oréal Are Investing More in CTV with Help from Retail Media Networks," *Ad Age*, https://adage.com, November 28, 2022; P&G blog, "Seven Habits for Market Growth," https://us.pg.com, November 18, 2022; A. Salgado, "P&G to Offset Rising Costs with Price Increases, Productivity Initiatives," *Supply Chain Dive*, www.supplychaindive.com, November 2, 2022; J. Neff, "Procter & Gamble Trims Ad Spending Again, but Still Beats Forecasts," *Advertising Age*, October 24, 2022, EBSCO, https://web.s.ebscohost.com; J. Neff, "Despite Pressure for Ads to Perform, P&G Isn't Giving Up on Purpose," *Advertising Age*, June 27, 2022, https://web.s.ebscohost.com; J. Stebbins, "Higher Prices Help Procter & Gamble Offset Commodity Costs, but Tide Maker Warns of More Challenges," *CNBC*, www.cnbc.com, July 29, 2022; N. Barsky, "Procter & Gamble's Tech Spending Boosts Supply Chain Resilience," *Forbes*, www.forbes.com, October 26, 2021; J. Neff, "P&G's Big Squeeze: Marketer Gets More with Less Spending," *Advertising Age*, August 2, 2021, EBSCO, https://web.s.ebscohost.com; V. Helias, "Force for Good," *Progressive Grocer*, January 30, 2021, 82.

Notes

1. D. Michels and K. Murphy, "How Good Is Your Company at Change?" *Harvard Business Review,* July–August 2021, 62–71.
2. S. McCartney, "What Delta's Big Bet on Blocking Middle Seats Means for Flying," *The Wall Street Journal,* www.wsj.com, February 10, 2021.
3. Michels and Murphy, "How Good Is Your Company?"
4. A. Sider, "Delta to Lift Block on Middle Seats Starting May 1," *The Wall Street Journal,* www.wsj.com, March 31, 2021.
5. L. Josephs, "Delta Expects 2023 Earnings to Nearly Double Thanks to 'Robust' Travel Demand," *CNBC,* www.cnbc.com, December 14, 2022; A. Sider, "Delta Reports Loss amid Omicron Wave but Expects to Make Recovery," *The Wall Street Journal,* www.wsj.com, January 13, 2022.
6. W.G. Ouchi, "Markets, Bureaucracies, and Clans," *Administrative Science Quarterly* 25 (1980), 129–41.
7. "2015 Executive Summary," www.caterpillar.com, accessed March 3, 2020; "Caterpillar Enterprise System Group: Lean: A Journey That Delivers Significant Results," http://reports.caterpillar.com.
8. Caterpillar, *2021 Annual Report,* www.caterpillar.com, accessed January 26, 2023.
9. P. Lorange, M. Morton, and S. Ghoshal, *Strategic Control* (St. Paul, MN: West, 1986).
10. H. Koontz and R.W. Bradspies, "Managing through Feedforward Control," *Business Horizons,* June 1972, 25–36.
11. E.E. Lawler III and J.G. Rhode, *Information and Control in Organizations* (Pacific Palisades, CA: Goodyear, 1976).
12. C.W.L. Hill and G.R. Jones, *Strategic Management: An Integrated Approach,* 6th ed. (Boston: Houghton Mifflin, 2011).
13. E. Flamholtz, "Organizational Control Systems as a Management Tool," *California Management Review,* Winter 1979, 50–58.
14. W.G. Ouchi, "The Transmission of Control through Organizational Hierarchy," *Academy of Management Journal* 21 (1978), 173–92.
15. P. Reynolds, "How Racial Bias Taints Customer Service: Evidence from 6,000 Hotels," Harvard Business School: Working Knowledge, https://hbswk.hbs.edu, February 28, 2022; A.C. Feldberg, "Fighting Bias on the Front Lines," *Harvard Business Review,* November–December 2021, 90–98; S. Carr, "Diagnosing Discrimination in Your Company's Customer Service," interview of Tami Kim, *Ideas to Action* (UVA Darden), https://ideas.darden.virginia.edu, September 2020; G. Mantica, "Racial Discrimination of Airline Customers on Twitter," Boston University Rafik B. Hariri Institute for Computing and Computational Science & Engineering, www.bu.edu/hic, November 10, 2021.
16. Feldberg, "Fighting Bias on the Front Lines"; Carr, "Diagnosing Discrimination."
17. Feldberg, "Fighting Bias on the Front Lines"; Reynolds, "How Racial Bias Taints Customer Service."
18. Ouchi, "Markets, Bureaucracies, and Clans."
19. W.H. Newman, *Constructive Control* (Englewood Cliffs, NJ: Prentice-Hall, 1975).
20. J.D. Thompson, *Organizations in Action* (New York: McGraw-Hill, 1967).
21. R.N. Anthony, *The Management Control Function* (Boston: Harvard Business School Press, 1988).
22. Ouchi, "Markets, Bureaucracies, and Clans."
23. Hill and Jones, *Strategic Management.*
24. K. Gray, "As Their Focus on GPA Fades, Employers Seek Key Skills on College Grads' Resumes," *National Association of Colleges and Employers (NACE),* www.naceweb.org, accessed January 26, 2023.
25. Ibid.
26. Indeed Editorial Team, "Why Is an Internship Important?" www.indeed.com, accessed January 26, 2023.
27. L. Ellis, "College Seniors Can Expect Lots of Job Offers Next Spring," *The Wall Street Journal,* www.wsj.com, October 25, 2022; M. Collins and K. Gray, "Employers Project 14.7% Increase in Hiring for Class of 2023 College Graduates," *NACE,* www.naceweb.org, October 24, 2022.
28. R. Simons, "Strategic Orientation and Top Management Attention to Control Systems," *Strategic Management Journal* 12 (1991), 49–62.
29. G. Schreyogg and H. Steinmann, "Strategic Control: A New Perspective," *Academy of Management Review* 12 (1987), 91–103.
30. B. Woolridge and S.W. Floyd, "The Strategy Process, Middle Management Involvement, and Organizational Performance," *Strategic Management Journal* 11 (1990), 231–41.
31. N. Trentmann, "Global Companies Extend Use of Zero-Based Budgeting to Slash Costs," *The Wall Street Journal,* https://blogs.wsj.com, February 27, 2018; K. Timmermans and R. Abdalla, *Beyond the ZBB Buzz,* Accenture, 2018, www.accenture.com; N. Trentmann, "European Companies Use Old-School Budget Tactic to Cut Costs," *The Wall Street Journal,* www.wsj.com, April 7, 2017; A. Loten, "Kraft Heinz CIO Spends on AI, Robots to Cut Costs," *The Wall Street Journal,* https://blogs.wsj.com, October 3, 2017.
32. K. Broughton, "Companies Turn to Zero-Based Budgeting to Cut Costs During the Pandemic," *The Wall Street Journal,* www.wsj.com, June 17, 2020.
33. Trentmann, "Global Companies Extend Use"; Timmermans and Abdalla, *Beyond the ZBB Buzz;* Trentmann, "European Companies Use Old-School Budget Tactic."
34. S. Callaghan, K. Hawke, and C. Mignerey, "Five Myths (and Realities) about Zero-Based Budgeting," *McKinsey & Company Insights,* www.mckinsey.com, accessed March 2, 2020.
35. K. Timmermans and S. Shuda, "Zero-Based Mindset: Getting Ahead by Cutting Back," www.accenture.com, October 25, 2019.
36. Hill and Jones, *Strategic Management.*
37. G.H.B. Ross, "Revolution in Management Control," *Management Accounting* 72 (1992), 23–27.
38. P.F. Drucker, *The Practice of Management* (New York: Harper & Row, 1954).
39. R. Rodgers and J.E. Hunter, "Impact of Management by Objectives on Organizational Productivity," *Journal of Applied Psychology* 76 (1991), 322–26.
40. M.B. Gavin, S.G. Green, and G.T. Fairhurst, "Managerial Control-Strategies for Poor Performance over Time and the Impact on Subordinate Reactions," *Organizational Behavior and Human Decision Processes* 63 (1995), 207–21.
41. T. Jackson, "A Brief History of the Balanced Scorecard–and 4 Critical Takeaways," www.clearpointstrategy.com, accessed March 2, 2020; R.S. Kaplan and D.P. Norton, "The Balanced Scorecard–Measures That Drive Performance," *Harvard Business Review,* January–February 1992, accessed at https://hbr.org.

42. M. Sailus, "20 Companies Using the Balanced Scorecard & Why," *Clear Point Strategy,* www.clearpointstrategy.com, accessed January 26, 2023.
43. P.M. Blau, *The Dynamics of Bureaucracy* (Chicago: University of Chicago Press, 1955).
44. G. Banerji, "Crypto's Onetime Fans Are Calling It Quits after FTX Collapse," *The Wall Street Journal,* www.wsj.com, December 18, 2022; A. Saeedy and J. Randles, "FTX Says Substantial Amount of Crypto Assets Stolen or Missing," *The Wall Street Journal,* www.wsj.com, November 22, 2022; G. Tsipursky, "FTX's Sam Bankman-Fried Gave Away His Flawed Decision-Making Philosophy Months Ago: A Behavioral Economist Explains," *Entrepreneur,* www.entrepreneur.com, November 14, 2022; J. J. Roberts, "The Conversation: Sam Bankman-Fried," *Fortune,* August/September 2022, 9–12.
45. "John Ray III, the Firefighter Drafted in to Quell the FTX Crisis," *Financial Times,* www.ft.com, December 16, 2022; M. Goldstein, A. Stevenson, M. Farrell, and D. Yaffe-Bellany, "How FTX's Sister Firm Brought the Crypto Exchange Down," *The New York Times,* www.nytimes.com, November 18, 2022.
46. A. Saeedy, S. Biswas, and E. Brown, "CEO in Charge of FTX Restructuring Calls Case an 'Unprecedented' Mess," *The Wall Street Journal,* www.wsj.com, November 17, 2022.
47. Saeedy et al., "CEO in Charge of FTX"; *Financial Times,* "John Ray III, the Firefighter"; B. Cohen, "Does FTX's New CEO Have the Worst Job in Corporate America?" *The Wall Street Journal,* www.wsj.com, December 15, 2022; D. Gura, "FTX's New CEO Reveals Just How Big a Mess He's Dealing With," *Morning Edition,* www.npr.org, November 23, 2022.
48. Testimony of Mr. John J. Ray III, CEO FTX Debtors, U.S. House Financial Services Committee, December 13, 2022; https://financialservices.house.gov.
49. Saeedy et al., "CEO in Charge of FTX"; Saeedy and Randles, "FTX Says Substantial Amount of Crypto Assets Stolen or Missing"; Testimony of Mr. John J. Ray III.
50. J. McGregor, "The World's Most Innovative Companies," www.businessweek.com, May 4, 2007.
51. T. Aquilina, "Iger's Big Disney Reorg Aims to Fix Problems He Helped Sow" *Variety,* https://variety.com, November 29, 2022.
52. L. Rizzo and S. Whitten, "Disney to Cut 7,000 Jobs and Slash $5.5 Billion in Costs as It Unveils Vast Restructuring," *CNBC,* www.cnbc.com, February 9, 2023; N. Gordon, "Poor Earnings, Power Struggles and Politics: The Forces That Pushed Disney to Replace CEO Bob Chapek after Just Two Years," *Fortune,* https://fortune.com, November 21, 2022; Associated Press, "Even Bob Iger Is Surprised by His Return as Disney CEO: 'I Must Admit, a Bit of Amazement,'" *Fortune,* https://fortune.com, November 21, 2022.
53. Ouchi, "Markets, Bureaucracies, and Clans."
54. "ORION Backgrounder," https://pressroom.ups.com, accessed March 3, 2020.
55. This section draws heavily on K. Lewin, *Field Theory in Social Science* (New York: Harper & Row, 1951).
56. L. Chung-Ming and R.W. Woodman, "Understanding Organizational Change: A Schematic Perspective," *Academy of Management Journal* 38, no. 2 (1995), 537–55.
57. D. Miller, "Evolution and Revolution: A Quantum View of Structural Change in Organizations," *Journal of Management Studies* 19 (1982), 131–151; D. Miller, "Momentum and Revolution in Organizational Adaptation," *Academy of Management Journal* 2 (1980), 591–614.
58. C.E. Lindblom, "The Science of Muddling Through," *Public Administration Review* 19 (1959), 79–88; P.C. Nystrom and W.H. Starbuck, "To Avoid Organizational Crises, Unlearn," *Organizational Dynamics* 12 (1984), 53–65.
59. L. Brown, "Research Action: Organizational Feedback, Understanding, and Change," *Journal of Applied Behavioral Research* 8 (1972), 697–711; P.A. Clark, *Action Research and Organizational Change* (New York: Harper & Row, 1972); N. Margulies and A.P. Raia, eds., *Conceptual Foundations of Organizational Development* (New York: McGraw-Hill, 1978).
60. M. Choi and W.E. Ruona, "Individual Readiness for Organizational Change and Its Implications for Human Resource and Organization Development," *Human Resource Development Review* 10, no. 1 (2011), 46–73.
61. M. Peiperl, "Resistance to Change," in N. Nicholson, P.G. Audia, and M.M. Pillutla (eds.), *The Blackwell Encyclopedia of Management,* Volume 11: *Organizational Behavior,* 2nd ed., (New York: Wiley, 2005), 348.
62. Choi and Ruona, "Individual Readiness for Organizational Change."
63. S.K. Piderit, "Rethinking Resistance and Recognizing Ambivalence: A Multidimensional View of Attitudes Toward an Organizational Change," *Academy of Management Review* 25, no. 4 (2000), 783–94.
64. W.L. French and C.H. Bell, *Organizational Development* (Englewood Cliffs, NJ: Prentice-Hall, 1990).
65. W.L. French, "A Checklist for Organizing and Implementing an OD Effort," in W.L. French, C.H. Bell, and R.A. Zawacki, eds., *Organizational Development and Transformation* (Homewood, IL: Irwin, 1994), 484–95.

CHAPTER 12

Human Resource Management

ferrantraite/Getty Images

Learning Objectives

After studying this chapter, you should be able to:

LO12-1 Explain why strategic human resource management can help an organization gain a competitive advantage.

LO12-2 Describe the steps managers take to recruit and select organizational members.

LO12-3 Discuss the training and development options that ensure organizational members can effectively perform their jobs.

LO12-4 Explain why performance appraisal and feedback are such crucial activities, and list the choices managers must make in designing effective performance appraisal and feedback procedures.

LO12-5 Explain the issues managers face in determining levels of pay and benefits.

LO12-6 Understand the role that labor relations play in the effective management of human resources.

A MANAGER'S CHALLENGE

Recruiting and Retaining Truck Drivers

How can managers effectively meet the need for human resources? For years, trucking companies and other organizations with truck fleets have struggled to find and keep enough qualified drivers. While the situation worsened during the economic and health disruptions of the COVID-19 pandemic, with reports of U.S. companies being short by 80,000 or more drivers, other factors had already been at work. Many truck drivers are reaching retirement age, and turnover in the industry is high. The work is tiring and can involve safety and health hazards and long stretches of time away from home.[1]

Employers have options for getting work done. Some employers use contractors to complete certain tasks. For example, a state or county might sign a contract with a company that provides snowplow drivers in the winter, when the need for drivers is high. However, contractors are competing in the same difficult labor market, so contract prices have risen. Technology also can help close the gap. For example, some state transportation departments have purchased "tow plows," which make it possible for one truck to plow two lanes at a time.[2]

Despite these options, most trucking companies have positions to fill, so they need to recruit qualified, interested candidates. In a competitive labor market, they must get creative in their recruitment. One approach is to speed up the hiring process with applicant tracking systems that collect information and communicate with job applicants on their mobile phones. The labor shortage also has sped up some companies' pursuit of diversity and inclusion. Many trucking firms are seeking out training programs and schools that target women and people of color. In some cases, employers are adjusting benefits packages and work schedules to accommodate the needs of drivers with family responsibilities. Drivers under 21 might become an additional source of diversity. These drivers are not allowed to cross state lines, but a federal program is testing a plan that prepares young drivers in trucks equipped with cameras, automated manual transmissions, systems designed to prevent collisions, and states that keep speeds under 65 miles per hour. If the test is successful, the safety technology and a change in regulations could expand the pool of young drivers.[3]

Training programs can make a company more attractive to job candidates. Young workers today are seen as being interested in working where there are clear career paths, and training can enable progress along those paths.

Hiring, training, and retaining competent drivers is an ongoing challenge for trucking companies and their HR staffs. Here, attendees at a Teamsters convention in Las Vegas use truck-driving simulator to hone their skills.
Jim West/Alamy Stock Photo

Programs for continuous learning also can help employees perform better, and that success can make work more satisfying. In addition, trucking companies may create or participate in apprenticeship programs for drivers. Apprenticeships enable would-be drivers to afford the steep cost of attending a private driving school.[4]

Success in meeting the need for good drivers is not just a matter of hiring and training; companies must keep people for the long run. Many workers are attracted to trucking for its earnings potential, so attractive pay and benefits are essential. Technology can help with retention too. Managers can use computer systems to track key measures such as the percentage of employees who quit within the first 90 days. Dissatisfaction commonly arises from not covering enough miles to reach goals for pay and time at home. Trucks can be equipped to provide managers with real-time digital feeds of information about mileage. Then the managers can reach out to employees who are struggling to meet their goals. For example, a breakdown is a true hardship, made worse if supply chain disruptions delay repairs. Intervention by managers—coupled with a commitment to proper equipment maintenance—plays a key role in keeping truck drivers behind the wheel.[5]

Overview

Managers are responsible for acquiring, developing, protecting, and utilizing the resources an organization needs to be efficient and effective. One of the most important resources in all organizations is human resources—the people involved in producing and distributing goods and services. Human resources include all members of an organization, ranging from top managers to entry-level employees. Effective managers realize how valuable human resources are and take active steps to make sure their organizations build and fully utilize their human resources to gain a competitive advantage.

human resource management (HRM) Activities that managers engage in to attract and retain employees and to ensure that they perform at a high level and contribute to the accomplishment of organizational goals.

This chapter examines how managers can tailor their human resource management system to their organization's strategy and structure. We discuss in particular the major components of human resource management: recruitment and selection, training and development, performance appraisal, and pay and benefits. We also discuss the topic of labor relations and how working with unions and the workers they represent can be integral to the process of effective human resource management. By the end of this chapter, you will understand the central role human resource management plays in creating a high-performing organization.

Strategic Human Resource Management

Organizational architecture (see Chapter 10) is the combination of organizational structure, control systems, culture, and a human resource management system that managers develop to use resources efficiently and effectively. **Human resource management (HRM)** includes all the activities managers engage in to attract and retain employees and to ensure that they perform at a high level and contribute to the accomplishment of organizational goals. These activities make up an organization's human resource management system, which has five major components: recruitment and selection, training and development, performance appraisal and feedback, pay and benefits, and labor relations (see Figure 12.1).

strategic human resource management The process by which managers design the components of an HRM system to be consistent with each other, with other elements of organizational architecture, and with the organization's strategy and goals.

Strategic human resource management is the process by which managers design the components of an HRM system to be consistent with each other, with other elements of organizational architecture, and with the organization's strategy and goals.[6] The objective of strategic HRM is the development of an HRM system that enhances an organization's efficiency, quality, innovation, and responsiveness to customers—the four building blocks of competitive advantage.

In today's highly competitive business environment, successful organizations understand that the HR function is no longer simply a part of the business that undertakes administrative

Figure 12.1

Components of a Human Resource Management System

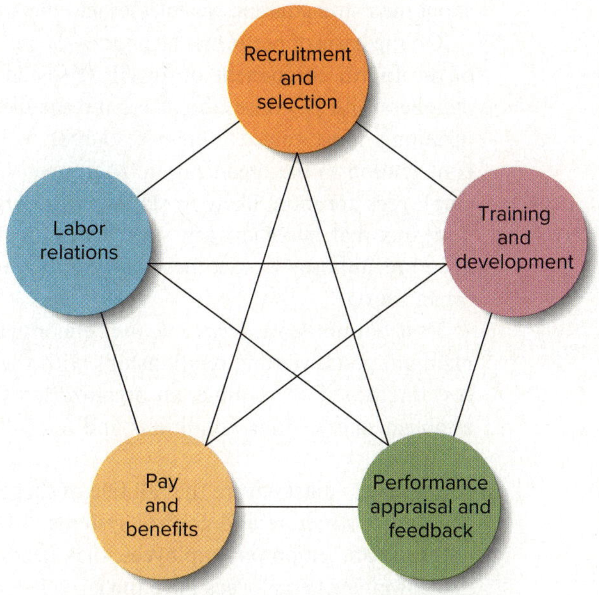

Each component of an HRM system influences the others, and all five must fit together.

LO12-1 Explain why strategic human resource management can help an organization gain a competitive advantage.

tasks, sets employee-related policies, or hires and fires employees. Rather, many companies believe that the HR function is a critical component of their strategic agenda and insist on HR managers not only understanding the critical tasks involved in running a business, but also taking an active role in helping senior management ensure that departmental strategies and goals align across the entire organization, that employee training and development remain a top organizational priority, and that the organization pursue a corporate culture that is competitive yet employee friendly.

Overview of the Components of HRM

Managers use *recruitment and selection,* the first component of an HRM system, to attract and hire new employees who have the abilities, skills, and experiences that will help an organization achieve its goals. Microsoft, for example, has the goal of becoming one of the top cloud-computing tech giants in the world. To achieve this goal, managers at Microsoft realize the importance of hiring only the best computer systems engineers: Hundreds of highly qualified candidates are interviewed and rigorously tested. Microsoft has little trouble recruiting top talent because candidates know they will be at the forefront of the cloud-computing industry if they work for Microsoft.[7]

After recruiting and selecting employees, managers use the second component, *training and development,* to ensure that organizational members develop the skills and abilities that will enable them to perform their jobs effectively in the present and the future. Training and development are an ongoing process. Changes in technology and the environment, as well as in an organization's goals and strategies, often require that organizational members learn new techniques and ways of working. For example, at Microsoft, newly hired systems engineers receive on-the-job training by joining small teams that include experienced employees who serve as mentors or advisers. New recruits learn firsthand from colleagues how to develop cloud-computing services that are responsive to customers' needs.[8]

The third component, *performance appraisal and feedback,* serves two purposes in HRM. First, performance appraisal can give managers the information they need to make good human resource decisions—decisions about how to train, motivate, and reward organizational members.[9] Thus, the performance appraisal and feedback component is a kind of *control system* that can be used with management by objectives (discussed in Chapter 11). Second, feedback from performance appraisal serves a developmental purpose for members of an organization. When managers regularly evaluate their subordinates' performance, they can give employees valuable information about their strengths and weaknesses and the areas in which they need to concentrate.

On the basis of performance appraisals, managers distribute *pay* to employees, which is part of the fourth component of an HRM system. By rewarding high-performing organizational members with pay raises, bonuses, and the like, managers increase the likelihood that an organization's most valued human resources will be motivated to continue their high levels of contribution to the organization. Moreover, if pay is linked to performance, high-performing employees are more likely to stay with the organization, and managers are more likely to fill positions that become open with highly talented individuals. *Benefits* such as health insurance are important outcomes that employees receive by virtue of their membership in an organization.

Last but not least, *labor relations* encompass the steps that managers take to develop and maintain good working relationships with the labor unions that may represent their employees' interests. For example, an organization's labor relations component can help managers establish safe working conditions and fair labor practices in their offices and manufacturing facilities.

Managers must ensure that all five of these components fit together and complement their company's structure and control systems.[10] For example, if managers decide to decentralize authority and empower employees, they need to invest in training and development to ensure that lower-level employees have the knowledge and expertise they need to make the decisions that top managers would make in a more centralized structure.

Each of the five components of HRM influences the others (see Figure 12.1).[11] The kinds of people the organization attracts and hires through recruitment and selection, for example, determine (1) the kinds of training and development that are necessary, (2) the way performance is appraised, and (3) the appropriate levels of pay and benefits. Managers at Microsoft ensure that their organization has highly qualified systems engineers by (1) recruiting and selecting the best candidates, (2) guiding new hires with experienced team members, (3) appraising performance in terms of individual contributions and team performance, and (4) basing pay on individual and team performance.

The Legal Environment of HRM

In the rest of this chapter, we focus in detail on the choices managers must make in strategically managing human resources to attain organizational goals and gain a competitive advantage. Effectively managing human resources is a complex undertaking for managers, and we provide an overview of some major issues they face. First, however, we need to look at how the legal environment affects human resource management.

The local, state, and national laws and regulations that managers and organizations must abide by add to the complexity of HRM. For example, the U.S. government's commitment to **equal employment opportunity (EEO)** has resulted in the creation and enforcement of a number of laws that managers must abide by. The goal of EEO is to ensure that all citizens have an equal opportunity to obtain employment regardless of their gender, race, country of origin, religion, age, or disabilities. Table 12.1 summarizes some of the major EEO laws affecting HRM. Other laws, such as the Occupational Safety and Health Act of 1970, require that managers ensure that employees are protected from workplace hazards and that safety standards are met.

equal employment opportunity (EEO) The equal right of all citizens to the opportunity to obtain employment regardless of their gender, age, race, country of origin, religion, or disabilities.

In Chapter 5, we explained how effectively managing diversity is an ethical and business imperative, and we discussed the many issues surrounding diversity. EEO laws and their enforcement make the effective management of diversity a legal imperative as well. The Equal Employment Opportunity Commission (EEOC) is the division of the Department of Justice that enforces most EEO laws and handles discrimination complaints. In addition, the EEOC issues guidelines for managers to follow to ensure that they are abiding by EEO laws. For example, the Uniform Guidelines on Employee Selection Procedures issued by the EEOC (in conjunction with the Departments of Labor and Justice and the Civil Service Commission) guide managers on how to ensure that the recruitment and selection component of human

Table 12.1

Major Equal Employment Opportunity Laws Affecting HRM

Year	Law	Description
1963	Equal Pay Act	Requires that workers be paid equally if they are performing equal work.
1964	Title VII of the Civil Rights Act	Prohibits employment discrimination on the basis of race, religion, sex, color, or national origin; covers a wide range of employment decisions, including hiring, firing, pay, promotion, and working conditions.
1967	Age Discrimination in Employment Act	Prohibits discrimination against workers over the age of 40 and restricts mandatory retirement.
1978	Pregnancy Discrimination Act	Prohibits employment discrimination against women on the basis of pregnancy, childbirth, and related medical decisions.
1986	Immigration Reform and Control Act	Prohibits discrimination on the basis of natural origin or citizenship, except for unauthorized immigrants, by employers having four or more employees.
1990	Americans with Disabilities Act	Prohibits employment discrimination against individuals with disabilities and requires that employers make accommodations for such workers to enable them to perform their jobs.
1991	Civil Rights Act	Prohibits discrimination (as does Title VII) and allows the awarding of punitive and compensatory damages, in addition to back pay, in cases of intentional discrimination.
1993	Family and Medical Leave Act	Requires that employers with 50 or more employees provide 12 weeks of unpaid leave for medical and family reasons, including paternity and illness of a family member.
1994	Uniformed Services Employment and Reemployment Rights Act	Requires rehiring of employees who are absent for military service, with training and accommodations as needed.
2009	Lilly Ledbetter Fair Pay Act	Allows employees to claim discriminatory compensation within a set time after receiving a discriminatory paycheck.

recruitment Activities that managers engage in to develop a pool of qualified candidates for open positions.

selection The process that managers use to determine the relative qualifications of job applicants and their potential for performing well in a particular job.

resource management complies with Title VII of the Civil Rights Act (which prohibits discrimination based on gender, race, color, religion, and national origin).[12]

Contemporary challenges that managers face related to the legal environment include how to eliminate sexual harassment, how to accommodate employees with disabilities, how to ensure LGBTQ (lesbian, gay, bisexual, transgender, and queer) employees are treated equally, how to address religious rights, how to minimize the wage gap between all workers, regardless of gender, how to deal with employees who have substance abuse problems, and mental health issues, and how to ensure inclusion for all employees.[13]

Recruitment and Selection

LO12-2 Describe the steps managers take to recruit and select organizational members.

Recruitment includes all the activities managers engage in to develop a pool of qualified candidates for open positions.[14] **Selection** is the process by which managers determine the relative qualifications of job applicants and their potential for performing well in a particular job. Before actually recruiting and selecting employees, managers need to engage in two important activities: human resource planning and job analysis (see Figure 12.2).

human resource planning Activities that managers engage in to forecast their current and future needs for human resources.

Human Resource Planning

Human resource planning includes all the activities managers engage in to forecast their current and future human resource needs. Current human resources are the employees an organization needs today to provide high-quality goods and services to customers. Future human

Figure 12.2

The Recruitment and Selection System

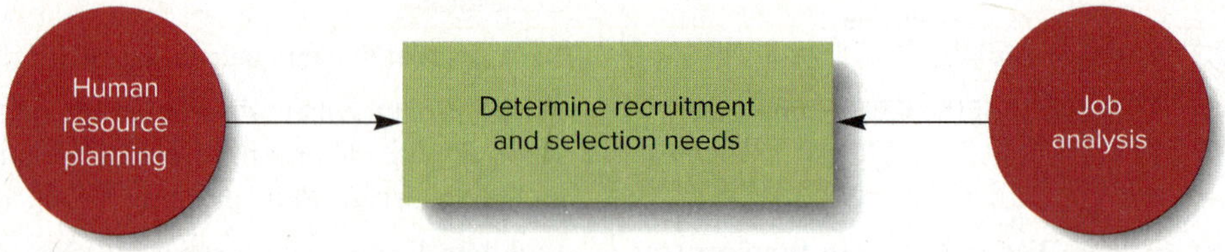

resource needs are the employees the organization will need at some later date to achieve its longer-term goals.

As part of human resource planning, managers must make both demand forecasts and supply forecasts. *Demand forecasts* estimate the qualifications and numbers of employees an organization will need, given its goals and strategies. *Supply forecasts* estimate the availability and qualifications of current employees now and in the future, as well as the supply of qualified workers in the external labor market.

outsource To use outside suppliers and manufacturers to produce goods and services.

As a result of their human resource planning, managers sometimes decide to **outsource** to fill some of their human resource needs. Instead of recruiting and selecting employees to produce goods and services, managers contract with people who are not members of their organization to produce goods and services. Managers in publishing companies, for example, often contract with freelance editors to copyedit books that they intend to publish. There are many companies and online platforms, such as LinkedIn, AngelList, Upwork, and others, that can link managers to the services of freelance professionals to help fill some of their HR requirements in these areas.[15]

Two reasons human resource planning sometimes leads managers to outsource are flexibility and cost. First, outsourcing can give managers increased flexibility, especially when accurately forecasting human resource needs is difficult, human resource needs fluctuate over time, or finding skilled workers in a particular area is difficult. Second, outsourcing can sometimes allow managers to use human resources at a lower cost. When work is outsourced, costs can be lower for a number of reasons: The organization does not have to provide benefits to these outside, temporary workers; managers can contract for work only when the work is needed; and managers do not have to invest in training. Outsourcing can be used for functional activities such as payroll, bookkeeping and accounting, and the management of information systems.[16]

Outsourcing has disadvantages, however. When work is outsourced, managers may lose some control over the quality of goods and services. Also, individuals performing outsourced work may have less knowledge of organizational practices, procedures, and goals and less commitment to an organization than regular employees. In addition, unions resist outsourcing because it has the potential to eliminate the jobs of some of their members. To gain some of the flexibility and cost savings of outsourcing and avoid some of its disadvantages, a number of organizations, such as Microsoft and IBM, rely on a pool of temporary employees to, for example, oversee cybersecurity threats.

A major trend reflecting the increasing globalization of business is the outsourcing of office work, computer programming, and technical jobs from the United States and countries in Western Europe, with high labor costs, to countries such as India and the Philippines, with lower labor costs.[17] For example, computer programmers in India earn a fraction of what their U.S. counterparts earn. Outsourcing (or *offshoring,* as it is also called when work is outsourced to other countries) has also expanded into knowledge-intensive work such as engineering, research and development, and the development of computer software. According to a study conducted by The Conference Board and Duke University's Offshoring Research Network, more than half of U.S. companies surveyed have some kind of offshoring strategy related to knowledge-intensive work and innovation.[18] Why are so many companies engaged in offshoring, and why are companies that already offshore work planning to increase the extent of offshoring? While cost savings continue to be a major motivation for offshoring, managers also want to take advantage of an increasingly talented global workforce and be closer to the growing global marketplace for goods and services.[19]

Major U.S. companies often earn a substantial portion of their revenues overseas. For example, Alphabet (parent company of Google), Apple, and Chevron, among others, earn over 50% of their revenues from overseas markets.[20] And many large companies employ thousands of workers overseas. Key challenges for managers who offshore are retaining sufficient managerial control over activities and employee turnover.[21]

As the application to outsourcing indicates, HR planning is about more than simply numbers of employees. Managers also have to consider the value that various combinations of human resources can deliver. Effective managers plan ways to develop and allocate that talent so the value of human resources increases.

Job Analysis

job analysis Identifying the tasks, duties, and responsibilities that make up a job and the knowledge, skills, and abilities needed to perform the job.

Job analysis is a second important activity that managers need to undertake prior to recruitment and selection.[22] **Job analysis** is the process of identifying (1) the tasks, duties, and responsibilities that make up a job (the *job description*) and (2) the knowledge, skills, and abilities needed to perform the job (the *job specifications*).[23] For each job in an organization, a job analysis needs to be done.

Job analysis can be done in a number of ways, including observing current employees as they perform the job or interviewing them. Often managers rely on questionnaires compiled by jobholders and their managers. The questionnaires ask about the skills and abilities needed to perform the job, job tasks and the amount of time spent on them, responsibilities, supervisory activities, equipment used, reports prepared, and decisions made. The Position Analysis Questionnaire (PAQ) is a comprehensive, standardized questionnaire that many managers rely on to conduct job analyses.[24] It focuses on behaviors jobholders perform, working conditions, and job characteristics and can be used for a variety of jobs. The PAQ contains 194 items organized into six divisions: (1) information input (where and how the jobholder acquires information to perform the job), (2) mental processes (reasoning, decision making, planning, and information processing activities that are part of the job), (3) work output (physical activities performed on the job and machines and devices used), (4) relationships with others (interactions with other people that are necessary to perform the job), (5) job context (the physical and social environment of the job), and (6) other job characteristics (such as work pace).[25] A trend, in some organizations, is toward more flexible jobs in which tasks and responsibilities change and cannot be clearly specified in advance. For these kinds of jobs, job analysis focuses more on determining the skills and knowledge workers need to be effective and less on specific duties.

After managers have completed human resource planning and job analyses for all jobs in an organization, they will know their human resource needs and the jobs they need to fill. They will also know what knowledge, skills, and abilities potential employees need to perform those jobs. At this point, recruitment and selection can begin.

External and Internal Recruitment

As noted earlier, recruitment is what managers do to develop a pool of qualified candidates for open positions. They traditionally have used two main types of recruiting, external and internal, which are now supplemented by recruiting over the Internet.

EXTERNAL RECRUITING When managers recruit externally to fill open positions, they look outside the organization for people who have not worked for the organization previously. There are multiple means through which managers can recruit externally: job postings on career websites, such as Indeed, Monster, and LinkedIn; job fairs in the community; career fairs at colleges; open houses for students and career counselors at high schools and on site at the organization; recruitment meetings with groups in the local community; and advertising on social media platforms and in local newspapers.

Many large organizations send teams of interviewers to college campuses to recruit new employees. External recruitment can also take place through informal networks, as occurs when current employees inform friends about open positions in their companies or recommend people they know to fill vacant spots. Some organizations use employment agencies for external recruitment, and some external recruitment takes place simply through walk-ins–job hunters going to an organization and inquiring about employment possibilities–or through job hunters going to the Careers page of a company's corporate website.

External recruiting has both advantages and disadvantages for managers. Advantages include having access to a potentially large applicant pool; being able to attract people who have the skills, knowledge, and abilities that an organization needs to achieve its goals; and being able to bring in newcomers who may have a fresh approach to problems and are up to date on the latest technology. These advantages have to be weighed against the disadvantages, including the relatively high costs of external recruitment. Employees recruited externally lack knowledge about the inner workings of the organization and may need to receive more training than those recruited internally. Finally, when employees are recruited externally, there is always uncertainty concerning whether they will actually be good performers. Nonetheless, managers can take steps to reduce some of the uncertainty surrounding external recruitment with methods such as tests, temporary jobs, and internships.

lateral moves Job changes that entail no major changes in responsibility or authority levels.

INTERNAL RECRUITING When recruiting is internal, managers turn to existing employees to fill open positions. Employees recruited internally are either seeking **lateral moves** (job changes that entail no major changes in responsibility or authority levels) or promotions. Internal recruiting has several advantages. First, internal applicants are already familiar with the organization (including its goals, structure, culture, rules, and norms). Second, managers already know the candidates; they have considerable information about their skills, abilities, and actual behavior on the job. Third, internal recruiting can help boost levels of employee motivation and morale, both for the employee who gets the job and for other workers. Those who are not seeking a promotion or who may not be ready for one can see that promotion is a possibility in the future; or a lateral move can alleviate boredom once a job has been fully mastered and can be a useful way to learn new skills. Finally, internal recruiting is normally less time-consuming and expensive than external recruiting.

Given the advantages of internal recruiting, why do managers rely on external recruiting as much as they do? The answer lies in the disadvantages of internal recruiting–among them, a limited pool of candidates and a tendency among those candidates to be set in the organization's ways. Often the organization simply does not have suitable internal candidates. Sometimes even when suitable internal applicants are available, managers may rely on external recruiting to find the very best candidate or to help bring new ideas and approaches into their organization. When organizations are in trouble and performing poorly, external recruiting is often relied on to bring in managerial talent with a fresh approach.

The lingering effects of the COVID-19 pandemic continue to have a profound effect on recruiting efforts by both large and small companies. The pandemic shifted priorities for many workers, including the ability to work remotely full time and the demand for increased pay and benefits. According to recent research, in 2021, more than 47 million people quit their jobs and 2022 was on track to surpass that number, despite fears of a recession and additional economic tightening. As HR professionals struggle to recruit new employees for their organizations, they are rethinking old strategies and devising innovative ways to attract new talent. For example, some employers are adapting their recruiting efforts to eliminate some educational and industry-experience requirements while offering greater flexibility in terms of schedules and remote work options.[26]

HONESTY IN RECRUITING At times, when trying to recruit the most qualified applicants, managers may be tempted to paint rosy pictures of both the open positions and the organization as a whole. They may worry that if they are honest about advantages and disadvantages, they either will not be able to fill positions or will have fewer or less qualified applicants. A manager trying to fill an administrative position, for example, may emphasize the high level of pay and benefits the job offers and fail to mention the fact that the position is usually a dead-end job offering few opportunities for promotion.

realistic job preview (RJP) An honest assessment of the advantages and disadvantages of a job and an organization.

Research suggests that painting a rosy picture of a job and the organization is not a wise recruiting strategy. Recruitment is more likely to be effective when managers give potential applicants an honest assessment of both the advantages and the disadvantages of the job and organization. Such an assessment is called a **realistic job preview (RJP)**.[27] RJPs can reduce the number of new hires who quit when their jobs and organizations fail to meet their unrealistic expectations, and they help applicants decide for themselves whether a job is right for them.

Figure 12.3
Selection Tools

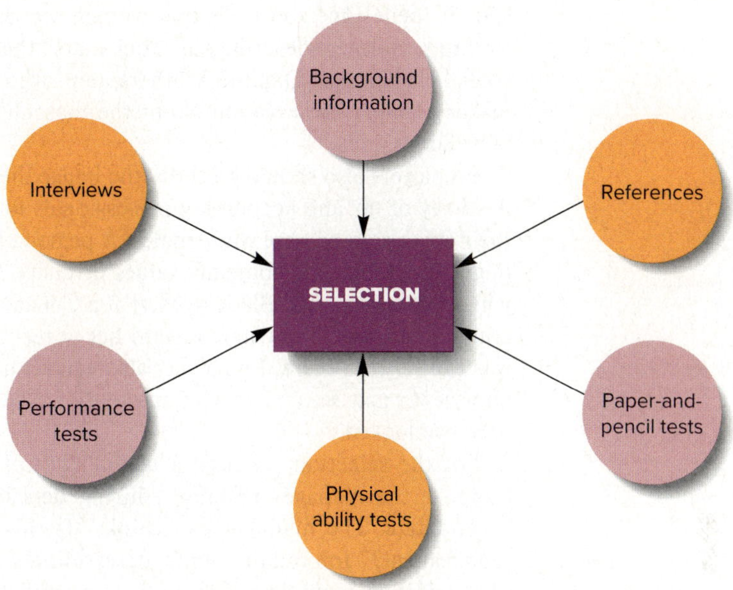

Take the earlier example of the manager trying to recruit an administrative assistant. The manager who paints a rosy picture of the job might have an easy time filling it but might hire a person who expects to be promoted quickly to an executive assistant position. After a few weeks on the job, the person may realize that a promotion is unlikely no matter how good their performance is, become dissatisfied, and look for and accept another job. The manager then has to recruit, select, and train another new administrative assistant. The manager could have avoided this waste of valuable organizational resources by using a realistic job preview. The RJP would have increased the likelihood of hiring a person who was comfortable with few promotional opportunities and subsequently would have been satisfied to remain on the job.

The Selection Process

Ideally, the recruiting efforts have been broad enough and equitable enough to meet the standard of equal opportunity and provide a pool of applicants who meet basic qualifications. (For a discussion on seeking diverse candidates, see the following "Focus on DEI&B" feature.) Managers then need to find out whether each applicant is qualified for the position and likely to be a good performer. If more than one applicant meets these two conditions, managers must further determine which applicants are likely to be better performers than others. They have several selection tools to help them sort out the relative qualifications of job applicants and appraise their potential for being good performers in a particular job. These tools include background information, interviews, paper-and-pencil tests, physical ability tests, performance tests, and references (see Figure 12.3).[28]

FOCUS ON DEI&B

Recruiting a Diverse Workforce

Many organizations have a policy of valuing diversity. Managers see advantages to including different perspectives, especially when employees reflect the diverse perspectives of the employer's customers and communities. Furthermore, a commitment to diversity widens the pool of potential talent, offering more ways to find the best people.[29]

A basic step is to review recruiting sources and messages. Recruiting in schools where many students are the same race or gender narrows the pool of candidates in terms of racial and gender diversity. Language also matters. Diversity-strategy consultant Joelle Emerson finds that women are less likely to respond to an ad looking for top performers described as "rock stars" than to an ad looking for someone who "seeks challenges." Daphne Wotherspoon, who helps companies find tech workers, makes a similar observation about the masculine appeal of a position described as "JavaScript ninja."[30]

Employers also should consider the image their recruiters and interviewers project. A survey of tax and accounting professionals found that most high-level managers in their organizations were white males. A person of color interviewed by these managers might doubt that the company values diversity. Conversely, Jessica Akue recalls that when she was the first Black woman at a Canadian law firm, students from a minority ethnic group would gravitate toward her at recruiting events, curious to know what it was like to work there. Employers also can set up panels of diverse interviewers. One interviewer may see and correct unintentional biases that a homogeneous panel would have overlooked.[31]

For the selection process, a useful control is to double-check one's opinions. Suppose the manager making a hiring decision likes a certain characteristic of a candidate. The manager can think, "Is this a preference, a tradition, or a job requirement?" Job requirements are essentials; preferences and traditions may be a plus, but they could limit selections to people who are so much alike that new ideas rarely surface.[32]

Similar issues arise with regard to physical or mental disabilities. Sean Casey, executive director of the Georgia Vocational Rehabilitation Agency, points out "everyone does things in life differently."[33] His point is that it is illogical as well as unjust to assume someone with a disability is less capable because they perform a task with accommodations. Casey adds that the person with a disability, simply by figuring out a way to adapt to the disability, has already demonstrated problem-solving skills.

BACKGROUND INFORMATION To aid in the selection process, managers obtain background information from job applications and from résumés. Such information might include the highest levels of education obtained, college majors and minors, type of college or university attended, years and type of work experience, and mastery of foreign languages. Background information can be helpful both to screen out applicants who are lacking key qualifications (such as a college degree) and to determine which qualified applicants are more promising than others. For example, applicants with a BS may be acceptable, but those who also have an MBA may be preferable.

Increasing numbers of organizations are performing background checks to verify the information prospective employees provide. In a recent study, nearly 96% of employers surveyed said their organization conducts one or more types of employment background screening.[34] In another recent report by HireRight, 85% of employers caught applicants fabricating or exaggerating information on their résumés or job applications–up from just 66% five years ago. Some HR analysts believe that the increase in bogus information is the result of some job applicants trying to trick a company's applicant tracking system by using key words that will help their résumés make it to the second round of résumé reviews, typically conducted by an HR staff member.[35]

INTERVIEWS Virtually all organizations use interviews during the selection process. Interviews may be structured or unstructured. In a *structured interview,* managers ask each applicant the same standard questions (such as "What are your unique qualifications for this position?" and "What characteristics of a job are most important to you?"). Particularly informative questions may be those that prompt an interviewee to demonstrate skills and abilities needed

Some managers find situational interview questions helpful in determining the right candidate for a specific job opening.
Ariel Skelley/Getty Images

for the job by answering the question. Sometimes called *situational interview questions,* these often present interviewees with a scenario they would likely encounter on the job and ask them to indicate how they would handle it.[36] For example, applicants for a sales job may be asked to indicate how they would respond to a customer who complained about waiting too long for service, a customer who was indecisive, and a customer whose order was lost.

An *unstructured interview* proceeds more like an ordinary conversation. The interviewer feels free to ask probing questions to discover what the applicant is like and does not ask a fixed set of questions determined in advance. In general, structured interviews are superior to unstructured interviews because they are more likely to yield information that will help identify qualified candidates, are less subjective, and may be less influenced by the interviewer's biases.

Even when structured interviews are used, however, the potential exists for the interviewer's biases to influence their judgment. Recall from Chapter 5 how implicit bias can cause people to perceive others who are similar to themselves more positively than those who are different and how stereotypes can result in inaccurate perceptions. Interviewers must be trained to avoid these biases and sources of inaccurate perceptions as much as possible. Many of the approaches to increasing diversity awareness and diversity skills described in Chapter 5 are used to train interviewers to avoid the effects of biases and stereotypes. In addition, using multiple interviewers can be advantageous because their individual biases and idiosyncrasies may cancel one another out.[37]

When conducting interviews, managers cannot ask questions that are irrelevant to the job in question; otherwise, their organizations run the risk of costly lawsuits. It is inappropriate and illegal, for example, to inquire about an interviewee's spouse or to ask questions about whether an interviewee plans to have children. Because questions such as these are irrelevant to job performance, they are discriminatory and violate EEO laws (see Table 12.1). Thus, interviewers need to be instructed in EEO laws and informed about questions that may violate those laws.

Managers can use interviews at various stages in the selection process. Some use interviews as initial screening devices; others use them as a final hurdle that applicants must jump. Regardless of when they are used, managers typically use other selection tools in conjunction with interviews because of the potential for bias and for inaccurate assessments of interviewees. Even though training and structured interviews can eliminate the effects of some biases, interviewers can still come to erroneous conclusions about interviewees' qualifications. Interviewees, for example, who make a bad initial impression or are overly nervous in the first minute or two of an interview tend to be judged more harshly than less nervous candidates, even if the rest of the interview goes well.

PAPER-AND-PENCIL TESTS The two main kinds of paper-and-pencil tests used for selection purposes are ability tests and personality tests; both kinds of tests can be administered in hard copy or electronic form. *Ability tests* assess the extent to which applicants possess the skills necessary for job performance, such as verbal comprehension or numerical skills. Workers hired by General Motors and Ford, for example, are typically tested for their ability to read and to do mathematics.

Personality tests measure personality traits and characteristics relevant to job performance. Some retail organizations, for example, give job applicants honesty tests to determine how trustworthy they are. The use of personality tests (including honesty tests) for hiring purposes is controversial. Some critics maintain that honesty tests do not really measure honesty (that is, they are not valid) and can be faked by job applicants. Before using any paper-and-pencil tests for selection purposes, managers must have sound evidence that the tests are actually good predictors of performance on the job in question. Managers who use tests without such evidence may be subject to costly discrimination lawsuits.

PHYSICAL ABILITY TESTS For jobs requiring physical abilities, such as firefighting, garbage collecting, and package delivery, managers use physical ability tests that measure physical strength and stamina as selection tools. Autoworkers are typically tested for mechanical dexterity because this physical ability is an important skill for high job performance in many auto plants.[38]

PERFORMANCE TESTS *Performance tests* measure job applicants' performance on actual job tasks. Applicants for secretarial positions, for example, typically are required to complete a keyboarding test that measures how quickly and accurately they type. Applicants for middle and top management positions are sometimes given short-term projects to complete–projects that mirror the kinds of situations that arise in the job being filled–to assess their knowledge and problem-solving capabilities.[39]

Assessment centers, first used by AT&T, take performance tests one step further. In a typical assessment center, about 10 to 15 candidates for managerial positions participate in a variety of activities over a few days. During this time they are assessed for the skills an effective manager needs–problem-solving, organizational, communication, and conflict resolution skills. Some of the activities are performed individually; others are performed in groups. Throughout the process, current managers observe the candidates' behavior and measure performance. Summary evaluations are then used as a selection tool.

REFERENCES Applicants for many jobs are required to provide references from former employers or other knowledgeable sources (such as a college instructor or adviser) who know the applicants' skills, abilities, and other personal characteristics. These people are asked to provide candid information about the applicant. References are often used at the end of the selection process to confirm a decision to hire. Yet the fact that many former employers are reluctant to provide negative information in references sometimes makes it difficult to interpret what a reference is really saying about an applicant.

In fact, several recent lawsuits filed by applicants who felt that they were unfairly denigrated or had their privacy invaded by unfavorable references from former employers have caused managers to be increasingly wary of providing any negative information in a reference, even if it is accurate. For jobs in which the jobholder is responsible for the safety and lives of other people, however, failing to provide accurate negative information in a reference does not just mean that the wrong person might get hired; it may also mean that other people's lives will be at risk.

reliability The degree to which a tool or test measures the same thing each time it is used.

validity The degree to which a tool or test measures what it purports to measure.

THE IMPORTANCE OF RELIABILITY AND VALIDITY Whatever selection tools a manager uses need to be both reliable and valid. **Reliability** is the degree to which a tool or test measures the same thing each time it is administered. Scores on a selection test should be similar if the same person is assessed with the same tool on two different days; if there is quite a bit of variability, the tool is unreliable. For interviews, determining reliability is more complex because the dynamic is personal interpretation. That is why the reliability of interviews can be increased if two or more qualified interviewers interview the same candidate. If the interviews are reliable, the interviewers should come to similar conclusions about the interviewee's qualifications.

Validity is the degree to which a tool measures what it purports to measure–for selection tools, it is the degree to which the test predicts performance on the tasks or job in question. Does a physical ability test used to select firefighters, for example, actually predict on-the-job performance? Do assessment center ratings actually predict managerial performance? Do keyboarding tests predict administrative assistant performance? These are all questions of validity. Honesty tests, for example, are controversial because it is not clear that they validly predict honesty in such jobs as retailing and banking.

Managers have an ethical and legal obligation to use reliable and valid selection tools. Yet reliability and validity are matters of degree rather than all-or-nothing characteristics. Thus, managers should strive to use selection tools in such a way that they can achieve the greatest degree of reliability and validity. For ability tests of a particular skill, managers should keep up to date on the latest advances in the development of valid paper-and-pencil tests and use the test with the highest reliability and validity ratings for their purposes. Regarding interviews, managers can improve reliability by having more than one person interview job candidates.

Training and Development

LO12-3 Discuss the training and development options that ensure organizational members can effectively perform their jobs.

Training and development help to ensure that organizational members have the knowledge and skills needed to perform jobs effectively, take on new responsibilities, and adapt to changing conditions. **Training** focuses primarily on teaching organizational members how to perform their current jobs and helping them acquire the knowledge and skills they need to be effective performers. **Development** focuses on building the knowledge and skills of organizational members so they are prepared to take on new responsibilities and challenges. Training tends to be used more often at lower levels of an organization; development tends to be used more often with professionals and managers.

Before creating training and development programs, managers should perform a **needs assessment** to determine which employees need training or development and what skills or knowledge they need to acquire (see Figure 12.4).[40]

training Teaching organizational members how to perform their current jobs and helping them acquire the knowledge and skills they need to be effective performers.

development Building the knowledge and skills of organizational members so they are prepared to take on new responsibilities and challenges.

needs assessment An assessment of which employees need training or development and what type of skills or knowledge they need to acquire.

Types of Training

There are two types of training: classroom instruction and on-the-job training.

CLASSROOM INSTRUCTION Through classroom instruction, employees acquire knowledge and skills in a classroom setting. This instruction may take place within the organization or outside it, such as through courses at local colleges and universities or through online classes. Many organizations establish their own formal instructional divisions–some are even called "colleges"–to provide needed classroom instruction. For example, at Disney, classroom instruction and other forms of training and development are provided to employees at Disney University.[41]

Classroom instruction frequently uses videos and role-playing in addition to traditional written materials, lectures, and group discussions. *Videos* can demonstrate appropriate and inappropriate job behaviors. For example, by watching an experienced salesperson effectively deal with a loud and angry customer, inexperienced salespeople can develop skills in handling similar situations. During *role-playing,* trainees either directly participate in or watch others perform actual job activities in a simulated setting. At McDonald's Hamburger University, for example, role-playing helps franchisees acquire the knowledge and skills they need to manage their restaurants.

Simulations also can be part of classroom instruction, particularly for complicated jobs that require an extensive amount of learning and in which errors carry a high cost. In a simulation, key aspects of the work situation and job tasks are duplicated as closely as possible in an artificial setting.[42] For example, air traffic controllers are trained by simulations because of the

Figure 12.4
Training and Development

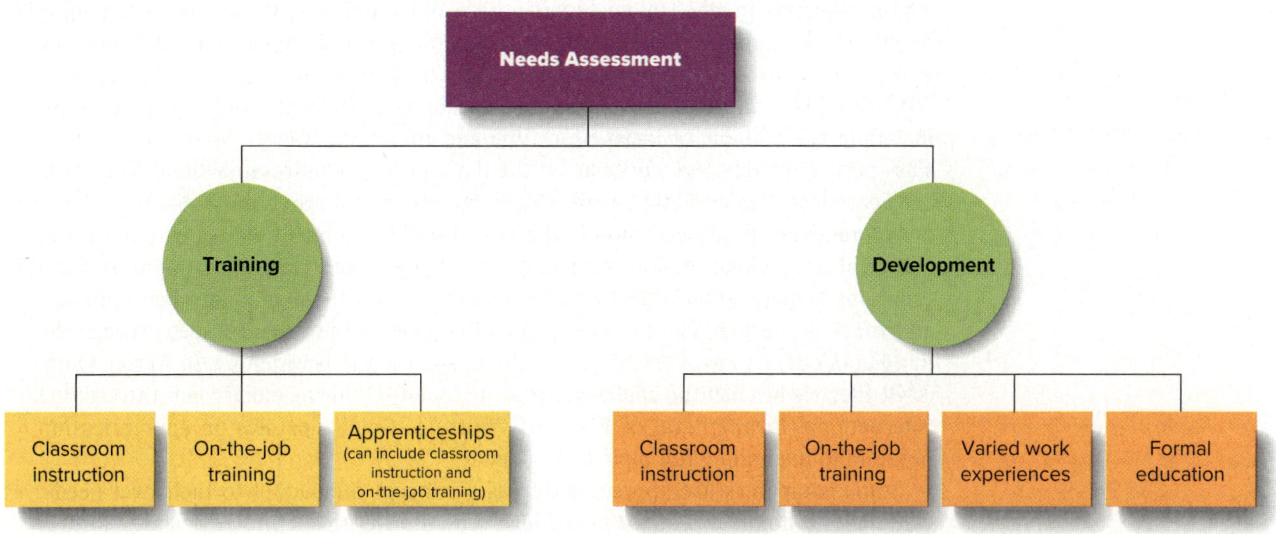

complicated nature of the work, the extensive amount of learning involved, and the very high costs of air traffic control errors.

Technology continues to expand the concept of classroom instruction to include classes of trainees scattered in various locations. With *distance learning,* trainees at different locations attend training programs online using computers and mobile devices to view lectures, participate in discussions, and share documents and other information. Technology applications in distant learning may include videoconferencing, email, instant messaging, document-sharing software, and web cameras.

on-the-job training Training that takes place in the work setting as employees perform their job tasks.

ON-THE-JOB TRAINING In **on-the-job training**, learning occurs in the work setting as employees perform their job tasks. On-the-job training can be provided by coworkers or supervisors or can occur simply as jobholders gain experience and knowledge from doing the work. Newly hired servers in chains such as Buffalo Wild Wings or Chili's often receive on-the-job training from experienced employees. The supervisor of a new bus driver for a campus bus system may ride the bus for a week to ensure that the driver has learned the routes and follows safety procedures. Chefs learn to create new and innovative dishes by experimenting with different combinations of ingredients and cooking techniques. For all on-the-job training, employees learn by doing.

Managers often use on-the-job training on a continuing basis to ensure that their employees keep up to date with changes in goals, technology, products, or customer needs and desires. For example, Medical Solutions, a health care staffing company based in Omaha, Nebraska, earned the top spot on *Training* magazine's 2022 APEX ranking for the best training programs in the country. The company offers programs focused on communication, transparency, diversity and inclusion, and career development, among others, to employees in eight offices across the country. In addition, the company's HR team believes a key component of learning within the organization is the visibility, accessibility, and communication methods of senior management, who actively participate in and facilitate various training opportunities.[43]

On-the-job training can be one part of a training program that also includes classroom instruction. For example, as described in the "Management Insight" feature, some companies hire apprentices–workers participating in an apprenticeship program sponsored by the company or a labor union, school, government agency, or other organization seeking to prepare the workforce by teaching highly demanded skills.

MANAGEMENT INSIGHT

More Companies Are Rediscovering Apprenticeships

Apprenticeships in the United States are an old training practice that is regaining popularity, sometimes taking new forms. According to the Department of Labor, the number of 16- to 24-year-olds in apprenticeship programs more than doubled between 2012 and 2022. The Labor Department sets standards for registered apprenticeships, including the amount of instruction time and minimum wages. Apprentices attend class part of the day and work part of the day, applying classroom lessons. They typically earn less than a full-time worker's pay but much more than minimum wage.[44]

Apprenticeships are common in the skilled trades, such as welding, carpentry, and electrical work. Construction companies are relying more than ever on apprenticeship programs as many experienced workers have retired and the demand for new buildings and roads is soaring. The number of jobs available in the skilled trades exceeds the number of qualified workers by half a million, and the gap is widening. In Akron, Ohio, ANR Electric has met the challenge, growing rapidly by hiring electricians through the International Brotherhood of Electrical Workers, which operates an apprenticeship program to maintain a full pipeline of talent.[45]

Some companies use apprenticeship as a concept they adapt to their own needs. Canon, for example, works with local high schools offering technology classes. It hires

Many companies have implemented apprenticeship programs to train new and less experienced workers in a variety of job skills.
Shutterstock

students to work part-time during their last two years of school and full-time during the summer in between, when they practice servicing the company's office equipment. At the end of the two-year program, Canon can hire young workers who already have experience. In the skilled trades, such high school programs can be a pathway to a registered apprenticeship program. In the Chicago Public Schools, a program called Chicago Builds prepares students to enter union-sponsored apprenticeship programs, where they can start out earning $20 or more per hour. Besides considering younger apprentices, companies are expanding the types of skills they consider for such programs, especially computer skills. IBM and Walmart have both set up their own apprenticeship programs to train employees in high-tech skills.[46]

Hiring apprentices gives companies access to a larger pool of talent, especially where apprenticeship programs are committed to bringing in underrepresented groups such as women and people of color. For the workers, apprenticeship programs offer an attractive alternative to years of college or settling for a low-wage job. They can earn a living wage following graduation, and their employers can hire people who already possess hard-to-find skills.[47]

Types of Development

Although both classroom instruction and on-the-job training can be used for development as well as training, development often includes additional activities such as varied work experiences and formal education.

VARIED WORK EXPERIENCES Top managers need to develop an understanding of, and expertise in, a variety of functions, products and services, and markets. To develop executives who will have this expertise, managers often make sure that employees with high potential have a wide variety of job experiences, some in line positions and some in staff positions. Varied work experiences broaden employees' horizons and help them think about the big picture. For example, one- to three-year stints overseas are being used increasingly to provide managers with international work experiences. With organizations becoming more global, managers need to understand the different values, beliefs, cultures, regions, and ways of doing business in different countries.

At many restaurants, new employees receive on-the-job training by shadowing more experienced waiters and waitresses as they go about their work.
Reza Estakhrian/Getty Images

Another development approach is mentoring. (Recall from Chapter 5 that a *mentor* is an experienced member of an organization who provides advice and guidance to a less experienced member, called a *protégé*.) Having a mentor can help managers seek out work experiences and assignments that will contribute to their development and can enable them to gain the most possible from varied work experiences.[48] Although some mentors and protégés create relationships informally, organizations have found that formal mentoring programs can be valuable ways to contribute to the development of managers and all employees. For example, Intel, Caterpillar, and Sodexo all have formal mentoring programs.[49]

Formal mentoring programs ensure that mentoring takes place in an organization and structure the process. Participants receive training, efforts are focused on matching mentors and protégés so meaningful developmental relationships ensue, and organizations can track reactions and assess the potential benefits of mentoring. Formal mentoring programs can also ensure that diverse members of an organization receive the benefits of mentoring. A study conducted at the Harvard Business School found that members of racial minority groups at three large corporations who were very successful in their careers had the benefit of mentors. Formal mentoring programs help organizations make this valuable development tool available to all employees.[50] In addition, mentoring programs can have a positive effect on a company's bottom line. For example, during the pandemic, companies with mentoring programs had profits nearly 20% better than average, while those without mentoring programs had profits that were 45% worse than average.[51]

When diverse members of an organization lack mentors, their progress in the organization and advancement to high-level positions can be hampered. In a recent survey of more than 1,000 professionals in North America, nearly three-quarters of the respondents from a minority ethnic group said they participated in their companies' formal mentoring programs because they believed the mentoring experience can be a key contributor to accelerating their careers and achieving professional growth. In addition, companies committed to attracting a diverse workforce find that mentoring programs help create a healthy corporate culture and retain top talent.[52]

FORMAL EDUCATION Many large corporations reimburse employees for tuition expenses they incur while taking college courses and obtaining advanced degrees. This is not just benevolence on the part of the employer or even a simple reward given to the employee; it is an effective way to develop employees who can take on new responsibilities and more challenging positions. For similar reasons, corporations spend thousands of dollars sending managers to executive development programs such as executive MBA programs. In these programs, experts teach managers the latest in business and management techniques and practices.

To save time and travel costs, some managers also rely on distance learning to formally educate and develop employees. Using videoconferencing technologies, business schools such as the Harvard Business School, the University of Michigan, and Babson College teach courses on video screens in corporate conference rooms. Business schools also customize courses and degrees to fit the development needs of employees in a particular company and/or a particular geographic region. Moreover, some employees and managers seek to advance their education through online degree programs.[53]

performance appraisal The evaluation of employees' job performance and contributions to their organization.

performance feedback The process through which managers share performance appraisal information with employees, give them an opportunity to reflect on their own performance, and develop, with employees, plans for the future.

Transfer of Training and Development

Whenever training and development take place off the job or in a classroom setting, it is vital for managers to promote the transfer of the knowledge and skills acquired *to the actual work situation.* Trainees should be encouraged and expected to use their newfound expertise on the job.

Performance Appraisal and Feedback

LO12-4 Explain why performance appraisal and feedback are such crucial activities, and list the choices managers must make in designing effective performance appraisal and feedback procedures.

The recruitment/selection and training/development components of a human resource management system ensure that employees have the knowledge and skills needed to be effective now and in the future. Performance appraisal and feedback complement recruitment, selection, training, and development. **Performance appraisal** is the evaluation of employees' job performance and contributions to the organization. **Performance feedback** is the process through which managers share performance appraisal information with their employees, give them an opportunity to reflect on their own performance, and develop, with employees' input, plans for the future. Before performance feedback, performance appraisal must take place. Performance appraisal could take place without providing performance feedback, but wise managers are careful to provide feedback because it can contribute to employee motivation and performance.

Performance appraisal and feedback contribute to the effective management of human resources in several ways. Performance appraisal gives managers important information on which to base human resource decisions. Decisions about pay raises, bonuses, promotions, and job moves all hinge on the accurate appraisal of performance. Performance appraisal can also help managers determine which workers are candidates for training and development and in what areas. Performance feedback encourages high levels of employee motivation and performance. It lets high performers know that their efforts are valued and appreciated. It also lets low performers know they need improvement. Performance feedback can give employees insight into their strengths and weaknesses and the ways in which they can improve their performance in the future.

Types of Performance Appraisal

Performance appraisal focuses on the evaluation of traits, behaviors, and results.[54]

TRAIT APPRAISALS When trait appraisals are used, managers assess employees on personal characteristics that are relevant to job performance, such as skills, abilities, or personality. A factory worker, for example, may be evaluated based on their ability to use computerized equipment and perform numerical calculations. A social worker may be appraised based on his empathy and communication skills.

Three disadvantages of trait appraisals often lead managers to rely on other appraisal methods. First, possessing a certain personal characteristic does not ensure that the personal characteristic will actually be used on the job and result in high performance. For example, a factory worker may possess superior computer and numerical skills but have low motivation. The second disadvantage of trait appraisals is linked to the first. Because traits do not always show a direct association with performance, workers and courts of law may view them as unfair and potentially discriminatory. The third disadvantage of trait appraisals is that they often do not enable managers to give employees feedback they can use to improve performance. Because trait appraisals focus on relatively enduring human characteristics that change only over the long term, employees can do little to change their behavior in response to performance feedback from a trait appraisal. Telling a social worker that they lack empathy says little about how they can improve interactions with clients, for example. These disadvantages suggest that managers should use trait appraisals only when they can demonstrate that the assessed traits are accurate and important indicators of job performance.

BEHAVIOR APPRAISALS Through behavior appraisals, managers assess how workers perform their jobs—the actual actions and behaviors that workers exhibit on the job. Whereas trait appraisals assess what workers *are like,* behavior appraisals assess what workers *do.* For example, with a behavior appraisal, a manager might evaluate a social worker on the extent to which they look clients in the eye when talking with them, express sympathy when they are upset, and refer them to community counseling and support groups geared toward the specific problems they are encountering. Behavior appraisals are especially useful when *how* workers perform their jobs is important. In educational organizations such as high schools, for example, the numbers of classes and students taught are important, but also important is how they are taught or the methods teachers use to ensure that learning takes place.

Behavior appraisals have the advantage of giving employees clear information about what they are doing right and wrong and how they can improve their performance. And because behaviors are much easier for employees to change than traits, performance feedback from behavior appraisals is more likely to lead to improved performance.

RESULTS APPRAISALS For some jobs, *how* people perform the job is not as important as *what* they accomplish or the results they obtain. With results appraisals, managers appraise performance by the results or the actual outcomes of work behaviors. Take the case of two new car salespeople. One salesperson strives to develop personal relationships with customers. They spend hours talking to customers and often call them to see how their decision-making process is going. The other salesperson has a much more hands-off approach. They are very knowledgeable, answer customers' questions, and then wait for the customer to initiate the next conversation. Both salespersons sell the same number of cars on average, and the customers of both are satisfied with the service they receive, according to the satisfaction ratings the dealership asks customers to provide. The manager of the dealership appropriately uses results appraisals (sales and customer satisfaction) to evaluate the salespeople's performance because it does not matter which behavior salespeople use to sell cars as long as they sell the desired number and satisfy customers. If one salesperson sells too few cars, however, the manager can give that person performance feedback about his or her low sales.

OBJECTIVE AND SUBJECTIVE APPRAISALS Whether managers appraise performance in terms of traits, behaviors, or results, the information they assess is either *objective* or *subjective.*

objective appraisal An appraisal that is based on facts and is likely to be numerical.

subjective appraisal An appraisal that is based on perceptions of traits, behaviors, or results.

Objective appraisals are based on facts and are likely to be numerical—the number of cars sold, the number of meals prepared, the number of times late, the number of audits completed. Managers often use objective appraisals when results are being appraised because results tend to be easier to quantify than traits or behaviors. When *how* workers perform their jobs is important, however, subjective behavior appraisals are more appropriate than results appraisals.

Subjective appraisals are based on managers' perceptions of traits, behaviors, or results. Because subjective appraisals rest on managers' perceptions, there is always the chance that they are inaccurate (see Chapter 5). This is why both researchers and managers have spent considerable time and effort on determining the best way to develop reliable and valid subjective measures of performance.

Some of the more popular subjective measures such as the graphic rating scale, the behaviorally anchored rating scale (BARS), and the behavior observation scale (BOS) are illustrated in Figure 12.5.[55] When graphic rating scales are used, performance is assessed along

Figure 12.5

Subjective Measures of Performance

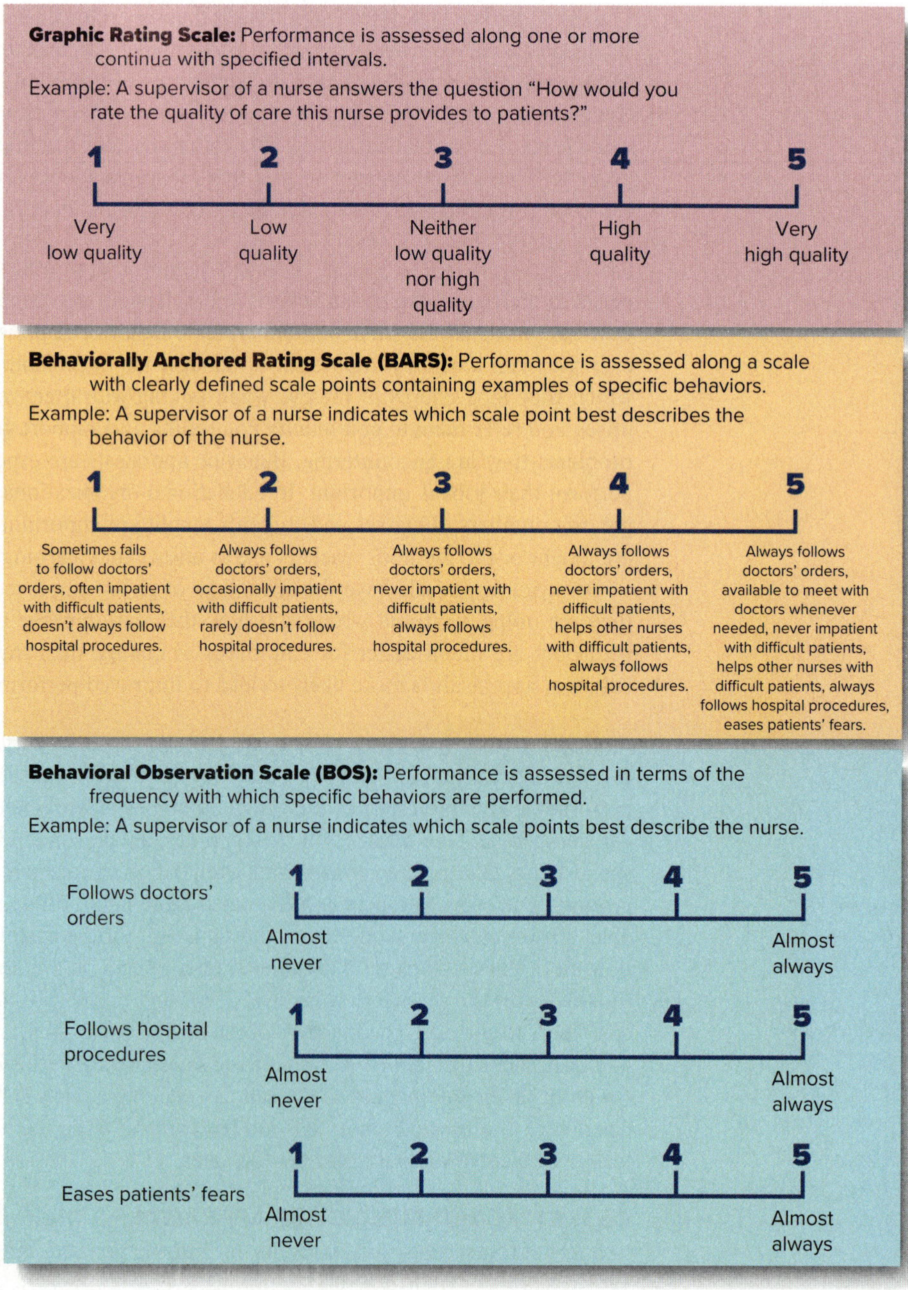

a continuum with specified intervals. With a BARS, performance is assessed along a scale with clearly defined scale points containing examples of specific behaviors. A BOS assesses performance by how often specific behaviors are performed. Many managers may use both objective and subjective appraisals. For example, a salesperson may be appraised both on the dollar value of sales (objective) and the quality of customer service (subjective).

In addition to subjective appraisals, some organizations employ *forced rankings,* whereby supervisors must rank their employees and assign them to different categories according to their performance (which is subjectively appraised). For example, managers and employees might be ranked by their superiors as a "1" (top 15% based on individual performance and goals), "2" (middle 75%), or "3" (bottom 10%). Some managers are proponents of forced rankings, but others strongly oppose the practice. Proponents believe that forced rankings help ensure that human resource decisions are made based on merit, top performers are recognized, and all employees know where they stand relative to others. Opponents of forced ranking believe that forced rankings can be demoralizing, lead to a competitive environment unsupportive of cooperation and teamwork, and result in favoritism. And forced ranking schemes that force managers to group percentages of employees in certain predetermined categories might not make sense if the predetermined categories do not match the distribution of employee performance. For example, a forced ranking system might require a manager to "force" 20% of their employees into the bottom ranking level when, in fact, only 5 to 10% of employees are poor performers. When forced rankings are applied on a regional basis, they can cause conflict and political maneuvering among managers, each of whom wants to ensure that their employees are ranked in the better categories.[56]

Who Appraises Performance?

We have been assuming that managers or the supervisors of employees evaluate performance. This is a reasonable assumption: Supervisors are the most common appraisers of performance. Performance appraisal is an important part of most managers' job duties. Managers are responsible for not only motivating their employees to perform at a high level but also making many decisions hinging on performance appraisals, such as pay raises or promotions. Appraisals by managers can be usefully augmented by appraisals from other sources (see Figure 12.6).

Figure 12.6

Who Appraises Performance?

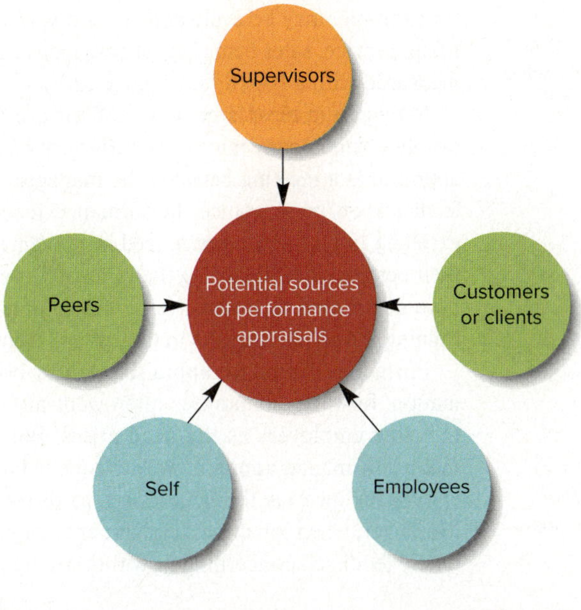

SELF, PEERS, EMPLOYEES, AND CLIENTS When self-appraisals are used, managers supplement their evaluations with an employee's assessment of their own performance. Peer appraisals are provided by an employee's coworkers. Especially when employees work in groups or teams, feedback from peer appraisals can motivate team members while giving managers important information for decision making. A growing number of companies are having employees appraise their managers' performance and leadership as well. And sometimes customers or clients assess employee performance in terms of responsiveness to customers and quality of service. Although appraisals from these sources can be useful, managers need to be aware of issues that may arise when they are used. Employees may be inclined to inflate self-appraisals, especially if organizations are downsizing and they are worried about job security. Managers who are appraised by their employees may fail to take needed but unpopular actions out of fear that their employees will appraise them negatively. Some of these potential issues can be mitigated to the extent that there are high levels of trust in an organization.

360-DEGREE PERFORMANCE APPRAISALS To improve motivation and performance, some organizations include 360-degree appraisals and feedback in their performance appraisal systems, especially for managers. In a **360-degree appraisal** a variety of people, beginning with the manager and including peers or coworkers, employees, superiors, and sometimes even customers or clients, appraise a manager's performance. The manager receives feedback based on evaluations from these multiple sources.

360-degree appraisal A performance appraisal by peers, employees, superiors, and sometimes clients who are in a position to evaluate a manager's performance.

Companies in a variety of industries rely on 360-degree appraisals and feedback.[57] For 360-degree appraisals and feedback to be effective, there has to be trust throughout an organization. More generally, trust is a critical ingredient in any performance appraisal and feedback procedure. In addition, research suggests that 360-degree appraisals should focus on behaviors rather than traits or results and that managers need to carefully select appropriate raters. Moreover, appraisals tend to be more honest when made anonymously and when raters have been trained in how to use 360-degree appraisal forms.[58] Additionally, managers need to think carefully about the extent to which 360-degree appraisals are appropriate for certain jobs and be willing to modify any appraisal system they implement if they become aware of unintended problems it creates, such as comments that seem too subjective on the part of the person rating the manager or employee.[59]

Effective Performance Feedback

For the appraisal and feedback component of a human resource management system to encourage and motivate high performance, managers must give their employees feedback. To generate useful information to feed back to their employees, managers can use both formal and informal appraisals. **Formal appraisals** are conducted at set times during the year and are based on performance dimensions and measures that have been specified in advance. A salesperson, for example, may be evaluated twice a year on the performance dimensions of sales and customer service, sales being objectively measured from sales reports, and customer service being measured with a BARS (see Figure 12.5).

formal appraisal An appraisal conducted at a set time during the year and based on performance dimensions and measures that were specified in advance.

Managers in most large organizations use formal performance appraisals on a fixed schedule dictated by company policy, such as every six months or every year. An integral part of a formal appraisal is a meeting between the manager and the employee in which the employee is given feedback on performance. Performance feedback lets employees know which areas they are excelling in and which areas need improvement; it should also tell them *how* they can improve their performance. Realizing the value of formal appraisals, managers in many large corporations have committed substantial resources to updating their performance appraisal procedures and training low-level managers in how to use them and provide accurate feedback to employees.[60]

Formal performance appraisals supply both managers and employees with valuable information; however, employees often want more frequent feedback, and managers often want to motivate employees as the need arises. For these reasons many companies supplement formal performance appraisal with frequent **informal appraisals**, for which managers and their employees meet as the need arises to discuss ongoing progress and areas for improvement. Moreover, when job duties, assignments, or goals change, informal appraisals can give workers timely feedback concerning how they are handling their new responsibilities.

informal appraisal An unscheduled appraisal of ongoing progress and areas for improvement.

Managers often dislike providing performance feedback, especially when the feedback is negative, but doing so is an important managerial activity.[61] Here are some guidelines for giving effective performance feedback that contributes to employee motivation and performance:

- *Be specific and focus on behaviors or outcomes that are correctable and within a worker's ability to improve.* Example: Telling a salesperson that they are too shy when interacting with customers is likely to lower the salesperson's self-confidence and prompt them to become defensive. A more effective approach would be to give the salesperson feedback about specific behaviors to engage in—greeting customers as soon as they enter the department, asking customers whether they need help, and volunteering to help customers find items.
- *Approach performance appraisal as an exercise in problem solving and solution finding, not criticizing.* Example: Rather than criticizing a financial analyst for turning in reports late, the manager helps the analyst determine why the reports are late and identify ways to better manage their time.
- *Express confidence in an employee's ability to improve.* Example: Instead of being skeptical, a first-level manager tells an employee that he is confident that the employee can increase quality levels.
- *Provide performance feedback both formally and informally.* Example: The staff of a preschool receives feedback from formal performance appraisals twice a year. The school director also provides frequent informal feedback such as complimenting staff members on creative ideas for special projects, noticing when they do a particularly good job handling a difficult child, and pointing out when they provide inadequate supervision.
- *Praise instances of high performance and areas of a job in which a worker excels.* Example: Rather than focusing on just the negative, a manager discusses the areas her employee excels in as well as the areas in need of improvement.
- *Avoid personal criticisms and treat employees with respect.* Example: An engineering manager acknowledges her employees' expertise and treats them as professionals. Even when the manager points out performance problems to employees, she refrains from criticizing them personally.
- *Agree to a timetable for performance improvements.* Example: A first-level manager and his employee decide to meet again in one month to determine whether quality levels have improved.

Recent Trends in Performance Appraisal

Performance reviews have always been a source of stress for both managers and employees. It's difficult to look back on an entire year's performance and come up with constructive feedback when situations or behaviors happened so far in the past.[62] When performance reviews take place on an annual basis, some employees are surprised and dismayed at some of the less-than-positive feedback they receive from supervisors, which may not have a positive impact on future employee performance.[63] In a recent Gallup survey, only 14% of respondents agreed that performance reviews motivated them to improve.[64]

Some companies have eliminated the annual performance review process all together, deciding instead that managers and their direct reports should discuss performance on an ongoing and informal basis.
mavo/Shutterstock

Over the last several years, major organizations, such as Adobe GE, and Deloitte, have changed the way they evaluate employee performance—by doing away with annual performance reviews.[65] Instead, these organizations have adopted a more informal and ongoing dialogue between manager and employee as a way of discussing performance and providing feedback that can help shape future behavior.[66]

For example, Adobe's "Check-in" program requires managers and employees to meet at least once a quarter to discuss expectations, feedback, and growth and development. The discussion is informal (with no script) and there is no paperwork to fill out. The Check-in program continues to work well: Morale increased significantly among both employees and managers, 30% fewer employees were leaving the company to take another job, and involuntary departures (people not meeting expectations) increased by 50%.[67]

Regardless of the approach they use, managers need to remember *why* they are giving performance feedback: to encourage high levels of motivation and performance. Moreover, the information that managers gather through performance appraisal and feedback helps them determine how to distribute pay raises and bonuses.

Pay and Benefits

LO12-5 Explain the issues managers face in determining levels of pay and benefits.

Pay includes employees' base salaries, pay raises, and bonuses and is determined by a number of factors such as the characteristics of the organization and the job and levels of performance. Employee *benefits* are based on membership in an organization (not necessarily on the particular job held) and include paid time off (PTO), company holidays, and medical and life insurance. In Chapter 13 we discuss how pay can motivate organizational members to perform at a high level, as well as the different kinds of pay plans managers can use to help an organization achieve its goals and gain a competitive advantage. As you will learn, it is important to link pay to behaviors or results that contribute to organizational effectiveness. Next we focus on establishing an organization's pay level and pay structure.

Pay Level

pay level The relative position of an organization's pay incentives in comparison with those of other organizations in the same industry employing similar kinds of workers.

Pay level is a broad, comparative concept that refers to how an organization's pay incentives compare, in general, to those of other organizations in the same industry employing similar kinds of workers. Managers must decide if they want to offer relatively high wages, average wages, or relatively low wages. High wages help ensure that an organization is going to be able to recruit, select, and retain high performers, but high wages also raise costs. Low wages give an organization a cost advantage but may undermine the organization's ability to select and recruit high performers and to motivate current employees to perform at a high level. Either of these situations may lead to inferior quality or inadequate customer service.

In determining pay levels, managers should take into account their organization's strategy. A high pay level may prohibit managers from effectively pursuing a low-cost strategy. But a high pay level may be worth the added costs in an organization whose competitive advantage lies in superior quality and excellent customer service. As one might expect, hotel and motel chains with a low-cost strategy, such as Days Inn and Hampton Inns, have lower pay levels than chains striving to provide high-quality rooms and services, such as the Four Seasons.

Pay Structure

pay structure The arrangement of jobs into categories, reflecting their relative importance to the organization and its goals, levels of skill required, and other characteristics.

After deciding on a pay level, managers have to establish a pay structure for the different jobs in the organization. A **pay structure** clusters jobs into categories, reflecting their relative importance to the organization and its goals, levels of skill required, and other characteristics managers consider important. Pay ranges are established for each job category. Individual jobholders' pay within job categories is then determined by factors such as performance, seniority, and skill levels.

There are some interesting global differences in pay structures. Large corporations based in the United States tend to pay their CEOs and top managers higher salaries than do their European or Japanese counterparts. Also, the pay differential between employees at the bottom of the corporate hierarchy and those higher up is much greater in U.S. companies than in European or Japanese companies.[68]

Concerns have been raised over whether it is equitable or fair for CEOs of large companies in the United States to be making millions of dollars in years when their companies have not performed well or are restructuring and laying off workers.[69] Additionally, the average CEO in the United States typically earns nearly 399 times what the average hourly worker earns.[70] Is a pay structure with such a huge pay differential ethical? Shareholders and the public are increasingly asking this very question as well as asking large corporations to rethink their pay structures. Also troubling are the millions of dollars in severance packages that some CEOs receive when they leave their organizations. When many workers are struggling to make ends meet, people are questioning whether it is ethical for some top managers to be making so much money.[71]

Benefits

Organizations are legally required to provide certain benefits to their employees, including workers' compensation, Social Security, and unemployment insurance. Workers' compensation helps employees financially if they become unable to work due to a work-related injury or illness. Social Security provides financial assistance to retirees and former employees with disabilities. Unemployment insurance provides financial assistance to workers who lose their jobs through no fault of their own. The legal system in the United States views these three benefits as ethical requirements for organizations and thus mandates that they be provided.

Other benefits such as health insurance, dental insurance, vacation time, pension plans, life insurance, flexible working hours, company-provided day care, and employee assistance and wellness programs have traditionally been provided at the option of employers. The Affordable Care Act signed into law by President Barack Obama in 2010 now requires employers with 50 or more employees to offer health insurance to employees or pay a penalty.[72] Benefits enabling workers to balance the demands of their jobs and of their lives away from the office or factory are of growing importance for many workers who have competing demands on their scarce time and energy. For an example of a company providing such benefits, see the "Manager as a Person" feature.

MANAGER AS A PERSON

Parenting Showed Bobbie's Founders How to Lead

At San Francisco–based Bobbie, employee benefits reflect the values and experiences of the founders, Sarah Hardy and Laura Modi. Hardy and Modi started the provider of organic infant formula in 2018. Three years later, Bobbie began distributing formula directly to consumers on a subscription basis. Hardy, the chief operating officer, and Modi, the CEO, expected revenues of $4 million that year but posted $18 million instead. By mid-2022, Bobbie's workforce surpassed 50 employees, 70% of whom are parents.[73]

Recognizing the demands weighing on new parents, Hardy and Modi decided to offer a benefit unusual at U.S. companies: paid parental leave. Bobbie grants new parents four months of paid leave plus an option to take eight additional months of unpaid leave—far beyond the 10 days taken by 25% of U.S. mothers and the one week taken by fathers. Also, a re-entry program allows returning parents to work three days per week at full salary for their first two weeks back on the job. For all employees, Bobbie employs a balance coordinator—someone employees can turn to when they need help juggling the demands of home and work.[74]

Recognizing the demands of caring for newborns while juggling job responsibilities, Bobbie offers new parents four months of paid leave plus an option to take eight additional months of unpaid leave—an unusual employee benefit at most U.S. companies.
JGI/Tom Grill/Getty Images

Behind this policy is a personal desire to support working parents. Before founding Bobbie, Hardy and Modi had worked for Airbnb, where Hardy became the first employee to return from maternity leave. She found the dual responsibilities of employee and parent to be a struggle. She and Modi concluded that removing such barriers could enable growth, so they aimed to "create an environment in which working parents can be successful." The founders also see a practical reason for spending on such benefits: attraction and retention of talented people who will contribute to the company's success.[75]

Early results of the benefits are encouraging. Hardy says Bobbie's launch of the benefits was quickly followed by a noticeable improvement in quality of people seeking jobs. Modi says she has observed impressive levels of efficiency. As of April 2022, the company reported that one-third of its employees had used the services of the balance coordinator, collectively relieving themselves of 50 hours they would have spent on those responsibilities each quarter. And investors have recently committed $50 million to enable additional growth. With busy parents increasingly shopping online and Bobbie's website being the only direct-to-consumer source of formula, any policy that keeps staff in place will be essential to Bobbie's future.[76]

cafeteria-style benefit plan A plan from which employees can choose the benefits they want.

In some organizations, top managers determine which benefits might best suit the employees and organization and offer the same benefit package to all employees. Other organizations, realizing that employees' needs and desires might differ, offer **cafeteria-style benefit plans** that let employees choose the benefits they want. Cafeteria-style benefit plans sometimes help managers deal with employees who feel unfairly treated because they cannot take advantage of certain benefits available to other employees who, for example, have children. Some organizations have success with cafeteria-style benefit plans; others find them difficult to manage.

As health care costs escalate and overstretched employees find it hard to take time to exercise and take care of their health, more companies are providing benefits and incentives to promote employee wellness. According to the Kaiser Family Foundation, more than 80% of large employers have some type of wellness program to help workers identify possible health problems and take steps to improve their overall health.[77] For working parents, family-friendly benefits are especially attractive. For example, access to on-site child care, the ability to telecommute and take time off to care for sick children, and provisions for emergency back-up child care can be valued benefits for working parents with young children.

Same-sex domestic partner benefits have been offered by some companies as a way to attract and retain valued employees. Workers in the LGBTQ community are reluctant to work for companies that do not provide the same kinds of benefits for their partners as those provided for partners of the opposite sex. In recent years, however, after the U.S. Supreme Court in 2015 ruled that same-sex marriage was legal in all 50 states, many companies have reduced same-sex domestic partner benefits in favor of covering married partners of all employees.[78]

Labor Relations

LO12-6 Understand the role that labor relations play in the effective management of human resources.

labor relations The activities managers engage in to ensure that they have effective working relationships with the labor unions that represent their employees' interests.

Labor relations are the activities managers engage in to ensure that they have effective working relationships with the labor unions that represent their employees' interests. Although the U.S. government has responded to the potential for unethical and unfair treatment of workers by creating and enforcing laws regulating employment (including the EEO laws listed in Table 12.1), some workers believe a union will ensure that their interests are fairly represented in their organizations.

Before we describe unions in more detail, let's take a look at some examples of important employment legislation. In 1938, the federal government passed the Fair Labor Standards Act, which prohibited child labor and provided for minimum wages, overtime pay, and maximum working hours to protect workers' rights. In 1963, the Equal Pay Act mandated that workers performing equal work (work requiring the same levels of skill, responsibility, and effort performed in the same kind of working conditions) receive equal pay (see Table 12.1). In 1970, the Occupational Safety and Health Act mandated procedures for managers to follow to ensure workplace safety. These are just a few of the U.S. government's efforts to protect workers' rights. State legislatures also have been active in promoting safe, ethical, and fair workplaces.

Unions

Unions exist to represent workers' interests in organizations. Given that managers have more power than workers and that organizations have multiple stakeholders, there is always the potential for managers to take steps that benefit one set of stakeholders, such as shareholders, while hurting another, such as employees. For example, managers may decide to speed up a production line to lower costs and increase production in the hopes of increasing returns to shareholders. Speeding up the line, however, could hurt employees forced to work at a rapid pace and may increase the risk of injuries. Also, employees receive no additional pay for the extra work they are performing. Unions would represent workers' interests in a scenario such as this one.

Congress acknowledged the role that unions could play in ensuring safe and fair workplaces when it passed the National Labor Relations Act of 1935. This act made it legal for workers to organize into unions to protect their rights and interests and declared certain unfair or unethical organizational practices to be illegal. The act also established the National Labor Relations Board (NLRB) to oversee union activity. Currently, the NLRB conducts certification elections, which are held among the employees of an organization to determine whether they want a union to represent their interests. The NLRB also makes judgments concerning unfair labor practices and specifies practices that managers must refrain from.

Employees might vote to have a union represent them for any number of reasons.[79] They may think their wages and working conditions need improvement. They may believe managers are not treating them with respect. They may think their working hours are unfair or they need more job security or a safer work environment. Or they may be dissatisfied with management and find it difficult to communicate their concerns to their bosses. Regardless of the specific reason, one overriding reason is power: A united group inevitably wields more power than an individual, and this type of power may be especially helpful to employees in some organizations.

Although these would seem to be potent forces for unionization, some workers are reluctant to join unions. Sometimes this reluctance is due to the perception that union leaders are corrupt. Some workers may simply believe that belonging to a union might not do them much good while costing them money in membership dues. Employees also might not want to be forced into doing something they do not want to, such as striking because the union thinks it is in their best interest. Moreover, although unions can be a positive force in organizations, sometimes they also can be a negative force, impairing organizational effectiveness. For example, when union leaders resist needed changes in an organization or are corrupt, organizational performance can suffer.

The percentage of U.S. workers represented by unions today is smaller than it was in the 1950s, an era when unions were especially strong. In the 1950s, around 35% of U.S. workers were union members; in 2022, 10.1% of workers were members of unions.[80] The American Federation of Labor–Congress of Industrial Organizations (AFL-CIO) includes 58 voluntary member unions representing more than 12.5 million workers.[81] Overall, approximately 14.3 million workers in the United States belong to unions. Union influence in manufacturing and heavy industries has been on the decline; more generally, approximately 6% of private-sector workers are union members, and 33.1% of government workers belong to unions.[82]

The COVID-19 pandemic may have contributed to an increased interest in unions. Countless health care, food service, grocery, and other frontline workers were forced to work long hours in 2020–2021 to the point where they felt abused by their managers and organizations. Some employees decided the only way to get management's attention about their working conditions (and lack of hazardous duty pay) was to take steps to unionize. For example, workers from various Starbucks, Trader Joe's, Apple Store, and Amazon locations voted for union representation over the past two years. According to the National Labor Relations Board, there were 1,249 union elections in 2022, and workers voted to unionize in 72% of those elections. According to a recent Gallup survey, more than 71% of Americans now approve of labor unions–the highest percentage Gallup has recorded on this topic since 1965.[83]

Collective Bargaining

collective bargaining
Negotiation between labor unions and managers to resolve conflicts and disputes about issues such as working hours, wages, benefits, working conditions, and job security.

Collective bargaining is negotiation between labor unions and managers to resolve conflicts and disputes about important issues such as working hours, wages, working conditions, and job security. Sometimes union members go on strike to drive home their concerns to managers. Once an agreement that union members support has been reached (sometimes with the help of a neutral third party called a *mediator*), union leaders and managers sign a contract spelling out the terms of the collective bargaining agreement. We discuss conflict and negotiation in depth in Chapter 17, but some brief observations are in order here because collective bargaining is an ongoing consideration in labor relations.

The signing of a contract, for example, does not finish the collective bargaining process. Disagreement and conflicts can arise over the interpretation of the contract. In such cases, a neutral third party called an *arbitrator* is usually called in to resolve the conflict. An important component of a collective bargaining agreement is a *grievance procedure* through which workers who believe they are not being fairly treated are allowed to voice their concerns and have their interests represented by the union. Workers who think they were unjustly fired in violation of a union contract, for example, may file a grievance, have the union represent them, and get their jobs back if an arbitrator agrees with them. Union members sometimes go on strike when managers make decisions that the members think will hurt them and are not in their best interests.

In 2023, more than 150 large union contracts were expected to expire, possibly giving rise to more unrest among dissatisfied workers and stalled negotiations. According to Bloomberg Law, union workers at UPS (256,000), Detroit autoworkers at Ford, GM, Fiat/Chrysler (150,000), and Kaiser Permanente health care workers (75,000), among others, may be involved in strikes if new contracts are not agreed upon by union members and organizations.[84]

Summary and Review

LO12-1 **STRATEGIC HUMAN RESOURCE MANAGEMENT** Human resource management (HRM) includes all the activities managers engage in to ensure that their organizations can attract, retain, and effectively use human resources. Strategic HRM is the process by which managers design the components of a human resource management system to be consistent with each other, with other elements of organizational architecture, and with the organization's strategies and goals.

LO12-2 **RECRUITMENT AND SELECTION** Before recruiting and selecting employees, managers must engage in human resource planning and job analysis. Human resource planning includes all the activities managers engage in to forecast their current and future needs for human resources. Job analysis is the process of identifying (1) the tasks, duties, and responsibilities that make up a job and (2) the knowledge, skills, and abilities needed to perform the job. Recruitment includes all the activities managers engage in to develop a pool of qualified applicants for open positions. Selection is the process by which managers determine the relative qualifications of job applicants and their potential for performing well in a particular job.

LO12-3 **TRAINING AND DEVELOPMENT** Training focuses on teaching organizational members how to perform effectively in their current jobs. Development focuses on broadening organizational members' knowledge and skills so they are prepared to take on new responsibilities and challenges.

LO12-4 **PERFORMANCE APPRAISAL AND FEEDBACK** Performance appraisal is the evaluation of employees' job performance and contributions to the organization. Performance feedback is the process through which managers share performance appraisal information with their employees, give them an opportunity to reflect on their own performance, and develop with them plans for the future. Performance appraisal gives managers useful information for decision making. Performance feedback can encourage high levels of motivation and performance. Recent trends suggest that some organizations are moving away from the annual performance review for employees, instead taking a more informal approach to evaluating workers with ongoing conversations between manager and employee on a regular basis to discuss expectations, feedback, and plans for growth and development.

LO12-5 **PAY AND BENEFITS** Pay level is the relative position of an organization's pay incentives in comparison with those of other organizations in the same industry employing similar workers. A pay structure clusters jobs into categories according to their relative importance to the organization and its goals, the levels of skill required, and other characteristics. Pay ranges are then established for each job category. Organizations are legally required to provide certain benefits to their employees; other benefits are provided at the discretion of employers.

LO12-6 **LABOR RELATIONS** Labor relations include all the activities managers engage in to ensure that they have effective working relationships with the labor unions that represent their employees' interests. The National Labor Relations Board oversees union activity. Collective bargaining is the process through which labor unions and managers resolve conflicts and disputes and negotiate agreements.

Management in Action

Topics for Discussion and Action

Discussion

1. Discuss why it is important for human resource management systems to be in sync with an organization's strategy and goals and with each other. [LO12-1]
2. Discuss why training and development are ongoing activities for all organizations. [LO12-3]
3. Describe the type of development activities you think middle managers are most in need of. [LO12-3]
4. Evaluate the pros and cons of 360-degree performance appraisals and feedback. Would you like your performance to be appraised in this manner? Why or why not? [LO12-4]
5. Discuss why two restaurants in the same community might have different pay levels. [LO12-5]
6. Explain why union membership is becoming more popular. [LO12-6]

Action

7. Interview a manager in a local organization to determine how that organization recruits and selects employees. [LO12-2]

Building Management Skills

Analyzing Human Resource Management Systems [LO12-1, 12-2, 12-3, 12-4, 12-5]

Think about your current job or a job you have had in the past. If you have never had a job, interview a friend or family member who is currently working. Answer the following questions about the job you have chosen:

1. How are people recruited and selected for this job? Are the recruitment and selection procedures the organization uses effective or ineffective? Why?
2. What training and development do people who hold this job receive? Are the training and development appropriate? Why or why not?
3. How is performance of this job appraised? Does performance feedback contribute to motivation and high performance on this job?
4. What levels of pay and benefits are provided on this job? Are these levels appropriate? Why or why not?

Managing Ethically [LO12-4, 12-5]

Some managers do not want to become overly friendly with their employees because they are afraid that doing so will impair their objectivity in conducting performance appraisals and making decisions about pay raises and promotions. Some employees resent it when they see one or more of their coworkers being very friendly with the boss; they are concerned about the potential for favoritism. Their reasoning runs something like this: If two employees are equally qualified for a promotion and one is a good friend of the boss and the other is a mere acquaintance, who is more likely to receive the promotion?

Questions

1. Either individually or in a group, think about the ethical implications of managers' becoming friendly with their employees.
2. Do you think managers should feel free to socialize and become good friends with their employees outside the workplace if they so desire? Why or why not?

Small Group Breakout Exercise

Building a Human Resource Management System [LO12-1, 12-2, 12-3, 12-4, 12-5]

Form groups of three or four people, and appoint one member as the spokesperson who will communicate your findings to the class when called on by the instructor. Then discuss the following scenario:

You and your three partners are engineers who minored in business at college and have decided to start a consulting business. Your goal is to provide manufacturing process engineering and other engineering services to large and small organizations. You forecast that there will be an increased use of outsourcing for these activities. You discussed with managers in several large organizations the services you plan to offer, and they expressed considerable interest. You have secured funding to start your business and now are building the HRM system. Your human resource planning suggests that you need to hire between five and eight experienced engineers with good communication skills, two administrative assistants, and two MBAs who between them have financial, accounting, and human resource skills. You are striving to develop your human resources in a way that will enable your new business to prosper.

1. Describe the steps you will take to recruit and select (a) the engineers, (b) the administrative assistants, and (c) the MBAs.
2. Describe the training and development the engineers, the administrative assistants, and the MBAs will receive.
3. Describe how you will appraise the performance of each group of employees and how you will provide feedback.
4. Describe the pay level and pay structure of your consulting firm.

Be the Manager [LO12-4]

You are Amy Boynton and just received some disturbing feedback. You are the director of human resources for Maxi Vision, a medium-size window and glass door manufacturer. You recently initiated a 360-degree performance appraisal system for all middle and upper managers at Maxi Vision, including yourself, but excluding the senior-most executives and top management team.

You were eagerly awaiting feedback about the new system from the managers who report directly to you. You recently implemented several important initiatives that affected them and their employees, including a complete overhaul of the company's appraisal system. While the managers who report to you were evaluated based on 360-degree appraisals, their employees were evaluated using a 20-question BARS scale you recently created that focuses on behaviors. Conducted annually, performance appraisals are an important consideration in determining pay raises and bonus decisions.

You were so convinced the new performance appraisal procedures would be highly effective and well received that you hoped your own managers would mention them in feedback to you. And boy, did they! You were amazed to learn that the managers and their employees thought the new performance appraisal system was unfair and a waste of time. In fact, several of the managers who report to you said their own performance was suffering based on the 360-degree appraisals they received from others in the organization. In addition, the managers told you their own employees hated the new appraisal system and partially blamed them for the new system because the employees viewed their bosses as part of the management team.

You couldn't believe the comments the managers conveyed as part of their own performance appraisals. You spent so much time developing what you thought was the ideal rating system for both managers and employees. Unfortunately, your enthusiasm for the new system wasn't shared by others in the company. Your own supervisor is aware of the complaints and told you it was a top priority for you to "fix this mess," which suggests she thinks you're responsible for creating a bad situation among employees and managers. What are you going to do?

Case in the News [LO12-1, 12-2, 12-3, 12-5, 12-6]

How Strategic HR Keeps Southwest Airlines Flying

Despite turbulence in its business environment, which included a global pandemic in 2020 and a recent horrific holiday meltdown in 2022, Southwest Airlines has a well-qualified, highly engaged workforce to keep the company aloft. Linda Rutherford, chief administration and communications officer of the Dallas-based company, leads efforts to provide this workforce. She promotes the culture espoused by the late Southwest founder Herb Kelleher: happy employees making customers happy, which makes shareholders happy. The HR strategy is to select, develop, and reward people who put that vision into practice, despite challenges like worsening storms and delays in the delivery of new jets. Southwest had been one of the biggest customers for Boeing's 737 MAX, so when that model was grounded because of safety problems, Southwest had to cancel flights, reduce revenue goals, and forgo the fuel savings promised by the new design.

Rutherford's team builds its engaged workforce by hiring based on people's commitment to ensuring that customers have a great experience. Rather than focusing just on technical skills, Southwest looks for people who want to be part of Southwest's fun- and people-oriented culture and then prepares them to move up in the organization as they gain experience. (Rutherford started her Southwest career more than 30 years ago.) Because these people love being part of Southwest, turnover has been low.

Analysis of the airline industry points to a shortage of pilots, because training is expensive, trainees must practice flying for 1,500 hours, and many current pilots are nearing the mandatory retirement age—65 in the United States. Southwest has responded with Destination 225°, a program that partners with established training organizations to create four pathways to a pilot's license while teaching Southwest's values. The cadet pathway is for interested candidates without previous flying experience, the university pathway partners with several universities to prepare students studying for a bachelor's degree, the military pathway gives military helicopter pilots experience with fixed-wing aircraft, and the employee pathway connects existing employees with pilot training appropriate for their background. Those who complete the training are eligible to apply to fly for Southwest.

Southwest also provides training for its employees. For pilots and flight attendants, training programs are critical and require sophisticated facilities. Southwest recently built a pilot training center in Dallas with 18 flight simulators, as well as a training center for flight attendants. Every year, thousands of employees visit Dallas for training.

Many of Southwest's employees are union members, so those workers' pay is based on the terms of their contract. Pilots, for example, are paid per trip and based on number of years with the company, plus an additional amount based on their time away from their home base. Pilots are guaranteed a certain number of trips each month, and they may trade with each other or give each other trips. The total compensation package at Southwest also includes retirement plan contributions and travel benefits for employees and dependents.

An employee benefit designed to be highly motivating is Southwest's profit-sharing plan, which allocates about 15% of profits before taxes to employees, divided according to the relative size of their pay. In 2019, when the grounding of Boeing's 737 MAX caused the company to cut flights, profits shrank through no fault of Southwest's people. However, Southwest negotiated with Boeing to pay damages for lost profits. Of the damages paid, Southwest allocated $125 million to profit sharing, bringing the total up to $667 million, higher than the year before. Each employee's profit sharing was equivalent to more than six weeks' pay, with most of it deposited in their retirement accounts.

In the same year, Southwest was dealing with the 737 MAX groundings, it was continuing contract negotiations with its mechanics, who have been worried about outsourcing. Southwest's management complained that during the negotiations, mechanics were finding minor maintenance issues (say, a missing row number in the cabin) just to cause flight cancellations. In the first half of the year, following a week of mediation, Southwest and the union reached an agreement calling for higher pay and promises to maintain a specified headcount.

While Southwest negotiated with Boeing for the hit to its profits, the Southwest Airlines Pilots Association sued Boeing for the pay lost when pilots' flight time was cut back. For pilots, the problems with the 737 MAX have been about more than money. Pilots are responsible for getting passengers safely to their destination, and their trust was shaken by what some describe as failure to provide proper training, which resulted in two fatal crashes.

As Southwest grappled with the impact of COVID-19 on its overall business, close to 28% of its workforce signed up for partially paid extended leave or outright buyouts, which helps reduce the airline's labor expense. While the company was grateful to employees who opted to take leave or company buyouts, management also realized that keeping passengers safe and employees satisfied would help the airline rebound as the virus became manageable and people got back to traveling. June 2021 was the first month since the previous March that the company made a net profit without funding from the federal government.

Southwest continued to recover from the effects of the pandemic in February 2022, as CEO Gary Kelly handed over the reins of the company to Bob Jordan, a 34-year company veteran.

Jordan already had several top priorities for the airline and the HR group, including hiring thousands of new employees and working with pilot and flight attendant unions to finalize contracts. However, the December 2022 holidays were a fiasco for the new CEO and Southwest. A combination of bad weather and crew rescheduling difficulties attributed to outdated technology caused the airline to cancel nearly half of its flight schedule for more than a week, leaving hundreds of thousands of passengers, crew, and baggage stranded in the wrong locations across the country. According to estimates, this major snafu could cause Southwest nearly $800 million, due to customer cancellations and expense reimbursements to affected passengers that included money for hotels and rental cars. Jordan has promised to make it right again, hiring an outside industry consulting firm to do an extensive review of the holiday meltdown, awarding 25,000 frequent flyer miles to passengers affected by cancellations, and giving all employees additional bonus points for going above and beyond, in the form of $400 worth of gift cards.

Questions for Discussion

1. What conditions present challenges to Southwest Airlines as it tries to fill its need for people who give customers a happy flying experience and to recover from its recent holiday issues? What conditions help Southwest meet the challenges?
2. Southwest used some of the settlement money from Boeing to increase employees' profit sharing above the previous year's amount, even though profits were down. Do you agree that this was a smart HR decision? Why or why not?
3. Besides the examples described in the case, what other HR efforts could enable or encourage Southwest employees to live out the vision of making customers happy?

Sources: "Destination 225°," https:careers .southwestair.com, accessed January 28, 2023; "Linda Rutherford: Chief Administration & Communications Officer," https://swamedia .com, accessed January 28, 2023; K. Arnold, "Southwest Airlines CEO Bob Jordan Talks about Holiday Meltdown and What Comes Next," *Dallas Morning News*, www.dallasnews.com, January 16, 2023; R. N. Velotta, "Southwest's Holiday Meltdown Was Decades in the Making," *Hastings Tribune*, www.hastingstribune.com, January 9, 2023; B. Schlapping, "Southwest Apologizes to Employees with Bonus Points," *One Mile at a Time*, https://onemileatatime.com, January 7, 2023; L. Josephs, "Southwest Airlines' Schedule Stabilizes after Holiday Meltdown But Costs Are Piling Up," *CNBC*, www.cnbc.com, January 4, 2023; L. Josephs, "Bob Jordan Is Now Southwest Airlines' New CEO. Here's What's on His Plate," *CNBC*, www.cnbc.com, February 2, 2022; J. Prohov, "Southwest Reports First Monthly Profit Since Pandemic Began with June Income," *WFAA*, www.wfaa.com, July 22, 2021; L. Josephs, "Nearly 17,000 Southwest Employees Sign Up for Buyouts, Voluntary Leave as Furlough Threat Looms," *CNBC*, www.cnbc.com, July 21, 2020; B. Tomasian, "Southwest Airlines Flies to the Top of the 2019 Workforce 100," *Workforce*, www .workforce.com, accessed March 4, 2020; L. Pratt, "Southwest Airlines Profit-Sharing Scheme Pays Out for 60,000 Employees," *Employee Benefits*, https://employeebenefits.co.uk, February 13, 2020; K. Arnold, "Southwest Is Building an Innovation Lab at Dallas Love Field," *Dallas Morning News*, www.dallasnews.com, January 15, 2020; A. Sider, "Southwest Airlines Pilots Union Sues Boeing, Alleging Lost Compensation," *The Wall Street Journal*, www.wsj.com, October 7, 2019; K. Arnold, "Southwest Airlines Partners with Universities, Flight Schools to Recruit Future Pilots," *Dallas Morning News*, www.dallasnews.com, August 2, 2019.

Notes

1. C. Commendatore, "How to Appeal to a Changing Truck Driver Demographic," *FleetOwner*, www.fleetowner.com, March 3, 2022; J. Fisher, "As Fleets Seek Future Drivers, TCA Backs Federal Apprenticeship Program," *FleetOwner*, www.fleetowner.com, March 21, 2022; "Equipment, Pay Issues Top Truck Driver Retention, Recruiting Report," *Trucker*, www.trucker.com, February 15, 2022; S. Avi-Yonah, "Short on Drivers, Shippers Shift Gears," *Bloomberg Businessweek*, August 30, 2021, 24–25.
2. Avi-Yonah, "Short on Drivers"; N. Austin, "Snowplow Driver Shortages Creating Avalanche of Issues for DOTs," *FreightWaves*, www.freightwaves.com, March 18, 2022.
3. Fisher, "As Fleets Seek Future Drivers"; S. Bennett, "How Fleets Are Winning the Race to Hire Drivers," *Transport Topics*, www.ttnews.com, March 4, 2022.
4. Commendatore, "How to Appeal"; Fisher, "As Fleets Seek Future Drivers."
5. Bennett, "How Fleets Are Winning"; *Trucker*, "Equipment, Pay Issues."
6. J.E. Butler, G.R. Ferris, and N.K. Napier, *Strategy and Human Resource Management* (Cincinnati: Southwestern, 1991); P.M. Wright and G.C. McMahan, "Theoretical Perspectives for Strategic Human Resource Management," *Journal of Management* 18 (1992), 295–320.
7. M. Murphy, "Microsoft Wants Anyone to Be a Developer, Whether They Code or Not," *Quartz*, https://qz.com, November 4, 2019.
8. "Reinventing the Employee Experience at Microsoft," www.microsoft.com, February 26, 2020.
9. J. Puckett, "The Importance of Performance Management," *Technology Advice*, https://technologyadvice.com, July 26, 2019; C.D. Fisher, L.F. Schoenfeldt, and J.B. Shaw, *Human Resource Management* (Boston: Houghton Mifflin, 1990).
10. Wright and McMahan, "Theoretical Perspectives for Strategic Human Resource Management."
11. L. Baird and I. Meshoulam, "Managing Two Fits for Strategic Human Resource Management," *Academy of Management Review* 13, no. 1 (1988), 116–28; J. Milliman, M. Von Glinow, and M. Nathan, "Organizational Life Cycles and Strategic International Human Resource Management in Multinational Companies: Implications for Congruence Theory," *Academy of Management Review* 16 (1991), 318–39; R.S. Schuler and S.E. Jackson, "Linking Competitive Strategies with Human Resource Management Practices," *Academy of Management Executive* 1 (1987), 207–19; P.M. Wright and S.A. Snell, "Toward an Integrative View of

Strategic Human Resource Management," *Human Resource Management Review* 1 (1991), 203–25.

12. Equal Employment Opportunity Commission, "Uniform Guidelines on Employee Selection Procedures," *Federal Register* 43 (1978), 38290–315.
13. E. Friedman, "Top 10 Issues Facing HR Leaders Heading into 2022," *Forbes,* www.forbes.com, accessed January 27, 2023; A. Burton and P. Confino, "6 HR Leaders Predict the Top Workforce Challenges in 2023," *Fortune,* https://fortune.com, January 19, 2023.
14. S.L. Rynes, "Recruitment, Job Choice, and Post-Hire Consequences: A Call for New Research Directions," in M.D. Dunnette and L.M. Hough, eds., *Handbook of Industrial and Organizational Psychology,* vol. 2 (Palo Alto, CA: Consulting Psychologists Press, 1991), 399–444.
15. S. Gerber, "Finding Talented Freelancers: 12 Websites Worth Searching," www.business.com, accessed March 4, 2020.
16. "Outsourcing Trends and Statistics for 2020 and Beyond," www.superstaff.com, October 13, 2019.
17. "Top 8 Countries for Outsourcing," *Time Doctor,* www.timedoctor.com, accessed January 27, 2023
18. "Report: Offshoring Evolving at Rapid Pace," https://today.duke.edu, accessed April 7, 2018; S. Minter, "Offshoring by US Companies Doubles," *Industry Week,* www.industryweek.com, accessed April 7, 2018.
19. D.Z. Morris, "How Outsourcing Tech Jobs Could Deepen Income Inequality in America," *Fortune,* http://fortune.com, September 3, 2017.
20. J. Butters, "S&P 500 Companies with More Global Exposure Reporting Higher Earnings Growth in Q3," *Factset,* https://insight.factset.com, October 25, 2021.
21. Deloitte, "The Risk Intelligent Approach to Outsourcing and Offshoring," www2.deloitte.com, accessed January 27, 2023.
22. R.J. Harvey, "Job Analysis," in M.D. Dunnette and L.M. Hough, eds., *Handbook of Industrial and Organizational Psychology,* vol. 2 (Palo Alto, CA: Consulting Psychologists Press, 1991), 71–163.
23. E.L. Levine, *Everything You Always Wanted to Know about Job Analysis: A Job Analysis Primer* (Tampa, FL: Mariner, 1983).
24. E.J. McCormick, P.R. Jeannerette, and R.C. Mecham, *Position Analysis Questionnaire* (West Lafayette, IN: Occupational Research Center, Department of Psychological Sciences, Purdue University, 1969).
25. E.J. McCormick, *Job Analysis: Methods and Applications* (New York: American Management Association, 1979); E.J. McCormick and P.R. Jeannerette, "The Position Analysis Questionnaire," in S. Gael, ed., *The Job Analysis Handbook for Business, Industry, and Government* (New York: Wiley, 1988).
26. "The Future of the Great Resignation: What Employers Need to Know for 2023," *Indeed,* www.indeed.com, accessed January 27, 2023.
27. S.L. Premack and J.P. Wanous, "A Meta-Analysis of Realistic Job Preview Experiments," *Journal of Applied Psychology* 70 (1985), 706–19; J.P. Wanous, "Realistic Job Previews: Can a Procedure to Reduce Turnover also Influence the Relationship between Abilities and Performance?" *Personnel Psychology* 31 (1978), 249–58; J.P. Wanous, *Organizational Entry: Recruitment, Selection, and Socialization of Newcomers* (Reading, MA: Addison-Wesley, 1980).
28. R.M. Guion, "Personnel Assessment, Selection, and Placement," in M.D. Dunnette and L.M. Hough, eds., *Handbook of Industrial and Organizational Psychology,* vol. 2 (Palo Alto, CA: Consulting Psychologists Press, 1991), 327–97.
29. M. Webb, "How to Alter Your Hiring Practices to Increase Diversity," *Forbes,* www.forbes.com, accessed March 4, 2020; C. Vargas, "Diversifying Tax Workforce Could Start with Hiring Practices," *Bloomberg BNA,* www.bna.com, March 22, 2018.
30. L. Stevens, "Small Changes Can Increase Corporate Diversity," *The Wall Street Journal,* www.wsj.com, March 13, 2018; Danielle Westermann King, "Unconscious Bias: Inside the Underbelly of Hiring," *Recruiting Trends,* www.recruitingtrends.com, April 2, 2018.
31. Vargas, "Diversifying Tax Workforce"; King, "Unconscious Bias."
32. King, "Unconscious Bias."
33. S.T. Casey, "From an Employer's View, Hiring Jobseekers with Disabilities," *Atlanta Business Chronicle,* www.bizjournals.com/atlanta, April 1, 2018.
34. J. Loffredi, "Before You Run an Employee Background Check You Need to Know These 6 Things," *Inc.,* www.inc.com, January 19, 2018.
35. J.T. O'Donnell, "85 Percent of Job Applicants Lie on Resumes. Here's How to Spot a Dishonest Candidate," *Inc.,* www.inc.com, accessed March 4, 2020.
36. R.A. Noe, J.R. Hollenbeck, B. Gerhart, and P.M. Wright, *Human Resource Management: Gaining a Competitive Advantage,* 13th ed. (Chicago: McGraw-Hill, 2023).
37. Noe et al, *Human Resource Management.*
38. D. Lechner, "Pre-Employment Physical Testing: What Skills Are You Looking For?" *Ergo Science,* http://info.ergoscience.com, accessed April 7, 2018.
39. "Screening by Means of Pre-Employment Testing," *Society for Human Resource Management,* www.shrm.org, September 10, 2018.
40. I.L. Goldstein, "Training in Work Organizations," in M.D. Dunnette and L.M. Hough, eds., *Handbook of Industrial and Organizational Psychology,* vol. 2 (Palo Alto, CA: Consulting Psychologists Press, 1991), 507–619.
41. "Disney University," *The Disney Wiki,* https://Disney.fandom.com, accessed January 27, 2023.
42. F. V. Cespedes, T. Aas, A. Hunt, and H. Newton-Hill, "Using Simulations to Upskill Employees," *Harvard Business Review,* https://hbr.org, November 15, 2022.
43. L. Freifeld, "A World-Class Operation," *Training,* March 2022, 20-24, accessed at https://pubs.royle.com; L. Freifeld, "Training Magazine Ranks the Winners of the 2022 Training APEX Awards," *Training,* https://trainingmag.com, March 1, 2022.
44. M. Smith and N. Querolo, "Apprenticeships Make a Comeback," *Bloomberg Businessweek,* August 8, 2022, 30, 32.
45. A. Van Dam, "Suddenly, Way More Women Are Working in Construction; Here's Why," *Washington Post,* www.washingtonpost.com, November 20, 2022; J. Bykowicz, "Labor Shortage Stymies Construction Work as $1 Trillion Infrastructure Spending Kicks In," *The Wall Street Journal,* www.wsj.com, June 20, 2022; T. Swartz, "'College Isn't for Everyone': CPS Grad, Face of Chicago Builds, Forgoing Scholarship Money to Train as a Welder," *Chicago Tribune,* www.chicagotribune.com, June 6, 2022; D. Shingler, "ANR Electric Has Found an Answer to Labor Shortages," *Crain's Cleveland Business,* February 7, 2022, EBSCOhost, https://web.p.ebscohost.com.
46. Smith and Querolo, "Apprenticeships Make a Comeback"; K. Tyler, "Alternative Methods," *HR Magazine,* Summer 2022, 38–44.
47. Van Dam, "Suddenly, Way More Women Are Working"; Swartz, "College Isn't for Everyone."
48. T.D. Allen, L.T. Eby, M.L. Poteet, E. Lentz, and L. Lima, "Career Benefits Associated with Mentoring for Protègès: A Meta-Analysis," *Journal of Applied Psychology* 89, no. 1 (2004), 127–36.
49. "9 Companies with Solid Mentorship Programs," *Monster,* www.monster.com, accessed January 27, 2023.
50. P. Garfinkel, "Putting a Formal Stamp on Mentoring," *The New York Times,* January 18, 2004, BU10.

51. G. Cantalupo, "Does Mentoring Still Matter for Fortune Companies?" *Forbes,* www.forbes.com, May 19, 2022.
52. C. Emrich, M.H. Livingston, D. Pruner, et al., *Creating a Culture of Mentorship,* www.heidrick.com, accessed March 4, 2020.
53. "Executive Education," https://michiganross.umich.edu, accessed March 4, 2020; "Best Online MBA Programs," *U.S. News & World Report,* www.usnews.com, accessed March 4, 2020.
54. G.P. Latham and K.N. Wexley, *Increasing Productivity through Performance Appraisal* (Reading, MA: Addison-Wesley, 1982).
55. T.A. DeCotiis, "An Analysis of the External Validity and Applied Relevance of Three Rating Formats," *Organizational Behavior and Human Performance* 19 (1977), 247–66.
56. G. Gupta, "Are You Still Using Force Rankings? Please Stop," *Forbes,* www.forbes.com, accessed January 28, 2023.
57. S.M. Heathfield, "360 Degree Feedback: See the Good, the Bad and the Ugly," *Balance Careers,* www.thebalancecareers.com, October 17, 2019.
58. C. Borman and D.W. Bracken, "360 Degree Appraisals," in C.L. Cooper and C. Argyris, eds., *The Concise Blackwell Encyclopedia of Management* (Oxford, England: Blackwell, 1998), 17; D.W. Bracken, "Straight Talk about Multi-Rater Feedback," *Training and Development* 48 (1994), 44–51; M.R. Edwards, W.C. Borman, and J.R. Sproul, "Solving the Double Bind in Performance Appraisal: A Saga of Solves, Sloths, and Eagles," *Business Horizons* 85 (1985), 59–68.
59. M. Buckingham, "The Fatal Flaws with 360 Surveys," *Harvard Business Review,* https://hbr.org, accessed January 28, 2023.
60. S.C. Twohill, "Make Performance Reviews Effective Again," *Workforce,* www.workforce.com, January 31, 2017.
61. S.E. Moss and J.I. Sanchez, "Are Your Employees Avoiding You? Managerial Strategies for Closing the Feedback Gap," *Academy of Management Executive* 18, no. 1 (2004), 32–46.
62. B. Wigert and A. Mann, "Give Performance Reviews That Actually Inspire Employees," *Gallup Blog,* http://news.gallup.com, September 25, 2017.
63. A. Sarkar, "Is It Time to Do Away with Annual Performance Appraisal System? Benefits and Challenges Ahead," *Human Resource Management International Digest* 24, no. 3 (2016), 7–10.
64. H.L. Kurter, "It's Time to Reinvent Your Performance Reviews. Here Are the 3 Best Practices," *Forbes,* www.forbes.com, November 27, 2021.
65. K. Doheny, "Annual Performance Review Bows Out," *Society for Human Resource Management,* www.shrm.org, January 12, 2021.
66. T. Koulopoulos, "Performance Reviews Are Dead. Here's What You Should Do Instead," *Inc.,* www.inc.com, February 25, 2018.
67. "The Story of Check-in," www.adobe.com, accessed January 28, 2023; D. Burkus, "How Adobe Scrapped Its Performance Review System and Why It Worked," *Forbes,* www.forbes.com, June 1, 2016.
68. D. Baker, J. Bivens, and J. Schieder, "Reining in CEO Compensation and Curbing the Rise of Inequality," *Economic Policy Institute,* www.epi.org, June 4, 2019.
69. R. DuBoff, "What Is Just When It Comes to CEO-to-Average Worker Pay?" *Forbes,* www.forbes.com, accessed March 4, 2020.
70. J. Bivens and J. Kandra, "CEO Pay Has Skyrocketed 1,460% Since 1978," *Economic Policy Institute,* www.epi.org, October 4, 2022.
71. F.J. Reh, "The Issues and Debates Surrounding CEO Compensation," *The Balance Careers,* www.thebalancecareers.com, December 23, 2018.
72. Cigna, "Employer Mandate," www.cigna.com, accessed January 28, 2023.
73. "Mom-Founded Infant Formula Company, Bobbie, Open-Sources New 12-Month Parental Leave Policy, TakeOurLeave," Bobbie news release, *Yahoo Finance,* https://finance.yahoo.com, April 7, 2022; C. Hall, "Bobbie Drinks Up $50 Million to Expand Infant Formula Product Line," *Tech Crunch,* https://techcrunch.com, March 15, 2022; C. Lagorio-Chafkin, "These Co-founders Nurture an Ideal Workplace for Ambitious Parents," *Inc.,* May/June 2022, 42.
74. Bobbie, "Mom-Founded Infant Formula Company."
75. Lagorio-Chafkin, "These Co-founders Nurture"; A. Donaldson, "How Smart Leaders Make Tough Decisions about Employee Benefits No Matter the Business," *Inc.,* www.inc.com, September 16, 2022.
76. "Bobbie, Mom-Founded Infant Formula Company"; Hall, "Bobbie Drinks Up $50 Million"; Donaldson, "How Smart Leaders Make Tough Decisions."
77. Kaiser Family Foundation, "2022 Employer Health Benefits Survey," www.kff.org, accessed January 28, 2023.
78. "Are Domestic Partner Benefits Mandatory?" www.paycor.com, August 21, 2019.
79. S. Premack and J.E. Hunter, "Individual Unionization Decisions," *Psychological Bulletin* 103 (1988), 223–34.
80. Bureau of Labor Statistics, "Union Members –2022" www.bls.gov, January 23, 2023.
81. AFL-CIO, "Our Unions and Allies," https://aflcio.org, accessed January 28, 2023.
82. Bureau of Labor Statistics, "Union Members–2022."
83. A. Hsu and A. Selyukh, "Union Wins Made Big News This Year. Here Are 5 Reasons Why It's Not the Full Story," *NPR,* www.npr.org, December 27, 2022; J. McCarthy, "U.S. Approval of Labor Unions at Highest Point Since 1965," *Gallup,* www.gallup.com, August 30, 2022; M. Kinder and L. Stateler, "Frontline Workers Were Excluded from Companies' Pandemic Windfalls. No Wonder So Many Are Forming Unions," *Brookings,* www.brookings.edu, May 4, 2022; "The Pandemic Could Be Leading to a Golden Age for Unions," *NPR,* www.npr.org, October 17, 2021.
84. I. Kullgreen and R. Rainey, "Expiring Labor Contracts Across Sectors Threaten Unrest in 2023," *Bloomberg Law,* https://news.bloomberglaw.com, accessed January 28, 2023.

CHAPTER 13

Motivation and Performance

SeventyFour/Shutterstock

Learning Objectives

After studying this chapter, you should be able to:

LO13-1 Explain what motivation is and why managers need to be concerned about it.

LO13-2 Describe from the perspectives of expectancy theory and equity theory what managers should do to have a highly motivated workforce.

LO13-3 Explain how goals and needs motivate people and what kinds of goals are especially likely to result in high performance.

LO13-4 Identify the motivation lessons that managers can learn from operant conditioning theory and social learning theory.

LO13-5 Explain why and how managers can use pay as a major motivation tool.

A MANAGER'S CHALLENGE

Chieh Huang Makes Working for Boxed More than Just a Job

Which ways of managing employees will motivate them best? After selling the first company he founded—Astro Ape, a creator of games for mobile devices—Chieh Huang wanted to try his hand at starting another kind of business. Looking for an unmet need, he realized that the low-cost advantage of buying goods in bulk at warehouse clubs like Sam's Club and Costco was unavailable to many people because they lived too far from an outlet or couldn't afford the membership fee. He applied his tech knowledge to developing a way to order bulk items like toilet paper and snacks on a mobile phone and have them delivered at an attractive price.[1]

Huang called his company Boxed and defined its mission as making shopping in bulk "easy, convenient and fun." Soon after its launch, the company landed a profile on the *Today* show, and orders began flowing in. Boxed has grown profitably through careful logistical planning, limiting inventory to the most popular products, and adding personal touches such as a handwritten note in each box. As the company scaled up, Huang pursued an additional opportunity: selling his software to other retailers seeking a presence on mobile devices. The company now has 500 employees, and in December 2021, it went public, valued at $900 million.[2]

For Huang, running a business is about much more than generating profits. He also prioritizes the treatment of Boxed's employees, saying, "What drives me personally is to show a future generation that you can be kind to the folks in your company and still do well."[3] This is immediately evident at the company's headquarters, where everyone, warehouse workers and executives alike, uses the same entrance, rest rooms, and break room. Huang's hiring practices include asking questions designed to screen out managerial candidates who might be inclined to look down on their workers.[4]

Kindness to employees at Boxed goes beyond treating all with dignity to recognizing that warehouse jobs pay at a level that meets industry norms but is insufficient for covering more than day-to-day needs. Huang can relate to the situation, having seen the hard work and tight budgets of his parents, who are immigrants from Taiwan. When he noticed that not all employees could get to company events because they lacked access to transportation, he considered how he could make their lives easier. His solutions include offering employees a $500 emergency fund, subsidies for life events such as weddings, and tuition benefits for their children. Huang also makes a point of

For Boxed CEO Chieh Huang, running a business is about much more than profits. Treating employees well helps the company thrive in the highly competitive e-commerce space.
Rick Kern/Getty Images Entertainment/Getty Images

visiting warehouses every week to stay in touch with employees there.[5]

Other employee benefits make total compensation generous for an e-commerce business. Employees receive health insurance, not always an option in low-wage occupations, as well as at-work amenities such as free food. Huang says the payoff for Boxed comes in the form of employee commitment and loyalty, with lower turnover among employees than is typical for his industry. This reduces the cost of constantly training new people.[6]

Huang's approach to creating a positive work climate is not always easy; e-commerce is under intense pressure to keep costs down. Huang recognizes that automation can make operations more efficient at the cost of some jobs. Boxed prioritizes creating new opportunities where possible, and key managers have worked their way up from warehouse positions. Huang says he considers Boxed a success if other companies follow its lead in treating employees well—and maybe they will. Target and Walmart each recently announced the addition of tuition reimbursement benefits for their employees.[7]

Overview

Even with the best strategy in place and an appropriate organizational architecture, an organization will be effective only if its members are motivated to perform at a high level. Chieh Huang, founder of Boxed, clearly realizes this. One reason that leading is such an important managerial activity is that it entails ensuring that each member of an organization is motivated to perform highly and help the organization achieve its goals. When managers are effective, the outcome of the leading process is a highly motivated workforce. A key challenge for managers of organizations both large and small is to encourage employees to perform at a high level.

In this chapter, we describe what motivation is, where it comes from, and why managers need to promote high levels of it for an organization to be effective and achieve its goals. We examine important theories of motivation: expectancy theory, need theories, equity theory, goal-setting theory, and learning theories. Each gives managers important insights into how to motivate organizational members. The theories are complementary in that each focuses on a different aspect of motivation. Considering all the theories together helps managers gain a rich understanding of the many issues and problems involved in encouraging high levels of motivation throughout an organization. Last, we consider the use of pay as a motivation tool. By the end of this chapter, you will understand what it takes to have a highly motivated workforce.

The Nature of Motivation

LO13-1 Explain what motivation is and why managers need to be concerned about it.

motivation Psychological forces that determine the direction of a person's behavior in an organization, a person's level of effort, and a person's level of persistence.

Motivation may be defined as psychological forces that determine the direction of a person's behavior in an organization, a person's level of effort, and a person's level of persistence in the face of obstacles.[8] The *direction of a person's behavior* refers to the many possible behaviors a person can engage in. For example, Boxed needs warehouse workers who will quickly but safely collect the correct products and pack them carefully to avoid damage during delivery. It wants to avoid behaviors going in other directions, such as horseplay or getting into arguments with coworkers. *Effort* refers to how hard people work. Warehouse work is physically demanding, and Boxed needs workers willing to put forth the necessary effort. *Persistence* refers to whether, when faced with roadblocks or other obstacles, people keep trying or give up. One of the major challenges recently facing e-commerce companies like Boxed is supply chain disruptions. When delivery of an item customers want does not come through, persistent workers will keep looking for another source or a similar product.

Motivation is central to management because it explains *why* people behave the way they do in organizations.[9] Motivation also explains why a waiter is polite or rude and why a kindergarten teacher really tries to get children to enjoy learning or just goes through the motions. It explains why some managers truly put their organizations' best interests first, whereas others are more concerned with maximizing their salaries and why—more generally—some workers put forth twice as much effort as others.

intrinsically motivated behavior Behavior that is performed for its own sake.

Motivation can come from either *intrinsic* or *extrinsic* sources. **Intrinsically motivated behavior** is behavior that is performed for its own sake; the source of motivation is actually performing the behavior, and motivation comes from doing the work itself. Many managers are intrinsically motivated; they derive a sense of accomplishment and achievement from helping the organization achieve its goals and gain competitive advantages. Jobs that are interesting and challenging or high on the five characteristics described by the job characteristics model (see Chapter 10) are more likely to lead to intrinsic motivation than are jobs that are boring or do not use a person's skills and abilities. An elementary school teacher who really enjoys teaching children, a software engineer who loves solving programming problems, and a commercial photographer who relishes taking creative photographs are all intrinsically motivated. For these people, motivation comes from performing their jobs—teaching children, finding bugs in computer programs, and taking pictures.

extrinsically motivated behavior Behavior that is performed to acquire material or social rewards or to avoid punishment.

Extrinsically motivated behavior is behavior that is performed to acquire material or social rewards or to avoid punishment; the source of motivation is the consequences of the behavior, not the behavior itself. A car salesperson who is motivated by receiving a commission on all cars sold, a lawyer who is motivated by the high salary and status that go along with the job, and a factory worker who is motivated by the opportunity to earn a secure income are all extrinsically motivated. Their motivation comes from the consequences they receive as a result of their work behaviors.

People can be intrinsically motivated, extrinsically motivated, or both intrinsically and extrinsically motivated.[10] A top manager who derives a sense of accomplishment and achievement from managing a large corporation and strives to reach year-end targets to obtain a hefty bonus is both intrinsically and extrinsically motivated. Similarly, a nurse who enjoys helping and taking care of clients and is motivated by having a secure job with good benefits is both intrinsically and extrinsically motivated.

Whether workers are intrinsically motivated, extrinsically motivated, or both depends on a wide variety of factors: (1) workers' own personal characteristics (such as their personalities, abilities, values, attitudes, and needs), (2) the nature of their jobs (such as whether they have been enriched or where they are on the five core characteristics of the job characteristics model), and (3) the nature of the organization (such as its structure, its culture, its control systems, its human resource management system, and the ways in which rewards such as pay are distributed to employees).

prosocially motivated behavior Behavior that is performed to benefit or help others.

In addition to being intrinsically or extrinsically motivated, some people are prosocially motivated by their work.[11] **Prosocially motivated behavior** is behavior that is performed to benefit or help others.[12] Behavior can be prosocially motivated in addition to being extrinsically and/or intrinsically motivated. An elementary school teacher who not only enjoys the process of teaching young children (has high intrinsic motivation) but also has a strong desire to give children the best learning experience possible and help those with learning disabilities overcome their challenges, and who keeps up with the latest research on child development and teaching methods in an effort to continually improve the effectiveness of their teaching, has high prosocial motivation in addition to high intrinsic motivation. A surgeon who specializes in organ transplants, enjoys the challenge of performing complex operations, has a strong desire to help patients regain their health and extend their lives through successful organ transplants, and is motivated by the relatively high income they earn has high intrinsic, prosocial, and extrinsic motivation. Recent preliminary research suggests that when workers have high prosocial motivation, also having high intrinsic motivation can be especially beneficial for job performance.[13]

outcome Anything a person gets from a job or an organization.

Regardless of whether people are intrinsically, extrinsically, or prosocially motivated, they join and are motivated to work in organizations to obtain certain outcomes. An **outcome** is anything a person gets from a job or an organization. Some outcomes, such as autonomy, responsibility, a feeling of accomplishment, and the pleasure of doing interesting or enjoyable work, result in intrinsically motivated behavior. Outcomes such as improving the lives or

Where are you more likely to find prosocial motivation? Here in the classroom as a teacher walks her student through that tricky math problem. Getting companies to foster this type of motivation is a bit trickier!
Blend Images - LWA/Dann Tardif/Getty Images

well-being of other people and doing good by helping others result in prosocially motivated behavior. Other outcomes, such as pay, job security, benefits, and vacation time, result in extrinsically motivated behavior.

Organizations hire people to obtain important inputs. An **input** is anything a person contributes to the job or organization, such as time, effort, education, experience, skills, knowledge, and actual work behaviors. Inputs such as these are necessary for an organization to achieve its goals. Managers strive to motivate members of an organization to contribute inputs—through their behavior, effort, and persistence—that help the organization achieve its goals. How do managers do this? They ensure that members of an organization obtain the outcomes they desire when they make valuable contributions to the organization. Managers use outcomes to motivate people to contribute their inputs to the organization. Giving people outcomes when they contribute inputs and perform well aligns the interests of employees with the goals of the organization as a whole because when employees do what is good for the organization, they personally benefit.

input Anything a person contributes to his or her job or organization.

This alignment between employees and organizational goals as a whole can be described by the motivation equation depicted in Figure 13.1. Managers seek to ensure that people are motivated to contribute important inputs to the organization, that these inputs are put to good use or focused in the direction of high performance, and that high performance results in workers' obtaining the outcomes they desire.

Each of the theories of motivation discussed in this chapter focuses on one or more aspects of this equation. Each theory focuses on a different set of issues that managers need to address to have a highly motivated workforce. Together the theories provide a comprehensive set of guidelines for managers to follow to promote high levels of employee motivation. Effective managers tend to follow many of these guidelines, whereas ineffective managers often fail to follow them and seem to have trouble motivating organizational members.

Figure 13.1

The Motivation Equation

INPUTS FROM ORGANIZATIONAL MEMBERS	PERFORMANCE CONTRIBUTES TO	OUTCOMES RECEIVED BY ORGANIZATIONAL MEMBERS
Time Effort Education Experience Skills Knowledge Work behaviors	Organizational efficiency Organizational effectiveness Attainment of organizational goals	Pay Job security Benefits Vacation time Job satisfaction Autonomy Responsibility A feeling of accomplishment The pleasure of doing interesting work Improving the lives or well-being of others

Expectancy Theory

LO13-2 Describe from the perspectives of expectancy theory and equity theory what managers should do to have a highly motivated workforce.

Expectancy theory, formulated by Victor H. Vroom in the 1960s, posits that motivation is high when workers believe high levels of effort lead to high performance and high performance leads to the attainment of desired outcomes. Expectancy theory is one of the most popular theories of work motivation because it focuses on all three parts of the motivation equation: inputs, performance, and outcomes. Expectancy theory identifies three major factors that determine a person's motivation: *expectancy, instrumentality,* and *valence* (see Figure 13.2).[14]

expectancy theory The theory that motivation will be high when workers believe that high levels of effort lead to high performance and high performance leads to the attainment of desired outcomes.

expectancy In expectancy theory, a perception about the extent to which effort results in a certain level of performance.

Expectancy

Expectancy is a person's perception about the extent to which effort (an input) results in a certain level of performance. A person's level of expectancy determines whether they believe that a high level of effort results in a high level of performance. People are motivated to put forth a lot of effort on their jobs only if they think that their effort will pay off in high performance—that is, if they have high expectancy. Think about how motivated you would be to study for a test if you thought that no matter how hard you tried, you would get a D. Think about how motivated a marketing manager would be who thought that no matter how hard they worked, there was no way to increase sales of an unpopular product. In these cases, expectancy is low, so overall motivation is also low.

Members of an organization are motivated to put forth a high level of effort only if they think that doing so leads to high performance.[15] In other words, in order for people's motivation to be high, expectancy must be high. Thus, in attempting to influence motivation, managers need to make sure their employees believe that if they do try hard, they can actually succeed. One way managers can boost expectancies is through expressing confidence in their employees' capabilities. Managers at The Container Store, for example, express high levels of confidence in their employees. As Container Store cofounder Garrett Boone put it, "Everybody we hire, we hire as a leader. Anybody in our store can take an action that you might think of typically being a manager's action."[16]

In addition to expressing confidence in employees, other ways for managers to boost employees' expectancy levels and motivation are by providing training so people have the expertise needed for high performance and increasing their levels of autonomy and responsibility as they gain experience so they have the freedom to do what it takes to perform at a high level.

Figure 13.2

Expectancy, Instrumentality, and Valence

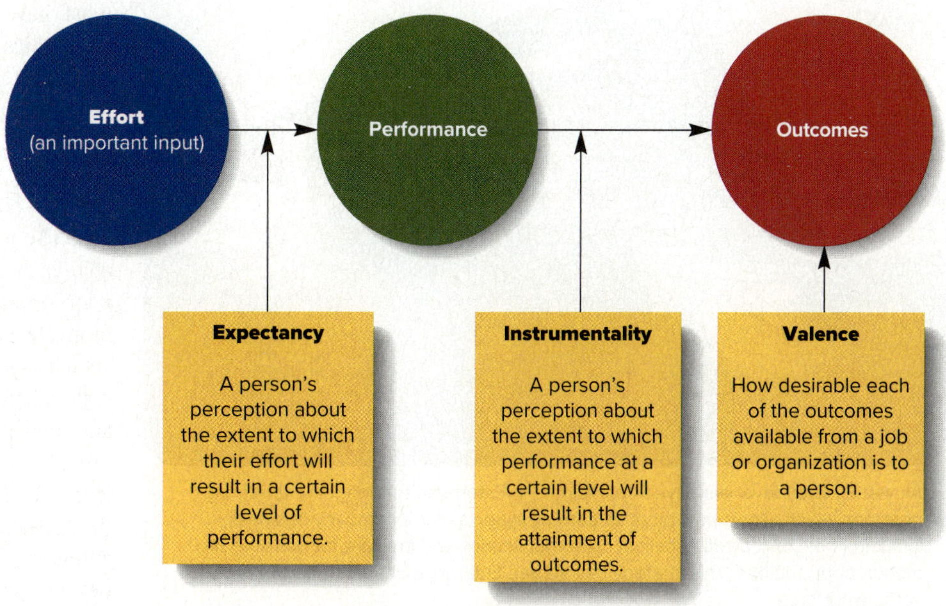

This strategy became critical during the recent era of "the great resignation," in which millions of U.S. employees in various industries quit their jobs in search of more meaningful and lucrative work during the COVID-19 pandemic.[17] Many organizations continue to struggle when it comes to retaining their top employees in a highly competitive labor market. According to Richard Branson, founder of the Virgin Group, companies must continue to invest in employee development and training and provide workers with a collaborative environment in which they can utilize their skills. Branson advises, "Train people well enough so they can leave and treat them well enough so they don't want to."[18]

Instrumentality

instrumentality In expectancy theory, a perception about the extent to which performance results in the attainment of outcomes.

Expectancy captures a person's perceptions about the relationship between effort and performance. **Instrumentality**, the second major concept in expectancy theory, is a person's perception about the extent to which performance at a certain level results in the attainment of outcomes (see Figure 13.2). According to expectancy theory, employees are motivated to perform at a high level only if they think high performance will lead to (or is *instrumental* in attaining) outcomes such as pay, job security, interesting job assignments, bonuses, or a feeling of accomplishment. In other words, instrumentalities must be high for motivation to be high—people must perceive that because of their high performance they will receive outcomes.[19]

Managers promote high levels of instrumentality when they link performance to desired outcomes. In addition, managers must clearly communicate this linkage to employees. By making sure that outcomes available in an organization are distributed to organizational members on the basis of their performance, managers promote high instrumentality and motivation. When outcomes are linked to performance in this way, high performers receive more outcomes than low performers.

Another example of high instrumentality contributing to high motivation can be found in the Cambodian immigrants who own, manage, and work in more than 80% of the doughnut shops in the Los Angeles area of California.[20] These immigrants see high performance as leading to many important outcomes such as income, a comfortable existence, family security, and the autonomy provided by working in a small business. Their high instrumentality contributes to their high motivation to succeed.

valence In expectancy theory, how desirable each of the outcomes available from a job or an organization is to a person.

Almost all entry-level employees participate in Enterprise's management training program, which allows new hires to learn all aspects of the company business, including how to provide excellent customer service and prepare for possible promotion opportunities. This strategy has helped Enterprise develop a highly motivated workforce.
Carlos Osorio/AP Images

Valence

Although all members of an organization must have high expectancies and instrumentalities, expectancy theory acknowledges that people differ in their preferences for outcomes. For many people, pay is the most important outcome of working. For others, a feeling of accomplishment or enjoying one's work is more important than pay. The term **valence** refers to how desirable each of the outcomes available from a job or an organization is to a person. To motivate organizational members, managers need to determine which outcomes have high valence for them—are highly desired—and make sure that those outcomes are provided when members perform at a high level. For example, at Enterprise Holdings, the largest car rental company in the world, autonomy, responsibility, and opportunities for promotion are highly valent outcomes for many employees. The company's

Figure 13.3
Expectancy Theory

management training program is touted not only for promoting a strong "promote-from-within" culture but also for developing new hires into the next generation of business leaders. According to Enterprise, the company has consistently been recognized as one of the largest recruiters of college graduates in the United States. On average, Enterprise hires more than 8,000 entry-level employees on an annual basis, along with more than 1,500 interns.[21]

Bringing It All Together

According to expectancy theory, high motivation results from high levels of expectancy, instrumentality, and valence (see Figure 13.3). If any one of these factors is low, motivation is likely to be low. No matter how tightly desired outcomes are linked to performance, if a person thinks it is practically impossible to perform at a high level, motivation to perform at a high level will be low. Similarly, if a person does not think outcomes are linked to high performance, or if a person does not want the outcomes that are linked to high performance, motivation to perform at a high level will be low. Effective managers realize the importance of high levels of expectancy, instrumentality, and valence and take concrete steps to ensure that their employees are highly motivated.

need A requirement or necessity for survival and well-being.

Need Theories

LO13-3 Explain how goals and needs motivate people and what kinds of goals are especially likely to result in high performance.

A **need** is a requirement or necessity for survival and well-being. The basic premise of **need theories** is that people are motivated to obtain outcomes at work that will satisfy their needs. Need theory complements expectancy theory by exploring in depth which outcomes motivate people to perform at a high level. Need theories suggest that to motivate a person to contribute valuable inputs to a job and perform at a high level, a manager must determine what needs the person is trying to satisfy at work and ensure that the person receives outcomes that help satisfy those needs when the person performs at a high level and helps the organization achieve its goals. As you read about the needs theories described in this chapter, consider how they relate to the needs described in the "Managing Globally" feature.

need theories Theories of motivation that focus on what needs people are trying to satisfy at work and what outcomes will satisfy those needs.

There are several need theories. Here we discuss Abraham Maslow's hierarchy of needs, Clayton Alderfer's ERG theory, Frederick Herzberg's motivator-hygiene theory, and David McClelland's needs for achievement, affiliation, and power. These theories describe needs that people try to satisfy at work. In doing so, they give managers insights into what outcomes motivate members of an organization to perform at a high level and contribute inputs to help the organization achieve its goals.

MANAGING GLOBALLY

Needs Vary—Sometimes—from Country to Country

While earning money is an obvious reason to work, other needs are important too. These may vary by country. Consultant Jeremy Pollack, who studies human needs, finds that the world's cultures vary in terms of employees seeking work that is stimulating, offers flexibility, and enables them to live out a deeper purpose.[22]

In a survey by the HR consulting firm Mercer, employees, managers, and top executives in 14 countries, Hong Kong, and the Middle East indicated what helps employees thrive. Employees in the United States said they need the ability to manage their work-life balance, followed by recognition for contributions. Those in Canada, Australia, and Singapore agreed, although work-life balance was ranked second in Canada. In contrast, employees in Germany most often cited working on meaningful projects, and in Italy, meaningful projects tied with work-life balance for first place. A fun work environment was a top-three need in four countries; it ranked first in France, second in Germany, and third in China and the United Kingdom.[23]

In the Mercer study, the need to balance work and personal life varied. For example, it was the top need in the United States but number three in France and Germany. One reason may involve how employees satisfy the need. Some countries require paid time off for vacations and for family and medical needs. Furthermore, employees may differ in what gives them work-life balance. Santander, a bank operating in 31 countries, analyzed work-life challenges. It found that most employees need workplace flexibility, but unmet needs—particularly for adjusted work schedules, reduced hours, and reduced business travel—were likelier in some countries.[24]

Other evidence for common needs across locations comes from the Mercer study. Work-life balance was a top-three contributor to thriving in every geographic segment except Brazil and Japan. Also, researchers from Harvard and the Boston Consulting Group found commonalities among employees. They surveyed employees in 11 countries and interviewed executives in eight countries about the changing work environment. Employees consistently said changes in technology and ways of working (such as gig work) will affect them. They were hopeful but saw a need to protect their job security, which employers could meet by enabling them to prepare for the workplace of the future. The executives in the study were largely unaware of employees' desire for learning. However, a few companies have initiatives to develop employees' skills and maintain data on how to meet future needs with their existing workforce.[25]

Maslow's Hierarchy of Needs

Maslow's hierarchy of needs An arrangement of five basic needs that, according to Maslow, motivate behavior. Maslow proposed that the lowest level of unmet needs is the prime motivator and that only one level of needs is motivational at a time.

Psychologist Abraham Maslow proposed that all people seek to satisfy five basic kinds of needs: physiological needs, safety needs, belongingness needs, esteem needs, and self-actualization needs (see Table 13.1).[26] He suggested that these needs constitute a **hierarchy of needs**, with the most basic or compelling needs—physiological and safety needs—at the bottom. Maslow argued that these lowest-level needs must be met before a person strives to satisfy needs higher up in the hierarchy, such as self-esteem needs. Once a need is satisfied, Maslow proposed, it ceases to operate as a source of motivation. The lowest level of *unmet* needs in the hierarchy is the prime motivator of behavior; if and when this level is satisfied, needs at the next highest level in the hierarchy motivate behavior.

Although this theory identifies needs that are likely to be important sources of motivation for many people, research does not support Maslow's contention that there is a need hierarchy or his notion that only one level of needs is motivational at a time.[27] Nevertheless, a key

Table 13.1
Maslow's Hierarchy of Needs

	Needs	Description	Examples of How Managers Can Help People Satisfy These Needs at Work
Highest-Level Needs ↑	**Self-actualization needs**	The needs to realize one's full potential as a human being.	Giving people the opportunity to use their skills and abilities to the fullest extent possible.
	Esteem needs	The needs to feel good about oneself and one's capabilities, to be respected by others, and to receive recognition and appreciation.	Granting promotions and recognizing accomplishments.
	Belongingness needs	Needs for social interaction, friendship, affection, and love.	Promoting good interpersonal relations and organizing social events such as company picnics and holiday parties.
	Safety needs	Needs for security, stability, and a safe environment.	Providing job security, adequate health care benefits, and safe working conditions.
↓ Lowest-Level Needs (Most Basic or Compelling)	**Physiological needs**	Basic needs for things such as food, water, and shelter that must be met in order for a person to survive.	Providing a level of pay that enables a person to buy food and clothing and have adequate housing.

The lowest level of unsatisfied needs motivates behavior; once this level of needs is satisfied, a person tries to satisfy the needs at the next level.

conclusion can be drawn from Maslow's theory: People try to satisfy different needs at work. To have a motivated workforce, managers must determine which needs employees are trying to satisfy in organizations and then make sure that individuals receive outcomes that satisfy their needs when they perform at a high level and contribute to organizational effectiveness. By doing this, managers align the interests of individual members with the interests of the organization as a whole. By doing what is good for the organization (that is, performing at a high level), employees receive outcomes that satisfy their needs.

In our increasingly global economy, managers must realize that citizens of different countries might differ in the needs they seek to satisfy through work.[28] Some research suggests, for example, that people in Greece and Japan are especially motivated by safety needs and that people in Sweden, Norway, and Denmark are motivated by belongingness needs.[29] In less developed countries, physiological and safety needs are likely to be the prime motivators of behavior. As countries become wealthier and have higher standards of living, needs related to personal growth and accomplishment (such as esteem and self-actualization) become important motivators of behavior.

Alderfer's ERG theory The theory that three universal needs—for existence, relatedness, and growth—constitute a hierarchy of needs and motivate behavior. Alderfer proposed that needs at more than one level can be motivational at the same time.

Alderfer's ERG Theory

Clayton **Alderfer's ERG theory** collapsed the five categories of needs in Maslow's hierarchy into three universal categories–existence, relatedness, and growth–also arranged in a hierarchy (see Table 13.2). Alderfer agreed with Maslow that as lower-level needs become satisfied, a person seeks to satisfy higher-level needs. Unlike Maslow, however, Alderfer believed that a person can be motivated by needs at more than one level at the same time. A cashier in a supermarket, for example, may be motivated by both existence needs and relatedness needs. The existence needs motivate the cashier to go to work regularly and not make mistakes so their job

Table 13.2
Alderfer's ERG Theory

	Needs	Description	Examples of How Managers Can Help People Satisfy These Needs at Work
Highest-Level Needs ↑	**Growth needs**	The needs for self-development and creative and productive work.	Allowing people to continually improve their skills and abilities and engage in meaningful work.
	Relatedness needs	The needs to have good interpersonal relations, to share thoughts and feelings, and to have open two-way communication.	Promoting good interpersonal relations and providing accurate feedback.
↓ **Lowest-Level Needs**	**Existence needs**	Basic needs for food, water, clothing, shelter, and a secure and safe environment.	Providing enough pay for the basic necessities of life and safe working conditions.

As lower-level needs are satisfied, a person is motivated to satisfy higher-level needs. When a person cannot satisfy higher-level needs (or is frustrated), motivation to satisfy lower-level needs increases.

will be secure and they will be able to pay rent and buy food. The relatedness needs motivate the cashier to become friends with some of the other cashiers and have a good relationship with the store manager. Alderfer also suggested that when people experience *need frustration* or are unable to satisfy needs at a certain level, they will focus more intently on satisfying the needs at the next lower level in the hierarchy.[30]

As with Maslow's theory, research does not support some of the specific ideas outlined in ERG theory, such as the existence of the three-level need hierarchy that Alderfer proposed.[31] However, for managers, the important message from ERG theory is the same as that from Maslow's theory: Determine what needs your employees are trying to satisfy at work, and make sure they receive outcomes that satisfy these needs when they perform at a high level to help the organization achieve its goals.

Herzberg's Motivator-Hygiene Theory

Herzberg's motivator-hygiene theory A need theory that distinguishes between motivator needs (related to the nature of the work itself) and hygiene needs (related to the physical and psychological context in which the work is performed) and proposes that motivator needs must be met for motivation and job satisfaction to be high.

Adopting an approach different from Maslow's and Alderfer's, Frederick Herzberg focused on two factors: (1) outcomes that can lead to high levels of motivation and job satisfaction and (2) outcomes that can prevent people from being dissatisfied. According to **Herzberg's motivator-hygiene theory**, people have two sets of needs or requirements: motivator needs and hygiene needs.[32] *Motivator needs* are related to the nature of the work itself and how challenging it is. Outcomes such as interesting work, autonomy, responsibility, the ability to grow and develop on the job, and a sense of accomplishment and achievement help to satisfy motivator needs. To have a highly motivated and satisfied workforce, Herzberg suggested, managers should take steps to ensure that employees' motivator needs are being met.

Hygiene needs are related to the physical and psychological context in which the work is performed. Hygiene needs are satisfied by outcomes such as pleasant and comfortable working conditions, pay, job security, good relationships with coworkers, and effective supervision. According to Herzberg, when hygiene needs are not met, workers are dissatisfied, and when hygiene needs are met, workers are not dissatisfied. Satisfying hygiene needs, however, does not result in high levels of motivation or even high levels of job satisfaction. For motivation and job satisfaction to be high, motivator needs must be met. Many research studies have tested Herzberg's propositions, and, by and large, the theory fails to receive support.[33] Nevertheless, Herzberg's formulations have contributed to our understanding of motivation in at least two ways. First, Herzberg helped to focus researchers' and managers' attention on the important distinction between intrinsic motivation (related to motivator needs) and extrinsic motivation (related to hygiene needs), covered earlier in the chapter. Second, his theory prompted researchers and managers to study how jobs could be designed or redesigned to be intrinsically motivating.

McClelland's Needs for Achievement, Affiliation, and Power

need for achievement The extent to which an individual has a strong desire to perform challenging tasks well and to meet personal standards for excellence.

need for affiliation The extent to which an individual is concerned about establishing and maintaining good interpersonal relations, being liked, and having other people get along.

need for power The extent to which an individual desires to control or influence others.

Psychologist David McClelland extensively researched the needs for achievement, affiliation, and power.[34] The **need for achievement** is the extent to which a person has a strong desire to perform challenging tasks well and to meet personal standards for excellence. People with a high need for achievement often set clear goals for themselves and like to receive performance feedback. The **need for affiliation** is the extent to which a person is concerned about establishing and maintaining good interpersonal relations, being liked, and having the people around them get along with each other. The **need for power** is the extent to which one wants to control or influence others.[35]

Although each of these needs is present in each of us to some degree, their importance in the workplace depends on the position one occupies. For example, research suggests that high needs for achievement and for power are assets for first-line and middle managers and that a high need for power is especially important for upper managers.[36] One study found that U.S. presidents with a relatively high need for power tended to be especially effective during their terms of office.[37] A high need for affiliation may not always be desirable in managers and other leaders because it might lead them to try too hard to be liked by others (including their employees) rather than doing all they can to ensure that performance is as high as it can and should be. Although most research on these needs has been done in the United States, some studies suggest that the findings may be applicable to people in other countries as well, such as India and New Zealand.[38]

Other Needs

Clearly, more needs motivate workers than the needs described by these four theories. For example, more and more workers are feeling the need for work-life balance and time to take care of their loved ones while being highly motivated at work. This need was particularly difficult to meet during the global pandemic, when most companies sent their employees home to work remotely and many people struggled with trying to do their jobs while taking care of children and other family members who were also at home.[39] Interestingly enough, recent research suggests that being exposed to nature (even just being able to see some trees from a window) has many valuable effects, and a lack of such exposure can impair well-being and performance.[40] Thus, having some time during the day when one can at least see nature may be another important need.

Equity Theory

LO13-2 Describe from the perspectives of expectancy theory and equity theory what managers should do to have a highly motivated workforce.

equity theory A theory of motivation that focuses on people's perceptions of the fairness of their work outcomes relative to their work inputs.

equity The justice, impartiality, and fairness to which all organizational members are entitled.

Equity theory is a theory of motivation that concentrates on people's perceptions of the fairness of their work *outcomes* relative to, or in proportion to, their work *inputs*. Equity theory complements expectancy and need theories by focusing on how people perceive the relationship between the outcomes they receive from their jobs and organizations and the inputs they contribute. Equity theory was formulated in the 1960s by J. Stacy Adams, who stressed that what is important in determining motivation is the *relative* rather than the *absolute* levels of outcomes a person receives and inputs a person contributes. Specifically, motivation is influenced by the comparison of one's own outcome-input ratio with the outcome-input ratio of a referent.[41] The *referent* might be another person or a group of people who are perceived to be similar to oneself; the referent also might be oneself in a previous job or one's expectations about what outcome-input ratios should be. In a comparison of one's own outcome-input ratio to a referent's ratio, one's *perceptions* of outcomes and inputs (not any objective indicator of them) are key.

Equity

Equity exists when a person perceives their own outcome-input ratio to be equal to a referent's outcome-input ratio. Under conditions of equity (see Table 13.3), if a referent receives more outcomes than you receive, the referent contributes proportionally more inputs to the

Table 13.3
Equity Theory

Condition	Person		Referent	Example
Equity	$\frac{\text{Outcomes}}{\text{Inputs}}$	=	$\frac{\text{Outcomes}}{\text{Inputs}}$	An engineer perceives that they contribute more inputs (time and effort) and receive proportionally more outcomes (a higher salary and choice job assignments) than their referent.
Underpayment inequity	$\frac{\text{Outcomes}}{\text{Inputs}}$	< (less than)	$\frac{\text{Outcomes}}{\text{Inputs}}$	An engineer perceives that they contribute more inputs but receive the same outcomes as their referent.
Overpayment inequity	$\frac{\text{Outcomes}}{\text{Inputs}}$	> (greater than)	$\frac{\text{Outcomes}}{\text{Inputs}}$	An engineer perceives that they contribute the same inputs but receive more outcomes than their referent.

organization, so their outcome–input ratio still equals your ratio. Consider, for example, two employees who work in a local hardware store. Employee A is paid more per hour than employee B but also contributes more inputs, including being responsible for some of the store's bookkeeping, opening or closing the store, and periodically depositing the store's cash receipts in the bank. When employee B compares their outcome–input ratio to employee A's ratio (employee B's referent), they perceive the ratios to be equitable because employee A's higher level of pay (an outcome) is proportional to their higher level of inputs (bookkeeping, opening/closing the store, and going to the bank).

Similarly, under conditions of equity, if you receive more outcomes than a referent, your inputs are perceived to be proportionally higher. Continuing with our example, when employee A compares their outcome–input ratio to employee B's ratio (employee A's referent), employee A perceives the two employees to be equitable because employee A's higher level of pay is proportional to their higher level of inputs. When equity exists, people are motivated to continue contributing their current level of inputs to their organizations to receive their current levels of outcomes. If people wish to increase their outcomes under conditions of equity, they are motivated to increase their inputs.

Inequity

inequity Lack of fairness.

Inequity, or lack of fairness, exists when a person's outcome–input ratio is not perceived to be equal to a referent's. Inequity creates pressure or tension inside people and motivates them to restore equity by bringing the two ratios back into balance.

underpayment inequity The inequity that exists when a person perceives that their own outcome–input ratio is less than the ratio of a referent.

overpayment inequity The inequity that exists when a person perceives that their own outcome–input ratio is greater than the ratio of a referent.

There are two types of inequity: underpayment inequity and overpayment inequity (see Table 13.3). **Underpayment inequity** exists when a person's own outcome–input ratio is perceived to be *less* than that of a referent. In comparing yourself to a referent, you think you are *not* receiving the outcomes you should be, given your inputs. **Overpayment inequity** exists when a person perceives that their own outcome–input ratio is *greater* than that of a referent. In comparing yourself to a referent, you think you are receiving *more* outcomes than you should be, given your inputs.

Ways to Restore Equity

According to equity theory, both underpayment inequity and overpayment inequity create tension that motivates most people to restore equity by bringing the ratios back into balance.[42] When people experience *underpayment* inequity, they may be motivated to lower their inputs by reducing their working hours, putting forth less effort on the job, or being absent; or they may be motivated to increase their outcomes by asking for a raise or a promotion. For example, a financial analyst at a large company noticed they were working longer hours and getting more work accomplished than a colleague who had the same position, yet they both received exactly the same pay and other outcomes. To restore equity, the financial analyst decided to stop going in early and staying late. An alternative approach to restoring equity would have been for the financial analyst to increase their outcomes—perhaps by asking the manager of the financial department for a raise.

When people experience underpayment inequity and other means of equity restoration fail, they can change their perceptions of their own or the referent's inputs or outcomes. For example, they may realize that their referent is really working on more difficult projects than they are or that they really take more time off from work than their referent does. Alternatively, if people who feel they are underpaid have other employment options, they may leave the organization. For example, an assistant principal in a high school experienced underpayment inequity when they realized all other high school assistant principals in the school district had received promotions to the position of principal even though they had been in their jobs for a shorter period of time. The assistant principal in question had always been evaluated as doing an excellent job, so after repeated requests for a promotion went unheeded, they found a job as a principal in a different school district.

When people experience *overpayment* inequity, they may try to restore equity by changing their perceptions of their own or their referent's inputs or outcomes. Equity can be restored when people realize they are contributing more inputs than they originally thought. Equity also can be restored by perceiving the referent's inputs to be lower or the referent's outcomes to be higher than one originally thought. When equity is restored in this way, actual inputs and outcomes are unchanged, and the person being overpaid takes no real action. What is changed is how people think about or view their or the referent's inputs and outcomes. For instance, an employee in a health food store experienced overpayment inequity when they realized they were being paid $2 an hour more than a coworker who had the same job. The employee restored equity by changing their perception of their own inputs, realizing they took on added responsibilities when asked and were the go-to employee on the floor when problems came up in the store or customers needed additional help.

Experiencing either overpayment or underpayment inequity, you might decide that your referent is not appropriate because, for example, the referent is too different from yourself. Choosing a more appropriate referent may bring the ratios back into balance. For example, a middle manager in the engineering department of a chemical company experienced overpayment inequity when they realized they were being paid quite a bit more than a friend who was a middle manager in the marketing department of the same company. After thinking about the discrepancy for a while, the middle manager decided that engineering and marketing were so different that they should not be comparing their jobs to each other even though they were both middle managers. The manager restored equity by changing the referent, choosing as a new referent another middle manager in the engineering department.

Motivation is highest when as many people as possible in an organization perceive that they are being equitably treated—their outcomes and inputs are in balance. Top contributors and performers are motivated to continue contributing a high level of inputs because they are receiving the outcomes they deserve. Mediocre contributors and performers realize that if they want to increase their outcomes, they have to increase their inputs. Managers of effective organizations realize the importance of equity for motivation and performance and continually strive to ensure that employees believe they are being equitably treated.

Over the past 20 years, the tech boom, its subsequent bust, and two recessions and a worldwide pandemic, along with increased global competition, have resulted in some workers putting in longer and longer working hours (increasing their inputs) without any increase in their outcomes. For those whose referents are not experiencing a similar change, perceptions of inequity are likely. According to Jill Andresky Fraser, author of *White Collar Sweatshop,* more than 25 million U.S. workers work more than 49 hours per week, almost 11 million work more than 60 hours per week, and many also put in additional work hours at home. Moreover, advances in technology, such as collaboration software and mobile devices, have resulted in work intruding on home time, vacation time, and even special occasions.[43] For another example of an issue related to equity, see the "Focus on DEI&B" feature.

FOCUS ON DEI&B

For Diversity to Motivate, It Must Come with Equity

Many organizations have sought to hire a diverse workforce to bring more points of view to their decision making and build stronger relationships with their customers and communities. Some are then surprised when people who differ from the majority group—say, women or nonbinary people in a male-dominated workplace or Black people in a predominantly white working environment—are quick to leave. One cause of the turnover may be that these employees are experiencing inequity. Quitting is one way to restore the equity balance.

This is a widely reported problem in the tech industry. For example, video game giant Activision Blizzard recently underwent multiple regulatory investigations into alleged sexual assaults and mistreatment of female employees over the past few years. In July 2021, the state of California filed a lawsuit alleging the company ignored numerous complaints by female employees of harassment, discrimination, and retaliation. Shortly thereafter, company employees staged a walkout to protest a company executive's statement playing down the lawsuit and to demand the CEO step down.[44]

Microsoft, for example, has made efforts to hire women and track their pay to make sure it is equitable. Even so, women there have reported pressure to act more like stereotypical college men in order to fit in with the culture. Aggression and criticism characterized the communication style, some have said. When everyone is expected to adopt a similar tone, the benefits of diversity get lost in the efforts at sameness, and some people are unable to contribute fully and receive the intrinsic and extrinsic rewards associated with valuable contributions. In an ironic twist, Microsoft recently announced it will acquire Activision Blizzard. However, the $69 billion deal is still being held up by federal regulators.[45]

Equitable treatment of all employees helps empower individuals and retain a company's workforce, which is a good business strategy.
Rawpixel.com/Shutterstock

Other companies also have focused on pay when considering their treatment of a diverse workforce. Starbucks, for example, spent 10 years adjusting pay to reach the point where pay for equal work in the United States is equal regardless of an employee's race or gender. The company continues to pursue pay equity for employees outside the United States. Intel measured its own achievement of pay equity one year earlier. The microchip maker also seeks to ensure equity in promoting and retaining workers. Lyft recently started annual audits of employee compensation, aiming to ensure that pay is equitable across race and gender. The ride-sharing company also hired a vice president of talent and inclusion, charged with ensuring the company welcomes diverse employees, so they can contribute fully.[46] Equitable treatment, because it empowers and helps retain an organization's workforce, is not only ethical but also good for business.

Equity and Justice in Organizations

distributive justice A moral principle calling for the use of fair procedures to determine how to distribute outcomes to organizational members.

Equity theory, given its focus on the fair distribution of outcomes in organizations to foster high motivation, is often labeled a theory of distributive justice.[47] **Distributive justice** refers to an employee's perception of the fairness of the distribution of outcomes (such as promotions, pay, job assignments, and working conditions) in an organization.[48] Employees are more likely to be highly motivated when they perceive distributive justice to be high rather than low.

procedural justice A moral principle calling for the use of fair procedures to determine how to distribute outcomes to organizational members.

interpersonal justice A person's perception of the fairness of the interpersonal treatment they receive from whoever distributes outcomes to them.

informational justice One's perception of the extent to which one's manager provides explanations for decisions and the procedures used to arrive at them.

Three other forms of justice are important for high motivation. **Procedural justice** refers to an employee's perception of the fairness of the procedures used to determine how to distribute outcomes in an organization.[49] For example, if important outcomes such as pay and promotions are distributed based on performance appraisals (see Chapter 12) and an employee perceives that the procedure that is used (i.e., the performance appraisal system) is unfair, then procedural justice is low and motivation is likely to suffer. More generally, motivation is higher when procedural justice is high rather than low.[50] **Interpersonal justice** refers to an employee's perception of the fairness of the interpersonal treatment they receive from whoever distributes outcomes to them (typically their manager).[51] Interpersonal justice is high when managers treat employees with dignity and respect and are polite and courteous.[52] Motivation is higher when interpersonal justice is high rather than low. **Informational justice** refers to an employee's perception of the extent to which their manager provides explanations for decisions and the procedures used to arrive at them.[53] For example, if a manager explains how performance is appraised and how decisions about the distribution of outcomes are made, informational justice (and motivation) are more likely to be high than if the manager does not do this.[54] All in all, it is most advantageous for distributive, procedural, interpersonal, and informational justice all to be high.

Goal-Setting Theory

LO13-3 Explain how goals and needs motivate people and what kinds of goals are especially likely to result in high performance.

Goal-setting theory focuses on motivating workers to contribute their inputs to their jobs and organizations; in this way it is similar to expectancy theory and equity theory. But goal-setting theory takes this focus a step further by considering as well how managers can ensure that organizational members focus their inputs in the direction of high performance and the achievement of organizational goals.

Ed Locke and Gary Latham, the leading researchers for goal-setting theory, suggested that the goals organizational members strive to attain are prime determinants of their motivation and subsequent performance. A *goal* is what someone is trying to accomplish through their efforts and behaviors.[55] Just as you may have a goal to get a good grade in this course, so do members of an organization have goals they strive to meet. For example, salespeople at Nordstrom retail stores strive to meet sales goals, while top managers pursue market share and profitability goals.

goal-setting theory A theory that focuses on identifying the types of goals that are most effective in producing high levels of motivation and performance and explaining why goals have these effects.

Goal-setting theory suggests that to stimulate high motivation and performance, goals must be *specific* and *difficult*.[56] Specific goals are often quantitative–a salesperson's goal to sell $750 worth of merchandise per day, a scientist's goal to finish a project in one year, a CEO's goal to reduce debt by 40% and increase revenues by 20%, a restaurant manager's goal to serve 150 customers per evening. In contrast to specific goals, vague goals such as "doing your best" or "selling as much as you can" do not have much motivational impact.

Difficult goals are hard but not impossible to attain. In contrast to difficult goals, easy goals are those that practically everyone can attain, and moderate goals are goals that about one-half of the people can attain. Both easy and moderate goals have less motivational power than difficult goals.

Regardless of whether specific, difficult goals are set by managers, workers, or teams of managers and workers, they lead to high levels of motivation and performance. When managers set goals for their employees, they must accept the goals or agree to work toward them; also, they should be committed to them or really want to attain them. Some managers find that having employees participate in the actual setting of goals boosts their acceptance of and commitment to the goals. In addition, organizational members need to receive *feedback* about how they are doing; feedback can often be provided by the performance appraisal and feedback component of an organization's human resource management system (see Chapter 12). More generally, goals and feedback are integral components of performance management systems such as management by objectives (see Chapter 11).

Specific, difficult goals affect motivation in two ways. First, they motivate people to contribute more inputs to their jobs. Specific, difficult goals cause people to put forth high levels of effort, for example. Just as you would study harder if you were trying to get an A in a course instead of a C, so will a salesperson work harder to reach a $750 sales goal instead of a $200 sales goal. Specific, difficult goals also cause people to be more persistent when they run into difficulties than do easy, moderate, or vague goals. Salespeople who are told to sell as much

Specific, difficult goals can encourage people to exert high levels of effort and to focus efforts in the right direction.
Stockbyte/Getty Images

as possible might stop trying on a slow day, whereas having a specific, difficult goal to reach causes them to keep trying.

A second way in which specific, difficult goals affect motivation is by helping people focus their inputs in the right direction. These goals let people know what they should be focusing their attention on, whether it is increasing the quality of customer service or sales or lowering new product development times. The fact that the goals are specific and difficult also often causes people to develop *action plans* for reaching them.[57] Action plans can include the strategies to attain the goals and timetables or schedules for the completion of different activities crucial to goal attainment. Like the goals themselves, action plans also help ensure that efforts are focused in the right direction and that people do not get sidetracked along the way.

Although specific, difficult goals have been found to increase motivation and performance in a wide variety of jobs and organizations both in the United States and abroad, recent research suggests that they may detract from performance under certain conditions. When people are performing complicated and challenging tasks that require them to focus on a considerable amount of learning, specific, difficult goals may actually impair performance.[58] Striving to reach such goals may direct some of a person's attention away from learning about the task and toward trying to figure out how to achieve the goal. Once a person has learned the task and it no longer seems complicated or difficult, then the assignment of specific, difficult goals is likely to have its usual effects. Additionally, for work that is very creative and uncertain, specific, difficult goals may be detrimental.

Learning Theories

LO13-4 Identify the motivation lessons that managers can learn from operant conditioning theory and social learning theory.

The basic premise of **learning theories** as applied to organizations is that managers can increase employee motivation and performance by how they link the outcomes that employees receive to the performance of desired behaviors and the attainment of goals. Thus, learning theory focuses on the linkage between performance and outcomes in the motivation equation (see Figure 13.1).

Learning can be defined as a relatively permanent change in a person's knowledge or behavior that results from practice or experience.[59] Learning takes place in organizations when people learn to perform certain behaviors to receive certain outcomes. For example, a person learns to perform at a higher level than in the past or to come to work earlier because they are motivated to obtain the outcomes that result from these behaviors, such as a pay raise or praise from a supervisor. As mentioned earlier, Enterprise's emphasis on training ensures that new hires learn how to provide excellent customer service and perform all the activities necessary for successful branch operations.

Of the different learning theories, operant conditioning theory and social learning theory provide the most guidance to managers in their efforts to have a highly motivated workforce.

learning theories Theories that focus on increasing employee motivation and performance by linking the outcomes that employees receive to the performance of desired behaviors and the attainment of goals.

learning A relatively permanent change in knowledge or behavior that results from practice or experience.

operant conditioning theory The theory that people learn to perform behaviors that lead to desired consequences and learn not to perform behaviors that lead to undesired consequences.

Operant Conditioning Theory

According to **operant conditioning theory**, developed by psychologist B. F. Skinner, people learn to perform behaviors that lead to desired consequences and learn not to perform behaviors that lead to undesired consequences.[60] Translated into motivation terms, Skinner's theory means that people will be motivated to perform at a high level and attain their work goals to the extent that high performance and goal attainment allow them to obtain outcomes they desire. Similarly, people avoid performing behaviors that lead to outcomes they do not desire. By linking the performance of *specific behaviors* to the attainment of *specific outcomes,* managers can motivate organizational members to perform in ways that help an organization achieve its goals.

Operant conditioning theory provides four tools that managers can use to motivate high performance and prevent workers from engaging in absenteeism and other behaviors that detract from organizational effectiveness. These tools are positive reinforcement, negative reinforcement, extinction, and punishment.[61]

No one pumps their fist over their laptop unless it's for a good reason—perhaps a congratulatory email from the boss, praising your efforts for leaving the competition in the dust with your exceptional sales numbers. This positive reinforcement helps motivate employees to do more and contributes to the company's overall success.
Jim Esposito/Getty Images

POSITIVE REINFORCEMENT **Positive reinforcement** gives people outcomes they desire when they perform organizationally functional behaviors. These desired outcomes, called *positive reinforcers,* include any outcomes that a person desires, such as pay, praise, or a promotion. Organizationally functional behaviors are behaviors that contribute to organizational effectiveness; they can include producing high-quality goods and services, providing high-quality customer service, and meeting deadlines. By linking positive reinforcers to the performance of functional behaviors, managers motivate people to perform the desired behaviors.

positive reinforcement Giving people outcomes they desire when they perform organizationally functional behaviors.

negative reinforcement Eliminating or removing undesired outcomes when people perform organizationally functional behaviors.

NEGATIVE REINFORCEMENT **Negative reinforcement** also can encourage members of an organization to perform desired or organizationally functional behaviors. Managers using negative reinforcement actually eliminate or remove undesired outcomes once the functional behavior is performed. These undesired outcomes, called *negative reinforcers,* can range from a manager's constant nagging or criticism to unpleasant assignments or the ever-present threat of losing one's job. When negative reinforcement is used, people are motivated to perform behaviors because they want to stop receiving or want to avoid undesired outcomes. Managers who try to encourage salespeople to sell more by threatening them with being fired are using negative reinforcement. In this case, the negative reinforcer is the threat of job loss, which is removed once the functional behavior is performed.

Whenever possible, managers should try to use positive reinforcement. Negative reinforcement can create a very unpleasant work environment and even a negative culture in an organization. No one likes to be nagged, threatened, or exposed to other kinds of negative outcomes. The use of negative reinforcement sometimes causes employees to resent managers and try to get back at them.

IDENTIFYING THE RIGHT BEHAVIORS FOR REINFORCEMENT Even managers who use positive reinforcement (and refrain from using negative reinforcement) can get into trouble if they are not careful to identify the right behaviors to reinforce–behaviors that are truly functional for the organization. Doing this is not always as straightforward as it might seem. First, it is crucial for managers to choose behaviors over which employees have control; in other words, employees must have the freedom and opportunity to perform the behaviors that are being reinforced. Second, it is crucial that these behaviors contribute to organizational effectiveness.

EXTINCTION Sometimes members of an organization are motivated to perform behaviors that detract from organizational effectiveness. According to operant conditioning theory, all behavior is controlled or determined by its consequences; one way for managers to curtail the performance of dysfunctional behaviors is to eliminate whatever is reinforcing the behaviors. This process is called **extinction**.

extinction Curtailing the performance of dysfunctional behaviors by eliminating whatever is reinforcing them.

Suppose a manager has an employee who often stops by their office to chat–sometimes about work-related matters but at other times about various topics ranging from politics to last night's football game. The manager and the employee share certain interests and views, so these conversations can get quite involved, and both seem to enjoy them. The manager, however, realizes that these frequent and sometimes lengthy conversations are causing them to stay at work later in the evening to make up for the time lost during the day. The manager also realizes that they are reinforcing the employee's behavior by acting interested in topics the employee brings up and responding at length to these topics. To extinguish this behavior, the manager stops acting interested in these non-work-related conversations and keeps responses polite and friendly but brief. No longer being reinforced with a pleasurable conversation, the employee eventually ceases to be motivated to interrupt the manager during work hours to discuss non-work-related issues.

PUNISHMENT Sometimes managers cannot rely on extinction to eliminate dysfunctional behaviors because they do not have control over whatever is reinforcing the behavior or because they cannot afford the time needed for extinction to work. When employees are

punishment Administering an undesired or negative consequence when dysfunctional behavior occurs.

performing dangerous behaviors or behaviors that are illegal or unethical, the behaviors need to be eliminated immediately. Sexual harassment, for example, is an organizationally dysfunctional behavior that cannot be tolerated. In such cases managers often rely on **punishment**, which is administering an undesired or negative consequence to employees when they perform the dysfunctional behavior. Punishments used by organizations include verbal reprimands, pay cuts, temporary suspensions, demotions, and firings. Punishment, however, can have some unintended side effects–resentment, loss of self-respect, a desire for retaliation–and should be used only when necessary.

To avoid the unintended side effects of punishment, managers should keep in mind these guidelines:

- Downplay the emotional element involved in punishment. Make it clear that you are punishing a person's performance of a dysfunctional behavior, not the person.
- Try to punish dysfunctional behaviors as soon as possible after they occur, and make sure the negative consequence is a source of punishment for the individuals involved. Be certain that organizational members know exactly why they are being punished.
- Try to avoid punishing someone in front of others because this can hurt a person's self-respect and lower esteem in the eyes of coworkers, as well as make coworkers feel uncomfortable.[62] Even so, making organizational members aware that someone who has committed a serious infraction has been punished can sometimes be effective in preventing future infractions and in teaching everyone in the organization that certain behaviors are unacceptable. For example, when organizational members are informed that a manager who has sexually harassed employees has been punished, it is reinforced that sexual harassment is not tolerated in the organization.

Managers and students alike often confuse negative reinforcement and punishment. To avoid such confusion, keep in mind the two major differences between them. First, negative reinforcement is used to promote the performance of functional behaviors in organizations; punishment is used to stop the performance of dysfunctional behaviors. Second, negative reinforcement entails the *removal* of a negative consequence when functional behaviors are performed; punishment entails the *administration* of negative consequences when dysfunctional behaviors are performed.

organizational behavior modification (OB MOD) The systematic application of operant conditioning techniques to promote the performance of organizationally functional behaviors and discourage the performance of dysfunctional behaviors.

ORGANIZATIONAL BEHAVIOR MODIFICATION When managers systematically apply operant conditioning techniques to promote the performance of organizationally functional behaviors and discourage the performance of dysfunctional behaviors, they are engaging in **organizational behavior modification (OB MOD)**.[63] OB MOD has been successfully used to improve productivity, efficiency, attendance, punctuality, safe work practices, customer service, and other important behaviors in a wide variety of organizations such as banks, department stores, factories, hospitals, and construction sites.[64] The five basic steps in OB MOD are described in Figure 13.4.

OB MOD works best for behaviors that are specific, objective, and countable, such as attendance and punctuality, making sales, or putting telephones together, all of which lend themselves to careful scrutiny and control. OB MOD may be questioned because of its lack of relevance to certain work behaviors (for example, the many work behaviors that are not specific, objective, and countable). Some people also have questioned it on ethical grounds. Critics of OB MOD suggest that it is overly controlling and robs workers of their dignity, individuality, freedom of choice, and even creativity. Supporters counter that OB MOD is a highly effective means of promoting organizational efficiency. There is some merit to both sides of this argument. What is clear, however, is that when used appropriately, OB MOD gives managers a technique to motivate the performance of at least some organizationally functional behaviors.[65]

Social Learning Theory

social learning theory A theory that takes into account how learning and motivation are influenced by people's thoughts and beliefs and their observations of other people's behavior.

Social learning theory proposes that motivation results not only from direct experience of rewards and punishments but also from a person's thoughts and beliefs. Social learning theory extends operant conditioning's contribution to managers' understanding of motivation by explaining (1) how people can be motivated by observing other people performing a behavior

Figure 13.4

Five Steps in OB MOD

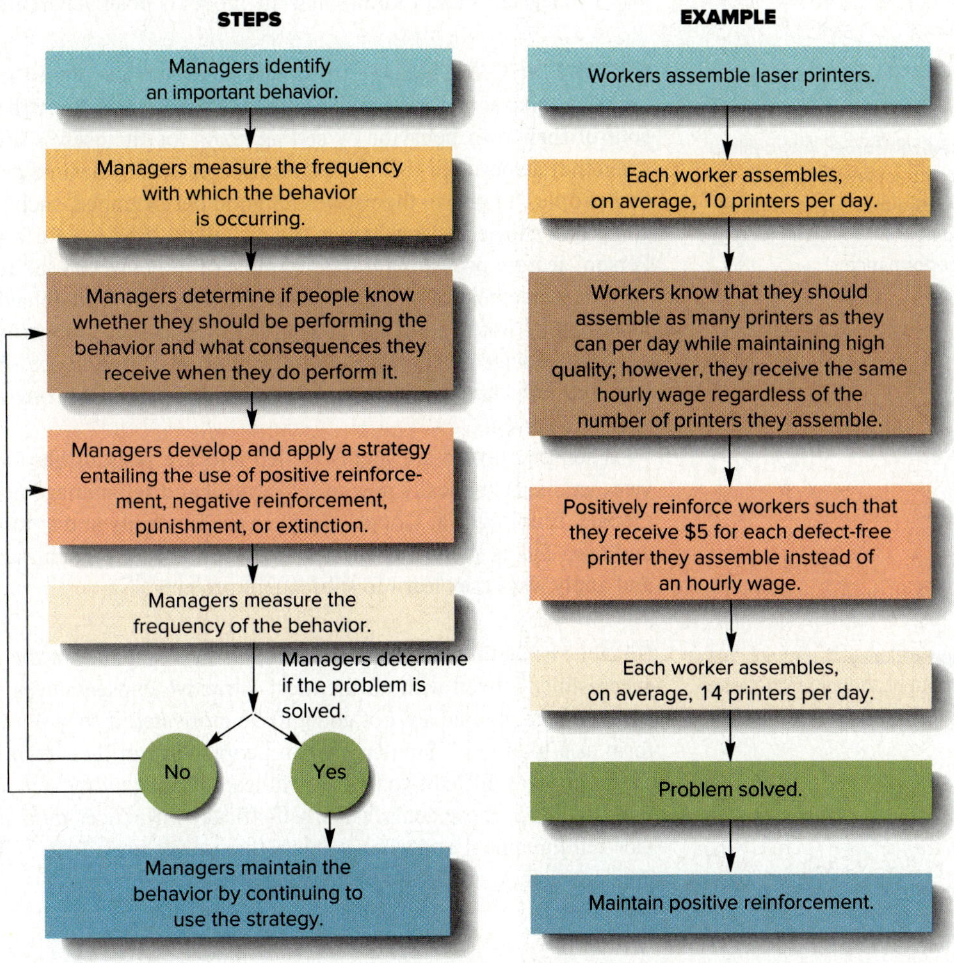

Adapted from F. Luthans and R. Kreitner, Organizational Behavior Modification and Beyond, Scott Foresman, 1985. Copyright 1985.

and being reinforced for doing so (*vicarious learning*), (2) how people can be motivated to control their behavior themselves (*self-reinforcement*), and (3) how people's beliefs about their ability to successfully perform a behavior affect motivation (*self-efficacy*).[66] We look briefly at each of these motivators.

vicarious learning Learning that occurs when the learner becomes motivated to perform a behavior by watching another person performing it and being reinforced for doing so; also called observational learning.

VICARIOUS LEARNING **Vicarious learning**, often called *observational learning,* occurs when a person (the learner) becomes motivated to perform a behavior by watching another person (the model) performing the behavior and being positively reinforced for doing so. Vicarious learning is a powerful source of motivation on many jobs in which people learn to perform functional behaviors by watching others. Salespeople learn how to help customers, medical school students learn how to treat patients, law clerks learn how to practice law, and nonmanagers learn how to be managers, in part, by observing experienced members of an organization perform these behaviors properly and be reinforced for them. In general, people are more likely to be motivated to imitate the behavior of models who are highly competent, are (to some extent) experts in the behavior, have high status, receive attractive reinforcers, and are friendly or approachable.[67]

To promote vicarious learning, managers should strive to have the learner meet the following conditions:

- The learner observes the model performing the behavior.
- The learner accurately perceives the model's behavior.

- The learner remembers the behavior.
- The learner has the skills and abilities needed to perform the behavior.
- The learner sees or knows that the model is positively reinforced for the behavior.[68]

self-reinforcer Any desired or attractive outcome or reward that a person gives to himself or herself for good performance.

SELF-REINFORCEMENT Although managers are often the providers of reinforcement in organizations, sometimes people motivate themselves through self-reinforcement. People can control their own behavior by setting goals for themselves and then reinforcing themselves when they achieve the goals.[69] **Self-reinforcers** are any desired or attractive outcomes or rewards that people can give to themselves for good performance, such as a feeling of accomplishment, going to a movie, having dinner out, or taking time out for a golf game. The "Manager as a Person" feature provides another example of the power of self-reinforcement.

When members of an organization control their own behavior through self-reinforcement, managers do not need to spend as much time as they ordinarily would trying to motivate and control behavior through the administration of consequences because employees are controlling and motivating themselves. In fact, this self-control is often referred to as the *self-management of behavior.*

When employees are highly skilled and are responsible for creating new goods and services, managers typically rely on self-control and self-management of behavior, as is the case at Google. Employees at Google are given the flexibility and autonomy to experiment, take risks, and even fail as they work on new projects. They are encouraged to learn from their failures and apply what they learn to subsequent projects.[70]

self-efficacy A person's belief about his or her ability to perform a behavior successfully.

SELF-EFFICACY **Self-efficacy** is a person's belief about their ability to perform a behavior successfully.[71] Even with all the most attractive consequences or reinforcers hinging on high performance, people are not going to be motivated if they do not think they can actually perform at a high level. Similarly, when people control their own behavior, they are likely to set for themselves difficult goals that will lead to outstanding accomplishments only if they think they can reach those goals. Thus, self-efficacy influences motivation both when managers provide reinforcement and when workers themselves provide it.[72] The greater the self-efficacy, the greater the motivation and performance.

MANAGER AS A PERSON

Bernard Olayo's Mission Is His Motivator

Bernard Olayo is a profound example that even company executives need motivation. Olayo, a physician and public-health specialist, formed Hewatele to provide affordable oxygen to hospitals in Kenya. About a year into the pandemic, he came down with COVID-19, and he later said, "If I didn't have a passion for this job, I would never have stepped back into a hospital."[73] He did, however, knowing that his innovative approach was saving lives.

The idea for Hewatele (which means "abundant air" in Swahili) came about when Olayo was working in maternal and child medicine in Kenya, Uganda, Tanzania, and Rwanda. In those programs, there was not always enough oxygen for his patients, especially children suffering from pneumonia. Deliveries were erratic, and the price charged by the sole supplier was high. Olayo had to make painful life-and-death choices, which motivated him to start a nonprofit called the Center for Public Health and Development (CPHD) to fund trials of his ideas. First he set up small oxygen-producing facilities in hospitals, but by the second year of the trial, the facilities were shutting down because the hospitals could not handle the maintenance. Undeterred, Olayo switched to what he calls a "milkman model," in which Hewatele, a CPHD affiliate, operates its own factories, fills cylinders with oxygen, and delivers them to local hospitals, charging less than the going rate–which is 13 times the average U.S. hospitals pay. The first plant launched in 2014 and is still operating.[74]

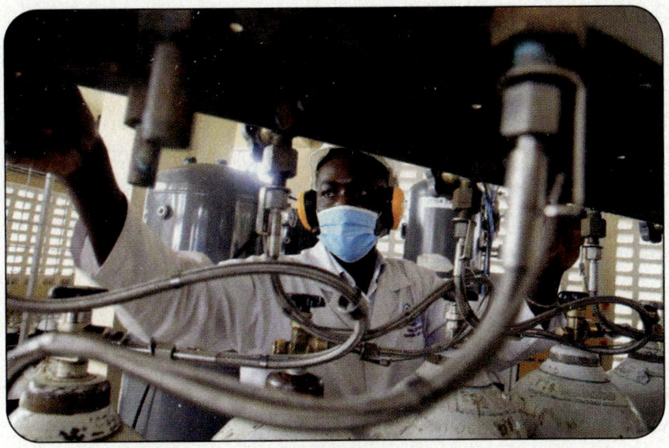

Dr. Bernard Olayo (pictured here) founded Hewatele with the goal of providing life-saving oxygen to hospital patients in Kenya. His motivation? That no health care worker will have to make the decision of who lives or who dies because there is not enough oxygen for all patients.
Thomas Mukoya/REUTERS/Alamy Stock Photo

Hewatele now serves about 250 hospitals, or one-tenth of Kenya's market. Before the pandemic, filling orders required 60 or 70% of Hewatele's production capacity. As cases mounted, demand doubled and then tripled, so the facilities moved to round-the-clock operations with twice the number of plant operators and drivers.[75]

Even as he reflects on the stress of those times, Olayo remains passionate about oxygen's potential to save lives. He has been raising funds to expand the number of oxygen plants and spread the milkman model to more of Kenya plus Uganda and Tanzania. He also is pursuing a more productive type of manufacturing, which could enable profitable sales at half the price.[76] What still keeps him going is his goal that "no health worker will ever have to make the painful decision I did between who lives and who dies."[77]

Pay and Motivation

LO13-5 Explain why and how managers can use pay as a major motivation tool.

In Chapter 12, we discussed how managers establish a pay level and structure for an organization as a whole. Here we focus on how, once a pay level and structure are in place, managers can use pay to motivate employees to perform at a high level and attain their work goals. Pay is used to motivate entry-level workers, first-line and middle managers, and even top managers such as CEOs. Pay can motivate people to perform behaviors that help an organization achieve its goals, and it can motivate people to join and remain with an organization.

Each of the theories described in this chapter alludes to the importance of pay and suggests that pay should be based on performance:

- *Expectancy theory:* Instrumentality, the association between performance and outcomes such as pay, must be high for motivation to be high. In addition, pay is an outcome that has high valence for many people.
- *Need theories:* People should be able to satisfy their needs by performing at a high level; pay can be used to satisfy several kinds of needs.
- *Equity theory:* Outcomes such as pay should be distributed in proportion to inputs (including performance levels).
- *Goal-setting theory:* Outcomes such as pay should be linked to the attainment of goals.
- *Learning theories:* The distribution of outcomes, such as pay, should be contingent on the performance of organizationally functional behaviors.

As these theories suggest, to promote high motivation, managers should base the distribution of pay to organizational members on performance levels so that high performers receive more pay than low performers (other things being equal).[78] A compensation plan basing pay on performance is often called a **merit pay plan**. This approach also addresses ethical issues related to motivation, as discussed earlier in the chapter in the context of equity theory.

merit pay plan A compensation plan that bases pay on performance.

In difficult and uncertain economic times, organizations may be forced to lay off employees, and pay levels and benefits of those still working may be cut while their responsibilities often increase. Unfortunately, managers are often limited in giving merit pay increases when this happens.[79] According to recent research conducted before and during the recent pandemic, employees (both in-office and working remotely), seem to acknowledge companies' inability to increase pay during these difficult times but would be pleased to receive thanks and appreciation for a job well done from their bosses and peers.

In the study, more than 200,000 employees worldwide took an online assessment, some pre-COVID-19 and some during COVID-19, to identify the primary language of appreciation in terms of acts of service, tangible gifts, words of affirmation, and quality time. Both before and during the pandemic, employees working remotely and in-office identified words of affirmation as the most desired form of appreciation (pre-COVID respondents 45.9%, respondents during COVID-19 45.1%), followed by quality time, acts of service, and tangible gifts. Not surprisingly, remote employees chose quality time (e.g., receiving advice from a mentor or hanging out with colleagues after work) slightly more often than their onsite colleagues. More than 46% of onsite employees and 39.5% of remote workers chose words of affirmation as their top choice for appreciation.[80]

Some of the effective ways companies can show appreciation include meeting and engaging with employees on a weekly basis; asking an employee's colleagues to be part of the appreciation efforts, whether in person or via videoconferencing; and sending employees care packages to let them know that their hard work is appreciated.[81]

Once managers have decided to use a merit pay plan, they face two important choices: whether to base pay on individual, group, or organizational performance and whether to use salary increases or bonuses.

Basing Merit Pay on Individual, Group, or Organizational Performance

Managers can base merit pay on individual, group, or organizational performance. When individual performance (such as the dollar value of merchandise a salesperson sells, the number of loudspeakers a factory worker assembles, or a lawyer's billable hours) can be accurately determined, individual motivation is likely to be highest when pay is based on individual performance.[82] When members of an organization work closely together and individual performance cannot be accurately determined (as in a team of computer programmers developing a single software package), pay cannot be based on individual performance, and a group- or organization-based plan must be used. When the attainment of organizational goals hinges on members' working closely together and cooperating with each other (as in a small construction company that builds custom homes), group- or organization-based plans may be more appropriate than individual-based plans.[83]

It is possible to combine elements of an individual-based plan with a group- or organization-based plan to motivate each person to perform highly and, at the same time, motivate everyone to work well together, cooperate with one another, and help one another as needed. Lincoln Electric, a leading manufacturer of welding machines, uses a combination individual- and organization-based plan.[84] Pay is based on individual performance. In addition, each year the size of a bonus fund depends on organizational performance. Money from the bonus fund is distributed to people on the basis of their contributions to the organization, attendance, levels of cooperation, and other indications of performance. Employees of Lincoln Electric are motivated to cooperate and help one another because when the firm as a whole performs well, everybody benefits by having a larger bonus fund. Employees also are motivated to contribute their inputs to the organization because their contributions determine their share of the bonus fund.

Salary Increase or Bonus?

Managers can distribute merit pay to people in the form of a salary increase or a bonus on top of regular salaries. Although the dollar amounts of a salary increase and of a bonus might be identical, bonuses tend to have more motivational impact for at least three reasons. First, salary levels are typically based on performance levels, cost-of-living increases, and so forth from the day people start working in an organization, which means the absolute level of the salary is based largely on factors unrelated to *current* performance. A 5% merit increase in salary, for example, may seem relatively small in comparison to one's total salary. Second, a current salary increase may be affected by other factors in addition to performance, such as cost-of-living increases or across-the-board market adjustments. Third, because organizations rarely reduce salaries, salary levels tend to vary less than performance levels do. Related to this point is the fact that bonuses give managers more flexibility in distributing outcomes. If an organization is doing well, bonuses can be relatively high to reward employees for their contributions. However, unlike salary increases, bonus levels can be reduced when an organization's performance lags. All in all, bonus plans have more motivational impact than salary increases because the amount of the bonus can be directly and exclusively based on performance.[85]

Consistent with the lessons from motivation theories, bonuses can be linked directly to performance and vary from year to year and employee to employee, as at Gradient Corporation, a Cambridge, Massachusetts, environmental consulting firm.[86] Another organization that successfully uses bonuses is Nucor Corporation. Steelworkers at Nucor tend to be much more productive than steelworkers in other companies–probably because they can receive bonuses tied to performance and quality that can range from 130% to 150% of their regular base pay.[87] During the economic downturn in 2007–2009, Nucor struggled, as did many other companies, and bonus pay for steelworkers dropped considerably. However, managers at Nucor avoided having to lay off employees by finding ways to cut costs and having employees work on maintenance activities and safety manuals, along with taking on tasks that used to be performed by independent contractors, such as producing specialty parts and mowing the grass.[88]

employee stock option A financial instrument that entitles the bearer to buy shares of an organization's stock at a certain price during a certain period or under certain conditions.

In addition to receiving pay raises and bonuses, high-level managers and executives are sometimes granted employee stock options. **Employee stock options** are financial instruments that entitle the bearer to buy shares of an organization's stock at a certain price during a certain period or under certain conditions.[89] For example, in addition to salaries, stock options are sometimes used to attract high-level managers. The exercise price is the stock price at which the bearer can buy the stock, and the vesting conditions specify when the bearer can actually buy the stock at the exercise price. The option's exercise price is generally set equal to the market price of the stock on the date it is granted, and the vesting conditions might specify that the manager has to have worked at the organization for 12 months or perhaps met some performance target (perhaps an increase in profits) before being able to exercise the option. In technology firms and start-ups, options are sometimes used in a similar fashion for employees at various levels in the organization.[90]

From a motivation standpoint, stock options are used not so much to reward past individual performance but, rather, to motivate employees to work in the future for the good of the company as a whole. This is true because stock options issued at current stock prices have value in the future only if an organization does well and its stock price appreciates; thus, giving employees stock options should encourage them to help the organization improve its performance over time.[91] At technology start-ups, stock options have often motivated potential employees to leave promising jobs in larger companies and work for the start-ups. Unfortunately, stock options have also led to unethical behavior; for example, some people seek to artificially inflate the value of a company's stock to increase the value of stock options.

Examples of Merit Pay Plans

Managers can choose among several merit pay plans, depending on the work that employees perform and other considerations. Using *piece-rate pay,* an individual-based merit plan, managers base employees' pay on the number of units each employee produces, whether televisions, computer components, or welded auto parts. Managers at Lincoln Electric use piece-rate pay to determine individual pay levels. Advances in information technology have dramatically simplified the administration of piece-rate pay in a variety of industries.

Using *commission pay,* another individual-based merit pay plan, managers base pay on a percentage of sales. Managers at the successful real estate company Re/Max International Inc. use commission pay for their agents, who are paid a percentage of their sales. Some department stores, such as Nordstrom, use commission pay for their salespeople.

Examples of organizational-based merit pay plans include the Scanlon plan and profit sharing. The *Scanlon plan* (developed by Joseph Scanlon, a union leader in a steel and tin plant in the 1920s) focuses on reducing expenses or cutting costs; members of an organization are motivated to propose and implement cost-cutting strategies because a percentage of the cost savings achieved during a specified time is distributed to the employees.[92] Under *profit sharing,* employees receive a share of an organization's profits. Regardless of the specific kind of plan that is used, managers should always strive to link pay to the performance of behaviors that help an organization achieve its goals.

Japanese managers in large corporations have long shunned merit pay plans in favor of plans that reward seniority. However, more and more Japanese companies are adopting merit-based pay due to its motivational benefits. According to recent reports, nearly 58% of Japanese companies have adopted merit-based pay, including auto giant Toyota and electronics maker Fujitsu.[93]

Summary and Review

LO13-1 **THE NATURE OF MOTIVATION** Motivation encompasses the psychological forces within a person that determine the direction of the person's behavior in an organization, the person's level of effort, and the person's level of persistence in the face of obstacles. Managers strive to motivate people to contribute their inputs to an organization, to focus these inputs in the direction of high performance, and to ensure that people receive the outcomes they desire when they perform at a high level.

LO13-2 **EXPECTANCY THEORY** According to expectancy theory, managers can promote high levels of motivation in their organizations by taking steps to ensure that expectancy is high (people think that if they try, they can perform at a high level), instrumentality is high (people think that if they perform at a high level, they will receive certain outcomes), and valence is high (people desire these outcomes).

LO13-3 **NEED THEORIES** Need theories suggest that to motivate their workforces, managers should determine what needs people are trying to satisfy in organizations and then ensure that people receive outcomes that satisfy these needs when they perform at a high level and contribute to organizational effectiveness.

LO13-2 **EQUITY THEORY** According to equity theory, managers can promote high levels of motivation by ensuring that people perceive that there is equity in the organization or that outcomes are distributed in proportion to inputs. Equity exists when a person perceives that their own outcome–input ratio equals the outcome–input ratio of a referent. Inequity motivates people to try to restore equity. Equity theory is a theory of distributive justice. It is most advantageous for distributive, procedural, interpersonal, and informational justice all to be high.

LO13-3 **GOAL-SETTING THEORY** Goal-setting theory suggests that managers can promote high motivation and performance by ensuring that people are striving to achieve specific, difficult goals. It is important for people to accept the goals, be committed to them, and receive feedback about how they are doing.

LO13-4 **LEARNING THEORIES** Operant conditioning theory suggests that managers can motivate people to perform highly by using positive reinforcement or negative reinforcement (positive reinforcement being the preferred strategy). Managers can motivate people to avoid performing dysfunctional behaviors by using extinction or punishment. Social learning theory suggests that people can also be motivated by observing how others perform behaviors and receive rewards, by engaging in self-reinforcement, and by having high levels of self-efficacy.

LO13-5 **PAY AND MOTIVATION** Each of the motivation theories discussed in this chapter alludes to the importance of pay and suggests that pay should be based on performance. Merit pay plans can be individual-, group-, or organization-based and can entail the use of salary increases or bonuses.

Management in Action

Topics for Discussion and Action

Discussion

1. Discuss why two people with similar abilities may have very different expectancies for performing at a high level. [LO13-2]
2. Describe why some people have low instrumentalities even when their managers distribute outcomes based on performance. [LO13-2]
3. Analyze how professors try to promote equity to motivate students. [LO13-2]
4. Describe three techniques or procedures that managers can use to determine whether a goal is difficult. [LO13-3]
5. Discuss why managers should always try to use positive reinforcement instead of negative reinforcement. [LO13-4]

Action

6. Interview three people who have the same kind of job (such as salesperson, waiter/waitress, or teacher), and determine what kinds of needs each is trying to satisfy at work. [LO13-3]
7. Interview a manager in an organization in your community to determine the extent to which the manager takes advantage of vicarious learning to promote high motivation among employees. [LO13-3]

Building Management Skills

Diagnosing Motivation [LO13-1, 13-2, 13-3, 13-4]

Think about the ideal job that you would like to obtain after graduation. Describe this job, the kind of manager you would like to report to, and the kind of organization you would be working in. Then answer the following questions:

1. What would be your levels of expectancy and instrumentality on this job? Which outcomes would have high valence for you on this job? What steps would your manager take to influence your levels of expectancy, instrumentality, and valence?
2. Whom would you choose as a referent on this job? What steps would your manager take to make you feel that you were being equitably treated? What would you do if, after a year on the job, you experienced underpayment inequity?
3. What goals would you strive to achieve on this job? Why? What role would your manager play in determining your goals?
4. What needs would you strive to satisfy on this job? Why? What role would your manager play in helping you satisfy these needs?
5. What behaviors would your manager positively reinforce on this job? Why? What positive reinforcers would your manager use?
6. Would there be any vicarious learning on this job? Why or why not?
7. To what extent would you be motivated by self-control on this job? Why?
8. What would be your level of self-efficacy on this job? Why would your self-efficacy be at this level? Should your manager take steps to boost your self-efficacy? If not, why not? If so, what would these steps be?

Managing Ethically [LO13-5]

Sometimes pay is so contingent upon performance that it creates stress for employees. Imagine a salesperson who knows that if sales targets are not met, they will not be able to make a house mortgage payment or pay the rent.

Questions

1. Either individually or in a group, think about the ethical implications of closely linking pay to performance.
2. Under what conditions might contingent pay be most stressful, and what steps can managers take to try to help their employees perform effectively and not experience excessive amounts of stress?

Small Group Breakout Exercise

Increasing Motivation [LO13-1, 13-2, 13-3, 13-4, 13-5]

Form groups of three or four people, and appoint one member as the spokesperson who will communicate your findings to the class when called on by the instructor. Then discuss the following scenario:

You and your partners own a chain of 15 dry-cleaning stores in a medium-size town. All of you are concerned about a problem in customer service that has surfaced recently. When any one of you spends the day, or even part of the day, in a particular store, clerks seem to provide excellent customer service, spotters make sure all stains are removed from garments, and pressers do a good job of pressing difficult items such as silk blouses. Yet during those same visits, customers complain to you about such things as stains not being removed and items being poorly pressed in some of their previous orders; indeed, several customers have brought garments in to be redone. Customers also sometimes comment on having waited too long for service on previous visits. You and your partners are meeting today to address this problem.

1. Discuss the extent to which you believe that you have a motivation problem in your stores.
2. Given what you have learned in this chapter, design a plan to increase the motivation of clerks to provide prompt service to customers even when they are not being watched by a partner.
3. Design a plan to increase the motivation of spotters to remove as many stains as possible even when they are not being watched by a partner.
4. Design a plan to increase the motivation of pressers to do a top-notch job on all clothes they press, no matter how difficult.

Be the Manager [LO13-1, 13-2, 13-3, 13-4, 13-5]

You supervise a team of marketing analysts who work on different snack products in a large food products company. The marketing analysts have recently received undergraduate degrees in business or liberal arts and have been on the job between one and three years. Their responsibilities include analyzing the market for their respective products, including competitors; tracking current marketing initiatives; and planning future marketing campaigns. They also need to prepare quarterly sales and expense reports for their products and estimated budgets for the next three quarters; to prepare these reports, they need to obtain data from financial and accounting analysts assigned to their products.

When they first started on the job, you took each marketing analyst through the reporting cycle, explaining what needs to be done and how to accomplish it and emphasizing the need for timely reports. Although preparing the reports can be tedious, you think the task is pretty straightforward and easily accomplished if the analysts plan ahead and allocate sufficient time for it. When reporting time approaches, you remind the analysts through email messages and emphasize the need for accurate and timely reports in team meetings.

You believe this element of the analysts' jobs couldn't be more straightforward. However, at the end of each quarter, the majority of the analysts submit their reports a day or two late, and, worse yet, your own supervisor (to whom the reports are eventually given) has indicated that information is often missing and sometimes the reports contain errors. Once you started getting flak from your supervisor about this problem, you decided you had better fix things quickly. You met with the marketing analysts, explained the problem, told them to submit the reports to you a day or two early so you could look them over, and more generally emphasized that they really needed to get their act together. Unfortunately, things have not improved much and you are spending more and more of your own time doing the reports. What are you going to do?

Case in the News [LO13-1, 13-2, 13-3, 13-4]

At Unilever, Motivation Is a Global Effort

For Unilever, a global marketer of consumer packaged goods, motivation is a massive challenge. The London-based company must motivate 148,000 employees in almost 200 countries as they innovate, distribute, and promote 400-plus brands, including Dove, Axe, and Ben & Jerry's.

Like other businesses, Unilever sets financial targets for profitability and growth. It aims to be in the top third of companies by total shareholder returns (what investors receive from dividends and gains in the value of their shares). To get there, Unilever's executives set the broad strategy, "where to play," as follows: business areas with growth potential; brands where the company can excel; geographic markets where it expects growth; and distribution channels it expects customers to embrace. The executives acquire or divest brands or companies to keep Unilever adhering to these criteria.

Unilever's strategy and structure help its people stay on track. The current structure includes five businesses: beauty and well-being, personal care, home care, nutrition, and ice cream. Business leaders are responsible for pursuing growth by investing in promising brands and markets. Managers make decisions about pricing, distribution, and other success factors. For example, facing rising costs in 2022, Unilever businesses raised prices and then measured the impact on sales. For ice cream, Unilever saw a 1.6% decline in volume sold, but because of the price increases, its sales revenue rose by 10.6%.

Unilever links its strategy to its purpose, "to make sustainable living commonplace," based on the idea that purposeful brands grow robustly because consumers appreciate them and gain from using them. Further, the chance to work for a company doing good can attract the best talent. Unilever has broad objectives for fulfilling its purpose: improve the planet's health; improve consumers' health, confidence, and well-being; and contribute to making the world fair and more socially inclusive. Specific targets establish how to do this—for example, by achieving net zero carbon emissions by 2030, cutting food wasted in manufacturing in half by 2025, and having 5% of Unilever's workforce be people with disabilities by 2025. Purpose can inspire employees. Gina Kiroff, who manages the Knorr brand of soups and condiments for North America, sees herself contributing to the mission to make nutritious food available to everyone, including by encouraging farming practices that regenerate the soil.

Unilever's purpose-related objectives include treatment of employees. For these stakeholders, the company aims to foster equity, diversity, and inclusion, partly by moving diverse employees into leadership roles. Unilever also aims to pioneer flexible work arrangements, making them widely available by 2030. In a pilot test of a four-day workweek in New Zealand, employees earned the same level of pay for doing their previous five-day jobs. Unilever provided new technology and tools to help them become more efficient—say, by spending less time in meetings. After the trial, employees reported less stress and a better work–life balance, so Unilever announced a larger trial in Australia.

Employee-related purpose also addresses how technology is enabling companies to do more with less—thereby transforming required skill sets. Rather than slashing the existing workforce to boost efficiency, Unilever has given employees an opportunity to learn skills the company expects to need. Employees participate in a process in which they explore their values and goals to define their purpose, which provides a basis for selecting training, planning a career path, and perhaps moving to contract work or even another employer. In the effort's early months, Unilever has retained most workers whose former jobs were automated.

Another group of stakeholders, Unilever's investors, play a motivational role, especially affecting top executives. Since the key measure of Unilever's performance is total shareholder returns, the price investors are willing to pay for Unilever's stock defines executives' success, and major investors sometimes pressure the company to focus more on growth. Such activist investors include Nelson Peltz, whose Trian Fund Management bought a stake in the company. Peltz pressed Unilever to focus on efficiency and to bring its value more in line with others in the industry. He obtained a seat on Unilever's board of directors, where he may influence decisions such as executive pay structure.

Despite its 2022 price increases, Unilever has posted growth in net sales. Other concerns include mixed forecasts for the global economy, especially since the company is heavily involved in high-inflation, low-income economies. Still, Unilever predicted it could maintain growth at 4.5 to 6.5% in 2023, versus 8% in 2022, by focusing on its faster-growing businesses.

Questions for Discussion

1. In this case, find one example of each: (a) intrinsic motivation, (b) extrinsic motivation, and (c) prosocial motivation.

2. For each of the following initiatives, what do the expectancy and equity theories of motivation suggest will be the initiative's impact on motivation—(a) testing and implementing a four-day workweek and (b) reskilling employees for a more automated workplace?

3. Based on the information given, do you think Unilever relies too much or not enough on financial goals to motivate top executives? Explain your reasoning.

Sources: Unilever, "The Unilever Compass for Sustainable Growth," infographic, www.unilever.com, accessed January 27, 2023; J. Brunner, "She Helps Make Food a Force for Good," *Forbes*, www.forbes.com, December 27, 2022; S. Harvey, "Unilever CEO Alan Jope Looks to 'Prune' Portfolio but Open to 'Bolt-On' Acquisitions," *Just Food*, www.just-food.com, December 12, 2022; "Four-Day Work Week Trial to Start in Australia," www.unilever.com, November 1, 2022; P. Stiff, "Dover Maker Unilever Boosted by Record Price Increases; Consumer-Goods Giant Pushes through Highest-Ever Price Rises to Offset Higher Costs," *The Wall Street Journal*, www.wsj.com, October 27, 2022; "Our Compass Organisation: Introducing Unilever's Five New Business Groups," www.unilever.com, October 7, 2022; P. Stiff, "Unilever CEO to End Rocky Tenure," *The Wall Street Journal*, www.wsj.com, September 27, 2022; S. Chaudhuri, "Peltz Faces Tricky Job in Energizing Unilever," *The Wall Street Journal*, June 2, 2022; C. Ryan, "P&G-Style Makeover Is a Big Ask for Unilever: Activist's Hopes for a Repeat May Be Too High," *The Wall Street Journal*, www.wsj.com, June 1, 2022; L. Nair, N. Dalton, P. Hull, and W. Kerr, "Use Purpose to Transform Your Workplace," *Harvard Business Review*, March–April 2022, 52–55.

Notes

1. J. Abdou, "Eight Leadership Lessons from Boxed Founder and CEO Chieh Huang," *33 Voices*, www.33voices.com, accessed January 27, 2023; E. Greenwood, "How to Go Public While Taking Care of Your People," *Entrepreneur*, January–February 2022, 40–43.
2. Boxed, "About Us," www.boxed.com, accessed January 27, 2023.
3. Greenwood, "How to Go Public."
4. T. Huddleston Jr., "CEO of $600 Million Company Boxed Asks This Sneaky Interview Question to Weed Out Jerks," *CNBC*, www.cnbc.com, February 27, 2019.
5. Abdou, "Eight Leadership Lessons."
6. Boxed, "About Us."
7. Greenwood, "How to Go Public."
8. R. Kanfer, "Motivation Theory and Industrial and Organizational Psychology," in M.D. Dunnette and L.M. Hough, eds., *Handbook of Industrial and Organizational Psychology*, 2nd ed., vol. 1 (Palo Alto, CA: Consulting Psychologists Press, 1990), 75–170.
9. G.P. Latham and M.H. Budworth, "The Study of Work Motivation in the 20th Century," in L.L. Koppes, ed., *Historical Perspectives in Industrial and Organizational Psychology* (Hillsdale, NJ: Erlbaum, 2006).
10. M.C. Bolino and A.C. Klotz, "How to Motivate Employees to Go Beyond Their Jobs," *Harvard Business Review*, https://hbr.org, September 15, 2017.
11. A.M. Grant, "Does Intrinsic Motivation Fuel the Prosocial Fire? Motivational Synergy in Predicting Persistence, Performance, and Productivity," *Journal of Applied Psychology* 93, no. 1 (2008), 48–58.
12. Grant, "Does Intrinsic Motivation Fuel the Prosocial Fire?"; C.D. Batson, "Prosocial Motivation: Is It Ever Truly Altruistic?" in L. Berkowitz, ed., *Advances in Experimental Social Psychology*, vol. 20 (New York: Academic Press, 1987), 65–122.
13. Grant, "Does Intrinsic Motivation Fuel the Prosocial Fire?"; Batson, "Prosocial Motivation."
14. J.P. Campbell and R.D. Pritchard, "Motivation Theory in Industrial and Organizational Psychology," in M.D. Dunnette, ed., *Handbook of Industrial and Organizational Psychology* (Chicago: Rand McNally, 1976), 63–130; T.R. Mitchell, "Expectancy Value Models in Organizational Psychology," in N.T. Feather, ed., *Expectations and Actions: Expectancy Value Models in Psychology* (Hillsdale, NJ: Erlbaum, 1982), 293–312; V.H. Vroom, *Work and Motivation* (New York: Wiley, 1964).
15. N. Shope Griffin, "Personalize Your Management Development," *Harvard Business Review* 8, no. 10 (2003), 113–19.
16. T.A. Stewart, "Just Think: No Permission Needed," *Fortune*, www.fortune.com, January 8, 2001, accessed June 26, 2001.
17. M. Leonhardt, "The Great Resignation Rages on as a Record 4.5 Million Americans Quit," *Fortune*, https://fortune.com, accessed January 28, 2023.
18. Young Entrepreneur Council, "8 Ways to Invest in Employee Training and Boost Retention," *Inc.*, www.inc.com, accessed January 28, 2023; E. Schurenberg, "Richard Branson: Why Customers Come Second at Virgin," *Inc.*, www.inc.com, February 6, 2020.
19. T.J. Maurer, E.M. Weiss, and F.G. Barbeite, "A Model of Involvement in Work-Related Learning and Development Activity: The Effects of Individual, Situational, Motivational, and Age Variables," *Journal of Applied Psychology* 88, no. 4 (2003), 707–24.
20. G. Chandra, "How One Cambodian Refugee Started Southern California's Donut Empire," *Food and Wine*, www.foodandwine.com, accessed September 29, 2022; D. Pierson, "Why Are Doughnut Boxes Pink? The Answer Could Only Come Out of Southern California," *Los Angeles Times*, www.latimes.com, May 25, 2017; E. Navales, "The Back Story Behind Cambodian-Owned Donut Shops," *Kore Asian Media*, http://kore.am, November 5, 2015.
21. Enterprise Holdings, "Recruiting & Management Training," www.enterpriseholdings.com, accessed March 10, 2022.
22. J. Pollack, "These Are Six Employee Needs that Companies Need to Serve," *Fast Company*, www.fastcompany.com, January 9, 2020.
23. Mercer, *Global Talent Trends 2019*, www.mercer.com, accessed March 9, 2020.
24. Mercer, *Global Talent Trends;* Society for Human Resource Management, "Do We Have to Offer the Same Benefits to Our Employees Who Work in Other Countries as to the Employees Working in the United States?" www.shrm.org, accessed March 9, 2020; "The Santander Way: Unlocking the Power of Employee Engagement with Big Data on Flexibility," Werk customer story, https://werk.co, accessed March 9, 2020.
25. J.B. Fuller, M. Raman, J.K. Wallenstein, and A. de Chalendar, "Your Workforce Is More Adaptable than You Think," *Harvard Business Review*, May–June 2019, 118–26.
26. A. H. Maslow, *Motivation and Personality* (New York: Harper & Row, 1954);

Campbell and Pritchard, "Motivation Theory in Industrial and Organizational Psychology."

27. Kanfer, "Motivation Theory and Industrial and Organizational Psychology."

28. S. Ronen, "An Underlying Structure of Motivational Need Taxonomies: A Cross-Cultural Confirmation," in H.C. Triandis, M.D. Dunnette, and L.M. Hough, eds., *Handbook of Industrial and Organizational Psychology,* vol. 4 (Palo Alto, CA: Consulting Psychologists Press, 1994), 241–69.

29. N.J. Adler, *International Dimensions of Organizational Behavior,* 2nd ed. (Boston: P.W.S. Kent, 1991); G. Hofstede, "Motivation, Leadership, and Organization: Do American Theories Apply Abroad?" *Organizational Dynamics,* Summer 1980, 42–63.

30. C.P. Alderfer, "An Empirical Test of a New Theory of Human Needs," *Organizational Behavior and Human Performance* 4 (1969), 142–75; C.P. Alderfer, *Existence, Relatedness, and Growth: Human Needs in Organizational Settings* (New York: Free Press, 1972); Campbell and Pritchard, "Motivation Theory in Industrial and Organizational Psychology."

31. Kanfer, "Motivation Theory and Industrial and Organizational Psychology."

32. F. Herzberg, *Work and the Nature of Man* (Cleveland: World, 1966).

33. N. King, "Clarification and Evaluation of the Two-Factor Theory of Job Satisfaction," *Psychological Bulletin* 74 (1970), 18–31; E.A. Locke, "The Nature and Causes of Job Satisfaction," in M.D. Dunnette, ed., *Handbook of Industrial and Organizational Psychology* (Cleveland: Rand McNally, 1976), 1297–349.

34. D.C. McClelland, *Human Motivation* (Glenview, IL: Scott, Foresman, 1985); D.C. McClelland, "How Motives, Skills, and Values Determine What People Do," *American Psychologist* 40 (1985), 812–25; D.C. McClelland, "Managing Motivation to Expand Human Freedom," *American Psychologist* 33 (1978), 201–10.

35. D.G. Winter, *The Power Motive* (New York: Free Press, 1973).

36. M.J. Stahl, "Achievement, Power, and Managerial Motivation: Selecting Managerial Talent with the Job Choice Exercise," *Personnel Psychology* 36 (1983), 775–89; D.C. McClelland and D.H. Burnham, "Power Is the Great Motivator," *Harvard Business Review* 54 (1976), 100–10.

37. R.J. House, W.D. Spangler, and J. Woycke, "Personality and Charisma in the U.S. Presidency: A Psychological Theory of Leader Effectiveness," *Administrative Science Quarterly* 36 (1991), 364–96.

38. G.H. Hines, "Achievement, Motivation, Occupations, and Labor Turnover in New Zealand," *Journal of Applied Psychology* 58 (1973), 313–17; P.S. Hundal, "A Study of Entrepreneurial Motivation: Comparison of Fast- and Slow-Progressing Small Scale Industrial Entrepreneurs in Punjab, India," *Journal of Applied Psychology* 55 (1971), 317–23.

39. J. Howington, "Attaining Work-Life Balance and Productivity When You Work from Home," *Flexjobs,* www.flexjobs.com, accessed January 27, 2023; I. Lupu and M. Ruiz-Castro, "Work-Life Balance Is a Cycle, Not an Achievement," *Harvard Business Review,* https://hbr.org, January 29, 2021.

40. C. Mooney, "Just Looking at Nature Can Help Your Brain Work Better, Study Finds," *The Washington Post,* www.washingtonpost.com, May 26, 2015; K.E. Lee et al., "40-Second Green Roof Views Sustain Attention," *Journal of Environmental Psychology* 42 (2015): 182–89.

41. J.S. Adams, "Toward an Understanding of Inequity," *Journal of Abnormal and Social Psychology* 67 (1963), 422–36.

42. Adams, "Toward an Understanding of Inequity"; J. Greenberg, "Approaching Equity and Avoiding Inequity in Groups and Organizations," in J. Greenberg and R.L. Cohen, eds., *Equity and Justice in Social Behavior* (New York: Academic Press, 1982), 389–435; J. Greenberg, "Equity and Workplace Status: A Field Experiment," *Journal of Applied Psychology* 73 (1988), 606–13; R.T. Mowday, "Equity Theory Predictions of Behavior in Organizations," in R.M. Steers and L.W. Porter, eds., *Motivation and Work Behavior* (New York: McGraw-Hill, 1987), 89–110.

43. N. Ismail, "5 Ways Mobility Is Impacting the Workplace Today," *Information Age,* www.information-age.com, October 17, 2017.

44. K. Grind, B. Fritz, and S. E. Needleman, "Activision CEO Bobby Kotick Knew for Years about Sexual-Misconduct Allegations at Videogame Giant," *The Wall Street Journal,* www.wsj.com, November 17, 2021; S. Liao, "Over 100 Activision Blizzard Employees Stage Walkout, Demand CEO Step Down," *The Washington Post,* www.washingtonpost.com, November 16, 2021.

45. K. Weise and D. McCabe, "Microsoft Gambles on 'Nice Guy' Strategy to Close Activation Megadeal," *The New York Times,* www.nytimes.com, December 22, 2022; M. Day, "'I Felt So Alone': What Women at Microsoft Face, and Why Many Leave," *Seattle Times,* www.seattletimes.com, April 12, 2018.

46. D. Kerr, "Lyft Pledges Equal Pay for Women, Men, People of Color," CNET, www.cnet.com, March 27, 2018; C. Connley, "Starbucks Has Closed Its Pay Gap in the US; Here Are 4 Other Companies That Have Done the Same," CNBC, www.cnbc.com, March 23, 2018.

47. L.J. Skitka and F.J. Crosby, "Trends in the Social Psychological Study of Justice," *Personality and Social Psychology Review* 7 (April 2003), 282–85.

48. J.A. Colquitt, J. Greenbery, and C.P. Zapata-Phelan, "What Is Organizational Justice? A Historical Overview," in J. Greenberg and J.A. Colquitt, eds., *Handbook of Organizational Justice* (Mahwah, NJ: Erlbaum, 2005), 12–45; J.A. Colquitt, "On the Dimensionality of Organizational Justice: A Construct Validation of a Measure," *Journal of Applied Psychology* 86 (March 2001), 386–400.

49. R. Folger and M.A. Konovsky, "Effects of Procedural and Distributive Justice on Reactions to Pay Raise Decisions," *Academy of Management Journal* 32 (1989), 115–30; J. Greenberg, "Organizational Justice: Yesterday, Today, and Tomorrow," *Journal of Management* 16 (1990), 339–432; M.L. Ambrose and A. Arnaud, "Are Procedural Justice and Distributive Justice Conceptually Distinct?" in J. Greenberg and J.A. Colquitt, eds., *Handbook of Organizational Justice* (Mahwah, NJ: Erlbaum, 2005), 60–78.

50. M.L. Ambrose and M. Schminke, "Organization Structure as a Moderator of the Relationship between Procedural Justice, Interactional Justice, Perceived Organizational Support, and Supervisory Trust," *Journal of Applied Psychology* 88 (February 2003), 295–305.

51. J.A. Colquitt, "On the Dimensionality of Organizational Justice: A Construct Validation of a Measure," *Journal of Applied Psychology* 86 (March 2001), 386–400.

52. Greenberg, "Organizational Justice"; E.A. Lind and T. Tyler, *The Social Psychology of Procedural Justice* (New York: Plenum, 1988).

53. R.J. Bies, "The Predicament of Injustice: The Management of Moral Outrage," in L.L. Cummings and B.M. Staw, eds, *Research in Organizational Behavior,* vol. 9 (Greenwich, CT: JAI Press, 1987), 289–319; R.J. Bies and D.L. Shapiro, "Interactional Fairness Judgments: The Influence of Casual Accounts," *Social Justice Research* 1 (1987), 199–218; J. Greenberg, "Looking Fair vs. Being Fair: Managing Impression of Organizational Justice," in B.M. Staw and L.L. Cummings, eds., *Research in Organizational Behavior,* vol. 12 (Greenwich, CT: JAI Press, 1990), 111–57; T.R. Tyler and R. J. Bies, "Beyond Formal Procedures: The Interpersonal Context of Procedural Justice," in J. Carroll, ed., *Advances in Applied Social Psychology: Business Settings* (Hillsdale, NJ: Erlbaum, 1989), 77–98; Colquitt, "On the Dimensionality of Organizational Justice."

54. Colquitt, "On the Dimensionality of Organizational Justice"; J.A. Colquitt and J.C. Shaw, "How Should Organizational

Justice Be Measured?" in J. Greenberg and J.A. Colquitt, eds., *Handbook of Organizational Justice* (Mahwah, NJ: Erlbaum, 2005), 115–41.

55. E.A. Locke and G.P. Latham, *A Theory of Goal Setting and Task Performance* (Englewood Cliffs, NJ: Prentice-Hall, 1990).

56. Locke and Latham, *A Theory of Goal Setting and Task Performance;* J.J. Donovan and D.J. Radosevich, "The Moderating Role of Goal Commitment on the Goal Difficulty-Performance Relationship: A Meta-Analytic Review and Critical Analysis," *Journal of Applied Psychology* 83 (1998), 308–15; M.E. Tubbs, "Goal Setting: A Meta Analytic Examination of the Empirical Evidence," *Journal of Applied Psychology* 71 (1986), 474–83.

57. E.A. Locke, K.N. Shaw, L.M. Saari, and G.P. Latham, "Goal Setting and Task Performance: 1969–1980," *Psychological Bulletin* 90 (1981), 125–52.

58. P.C. Earley, T. Connolly, and G. Ekegren, "Goals, Strategy Development, and Task Performance: Some Limits on the Efficacy of Goal Setting," *Journal of Applied Psychology* 74 (1989), 24–33; R. Kanfer and P.L. Ackerman, "Motivation and Cognitive Abilities: An Integrative/Aptitude-Treatment Interaction Approach to Skill Acquisition," *Journal of Applied Psychology* 74 (1989), 657–90.

59. W.C. Hamner, "Reinforcement Theory and Contingency Management in Organizational Settings," in H. Tosi and W.C. Hamner, eds., *Organizational Behavior and Management: A Contingency Approach* (Chicago: St. Clair Press, 1974).

60. B.F. Skinner, *Contingencies of Reinforcement* (New York: Appleton-Century-Crofts, 1969).

61. H.W. Weiss, "Learning Theory and Industrial and Organizational Psychology," in M.D. Dunnette and L.M. Hough, eds., *Handbook of Industrial and Organizational Psychology* (Palo Alto, CA: Consulting Psychologists Press, 1991), 171–221.

62. Hamner, "Reinforcement Theory and Contingency Management."

63. F. Luthans and R. Kreitner, *Organizational Behavior Modification and Beyond* (Glenview, IL: Scott, Foresman, 1985); A.D. Stajkovic and F. Luthans, "A Meta-Analysis of the Effects of Organizational Behavior Modification on Task Performance, 1975–95," *Academy of Management Journal* 40 (1997), 1122–49.

64. A.D. Stajkovic and F. Luthans, "Behavioral Management and Task Performance in Organizations: Conceptual Background, Meta Analysis, and Test of Alternative Models," *Personnel Psychology* 56 (2003), 155–94.

65. Ibid.; F. Luthans and A.D. Stajkovic, "Reinforce for Performance: The Need to Go beyond Pay and Even Rewards," *Academy of Management Executive* 13, no. 2 (1999), 49–56; G. Billikopf and M.V. Norton, "Pay Method Affects Vineyard Pruner Performance," *California Agriculture,* September–October 1992, 12–13.

66. A. Bandura, *Principles of Behavior Modification* (New York: Holt, Rinehart and Winston, 1969); A. Bandura, *Social Learning Theory* (Englewood Cliffs, NJ: Prentice-Hall, 1977); T.R.V. Davis and F. Luthans, "A Social Learning Approach to Organizational Behavior," *Academy of Management Review* 5 (1980), 281–90.

67. A.P. Goldstein and M. Sorcher, *Changing Supervisor Behaviors* (New York: Pergamon Press, 1974); Luthans and Kreitner, *Organizational Behavior Modification and Beyond.*

68. Bandura, *Social Learning Theory;* Davis and Luthans, "A Social Learning Approach to Organizational Behavior"; Luthans and Kreitner, *Organizational Behavior Modification and Beyond.*

69. A. Bandura, "Self-Reinforcement: Theoretical and Methodological Considerations," *Behaviorism* 4 (1976), 135–55.

70. M. Schneider, "Google Increased New Employee Productivity by 25 Percent with 1 Email. Here's What You Need to Know," *Inc.*, www.inc.com, accessed March 9, 2020.

71. A. Bandura, *Self-Efficacy: The Exercise of Control* (New York: W.H. Freeman, 1997); J.B. Vancouver, K.M. More, and R.J. Yoder, "Self-Efficacy and Resource Allocation: Support for a Nonmonotonic, Discontinuous Model," *Journal of Applied Psychology* 93, no. 1 (2008), 35–47.

72. A. Bandura, "Self-Efficacy Mechanism in Human Agency," *American Psychologist* 37 (1982), 122–27; M.E. Gist and T.R. Mitchell, "Self-Efficacy: A Theoretical Analysis of Its Determinants and Malleability," *Academy of Management Review* 17 (1992), 183–211.

73. "Bernard Olayo," *Aspen Ideas,* www.aspenideas.org, accessed January 28, 2023; "'Milkman' Expands Kenya's Medical Oxygen Supplies," *Africa Defense Forum* (ADF), https://adf-magazine.com, October 12, 2021; D. Herbling, "A Breath of Life for Africa," *Bloomberg Businessweek,* October 4, 2021, 40–41.

74. "'Milkman Expands Kenya's Medical Oxygen Supplies"; Hewatele, "About Us," https://hewatele.org, accessed January 28, 2023; "Kenyan Oxygen Maker to Double Production as COVID-19 Fuels Demand," *Reuters,* www.reuters.com, August 12, 2021.

75. Herbling, "A Breath of Life"; Reuters, "Kenyan Oxygen Maker."

76. Reuters, "Kenyan Oxygen Maker"; "'Milkman, Expands Kenya's Medical Oxygen Supplies."

77. "'Milkman' Expands Kenya's Medical Oxygen Supplies."

78. E.E. Lawler III, *Pay and Organization Development* (Reading, MA: Addison-Wesley, 1981).

79. S. Miller, "Pandemic Forces Employers to Cut Pay," *Society for Human Resource Management,* www.shrm.org, April 1, 2020.

80. "MBA Inventory: Motivating by Appreciation," https://mbainventory.com, accessed January 28, 2023.

81. Forbes Human Resources Council, "13 Clever Ways to Show Appreciation for Remote Workers," *Forbes,* www.forbes.com, May 24, 2021; P. White, "The COVID-19 Pandemic Changed Everything about Work...Except How People Want to Be Shown Appreciation," *Training Industry,* https://trainingindustry.com, May 7, 2021.

82. Lawler, *Pay and Organization Development.*

83. Ibid.

84. "Employee Engagement," https://sustainability.lincolnelectric.com, accessed March 10, 2020; J.F. Lincoln, *Incentive Management* (Cleveland: Lincoln Electric Company, 1951); R. Zager, "Managing Guaranteed Employment," *Harvard Business Review* 56 (1978), 103–15.

85. Lawler, *Pay and Organization Development.*

86. "Benefits," https://gradientcorp.com, accessed March 10, 2020; M. Gendron, "Gradient Named 'Small Business of Year,'" *Boston Herald,* May 11, 1994, p. 35.

87. "Careers," https://nucor.com, accessed January 28, 2023; W. Zeller, R.D. Hof, R. Brandt, S. Baker, and D. Greising, "Go-Go Goliaths," *BusinessWeek,* February 13, 1995, 64–70.

88. "Nucor Fact Sheet—National," https://nucor.com/newsroom, accessed March 10, 2020; N. Byrnes, "A Steely Resolve," *BusinessWeek,* April 6, 2009, 54.

89. "Stock Option," *Encarta World English Dictionary,* www.dictionary.msn.com, June 28, 2001; personal interview with Professor Bala Dharan, Jones Graduate School of Business, Rice University, June 28, 2001.

90. Personal interview with Professor Bala Dharan.

91. Ibid.

92. C.D. Fisher, L.F. Schoenfeldt, and J.B. Shaw, *Human Resource Management* (Boston: Houghton Mifflin, 1990); B.E. Graham-Moore and T.L. Ross, *Productivity Gainsharing* (Englewood Cliffs, NJ: Prentice-Hall, 1983); A.J. Geare, "Productivity from Scanlon Type Plans," *Academy of Management Review* 1 (1976), 99–108.

93. R. Stevenson, "Japan CEOs Facing Inflation Are Talking More about Merit-Based Pay," *Bloomberg,* www.bloomberg.com, January 15, 2023; T. Kajimoto and I. Nakagawa, "Japan's Efforts to Raise Wages Wane as Firms Embrace Merit-Based Pay," *Reuters,* www.reuters.com, February 11, 2020.

CHAPTER 14

Leadership

mentatdgt/Shutterstock

Learning Objectives

After studying this chapter, you should be able to:

LO14-1 Explain what leadership is, when leaders are effective and ineffective, and the sources of power that enable managers to be effective leaders.

LO14-2 Identify the traits that show the strongest relationship to leadership, the behaviors leaders engage in, and the limitations of the trait and behavior models of leadership.

LO14-3 Explain how contingency models of leadership enhance our understanding of effective leadership and management in organizations.

LO14-4 Describe what transformational leadership is, and explain how managers can engage in it.

LO14-5 Characterize the relationship between gender and leadership, and explain how emotional intelligence may contribute to leadership effectiveness.

A MANAGER'S CHALLENGE

How Julie Sweet Leads Accenture

What does effective leadership look like? Julie Sweet brought an atypical background to her executive role at management consulting firm Accenture. A lawyer, she joined the firm as its general counsel and chief compliance officer. Five years later, she was promoted to CEO of Accenture's North America business, and in 2019, the board selected her to be CEO of the entire 700,000-employee company, which serves clients in more than 120 countries. As Accenture's top executive, Sweet leads by example and by teaching the company's values.[1]

Sweet wants to see leadership at all levels of Accenture. She has defined a set of essential leadership behaviors that she attempts to model and expects others to emulate. Two such leadership behaviors are to "have the courage to change and the ability to bring people along the journey."[2] Other leadership essentials are to lead with confidence, excellence, and humility and to care for one's people personally and professionally.[3]

From the start, Sweet made learning a priority for herself and the firm. She regularly includes learning objectives in the goals she sets for herself each quarter. Appreciating from the start that she lacked knowledge of the technology Accenture uses and helps clients implement, she emphasizes learning technologies such as digital manufacturing, 5G, and artificial intelligence. She shares the learning objectives with her team, and the company has built a "learning board" online, where employees can participate in learning along with her. Sweet notes that expressing a need for learning requires humility, and she embodies it. She is transparent about her need to learn and openly asks questions when she doesn't understand something. Now Sweet considers learning one of Accenture's core competencies.[4]

Transparency is another key value in Sweet's leadership; she says being transparent with employees can be uncomfortable but builds trust. This is relevant to Accenture's view of the future—one in which applications for technology, including artificial intelligence, will change the nature of work. Sweet insists that Accenture be open with employees about this. Applying the value placed on continuous learning, Accenture invites employees to participate in identifying what can be automated, how jobs will change, and what new skills will be needed. Then she gives the employees opportunities to learn the new skills they will need in the future. According to Sweet, this approach has not only made the firm more agile, it also motivates employees, who see that Accenture values them enough to invest in them.[5]

Finally, Sweet observes that more than half a million employees advising companies across industries around the world about every aspect of business will necessarily be highly

Accenture CEO Julie Sweet guides the organization with essential leadership behaviors that include humility, transparency, and continuous learning.
Cindy Ord/Getty Images

diverse. Some people have deep expertise in operations, others in data management; some in industrials, others in banking; some in medicine, others in accounting. So Sweet describes her workforce as a "culture of cultures" where individuals are united by the goal of sharing success as a company and with their clients. They also are united by the values Sweet models and teaches, including integrity and meritocracy. Under Sweet, Accenture values diversity and actively widens its pool of talent. For example, the firm reevaluated its assumption that most of its positions require a four-year college degree. It has set up what it calls "professional apprenticeships" that bring in high school and junior college students. The firm's hiring decisions focus less on years of education and more on evidence that candidates are eager and able to learn. This way, Sweet says, Accenture recruits a wider variety of employees, and nontraditional hires have often been the best performers because they are loyal and learn fast.[6]

Overview

Accenture's Julie Sweet exemplifies the many facets of effective leadership. In Chapter 1, we explained that one of the four primary tasks of managers is leading. Thus, it should come as no surprise that leadership is a key ingredient in effective management. When leaders are effective, their employees or followers are highly motivated, committed, and high-performing. When leaders are ineffective, chances are good that their employees do not perform up to their capabilities, are demotivated, and may be dissatisfied as well. Sweet is a leader at the top of an organization, but leadership is an important ingredient for managerial success at all levels of organizations: top management, middle management, and first-line management. Moreover, leadership is a key ingredient of managerial success for organizations large and small.

leadership The process by which an individual exerts influence over other people and inspires, motivates, and directs their activities to help achieve group or organizational goals.

In this chapter, we describe what leadership is and examine the major leadership models that shed light on the factors that contribute to a manager being an effective leader. We look at trait and behavior models, which focus on what leaders are like and what they do, and contingency models–Fiedler's contingency model, path–goal theory, and the leader substitutes model–each of which takes into account the complexity surrounding leadership and the role of the situation in leader effectiveness. We also describe how managers can use transformational leadership to dramatically affect their organizations. By the end of this chapter, you will appreciate the many factors and issues that managers face in their quest to be effective leaders.

The Nature of Leadership

LO14-1 Explain what leadership is, when leaders are effective and ineffective, and the sources of power that enable managers to be effective leaders.

Leadership is the process by which a person exerts influence over other people and inspires, motivates, and directs their activities to help achieve group or organizational goals.[7] The person who exerts such influence is a **leader**. When leaders are effective, the influence they exert over others helps a group or an organization achieve its performance goals. When leaders are ineffective, their influence does not contribute to, and often detracts from, goal attainment. As "A Manager's Challenge" makes clear, CEO Sweet inspires and motivates Accenture employees at all levels of the company so they can help the organization achieve its goals.

Beyond facilitating the attainment of performance goals, effective leadership increases an organization's ability to meet all the contemporary challenges discussed throughout this book, including the need to obtain a competitive advantage, the need to foster ethical behavior, and the need to manage a diverse workforce fairly and equitably. Leaders who exert influence over organizational members to help meet these goals increase their organizations' chances of success.

leader An individual who is able to exert influence over other people to help achieve group or organizational goals.

In considering the nature of leadership, we first look at leadership styles and how they affect managerial tasks and at the influence of culture on leadership styles. We then focus on the key to leadership, *power,* which can come from a variety of sources. Finally, we consider the contemporary dynamic of empowerment and how it relates to effective leadership.

Personal Leadership Style and Managerial Tasks

A manager's *personal leadership style*–that is, the specific ways in which a manager chooses to influence other people–shapes how that manager approaches planning, organizing, and controlling (the other principal tasks of managing). Consider Julie Sweet's personal leadership style as described in "A Manager's Challenge." She models values like learning and transparency and fosters an environment in which learning is continuously preparing the company for its new skill needs in a rapidly changing environment.

Managers at all levels and in all kinds of organizations have their own personal leadership styles, which determine not only how they lead their employees but also how they perform the other management tasks. Abby Woods, owner and manager of a spice and tea shop in suburban Chicago, for example, takes a hands-on approach to leadership. She has the sole authority for determining work schedules and job assignments for the 11 employees in her store (an organizing task), makes all important decisions by herself (a planning task), and closely monitors her employees' performance and rewards top performers with pay increases (a control task). Woods's personal leadership style is effective in her organization. Her employees are generally motivated, perform highly, and are satisfied–and the store continues to be profitable.

Developing an effective personal leadership style often is a challenge for managers at all levels in an organization. This challenge is often exacerbated when times are tough, due, for example, to an economic downturn or a decline in customer demand. The recent COVID-19 pandemic provided many managers with just such a challenge.

Although leading is one of the four principal tasks of managing, a distinction is often made between managers and leaders. When this distinction is made, managers are thought of as those organizational members who establish and implement procedures and processes to ensure smooth functioning and are accountable for goal accomplishment. Leaders look to the future, chart the course for the organization, and attract, retain, motivate, inspire, and develop relationships with employees based on trust and mutual respect. They also provide meaning and purpose, seek innovation rather than stability, and impassion employees to work together to achieve the leaders' vision.[8]

Servant Leadership

servant leader A leader who has a strong desire to serve and work for the benefit of others.

As part of their personal leadership style, some leaders strive to serve others. Robert Greenleaf–who was director of management research at AT&T and upon his retirement embarked on a second career focused on writing, speaking, and consulting–came up with the term *servant leadership* to describe these leaders.[9] **Servant leaders**, above all else, have a strong desire to work for the benefit of others. Servant leaders share power with followers and strive to ensure that followers' most important needs are met, that they are able to develop as individuals, that their well-being is enhanced, and that attention is paid to those who are least well-off in a society.[10] Servant leadership is unique as a leadership approach because the leader views their role more as a motivator and listener, someone who empowers followers to act as collaborators and innovators within the organization.[11] Greenleaf founded a nonprofit organization called the Greenleaf Center for Servant Leadership (formerly called the Center for Applied Ethics) to foster leadership focused on service to others, power sharing, and a sense of community between organizations and their multiple stakeholders.[12]

Leadership Styles across Cultures

Some evidence suggests that leadership styles vary not only among individuals but also among countries or cultures. Some research indicates that European managers tend to be more humanistic, or people-oriented, than both Japanese and American managers. The collectivistic culture in Japan places prime emphasis on the group rather than the individual, so the importance of individuals' own personalities, needs, and desires is minimized. Organizations in the United States tend to be very profit-oriented and thus tend to downplay the importance of individual employees' needs and desires. Many countries in Europe have a more individualistic perspective than Japan and a more humanistic perspective than the United States, and this may result in some European managers' being more people-oriented than their Japanese or American counterparts. European managers, for example, tend to be reluctant to lay off employees, and when a layoff is absolutely necessary, they take careful steps to make it as painless as possible.[13]

Another cross-cultural difference occurs in time horizons. While managers in any one country often differ in their time horizons, there are also national differences. For example, U.S. organizations tend to have a short-term profit orientation; thus, U.S. managers' personal leadership styles emphasize short-term performance. Japanese organizations tend to have a long-term growth orientation, so Japanese managers' personal leadership styles emphasize long-term performance. Justus Mische, a personnel manager at the European organization Hoechst, suggested that "Europe, at least the big international firms in Europe, have a philosophy between the Japanese, long term, and the United States, short term."[14] Research on these and other global aspects of leadership is ongoing; as it continues, more cultural differences in managers' personal leadership styles may be discovered.[15]

Power: The Key to Leadership

No matter what one's leadership style, a key component of effective leadership is found in the *power* the leader has to affect other people's behavior and to get them to act in certain ways.[16] There are several types of power: legitimate, reward, coercive, expert, and referent power (see Figure 14.1).[17] Effective leaders take steps to ensure that they have sufficient levels of each type and that they use their power in beneficial ways.

legitimate power The authority that a manager has by virtue of their position in an organization's hierarchy.

LEGITIMATE POWER **Legitimate power** is the authority a manager has by virtue of their position in an organization's hierarchy. Personal leadership style often influences how a manager exercises legitimate power. Consider the case of a first-line manager in a greeting card company who leads a group of 15 artists and designers. The manager has the legitimate power to hire new employees, assign projects to the artists and designers, monitor their work, and appraise their performance. The manager uses this power effectively by making sure project assignments match the interests of the employees as much as possible so they will enjoy their work and monitoring their work to be sure they are on track but stopping short of engaging in close supervision, which can hamper creativity. The manager also makes sure that employee performance appraisals are developmental in nature, providing concrete advice for areas where improvements could be made. In addition, the manager recently negotiated for an increase in the level of legitimate power, so the manager can now initiate and develop proposals for new product lines.

Figure 14.1
Sources of Managerial Power

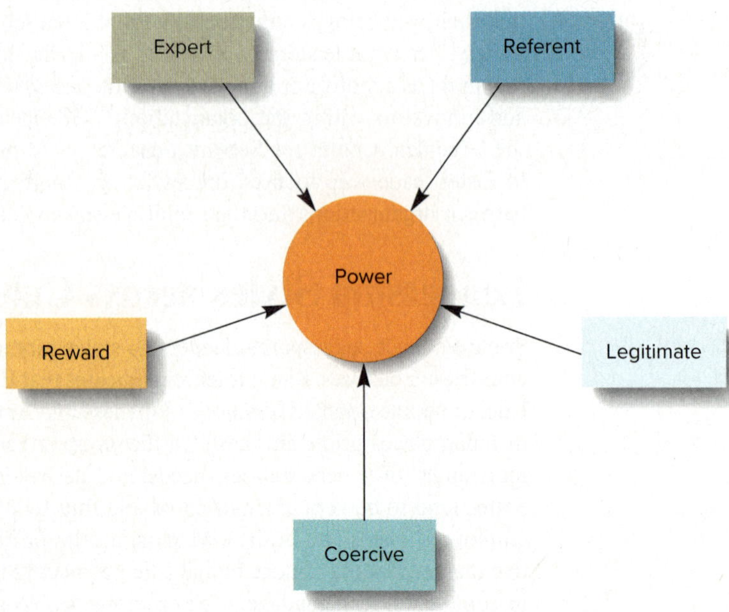

A manager can have significant impact by wielding legitimate power. However, exercising legitimate power does not necessarily make followers enthusiastic about or committed to following a directive. For an example of the limits of legitimate power, see the "Focus on DEI&B" feature.

FOCUS ON DEI&B

Leading Across the Divide Between Right and Left

Despite its significant benefits, diversity can introduce conflict. In the U.S. workplace, this certainly applies to politics. With news outlets reporting issues as right-versus-left-wing debates and social media enabling near-anonymity for commenting, some issues seem to be impossible to discuss civilly. Yet issues with political aspects arise when employees have concerns about fair employment, advertising messages, or where to open a new facility. Companies including Basecamp, Facebook, Netflix, and Pinterest have endured protests, walkouts, and employee turnover when employees clashed about such issues. Furthermore, research suggests that a growing share of workers have experienced mistreatment because of their political views, and where managers are aware of political positions, employment decisions may be shaped as much by politics as by race or sex.[18]

Leaders may be tempted to invoke their legitimate power and ban workplace discussion of politics. However, employees want to bring their whole selves to work. Those who already feel unheard or unappreciated may experience a policy of silence as further injustice. Also, banning topics conflicts with work models using teamwork to generate new ideas through the exchange of diverse perspectives. A more effective option is to develop teamwork skills and use them to lead across the political divide.[19]

Leading in this context requires knowledge of human behavior plus humility. A body of evidence indicates that political perspectives generate perception biases. This is not a problem of the left or of the right but a human behavior. No one is immune. In an experiment involving staged interactions, people concerned about social equality (categorized as left-leaners) were likelier to see inequities if these affected underrepresented groups. People categorized as right-leaners tended not to see inequities, regardless of demographics. People who don't agree on what happened will draw different conclusions. It can help if group members, including the leader, agree that perception biases exist.[20]

To prevent disputes, leaders can model humility and attentive listening and establish norms for respectful, productive discourse. They can require training, starting with orientation, in which employees learn what is unacceptable (e.g., hate speech, insults, purposeless arguing) and is valued (e.g., listening to understand, pursuing shared goals). Training should cover perception biases and ways to address them: For example, feeling indignant and righteous may signal that a bias is in play. One company allowed employees to post political content on its internal messaging system as long as such comments included a video in which they explained their opinions. Employees then became more selective in their posts.[21]

reward power The ability of a manager to give or withhold tangible and intangible rewards.

REWARD POWER **Reward power** is the ability of a manager to give or withhold tangible rewards (pay raises, bonuses, choice job assignments) and intangible rewards (verbal praise, a pat on the back, respect). As you learned in Chapter 13, members of an organization are motivated to perform at a high level by a variety of rewards. Being able to give or withhold rewards based on performance is a major source of power, which allows managers to have a highly motivated workforce. Managers of salespeople in retail organizations, like Neiman Marcus, Nordstrom, and Macy's, and in car dealerships, such as Mazda, Ford, and Volvo, often use their reward power to motivate their employees. Employees in organizations such as these often receive commissions on whatever they sell and rewards for the quality of their customer service, which motivate them to do the best they can.[22]

Effective managers use their reward power to show appreciation for employees' good work and efforts. Ineffective managers use rewards in a more controlling manner that signals to employees that the manager has the upper hand. Managers also can take steps to increase their reward power. For example, the manager in the greeting card company we discussed earlier had the legitimate power to appraise employees' performance, but they lacked the reward power to distribute raises and end-of-year bonuses until they discussed with their own manager why this would be a valuable motivational tool for the manager to use. The manager now receives a pool of money each year for salary increases and bonuses and has the reward power to distribute them as they see fit.

coercive power The ability of a manager to punish others.

COERCIVE POWER **Coercive power** is the ability of a manager to punish others. Punishment can range from verbal reprimands to reductions in pay or working hours to actual dismissal. In the previous chapter, we discussed how punishment can have negative side effects, such as resentment and retaliation, and should be used only when necessary (for example, to curtail a dangerous behavior). Managers who rely heavily on coercive power tend to be ineffective as leaders and sometimes even get fired or sent to prison. Didier Lombard, former CEO of a French communications company, was recently convicted, along with two other top executives, of "collective moral harassment" for creating a toxic work environment that resulted in the suicides of 35 employees. When Didier took the company private, he and his management team devised a plan to cut nearly 22,000 workers as part of an overall restructuring to reduce costs. Because of French labor laws, Didier could not just fire the workers; instead, he and his managers hatched a plan to create an "atmosphere of fear," making workers' lives miserable and intolerable. Their use of power caused severe anxiety among workers, causing some employees to take their own lives. Ten years after the company restructuring, the French courts found Didier guilty of masterminding the plot and sentenced him to jail time and a $16,000 fine for abuse of power.[23]

Excessive use of coercive power seldom produces high performance and is questionable ethically. Sometimes it amounts to a form of mental abuse, robbing workers of their dignity and causing excessive levels of stress. Overuse of coercive power can even result in dangerous working conditions. Better results and, importantly, an ethical workplace that respects employee dignity can be obtained by using reward power.

expert power Power that is based on the special knowledge, skills, and expertise that a leader possesses.

EXPERT POWER **Expert power** is based on the special knowledge, skills, and expertise that a leader possesses. The nature of expert power varies, depending on the leader's level in the hierarchy. First-level and middle managers often have technical expertise relevant to the tasks their employees perform. Their expert power gives them considerable influence over employees. Some top managers derive expert power from their technical expertise. Other top-level managers lack technical expertise and derive their expert power from their abilities as decision makers, planners, and strategists. Jack Welch, the former leader and CEO of General Electric, summed it up this way: "The basic thing that we at the top of the company know is that we don't know the business. What we have, I hope, is the ability to allocate resources, people, and dollars."[24]

Effective leaders take steps to ensure that they have an adequate amount of expert power to perform their leadership roles. They may obtain additional training or education in their fields, make sure they keep up with the latest developments and changes in technology, stay abreast of changes in their fields through involvement in professional associations, and read widely to be aware of momentous changes in the organization's task and general environments. Expert power tends to be best used in a guiding or coaching manner rather than in an arrogant, high-handed way.

referent power Power that comes from employees' and coworkers' respect, admiration, and loyalty.

REFERENT POWER **Referent power** is more informal than the other kinds of power. Referent power is a function of the personal characteristics of a leader; it is the power that comes from employees' and coworkers' respect, admiration, and loyalty. Leaders who are likable and whom employees wish to use as a role model are especially likely to possess referent power.

In addition to being a valuable asset for top managers, referent power can help first-line and middle managers be effective leaders as well. Consider, for example, the manager of a group of administrative assistants in the finance department of a large university. The assistants in the group are known to be among the best employees in the university. Much of their willingness to go above and beyond the call of duty has been attributed to their manager's caring and empathetic nature, which makes them feel important and valued. Managers can take steps to increase their referent power, such as taking time to get to know their employees and showing interest and concern for them.

Empowerment: An Ingredient in Modern Management

empowerment The expansion of employees' knowledge, tasks, and decision-making responsibilities.

More and more managers today are incorporating into their personal leadership styles an aspect that at first glance seems to be the opposite of being a leader. In Chapter 1 we described how **empowerment**–the process of giving employees at all levels the authority to make decisions, be responsible for their outcomes, improve quality, and cut costs–is becoming increasingly popular in organizations. When leaders empower their employees, the employees typically take over some responsibilities and authority that used to reside with the leader or manager, such as the right to reject parts that do not meet quality standards, the right to check one's own work, and the right to schedule work activities. Empowered employees are given the power to make some decisions that their leaders or supervisors used to make.

Empowerment might seem to be the opposite of effective leadership because managers are allowing employees to take a more active role in leading themselves. In actuality, however, empowerment can contribute to effective leadership for several reasons:

- Empowerment increases a manager's ability to get things done because the manager has the support and help of employees who may have special knowledge of work tasks.
- Empowerment often increases workers' involvement, motivation, and commitment; and this helps ensure that they are working toward organizational goals.
- Empowerment gives managers more time to concentrate on their pressing concerns because they spend less time on day-to-day supervision.

Effective managers, like Accenture's Julie Sweet, realize the benefits of empowerment. The personal leadership style of managers who empower employees often entails developing employees' ability to make good decisions as well as being their guide, coach, and source of inspiration. The COVID-19 pandemic continues to influence how managers and employees view empowerment. In a recent survey, more than 63% of 1,000 full-time U.S. employees cited the flexibility to work when and how they want as the most empowering benefit they desire from organizations. One takeaway from the pandemic is that employees working for companies that encourage flexibility feel empowered to exceed expectations at work while gaining control over their work-life balance.[25]

Trait and Behavior Models of Leadership

Leading is such an important process in all organizations–nonprofit organizations, government agencies, and schools, as well as for-profit corporations–that it has been researched for decades. Early approaches to leadership, called the *trait model* and the *behavior model,* sought to determine what effective leaders are like as people and what they do that makes them so effective.

The Trait Model

LO14-2 Identify the traits that show the strongest relationship to leadership, the behaviors leaders engage in, and the limitations of the trait and behavior models of leadership.

The trait model of leadership focused on identifying the personal characteristics that cause effective leadership. Researchers thought effective leaders must have certain personal qualities that set them apart from ineffective leaders and from people who never become leaders. Decades of research (beginning in the 1930s) and hundreds of studies indicate that certain personal characteristics do appear to be associated with effective leadership. (See Table 14.1 for a list of these.[26]) Notice that although this model is called the "trait" model, some of the personal characteristics that it identifies are not personality traits per se but, rather, are concerned with a leader's skills, abilities, knowledge, and expertise. As "A Manager's Challenge" shows, Accenture CEO Julie Sweet appears to have many of these characteristics (such as intelligence, self-confidence, and integrity and honesty). Leaders who do not have these traits may be ineffective.

Traits alone are not the key to understanding leader effectiveness, however. Some effective leaders do not possess all these traits, and some leaders who possess them are not effective in

Table 14.1
Traits Related to Effective Leadership

Trait	Description
Intelligence	Helps managers understand complex issues and solve problems.
Knowledge and expertise	Help managers make good decisions and discover ways to increase efficiency and effectiveness.
Dominance	Helps managers influence their employees to achieve organizational goals.
Self-confidence	Contributes to managers' effectively influencing employees and persisting when faced with obstacles or difficulties.
High energy	Helps managers deal with the many demands they face.
Tolerance for stress	Helps managers deal with uncertainty and make difficult decisions.
Integrity and honesty	Help managers behave ethically and earn their employees' trust and confidence.
Maturity	Helps managers avoid acting selfishly, control their feelings, and admit when they have made a mistake.

their leadership roles. This lack of a consistent relationship between leader traits and leader effectiveness led researchers to shift their attention away from traits and to search for new explanations for effective leadership. Rather than focusing on what leaders are like (the traits they possess), researchers began looking at what effective leaders actually do—in other words, at the behaviors that allow effective leaders to influence their employees to achieve group and organizational goals.

The Behavior Model

After extensive study in the 1940s and 1950s, researchers at The Ohio State University identified two basic kinds of leader behaviors that many leaders in the United States, Germany, and other countries engaged in to influence their employees: *consideration* and *initiating structure*.[27]

consideration Behavior indicating that a manager trusts, respects, and cares about employees.

CONSIDERATION Leaders engage in **consideration** when they show their employees that they trust, respect, and care about them. Managers who truly look out for the well-being of their employees, and do what they can to help them feel good and enjoy their work, perform consideration behaviors.

At Costco, not only is consideration an ethical imperative, but it also makes good business sense to take care of employees with generous benefits, sizable contributions to retirement plans, competitive time-off policies, and pay equity for all workers.
Paul Kane/Stringer/Getty Images

At Costco Wholesale Corporation, consideration is not only an ethical imperative, but it makes good business sense. In fact, the warehouse retailer believes consideration is so important that it is one of five principles in Costco's code of ethics: "Take care of our employees."[28] In addition to paying its employees substantially more than most other U.S. retailers, Costco also offers other generous benefits to its more than 250,000 employees worldwide, including affordable health care coverage for full- and part-time employees, sizable contributions to employees' company-sponsored retirement plans based on years of service, competitive paid sick and vacation time policies, and pay equity for men and women. In the United States, Costco employees average almost nine years of service with the company, and more than 70% of its managers began their careers as hourly employees. In 2022, Costco ranked 17 out of 500 organizations on *Forbes* 2022 America's Best Large Employers list.[29]

initiating structure Behavior that managers engage in to ensure that work gets done, employees perform their jobs acceptably, and the organization is efficient and effective.

INITIATING STRUCTURE Leaders engage in **initiating structure** when they take steps to make sure that work gets done, employees perform their jobs acceptably, and the organization is efficient and effective. Assigning tasks to individuals or work groups, letting employees know what is expected of them, deciding how work should be done, making schedules, encouraging adherence to rules and regulations, and motivating employees to do a good job are all examples of initiating structure.[30] For an example of how leaders have an impact by initiating structure, read the "Ethics in Action" feature about Salesforce's decision to hire an ethics officer.

ETHICS IN ACTION

Initiating Structure for Ethics at Salesforce

Salesforce, which makes business software for marketing, sales, and customer service, hired Paula Goldman as its chief ethical and humane use officer.[31] Goldman, possibly the first manager with this title, equips the company to make ethical decisions. She was selected from another Salesforce innovation: its ethical-use advisory council, consisting of technical experts from inside and outside the company. Goldman maintains and consults with the council to ensure that many perspectives on ethics are considered. The council issues recommendations to decision makers. Goldman also set up a thought process called consequence scanning. When employees plan a new idea or product, consequence scanning asks what consequences the planners expect and what might be unintended consequences. Often, new and surprising issues arise.[32]

Goldman's work affects decisions about products and company policies. Some involve concerns brought by employees to the advisory council, including questions about restrictions on customers or customer activities. In one case, the council's guidance persuaded management that customers must agree not to use its software to sell military-style firearms to private citizens. In other cases, products have been modified so that software guides personnel decisions away from discrimination.[33]

More so than other technology, artificial intelligence has potential to guide decisions in unintended directions. Salesforce therefore created another position, architect of ethical AI. Kathy Baxter, first to hold this job, works with product teams to consider ethical implications, so they can prepare customers to use products responsibly. For example, AI might flag a process that systematically selects or unselects people of a certain race–not only those categories themselves, but tightly linked categories, such as race and zip code. Seeing these flagged, the customer can adjust the program to behave more inclusively. Other ethical issues involve invasion of privacy, such as data gathering with cameras.[34]

Unethical technology uses may damage a business's reputation with customers, employees, and governments. Salesforce's CEO, Marc Benioff, has noted that what makes technology good or bad is the way it is used, not the technology itself. When Benioff makes certain managers responsible for establishing processes that push decisions toward the good uses, he exercises leadership by making ethics part of the management structure. Goldman and Baxter then lead by using Salesforce's own stated values–responsibility, accountability, transparency, empowerment, and inclusivity–as a starting point. By applying these values to decision-making processes, leaders align followers' actions with the company's purpose.[35]

Initiating structure and consideration are independent leader behaviors. Leaders can be high on both, low on both, or high on one and low on the other. Many effective leaders, like Accenture's Julie Sweet, engage in both of these behaviors.

Leadership researchers have identified leader behaviors similar to consideration and initiating structure. Researchers at the University of Michigan, for example, identified two categories of leadership behaviors, *employee-centered behaviors* and *job-oriented behaviors,* that correspond roughly to consideration and initiating structure, respectively.[36] Models of leadership popular with consultants also tend to zero in on these two kinds of behaviors. For example, Robert Blake and Jane Mouton's Managerial Grid focuses on *concern for people* (similar to consideration) and *concern for production* (similar to initiating structure). Blake and Mouton advise that effective leadership often requires both a high level of concern for people and a high level of concern for production.[37] As another example, Paul Hersey and Kenneth Blanchard's model focuses on *supportive behaviors* (similar to consideration) and *task-oriented behaviors* (similar to initiating structure). According to Hersey and Blanchard, leaders need to consider the nature of their employees when trying to determine the extent to which they should perform these two behaviors.[38]

You might expect that effective leaders and managers would perform both kinds of behaviors, but research has found that this is not necessarily the case. The relationship between performance of consideration and initiating-structure behaviors and leader effectiveness is not clear-cut. Some leaders are effective even when they do not perform consideration or initiating-structure behaviors, and some leaders are ineffective even when they perform both kinds of behaviors. Like the trait model of leadership, the behavior model alone cannot explain leader effectiveness. Realizing this, researchers began building more complicated models of leadership, focused not only on the leader and what they do but also on the situation or context in which leadership occurs.

Contingency Models of Leadership

LO14-3 Explain how contingency models of leadership enhance our understanding of effective leadership and management in organizations.

Simply having certain traits or performing certain behaviors does not ensure that a manager will be an effective leader in all situations calling for leadership. Some managers who seem to have the right traits and perform the right behaviors turn out to be ineffective leaders. Managers lead in a wide variety of situations and organizations and have various kinds of employees performing diverse tasks in a multiplicity of environmental contexts. Given the wide variety of situations in which leadership occurs, what makes a manager an effective leader in one situation (such as certain traits or behaviors) is not necessarily what that manager needs to be equally effective in a different situation. An effective army general might not be an effective university president; an effective restaurant manager might not be an effective clothing store manager; an effective football team coach might not be an effective fitness center manager; an effective first-line manager in a manufacturing company might not be an effective middle manager. The traits or behaviors that may contribute to a manager's being an effective leader in one situation might actually result in the same manager being an ineffective leader in another situation.

Contingency models of leadership take into account the situation, or context, within which leadership occurs. According to contingency models, whether or not a manager is an effective leader is the result of the interplay among what the manager is like, what they do, and the situation in which leadership takes place. Contingency models propose that whether a leader with certain traits or certain behaviors is effective depends on, or is contingent on, the situation, or context. In this section we discuss three prominent contingency models developed to shed light on what makes managers effective leaders: Fred Fiedler's contingency model, Robert House's path–goal theory, and the leader substitutes model. As you will see, these leadership models are complementary; each focuses on a somewhat different aspect of effective leadership in organizations.

Fiedler's Contingency Model

Fred E. Fiedler was among the first leadership researchers to acknowledge that effective leadership is contingent on, or depends on, the characteristics of the leader *and* of the situation. Fiedler's contingency model helps explain why a manager may be an effective leader in one situation and ineffective in another; it also suggests which kinds of managers are likely to be most effective in which situations.[39]

LEADER STYLE As with the trait approach, Fiedler hypothesized that personal characteristics can influence leader effectiveness. He used the term *leader style* to refer to a manager's characteristic approach to leadership and identified two basic leader styles: *relationship-oriented* and *task-oriented.* All managers can be described as having one of these styles.

relationship-oriented leaders Leaders whose primary concern is to develop good relationships with their employees and to be liked by them.

task-oriented leaders Leaders whose primary concern is to ensure that employees perform at a high level.

Relationship-oriented leaders are primarily concerned with developing good relationships with their employees and being liked by them. Relationship-oriented managers focus on having high-quality interpersonal relationships with employees. This does not mean, however, that the job does not get done when such leaders are at the helm. But it does mean that the quality of interpersonal relationships with employees is a prime concern for relationship-oriented leaders.

Task-oriented leaders are primarily concerned with ensuring that employees perform at a high level and focus on task accomplishment. While task-oriented leaders also may be concerned about having good interpersonal relationships with their employees, task accomplishment is their prime concern.

In his research, Fiedler measured leader style by asking leaders to rate the coworker with whom they have had the most difficulty working (called the least preferred coworker, or LPC) on a number of dimensions, such as whether the person is boring or interesting, gloomy or cheerful, enthusiastic or unenthusiastic, cooperative or uncooperative. Relationship-oriented leaders tend to describe the LPC in relatively positive terms; their concern for good relationships leads them to think well of others. Task-oriented leaders tend to describe the LPC in negative terms; their concern for task accomplishment causes them to think badly about others who make getting the job done difficult. Thus, relationship-oriented and task-oriented leaders are sometimes referred to as high-LPC and low-LPC leaders, respectively.

SITUATIONAL CHARACTERISTICS According to Fiedler, leadership style is an enduring characteristic; managers cannot change their style, nor can they adopt different styles in different kinds of situations. With this in mind, Fiedler identified three situational characteristics that are important determinants of how favorable a situation is for leading: leader–member relations, task structure, and position power. When a situation is favorable for leading, it is relatively easy for a manager to influence employees so they perform at a high level and contribute to organizational efficiency and effectiveness. In a situation unfavorable for leading, it is much more difficult for a manager to exert influence.

leader–member relations The extent to which followers like, trust, and are loyal to their leader; a determinant of how favorable a situation is for leading.

LEADER–MEMBER RELATIONS The first situational characteristic Fiedler described, **leader–member relations**, is the extent to which followers like, trust, and are loyal to their leader. Situations are more favorable for leading when leader–member relations are good.

task structure The extent to which the work to be performed is clear-cut so that a leader's employees know what needs to be accomplished and how to go about doing it; a determinant of how favorable a situation is for leading.

TASK STRUCTURE The second situational characteristic Fiedler described, **task structure**, is the extent to which the work to be performed is clear-cut so that a leader's employees know what needs to be accomplished and how to go about doing it. When task structure is high, the situation is favorable for leading. When task structure is low, goals may be vague, employees may be unsure of what they should be doing or how they should do it, and the situation is unfavorable for leading.

Task structure was low for Geraldine Laybourne when she was a top manager at Nickelodeon, the children's television network. It was never precisely clear what would appeal to her young viewers, whose tastes can change dramatically, or how to motivate her employees to come up with creative and novel ideas.[40] In contrast, Herman Mashaba, founder of Black Like Me, a hair care products company based in South Africa, seemed to have relatively high task structure when he started his company. His company's goals were to produce and sell inexpensive hair care products to native Africans, and managers accomplished these goals by using simple yet appealing packaging and distributing the products through neighborhood beauty salons.[41]

position power The amount of legitimate, reward, and coercive power that a leader has by virtue of their position in an organization; a determinant of how favorable a situation is for leading.

POSITION POWER The third situational characteristic Fiedler described, **position power**, is the amount of legitimate, reward, and coercive power a leader has by virtue of their position in an organization. Leadership situations are more favorable for leading when position power is strong.

COMBINING LEADER STYLE AND THE SITUATION By considering all possible combinations of good and poor leader–member relations, high and low task structure, and strong and weak position power, Fiedler identified eight leadership situations that vary in their favorability

Figure 14.2

Fielder's Contingency Theory of Leadership

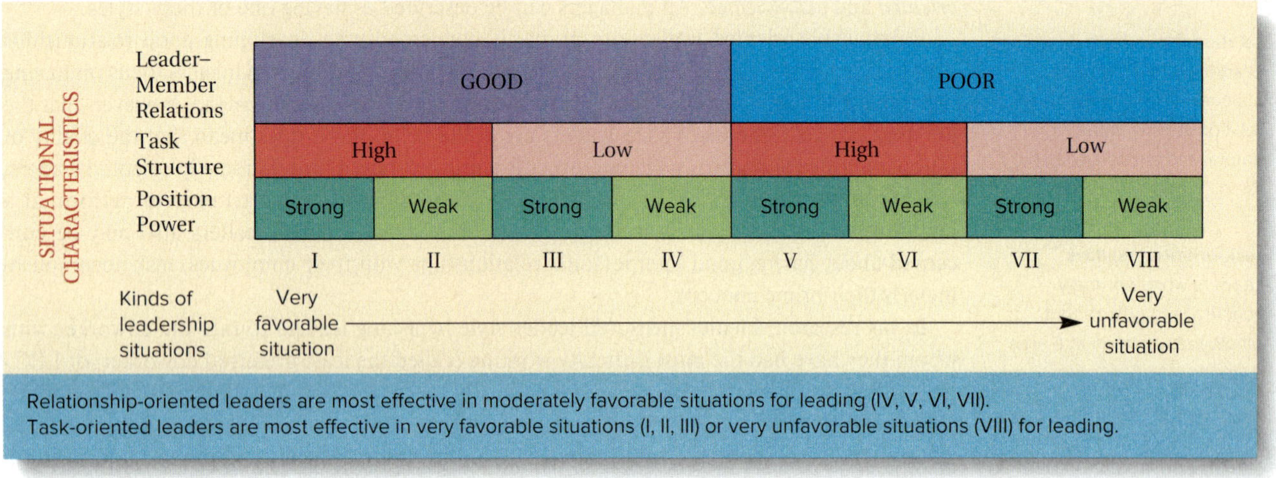

for leading (see Figure 14.2). After extensive research, he determined that relationship-oriented leaders are most effective in moderately favorable situations (IV, V, VI, and VII in Figure 14.2), and task-oriented leaders are most effective in situations that are either very favorable (I, II, and III) or very unfavorable (VIII).

PUTTING THE CONTINGENCY MODEL INTO PRACTICE Recall that according to Fiedler, leader style is an enduring characteristic that managers cannot change. This suggests that for managers to be effective, either managers need to be placed in leadership situations that fit their style or situations need to be changed to suit the managers. Situations can be changed, for example, by giving a manager more position power or by taking steps to increase task structure, such as by clarifying goals.

Consider the case of a relationship-oriented leader employed by a small construction company. The leader was in a very unfavorable situation and was having a tough time leading the crew. Employees did not trust the leader to look out for their well-being (poor leader–member relations); the projects the leader supervised tended to be unique and complex (low task structure); and the leader had no control over the rewards and disciplinary actions employees received (weak position power). Recognizing the need to improve matters, the leader's supervisor gave them the power to reward crew members with bonuses and overtime work and to discipline crew members for poor-quality work and unsafe on-the-job behavior. As the leadership situation improved to moderately favorable, so did the leader's effectiveness and the crew's performance.

Research studies tend to support some aspects of Fiedler's model but also suggest that, like most theories, it needs some modifications.[42] Some researchers have questioned what the LPC scale really measures. Others find fault with the model's premise that leaders cannot alter their styles. That is, it is likely that at least some leaders can diagnose the situation they are in and, when their style is inappropriate for the situation, modify their style so that it is more in line with what the leadership situation calls for. The ability to modify one's leadership style is especially important in today's global business environment because the expectations of leaders and followers differ from one culture to another (see the "Managing Globally" feature).

MANAGING GLOBALLY

International Differences in Leadership

Erin Meyer, a professor of international management, has observed that expectations of a leader differ from one country to another. If employees perceive that a manager is not acting like their idea of a leader, they may feel confused or upset. Meyer has seen misunderstandings related to cultural ideas of authority, decision making, and the interactions between them. Authority has to do with how much importance people place on rank and how much they show respect based on rank. Decision making refers to whether leaders issue decisions or the group arrives at a consensus.[43]

These differences become more complex when combined. For example, in China and Indonesia, hierarchy is important, and leaders make top-down decisions. The Scandinavian countries downplay hierarchy, and decisions are reached through consensus. But in the United States and Great Britain, which also are egalitarian, a leader is typically expected to listen to views and then decide. And in Japan, although hierarchy is important, employees at lower levels of the organization confer, reach a consensus, and present their proposal to the next level up. The process can be slow, but once an idea has worked its way up through the hierarchy, it already has buy-in, the decision is firm, and the people are committed to implementing it.[44]

How can leaders navigate these differences? An important start is to learn about the cultures of followers' countries. A culturally agile leader can recognize and name those differences in order to identify which cultural style will be effective for particular decisions. Then the leader should clarify expectations–for example, by saying, "I want to hear three ideas from the team before I express my views" or "Here's our decision, but it's not firm until we get approval from the finance department." In addition to learning general cultural patterns, leaders should gather information from the group being led, according to Jo Owen, who has led international business and nonprofit groups. Owen advises that the best way to observe cultural norms and personal differences is to engage with people face-to-face. Like Meyer, Owen advises talking about norms, so people understand their group's dynamics. Leadership coach Amir Ghannad takes Owen's thinking one step further, urging leaders to see their followers first as unique individuals, rather than generic members of a culture. This prepares leaders to expect differences while seeing the other person's shared humanity.[45]

House's Path-Goal Theory

path-goal theory A contingency model of leadership proposing that leaders can motivate employees by identifying their desired outcomes, rewarding them for high performance and the attainment of work goals with these desired outcomes, and clarifying for them the paths leading to the attainment of work goals.

In what he called **path-goal theory**, leadership researcher Robert House focused on what leaders can do to motivate their employees to achieve group and organizational goals.[46] The premise of path-goal theory is that effective leaders motivate employees to achieve goals by (1) clearly identifying the outcomes that employees are trying to obtain from the workplace, (2) rewarding employees with these outcomes for high performance and the attainment of work goals, and (3) clarifying for employees the *paths* leading to the attainment of work *goals.* Path-goal theory is a contingency model because it proposes that the steps managers should take to motivate employees depend on both the nature of the employees and the type of work they do.

Based on the expectancy theory of motivation (see Chapter 13), path-goal theory gives managers three guidelines to being effective leaders:

1. *Find out what outcomes your employees are trying to obtain from their jobs and the organization.* These outcomes can range from satisfactory pay and job security to reasonable working hours and interesting and challenging job assignments. After identifying these outcomes, the manager should have the *reward power* needed to distribute or withhold the outcomes. Mark Crane, for example, is the vice principal of a large elementary school. Crane determined that the teachers he leads are trying to obtain the following outcomes from their jobs: pay raises, autonomy in the classroom, and the choice of which grades they teach. Crane had reward power for the last two outcomes, but the school's principal determined how the pool of money for raises was to be distributed each year. Because Crane was the first-line manager who led the teachers and was most familiar with their performance, he asked the principal (his boss) to give him some say in determining pay raises. Realizing that this made a lot of sense, his principal gave Crane full power to distribute raises and requested only that Crane review his decisions with him before informing the teachers about them.

2. *Reward employees for high performance and goal attainment with the outcomes they desire.* The teachers and administrators at Crane's school considered several dimensions of teacher performance to be critical to achieving their goal of providing high-quality education: excellent in-class instruction, special programs to enhance student interest and learning (such as science and computer projects), and availability for meetings with parents to discuss their children's progress and special needs. Crane distributed pay raises to the teachers based on the extent to which they performed highly on each of these dimensions. The top-performing teachers were given first choice of grade assignments and had practically complete autonomy in their classrooms.
3. *Clarify the paths to goal attainment for employees, remove any obstacles to high performance, and express confidence in employees' capabilities.* This does not mean that a manager needs to tell employees what to do. Rather, it means that a manager needs to make sure employees are clear about what they should be trying to accomplish and have the capabilities, resources, and confidence levels needed to be successful. Crane made sure all the teachers understood the importance of the three targeted goals and asked them whether, to reach them, they needed any special resources or supplies for their classes. Crane also gave additional coaching and guidance to teachers who seemed to be struggling. For example, Patrick Conolly, in his first year of teaching after graduate school, was unsure how to use special projects in a third grade class and how to react to parents who were critical. Conolly's teaching was excellent, but he felt insecure about how he was doing on this dimension. To help build Conolly's confidence, Crane told Conolly that he thought he could be one of the school's top teachers (which was true). He gave Conolly some ideas about special projects that worked particularly well with the third grade, such as a writing project. Crane also role-played teacher–parent interactions with Conolly. Conolly played the role of a particularly dissatisfied or troubled parent, while Crane played the role of a teacher trying to solve the underlying problem while making the parent feel that their child's needs were being met. Crane's efforts to clarify the paths to goal attainment for Conolly paid off: Within two years the local PTS voted Conolly teacher of the year.

You could stand over your employees or you could empower them to find the solution by working to see where the issue developed. Supportive managers make a world of difference in retaining and motivating employees.
Stockbyte/Getty Images

Path–goal theory identifies four kinds of leadership behaviors that motivate employees:

- *Directive behaviors* are similar to initiating structure and include setting goals, assigning tasks, showing employees how to complete tasks, and taking concrete steps to improve performance.
- *Supportive behaviors* are similar to consideration and include expressing concern for employees and looking out for their best interests.
- *Participative behaviors* give employees a say in matters and decisions that affect them.
- *Achievement-oriented behaviors* motivate employees to perform at the highest level possible by, for example, setting challenging goals, expecting that they be met, and believing in employees' capabilities.

Which of these behaviors should managers use to lead effectively? The answer to this question depends, or is contingent, on the nature of the employees and the kind of work they do.

Directive behaviors may be beneficial when employees are having difficulty completing assigned tasks, but they might be detrimental when employees are independent thinkers who work best when left alone. *Supportive* behaviors are often advisable when employees are experiencing high levels of stress. *Participative* behaviors can be particularly effective when employees' support of a decision is required. *Achievement-oriented* behaviors may increase motivation levels of highly capable employees who are bored from having too few challenges, but they might backfire if used with employees who are already pushed to their limit.

The Leader Substitutes Model

leadership substitute A characteristic of a subordinate or of a situation, or context, that acts in place of the influence of a leader and makes leadership unnecessary.

The leader substitutes model suggests that leadership is sometimes unnecessary because substitutes for leadership are present. A **leadership substitute** is something that acts in place of the influence of a leader and makes leadership unnecessary. This model suggests that under certain conditions managers do not have to play a leadership role—members of an organization sometimes can perform at a high level without a manager exerting influence over them.[47] The leader substitutes model is a contingency model because it suggests that in some situations leadership is unnecessary.

Consider the case of someone who teaches English at a foreign language school in Cyprus, an island in the Mediterranean Sea. The instructor is fluent in Greek, English, and French; is an excellent teacher; and is highly motivated. Many of the students are business professionals who have some basic English skills and wish to improve their fluency to conduct more of their business in English. The instructor not only enjoys teaching the students English but also enjoys learning about the work they do and often keeps in touch with the students after they finish the classes. The instructor meets with the director of the school twice a year to discuss class schedules and enrollments.

With practically no influence from a leader, the teacher is a highly motivated top performer at the school. In this situation, leadership is unnecessary because substitutes for leadership are present. The instructor's teaching expertise, motivation, and enjoyment of the work are substitutes for the influence of a leader—in this case, the school's director. If the school's director were to try to influence how the instructor performs the job, the instructor would probably resent this infringement on their autonomy, and it is unlikely that their performance would improve because the instructor is already one of the school's best teachers.

As in the preceding example, *characteristics of employees*—such as their skills, abilities, experience, knowledge, and motivation—can be substitutes for leadership.[48] *Characteristics of the situation, or context*—such as the extent to which the work is interesting and enjoyable—also can be substitutes. When work is interesting and enjoyable, as it is for the instructor described in the previous example, jobholders do not need to be coaxed into performing because performing is rewarding in its own right. Similarly, when managers *empower* their employees or use *self-managed work teams* (discussed in detail in Chapter 15), the need for leadership influence from a manager is decreased because team members manage themselves.

The concept of shared leadership is an effective example of a leadership substitute. In this situation, leadership is distributed among team members rather than being exhibited by one single leader. Research suggests teams that successfully share the leadership role among members may provide higher-quality outcomes to their customers.[49] Substitutes for leadership can increase organizational efficiency and effectiveness because they free up some of managers' valuable time and allow managers to focus their efforts on discovering new ways to improve organizational effectiveness. In the scenario described earlier, the director of the foreign language school in Cypress was able to spend time making arrangements to open a second school in Rhodes, an island in the Aegean Sea, because of the presence of leadership substitutes for many of the school's instructors.

Bringing It All Together

Effective leadership in organizations occurs when managers take steps to lead in a way that is appropriate for the situation, or context, in which leadership occurs and for the employees who are being led. The three contingency models of leadership just discussed help managers focus on the necessary ingredients for effective leadership. They are complementary in that each one looks at the leadership question from a different angle. Fiedler's contingency model explores how a manager's leadership style needs to be matched to that person's leadership situation for maximum effectiveness. House's path-goal theory focuses on how managers should motivate employees and describes the specific kinds of behaviors managers can engage in to have a highly motivated workforce. The leadership substitutes model alerts managers to the fact that sometimes they do not need to exert influence over employees and thus can free up their time for other important activities. Table 14.2 recaps these three contingency models of leadership.

Table 14.2
Contingency Models of Leadership

Model	Focus	Key Contingencies
Fiedler's contingency model	Describes two leader styles, relationship-oriented and task-oriented, and the kinds of situations in which each kind of leader will be most effective.	Whether a relationship-oriented or a task-oriented leader is effective is contingent on the situation.
House's path–goal theory	Describes how effective leaders motivate their followers.	The behaviors that managers should engage in to be effective leaders are contingent on the nature of the employees and the work they do.
Leader substitutes model	Describes when leadership is unnecessary.	Whether leadership is necessary for employees to perform highly is contingent on characteristics of the employees and the situation.

Transformational Leadership

LO14-4 Describe what transformational leadership is, and explain how managers can engage in it.

Time and time again, throughout business history, certain leaders seem to transform their organizations, making sweeping changes to revitalize and renew operations. For example, Reed Hastings, co-founder of Netflix, began his career in the software industry, where he honed his leadership and managerial skills. He started a company in 1991 called Pure Software, which eventually went public and was bought by another tech company, giving Hastings more than $750 million from the company's sale to invest in other entrepreneurial efforts.[50] In the late 1990s Hastings and Marc Rudolph came up with the idea of offering movie rentals over the Internet, which led to the founding of Netflix.com in 1998, a company focused on DVD movie rentals delivered to customers via snail mail. In the following year, Netflix offered a subscription service, which allowed customers to have unlimited DVD rentals per month. Netflix's disruption of the DVD rental business (and local video retail stores) made the company a huge success.[51]

Based on his knowledge and experience in software development and other technologies, Hastings believed that the DVD-by-mail service was merely a stepping stone to the next technological advance, although he was fearful that it would be difficult to make the leap from movies by mail to online content streaming. More than a dozen years ago, Hastings laid the groundwork for the eventual success of content streaming by negotiating deals with entertainment companies to test online streaming of movies and TV shows. Not one to make excuses or to point the finger at others, however, Hastings made a crucial decision in 2011, which almost derailed Netflix altogether: He decided to spin off the core business of DVD rentals by mail (a short-lived business called Qwikster) and concentrate Netflix on streaming content.[52]

The backlash from Netflix customers was swift and angry—the company lost more than 800,000 subscribers in three months. Realizing his decision to split the operation into separate companies was a huge mistake, Hastings offered a humble apology to customers, saying that he and the company had become "overconfident" and were "moving too quickly," and reinstated the DVD-by-mail portion of the Netflix business, which today still has nearly 3 million subscribers. (Netflix recently announced it would end the DVDs-by-mail service in late 2023).[53] At the same time, he and his management team worked in parallel to get the streaming portion of the business up and running while keeping DVD customers happy—a decision that helped the company fund the new streaming business.[54] By 2013, Netflix turned its attention to the streaming of original content, including such hits as *House of Cards* and *Orange Is the New Black,* to its monthly subscribers.[55] Today, the company has more than 231 million paid memberships in more than 190 countries.[56]

Hastings transformed Netflix into a company in which satisfied employees provide excellent service to customers. The company is well known for its culture and what it expects from employees and what Netflix provides them in return. For example, on the Jobs page of its corporate website, Netflix describes the "real values" it expects from its employees, including in the areas of judgment, communication, courage, and passion, among others.[57] When managers have such dramatic effects on their employees and on an organization as a whole, they are engaging in transformational leadership. **Transformational leadership** occurs when managers change (or transform) their employees in three important ways:[58]

transformational leadership Leadership that makes employees aware of the importance of their jobs and performance to the organization and aware of their own needs for personal growth and that motivates employees to work for the good of the organization.

1. *Transformational managers make employees aware of how important their jobs are for the organization and how necessary it is for them to perform those jobs as best they can so the organization can attain its goals.* More than a decade ago, Hastings and Netflix's then chief talent officer, Patty McCord, put together a PowerPoint presentation that became known as the Netflix Culture Deck, which describes the organizational practices the company believes in and helps employees understand their pivotal role in creating value for customers as well as for the organization. The slide deck was a collaborative effort on the part of managers, employees, and others who worked in the Netflix organization at various times. For example, one of the practices involves being a culture of freedom and responsibility, which encourages employees to do the right thing because they are "smart people with good judgment."[59]
2. *Transformational managers make their employees aware of the employees' own needs for personal growth, development, and accomplishment.* Hastings decided long ago to eliminate formal performance reviews at Netflix because they seemed too infrequent and ritualistic. Instead, managers and their direct reports have conversations about performance as part of their work. One of the important themes that run through these discussions is honesty; in some instances, technology changes implemented at Netflix have caused people's jobs to change dramatically or become obsolete. When this happens, Netflix managers are expected to have heart-to-heart conversations with the employees in question about losing their jobs and to provide them with a great severance package that will give them time (and money) to go look for another career path outside the company that makes sense for the employee and helps them grow on a personal and professional level.[60]
3. *Transformational managers motivate their employees to work for the good of the organization as a whole, not just for their own personal gain or benefit.* Part of Hastings's approach to employees and their important role in the company's success is the vision of a "dream team," one in which *every* colleague is the best at their job and work really well as collaborators to move the company forward in terms of innovation and overall success. As part of this scenario, the company believes in providing very competitive salaries, unlimited vacation days, generous parental leave for all new parents, and fully vested stock options. In return, Hastings expects Netflix employees to act in its best interest, use good judgment, behave like adults, and have fun while doing it. Hastings recently announced he would step down as CEO but remain as chairman. Over the past several years, Hastings put plans in place to have other leaders take over day-to-day operations at the company. Ted Sarandos was promoted to co-chief executive in 2020 and Greg Peters was the company's COO. Peters will now join Sarandos as co-CEO of the streaming service.[61]

Co-founder Reed Hastings demonstrates transformational leadership at Netflix. He recently stepped down as CEO but remains chairman of the streaming service.
Ore Huiying/Stringer/Getty Images

When managers transform their employees in these three ways, employees trust the managers, are highly motivated, and help the organization achieve its goals. How do managers such as Hastings transform employees and produce dramatic effects in their organizations? There are at least three ways in which transformational leaders can influence their followers: by being a charismatic leader, by intellectually stimulating employees, and by engaging in developmental consideration (see Table 14.3).

Being a Charismatic Leader

charismatic leader An enthusiastic, self-confident leader who is able to clearly communicate his or her vision of how good things could be.

Transformational managers such as Reed Hastings are **charismatic leaders**. They have a vision of how good things could be in their work groups and organizations that is in contrast with the status quo. Their vision usually entails dramatic improvements in group and organizational

Table 14.3

Transformational Leadership

Transformational managers
- Are charismatic.
- Intellectually stimulate employees.
- Engage in developmental consideration.

Employees of transformational managers
- Have increased awareness of the importance of their jobs and high performance.
- Are aware of their own needs for growth, development, and accomplishment.
- Work for the good of the organization and not just their own personal benefit.

performance as a result of changes in the organization's structure, culture, strategy, decision making, and other critical processes and factors. This vision paves the way for gaining a competitive advantage.

Charismatic leaders are excited and enthusiastic about their vision and clearly communicate it to their employees. The excitement, enthusiasm, and self-confidence of a charismatic leader contribute to the leader's being able to inspire followers to enthusiastically support their vision.[62] People often think of charismatic leaders or managers as being "larger than life." The essence of charisma, however, is having a vision and enthusiastically communicating it to others. Thus, managers who appear to be quiet and earnest can also be charismatic.

Stimulating Employees Intellectually

Transformational managers openly share information with their employees so they are aware of problems and the need for change. The manager causes employees to view problems in their groups and throughout the organization from a different perspective, consistent with the manager's vision. Whereas in the past employees may not have been aware of some problems, may have viewed problems as a "management issue" beyond their concern, or may have viewed problems as insurmountable, the transformational manager's **intellectual stimulation** leads employees to view problems as challenges that they can and will meet and conquer. The manager engages and empowers employees to take personal responsibility for helping to solve problems, as Reed Hastings has done at Netflix.[63]

intellectual stimulation Behavior a leader engages in to make followers aware of problems and view these problems in new ways, consistent with the leader's vision.

Engaging in Developmental Consideration

When managers engage in **developmental consideration**, they not only perform the consideration behaviors described earlier, such as demonstrating true concern for the well-being of employees, but also go one step further. The manager goes out of their way to support and encourage employees, giving them opportunities to enhance their skills and capabilities and to grow and excel on the job.[64]

developmental consideration Behavior a leader engages in to support and encourage followers and help them develop and grow on the job.

All organizations, no matter how large or small, successful or unsuccessful, can benefit when their managers engage in transformational leadership. Moreover, while the benefits of transformational leadership are often most apparent when an organization is in trouble, transformational leadership can be an enduring approach to leadership, leading to long-term organizational effectiveness.

The Distinction between Transformational and Transactional Leadership

Transformational leadership is often contrasted with transactional leadership. In **transactional leadership**, managers use their reward and coercive powers to encourage high performance. When managers reward high performers, reprimand or otherwise punish low performers, and motivate employees by reinforcing desired behaviors and extinguishing or punishing undesired ones, they are engaging in transactional leadership.[65] Managers who effectively influence their employees to achieve goals, yet do not seem to be making the kind of dramatic changes that are part of transformational leadership, are engaging in transactional leadership.

transactional leadership Leadership that motivates employees by rewarding them for high performance and reprimanding them for low performance.

Many transformational leaders engage in transactional leadership. They reward employees for a job well done and notice and respond to substandard performance. But they also have their eyes on the bigger picture of how much better things could be in their organizations, how much more their employees are capable of achieving, and how important it is to treat their employees with respect and help them reach their full potential.

Research has found that when leaders engage in transformational leadership, their employees tend to have higher levels of job satisfaction and performance.[66] Additionally, employees of transformational leaders may be more likely to trust their leaders and their organizations and feel that they are being fairly treated, and this in turn may positively influence their work motivation (see Chapter 13).[67]

Gender and Leadership

LO14-5 Characterize the relationship between gender and leadership, and explain how emotional intelligence may contribute to leadership effectiveness.

The increasing number of women entering the ranks of management, as well as the problems some women face in their efforts to be hired as managers or promoted into management positions, has prompted researchers to explore the relationship between gender and leadership. Although there are relatively more women in management positions today than there were 10 years ago, there are still relatively few women in top management and, in some organizations, even in middle management.

When women do advance to top management positions, special attention often is focused on them and the fact that they are women. For example, women CEOs of large companies are still rare; those who make it to the top post, such as Michele Buck of Hershey and Mary Barra of General Motors, are still scarce.[68] Although women have made inroads into leadership positions in many organizations, they continue to be underrepresented in top leadership posts. As indicated in Chapter 5, for example, while almost 42% of the employees in managerial and professional jobs are women, only 30% of corporate officers in the *Fortune* 500 are women.[69]

A widespread stereotype of women is that they are nurturing, supportive, and concerned with interpersonal relations. Men are stereotypically viewed as being directive and focused on task accomplishment. Such stereotypes suggest that women tend to be more relationship-oriented as managers and engage in more consideration behaviors, whereas men are more task-oriented and engage in more initiating-structure behaviors. Does the behavior of men and women in managerial roles bear out these stereotypes? Does a manager's gender affect leadership? Is any gender more effective at leadership?

Research suggests that managers of any gender who have leadership positions in organizations behave in similar ways.[70] Women do not engage in more consideration than men, and men do not engage in more initiating structure than women. Research does suggest, however, that leadership style may vary between genders. Women tend to be somewhat more participative as leaders, involving employees in decision making and seeking their input.[71] Men as managers tend to be less participative, making more decisions on their own and wanting to do things their own way.

There are at least two reasons that managers who are women may be more participative as leaders than managers who are men.[72] First, employees may try to resist the influence of managers who are women more than they do the influence of managers who are men. Some employees may never have reported to a woman before, some may incorrectly see a management role as being more appropriate for a man than for a woman, and some may just resist being managed by a woman. To overcome this resistance and encourage employees' trust and respect, managers who are women may adopt a participative approach.

A second reason that women who are managers may be more participative is that they sometimes have better interpersonal skills than their male counterparts.[73] A participative approach to leadership requires high levels of interaction and involvement between managers and their employees, sensitivity to employees' feelings, and the ability to make decisions that may be unpopular with employees but necessary for goal attainment. Good interpersonal skills may help managers who are women have the effective interactions with their employees that are crucial to a participative approach.[74] To the extent that managers who are men have more difficulty managing interpersonal relationships, they may shy away from the high levels of interaction with employees necessary for true participation.

Research suggests that managers with leadership positions in organizations behave in similar ways regardless of gender.
michaeljung/Shutterstock

The key finding from research on leader behaviors, however, is that male and female managers do *not* differ significantly in their propensities to perform different leader behaviors based on their gender. In addition, research suggests that across different kinds of organizational settings, managers, regardless of their gender, tend to be *equally effective* as leaders.[75] Thus, there is no logical basis for stereotypes favoring male managers and leaders or for the existence of the "glass ceiling" (an invisible barrier that prevents women and other underrepresented groups from advancing as far as they should in some organizations). Because all genders are equally effective as leaders, the increasing number of women in the workforce should result in a larger pool of highly qualified candidates for management positions, ultimately enhancing organizational effectiveness.[76]

Emotional Intelligence and Leadership

Do the moods and emotions leaders experience on the job influence their behavior and effectiveness as leaders? Research suggests this is likely to be the case. For example, one study found that when store managers experienced positive moods at work, salespeople in their stores provided high-quality customer service and were less likely to quit.[77] Another study found that groups whose leaders experienced positive moods had better coordination, whereas groups whose leaders experienced negative moods exerted more effort; members of groups with leaders in positive moods also tended to experience more positive moods themselves; and members of groups with leaders in negative moods tended to experience more negative moods.[78]

A leader's level of emotional intelligence (see Chapter 3) may play a particularly important role in leadership effectiveness.[79] For example, emotional intelligence may help leaders develop a vision for their organizations, motivate their employees to commit to this vision, and energize them to enthusiastically work to achieve this vision. Moreover, emotional intelligence may enable leaders to develop a significant identity for their organization and instill high levels of trust and cooperation throughout the organization while maintaining the flexibility needed to respond to changing conditions.[80]

Emotional intelligence also plays a crucial role in how leaders relate to and deal with their followers, particularly when it comes to encouraging followers to be creative.[81] Creativity in organizations is an emotion-laden process; it often entails challenging the status quo, being willing to take risks and accept and learn from failures, and doing much hard work to bring creative ideas to fruition in terms of new products, services, or procedures and processes when uncertainty is bound to be high.[82] Leaders who are high on emotional intelligence are more likely to understand all the emotions surrounding creative endeavors, to be able to awaken and support the creative pursuits of their followers, and to provide the kind of support that enables creativity to flourish in organizations.[83]

The "Management Insight" feature provides some guidelines for applying the concept of emotional intelligence to the practice of leadership.

MANAGEMENT INSIGHT

How to Be a High-EQ Leader

What behaviors should a manager practice in order to lead with emotional intelligence (EQ)? A good starting point is to become aware of one's emotions. When someone puts forth an idea different from what you were advocating, what do you feel? Are you curious to learn more or defensive of an idea you were proud of? Or when you hear a critical remark, do you feel hurt, angry, or interested you might have information that

To lead with emotional intelligence, practice empathy, through the skill of active listening.
fizkes/Getty Images

will help you do better in the future? Defining these feelings can help you evaluate your options for action more accurately and fully.[84]

Another essential behavior to practice is empathy. The objective is to understand how people feel, not to encourage negative behavior or even necessarily to agree. To practice empathy, when you observe others, try to imagine yourself in their place. If you aren't sure how another person feels, ask and try to understand the answer. Even when you cannot–or do not think it is appropriate to–solve another person's problem, you demonstrate respect when you try to understand.[85]

Empathy increases when you practice listening. Communication skills are a mark of a high-EQ leader, and listening is among the most important of those skills. While listening, practice focusing on understanding rather than judging what the person says. Jumping to a judgment makes it harder to get the full message. Listening to learn about others, in contrast, is motivational as well as informative. When Tom Gartland became president of Avis Budget Group, he spent weeks on a bus tour to meet the company's employees face-to-face. Focusing on others and learning how he could help them resulted in the employees being highly committed to the company.[86]

Finally, emotionally intelligent leaders manage their emotions. The other practices can help with this. For example, anger at an employee is easier to manage if you have listened and practiced empathy, so that you have some understanding of what behavior to expect and why it is occurring. Learning to recognize your emotions alerts you to situations in which self-control will help you. For example, if conflict erupts during a meeting, awareness of one's own and others' feelings can put you on guard to keep your own anger or dismay under control. Then you can explore the ideas in play and perhaps even steer the group to a creative solution built on a variety of perspectives.[87]

Summary and Review

LO14-1 **THE NATURE OF LEADERSHIP** Leadership is the process by which a person exerts influence over other people and inspires, motivates, and directs their activities to help achieve group or organizational goals. Leaders can influence others because they possess power. The five types of power available to managers are legitimate power, reward power, coercive power, expert power, and referent power. Many managers are using empowerment as a tool to increase their effectiveness as leaders.

LO14-2 **TRAIT AND BEHAVIOR MODELS OF LEADERSHIP** The trait model of leadership describes personal characteristics, or traits, that contribute to effective leadership. However, some managers who possess these traits are not effective leaders, and some managers who do not possess all the traits are nevertheless effective leaders. The behavior model of leadership describes two kinds of behavior that most leaders engage in: consideration and initiating structure.

LO14-3 **CONTINGENCY MODELS OF LEADERSHIP** Contingency models take into account the complexity surrounding leadership and the role of the situation in determining whether a manager is an effective leader. Fiedler's contingency model explains why managers may be effective leaders in one situation and ineffective in another. According to Fiedler's model, relationship-oriented leaders are most effective in situations that are moderately favorable for leading, and task-oriented leaders are most effective in situations that are very favorable or very unfavorable for leading. House's path-goal theory describes how effective managers motivate their employees by determining what outcomes their employees want, rewarding employees with these outcomes when they achieve their goals and perform at a high level, and clarifying the paths to goal attainment. Managers can engage in four kinds of behaviors to motivate employees: directive, supportive, participative, and achievement-oriented behaviors. The leader substitutes model suggests that sometimes managers do not have to play a leadership role because their employees perform at a high level without the manager's having to exert influence over them.

LO14-4 **TRANSFORMATIONAL LEADERSHIP** Transformational leadership occurs when managers have dramatic effects on their employees and on the organization as a whole and they inspire and energize employees to solve problems and improve performance. These effects include making employees aware of the importance of their own jobs and high performance; making employees aware of their own needs for personal growth, development, and accomplishment; and motivating employees to work for the good of the organization and not just their own personal gain. Managers can engage in transformational leadership by being charismatic leaders, by intellectually stimulating employees, and by engaging in developmental consideration. Transformational managers also often engage in transactional leadership by using their reward and coercive powers to encourage high performance.

LO14-5 **GENDER AND LEADERSHIP** Managers do not differ in the leadership behaviors they perform based on gender, contrary to stereotypes suggesting that women are more relationship-oriented and men more task-oriented. Female managers sometimes are more participative than male managers, however. Research has found that women and men are equally effective as managers and leaders.

LO14-5 **EMOTIONAL INTELLIGENCE AND LEADERSHIP** The moods and emotions leaders experience on the job, and their ability to effectively manage these feelings, can influence their effectiveness as leaders. Moreover, emotional intelligence can contribute to leadership effectiveness in multiple ways, including encouraging and supporting creativity among followers.

Management in Action

Topics for Discussion and Action

Discussion

1. Describe the steps managers can take to increase their power and ability to be effective leaders. [LO14-1]
2. Think of specific situations in which it might be especially important for a manager to engage in consideration and in initiating structure. [LO14-2]
3. For your current job or for a future job you expect to hold, describe what your supervisor could do to strongly motivate you to be a top performer. [LO14-3]
4. Discuss why managers might want to change the behaviors they engage in, given their situation, their employees, and the nature of the work being done. Do you think managers can readily change their leadership behaviors? Why or why not? [LO14-3]
5. Discuss why substitutes for leadership can contribute to organizational effectiveness. [LO14-3]
6. Describe what transformational leadership is, and explain how managers can engage in it. [LO14-4]
7. Discuss why some people still think men make better managers than women, even though research indicates that men and women are equally effective as managers and leaders. [LO14-5]
8. Imagine that you are working in an organization in an entry-level position after graduation and have come up with what you think is a great idea for improving a critical process in the organization that relates to your job. In what ways might your supervisor encourage you to implement your idea? How might your supervisor discourage you from even sharing your idea with others? [LO14-4, 14-5]

Action

9. Interview a manager to find out how the three situational characteristics that Fiedler identified affect their ability to provide leadership. [LO14-3]
10. Find a company that has dramatically turned around its fortunes and improved its performance. Determine whether a transformational manager was behind the turnaround and, if one was, what this manager did. [LO14-4]

Building Management Skills

Analyzing Failures of Leadership [LO14-1, 14-2, 14-3, 14-4]

Think about a situation you are familiar with in which a leader was very ineffective. Then answer the following questions:

1. What sources of power did this leader have? Did the leader have enough power to influence their followers?
2. What kinds of behaviors did this leader engage in? Were they appropriate for the situation? Why or why not?
3. From what you know, do you think this leader was a task-oriented leader or a relationship-oriented leader? How favorable was this leader's situation for leading?
4. What steps did this leader take to motivate followers? Were these steps appropriate or inappropriate? Why?
5. What signs, if any, did this leader show of being a transformational leader?

Managing Ethically [LO14-1]

Managers who verbally criticize their employees, put them down in front of their coworkers, or use the threat of job loss to influence behavior are exercising coercive power. Some employees subject to coercive power believe that using it is unethical.

Questions

1. Either alone or in a group, think about the ethical implications of the use of coercive power.
2. To what extent do managers and organizations have an ethical obligation to put limits on the amount of coercive power that is exercised?

Small Group Breakout Exercise

Improving Leadership Effectiveness [LO14-1, 14-2, 14-3, 14-4]

Form groups of three to five people, and appoint one member as the spokesperson who will communicate your findings and conclusions to the class when called on by the instructor. Then discuss the following scenario:

You are a team of human resource consultants who have been hired by Carla Caruso, an entrepreneur who has started her own interior design business. A highly competent and creative interior designer, Caruso has established a working relationship with most of the major home builders in her community. At first, she worked on her own as an independent contractor. Then because of a dramatic increase in the number of new homes being built, she became swamped with requests for her services and decided to start her own company.

She hired an administrative assistant/bookkeeper and four interior designers, all of whom are highly competent. Caruso still does decorating jobs herself and has adopted a hands-off approach to leading the four designers who report to her because she feels that interior design is a very personal, creative endeavor. Rather than pay the designers on some kind of commission basis (such as a percentage of their customers' total billings), she pays them a premium salary, higher than average, so they are motivated to do what's best for a customer's needs and not what will result in higher billings and commissions.

Caruso thought everything was going smoothly until customer complaints started coming in. The complaints ranged from the designers' being hard to reach, promising unrealistic delivery times, and being late for or failing to keep appointments to their being impatient and rude when customers had trouble making up their minds. Caruso knows her designers are competent and is concerned that she is not effectively leading and managing them. She wonders, in particular, if her hands-off approach is to blame and if she should change the manner in which she rewards or pays her designers. She has asked for your advice.

1. Analyze the sources of power that Caruso has available to her to influence the designers. What advice can you give her to either increase her power base or use her existing power more effectively?
2. Given what you have learned in this chapter (for example, from the behavior model and path–goal theory), does Caruso seem to be performing appropriate leader behaviors in this situation? What advice can you give her about the kinds of behaviors she should perform?
3. What steps would you advise Caruso to take to increase the designers' motivation to deliver high-quality customer service?
4. Would you advise Caruso to try to engage in transformational leadership in this situation? If not, why not? If so, what steps would you advise her to take?

Be the Manager [LO14-1, 14-2, 14-3, 14-4, 14-5]

You are the CEO of a medium-size company that makes window coverings such as blinds and shutters. Your company has a cost advantage in terms of being able to make custom window coverings at costs that are relatively low in the industry. However, the performance of your company has been lackluster. To make needed changes and improve performance, you met with the eight other top managers in your company and charged them with identifying problems and missed opportunities in each of their areas and coming up with an action plan to address the problems and take advantage of opportunities.

Once you gave the managers the okay, they were charged with implementing their action plans in a timely fashion and monitoring the effects of their initiatives monthly for the next 8 to 12 months.

You approved each of the managers' action plans, and a year later most of the managers were reporting that their initiatives had been successful in addressing the problems and opportunities they had identified a year ago. However, overall company performance continues to be lackluster and shows no signs of improvement. You are confused and are starting to question your leadership capabilities and your approach to change. What are you going to do to improve the performance and effectiveness of your company?

Case in the News [LO14-1, 14-2, 14-5]

People-First Leadership at WM

At WM, leaders try to express their values, even with the company's name. The Houston-based company shortened its former name, Waste Management, to WM after someone asked CEO Jim Fish why a company seeking growth in the recycling business had a name referring to waste. Fish saw the point: WM is both the largest landfill operator and the biggest recycler in North America, and it wasn't seeking to open more landfills. For one thing, this would be less profitable. Collecting plastics for burial in a landfill doesn't add much to WM's bottom line because the company charges by weight. But if it can sell used plastic to a business that converts it into roofing board or shopping bags, WM earns more money on the sale.

At the end of 2018, Fish announced that he wanted WM to shift its focus "from profits first to people first." Leaders would seek both profitability and people's well-being, but putting people first would better equip them to generate profits. Around the same time, Fish elevated the professional credentials of WM's human resources team by hiring an experienced leader, Tamla Oates-Forney, as chief people officer to bring HR functions in line with corporate strategy.

That role became even more critical in March 2020, when the U.S. government declared a state of emergency in response to the COVID-19 pandemic. Hearing the declaration, Fish realized that WM needed to take its leadership to a new level. He thought about the fear such an announcement could invoke in WM's 50,000-member workforce as they contemplated business shutdowns, job losses, health crises, and endless uncertainty. Collectively, the stress employees were undergoing could amount to a trauma. Fish's first and immediate response was to call a companywide meeting at which he announced that whether or not any operations would have to pause, employees would be paid throughout the national emergency. Fish had considered evaluating the economic impact first but instead prioritized employees' well-being, as he had promised to do less than two years before.

WM's human resources team, ever ready to contribute to strategy, saw their role as equipping leaders for this new type of leadership. The usual leadership models seemed inadequate for addressing the needs of employees and managers who felt traumatized. The staff responsible for learning and development therefore created a new curriculum for "trauma-informed" leadership, placing heavy emphasis on workers' emotional needs without shortchanging task-related capabilities. They began by identifying the capabilities that would be necessary for this type of leadership: self-awareness, ability to foster trust, emotional intelligence, active listening, adaptable communication styles, acceptance of accountability, and ability to foster an inclusive work environment. Then they built a curriculum that combines training in these capabilities with a one-on-one coaching program and education about how to recognize and address trauma. Feedback from the pilot tests and full rollout of the program indicated that managers were applying the new leadership behaviors and improving the work experience of their employees and themselves.

Even as the pandemic recedes into the background of employees' lives, the exercise of trauma-informed leadership still seems relevant to management for other reasons. Jobs at WM are changing dramatically as automation spreads. The company expects that automation of work can end the need for many hard-to-fill positions while improving efficiency. In many cases, WM expects it simply won't fill empty positions, but some workers may have to find new jobs. The company's approach is to be transparent about the change and to offer opportunities for learning new skills that will be needed. Technology also is helping WM's managers lead better. The company has been developing a system employees can use to send their leaders feedback—anonymously if they choose to do so. The idea is that managers can obtain a real-time look at what is on people's minds, which should enable small, informed course corrections, instead of waiting for a big dump of data from, say, an annual survey of employee satisfaction.

This people-first approach reflects the CEO's broader concern for sustainability. Fish joined WM in 2001 as its financial director and then worked in various executive roles before being promoted to CEO in 2016. At the helm of the company, he identified recycling and energy generation as key growth areas. That approach has enabled WM to reach or exceed earnings targets almost every quarter and to double in corporate value. WM's strategy also includes the company being considered what Fish calls "the best workplace."

Questions for Discussion

1. Based on the information given, how do WM's leaders exercise the two major categories of leader behavior (consideration and initiating structure)? In your opinion, is there an appropriate balance of the two? Why or why not?
2. What impact did the COVID-19 pandemic have on leadership at WM? Choose one of the contingency models and apply it to describe and evaluate the leadership changes.
3. Describe the role of emotional intelligence in leadership at WM.

Sources: P. Rhodes and D. Martoccia, "From Struggle Comes Growth," *TD*, December 2022, 21–23; J. A. Miller, "Exit Interview: WM's Former HR Chief on Her Move to USAA and the Profession's Evolution," *HR Dive*, www.hrdive.com, October 4, 2022; B. R. Fischer, "A Great Place to Work," *Chicago Booth Magazine*, www.chicagobooth.edu, September 19, 2022; C. Cutter, "Bosses Swear by the 90-Day Rule to Keep Workers Long Term," *The Wall Street Journal*, www.wsj.com, June 25, 2022; M. Rachal, "WM Explains Plans to Accelerate Automation amid a 'War for Talent,'" *Waste Dive*, www.wastedive.com, June 15, 2022.

Notes

1. Accenture, "Leadership: Julie Sweet," www.accenture.com, accessed January 30, 2023; "Accelerating Equality for All in the Workplace: In Conversation with Julie Sweet, CEO, Accenture," transcript, *Great Place to Work,* For All Summit, www.greatplacetowork.com, accessed January 30, 2023; "Accenture CEO Julie Sweet on the Most Important Skill Job Seekers Need Today," interview by Adi Ignatius, *The New World of Work* (Harvard Business Review), podcast transcript, May 8, 2022, https://hbr.org.
2. *Great Place to Work,* "Accelerating Equality for All."
3. Ibid.; "Julie Sweet on Understanding Technology and Dreaming Big," *Fuqua Insights* (Fuqua School of Business, Duke University), www.fuqua.duke.edu, December 15, 2022; A. Ignatius, "Accenture CEO Julie Sweet."
4. *Great Place to Work,* "Accelerating Equality for All"; *Fuqua Insights,* "Julie Sweet on Understanding Technology and Dreaming Big."
5. *Great Place to Work,* "Accelerating Equality for All"; Ignatius, "Accenture CEO Julie Sweet."
6. *Great Place to Work,* "Accelerating Equality for All"; J. F. Kovar, "Accenture CEO Julie Sweet: IT Growth to Exceed Macro Impacts," *CRN,* www.crn.com, December 16, 2022.
7. G. Yukl, *Leadership in Organizations,* 2nd ed. (New York: Academic Press, 1989); R.M. Stogdill, *Handbook of Leadership: A Survey of the Literature* (New York: Free Press, 1974).
8. W. D. Spangler, R. J. House, and R. Palrecha, "Personality and Leadership," in B. Schneider and D. B. Smith, eds. *Personality and Organizations* (Mahwah, NJ): Erlbaum, 2004), 251–90; "10 Differences between a Manager and a Leader," *Business 2 Community,* www.business-2community.com, accessed March 11, 2020; V. Nayar, "Three Differences between Managers and Leaders," *Harvard Business Review,* https://hbr.org, August 2, 2013.
9. Greenleaf Center for Servant Leadership, "Our History," www.greenleaf.org, accessed January 30, 2023.
10. Greenleaf Center for Servant Leadership, "What Is Servant Leadership?"; Review by F. Hamilton of L. Spears and M. Lawrence, *Practicing Servant Leadership: Succeeding through Trust, Bravery, and Forgiveness* (San Francisco: Jossey-Bass, 2004), in *Academy of Management Review* 30 (October 2005), 875–87; R.R. Washington, "Empirical Relationships between Theories of Servant, Transformational, and Transactional Leadership," *Academy of Management,* Best Paper Proceedings, 2007, 1–6.
11. C. Williamson, "Servant Leadership: How to Put Your People Before Yourself," *Forbes,* www.forbes.com, accessed March 11, 2020; J.E. Hoch, W.H. Bommer, J.H. Dulebohn, and D. Wu, "Do Ethical, Authentic, and Servant Leadership Explain Variance Above and Beyond Transformational Leadership? A Meta-Analysis," *Journal of Management,* http://journals.sagepub.com, August 31, 2016.
12. "What Is Servant Leadership?" www.greenleaf.org, accessed January 30, 2023.
13. R. Calori and B. Dufour, "Management European Style," *Academy of Management Executive* 9, no. 3 (1995), 61–70.
14. Ibid.
15. M. Symonds, "Game of European Thrones: An Essential Guide to Management Styles in Europe," *Forbes,* www.forbes.com, April 5, 2019.
16. H. Mintzberg, *Power in and around Organizations* (Englewood Cliffs, NJ: Prentice-Hall, 1983); J. Pfeffer, *Power in Organizations* (Marshfield, MA: Pitman, 1981).
17. R.P. French, Jr., and B. Raven, "The Bases of Social Power," in D. Cartwright and A.F. Zander, eds., *Group Dynamics* (Evanston, IL: Row, Peterson, 1960), 607–23.
18. N. Kteily and E. J. Finkel, "Leadership in a Politically Charged Age," *Harvard Business Review,* July–August 2022, 109–117; M. Bomgardner, "Could Your Political Views Stymie Your Career?" *Kellogg Insight* (Kellogg School of Management, Northwestern University), https://insight.kellogg.northwestern.edu, September 1, 2022; "SHRM Study Reveals 20% of Workers Mistreated Due to Political Views," *Society for Human Resource Management,* www.shrm.org, October 5, 2022; R. Knight, "Managing a Team with Conflicting Political Views," *Harvard Business Review,* https://hbr.org, October 22, 2020.
19. Kteily and Finkel, "Leadership in a Politically Charged Age"; Knight, "Managing a Team with Conflicting Political Views."
20. Kteily and Finkel, "Leadership in a Politically Charged Age."
21. Kteily and Frankel, "Leadership in a Politically Charged Age"; Knight, "Managing a Team with Conflicting Political Views."
22. D.J. Chung, "How to Really Motivate Salespeople," *Harvard Business Review,* https://hbr.org, April 2015 issue.
23. J. Kelly, "French CEO Sent to Prison after His Policies Resulted in the Suicides of 35 Employees," *Forbes,* www.forbes.com, December 23, 2019.
24. M. Loeb, "Jack Welch Lets Fly on Budgets, Bonuses, and Buddy Boards," *Fortune,* May 29, 1995, 146.
25. E. Segal, "Flexibility Is the Most Empowering Benefit for Employees: New Poll," *Forbes,* www.forbes.com, February 4, 2022; A. Marks, "Envoy Return to the Workplace Report Reveals Work Flexibility Is the New Employee Benefit," *Envoy,* https://envoy.com/blog, January 24, 2022.
26. B.M. Bass, *Bass and Stogdill's Handbook of Leadership: Theory, Research, and Managerial Applications,* 3rd ed. (New York: Free Press, 1990); R.J. House and M.L. Baetz, "Leadership: Some Empirical Generalizations and New Research Directions," in B.M. Staw and L.L. Cummings, eds., *Research in Organizational Behavior,* vol. 1 (Greenwich, CT: JAI Press, 1979), 341–423; S.A. Kirpatrick and E.A. Locke, "Leadership: Do Traits Matter?" *Academy of Management Executive* 5, no. 2 (1991), 48–60; Yukl, *Leadership in Organizations;* G. Yukl and D.D. Van Fleet, "Theory and Research on Leadership in Organizations," in M.D. Dunnette and L.M. Hough, eds., *Handbook of Industrial and Organizational Psychology,* 2nd ed., vol. 3 (Palo Alto, CA: Consulting Psychologists Press, 1992), 147–97.
27. E.A. Fleishman, "Performance Assessment Based on an Empirically Derived Task Taxonomy," *Human Factors* 9 (1967), 349–66; E.A. Fleishman, "The Description of Supervisory Behavior," *Personnel Psychology* 37 (1953), 1–6; A.W. Halpin and B.J. Winer, "A Factorial Study of the Leader Behavior Descriptions," in R.M. Stogdill and A.I. Coons, eds., *Leader Behavior: Its Description and Measurement* (Columbus Bureau of Business Research, Ohio State University, 1957); D. Tscheulin, "Leader Behavior Measurement in German Industry," *Journal of Applied Psychology* 56 (1971), 28–31.
28. Costco Wholesale, "Sustainability Commitment: 2019 Update," www.costco.com, accessed March 11, 2020.
29. S. Todd, "America's Best Large Employers: 2022," *Forbes,*www.forbes.com, accessed January 29, 2023; "Compensation and Benefits," www.costco.com, accessed January 29, 2023.
30. E.A. Fleishman and E.F. Harris, "Patterns of Leadership Behavior Related to Employee Grievances and Turnover," *Personnel Psychology*15 (1962), 43–56.

31. "Technology as a Force for Good: Salesforce's Paula Goldman," *MIT Sloan Management Review,* https://sloanreview.mit.edu, November 30, 2021.
32. K. Broughton, "How Salesforce Makes Decisions on Ethics and Social Issues," *The Wall Street Journal,*www.wsj.com, February 17, 2020; B. Detwiler, "Dreamforce 2019: Salesforce Wants Ethics to Be Baked In to Their Business," *TechRepublic,* November 26, 2019, www.techrepublic.com, November 26, 2019.
33. Broughton, "How Salesforce Makes Decisions"; Detwiler, "Dreamforce 2019."
34. J. Murawski, "Need for AI Ethicists Becomes Clearer as Companies Admit Tech's Flaws," *The Wall Street Journal,* www.wsj.com, March 1, 2019.
35. P. Goldman, "Ethical Leadership and Business in the Fourth Industrial Revolution: New Consumer Research," Salesforce.com blog, www.salesforce.com, February 4, 2019.
36. R. Likert, *New Patterns of Management* (New York: McGraw-Hill, 1961); N.C. Morse and E. Reimer, "The Experimental Change of a Major Organizational Variable," *Journal of Abnormal and Social Psychology* 52 (1956), 120–29.
37. R.R. Blake and J.S. Mouton, *The New Managerial Grid* (Houston: Gulf, 1978).
38. P. Hersey and K. Blanchard, *Management of Organizational Behavior: Utilizing Human Resources* (Englewood Cliffs, NJ: Prentice-Hall, 1982).
39. F.E. Fiedler, *A Theory of Leadership Effectiveness* (New York: McGraw-Hill, 1967); F.E. Fiedler, "The Contingency Model and the Dynamics of the Leadership Process," in L. Berkowitz, ed., *Advances in Experimental Social Psychology* (New York: Academic Press, 1978).
40. "Geraldine Laybourne," https://allwomeninmedia.org, accessed March 11, 2020; J. Fierman, "Winning Ideas from Maverick Managers," *Fortune,* February 6, 1995, 66–80.
41. "Who Is Herman Mashaba?" www.enca.com, accessed March 11, 2020; M. Schuman, "Free to Be," *Forbes,* May 8, 1995, 78–80.
42. House and Baetz, "Leadership"; L.H. Peters, D.D. Hartke, and J.T. Pohlmann, "Fiedler's Contingency Theory of Leadership: An Application of the Meta-Analysis Procedures of Schmidt and Hunter," *Psychological Bulletin* 97 (1985), 274–85; C.A. Schriesheim, B.J. Tepper, and L.A. Tetrault, "Least Preferred Co-Worker Score, Situational Control, and Leadership Effectiveness: A Meta-Analysis of Contingency Model Performance Predictions," *Journal of Applied Psychology* 79 (1994), 561–73.
43. E. Meyer, "Being the Boss in Brussels, Boston, and Beijing," *Harvard Business Review,* July–August 2017, 70–77.
44. Ibid., 75–77.
45. Ibid., 77; J. Owen, "How to Be a Global Leader," *Director,* November 2017, 56–57; A. Ghannad, "The Simple Key to Cross-Cultural Leadership," Association for Talent Development blog, www.td.org, February 5, 2018.
46. M.G. Evans, "The Effects of Supervisory Behavior on the Path–Goal Relationship," *Organizational Behavior and Human Performance* 5 (1970), 277–98; R.J. House, "A Path–Goal Theory of Leader Effectiveness," *Administrative Science Quarterly* 16 (1971), 321–38; J.C. Wofford and L.Z. Liska, "Path–Goal Theories of Leadership: A Meta-Analysis," *Journal of Management* 19 (1993), 857–76.
47. S. Kerr and J.M. Jermier, "Substitutes for Leadership: Their Meaning and Measurement," *Organizational Behavior and Human Performance* 22 (1978), 375–403; P. M. Podsakoff, B.P. Niehoff, S.B. MacKenzie, and M.L. Williams, "Do Substitutes for Leadership Really Substitute for Leadership? An Empirical Examination of Kerr and Jermier's Situational Leadership Model," *Organizational Behavior and Human Decision Processes* 54 (1993), 1–44.
48. Kerr and Jermier, "Substitutes for Leadership"; Podsakoff et al., "Do Substitutes for Leadership Really Substitute for Leadership?"
49. J.B. Carson, P.E. Tesluk, and J.A. Marrone, "Shared Leadership in Teams: An Investigation of Antecedent Conditions and Performance," *Academy of Management Journal* 50, no. 5 (2007), 1217–34.
50. T. Loudenbeck, "Meet Reed Hastings, the Man Who Built Netflix," *Business Insider,* www.businessinsider.com, accessed March 11, 2020.
51. D. Butler, "History of Netflix: Timeline and Facts," *The Street,* www.thestreet.com, September 16, 2019.
52. S.D. Anthony and E.I. Schwartz, "What the Best Transformational Leaders Do," *Harvard Business Review,* https://hbr.org, accessed March 11, 2020.
53. "Netflix DVD Subscribers Mourn Service's Imminent Demise," *CBS News,* April 21, 2023, https://www.cbsnews.com; N. Wingfield and B. Stelter, "How Netflix Lost 800,000 Members, and Good Will," *The New York Times,* www.nytimes.com, accessed March 11, 2020; J. Roettgers, "Netflix Has Now Shipped 5 Billion DVDs to Its Members," *Variety,* https://variety.com, August 26, 2019.
54. Anthony and E.I. Schwartz, "What the Best Transformational Leaders Do."
55. Butler, "History of Netflix."
56. J. Stoll, "Netflix Subscribers Count Worldwide 2021–2022," *Statista,* www.statista.com, January 20, 2023.
57. Netflix, "Real Values," https://jobs.netflix.com, accessed March 11, 2020.
58. B.M. Bass, *Leadership and Performance beyond Expectations* (New York: Free Press, 1985); Bass, *Bass and Stogdill's Handbook of Leadership;* Yukl and Van Fleet, "Theory and Research on Leadership."
59. "Learning from Netflix: How to Build a Culture of Freedom and Responsibility," *Knowledge@Wharton,* https://knowledge.wharton.upenn.edu, May 29, 2018.
60. P. McCord, "How Netflix Reinvented HR," *Harvard Business Review,* https://hbr.org, accessed March 11, 2020; "Dream Team," https://jobs.netflix.com, accessed March 11, 2020.
61. "Freedom and Responsibility," https://jobs.netflix.com, accessed January 29, 2023; R. Picciotto, "Netflix Founder Reed Hastings Is Giving Up His CEO Role," *CNBC,* www.cnbc.com, January 19, 2023.
62. K. Shonk, "Charismatic Leadership: Weighing the Pros and Cons," Harvard Law School's Program on Negotiation Daily Blog, www.pon.harvard.edu, accessed January 30, 2023.
63. Bass, *Leadership and Performance beyond Expectations;* Bass, *Bass and Stogdill's Handbook of Leadership;* Yukl and Van Fleet, "Theory and Research on Leadership."
64. Ibid.
65. Bass, *Leadership and Performance beyond Expectations.*
66. Bass, *Bass and Stogdill's Handbook of Leadership;* B.M. Bass and B.J. Avolio, "Transformational Leadership: A Response to Critiques," in M.M. Chemers and R. Ayman, eds., *Leadership Theory and Research: Perspectives and Directions* (San Diego: Academic Press, 1993), 49–80; B.M. Bass, B.J. Avolio, and L. Goodheim, "Biography and the Assessment of Transformational Leadership at the World Class Level," *Journal of Management* 13 (1987), 7–20; J.J. Hater and B.M. Bass, "Supervisors' Evaluations and Subordinates' Perceptions of Transformational and Transactional Leadership," *Journal of Applied Psychology* 73 (1988), 695–702; R. Pillai, "Crisis and Emergence of Charismatic Leadership in Groups: An Experimental Investigation," *Journal of Applied Psychology* 26 (1996), 543–62; J. Seltzer and B.M. Bass, "Transformational Leadership: Beyond Initiation and Consideration," *Journal of Management* 16 (1990), 693–703; D.A. Waldman, B.M. Bass, and W.O. Einstein, "Effort, Performance, Transformational Leadership in Industrial and Military Service," *Journal of Occupation Psychology* 60 (1987), 1–10.

67. W. Jiang, X. Zhao, and J. Ni, "The Impact of Transformational Leadership on Employee Sustainable Performance: The Mediating Role of Organizational Citizenship Behavior," *Sustainability* 9 (2017), 1567–83; R. Pillai, C.A. Schriesheim, and E.S. Williams, "Fairness Perceptions and Trust as Mediators of Transformational and Transactional Leadership: A Two-Sample Study," *Journal of Management* 25 (1999), 897–933.

68. Catalyst, "Women CEOs of the S&P 500," www.catalyst.org, March 5, 2020; J. Carpenter, "This Is What Women Have to Do to Become CEO," *CNNMoney*, http://money.cnn.com, February 1, 2018.

69. Catalyst, "Pyramid: Women in the United States Workforce (Infographic)," www.catalyst.org, accessed January 30, 2023.

70. A.H. Eagly and B.T. Johnson, "Gender and Leadership Style: A Meta-Analysis," *Psychological Bulletin* 108 (1990), 233–56.

71. Eagly and Johnson, "Gender and Leadership Style."

72. V. Lipman, "Are Women Better Managers Than Men?" *Psychology Today*, www.psychologytoday.com, April 23, 2015.

73. J. Baldoni, "Few Executives Are Self-Aware, But Women Have the Edge," *Harvard Business Review*, https://hbr.org, May 9, 2013.

74. Ibid.

75. A.H. Eagly, S.J. Karau, and M.G. Makhijani, "Gender and the Effectiveness of Leaders: A Meta-Analysis," *Psychological Bulletin* 117 (1995), 125–45.

76. Ibid.

77. J.M. George and K. Bettenhausen, "Understanding Prosocial Behavior, Sales Performance, and Turnover: A Group-Level Analysis in a Service Context," *Journal of Applied Psychology* 75 (1990), 698–709.

78. T. Sy, S. Cote, and R. Saavedra, "The Contagious Leader: Impact of the Leader's Mood on the Mood of Group Members, Group Affective Tone, and Group Processes," *Journal of Applied Psychology* 90, no. 2 (2005), 295–305.

79. J.M. George, "Emotions and Leadership: The Role of Emotional Intelligence," *Human Relations* 53 (2000), 1027–55.

80. George, "Emotions and Leadership"; G. Chan, "5 Ways Emotional Intelligence Can Make You a Better Leader," *Forbes*, www.forbes.com, August 22, 2022.

81. J. Zhou and J.M. George, "Awakening Employee Creativity: The Role of Leader Emotional Intelligence," *The Leadership Quarterly* 14, no. 45 (August–October 2003), 545–68.

82. Zhou and George, "Awakening Employee Creativity."

83. Ibid.

84. J. Garfinkle, "Five Qualities of Emotionally Intelligent Leaders," *Smart Brief*, www.smartbrief.com, January 15, 2018; B. Tracy, "Why Emotional Intelligence Is Indispensable for Leaders," *Forbes*, October 30, 2017, www.forbes.com; S.T.A. Phipps, "Why Emotional Intelligence Is Necessary for Effective Leadership," *Leadership Excellence Essentials*, June 2017, 56–57.

85. Garfinkle, "Five Qualities"; S. Bawany, "The Art and Practice of Servant Leadership," *Leadership Excellence Essentials*, November 2017, 34–35.

86. Tracy, "Why Emotional Intelligence Is Indispensable"; M. Prokopeak, "Building the Leader of the Future," *Chief Learning Officer*, www.clomedia.com, March 22, 2018.

87. S. Goldstein, "EQ Is Massively More Important Than IQ for Leaders. Here's Why," *Inc.*, www.inc.com, September 26, 2017.

CHAPTER 15

Effective Groups and Teams

El Nariz/Shutterstock

Learning Objectives

After studying this chapter, you should be able to:

LO15-1 Explain why groups and teams are key contributors to organizational effectiveness.

LO15-2 Identify the different types of groups and teams that help managers and organizations achieve their goals.

LO15-3 Explain how different elements of group dynamics influence the functioning and effectiveness of groups and teams.

LO15-4 Explain why it is important for groups and teams to have a balance of conformity and deviance and a moderate level of cohesiveness.

LO15-5 Describe how managers can motivate group members to achieve organizational goals and reduce social loafing in groups and teams.

A MANAGER'S CHALLENGE

How NI's CEO Ignited Teamwork

How can managers use teams to enhance performance? When Eric Starkloff accepted a promotion to CEO of NI (then called National Instruments), he wanted to generate faster growth by making the company more flexible. NI started in the 1970s as a manufacturer of testing and measurement hardware, but customer needs were rapidly shifting to full systems with automated capabilities, data analytics, and support. An engineer by training, Starkloff wanted to keep the company at the forefront of testing technology and elevate the role of testing engineers in customers' companies. This strategy would require a new corporate culture, making it essential for the change to start at the top, with Starkloff's leadership team.[1]

Making his job more difficult, Starkloff took the helm in February 2020, just a month before COVID-19 was declared a global pandemic. He moved the process forward even as activity shifted to remote work. For help, he brought in a consulting firm to guide the process. The consultants led off with an assessment of the leadership team. They found that NI's executives tended to tackle their challenges independently, avoiding the engagement and honesty that could build trust and collaboration.[2]

With facilitation and coaching from NI's chief people officer, Cate Prescott, the leadership team began to learn a set of practices that the consultant said would deliver high returns. They engaged in 60- to 90-minute team meetings focused on a single topic, with half the time devoted to breakout sessions in which groups of three team members arrive at ideas to recommend. To keep team cohesion strong in spite of physical distancing, meetings took time for hearing what is going on in team members' lives.[3]

Especially while the leadership team worked remotely, effective methods of collaboration were essential. Online meetings used conferencing software that allows for dividing a larger group into breakout groups and reconvening them later. A three-person group can build candor and trust quickly, and that spirit tends to carry over when the larger group reconvenes. Another tool, called "bulletproofing," aims to promote collaboration. One team member presents a description of a project, what has been achieved so far, what the project is struggling with, and what it aims to do next. That team member then invites feedback, and the meeting divides into three-member groups to develop the feedback and present it in the reconvened meeting. A third practice, which improves accountability and employee development, is "open 360" meetings in which one team member receives performance feedback from the others, including praise and ideas for improvement. Finally, in any team meeting, participants

NI CEO Eric Starkloff championed a new approach to encouraging collaboration among the company's leadership team, which helped build trust among team members.
10'000 Hours/Getty Images

can call for "candor break" breakout sessions whenever team members seem to be holding back; the breakout teams are asked to come back with answers to "What is not being said?"[4]

Within a few months, NI's executives were seeing improvements in their ability to work as a team. The small-group discussions with meeting records prepared by the facilitator increased their trust in one another, and the bulletproofing method showed them the potential of getting fresh insight from colleagues. The leadership team was making decisions faster and getting more buy-in from those affected. Seeing these improvements, team members began spreading the positive attitudes and high-return practices throughout the organization, increasing the number of people who understood and were on board with what the leadership team wanted to accomplish. These outcomes are consistent with NI's corporate values, "Be bold; be kind; and be connectors," which apply to customer as well as coworker relationships. The benefits flowed to NI's financial statement, including a 9% increase in revenues from 2019 to 2021.[5]

Overview

In addition to NI featured in "A Manager's Challenge," many organizations use groups and teams to innovate and improve organizational effectiveness. Managers in companies large and small are using groups and teams to enhance performance, increase responsiveness to customers, spur innovation, and motivate employees. In this chapter, we look in detail at how groups and teams can contribute to organizational effectiveness and the types of groups and teams used in organizations. We discuss how different elements of group dynamics influence the functioning and effectiveness of groups, and we describe how managers can motivate group members to achieve organizational goals and reduce social loafing in groups and teams. By the end of this chapter, you will understand why the effective management of groups and teams is a key ingredient in organizational performance and effectiveness.

Groups, Teams, and Organizational Effectiveness

LO15-1 Explain why groups and teams are key contributors to organizational effectiveness.

group Two or more people who interact with each other to accomplish certain goals or meet certain needs.

team A group whose members work intensely with one another to achieve a specific common goal or objective.

A **group** may be defined as two or more people who interact with each other to accomplish certain goals or meet certain needs.[6] A **team** is a group whose members work *intensely* with one another to achieve a specific common goal or objective. As these definitions imply, all teams are groups, but not all groups are teams. The two characteristics that distinguish teams from groups are the *intensity* with which team members work together and the presence of a *specific, overriding team goal or objective.*

As detailed in "A Manager's Challenge," NI's leadership team met regularly to redefine the company's strategy for a high-tech future, motivated by the awareness that they needed a high degree of collaboration. In contrast, the accountants who work in a small CPA firm are a group: They may interact with one another to achieve goals such as keeping up-to-date on the latest changes in accounting rules and regulations, maintaining a smoothly functioning office, satisfying clients, and attracting new clients, but they are not a team because they do not work closely with one another. Each accountant concentrates on serving the needs of their own clients.

Because all teams are also groups, whenever we use the term *group* in this chapter, we are referring to both groups *and* teams. As you might imagine, because members of teams work intensely together, teams can sometimes be difficult to form, and it may take time for members to learn how to work effectively together. Under these conditions, for team development and performance to succeed, team members need "soft" skills, as described in the "Management Insight" feature.

Groups and teams can help an organization gain a competitive advantage because they can (1) enhance its performance, (2) increase its responsiveness to customers, (3) increase innovation, and (4) increase employees' motivation and satisfaction (see Figure 15.1). In this section we look at each of these contributions in turn.

MANAGEMENT INSIGHT

Soft Skills Critical to Team Success

Teams are often formed for challenging activities: developing products, rolling out software systems, or planning a marketing campaign. These require the expertise of engineers, software developers, marketing researchers, finance professionals, and others. Besides this technical expertise, all teams require "soft" skills. These are the people-related skills that get team members connected with each other and aligned on carrying out a shared purpose. Soft skills include showing empathy, organizing, collaborating, solving interpersonal problems, and communicating (speaking, writing, and above all, listening).[7]

On teams with soft skills, members share ideas, pool their knowledge to solve problems, and keep each other updated on their progress. People are unafraid to make mistakes, are open to learning from one another, and listen to one another's ideas. Team members with soft skills benefit the team by connecting with the rest of the organization to gather information and other resources. These individuals bring out other members' ideas and get them motivated.[8]

However, soft skills are hard to measure, so it is difficult to select job candidates with soft skills. Furthermore, employers struggle to teach these skills. Annie Healy, recruiting manager for the Motley Fool, a media company focused on investing, recalls interviewing a candidate whose technical skills were so impressive that she did not fully explore the candidate's soft skills. The company made the hire but has since needed to intervene a great deal to make up for the person's lack of focus on teamwork.[9]

The first and most important way to form teams with soft skills is to hire people who have those skills or at least have shown potential to develop them. This requires identifying which soft skills will contribute to the team's success and developing questions that ask job candidates to describe situations in which they have used or would use the particular skills. Commercially available tests can screen for particular qualities such as empathy or emotional intelligence. Other tests measure individual differences such as problem-solving styles. Team leaders can be taught to use information from these tests to ensure that each person is contributing effectively according to their style.[10]

In addition, training should address development of soft skills. It should extend beyond classroom or coaching sessions by assigning behaviors to practice and situations in which to practice them. Along with training, the employee should have measurable goals, such as giving presentations or restructuring meetings to ensure all voices are heard.[11]

Figure 15.1

Groups' and Teams' Contributions to Organizational Effectiveness

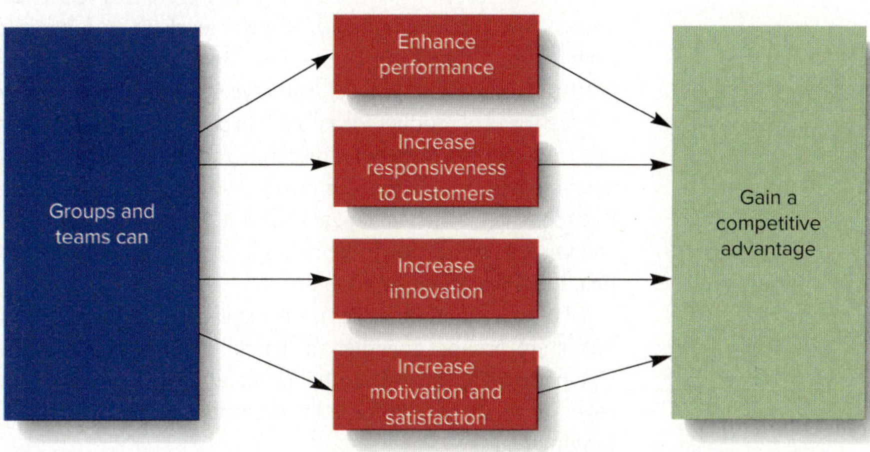

Groups and Teams as Performance Enhancers

synergy Performance gains that result when individuals and departments coordinate their actions.

One of the main advantages of using groups is the opportunity to obtain a type of **synergy**: People working in a group can produce more or higher-quality outputs than would have been produced if each person had worked separately and all their individual efforts were later combined. The essence of synergy is captured in the saying "The whole is more than the sum of its parts." Factors that can contribute to synergy in groups include the abilities of group members to bounce ideas off one another, to correct one another's mistakes, to solve problems immediately as they arise, to bring a diverse knowledge base to bear on a problem or goal, and to accomplish work that is too vast or all-encompassing for any person to achieve alone.

To take advantage of the potential for synergy in groups, managers need to make sure that groups are composed of members who have complementary skills and knowledge relevant to the group's work. For example, at Hallmark Cards Inc., the company division that sells cards, gift wrap, and related products in more than 30 languages in 100 countries, synergies are created by bringing together all the different functions needed to create and produce a greeting card in a cross-functional team (a team composed of members from different departments or functions) (see Chapter 10). For instance, artists, writers, designers, and marketing experts work together as team members to develop new cards and other products.[12]

At Hallmark, the skills and expertise of the artists complement the contributions of the writers and vice versa. Managers also need to give groups enough autonomy so that the groups, rather than the manager, are solving problems and determining how to achieve goals and objectives, as is true in the cross-functional teams at Hallmark. To promote synergy, managers need to empower their employees and to be coaches, guides, and resources for groups while refraining from playing a more directive or supervisory role. The potential for synergy in groups may be one reason more managers are incorporating empowerment into their personal leadership styles (see Chapter 14).

When tasks are complex and involve highly sophisticated and rapidly changing technologies, achieving synergies in teams often hinges on having the appropriate mix of backgrounds and areas of expertise represented on the team. In large organizations with operations in many states and countries, managers can rely on databases and software applications to determine which employees might have the expertise needed on a particular team or for a certain project.

Groups, Teams, and Responsiveness to Customers

Being responsive to customers is not always easy. In manufacturing organizations, for example, customers' needs and desires for new and improved products have to be balanced against engineering constraints, production costs and feasibilities, government safety regulations, and marketing challenges. In service organizations such as health care organizations, being responsive to patients' needs and desires for prompt, high-quality medical care and treatment has to be balanced against meeting physicians' needs and desires and keeping health care costs under control. Being responsive to customers often requires the wide variety of skills and expertise found in different departments and at different levels in an organization's hierarchy. Sometimes, for example, employees at lower levels in an organization's hierarchy, such as sales representatives for a software company, are closest to its customers and the most attuned to their needs. However, lower-level employees, like salespeople, often lack the technical expertise needed for new product ideas; such expertise is found in the research and development department. Bringing salespeople, research and development experts, and members of other departments together in a group or cross-functional team can enhance responsiveness to customers. Consequently, when managers form a team, they must make sure the diversity of expertise and knowledge needed to be responsive to customers exists within the team; this is why cross-functional teams are so popular.

In a cross-functional team, the expertise and knowledge in different organizational departments are brought together in the skills and knowledge of the team members. Managers of high-performing organizations are careful to determine which types of expertise and knowledge are required for teams to be responsive to customers, and they use this information in forming teams.

Teams and Innovation

Innovation—the creative development of new products, new technologies, new services, or even new organizational structures—is a topic we introduced in Chapter 1. Often an individual working alone does not have the extensive and diverse skills, knowledge, and expertise required for successful innovation. Managers can better encourage innovation by creating teams of diverse individuals who together have the knowledge relevant to a particular type of innovation—as when NI's leaders, described in "A Manager's Challenge," brought together executives across business lines and functions to transform the company's business model—rather than relying on individuals working alone.

Using teams to innovate has other advantages. First, team members can often uncover one another's errors or false assumptions; one person acting alone would not be able to do this. Second, team members can critique one another's approaches and build off one another's strengths while compensating for weaknesses—an advantage of devil's advocacy and dialectical inquiry, discussed in Chapter 7.

To further promote innovation, managers can empower teams and make their members fully responsible and accountable for the innovation process. The manager's role is to provide guidance, assistance, coaching, and the resources that team members need, *not* to closely direct or supervise their activities. To speed innovation, managers also need to form teams in which each member brings a unique resource to the team, such as engineering prowess, knowledge of production, marketing expertise, or financial savvy. Successful innovation sometimes requires that managers form teams with members from different countries and cultures.

Groups and Teams as Motivators

Managers often form groups and teams to accomplish organizational goals and then find that using groups and teams brings additional benefits. Members of groups, and especially members of teams (because of the higher intensity of interaction in teams), are likely to be more satisfied than they would have been if they had been on their own. The experience of working alongside other highly charged and motivated people can be stimulating and motivating: Team members can see how their efforts and expertise directly contribute to the achievement of team and organizational goals, and they feel personally responsible for the outcomes or results of their work. This has been the case at Hallmark.

The increased motivation and satisfaction that can accompany the use of teams can also lead to other outcomes, such as increased efficiency and talent retention. These were common outcomes for many teams and organizations during the global pandemic.[13] For example, working remotely forced many teams to meet less often but accomplish more in each meeting, focusing "team time" to help junior members review projects and seek informal guidance from senior members. In addition, fostering this type of strong collaboration may provide organizations with a competitive advantage when it comes to hiring and retaining top talent. Although some organizations continue to bring employees back to the office, others say they will continue to allow regular remote workdays, which may increase motivation and help recruit talent from distant locations.[14]

Working in a group or team can also satisfy organizational members' needs for engaging in social interaction and feeling connected to other people. For workers who perform highly stressful jobs, such as health care workers, group membership can be an important source of social support and motivation. Family members or friends may not be able to fully understand or appreciate some sources of work stress that these group members experience firsthand. Moreover, group members may cope better with work stressors when they can share them with other members of their group. In addition, groups often devise techniques to relieve stress, such as telling jokes among hospital operating room staff.

Why do managers in all kinds of organizations rely so heavily on groups and teams? Effectively managed groups and teams can help managers in their quest for high performance, responsiveness to customers, and employee motivation. Before explaining how managers can effectively manage groups, however, we will describe the types of groups that are formed in organizations.

Types of Groups and Teams

LO15-2 Identify the different types of groups and teams that help managers and organizations achieve their goals.

To achieve their goals of high performance, responsiveness to customers, innovation, and employee motivation, managers can form various types of groups and teams (see Figure 15.2). **Formal groups** are those that managers establish to achieve organizational goals. The formal work groups are *cross-functional* teams composed of members from different departments, such as those at Hallmark, and *cross-cultural* teams composed of members from different cultures or countries, such as the teams at global car makers. As you will see, some of the groups discussed in this section also can be considered to be cross-functional (if they are composed of members from different departments) or cross-cultural (if they are composed of members from different countries or cultures).

Sometimes organizational members, managers or nonmanagers, form groups because they feel that groups will help them achieve their own goals or meet their own needs (for example, the need for social interaction). Groups formed in this way are **informal groups**. For example, four nurses who work in a hospital and have lunch together twice a week constitute an informal group.

formal groups Groups that managers establish to achieve organizational goals.

informal groups Groups that managers or nonmanagerial employees form to help them achieve their own goals or meet their own needs.

The Top Management Team

A central concern of the CEO and president of a company is to form a **top management team** to help the organization achieve its mission and goals. Top management teams are responsible for developing the strategies that result in an organization's competitive advantage; most have between five and seven members. In forming their top management teams, CEOs are well advised to stress diversity in expertise, skills, knowledge, and experience. Thus, many top management teams are also cross-functional teams: They are composed of members from different departments, such as finance, marketing, production, and engineering. Diversity helps ensure that the top management team will have all the background and resources it needs to make good decisions. Diversity also helps guard against *groupthink*–faulty group decision making that results when group members strive for agreement at the expense of an accurate assessment of the situation (see Chapter 7).

top management team A group composed of the CEO, the president, and the heads of the most important departments.

Research and Development Teams

Managers in pharmaceuticals, computers, electronics, electronic imaging, and other high-tech industries often create **research and development teams** to develop new products. Managers select research and development (R&D) team members on the basis of their expertise and experience in a certain area. Sometimes R&D teams are cross-functional, with members from departments such as engineering, marketing, and production in addition to members from the research and development department.

research and development teams Teams whose members have the expertise and experience needed to develop new products.

Figure 15.2

Types of Groups and Teams in Organizations

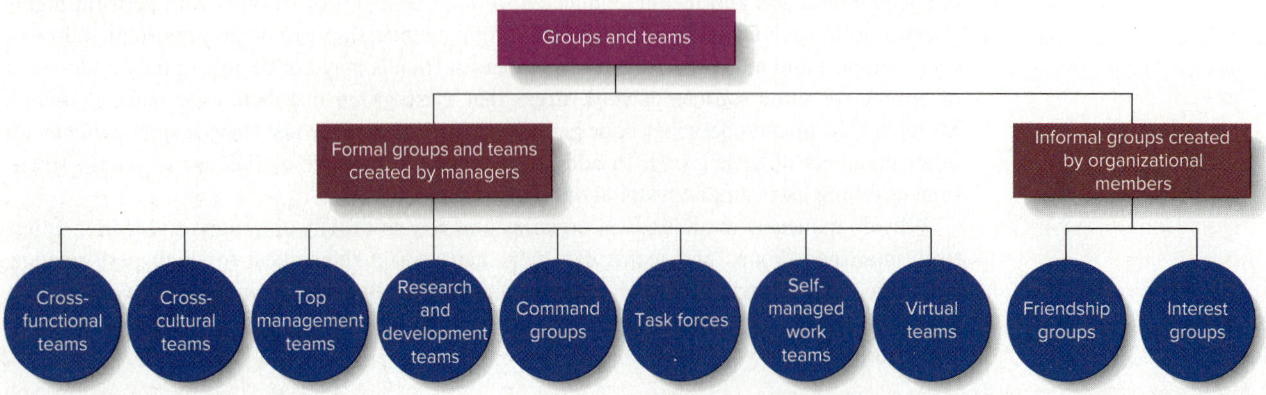

Command Groups

command group A group composed of employees who report to the same supervisor; also called department or unit.

Employees who report to the same supervisor compose a **command group**. When top managers design an organization's structure and establish reporting relationships and a chain of command, they are essentially creating command groups. Command groups, often called *departments* or *units,* perform a significant amount of the work in many organizations. In order to have command groups that help an organization gain a competitive advantage, managers not only need to motivate group members to perform at a high level but also must be effective leaders. Examples of command groups include the salespeople in a large department store in New York who report to the same supervisor, the employees of a small swimming pool sales and maintenance company in Florida who report to a general manager, the customer service representatives at the MetLife insurance company who report to the same supervisor, and workers on an automobile assembly line in the Ford Motor Company who report to the same first-line manager.

Task Forces

task forces Committees of managers or nonmanagerial employees from various departments or divisions who meet to solve a specific, mutual problem; also called ad *hoc committees.*

Managers form **task forces** to accomplish specific goals or solve problems in a certain time period; task forces are sometimes called *ad hoc committees.* For example, the owner and top manager of a chain of six gyms and fitness centers in the Midwest created a task force composed of the general managers of the six gyms to determine whether the fitness centers should institute a separate fee schedule for customers who wanted to use the centers only for exercise classes (and not use other facilities such as weights and swimming pools). The task force was given three months to prepare a report summarizing the pros and cons of the proposed change in fee schedules. After the task force completed its report and reached the conclusion that the change in fee structure probably would reduce revenues rather than increase them and thus should not be implemented, the task force was disbanded. As in this case, task forces can be a valuable tool for busy managers who do not have the time to personally explore an important issue in depth.

Sometimes managers need to form task forces whose work, so to speak, is never done. The task force may be addressing a long-term or enduring problem or issue facing an organization, such as how to most usefully contribute to the local community or how to make sure the organization provides opportunities for potential employees with disabilities. Task forces that are relatively permanent are often referred to as *standing committees.* Membership in standing committees changes over time. Members may have, for example, a two- or three-year term on the committee, and memberships expire at varying times so there are always some members with experience on the committee. Managers often form and maintain standing committees to make sure important issues continue to be addressed.

Self-Managed Work Teams

self-managed work teams Groups of employees who supervise their own activities and monitor the quality of the goods and services they provide.

Self-managed work teams are teams in which members are empowered and have the responsibility and autonomy to complete identifiable pieces of work. On a day-to-day basis, team members decide what the team will do, how it will do it, and which members will perform which specific tasks.[15] Managers can assign self-managed work teams' overall goals (such as assembling defect-free computer keyboards) but let team members decide how to meet those goals. Managers usually form self-managed work teams to improve quality, increase motivation and satisfaction, and lower costs. Often, by creating self-managed work teams, they combine tasks that individuals working separately used to perform, so the team is responsible for the whole set of tasks that yields an identifiable output or end product.

Managers can take a number of steps to ensure that self-managed work teams are effective and help an organization achieve its goals:[16]

- Give teams enough responsibility and autonomy to be truly self-managing. Refrain from telling team members what to do or solving problems for them, even if you (as a manager) know what should be done.

- Make sure a team's work is sufficiently complex so that it entails a number of different steps or procedures that must be performed and results in some kind of finished end product.
- Carefully select members of self-managed work teams. Team members should have the diversity of skills needed to complete the team's work, have the ability to work with others, and want to be part of a team.
- As a manager, realize that your role with self-managed work teams calls for guidance, coaching, and supporting, not supervising. You are a resource for teams to turn to when needed.
- Analyze what type of training team members need, and provide it. Working in a self-managed work team often requires that employees have more extensive technical and interpersonal skills.

Sometimes employees have individual jobs but also are part of a self-managed team that is formed to accomplish a specific goal or work on an important project. Employees need to perform their own job tasks as well as actively contribute to the self-managed team so that the team achieves its goal.

Sometimes self-managed work teams run into trouble. Members may be reluctant to discipline one another by firing members or withholding bonuses from members who are not performing up to par.[17] For example, a manager who oversaw self-managed work teams in AES Corporation's Houston plant found that although the self-managed work teams were highly effective, they had a difficult time firing team members who were performing poorly.[18]

The Dallas office of the New York Life Insurance Company experimented with having members of self-managed teams evaluate one another's performance and determine pay levels. Team members did not feel comfortable assuming this role, however, and managers ended up handling these tasks.[19] One reason for team members' discomfort may be the close personal relationships they sometimes develop with one another. In addition, members of self-managed work teams may sometimes take longer to accomplish tasks, such as when team members have difficulties coordinating their efforts.

Virtual Teams

virtual teams Teams whose members rarely or never meet in person but, rather, interact by using various forms of information technology such as email, cloud computing, videoconferences, and various meeting and management apps.

Virtual teams are teams whose members rarely or never meet face-to-face but, rather, interact by using various forms of information technology such as email, text messaging, collaborative software programs, videoconferences, and various meeting and management apps. This was the situation for better part of two years during the global pandemic when most managers and their employees were forced to work remotely. As COVID-19 becomes more manageable and more people are vaccinated against the virus, companies continue to struggle with the question of requiring employees to return to the office rather than allowing them to work virtually. In a recent survey of company executives by consulting firm PwC, 83% now say the "temporary" shift to remote work was successful for their organizations; however, they continue to grapple with how widely to extend virtual/remote work options for their employees.[20] Research conducted by the Pew Research Center in 2022 revealed that nearly 60% of the 6,000 workers surveyed said their jobs could be done virtually, and they would prefer not to work in the office.[21] Organizations and their managers will continue to address how work gets done in light of the ongoing effects of the pandemic.

As organizations become increasingly global, and as the need for specialized knowledge increases due to advances in technology, managers can create virtual teams to solve problems or explore opportunities without being limited by team members' needing to work in the same geographic location.[22] Take the case of an organization that has manufacturing facilities in Australia, Canada, the United States, and Mexico and is encountering a quality problem in a complex manufacturing process. Each of its facilities has a quality control team headed by a quality control manager. The vice president for production does not try to solve the problem by forming and leading a team at one of the four manufacturing facilities; instead, she forms and leads a virtual team composed of the quality control managers of the four plants and the plants' general managers. When these team members communicate via email, the company's networking site, and videoconferencing, a wide array of knowledge and experience is brought together to solve the problem.

Virtual teams enable managers to disregard geographic distances and form teams whose member have the knowledge and expertise to tackle a particular problem. Videoconferencing helps virtual teams stay connected.
Andrey_Popov/Shutterstock

The principal advantage of virtual teams is that they enable managers to disregard geographic distances and form teams whose members have the knowledge, expertise, and experience to tackle a particular problem or take advantage of a specific opportunity.[23] Virtual teams also can include members who are not actually employees of the organization itself; a virtual team might include members of a company that is used for outsourcing.

Along with increased globalization, the pandemic, with its social distancing requirements, contributed to greater reliance on virtual teamwork over the past few years, so managers are increasingly required to meet the challenges of this way of working. One such challenge that members of virtual teams face is building a sense of camaraderie and trust among team members who rarely, if ever, meet in person. In fact, recent research suggests that the link between trust and team effectiveness was even stronger for virtual teams than for teams that work in the same location. This finding underscores the need for managers of virtual teams to focus on building trust among team members.[24] To address this challenge, some organizations make sure virtual team members have a chance to meet in person soon after the team is formed and then schedule periodic in-person meetings to promote trust, understanding, and cooperation in the teams.[25] The need for such meetings is underscored by research suggesting that while some virtual teams can be as effective as teams that meet in-person, virtual team members might be less satisfied with teamwork efforts and have fewer feelings of camaraderie or cohesion. (Group cohesiveness is discussed in more detail later in the chapter.)[26] In addition, because in-person meetings are not always possible, team leaders and members need relationship-building skills for online interactions, as described in the "Manager as a Person" feature.

MANAGER AS A PERSON

Building Strong Relationships on Virtual Teams

The COVID-19 pandemic launched a sudden experiment in remote teamwork. Managers can be proud that they succeeded well enough in deploying new processes and technology that many workers want to continue working remotely at least part of the time. But one aspect of work has suffered: the sense of trust that builds when people learn about each other in person. Remote workers report feeling less of a connection, and their pattern of interactions shifted to smaller networks–a few people they know best. The situation is especially hard on employees who are starting their careers and haven't already built strong networks.[27]

Fortunately, people can build strong relationships online, but it may take extra planning, leadership, and time. Team members should pay more attention to how they interact with one another and how often. They should keep teammates informed about the status of their contributions to team projects–say, by setting a status message on a team page or employee profile. Another way to build trust is to disclose information about yourself that will help others understand your situation–for example, that you have soccer practice on Thursday evenings or are anticipating a call to hear about a parent's well-being after surgery. The flip side is equally important: Team members should listen attentively, especially when others are sharing sensitive information, so they can empathize with and help one another. Perhaps surprisingly, a helpful team member also can build empathy and trust by asking for help at times.[28]

Team leaders can support these efforts by frequently checking in one-on-one with team members. They also should foster good teamwork when they lead online and hybrid meetings. They should observe members' participation levels and invite thoughts from quieter participants. An option to type comments in a chat function can draw more responses from introverted team members than they might offer in person. Also, leaders should schedule time in meetings for getting acquainted and learning more about one another.[29]

Organizations benefit from creative teamwork, so they should support remote collaboration with policies and technology. Companies that have succeeded with virtual teamwork treat it as something worth planning. They prepare guides for using communication tools and set up mentor relationships that ensure someone is hearing team members' questions and concerns. They also supply adequate hardware and software, so that no one is excluded for lack of messaging software or a large enough screen to see everyone on the team during a meeting.[30]

Not surprisingly, members of successful virtual teams exhibit certain skills and abilities that help make these long-distance groups so effective. Researchers point out that leadership behaviors such as taking personal initiative and working independently are more beneficial to virtual teams than to teams that work face-to-face on a daily basis. In addition, studies point out that members' strong analytical and written communication skills provide competitive advantage to a company's virtual teams. These findings suggest that managers hiring employees for virtual teams might focus on some of these specific skills that have proved successful.[31]

Research also suggests that it is important for managers to keep track of virtual teams and intervene when necessary by, for example, encouraging members of teams who do not communicate often enough to monitor their team's progress and making sure team members actually have the time, and are recognized, for their virtual teamwork. Additionally, when virtual teams are experiencing downtime or rough spots, managers might try to schedule in-person team time to bring team members together and help them focus on their goals.[32]

Researchers at the London Business School, including Professor Lynda Gratton, studied global virtual teams to try to identify factors that might help such teams be effective. Based on their research, Gratton suggests that when forming virtual teams, it is helpful to include a few members who already know each other, other members who are well connected to people outside the team, and when possible, members who have volunteered to be a part of the team. It is also advantageous for companies to have some kind of online site where team members can learn more about each other and the kinds of work they are engaged in and, in particular, a shared online workspace that team members can access around the clock. Frequent communication is beneficial. Additionally, virtual team members should perceive their projects as meaningful, interesting, and important to promote and sustain their motivation.[33]

Today, members of virtual teams rely on many different technology tools to help them with their work activities. These may include Zoom (a videoconferencing/screen-sharing tool); Microsoft Teams (a secure platform that allows users to chat, share files, and collaborate in real time); Google Drive (centralized location where teams can share, edit, and collaborate on various documents); Slack (a group chat and notifications app); and Every Time Zone (a program that allows workers to find optimal times to schedule calls and meetings).[34]

Friendship Groups

friendship groups Informal groups of employees who enjoy one another's company and socialize with one another.

The groups described so far are formal groups created by managers. **Friendship groups** are informal groups of employees who enjoy one another's company and socialize with one another. Members of friendship groups may have lunch together, take breaks together, or meet after work for meals, sports, or other activities. Friendship groups help satisfy employees' needs for interpersonal interaction, can provide needed social support in times of stress, and can contribute to people's feeling good at work and being satisfied with their jobs. Managers themselves often form friendship groups. The informal relationships that managers build in friendship groups can often help them solve work-related problems because members of these groups typically discuss work-related matters and offer advice.

Interest Groups

interest groups Informal groups of employees seeking to achieve a common goal related to their membership in an organization.

Employees form informal **interest groups** when they seek to achieve a common goal related to their membership in an organization. Employees may form interest groups, for example, to encourage managers to consider instituting flexible working hours, providing on-site child care, improving working conditions, or more proactively supporting environmental protection. Interest groups can give managers valuable insights into the issues and concerns that are foremost in employees' minds. They also can signal the need for change.

Group Dynamics

LO15-3 Explain how different elements of group dynamics influence the functioning and effectiveness of groups and teams.

How groups function and, ultimately, their effectiveness hinge on group characteristics and processes known collectively as *group dynamics.* In this section we discuss five key elements of group dynamics: group size, tasks, and roles; group leadership; group development; group norms; and group cohesiveness.

Group Size, Tasks, and Roles

Managers need to take group size, group tasks, and group roles into account as they create and maintain high-performing groups and teams.

GROUP SIZE The number of members in a group can be an important determinant of members' motivation and commitment and group performance. There are several advantages to keeping a group relatively small–between two and nine members. Compared with members of large groups, members of small groups tend to (1) interact more with each other and find it easier to coordinate their efforts; (2) be more motivated, satisfied, and committed; (3) find it easier to share information; and (4) be better able to see the importance of their personal contributions for group success. A disadvantage of small rather than large groups is that members of small groups have fewer resources available to accomplish their goals.

Large groups–with 10 or more members–also offer some advantages. They have more resources at their disposal to achieve group goals than small groups do. These resources include the knowledge, experience, skills, and abilities of group members as well as their actual time and effort. Large groups also let managers obtain the advantages stemming from the **division of labor**–splitting the work to be performed into particular tasks and assigning tasks to individual workers. Workers who specialize in particular tasks are likely to become skilled at performing those tasks and contribute significantly to high group performance.

division of labor Splitting the work to be performed into particular tasks and assigning tasks to individual workers.

The disadvantages of large groups include the problems of communication and coordination and the lower levels of motivation, satisfaction, and commitment that members of large groups sometimes experience. It is clearly more difficult to share information with, and coordinate the activities of, 16 people rather than 8 people. Moreover, members of large groups might not think their efforts are really needed and sometimes might not even feel a part of the group.

Sometimes groups are too large to be effective–communication and coordination problems may prove to be a challenge in large groups trying to work together.
Stockbroker/123RF

In deciding on the appropriate size for any group, managers try to gain the advantages of small group size and, at the same time, form groups with sufficient resources to accomplish their goals and have a well-developed division of labor. As a general rule of thumb, groups should have no more members than necessary to achieve a division of labor and provide the resources needed to achieve group goals. In R&D teams, for example, group size is too large when (1) members spend more time communicating what they know to others than applying what they know to solve problems and create new products, (2) individual productivity decreases, and (3) group performance suffers.[35]

task interdependence The degree to which the work performed by one member of a group influences the work performed by other members.

GROUP TASKS The appropriate size of a high-performing group is affected by the kinds of tasks the group is to perform. An important characteristic of group tasks that affects performance is **task interdependence**—the degree to which the work performed by one member of a group influences the work performed by other members.[36] As task interdependence increases, group members need to interact more often and intensely with one another, and their efforts have to be more closely coordinated if they are to perform at a high level. Recent research underscores this point. Findings suggest that frequent and repeated interaction among team members results in greater familiarity, which in turn results in higher levels of information sharing, work coordination, and joint decision making. In addition, teams with higher levels of task interdependence should focus their interactions toward planning and orchestrating how tasks get done.[37] Management expert James D. Thompson identified three types of task interdependence: pooled, sequential, and reciprocal (see Figure 15.3).[38]

pooled task interdependence The task interdependence that exists when group members make separate and independent contributions to group performance.

Pooled task interdependence exists when group members make separate and independent contributions to group performance; overall group performance is the sum of the performance of the individual members (see Figure 15.3A). Examples of groups that have pooled task interdependence include a group of teachers in an elementary school, a group of salespeople in a department store, a group of administrative assistants in an office, and a group of custodians in an office building. In these examples, group performance, whether it is the number of children who are taught and the quality of their education, the dollar value of sales, the amount of work completed, or the number of offices cleaned, is determined by summing the individual contributions of group members.

For groups with pooled interdependence, managers should determine the appropriate group size primarily from the amount of work to be accomplished. Large groups can be effective because group members work independently and do not have to interact often with one another. Motivation in groups with pooled interdependence will be highest when managers reward group members based on individual performance.

Figure 15.3

Types of Task Interdependence

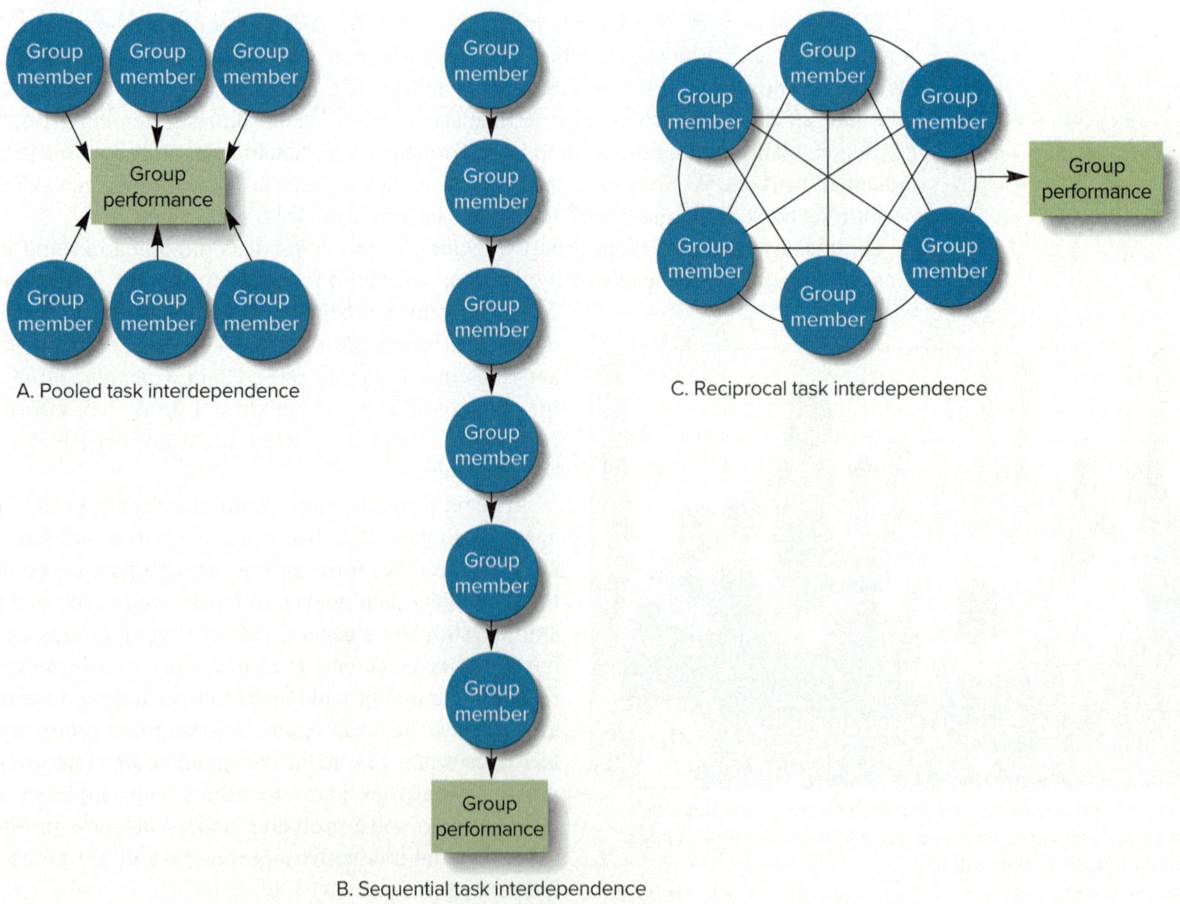

sequential task interdependence The task interdependence that exists when group members must perform specific tasks in a predetermined order.

Sequential task interdependence exists when group members must perform specific tasks in a predetermined order; certain tasks have to be performed before others, and what one worker does affects the work of others (see Figure 15.3B). Assembly lines and mass-production processes are characterized by sequential task interdependence.

When group members are sequentially interdependent, group size is usually dictated by the needs of the production process—for example, the number of steps needed in an assembly line to efficiently produce a mobile phone or tablet. With sequential interdependence, it is difficult to identify individual performance, because one group member's performance depends on how well others perform their tasks. A slow worker at the start of an assembly line, for example, causes all workers farther down the line to work slowly. Thus, managers are often advised to reward group members for group performance. Group members will be motivated to perform at a high level because if the group performs well, each member will benefit. In addition, group members may put pressure on poor performers to improve so that group performance and rewards do not suffer.

reciprocal task interdependence The task interdependence that exists when the work performed by each group member is fully dependent on the work performed by other group members.

Reciprocal task interdependence exists when the work performed by each group member is fully dependent on the work performed by other group members; group members have to share information, intensely interact with one another, and coordinate their efforts in order for the group to achieve its goals (see Figure 15.3C). In general, reciprocal task interdependence characterizes the operation of teams, rather than other kinds of groups. The task interdependence of R&D teams, top management teams, and many self-managed work teams is reciprocal.

group role A set of behaviors and tasks that a member of a group is expected to perform because of their position in the group.

When group members are reciprocally interdependent, managers are advised to keep group size relatively small because of the necessity of coordinating team members' activities. Communication difficulties can arise in teams with reciprocally interdependent tasks because team members need to interact often with one another and be available when needed. As group size increases, communication difficulties increase and can impair team performance.

When a group's members are reciprocally interdependent, managers also are advised to reward group members on the basis of group performance. Individual levels of performance are often difficult for managers to identify, and group-based rewards help ensure that group members will be motivated to perform at a high level and make valuable contributions to the group. Of course, if a manager can identify instances of individual performance in such groups, they, too, can be rewarded to maintain high levels of motivation. Many companies reward group members for their individual performance as well as for the performance of their group.

Goal interdependence is another important aspect of group dynamics. This concept refers to the interconnection among group members as it pertains to the type of goal (individual or group) that guides the team's overall performance.[39] Research suggests collective goals can foster the development of effective strategies and team processes, while implementation of individual goals does not encourage cooperative team processes.[40] In addition, research has shown that teams with higher task interdependence can achieve better performance when they also incorporate higher goal interdependence—which serves to encourage increased social activity among team members.[41]

First the steak, then the asparagus, then the carefully drizzled béarnaise sauce; gourmet kitchens where the presentation is an integral part of the experience exemplify sequential task interdependence.
Digital Vision/Getty Images

GROUP ROLES A **group role** is a set of behaviors and tasks that a member of a group is expected to perform because of their position in the group. Members of cross-functional teams, for example, are expected to perform roles relevant to their special areas of expertise. In our earlier example of cross-functional teams at Hallmark Cards, it is the role of writers on the teams to create verses for new cards, the role of artists to draw illustrations, and the role of designers to put verse and artwork together in an attractive and appealing card design. The roles of members of top management teams are shaped primarily by their areas of expertise—production, marketing, finance, research and development—but members of top management teams also typically draw on their broad expertise as planners and strategists.

In forming groups and teams, managers need to clearly communicate to group members the expectations for their roles in the group, what is required of them, and how the different roles in the group fit together to accomplish group goals. Managers also need to realize that group roles often change and evolve as a group's tasks and goals change and as group members gain experience and knowledge. Thus, to get the performance gains that come from experience, or "learning by doing," managers should encourage group members to take the initiative to assume additional responsibilities as they see fit and modify their assigned roles. This process, called **role making**, can enhance individual and group performance.

role making Taking the initiative to modify an assigned role by assuming additional responsibilities.

In self-managed work teams and some other groups, group members themselves are responsible for creating and assigning roles. Many self-managed work teams also pick their own team leaders. When group members create their own roles, managers should be available to group members in an advisory capacity, helping them effectively settle conflicts and disagreements. At Johnsonville Foods, for example, the position titles of first-line managers were changed to "advisory coach" to reflect the managers' role with the self-managed work teams they oversaw.[42]

Group Leadership

All groups and teams need leadership. Indeed, as we discussed in detail in Chapter 14, effective leadership is a key ingredient in high-performing groups, teams, and organizations. Sometimes managers assume the leadership role in groups and teams, as is the case in many command groups and top management teams. Or a manager may appoint a member of a group who is not a manager to be group leader or chairperson, as is the case in a task force or standing committee. In other cases, group or team members may choose their own leaders, or a leader may emerge naturally as group members work together to achieve group goals. When managers empower members of self-managed work teams, they often let group members choose their own leaders. Some self-managed work teams find it effective to rotate the leadership role among their members. Whether or not leaders of groups and teams are managers, and whether they are appointed by managers (often referred to as *formal leaders*) or emerge naturally in a group (often referred to as *informal leaders*), they play an important role in ensuring that groups and teams perform up to their potential.

Group Development over Time

As many managers overseeing self-managed teams have learned, it sometimes takes a self-managed work team two or three years to perform up to its capabilities.[43] As their experience suggests, what a group is capable of achieving depends in part on its stage of development. Knowing that it takes considerable time for self-managed work teams to get up and running has helped managers to have realistic expectations for new teams and to know that they need to give new team members considerable training and guidance.

Although every group's development over time is unique, researchers have identified five stages of group development that many groups seem to pass through (see Figure 15.4).[44] In the first stage, *forming,* members try to get to know one another and reach a common understanding of what the group is trying to accomplish and how group members should behave. During this stage, managers should strive to make each member feel that they are a valued part of the group.

Figure 15.4

Five Stages of Group Development

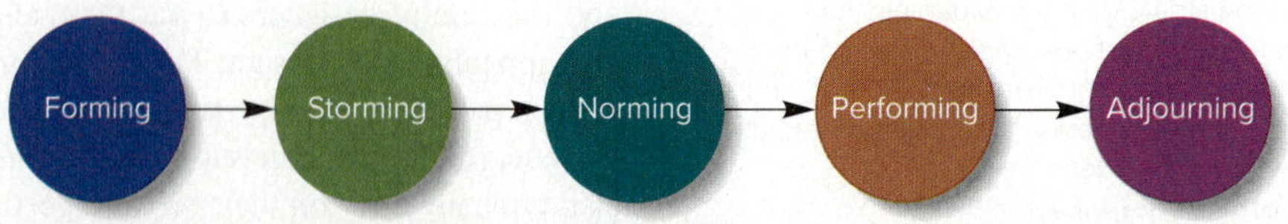

In the second stage, *storming,* group members experience conflict and disagreements because some members do not wish to submit to the demands of other group members. Disputes may arise over who should lead the group. Self-managed work teams can be particularly vulnerable during the storming stage. Managers need to keep an eye on groups at this stage to make sure conflict does not get out of hand.

During the third stage, *norming,* close ties between group members develop, and feelings of friendship and camaraderie emerge. Group members arrive at a consensus about what goals they should seek to achieve and how group members should behave toward one another. In the fourth stage, *performing,* the real work of the group is accomplished. Depending on the type of group in question, managers need to take different steps at this stage to help ensure that groups are effective. Managers of command groups need to make sure that group members are motivated and that they are effectively leading group members. Managers overseeing self-managed work teams have to empower team members and make sure teams are given enough responsibility and autonomy at the performing stage.

The last stage, *adjourning,* applies only to groups that eventually are disbanded, such as task forces. During adjourning, a group is dispersed. Sometimes adjourning takes place when a group completes a finished product, such as when a task force evaluating the pros and cons of providing on-site child care produces a report supporting its recommendation.

Managers should have a flexible approach to group development and should keep attuned to the different needs and requirements of groups at the various stages.[45] Above all else, and regardless of the stage of development, managers need to think of themselves as *resources* for groups. Thus, managers always should strive to find ways to help groups and teams function more effectively. For some ideas about how to do this, see the "Management Insight" feature.

MANAGEMENT INSIGHT

How to Help a Team Develop

According to Edward Marshall, former senior partner of the Center for Creative Leadership, when managers want a team to improve, "the members need to take care of it." Why? Because, says Marshall, "People take care of what they own."[46] In Marshall's experience, team members often need to work on a shortage of trust. Trust can flourish when team leaders and members act with integrity and work on resolving conflict. Teams also get better at collaborating when they focus on shared principles, such as mutual respect and taking responsibility, rather than on personalities and politics.

Given the power of effective teams, many researchers studying management have investigated which behaviors are associated with high-performing teams. At the Gallup organization, studies have identified conditions associated with highly engaged team members. The results suggest ways in which managers can help teams develop. For example, high-performing teams have a shared purpose, and managers can shape this in the way a team's goals are developed and expressed. Also, team members need to connect with one another, whether or not they work in the same location. Managers can direct teams to develop routines and practices that ensure everyone checks in to share ideas and accomplishments. A third, and related, necessity for high performance is communication; managers should select and train team members with this in mind.[47]

Francesca Gino, a professor at Harvard Business School, has applied psychology to the question of teamwork effectiveness. She concludes that collaborating as a team requires skills that can be taught. Among her lessons, team members need to listen. Teamwork involves talking, but too often, people focus not on listening but on preparing a reply. Gino advocates learning to focus on the speaker's message, including body language, and to ask questions as needed to gain a full understanding. A related lesson is to practice empathy, or openness to understanding another person's perspective.

One way is to start with the assumption that team members are intelligent and invested in the team's mission. Then when differences arise, they can be approached more from a standpoint of curiosity than mistrust and judgment.[48]

Another idea from Gino is to learn to feel comfortable with receiving feedback. This can start with team leaders openly acknowledging that hearing feedback can feel uncomfortable. The team can also practice giving feedback that is constructive–for example, specific and related to behavior, not broad statements about people. Another way to create a favorable environment for feedback is to teach team members to avoid reacting to ideas with criticism ("No, if we do that, we'll miss the deadline"), but instead add to the idea ("Yes, and how can we improve the process so we deliver that on time?").[49]

Group Norms

LO15-4 Explain why it is important for groups and teams to have a balance of conformity and deviance and a moderate level of cohesiveness.

All groups, whether top management teams, self-managed work teams, or command groups, need to control their members' behaviors to ensure that the group performs at a high level and meets its goals. Assigning roles to each group member is one way to control behavior in groups. Another important way in which groups influence members' behavior is through the development and enforcement of group norms.[50] **Group norms** are shared guidelines or rules for behavior that most group members follow. Groups develop norms concerning a wide variety of behaviors, including working hours, the sharing of information among group members, how certain group tasks should be performed, and even how members of a group should dress.

group norms Shared guidelines or rules for behavior that most group members follow.

Managers should encourage members of a group to develop norms that contribute to group performance and the attainment of group goals. For example, group norms dictating that each member of a cross-functional team should always be available for the rest of the team when their input is needed, return phone calls as soon as possible, inform other team members of travel plans, and give team members a phone number at which they can be reached when traveling on business help to ensure that the team is efficient, performs at a high level, and achieves its goals. A norm in a command group of executive assistants that dictates that executive assistants who happen to have a light workload in any given week should help out executive assistants with heavier workloads helps to ensure that the group completes all assignments in a timely and efficient manner. And a norm in a top management team that dictates that team members should always consult with one another before making major decisions helps to ensure that good decisions are made with a minimum of errors.

CONFORMITY AND DEVIANCE Group members conform to norms for three reasons: (1) They want to obtain rewards and avoid punishments. (2) They want to imitate group members whom they like and admire. (3) They have internalized the norms and believe they are the right and proper ways to behave.[51] Consider the case of an employee who conformed to the department's norm of attending a fundraiser for a community food bank. This person's conformity could be due to (1) the desire to be a member of the group in good standing and to have friendly relationships with other group members (rewards); (2) copying the behavior of other members of the department whom they respect and who always attend the fundraiser (imitating other group members); or (3) the person's belief in the merits of supporting the activities of the food bank (believing that is the right and proper way to behave).

Failure to conform, or deviance, occurs when a member of a group violates a group norm. Deviance signals that a group is not controlling the behaviors of one of its members. Groups generally respond to members who behave deviantly in one of three ways:[52]

1. The group might try to get deviant members to change their behavior and conform to the norm. Group members might try to convince the member of the need to conform, or they might ignore or even punish the deviant. For example, in a Jacksonville Foods plant, a member of a self-managed work team responsible for weighing sausages failed to conform to a group norm dictating that group members should periodically clean up an untidy interview room. Because the employee refused to take part in the team's cleanup

efforts, team members reduced the member's monthly bonus by about $225 for a two-month period.[53] The person clearly learned the costs of deviant behavior within the team.

2. The group might expel the member.
3. The group might change the norm to be consistent with the member's behavior.

This last alternative suggests that some deviant behavior can be functional for groups. Deviance is functional when it causes group members to evaluate norms that may be dysfunctional but are taken for granted by the group. Often group members do not think about why they behave in a certain way or why they follow certain norms. Deviance can cause group members to reflect on their norms and change them when appropriate.

Consider a group of receptionists in a day spa who followed the norm that all appointments would be handwritten in an appointment book and, at the end of each day, the receptionist on duty would enter the appointments into the spa's computer system, which printed out the massage therapists' and estheticians' daily schedules. One day a receptionist decided to enter appointments directly into the computer system when they were being made, bypassing the appointment book. This deviant behavior caused the other receptionists to think about why they were using the appointment book at all. After consulting with the owner of the day spa, the group changed its norm. Now appointments are entered directly into the computer, which saves time and reduces scheduling errors.

ENCOURAGING A BALANCE OF CONFORMITY AND DEVIANCE To effectively help an organization gain a competitive advantage, groups and teams need the right balance of conformity and deviance (see Figure 15.5). A group needs a certain level of conformity to ensure that it can control members' behavior and channel it in the direction of high performance and group goal accomplishment. A group also needs a certain level of deviance to

Figure 15.5

Balancing Conformity and Deviance in Groups

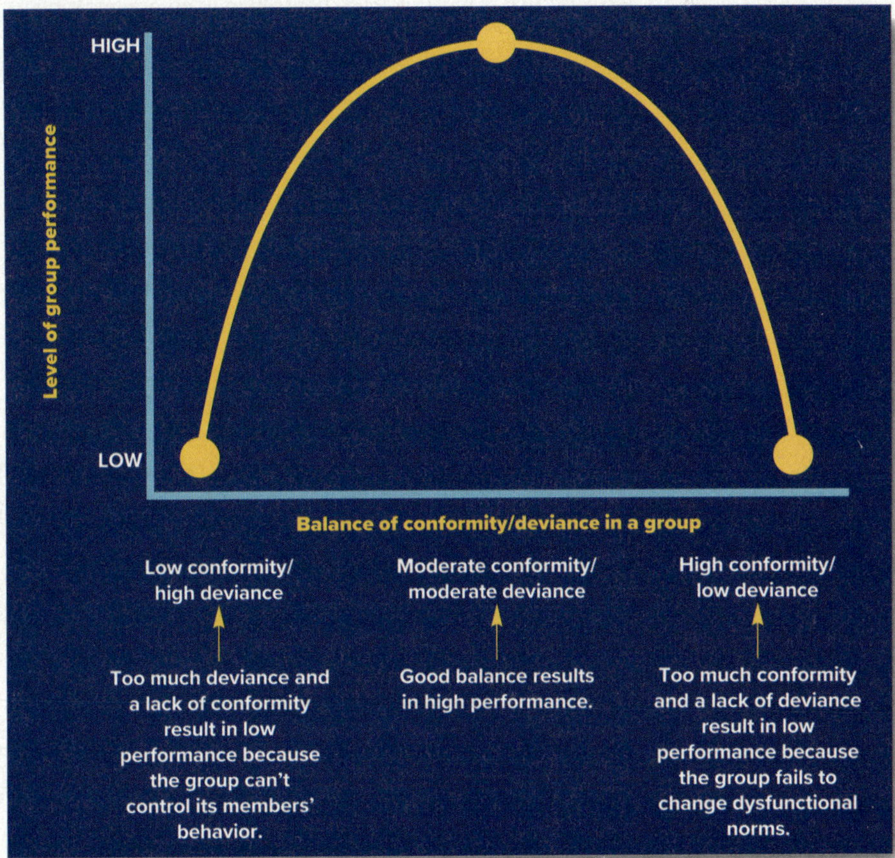

ensure that dysfunctional norms are discarded and replaced with functional ones. Balancing conformity and deviance is a pressing concern for all groups, whether they are top management teams, R&D teams, command groups, or self-managed work teams.

The extent of conformity and reactions to deviance within groups are determined by group members themselves. The three bases for conformity just described are powerful forces that more often than not result in group members' conforming to norms. Sometimes these forces are so strong that deviance rarely occurs in groups, and when it does, it is stamped out.

Managers can take several steps to ensure adequate tolerance of deviance in groups so that group members are willing to deviate from dysfunctional norms and, when deviance occurs in their group, reflect on the appropriateness of the violated norm and change the norm if necessary. First, managers can be role models for the groups and teams they oversee. When managers encourage and accept employees' suggestions for changes in procedures, do not rigidly insist that tasks be accomplished in a certain way, and admit when a norm they once supported is no longer functional, they signal to group members that conformity should not come at the expense of needed changes and improvements. Second, managers should let employees know that there are always ways to improve group processes and performance levels and, thus, opportunities to replace existing norms with norms that will better enable a group to achieve its goals and perform at a high level. Third, managers should encourage members of groups and teams to periodically assess the appropriateness of their norms.

Group Cohesiveness

group cohesiveness The degree to which members are attracted to or loyal to their group.

Another important element of group dynamics that affects group performance and effectiveness is **group cohesiveness**, which is the degree to which members are attracted to or loyal to their group or team.[54] When group cohesiveness is high, people strongly value their group membership, find the group appealing, and have strong desires to remain a part of the group. When group cohesiveness is low, group members do not find their group particularly appealing and have little desire to retain their group membership. Research suggests that managers should strive to have a moderate level of cohesiveness in the groups and teams they manage because that is most likely to contribute to an organization's competitive advantage.

CONSEQUENCES OF GROUP COHESIVENESS There are three major consequences of group cohesiveness: level of participation within a group, level of conformity to group norms, and emphasis on group goal accomplishment (see Figure 15.6).[55]

Figure 15.6

Sources and Consequences of Group Cohesiveness

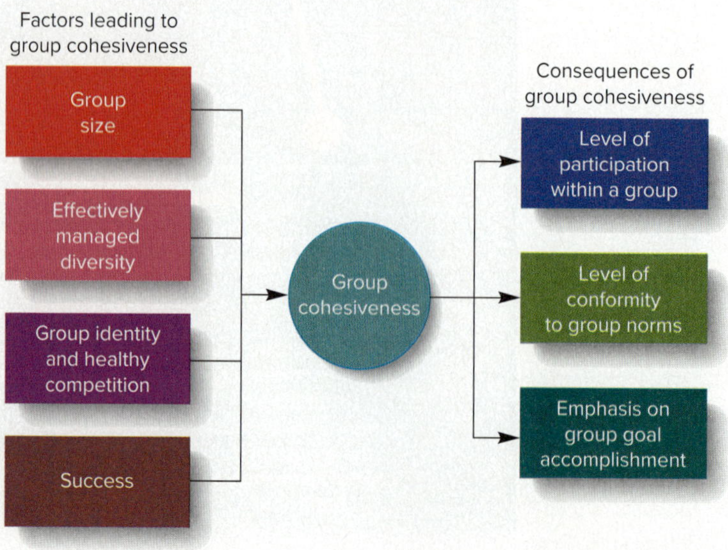

LEVEL OF PARTICIPATION WITHIN A GROUP As group cohesiveness increases, the extent of group members' participation within the group increases. Participation contributes to group effectiveness because group members are actively involved in the group, ensure that group tasks get accomplished, readily share information with each other, and have frequent and open communication (the important topic of communication is covered in depth in Chapter 16).

A moderate level of group cohesiveness helps ensure that group members actively participate in the group and communicate effectively with one another. The reason that managers may not want to encourage high levels of cohesiveness is illustrated by the example of two cross-functional teams responsible for developing new toys. Members of the highly cohesive Team Alpha often have lengthy meetings that usually start with nonwork-related conversations and jokes, meet more often than most of the other cross-functional teams in the company, and spend a good portion of their time communicating the ins and outs of their department's contribution to toy development to other team members. Members of the moderately cohesive Team Beta generally have efficient meetings in which ideas are communicated and discussed as needed, do not meet more often than necessary, and share the ins and outs of their expertise with one another to the extent needed for the development process. Teams Alpha and Beta have both developed some top-selling toys. However, it generally takes Team Alpha 30% longer to do so than Team Beta. This is why too much cohesiveness can be too much of a good thing.

LEVEL OF CONFORMITY TO GROUP NORMS Increasing levels of group cohesiveness result in increasing levels of conformity to group norms, and when cohesiveness becomes high, there may be so little deviance in groups that group members conform to norms even when they are dysfunctional. In contrast, low cohesiveness can result in too much deviance and undermine the ability of a group to control its members' behaviors to get things done.

Both teams in the toy company had the same norm for toy development. It dictated that members of each team would discuss potential ideas for new toys, decide on a line of toys to pursue, and then have the team member from R&D design a prototype. Recently, a new animated movie featuring a family of rabbits produced by a small film company was an unexpected hit, and major toy companies were scrambling to reach licensing agreements to produce toy lines featuring the rabbits. The top management team in the toy company assigned these teams to develop the new toy lines quickly to beat the competition.

Members of Team Alpha followed their usual toy development norm, even though the marketing expert on the team believed the process could have been streamlined to save time. The marketing expert on Team Beta urged the team to deviate from its toy development norm. She suggested that the team not have R&D develop prototypes but, instead, modify top-selling toys the company already made to feature rabbits and then reach a licensing agreement with the film company based on the high sales potential (given the company's prior success). Once the licensing agreement was signed, the company could take the time needed to develop innovative and unique rabbit toys with more input from R&D.

As a result of the willingness of the marketing expert on Team Beta to deviate from the norm for toy development, the toy company obtained an exclusive licensing agreement with the film company and had its first rabbit toys on store shelves in a record three months. Groups need a balance of conformity and deviance, so a moderate level of cohesiveness often yields the best outcome, as it did in the case of Team Beta.

How much cohesiveness is too much? You can answer that question when you evaluate whether a group actually gets something done in its meetings or whether most of the conversation drifting out of the room consists of jokes, life experiences, or comparisons of the last company outing.
Aleksandr Davydov/Alamy Stock Photo

EMPHASIS ON GROUP GOAL ACCOMPLISHMENT As group cohesiveness increases, the emphasis placed on group goal accomplishment also increases within a group. A strong emphasis on group goal accomplishment, however, does not always lead to organizational effectiveness. For an organization to be effective and gain a competitive advantage, the different groups and teams in the organization must cooperate with one another and be motivated to achieve *organizational goals,* even if doing so sometimes comes at the expense of the achievement of group goals. A moderate level of cohesiveness motivates group members to accomplish both group and organizational goals. High levels of cohesiveness can cause group members to be so focused on group goal accomplishment that they may strive to achieve group goals no matter what—even when doing so jeopardizes organizational performance.

At the toy company, the major goal of the cross-functional teams was to develop new toy lines that were truly innovative, that utilized the latest in technology, and that were in some way fundamentally distinct from other toys on the market. When it came to the rabbit project, Team Alpha's high level of cohesiveness contributed to its continued emphasis on its group goal of developing an innovative line of toys; thus, the team stuck with its usual design process. Team Beta, in contrast, realized that developing the new line of toys quickly was an important organizational goal that should take precedence over the group's goal of developing groundbreaking new toys, at least in the short term. Team Beta's moderate level of cohesiveness contributed to team members' doing what was best for the toy company in this case.

FACTORS LEADING TO GROUP COHESIVENESS Four factors contribute to the level of group cohesiveness (see Figure 15.6).[56] By influencing these *determinants of group cohesiveness,* managers can raise or lower the level of cohesiveness to promote moderate levels of cohesiveness in groups and teams.

GROUP SIZE As we mentioned earlier, members of small groups tend to be more motivated and committed than members of large groups. Thus, to promote cohesiveness in groups, when feasible, managers should form groups that are small to medium in size (about 2 to 15 members). If a group is low in cohesiveness and large in size, managers might want to consider dividing the group in half and assigning different tasks and goals to the two newly formed groups.

EFFECTIVELY MANAGED DIVERSITY In general, people tend to like and get along with others who are similar to themselves. It is easier to communicate with someone, for example, who shares your values, has a similar background, and has had similar experiences. However, as discussed in Chapter 5, diversity in groups, teams, and organizations can help an organization gain a competitive advantage. Diverse groups often come up with more innovative and creative ideas. One reason cross-functional teams are so popular in organizations such as Hallmark Greetings is that the diverse expertise represented in the teams results in higher levels of team performance.

In forming groups and teams, managers need to make sure the diversity in knowledge, experience, expertise, and other characteristics necessary for group goal accomplishment is represented in the new groups. Managers then have to make sure this diversity in group membership is effectively managed so groups will be cohesive (see Chapter 5). The "Focus on DEI&B" feature describes how an assessment tool developed by Deloitte is helping organizations do this with regard to diverse work styles.

FOCUS ON DEI&B

Leveraging Diverse Team Perspectives

Anyone with teamwork experience has at times noticed another team member focus on what seems unimportant or seen a few team members dominate a meeting. In these situations, the team is not fully drawing upon every team member, so the organization is not fully benefiting from the team. Consultants at Deloitte wanted to address this problem. They believed they were seeing a failure to consider different work styles and perspectives. If team members could readily understand this diversity, they could treat it as a resource rather than an obstacle to cooperation.[57]

Deloitte built on research about brain chemistry to develop and test profiles of four primary ways that people work. The resulting system, named Business Chemistry, defines four styles: *Pioneers* inspire creativity; they look at the big picture and are open to new ideas, willing to take risks, and comfortable basing decisions on intuition.

Management consulting firm Deloitte developed a profile of four different ways people work: Pioneers, Guardians, Drivers, and Integrators. Which profile do you fit, and how can you use this style to work more effectively in a team setting?
Adam Hester/Blend Images

Guardians are cautious about risk and value stability; they want to learn from experience and look for detailed data to back decisions. *Drivers* care about results and winning; they get the team moving and want data so they can solve problems and tackle challenges. *Integrators* focus on relationships; they seek consensus and try to strengthen the team. This model assumes that teams need all of these perspectives at various times.[58]

Teams with diverse profiles should be creative, and their decisions should be well thought out. In practice, diversity poses challenges. For example, if a Driver opens the floor to debate an issue, an Integrator might hesitate to speak up and provoke an argument. If Guardians raise concerns about an idea, a Driver might feel frustrated about being slowed down, even though the concerns might be valid and significant. Team members who are unaware of these differences might work ineffectively. A Guardian might come prepared with pages of data that won't capture the imaginations of the team's Pioneers.[59]

Business Chemistry can help team members address these issues constructively. They can be aware of the strengths and limitations of their view and the other views. They can practice imagining how people in other categories would think about situations. Also, team leaders can notice which kinds of perspectives aren't being addressed by the team and then seek out those perspectives. For example, if everyone is immediately excited about an idea, perhaps everyone is thinking like a Pioneer. The leader should pause and invite the team to consider what a Guardian-style team member would say about the idea.[60]

GROUP IDENTITY AND HEALTHY COMPETITION When group cohesiveness is low, managers can often increase it by encouraging groups to develop their own identities or personalities and engage in healthy competition. This is precisely what managers at Eaton Corporation's manufacturing facility in Lincoln, Illinois, did. Eaton's employees manufacture products such as engine valves, gears, truck axles, and circuit breakers. Managers at Eaton created self-managed work teams to cut costs and improve performance. They realized, however, that the teams would have to be cohesive to ensure that they would strive to achieve their goals. Managers promoted group identity by having the teams give themselves names such as "The Hoods," "The Worms," and "Scrap Attack" (a team striving to reduce costly scrap metal waste by 50%). Healthy competition among groups was promoted by displaying measures of each team's performance and the extent to which teams met their goals on a large TV screen in the cafeteria and by rewarding team members for team performance.[61]

If groups are too cohesive, managers can try to decrease cohesiveness by promoting organizational (rather than group) identity and making the organization as a whole the focus of the group's efforts. Organizational identity can be promoted by making group members feel that they are valued members of the organization and by stressing cooperation across groups to promote the achievement of organizational goals. Excessive levels of cohesiveness also can be reduced by reducing or eliminating competition among groups and rewarding cooperation.

SUCCESS When it comes to promoting group cohesiveness, there is more than a grain of truth to the saying "Nothing succeeds like success." As groups become more successful, they become increasingly attractive to their members, and their cohesiveness tends to increase. When cohesiveness is low, managers can increase cohesiveness by making sure a group can achieve some noticeable and visible successes.

Consider a group of salespeople in the housewares department of a medium-size department store. The housewares department had recently been moved to a corner of the store's basement. Its remote location resulted in low sales because of infrequent customer traffic in that part of the store. The salespeople, who were generally evaluated favorably by their supervisors and were valued members of the store, tried various initiatives to boost sales, but to no avail. As a result of this lack of success and the poor performance of their department, their cohesiveness started to plummet. To increase and preserve the cohesiveness of the group, the store manager implemented a group-based incentive across the store. In any month, members of the group with the best attendance and punctuality records would have their names and pictures posted on a bulletin board in the cafeteria and would each receive a $50 gift certificate. The housewares group frequently had the best records, and their success on this dimension helped to build and maintain their cohesiveness. Moreover, this initiative boosted attendance and discouraged lateness throughout the store.

Managing Groups and Teams for High Performance

Now that you understand why groups and teams are so important for organizations, the types of groups managers create, and group dynamics, we consider some additional steps managers can take to make sure groups and teams perform at a high level and contribute to organizational effectiveness. Before discussing these strategies, however, we highlight some of the traits and characteristics associated with high-performing work groups.

LO15-5 Describe how managers can motivate group members to achieve organizational goals and reduce social loafing in groups and teams.

The concept of high-performing work teams is not new; it has been used by successful organizations for more than 20 years. High-performing work teams can be defined as groups that consistently satisfy the needs of customers, employees, investors, and other stakeholders and that frequently outperform other teams that produce similar products or services.[62] Recent research into what constitutes a high-performing work group identifies several key factors that may contribute to the team's success, including a highly developed team culture; clearly defined norms that encourage effective behavior and high performance; and results-oriented meetings that include information sharing, problem solving, and decision making.[63] Understanding what it takes to assemble and manage such top-performing groups is an ongoing challenge for any organization. Ways to create such high performance begin with three key strategies: (1) motivating group members to work toward the achievement of organizational goals, (2) reducing social loafing, and (3) helping groups manage conflict effectively.

Motivating Group Members to Achieve Organizational Goals

When work is difficult, is tedious, or requires a high level of commitment and energy, managers cannot assume group members will always be motivated to work toward the achievement of organizational goals. Consider, for example, a house painting service that paints the interiors and exteriors of new homes for a construction company and are paid on an hourly basis. Why should they strive to complete painting jobs quickly and efficiently if doing so will just make them feel more tired at the end of the day and they will not receive any tangible benefits, such as additional pay or performance bonuses? There is no motivation for the painters to speed up their work; it seems logical for the painters to adopt a relaxed approach, to take frequent breaks, and to work at a leisurely pace. This relaxed approach, however, impairs the construction company's ability to gain a competitive advantage because it increases the time needed to complete a new home.

Managers can motivate members of groups and teams to achieve organizational goals by making sure the members themselves benefit when the group or team performs highly. For example, if members of a self-managed work team know they will receive a weekly bonus based on team performance, they will be motivated to perform at a high level.

Managers often rely on some combination of individual and group-based incentives to motivate members of groups and teams to work toward the achievement of organizational goals. When individual performance within a group can be assessed, pay is often determined by individual performance or by both individual and group performance. When individual performance within a group cannot be accurately assessed, group performance should be

Figure 15.7

Three Ways to Reduce Social Loafing

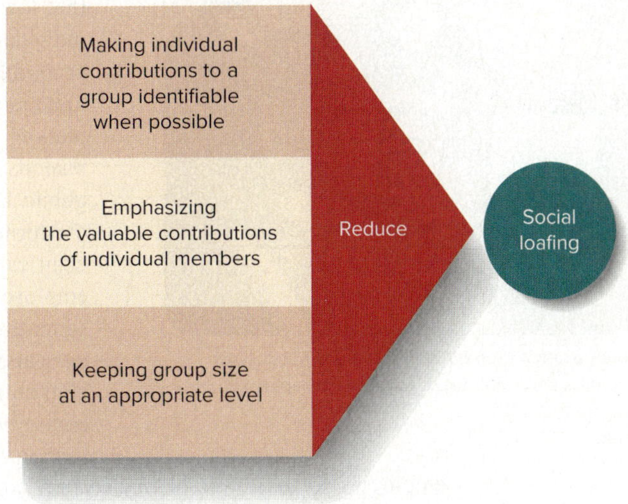

the key determinant of pay levels. Many companies that use self-managed work teams base team members' pay in part on team performance.[64] A major challenge for managers is to develop a fair pay system that will lead to both high individual motivation and high group or team performance.

Other benefits managers can make available to high-performing group members–in addition to monetary rewards–include extra resources such as equipment and computer software, awards and other forms of recognition, and choice of future work assignments. For example, members of self-managed work teams that develop new software at companies such as Microsoft often value working on interesting and important projects; members of teams that have performed at a high level are rewarded by being assigned to interesting and important new projects.

Reducing Social Loafing in Groups

social loafing The tendency of individuals to put forth less effort when they work in groups than when they work alone.

We have been focusing on the steps managers can take to encourage high levels of performance in groups. Managers, however, need to be aware of an important downside to group and team work: the potential for social loafing, which reduces group performance. **Social loafing** is the tendency of individuals to put forth less effort when they work in groups than when they work alone.[65] Have you ever worked on a group project in which one or two group members never seemed to be contributing? Have you ever worked in a student club or committee in which some members always seemed to be missing meetings and never volunteered for activities? Have you ever had a job in which one or two of your coworkers seemed to be slacking off because they knew you or other members of your work group would make up for their low levels of effort? If so, you have witnessed social loafing in action.

Social loafing can occur in all kinds of groups and teams and in all kinds of organizations. It can result in lower group performance and may even prevent a group from attaining its goals. Fortunately, managers can take steps to reduce social loafing and sometimes completely eliminate it; we will look at three (see Figure 15.7).

1. *Make individual contributions to a group identifiable.* Some people may engage in social loafing when they work in groups because they think they can hide in the crowd–no one will notice if they put forth less effort than they should. Other people may think that if they put forth high levels of effort and make substantial contributions to the group, their contributions will not be noticed and they will receive no rewards for their work–so why bother?[66]

Social loafing occurs when members of a group are not pulling their weight on projects and other tasks and are content to let others in the group do the work.
fizkes/iStock/Getty Images

One way that managers can effectively eliminate social loafing is by making individual contributions to a group identifiable so that group members perceive that low and high levels of effort will be noticed and individual contributions evaluated.[67] Managers can accomplish this by assigning specific tasks to group members and holding them accountable for their completion. Take the case of a group of eight employees responsible for reshelving returned books in a large public library in New York. The head librarian was concerned that there was always a backlog of seven or eight carts of books to be reshelved, even though the employees never seemed to be particularly busy and some even found time to sit down and read newspapers and magazines. The librarian decided to try to eliminate the apparent social loafing by assigning each employee sole responsibility for reshelving a particular section of the library. Because the library's front desk employees sorted the books by section on the carts as they were returned, holding the shelvers responsible for particular sections was easily accomplished. Once the shelvers knew the librarian could identify their effort or lack thereof, there were rarely any backlogs of books to be reshelved.

Sometimes the members of a group can cooperate to eliminate social loafing by making individual contributions identifiable. For example, in a small security company, members of a self-managed work team who assemble control boxes for home alarm systems start each day by deciding who will perform which tasks that day and how much work each member and the group as a whole should strive to accomplish. Each team member knows that, at the end of the day, the other team members will know exactly how much they have accomplished. With this system in place, social loafing never occurs in the team. Remember, however, that in some teams, individual contributions cannot be made identifiable, as in teams whose members are reciprocally interdependent.

2. *Emphasize the valuable contributions of individual members.* Another reason social loafing may occur is that people sometimes think their efforts are unnecessary or unimportant when they work in a group. They feel the group will accomplish its goals and perform at an acceptable level whether or not they personally perform at a high level. To counteract this belief, when managers form groups, they should assign individuals to a group on the basis of the valuable contributions that *each* person can make to the group as a whole. Clearly communicating to group members why each person's contributions are valuable to the group is an effective means by which managers and group members themselves can reduce or eliminate social loafing.[68] This is most clearly illustrated in cross-functional teams, where each member's valuable contribution to the team derives from a personal area of expertise. By emphasizing why each member's skills are important, managers can reduce social loafing in such teams.
3. *Keep group size at an appropriate level.* Group size is related to the causes of social loafing we just described. As size increases, identifying individual contributions becomes increasingly difficult, and members are increasingly likely to think their individual contributions are not important. To overcome this, managers should form groups with no more members than are needed to accomplish group goals and perform at a high level.[69]

Helping Groups to Manage Conflict Effectively

At some point, practically all groups experience conflict either within the group (*intragroup* conflict) or with other groups (*intergroup* conflict). In Chapter 17, we discuss conflict in depth and explore ways to manage it effectively. As you will learn, managers can take several steps to help groups manage conflict and disagreements.

Summary and Review

LO15-1 **GROUPS, TEAMS, AND ORGANIZATIONAL EFFECTIVENESS** A group consists of two or more people who interact with each other to accomplish certain goals or meet certain needs. A team is a group whose members work intensely with one another to achieve a specific common goal or objective. Groups and teams can contribute to organizational effectiveness by enhancing performance, increasing responsiveness to customers, increasing innovation, and being a source of motivation for their members.

LO15-2 **TYPES OF GROUPS AND TEAMS** Formal groups are groups that managers establish to achieve organizational goals; they include cross-functional teams, cross-cultural teams, top management teams, research and development teams, command groups, task forces, self-managed work teams, and virtual teams. Informal groups are groups that employees form because they believe the groups will help them achieve their own goals or meet their needs; they include friendship groups and interest groups.

LO15-3, 15-4 **GROUP DYNAMICS** Key elements of group dynamics are group size, tasks, and roles; group leadership; group development; group norms; and group cohesiveness. The advantages and disadvantages of large and small groups suggest that managers should form groups with no more members than are needed to provide the group with the human resources it needs to achieve its goals and use a division of labor. The type of task interdependence that characterizes a group's work gives managers a clue about the appropriate size of the group. A group role is a set of behaviors and tasks that a member of a group is expected to perform because of their position in the group. All groups and teams need leadership.

Five stages of development that many groups pass through are forming, storming, norming, performing, and adjourning. Group norms are shared rules for behavior that most group members follow. To be effective, groups need a balance of conformity and deviance. Conformity allows a group to control its members' behavior to achieve group goals; deviance provides the impetus for needed change.

Group cohesiveness is the attractiveness of a group or team to its members. As group cohesiveness increases, so do the level of participation and communication within a group, the level of conformity to group norms, and the emphasis on group goal accomplishment. Managers should strive to achieve a moderate level of group cohesiveness in the groups and teams they manage.

LO15-5 **MANAGING GROUPS AND TEAMS FOR HIGH PERFORMANCE** To make sure groups and teams perform at a high level, managers need to motivate group members to work toward the achievement of organizational goals, reduce social loafing, and help groups to effectively manage conflict. Managers can motivate members of groups and teams to work toward the achievement of organizational goals by making sure members personally benefit when the group or team performs at a high level.

Management in Action

Topics for Discussion and Action

Discussion

1. Why do all organizations need to rely on groups and teams to achieve their goals and gain a competitive advantage? [LO15-1]
2. What kinds of employees would prefer to work in a virtual team? What kinds of employees would prefer to work in a team that meets in person? [LO15-2]
3. Think about a group that you are a member of, and describe that group's current stage of development. Does the development of this group seem to be following the forming, storming, norming, performing, and adjourning stages described in the chapter? [LO15-3]
4. Think about a group of employees who work in a McDonald's restaurant. What type of task interdependence characterizes this group? What potential problems in the group should the restaurant manager be aware of and take steps to avoid? [LO15-3]
5. Discuss the reasons that too much conformity can hurt groups and their organizations. [LO15-4]
6. Why do some groups have very low levels of cohesiveness? [LO15-4]
7. Imagine that you are the manager of a hotel. What steps will you take to reduce social loafing by members of the cleaning staff who are responsible for keeping all common areas and guest rooms spotless? [LO15-5]

Action

8. Interview one or more managers in an organization in your local community to identify the types of groups and teams that the organization uses to achieve its goals. What challenges do these groups and teams face? [LO15-2]

Building Management Skills

Diagnosing Group Failures [LO15-1, 15-2, 15-3, 15-4, 15-5]

Think about the last dissatisfying or discouraging experience you had as a member of a group or team. Perhaps the group did not accomplish its goals, perhaps group members could agree about nothing, or perhaps there was too much social loafing. Now answer the following questions:

1. What type of group was this?
2. Were group members motivated to achieve group goals? Why or why not?
3. How large was the group, what type of task interdependence existed in the group, and what group roles did members play?
4. What were the group's norms? How much conformity and deviance existed in the group?
5. How cohesive was the group? Why do you think the group's cohesiveness was at this level? What consequences did this level of group cohesiveness have for the group and its members?
6. Was social loafing a problem in this group? Why or why not?
7. What could the group's leader or manager have done differently to increase group effectiveness?
8. What could group members have done differently to increase group effectiveness?

Managing Ethically [LO15-1, 15-2, 15-3, 15-4, 15-5]

Some self-managed teams encounter a troubling problem: One or more members engage in social loafing, and other members are reluctant to try to rectify the situation. Social loafing can be especially troubling if team members' pay is based on team performance and social loafing reduces the team's performance and, thus, the pay of all members (even the highest performers). Even if managers are aware of the problem, they may be reluctant to take action because the team is supposedly self-managing.

Questions

1. Either individually or in a group, think about the ethical implications of social loafing in a self-managed team.
2. Do managers have an ethical obligation to step in when they are aware of social loafing in a self-managed team? Why or why not? Do other team members have an obligation to try to curtail the social loafing? Why or why not?

Small Group Breakout Exercise

Creating a Cross-Functional Team [LO15-1, 15-2, 15-3, 15-4, 15-5]

Form groups of three or four people, and appoint one member as the spokesperson who will communicate your findings to the class when called on by the instructor. Then discuss the following scenario:

You are a group of managers in charge of food services for a large state university in the Midwest. Recently, a survey of students, faculty, and staff was conducted to evaluate customer satisfaction with the food services provided by the university's eight cafeterias. The results were disappointing, to put it mildly. Complaints ranged from dissatisfaction with the type and range of meals and snacks provided, operating hours, and food temperature to frustration about unresponsiveness to current concerns about healthful diets and the needs of vegetarians. You have decided to form a cross-functional team that will further evaluate reactions to the food services and will develop a proposal for changes to be made to increase customer satisfaction.

1. Indicate who should be on this important cross-functional team, and explain why.
2. Describe the goals the team should strive to achieve.
3. Describe the different roles that will need to be performed on this team.
4. Describe the steps you will take to help ensure that the team has a good balance between conformity and deviance and has a moderate level of cohesiveness.

Be the Manager [LO15-1, 15-2, 15-3, 15-4, 15-5]

You were recently hired in a boundary-spanning role for the global unit of an educational and professional publishing company. The company is headquartered in New York (where you work) and has divisions in multiple countries. Each division is responsible for translating, manufacturing, marketing, and selling a set of books in its country. Your responsibilities include interfacing with managers in each of the divisions in your region (Central and South America), overseeing their budgeting and financial reporting to headquarters, and leading a virtual team consisting of the top managers in charge of each of the divisions in your region. The virtual team's mission is to promote global learning, explore new potential opportunities and markets, and address ongoing problems. You communicate directly with division managers via telephone and email, as well as written reports and memos. When virtual team meetings are convened, videoconferencing is often used.

After your first few virtual team meetings, you noticed that the managers seemed to be reticent about speaking up. Interestingly enough, when each manager communicates with you individually, primarily in telephone conversations and emails, they tend to be forthcoming and frank, and you feel you have a good rapport with each of them. However, getting the managers to communicate with one another as a virtual team has been a challenge. At the last meeting, you tried to prompt some of the managers to raise issues relevant to the agenda that you knew were on their minds from your individual conversations with them. Surprisingly, the managers skillfully avoided informing their teammates about the heart of the issues in question. You are confused and troubled. Although you feel your other responsibilities are going well, you know your virtual team is not operating like a team at all; and no matter what you try, discussions in virtual team meetings are forced and generally unproductive. What are you going to do to address this problem?

Case in the News [LO15-1, 15-2, 15-3, 15-4, 15-5]

Novartis Speeds Up R&D with Project Teams

Novartis, an international pharmaceutical company, has an innovation-based strategy. According to the company, its purpose is "to reimagine medicine to improve and extend people's lives," using science and technology to "develop breakthrough treatments and find new ways to deliver them." Among its products are gene therapies and cancer treatments. To enable this kind of work, Novartis fosters a culture in which people are "Inspired, Curious, and Unbossed." The inspiration comes from the company's mission, its emphasis on innovation and training makes the company attractive for curious employees, and "unbossed" means employees can choose flexible work arrangements and are encouraged to promote their ideas.

This context presented an opportunity for Jay Bradner when he became Novartis's head of research and development. While the company had been innovating, Bradner thought it could be missing great ideas in the heads of its many scientists. Some had already left to start their own companies. Were they and others generating ideas that Novartis should be pursuing? Bradner wanted to find out—and then fund some of the ideas uncovered.

Building on a suggestion from a Novartis scientist named Ian Hunt, Bradner launched Project Genesis, a team-based process for accelerating innovation. The project invites R&D employees to network with colleagues across scientific disciplines, sharing their dream research projects. Those who build interest in their ideas can form teams to prepare project proposals, and on a predetermined day, all the teams present their ideas to a panel of scientists, including Bradner, in front of the whole company. The panel selects a few ideas with the greatest potential, and the company funds those projects to move forward within Novartis for 18 months. If a team's progress is favorable, their project can earn a place in Novartis's R&D pipeline.

Coordinating this effort is the Genesis Labs program lead—currently Ian Hunt, the scientist who had suggested the idea to Bradner. Besides designing and launching each round of invitations to submit and promote ideas, the program lead fosters collaboration across Novartis's divisions and with scientists in academia. For example, a Novartis researcher saw a new technology at MIT that he thought would have applications to pharmaceutical research. MIT researchers in computer science had developed a device that can measure heartbeats wirelessly, which the Novartis researcher realized could improve drug trials; research subjects could do their normal activities instead of driving to a lab to be hooked up to measuring instruments. The researcher succeeded in winning funding from Project Genesis to see how Novartis could combine its knowledge of drug research with the MIT computer scientists' understanding of wireless measurement.

Project Genesis is much more than a contest on the sidelines of Novartis. Rather, the organization provides resources with which the teams can maximize their chances of success. The contest has clear rules and a schedule. To help people with ideas to find potential team members across disciplines, Novartis created an internal social media platform and hosts practice sessions for idea generation. Before the day of the presentations, the panel reviews all the ideas and creates a short list of contenders; for these teams, the company offers coaching on writing a business plan and training in presentation skills. After the presentations are made and the panel selects teams to fund, Novartis assigns a mentor to guide each team. Within weeks of being selected, teams have the resources they need to get started, which stimulates rapid innovation at little cost to Novartis.

In 2016, its first year, Project Genesis yielded 90 proposals, of which the scientist panel chose five to receive funding. The second round of competition generated more than 150 proposals, of which six were selected. The COVID-19 pandemic disrupted the initial plans for a third round. It took place remotely, with networking and presentations online. However, Novartis's internal social media helped Project Genesis make this round broader than before, extending beyond the research division to the more than 20,000 clinicians, engineers, and scientists throughout the company. In this round, 3,870 employees participated in the generation and discussion of ideas, and 160 proposals were presented online. Not only are more projects now moving through the company's pipeline, but Novartis also observes a greater degree of collaboration across disciplines and improved employee engagement. The company's leaders are optimistic about the future, pointing to more than 20 potential new products on track to enter the market over the next few years.

Questions for Discussion

1. In general, how can teams increase a company's innovation performance? In the description of Novartis, what evidence do you see of Project Genesis teams contributing to greater innovation?
2. How can the program lead who manages Genesis Labs contribute to the cohesiveness of the teams selected to receive funding?
3. What factors do you think would be important for motivating the members of the Project Genesis team?

Sources: "About Novartis," www.novartis.com, accessed January 31, 2023; "Novartis Delivers Mid Single Digit Sales Growth, Margin Expansion and Advancement of Robust Pipeline in 2021," news release, www.novartis.com, February 2, 2022; "Genesis Labs Program Lead Job," *Lensa*, https://lensa.com, December 22, 2021; A.C. Edmondson, "Agility Hacks," *Harvard Business Review*, November–December 2021, 46–49; "Building, Scaling and 'Unbossing' Innovation at Novartis' Genesis Labs," *Innovation Leader*, www.innovationleader.com, January 28, 2021; E. Dougherty, "Tracking Patients' Progress with Radio Signals and Machine Learning," www.novartis.com, January 29, 2018.

Notes

1. Corporate website, "About NI," www.ni.com, accessed February 1, 2023; K. Ferrazzi, "A New Social Contract for Teams," *Harvard Business Review*, September-October 2022, 88–97; M. Cronin, "National Instruments, Now NI, Transforms Itself in More Than Name," *Austin (TX) Business Journal*, www.bizjournals.com, June 17, 2020.
2. Ferrazzi, "A New Social Contract for Teams."
3. K. Ferrazzi, "Remote Meetings: The New Work Rules for High-Performing Teams in the Remote Work Field," *Forbes*, www.forbes.com, December 13, 2021.
4. Ferrazzi, "A New Social Contract for Teams"; Ferrazzi, "Remote Meetings."
5. "About NI"; "Ferrazzi, "A New Social Contract for Teams"; Ferrazzi, "Remote Meetings."
6. T.M. Mills, *The Sociology of Small Groups* (Englewood Cliffs, NJ: Prentice-Hall, 1967); M.E. Shaw, *Group Dynamics* (New York: McGraw-Hill, 1981).
7. J. Richmond, "Eager to Boost Your Team's Soft Skills? Focus on This," *Fast Company*, www.fastcompany.com, accessed February 1, 2023.
8. L. Smith, "Soft Skills: Unlock Your Team's Success," *Training Journal*, www.trainingjournal.com, February 25, 2022.
9. M. Feffer, "HR's Hard Challenge: When Employees Lack Soft Skills," *Society for Human Resource Management*, www.shrm.org, April 1, 2016.
10. K. Cases, "How to Cultivate Soft Skills in Your IT Team," *The Enterprisers Project*, https://enterprisersproject.com, February 12, 2018; M. Fouts, "Improve Team Collaboration with These Key Skills," *Forbes*, www.forbes.com, June 22, 2017.
11. Feffer, "HR's Hard Challenge"; T. Rahschulte, "Investing for Soft Skills: Build, Buy or Both," *Chief Learning Officer*, www.clomedia.com, January 3, 2018.
12. "About Hallmark," https://corporate.hallmark.com, accessed February 1, 2023; R.S. Buday, "Reengineering One Firm's Product Development and Another's Service Delivery," *Planning Review*, March–April 1993, 14–19; J.M. Burcke, "Hallmark's Quest for Quality Is a Job Never Done," *Business Insurance*, April 26, 1993, 122; M. Hammer and J. Champy, *Reengineering the Corporation* (New York: HarperBusiness, 1993); T.A. Stewart, "The Search for the Organization of Tomorrow," *Fortune*, May 18, 1992, 92–98.
13. B. Steenbarger, "Returning to Work, Redefining Teamwork," *Forbes*, www.forbes.com, April 29, 2021.
14. McKinsey and Company, "Americans Are Embracing Flexible Work–and They Want More of It," www.mckinsey.com, June 23, 2022; R. Carucci, "How to Lead Your Team Through the Transition Back to the Office," *Harvard Business Review*, https://hbr.org, June 16, 2021.
15. J.A. Pearce II and E.C. Ravlin, "The Design and Activation of Self-Regulating Work Groups," *Human Relations* 11 (1987), 751–82.
16. B. Dumaine, "Who Needs a Boss?" *Fortune*, May 7, 1990, 52–60; Pearce and Ravlin, "The Design and Activation of Self-Regulating Work Groups."
17. T.D. Wall, N.J. Kemp, P.R. Jackson, and C.W. Clegg, "Outcomes of Autonomous Work Groups: A Long-Term Field Experiment," *Academy of Management Journal* 29 (1986), 280–304.
18. A. Markels, "A Power Producer Is Intent on Giving Power to Its People," *The Wall Street Journal*, July 3, 1995, A1, A12; "AES Corporation/The Power of Being Global," www.aes.com/aes/index?page5home, April 15, 2008.
19. J.S. Lublin, "My Colleague, My Boss," *The Wall Street Journal*, April 12, 1995, R4, R12.
20. PwC, "It's Time to Reimagine Where and How Work Will Get Done: PwC's US Remote Work Survey," www.pwc.com, January 12, 2021.
21. K. Parker, J. M. Horowitz, and R. Minkin, "COVID-19 Pandemic Continues to Reshape Work in America," *Pew Research Center*, www.pewresearch.org, February 16, 2022.
22. W.R. Pape, "Group Insurance," *Inc.* (Technology Supplement), June 17, 1997, 29–31; A.M. Townsend, S.M. DeMarie, and A.R. Hendrickson, "Are You Ready for Virtual Teams?" *HR Magazine*, September 1996, 122–26; A.M. Townsend, S.M. DeMarie, and A.M. Hendrickson, "Virtual Teams: Technology and the Workplace of the Future," *Academy of Management Executive* 12, no. 3 (1998), 17–29.
23. Townsend et al., "Virtual Teams."
24. C. Breuer, J. Hüffmeier, and G. Hertel, "Does Trust Matter More in Virtual Teams? A Meta-Analysis of Trust and Team Effectiveness Considering Virtuality and Documentation as Moderators," *Journal of Applied Psychology* 101, no. 8 (2016), 1151–77.
25. V. Maza, "Are Your Remote Workers Happy? How to Keep Teams Connected from Afar," *Forbes*, www.forbes.com, accessed March 13, 2020.
26. E.J. Hill, B.C. Miller, S.P. Weiner, and J. Colihan, "Influences of the Virtual Office on Aspects of Work and Work/Life Balance," *Personnel Psychology* 31 (1998), 667–83; S.G. Strauss, "Technology, Group Process, and Group Outcomes: Testing the Connections in Computer-Mediated and Face-to-Face Groups," *Human-Computer Interaction* 12 (1997), 227–66; M.E. Warkentin, L. Sayeed, and R. Hightower, "Virtual Teams versus Face-to-Face Teams: An Exploratory Study of a Web-Based Conference System," *Decision Sciences* 28, no. 4 (Fall 1997), 975–96.
27. Microsoft, "The Next Great Disruption Is Hybrid Work–Are We Ready?" *2021 Work Trend Index: Annual Report*, www.microsoft.com, March 22, 2022; C. Purtill, "Can Workers Climb the Career Ladder from Outside the Office?" *The New York Times*, www.nytimes.com, March 3, 2022; N. Baym, J. Larson, and R. Martin, "What a Year of WFH Has Done to Our Relationships at Work," *Harvard Business Review*, https://hbr.org, March 22, 2021.

28. S. Oliver, "How to Build Stronger Relationships with Colleagues in the Zoom Era," *The Wall Street Journal,* www.wsj.com, November 26, 2021.

29. Baym et al., "What a Year of WFH Has Done"; Purtill, "Can Workers Climb the Career Ladder?"

30. Baym et al., "What a Year of WFH Has Done"; Microsoft, "The Next Great Disruption."

31. S. Krumm, J. Kanthak, K. Hartmann, and G. Hertel, "What Does It Take to Be a Virtual Team Player? The Knowledge, Skills, Abilities, and Other Characteristics Required in Virtual Teams," *Human Performance* 29, no. 2 (2016), 123–42.

32. S.A. Furst, M. Reeves, B. Rosen, and R.S. Blackburn, "Managing the Life Cycle of Virtual Teams," *Academy of Management Executive* 18, no. 2 (May 2004), 6–20.

33. L. Gratton, "Work Together. . . . When Apart," *The Wall Street Journal,* June 16–17, 2007, R4.

34. M. Rollings, "36 Remote Work Tools & Software for Teams Working from Home in 2023," *Hive,* https://hive.com, January 27, 2023.

35. D. Wang and J.A. Evans, "Research: When Small Teams Are Better than Big Ones," *Harvard Business Review,* https://hbr.org, February 21, 2019.

36. J.D. Thompson, *Organizations in Action* (New York: McGraw-Hill, 1967).

37. S.H. Courtright, G.R. Thurgood, G.L. Stewart, and A. J. Pierotti, "Structural Interdependence in Teams: An Integrative Framework and Meta-Analysis," *Journal of Applied Psychology* 100, no. 6 (2015), 1825–46.

38. Thompson, *Organizations in Action.*

39. R. Saavedra, P.C. Earley, and L. Van Dyne, "Complex Interdependence in Task-Performing Groups," *Journal of Applied Psychology* 78, no. 1 (1993), 61–72.

40. S.M. Gully, K.A. Incalcaterra, A. Joshi, and J.M. Beaubien, "A Meta-Analysis of Team-Efficacy, Potency, and Performance: Interdependence and Level of Analysis as Moderators of Observed Relationships," *Journal of Applied Psychology* 87, no. 5 (2002), 819–32.

41. Courtright et al., "Structural Interdependence in Teams."

42. Lublin, "My Colleague, My Boss."

43. R.G. LeFauve and A.C. Hax, "Managerial and Technological Innovations at Saturn Corporation," *MIT Management,* Spring 1992, 8–19.

44. B.W. Tuckman, "Developmental Sequences in Small Groups," *Psychological Bulletin* 63 (1965), 384–99; B.W. Tuckman and M.C. Jensen, "Stages of Small Group Development," *Group and Organizational Studies* 2 (1977), 419–27.

45. C.J.G. Gersick, "Time and Transition in Work Teams: Toward a New Model of Group Development," *Academy of Management Journal* 31 (1988), 9–41; C.J.G. Gersick, "Marking Time: Predictable Transitions in Task Groups," *Academy of Management Journal* 32 (1989), 274–309.

46. "How to Lead a Collaborative Team," Center for Creative Leadership, www.ccl.org, accessed March 13, 2020.

47. A. Hickman, "The Five Tactics of Teamwork: A Blueprint for Team Management," *Gallup,* www.gallup.com, January 9, 2020.

48. F. Gino, "Cracking the Code of Sustained Collaboration," *Harvard Business Review,* November–December 2019, 73–81.

49. Ibid., 77–79.

50. J.R. Hackman, "Group Influences on Individuals in Organizations," in M.D. Dunnette and L.M. Hough, eds., *Handbook of Industrial and Organizational Psychology,* 2nd ed., vol. 3 (Palo Alto, CA: Consulting Psychologists Press, 1992), 199–267.

51. Hackman, "Group Influences on Individuals."

52. Ibid.

53. Lublin, "My Colleague, My Boss."

54. L. Festinger, "Informal Social Communication," *Psychological Review* 57 (1950), 271–82; Shaw, *Group Dynamics.*

55. Hackman, "Group Influences on Individuals in Organizations"; Shaw, *Group Dynamics.*

56. D. Cartwright, "The Nature of Group Cohesiveness," in D. Cartwright and A. Zander, eds., *Group Dynamics,* 3rd ed. (New York: Harper & Row, 1968); L. Festinger, S. Schacter, and K. Black, *Social Pressures in Informal Groups* (New York: Harper & Row, 1950); Shaw, *Group Dynamics.*

57. "About the Business Chemistry Types," www2.deloitte.com, accessed February 1, 2023; K. Christfort, "The Power of Business Chemistry," Deloitte, www2.deloitte.com, accessed April 23, 2018; K. Christfort and S. Vickberg, "Business Chemistry in the C-Suite," *The Wall Street Journal,* November 2, 2017, http://deloitte.wsj.com; S.M. Johnson Vickberg and K. Christfort, "Pioneers, Drivers, Integrators, and Guardians," *Harvard Business Review,* March–April 2017, 50–57.

58. Vickberg and Christfort, "Pioneers, Drivers, Integrators, and Guardians"; T. Williams, "Business Chemistry: Are You a Driver, Guardian, Integrator, or Pioneer," *Economist,* https://exceed.economist.com, accessed March 6, 2020; Christfort and Vickberg, "Business Chemistry in the C-Suite."

59. Vickberg and Christfort, "Pioneers, Drivers, Integrators, and Guardians"; Christfort and Vickberg, "Business Chemistry in the C-Suite"; Christfort, "The Power of Business Chemistry."

60. Vickberg and Christfort, "Pioneers, Drivers, Integrators, and Guardians"; Christfort and Vickberg, "Business Chemistry in the C-Suite"; A. Beard, "How Work Styles Inform," *Harvard Business Review,* March–April 2017, 58–59; Christfort, "The Power of Business Chemistry."

61. T.F. O'Boyle, "A Manufacturer Grows Efficient by Soliciting Ideas from Employees," *The Wall Street Journal,* June 5, 1992, A1, A5.

62. E. Kur, "The Faces Model of High Performing Team Management," *Leadership & Organizational Development Journal* 17, no. 1 (1996), 32–41.

63. D.D. Warrick, "What Leaders Can Learn about Teamwork and Developing High Performance Teams from Organization Development Practitioners," *Performance Improvement* 55(3): 13–21, 2016.

64. Lublin, "My Colleague, My Boss."

65. P.C. Earley, "Social Loafing and Collectivism: A Comparison of the United States and the People's Republic of China," *Administrative Science Quarterly* 34 (1989), 565–81; J.M. George, "Extrinsic and Intrinsic Origins of Perceived Social Loafing in Organizations," *Academy of Management Journal* 35 (1992), 191–202; S.G. Harkins, B. Latane, and K. Williams, "Social Loafing: Allocating Effort or Taking It Easy," *Journal of Experimental Social Psychology* 16 (1980), 457–65; B. Latane, K.D. Williams, and S. Harkins, "Many Hands Make Light the Work: The Causes and Consequences of Social Loafing," *Journal of Personality and Social Psychology* 37 (1979), 822–32; J.A. Shepperd, "Productivity Loss in Performance Groups: A Motivation Analysis," *Psychological Bulletin* 113 (1993), 67–81.

66. George, "Extrinsic and Intrinsic Origins of Perceived Social Loafing in Organizations"; G.R. Jones, "Task Visibility, Free Riding, and Shirking: Explaining the Effect of Structure and Technology on Employee Behavior," *Academy of Management Review* 9 (1984), 684–95; K. Williams, S. Harkins, and B. Latane, "Identifiability as a Deterrent to Social Loafing: Two Cheering Experiments," *Journal of Personality and Social Psychology* 40 (1981), 303–11.

67. S. Harkins and J. Jackson, "The Role of Evaluation in Eliminating Social Loafing," *Personality and Social Psychology Bulletin* 11 (1985), 457–65; N.L. Kerr and S.E. Bruun, "Ringelman Revisited: Alternative Explanations for the Social Loafing Effect," *Personality and Social Psychology Bulletin* 7 (1981), 224–31; Williams et al., "Identifiability as a Deterrent to Social Loafing"; Harkins and Jackson, "The Role of Evaluation in Eliminating Social Loafing."
68. M.A. Brickner, S.G. Harkins, and T.M. Ostrom, "Effects of Personal Involvement: Thought-Provoking Implications for Social Loafing," *Journal of Personality and Social Psychology* 51 (1986), 763–69; S.G. Harkins and R.E. Petty, "The Effects of Task Difficulty and Task Uniqueness on Social Loafing," *Journal of Personality and Social Psychology* 43 (1982), 1214–29.
69. B. Latane, "Responsibility and Effort in Organizations," in P.S. Goodman, ed., *Designing Effective Work Groups* (San Francisco: Jossey-Bass, 1986); Latane et al., "Many Hands Make Light the Work"; I.D. Steiner, *Group Process and Productivity* (New York: Academic Press, 1972).

CHAPTER 16

Promoting Effective Communication

Peopleimages/Getty Images

Learning Objectives

After studying this chapter, you should be able to:

LO16-1 Explain why effective communication helps an organization gain a competitive advantage.

LO16-2 Describe the communication process, and explain the role of perception in communication.

LO16-3 Define information richness, and describe the information richness of communication media available to managers.

LO16-4 Describe the communication networks that exist in groups and teams.

LO16-5 Explain how advances in technology have given managers new options for managing communication.

LO16-6 Describe important communication skills that managers need as senders and as receivers of messages and why it is important to understand differences in linguistic styles.

A MANAGER'S CHALLENGE

Insights on Communicating in the Digital Age

How can managers communicate effectively as media tools proliferate? As technology adds to the options for sending and receiving messages, human beings still inhabit the bodies that evolved to gather information through in-person interactions. Whether we silently watch others or engage in conversation, we observe facial expressions, tone of voice, and gestures for signs of others' attitudes and intentions. Nowadays, however, business communications often travel through digital channels that omit these sources of information, resulting in misunderstandings, anxiety, and wasted time.[1]

Erica Dhawan has made it her life's work to study technology's impact on workplace communication and to teach others what she learns. She developed this interest as a child of immigrants, navigating life between a home where the family spoke Hindi and a school where the children and teachers spoke English. As she struggled to master both languages, she observed others' body language—gestures, postures, and so on. Later, at MIT and Harvard, she made this topic the object of her research and began applying what she learned by consulting with organizations.[2]

In her consulting work, Dhawan observed that many communication challenges involve the use of online tools such as texting, instant messaging, and online meeting apps that combine video, audio, and messaging. For example, some employees worry that an unanswered text means someone is angry, or they look for emotional clues in an email's exclamation points. Participants in an online meeting may be confused about where to direct their gaze. And employees either don't consider or can't decide when to send an email instead of texting.[3]

Dhawan concluded that our online behaviors send messages that take the place of body language in face-to-face interactions. She calls these behaviors "digital body language" and developed four principles for using it effectively. The first principle is to "value others visibly," because employees who don't see nods and smiles of approval will look for other cues—for example, a coworker respects people's time

Consultant Erica Dhawan observed that many communication challenges involve the use of online tools such as texting, instant messaging, and online meeting apps that combine video, audio, and messaging. She suggests managers establish norms for communication among members of an organization.
Larry Busacca/Staff/Getty Images Entertainment/Getty Images

when scheduling meetings, or a manager makes a point of inviting remote participants in a meeting to share their thoughts. Second is to use care in communicating. Managers demonstrate care when they read employees' messages carefully, not jumping to conclusions, and construct requests and questions clearly. Dhawan recommends thoughtful use of emojis to clarify emotional content (although other researchers caution that people differ in how they interpret emojis, with women more likely to see a negative connotation). Third, managers and employees should collaborate well. At one company where Dhawan consulted, the team appointed "channel advocates" to encourage best practices in communication. Finally, communicators need to foster and show trust. Being open and honest with information builds trust, as does keeping promises, such as scheduling a meeting at a specific time.[4]

Managers can enable better digital body language by establishing norms for online communication. For example, people may worry when they don't get a same-day answer to a message, but if the department has a norm to respond to phone calls the same day and to texts within an hour, people understand what to prioritize and when to be patient. At one organization that brought in Dhawan to improve communication, team members would send instant messaging comments so short that employees couldn't tell whether they were expected to act. Team members also would send documents through multiple channels, creating waves of unnecessary information. Dhawan guided teams in establishing norms such as sending documents through just one channel and limiting IMs to simple questions for six or fewer recipients. Dhawan sees a major payoff from such efforts: online channels can include employees from wide geographic areas and remove the significance of cultural differences in body language, so creative, inclusive thinking can flourish.[5]

Overview

Even with all the advances in technology that are available to managers, ineffective communication continues to take place in organizations. Ineffective communication is detrimental for managers, employees, and organizations; it can lead to poor performance, strained interpersonal relations, poor service, and dissatisfied customers. For an organization to be effective and gain a competitive advantage, managers at all levels need to be good communicators.

In this chapter, we describe the nature of communication and the communication process and explain why all managers and their employees need to be effective communicators. We describe the communication media available to managers and the factors they need to consider in selecting a communication medium for each message they send. We consider the communication networks organizational members rely on, and we explore how advances in technology have expanded managers' range of communication options. We describe the communication skills that help managers to be effective senders and receivers of messages. By the end of this chapter, you will appreciate the nature of communication and the steps managers can take to ensure that they are effective communicators.

communication The sharing of information between two or more individuals or groups to reach a common understanding.

Communication and Management

Communication is the sharing of information between two or more individuals or groups to reach a common understanding.[6] First and foremost, no matter how electronically based, communication is a human endeavor and involves individuals and groups. Second, communication does not take place unless a common understanding is reached. Thus, when you call a business to speak to a person in customer service or billing and are bounced between endless automated messages and menu options and eventually hang up in frustration, communication has not taken place.

The Importance of Good Communication

LO16-1 Explain why effective communication helps an organization gain a competitive advantage.

In Chapter 1, we described how an organization can gain a competitive advantage when managers strive to increase efficiency, quality, responsiveness to customers, and innovation. Good communication is essential for attaining each of these four goals and, thus, is a necessity for gaining a competitive advantage.

Managers can *increase efficiency* by updating the production process to take advantage of new and more efficient technologies and by training workers to operate the new technologies and to expand their skills. Good communication is necessary for managers to learn about new technologies, implement them in their organizations, and train workers in how to use them. Similarly, *improving quality* hinges on effective communication. Managers need to communicate to all members of an organization the meaning and importance of high quality and the routes to attaining it. Employees need to communicate quality problems and suggestions for increasing quality to their superiors, and members of self-managed work teams need to share their ideas on improving quality.

Good communication can also help increase *responsiveness to customers.* When the organizational members who are closest to customers, such as department store salespeople and customer service reps, are empowered to communicate customers' needs and desires to managers, managers can better respond to these needs. Managers, in turn, must communicate with other organizational members to determine how best to respond to changing customer preferences.

Innovation, which often takes place in cross-functional teams, also requires effective communication. Members of a cross-functional team developing a new video game, for example, must effectively communicate with one another to develop a game that customers will want to play; that will be engaging, interesting, and fun; and that can lead to sequels. Members of the team also must communicate with managers to secure the resources they need for developing the game and to keep managers informed of progress on the project. Innovation, whether in products or processes, is likeliest in a culture where employees share ideas, rather than merely waiting for direction from their managers.

LO16-2 Describe the communication process, and explain the role of perception in communication.

In addition, to maintain or increase competitive advantage, companies are turning to technology to gather information from their own employees about what works and what doesn't when it comes to company processes and procedures. For example, Betterworks is a technology platform that lets businesses gather and analyze anonymous communications from their employees. The purpose is to communicate to employees that their opinions matter and to make these sentiments available quickly and easily through a variety of methods, including quick surveys via mobile device. Betterworks's system gathers the responses, analyzes them, and then submits information and alerts to management about what employees are thinking–and saying.[7]

Effective communication is necessary for managers and all members of an organization to increase efficiency, quality, responsiveness to customers, and innovation and, thus, gain a competitive advantage for the organization. Managers therefore must understand the communication process well if they are to perform effectively.

sender The person or group wishing to share information.

message The information that a sender wants to share.

encoding Translating a message into understandable symbols or language.

noise Anything that hampers any stage of the communication process.

receiver The person or group for whom a message is intended.

medium The pathway through which an encoded message is transmitted to a receiver.

decoding Interpreting and trying to make sense of a message.

The Communication Process

The communication process consists of two phases. In the *transmission phase,* information is shared between two or more individuals or groups. In the *feedback phase,* a common understanding is ensured. In both phases, a number of distinct stages must occur for communication to take place (see Figure 16.1).[8]

Starting the transmission phase, the **sender**, the person or group wishing to share information with some other person or group, decides on the **message**, what information to communicate. Then the sender translates the message into symbols or language, a process called **encoding**; often messages are encoded into words. **Noise** is a general term that refers to anything that hampers any stage of the communication process.

Once encoded, a message is transmitted through a medium to the **receiver**, the person or group for whom the message is intended. The **medium** is simply the pathway, such as a phone call, a letter, a memo, or face-to-face communication in a meeting, through which an encoded message is transmitted to a receiver. At the next stage, the receiver interprets and tries to make sense of the message, a process called **decoding**. This is a critical point in communication.

Figure 16.1
The Communication Process

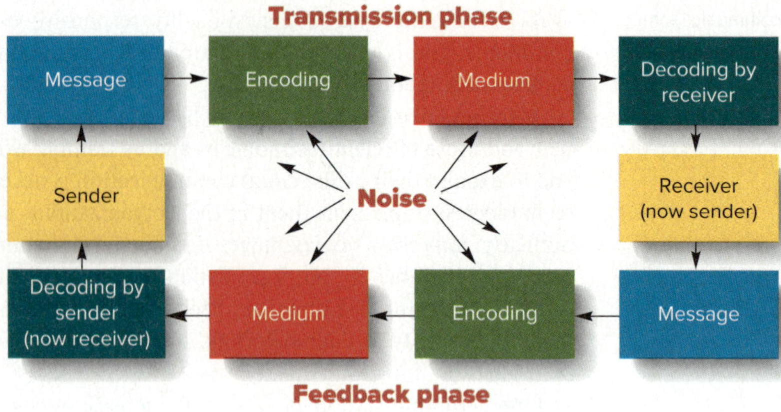

The feedback phase is initiated by the receiver (who becomes a sender). The receiver decides what message to send to the original sender (who becomes a receiver), encodes it, and transmits it through a chosen medium (see Figure 16.1). The message might contain a confirmation that the original message was received and understood, a restatement of the original message to make sure it has been correctly interpreted, or a request for more information. The original sender decodes the message and makes sure a common understanding has been reached. If the original sender determines that a common understanding has not been reached, sender and receiver cycle through the whole process as many times as needed to reach a common understanding. Feedback eliminates misunderstandings, ensures that messages are correctly interpreted, and enables senders and receivers to reach a common understanding.

verbal communication The encoding of messages into words, either written or spoken.

nonverbal communication The encoding of messages by means of facial expressions, body language, and style of dress.

The encoding of messages into words, written or spoken, is **verbal communication**. We can also encode messages without using written or spoken language.

Nonverbal communication shares information by means of facial expressions (smiling, raising an eyebrow, frowning), body language (posture, gestures, nods, and shrugs), and even style of dress (casual, formal, conservative). The trend toward increasing empowerment of the workforce has led some managers to dress informally to communicate that all employees of an organization are team members, working together to create value for customers.

Nonverbal communication can be used to reinforce verbal communication. Just as a warm and genuine smile can back up words of appreciation for a job well done, a concerned facial expression can back up words of sympathy for a personal problem. In such cases, the balance between the verbal and the nonverbal communication helps to ensure that a common understanding is reached.

Sometimes when members of an organization decide not to express a message verbally, they inadvertently do so nonverbally. People tend to have less control over nonverbal communication, and often a verbal message that is withheld gets expressed through body language or facial expressions. A manager who agrees to a proposal they actually do not like may unintentionally communicate disfavor by grimacing.

Sometimes nonverbal communication is used to send messages that cannot be sent through verbal channels. Many lawyers are well aware of this communication tactic. Lawyers are often schooled in techniques of nonverbal communication, such as choosing where to stand in the courtroom for maximum effect and using eye contact during different stages of a trial. Lawyers sometimes get into trouble for using inappropriate nonverbal communication in an attempt to influence juries.[9]

If a picture is worth a thousand words, so too is nonverbal communication. Facial expressions, body language, posture, and eye contact all send powerful messages.
Christopher Robbins/Digital Vision/Getty Images

The Role of Perception in Communication

Perception plays a central role in communication and affects both transmission and feedback. In Chapter 5, we defined *perception* as the process through which people select, organize, and interpret sensory input to give meaning and order to the world around them. We mentioned that perception is inherently subjective and is influenced by people's personalities, values, attitudes, and moods as well as by their experience and knowledge. When senders and receivers communicate with each other, they do so based on their subjective perceptions. The encoding and decoding of messages and even the choice of a medium hinge on the perceptions of senders and receivers.

In addition, perceptual biases can hamper effective communication. Recall from Chapter 5 that *biases* are systematic tendencies to use information about others in ways that result in inaccurate perceptions. In Chapter 5, we described a number of biases that can cause unfair treatment of diverse members of an organization. The same biases also can lead to ineffective communication. For example, *stereotypes*—simplified and often inaccurate beliefs about the characteristics of particular groups of people—can interfere with the encoding and decoding of messages.

Suppose a manager stereotypes older workers as being fearful of change. When this manager encodes a message to an older worker about an upcoming change in the organization, she may downplay the extent of the change so as not to make the older worker feel stressed. The older worker, however, fears change no more than do his younger colleagues and, thus, decodes the message to mean that only a minor change is going to be made. The older worker fails to prepare adequately for the change, and his performance subsequently suffers because of his lack of preparation. Clearly, this ineffective communication was due to the manager's inaccurate assumptions about older workers. Instead of relying on stereotypes, effective managers strive to perceive other people accurately by focusing on their actual behaviors, knowledge, skills, and abilities. Accurate perceptions, in turn, contribute to effective communication.

The Dangers of Ineffective Communication

Because managers must communicate with others to perform their various roles and tasks, managers spend most of their time communicating, whether in meetings, in telephone conversations, through email, or in face-to-face interactions in person or online. Indeed, some experts estimate that managers spend approximately 80% of their time engaged in some form of communication.[10]

Effective communication is so important that managers cannot just be concerned that they themselves are effective communicators; they also have to help their employees be effective communicators. When all members of an organization can communicate effectively with one another and with people outside the organization, the organization is much more likely to perform highly and gain a competitive advantage. The "Ethics in Action" feature explores how this applies to the use of questions to foster effective communication.

When managers and other members of an organization are ineffective communicators, organizational performance suffers, and any competitive advantage the organization might have is likely to be lost. Moreover, poor communication can be downright dangerous and even lead to tragic and unnecessary loss of human life. For example, a recent study by Harvard University researchers found that changing how doctors communicate during shift changes reduced the risk of adverse events in patients by 30%. In addition, researchers found that improving communication methods could also reduce the rate of medical errors by almost 25%.[11]

ETHICS IN ACTION

Questions Can Lead to Honest, Open Communication

Managers might assume that their most valuable communications deliver information and instructions. Research, however, supports the value of asking questions, listening to answers, and probing for details. Question-oriented communication builds trust and rapport, so it motivates employees, strengthens teamwork, and stimulates creativity. Even non-management employees can gain power by asking questions, along with demonstrating respect and seeking opportunities to help. These behaviors build strong social networks, which become a source of opportunities for development and

Asking questions as a form of communication builds trust and rapport, which can lead to motivated employees, effective teamwork, and increased creativity.
Aleksandr Davydov/fizkes/123RF

advancement. Thoughtful use of questioning also is associated with greater effectiveness in personal selling.[12]

Some techniques improve the impact of questions. For getting people to share information, open-ended questions are more effective than multiple-choice or yes/no questions. Asking questions in a casual, conversational way causes people to open up. When questions aim to generate ideas, reassuring people that they can change their answers tends to free them to speak. Think of brainstorming sessions, where everyone is encouraged to toss out ideas. It may help to think of questions not as a debate with winners and losers, but as a dialogue aimed at achieving a meeting of the minds, bringing the participants together on an idea, goal, or solution.[13]

Of course, the benefits of asking questions are achievable only with a person giving honest answers. Ideally, managers and employees function in an ethical environment that encourages honesty. But sometimes the context is competitive, such as when negotiating a high-stakes deal with a counterpart trying to withhold information. In that case, honesty may be more likely with closed-ended questions and pessimistic assumptions–for example, in negotiating an acquisition, "Your sales growth has flattened out over the past two years, hasn't it?"[14]

A practice of asking questions and listening respectfully builds one's character because it demonstrates concern for others. Ken Sterling, executive vice president of BigSpeak, embraces questions as part of his policy of "radical candor," which involves caring about employees personally and challenging them directly. For the first objective, Sterling's meeting agendas include time for questions about employees' personal goals and concerns. The second objective, to challenge directly, involves offering honest feedback about what is and is not working. Here, too, Sterling asks questions in regular meetings. Specifically, he has teams identify areas of success, problems, and ideas for improvement. Making these questions routine teaches team members that questions are about problem solving, not criticism. This frees them to be honest.[15]

Information Richness and Communication Media

To be effective communicators, managers (and other members of an organization) need to select an appropriate communication medium for each message they send. Should a change in procedures be communicated to employees in an email? Should a congratulatory message about a major accomplishment be communicated in a letter, in a phone call, or over lunch? Should a layoff announcement be made in a memo or at a plant meeting? Should the members of a purchasing team travel to Europe to cement a major agreement with a new supplier, or should they do so through Zoom meetings and email messages? Managers deal with these questions day in and day out.

LO16-3 Define information richness, and describe the information richness of communication media available to managers.

There is no one best communication medium for managers to rely on. In choosing a medium for any message, managers need to consider three factors. The first and most important is the level of information richness that is needed. **Information richness** is the amount of information a communication medium can carry and the extent to which the medium enables the sender and receiver to reach a common understanding.[16] The communication media that managers use vary in their information richness (see Figure 16.2).[17] Media high in information richness can carry an extensive amount of information and generally enable receivers and senders to come to a common understanding.

information richness The amount of information that a communication medium can carry and the extent to which the medium enables the sender and receiver to reach a common understanding.

The second factor that managers need to take into account in selecting a communication medium is the *time* needed for communication, because managers' and other organizational members' time is valuable. During the global COVID-19 pandemic, online videoconferencing via Zoom, Microsoft Teams, and other platforms became a critical time saver and allowed managers and employees alike to communicate and even collaborate efficiently as most people

Figure 16.2
The Information Richness of Communication Media

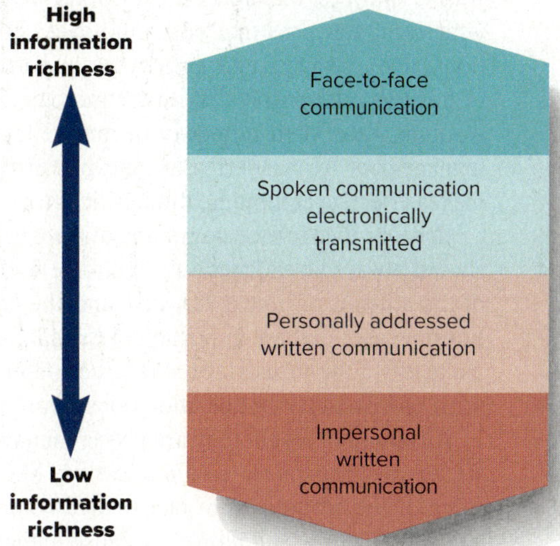

worked from home. As the pandemic began to wane, many organizations shifted their thinking about remote work and mandating in-office work five days a week for employees. In a recent study of 125 corporate leaders that explored the changing approach to communication in business, when surveyed at the start of the pandemic in 2020, 71% believed that flexible working schedules had a negative impact on work. Two years later, that percentage had dropped dramatically to 16%.[18]

The third factor that affects the choice of a communication medium is the *need for a paper or electronic trail* or some kind of written documentation that a message was sent and received. A manager may wish to document in writing, for example, that an employee was given a formal warning about excessive lateness.

In the remainder of this section, we examine four types of communication media that vary along these three dimensions (information richness, time, and paper or electronic trail).[19]

Face-to-Face Communication

Despite the popularity of electronic communication, face-to-face communication is still the medium that is highest in information richness.
Digital Vision/Getty Images

Face-to-face communication is the medium that is highest in information richness. When managers communicate face-to-face, they not only can take advantage of verbal communication but also can interpret each other's nonverbal signals such as facial expressions and body language. A look of concern or puzzlement can sometimes say more than a thousand words, and managers can respond to such nonverbal signals on the spot. Face-to-face communication also enables managers to receive instant feedback. Points of confusion, ambiguity, or misunderstanding can be resolved, and managers can cycle through the communication process as many times as needed to reach a common understanding.

With the growing proliferation of electronic forms of communication, some managers fear that face-to-face communication is being shortchanged to the detriment of building common understandings and rapport. Moreover, some messages that should be communicated face-to-face or at least in a phone conversation, and messages that are more efficiently communicated in this manner, are nonetheless sent electronically.[20]

Creating opportunities for face-to-face communication can be especially important when trying to communicate effectively with employees located in other countries. For example, ProQuest, a technology company, has remote teams scattered in cities around the world that communicate daily via various forms of media. However, the teams come together face-to-face every four months to plan the projects they will carry out in the coming year.[21]

management by wandering around A face-to-face communication technique in which a manager walks around a work area and talks informally with employees about issues and concerns.

Management by wandering around is a face-to-face communication technique that is effective for many managers at all levels in an organization. Rather than scheduling formal meetings with employees, managers walk around work areas and talk informally with employees about issues and concerns that both employees and managers may have. These informal conversations give managers and employees important information while fostering the development of positive relationships. With technology changing at breakneck speed and more employees working out of their homes or in remote locations, some experts suggest that in recent years, management by wandering around has evolved into management by weekly check-in, which makes effective communication critical to an organization's success.[22]

Because face-to-face communication is highest in information richness, you might think it should always be the medium of choice for managers. This is not the case, however, because of the amount of time it can take and the lack of a paper or electronic trail resulting from it. For messages that are important, personal, or likely to be misunderstood, it is often well worth managers' time to use face-to-face communication and, if need be, supplement it with some form of written communication documenting the message.

Advances in technology are giving managers new communication media that are close substitutes for face-to-face communication. Many organizations use videoconferences to capture some of the advantages of face-to-face communication (such as access to facial expressions) while saving time and money, because managers in different locations do not have to travel to meet with one another. In addition to saving travel costs, videoconferences sometimes have other advantages. Managers have found that decisions get made more quickly when videoconferences are used, because more managers can be involved in the decision-making process, and therefore, fewer managers have to be consulted outside the meeting itself. Videoconferences also seem to lead to more efficient meetings. Some managers have found meetings are 20–30% shorter when videoconferences are used instead of face-to-face meetings.

Spoken Communication Electronically Transmitted

After face-to-face communication, spoken communication electronically transmitted over phone lines or via the Internet is second highest in information richness (see Figure 16.2). Although managers communicating over the telephone do not see body language and facial expressions, they do have access to the tone of voice in which a message is delivered, the parts of the message the sender emphasizes, and the general manner in which the message is spoken, in addition to the words themselves. Thus, telephone conversations can convey extensive amounts of information. Managers can ensure mutual understanding because they can get quick feedback over the phone and answer questions.

Many organizations also enable communication via software such as Zoom or Slack. With these apps, participants can see one another's faces and hear one another's voices–if participants enable these capabilities. The apps also enable the host to share documents or web pages with a screen-share feature and to create a recording, which addresses a shortcoming of other forms of communication. In addition, some companies use these tools to interview job applicants, which was particularly useful during the pandemic.[23] However, with a large group, this channel may not be suitable for personal or emotional messages, as described in the "Manager as a Person" feature.

MANAGER AS A PERSON

A Tough Lesson in Communication

Vishal Garg, founder and CEO of Better, which provides home buying services including mortgage lending, shocked employees by announcing in a Zoom meeting that he was laying them off. Millions more people watched a replay of this episode after someone posted a recording of the meeting on social media. In the recording, Garg said, "This is the second time in my career that I'm doing this, and I do not, do not, want to do this. The last time I did it, I cried." He announced that the employees were

Many organizations enable communication among their members via software such as Zoom or Slack. However, as Vishal Garg discovered, this online communication channel may not be the best way to tell employees they are being terminated.
Alistair Berg/DigitalVision/Getty Images

"part of the unlucky group that is being laid off. Your employment here is terminated effective immediately." Some of the 900 employees laid off (9% of Better's workforce) missed the meeting; one posted on LinkedIn that she discovered something was happening when her computer shut down while she was communicating with a client.[24]

The next day, Better's website posted a letter from Garg in which he apologized for how he had communicated the layoffs. He said, "I own the decision" but "blundered the execution." A week later, the company's board of directors announced Garg would be taking time off and an outside firm would analyze Better's culture and leadership.[25] One month later, the board announced in an email to employees that Garg would be returning to his position after reflecting on his leadership and working with a coach. Separately, Garg wrote a letter in which he apologized again and promised to be more conscious of the impact of his words. He promised, "I am committed to being more thoughtful and communicating more effectively." To back up the words, the company planned to hire a chief human resource officer and provide training in building a respectful workplace.[26]

These efforts were tested two months later: Better announced another round of layoffs in response to a slowing of the real estate market. This time, a letter to employees announced the company would lay off 35% of its workforce, saying those terminated employees would be contacted personally. The announcement described plans to provide severance pay and medical insurance. Despite the promise to reach out personally, some employees received severance payments before they learned they would be laid off. However, in a possible sign of the CEO's new leadership style, the head of HR announced that Garg would "personally cover" health insurance costs of expecting parents who were let go and couldn't find employment or health insurance.[27]

Personally Addressed Written Communication

Lower in information richness than electronically transmitted verbal communication is personally addressed written communication (see Figure 16.2). One advantage of face-to-face communication and electronically transmitted verbal communication is that they both tend to demand attention, which helps ensure that receivers pay attention. Personally addressed written communications, such as memos and letters, also have this advantage. Because they are addressed to a particular person, the chances are good that the person will pay attention to (and read) them. Moreover, the sender can write the message in a way that the receiver is most likely to understand. However, unlike spoken communication electronically transmitted, receivers of personally addressed written communication do not have access to the sender's tone of voice, parts of the message the sender emphasizes, and the general manner in which the message is spoken. Additionally, like voice mail, written communication does not enable a receiver to have their questions answered immediately; however, when messages are clearly written and feedback is provided, common understandings can still be reached.

Even if managers use face-to-face communication, sending a follow-up in writing is often necessary for messages that are important or complicated and need to be referred to later on. This is precisely what a hospital administrator did when she needed to tell one of her employees about an important change in how the hospital would be handling denials of insurance benefits. The administrator met with the individual and described the changes in person. Once the administrator was sure the employee understood them, she handed the employee a sheet of instructions to follow, which essentially summarized the information they had discussed.

Email and text messages also fit into this category of communication media, because senders and receivers are communicating through personally addressed written words. The words, however, appear on computer screens, laptops, or mobile devices rather than on paper. Email is so widespread in the business world that some managers find they have to deliberately take time out from managing their email to get their work done, including taking action on business strategies and coming up with new and innovative ideas. According to the Radicati Group, a technology market research firm, by 2026, worldwide email traffic will surpass 396 *billion* emails every day–including both business and consumer communications.[28] To help employees manage their email effectively, many organizations provide in-house training programs or other guidance to help workers (and managers) use email effectively as part of their daily work activities.[29]

The use of email and other tools has also enabled many workers and managers to become telecommuters, people employed by organizations who work out of their homes on a regular basis. Once the global pandemic spread in 2020, most workers and managers routinely worked remotely and now nearly three years later, many organizations have rethought their original mandate that workers needed to return to the office in 2022. As companies continue to adopt more online communication and collaboration tools, workers are expecting their employers to allow them to work a hybrid workweek–with limited time in the office. A recent Gallup survey found that 8 out of 10 people are working a hybrid schedule (limited time in the office on a weekly basis). This hybrid work model is expected to grow from 42% in 2021 to more than 80% over the next few years.[30]

Today email continues to be the most used form of business communication in the workplace. Managers need to develop a clear, written policy specifying what company email can and should be used for–and what is out of bounds. Managers should clearly communicate this policy to all members of the organization, as well as tell them what procedures will be used when email abuse is suspected and what consequences will result if abuse is confirmed.[31]

In addition, email policies should specify how much personal email is appropriate and when those bounds have been overstepped. Clearly banning all personal email is impractical and likely to have negative consequences for employees and their organizations (such as lower levels of job satisfaction and increased personal phone conversations). Some companies urge employees to use other web-based systems such as Gmail for personal communications rather than the corporate email system.[32]

Impersonal Written Communication

Impersonal written communication is lowest in information richness but is well suited for messages that need to reach many receivers. Because such messages are not addressed to particular receivers, feedback is unlikely, so managers must make sure messages sent by this medium are written clearly in language that all receivers will understand.

Managers often find company newsletters useful vehicles for reaching large numbers of employees. Many managers give their newsletters catchy names to spark employee interest and to inject a bit of humor into the workplace. Today, most companies distribute their newsletters online. For example, IBM's employee communications typically are available through the company's intranet, known internally as W3, and it has led a transformation from professional to user-generated content within the company.[33]

Managers can use impersonal written communication for various messages, including announcements of rules, regulations, policies, newsworthy information, changes in procedures, and the arrival of new organizational members. Impersonal written communication also can convey instructions about how to use machinery or how to process work orders or customer requests. For these kinds of messages, the paper or electronic trail left by this communication medium can be valuable for employees.

information overload The potential for important information to be ignored or overlooked while tangential information receives attention.

Just as with personal written communication, impersonal written communication can be delivered and retrieved electronically, and this is increasingly the case in companies large and small. Unfortunately, the ease with which electronic messages can spread has led to their proliferation. Many managers' and workers' electronic inboxes are so backlogged that often they do not have time to read all the electronic work-related information available to them. The problem with such **information overload** is the potential for important information to be ignored or overlooked (even that which is personally addressed) while tangential information receives attention. Moreover, information overload can result in thousands of hours and millions of dollars in lost productivity.

blog A website on which an individual, a group, or an organization posts information, commentary, and opinions and to which readers can often respond with their own commentary and opinions.

social networking site A website that enables people to communicate with others with whom they have some common interest or connection.

Some managers and organizations use blogs to communicate with employees, investors, customers, and the general public. A **blog** is a website on which an individual, a group, or an organization posts information, commentary, and opinions and to which readers can often respond with their own commentary and opinions. Some top managers write their own blogs, and some companies such as Disney, Dell, Zillow, and Marriott have corporate blogs.[34]

A **social networking site** such as Instagram, Facebook, Twitter, YouTube, or LinkedIn enables people to communicate with others with whom they might have some common personal or professional interest or connection. Billions of people in the United States and around the world create custom profiles and communicate with networks of other participants through these sites. While communication through social networks may be work related, some managers are concerned that employees are wasting time at work communicating with their personal group of acquaintances through these sites. A recent study found that 77% of workers use social media at work, and the average employee spends 12% of their working hours using unproductive social media applications.[35]

Communication Networks

LO16-4 Describe the communication networks that exist in groups and teams.

communication networks The pathways along which information flows in groups and teams and throughout the organization.

Although various communication media are used, communication in organizations tends to flow in certain patterns. The pathways along which information flows in groups and teams and throughout an organization are called **communication networks**. The type of communication network that exists in a group depends on the nature of the group's tasks and the extent to which group members need to communicate with one another to achieve group goals.

Communication Networks in Groups and Teams

As you learned in Chapter 15, groups and teams, whether they are cross-functional teams, top management teams, command groups, self-managed work teams, or task forces, are the building blocks of organizations. Four kinds of communication networks can develop in groups and teams: the wheel, the chain, the circle, and the all-channel network (see Figure 16.3).

WHEEL NETWORK In a wheel network, information flows to and from one central member of the group. Other group members do not need to communicate with one another to perform at a high level, so the group can accomplish its goals by directing all communication to and from the central member. Wheel networks are often found in command groups with pooled task interdependence. Picture a group of taxi drivers who report to the same dispatcher, who is also their supervisor. Each driver needs to communicate with the dispatcher, but the drivers do not need to communicate with one another. In groups such as this, the wheel network results in efficient communication, saving time without compromising performance. Although found in groups, wheel networks are not found in teams because they do not allow the intense interactions characteristic of teamwork.

CHAIN NETWORK In a chain network, members communicate with one another in a predetermined sequence. Chain networks are found in groups with sequential task interdependence, such as assembly-line groups. When group work has to be performed in a predetermined order, the chain network is often found because group members need to communicate with those whose work directly precedes and follows their own. Like wheel networks, chain networks tend not to exist in teams because of the limited amount of interaction among group members.

CIRCLE NETWORK In a circle network, group members communicate with others who are similar to them in experiences, beliefs, areas of expertise, background, office location, or even where they sit when the group meets. Members of task forces and standing committees, for example, tend to communicate with others who have similar experiences or backgrounds.

Figure 16.3

Communication Networks in Groups and Teams

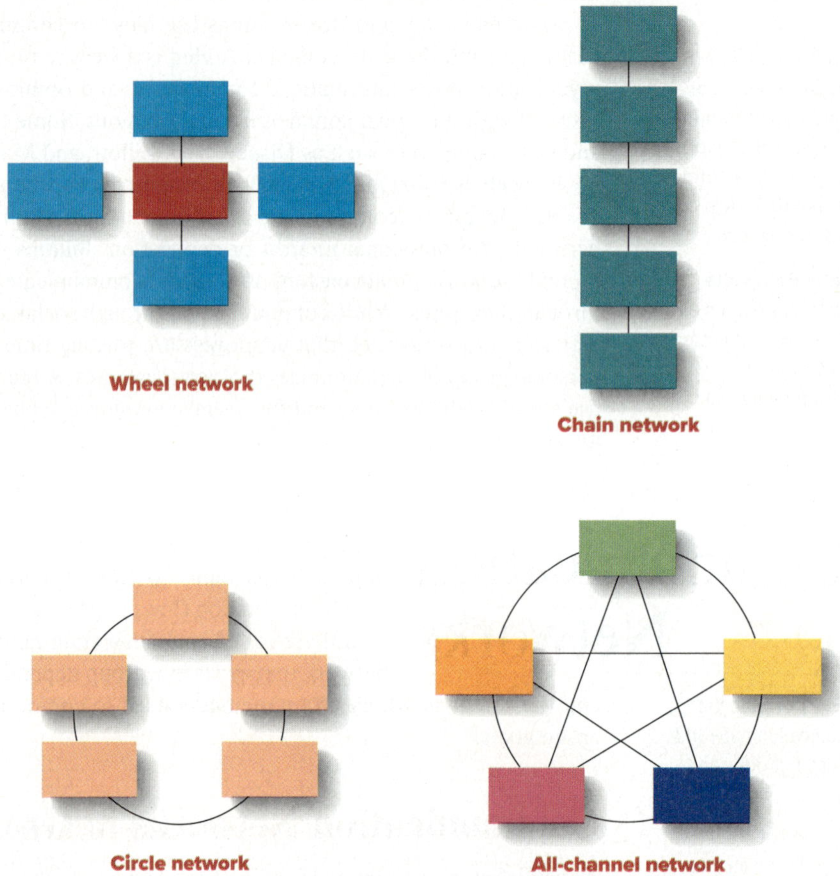

People also tend to communicate with those whose offices are next to their own. Like wheel and chain networks, circle networks are most often found in groups that are not teams.

ALL-CHANNEL NETWORK An all-channel network is found in teams. It is characterized by high levels of communication: Every team member communicates with every other team member. Top management teams, cross-functional teams, and self-managed work teams often have all-channel networks. The reciprocal task interdependence often found in such teams requires that information flows in all directions. Software designed for use by work groups can help maintain effective communication in teams with all-channel networks because it gives team members an efficient way to share information.

Organizational Communication Networks

An organization chart may seem to be a good summary of an organization's communication network, but often it is not. An organization chart summarizes the *formal* reporting relationships in an organization and the formal pathways along which communication takes place. Often, however, communication is *informal* and flows around issues, goals, projects, and ideas instead of moving up and down the organizational hierarchy in an orderly fashion. Thus, an organization's communication network includes not only the formal communication pathways summarized in an organization chart but also informal communication pathways along which a great deal of communication takes place (see Figure 16.4).

Communication can and should occur across departments and groups as well as within them and up and down and sideways in the corporate hierarchy. Communication up and down the corporate hierarchy is often called *vertical* communication. Communication among

Figure 16.4

Formal and Informal Communication Networks in an Organization

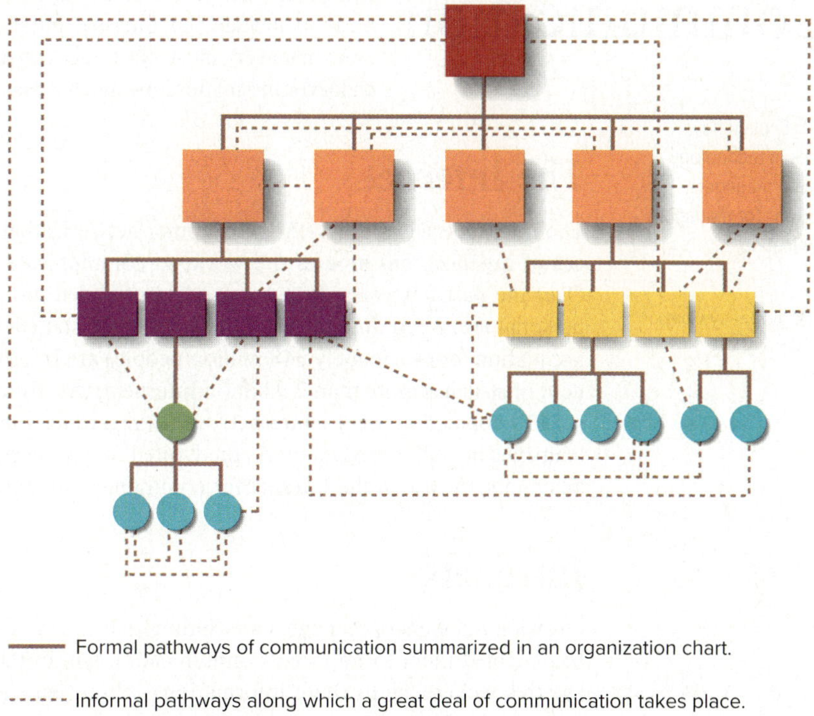

employees at the same level in the hierarchy, or sideways, is called *horizontal* communication. Managers obviously cannot determine in advance what an organization's communication network will be, nor should they try to. Instead, to accomplish goals and perform at a high level, organizational members should be free to communicate with whomever they need to contact. Because organizational goals change over time, so do organizational communication networks. Informal communication networks can contribute to an organization's competitive advantage, because they help ensure that organizational members have the information they need when they need it to accomplish their goals.

grapevine An informal communication network along which unofficial information flows.

The **grapevine** is an informal organizational communication network along which unofficial information flows quickly, if not always accurately.[36] People in an organization who seem to know everything about everyone are prominent in the grapevine. Information spread over the grapevine can be about issues of either a business nature (such as an impending merger) or a personal nature (such as the CEO's separation from his wife).

External Networks

In addition to participating in networks within an organization, managers, professional employees, and those with work-related ties outside their organization often are part of external networks whose members span a variety of companies. For example, scientists working in universities and corporations often communicate in networks formed around common underlying interests in a particular topic or subfield. As another example, physicians working throughout the country belong to specialty professional associations that help them keep up-to-date on the latest advances in their fields. For some managers and professionals, participation in such interest-oriented networks is as important as, or even more important than, participation in internal company networks. Networks of contacts who are working in the same discipline or field or who have similar expertise and knowledge can be very helpful, for example, when one wants to change jobs, recruit top talent to the organization, locate new suppliers, or find a new job after a layoff.

Technology and Communication

Advances in technology have dramatically increased managers' abilities to communicate with others as well as to quickly access information to make decisions. Advances that are having major impacts on managerial communication include the Internet, intranets, and collaboration software. However, managers must not forget that communication is essentially a human endeavor, no matter how much it may be facilitated by technology.

LO16-5 Explain how advances in technology have given managers new options for managing communication.

The Internet

Internet A global system of computer networks.

The **Internet** is a global system of computer networks that is easy to join and is used by employees of organizations around the world to communicate inside and outside their companies. Over the past few years, Internet use has exploded around the world, both for business and personal use. According to recent Internet usage statistics, nearly 95% of the North American population (approximately 348 million people) are Internet users. In sheer numbers, the continent of Asia has more than 2.9 billion Internet users. Across the globe, nearly 70% of the entire world's population use the Internet.[37] With regard to competitiveness in the digital era, the top countries in 2022 were Denmark, the United States, Sweden, Singapore, and Switzerland.[38] By all counts, the use of the Internet for communication continues to expand.

Intranets

intranet A companywide system of computer networks.

Growing numbers of managers are finding that the technology on which the Internet is based has enabled them to improve communication within their own companies. These managers use this technology to share information within their own companies through company networks called **intranets**.

Intranets allow employees to have many kinds of information at their fingertips. Directories, manuals, inventory figures, product specifications, information about customers, biographies of top managers and the board of directors, global sales figures, meeting minutes, annual reports, delivery schedules, and up-to-the-minute revenue, cost, and profit figures are just a few examples of the information that can be shared through intranets. Intranets can be accessed with different kinds of computers so that all members of an organization can be linked together. Intranets are protected from unwanted intrusions–of hackers or competitors–by firewall security systems that ask users to provide passwords and other identification before they are allowed access.

The advantage of intranets lies in their versatility as a communication medium. They can be used for a number of different purposes by people who may have little expertise in computer software and programming. While some managers complain that the Internet is too crowded, informed managers are realizing that using the Internet's technology to create their own computer networks may be one of the Internet's biggest contributions to organizational effectiveness.

Collaboration Software

collaboration software Programs that promote and facilitate collaborative, highly interdependent interactions and provide an electronic meeting site for communication among team members.

For an organization to gain a competitive advantage, managers need to keep up-to-date on advances in technology. **Collaboration software** aims to promote collaborative, highly interdependent interactions among members of a team and to provide the team with an electronic meeting site for communication. Collaboration software gives team members an online work site where they can post, share, and save data, reports, sketches, and other documents; keep calendars; have team-based online conferences; and send and receive messages. The software can also keep and update progress reports, survey team members about various issues, forward documents to managers, and let users know which of their team members are also online and at the site. Having an integrated online work area can help organize and centralize the work of a team, help ensure that information is readily available as needed, and help team members make sure important information is not overlooked.

Collaboration software can be much more efficient than email or instant messaging for managing ongoing team collaboration and interaction that is not face-to-face. Moreover, when a team does meet face-to-face, all documents the team might need in the meeting are just a click away. For work that is truly team-based, that entails a number of highly interdependent yet distinct components, and that involves team members with distinct areas of expertise who need to closely coordinate their efforts, collaboration software can be a powerful communication tool. There are many collaboration apps currently being used by managers and their employees when it comes to project management, workflow management, and overall productivity and messaging processes. Several of the more popular programs include Zoho Projects, Slack, and Basecamp, all of which can be customized and used in coordination with other programs such as Smartsheets.[39] When adopting collaborative tools to improve team and company performance, managers must continue to consider how the tools in question might improve communication, recognizing they are not replacements for face-to-face communication.

Communication Skills for Managers

LO16-6 Describe important communication skills that managers need as senders and as receivers of messages and why it is important to understand differences in linguistic styles.

Some of the barriers to effective communication in organizations have their origins in senders. Communication suffers when messages are unclear, incomplete, or difficult to understand; when they are sent over an inappropriate medium; or when no provision for feedback is made. Other communication barriers have their origins in receivers. When receivers pay no attention to or do not listen to messages or when they make no effort to understand the meaning of a message, communication is likely to be ineffective. Sometimes advanced technology, such as automated phone systems, can hamper effective communication to the extent that the human element is missing.

To overcome these barriers and effectively communicate with others, managers (as well as other organizational members) must possess or develop certain communication skills. Some of these skills are particularly important when managers *send* messages; others are critical when managers *receive* messages. These skills help ensure that managers will be able to share information, will have the information they need to make good decisions and take action, and will be able to reach a common understanding with others.

Communication Skills for Managers as Senders

Organizational effectiveness depends on the ability of managers (as well as other organizational members) to effectively send messages to people both inside and outside the organization. Table 16.1 summarizes seven communication skills that help ensure that when managers send messages, they are properly understood and the transmission phase of the communication process is effective. Let's see what each skill entails.

SEND CLEAR AND COMPLETE MESSAGES Managers need to learn how to send a message that is clear and complete. A message is clear when it is easy for the receiver to understand and interpret, and it is complete when it contains all the information the sender and receiver need to reach a common understanding. In striving to send messages that are both clear and complete, managers must learn to anticipate how receivers will interpret messages and must adjust them to eliminate sources of misunderstanding or confusion.

Table 16.1
Seven Communication Skills for Managers as Senders of Messages

- Send messages that are clear and complete.
- Encode messages in symbols that the receiver understands.
- Select a medium that is appropriate for the message.
- Select a medium that the receiver monitors.
- Avoid filtering and information distortion.
- Ensure that a feedback mechanism is built into messages.
- Provide accurate information to ensure that misleading rumors are not spread.

Clear and complete messages include any nonverbal components. Messages are unclear if the tone of voice does not match the content of the words. Likewise, as described in the "Management Insight" feature, a person's nonverbal cues are very important when the manager is first meeting the person they are communicating with.

MANAGEMENT INSIGHT

Make Sure That First Impression Counts

Many business and daily life situations involve introducing yourself to others. Some examples are job interviews, first meetings with customers or clients, and presentations to a group including strangers. In these contexts, a first impression carries a great deal of weight. What the other person observes in the first few seconds will shape how the person interprets the communicator and the message.[40]

Managers cannot control every aspect of a first impression. They cannot overcome prejudices by changing their sex, race, or age, and they cannot change their facial features. But there are other ways to communicate a message of being trustworthy and agreeable.[41]

Facial expressions matter. A relaxed and smiling face is appealing. However, it is important to be consistent and sincere, not just flashing a smile when making eye contact. As for eye contact, it is necessary for building trust in a business context. Some experts suggest looking in the other person's eyes during 60–70% of the interaction. Those who are uncomfortable making prolonged eye contact can practice by looking at the other person's eyebrows or space between the eyes until eye contact feels more natural.[42]

Posture and gestures make a difference as well. People tend to respond well to erect but not stiff posture, with hands visible and arms uncrossed. Taking a minute to slow one's breathing, stand firmly, and think confident thoughts can help. Then, while talking, the speaker can increase trust by leaning in a little toward the other person. Also, researchers have found greater appeal in presentations where the presenters used more hand gestures to emphasize points. In the same way, shaking hands firmly is a gesture that builds rapport.[43]

Making a good first impression carries a great deal of weight in both business and personal situations.
Monkeybusinessimages/Getty Images

Clothing also plays a role. Those seeking to make a good first impression should, within their means, seek clothes that fit well in a flattering style and are suitable for the situation. At a minimum, it is essential to be clean and neat.[44]

First impressions include verbal communication, too. One way to make a positive and lasting impression is to greet people with questions that demonstrate a genuine interest. For example, if appropriate for the situation, a person might ask, "What has been the highlight of your day so far?" or "Has anything exciting been happening in your life?"[45] And then, of course, the questioner should listen carefully to the answer.

ENCODE MESSAGES IN SYMBOLS THE RECEIVER UNDERSTANDS Managers need to appreciate that when they encode messages, they should use symbols or language that the receiver understands. When sending messages in English to receivers whose native language is not English, for example, it is important to use common vocabulary and to avoid clichés and idioms that, when translated, may make little sense or are either comical or insulting. **Jargon**, specialized language that members of an occupation, a group, or an organization develop to facilitate communication among themselves, should never be used when communicating with people outside the occupation, group, or organization.

jargon Specialized language that members of an occupation, group, or organization develop to facilitate communication among themselves.

SELECT A MEDIUM APPROPRIATE FOR THE MESSAGE As you have learned, when relying on verbal communication, managers can choose from a variety of communication media, including in-person communication, written letters, memos, newsletters, phone conversations, email, voice mail, and videoconferences. When choosing among these media, managers need to take into account the level of information richness required, the time constraints, and the need for a paper or electronic trail. A primary concern in choosing an appropriate medium is the nature of the message. Is it personal, important, nonroutine, or likely to be misunderstood and in need of further clarification? If it is, face-to-face communication is likely to be in order.

SELECT A MEDIUM THE RECEIVER MONITORS Another factor that managers need to take into account when selecting a communication medium is whether the medium is one that the receiver monitors. Managers differ in the communication media they pay attention to. Many managers simply select the medium they themselves use the most and are most comfortable with, but doing this can lead to ineffective communication. Managers who dislike telephone conversations and too many face-to-face interactions may prefer to use email, send many email messages per day, and check their own email often. Managers who prefer to communicate with people in person or over the phone may have email addresses but are less likely to respond to email messages. No matter how much a manager likes email, sending email to someone who does not respond to email is futile. Learning which managers like things in writing and which prefer face-to-face interactions and then using the appropriate medium enhances the chance that receivers will actually receive and pay attention to messages.

A related consideration is whether receivers have disabilities that hamper their ability to decode certain messages. A receiver with a loss of vision, for example, cannot read a written message. Managers should ensure that employees with disabilities have resources available to communicate effectively with others.[46]

filtering Withholding part of a message because of the mistaken belief that the receiver does not need or will not want the information.

AVOID FILTERING AND INFORMATION DISTORTION **Filtering** occurs when a sender withholds part of a message because they mistakenly think the receiver does not need the information or will not want to receive it. Filtering can occur at all levels in an organization and in both vertical and horizontal communication. Workers may filter messages they send to first-line managers, first-line managers may filter messages to middle managers, and middle managers may filter messages to top managers. Such filtering is most likely to take place when messages contain bad news or problems that employees are afraid they will be blamed for. Managers need to hear bad news and be aware of problems as soon as they occur so they can take swift steps to rectify the problem and limit the damage it may have caused.

Some filtering takes place because of internal competition in organizations or because organizational members fear their power and influence will be diminished if others have access to some of their specialized knowledge. By increasing levels of trust in an organization, taking steps to motivate all employees (and the groups and teams they belong to) to work together to achieve organizational goals, and ensuring that employees realize that when the organization reaches its goals and performs effectively, they will benefit as well, this kind of filtering can be reduced.

information distortion Changes in the meaning of a message as the message passes through a series of senders and receivers.

Information distortion occurs when the meaning of a message changes as the message passes through a series of senders and receivers. Some information distortion is accidental—due to faulty encoding and decoding or to a lack of feedback. Other information distortion is deliberate. Senders may alter a message to make themselves or their groups look good and to receive special treatment.

Managers themselves should avoid filtering and distorting information. But how can they eliminate these barriers to effective communication throughout their organizations? They need to establish trust throughout the organization. Employees who trust their managers believe they will not be blamed for things beyond their control and will be treated fairly. Managers who trust their employees give them clear and complete information and do not hold things back.

INCLUDE A FEEDBACK MECHANISM IN MESSAGES Because feedback is essential for effective communication, managers should build a feedback mechanism into the messages they send. They should either include a request for feedback or indicate when and how they will follow up on the message to make sure it was received and understood. When managers write letters and memos or send faxes, they can request that the receiver respond with comments and suggestions in a letter, memo, or fax; schedule a meeting to discuss the issue; or follow up with a phone call. By building feedback mechanisms such as these into their messages, managers ensure that they have been heard and are understood.

rumors Unofficial pieces of information of interest to organizational members but with no identifiable source.

PROVIDE ACCURATE INFORMATION **Rumors** are unofficial pieces of information of interest to organizational members but with no identifiable source. Rumors spread quickly once they are started, and usually they concern topics that organizational members think are important, interesting, or amusing. Rumors, however, can be misleading and can harm individual employees and their organizations when they are false, malicious, or unfounded. Managers can halt the spread of misleading rumors by giving organizational members accurate information about matters that concern them.

Providing accurate information is especially important in tough economic times like the recent global pandemic, in which some employees were laid off and others were sent home to work remotely. When managers give employees accurate information, this can help reduce their stress levels as well as motivate them to find ways to help their companies weather challenging times.[47] Moreover, when business turns around, employees who received accurate information from their bosses may be more likely to remain with their organizations rather than pursue other opportunities.

Communication Skills for Managers as Receivers

Managers receive as many messages as they send. Thus, managers must possess or develop communication skills that allow them to be effective receivers. Table 16.2 summarizes three of these important skills, which we examine here in greater detail.

PAY ATTENTION Because of their multiple roles and tasks, managers often are overloaded and forced to think about several things at once. Pulled in many different directions, they sometimes do not pay sufficient attention to the messages they receive. To be effective, however, managers should always pay attention to messages they receive, no matter how busy they are. When discussing a project with an employee, for example, an effective manager focuses on the project, not on an upcoming meeting with their own boss. Similarly, when managers are reading written communication, they should focus on understanding what they are reading; they should not be sidetracked into thinking about other issues.

BE A GOOD LISTENER Managers (and all other members of an organization) can do several things to be good listeners. First, managers should refrain from interrupting senders in the middle of a message so that senders do not lose their train of thought and managers do not jump to erroneous conclusions based on incomplete information. Second, managers should maintain eye contact with senders so that senders feel their listeners are paying attention; doing this also helps managers focus on what they are hearing. Third, after receiving a message, managers should ask questions to clarify points of ambiguity or confusion. Fourth, managers should paraphrase, or restate in their own words, points senders make that are important, complex, or open to alternative interpretations; this is the feedback component so critical to successful communication.

Managers, like most people, often like to hear themselves talk rather than listen to others. Part of being a good communicator, however, is being a good listener–an essential communication skill for managers as receivers of messages transmitted face-to-face and over the telephone.

Table 16.2

Three Communication Skills for Managers as Receivers of Messages

- Pay attention.
- Be a good listener.
- Be empathetic.

BE EMPATHETIC Receivers are empathetic when they try to understand how the sender feels and try to interpret a message from the sender's perspective, rather than viewing the message from only their own point of view. For example, the chief psychologist in a public school system in the Northwest learned this lesson after interacting with a new psychologist on staff. The new psychologist was distraught after meeting with the parent of a child they had been working with extensively. The parent was argumentative, difficult to talk to, and unsupportive of their own child. The psychologist told the chief psychologist how upset they were, and the chief psychologist responded by reminding the new psychologist that they were a professional and that dealing with such situations was part of the job. This feedback from their supervisor further upset the new psychologist and caused them to storm out of the room.

In hindsight, the chief psychologist realized that the response to the employee had been inappropriate. They had failed to empathize with the new psychologist, who had spent so much time with the child and was deeply concerned about the child's well-being. Rather than dismissing the new psychologist's concerns, the chief psychologist realized they should have tried to understand how the employee felt and given them some support and advice for dealing positively with the situation.

Understanding Linguistic Styles

Consider the following scenarios:

- A manager from New York is having a conversation with a manager from Iowa City. The Iowa City manager never seems to get a chance to talk. He keeps waiting for a pause to signal his turn to talk, but the New York manager never pauses long enough. The New York manager wonders why the Iowa City manager does not say much. He feels uncomfortable when he pauses and the Iowa City manager says nothing, so he starts talking again.
- Elizabeth compliments Bob on his presentation to upper management and asks Bob what he thought of her presentation. Bob launches into a lengthy critique of Elizabeth's presentation and describes how he would have handled it differently. This is hardly the response Elizabeth expected.
- Catherine shares with co-members of a self-managed work team a new way to cut costs. Michael, another team member, thinks her idea is a good one and encourages the rest of the team to support it. Catherine is quietly pleased by Michael's support. The group implements "Michael's" suggestion, and it is written up as such in the company newsletter.
- Robert was recently promoted and transferred from his company's Oklahoma office to its headquarters in New Jersey. Robert is perplexed because he never seems to get a chance to talk in management meetings; someone else always seems to get the floor. Robert's new boss wonders whether Robert's new responsibilities are too much for him, although Robert's supervisor in Oklahoma rated him highly and said he is a real "go-getter." Robert is timid in management meetings and rarely says a word.

linguistic style A person's characteristic way of speaking.

What do these scenarios have in common? Essentially, they all describe situations in which a misunderstanding of linguistic styles leads to a breakdown in communication. The scenarios are based on the research of linguist Deborah Tannen, who describes **linguistic style** as a person's characteristic way of speaking. Elements of linguistic style include tone of voice, speed, volume, use of pauses, directness or indirectness, choice of words, credit taking, and use of questions, jokes, and other manners of speech.[48] When people's linguistic styles differ and these differences are not understood, ineffective communication is likely.

The first and last scenarios illustrate regional differences in linguistic style.[49] The Iowa City manager and Robert from Oklahoma expect the pauses that signal turn taking in conversations to be longer than the pauses made by their colleagues in New York and New Jersey. This difference causes communication problems. The Iowan and transplanted Oklahoman think their Eastern colleagues never let them get a word in edgewise, and the Easterners cannot figure out why their colleagues from the Midwest and South do not get more actively involved in conversations.

Differences in linguistic style can be a particularly insidious source of communication problems because linguistic style is often taken for granted. People rarely think about their own linguistic styles and often are unaware of how linguistic styles can differ. In the example

Cross-cultural differences in linguistic style can lead to misunderstandings in business meetings and other communications.
MIXA/Getty Images

here, Robert did not realize that when dealing with his New Jersey colleagues, he could and should jump into conversations more quickly than he used to do in Oklahoma, and his boss never realized that Robert felt he was not being given a chance to speak in meetings.

The aspect of linguistic style just described, length of pauses, differs by region in the United States. Much more dramatic differences in linguistic style occur cross-culturally.

CROSS-CULTURAL DIFFERENCES Cultural differences play an important role in both verbal and nonverbal communication. Some cultures prefer an indirect method of communication while others prefer a direct style. For example, high-context cultures–typically those found in Asia, South America, and Arab countries–tend to communicate indirectly, talking around the point they're trying to make. Low-context cultures–those found in the United States, German, Scandinavia, and Australia–tend to communicate directly, valuing the content of the message and getting to the point quickly.[50] In addition, a nonverbal gesture such as eye contact is very important to individuals from low-context cultures when communicating with others, while those from high-context cultures tend to avoid eye contact because it is viewed as aggressive and impolite.[51]

Managers from Japan tend to be more formal in their conversations and more deferential toward upper-level managers and people with high status than are managers from the United States. Japanese managers do not mind extensive pauses in conversations when they are thinking things through or when they think further conversation might be detrimental. In contrast, U.S. managers (even managers from regions of the United States where pauses tend to be long) find lengthy pauses disconcerting and feel obligated to talk to fill the silence.[52]

Another cross-cultural difference in linguistic style concerns the appropriate physical distance separating speakers and listeners in business-oriented conversations.[53] The distance between speakers and listeners is greater in the United States, for example, than it is in Brazil or Saudi Arabia. Citizens of different countries also vary in how direct or indirect they are in conversations and the extent to which they take individual credit for accomplishments. Japanese culture, with its collectivist, or group, orientation, tends to encourage linguistic styles in which group rather than individual accomplishments are emphasized. The opposite tends to be true in the United States.

These and other cross-cultural differences in linguistic style can and often do lead to misunderstandings. For example, when a team of American managers presented a proposal for a joint venture to Japanese managers, the Japanese managers were silent as they thought about the implications of what they had just heard. The American managers took this silence as a sign that the Japanese managers wanted more information, so they went into more detail about the proposal. When they finished, the Japanese were silent again, not only frustrating the Americans but also making them wonder whether the Japanese were interested in the project. The American managers suggested that if the Japanese already had decided they did not want to pursue the project, there was no reason for the meeting to continue. The Japanese were bewildered. They were trying to carefully think out the proposal, yet the Americans thought they were not interested!

Communication misunderstandings and problems like this can be overcome if managers learn about cross-cultural differences in linguistic styles. If the American managers and the Japanese managers had realized that periods of silence are viewed differently in Japan and in the United States, their different linguistic styles might have been less troublesome barriers to communication. Before managers communicate with people from abroad, they should try to find out as much as they can about the aspects of linguistic style that are specific to the country or culture in question. Expatriate managers who have lived in the country in question for an extended time can be good sources of information about linguistic styles because they are likely to have experienced firsthand some of the differences that citizens of a country are not aware of. Finding out as much as possible about cultural differences also can help managers learn about differences in linguistic styles because the two are often closely linked.

GENDER DIFFERENCES In the four scenarios that open this section, you may be wondering why Bob launched into a lengthy critique of Elizabeth's presentation after she paid him a routine compliment on his presentation, or you may be wondering why Michael got the credit for Catherine's idea in the self-managed work team. Research conducted by Tannen and other linguists has found that the linguistic styles of men and women differ in practically every culture or language.[54] Men and women take their own linguistic styles for granted and thus do not realize when they are talking with someone of a different gender that differences in their styles may lead to ineffective communication.

In the United States, women tend to downplay differences between people, are not overly concerned about receiving credit for their own accomplishments, and want to make everyone feel more or less on an equal footing so that even poor performers or low-status persons feel valued. Men, in contrast, tend to emphasize their own superiority and are not reluctant to acknowledge differences in status. These differences in linguistic style led Elizabeth to routinely compliment Bob on his presentation even though she thought he had not done a particularly good job. She asked him how her presentation was so he could reciprocate and give her a routine compliment, putting them on an equal footing. Bob took Elizabeth's compliment and question about her own presentation as an opportunity to confirm his superiority, never realizing that all she was expecting was a routine compliment. Similarly, Michael's enthusiastic support for Catherine's cost-cutting idea and her apparent surrender of ownership of the idea after she described it led team members to assume incorrectly that the idea was Michael's.[55]

Do some women try to prove they are better than everyone else, and are some men unconcerned about taking credit for ideas and accomplishments? Of course. The gender differences in linguistic style that Tannen and other linguists have uncovered are general tendencies evident in *many* women and men, not in *all* women and men.

Where do gender differences in linguistic style come from? Tannen suggests they begin developing in early childhood. Girls and boys tend to play with children of their own gender, and the ways in which girls and boys play are quite different. Girls play in small groups, engage in a lot of close conversation, emphasize how similar they are to one another, and view boastfulness negatively. Boys play in large groups, emphasize status differences, expect leaders to emerge who boss others around, and give one another challenges to try to meet. These differences in styles of play and interaction result in different linguistic styles when boys and girls grow up and communicate as adults. The ways in which men communicate emphasize status differences and play up relative strengths; the ways in which women communicate emphasize similarities and downplay individual strengths.[56]

Interestingly, gender differences are also turning up in how women and men use email and electronic forms of communication. For example, Susan Herring, a researcher at Indiana University, has found that in public electronic forums such as message boards and chat rooms, men tend to make stronger assertions, be more sarcastic, and be more likely to use insults and profanity than women, whereas women are more likely to be supportive, agreeable, and polite.[57] David Silver, a researcher at the University of Washington, has found that women are more expressive electronic communicators and encourage others to express their thoughts and feelings, while men are briefer and more to the point.[58] Interestingly enough, some men find email to be a welcome way to express their feelings to people they care about. For example, real estate broker Mike Murname finds it easier to communicate with, and express his love for, his grown children via email.[59]

MANAGING DIFFERENCES IN LINGUISTIC STYLES Managers should not expect to change people's linguistic styles and should not try to. To be effective, managers need to understand differences in linguistic styles. Knowing, for example, that some women are reluctant to speak up in meetings, not because they have nothing to contribute but because of their linguistic style, should lead managers to ensure that these women have a chance to talk. And a manager who knows certain people are reluctant to take credit for ideas can be careful to give credit where it is deserved. As Tannen points out, "Talk is the lifeblood of managerial work, and understanding that different people have different ways of saying what they mean will make it possible to take advantage of the talents of people with a broad range of linguistic styles."[60]

Summary and Review

LO16-1, 16-2 **COMMUNICATION AND MANAGEMENT** Communication is the sharing of information between two or more individuals or groups to reach a common understanding. Good communication is necessary for an organization to gain a competitive advantage. Communication occurs in a cyclical process that entails two phases: transmission and feedback.

LO16-3 **INFORMATION RICHNESS AND COMMUNICATION MEDIA** Information richness is the amount of information a communication medium can carry and the extent to which the medium enables the sender and receiver to reach a common understanding. Four categories of communication media, in descending order of information richness, are face-to-face communication (includes videoconferences), electronically transmitted spoken communication (includes voice mail), personally addressed written communication (includes email), and impersonal written communication (includes corporate newsletters and blogs).

LO16-4 **COMMUNICATION NETWORKS** Communication networks are the pathways along which information flows in an organization. Four communication networks found in groups and teams are the wheel, the chain, the circle, and the all-channel network. An organization chart summarizes formal pathways of communication, but communication in organizations is often informal, as is true of communication through the grapevine.

LO16-5 **TECHNOLOGY AND COMMUNICATION** The Internet is a global system of computer networks that managers around the world use to communicate within and outside their companies. Intranets are internal communication networks that managers can create to improve communication, performance, and customer service. Intranets use the same technology that the Internet is based on. Collaboration software enables members of groups and teams to share information with one another to improve their communication and performance.

LO16-6 **COMMUNICATION SKILLS FOR MANAGERS** There are various barriers to effective communication in organizations. To overcome these barriers and effectively communicate with others, managers must possess or develop certain communication skills. As senders of messages, managers should send messages that are clear and complete, encode messages in symbols the receiver understands, choose a medium that is appropriate for the message and is monitored by the receiver, avoid filtering and information distortion, include a feedback mechanism in the message, and provide accurate information to ensure that misleading rumors are not spread. Communication skills for managers as receivers of messages include paying attention, being a good listener, and being empathetic. Understanding linguistic styles is also an essential communication skill for managers. Linguistic styles can vary by geographic region, gender, and country or culture. When these differences are not understood, ineffective communication can occur.

Management in Action

Topics for Discussion and Action

Discussion

1. Which medium (or media) do you think would be appropriate for each of the following kinds of messages that an employee could receive from their boss: (a) a raise, (b) not receiving a promotion, (c) an error in a report prepared by the employee, (d) additional job responsibilities, and (e) the schedule for company holidays for the upcoming year? Explain your choices. [LO16-3]
2. Discuss the pros and cons of using the Internet for communication within and between organizations. [LO16-1, 16-2, 16-3, 16-5]
3. How can collaboration software help managers and their teams communicate more efficiently? [LO16-5]
4. Why do some managers find it difficult to be good listeners? [LO16-6]
5. Explain why employees might filter and distort information about problems and performance shortfalls when communicating with their bosses. What steps can managers take to eliminate filtering and information distortion? [LO16-6]
6. Explain why differences in linguistic style, when not understood by message senders and receivers, can lead to ineffective communication. [LO16-6]

Action

7. Interview a manager in an organization in your community to determine with whom they communicate on a typical day, what communication media they use, and which typical communication problems the manager experiences. [LO16-1, 16-2, 16-3, 16-4, 16-5, 16-6]

Building Management Skills

Diagnosing Ineffective Communication [LO16-1, 16-2, 16-3, 16-4, 16-5, 16-6]

Think about the last time you experienced very ineffective communication with another person—someone you work with, a classmate, a friend, or a member of your family. Describe the incident. Then answer the following questions:

1. Why was your communication ineffective in this incident?
2. What stages of the communication process were particularly problematic, and why?
3. Describe any filtering or information distortion that occurred.
4. Do you think differences in linguistic styles adversely affected the communication that took place? Why or why not?
5. How could you have handled this situation differently so communication would have been effective?

Managing Ethically [LO16-3, 16-5]

Many employees use their company's Internet connections and email systems to visit websites and send personal email and instant messages.

Questions

1. Either individually or in a group, explore the ethics of using an organization's Internet connection and email system for personal purposes at work and while away from the office. Should employees have some rights to use this resource? When does their behavior become unethical?
2. Some companies track how their employees use the company's Internet connection and email system. Is it ethical for managers to read employees' personal email or to record websites that employees visit? Why or why not?

Small Group Breakout Exercise

Reducing Resistance to Advances in Technology [LO16-5]

Form groups of three or four people, and appoint one member as the spokesperson who will communicate your findings to the class when called on by the instructor. Then discuss the following scenario:

You are a team of managers in charge of information and communication in a large consumer products corporation. Your company has already implemented many advances in technology. Managers and workers have access to email, the Internet, your company's own intranet, and collaboration software.

Many employees use the technology, but the resistance of some is causing communication problems. A case in point is the use of collaboration software. Many teams in your organization have access to collaboration software and are encouraged to use it. While some teams welcome this communication tool and actually have made suggestions for improvements, others are highly resistant to sharing documents in their teams' online workspaces.

Although you do not want to force people to use the technology, you want them to at least try it and give it a chance. You are meeting today to develop strategies for reducing resistance to the new technologies.

1. One resistant group of employees is made up of top managers. Some of them seem computer-phobic and are highly resistant to sharing information online, even with sophisticated security precautions in place. What steps will you take to get these managers to have more confidence in electronic communication?
2. A second group of resistant employees consists of middle managers. Some middle managers resist using your company's intranet. Although these managers do not resist the technology per se and do use electronic communication for multiple purposes, they seem to distrust the intranet as a viable way to communicate and get things done. What steps will you take to get these managers to take advantage of the intranet?
3. A third group of resistant employees is made up of members of groups and teams who do not want to use the collaborative software tools that have been provided to them. You think the tools could improve their communication and performance, but they seem to think otherwise. What steps will you take to get these members of groups and teams to start using the collaborative tools?

Be the Manager [LO16-1, 16-2, 16-3, 16-6]

You supervise support staff for an online company that sells furniture over the Internet. You always thought that you needed to expand your staff, and just when you were about to approach your boss with such a request, business slowed. Thus, your plan to try to add new employees to your staff is on hold.

However, you have noticed a troubling pattern of communication with your staff. Ordinarily, when you want a staff member to work on a task, you email that employee the pertinent information. For the last few months, your email requests have gone unheeded, and your employees seem to respond to your requests only after you visit them in person and give them a specific deadline. Each time they apologize for not getting to the task sooner but say they are so overloaded with requests that they sometimes even stop reviewing and answering their emails. Unless someone asks for something more than once, your staff seems to feel the request is not that urgent and can be put on hold. You think this state of affairs is dysfunctional and could lead to serious problems down the road. Also, you are starting to realize that your employees seem to have no way of prioritizing tasks—hence, some very important projects you asked them to complete were put on hold until you followed up with them about the tasks. Knowing you cannot add employees to your staff in the short term, what are you going to do to improve communication with your overloaded staff?

Case in the News [LO16-1, 16-2, 16-6]

ExxonMobil Rides a Communication Wave in Turbulent Waters

In the oil industry, demand can swing abruptly in either direction at any time. The industry also faces public pressure to address climate change, along with the impacts of a global pandemic and Russia's invasion of Ukraine. For managers, uncertainty and change on this scale make communication effectiveness critical. Managers must communicate with their employees and investors about how the company intends to weather change. Neither group likes to be caught by surprise, and the company will suffer if employees lose faith and quit or if investors lose faith and take their money elsewhere.

ExxonMobil has been whipsawed by these changes. In 2020, when COVID-19 began its rapid spread, petroleum prices plummeted as the economy contracted and commuters started working from home. Exxon posted its greatest loss ever and borrowed money to help pay dividends to investors. To contain costs during a cycle of low demand, Exxon's managers prepared a strategy of reduced spending on capital projects.

Exxon's low-spending approach included staff reductions. The company announced in 2020 that it would reduce its workforce by 14,000 during the following year. At the same time, performance reviews would identify 5 to 10% of the lowest-performing employees, who would be tasked with improving their performance. Although the performance reviews were not strictly for workforce reduction, those who fell short were candidates for layoffs. Reducing the workforce would enable additional savings from closing two office towers near Houston and relocating the employees to the main Houston-area campus. In an email message to employees, Exxon CEO Darren Woods said, "We look forward to bringing our teams together and having them collaborate."

Despite the positive tone of Woods's message, voluntary employee departures at Exxon rose during this period of job cuts. Woods held a town hall meeting to bring his message to employees in person. He called on them to be encouraged by the changes being made and to see those actions as putting Exxon on a new and better path after 2020's troubling loss. In addition, he said the company was evaluating the use of salary increases to retain employees. (It later announced raises averaging 3.6% for its nonunion employees.) But when employees asked about the causes of employees quitting, Woods said they should view the departures in the context of the overall high turnover among employees as Exxon emerges from the pandemic-related recession.

One year later, demand had surged in a fast-rebounding economy, and oil prices quickly rebounded to pre-pandemic levels. Then Russia invaded Ukraine, and the resulting disruption in oil supplies sent prices skyrocketing. Even so, Exxon, like other large oil companies, announced to investors that it had no plans to increase capital spending. Instead, it would use earnings to pay off debt—a decision expected to appeal to investors looking for strong financial results in the short term. Opening new rigs to pump oil is a costly process for meeting long-term demand. As long as managers were uncertain about whether a new coronavirus variant would slam the brakes on the economy, they preferred to remain cautious. Even after 2021 turned out to be a growth year, the company announced to investors that it would continue budgeting conservatively over the next five years.

Like other high-level executives, Woods represents the company to outsiders such as investors and society at large. Woods recently shifted from his predecessors' reluctance to discuss climate change. He acknowledged that society is seeking alternative sources of energy and said Exxon was working on addressing that demand and hoped to someday be able to keep its emissions of greenhouse gases below the amount it removes from the atmosphere by capturing and burying carbon dioxide. This sets a high bar for Exxon, which has invested heavily in deep-water oil exploration and shale drilling.

These announcements came at a time when Exxon was feeling pressure from some investors who want companies to move away from fossil fuels. At the company's 2021 board meeting, investors voted to appoint three of these "activist investors" to Exxon's board of directors. Exxon's management needs a response to board members who say demand for fossil fuels is not sustainable in the long run, so companies need to pursue other avenues of growth. Following the vote, the company announced it would add a climate expert to its board of directors. And at the end of the year, Exxon announced a strong return to profitability—and a goal of achieving net-zero greenhouse gas emissions from its operations by 2050.

Questions for Discussion

1. Based on the examples given, how does managers' communication with employees and investors support Exxon's strategy (or interfere with it)?
2. What communication media are described in the case? What, if any, other media would you recommend that Exxon managers use for these messages?
3. Suggest two ways CEO Woods could improve his communication effectiveness.

Sources: D. Blackmon, "ExxonMobil Strives to Please Everyone in New Strategic Plan," *Forbes*, www.forbes.com, accessed February 6, 2023; J. Strasburg, C. M. Matthews, and E. Glazer, "How Oil Giants' Bets on Russia, Years in the Making, Crumbled in Days," *The Wall Street Journal*, www.wsj.com, March 7, 2022; J. Lee, "Exxon Mobil's Gusher of Cash Means Harder Decisions Ahead," *The Wall Street Journal*, www.wsj.com, February 1, 2022; C. Krauss, "Exxon Sets a 2050 Goal for Net-Zero Greenhouse Gas Emissions," *The New York Times*, www.nytimes.com, January 18, 2022; K. Crowley, "Exxon Plans Below-Inflation U.S. Pay Raises Despite Banner Year," *Bloomberg*, www.bloomberg.com, December 2, 2021; C. M. Matthews, "Exxon to Continue Leaner Spending as Covid-19 Threat Lingers," *The Wall Street Journal*, www.wsj.com, December 1, 2021; K. Crowley, "Exxon CEO Floats Pay Hikes to Combat 'Major' Employee Attrition," *Bloomberg*, www.bloomberg.com, October 25, 2021; K. Crowley, "Exxon to Shutter Two Houston Office Towers after Worker Exodus," *Bloomberg*, www.bloomberg.com, October 22, 2021; J. Lee, "Exxon Can't Catch a Break," *The Wall Street Journal*, www.wsj.com, July 30, 2021; C. M. Matthews, "Exxon, Chevron Report Billions in Profits But Plan to Keep Spending Tight," *The Wall Street Journal*, www.wsj.com, July 30, 2021; J. Hiller and S. Khan, "Angst at Exxon as Managers Begin Employee Performance Reviews," *Reuters*, www.reuters.com, June 21, 2021; C. Krauss and P. Eavis, "Activist Wins Battle to Join Exxon's Board," *The New York Times*, www.nytimes.com, May 27, 2021; C. Krauss, "The Chief of Exxon Mobil Shifts His Tone on Emissions," *The New York Times*, www.nytimes.com, March 4, 2021.

Notes

1. K. Baskin, "Digital Body Language for the Post-Pandemic Era," *MIT Technology Review*, www.technologyreview.com, accessed February 5, 2023; E. Dhawan, "Seeing Yourself on Screen," *Marketing News*, Summer 2021, 6–7; E. Dhawan, "Did You Get My Slack/Email/Text?" *Harvard Business Review*, https://hbr.org, May 7, 2021.
2. Baskin, "Digital Body Language for the Post-Pandemic Era"; L. Scheier, "Through a Screen Darkly," *Publisher's Weekly*, May 10, 2021, 26–27.
3. Dhawan, "Did You Get My Slack?"; Scheier, "Through a Screen Darkly."
4. E. Dhawan, "The 3 Biggest Signs of 'Passive Aggressive' and 'Childish Behavior': Harvard-Trained Body Language Expert," *CNBC*, www.cnbc.com, September 27, 2022; H. Mitchell, "Why You Shouldn't Use Emojis in Work Messages," *The Wall Street Journal*, www.wsj.com, November 27, 2021; J. Fantozzi, "Cotential CEO Erica Dhawan on How We Need to Change Communication in the Age of Connectional Intelligence," *Nation's Restaurant News*, www.nrn.com, October 8, 2020.
5. Baskin, "Digital Body Language for the Post-Pandemic Era"; Dhawan, "Did You Get My Slack?"; Dhawan, "Seeing Yourself on Screen."
6. C.A. O'Reilly and L.R. Pondy, "Organizational Communication," in S. Kerr, ed., *Organizational Behavior* (Columbus, OH: Grid, 1979).
7. Betterworks, "Employee Engagement" and "Insight & Analytics," www.betterworks.com, accessed February 5, 2023.
8. E.M. Rogers and R. Agarwala-Rogers, *Communication in Organizations* (New York: Free Press, 1976).
9. N. McDermott, "6 Types of Nonverbal Communication, What They Mean and How to Spot Them," *Forbes*, www.forbes.com, January 19 2023; "Listening to Nonverbal Cues," https://listenlikealawyer.com, accessed March 17, 2020.
10. N. Zandan, "How Much of Our Workdays Do We Spend Communicating?" *Quantified Communications*, www.quantifiedcommunications.com, accessed March 17, 2020.
11. S. Reinberg, "A Key Thing Doctors Can Do to Reduce Hospital Errors," *CBS News*, www.cbsnews.com, accessed April 20, 2018.
12. A.W. Brooks and L.K. John, "The Surprising Power of Questions," *Harvard Business Review*, May–June 2018, 60–67; S. Shellenbarger, "How to Gain Power at Work When You Have None," *The Wall Street Journal*, www.wsj.com, March 6, 2018.
13. K. Eikenberry, "The Mess of Discussion and the Magic of Dialogue," *TD*, January 2018, 48–53.
14. Brooks and John, "The Surprising Power of Questions."
15. Shellenbarger, "How to Gain Power at Work"; Ken Sterling, "How You Can Use Honesty to Be a Great Boss," *Inc.*, www.inc.com, April 16, 2018.
16. R.L. Daft, R.H. Lengel, and L.K. Trevino, "Message Equivocality, Media Selection, and Manager Performance: Implications for Information Systems," *MIS Quarterly* 11 (1987), 355–66; R.L. Daft and R.H. Lengel, "Information Richness: A New Approach to Managerial Behavior and Organization Design," in B.M. Staw and L.L. Cummings, eds., *Research in Organizational Behavior* (Greenwich, CT: JAI Press, 1984).
17. R.L. Daft, *Organization Theory and Design* (St. Paul, MN: West, 1992).
18. A. Simonian, "How COVID-19 Has Changed Workplace Communications," *Insight for Professionals*, www.insightforprofessionals.com, August 4, 2022.
19. Daft, *Organization Theory and Design*.
20. C.K. Goman, "Has Technology Killed Face-to-Face Communication?" *Forbes*, www.forbes.com, accessed March 17, 2020.
21. N. Dixon, "Combining Virtual and Face-to-Face Work," *Harvard Business Review*, https://hbr.org, accessed March 17, 2020.
22. D. Hassell, "Management by Weekly Check-In Is the New 'Wandering Around,'" *Entrepreneur*, www.entrepreneur.com, June 9, 2016.
23. E. A. Almazora, "How VoIP Technology Prevented a Mass Work Stoppage," *Market Scale*, https://marketscale.com, accessed February 5, 2023; "Video Interview Guide: Tips for a Successful Interview," *Indeed*, www.indeed.com, accessed February 5, 2023; K. Gurchiek, "Small Businesses Get Creative to Survive during the Pandemic," *Society for Human Resource Management*, www.shrm.org, September 19, 2020.
24. E. Goldberg, "Better.com's Founder Returns as C.E.O. after Firing 900 Workers on Zoom," *The New York Times*, www.nytimes.com, January 18, 2022; J. Pisani, "Better.com CEO to Take Time Off after Zoom Firings," *The Wall Street Journal*, www.wsj.com, December 10, 2021.
25. Pisani, "Better.com CEO to Take Time Off."
26. J. Pisani, "The CEO Who Fired 900 People on Zoom Is Back," *The Wall Street Journal*, www.wsj.com, January 19, 2022; J. Bote, "Better.com CEO Vishal Garg to Be Reinstated after Mass Zoom Layoff Controversy," *SFGate*, www.sfgate.com, January 19, 2022.

27. "Vishal Garg-Led Better.com to Cover Insurance for Sacked Expecting Parents," *Mint,* www.livemint.com, March 11, 2022; C. Furst and J. Calfas, "Better.com to Lay Off More Employees—This Time Not on Zoom," *The Wall Street Journal,* www.wsj.com, March 8, 2022.
28. The Radicati Group, "Email Statistics Report, 2022–2026," www.radicati.com, accessed February 5, 2023.
29. A. Blackman, "The Smartest Ways to Use Email at Work," *The Wall Street Journal,* www.wsj.com, accessed March 18, 2020.
30. L. Paulise, "The 2022 Status of Remote Work and Top Future Predictions," *Forbes,* www.forbes.com, December 8, 2022.
31. M. Bose, "How to Communicate Effectively over Emails at Workplace," *Entrepreneur,* www.entrepreneur.com, accessed March 18, 2020.
32. S.M. Heathfield, "Company Internet and Email Policy Sample," *The Balance Careers,* www.thebalancecareers.com, November 22, 2019.
33. "Three Major Internal Communication Trends for 2016 According to IBM," www.orteccommunications.com, January 12, 2016; S. Rodenbaum, "IBM: Communication and Curation Go Hand in Hand," *Forbes,* www.forbes.com, accessed April 30, 2015.
34. Evolve Media, "15 Excellent Corporate Blogs to Learn From," https://evolvemedia.com, accessed February 5, 2023.
35. C. Kolmar, "30 Surprising Social Media at Work Statistics [2023]: What Every Manager Should Know," *Zippia,* www.zippia.com, February 2, 2023.
36. O.W. Baskin and C.E. Aronoff, *Interpersonal Communication in Organizations* (Santa Monica, CA: Goodyear, 1989).
37. "Internet Usage Statistics: World Internet Users and 2023 Population Stats," www.internetworldstats.com, accessed February 6, 2023.
38. P. Taylor, "Digital Competitiveness Rankings by Country Worldwide 2022," *Statista,* www.statista.com, December 22, 2022.
39. J. Duffy, "The Best Online Collaboration Software for 2023," *PC Magazine,* www.pcmag.com, January 11, 2023.
40. C. Sun, "The Science of the First Impression: Five Elements of a Great First Impression," *Entrepreneur,* www.entrepreneur.com, accessed March 18, 2020; S. Shellenberger, "The Mistakes You Make in a Meeting's First Milliseconds," *The Wall Street Journal,* www.wsj.com, January 30, 2018; V. Van Edwards, "How to Hack a First Impression," *Entrepreneur,* May 2017, 46–48.
41. C. DesMarais, "12 Tips on How to Make a Great First Impression, According to Executives," *Inc.,* www.inc.com, accessed March 18, 2020.
42. Sun, "The Science of the First Impression."
43. Schellenberger, "The Mistakes You Make."
44. DesMarais, "12 Tips on How to Make a Great First Impression."
45. Van Edwards, "How to Hack a First Impression"; Sun, "The Science of the First Impression."
46. D. Zielinski, "New Assistive Technologies Aid Employees with Disabilities," Society for Human Resource Management, www.shrm.org, accessed March 18, 2020.
47. A. Mendy, M. L. Stewart, and K. Van Akin, "A Leader's Guide: Communicating with Teams, Stakeholders, and Communities during COVID-19," *McKinsey and Company,* www.mckinsey.com, accessed February 6, 2023.
48. D. Tannen, "The Power of Talk," *Harvard Business Review,* September–October 1995, 138–48; D. Tannen, *Talking from 9 to 5* (New York: Avon Books, 1995).
49. Tannen, "The Power of Talk."
50. E.T. Hall, *Beyond Culture* (New York: Anchor Books, 1989).
51. M. de Mooji, *Human and Mediated Communication Around the World* (New York: Springer, 2014).
52. R. Bernstein, "7 Cultural Differences in Nonverbal Communication," https://pointpark.edu, November 28, 2017.
53. Ibid.
54. Tannen, "The Power of Talk"; C. Wakslak and P. Joshi, "Research: Men Speak More Abstractly Than Women," *Harvard Business Review,* https://hbr.org, December 2, 2022.
55. Ibid.; Tannen, *Talking from 9 to 5.*
56. Organisation for Economic Co-operation and Development, "Bridging the Digital Divide," www.oecd.org, accessed March 18, 2020.
57. J. Cohen, "He Writes, She Writes," *Houston Chronicle,* July 7, 2001, C1–C2.
58. Ibid.
59. Ibid.
60. Tannen, "The Power of Talk," 148.

CHAPTER 17

Managing Conflict, Politics, and Negotiation

Thomas Barwick/Getty Images

Learning Objectives

After studying this chapter, you should be able to:

LO17-1 Explain why conflict arises, and identify the types and sources of conflict in organizations.

LO17-2 Describe conflict management strategies that managers can use to resolve conflict effectively.

LO17-3 Understand the nature of negotiation and why integrative bargaining is more effective than distributive negotiation.

LO17-4 Describe ways in which managers can promote integrative bargaining in organizations.

LO17-5 Explain why managers need to be attuned to organizational politics, and describe the political strategies that managers can use to become politically skilled.

A MANAGER'S CHALLENGE

Daymond John: From FUBU to the Sharks

How do managers effectively negotiate and influence people? Negotiations and influence play a central role in Daymond John's career as a business founder, investor, and motivational speaker. As a young man in New York City, John started the FUBU clothing line, of which he is the CEO. He later accepted an offer to be a "Shark," or potential investor, on the *Shark Tank* TV show. Along the way, he has built a wide-ranging network of friends and contacts through his curiosity and willingness to mentor others.[1]

John started FUBU in his working-class neighborhood in New York's borough of Queens. In 1992, he taught himself to make a hat like one he saw in a music video, and he began selling the hats outside a local mall. The hats sold briskly, so he extended the product line, hired trusted friends, and came up with a meaningful brand: FUBU stands for "For Us, By Us," expressing John's and his neighbors' pride in their culture. John and his friends marketed through their relationships with local stores and by visiting sets of music videos, where hip-hop artists accepted FUBU merchandise to wear on camera. Despite the initial sales, 27 banks turned down John's request to borrow money for expansion.[2]

FUBU turned the corner when LL Cool J wore a FUBU hat in a commercial filmed for Gap, rapping lyrics that happened to include the phrase "for us, by us." Then John's mother posted a newspaper ad, "Millions of dollars in orders. Need financing," and Samsung's textile division was one of 33 respondents. Samsung offered to provide financing if FUBU could earn $5 million over three years, a goal the company surpassed within months. FUBU's sales peaked in 1998, at $350 million. Now John's role at FUBU involves mainly negotiating partnership and licensing deals.[3]

John's networking crosses economic classes and has provided him with life lessons and many opportunities to share them. Near the start of his career, executive coach Jay Abraham told him that ideas and opportunities can come from anything, so John spends much of each day meeting and listening to others. This approach to life also contributes to his resilience when he, as a Black man, encounters racist behavior. John interprets such behavior

Negotiations and influence play a central role in Daymond John's career as a business founder, investor, and motivational speaker.
Efren Landaos/SOPA Images/Sipa USA/Alamy Stock Photo

as hurting the perpetrator because it limits one's exposure to new perspectives. Other mentors have revealed that struggles and mistakes are a normal part of business and a learning opportunity.[4]

When John received an offer to appear on *Shark Tank*, his first instinct was to decline because any investment he made would have to come from his own assets. On further reflection, John concluded that investing was an opportunity: Others work to build a business while he shares his hard-earned knowledge. On *Shark Tank*, John now negotiates deals in which he is the investor. Any offer he makes is only the beginning of the investor's relationship with an entrepreneur. John formed a company, Shark Group, through which he and others consult with the businesses he funds. The group also has negotiated sponsorships and recruited donors for an annual Black Entrepreneurs Day featuring motivational talks and grants to start-ups.[5]

Today, as a public speaker and mentor, John shares what he has learned about influencing others and negotiating deals. He advises displaying confidence, based on knowing about one's own motivation and business and the negotiation partner's goals. He encourages negotiators to see the process as the start of a relationship in which they have conversations to learn what each party can offer and whether the deal can benefit both.[6]

Overview

Successful leaders, such as Daymond John profiled in "A Manager's Challenge," can effectively use their power to influence others and to manage conflict to achieve win-win solutions. In Chapter 14, we described how managers, as leaders, influence other people to achieve group and organizational goals and how managers' sources of power enable them to exert such influence. In this chapter, we describe why managers need to develop the skills necessary to manage organizational conflict, politics, and negotiation if they are going to be effective and achieve their goals.

We describe conflict and the strategies managers can use to resolve it effectively. We discuss one major conflict resolution technique, negotiation, in detail, outlining the steps managers can take to be good negotiators. Then we discuss the nature of organizational politics and the political strategies managers can use to maintain and expand their power and use it effectively. By the end of this chapter, you will appreciate why managers must develop the skills necessary to manage these important organizational processes if they are to be effective and achieve organizational goals.

Organizational Conflict

LO17-1 Explain why conflict arises, and identify the types and sources of conflict in organizations.

organizational conflict The discord that arises when the goals, interests, or values of different individuals or groups are incompatible and those individuals or groups block or thwart one another's attempts to achieve their objectives.

Organizational conflict is the discord that arises when the goals, interests, or values of different individuals or groups are incompatible and those individuals or groups block or thwart one another's attempts to achieve their objectives.[7] Conflict is an inevitable part of organizational life because the goals of different stakeholders such as managers and workers are often incompatible. Organizational conflict also can exist between departments and divisions that compete for resources or even between managers who may be competing for promotion to the next level in the organizational hierarchy.

Not surprisingly, the current business environment continues to evolve at a rapid pace, which intensifies the existence of conflict throughout various parts of any organization. Factors often cited for why finely tuned conflict resolution skills are essential for today's managers include (1) increased pressure on organizations to change and adapt quickly to maintain competitive advantage; (2) increased diversity due to global business expansion, which may cause more conflict; (3) intense use of technology and flexible working arrangements that have reduced face-to-face communications among supervisors, employees, senior management, and business colleagues, which may increase the opportunity for misunderstanding and communication gaps; and (4) increased conflict among members of self-managed teams, who are now making decisions previously the responsibility of other managers in the organization. All of these factors, among others, require greater conflict resolution and negotiation skills at all levels of the organization.[8]

It is important for managers to develop the skills necessary to manage conflict effectively. In addition, the level of conflict present in an organization has important implications for

Figure 17.1

The Effect of Conflict on Organizational Performance

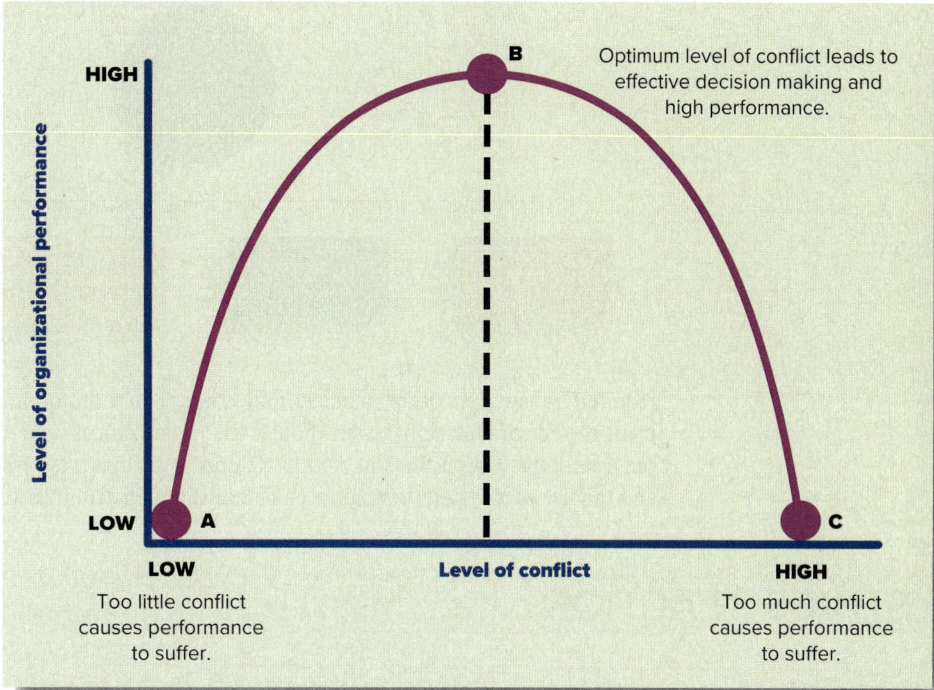

organizational performance. Figure 17.1 illustrates the relationship between organizational conflict and performance. At point A, there is little or no conflict, and organizational performance suffers. Lack of conflict in an organization often signals that managers emphasize conformity at the expense of new ideas, resist change, and strive for agreement rather than effective decision making. As the level of conflict increases from point A to point B, organizational effectiveness is likely to increase. When an organization has an optimum level of conflict, managers are likely to be open to, and encourage, a variety of perspectives; look for ways to improve organizational functioning and effectiveness; and view debates and disagreements as a necessary ingredient of effective decision making and innovation. As the level of conflict increases from point B to point C, conflict escalates to the point where organizational performance suffers. When an organization has a dysfunctionally high level of conflict, managers are likely to waste organizational resources to achieve their own ends, to be more concerned about winning political battles than about doing what will lead to a competitive advantage for their organizations, and to try to get even with their opponents rather than make good decisions.

Conflict is a force that needs to be managed rather than eliminated.[9] Managers should never try to eliminate all conflict but, rather, should try to keep conflict at a moderate and functional level to promote change efforts that benefit the organization. Additionally, managers should strive to keep conflict focused on substantive, task-based issues and minimize conflict based on personal disagreements and animosities. To manage conflict, managers must understand the types and sources of conflict and be familiar with strategies that can be effective in dealing with it.[10]

Types of Conflict

There are several types of conflict in organizations: interpersonal, intragroup, intergroup, and interorganizational (see Figure 17.2).[11] Understanding how these types differ can help managers deal with conflict.

INTERPERSONAL CONFLICT Interpersonal conflict is conflict between individual members of an organization, occurring because of differences in their goals or values. Two managers may experience interpersonal conflict, for example, when their values concerning protection of the environment differ. One manager may argue that the organization should do only what is

Figure 17.2

Types of Conflict in Organizations

required by law. The other manager may counter that the organization should invest in equipment to reduce emissions, even though the organization's current level of emissions is below the legal limit. The "Ethics in Action" feature describes ways this kind of conflict can play out and the use of a system to channel such conflict constructively.

ETHICS IN ACTION

Giving Voice to Values

Organization members often see financial goals as conflicting with values. For example, profits might seem to conflict with protecting the environment or offering health insurance to part-time employees. When trade-offs are assumed, ethical decisions tend to boil down to the minimum legal standard or personal opinions about who is moral. Such thinking tends to shut down creativity and can escalate a choice into a divisive personality conflict.[12]

Business professor Mary Gentile wanted to promote more thoughtful conversations, so she developed a method she calls Giving Voice to Values (GVV). According to Gentile, GVV starts not with choosing sides for a debate, but with an invitation to identify the underlying values that underlie each perspective on the issue. This exercise tends to unearth some shared values. Then GVV asks decision makers not *whether* to perform an action, but assuming they perform a given action, *how* they could do so in a way that succeeds while upholding shared values. Ideally, this gets the parties thinking about how they can move forward without compromising their principles. It thus focuses on actions, not personalities.[13]

In practice, GVV is more than questions. Like other decision processes, it involves gathering evidence, building a coalition of support, rehearsing a presentation of the idea, and explaining expected benefits. Thus, GVV involves the same care in presenting an ethics argument as one would use with the financial return on an investment decision.[14]

John Heiser learned about GVV while he was working on his doctorate degree and applied it to his work as president and chief operating officer of Magnetrol, which makes systems for controlling flow and volume in manufacturing. As a former corporate attorney, Heiser appreciates the way GVV brings together business methods with the company's values. In one situation at Magnetrol, salespeople wanted to change the standard sales agreement in a way that would be inconsistent with the company's values. The administrative assistant who was asked to make this change recognized the issue. Having been trained in GVV, she prepared her message and took her concerns first to the salespeople, then to their supervisor, and finally to Heiser. He agreed with her, overruled the change, and explained it to the sales team. GVV gave the whole group a chance to discuss the issue in terms of shared corporate values without blame or punishment. In this and other situations, Magnetrol's use of GVV has nurtured a culture of reflection, rather than one of personal attacks.[15]

INTRAGROUP CONFLICT Intragroup conflict arises within a group, team, or department. When members of the marketing department in a clothing company disagree about how they should spend budgeted advertising dollars for a new line of designer jeans, they are experiencing intragroup conflict. Some of the members want to spend all the money on advertisements in magazines; others want to devote half of the money to ads on social media platforms like Instagram and Twitter.

INTERGROUP CONFLICT Intergroup conflict occurs between groups, teams, or departments. R&D departments, for example, sometimes experience intergroup conflict with production departments. Members of the R&D department may develop a new product that they think production can make inexpensively by using existing manufacturing capabilities. Members of the production department, however, may disagree and believe that the costs of making the product will be much higher. Managers of departments usually play a key role in managing intergroup conflicts such as this.

INTERORGANIZATIONAL CONFLICT Interorganizational conflict arises across organizations. Sometimes interorganizational conflict occurs when managers in one organization feel that another organization is not behaving ethically and is threatening the well-being of certain stakeholder groups. Interorganizational conflict also can occur between government agencies and corporations.

Sources of Conflict

Conflict in organizations springs from a variety of sources. The ones we examine here are different goals and time horizons, overlapping authority, task interdependencies, different evaluation or reward systems, scarce resources, and status inconsistencies (see Figure 17.3).[16]

DIFFERENT GOALS AND TIME HORIZONS Recall from Chapter 10 that an important managerial activity is organizing people and tasks into departments and divisions to accomplish an organization's goals. Almost inevitably this grouping creates departments and divisions that have different goals and time horizons, and the result can be conflict. Production managers, for example, usually concentrate on efficiency and cost cutting; they have a relatively short time horizon and focus on producing quality goods or services in a timely and efficient manner. In contrast, marketing managers focus on sales and responsiveness to customers. Their time horizon is longer than that of production because they are trying to be responsive

Figure 17.3
Sources of Conflict in Organizations

Conflict in organizations can arise from a variety of sources, including specific goals and timelines put forth by different departments.
fizkes/Shutterstock

not only to customers' needs today but also to their changing needs in the future to build long-term customer loyalty. These fundamental differences between marketing and production often breed conflict.

Suppose production is behind schedule in its plan to produce a specialized product for a key customer. The marketing manager believes the delay will reduce sales of the product and therefore insists that the product be delivered on time even if saving the production schedule means increasing costs by paying production workers overtime. The production manager says they will happily schedule overtime if marketing will pay for it. Both managers' positions are reasonable from the perspective of their own departments, and conflict is likely.

OVERLAPPING AUTHORITY When two or more managers, departments, or functions claim authority for the same activities or tasks, conflict is likely.[17] This is precisely what happened when heirs of the Forman liquor distribution company, based in Washington, DC, inherited the company from their parents. One of the heirs, Barry Forman, wanted to control the company and was reluctant to share power with the other heirs. Several of the heirs felt they had authority over certain tasks crucial to Forman's success (such as maintaining good relationships with the top managers of liquor companies). What emerged was a battle of wills and considerable conflict, which escalated to the point of being dysfunctional, requiring that the family hire a consulting firm to help resolve it.[18]

TASK INTERDEPENDENCIES Have you ever been assigned a group project for one of your classes and had one group member who consistently failed to get things done on time? This probably created some conflict in your group because other group members were dependent on the late member's contributions to complete the project. Whenever individuals, groups, teams, or departments are interdependent, the potential for conflict exists.[19] With differing goals and time horizons, the managers of marketing and production come into conflict precisely because the departments are interdependent. Marketing is dependent on production for the goods it markets and sells, and production is dependent on marketing to create demand for the things it makes.

DIFFERENT EVALUATION OR REWARD SYSTEMS How interdependent groups, teams, or departments are evaluated and rewarded can be another source of conflict.[20] Production managers, for example, are evaluated and rewarded for their success in staying within budget or lowering costs while maintaining quality. So they are reluctant to take any steps that will increase costs, such as paying workers high overtime rates to finish a late order for an important customer. Marketing managers, in contrast, are evaluated and rewarded for their success in generating sales and satisfying customers. So they often think overtime pay is a small price to pay for responsiveness to customers. Thus, conflict between production and marketing is rarely unexpected.

SCARCE RESOURCES Management is the process of acquiring, developing, protecting, and using the resources that allow an organization to be efficient and effective (see Chapter 1). When resources are scarce, management is more difficult and conflict is likely.[21] For example, divisional managers may be in conflict over who has access to financial capital, and organizational members at all levels may be in conflict over who gets raises and promotions.

STATUS INCONSISTENCIES The fact that some individuals, groups, teams, or departments within an organization are more highly regarded than others in the organization can also create conflict. In some restaurants, for example, the chefs have relatively higher status than the people who wait on tables. Nevertheless, the chefs receive customers' orders from the waitstaff, and the waitstaff can return to the chefs food that their customers or they think is not acceptable. This status inconsistency–high-status chefs taking orders from low-status waitstaff—can be the source of considerable conflict between chefs and the waitstaff. For this reason, many restaurants require the waitstaff to input food orders directly into an electronic system via iPad or another type of mobile device, thereby reducing the amount of direct ordering from the waitstaff to the chef.[22]

Conflict Management Strategies

LO17-2 Describe conflict management strategies that managers can use to resolve conflict effectively.

If an organization is to achieve its goals, managers must be able to resolve conflicts in a functional manner. *Functional conflict resolution* means the conflict is settled by compromise or by collaboration between the parties in conflict (later in the chapter, we discuss other typically less functional ways in which conflicts are sometimes resolved).[23] **Compromise** is possible when each party is concerned about not only its own goal accomplishment but also the goal accomplishment of the other party and is willing to engage in a give-and-take exchange and to make concessions until a reasonable resolution of the conflict is reached. **Collaboration** is a way of handling conflict in which the parties try to satisfy their goals without making any concessions but, instead, come up with a way to resolve their differences that leaves them both better off.[24]

compromise A way of managing conflict in which each party is concerned about not only its own goal accomplishment but also the goal accomplishment of the other party and is willing to engage in a give-and-take exchange and make concessions.

collaboration A way of managing conflict in which both parties try to satisfy their goals by coming up with an approach that leaves them better off and does not require concessions on issues that are important to either party.

accommodation A conflict-handling approach in which one party, typically with weaker power, gives in to the demands of the other, typically more powerful party.

avoidance A conflict-handling approach in which the parties try to ignore the problem and do nothing to resolve their differences.

competition A conflict-handling approach in which each party tries to maximize its own gain and has little interest in understanding the other party's position and arriving at a solution that will allow both parties to achieve their goals.

In addition to compromise and collaboration, there are three other ways in which conflicts are sometimes handled: accommodation, avoidance, and competition.[25] When **accommodation** takes place, one party to the conflict simply gives in to the demands of the other party. Accommodation typically takes place when one party has more power than the other and can pursue its goal attainment at the expense of the weaker party. From an organizational perspective, accommodation is often ineffective: The two parties are not cooperating with each other, they are unlikely to want to cooperate in the future, and the weaker party who gives in or accommodates the more powerful party might look for ways to get back at the stronger party in the future.

When conflicts are handled by **avoidance**, the parties to a conflict try to ignore the problem and do nothing to resolve the disagreement. Avoidance is often ineffective because the real source of the disagreement has not been addressed, conflict is likely to continue, and communication and cooperation are hindered.

Competition occurs when each party to a conflict tries to maximize its own gain and has little interest in understanding the other party's position and arriving at a solution that will allow both parties to achieve their goals. Competition can actually escalate levels of conflict as each party tries to outmaneuver the other. As a way of handling conflict, competition is ineffective for the organization because the two sides to a conflict are more concerned about winning the battle than cooperating to arrive at a solution that is best for the organization and acceptable to both sides. Handling conflicts through accommodation, avoidance, or competition is ineffective from an organizational point of view because the parties do not cooperate with each other and work toward a mutually acceptable solution to their differences.

Another strategy that has been successful in resolving conflict is the problem-solving approach because it focuses on objective outcomes—not individual opinions or views—thus respecting and preserving social relationships within a group. This approach also helps reduce the stress of interpersonal conflict among employees.[26]

When the parties to a conflict are willing to cooperate with each other and devise a solution that each finds acceptable, an organization is more likely to achieve its goals.[27] Conflict management strategies managers can use to ensure that conflicts are resolved in a functional manner focus on individuals and on the organization as a whole. Next we describe four strategies that focus on individuals: increasing awareness of the sources of conflict, increasing diversity awareness and skills, practicing job rotation or temporary assignments, and using permanent transfers or dismissals when necessary. We also describe two strategies that focus on the organization as a whole: changing an organization's structure or culture and directly altering the source of conflict.

STRATEGIES FOCUSED ON INDIVIDUALS

INCREASING AWARENESS OF THE SOURCES OF CONFLICT Sometimes conflict arises because of communication problems and interpersonal misunderstandings. For example, different linguistic styles (see Chapter 16) may lead some men in work teams to talk more and take more credit for ideas than women in those teams. These communication differences can cause conflict when the men incorrectly assume that the women are uninterested or less capable because they participate less, and the women incorrectly assume that the men are bossy and are not interested in their ideas because they seem to do all the talking. By increasing people's awareness of this source of conflict, managers can help resolve conflict functionally. Once men and women realize that the source of their conflict is different linguistic styles, they can take steps to interact with each other more effectively. The men can give the women more chances to provide input, and the women can be more proactive in providing this input.

Sometimes personalities clash in an organization. In these situations, too, managers can help resolve conflicts functionally by increasing organizational members' awareness of the source of their difficulties. For example, some people who are not inclined to take risks may come into conflict with those who are prone to taking risks. The non-risk takers might complain that those who welcome risk propose outlandish ideas without justification, whereas the risk takers might complain that their innovative ideas are always getting shot down. When both types of people are made aware that their conflicts are due to fundamental differences in their ways of approaching problems, they will likely be better able to cooperate in coming up with innovative ideas that entail only moderate levels of risk.

In addition, work teams can get sidetracked when trying to resolve conflict within the group and between individual members. Recent research suggests that one possible approach to dealing with conflict within a work group includes assigning work tasks based on skill and relevance, not necessarily on who volunteers to do the task; acknowledging that team members' ability to compromise is an important, positive step toward reaching the team's overall goal; anticipating possible conflicts and working proactively to resolve them rather than reacting to them; and focusing on evidence-based decisions through analysis rather than getting distracted by conflicting views of individual team members.[28]

INCREASING DIVERSITY AWARENESS AND SKILLS Interpersonal conflicts also can arise because of diversity. Older workers may feel uncomfortable or resentful about reporting to a younger supervisor, a Hispanic worker may feel singled out in a group of non-Hispanic workers, or a female top manager may feel that members of her predominantly male top management team band together whenever one of them disagrees with one of her proposals. Whether or not these feelings are justified, they are likely to cause recurring conflicts.

Many of the techniques described in Chapter 5 for increasing diversity awareness and skills can help managers effectively manage diversity and resolve conflicts that originate in differences among organizational members. The "Focus on DEI&B" feature describes one way interpersonal conflict affects employees of different ages, including measures that managers can take to realize the benefits of a diverse workforce.

FOCUS ON DEI&B

When Experience Becomes a Pitfall

Managers become managers after gaining experience in their field or industry and accomplishing some successes. Upper-level managers often have an impressive record of achievements gained over the course of many years. They rightly see themselves as intelligent. But with greater age and experience comes the risk of falling into a pattern of mistakes. It becomes easy for managers to see themselves as smarter than their younger colleagues and to assume that what led to success in the past will lead there in the future. This attitude can yield poor decisions when circumstances change, and it can create conflict that drives away creative, intelligent younger employees.[29]

Managers can prevent or address this kind of intergenerational conflict by rethinking how they view themselves and their role. A starting point is to notice when younger employees aren't sticking around and when you automatically react to new ideas by criticizing them or thinking the old ways have worked just fine. Instead of jumping to the conclusion that you already know what will work, think about what

Valuing input from a younger, diverse workforce helps experienced managers retain key employees.
Life_imageS/Shutterstock

assumptions are behind that conclusion, and ask how well they apply to the new situation. Taking this to a deeper level, experienced managers can ask themselves why they feel they need to be right and what will happen if someone else's idea is better. Often, managers add the most value through their ability to enable others to reach their full potential.[30]

Besides cultivating an open mind, managers can improve intergenerational relations by inviting employees to contribute fully. Ways to do this include assigning younger colleagues to present ideas on emerging issues or new trends they care about. Another tactic is to react to ideas with interest and open-ended questions rather than objections. In a meeting, when a less-experienced employee volunteers an opinion or idea, praise ideas or at least the effort to speak up, and provide opportunities to investigate the potential of doing things differently.[31]

Practicing inclusiveness begins with recognizing less-experienced employees' strengths. Viewing these employees as having unique perspectives to contribute creates an environment that is engaging for all ages, particularly younger workers, who tend to value coaching. Providing assignments related to employees' strengths enables them to be the best version of themselves as employees, not a clone of their experienced manager. This is gratifying for the employee, better for the organization, and a sign of a wise and effective manager.[32]

PRACTICING JOB ROTATION OR TEMPORARY ASSIGNMENTS Sometimes conflicts arise because individual organizational members simply do not understand the work activities and demands that others in an organization face. A financial analyst, for example, may be required to submit monthly reports to a member of the accounting department. These reports have a low priority for the analyst, who typically turns them in a couple of days late. On each due date the accountant calls the financial analyst, and conflict ensues as the accountant describes in detail why she must have the reports on time and the financial analyst describes everything else he needs to do. In situations such as this, job rotation or temporary assignments, which expand organizational members' knowledge base and appreciation of other departments, can be a useful way of resolving the conflict. If the financial analyst spends some time working in the accounting department, he may appreciate better the need for timely reports. Similarly, a temporary assignment in the finance department may help the accountant realize the demands a financial analyst faces and the need to streamline unnecessary aspects of reporting.

USING PERMANENT TRANSFERS OR DISMISSALS WHEN NECESSARY Sometimes when other conflict resolution strategies do not work, managers need to take more drastic steps, including permanent transfers or dismissals.

Suppose two first-line managers who work in the same department are always at each other's throats; frequent, bitter conflicts arise between them even though they both seem to get along well with other employees. No matter what their supervisor does to increase their understanding of each other, the conflicts keep occurring. In this case the supervisor may want to transfer one or both managers so they do not have to interact as often.

When dysfunctionally high levels of conflict occur among top managers who cannot resolve their differences and understand each other, it may be necessary for one of them to leave the company. This is what happened when Adam Neumann, co-founder and CEO of WeWork, was forced to resign over his unethical behavior while running the communal office space company. Known for his magnetic personality and WeWork's trendy design spaces, Neumann delayed a planned initial public offering (IPO) for the company in late 2019 after Wall Street analysts

Adam Neumann, co-founder of WeWork, was forced to resign due to his unethical behavior while running the communal office space company.
Michael Kovac/Contributor/Getty Images

questioned the company's "real value" after reviewing massive financial losses listed in its IPO filings.[33] WeWork employees and others were furious to learn Japan's SoftBank, a major investor in WeWork, approved Neumann's severance package of $1.7 billion to leave the company.[34]

STRATEGIES FOCUSED ON THE WHOLE ORGANIZATION

CHANGING AN ORGANIZATION'S STRUCTURE OR CULTURE Conflict can signal the need for changes in an organization's structure or culture. Sometimes managers can effectively resolve conflict by changing the organizational structure they use to group people and tasks.[35] As an organization grows, for example, the *functional structure* (composed of departments such as marketing, finance, and production) that was effective when the organization was small may cease to be effective, and a shift to a *product structure* might effectively resolve conflicts (see Chapter 10).

negotiation A method of conflict resolution in which the parties consider various alternative ways to allocate resources to come up with a solution acceptable to all of them.

third-party negotiator An impartial individual with expertise in handling conflicts and negotiations who helps parties in conflict reach an acceptable solution.

mediator A third-party negotiator who facilitates negotiations but has no authority to impose a solution.

arbitrator A third-party negotiator who can impose what they think is a fair solution to a conflict, which both parties are obligated to abide by.

Managers also can effectively resolve conflicts by increasing levels of integration in an organization. Recall from Chapter 15 that Hallmark Cards increased integration by using cross-functional teams to produce new cards. The use of cross-functional teams sped new card development and helped resolve conflicts between departments. Now when a writer and an artist have a conflict over the appropriateness of the artist's illustrations, they do not pass criticisms back and forth from one department to another because they are on the same team and can directly resolve the issue on the spot.

Sometimes managers need to take steps to change an organization's culture to resolve conflict (see Chapter 3). Norms and values in an organizational culture might inadvertently promote dysfunctionally high levels of conflict that are difficult to resolve. For instance, norms that stress respect for formal authority may create conflict that is difficult to resolve when an organization creates self-managed work teams and managers' roles and the structure of authority in the organization change. Values stressing individual competition may make it difficult to resolve conflicts when organizational members need to put others' interests ahead of their own. In circumstances such as these, taking steps to change norms and values can be an effective conflict resolution strategy.

ALTERING THE SOURCE OF CONFLICT When the source of conflict is overlapping authority, different evaluation or reward systems, or status inconsistencies, managers can sometimes effectively resolve the conflict by directly altering its source. For example, managers can clarify the chain of command and reassign tasks and responsibilities to resolve conflicts due to overlapping authority.

Negotiation

LO17-3 Understand the nature of negotiation and why integrative bargaining is more effective than distributive negotiation.

Negotiation is a particularly important conflict resolution technique for managers and other organizational members in situations where the parties to a conflict have approximately equal levels of power. During **negotiation** the parties to a conflict try to come up with a solution acceptable to themselves by considering various alternative ways to allocate resources to each other.[36] Sometimes the sides involved in a conflict negotiate directly with each other. Other times a **third-party negotiator** is relied on. Third-party negotiators are impartial individuals who are not directly involved in the conflict and have special expertise in handling conflicts and negotiations; they are relied on to help the two negotiating parties reach an acceptable resolution of their conflict.[37] When a third-party negotiator acts as a **mediator**, their role in the process is to facilitate an effective negotiation between the two parties; mediators do not force either party to make concessions, nor can they force an agreement to resolve a conflict. **Arbitrators**, on the other hand, are third-party negotiators who can impose what they believe is a fair solution to a dispute, which both parties are obligated to abide by.[38]

In integrative bargaining, conflicts are handled by avoiding a win–lose competitive mindset, and creating a win–win situation for both parties.
moodboard/SuperStock

Distributive Negotiation and Integrative Bargaining

There are two major types of negotiation—distributive negotiation and integrative bargaining. In **distributive negotiation**, the two parties perceive that they have a "fixed pie" of resources they need to divide. They take a competitive, adversarial stance. Each party realizes that they must concede something, but each is out to get the lion's share of the resources.[39] The parties see no need to interact with each other in the future and do not care if their interpersonal relationship is damaged or destroyed by their competitive negotiation.[40] In distributive negotiations, conflicts are handled by competition.

distributive negotiation Adversarial negotiation in which the parties in conflict compete to win the most resources while conceding as little as possible.

integrative bargaining Cooperative negotiation in which the parties in conflict work together to achieve a resolution that is good for them both.

In **integrative bargaining**, the parties perceive that they might be able to increase the resource pie by trying to come up with a creative solution to the conflict. They do not view the conflict competitively as a win-or-lose situation; instead, they view it cooperatively, as a win-win situation in which both parties can gain. Trust, information sharing, and the desire of both parties to achieve a good resolution of the conflict characterize integrative bargaining.[41] In integrative bargaining, conflicts are handled through collaboration and/or compromise.

Consider how Adrian Hofbeck and Joseph Steinberg, partners in a successful German restaurant in the Midwest, resolved their conflict. Hofbeck and Steinberg founded the restaurant 15 years ago, share management responsibilities, and share equally in the restaurant's profits. Hofbeck recently decided that he wanted to retire and sell the restaurant, but retirement was the last thing Steinberg had in mind; he wanted to continue to own and manage the restaurant. Distributive negotiation was out of the question because Hofbeck and Steinberg were close friends and valued their friendship; neither wanted to do something that would hurt the other or their continuing relationship. So they opted for integrative bargaining, which they thought would help them resolve their conflict so both could achieve their goals and maintain their friendship.

Strategies to Encourage Integrative Bargaining

LO17-4 Describe ways in which managers can promote integrative bargaining in organizations.

Managers in all kinds of organizations can rely on five strategies to facilitate integrative bargaining and avoid distributive negotiation: emphasizing superordinate goals; focusing on the problem, not the people; focusing on interests, not demands; creating new options for joint gain; and focusing on what is fair (see Table 17.1).[42] Hofbeck and Steinberg used each of these strategies to resolve their conflict.

EMPHASIZING SUPERORDINATE GOALS *Superordinate goals* are goals that both parties agree to, regardless of the source of their conflict. Increasing organizational effectiveness, increasing responsiveness to customers, and gaining a competitive advantage are just a few of the many superordinate goals that members of an organization can emphasize during integrative bargaining. Superordinate goals help parties in conflict to keep in mind the big picture and the fact that they are working together for a larger purpose or goal despite their disagreements. Hofbeck and Steinberg emphasized three superordinate goals during their bargaining: ensuring that the restaurant continued to survive and prosper, allowing Hofbeck to retire, and allowing Steinberg to remain an owner and manager as long as he wished.

FOCUSING ON THE PROBLEM, NOT THE PEOPLE People who are in conflict may not be able to resist the temptation to focus on the other party's shortcomings and weaknesses,

Table 17.1
Negotiation Strategies for Integrative Bargaining

- Emphasize superordinate goals.
- Focus on the problem, not the people.
- Focus on interests, not demands.
- Create new options for joint gain.
- Focus on what is fair.

thereby personalizing the conflict. Instead of attacking the problem, the parties to the conflict attack each other. This approach is inconsistent with integrative bargaining and can easily lead both parties into a distributive negotiation mode. All parties to a conflict need to keep focused on the problem or on the source of the conflict and avoid the temptation to discredit one another.

Given their strong friendship, this was not much of an issue for Hofbeck and Steinberg, but they still had to be on their guard to avoid personalizing the conflict. Steinberg recalls that when they were having a hard time coming up with a solution, he started thinking that Hofbeck, a healthy 57-year-old, was lazy to want to retire so young: "If only he wasn't so lazy, we would never be in the mess we're in right now." Steinberg never mentioned these thoughts to Hofbeck (who later admitted that sometimes he was annoyed with Steinberg for being such a workaholic) because he realized that doing so would hurt their chances for reaching an integrative solution.

FOCUSING ON INTERESTS, NOT DEMANDS Demands are *what* a person wants; interests are *why* the person wants them. When two people are in conflict, it is unlikely that the demands of both can be met. Their underlying interests, however, can be met, and meeting them is what integrative bargaining is all about.

Hofbeck's demand was that they sell the restaurant and split the proceeds. Steinberg's demand was that they keep the restaurant and maintain the status quo. Obviously, both demands could not be met, but perhaps their interests could be. Hofbeck wanted to be able to retire, invest his share of the money from the restaurant, and live off the returns on the investment. Steinberg wanted to continue managing, owning, and deriving income from the restaurant.

CREATING NEW OPTIONS FOR JOINT GAIN Once two parties to a conflict focus on their interests, they are on the road to achieving creative solutions to the conflict that will benefit them both. This win-win scenario means that rather than having a fixed set of alternatives from which to choose, the two parties can come up with new alternatives that might even expand the resource pie.

Hofbeck and Steinberg came up with three such alternatives. First, even though Steinberg did not have the capital, he could buy out Hofbeck's share of the restaurant. Hofbeck would provide the financing for the purchase, and in return Steinberg would pay him a reasonable return on his investment (the same kind of return he could have obtained had he taken his money out of the restaurant and invested it). Second, the partners could seek to sell Hofbeck's share in the restaurant to a third party under the stipulation that Steinberg would continue to manage the restaurant and receive income for his services. Third, the partners could continue to jointly own the restaurant. Steinberg would manage it and receive a proportionally greater share of its profits than Hofbeck, who would be an absentee owner not involved in day-to-day operations but would still receive a return on his investment in the restaurant.

FOCUSING ON WHAT IS FAIR Focusing on what is fair is consistent with the principle of distributive justice, which emphasizes the fair distribution of outcomes based on the meaningful contributions that people make to organizations (see Chapter 5). It is likely that two parties in conflict will disagree on certain points and prefer different alternatives that each party believes may better serve their own interests or maximize their own outcomes. Emphasizing fairness and distributive justice will help the two parties come to a mutual agreement about what the best solution is to the problem.

Steinberg and Hofbeck agreed that Hofbeck should be able to cut his ties with the restaurant if he chose to do so. They decided to pursue the second alternative described and seek a suitable buyer for Hofbeck's share. They were successful in finding an investor who was willing to buy out Hofbeck's share and let Steinberg continue managing the restaurant. And they remained good friends.

When managers pursue these five strategies and encourage other organizational members to do so, they are more likely to be able to effectively resolve their conflicts through integrative bargaining. These skills result in outcomes that benefit the individual participants and the organization as a whole. Furthermore, managers who learn these skills are well prepared for many practical career challenges, including the negotiation of job offers, as described in the "Manager as a Person" feature. In addition, throughout the negotiation process, managers and other organizational members need to be aware of, and on their guard against, the biases that can lead to faulty decision making (see Chapter 7).[43]

MANAGER AS A PERSON

Negotiating a job offer can be nerve-racking—for both experienced workers and recent grads. Learning how to negotiate is a legitimate skill that comes in handy during both professional and personal situations.
fizkes/Shutterstock

Negotiating a Job Offer

A manager's role involves advancing the organization's well being and its overall business success. But like any other person looking for work, managers also find themselves in the labor market, negotiating for a new position. The negotiation skills they apply at work can help them reach employment agreements that benefit both parties. The company acquires talent, and the manager finds an attractive position in exchange for compensation that both parties consider fair.

Especially when currently unemployed, a job seeker might feel safest accepting all the terms in a job offer, thinking the risk of an employer losing interest in them might seem too great. But successful managers understand that negotiation is part of decision making. Furthermore, the fact that the company made an offer signals they see the candidate as someone who will add value to the organization. Negotiation is a legitimate skill that can make a major difference in a manager's lifetime earnings.[44]

Negotiation requires information about the situation and the other party, including the going rate of pay for the position. The effective negotiator has in mind a desired salary that is realistic, given the job market and the person's qualifications. If the initial offer is below that amount, the negotiator should respond as objectively as possible, indicating the desired amount and giving reasons why it is reasonable. Reasons should emphasize how the person will contribute to the company's success, including specific examples if possible. If the company representative says the amount of pay is firm, it might help to ask whether demonstrating success on certain measures could be tied to a raise in six months or a year.[45]

Job seekers should look at the complete offer, not just salary. Employee benefits, such as insurance, student-loan repayment, retirement accounts, training or tuition reimbursement, and paid time off, also have value. People in high-demand jobs might get a signing bonus. If a job requires moving to a new location, then a generous relocation package also can make the offer appealing. Negotiators should consider whether trade-offs on some of these could result in an acceptable offer. If so, the key to a resolution might be a statement such as "If you can get me tuition reimbursement along with that salary, I'll accept your offer today." Human resource professionals advise that candidates using this approach focus on one or two changes that matter most. Picking apart every detail will not win over a team that spent hours putting together what they thought was a fair offer.[46]

Organizational Politics

LO17-5 Explain why managers need to be attuned to organizational politics, and describe the political strategies that managers can use to become politically skilled.

Managers must develop the skills necessary to manage organizational conflict for an organization to be effective. Suppose, however, that top managers are in conflict over the best strategy for an organization to pursue or the best structure to adopt to use organizational resources efficiently. In such situations, resolving conflict is often difficult, and the parties to the conflict resort to organizational politics and political strategies to try to resolve the conflict in their favor.

Organizational politics are the activities that managers (and other members of an organization) engage in to increase their power and to use power effectively to achieve their goals and overcome resistance or opposition.[47] Managers often engage in organizational politics to resolve conflicts in their favor.

Political strategies are the specific tactics that managers (and other members of an organization) use to increase their power and to use power effectively to influence and gain the support

organizational politics Activities that managers engage in to increase their power and to use power effectively to achieve their goals and overcome resistance or opposition.

political strategies Tactics that managers use to increase their power and to use power effectively to influence and gain the support of other people while overcoming resistance or opposition.

of other people while overcoming resistance or opposition. Political strategies are especially important when managers are planning and implementing major changes in an organization: Managers not only need to gain support for their change initiatives and influence organizational members to behave in new ways but also need to overcome often strong opposition from people who feel threatened by the change and prefer the status quo. By increasing their power, managers are better able to make needed changes. In addition to increasing their power, managers also must make sure they use their power in a way that actually enables them to influence others.

The Importance of Organizational Politics

The term *politics* has a negative connotation for many people. Some think that managers who are political have risen to the top not because of their own merit and capabilities but because of whom they know. Or people may think that political managers are self-interested and wield power to benefit themselves, not their organizations. There is a grain of truth to this negative connotation. Some managers do appear to misuse their power for personal benefit at the expense of their organizations' effectiveness.

Nevertheless, organizational politics are often a positive force. Managers striving to make needed changes often encounter resistance from individuals and groups who feel threatened and wish to preserve the status quo. Effective managers engage in politics to gain support for and implement needed changes. Similarly, managers often face resistance from other managers who disagree with their goals for a group or for the organization and with what they are trying to accomplish. Engaging in organizational politics can help managers overcome this resistance and achieve their goals.

Indeed, managers cannot afford to ignore organizational politics. Everyone engages in politics to a degree—other managers, coworkers, and employees, as well as people outside an organization, such as suppliers. Those who try to ignore politics might as well bury their heads in the sand because in all likelihood they will be unable to gain support for their initiatives and goals.

Political Strategies for Gaining and Maintaining Power

Managers who use political strategies to increase and maintain their power are better able to influence others to work toward the achievement of group and organizational goals. (Recall from Chapter 14 that legitimate, reward, coercive, expert, and referent power help managers influence others as leaders.) By controlling uncertainty, making themselves irreplaceable, being in a central position, generating resources, and building alliances, managers can increase their power (see Figure 17.4).[48] We next look at each of these strategies.

CONTROLLING UNCERTAINTY Uncertainty is a threat for individuals, groups, and entire organizations and can interfere with effective performance and goal attainment. For example, uncertainty about job security is threatening for many workers and may cause top performers (who have the best chance of finding another job) to quit and take a more secure position with another organization. When an R&D department faces uncertainty about customer preferences, its members may waste valuable resources to develop a product that customers do not want. When top managers face uncertainty about global demand, they may fail to export products to countries that want them and, thus, may lose a source of competitive advantage.

Managers who can control and reduce uncertainty for other managers, teams, and departments as well as the organization as a whole are likely to see their power increase.[49] Managers of labor unions gain power when they can eliminate uncertainty over job security for workers. Marketing and sales managers gain power when they can eliminate uncertainty for other departments, such as R&D, by accurately forecasting customers' changing preferences. Top managers gain power when they are knowledgeable about global demand for an organization's products. Managers who can control uncertainty are likely to be in demand and sought after by other organizations.

MAKING ONESELF IRREPLACEABLE Managers gain power when they have valuable knowledge and expertise that allow them to perform activities no one else can handle. This

Figure 17.4
Political Strategies for Increasing Power

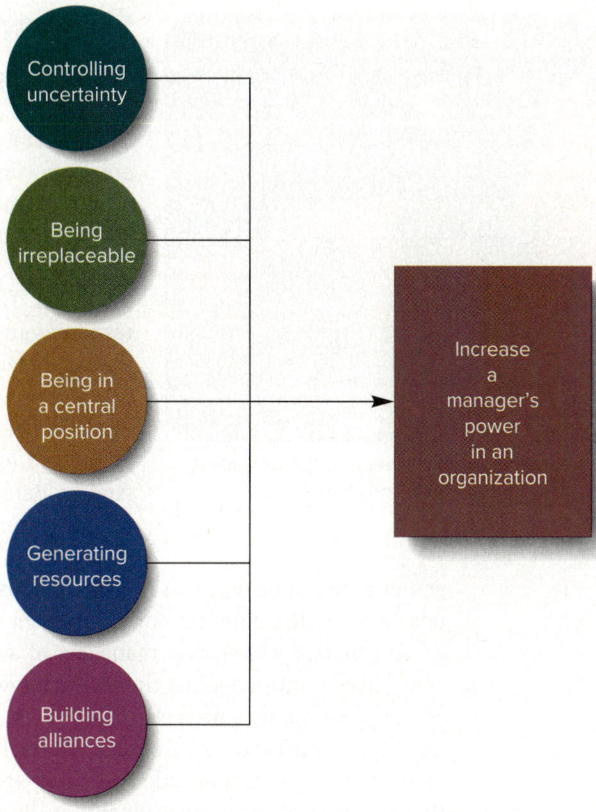

is the essence of being irreplaceable.[50] The more central these activities are to organizational effectiveness, the more power managers gain from being irreplaceable.

BEING IN A CENTRAL POSITION Managers in central positions are responsible for activities that are directly connected with an organization's goals and sources of competitive advantage and often are located in central positions in important communication networks in an organization.[51] Managers in key positions have control over crucial organizational activities and initiatives and have access to important information. Other organizational members depend on them for their knowledge, expertise, advice, and support, and the success of the organization as a whole is seen as riding on these managers. These consequences of being in a central position are likely to increase managers' power.

Managers who are outstanding performers, have a wide knowledge base, and have made important and visible contributions to their organizations are likely to be offered central positions that will increase their power.

GENERATING RESOURCES Organizations need three kinds of resources to be effective: (1) input resources such as raw materials, skilled workers, and financial capital; (2) technical resources such as machinery and computers; and (3) knowledge resources such as marketing, information technology, or engineering expertise. To the extent that a manager can generate one or more of these kinds of resources for an organization, that manager's power is likely to increase.[52] In universities, for example, professors who win large grants to fund their research, from associations such as the National Science Foundation and the Army Research Institute, gain power because of the financial resources they generate for their departments and the university as a whole.

In a knowledge economy, some of the most important resources are the organization's people and what they know. Thus, generating resources often is not a solo activity, and managers increasingly find they are most powerful when they empower others. The "Managing Globally" feature describes how this applies to aid organizations.

MANAGING GLOBALLY

Working with resources and community leaders on a local level can help businesses and other organizations thrive.
Farm Images/Contributor/Getty Images

Grassroots Knowledge Is Power

For government and private aid organizations, programs are often run far from headquarters, under difficult conditions such as extreme poverty or the aftermath of a major disaster. The headquarters is near the founders and funders, and the programs could be halfway around the world. This poses difficulties in obtaining knowledge resources about the needs of the people being served and the performance of the program. Sometimes initiatives break down. Public restrooms built to serve residents of poor neighborhoods in Kibera, Kenya, were never connected to the sewage system, so they were unusable. And in Bangladesh, storm shelters built to house poor people during cyclones were ill-suited for the local culture because the design assumed women and men would gather in the same dimly lit room. This was considered improper for women, as well as unsafe, given the potential for harassment in the shadows.[53]

To generate knowledge, managers of aid organizations must weigh the benefits of centralized control against those of empowering locals. An examination of more than 14,000 development projects in 180 countries found that programs in which decision making is entrusted to local leaders are better able to weather an unstable environment. For example, a decade and a half ago, two agencies set up programs to improve the practices of local governments in South Africa. One program involved traveling from town to town and delivering a training program. In the other, advisers lived in an area and worked alongside the government officials to build skills. The first program met its measurable goals to deliver training, but it had little impact on the governments. The second program let local advisers set goals and report performance as they saw fit. The advisers described a variety of interventions and ways they made a difference. The second program demonstrated results but required a high degree of trust in the advisers.[54]

Local decision making works best when managers establish long-term relationships founded on local knowledge, commitment to the organization's mission and values, and mutual trust. This requires careful hiring decisions and respectful long-term engagement with local people. In the case of the Bangladesh storm shelters, Oxfam learned about the problem because it partnered with Bangladeshi women who had formed a Gender Task Team that works with local governments. They redesigned the shelters to make them welcoming and safe for women, including those who are pregnant, breastfeeding, or have a disability.[55]

BUILDING ALLIANCES When managers build alliances, they develop mutually beneficial relationships with people both inside and outside the organization, as does FUBU's Daymond John, profiled in "A Manager's Challenge." The parties to an alliance support one another because doing so is in their best interests, and all parties benefit from the alliance. Alliances give managers power because they provide the managers with support for their initiatives. Partners to alliances provide support because they know the managers will reciprocate when their partners need support. Alliances can help managers achieve their goals and implement needed changes in organizations because they increase managers' levels of power.

Many powerful top managers focus on building alliances not only inside their organizations but also with individuals, groups, and organizations in the task and general environments on which their organizations depend for resources. These individuals, groups, and organizations enter alliances with managers because doing so is in their best interests and they know they can count on the managers' support when they need it. When managers build alliances, they need to be on their guard to ensure that everything is aboveboard, ethical, and legal.

Political Strategies for Exercising Power

Politically skilled managers not only understand, and can use, the five strategies to increase their power; they also appreciate strategies for exercising their power. These strategies generally focus on how managers can use their power quietly or *unobtrusively*.[56] When managers exercise power unobtrusively, other members of an organization may not be aware that the managers are using their power to influence them. They may think they support these managers for a variety of reasons: because they believe it is the rational or logical thing to do, because they believe doing so is in their own best interests, or because they believe the position or decision the managers are advocating is legitimate or appropriate.

The unobtrusive use of power may sound devious, but managers typically use this strategy to bring about change and achieve organizational goals. Political strategies for exercising power to gain the support and agreement of others include relying on objective information, bringing in an outside expert, controlling the agenda, and making everyone a winner (see Figure 17.5).[57]

RELYING ON OBJECTIVE INFORMATION Managers require the support of others to achieve their goals, implement changes, and overcome opposition. One way for a manager to gain this support and overcome opposition is to rely on objective information that supports the manager's initiatives. Reliance on objective information leads others to support the manager because of the facts; objective information causes others to believe that what the manager is proposing is the proper course of action. By relying on objective information, politically skilled managers unobtrusively exercise their power to influence others.

Figure 17.5

Political Strategies for Exercising Power

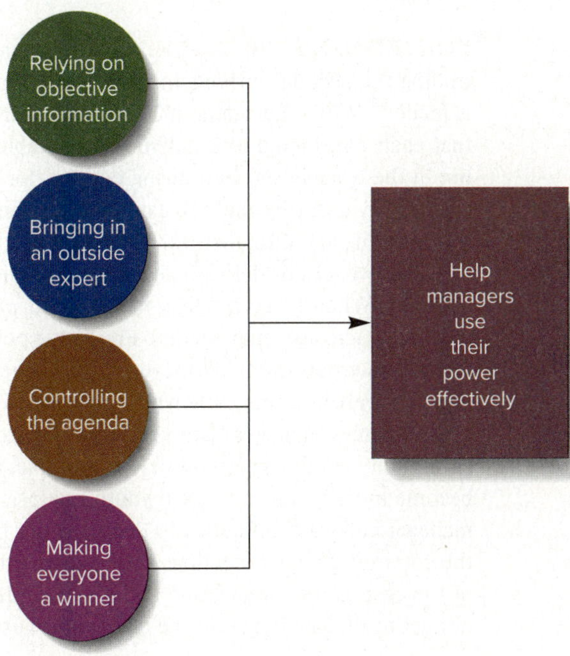

Take the case of Mary Callahan, vice president of Better Built Cabinets, a small cabinet company in the Southeast. Callahan is extremely influential in the company; practically every new initiative that she proposes to the president and owner of the company is implemented. Why is Callahan able to use her power in the company so effectively? Whenever she has an idea for a new initiative that she thinks the company might pursue, she and her employees begin by collecting objective information supporting the initiative. Recently, Callahan decided that Better Built should develop a line of high-priced, European-style kitchen cabinets. Before presenting her proposal to Better Built's president, she compiled objective information showing that (1) there was a strong, unmet demand for these kinds of cabinets; (2) Better Built could manufacture them in its existing production facilities; and (3) the new line had the potential to increase Better Built's sales by 20% while not detracting from sales of the company's other cabinets. Presented with this information, the president agreed to Callahan's proposal. Moreover, the president and other members of Better Built whose cooperation was needed to implement the proposal supported it because they thought it would help Better Built gain a competitive advantage. Using objective information to support her position enabled Callahan to unobtrusively exercise her power and influence others to support her proposal.

BRINGING IN AN OUTSIDE EXPERT Bringing in an outside expert to support a proposal or decision can, at times, provide managers with some of the same benefits that the use of objective information does. It lends credibility to a manager's initiatives and causes others to believe that what the manager is proposing is the appropriate or rational thing to do. Suppose Callahan had hired a consultant to evaluate whether her idea was a good one. The consultant reports back to the president that the new European-style cabinets are likely to fulfill Callahan's promises and increase Better Built's sales and profits. As with objective information, this information provided by an objective expert can lend a sense of legitimacy to Callahan's proposal and allow her to unobtrusively exercise power to influence others.

Although you might think consultants and other outside experts are neutral or objective, they sometimes are hired by managers who want them to support a certain position or decision in an organization. For instance, when managers face strong opposition from others who fear that a decision will harm their interests, the managers may bring in an outside expert. They hope this expert will be perceived as a neutral observer to lend credibility and "objectivity" to their point of view. The support of an outside expert may cause others to believe that a decision is indeed the right one. Of course, sometimes consultants and other outside experts actually are brought into organizations to be objective and guide managers on the appropriate course of action.

CONTROLLING THE AGENDA Managers also can exercise power unobtrusively by controlling the agenda–influencing which alternatives are considered or even whether a decision is made.[58] When managers influence the alternatives that are considered, they can make sure that each considered alternative is acceptable to them and that undesirable alternatives are not in the feasible set. In a hiring context, for example, managers can exert their power unobtrusively by ensuring that job candidates whom they do not find acceptable do not make their way onto the list of finalists for an open position. They do this by making sure that these candidates' drawbacks or deficiencies are communicated to everyone involved in making the hiring decision. When three finalists for an open position are discussed and evaluated in a hiring meeting, a manager may seem to exert little power or influence and just go along with what the rest of the group wants. However, the manager may have exerted power in the hiring process unobtrusively by controlling which candidates have made it to the final stage.

Sometimes managers can prevent a decision from being made. A manager in charge of a community relations committee, for example, may not favor a proposal for the organization to become more involved in local youth groups such as the Boy Scouts and the Girl Scouts. The manager can exert influence in this situation by not including the proposal on the agenda for the committee's next meeting. Alternatively, the manager could place the proposal at the end of the agenda for the meeting and feel confident that the committee will run out of time and not get to the last items on the agenda because that is what always happens. Either approach enables the manager to unobtrusively exercise power. Committee members do not perceive this manager as trying to influence them to turn down the proposal. Rather, the manager has turned the proposal into a nonissue that is not even considered by the committee.

MAKING EVERYONE A WINNER Often, politically skilled managers can exercise their power unobtrusively because they make sure that everyone whose support they need benefits personally from providing that support. By making everyone a winner, a manager can influence other organizational members because these members see supporting the manager as being in their best interest.

When top managers turn around troubled companies, some organizational members and parts of the organization are bound to suffer due to restructurings that often entail painful layoffs. However, the power of the turnaround CEO often accelerates as it becomes clear that the future of the company is now on solid footing and the organization and its stakeholders are winners as a result of the change effort.

Making everyone a winner not only is an effective way of exercising power but, when used consistently and openly, also can increase managers' power and influence over time. That is, when a manager actually does make everyone a winner, all stakeholders will see it as in their best interests to support the manager and their initiatives.

Summary and Review

LO17-1, 17-2

ORGANIZATIONAL CONFLICT Organizational conflict is the discord that arises when the goals, interests, or values of different individuals or groups are incompatible and those individuals or groups block or thwart each other's attempts to achieve their objectives. Four types of conflict arising in organizations are interpersonal conflict, intragroup conflict, intergroup conflict, and interorganizational conflict. Sources of conflict in organizations include different goals and time horizons, overlapping authority, task interdependencies, different evaluation or reward systems, scarce resources, and status inconsistencies. Conflict management strategies focused on individuals include increasing awareness of the sources of conflict, increasing diversity awareness and skills, practicing job rotation or temporary assignments, and using permanent transfers or dismissals when necessary. Strategies focused on the whole organization include changing an organization's structure or culture and altering the source of conflict.

LO17-3, 17-4

NEGOTIATION Negotiation is a conflict resolution technique used when parties to a conflict have approximately equal levels of power and try to come up with an acceptable way to allocate resources to each other. In distributive negotiation, the parties perceive that there is a fixed level of resources for them to allocate, and they compete to receive as much as possible at the expense of the other party, not caring about their relationship in the future. In integrative bargaining, both parties perceive that they may be able to increase the resource pie by coming up with a creative solution to the conflict, trusting each other, and cooperating with each other to achieve a win–win resolution. Five strategies that managers can use to facilitate integrative bargaining are to emphasize superordinate goals; focus on the problem, not the people; focus on interests, not demands; create new options for joint gain; and focus on what is fair.

LO17-5

ORGANIZATIONAL POLITICS Organizational politics are the activities that managers (and other members of an organization) engage in to increase their power and to use power effectively to achieve their goals and overcome resistance or opposition. Effective managers realize that politics can be a positive force that enables them to make needed changes in an organization. Five important political strategies for gaining and maintaining power are controlling uncertainty, making oneself irreplaceable, being in a central position, generating resources, and building alliances. Political strategies for effectively exercising power focus on how to use power quietly and unobtrusively and include relying on objective information, bringing in an outside expert, controlling the agenda, and making everyone a winner.

Management in Action

Topics for Discussion and Action

Discussion

1. Discuss why too little conflict in an organization can be just as detrimental as too much conflict. [LO17-1]
2. Why are compromise and collaboration more effective ways of handling conflict than accommodation, avoidance, and competition? [LO17-2]
3. Why should managers promote integrative bargaining rather than distributive negotiation? [LO17-3]
4. How can managers promote integrative bargaining? [LO17-4]
5. Why do organizational politics affect practically every organization? [LO17-5]
6. Why do effective managers need good political skills? [LO17-5]
7. What steps can managers take to ensure that organizational politics are a positive force leading to a competitive advantage, not a negative force leading to personal advantage at the expense of organizational goal attainment? [LO17-5]
8. Think of a member of an organization whom you know and who is particularly powerful. What political strategies does this person use to increase their power? [LO17-5]
9. Why is it best to use power unobtrusively? How are people likely to react to power that is exercised obtrusively? [LO17-5]

Action

10. Interview a manager in a local organization to determine the kinds of conflicts that occur in their organization and the strategies that are used to manage them. [LO17-1, 17-2]

Building Management Skills

Effective and Ineffective Conflict Resolution [LO17-1, 17-2]

Think about two recent conflicts that you had with other people—one conflict that you felt was effectively resolved (C1) and one that you felt was ineffectively resolved (C2). The other people involved could be coworkers, students, family members, friends, or members of an organization that you are a member of. Answer the following questions:

1. Briefly describe C1 and C2. What type of conflict was involved in each of these incidents?
2. What was the source of the conflict in C1 and in C2?
3. What conflict management strategies were used in C1 and in C2?
4. What could you have done differently to more effectively manage conflict in C2?
5. How was the conflict resolved in C1 and in C2?

Managing Ethically [LO17-5]

One political strategy managers can engage in is controlling the agenda by subtly influencing which alternatives are considered or even whether a decision is up for discussion. Some employees believe this can be unethical and can prevent important issues from being raised and points of view from being expressed.

Questions

1. Either individually or in a group, think about the ethical implications of controlling the agenda as a political strategy.
2. What steps can managers and organizations take to ensure that this strategy does not result in important issues and differing points of view being suppressed in an organization?

Small Group Breakout Exercise

Negotiating a Solution [LO17-3, 17-4]

Form groups of three or four people. One member of your group will play the role of Jane Rister, one member will play the role of Michael Schwartz, and one or two members will be observer(s) and spokesperson(s) for your group.

Jane Rister and Michael Schwartz are assistant managers in a large home improvement store. They report directly to the store manager. Today they are meeting to discuss some important problems they need to solve but about which they disagree.

The first problem hinges on the fact that either Rister or Schwartz needs to be on duty whenever the store is open. For the last six months, Rister has taken most of the least desirable hours (nights and weekends). They are planning their schedules for the next six months. Rister thought Schwartz would take more of the undesirable times, but Schwartz has informed Rister that his wife has just gotten a nursing job that requires her to work weekends, so he needs to stay home weekends to take care of their infant daughter.

The second problem concerns a department manager who has had a hard time retaining salespeople in their department. The turnover rate in the department is twice that in the other store departments. Rister thinks the manager is ineffective and wants to fire him. Schwartz thinks the high turnover is just a fluke and the manager is effective.

The last problem concerns Rister's and Schwartz's vacation schedules. Both managers want to take off the week of July 4, but one of them needs to be in the store whenever it is open.

1. The group members playing Rister and Schwartz assume their roles and negotiate a solution to these three problems.
2. Observers take notes on how Rister and Schwartz negotiate solutions to their problems.
3. Observers determine the extent to which Rister and Schwartz use distributive negotiation or integrative bargaining to resolve their conflicts.
4. When called on by the instructor, observers communicate to the rest of the class how Rister and Schwartz resolved their conflicts, whether they used distributive negotiation or integrative bargaining, and their actual solutions.

Be the Manager [LO17-1, 17-2, 17-3, 17-4, 17-5]

You are a middle manager in a large corporation, and lately you have felt that you are caught between a rock and a hard place. Times are tough; your unit has experienced layoffs; your surviving employees are overworked and demoralized; and you feel that you have no meaningful rewards, such as the chance for a pay raise, bonus, or promotion, to motivate them. Your boss keeps increasing the demands on your unit as well as the unit's responsibilities. Moreover, you believe that you and your employees are being unfairly blamed for certain problems beyond your control. You believe that you have the expertise and skills to perform your job effectively and that your employees are capable and effective in their jobs. Yet you feel that you are on shaky ground and powerless, given the current state of affairs. What are you going to do?

Case in the News [LO17-1, 17-2, 17-5]

Disastrous Conflict at Boeing

In 2010, Boeing was caught by surprise when its competitor, Airbus, announced it would introduce a new version of its A320 jet with fuel-saving engines. The new model would be otherwise so similar that customer airlines could skip the expense of retraining pilots. Boeing quickly announced that it would similarly update its popular 737 plane. When the 737 MAX made its first flight in 2016, Boeing recommended that training could safely be limited to computer-based education in place of a flight simulator. Less than three years later, tragedy struck twice: 737 MAX jets taking off from Indonesia and Ethiopia crashed soon after takeoff, killing their crews and passengers. In both cases, a faulty stabilizer pushed down the jet's nose, triggering multiple warning devices that pilots were unprepared to deal with.

The circumstances are still being investigated, but various conflicts may have played a role. Some involved tensions between management and employees regarding cost cutting as Boeing moved to get the 737 MAX into production and into customers' hangars. Boeing uses pilots to test its planes and train customers' pilots to fly them. Training started as a service accompanying sales, but Boeing more recently saw potential in making it profitable. Boeing shifted work from employee pilots to contractors. Saying this would compromise quality, the pilots formed a union. The company then moved its flight simulators from Seattle, where the unionized pilots were, to Miami.

When they were in Seattle, the pilots who work for Boeing would consult with engineers and tell them about situations they experienced in the cockpit. Moving training to Miami disrupted these informal exchanges of information. In addition, Boeing saw a departure of other skilled labor, including experts in human factors, or the way people interact with machines. Their absence became another risk to designing a safe jet. One glaring omission: Apparently no one tested pilots' reaction to the type of malfunction that caused the crashes.

Other conflicts emerged after the crashes. CEO Dennis Muilenburg met with other executives to decide on a path forward. Muilenburg, trained as an engineer and with experience in Boeing's defense division, is said to have focused on how to ensure the 737 MAX—by far the company's biggest source of revenue—could keep flying. He noted there was not yet proof that the crashes had the same cause. Some in the Federal Aviation Administration wanted to ground the plane, but senior FAA officials agreed with Muilenburg's preference to allow the plane to fly. Over the following weeks, as more data became available, the FAA joined other countries' regulators in banning the 737 MAX from the air.

From there, however, the conflict with regulators deepened as statements by Muilenburg made presumptions about the FAA's position. He said that within weeks, the FAA would approve what he called a software enhancement to the flight control system, making an "already safe aircraft even safer." He observed that the company had properly sought the initial approval to fly and that the FAA had granted it. Muilenburg repeatedly made public statements estimating when the planes would be allowed to fly again, even after FAA acting administrator Dan Elwell asked him not to keep making promises. Critics had been noting that the FAA had relaxed its regulation of Boeing in the past, and Elwell was concerned about the agency's reputation.

Later, as the Justice Department investigated whether laws had been broken, Boeing discovered instant messages in which one of its pilots mentioned having unintentionally "basically lied" to regulators. Boeing shared the information with the investigators but not the FAA. This led the agency's new administrator, Steve Dickson, to warn Boeing of stricter regulation if it continued to undermine the FAA. After Muilenburg made another prediction that Boeing would have the 737 MAX flying soon, Dickson firmly indicated that his agency would not be following a schedule and would not be allowing the 737 MAX to fly that year.

During this time, Boeing had continued to assemble 737 MAX jets to fill a backlog of orders. But after Dickson's statement, Muilenburg announced that the company would suspend production. One week later, the board of directors asked Muilenburg to resign, saying the company needed new leadership in order to restore confidence and repair relationships with customers and the FAA. The following month, Dave Calhoun became CEO, and Boeing announced it recommended 737 MAX pilots undergo training in the flight simulator. In September 2022, Boeing agreed to pay a fine of $200 million to settle charges made by the U.S. Securities and Exchange Commission that the company and former CEO Muilenburg misled investors and the public about the safety of the 737 MAX.

Questions for Discussion

1. Categorize the conflicts discussed in this case as interpersonal, intragroup, intergroup, and interorganizational conflicts.
2. Review the conflict management strategies. Pick two and describe briefly how Muilenburg could have used them to handle conflict more effectively.
3. Muilenburg was in a position of power, but he did not maintain power effectively enough to keep his job after the 737 MAX jets crashed. Of the political strategies for gaining and maintaining power, identify one that could have helped Muilenburg fulfill his role more effectively. How could he have used this strategy? Who would have benefited?

Sources: D. Gates, "Final Report on Boeing 737 MAX Crash Sparks Dispute over Pilot Error," *Seattle Times*, www.seattletimes.com, January 6, 2023; D. Schaper, "Boeing Will Pay $200 Million to Settle SEC Charges over 737 Max Crashes," *NPR*, www.npr.org, September 22, 2022; G. Rapier, "Boeing Burned through $13.8 Billion of Loans in Just over a Month as Coronavirus Derails Its 737 Max Recovery," *Business Insider*, www.businessinsider.com, March 17, 2020; A. Tangel, "Botched Predictions, Strife with Regulators Cost Boeing CEO His Job," *The Wall Street Journal*, www.wsj.com, January 7, 2020; A. Pasztor, D. Cameron, and A. Sider, "Boeing Backs MAX Simulator Training in Reversal of Stance," *The Wall Street Journal*, www.wsj.com, January 7, 2020; A. Tangel, A. Sider, and A. Pasztor, "'We've Been Humbled': Boeing's CEO Struggles to Contain 737 MAX Crisis," *The Wall Street Journal*, www.wsj.com, December 22, 2019; P. Robison and J. Johnsson, "Boeing's Push to Make Training Profitable May Have Left 737 Max Pilots Unprepared," *Bloomberg Businessweek*, www.bloomberg.com, December 20, 2019; A. Tangel, D. Cameron, and A. Sider, "Boeing to Suspend 737 MAX Production in January," *The Wall Street Journal*, www.wsj.com, December 16, 2019.

Notes

1. K.J. Ryan, "Daymond John Is Gone Fishin'," *Inc.,* November 2022, 42–49; J. Hilburn, "Daymond John Is on a Mission," *Forbes,* www.forbes.com, January 17, 2022.
2. Ryan, "Daymond John Is Gone Fishin'"; C. Massa, "How Daymond John Went from Selling T-Shirts on the Street to Running a $350 Million Company," *Entrepreneur,* www.entrepreneur.com, March 23, 2022.
3. Hilburn, "Daymond John Is on a Mission"; Massa, "How Daymond John Went from Selling T-Shirts"; O. Blanco, "Daymond John on Hip-Hop, His Mom, and Making It Big," *CNN Money,* https://money.cnn.com, accessed February 7, 2023.
4. Ryan, "Daymond John Is Gone Fishin'"; B. Gomez, "Daymond John: Successful People Have No 'Magic Wand'–Here's What It Takes," *CNBC,* www.cnbc.com, October 13, 2021.
5. Ryan, "Daymond John Is Gone Fishin'"; Hilburn, "Daymond John Is on a Mission."
6. "Daymond John on Harnessing Your Unseen Negotiating Power," *Chase for Business,* www.chase.com, accessed February 7, 2023; T. Locke, "Daymond John Says You Can Shift the Power in Any Room–As Long as You Master These Skills," *CNBC,* www.cnbc.com, February 1, 2021.
7. J.A. Litterer, "Conflict in Organizations: A Reexamination," *Academy of Management Journal* 9 (1966), 178–86; S.M. Schmidt and T.A. Kochan, "Conflict: Towards Conceptual Clarity," *Administrative Science Quarterly* 13 (1972), 359–70; R.H. Miles, *Macro Organizational Behavior* (Santa Monica, CA: Goodyear, 1980).
8. C.K.W. De Dreu and M.J. Gelfand (eds.), *The Psychology of Conflict and Conflict Management in Organizations* (New York: Lawrence Erlbaum Associates, 2008).
9. P. Haapaniemi, "Senior Teams: The Positive Power of Conflict," *Chief Executive,* https://chiefexecutive.net, December 1, 2017; S.P. Robbins, *Managing Organizational Conflict: A Nontraditional Approach* (Englewood Cliffs, NJ: Prentice-Hall, 1974).
10. K.A. Jehn, "A Qualitative Analysis of Conflict Types and Dimensions in Organizational Groups," Cornell University, 1997; K.A. Jehn, "A Multimethod Examination of the Benefits and Detriments of Intragroup Conflict," Cornell University, 1995.
11. L.L. Putnam and M.S. Poole, "Conflict and Negotiation," in F.M. Jablin, L.L. Putnam, K.H. Roberts, and L.W. Porter, eds., *Handbook of Organizational Communication: An Interdisciplinary Perspective* (Newbury Park, CA: Sage, 1987), 549–99.
12. M.C. Gentile, "Giving Voice to Values," *Stanford Social Innovation Review,* https://ssir.org, September 11, 2018.
13. C. Plump, "How Giving Voice to Values Can Transform a Toxic Workplace Culture," *People + Strategy,* Summer 2019, 40–45.
14. Gentile, "Giving Voice to Values"; Plump, "How Giving Voice to Values Can Transform a Toxic Workplace Culture."
15. Company website, "About Magnetrol," www.magnetrol.com, accessed March 19, 2020; M. Gentile, "Developing a Dialogue across Conflict," interview of John Heiser, *People + Strategy,* Summer 2019, 53–55.
16. L.R. Pondy, "Organizational Conflict: Concepts and Models," *Administrative Science Quarterly* 2 (1967), 296–320; R.E. Walton and J.M. Dutton, "The Management of Interdepartmental Conflict: A Model and Review," *Administrative Science Quarterly* 14 (1969), 62–73.
17. G.R. Jones and J.E. Butler, "Managing Internal Corporate Entrepreneurship: An Agency Theory Perspective," *Journal of Management* 18 (1992), 733–49.
18. T. Petzinger, Jr., "All Happy Businesses Are Alike, but Heirs Bring Unique Conflicts," *The Wall Street Journal,* November 17, 1995, B1.
19. J.A. Wall, Jr., "Conflict and Its Management," *Journal of Management* 21 (1995), 515–58.
20. Walton and Dutton, "The Management of Interdepartmental Conflict."
21. Pondy, "Organizational Conflict."
22. "Restaurant Management Software with Mobile Ordering System," https://possector.com, accessed March 20, 2020.
23. K. Shonk, "5 Conflict Resolution Strategies," *Harvard Law School Daily Blog,* www.pon.harvard.edu, October 7, 2019; R.L. Pinkley and G.B. Northcraft, "Conflict Frames of Reference: Implications for Dispute Processes and Outcomes," *Academy of Management Journal* 37 (February 1994), 193–206.
24. K.W. Thomas, "Conflict and Negotiation Processes in Organizations," in M.D. Dunnette and L.M. Hough, eds., *Handbook of Industrial and Organizational Psychology,* 2nd ed., vol. 3 (Palo Alto, CA: Consulting Psychologists Press, 1992), 651–717.
25. Thomas, "Conflict and Negotiation Processes in Organizations."
26. M.T.M. Dijkstra, B. Beersma, and A. Evers, "Reducing Conflict-Related Employee Strain: The Benefits of an Internal Locus of Control and a Problem-Solving Conflict Management Strategy," *Work & Stress* 25, no. 2 (2011), 167–84.
27. Pinkley and Northcraft, "Conflict Frames of Reference."
28. K.J. Behfar, "Clash of the Teammates: How the Ideal Team Works Through Conflict," *Darden Ideas to Action,* https://ideas.darden.virginia.edu, accessed May 2, 2018.
29. S. Finkelstein, "Don't Be Blinded by Your Own Expertise," *Harvard Business Review,* May–June 2019, 153–58; T. Bradberry, "Six Reasons Smart People Fail," *Inc.,* www.inc.com, February 17, 2017.
30. S. Finkelstein, "What Kind of Boss Are You?" *Thrive Global,* https://thriveglobal.com, February 8, 2019.
31. Finkelstein, "Don't Be Blinded"; Finkelstein, "What Kind of Boss Are You?"
32. S.A. Hocking, "How to Be a Good Boss (that People Actually Want to Work For)," *Ladders,* www.theladders.com, accessed March 19, 2020; "Is This the Biggest Shift Needed When Managing Millennials?" Chartered Management Institute, www.managers.org.uk, February 6, 2018.
33. D. Rushe, "WeWork Set to Sack 2,000 Staff as Anger towards Founder Adam Neumann Grows," *The Guardian,* www.theguardian.com, October 15, 2019; D. Durbin, "WeWork Founder Leaving CEO Post after Controversy over His Conduct, Skepticism about Company," *Chicago Tribune,* www.chicagotribune.com, September 24, 2019.
34. L. Hoffman and E. Brown, "SoftBank Backs Away from Part of Planned WeWork Bailout," *The Wall Street Journal,* www.wsj.com, March 18, 2020; M. Binder, "WeWork's Adam Neumann Got $1.7 Billion. 2,400 Employees Just Got Fired," *Mashable,* https://mashable.com, November 21, 2019; M. Farrell, L. Hoffman, E. Brown, and D. Benoit, "The Fall of WeWork: How a Startup Darling Came Unglued," *The Wall Street Journal,* www.wsj.com, October 24, 2019.
35. P.R. Lawrence, L.B. Barnes, and J.W. Lorsch, *Organizational Behavior and Administration* (Homewood, IL: Irwin, 1976).

36. L.K. Stroh, G.B. Northcraft, and M.A. Neale, *Organizational Behavior,* 3rd ed. (Mahwah, NJ: Lawrence Erlbaum Associates, 2002).
37. C. Bendersky, "Organizational Dispute Resolution Systems: A Complementarities Model," *Academy of Management Review* 28 (October 2003), 643–57.
38. "Using Arbitration to Resolve Legal Disputes," https://adr.findlaw.com, accessed February 7, 2023.
39. R.J. Lewicki, S.E. Weiss, and D. Lewin, "Models of Conflict, Negotiation, and Third Party Intervention: A Review and Synthesis," *Journal of Organizational Behavior* 13 (1992), 209–52.
40. Stroh et al., *Organizational Behavior.*
41. Ibid.; Lewicki et al., "Models of Conflict, Negotiation, and Third Party Intervention."
42. "Expanding the Pie-Integrative versus Distributive Bargaining Negotiation Strategies," *Harvard Law School Daily Blog,* www.pon.harvard.edu, accessed February 7, 2023.
43. P.J. Carnevale and D.G. Pruitt, "Negotiation and Mediation," *Annual Review of Psychology* 43 (1992), 531–82.
44. D. Malhotra, "15 Rules for Negotiating a Job Offer," *Harvard Business Review,* https://hbr.org, accessed March 20, 2020.
45. "How to Negotiate Salary after You Get a Job Offer," Robert Half, www.roberthalf.com, February 19, 2020.
46. A. Martin, "10 Tips for Negotiating Your First Job Offer (and Every One After That!)," *CNBC,* www.cnbc.com, April 9, 2022.
47. M. Jarrett, "The 4 Types of Organizational Politics," *Harvard Business Review,* https://hbr.org, April 24, 2017.
48. D.J. Hickson, C.R. Hinings, C.A. Lee, R.E. Schneck, and D.J. Pennings, "A Strategic Contingencies Theory of Intraorganizational Power," *Administrative Science Quarterly* 16 (1971), 216–27; C.R. Hinings, D.J. Hickson, J.M. Pennings, and R.E. Schneck, "Structural Conditions of Interorganizational Power," *Administrative Science Quarterly* 19 (1974), 22–44; J. Pfeffer, *Power in Organizations* (Boston: Pitman, 1981).
49. Pfeffer, *Power in Organizations.*
50. K. Ashford, "6 Ways to Become Irreplaceable at Work," *Monster,* www.monster.com, accessed March 20, 2020.
51. M. Crozier, "Sources of Power of Lower Level Participants in Complex Organizations," *Administrative Science Quarterly* 7 (1962), 349–64; A.M. Pettigrew, "Information Control as a Power Resource," *Sociology* 6 (1972), 187–204.
52. Pfeffer, *Power in Organizations;* G.R. Salancik and J. Pfeffer, "The Bases and Uses of Power in Organizational Decision Making," *Administrative Science Quarterly* 19 (1974), 453–73; J. Pfeffer and G.R. Salancik, *The External Control of Organizations: A Resource Dependence View* (New York: Harper & Row, 1978).
53. A. Higgins, "When Aid Fails," *Stanford Social Innovation Review,* Summer 2019, 6; E. Stevens, "Local Women Know Best When It Comes to Ensuring Women's Safety in a Disaster," *Oxfam,* www.oxfamamerica.org, February 24, 2020.
54. D. Honig, "The Power of Letting Go," *Stanford Social Innovation Review,* Winter 2019, 43–47.
55. E. Stevens, "Local Women Know Best"; Y. Eyoel, T. Montgomery, and J. Walker, "Social Change Won't Happen Unless Philanthropy Gives More Power to Grassroots Leaders," *Chronicle of Philanthropy,* May 2019, EBSCOhost, http://web.b.ebscohost.com.
56. Pfeffer, *Power in Organizations.*
57. Ibid.
58. J.R. Galosy, "Power Tactics," *TD magazine,* www.td.org, accessed March 20, 2020.

CHAPTER 18

Using Advanced Information Technology to Increase Performance

Rawpixel.com/Shutterstock

Learning Objectives

After studying this chapter, you should be able to:

LO18-1 Differentiate between data and information, and explain how the attributes of useful information allow managers to make better decisions.

LO18-2 Describe three reasons managers must have access to information to perform their tasks and roles effectively.

LO18-3 Describe the hardware and software innovations that created the IT revolution and changed the way managers behave.

LO18-4 Compare six performance-enhancing kinds of management information systems.

LO18-5 Explain how IT is helping managers build strategic alliances and network structures to increase efficiency and effectiveness.

A MANAGER'S CHALLENGE

AI Is Changing the Way We Work

How can information technology enable managers to get better results? Imagine, for example, the challenges a fast-growing company faces in managing employees. When the company is small, a few people handle their areas of expertise independently. As it grows, those people need help, individual projects become group projects, and someone familiar with the work becomes the manager. The demand for operating on a larger scale often outstrips the new manager's ability to pick up the people skills necessary for leadership, motivation, and control. The organization then wants to develop its managers, but doing so takes time, and training efforts can be difficult to target to the specific needs of a leader at a particular time.[1]

Information technology offers solutions, including software that applies *artificial intelligence* (AI)—typically software that has "learned," through massive amounts of trial and error, to analyze situations and propose responses that are associated with good outcomes. The more data the software processes, the better its recommendations become. For example, Butterfly is software that gathers anonymous data from an organization's instant-messaging system and analyzes the data to identify situations calling for more active leadership from the organization's managers. The three partners who founded Butterfly were inspired by their own difficulties in learning to lead their teams in prior jobs.[2]

Butterfly's creators describe their product as a management coaching system; the feedback from employees becomes the basis for defining the areas in which managers need to improve their leadership. This analysis, in turn, becomes the basis of recommendations for improvement. The system also can be set up to deliver alerts when managers need additional support. Because the software uses AI to improve its results based on experience, it is designed to increase in value as the company signs on more clients. In its early years, Butterfly has signed up notable clients including Citibank, Live Nation, and Ticketmaster. And the frequency of feedback—daily or weekly one-question surveys—also contributes to the pool of data. Cofounder Simon Rakosi says companies using Butterfly have measured increased productivity, decreased absenteeism, and higher levels of employee engagement.[3]

Another area where AI is changing the way managers and employees work is at company call centers. For example, HomeServe USA Corp. sells repair plans for plumbing, heating, cooling, and electrical systems to millions of customers through its sales agents in Chattanooga, Tennessee. As business continues to expand, HomeServe has added an AI-powered virtual assistant named Charlie to the call center staff.

Charlie answers thousands of calls a day, routes them to the appropriate department,

Technology continues to change the way managers and employees do their jobs. The impact of artificial intelligence on work is likely to change jobs, not eliminate them all together.
chaoguay/Getty Images

processes claims, and schedules repair appointments. While a human sales agent is on the phone with a customer, Charlie can whisper to the agent whether the customer is eligible for a specific coverage, and she can even type on the agent's screen the reason why the customer is calling. But Charlie's performance is not without its critics—some of them the sales agents Charlie is assisting. While HomeServe managers are thrilled about Charlie's efficiencies, some sales agents find Charlie's assistance to be frustrating and overreaching. A top sales agent told *The Wall Street Journal,* "She's supposed to make my job easier, not just make us do what she said."[4]

Despite grumblings about advances in technology such as AI, the biggest impact on the workplace will be changing jobs, not replacing them. McKinsey estimates that by 2030, 25% of U.S. jobs will be fully automated, which will require workers to increase their skill sets, acquire new ones, and be ready (and willing) to adapt to evolving technologies.[5]

Overview

In a world in which business activities of all kinds are increasingly conducted through the Internet, the challenge facing managers is to continually update and improve their use of advancing technology to increase organizational performance. Managers must utilize the most effective technological solutions such as cloud computing and artificial intelligence (AI) to assist their employees and customers, or risk being surpassed by more effective rivals who have developed superior technology competencies. Google and Apple are two of the most valuable companies in the world because they provide advanced solutions that increase people's ability to access, search, and use the potential of the web and communicate with others. The most successful brick-and-mortar and online companies, such as Walmart, Samsung, and Amazon, excel in developing improved company-specific technology solutions. The implication is clear: There are enormous opportunities for managers of all kinds of organizations to find new ways to employ technology to use organizational resources more efficiently and effectively.

In this chapter, we begin by looking at the relationship between information and the manager's job and then examine the ongoing technological revolution. Next we examine the impact of rapidly evolving technology on managers' jobs and on an organization's competitive advantage. Then we discuss six types of management information systems, each of which is based on a different sort of information technology, which can help managers perform their jobs more efficiently and effectively. By the end of this chapter, you will understand how new developments in technology are profoundly shaping managers' tasks and roles and the way organizations operate.

Information and the Manager's Job

LO18-1 Differentiate between data and information, and explain how the attributes of useful information allow managers to make better decisions.

data Raw, unsummarized, and unanalyzed facts.

information Data that are organized in a meaningful fashion.

Managers cannot plan, organize, lead, and control effectively unless they have access to information. Information is the source of the knowledge and intelligence they need to make the right decisions. Information, however, is not the same as data.[6] **Data** are raw, unsummarized, and unanalyzed facts such as volume of sales, level of costs, or number of customers. **Information** is data that are organized in a meaningful fashion, such as in a graph showing the changes in sales volume or costs over time. Data alone do not tell managers anything; information, in contrast, can communicate a great deal of useful knowledge to the person who receives it–such as a manager who sees sales falling or costs rising. The distinction between data and information is important because one purpose of technology is to help managers transform data into information to make better managerial decisions.

To further clarify the difference between data and information, consider a supermarket manager who must decide how much shelf space to allocate to two breakfast cereal brands: Dentist's Delight and Sugar Supreme. Most supermarkets use checkout scanners to record individual sales and store the data in an online program. Accessing this program, the manager might find that Dentist's Delight sells 50 boxes per day and Sugar Supreme sells 25 boxes per day. These raw data, however, are of little value in helping the manager decide how to allocate shelf space. The manager also needs to know how much shelf space each cereal currently occupies and how much profit each cereal generates for the supermarket.

Suppose the manager discovers that Dentist's Delight occupies 10 feet of shelf space and Sugar Supreme occupies 4 feet and that Dentist's Delight generates 20 cents of profit a box, while Sugar Supreme generates 40 cents of profit a box. By putting these three bits of data together (number of boxes sold, amount of shelf space, and profit per box), the manager gets some useful information on which to base a decision: Dentist's Delight generates $1 of profit per foot of shelf space per day [(50 boxes × $.20)/10 feet], and Sugar Supreme generates $2.50 of profit per foot of shelf space per day [(25 boxes × $.40)/4 feet]. Armed with this information, the manager might decide to allocate less shelf space to Dentist's Delight and more to Sugar Supreme.

Attributes of Useful Information

Four factors determine the usefulness of information to a manager: quality, timeliness, completeness, and relevance (see Figure 18.1).

QUALITY Accuracy and reliability determine the quality of information.[7] The greater its accuracy and reliability, the higher the quality of information. Technology gives managers access to high-quality, real-time information that they can use to improve long-term decision making and alter short-term operating decisions, such as how much of a particular product to make daily or monthly. Supermarket managers, for example, use handheld barcode readers that are wireless (using Bluetooth technology) or are linked to a server to monitor and record how demand for particular products such as milk, chicken, or bread changes daily so they know how to restock their shelves to ensure the products are always available.

TIMELINESS Information that is timely is available when it is required to allow managers to make the optimal decision—not after the decision has been made. In today's rapidly changing world, the need for timely information often means information must be available on a real-time basis—hence the enormous growth in the demand for mobile devices.[8] **Real-time information** is information that reflects current changes in business conditions. In an industry that experiences rapid changes, real-time information may need to be updated frequently.

real-time information Frequently updated information that reflects current conditions.

Local transportation systems (buses, subway trains, commuter rail) use real-time information to help commuters track when they can expect their next transit ride. For example, the Transit app (available for Android and iOS devices) helps simplify daily commutes for people in 269 cities in more than 16 countries around the world, including the United States, Australia, Iceland, Canada, France, Germany, and the UK. The app updates arrival times of public transportation in your area (thanks to the locations setting/geo-tracking feature of your mobile

Figure 18.1

Factors Affecting the Usefulness of Information

device), monitors your walking speed, and tells you whether you're going to get to your ride on time. In addition, the app will suggest changing your transit connections based on detours or transportation delays to help you get to your destination on time. And it can even wake you up on your ride before you get to where you're going if you take a quick nap on your journey.[9]

COMPLETENESS Information that is complete gives managers all the information they need to exercise control, achieve coordination, or make an effective decision. Recall from Chapter 7, however, that managers rarely have access to complete information. Instead, because of uncertainty, ambiguity, and bounded rationality, they have to make do with incomplete information.[10] One function of technology is to increase the completeness of managers' information.

RELEVANCE Information that is relevant is useful and suits a manager's particular needs and circumstances. Irrelevant information is useless and may actually hurt the performance of a busy manager who has to spend valuable time determining whether information is relevant. Given the massive amounts of information that managers are now exposed to and their limited information-processing capabilities, a company's information systems designers need to ensure that managers receive only relevant information.

What Is Information Technology?

information technology (IT) The set of methods or techniques for acquiring, organizing, storing, manipulating, and transmitting information.

management information system (MIS) A specific form of IT that managers utilize to generate the specific, detailed information they need to perform their roles effectively.

Information technology (IT) is the set of methods or techniques for acquiring, organizing, storing, manipulating, and transmitting information.[11] A **management information system (MIS)** is a specific form of IT that managers select and use to generate the specific, detailed information they need to perform their roles effectively. Management information systems have existed for as long as there have been organizations, which is a long time indeed–merchants in ancient Egypt used clay tablets to record their transactions. Before the computing age, most systems were paper-based: Clerks recorded important information on paper documents (often in duplicate or triplicate) in words and numbers; sent copies of the documents to superiors, customers, or suppliers; and stored other copies in filing cabinets for future reference.

Rapid advances in the power of technology–specifically, the development of ever more powerful and sophisticated hardware and software–have had a fundamental impact on organizations, managers, and employees, as suggested by the discussion of artificial intelligence in "A Manager's Challenge." Some IT developments, such as inventory management and customer relationship management (CRM) systems, contribute so much to performance that organizations that do *not* adopt them, or that adopt them ineffectively, become less competitive compared with organizations that do adopt them.[12] IT predictions for the near future include increased use of blockchain technology; continuing advances in AI and augmented and virtual reality; additional success with quantum computing to create new ways of processing and storing information; and progress in green technology including green hydrogen–a new source of energy that produces nearly zero greenhouse emissions.[13]

Managers need information for three reasons: to make effective decisions, to control the activities of the organization, and to coordinate the activities of the organization. Next we examine these uses of information in detail.

Information and Decisions

LO18-2 Describe three reasons managers must have access to information to perform their tasks and roles effectively.

Much of management (planning, organizing, leading, and controlling) is about making decisions. For example, the marketing manager must decide what price to charge for a product, what distribution channels to use, and what promotional messages to emphasize to maximize sales. The manufacturing manager must decide how much of a product to make and how to make it so that the company makes a profit. The purchasing manager must decide from whom to purchase inputs and what inventory of inputs to hold. The human relations manager must decide how much employees should be paid, how they should be trained, what benefits they should be given, and when it makes sense to hire more workers. The engineering manager must make decisions about new product design. Top managers must decide how to allocate scarce financial resources among competing projects, how best to structure and control the organization, and what business-level strategy the organization should be pursuing. And regardless of

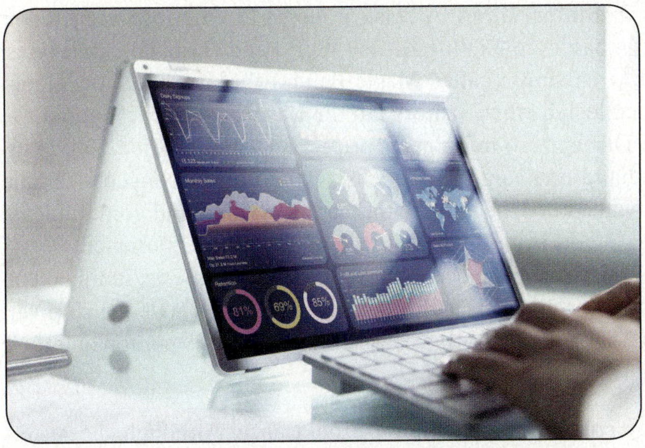

Although technology has changed the way key data are shared with managers, the information is still critical to making informed decisions.
Andrey_Popov/Shutterstock

their functional orientation, all managers have to make decisions about matters such as what performance evaluation to give to an employee.

To make effective decisions, managers need information both from inside the organization and from external stakeholders. When deciding how to price a product, for example, marketing managers need information about how consumers will react to different price points. They need information about unit costs because they do not want to set the price below the cost of production. And they need information about competitive strategy because pricing strategy should be consistent with an organization's competitive strategy. Some of this information will come from outside the organization (for example, from gathering consumer data) and some from inside the organization (information about production costs comes from manufacturing). As this example suggests, managers' ability to make effective decisions rests on their ability to acquire and process information.

BIG DATA The collection and analysis of large sets of data from consumers, competitors, employees, suppliers, and others has become a global industry, with the big data sector expected to top the $655 billion mark by 2029.[14] *Analytics* is the process of examining all these data to uncover hidden patterns, unknown correlations, market trends, customer preferences, and the like which can help managers make decisions that will advance the organization's business.[15] Analyzing data is no longer done by reviewing a spreadsheet and manually highlighting key bits of information. Instead, powerful software can provide real-time information that assists managers at all levels of an organization in making faster, more effective decisions to help develop new products and services, while reducing costs.[16]

Information and Control

As discussed in Chapter 11, controlling is the process through which managers regulate how efficiently and effectively an organization and its members perform the activities necessary to achieve its stated goals.[17] Managers achieve control over organizational activities by taking four steps (see Figure 11.2): (1) They establish measurable standards of performance or goals, (2) they measure actual performance, (3) they compare actual performance against established goals, and (4) they evaluate the results and take corrective action if necessary.[18] UPS, for example, has a delivery goal to deliver 99% of the overnight packages it picks up by noon the next day.[19] UPS has thousands of U.S. ground stations (branch offices that coordinate the pickup and delivery of packages in a particular area) that are responsible for the physical pickup and delivery of packages. UPS managers monitor the delivery performance of these stations regularly; if they find that the 99% goal is not being attained, they determine why and take corrective action if necessary.

To achieve control over any organizational activity, managers must have information. To control ground station activities, a UPS manager might need to know what percentage of packages each station delivers by noon. To obtain this information, the manager uses UPS's own information systems; UPS is also a leader in developing proprietary in-house IT. All packages to be shipped to the stations have been scanned with wireless scanners by the UPS drivers who pick them up; then all this information is sent through UPS servers to its headquarters' mainframe computer. When the packages are scanned again at delivery, this information is also transmitted through its computer network. Managers can access this information to quickly discover what percentage of packages were delivered by noon of the day after they were picked up, as well as how this information breaks down station by station so they can take corrective action if necessary.

Management information systems are used to control all divisional and functional operations. In accounting, for example, information systems are used to monitor expenditures and compare them against budgets. To track expenditures against budgets, managers need information about current expenditures, broken down by relevant organizational units; accounting

IT is designed to give managers this information. A twist on using IT to improve customer service is being used by several companies, including Disney World and Carnival cruise lines. Disney guests can now purchase wristbands (called Magic Bands) that work as hotel room keys and charge cards. The data collected when visitors tap the Magic Bands throughout the theme park and resorts will help Disney zero in on guest preferences and provide better customer service.[20] Taking the wristband one step further, Carnival Corp. introduced wearable Ocean Medallions, quarter-size, waterproof medallions that are encrypted and communicate with thousands of sensors on board and in port to enhance guests' travel experiences. Crew members on Carnival's Princess cruise line can access information about guests, family members can use the medallions to track each other, and touch screens throughout the ship will display recommended entertainment or dining options based on guests' information and their interests and activities.[21]

CYBERSECURITY Technology continues to evolve at a rapid pace. Although the results of such innovations have changed both business and daily life, these changes are not without challenges, particularly when it comes to controlling the information. With advanced technology comes the need for *cybersecurity* to keep all of this information safe and protected against unauthorized use.[22] Consider some recent statistics. According to the Allianz Risk Barometer, cyber incidents and business interruptions top global business worries in 2023 (34% of survey responses), followed by macroeconomic developments, such as inflation, deflation, monetary policies, and austerity programs (25% of survey respondents), and energy issues (22%).[23]

Another form of cybercrime has become commonplace as businesses collect large amounts of data from individuals. Over the past few years, data breaches have occurred in which information about millions of consumers has been stolen by cyber thieves who figured out how to infiltrate companies', so-called secure information systems. For example, in November 2022, T-Mobile suffered a data breach affecting 37 million current customers that was not discovered by the company until early January 2023. In a filing with the U.S. Securities and Exchange Commission, the mobile giant said that a "bad actor" manipulated one of the company's programming interfaces to steal customers' names, email addresses, phone numbers, billing addresses, birthdates, and account numbers.[24] This is not the first time data breaches have occurred at T-Mobile; in August 2021, a data breach cost the company more than $350 million in a class action lawsuit payout to customers. At the time of the settlement, T-Mobile committed to a $150 million initiative to improve its digital security efforts.[25]

Small businesses, in particular, are vulnerable to cyberattacks because they typically do not employ a cybersecurity staff to monitor and protect company data and other vital information. According to the Information Security Forum, as real-time data collection via devices controlled by the Internet of Things (IoT) continues to play an important role in business operations, data leaks from industrial equipment and other digital products such as digital doorbells, web cameras, printers, and garage door openers are easy targets for hackers.[26] The IoT is a network of devices, vehicles, home appliances, and other products embedded with electronics, sensors, and connectivity, which allow these "things" to collect and share data via the Internet. Estimates suggest more than 43 billion devices are currently connected to the Internet that generate, share, and collect data.[27]

Home security products such as doorbells fitted with security cameras can be easy targets for hackers and other cybersecurity thieves.
BrandonKleinVideo/Shutterstock

DATA PRIVACY Another aspect of controlling information within an organization concerns keeping data private and secure. While many companies are taking steps to make sure security measures outside the company's internal systems are solid, some firms do not use the same aggressive approach to keep their internal networks safe. Once a hacker infiltrates a company's internal networks, it may be difficult for the cyber thief to be detected.[28] In addition, some well-known tech companies seem to be in the news lately for security lapses when it comes to protecting consumers' private data. The "Ethics in Action" feature discusses strategic and ethical implications of supermarkets collecting and analyzing data about consumers.

ETHICS IN ACTION

Supermarket chains such as Kroger collect data from shoppers in a variety of ways, which allows retailers to determine which shelf displays of products will generate the best sales growth in a particular location.
Dave and Les Jacobs/Blend Images LLC

Kroger Uses Consumer Data to Spur Growth

Kroger, the largest U.S. supermarket chain, operates under its own name and several others, including Fred Meyer, Harris Teeter, and Ralphs. It has about 2,800 stores plus websites for its chains, together generating millions of transactions every day. In the past, the record keeping for this sales volume would have been just a major expense, but with today's advanced information technology, it generates valuable insights into customer behavior.[29]

Kroger treats data as a key part of its growth strategy. The company operates a data intelligence division called 84.51°, the longitude of its location in Cincinnati. The name alludes to the division's use of "longitudinal" research, looking at the activities of consumers or stores over a stretch of time. In its stores, Kroger collects data from customers on sales, loyalty card use, and videos of their behavior in front of shelves, such as the time they spend looking for but not finding items. Consumers who visit Kroger-owned websites generate data about which products they view and purchase.[30]

Analyzing the data increases Kroger's power relative to its suppliers: consumer packaged goods (CPG) companies. CPG makers used to be the experts, with insights into what consumers buy and when. They would plan how their products should be arranged on the shelves and would pay for a desired bit of store real estate. But Kroger today sees better growth opportunity from using its own data to determine the shelf displays that will generate the best sales growth–including of its own store brands, made in dozens of Kroger-owned factories. It also sells data to suppliers. For example, CPG companies can purchase data showing how ads on Kroger-owned websites are associated with purchases of their products online or in stores. With Kroger's Stratum tool, they can learn about their products' sales, inventory levels, customer segments, and more. And through a Kroger alliance with Pinterest, a CPG company can purchase data about how Pinterest users react to the company's ads on the site.[31]

All this data collection, analysis, and selling has obvious benefits for Kroger, but how are consumers affected? They may not even realize that Kroger is tracking their Pinterest searches, purchases of over-the-counter remedies, or time spent perusing the cereal aisle. Emily Gibbons, the vice president of data science for 84.51°, agrees about the advantages to Kroger but adds that providing an optimal assortment at the right price ultimately results in a better shopping experience for customers.[32]

Information and Coordination

Coordinating department and divisional activities to achieve organizational goals is another basic task of management. As an example of the size of the coordination task that managers face, consider the coordination effort necessary to prepare between 500,000 and 1 million meals for the people who visit Disney parks and resorts every day. Combine that type of volume with Disney's efforts to get food locally, and logistics get complicated fast. For example, the supply chain at the Disney parks and resorts worldwide depends on the location of the resort and what local growers and producers can provide. In Florida, for example, the company works with "Fresh from Florida" to find out what fruits and vegetables are in season and available. In Southern California, Disney works with local growers who provide organic produce for food operations at Disneyland. Disney's culinary team creates their magic in the Flavor Lab, a top-secret Orlando facility where they devise, create, and execute every new food and beverage concept for Disney properties around the world.[33]

Starbucks has a program called "Origin Experience" that allows its employees to get involved in the logistics of the supply chain. This experience allows associates to travel overseas and meet Starbucks partners where the coffee beans are grown. The trips provide associates with a new perspective on the supply chain and the coffee that ends up in their stores.

The supply chain at Starbucks runs from the field where the coffee beans are grown to the cup of coffee poured by a friendly barista at a local shop. The supply chain spans 19 countries. From the field, the beans travel to one of six roasting centers, where they are prepared and then shipped to one of 48 regional distribution centers and then on to their final destination. The distribution centers make roughly 70,000 deliveries each week.[34]

These visits help Starbucks employees learn about the supply chain and how to make it run more smoothly. The visits provide employees at the end of the supply chain with information about how things work at the beginning. The coffee giant recently announced a pilot program with select coffee growers in Costa Rica, Colombia, and Rwanda to develop advanced data technology to share real-time information about the status of coffee bean shipments from the field to Starbucks distribution centers around the world. According to the company, digital communications seem to be everywhere, even within small family farms in faraway places due to the availability of mobile phones.[35]

Starbucks experienced a coffee shortage in 2022, mainly due to unfavorable weather conditions in Brazil, one of the world's largest coffee producers. This issue caused Starbucks to increase prices for their products. In addition, continuing supply-chain issues caused the company to temporarily halt the sale of 25 items, including chai tea and hazelnut-flavored beverages.[36]

The IT Revolution

LO18-3 Describe the hardware and software innovations that created the IT revolution and changed the way managers behave.

Advances in IT have enabled managers to make gigantic leaps in the way they can collect more timely, complete, relevant, and high-quality information and use it in more effective ways. To better understand the ongoing revolution in IT that has transformed companies, allowing them to improve their responsiveness to customers, minimize costs, and improve their competitive position, we need to examine several key aspects of advanced IT.

The Effects of Advancing IT

The IT revolution began with the development of the first computers—the hardware of IT—in the 1950s. The language of computers is a digital language of zeros and ones. Words, numbers, images, and sound can all be expressed in zeros and ones. Each letter in the alphabet has its own unique code of zeros and ones, as does each number, each color, and each sound. For example, the digital code for the number 20 is 10100. In the language of computers, it takes a lot of zeros and ones to express even a simple sentence, to say nothing of complex color graphics or moving video images. Nevertheless, modern computers can read, process, and store trillions of instructions per second (an *instruction* is a line of software code) and, thus, vast amounts of zeros and ones. This awesome number-crunching power forms the foundation of the ongoing IT revolution.

The products and services that result from advancing IT are all around us—ever more powerful microprocessors and PCs, high-bandwidth smartphones, sophisticated word-processing software, ever-expanding computer networks, and more and more useful online information and retailing services that did not exist a generation ago. These products are commonplace and are being continuously improved. Many managers and companies that helped develop the new IT have reaped enormous gains.

However, while many companies have benefited from advancing IT, others have been threatened. Traditional landline telephone companies have seen their market dominance evaporate, overtaken by new companies offering Internet, broadband, and wireless technology. They have been forced to respond by buying wireless cell phone companies, building their own high-powered broadband networks, and forming alliances with companies such as Apple and Samsung to make smartphones that will work on their networks. So advancing IT is both an opportunity and a threat, and managers have to move quickly to protect or reinvent their companies and maintain their competitive advantage.

On one hand, IT helps create new product opportunities that managers and their organizations can take advantage of–such as online travel and vacation booking. On the other hand, IT creates new and improved products that reduce or destroy demand for older, established products–such as the services provided by brick-and-mortar travel agents. Walmart, by developing its own sophisticated proprietary IT, has been able to reduce retailing costs so much that it has put hundreds of thousands of small and medium-size stores out of business. Similarly, thousands of small, specialized U.S. bookstores have closed in the past decade as a result of advances in IT that made online bookselling possible.

IT and the Product Life Cycle

product life cycle The way demand for a product changes in a predictable pattern over time.

When IT is advancing, organizational survival requires that managers quickly adopt and apply it. One reason for this is how IT affects the length of the **product life cycle**, which is the way demand for a product changes in a predictable pattern over time.[37] In general, the product life cycle consists of four stages: the introduction, growth, maturity, and decline stages (see Figure 18.2). In the introduction stage, a product has yet to gain widespread acceptance; customers are unsure what a product, such as a new smartphone, has to offer, and demand for it is minimal.

As a product, like Apple's iPad, becomes accepted by customers (although many products do not, like BlackBerry's tablet), demand takes off and the product enters its growth stage. In

Figure 18.2

A Product Life Cycle

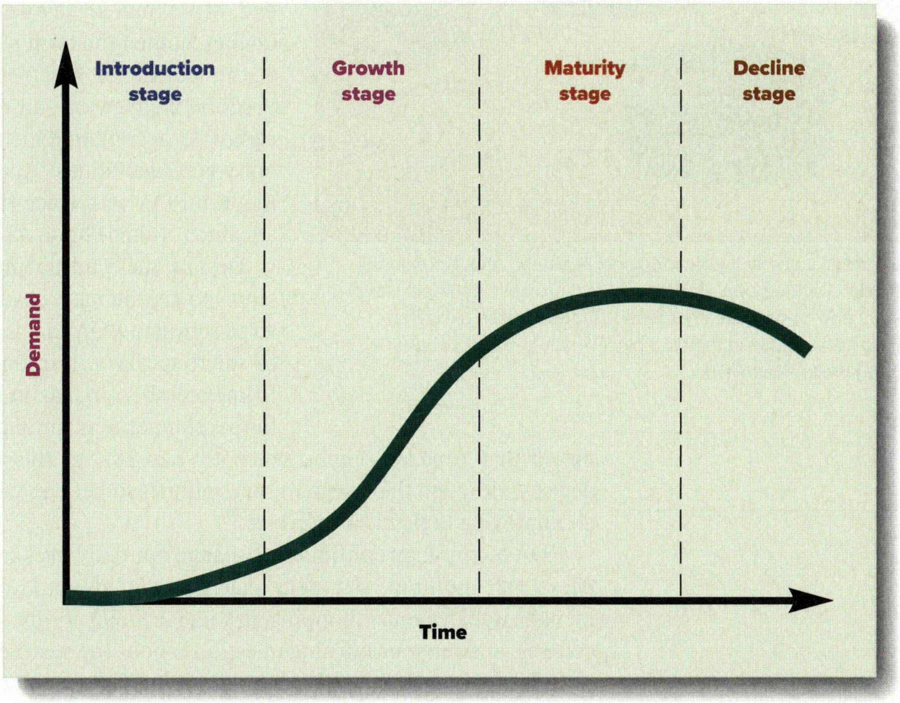

the growth stage, many consumers are entering the market and buying the product for the first time, and demand increases rapidly. This is the stage iPhones and iPads passed through with great success. Of course, the future success of these products will depend on the value customers see in the array of apps the products offer–and how quickly competitors such as Samsung and Google move to offer similar and less expensive tablets and smartphones.

The growth stage ends and the maturity stage begins when market demand peaks because most customers have already bought the product (there are relatively few first-time buyers left). At this stage, demand is typically replacement demand. Once demand for a product starts to fall, the decline stage begins. This typically occurs when advancing technology leads to the development of a more advanced product, making the old one obsolete. For example, Apple's iPod music player went into decline when the company developed the iPhone, which could also play music. In 2015, the company introduced the Apple Watch, and its Series 8 was released in September 2022. The watch continues to be solidly in the growth stage with a more than 50% share of the digital watch sector for high-level operating system watches.[38]

In general, demand for every generation of a digital device such as a smartphone or tablet falls off when the current leaders' technology is superseded by new products that incorporate the most recent IT advances. One reason the IT revolution has been so important for managers is that advances in IT are one of the most significant determinants of the length of a product's life cycle and, therefore, of competition in an industry.[39] One product strongly in the growth stage that has created intense competition among several tech leaders is the digital personal assistant, as described in the following "Management Insight" feature.

MANAGEMENT INSIGHT

Amazon's voice-activated personal assistant, Alexa, continues to help change people's personal and professional lives. Developers and companies are creating individualized skills that Alexa can take on in the workplace.
Charles Brutlag/Shutterstock

Alexa Works at Home and in the Office

The technology revolution continues to change the way we live and do business–and innovation never seems to end. More than 25 years ago, then CEO of Apple, John Sculley, coined the term *personal digital assistant* (PDA) at the Consumer Electronics Show, which he used to describe the Newton–an Apple device that was the precursor to a combination tablet and smartphone without voice capabilities. Apple's Siri, considered the first modern PDA with voice recognition, was introduced as a feature of the iPhone 4S back in 2011.[40]

Despite these advancing technologies, the PDA that seems to get the most coverage and interest is Alexa, the voice-activated PDA that is part of the Amazon Echo line of smart speakers. Introduced in 2014, first to Amazon Prime members, Amazon Echo and Alexa have sparked fierce competition among tech companies. It is estimated that Amazon's Echo currently has 28% of the global market for AI-assisted devices, although the competition continues to heat up with Google, Apple, and Sonos all improving their PDA offerings.[41]

PDA technology continues to change our daily lives in so many ways. For example, Alexa can monitor your daily calendar and remind you about important appointments; prepare your shopping list and actually order food items (via Amazon, of course); answer your burning questions about the weather, the time, and even football stats from your fantasy league; and control lighting and temperature in your home. Amazon has set up a rewards program to pay developers around the world to come up with "skills" for Alexa in seven key categories, such as education and reference or trivia and accessories. Already the company has paid out millions to developers for these time-saving apps.[42]

And Alexa's talents are no longer limited to personal activities; the voice-activated device is now taking over duties in the office. Recently Amazon rolled out its "Alexa for Business" program, encouraging use of the AI device in the workplace for tasks such as setting up meetings (including reserving the conference room, managing videoconferencing equipment, and alerting meeting attendees you're running late), automatically dialing into conference calls, sending messages and managing calendars, helping people track billable hours, reordering supplies, streaming music, and even reading you your emails while you're enjoying a cup of coffee.[43]

Business applications for Alexa will continue to expand as more and more companies create individualized "skills" for Alexa within their own work environment. Companies already putting Alexa to work include Condé Nast, GE, Seattle Children's Hospital, and Propel Insurance.[44]

The message for managers is clear: The shorter a product's life cycle because of advancing IT, the more important it is to innovate products quickly and continuously. A company that cannot develop a new and improved product line every three to six months will soon find itself in trouble. Increasingly, managers are trying to outdo their rivals by being the first to market with a product that incorporates some advance in IT, such as advanced stability or steering control that prevents vehicle wrecks.[45] In sum, the tumbling price of information brought about by advances in IT is at the heart of the IT revolution. So how can managers use all this computing power to their advantage?

The Network of Computing Power

The tumbling price of computing power and applications has allowed all kinds of organizations, large and small, to invest more to develop networks of servers that are customized with the mix of hardware and software applications that best meets the needs of their current value chain management.

network Interlinked computers that exchange information.

The typical organizationwide computing **network** that has emerged over time is a four-tier network solution that consists of "external" mobile computing devices such as laptops, smartphones, and tablets, connected to desktops, and then through servers to a company's mainframe or to remote access on the cloud (see Figure 18.3). Through wireless and wired communication, an employee with the necessary permissions can access a company's IT system from any location—in the office, at home, on a boat, on the beach, in the air—anywhere a wireless or wired link can be established.

The internal network is composed of "client" desktop and laptop PCs connected by ethernet or wirelessly to the company's system of servers. The client computers that are linked directly to a server constitute a *local area network* (LAN), and most companies have many LANs—for example, one in every division and function. Large companies that need immense processing power have a mainframe computer at the center or hub of the network that can quickly process vast amounts of information, issue commands, and coordinate computing devices at the other levels. The mainframe can also handle electronic communications between servers and PCs situated in different LANs, and the mainframe can connect to the mainframes of other companies. The mainframe is the master computer that controls the operations of all the other types of computers and digital devices as needed and can link them into one integrated system. It also provides the connection to the *external* IT networks outside the organization; for example, it gives a user access to an organization's cloud computing services—but with high security and reliability and only from recognized and protected computing devices. For instance, a manager with a mobile device or laptop can connect to a four-tier system, accessing data and software stored in the local server, in the mainframe, or through the Internet to a cloud-based computing solution hosted by a third party whose database might be located anywhere in the world.

Figure 18.3

A Four-Tier Information System with Cloud Computing

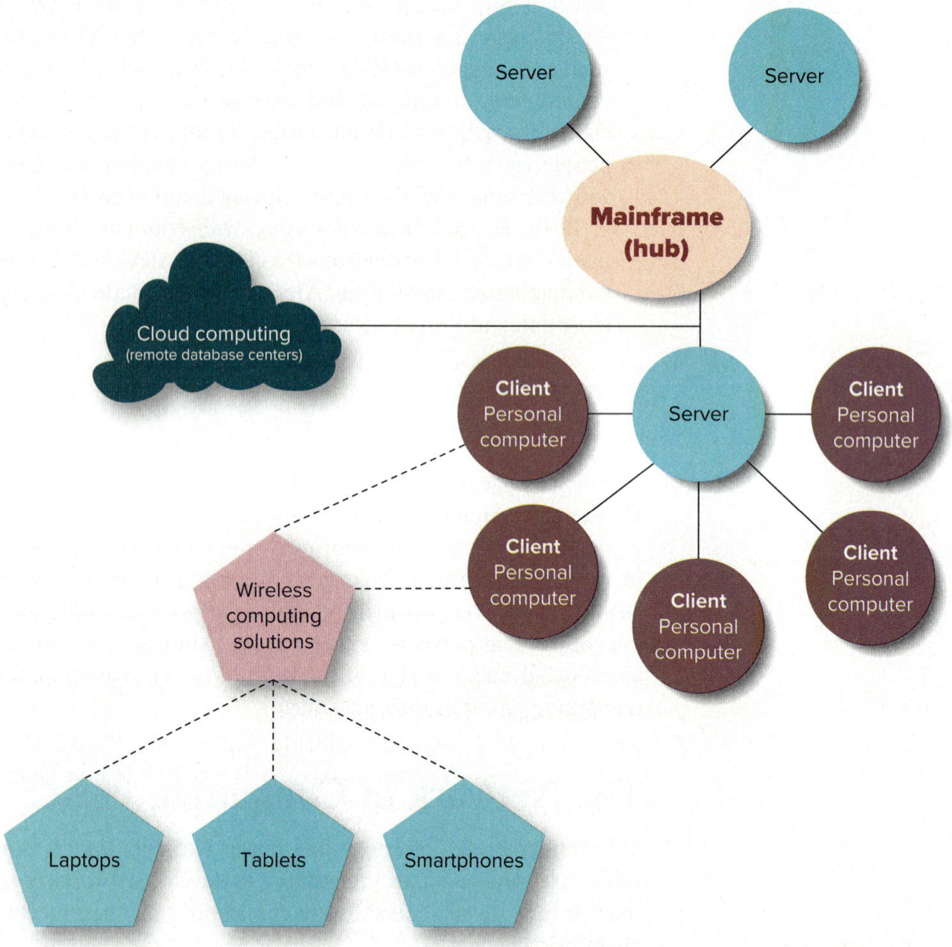

Just as computer hardware has been advancing rapidly, so has computer software. *Operating system software* tells the computer hardware how to run. *Applications software,* such as programs for word processing, spreadsheets, graphics, and database management, is developed for a specific task or use. The increase in the power of computer hardware has allowed software developers to write increasingly powerful programs that are also increasingly user-friendly. By harnessing the rapidly growing power of microprocessors, applications software has vastly increased the ability of managers to acquire, organize, and transmit information. In doing so, it also has improved the ability of managers to coordinate and control the activities of their organization and to make better decisions.

Types of Management Information Systems

LO18-4 Compare six performance-enhancing kinds of management information systems.

Advances in IT have continuously increased managers' ability to obtain the information they need to make better decisions and coordinate and control organizational resources. Next we discuss six types of management information systems (MIS) that have been particularly helpful to managers as they perform their management tasks: transaction-processing systems, operations information systems, decision support systems, expert systems, enterprise resource planning systems, and e-commerce systems (see Figure 18.4). These MIS systems are arranged along a continuum according to the sophistication of the IT they are based on—technology that determines their ability to give managers the information they need to make nonprogrammed decisions. (Recall from Chapter 7 that nonprogrammed decision making occurs in response to unusual, unpredictable opportunities and threats.)

Figure 18.4
Six Management Information Systems

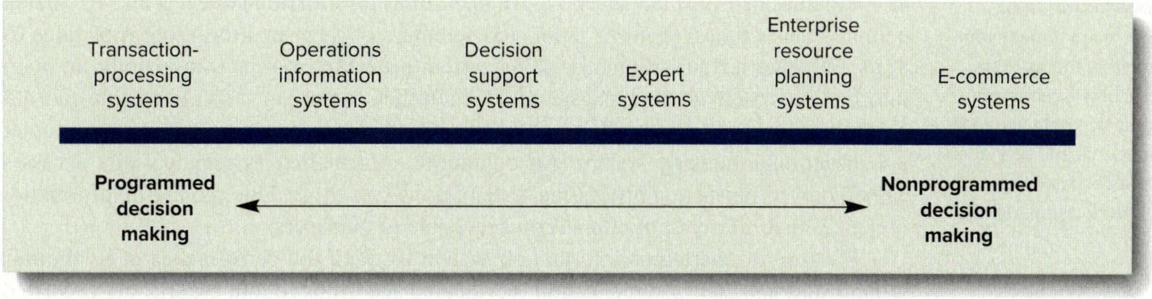

We examine each of these systems after focusing on the management information system that preceded them all: the organizational hierarchy.

The Organizational Hierarchy: The Traditional Information System

Traditionally, managers have used the organizational hierarchy as the main way to gather the information necessary to make decisions and coordinate and control organizational activities (see Chapter 10 for a detailed discussion of organizational structure and hierarchy). According to business historian Alfred Chandler, the use of the hierarchy as an information network was perfected by U.S. railroad companies in the 1850s.[46] At that time, railroads were among the largest U.S. companies, and because of the size of their geographic footprint they faced unique problems of coordination and control. Railroad companies started to solve these problems by designing hierarchical management structures that gave top managers the information they needed to coordinate and control their nationwide operations.

Although hierarchy is a useful information system, it has several drawbacks, as we noted in Chapter 10. First, when too many layers of managers exist, it takes a long time for information and requests to travel up the hierarchy and for decisions and answers to travel back down. The slow communication can reduce the timeliness and usefulness of the information and prevent a quick response to changing market conditions.[47] Second, information can be distorted as it moves from one layer of management to another, and information distortion reduces the quality of information. Third, managers have only a limited span of control, so as an organization grows larger and its hierarchy lengthens, more managers must be hired, and this makes the hierarchy an expensive information system. The popular idea that companies with tall management hierarchies are bureaucratic and unresponsive to the needs of their customers arises from the inability of tall hierarchies to effectively process data and give managers timely, complete, relevant, and high-quality information. The management hierarchy is still the best information system available today—the one that results in the best decisions—*if* managers have access to the other kinds of MIS systems discussed next.

Transaction-Processing Systems

transaction-processing system A management information system designed to handle large volumes of routine, recurring transactions.

A **transaction-processing system** is an MIS designed to handle large volumes of routine, recurring transactions (see Figure 18.4). Transaction-processing systems began to appear in the early 1960s with the advent of commercially available mainframe computers. They were the first type of computer-based IT adopted by many organizations, and today they are commonplace. Bank managers use a transaction-processing system to record deposits into, and payments out of, bank accounts. Supermarket managers use a transaction-processing system to record the sale of items and to track inventory levels. More generally, most managers in large organizations use a transaction-processing system to handle tasks such as payroll preparation and payment, customer billing, and payment of suppliers.

Operations Information Systems

operations information system A management information system that gathers, organizes, and summarizes comprehensive data in a form that managers can use in their nonroutine coordinating, controlling, and decision-making tasks.

Many types of MIS followed hard on the heels of transaction-processing systems in the 1960s as companies like IBM advanced IT. An **operations information system** is an MIS that gathers comprehensive data, organizes them, and summarizes them in a form that is of value to managers. Whereas a transaction-processing system processes routine transactions, an operations information system gives managers information they can use in their nonroutine coordinating, controlling, and decision-making tasks. Most operations information systems are coupled with a transaction-processing system. An operations information system typically accesses data gathered by a transaction-processing system, processes those data into useful information, and organizes that information into a form accessible to managers.

UPS uses an operations information system to track the performance of its thousands of ground stations. Each ground station is evaluated according to four criteria: delivery (to deliver 99% of all packages within the agreed-upon time period), productivity (measured by the number of packages shipped per employee-hour), cost control and efficiency, and station profitability. Each ground station also has specific delivery, efficiency, cost, and profitability targets that it must attain. Every month UPS's operations information system gathers information about these four criteria and summarizes it for top managers, who can then compare the performance of each station against its previously established targets. The system quickly alerts senior managers to underperforming ground stations so they can intervene selectively to help solve any problems that may have given rise to the poor performance.

Decision Support Systems

decision support system An interactive, computer-based management information system that managers can use to make nonroutine decisions.

A **decision support system** provides computer-built models that help managers make better nonprogrammed decisions.[48] Recall from Chapter 7 that nonprogrammed decisions are those that are relatively unusual or novel, such as decisions to invest in new productive capacity, develop a new product, launch a new promotional campaign, enter a new market, or expand internationally. Whereas an operations information system organizes important information for managers, a decision support system gives managers model-building capability and the chance to manipulate information in a variety of ways. Managers might use a decision support system to help them decide whether to cut prices for a product. The decision support system might contain models of how customers and competitors would respond to a price cut. Managers could run these models and use the results as an *aid* to decision making.

The stress on the word *aid* is important–in the final analysis a decision support system is not meant to make decisions for managers. Rather, its function is to give managers valuable information they can use to improve the quality of their decisions.

A good example of a sophisticated decision support system is one developed by DTN, an operational intelligence company, that provides companies in agriculture, aviation, and other industries with valuable insights to assist them in their business operations. One of its decision support systems, ClearPath Weather, helps government agencies, local municipalities, and facility managers develop road maintenance strategies that optimize the use of personnel, equipment, and chemicals to keep roadways clear in snowy conditions. In addition, the system uses proprietary algorithms and several prediction systems to give managers the information needed to make good decisions about when to plow, the quantity of chemicals to buy, and other key decisions.[49]

Most decision support systems are geared toward aiding middle managers in the decision-making process. For example, a loan manager at a bank might use a decision support system to evaluate the credit risk involved in lending money to a particular client. Rarely does a top manager use a decision support system. One reason for this is that most electronic management information systems have not yet become sophisticated enough to effectively handle the ambiguous types of problems facing top managers. To improve this situation, IT experts have been developing a variant of the decision support system: an executive support system.

executive support system A sophisticated version of a decision support system that is designed to meet the needs of top managers.

An **executive support system** is a sophisticated version of a decision support system that is designed to meet the needs of top managers. One defining characteristic of executive support systems is user-friendliness. Many of them include simple pull-down menus to take a manager through a decision analysis problem. Moreover, they may contain stunning graphics and other visual and interactive features to encourage top managers to use them.[50] Increasingly, executive support systems are used to link top managers virtually so they can function as a team; this type of executive support system is called a **group decision support system**.

group decision support system An executive support system that links top managers so they can function as a team.

Ultimately top managers' intuition, judgment, and integrity will always be needed to decide whether to pursue the course of action suggested by an MIS. There are always many different issues to be factored into a decision, not least of which are its ethical implications.

Artificial Intelligence and Expert Systems

As described in "A Manager's Challenge," artificial intelligence (AI) is the capability of a machine to imitate intelligent human behavior.[51] AI has already made it possible to write programs that can solve problems and perform tasks. For example, Google Maps uses artificial intelligence (via location data from smartphones) to analyze the speed of traffic and suggest the fastest routes to and from a destination to reduce driving time behind the wheel.[52] Software programs can be used to perform simple managerial tasks such as sorting through reams of data or incoming email messages to look for important ones. The interesting feature of such technology is that from "watching" a manager sort through data, it can "learn" what the manager's preferences are. Having done this, the software program can take over some of this work from the manager, freeing time for them to work on other tasks. Although AI is an ever-evolving technology, many applications have become commonplace in everyday life.[53]

Expert systems, the most advanced management information systems available, incorporate artificial intelligence in their design.[54] An **expert system** is a system that employs human knowledge, embedded in computer software, to solve problems that ordinarily require human expertise.[55] Mimicking human expertise (and intelligence) requires IT that can at a minimum (1) recognize, formulate, and solve a problem; (2) explain the solution; and (3) learn from experience. A basic expert system can apply decision rules to repeated situations like whether to offer a loan or how much material to order for a production process. A human decision maker typically reviews the expert system's recommendation. But as expert systems apply more artificial intelligence and improve their predictive ability, they are replacing more of the work of human decision makers. The "Managing Globally" feature describes an example of using artificial intelligence at a financial company in China.

expert system A management information system that employs human knowledge, embedded in a computer, to solve problems that ordinarily require human expertise.

MANAGING GLOBALLY

China's Ant Group Runs on AI

At China-based Ant Group, artificial intelligence isn't just a way to improve how work is done; it *is* how work is done. AI-based systems accept deposits, approve loans, assign credit ratings, and deliver financial advice. These automated decisions are based on massive amounts of data because Ant is an expansion of Alipay, the online-payments system developed to enable transactions on Alibaba, the e-commerce platform that dwarfs U.S.-based Amazon. Ant Group's roots also help explain its rapid growth: Alipay offered customers the option to deposit extra cash in a money market fund, and this easy, relatively high-interest form of saving attracted hundreds of millions of customers. Once Ant had customers, it wrote more software to add services, such as lending and asset management, based on what it learned about customers from their interactions with the entire Alibaba company.[56]

In terms of technology, Ant Group is a kind of "AI factory." Its computer systems gather data systematically, apply algorithms to make predictions about the business, test hypotheses about various decisions, and connect all of this analysis to employees and customers. This model integrates the various lines of work in a way that has been impossible for traditional companies built on the expertise of human specialists in different departments.[57]

An AI factory has advantages for Ant Group and its customers. The company can expand without a lot of hiring and construction. Further, the bigger it gets, the more data it acquires for machine learning about its own industry and about customers' needs that could be served through new kinds of services. For customers, Ant offers an easy way into building wealth and obtaining credit in China and other markets where these services have been limited or even nonexistent.[58]

However, risks can arise when a company grows so fast with AI at its core. The company's behavior is only as good as its algorithms. If there is a flaw in an algorithm, its impact can be amplified by the company's size. Over just a few years, Ant Group's money market fund became one of the world's largest. Such funds are low risk compared with holding stock but riskier than savings accounts, which most countries insure up to some level. Not surprisingly, then, China's government has begun to explore regulation of money market funds within the country and forced Ant Group to restructure to ensure the firm's business is brought under government regulatory limits. As a result, Ant Group has shifted its focus toward selling information technology and consulting services to other financial institutions.[59]

Enterprise Resource Planning Systems

To achieve high performance, it is not sufficient just to develop an MIS inside each of a company's functions or divisions to provide better information and knowledge. It is also vital that managers in the different functions and divisions have access to information about the activities of managers in other functions and divisions. The greater the flow of information and knowledge among functions and divisions, the more learning can take place, and this builds a company's stock of knowledge and expertise. This knowledge and expertise are the source of its competitive advantage and profitability.

Over the past 25 years, another revolution has taken place in IT as software companies have worked to develop enterprise resource planning systems, which essentially incorporate most MIS aspects just discussed, as well as much more. **Enterprise resource planning (ERP) systems** are multimodule application software packages that allow a company to link and coordinate the entire set of functional activities and operations necessary to move products from the initial design stage to the final customer stage. Essentially, ERP systems (1) help each individual function improve its functional-level skills and (2) improve integration among all functions so they work together to build a competitive advantage for the company. Today choosing and designing an ERP system to improve how a company operates is the biggest challenge facing the IT function inside a company. To understand why almost every large global company has installed an ERP system in the last few decades, it is necessary to return to the concept of the value chain, introduced in Chapter 9.

enterprise resource planning (ERP) systems Multimodule application software packages that coordinate the functional activities necessary to move products from the design stage to the final customer stage.

Recall that a company's value chain is composed of the sequence of functional activities that are necessary to make and sell a product. The value chain idea focuses attention on the fact that each function, in sequence, performs its activities to add or contribute value to a product. After one function has made its contribution, it hands the product over to the next function, which makes its own contribution, and so on down the line.

The primary activity of marketing, for example, is to uncover new or changing customer needs or new groups of customers and then decide what kinds of products should be developed to appeal to those customers. It shares, or "hands off," its information to product development, where engineers and scientists work to develop and design the new products. In turn, manufacturing and materials management work to find ways to make the new products as efficiently as possible. Then sales is responsible for finding the best way to convince customers to buy these products.

The value chain is useful in demonstrating the sequence of activities necessary to bring products to the market successfully. In an IT context, however, it suggests the enormous amount of information and communication that needs to link and coordinate the activities of all the various functions. Installing an ERP system for a large company can cost tens of millions of dollars.

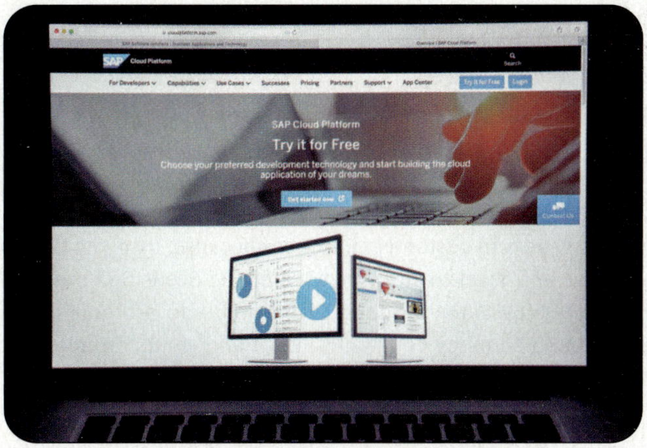

A leading supplier of ERP software, SAP provides businesses with application software to link and coordinate cross-functional activities.
Casimiro PT/Shutterstock

As an example of how an ERP system works, let's examine how SAP, one of the world's leading suppliers of ERP software, helps management coordinate activities to speed product development. Suppose marketing has discovered some new unmet customer need, has suggested what kind of product needs to be developed, and forecasts that the demand for the product will be 40,000 units a year. With SAP's IT, engineers in product development use their expert system to work out how to design the new product in a way that builds in quality at the lowest possible cost. Manufacturing managers, watching product development's progress, work simultaneously to find the best way to make the product and thus use their expert system to find out how to keep operating costs at a minimum.

SAP's IT gives all the other functions access to this information; they can tap into what is going on between marketing and manufacturing in real time. So materials management managers, watching manufacturing make its plans, can simultaneously plan how to order supplies of inputs or components from global suppliers or how and when to ship the final product to customers to keep costs at a minimum. At the same time, HRM is tied into the ERP system and uses its expert system to forecast the type and cost of the labor that will be required to carry out the activities in the other functions–for example, the number of manufacturing employees who will be required to make the product or the number of salespeople who will be needed to sell the product to achieve the 40,000 sales forecast.

How does this build competitive advantage and profitability? First, it speeds up product development; companies can bring products to market much more quickly, thereby generating higher sales revenues. Second, SAP's IT focuses on how to drive down operating costs while keeping quality high. Third, SAP's IT is oriented toward the final customer; its customer relationship management (CRM) module watches how customers respond to the new product and then feeds back this information quickly to the other functions.

To see what this means in practice, let's jump ahead three months and suppose that the CRM component of SAP's ERP software reports that actual sales are 20% below target. Further, the software has reasoned that the problem is occurring because the product lacks a crucial feature that customers want. The product is a smartphone, for example, and customers demand a built-in digital camera. The sales group decides this issue deserves major priority and alerts managers in all the other functions about the problem. Now managers can begin to decide how to manage this unexpected situation.

Engineers in product development, for example, use their expert system to work out how much it would cost, and how long it would take, to modify the product so that it includes the missing feature, the digital camera, that customers require. Managers in other functions watch the engineers' progress through the ERP system and can make suggestions for improvement. In the meantime, manufacturing managers know about the slow sales and have already cut back on production to avoid a buildup of the unsold product in the company's warehouse. They are also planning how to phase out this product and introduce the next version, with the digital camera, to keep costs as low as possible. Similarly, materials management managers are contacting digital camera makers to find out how much such a camera will cost and when it can be supplied. Meanwhile marketing managers are researching how they missed this crucial product feature and are developing new sales forecasts to estimate demand for the modified product. They announce a revised sales forecast of 75,000 units of the modified product.

It takes the engineers one month to modify the product; but because SAP's IT has been providing information about the modified product to managers in manufacturing and materials management, the product reaches the market only two months later. Within weeks, the sales function reports that early sales figures for the product have greatly exceeded even marketing's revised forecast. The company knows it has a winning product, and top managers give the go-ahead for manufacturing to build a second production line to double production of the product. All the other functions are expecting this decision; in fact, they have already been experimenting with their SAP modules to find out how long it will take them to respond to such a move. Each function gives the others its latest information so they can all adjust their functional activities accordingly.

This quick and responsive action is possible because of the ERP system that gives a company better control of its manufacturing and materials management activities. Quality is increased because a greater flow of information between functions allows a better-designed product. Innovation is accelerated because a company can rapidly change its products to suit the needs of customers. Finally, responsiveness to customers improves because, using its CRM software module, sales can better manage and react to customers' changing needs and provide better service and support to back up the sales of the product. ERP's ability to promote competitive advantage is the reason managers in so many companies, large and small, are moving to find the best ERP solution for their particular companies.

E-Commerce Systems

e-commerce The trading of goods and services on the Internet.

business-to-business (B2B) commerce Trade that takes place between companies using IT and the Internet to link and coordinate the value chains of different companies.

B2B marketplace An Internet-based trading platform set up to connect buyers and sellers in an industry.

business-to-customer (B2C) commerce Trade that takes place between a company and individual customers using IT and the Internet.

E-commerce is trade that takes place between companies, and between companies and individual customers, using IT and the Internet. **Business-to-business (B2B) commerce** is trade that takes place between companies using IT and the Internet to link and coordinate the value chains of different companies. (See Figure 18.5.) The goal of B2B commerce is to increase the profitability of making and selling goods and services. B2B commerce increases profitability because it lets companies reduce operating costs and may improve product quality. Recent estimates suggest that B2B e-commerce sales in the United States could top $2.45 trillion by 2025. In addition, more than 70% of B2B customers use mobile devices for their purchases.[60] A principal B2B software application is **B2B marketplaces**, which are Internet-based trading platforms that have been set up in many industries to connect buyers and sellers. To participate in a B2B marketplace, companies adopt a common software standard that allows them to search for and share information with one another. Then companies can work together over time to find ways to reduce costs or improve quality.

Business-to-customer (B2C) commerce is trade that takes place between a company and individual customers using IT and the Internet. Using IT to connect directly to the customer means companies can avoid having to use intermediaries, such as wholesalers and retailers, who capture a significant part of the profit in the value chain. The use of websites and online stores also lets companies give their customers much more information about the value of their products.

Figure 18.5

Types of E-Commerce

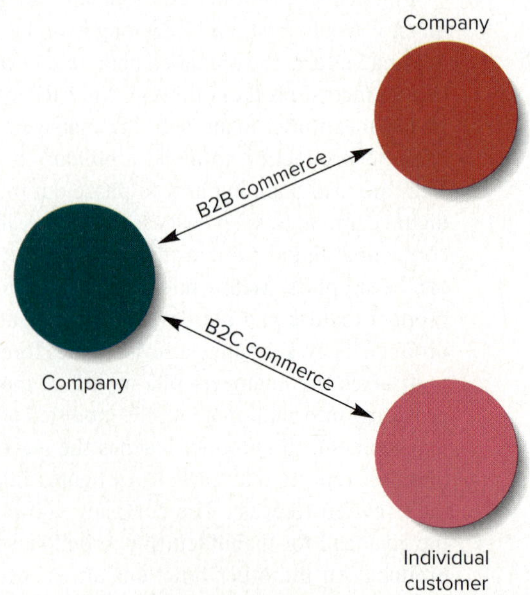

This often allows them to attract more customers and thus generate higher sales revenues. Recent estimates suggest that B2C e-commerce sales globally will exceed $8 trillion by 2026.[61]

Software makers, including Microsoft, Oracle, SAP, and IBM, have rushed to use cloud computing to make their products work seamlessly with the Internet and thus respond to global companies' growing demand for e-commerce software. Previously, their software was configured to work only on a particular company's intranet; today their software must be able to network a company's IT systems to other companies, such as their suppliers and distributors. At the same time, as we discussed earlier, companies also need to use software to establish a secure platform their employees can use to share information inside their organizations.

The challenge facing managers now is to select e-commerce software that allows seamless exchange of information between companies anywhere in the world. The stakes are high because global competitive advantage goes to the company first with a major new technological advance. For example, SAP rushed to update its ERP modules to allow transactions over the Internet, and today all its modules have full cloud computing capability. However, Oracle, IBM, and many small specialist companies have also developed ways to provide advanced cloud computing and Internet applications at a lower price, so SAP faces increased global competition.

In summary, by using advanced types of MIS, managers have more control over a company's activities and operations and can work to improve its competitive advantage and profitability. Today the IT function is becoming increasingly important because IT managers select which kind of hardware and software a company will use and then train other functional managers and employees to use it effectively as part of daily business operations.

The Impact and Limitations of Information Technology

Advances in IT and management information systems are having important effects on managers and organizations. By improving the ability of managers to coordinate and control the activities of the organization and by helping managers make more effective decisions, modern IT has become a central component of any organization's structure. And evidence that IT can be a source of competitive advantage is growing; organizations that do not adopt leading-edge IT are likely to be at a competitive disadvantage. In this section, we examine how the rapid advances in IT are affecting organizational structure and competitive advantage. We also examine problems associated with implementing management information systems effectively, as well as the limitations of MIS.

LO18-5 Explain how IT is helping managers build strategic alliances and network structures to increase efficiency and effectiveness.

Strategic Alliances, B2B Network Structures, and IT

Increasing globalization and the use of new IT have brought about two innovations that are sweeping through global companies: electronically managed strategic alliances and B2B network structures. A **strategic alliance** is a formal agreement that commits two or more companies to exchange or share their resources in order to produce and market a product.[62] Most commonly, strategic alliances are formed because the companies share similar interests and believe they can benefit from cooperating. For example, Disney recently entered into a strategic alliance with McDonald's that will bring Disney movie toys back to Happy Meals for the first time in more than a decade. This strategic move will give both global brands new ways to market their products to families over the next several years. In 2006, Disney ended an agreement with the fast-food giant because the children's meals didn't meet Disney's nutritional guidelines.[63]

strategic alliance An agreement in which managers pool or share their organization's resources and know-how with a foreign company, and the two organizations share the rewards and risks of starting a new venture.

Throughout the 2000s, the growing sophistication of IT using global intranets, cloud computing, and teleconferencing made it much easier to manage strategic alliances and allow managers to share information and cooperate. One outcome of this has been the growth of strategic alliances into an IT-based network structure. A **B2B network structure** is a formal series of global strategic alliances that one or several organizations create with suppliers, manufacturers, and distributors to produce and market a product. Network structures allow an organization to manage its global value chain in order to find new ways to reduce costs and increase the quality of products—without incurring the high costs of operating a complex organizational

B2B network structure A series of global strategic alliances that an organization creates with suppliers, manufacturers, and distributors to produce and market a product.

structure (such as the costs of employing many managers). More and more companies are relying on global network structures to gain access to low-cost foreign sources of inputs, as discussed in Chapter 6.

Nike is the largest and most profitable sports shoe manufacturer in the world. The key to Nike's success is the network structure that Nike founder Philip Knight created to allow his company to produce and market shoes. As noted in Chapter 8, the most successful companies today are trying to pursue simultaneously a low-cost and a differentiation strategy. Knight decided early that to do this at Nike he needed to focus his company's efforts on the most important functional activities, such as product design and engineering, and leave the others, such as manufacturing, to other organizations.

By far the largest function at Nike's Oregon headquarters is the design and engineering function, whose members pioneered innovations in sports shoe design such as the air pump and Air Jordans that Nike introduced so successfully. Designers use computer-aided design (CAD) to design Nike shoes, and they electronically store all new product information, including manufacturing instructions. When the designers have finished their work, they electronically transmit the blueprints for the new products to a network of Southeast Asian suppliers and manufacturers with which Nike has formed strategic alliances.[64] Instructions for the design of a new sole may be sent to a supplier in Taiwan, instructions for the leather uppers to a supplier in Malaysia. The suppliers produce the shoe parts and send them for final assembly to a manufacturer in China with which Nike has established another strategic alliance. From China the shoes are shipped to distributors throughout the world. Ninety-nine percent of the over 780 million pairs of shoes that Nike makes each year are made in Southeast Asia.[65]

This network structure gives Nike two important advantages. First, Nike can quickly respond to changes in sports shoe fashion. Using its global IT system, Nike literally can change the instructions it gives each of its suppliers overnight, so that within a few weeks its foreign manufacturers are producing new kinds of shoes.[66] Any alliance partners that fail to perform up to Nike's standards are replaced with new partners through the regular B2B marketplace.

Second, Nike's costs are low because wages in Southeast Asia are a fraction of what they are in the United States, and this difference gives Nike a low-cost advantage. Also, Nike's ability to outsource and use foreign manufacturers to produce all its shoes abroad allows the company to keep the organization's U.S. structure flat and flexible. Nike can use a relatively inexpensive functional structure to organize its activities.

The use of network structures is increasing rapidly as organizations recognize the many opportunities they offer to reduce costs and increase organizational flexibility. Supply chain spending by U.S. firms exceeded $1.85 trillion in 2021.[67] The push to lower costs has led to the development of B2B marketplaces in which most or all of the companies in an industry (for example, carmakers) use the same software platform to link to each other and establish industry specifications and standards. Then these companies jointly list the quantity and specifications of the inputs they require and invite bids from the thousands of potential suppliers around the world. Suppliers also use the same software platform, so electronic bidding, auctions, and transactions are possible between buyers and sellers around the world. The idea is that high-volume standardized transactions can help drive down costs at the industry level. Also, quality will increase as these relationships become more stable as a B2B network structure develops.

Flatter Structures and Horizontal Information Flows

Rapid advances in IT have been associated with a "delayering," or flattening, of the organizational hierarchy, a move toward greater decentralization and horizontal information flows within organizations, and the concept of the boundaryless organization.[68] By electronically giving managers high-quality, timely, relevant, and relatively complete information, modern management information systems have reduced the need for tall management hierarchies. Modern IT has reduced the need for a hierarchy to function as a means of coordinating and controlling organizational activities. Also, by reducing the need for hierarchy, modern IT can directly increase an organization's efficiency because fewer employees are required to perform organizational activities.

boundaryless organization An organization linked by computers, mobile technology, and video teleconferencing and whose employees and associates rarely, if ever, see one another face-to-face.

knowledge management system A company-specific virtual information system that systematizes the knowledge of its employees and facilitates the sharing and integration of their expertise.

The ability of IT to flatten structure and facilitate the flow of horizontal information between employees has led many researchers and consultants to popularize the idea of a **boundaryless organization**. Such an organization is composed of people linked by IT—computers, mobile technology, and videoconferencing—who may rarely, if ever, see one another face-to-face. People are used when their services are needed, but they are not formal members of an organization; they are functional experts who form an alliance with an organization, fulfill their contractual obligations, and then move on to the next project.

Large consulting companies, such as Accenture, IBM, and McKinsey & Co., use their global consultants in this way. Consultants are connected to an organization's **knowledge management system**—its company-specific virtual information system that systematizes the knowledge of its employees and facilitates the sharing and integration of expertise within and between functions and divisions through real-time interconnected IT. Knowledge management systems let employees share their knowledge and expertise and give them virtual access to other employees who have the expertise to solve the problems they encounter as they perform their jobs.

Some organizations, especially those that provide complex services and employ highly trained workers, have gone one step further and created what has been called a virtual organization. A *virtual organization* is one in which employees are linked to an organization's centralized information system and rarely see one another in person, if ever. These employees might only infrequently visit the physical locations of their companies; they receive their assignments electronically, report back to their superiors electronically, and operate autonomously. Almost all their employees are out in the field, working anywhere around the globe with clients to solve their problems. According to Virtual Vocations, the top companies in 2022 for remote work included UnitedHealth Group, Amazon, Liberty Mutual Insurance, and U.S. Bank.[69]

Despite their usefulness, IT in general, and management information systems, in particular, have some limitations. A serious potential problem is that in all the enthusiasm for MIS, communication via computer networks might lose the vital human element of communication. There is a strong argument that electronic communication should support face-to-face communication rather than replacing it. For example, it would be wrong to make a judgment about an individual's performance merely by "reading the numbers" provided by an MIS. Instead, the numbers should be used to alert managers to individuals who may have a performance problem. The nature of this problem should then be explored in a face-to-face meeting, during which more detailed information can be gathered. One drawback of using IT, such as email and teleconferencing, is that employees may spend too much time watching their computer screens and communicating electronically—and little time interacting directly with other employees.[70] If this occurs, important and relevant information may not be obtained because of the lack of face-to-face contact, and the quality of decision making may suffer.

Summary and Review

LO18-1, 18-2 **INFORMATION AND THE MANAGER'S JOB** Computer-based technology is central to the operation of most organizations. By giving managers high-quality, timely, relevant, and relatively complete information, properly implemented technology can improve managers' ability to coordinate and control the operations of an organization and to make effective decisions. Moreover, IT can help the organization attain a competitive advantage through its beneficial impact on productivity, quality, innovation, and responsiveness to customers. Technology is an indispensable management tool; however, it comes with several consequences that require managers to control these technological advances. The increase in cybercrimes—events in which data hackers leverage weak security measures and steal company and customer data—have become common in this digital age. In addition, consumers and organizations alike must be vigilant when it comes to ensuring the privacy of key data and information.

LO18-3 **THE TECHNOLOGY REVOLUTION** Over the last 30 years, there have been rapid advances in the power and rapid declines in the cost of technology. Falling prices, wireless communication, computer networks, and software developments have all radically improved the power and efficacy of computer-based technology.

LO18-4 TYPES OF MANAGEMENT INFORMATION SYSTEMS Traditionally, managers used the organizational hierarchy as the main system for gathering the information they needed to coordinate and control the organization and to make effective decisions. Today managers use six main types of computer-based information systems. Listed in ascending order of sophistication, they are transaction-processing systems, operations information systems, decision support systems, expert systems, enterprise resource planning systems, and e-commerce systems.

LO18-5 THE IMPACT AND LIMITATIONS OF INFORMATION TECHNOLOGY Advances in technology have changed organizational structure in many ways. Using technology, managers can create electronic strategic alliances and form a B2B network structure. A network structure, based on some shared form of technology, can be formed around one company, or a number of companies can join together to create an industry B2B network. Technology also makes organizations flatter and encourages more horizontal cross-functional communication. As this increasingly happens across the organizational boundary, the term *boundaryless organizations* has been coined to refer to virtual organizations whose members are linked electronically.

Management in Action

Topics for Discussion and Action

Discussion

1. To be useful, information must be of high quality, be timely, be relevant, and be as complete as possible. Why does a tall management hierarchy, when used as a management information system, have negative effects on these desirable attributes? [LO18-1]
2. What is the relationship between technology and competitive advantage? [LO18-2]
3. Because of the growth of high-powered, low-cost wireless communications and technology such as videoconferencing, many managers may not need to go into the office to do their jobs. They will be able to work at home. What are the pros and cons of such an arrangement? [LO18-3, 18-4, 18-5]
4. Many companies have reported that it is difficult to implement advanced management information systems such as ERP systems. Why do you think this is so? How might the roadblocks to implementation be removed? [LO18-4]
5. How can IT help in the new product development process? [LO18-4]
6. Why is face-to-face communication between managers still important in an organization? [LO18-4, 18-5]

Action

7. Ask a manager to describe the main kinds of technology that they use on a routine basis at work. [LO18-1, 18-4]
8. Compare the pros and cons of using a network structure to perform organizational activities versus performing all activities in-house or within one organizational hierarchy. [LO18-3, 18-4, 18-5]
9. What are the advantages and disadvantages of business-to-business networks? [LO18-5]

Building Management Skills

Analyzing Management Information Systems [LO18-3, 18-4]

Pick an organization about which you have some direct knowledge. It may be an organization you worked for in the past or are in contact with now (such as the college or school you attend). For this organization, answer the following questions:

1. Describe the management information systems that are used to coordinate and control organizational activities and to help make decisions.
2. Do you think that the organization's existing MIS gives managers high-quality, timely, relevant, and relatively complete information? Why or why not?
3. How might advanced technology improve the competitive position of this organization? In particular, try to identify the impact that a new MIS might have on the organization's efficiency, quality, innovation, and responsiveness to customers.

Managing Ethically [LO18-1, 18-2]

The use of management information systems, such as ERPs, often gives employees access to confidential information from all functions and levels of an organization. Employees can see important information about the company's products that is of great value to competitors. As a result, many companies monitor employees' use of the intranet and Internet to prevent employees from acting unethically, such as by selling product information to competitors. On the other hand, with access to this information, employees might discover that their company has been engaging in unethical or even illegal practices.

Questions

1. Ethically speaking, how far should a company go to protect its proprietary information, given that it also needs to protect the privacy of its employees? What steps can it take?
2. When is it ethical for employees to give information about a company's unethical or illegal practices to a third party, such as a newspaper or government agency?

Small Group Breakout Exercise

Using New Management Information Systems [LO18-2, 18-4]

Form groups of three or four people, and appoint one member as the spokesperson who will communicate your findings to the class when called on by the instructor. Then discuss the following scenario:

You are a team of managing partners of a large management consulting company. You are responsible for auditing your firm's MIS to determine whether it is appropriate and up to date. To your surprise, you find that although your organization has a wireless email system in place and consultants are connected into a powerful local area network (LAN) at all times, most of the consultants (including partners) are not using this technology. It seems that most important decision making still takes place through the organizational hierarchy.

Given this situation, you are concerned that your organization is not exploiting the opportunities offered by new IT to obtain a competitive advantage. You have discussed this issue and are meeting to develop an action plan to get consultants to appreciate the need to learn about and use the new IT.

1. What advantages can you tell consultants they will obtain when they use the new IT?
2. What problems do you think you may encounter in convincing consultants to use the new IT?
3. What steps might you take to motivate consultants to learn to use the new technology?

Be the Manager [LO18-4]

You are one of the managers of a small specialty maker of custom tables, chairs, and cabinets. You have been charged with finding ways to use IT and the Internet to identify new business opportunities that can improve your company's competitive advantage, such as ways to reduce costs or attract customers.

Questions

1. What are the various forces in a specialty furniture maker's task environment that have the most effect on its performance?
2. What kinds of IT or MIS can help the company better manage these forces?
3. In what ways can the Internet help this organization improve its competitive position?

Case in the News [LO18-1, 18-2, 18-4]

AI Fuels a Transformation at Shell

Royal Dutch Shell covers the supply chain for oil and gas, from extracting to refining to retailing. Oil demand is expected to peak during the 2030s, and international pressure for reducing carbon emissions is intensifying, so Shell developed a strategy to become a cleaner but more profitable player in the energy industry. Its core business will remain oil and gas, but to reduce fossil-fuel emissions and benefit from the shift to electrically powered vehicles and processes, Shell will pursue greater involvement in the electricity sector, aiming to become the world's largest electric power company.

To carry out this business transformation, Shell is investing in artificial intelligence. By a recent count, Shell had embarked on about 280 AI projects with potential to increase the efficiency of all areas of business while promoting safety and reducing carbon emissions. Many projects involve machine learning in which the AI software uses decades of data from the company's sensor-equipped processes and information systems. The learning process includes a reward system that signals when the AI decisions achieve outcomes the company is seeking, such as reductions in downtime, accidents, or pollution. As the system generates decisions, it applies what it learned from the past data and continues to learn from new outcomes.

AI at Shell is speeding up oil exploration and increasing the efficiency of drilling. Exploration relies on surveys of the land under which the company hopes to find oil and gas deposits. Especially for surveys of the ocean floor, imaging can suffer from "noisy data," or irrelevant inputs such as ocean currents. Shell uses machine learning to create algorithms for filtering out the noise and creating a clearer image. When human workers carried out that work, they took months to interpret images; with AI, they can do it a few weeks, so they can scan more locations and potentially find better options for drilling. In drilling, the systems apply knowledge from drilling records and data from land surveys and drill bits to guide the drills. The human operator of the equipment uses guidance from AI to work faster and more accurately, reducing wear and tear on the equipment.

Many of Shell's operations involve expensive and complex equipment. AI is helping to keep it running efficiently with applications for predictive maintenance. Wired or wireless sensors gather performance data from the equipment—for example, temperature and pressure of specific parts. Based on machine learning, the system can identify conditions that have been associated with a malfunction in the past and trigger an alert to carry out maintenance days or weeks before a system failure. In the first two weeks of predictive maintenance at Shell's Pernis oil refinery in the Netherlands, AI prevented two malfunctions, saving the company an estimated $2 million.

In the retail sector, Shell's recent acquisitions have included makers of electric-vehicle charging stations. At test sites in California, AI monitors the demand for them, helping Shell plan how to distribute the electrical load and ensure that these services are efficient. In another trial, at Shell gas stations in Singapore and Thailand, computers monitor consumer behavior at the pumps to detect scenes matching the image of a person smoking. When analysis of an image identifies this hazardous behavior, the system sends an alert to the station manager. Future applications could send alerts for detection of reckless driving or criminal activity. AI about consumer behavior also may help Shell better target rewards to customers who join its loyalty program.

Introducing AI into the business requires talent that is in high demand. Shell's payroll includes more than 150 data scientists, but it needs more people who can apply the technology. The company has invited employees to sign up for free AI training on company time; so far, about 2,000 have enrolled or been asked. Shell also has a residency program in which people with relevant educational backgrounds can work on AI projects for two years, after which they may be considered for a permanent position.

Another management challenge is selecting the projects to fund, given that data analytics and AI have so many possible applications. Shell's chief technology officer aims to focus on projects that can give the company a competitive advantage. Shell's vice president in charge of digitization steers decision makers toward starting with the problem, such as downtime or emissions reduction, then looking for the best technology, rather than starting with AI methods and looking for applications.

Questions for Discussion

1. Based on the information given, how well would you say Shell's move to AI-based information systems provides the attributes of useful information (quality, timeliness, completeness, and relevance)? Briefly explain your assessment.

2. How could cybersecurity and data privacy risks affect Shell as it transitions to greater use of AI in its information systems?

3. If you were a manager of a Shell oil rig or planning the rollout of more electric-vehicle charging stations, would you expect the use of AI to make your work more interesting or less so? Why?

Sources: "Shell.ai Residency Programme," and "Artificial Intelligence," Shell Global, www.shell.com, accessed February 23, 2023; N. Naoum, "For Shell, AI and Data Is as Critical as Oil," *Venture Beat*, https://venturebeat.com, June 24, 2022; P. Rooney, "Shell Sees AI as Fuel for Its Sustainability Goals," *CIO Magazine*, www.cio.com, February 28, 2022; N. Coleman, "Technology, AI Transforming All Parts of Shell: CTO," S&P Global, www.spglobal.com, February 21, 2020; S. Castellanos, "Shell Aims to Enroll Thousands in Online Artificial-Intelligence Training," *The Wall Street Journal*, www.wsj.com, February 13, 2020; J. Council, "Shell's Companywide AI Effort Shows Early Returns," *The Wall Street Journal*, www.wsj.com, November 26, 2019; N. Thomas, "AI Sensors Keep Fuel Flowing at Europe's Largest Refinery," *Financial Times*, www.ft.com, November 10, 2019; G. Petroni, "Oil Giant Shell's Pivot to Electricity Could Bring Investors Less Sizzle," *The Wall Street Journal*, July 13, 2019, www.wsj.com, July 13, 2019; B. Marr, "The Incredible Ways Shell Uses Artificial Intelligence to Help Transform the Oil and Gas Giant," *Forbes*, www.forbes.com, January 18, 2019.

Notes

1. E. Loutfi, "What Does the Future Hold for AI-Enabled Coaching?" *Chief Learning Officer*, www.chieflearningofficer.com, November 25, 2019; K. Ang, "Companies Use AI to Help Managers Become More Human," *The Wall Street Journal*, www.wsj.com, April 29, 2018; J. Mannes, "Butterfly Nabs $2.4M Seed Round to Improve Managers with Targeted Tips," *TechCrunch*, http://techcrunch.com, October 6, 2017; S.F. Gale, "Robot Coaches: New Model for Leadership Training?" *Chief Learning Officer*, www.chieflearningofficer.com, August 25, 2017.

2. S. Shellenbarger, "The Robots That Manage the Managers," *The Wall Street Journal*, www.wsj.com, April 15, 2019.

3. "Work of the Future: Butterfly a.i.," *MIT Solve*, https://solve.mit.edu, accessed February 23, 2023; "Why Butterfly?" www.butterfly.ai, accessed March 20, 2020.

4. L. Bannon, "AI in the Workplace Is Already Here. The First Battleground? Call Centers," *The Wall Street Journal*, www.wsj.com, February 18, 2023.

5. J. Bughin, E. Hazan, S. Lund, et al., "Skill Shift: Automation and the Future of the Workforce," *McKinsey and Company*, www.mckinsey.com, accessed February 23, 2023; C. Mims, "Meet the Army of Robots Coming to Fill In for Scarce Workers," *The Wall Street Journal*, www.wsj.com, October 15, 2022.
6. "What Is the Difference between Data and Information?" www.computerhope.com, accessed March 20, 2020.
7. J. Cotton, "Data: The Importance of Accuracy, Integrity and Real-Time Integration," ww2.informationbuilders.com, accessed May 5, 2018.
8. T. Chen, L. Ravindranath, S. Deng, P. Bahl, and H. Balakrishnan, "Glimpse: Continuous, Real-Time Object Recognition on Mobile Devices," www.microsoft.com, accessed May 5, 2018.
9. "About Transit" and "Supported Regions," https://transitapp.com, accessed February 23, 2023.
10. A. Ranadive, "Making Decisions under Uncertainty," https://medium.com, accessed March 19, 2020.
11. E. Turban, *Decision Support and Expert Systems* (New York: Macmillan, 1988).
12. W.H. Davidow and M.S. Malone, *The Virtual Corporation* (New York: Harper Business, 1992); M. E. Porter, *Competitive Advantage* (New York: Free Press, 1984).
13. B. Marr, "The Top 10 Tech Trends in 2023 Everyone Must Be Ready For," *Forbes*, www.forbes.com, November 21, 2022.
14. "Big Data—Statistics & Facts," *Statista*, www.statista.com, October 19, 2022.
15. "What Is Big Data Analytics?" https://searchbusinessanalytics.techtarget.com, accessed March 19, 2020.
16. "Big Data Analytics: What It Is and Why It Matters," https://www.sas.com, accessed March 19, 2020.
17. S.M. Dornbusch and W.R. Scott, *Evaluation and the Exercise of Authority* (San Francisco: Jossey-Bass, 1975).
18. J. Child, *Organization: A Guide to Problems and Practice* (London: Harper & Row, 1984).
19. "UPS Shipping Services," www.ups.com, accessed February 23, 2023.
20. "Disney Magic Band 101: Everything You Need to Know," *The Frugal South*, www.thefrugalsouth.com, February 14, 2023; J. Hollander, "Disney's MagicBand: Breaking Down One of Hospitality's Greatest Innovations," *Hotel Tech Report*, https://hoteltechreport.com, October 28, 2022.
21. "Princess Cruises' Ocean Medallion FAQs," *Cruise Web*, https://cruiseweb.com, accessed February 23, 2023.
22. "What Is Cybersecurity?" *Palo Alto Networks*, www.paloaltonetworks.com, accessed May 3, 2018.
23. "10 Most Important Global Business Risks for 2023 per Allianz Risk Barometer," *BeInsure*, https://beinsure.com, January 17, 2023.
24. J. Weatherbed, "T-Mobile Announces Another Data Breach, Impacting 37 Million Accounts," *The Verge*, www.theverge.com, January 20, 2023.
25. L.H. Newman, "T-Mobile's $150 Million Security Plan Isn't Cutting It," *Wired*, www.wired.com, January 28, 2023.
26. E. MacBride, "The Dark Web's Criminal Minds See Internet of Things as Next Big Hacking Prize," *CNBC*, www.cnbc.com, January 9, 2023.
27. B. Marr, "The Top 4 Internet of Things Trends in 2023," *Forbes*, www.forbes.com, accessed February 23, 2023.
28. K.S. Nash, "Tech Cyber Companies Launch Security Standard to Monitor Hacking Attempts," *The Wall Street Journal*, www.wsj.com, August 10, 2022.
29. A. Gasparro and J. Kang, "Grocers Wrest Control of Shelf Space from Struggling Food Giants," *The Wall Street Journal*, www.wsj.com, February 19, 2020; R. Redman, "Kroger's 84.51° Launches Omnichannel Analytics Tool for CPGs," *Supermarket News*, www.supermarketnews.com, July 18, 2019.
30. M. O'Brien, "Kroger's 84.51° Labs: Pushing the Boundaries of Data Science (podcast)," *Multichannel Merchants*, https://multichannelmerchant.com, October 11, 2022.
31. J. Davis, "Grocery Giant Kroger's Data Side Hustle," *Information Week*, www.informationweek.com, January 9, 2023; D. Berthiaume, "Kroger Offers Brands Deeper Marketing Analytics," *Chain Store Age*, https://chainstoreage.com, February 13, 2020.
32. Davis, "Kroger's Data Side Hustle"; A. Kleckler, "Fresh Tech Perspectives: Three GenNext Award Winners Talk about What's Next for Grocery," *Progressive Grocer*, https://progressivegrocer.com, February 11, 2020.
33. K. Schink, "The Super New Bowl Trend Coming to Disney Parks," *D23*, https://d23.com, accessed February 23, 2023; S. Porges, "Inside the Backstage Lab Where Disney Mixes Story and Tech into Food," Forbes, www.forbes.com, January 26, 2018.
34. J. Trujillo, "Starbucks Origin Trip Builds a Bridge between Partners and Rwandan Farmers," https://news.starbucks.com, May 1, 2017.
35. K. Yuan, "How Starbucks Changed Its Take on the Supply Chain (and What Ariana Grande Fans Taught the Company)," *Fortune*, https://fortune.com, October 21, 2019.
36. M. Meisenzahl, "Starbucks Cup Lids Are Falling Off—It's Not Your Imagination. Workers Say It's a Problem," *Business Insider*, www.businessinsider.com, January 20, 2023; "Starbucks Is Running Out of Coffee," *The Commons Cafe*, www.thecommonscafe.com, December 10, 2022.
37. A. Sraders, "What Is the Product Life Cycle? Stages and Examples," *The Street*, www.thestreet.com, March 4, 2019.
38. A. Orr, "Apple Watch Series 8 Accounted for Half of Smartwatch Market in Q3 2022," *Apple Insider*, https://appleinsider.com, November 29, 2022.
39. See M.M.J. Berry and J.H. Taggart, "Managing Technology and Innovation: A Review," *R & D Management* 24 (1994), 341–53; K.B. Clark and S.C. Wheelwright, *Managing New Product and Process Development* (New York: Free Press, 1993).
40. A. Mutchler, "Voice Assistant Timeline: A Short History of the Voice Revolution," https://voicebot.ai, accessed February 23, 2023.
41. F. Laricchia, "Market Share of Global Smart Speaker Shipments from 3rd Quarter 2016 to First Quarter 2022 by Vendor," *Statista*, www.statista.com, February 8, 2023.
42. A. Montag, "This 22-Year-Old College Student Makes $10,000 a Month Off Amazon's Alexa," *CNBC*, www.cnbc.com, April 12, 2018.
43. K. Teague, "6 Surprising Ways to Use Your Amazon Echo at Work," *CNET*, www.cnet.com, accessed February 23, 2023.
44. "Alexa for Business: Overview," https://aws.amazon.com, accessed February 23, 2023.
45. See Berry and Taggart, "Managing Technology and Innovation"; M. Gort and J. Klepper, "Time Paths in the Diffusion of Product Innovations," *Economic Journal* (September 1982), 630–53. Looking at the history of 46 products, Gort and Klepper found that the length of time before other companies entered the markets created by a few inventive companies declined from an average of 14.4 years for products introduced before 1930 to 4.9 years for those introduced after 1949—implying that product life cycles were being compressed. Also see A. Griffin, "Metrics for Measuring Product Development Cycle Time," *Journal of Production and Innovation Management* 10 (1993), 112–25.
46. A.D. Chandler, *The Visible Hand* (Cambridge, MA: Harvard University Press, 1977).
47. C.W.L. Hill and J.F. Pickering, "Divisionalization, Decentralization, and

Performance of Large United Kingdom Companies," *Journal of Management Studies* 23 (1986), 26–50.

48. Turban, *Decision Support and Expert Systems.*
49. Corporate website, "Weather Solutions," www.dtn.com, accessed February 23, 2023.
50. Turban, *Decision Support and Expert Systems.*
51. B. Marr, "The Key Definitions of Artificial Intelligence (AI) That Explain Its Importance," *Forbes,* www.forbes.com, February 14, 2018.
52. G. Narula, "Everyday Examples of Artificial Intelligence and Machine Learning," www.techemergence.com, March 29, 2018.
53. G. Kesari, "AI Trends for 2023: Industry Experts (and Chat GPT AI) Make Their Predictions," *Forbes,* www. forbes.com, accessed February 23, 2023.
54. Narula, "Everyday Examples of Artificial Intelligence and Machine Learning."
55. Turban, *Decision Support and Expert Systems.*
56. J. Wong, "China's Ant Group Will Bestride Chinese Markets," *The Wall Street Journal,* July 21, 2020, www.wsj.com; J. Detrixhe, "China No Longer Runs the World's Largest Money Market Fund," *Quartz,* https://qz.com, January 28, 2020; M. Iansiti and K. R. Lakhani, "Competing in the Age of AI," *Harvard Business Review,* January–February 2020, 61–67; "Ant Financial: How a Bug Took on the World," *Euromoney,* www.euromoney.com, September 26, 2019.
57. Iansiti and Lakhani, "Competing in the Age of AI."
58. Ibid.; *Euromoney,* "Ant Financial."
59. M. Shrivastava, "The Continuing Saga of China's Ant Group," *The Diplomat,* https://thediplomat.com, January 12, 2023; Detrixhe, "China No Longer Runs the World's Largest Money Market Fund"; Y. Wang, "China's $7.6 Trillion Online Payments Market Is No Longer Enough for Jack Ma's Ant Financial," *Forbes,* www.forbes.com, January 17, 2020.
60. S. Bennett, "Mobile Marketing Statistics 2023—Everything You Need to Know," *Webinar Care,* https://webinarcare.com, February 20, 2023; A. Phaneuf, "Ecommerce Statistics: Industry Benchmarks & Growth," *Insider Intelligence,* www.insiderintelligence.com, January 8, 2023.
61. S. Chevalier, "Retail e-Commerce Sales Worldwide from 2014 to 2026," *Statista,* www.statista.com, September 21, 2022.
62. B. Kogut, "Joint Ventures: Theoretical and Empirical Perspectives," *Strategic Management Journal* 9 (1988), 319–32.
63. J. Wohl, "Disney, Now Happy with Happy Meals, Reunites with McDonald's," *Advertising Age,* http://adage.com, February 27, 2018.
64. M. Oberoi, "Analyzing Nike's Distribution Channels and Retail Strategy," *Market Realist,* www.marketrealist.com, October 17, 2019; G. S. Capowski, "Designing a Corporate Identity," *Management Review,* June 1993, 37–38.
65. "How Many Shoes Does Nike Sell a Year?" *Shoe Ops,* https://shoeops.com, accessed March 20, 2020.
66. J. Marcia, "Just Doing It," *Distribution,* January 1995, 36–40.
67. L. Young, "Companies Face Rising Supply-Chain Costs Amid Inventory Challenges," *The Wall Street Journal,* www.wsj.com, June 21, 2022.
68. T. Kastelle, "Hierarchy Is Overrated," *Harvard Business Review,* https://hbr.org, accessed March 20, 2020.
69. "Top 100 Companies to Watch for Fully Remote Jobs in 2023," *PR Web,* www.prweb.com, February 21, 2023.
70. "Advantages and Disadvantages of Remote Work," *Next Technology,* https://nexttechnology.io, accessed February 23, 2023.

CHAPTER 19

Starting a New Business

Dragana Gordic/Shutterstock

Learning Objectives

After studying this chapter, you should be able to:

LO19-1 Understand the role of entrepreneurship in today's business environment, and compare the characteristics of entrepreneurs and managers.

LO19-2 Explain the entrepreneurial process from opportunity identification to harvesting, and understand the principles of a sound business plan.

LO19-3 Explain new business creation, and describe the different types of legal structures, financing options, and contemporary business models.

LO19-4 Describe social entrepreneurship and how businesses can do good while still making a profit, and differentiate between the types of social entrepreneurs.

LO19-5 Explain how to successfully utilize corporate entrepreneurship in existing businesses.

A MANAGER'S CHALLENGE

Supergoop! Is Super Entrepreneurial

How can a business do good and prosper? Holly Thaggard was astonished when she learned about the impact the sun has on our skin. Her close friend was diagnosed with skin cancer at the young age of 29, leading Thaggard to spend many sleepless nights researching how this could have happened. She learned that our daily exposure to the sun, starting in our youth, affects our health, even as early as our twenties. As a third grade teacher, Thaggard wanted to ensure the next generation of kids didn't grow up absorbing the sun's harmful rays, so she created the skincare brand Supergoop!.[1]

Supergoop! didn't invent sunscreen, but it did invent a new way to produce and think about this important product. This is because Holly Thaggard believes that entrepreneurs innately refuse to accept the norm and feel that they have the power to inspire change for the better. She started by finding out that people didn't typically wear sunscreen on a daily basis because of the way it felt on their skin.[2] This led Thaggard to create the first oxybenzone-free sunscreen. (Oxybenzone is an irritant and allergen and also damages coral reefs.) Supergoop!'s formula provides full-spectrum protection from the sun's ultraviolet rays, blue light, and infrared radiation while also nourishing the skin.[3]

Thaggard started to market Supergoop! to schools in 2008 because she believed that was the best way to reach a large audience across the country. She soon found out that this approach would be challenging. At the time, because it was classified as an over-the-counter drug, only California allowed sunscreen in public schools. She didn't let this setback doom Supergoop! and instead focused on retail.[4] Using her elementary school teaching skills, Thaggard messaged her product as a feel-good, game-changing innovation to build excitement around it instead of using cancer-based scare tactics.[5] This got the attention of leading retailers like Sephora, which agreed to allow her to stock their shelves year-round instead of just during the summer months. This was important to Thaggard because her business model was built on daily UV protection instead of just using sunscreen when the weather is hot.[6]

Thaggard didn't stop innovating just because Supergoop! was landing on store shelves. She brought in executive talent who knew how to grow a business, launched new skincare products, and increased sales to $40 million by 2016. Then in 2021, the company was able to raise additional financing from Blackstone so that it could fuel its growing product line and production.[7] Blackstone even brought in actor Hugh Jackman, golfer Michelle Wie, and Spanx founder Sara Blakely as investors.[8]

Supergoop! founder Holly Thaggard (*right*) started her business to help others avoid the deadly effects of the sun's rays year-round. She is pictured here with Maria Sharapova, tennis champion and Supergoop! investor.
Rachel Murray/Stringer/Getty Images

Thaggard started her business to help the next generation avoid the sun's deadly rays, but through her innovative spirit, she was also able to create a profitable sunscreen empire. She continues to give back to the community in partnership with foundations, such as the LeBron James Family Foundation, by donating educational materials and products. In fact, Supergoop! has donated more than 4,300 sunscreen pumps to over 1,600 schools and youth organizations nationwide. Thaggard and Supergoop! CEO Amanda Baldwin were named 2022 National Entrepreneur Of The Year® by consulting firm Ernst & Young in an annual competition among more than 200 regional winners.[9]

Overview

As the opening story suggests, entrepreneurship can change the way we live and work. It helps solve daily challenges with the help of innovative products and services, creates an abundance of jobs, and accelerates a nation's overall economic development. Yet the journey to becoming a successful entrepreneur isn't an easy one.

LO19-1 Understand the role of entrepreneurship in today's business environment, and compare the characteristics of entrepreneurs and managers.

In this chapter, we examine the role of entrepreneurship in today's business environment and differentiate between entrepreneurs and managers. We'll then outline the entrepreneurial process, from the development of a business idea, to drafting a business plan and seeking financial backing, successfully managing daily operations, and finally to harvesting or exiting the venture. Next, we'll explore new business creation and important decisions surrounding legal structure, financing, and contemporary business models. The focus then turns to social entrepreneurship, a growing area of entrepreneurship focused on beneficial changes in society (while still making a profit), and the different types of social entrepreneurs in business today. Finally, we'll discuss the important role that corporate entrepreneurship plays in existing organizations and how managers can foster innovation in the workplace. By the end of this chapter, you will appreciate the critical role entrepreneurship plays in the economy today and understand how you can develop your own new business.

Modern Entrepreneurship

entrepreneurs Individuals who notice opportunities and decide how to mobilize resources to produce new or improved goods and services.

entrepreneurship Mobilization of resources to take advantage of an opportunity to provide consumers with new or improved goods and services.

Entrepreneurs are individuals who notice opportunities and decide how to mobilize the resources necessary to produce new and improved goods and services. They make all of the planning, organizing, leading, and controlling decisions needed to start new business ventures. In doing so, entrepreneurs are an important source of creativity in the organizational world. These people, such as Sergey Brin and Larry Page (founders of Google) and Sara Blakely (founder of Spanx), make vast fortunes when their businesses succeed. Or they are among the millions of people who start new business ventures only to lose money when the business fails. Despite the fact that many small businesses fail in the first few years, 6 out of 10 Americans believe that entrepreneurship is a sound career choice.[10] In 2022, small businesses accounted for 99.9% of all U.S. businesses and employed approximately half of the nation's workforce.[11]

Entrepreneurship is the mobilization of resources to take advantage of an opportunity to provide consumers with new or improved goods and services. As you'll read about in this chapter, being an entrepreneur isn't for everyone. A healthy entrepreneurial atmosphere, however, is extremely important for a strong national economy. Here are three reasons why:[12]

- *Improved productivity.* As more firms are introduced to the economy, there is increased competition, and less productive businesses are forced out.
- *Increased innovation.* New firms lead to the commercialization of new innovations, some of which create entirely new markets or disrupt existing ones.
- *Job creation.* New and young businesses create jobs and are responsible for developing entirely new jobs that were never thought of before.

Entrepreneurs can follow different paths to success. For example, Henry Ford took a classic approach, developing new technologies to improve the quality of life and create global economic success for the Ford Motor Company.
Shawshots/Alamy Stock Photo

A 21st Century Entrepreneur

Today's entrepreneurs can follow different paths to success. Some will take a more classical approach and develop new technologies to improve quality of life and create global economic powerhouses. For example, Henry Ford, the founder of the Ford Motor Company, created the Model T automobile in 1908 and revolutionized America's transportation industry.[13] Others may take a different approach and use entrepreneurship to drive social change or fight for social justice. For instance, Muhammad Yunus established Grameen Bank to provide economically challenged people with small loans on easy terms (known as microcredit). These loans helped bring many out of poverty and earned Yunus a Nobel Peace Prize in 2006.[14] We discuss this social approach to entrepreneurship later in the chapter.

It's important to differentiate Ford and Yunus, two successful entrepreneurs, from managers. Some entrepreneurs who start a new business have difficulty deciding how to manage the organization as it grows; entrepreneurship is not the same as management (see Figure 19.1).

Entrepreneurship is noticing an opportunity to satisfy a customer need and then deciding how to find and use resources to make a product or service that satisfies that need. When an entrepreneur has created something customers want, entrepreneurship gives way to management because the pressing need becomes providing

Figure 19.1

The Differences Between an Entrepreneur and a Manager[15]

the product both efficiently and effectively. Management thus encompasses all the decisions involved in planning, organizing, leading, and controlling resources.

Often, a founding entrepreneur lacks the skills, patience, and experience to engage in the difficult and challenging work of management. Some entrepreneurs find it hard to delegate authority because they are afraid to risk their company by letting others manage it. As a result, they become overloaded, and the quality of their decision making declines, putting their business in jeopardy. Other entrepreneurs lack the detailed knowledge needed to establish state-of-the-art information systems and technology or to create the operations management procedures that are vital to increase the efficiency of their organizations' production systems. Thus, to succeed, it is necessary to do more than create a new product or service; an entrepreneur must hire managers who can create and oversee operations that will allow a new venture to survive and prosper.

Characteristics of Entrepreneurs

Entrepreneurs are likely to have a particular set of the personality characteristics we discussed in Chapter 3. We will focus on three here.

OPENNESS TO EXPERIENCE Entrepreneurs are likely to be high on the personality trait of openness to experience, meaning they are predisposed to be original, to be open to a wide range of stimuli, to be daring, and to take risks. Entrepreneurs have a sense of curiosity, which allows them to always be on the lookout for new opportunities.

LOCUS OF CONTROL Entrepreneurs are likely to have an internal locus of control, believing that they are responsible for what happens to them and that their own actions determine important outcomes such as the success or failure of a new business. People with an external locus of control, in contrast, would be unlikely to leave a secure job in an organization and assume the risk associated with a new venture.

SELF-ESTEEM Entrepreneurs are likely to have a high level of self-esteem and feel competent and capable of handling most situations—including the stress and uncertainty of a risky new venture. They are also likely to have a high need for achievement and have a strong desire to perform challenging tasks and meet high personal standards of excellence.

LO19-2 Explain the entrepreneurial process from opportunity identification to harvesting, and understand the principles of a sound business plan.

Not everyone in an entrepreneurial venture needs to have the same personality characteristics. Although leaders tend to hire employees who have the same personalities as they do, it's important for entrepreneurs to partner with or hire those who complement their own personality traits. These people can fill in weak spots and may excel in the tasks that the entrepreneur finds challenging. This will relieve the mental and emotional strain on entrepreneurs and will enable them to focus on the work they do well.[16]

The Entrepreneurial Process

Have an idea for a business? Great! Entrepreneurs looking to launch a business need to follow a step-by-step method to success. These steps, provided in Figure 19.2, include opportunity identification, the business plan, operations, and harvesting.

Opportunity Identification

entrepreneurial creativity Ability to develop new ideas as solutions to the world's problems.

The entrepreneurial process starts with an idea, but not just any idea will do. Successful ventures are launched by entrepreneurs who have thought critically about a problem or need and who have found creative solutions. **Entrepreneurial creativity** is thus defined as the ability to develop new ideas as solutions to the world's problems.[17] Sometimes these solutions are meant to address existing problems and challenges, such as climate change and disease. At other times, an entrepreneur needs to come up with solutions to problems that don't seem to exist. For example, consider the problem of snow on car windshields. By the turn of the 20th century, every time it snowed, people had to stop their cars in order to clean their windshields.

Figure 19.2

The Steps in the Entrepreneurial Process

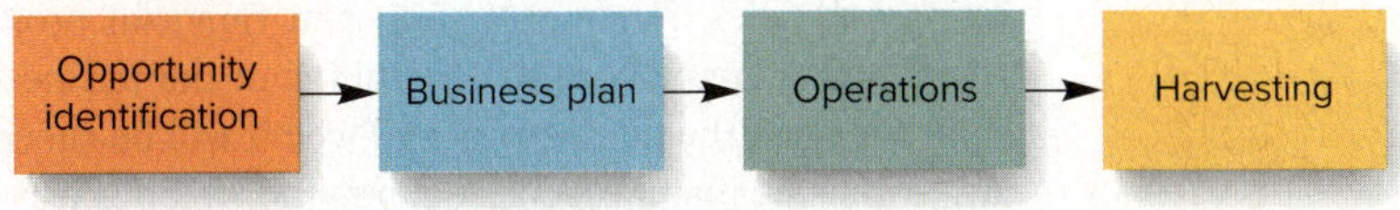

Drivers defined the problem as snow, not the snow sticking on their windshields. Although it was a chore to clean windshields in this way, what else could they do–stop it from snowing? Mary Anderson, who was visiting New York one winter, saw it differently, and in 1903, she patented a blade system that could clean a windshield without requiring drivers to leave the automobile.[18] Anderson's ability to think of the problem in a different way hasn't just kept people drier while driving in the cold, it's made the roads safer during inclement weather.

feasibility study A detailed analysis to determine the likelihood that an idea will become successful as the basis for a new business.

After coming up with a new idea, an entrepreneur would be wise to conduct a **feasibility study**, which is a detailed analysis to determine the likelihood that an idea will become successful as the basis for a new business. There are different variations of feasibility studies, but most focus on technology, the market, and resources required. Table 19.1 highlights these dimensions, what they seek to determine, and a sampling of questions that need to be answered.[19]

The Business Plan

Feasibility studies look at the possibility that an idea can be turned into a successful business. They are investigative in nature and don't explain how a business idea can become reality. Once an entrepreneur has decided an idea is feasible, a business plan for the new venture can be drafted. Business plans can be long or short, although recent ones tend to be on the shorter side. They are fairly standardized documents that can be customized based on the business idea and the intended audience that will review the information. Let's consider the business plan's audience and key components.

AUDIENCE Various stakeholders will take an interest in your business plan. For example, an investor or bank looking to fund your idea would want to know how you plan on bringing the new product or service to market and what risks are associated with your new venture. Potential partners or employees would want to know how the organization would be structured for success and what role they would play. Finally, if your business requires suppliers or distributors, they may want to know how your business is going to operate before they agree to work with you. This may include everyone from a landlord to a manufacturer to a shipping company.

Table 19.1

Feasibility Study Dimensions

Dimension	Determination	Sampling of Questions
Technology	Whether or not the idea can actually work	• What type of technology is required? • Is this a novel idea, or does it build on or change an existing product or service?
Market	Demand for a product or service and the price customers will be willing to pay	• Does this idea solve a current or future problem? • Who else is competing in this market? • What would customers pay for such a product or service?
Resources	Monetary and nonmonetary resources required	• How much money is required to start this business? • What type of expertise do I need to have or acquire? • How should the organization be structured? • What are the return on investment benchmarks?

KEY COMPONENTS There are different variations of what goes into a business plan. The U.S. Small Business Administration recommends including a combination of these sections: company description, market analysis, organizational structure, service or product line, marketing and sales, funding request, and financial projections. In addition, you should include an executive summary at the beginning of the business plan. The summary will briefly tell the audience what the company is and why it will be successful.[20] Some potential stakeholders will just review the plan's executive summary, which is why it's important that it resonate with them.

Your business plan should provide you with a roadmap that aligns with your overall business strategy. Keep in mind, however, that a business plan is a living document and may sometimes need to be changed based on what you're experiencing as the business progresses (for example, changes in market environment, additional opportunities).

Operations

Once the relevant stakeholders have bought into your plan, you're ready to launch. Here are three recommendations to consider as you work on growing your business:[21]

Manage Your Time Wisely. Effective time management is an important business skill, but it's even more crucial for entrepreneurs because they often wear more than one hat in setting up and running a new business. Consider using a digital calendar or time chart to fill in daily activities. Remember that selecting the optimal tasks to be accomplished during a time period requires conscious effort.

Delegate as Needed. Entrepreneurs often have difficulty letting go of responsibilities. To optimize their time, successful entrepreneurs will need to learn when and how to delegate time-consuming tasks that others can handle. This is another reason why it's important to select partners and employees who have the right set of skills to help make the venture successful.

Practice Reflection. Starting a business takes a lot of work, and often entrepreneurs are so occupied thinking about the next task that they don't have much time to be mindful about what they're actually doing. It's important to schedule some time during the day to reflect on what you've done and what you are planning to do. Then, at the end of the day, you should reflect on what you've accomplished and if you would do anything differently tomorrow.

harvesting The method for withdrawing from a business and capturing the value of investment in the firm.

privately held company Organization that has not offered ownership via a public stock exchange.

publicly held company Organization that offers shares of the business to others via a public stock exchange.

Harvesting

Eventually, most entrepreneurs need a strategy for exiting the business. This plan, known as **harvesting**, is the method for withdrawing from a business and capturing the value of investment in the firm. Harvesting can occur for a variety of reasons. For example, the business may be doing very well and the founder has decided to cash out. If the business is doing poorly, the entrepreneur may be looking to bring in others to change things around, or it may be time to close the business and cut losses. We will focus on three harvesting strategies: initial public offerings, sale, and closure.

Many successful businesses will offer shares of the business to the public for the first time through an initial public offering (IPO) on a stock exchange, such as the New York Stock Exchange pictured here.
ANGELA WEISS/Contributor/AFP/Getty Images

INITIAL PUBLIC OFFERING Most new business ventures are owned by their founders and other initial investors. This type of business is called a **privately held company**, which is an organization that has not offered ownership via a public stock exchange. Many successful businesses will opt to go through an initial public offering (IPO) and offer shares of the business to the public for the first time on a stock exchange, such as the New York Stock Exchange or Nasdaq. An organization that proceeds with an IPO becomes a **publicly held company**. This means that shareholders now have claim to the company's assets and profits. IPOs allow organizations to raise capital for expansion, research and development, and other purposes. They also allow most equity holders in the company to sell their holdings. It's important to understand that once an organization goes public, it is required to abide by Securities and Exchange Commission regulations, which include extensive reporting requirements and additional fiduciary responsibilities to shareholders.[22]

SALE Some business owners opt to sell their business to new potential owners. This can be for a variety of reasons, such as retirement, health, or challenges that require specific expertise. Before listing the business for sale, an owner will need a proper valuation of the business so that a reasonable asking price can be set. This valuation will be verified during a due diligence period, which is when the business reveals its financials to potential buyers. Just like in the real estate market, there are business brokers who can assist in the listing, negotiation, and eventual sale of a business in return for a fee or commission.

CLOSURE Unfortunately, despite herculean efforts on the part of business owners, many companies just don't make it. In fact, according to data from the U.S. Bureau of Labor Statistics, around 20% of small businesses fail within their first year. By the end of their second year, that number increases to 30%. After five years, about 50% of businesses will fail, and that number rises to 70% by the end of a decade. In essence, only around 30% of businesses end up surviving.[23] Entrepreneurs need to be prepared for failure because starting a new business is a risky endeavor. Effective preparation includes understanding when and how to liquidate a company's assets, and whether the entrepreneur may need to declare bankruptcy. **Bankruptcy** occurs when a business has become insolvent and needs a legal way to reorganize or liquidate.

bankruptcy Legal process that occurs when a person or business cannot repay outstanding debts or obligations.

New Business Formation

LO19-3 Explain new business creation, and describe the different types of legal structures, financing options, and contemporary business models.

Starting a new venture is an exciting time, but it requires careful work upfront in order to maximize your chances of success. In fact, recent research finds that after the idea itself, leadership decisions and business model choices are two of the most important factors leading to entrepreneurial success.[24] There are various considerations when launching a venture, and one's business plan should serve as a guide for early decisions. In this section we will focus on three important considerations: legal structure, financing, and contemporary business models.

Legal Structure

One of the most important decisions an entrepreneur can make is what legal structure to pursue for the new business. An organization's legal structure affects the liability owners face if there's a lawsuit, required filings with government authorities, tax rates, fund-raising ability, and more. In the United States, legal structures are usually determined at the state level, meaning each state has its own set of initial and annual requirements for different legal structures. Here we will focus on the general benefits and drawbacks of four popular structures: sole proprietorships, partnerships, corporations, and limited liability companies.

SOLE PROPRIETORSHIPS The simplest business entity is a **sole proprietorship**, which is when an individual owns an unincorporated business by themselves.[25] In this structure, the sole proprietor makes all the business decisions and is responsible for the company's profits and debts. Sole proprietorships have few paperwork requirements, are usually inexpensive to start up, and allow for easy dissolution. The sole proprietor, however, is usually completely liable for the business's actions and is individually taxed on profits because the business and owner are essentially one entity. This increased exposure to risk means that financial backing from investors and banks may be harder to come by.[26]

sole proprietorship Form of business in which an individual owns an unincorporated business by themselves.

PARTNERSHIPS When an unincorporated business is owned by two or more people, it is categorized as a **partnership**.[27] Partnerships resemble sole proprietorships, but in a partnership, more than one person may make the business decisions. Partners usually split profits, debt, and taxes in this arrangement, but as in sole proprietorships, partners are usually liable for the business's actions, although the liability is typically divided between the partners. Individuals involved in a partnership should draft a partnership agreement listing each person's responsibilities and authority in the business in order to limit ambiguity and conflict in the future.[28]

partnership Form of business in which two or more people are owners of an unincorporated business.

corporation Form of business that is a separate legal entity from its owners and is responsible for its own business affairs.

CORPORATIONS Unlike sole proprietorships and partnerships, a **corporation** is a separate legal entity from its owners and responsible for its own business affairs.[29] Generally, corporations have separate legal liability from their owners, can own property in their own name, and can sell ownership through stock. Two widely utilized types of corporations are C corporations and S corporations. C corporations are owned by shareholders and are taxed as separate entities. They can have unlimited numbers of shareholders but they are taxed once on profit earned and again when distributing profits as dividends (the "double taxation rule"). S corporations, on the other hand, provide the liability-shielding benefits of C corporations, but income passes through to shareholders, which means double taxation is avoided. S corporations are a better fit for small businesses because the number and types of shareholders are more restricted than for C corporations.[30]

limited liability company (LLC) Form of business with a hybrid structure that combines the benefits of unincorporated businesses and corporations.

LIMITED LIABILITY COMPANIES One of the newer types of legal structures, a **limited liability company (LLC)**, is a hybrid structure that combines the benefits of both unincorporated businesses and corporations. Although regulations vary by state, LLCs typically shield their shareholders (known as members) from liability while avoiding double taxation. LLCs that have multiple members can elect to be taxed as partnerships, and like partnerships, an LLC operating agreement, specifying member responsibilities and authority, is suggested. Similar to corporations, LLCs are usually considered separate entities from their members. However, they typically do not have the same record-keeping and reporting requirements as corporations.[31] Table 19.2 provides a comparison of the various legal structures available for businesses.

You can see that there is no single "best" legal entity; each has its own advantages and drawbacks. There are also additional differences between the legal structures discussed, and government regulations vary by state and may be amended. With this in mind, it's important that you do your own research and consult with professionals before choosing a legal structure for your new venture.

Financing

debt financing Money borrowed by an individual or business that needs to be paid back, usually with interest.

equity financing Money that is exchanged for an ownership stake in a business.

No matter what type of legal structure you choose for your new business, you'll most likely need funding in order to start. Whether for raw materials, prototypes, office space, or employee salaries, start-up capital will allow you to get up and running. Depending on your own personal circumstances and the type of business you are looking to start, you may be able to get away with using your own capital to start your venture. Most business ideas, however, will need additional funding in order to be successful. There are two types of financing available for new ventures: debt and equity. **Debt financing** involves a sum of money that is borrowed and needs to be paid back, usually with interest. These are usually known as loans. On the other hand, **equity financing** involves a sum of money that is exchanged for an ownership stake in the

Table 19.2

Legal Structures Comparison[32]

Structure	Owners	Filing Requirements and Fees	Liability	Taxation
Sole Proprietorship	One	Minimal	Unlimited personal	Owner reports profit or loss on personal taxes.
Partnership	Two or more	Moderate (partnership agreement)	Generally unlimited personal	Partners report profit or loss on personal taxes.
Corporation	One or more	Extensive	Limited	C Corp: Files own taxes; double taxation. S Corp: Shareholders report profit or loss on personal taxes.
Limited Liability Company	One or more	Moderate (operating agreement)	Limited	Members usually report profit or loss on personal taxes.

company. Although equity financing typically doesn't involve interest payments, entrepreneurs may be giving up ownership and decision-making rights in the organization. We discuss three ways entrepreneurs obtain debt or equity financing for business ventures: family and friends, banks, and investors.[33]

FAMILY AND FRIENDS Parents, siblings, other relatives, and friends are examples of individuals who may invest in a business idea. These individuals may provide debt or equity financing, depending on their personal circumstances as well as the business itself. Funding by family and friends should be treated the same way as it would be if it were coming from strangers: the appropriate paperwork (for example, promissory note, stock certificate) should be executed. This will help separate the business nature of the investment from personal relationships.

venture capitalists (VCs) Individuals or organizations that use their firm's capital to invest in growing startups.

angel investor Individual who uses their own wealth to fund businesses.

crowdfunding Process of using small contributions from many people to fund a new or existing business.

BANKS Banks typically provide debt financing, in the form of loans, to well-qualified businesses. The chances of being approved for a loan with a competitive interest rate depends on many factors, including the strength of the company's business plan, owners' credit scores, collateral provided (if any), and existing/anticipated cash flows.[34] The U.S. Small Business Administration (SBA) also provides loans to startup businesses. In fact, the organization provided more than 14 million loans worth $764 billion to small businesses in 2020.[35]

INVESTORS In contrast to banks, investors are more focused on equity financing. **Venture capitalists (VCs)** are one type of investor. They use their firm's capital, which comes from other investors, foundations, pension funds, and others to invest in growing startups. This was the case with Blackstone's investment in Supergoop! as described in the Manager's Challenge at the beginning of the chapter. Typically, VCs bet on growing companies, nurture them, and then look to get a sizable return on investment when the startup is acquired or goes public through an IPO. Another type of investor is an **angel investor**. Angel investors typically use their own wealth to fund businesses and are interested in mentoring entrepreneurs.[36] On average, VCs invest larger sums of money into new businesses and thus require greater control over them than angel investors do.[37] A more contemporary investment method is known as **crowdfunding**. This is when a business utilizes small contributions from many people (the "crowd"). These contributions can be either debt or equity based. The Internet, with its large reach, is usually the means by which an entrepreneur seeks crowdfunding.[38]

Crowdfunding sites such as Kickstarter are used by entrepreneurs to obtain funding for their new business ventures from many different types of investors.
M4OS Photos/Alamy Stock Photo

As when choosing a legal structure, deciding on the type or mix of funding for your business is a complex decision. It should be made based on thorough research, individual circumstances, and consultation with a financial professional in order to ensure success. However, some entrepreneurs face additional challenges when it comes to funding their startups, as described in the "Focus on DEI&B" feature.

FOCUS ON DEI&B

Raising Money as a Female Entrepreneur

More than 5.4 million businesses were started in 2021. According to the World Economic Forum, almost half of these businesses were formed by women, up from 28% in 2019. Although these numbers are going in a positive direction, many obstacles remain for female entrepreneurs, and men still outnumber women three to one in business ownership.[39] Studies have shown that one reason for this phenomenon is gender stereotypes, particularly in raising money for the new venture.[40]

According to *Harvard Business Review,* a significant gender gap exists between what male and female entrepreneurs can raise in venture capital. In 2017, for example, female entrepreneurs received only about 2% of all available venture funding, although they owned 38% of businesses in the United States.[41] Women and men even get asked different questions from potential investors. When men pitch startups, they get asked how they'll make money, but women often are asked how they'll prevent the loss of the investor's investment. A team of researchers evaluated 200 videos of entrepreneurs pitching at a TechCrunch funding competition. Potential investors used words like "gain," "hope," and "achieve" with men, but women mostly heard words such as "afraid," "anxious," and "avoid." Interestingly, both female and male investors used the same biased language.[42]

Is this difference in questioning warranted? Studies say no. Data from the U.S. Census Bureau show that female-owned startups generated higher revenues and created more jobs on average than male-owned startups in 2018.[43] Women-led startups also used two-thirds less capital than their male counterparts.[44] Finally, a 2021 Women's Entrepreneurship Report found that men and women entrepreneurs are about equally likely to offer genuinely innovative products or services.[45]

Indeed, gender bias does not contribute to a sound entrepreneurial ecosystem. According to *Forbes,* addressing these funding gaps between men and women entrepreneurs will accelerate economic growth by increasing innovation, creating jobs, improving productivity, boosting competitiveness, and growing wealth.[46]

Contemporary Business Models

Thanks to a greater interest in entrepreneurship and advancements in technology, more opportunities for aspiring entrepreneurs exist today than ever before. "We're living in a digitally connected global economy. So, you need to ask yourself: Can I do it? Is entrepreneurship right for me? More and more young people are saying 'yes,'" according to *Forbes.*[47] Two contemporary business models fueling this growth in entrepreneurial ambition are e-commerce and franchising.

e-commerce The trading of goods and services on the Internet.

E-COMMERCE The trading of goods and services on the Internet, known as **e-commerce**, or electronic commerce, has been growing exponentially for a number of years.[48] In 2021, retail e-commerce sales were around $5.2 trillion, and this figure is expected to reach $8.1 trillion by 2026.[49] Among the primary reasons why e-commerce has grown so quickly are advancements in technology and an increase in online marketplaces. Thanks to websites such as Alibaba and eBay, anyone can list their products online and sell them to consumers around the world. Amazon, the largest e-commerce organization in the world by revenue, even allows vendors to ship their products to the company's warehouses.[50] The Internet giant handles the entire commercial process, from packing and shipping to payment and advertising. Another e-commerce company, Etsy, focuses on handmade or vintage items for sale. Consumers can order customized products from their website, and vendors don't need to worry about leasing retail space and staying open throughout the day or investing in a tremendous amount of inventory.

The COVID-19 pandemic is another reason why e-commerce is booming. According to the U.S. Department of Commerce, global e-commerce revenue jumped an additional 19% and 22% on top of the 9% and 12% expected growth rates for 2020 and 2021, respectively.[51] The food delivery market is a good example of pandemic-inspired growth. According to McKinsey and Co., the global food delivery market, led by the likes of Uber Eats and DoorDash, more than doubled during the pandemic. And it looks like this growth is here to stay.[52] Post pandemic, "Customers are now eating at restaurants again, but many also are still ordering takeout and delivery because of the convenience.. . .We're seeing online and takeout not go down as things open up, but stay steady," according to MiBiz.[53]

FRANCHISING Sometimes entrepreneurs prefer running with the ideas of others instead of coming up with something new. And this model of entrepreneurship continues to be

franchising Form of business in which an owner of a product or service (franchisor) obtains distribution through affiliated dealers (franchisees), who pay an initial setup fee and a share of their profits to the franchisor.

successful. **Franchising** is when the owner of a product or service (franchisor) obtains distribution through affiliated dealers (franchisees). In this setup, the franchisor helps in organizing, training, merchandising, marketing, and managing a business in exchange for an initial fee and a share of profits.[54] Franchises grew at a rate of 2.8% year-over-year in 2021 and are expected to continue their growth trajectory, especially in the gym, beauty salon, and entertainment venue sectors.[55]

Franchise ownership is beneficial because franchisees can take advantage of proven brands and methods. Often they will have access to superior suppliers at steeper discounts as well as marketing and technology support. Franchises do have drawbacks though. Franchisors are typically able to limit what their franchisees can do, and there is the added cost of franchise fees. Take for instance McDonald's, one of the largest franchises with more than 36,000 locations around the world. The company's initial franchise fee starts at $45,000, and it charges another fee, known as royalty, of 4% of monthly gross sales. Total investment for someone owning a McDonald's franchise ranges between $1.4 and $2.5 million.[56] Of course, you could avoid these costs if you started your own hamburger joint, but you wouldn't have the McDonald's brand behind you or McDonald's assistance with marketing and training, which is part of the package franchisees pay for when they do business with companies such as the fast-food giant. In 2022, along with McDonald's, 7-Eleven, KFC, and Ace Hardware were some of the top franchise systems in the United States.[57] If you don't have millions to spend on buying a franchise, there are less-expensive options with initial investments running anywhere from $5,000 to $100,000 for commercial cleaning, insurance, real estate, and travel services.[58]

LO19-4
Describe social entrepreneurship and how businesses can do good while still making a profit, and differentiate between the types of social entrepreneurs.

Social Entrepreneurship

social entrepreneurship Process by which entrepreneurs develop innovative solutions to address social issues.

As the story of Holly Thaggard and Supergoop! at the beginning of the chapter showed, aspiring entrepreneurs are motivated for a variety of reasons. Some just want to be their own boss, while others want to make a lot of money and build their own empire. Recently, the social entrepreneur has also emerged. These people are focused on making a positive impact on society. **Social entrepreneurship** is the process by which entrepreneurs develop innovative solutions to address social issues.[59] Bill Drayton, the founder and CEO of Ashoka, a social entrepreneurship association, believes that social entrepreneurs ". . .are the essential corrective force. They are system-changing entrepreneurs. And from deep within they, and therefore their work, are committed to the good of all."[60] Indeed, research shows that social entrepreneurs have great confidence in their important work because of the belief that they aren't enriching only themselves, but also the community, the society, and the world around them.[61]

TOMS has expanded its philanthropic efforts from giving away shoes to children in need to donating a third of its profits to support issues such as ending gun violence and promoting mental health.
Ael/Alamy Stock Photo

Being Good and Making a Profit

Social entrepreneurship is at times confused with nonprofit ventures, but this isn't always the case. Firms focused on social entrepreneurship may be in the for-profit business, it's just that they place a greater emphasis on social changes. Shoemaker TOMS is such an example. The for-profit company, founded in 2006, was founded on a "one for one" model: for each pair of shoes the organization sold, it would provide a pair of shoes to children in need. TOMS has given over 95 million pairs of shoes to people in need to date and has expanded its model to include access to safe drinking water, eye surgery, and other important initiatives.[62] Now the company has evolved its model and provides a third of its profits to support grassroots issues such as ending gun violence and promoting mental health. In 2022, TOMS gave $1.7 million to support these important causes.[63]

TOMS has good reason to be involved with social issues. Not only is it the right thing to do, but it attracts customers. Consider these statistics from a Zeno group 2020 study on American consumers:[64]

- They are four to six times more likely to buy products from companies they believe are purpose driven.
- They would advertise a company they perceive to be making honest and ethical decisions.
- They would stop buying from brands they believe are unethical.

Indeed, supporting social issues provides organizations with a unique value proposition for their products and services and can safeguard against competitors who aren't doing the same. See the "Manager as a Person" feature to learn more about another successful social entrepreneur.

MANAGER AS A PERSON

From Worms to Riches

Hungarian-born Tom Szaky isn't your typical social entrepreneur. While an economics student at Princeton, he came up with the idea of using worm droppings as fertilizer. His first test consisted of using scraps from one of the university's cafeterias and vermicomposting, or worm composting, them in his dorm room over the summer.[65] Szaky collected money from family and friends, and used his own savings, to purchase a $20,000 "worm gin," which could store hundreds of thousands of worms. He then dropped out of college, secured a $2,000 angel investment, and started packaging his fertilizer in used soda bottles, which he sold to local gardening centers from the back of his car.[66]

TerraCycle founder and CEO Tom Szaky, pictured here at the company's Trenton, New Jersey, headquarters, is considered a social entrepreneur whose recycling business continues to be successful by finding creative ways to repurpose trash into usable items.

David Williams/Bloomberg/Getty Images

Szaky's grit and persistence paid off in 2004 when he was able to convince a buyer for Home Depot to take a chance on his fertilizer. Target and Walmart followed, and his company, TerraCycle, was born.[67] The multimillion-dollar organization focuses on recycling and repurposing objects that are often challenging to recycle. According to Szaky, "99% of the things people buy, they don't actually want to own."[68] In fact, it's estimated that we dump around 2.12 billion tons of waste a year, most of which is thrown away after six months of use.[69]

TerraCycle is now one of the most influential recycling businesses with operations in over 20 countries and 2021 revenues of $33.5 million, up 36% from the year before.[70] Its bright and innovative office space in Trenton, New Jersey, is made of recycled garbage, and employees are encouraged to socialize through activities such as weekly rock climbing. "Creativity is demanded by the industry and the challenges we're taking on, and in order to deal with unknown obstacles and questions, we need the creativity this office culture encourages," Szaky tells *Business Insider.*[71]

"Garbage Mogul" Szaky has advanced past simple recycling and now takes trash, such as used beverage packages, and repurposes them into classy messenger bags. He also donates two cents to charity for each object the company recycles, contributing over $3.2 million to date.[72]

Types of Social Entrepreneurs

Tom Szaky is an ambitious social entrepreneur, but he doesn't represent the entire population of these socially minded new venture creators. Today, social entrepreneurs differ in both the way they conduct business and their goals. Dr. Joe Johnson, an entrepreneur and CEO of OXLOS, a life-enriching business, arranges social entrepreneurs into four distinct categories: community, nonprofit, transformational, and global.[73] Let's examine each more closely.

COMMUNITY SOCIAL ENTREPRENEURS These entrepreneurs focus on the social needs of individuals in a relatively narrow geographical area, and the enterprise is typically based on the participation of people living in that small area. An advantage to this focus is that ventures can become more sustainable over time as the community can directly see the benefits of the enterprise. Example: Building a local community center.

NONPROFIT SOCIAL ENTREPRENEURS These entrepreneurs are more focused on social, rather than material wealth. Consequently, profits are reinvested into the enterprise to expand the products and services provided. Since they can generate their own funding through profits, nonprofits have an advantage in meeting their stated goals. Example: Goodwill Industries.

TRANSFORMATIONAL SOCIAL ENTREPRENEURS Transformational entrepreneurs are looking to meet societal needs that the government and others aren't satisfying. These enterprises often start out as nonprofits and then evolve into institutions that can make an even greater societal impact, but they can be bound by rules, regulations, and politics. Example: Unilever's TRANSFORM initiative, a joint venture with the United Kingdom's Foreign and Commonwealth Development Office and Ernst & Young.

GLOBAL SOCIAL ENTREPRENEUR These individuals or firms are focused on the complete transformation of a social system. Often they have lofty goals, such as access to clean drinking water or education for all, and their success depends on their ability to work with a network of other social entrepreneurs.[74] Example: Bill & Melinda Gates Foundation.

Figure 19.3 illustrates how the need to network with other social entrepreneurs grows as the enterprise evolves. For example, after continued business success, Danish pharmaceutical company Novo Nordisk started a nonprofit called the Novo Nordisk Foundation, which evolved into a global social venture focused on improving "people's health and the sustainability of society and the planet."[75] The organization is now valued at more than $93 billion,

Figure 19.3

Evolution of Social Entrepreneurs

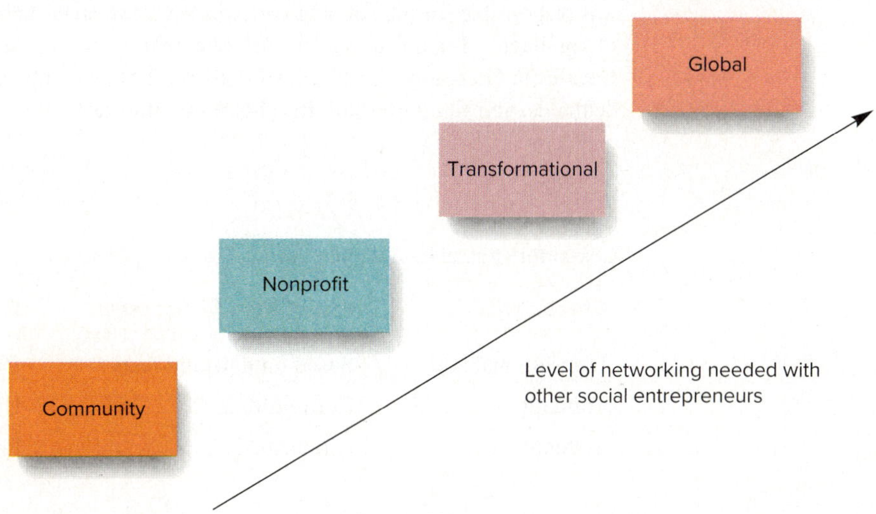

making it the world's wealthiest charitable foundation.[76] Even though it has extensive wealth, the Novo Nordisk Foundation partners with other social ventures, such as Open Philanthropy and the Bill & Melinda Gates Foundation, on projects such as discovering and developing antiviral medicines for future pandemics, because it understands the advantage of collaborating with other entrepreneurial enterprises.[77]

The Internal Entrepreneur

LO19-5 Explain how to successfully utilize corporate entrepreneurship in existing businesses.

Innovation isn't limited to individuals looking to start new businesses. Many managers, scientists, and researchers employed by various companies engage in entrepreneurship, and they are an important source of organizational creativity. In fact, a recent study found that more than 20% of employees exhibited some entrepreneurial activity in the workplace.[78] They are involved in innovation, developing new and improved products and services, and determining ways to make or implement them. These employees notice opportunities for either quantum or incremental product improvements and are responsible for managing the product development process. They are known as **corporate entrepreneurs**, or intrapreneurs, to distinguish them from entrepreneurs, who start their own businesses.

Challenges to Corporate Entrepreneurship

corporate entrepreneurs Individuals working for corporations who develop new and improved products or services and determine ways to make or implement these innovations.

Coming up with the right idea may not be the hardest part of innovation in the workplace. Instead, corporate entrepreneurs may find that implementing change within an established organization may pose the greater challenge. Established businesses aren't inherently receptive to change. They have well-established systems, processes, and cultures and typically are not known for their agility or entrepreneurial mindset when it comes to developing new product lines or new businesses.

Managers at traditional firms are trained to make decisions based on information, but emerging businesses often lack hard data. You can't find marketplace data for markets that may not exist, and financial forecasts are often not dependable. Emerging businesses also require fresh ideas, but employees are often stuck in conventional thinking out of fear of retaliation by their supervisors. As Robert Nardelli, Home Depot's former CEO, put it, "there's only a fine line between entrepreneurship and insubordination."[79] Finally, there's usually a poor fit between an established organization's systems and the needs of an emerging business. For example, accounting, human resources, and operations systems and software are usually customized for a firm's existing capabilities and are not designed to capture a disruptive business's needs.[80] Table 19.3 summarizes the often-opposing characteristics of established versus emerging businesses.

The Coca-Cola Company is an example of an organization that is all in on corporate entrepreneurship. The company has a team of experts called the Transformational Innovation Team, which is responsible for launching new beverages in record time. The team, for instance, was responsible for introducing Cidewinder, a low-sugar beverage with health benefits similar to kombucha. Team lead Susan Zaripheh believes that Cidewinder is an example of how The Coca-Cola Company is using corporate entrepreneurship to stay nimble, respond to market demands, and gain important insights for the future.[81]

Table 19.3

Characteristics of Established versus Emerging Businesses

Characteristic	Established Businesses	Emerging Businesses
Decision making	Based on data and facts	Usually lack hard data
Thinking	Conventional	Unconventional
Systems	Established	Primitive (if they even exist)

There is an interesting relationship between entrepreneurs and corporate entrepreneurs. Many managers with intrapreneurial talents become dissatisfied if their superiors decide not to support or fund new product ideas and development efforts the managers think will succeed. What do intrapreneurial managers do who feel they are getting nowhere? Often they decide to leave their current organizations and start their own companies to take advantage of their new product ideas! In other words, intrapreneurs become entrepreneurs and start businesses that often compete with the companies they left. To avoid losing these people, top managers must find ways to facilitate the entrepreneurial spirit of their most creative employees.

Fostering an Entrepreneurial Culture

A culture of corporate entrepreneurship starts at the top of the organization. Without C-suite buy-in, employees will not feel free or incentivized to be innovative. Procter and Gamble (P&G) is an example of a company with corporate entrepreneurship built into its DNA. By the early 2000s, the company started encouraging an entrepreneurial mindset in senior management. Executives attended training on product demand and disruptive innovation, and from there they developed new-growth business guides and an organizational structure to support and enhance innovation.[82] "We know from our history that while promotions may win quarters, innovation wins decades," said P&G ex-CEO and Chairman Bob McDonald. The company created the "new growth factory" in 2004 to churn out innovative and disruptive products that could drive growth. Thanks to this growth factory, profits from the company's Tide detergent line doubled from $12 billion to $24 billion in 10 years.[83]

Creating an entrepreneurial mindset among managers has helped Procter & Gamble create innovative and disruptive products that drive growth, such as Tide's line of detergents.
Ron Adar/SOPA Images/Shutterstock

A focus on innovation is not only important for increasing profits but is also fundamental for staying relevant in the marketplace, especially after a crisis. McKinsey stated in a 2020 report that ". . .90% of executives believed the COVID-19 crisis would fundamentally change how they do business in the next five years. Yet, only 21% reported having the expertise, commitment and resources to accomplish the necessary changes."[84] Here are three ways managers can foster corporate entrepreneurship to gain competitive advantage:

EMPOWER EMPLOYEES It's important that workers know their ideas matter. Managers need to be proactive and recognize employees' contributions (even the simple ones), welcome input, and reward risk-taking. Moreover, first-line supervisors should receive training on how to provide feedback because they are usually the ones employees go to first with ideas.[85]

EMBRACE UPSKILLING Teaching employees new ways of doing things promotes creativity and innovation. In fact, more than half of the respondents to a recent PwC global CEO survey agreed that upskilling programs led to greater innovation and the acceleration of the organization's digital transformation. In order to promote upskilling, managers should define key skills employees need to focus on, create training programs, and provide support for employees to learn while performing their regular responsibilities.[86]

ADAPT QUICKLY Businesses need to stay nimble by reacting thoughtfully yet quickly in response to changing circumstances. Whether the change is inspired by a new employee's creativity, a global pandemic such as COVID-19, or a competitor's actions, employees need to have faith that their employer can evolve at a healthy pace. Managers can support organizational agility by encouraging cross-department collaboration and communication, developing rotating positions, and minimizing burnout at all levels of the organization.[87]

Summary and Review

LO19-1 **MODERN ENTREPRENEURSHIP** Entrepreneurs are individuals who notice opportunities and decide how to mobilize the resources needed to produce new and improved goods and services. When an entrepreneur has created something customers want, entrepreneurship gives way to management because the pressing need becomes providing the product both efficiently and effectively. Management thus encompasses all the decisions involved in planning, organizing, leading, and controlling resources. Entrepreneurs are likely to be high on the personality trait of openness and to possess an internal locus of control and a high level of self-esteem.

LO19-2 **THE ENTREPRENEURIAL PROCESS** The entrepreneurial process includes opportunity identification, the business plan, operations, and harvesting. Opportunity identification includes entrepreneurial creativity or the ability to develop new ideas as solutions to the world's problems. After coming up with a new idea, an entrepreneur would be wise to conduct a feasibility study, which is a detailed analysis to determine the likelihood that an idea will become successful as the basis for a new business. Once an entrepreneur has decided an idea is feasible, they would proceed with drafting a business plan for the new venture. When operating the business, you should manage your time wisely, delegate as needed, and practice reflection. Harvesting is the method for withdrawing from a business and capturing the value of investment in the firm; three methods include an initial public offering, sale, and closure.

LO19-3 **NEW BUSINESS FORMATION** There are various considerations when launching a venture, and one's business plan should serve as a guide for early decisions. One of the most important decisions an entrepreneur can make is what legal structure to pursue for the new business: sole proprietorship, partnership, corporation, or limited liability company. There are also two types of financing. Debt financing involves a sum of money that is borrowed and needs to be paid back, usually with interest. These are usually known as loans. Equity financing involves a sum of money that is exchanged for an ownership stake in the company. There are two types of contemporary business models: e-commerce, or electronic commerce, and franchising, which is when the owner of a product or service (franchisor) obtains distribution through affiliated dealers (franchisees).

LO19-4 **SOCIAL ENTREPRENEURSHIP** Social entrepreneurship is the process by which entrepreneurs develop innovative solutions to address social issues. There are four types of social entrepreneurs: community, nonprofit, transformational, and global.

LO19-5 **CORPORATE ENTREPRENEURSHIP** Entrepreneurs start their own businesses, while corporate entrepreneurs, or intrapreneurs, notice opportunities within their companies for either quantum or incremental product improvements and are responsible for managing the product development process. There are three ways that managers can foster corporate entrepreneurship to gain a competitive advantage: they can empower employees, embrace upskilling, and adapt quickly.

Management in Action

Topics for Discussion and Action

Discussion

1. What are the differences between an entrepreneur and a manager? [LO19-1]
2. What are the differences between the four legal structures typically used by new businesses? [LO19-2]
3. Describe the ways entrepreneurs can secure funding for their businesses. [LO19-2]
4. What are the advantages and disadvantages of franchising? [LO19-3]
5. What is social entrepreneurship, and what types of social entrepreneurs exist? [LO19-4]
6. What is the difference between an entrepreneur and a corporate entrepreneur? [LO19-5]

Action

7. Interview a local entrepreneur who owns a franchise business and get their take on the advantages and disadvantages of being a franchisee. [LO19-3]

Building Management Skills

Analyzing Successful Entrepreneurs [LO19-1, 19-2, 19-3, 19-4]

Think about a successful entrepreneur who started a business in the 21st century. Then answer the following questions:

1. Did this person show more entrepreneurial or managerial skills? Provide examples.
2. What personality characteristics did this person have? Were these traits appropriate for starting a new business? Why or why not?
3. How did this person handle the operations of their business? What kinds of behaviors did they engage in?
4. How did this person finance their new business? Was this the most effective method? Why or why not?
5. Was this person a social entrepreneur? Why or why not?

Managing Ethically [LO19-4]

Many social entrepreneurs include both profit-making motives and social impact in their businesses, but these goals aren't always harmonious. For example, a growing business may have to decide between greater societal impact or making a profit. This includes prioritizing which organizations or individuals may receive its assistance, the amount of its operating expenses, and strategic investments, all of which may impact the amount of earnings retained by ownership. As a result, business owners may find themselves at odds with other stakeholders, such as investors and employees.

Questions

1. Either alone or in a group, think about the ethical implications of these business decisions.
2. What responsibilities do social entrepreneurs have to society versus their responsibilities to make sure their business survives? Explain.

Small Group Breakout Exercise

Opportunity Identification [LO19-1, 19-2]

Form groups of three or four people, and appoint one member as the spokesperson who will communicate your findings to the class when called on by the instructor. Then discuss the following scenario:

You and your partners are trying to decide which kind of gym or fitness center to open in a large metropolitan area. The problem you face is that the city already has many similar businesses that provide memberships at all price ranges. You have the resources to open any type of gym or fitness center, but your challenge is to decide which type is most likely to succeed. Follow these steps:

1. As a group, spend 5 to 10 minutes generating ideas about the different businesses that the members think will be most likely to succeed. Each group member should be as innovative and creative as possible (that is, consider franchising, use of e-commerce, etc.).
2. Appoint one group member to take notes of all the ideas.
3. Spend the next 10 to 15 minutes debating the pros and cons of each business. As a group, try to reach a consensus on which type of gym or fitness center is most likely to succeed.

When called on by the instructor, the spokesperson should be prepared to share your group's decision with the class, as well as the reasons for the group's decision.

Be the Manager [LO19-1, 19-2, 19-4]

Your friend approaches you with a proposal to partner with them and start a new mobile car washing and detailing service. The business will involve the creation of a website to advertise your services and book appointments. You and your friend, whom you worked with at a carwash as teenagers, will then travel locally to homes and workplaces and wash and detail customers' vehicles. Here are some details in the proposal:

- You'll need a vehicle to travel with and store your tools. Neither of you currently has a car or savings to purchase a car.
- Local customers are very sensitive about damage to the inside or outside of their vehicles.
- There are other local businesses offering the same type of service.

Assume that after reviewing the proposal, you like the business idea and think your organization can offer superior service and capture the market. Nevertheless, you ask your friend for some time to think about the business.

Questions

1. What types of characteristics do you want to ensure your friend has before getting into business with them? Explain.
2. What type of fund-raising would you need to pursue? Why?
3. What type of legal structure would work best for this business? Explain.
4. How could this potential business incorporate elements of social entrepreneurship?

Case in the News [LO19-2, 19-3, 19-4]

Kinly Advocates for the Underrepresented

Black Americans have continued to face limited access to building wealth since the abolishment of slavery in 1865. According to the Kaiser Family Foundation, the national Black poverty rate in 2019 was more than double the white poverty rate (the 2020 COVID-19 pandemic increased this disparity even more). Moreover, the Federal Reserve reports that the average white family's wealth is eight times more than a Black family's. Black representation in America's financial system does not fare much better either. According to the U.S. Equal Employment Opportunity Commission, 82% of loan officers are white, while only 9% are Black. Higher up in the ranks, Black employees only make up 2% of bank executives.

Entrepreneur Donald Hawkins set out to reverse this racial wealth disparity by establishing Kinly, a "neobank." Neobanks are financial technology startups that offer digital, nontraditional banking services. They typically don't have branch locations, and they provide checking and savings accounts through a mobile app or website, offer tools to help customers budget and reach financial goals, and maintain lower fees and higher interest rates than traditional banks. As a neobank, Kinly partners with Bancorp, an FDIC-insured bank, so its members' deposits are insured up to $250,000.

Hawkins started Kinly in 2020 in order to gain the trust of Black America and help this community build generational wealth. He followed the models of other historically underserved communities that established their own banks to serve their interests—for example, the Jewish community, which formed Goldman Sachs in 1869, and Italian immigrants, who established the Bank of Italy in 1904. Hawkins was successful in blending the importance of serving the Black community with the potential of high growth and profitability. The Bank of Italy, after all, eventually became Bank of America in 1930, showing how a community bank could actually become one of the largest financial institutions in the world. Investors bought in to Kinly, with Barclays leading an initial $5 million round of fund-raising in 2021 and venture capital firm Point72 Ventures bringing in another $15 million later that year.

With $20 million in funding in hand, Kinly started by providing financial education to Black communities, who annually spend $1.6 trillion, although around 18% have no banking relationships. Hawkins is determined to create and enhance relationships with these communities by actively engaging with them and building trust. Once trust is developed, Kinly then provides services such as high-yield savings accounts, Visa debit cards, business banking, and credit lending to help communities raise and maintain wealth.

Kinly didn't stop at providing banking services to Black America. It grew its lines of business through partnerships with other organizations, such as Haven Life, a customer-focused life insurance company owned by MassMutual. The two organizations formed a partnership in 2022 to offer life insurance products through Kinly's mobile app. Wade Seward, Haven Life's Head of Distribution Strategy, believes that the partnership with Kinly is central to Haven Life's founding mission and helps break down barriers for Black Americans, who on average have one-third as much life insurance coverage as white policyholders.

Hawkins believes that the COVID-19 pandemic has accelerated the digital-first movement and that neobanks like his are in a strong position to increase their customer base. His hope is that he can continue to do good for Black communities along the way too.

Questions for Discussion

1. What type of social entrepreneur is Donald Hawkins? Why?

2. Which stage of the entrepreneurial process is Kinly in? Explain.

3. What type(s) of fund-raising did Hawkins pursue? Explain.

Sources: Kinly, "Who We Are," https://bekinly.com, accessed January 15, 2023; Rosenblatt Securities, "About Kinly," www.rbit.com, accessed January 15, 2023; E. Perkins, "Tackling Disparities in Finance for Black and African Americans," *MoneyGeek*, www.moneygeek.com, November 21, 2022; S. Roderick, "Kinly Is Looking to Uplift Black Communities through Financial Education and Beneficial Banking Products," *CardRates*, www.cardrates.com, August 4, 2022; J. Woods, "Kinly App Founder Motivated to Balance the Financial Scales for Black America," *Rollingout*, https://rollingout.com, June 14, 2022; "Haven Life and Kinly Partner to Make Term Life Insurance More Accessible to Black Americans," *PR Newswire*, www.prnewswire.com, June 1, 2022; C. Steinmetz, "Fintech Revolution Follows Historical Abuse of Black Wealth: 'We're Already Late, But We've Got to Do Something,'" *Startland News*, www.startlandnews.com, March 11, 2022; A. Tilford, "What Is a Neobank?" Definition and Examples of Popular Neobanks," *Bankrate*, www.bankrate.com, February 11, 2022; A. Florant et al., "The Case for Accelerating Financial Inclusion in Black Communities," *McKinsey & Company*, www.mckinsey.com, February 25, 2020.

Notes

1. R. Tuchman, "How Success Happened for Holly Thaggard, Founder of Supergoop," *Entrepreneur*, www.entrepreneur.com, February 10, 2022.
2. S. Grinnell, "Meet the 'Norma Rae' of Sunscreen: Holly Thaggard, Founder and CEO of Supergoop!," *Vanity Fair*, www.vanityfair.com, January 4, 2018.
3. Tuchman, "How Success Happened for Holly Thaggard."
4. Grinnell, "Meet the 'Norma Rae' of Sunscreen."
5. Tuchman, "How Success Happened for Holly Thaggard."
6. M. Angell, "What Supergoop!'s Founder Learned When She Reinvented the Sunscreen Industry," *Inc.*, www.inc.com, January 9, 2023.
7. Ibid.
8. Happi, "New Investors for SPF Brand Supergoop!," www.happi.com, May 25, 2022.
9. EY Americas, "Entrepreneur Of the Year National Overall Award Winners," www.ey.com, November 13, 2022; Happi, "New Investors for Supergoop!"
10. C. Kolman, "25+ Important Entrepreneur Statistics [2022]: What to Know Before You Start a Business," *Zippia*, https://zippia.com, November 17, 2022.
11. K. Main, "Small Business Statistics of 2023," *Forbes*, www.forbes.com, accessed January 19, 2023; A. Stahl, "Entrepreneurship Is Booming—Here's Why That's Great News," *Forbes*, www.forbes.com, July 8, 2022.
12. Center for American Entrepreneurship, "Why Is Entrepreneurship Important?" https://startupsusa.org, accessed January 2, 2023.
13. Ford, "The Model T," https://corporate.ford.com, accessed January 2, 2023.

14. The Nobel Prize, "Muhammad Yunus," www.nobelprize.org, accessed January 2, 2023.
15. See E. Natter, "Traits of an Entrepreneur vs. a Manager," *Chron*, https://smallbusiness.chron.com, accessed January 19, 2023; ClearTax, "Difference Between Entrepreneur and Manager: Example, Meaning," https://cleartax.in, November 3, 2022.
16. L. Okwatch, "Research Shows That Entrepreneurs Are More Depressed Than Everyone Else," *Medium*, https://medium.com, July 24, 2021.
17. G. Kaur, "How to Use Entrepreneurial Creativity for Innovation," *Entrepreneur*, www.entrepreneur.com, July 27, 2022.
18. J. Palca, "Alabama Woman Stuck in NYC Traffic in 1902 Invented the Windshield Wiper," *NPR*, www.npr.org, July 25, 2017.
19. Iowa State University, "What Is a Feasibility Study," www.extension.iastate.edu, accessed January 2, 2023; "Feasibility Study," *Investopedia*, www.investopedia.com, accessed January 2, 2023.
20. U.S. Small Business Administration, "Write Your Business Plan," www.sba.gov, accessed January 2, 2023.
21. S. Gibbons, "Why Entrepreneurs Should Prioritize Time Management Within Their Businesses," *Forbes*, www.forbes.com, July 16, 2020.
22. J. Bowman, "IPO Meaning: What Does IPO Stand For?" *The Motley Fool*, www.fool.com, September 6, 2022.
23. T. Carter, "The True Failure Rate of Small Businesses," *Entrepreneur*, www.entrepreneur.com, January 3, 2021.
24. J. Sevilla-Bernardo, B. Sanchez-Robles, and T.C. Herrador-Alcaide, "Success Factors of Startups in Research Literature within the Entrepreneurial Ecosystem," *Administrative Sciences*, https://doi.org/10.3390/admsci12030102, August 12, 2022.
25. Internal Revenue Service, "Sole Proprietorships," www.irs.gov, accessed January 3, 2023.
26. J. Stowers, "How to Choose the Best Legal Structure for Your Business," *Business News Daily*, www.businessnewsdaily.com, August 3, 2022.
27. Internal Revenue Service, "Partnerships," www.irs.gov, accessed January 3, 2023.
28. J. Stowers, "How to Choose the Best Legal Structure for Your Business," *Business News Daily*, www.businessnewsdaily.com, August 3, 2022.
29. Internal Revenue Service, "Corporations," www.irs.gov, accessed January 3, 2023.
30. J. Stowers, "How to Choose the Best Legal Structure for Your Business," *Business News Daily*, www.businessnewsdaily.com, August 3, 2022.
31. Ibid.
32. See U.S. Small Business Administration, "Choose a Business Structure," www.sbs.gov, accessed January 3, 2023.
33. S. Nicastro and R. Lane, "Debt vs. Equity Financing: What Option Is Best for You?" *Nerd Wallet*, www.nerdwallet.com, June 15, 2022.
34. J. Jones, "How Hard Is It to Get a Business Loan?" *Lending Tree*, www.lendingtree.com, May 13, 2022.
35. J. Flynn, "25+ Essential Small Business Lending Statistics [2022]: What Percentage of SBA Loans Get Approved," *Zippia*, www.zippia.com, November 3, 2022.
36. Z. Kaplan, "What Is a Venture Capitalist?" *Forage*, www.theforage.com, July 28, 2022.
37. E. Dure, "Angel Investors vs. Venture Capitalists," *J.P. Morgan Chase*, www.chase.com, January 24, 2022.
38. S. Johnson, "What Is Crowdfunding?" *Business News Daily*, www.businessnews-daily.com, June 29, 2022.
39. V. Masterson, "Here's What Women's Entrepreneurship Looks Like around the World," *World Economic Forum*, www.weforum.org, July 20, 2022.
40. K. Snellman and I. Solal, "Does Investor Gender Matter for the Success of Female Entrepreneurs? Gender Homophily and the Stigma of Incompetence in Entrepreneurial Finance," *Organization Science*, https://doi.org/10.1287/orsc.2022.1594, May 19, 2022.
41. D. Kanze, L. Huang, M. Conley, and E.T. Higgins, "Male and Female Entrepreneurs Get Asked Different Questions by VCs – and It Affects How Much Funding They Get," *Harvard Business Review*, https://hbr.org, June 27, 2017.
42. S. Herships, "Why Female Entrepreneurs Get Less Funding than Men," *Marketplace*, www.marketplace.org, October 25, 2017.
43. Atina, "Why Women Make the Best Entrepreneurs," www.atina.org.rs, accessed January 14, 2023.
44. S. Hollenbeck, "41+ Women in Business Statistics," *incfile*, https://www.incfile.com, August 18, 2022.
45. G. Stengel, "Addressing Gaps Between Men and Women Entrepreneurs Can Drive Economic Growth Globally, Report Finds," *Forbes*, www.forbes.com, November 17, 2021.
46. Ibid.
47. A. Stahl, "Entrepreneurship Is Booming–Here's Why That's Great News," *Forbes*, www.forbes.com, July 8, 2022.
48. Amazon, "What Is ecommerce? Definition, Types, Advantages, and Disadvantages," https://sell.amazon.com, accessed January 3, 2023.
49. Statista, "Retail e-Commerce Sales Worldwide from 2014 to 2026," www.statista.com, accessed January 3, 2023.
50. J. Bowman, "Investing in Top E-Commerce Companies," *The Motley Fool*, www.fool.com, August 12, 2022.
51. United States Department of Commerce, "Impact of COVID Pandemic on eCommerce," www.trade.gov, accessed January 3, 2023.
52. McKinsey, "Next on the Menu for Food Delivery," https://www.mckinsey.com, March 29, 2022.
53. K. Carlson, "Restaurants Embrace e-Commerce as Consumer Habits Permanently Shift," *MiBiz*, https://mibiz.com, March 27, 2022.
54. Entrepreneur, "Franchising," www.entrepreneur.com, accessed January 3, 2023.
55. M. Haller, "Franchise Trends That Make 2022 the Year of Opportunity," *Entrepreneur*, www.entrepreneur.com, February 17, 2022.
56. C. Kibet, "Who Owns McDonald's? Can You Afford the McDonald's Franchise Cost? (2023)," *Vetted Biz*, www.vettedbiz.com, December 14, 2022.
57. "The Top 500," *Franchise Times*, www.franchisetimes.com, accessed January 10, 2023.
58. "2022 Top Franchises for Less Than $50,000 Ranking," *Entrepreneur*, www.entrepreneur.com, accessed January 10, 2023.
59. S. Peek, "What Is Social Entrepreneurship? 5 Examples of Businesses with a Purpose," *U.S. Chamber of Commerce*, www.uschamber.com, accessed January 4, 2023.
60. Ashoka, "Social Entrepreneurship," www.ashoka.org, accessed January 4, 2023.
61. See T. Konakll, "Effects of Self-Efficacy on Social Entrepreneurship in Education: A Correlational Research," *Sage*, https://journals.sagepub.com/doi/10.7227/RIE.0019, November 1, 2015.
62. Peek, "What Is Social Entrepreneurship?"
63. TOMS, "2022 TOMS Impact Report," www.toms.com, accessed January 10, 2023; T. Ryan, "Toms Finds One-for-One Charitable Model Doesn't Add Up for Its Business," *RetailWire*, https://retailwire.com, April 13, 2021.

64. Loyola University Chicago, "The Rise of Social Entrepreneurship: Why American Consumers Want Action," www.luc.edu, accessed January 4, 2023.

65. E. Daugherty, "PAWcast: Tom Szaky '05 on the World's Overwhelming Waste Problem," *Princeton Alumni Weekly,* https://paw.princeton.edu, August 15, 2022.

66. Forbes, "Tom Szaky," https://www.forbes.com, accessed January 4, 2023.

67. Ibid.

68. Calcalist, "Mind the Tech NY 99% of What We Buy, We Don't Actually Want to Own, Says TerraCycle CEO," www.calcalistech.com, April 16, 2019.

69. T. Parker, "TerraCycle CEO Tom Szaky on How Businesses and Consumers Must Cut Waste," *NS Packaging,* www.nspackaging.com, June 5, 2020.

70. Ibid; J. Paben, "COVID-19 Hurt TerraCycle's Recycled Materials Sales in '21," *Resource Recycling,* https://resource-recycling.com, May 18, 2022.

71. K. Bhasin, The Incredible Story of How TerraCycle CEO Tom Szaky Became a Garbage Mogul," *Business Insider,* www.businessinsider.com, August 29, 2011.

72. D. Buckley, "8 Famous Social Entrepreneurs Doing Good and Making Money," *Change Creator,* https://change-creator.com, accessed January 4, 2023; Forbes, "Tom Szaky."

73. J. Johnson, "Types of Social Entrepreneurs," *Medium,* https://medium.com, April 11, 2018.

74. Net Impact, "The Four Types of Social Entrepreneurship," https://netimpact.org, April 26, 2021.

75. Novo Nordisk Foundation, "Who Are We?" https://novonordiskfonden.dk, accessed January 4, 2023.

76. B.W. Christensen, "Novo Money Tank Breaks All Records: Now Has Assets Worth a Staggering DKK 697 Billion. DKK," *FINANS,* https://finans.dk, March 28, 2022.

77. Novo Nordisk Foundation, Pandemic Antiviral Discovery (PAD)," https://novonordiskfonden.dk, accessed January 4, 2023.

78. Deloitte, "Five Insights into Intrapreneurship," www2.deloitte.com, accessed January 5, 2023.

79. D.A. Garvin and L.C. Levesque, "Meeting the Challenge of Corporate Entrepreneurship," *Harvard Business* Review, https://hbr.org, accessed January 10, 2023.

80. D.A. Garvin and L.C. Levesque, "Meeting the Challenge of Corporate Entrepreneurship," *Harvard Business Review,* https://hbr.org, October 2006.

81. The Coca-Cola Company, "How Coca-Cola Is Rethinking Disruptive Innovation to Anticipate Tomorrow's Tastes," https://www.coca-colacompany.com, February 18, 2020.

82. B. Brown and S.D. Anthony, "How P&G Tripled Its Innovation Success Rate," *Harvard Business Review,* https://hbr.org, June 2011.

83. L. Maurer, "Examples of Corporate Entrepreneurship," *Noodle,* www.noodle.com, February 28, 2022.

84. S. Arizpe, "5 Key Ways to Create an Innovation Culture," *Entrepreneur,* https://www.entrepreneur.com, November 18, 2022.

85. Ibid; R. Power, "How to Empower Your Teams to Innovate," *Forbes,* www.forbes.com, January 23, 2022.

86. C. Windham-Bradstock, "Why Upskilling Employees Is So Important Right Now," *Forbes,* www.forbes.com, June 17, 2022.

87. J. Khuri, "5 Ways to Adapt to Change and Build a More Resilient Business Model," *Entrepreneur,* www.entrepreneur.com, September 22, 2022.

NAME INDEX

C

D

H

I

J

N

O

P

Q

R

S

T

ORGANISATION INDEX

G

H

I

J

K

L

M

N

X

Y

Z

SUBJECT GLINDEX

A

B

C

F

J

K

L

M

O

P

Q

R

S

T

U

V

W

Z